T0180816

Lecture Notes in Computer Science 11207

Commenced Publication in 1973
Founding and Former Series Editors:
Gerhard Goos, Juris Hartmanis, and Jan van Leeuwen

More information about this series at http://www.springer.com/series/7412

Vittorio Ferrari · Martial Hebert
Cristian Sminchisescu · Yair Weiss (Eds.)

Computer Vision – ECCV 2018

15th European Conference
Munich, Germany, September 8–14, 2018
Proceedings, Part III

Editors
Vittorio Ferrari
Google Research
Zurich
Switzerland

Cristian Sminchisescu
Google Research
Zurich
Switzerland

Martial Hebert
Carnegie Mellon University
Pittsburgh, PA
USA

Yair Weiss
Hebrew University of Jerusalem
Jerusalem
Israel

ISSN 0302-9743 ISSN 1611-3349 (electronic)
Lecture Notes in Computer Science
ISBN 978-3-030-01218-2 ISBN 978-3-030-01219-9 (eBook)
https://doi.org/10.1007/978-3-030-01219-9

Library of Congress Control Number: 2018955489

LNCS Sublibrary: SL6 – Image Processing, Computer Vision, Pattern Recognition, and Graphics

This Springer imprint is published by the registered company Springer Nature Switzerland AG
The registered company address is: Gewerbestrasse 11, 6330 Cham, Switzerland

Foreword

It was our great pleasure to host the European Conference on Computer Vision 2018 in Munich, Germany. This constituted by far the largest ECCV event ever. With close to 2,900 registered participants and another 600 on the waiting list one month before the conference, participation more than doubled since the last ECCV in Amsterdam. We believe that this is due to a dramatic growth of the computer vision community combined with the popularity of Munich as a major European hub of culture, science, and industry. The conference took place in the heart of Munich in the concert hall Gasteig with workshops and tutorials held at the downtown campus of the Technical University of Munich.

One of the major innovations for ECCV 2018 was the free perpetual availability of all conference and workshop papers, which is often referred to as open access. We note that this is not precisely the same use of the term as in the Budapest declaration. Since 2013, CVPR and ICCV have had their papers hosted by the Computer Vision Foundation (CVF), in parallel with the IEEE Xplore version. This has proved highly beneficial to the computer vision community.

We are delighted to announce that for ECCV 2018 a very similar arrangement was put in place with the cooperation of Springer. In particular, the author's final version will be freely available in perpetuity on a CVF page, while SpringerLink will continue to host a version with further improvements, such as activating reference links and including video. We believe that this will give readers the best of both worlds; researchers who are focused on the technical content will have a freely available version in an easily accessible place, while subscribers to SpringerLink will continue to have the additional benefits that this provides. We thank Alfred Hofmann from Springer for helping to negotiate this agreement, which we expect will continue for future versions of ECCV.

September 2018

Horst Bischof
Daniel Cremers
Bernt Schiele
Ramin Zabih

Preface

Welcome to the proceedings of the 2018 European Conference on Computer Vision (ECCV 2018) held in Munich, Germany. We are delighted to present this volume reflecting a strong and exciting program, the result of an extensive review process. In total, we received 2,439 valid paper submissions. Of these, 776 were accepted (31.8%): 717 as posters (29.4%) and 59 as oral presentations (2.4%). All oral presentations were presented as posters as well. The program selection process was complicated this year by the large increase in the number of submitted papers, +65% over ECCV 2016, and the use of CMT3 for the first time for a computer vision conference. The program selection process was supported by four program co-chairs (PCs), 126 area chairs (ACs), and 1,199 reviewers with reviews assigned.

We were primarily responsible for the design and execution of the review process. Beyond administrative rejections, we were involved in acceptance decisions only in the very few cases where the ACs were not able to agree on a decision. As PCs, and as is customary in the field, we were not allowed to co-author a submission. General co-chairs and other co-organizers who played no role in the review process were permitted to submit papers, and were treated as any other author is.

Acceptance decisions were made by two independent ACs. The ACs also made a joint recommendation for promoting papers to oral status. We decided on the final selection of oral presentations based on the ACs' recommendations. There were 126 ACs, selected according to their technical expertise, experience, and geographical diversity (63 from European, nine from Asian/Australian, and 54 from North American institutions). Indeed, 126 ACs is a substantial increase in the number of ACs due to the natural increase in the number of papers and to our desire to maintain the number of papers assigned to each AC to a manageable number so as to ensure quality. The ACs were aided by the 1,199 reviewers to whom papers were assigned for reviewing. The Program Committee was selected from committees of previous ECCV, ICCV, and CVPR conferences and was extended on the basis of suggestions from the ACs. Having a large pool of Program Committee members for reviewing allowed us to match expertise while reducing reviewer loads. No more than eight papers were assigned to a reviewer, maintaining the reviewers' load at the same level as ECCV 2016 despite the increase in the number of submitted papers.

Conflicts of interest between ACs, Program Committee members, and papers were identified based on the home institutions, and on previous collaborations of all researchers involved. To find institutional conflicts, all authors, Program Committee members, and ACs were asked to list the Internet domains of their current institutions. We assigned on average approximately 18 papers to each AC. The papers were assigned using the affinity scores from the Toronto Paper Matching System (TPMS) and additional data from the OpenReview system, managed by a UMass group. OpenReview used additional information from ACs' and authors' records to identify collaborations and to generate matches. OpenReview was invaluable in refining conflict definitions and in generating quality matches. The only glitch is that, once the matches were generated, a small percentage of papers were unassigned because of discrepancies between the OpenReview conflicts and the conflicts entered in CMT3. We manually assigned these papers. This glitch is revealing of the challenge of using multiple systems at once (CMT3 and OpenReview in this case), which needs to be addressed in future.

After assignment of papers to ACs, the ACs suggested seven reviewers per paper from the Program Committee pool. The selection and rank ordering were facilitated by the TPMS affinity scores visible to the ACs for each paper/reviewer pair. The final assignment of papers to reviewers was generated again through OpenReview in order to account for refined conflict definitions. This required new features in the OpenReview matching system to accommodate the ECCV workflow, in particular to incorporate selection ranking, and maximum reviewer load. Very few papers received fewer than three reviewers after matching and were handled through manual assignment. Reviewers were then asked to comment on the merit of each paper and to make an initial recommendation ranging from definitely reject to definitely accept, including a borderline rating. The reviewers were also asked to suggest explicit questions they wanted to see answered in the authors' rebuttal. The initial review period was five weeks. Because of the delay in getting all the reviews in, we had to delay the final release of the reviews by four days. However, because of the slack included at the tail end of the schedule, we were able to maintain the decision target date with sufficient time for all the phases. We reassigned over 100 reviews from 40 reviewers during the review period. Unfortunately, the main reason for these reassignments was reviewers declining to review, after having accepted to do so. Other reasons included technical relevance and occasional unidentified conflicts. We express our thanks to the emergency reviewers who generously accepted to perform these reviews under short notice. In addition, a substantial number of manual corrections had to do with reviewers using a different email address than the one that was used at the time of the reviewer invitation. This is revealing of a broader issue with identifying users by email addresses that change frequently enough to cause significant problems during the timespan of the conference process.

The authors were then given the opportunity to rebut the reviews, to identify factual errors, and to address the specific questions raised by the reviewers over a seven-day rebuttal period. The exact format of the rebuttal was the object of considerable debate among the organizers, as well as with prior organizers. At issue is to balance giving the author the opportunity to respond completely and precisely to the reviewers, e.g., by including graphs of experiments, while avoiding requests for completely new material or experimental results not included in the original paper. In the end, we decided on the two-page PDF document in conference format. Following this rebuttal period, reviewers and ACs discussed papers at length, after which reviewers finalized their evaluation and gave a final recommendation to the ACs. A significant percentage of the reviewers did enter their final recommendation if it did not differ from their initial recommendation. Given the tight schedule, we did not wait until all were entered.

After this discussion period, each paper was assigned to a second AC. The AC/paper matching was again run through OpenReview. Again, the OpenReview team worked quickly to implement the features specific to this process, in this case accounting for the existing AC assignment, as well as minimizing the fragmentation across ACs, so that each AC had on average only 5.5 buddy ACs to communicate with. The largest number was 11. Given the complexity of the conflicts, this was a very efficient set of assignments from OpenReview. Each paper was then evaluated by its assigned pair of ACs. For each paper, we required each of the two ACs assigned to certify both the final recommendation and the metareview (aka consolidation report). In all cases, after extensive discussions, the two ACs arrived at a common acceptance decision. We maintained these decisions, with the caveat that we did evaluate, sometimes going back to the ACs, a few papers for which the final acceptance decision substantially deviated from the consensus from the reviewers, amending three decisions in the process.

We want to thank everyone involved in making ECCV 2018 possible. The success of ECCV 2018 depended on the quality of papers submitted by the authors, and on the very hard work of the ACs and the Program Committee members. We are particularly grateful to the OpenReview team (Melisa Bok, Ari Kobren, Andrew McCallum, Michael Spector) for their support, in particular their willingness to implement new features, often on a tight schedule, to Laurent Charlin for the use of the Toronto Paper Matching System, to the CMT3 team, in particular in dealing with all the issues that arise when using a new system, to Friedrich Fraundorfer and Quirin Lohr for maintaining the online version of the program, and to the CMU staff (Keyla Cook, Lynnetta Miller, Ashley Song, Nora Kazour) for assisting with data entry/editing in CMT3. Finally, the preparation of these proceedings would not have been possible without the diligent effort of the publication chairs, Albert Ali Salah and Hamdi Dibeklioğlu, and of Anna Kramer and Alfred Hofmann from Springer.

September 2018   Vittorio Ferrari
                                                                 Martial Hebert
                                                        Cristian Sminchisescu
                                                                    Yair Weiss

Organization

General Chairs

Horst Bischof	Graz University of Technology, Austria
Daniel Cremers	Technical University of Munich, Germany
Bernt Schiele	Saarland University, Max Planck Institute for Informatics, Germany
Ramin Zabih	CornellNYCTech, USA

Program Committee Co-chairs

Vittorio Ferrari	University of Edinburgh, UK
Martial Hebert	Carnegie Mellon University, USA
Cristian Sminchisescu	Lund University, Sweden
Yair Weiss	Hebrew University, Israel

Local Arrangements Chairs

Björn Menze	Technical University of Munich, Germany
Matthias Niessner	Technical University of Munich, Germany

Workshop Chairs

Stefan Roth	TU Darmstadt, Germany
Laura Leal-Taixé	Technical University of Munich, Germany

Tutorial Chairs

Michael Bronstein	Università della Svizzera Italiana, Switzerland
Laura Leal-Taixé	Technical University of Munich, Germany

Website Chair

Friedrich Fraundorfer	Graz University of Technology, Austria

Demo Chairs

Federico Tombari	Technical University of Munich, Germany
Joerg Stueckler	Technical University of Munich, Germany

Publicity Chair

Giovanni Maria   University of Catania, Italy
  Farinella

Industrial Liaison Chairs

Florent Perronnin   Naver Labs, France
Yunchao Gong   Snap, USA
Helmut Grabner   Logitech, Switzerland

Finance Chair

Gerard Medioni   Amazon, University of Southern California, USA

Publication Chairs

Albert Ali Salah   Boğaziçi University, Turkey
Hamdi Dibeklioğlu   Bilkent University, Turkey

Area Chairs

Kalle Åström   Lund University, Sweden
Zeynep Akata   University of Amsterdam, The Netherlands
Joao Barreto   University of Coimbra, Portugal
Ronen Basri   Weizmann Institute of Science, Israel
Dhruv Batra   Georgia Tech and Facebook AI Research, USA
Serge Belongie   Cornell University, USA
Rodrigo Benenson   Google, Switzerland
Hakan Bilen   University of Edinburgh, UK
Matthew Blaschko   KU Leuven, Belgium
Edmond Boyer   Inria, France
Gabriel Brostow   University College London, UK
Thomas Brox   University of Freiburg, Germany
Marcus Brubaker   York University, Canada
Barbara Caputo   Politecnico di Torino and the Italian Institute
                          of Technology, Italy
Tim Cootes   University of Manchester, UK
Trevor Darrell   University of California, Berkeley, USA
Larry Davis   University of Maryland at College Park, USA
Andrew Davison   Imperial College London, UK
Fernando de la Torre   Carnegie Mellon University, USA
Irfan Essa   GeorgiaTech, USA
Ali Farhadi   University of Washington, USA
Paolo Favaro   University of Bern, Switzerland
Michael Felsberg   Linköping University, Sweden

Sanja Fidler	University of Toronto, Canada
Andrew Fitzgibbon	Microsoft, Cambridge, UK
David Forsyth	University of Illinois at Urbana-Champaign, USA
Charless Fowlkes	University of California, Irvine, USA
Bill Freeman	MIT, USA
Mario Fritz	MPII, Germany
Jürgen Gall	University of Bonn, Germany
Dariu Gavrila	TU Delft, The Netherlands
Andreas Geiger	MPI-IS and University of Tübingen, Germany
Theo Gevers	University of Amsterdam, The Netherlands
Ross Girshick	Facebook AI Research, USA
Kristen Grauman	Facebook AI Research and UT Austin, USA
Abhinav Gupta	Carnegie Mellon University, USA
Kaiming He	Facebook AI Research, USA
Martial Hebert	Carnegie Mellon University, USA
Anders Heyden	Lund University, Sweden
Timothy Hospedales	University of Edinburgh, UK
Michal Irani	Weizmann Institute of Science, Israel
Phillip Isola	University of California, Berkeley, USA
Hervé Jégou	Facebook AI Research, France
David Jacobs	University of Maryland, College Park, USA
Allan Jepson	University of Toronto, Canada
Jiaya Jia	Chinese University of Hong Kong, SAR China
Fredrik Kahl	Chalmers University, USA
Hedvig Kjellström	KTH Royal Institute of Technology, Sweden
Iasonas Kokkinos	University College London and Facebook, UK
Vladlen Koltun	Intel Labs, USA
Philipp Krähenbühl	UT Austin, USA
M. Pawan Kumar	University of Oxford, UK
Kyros Kutulakos	University of Toronto, Canada
In Kweon	KAIST, South Korea
Ivan Laptev	Inria, France
Svetlana Lazebnik	University of Illinois at Urbana-Champaign, USA
Laura Leal-Taixé	Technical University of Munich, Germany
Erik Learned-Miller	University of Massachusetts, Amherst, USA
Kyoung Mu Lee	Seoul National University, South Korea
Bastian Leibe	RWTH Aachen University, Germany
Aleš Leonardis	University of Birmingham, UK
Vincent Lepetit	University of Bordeaux, France and Graz University of Technology, Austria
Fuxin Li	Oregon State University, USA
Dahua Lin	Chinese University of Hong Kong, SAR China
Jim Little	University of British Columbia, Canada
Ce Liu	Google, USA
Chen Change Loy	Nanyang Technological University, Singapore
Jiri Matas	Czech Technical University in Prague, Czechia

Yasuyuki Matsushita	Osaka University, Japan
Dimitris Metaxas	Rutgers University, USA
Greg Mori	Simon Fraser University, Canada
Vittorio Murino	Istituto Italiano di Tecnologia, Italy
Richard Newcombe	Oculus Research, USA
Minh Hoai Nguyen	Stony Brook University, USA
Sebastian Nowozin	Microsoft Research Cambridge, UK
Aude Oliva	MIT, USA
Bjorn Ommer	Heidelberg University, Germany
Tomas Pajdla	Czech Technical University in Prague, Czechia
Maja Pantic	Imperial College London and Samsung AI Research Centre Cambridge, UK
Caroline Pantofaru	Google, USA
Devi Parikh	Georgia Tech and Facebook AI Research, USA
Sylvain Paris	Adobe Research, USA
Vladimir Pavlovic	Rutgers University, USA
Marcello Pelillo	University of Venice, Italy
Patrick Pérez	Valeo, France
Robert Pless	George Washington University, USA
Thomas Pock	Graz University of Technology, Austria
Jean Ponce	Inria, France
Gerard Pons-Moll	MPII, Saarland Informatics Campus, Germany
Long Quan	Hong Kong University of Science and Technology, SAR China
Stefan Roth	TU Darmstadt, Germany
Carsten Rother	University of Heidelberg, Germany
Bryan Russell	Adobe Research, USA
Kate Saenko	Boston University, USA
Mathieu Salzmann	EPFL, Switzerland
Dimitris Samaras	Stony Brook University, USA
Yoichi Sato	University of Tokyo, Japan
Silvio Savarese	Stanford University, USA
Konrad Schindler	ETH Zurich, Switzerland
Cordelia Schmid	Inria, France and Google, France
Nicu Sebe	University of Trento, Italy
Fei Sha	University of Southern California, USA
Greg Shakhnarovich	TTI Chicago, USA
Jianbo Shi	University of Pennsylvania, USA
Abhinav Shrivastava	UMD and Google, USA
Yan Shuicheng	National University of Singapore, Singapore
Leonid Sigal	University of British Columbia, Canada
Josef Sivic	Czech Technical University in Prague, Czechia
Arnold Smeulders	University of Amsterdam, The Netherlands
Deqing Sun	NVIDIA, USA
Antonio Torralba	MIT, USA
Zhuowen Tu	University of California, San Diego, USA

Tinne Tuytelaars	KU Leuven, Belgium
Jasper Uijlings	Google, Switzerland
Joost van de Weijer	Computer Vision Center, Spain
Nuno Vasconcelos	University of California, San Diego, USA
Andrea Vedaldi	University of Oxford, UK
Olga Veksler	University of Western Ontario, Canada
Jakob Verbeek	Inria, France
Rene Vidal	Johns Hopkins University, USA
Daphna Weinshall	Hebrew University, Israel
Chris Williams	University of Edinburgh, UK
Lior Wolf	Tel Aviv University, Israel
Ming-Hsuan Yang	University of California at Merced, USA
Todd Zickler	Harvard University, USA
Andrew Zisserman	University of Oxford, UK

Technical Program Committee

Hassan Abu Alhaija	Peter Anderson	Arunava Banerjee
Radhakrishna Achanta	Juan Andrade-Cetto	Atsuhiko Banno
Hanno Ackermann	Mykhaylo Andriluka	Aayush Bansal
Ehsan Adeli	Anelia Angelova	Yingze Bao
Lourdes Agapito	Michel Antunes	Md Jawadul Bappy
Aishwarya Agrawal	Pablo Arbelaez	Pierre Baqué
Antonio Agudo	Vasileios Argyriou	Dániel Baráth
Eirikur Agustsson	Chetan Arora	Adrian Barbu
Karim Ahmed	Federica Arrigoni	Kobus Barnard
Byeongjoo Ahn	Vassilis Athitsos	Nick Barnes
Unaiza Ahsan	Mathieu Aubry	Francisco Barranco
Emre Akbaş	Shai Avidan	Adrien Bartoli
Eren Aksoy	Yannis Avrithis	E. Bayro-Corrochano
Yağız Aksoy	Samaneh Azadi	Paul Beardlsey
Alexandre Alahi	Hossein Azizpour	Vasileios Belagiannis
Jean-Baptiste Alayrac	Artem Babenko	Sean Bell
Samuel Albanie	Timur Bagautdinov	Ismail Ben
Cenek Albl	Andrew Bagdanov	Boulbaba Ben Amor
Saad Ali	Hessam Bagherinezhad	Gil Ben-Artzi
Rahaf Aljundi	Yuval Bahat	Ohad Ben-Shahar
Jose M. Alvarez	Min Bai	Abhijit Bendale
Humam Alwassel	Qinxun Bai	Rodrigo Benenson
Toshiyuki Amano	Song Bai	Fabian Benitez-Quiroz
Mitsuru Ambai	Xiang Bai	Fethallah Benmansour
Mohamed Amer	Peter Bajcsy	Ryad Benosman
Senjian An	Amr Bakry	Filippo Bergamasco
Cosmin Ancuti	Kavita Bala	David Bermudez

Jesus Bermudez-Cameo
Leonard Berrada
Gedas Bertasius
Ross Beveridge
Lucas Beyer
Bir Bhanu
S. Bhattacharya
Binod Bhattarai
Arnav Bhavsar
Simone Bianco
Adel Bibi
Pia Bideau
Josef Bigun
Arijit Biswas
Soma Biswas
Marten Bjoerkman
Volker Blanz
Vishnu Boddeti
Piotr Bojanowski
Terrance Boult
Yuri Boykov
Hakan Boyraz
Eric Brachmann
Samarth Brahmbhatt
Mathieu Bredif
Francois Bremond
Michael Brown
Luc Brun
Shyamal Buch
Pradeep Buddharaju
Aurelie Bugeau
Rudy Bunel
Xavier Burgos Artizzu
Darius Burschka
Andrei Bursuc
Zoya Bylinskii
Fabian Caba
Daniel Cabrini Hauagge
Cesar Cadena Lerma
Holger Caesar
Jianfei Cai
Junjie Cai
Zhaowei Cai
Simone Calderara
Neill Campbell
Octavia Camps

Xun Cao
Yanshuai Cao
Joao Carreira
Dan Casas
Daniel Castro
Jan Cech
M. Emre Celebi
Duygu Ceylan
Menglei Chai
Ayan Chakrabarti
Rudrasis Chakraborty
Shayok Chakraborty
Tat-Jen Cham
Antonin Chambolle
Antoni Chan
Sharat Chandran
Hyun Sung Chang
Ju Yong Chang
Xiaojun Chang
Soravit Changpinyo
Wei-Lun Chao
Yu-Wei Chao
Visesh Chari
Rizwan Chaudhry
Siddhartha Chaudhuri
Rama Chellappa
Chao Chen
Chen Chen
Cheng Chen
Chu-Song Chen
Guang Chen
Hsin-I Chen
Hwann-Tzong Chen
Kai Chen
Kan Chen
Kevin Chen
Liang-Chieh Chen
Lin Chen
Qifeng Chen
Ting Chen
Wei Chen
Xi Chen
Xilin Chen
Xinlei Chen
Yingcong Chen
Yixin Chen

Erkang Cheng
Jingchun Cheng
Ming-Ming Cheng
Wen-Huang Cheng
Yuan Cheng
Anoop Cherian
Liang-Tien Chia
Naoki Chiba
Shao-Yi Chien
Han-Pang Chiu
Wei-Chen Chiu
Nam Ik Cho
Sunghyun Cho
TaeEun Choe
Jongmoo Choi
Christopher Choy
Wen-Sheng Chu
Yung-Yu Chuang
Ondrej Chum
Joon Son Chung
Gökberk Cinbis
James Clark
Andrea Cohen
Forrester Cole
Toby Collins
John Collomosse
Camille Couprie
David Crandall
Marco Cristani
Canton Cristian
James Crowley
Yin Cui
Zhaopeng Cui
Bo Dai
Jifeng Dai
Qieyun Dai
Shengyang Dai
Yuchao Dai
Carlo Dal Mutto
Dima Damen
Zachary Daniels
Kostas Daniilidis
Donald Dansereau
Mohamed Daoudi
Abhishek Das
Samyak Datta

Achal Dave
Shalini De Mello
Teofilo deCampos
Joseph DeGol
Koichiro Deguchi
Alessio Del Bue
Stefanie Demirci
Jia Deng
Zhiwei Deng
Joachim Denzler
Konstantinos Derpanis
Aditya Deshpande
Alban Desmaison
Frédéric Devernay
Abhinav Dhall
Michel Dhome
Hamdi Dibeklioğlu
Mert Dikmen
Cosimo Distante
Ajay Divakaran
Mandar Dixit
Carl Doersch
Piotr Dollar
Bo Dong
Chao Dong
Huang Dong
Jian Dong
Jiangxin Dong
Weisheng Dong
Simon Donné
Gianfranco Doretto
Alexey Dosovitskiy
Matthijs Douze
Bruce Draper
Bertram Drost
Liang Du
Shichuan Du
Gregory Dudek
Zoran Duric
Pınar Duygulu
Hazım Ekenel
Tarek El-Gaaly
Ehsan Elhamifar
Mohamed Elhoseiny
Sabu Emmanuel
Ian Endres

Aykut Erdem
Erkut Erdem
Hugo Jair Escalante
Sergio Escalera
Victor Escorcia
Francisco Estrada
Davide Eynard
Bin Fan
Jialue Fan
Quanfu Fan
Chen Fang
Tian Fang
Yi Fang
Hany Farid
Giovanni Farinella
Ryan Farrell
Alireza Fathi
Christoph Feichtenhofer
Wenxin Feng
Martin Fergie
Cornelia Fermuller
Basura Fernando
Michael Firman
Bob Fisher
John Fisher
Mathew Fisher
Boris Flach
Matt Flagg
Francois Fleuret
David Fofi
Ruth Fong
Gian Luca Foresti
Per-Erik Forssén
David Fouhey
Katerina Fragkiadaki
Victor Fragoso
Jan-Michael Frahm
Jean-Sebastien Franco
Ohad Fried
Simone Frintrop
Huazhu Fu
Yun Fu
Olac Fuentes
Christopher Funk
Thomas Funkhouser
Brian Funt

Ryo Furukawa
Yasutaka Furukawa
Andrea Fusiello
Fatma Güney
Raghudeep Gadde
Silvano Galliani
Orazio Gallo
Chuang Gan
Bin-Bin Gao
Jin Gao
Junbin Gao
Ruohan Gao
Shenghua Gao
Animesh Garg
Ravi Garg
Erik Gartner
Simone Gasparin
Jochen Gast
Leon A. Gatys
Stratis Gavves
Liuhao Ge
Timnit Gebru
James Gee
Peter Gehler
Xin Geng
Guido Gerig
David Geronimo
Bernard Ghanem
Michael Gharbi
Golnaz Ghiasi
Spyros Gidaris
Andrew Gilbert
Rohit Girdhar
Ioannis Gkioulekas
Georgia Gkioxari
Guy Godin
Roland Goecke
Michael Goesele
Nuno Goncalves
Boqing Gong
Minglun Gong
Yunchao Gong
Abel Gonzalez-Garcia
Daniel Gordon
Paulo Gotardo
Stephen Gould

Venu Govindu	Wolfgang Heidrich	Evren Imre
Helmut Grabner	Janne Heikkila	Eldar Insafutdinov
Petr Gronat	Jared Heinly	Go Irie
Steve Gu	Mattias Heinrich	Hossam Isack
Josechu Guerrero	Lisa Anne Hendricks	Ahmet Işcen
Anupam Guha	Dan Hendrycks	Daisuke Iwai
Jean-Yves Guillemaut	Stephane Herbin	Hamid Izadinia
Alp Güler	Alexander Hermans	Nathan Jacobs
Erhan Gündoğdu	Luis Herranz	Suyog Jain
Guodong Guo	Aaron Hertzmann	Varun Jampani
Xinqing Guo	Adrian Hilton	C. V. Jawahar
Ankush Gupta	Michael Hirsch	Dinesh Jayaraman
Mohit Gupta	Steven Hoi	Sadeep Jayasumana
Saurabh Gupta	Seunghoon Hong	Laszlo Jeni
Tanmay Gupta	Wei Hong	Hueihan Jhuang
Abner Guzman Rivera	Anthony Hoogs	Dinghuang Ji
Timo Hackel	Radu Horaud	Hui Ji
Sunil Hadap	Yedid Hoshen	Qiang Ji
Christian Haene	Omid Hosseini Jafari	Fan Jia
Ralf Haeusler	Kuang-Jui Hsu	Kui Jia
Levente Hajder	Winston Hsu	Xu Jia
David Hall	Yinlin Hu	Huaizu Jiang
Peter Hall	Zhe Hu	Jiayan Jiang
Stefan Haller	Gang Hua	Nianjuan Jiang
Ghassan Hamarneh	Chen Huang	Tingting Jiang
Fred Hamprecht	De-An Huang	Xiaoyi Jiang
Onur Hamsici	Dong Huang	Yu-Gang Jiang
Bohyung Han	Gary Huang	Long Jin
Junwei Han	Heng Huang	Suo Jinli
Xufeng Han	Jia-Bin Huang	Justin Johnson
Yahong Han	Qixing Huang	Nebojsa Jojic
Ankur Handa	Rui Huang	Michael Jones
Albert Haque	Sheng Huang	Hanbyul Joo
Tatsuya Harada	Weilin Huang	Jungseock Joo
Mehrtash Harandi	Xiaolei Huang	Ajjen Joshi
Bharath Hariharan	Xinyu Huang	Amin Jourabloo
Mahmudul Hasan	Zhiwu Huang	Frederic Jurie
Tal Hassner	Tak-Wai Hui	Achuta Kadambi
Kenji Hata	Wei-Chih Hung	Samuel Kadoury
Soren Hauberg	Junhwa Hur	Ioannis Kakadiaris
Michal Havlena	Mohamed Hussein	Zdenek Kalal
Zeeshan Hayder	Wonjun Hwang	Yannis Kalantidis
Junfeng He	Anders Hyden	Sinan Kalkan
Lei He	Satoshi Ikehata	Vicky Kalogeiton
Varsha Hedau	Nazlı Ikizler-Cinbis	Sunkavalli Kalyan
Felix Heide	Viorela Ila	J.-K. Kamarainen

Martin Kampel
Kenichi Kanatani
Angjoo Kanazawa
Melih Kandemir
Sing Bing Kang
Zhuoliang Kang
Mohan Kankanhalli
Juho Kannala
Abhishek Kar
Amlan Kar
Svebor Karaman
Leonid Karlinsky
Zoltan Kato
Parneet Kaur
Hiroshi Kawasaki
Misha Kazhdan
Margret Keuper
Sameh Khamis
Naeemullah Khan
Salman Khan
Hadi Kiapour
Joe Kileel
Chanho Kim
Gunhee Kim
Hansung Kim
Junmo Kim
Junsik Kim
Kihwan Kim
Minyoung Kim
Tae Hyun Kim
Tae-Kyun Kim
Akisato Kimura
Zsolt Kira
Alexander Kirillov
Kris Kitani
Maria Klodt
Patrick Knöbelreiter
Jan Knopp
Reinhard Koch
Alexander Kolesnikov
Chen Kong
Naejin Kong
Shu Kong
Piotr Koniusz
Simon Korman
Andreas Koschan

Dimitrios Kosmopoulos
Satwik Kottur
Balazs Kovacs
Adarsh Kowdle
Mike Krainin
Gregory Kramida
Ranjay Krishna
Ravi Krishnan
Matej Kristan
Pavel Krsek
Volker Krueger
Alexander Krull
Hilde Kuehne
Andreas Kuhn
Arjan Kuijper
Zuzana Kukelova
Kuldeep Kulkarni
Shiro Kumano
Avinash Kumar
Vijay Kumar
Abhijit Kundu
Sebastian Kurtek
Junseok Kwon
Jan Kybic
Alexander Ladikos
Shang-Hong Lai
Wei-Sheng Lai
Jean-Francois Lalonde
John Lambert
Zhenzhong Lan
Charis Lanaras
Oswald Lanz
Dong Lao
Longin Jan Latecki
Justin Lazarow
Huu Le
Chen-Yu Lee
Gim Hee Lee
Honglak Lee
Hsin-Ying Lee
Joon-Young Lee
Seungyong Lee
Stefan Lee
Yong Jae Lee
Zhen Lei
Ido Leichter

Victor Lempitsky
Spyridon Leonardos
Marius Leordeanu
Matt Leotta
Thomas Leung
Stefan Leutenegger
Gil Levi
Aviad Levis
Jose Lezama
Ang Li
Dingzeyu Li
Dong Li
Haoxiang Li
Hongdong Li
Hongsheng Li
Hongyang Li
Jianguo Li
Kai Li
Ruiyu Li
Wei Li
Wen Li
Xi Li
Xiaoxiao Li
Xin Li
Xirong Li
Xuelong Li
Xueting Li
Yeqing Li
Yijun Li
Yin Li
Yingwei Li
Yining Li
Yongjie Li
Yu-Feng Li
Zechao Li
Zhengqi Li
Zhenyang Li
Zhizhong Li
Xiaodan Liang
Renjie Liao
Zicheng Liao
Bee Lim
Jongwoo Lim
Joseph Lim
Ser-Nam Lim
Chen-Hsuan Lin

Shih-Yao Lin
Tsung-Yi Lin
Weiyao Lin
Yen-Yu Lin
Haibin Ling
Or Litany
Roee Litman
Anan Liu
Changsong Liu
Chen Liu
Ding Liu
Dong Liu
Feng Liu
Guangcan Liu
Luoqi Liu
Miaomiao Liu
Nian Liu
Risheng Liu
Shu Liu
Shuaicheng Liu
Sifei Liu
Tyng-Luh Liu
Wanquan Liu
Weiwei Liu
Xialei Liu
Xiaoming Liu
Yebin Liu
Yiming Liu
Ziwei Liu
Zongyi Liu
Liliana Lo Presti
Edgar Lobaton
Chengjiang Long
Mingsheng Long
Roberto Lopez-Sastre
Amy Loufti
Brian Lovell
Canyi Lu
Cewu Lu
Feng Lu
Huchuan Lu
Jiajun Lu
Jiasen Lu
Jiwen Lu
Yang Lu
Yujuan Lu

Simon Lucey
Jian-Hao Luo
Jiebo Luo
Pablo Márquez-Neila
Matthias Müller
Chao Ma
Chih-Yao Ma
Lin Ma
Shugao Ma
Wei-Chiu Ma
Zhanyu Ma
Oisin Mac Aodha
Will Maddern
Ludovic Magerand
Marcus Magnor
Vijay Mahadevan
Mohammad Mahoor
Michael Maire
Subhransu Maji
Ameesh Makadia
Atsuto Maki
Yasushi Makihara
Mateusz Malinowski
Tomasz Malisiewicz
Arun Mallya
Roberto Manduchi
Junhua Mao
Dmitrii Marin
Joe Marino
Kenneth Marino
Elisabeta Marinoiu
Ricardo Martin
Aleix Martinez
Julieta Martinez
Aaron Maschinot
Jonathan Masci
Bogdan Matei
Diana Mateus
Stefan Mathe
Kevin Matzen
Bruce Maxwell
Steve Maybank
Walterio Mayol-Cuevas
Mason McGill
Stephen Mckenna
Roey Mechrez

Christopher Mei
Heydi Mendez-Vazquez
Deyu Meng
Thomas Mensink
Bjoern Menze
Domingo Mery
Qiguang Miao
Tomer Michaeli
Antoine Miech
Ondrej Miksik
Anton Milan
Gregor Miller
Cai Minjie
Majid Mirmehdi
Ishan Misra
Niloy Mitra
Anurag Mittal
Nirbhay Modhe
Davide Modolo
Pritish Mohapatra
Pascal Monasse
Mathew Monfort
Taesup Moon
Sandino Morales
Vlad Morariu
Philippos Mordohai
Francesc Moreno
Henrique Morimitsu
Yael Moses
Ben-Ezra Moshe
Roozbeh Mottaghi
Yadong Mu
Lopamudra Mukherjee
Mario Munich
Ana Murillo
Damien Muselet
Armin Mustafa
Siva Karthik Mustikovela
Moin Nabi
Sobhan Naderi
Hajime Nagahara
Varun Nagaraja
Tushar Nagarajan
Arsha Nagrani
Nikhil Naik
Atsushi Nakazawa

P. J. Narayanan
Charlie Nash
Lakshmanan Nataraj
Fabian Nater
Lukáš Neumann
Natalia Neverova
Alejandro Newell
Phuc Nguyen
Xiaohan Nie
David Nilsson
Ko Nishino
Zhenxing Niu
Shohei Nobuhara
Klas Nordberg
Mohammed Norouzi
David Novotny
Ifeoma Nwogu
Matthew O'Toole
Guillaume Obozinski
Jean-Marc Odobez
Eyal Ofek
Ferda Ofli
Tae-Hyun Oh
Iason Oikonomidis
Takeshi Oishi
Takahiro Okabe
Takayuki Okatani
Vlad Olaru
Michael Opitz
Jose Oramas
Vicente Ordonez
Ivan Oseledets
Aljosa Osep
Magnus Oskarsson
Martin R. Oswald
Wanli Ouyang
Andrew Owens
Mustafa Özuysal
Jinshan Pan
Xingang Pan
Rameswar Panda
Sharath Pankanti
Julien Pansiot
Nicolas Papadakis
George Papandreou
N. Papanikolopoulos

Hyun Soo Park
In Kyu Park
Jaesik Park
Omkar Parkhi
Alvaro Parra Bustos
C. Alejandro Parraga
Vishal Patel
Deepak Pathak
Ioannis Patras
Viorica Patraucean
Genevieve Patterson
Kim Pedersen
Robert Peharz
Selen Pehlivan
Xi Peng
Bojan Pepik
Talita Perciano
Federico Pernici
Adrian Peter
Stavros Petridis
Vladimir Petrovic
Henning Petzka
Tomas Pfister
Trung Pham
Justus Piater
Massimo Piccardi
Sudeep Pillai
Pedro Pinheiro
Lerrel Pinto
Bernardo Pires
Aleksis Pirinen
Fiora Pirri
Leonid Pischulin
Tobias Ploetz
Bryan Plummer
Yair Poleg
Jean Ponce
Gerard Pons-Moll
Jordi Pont-Tuset
Alin Popa
Fatih Porikli
Horst Possegger
Viraj Prabhu
Andrea Prati
Maria Priisalu
Véronique Prinet

Victor Prisacariu
Jan Prokaj
Nicolas Pugeault
Luis Puig
Ali Punjani
Senthil Purushwalkam
Guido Pusiol
Guo-Jun Qi
Xiaojuan Qi
Hongwei Qin
Shi Qiu
Faisal Qureshi
Matthias Rüther
Petia Radeva
Umer Rafi
Rahul Raguram
Swaminathan Rahul
Varun Ramakrishna
Kandan Ramakrishnan
Ravi Ramamoorthi
Vignesh Ramanathan
Vasili Ramanishka
R. Ramasamy Selvaraju
Rene Ranftl
Carolina Raposo
Nikhil Rasiwasia
Nalini Ratha
Sai Ravela
Avinash Ravichandran
Ramin Raziperchikolaei
Sylvestre-Alvise Rebuffi
Adria Recasens
Joe Redmon
Timo Rehfeld
Michal Reinstein
Konstantinos Rematas
Haibing Ren
Shaoqing Ren
Wenqi Ren
Zhile Ren
Hamid Rezatofighi
Nicholas Rhinehart
Helge Rhodin
Elisa Ricci
Eitan Richardson
Stephan Richter

Gernot Riegler
Hayko Riemenschneider
Tammy Riklin Raviv
Ergys Ristani
Tobias Ritschel
Mariano Rivera
Samuel Rivera
Antonio Robles-Kelly
Ignacio Rocco
Jason Rock
Emanuele Rodola
Mikel Rodriguez
Gregory Rogez
Marcus Rohrbach
Gemma Roig
Javier Romero
Olaf Ronneberger
Amir Rosenfeld
Bodo Rosenhahn
Guy Rosman
Arun Ross
Samuel Rota Bulò
Peter Roth
Constantin Rothkopf
Sebastien Roy
Amit Roy-Chowdhury
Ognjen Rudovic
Adria Ruiz
Javier Ruiz-del-Solar
Christian Rupprecht
Olga Russakovsky
Chris Russell
Alexandre Sablayrolles
Fereshteh Sadeghi
Ryusuke Sagawa
Hideo Saito
Elham Sakhaee
Albert Ali Salah
Conrad Sanderson
Koppal Sanjeev
Aswin Sankaranarayanan
Elham Saraee
Jason Saragih
Sudeep Sarkar
Imari Sato
Shin'ichi Satoh

Torsten Sattler
Bogdan Savchynskyy
Johannes Schönberger
Hanno Scharr
Walter Scheirer
Bernt Schiele
Frank Schmidt
Tanner Schmidt
Dirk Schnieders
Samuel Schulter
William Schwartz
Alexander Schwing
Ozan Sener
Soumyadip Sengupta
Laura Sevilla-Lara
Mubarak Shah
Shishir Shah
Fahad Shahbaz Khan
Amir Shahroudy
Jing Shao
Xiaowei Shao
Roman Shapovalov
Nataliya Shapovalova
Ali Sharif Razavian
Gaurav Sharma
Mohit Sharma
Pramod Sharma
Viktoriia Sharmanska
Eli Shechtman
Mark Sheinin
Evan Shelhamer
Chunhua Shen
Li Shen
Wei Shen
Xiaohui Shen
Xiaoyong Shen
Ziyi Shen
Lu Sheng
Baoguang Shi
Boxin Shi
Kevin Shih
Hyunjung Shim
Ilan Shimshoni
Young Min Shin
Koichi Shinoda
Matthew Shreve

Tianmin Shu
Zhixin Shu
Kaleem Siddiqi
Gunnar Sigurdsson
Nathan Silberman
Tomas Simon
Abhishek Singh
Gautam Singh
Maneesh Singh
Praveer Singh
Richa Singh
Saurabh Singh
Sudipta Sinha
Vladimir Smutny
Noah Snavely
Cees Snoek
Kihyuk Sohn
Eric Sommerlade
Sanghyun Son
Bi Song
Shiyu Song
Shuran Song
Xuan Song
Yale Song
Yang Song
Yibing Song
Lorenzo Sorgi
Humberto Sossa
Pratul Srinivasan
Michael Stark
Bjorn Stenger
Rainer Stiefelhagen
Joerg Stueckler
Jan Stuehmer
Hang Su
Hao Su
Shuochen Su
R. Subramanian
Yusuke Sugano
Akihiro Sugimoto
Baochen Sun
Chen Sun
Jian Sun
Jin Sun
Lin Sun
Min Sun

Qing Sun
Zhaohui Sun
David Suter
Eran Swears
Raza Syed Hussain
T. Syeda-Mahmood
Christian Szegedy
Duy-Nguyen Ta
Tolga Taşdizen
Hemant Tagare
Yuichi Taguchi
Ying Tai
Yu-Wing Tai
Jun Takamatsu
Hugues Talbot
Toru Tamak
Robert Tamburo
Chaowei Tan
Meng Tang
Peng Tang
Siyu Tang
Wei Tang
Junli Tao
Ran Tao
Xin Tao
Makarand Tapaswi
Jean-Philippe Tarel
Maxim Tatarchenko
Bugra Tekin
Demetri Terzopoulos
Christian Theobalt
Diego Thomas
Rajat Thomas
Qi Tian
Xinmei Tian
YingLi Tian
Yonghong Tian
Yonglong Tian
Joseph Tighe
Radu Timofte
Massimo Tistarelli
Sinisa Todorovic
Pavel Tokmakov
Giorgos Tolias
Federico Tombari
Tatiana Tommasi

Chetan Tonde
Xin Tong
Akihiko Torii
Andrea Torsello
Florian Trammer
Du Tran
Quoc-Huy Tran
Rudolph Triebel
Alejandro Troccoli
Leonardo Trujillo
Tomasz Trzcinski
Sam Tsai
Yi-Hsuan Tsai
Hung-Yu Tseng
Vagia Tsiminaki
Aggeliki Tsoli
Wei-Chih Tu
Shubham Tulsiani
Fred Tung
Tony Tung
Matt Turek
Oncel Tuzel
Georgios Tzimiropoulos
Ilkay Ulusoy
Osman Ulusoy
Dmitry Ulyanov
Paul Upchurch
Ben Usman
Evgeniya Ustinova
Himanshu Vajaria
Alexander Vakhitov
Jack Valmadre
Ernest Valveny
Jan van Gemert
Grant Van Horn
Jagannadan Varadarajan
Gul Varol
Sebastiano Vascon
Francisco Vasconcelos
Mayank Vatsa
Javier Vazquez-Corral
Ramakrishna Vedantam
Ashok Veeraraghavan
Andreas Veit
Raviteja Vemulapalli
Jonathan Ventura

Matthias Vestner
Minh Vo
Christoph Vogel
Michele Volpi
Carl Vondrick
Sven Wachsmuth
Toshikazu Wada
Michael Waechter
Catherine Wah
Jacob Walker
Jun Wan
Boyu Wang
Chen Wang
Chunyu Wang
De Wang
Fang Wang
Hongxing Wang
Hua Wang
Jiang Wang
Jingdong Wang
Jinglu Wang
Jue Wang
Le Wang
Lei Wang
Lezi Wang
Liang Wang
Lichao Wang
Lijun Wang
Limin Wang
Liwei Wang
Naiyan Wang
Oliver Wang
Qi Wang
Ruiping Wang
Shenlong Wang
Shu Wang
Song Wang
Tao Wang
Xiaofang Wang
Xiaolong Wang
Xinchao Wang
Xinggang Wang
Xintao Wang
Yang Wang
Yu-Chiang Frank Wang
Yu-Xiong Wang

Zhaowen Wang
Zhe Wang
Anne Wannenwetsch
Simon Warfield
Scott Wehrwein
Donglai Wei
Ping Wei
Shih-En Wei
Xiu-Shen Wei
Yichen Wei
Xie Weidi
Philippe Weinzaepfel
Longyin Wen
Eric Wengrowski
Tomas Werner
Michael Wilber
Rick Wildes
Olivia Wiles
Kyle Wilson
David Wipf
Kwan-Yee Wong
Daniel Worrall
John Wright
Baoyuan Wu
Chao-Yuan Wu
Jiajun Wu
Jianxin Wu
Tianfu Wu
Xiaodong Wu
Xiaohe Wu
Xinxiao Wu
Yang Wu
Yi Wu
Ying Wu
Yuxin Wu
Zheng Wu
Stefanie Wuhrer
Yin Xia
Tao Xiang
Yu Xiang
Lei Xiao
Tong Xiao
Yang Xiao
Cihang Xie
Dan Xie
Jianwen Xie

Jin Xie
Lingxi Xie
Pengtao Xie
Saining Xie
Wenxuan Xie
Yuchen Xie
Bo Xin
Junliang Xing
Peng Xingchao
Bo Xiong
Fei Xiong
Xuehan Xiong
Yuanjun Xiong
Chenliang Xu
Danfei Xu
Huijuan Xu
Jia Xu
Weipeng Xu
Xiangyu Xu
Yan Xu
Yuanlu Xu
Jia Xue
Tianfan Xue
Erdem Yörük
Abhay Yadav
Deshraj Yadav
Payman Yadollahpour
Yasushi Yagi
Toshihiko Yamasaki
Fei Yan
Hang Yan
Junchi Yan
Junjie Yan
Sijie Yan
Keiji Yanai
Bin Yang
Chih-Yuan Yang
Dong Yang
Herb Yang
Jianchao Yang
Jianwei Yang
Jiaolong Yang
Jie Yang
Jimei Yang
Jufeng Yang
Linjie Yang

Michael Ying Yang
Ming Yang
Ruiduo Yang
Ruigang Yang
Shuo Yang
Wei Yang
Xiaodong Yang
Yanchao Yang
Yi Yang
Angela Yao
Bangpeng Yao
Cong Yao
Jian Yao
Ting Yao
Julian Yarkony
Mark Yatskar
Jinwei Ye
Mao Ye
Mei-Chen Yeh
Raymond Yeh
Serena Yeung
Kwang Moo Yi
Shuai Yi
Alper Yılmaz
Lijun Yin
Xi Yin
Zhaozheng Yin
Xianghua Ying
Ryo Yonetani
Donghyun Yoo
Ju Hong Yoon
Kuk-Jin Yoon
Chong You
Shaodi You
Aron Yu
Fisher Yu
Gang Yu
Jingyi Yu
Ke Yu
Licheng Yu
Pei Yu
Qian Yu
Rong Yu
Shoou-I Yu
Stella Yu
Xiang Yu

Yang Yu
Zhiding Yu
Ganzhao Yuan
Jing Yuan
Junsong Yuan
Lu Yuan
Stefanos Zafeiriou
Sergey Zagoruyko
Amir Zamir
K. Zampogiannis
Andrei Zanfir
Mihai Zanfir
Pablo Zegers
Eyasu Zemene
Andy Zeng
Xingyu Zeng
Yun Zeng
De-Chuan Zhan
Cheng Zhang
Dong Zhang
Guofeng Zhang
Han Zhang
Hang Zhang
Hanwang Zhang
Jian Zhang
Jianguo Zhang
Jianming Zhang
Jiawei Zhang
Junping Zhang
Lei Zhang
Linguang Zhang
Ning Zhang
Qing Zhang

Quanshi Zhang
Richard Zhang
Runze Zhang
Shanshan Zhang
Shiliang Zhang
Shu Zhang
Ting Zhang
Xiangyu Zhang
Xiaofan Zhang
Xu Zhang
Yimin Zhang
Yinda Zhang
Yongqiang Zhang
Yuting Zhang
Zhanpeng Zhang
Ziyu Zhang
Bin Zhao
Chen Zhao
Hang Zhao
Hengshuang Zhao
Qijun Zhao
Rui Zhao
Yue Zhao
Enliang Zheng
Liang Zheng
Stephan Zheng
Wei-Shi Zheng
Wenming Zheng
Yin Zheng
Yinqiang Zheng
Yuanjie Zheng
Guangyu Zhong
Bolei Zhou

Guang-Tong Zhou
Huiyu Zhou
Jiahuan Zhou
S. Kevin Zhou
Tinghui Zhou
Wengang Zhou
Xiaowei Zhou
Xingyi Zhou
Yin Zhou
Zihan Zhou
Fan Zhu
Guangming Zhu
Ji Zhu
Jiejie Zhu
Jun-Yan Zhu
Shizhan Zhu
Siyu Zhu
Xiangxin Zhu
Xiatian Zhu
Yan Zhu
Yingying Zhu
Yixin Zhu
Yuke Zhu
Zhenyao Zhu
Liansheng Zhuang
Zeeshan Zia
Karel Zimmermann
Daniel Zoran
Danping Zou
Qi Zou
Silvia Zuffi
Wangmeng Zuo
Xinxin Zuo

Contents – Part III

Computational Photography

Light Structure from Pin Motion: Simple and Accurate Point Light Calibration for Physics-Based Modeling

Hiroaki Santo[✉], Michael Waechter, Masaki Samejima, Yusuke Sugano,
and Yasuyuki Matsushita

Osaka University, Osaka, Japan
{santo.hiroaki,waechter.michael,samejima,sugano,
yasumat}@ist.osaka-u.ac.jp

Abstract. We present a practical method for geometric point light source calibration. Unlike in prior works that use Lambertian spheres, mirror spheres, or mirror planes, our calibration target consists of a Lambertian plane and small shadow casters at unknown positions above the plane. Due to their small size, the casters' shadows can be localized more precisely than highlights on mirrors. We show that, given shadow observations from a moving calibration target and a fixed camera, the shadow caster positions and the light position or direction can be simultaneously recovered in a structure from motion framework. Our evaluation on simulated and real scenes shows that our method yields light estimates that are stable and more accurate than existing techniques while having a considerably simpler setup and requiring less manual labor.

This project's source code can be downloaded from: https://github.com/hiroaki-santo/light-structure-from-pin-motion.

Keywords: Light source calibration · Photometric stereo Shape-from-shading · Appearance modeling · Physics-based modeling

1 Introduction

Estimating the position or direction of a light source *accurately* is essential for many physics-based techniques such as shape from shading, photometric stereo, or reflectance and material estimation. In these, inaccurate light positions immediately cause errors. Figure 1 shows the relation between light calibration error and normal estimation error in a synthetic experiment with directional light, a Lambertian sphere as target object, and a basic photometric stereo method [1, 2]. We can see the importance of accurate light calibration: Working on algorithmic improvements in photometric stereo that squeeze out the last few percent in accuracy is futile if the improvements are overshadowed by the calibration inaccuracy. Despite the importance of accurate light calibration, it remains laborious as researchers have not yet come up with accurate *and* easy to use techniques.

This paper proposes a method for calibrating both distant and near point lights. We introduce a calibration target, shown in Fig. 2, that can be made

© Springer Nature Switzerland AG 2018
V. Ferrari et al. (Eds.): ECCV 2018, LNCS 11207, pp. 3–19, 2018.
https://doi.org/10.1007/978-3-030-01219-9_1

from off-the-shelf items for $< \$ 5$ within 1–2 min. Instead of specular highlights on spheres we use a planar board (shadow receiver) and pins (shadow casters) stuck on it that cast small point shadows on the board. Moving the board around in front of a static camera and light source and observing the pin head shadows under various board poses lets us derive the light position/direction.

The accuracy with which we can localize the point shadows is the key factor in the overall calibration accuracy. We can control this through the pin head size. Ideally the shadows should be about 1 px wide, but even with off-the-shelf pins we can automatically localize their centers with an accuracy of about 1–2 px (Fig. 3, *right*), which is in marked contrast to how accurately we can detect specular highlights. Further, since our target is planar, it translates small shadow localization errors only into small light direction errors.

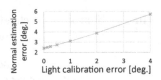

Fig. 1. Light calibration error vs. normal error in photometric stereo. Each data point is the mean of 100 runs.

This is in contrast to mirror sphere methods where the surface normal, which determines the light reflection angle, changes across the sphere and thus amplifies errors. We will come back to these advantages of our method in Sect. 2.

Geometrically, point lights are inverse pinhole cameras [3] (see Fig. 4). We can thus build upon past studies on projective geometry. In particular we show that, analogous to structure from motion (SfM) which jointly estimates camera poses and 3D feature positions, we can jointly estimate light position/direction and shadow caster pin positions from moving our calibration target and observing the pin shadows, *i.e.*, we can estimate light (and pin) *structure from* pin *motion*.

In this paper we clarify the relationship between our problem and conventional SfM and develop a solution technique for our context. Interestingly, our method's connection to SfM allows users to place the pins arbitrarily on the board because their positions will be estimated in the calibration process. This means that – in contrast to many previous works – we do not need to carefully manufacture or measure our calibration target. Further, in contrast to some previous methods, we require no hand annotations in the captured imagery. All required information can be inferred automatically with sufficient accuracy.

The primary contributions of our work are twofold. First, it introduces a practical light source calibration method that uses an easy-to-make calibration target. Instead of requiring a carefully designed calibration target, our method

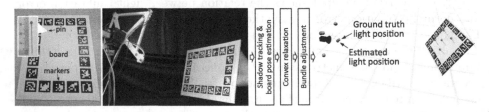

Fig. 2. Our calibration board, a camera observing the movement of shadows cast by a point light while the board moves, our algorithm's workflow, and the estimation result.

Fig. 3. *Left and center:* Specular highlights on a mirror plane [4] and a mirror sphere. *Right:* The pin head shadows on our planar board.

only uses needle pins that are stuck at unknown locations on a plane. Second, we show that the calibration of point light source positions/directions can be formulated as a bundle adjustment problem using the observations of cast shadows, and develop a robust solution technique for accurately achieving the calibration.

The benefits from the new calibration target and associated solution method are an extremely simple target construction process (shown in the supplemental video), a calibration process that requires no manual intervention other than moving the board, and improved accuracy compared to prior work.

2 Related Work

Light source calibration methods can be roughly divided into three categories: (1) estimating light source directions for scenes with a distant point light source, (2) estimating illumination distributions in natural light source environments, and (3) estimating light source positions in scenes with a near point light source.

In the first category, Zhang and Yang [5] (and Wei [6] with a more robust implementation) proposed a method to estimate multiple distant light directions based on a Lambertian sphere's shadow boundaries and their intensities. Wang and Samaras [7] extended this to objects of arbitrary but known shape, combining information from the object's shading and the shadows cast on the scene. Zhou and Kambhamettu [8] used stereo images of a reference sphere with specular reflection to estimate light directions. Cao and Shah [9] proposed a method for estimating camera parameters and the light direction from shadows cast by common vertical objects such as walls instead of special, precisely fabricated objects, which can be used for images from less restricted settings.

In the second category, Sato *et al.* [10,11] used shadows of an object of known shape to estimate illumination distributions of area lights while being restricted to distant light and having to estimate the shadow receiver's reflectance.

In the third category, Powell *et al.* [12] triangulate multiple light positions from highlights on three specular spheres at known positions. Other methods also use reflective spheres [13–16] or specially designed geometric objects [17–19]. In contrast to some of these methods' simple triangulation schemes, Ackermann *et al.* [20] model the light estimation as nonlinear least squares minimization of highlight reprojection errors, yielding improved accuracy. Park *et al.* [21] handle non-isotropic lights and estimate light position and radiant intensity distribution from multi-view imagery of the shading and specular reflections on a plane. Further, some methods are based on planar mirrors [4, 22]. They model the mirror by perspective projection and infer parameters similar to camera calibration.

In highlight-based calibration methods, precisely localizing the light source center's reflection on the specular surface is problematic in practice: Even with the shortest exposure at which we can still barely detect or annotate other parts of the calibration target (pose detection markers, sphere outline, *etc.*), the highlight is much bigger than the light source's image itself (see Fig. 3, *left* and *center*). Lens flare, noise, *etc.* further complicate segmenting the highlight.

Also, since the highlight is generally not a circle but a conic section on a mirror plane or an even more complicated shape on a mirror sphere, the light source center's image (*i.e.*, the intersection of the mirror and the light cone's axis) cannot be found by computing the highlight's centroid, as for example Shen *et al.* [4] do. We thus argue that it is extremely hard to reliably localize light source centers on specular surfaces with pixel accuracy – even with careful manual annotation. Instead, we employ small cast shadows for stable localization.

Mirror sphere-based calibration methods suffer from the fact that the sphere curvature amplifies highlight localization errors into larger light direction errors because the surface orientation, which determines the reflection angle, differs between erroneous and correct highlight location. Also, the spheres need to be very precise since "even slight geometric inaccuracies on the surface can lead to highlights that are offset by several pixels and markedly influence the stability of the results" (Ackermann *et al.* [20]). The prices of precise spheres (~$40 for a high-quality 60 mm bearing ball of which we need 3–8 for accurate calibration) rules out high-accuracy sphere-based calibration for users on a tight budget.

Further, sphere methods typically require annotating the sphere outline in the image which is highly tedious if done accurately, as anyone who has done it can confirm. This is because one has to fit a conic section into the sphere's image and the sphere's exact outline is hard to distinguish from the background, especially in dark images, since the sphere also mirrors the background.

The connection between pinhole cameras and point lights has already been shown by others: Hu *et al.* [3] use it in a theoretical setting similar to ours with point objects and shadows. Each shadow yields a line constraint for the light position and they triangulate multiple such constraints by computing the point closest to all lines. However, they only discuss the idea with geometric sketches.

We push the idea further by deriving mathematical solutions, extending it to distant light, embedding it in an SfM framework [23,24] that minimizes reprojection error, deriving an initialization for the non-convex minimization, devising a simple calibration target that leverages our method in the real world, and demonstrating our method's accuracy in simulated and real-world experiments. Given noisy observations, minimizing reprojection error as we do gives better results (see Szeliski [25, Sect. 7.1] or Hartley and Sturm [26]) than the point-closest-to-all-rays triangulation used by Hu *et al.* [3], Shen and Cheng's mirror plane method [4], and most sphere methods prior to Ackermann's [20].

3 Proposed Method

Our method estimates a nearby point light's position or a distant light's direction using a simple calibration target consisting of a shadow receiver plane and shadow casters above the plane. Our method automatically achieves the point light source calibration by observing the calibration target multiple times from a fixed viewpoint under a fixed point light source while changing the calibration target's pose. The positions of the shadow casters on the calibration board are treated *unknown*, which makes it particularly easy to build the target while the problem remains tractable as we will see later in this section.

To illustrate the relationship between light source, shadow caster, and observed shadow, we begin with the shadow formation model which is connected to perspective camera geometry. We then describe our proposed calibration method that is based on bundle adjustment, as well as its implementation details.

We denote matrices and vectors with bold upper and lower case and the homogeneous representation of $\mathbf{v}$ with $\hat{\mathbf{v}}$. Due to space constraints we show the exact derivations of Eqs. (2), (4), (7), and (9) in the supplemental material.

3.1 Shadow Formation Model

Let us for now assume that the pose of the shadow receiver plane Π is fixed to the world coordinate system's x-y plane.

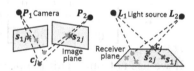

Let a *nearby point light* be located at $\mathbf{l} = [l_x, l_y, l_z]^\top \in \mathbb{R}^3$ in world coordinates. An infinitesimally small caster located at $\mathbf{c} \in \mathbb{R}^3$ in world coordinates casts a shadow on Π at $\mathbf{s} \in \mathbb{R}^2$ in Π's 2D coordinate system which is $\bar{\mathbf{s}} = [\mathbf{s}^\top, 0]^\top$ in world coordinates (because Π coincides with the world's x-y plane). Since $\mathbf{l}$, $\mathbf{c}$ and $\bar{\mathbf{s}}$ are all on one line, the lines $\overline{\mathbf{c}\bar{\mathbf{s}}}$ and $\overline{\mathbf{l}\bar{\mathbf{s}}}$ are parallel:

Fig. 4. Cameras vs. point lights. Camera matrix $\mathbf{P}_i$ projects a scene point $\mathbf{c}_j$ to $\mathbf{s}_{ij}$ just like light matrix $\mathbf{L}_i$ projects $\mathbf{c}_j$ to $\mathbf{s}_{ij}$. SfM estimates $\mathbf{P}_i$ and $\mathbf{c}_j$ from $\{\mathbf{s}_{ij}\}$ and we estimate $\mathbf{L}_i$ and $\mathbf{c}_j$.

$$(\mathbf{c} - \bar{\mathbf{s}}) \times (\mathbf{l} - \bar{\mathbf{s}}) = \mathbf{0}. \tag{1}$$

From this it follows that the shadow formation can be written as

$$\lambda\hat{\mathbf{s}} = \begin{bmatrix} -l_z & 0 & l_x \\ 0 & -l_z & l_y \\ 0 & 0 & 1 \end{bmatrix} \begin{bmatrix} 1 & 0 & 0 & -l_x \\ 0 & 1 & 0 & -l_y \\ 0 & 0 & 1 & -l_z \end{bmatrix} \hat{\mathbf{c}} = \begin{bmatrix} -l_z & 0 & l_x & 0 \\ 0 & -l_z & l_y & 0 \\ 0 & 0 & 1 & -l_z \end{bmatrix} \hat{\mathbf{c}} = \mathbf{L}\hat{\mathbf{c}}. \tag{2}$$

As such, point lights and pinhole cameras can be described by similar mathematical models with the following correspondences: (light source $\Leftrightarrow$ camera), (shadow receiver plane $\Leftrightarrow$ image plane), (shadow caster $\Leftrightarrow$ observed point), and (first two matrices of Eq. (2) $\Leftrightarrow$ camera intrinsics and extrinsics), see Fig. 4.

For *distant light* all light rays in the scene are parallel, $\mathbf{l} = [l_x, l_y, l_z]^\top$ is a light direction instead of a position, and the line $\overline{\mathbf{cs}}$ is parallel to $\mathbf{l}$:

$$(\mathbf{c} - \bar{\mathbf{s}}) \times \mathbf{l} = \mathbf{0}. \tag{3}$$

From this follows an expression that resembles orthographic projection:

$$\lambda \hat{\mathbf{s}} = \begin{bmatrix} -l_z & 0 & l_x & 0 \\ 0 & -l_z & l_y & 0 \\ 0 & 0 & 0 & -l_z \end{bmatrix} \hat{\mathbf{c}} = \mathbf{L}\hat{\mathbf{c}}. \tag{4}$$

3.2   Light Source Calibration as Bundle Adjustment

Our goal is to determine the light source position or direction $\mathbf{l}$ in Eqs. (2) or (4) by observing the shadows cast by unknown casters. A single shadow observation $\mathbf{s}$ does not provide sufficient information to solve this. We thus let the receiver plane undergo multiple poses $\{[\mathbf{R}_i|\mathbf{t}_i]\}$. In pose i, the light position $\mathbf{l}_i$ in receiver plane coordinates is related to $\mathbf{l}$ in world coordinates as

$$\mathbf{l}_i = \left[l_x^{(i)}\ l_y^{(i)}\ l_z^{(i)}\right]^\top = \mathbf{R}_i^\top \mathbf{l} - \mathbf{R}_i^\top \mathbf{t}_i.$$

With this index i the matrices $\{\mathbf{L}_i\}$ for nearby and distant light, resp., become

$$\mathbf{L}_i = \begin{bmatrix} -l_z^{(i)} & 0 & l_x^{(i)} & 0 \\ 0 & -l_z^{(i)} & l_y^{(i)} & 0 \\ 0 & 0 & 1 & -l_z^{(i)} \end{bmatrix}, \quad \text{and} \quad \mathbf{L}_i = \begin{bmatrix} -l_z^{(i)} & 0 & l_x^{(i)} & 0 \\ 0 & -l_z^{(i)} & l_y^{(i)} & 0 \\ 0 & 0 & 0 & -l_z^{(i)} \end{bmatrix}.$$

If we use not only multiple poses $\{[\mathbf{R}_i|\mathbf{t}_i]\}$ but also multiple shadow casters $\{\mathbf{c}_j\}$ (to increase the calibration accuracy as we show later), we obtain shadows $\{\mathbf{s}_{ij}\}$ for each combination of pose i and caster j. Equations (2) and (4) then become

$$\lambda_{ij}\hat{\mathbf{s}}_{ij} = \mathbf{L}_i\hat{\mathbf{c}}_j.$$

Assuming that the target poses $\{[\mathbf{R}_i|\mathbf{t}_i]\}$ are known, our goal is to estimate the light position $\mathbf{l}$ in world coordinates and the shadow caster locations $\{\mathbf{c}_j\}$. We formulate this as a least-squares objective function of the reprojection error:

$$\min_{\mathbf{l},\mathbf{c}_j,\lambda_{ij}} \sum_{i,j} \|\lambda_{ij}\hat{\mathbf{s}}_{ij} - \mathbf{L}_i\hat{\mathbf{c}}_j\|_2^2 \quad \text{s.t.} \quad \mathbf{l} = \mathbf{R}_i\mathbf{l}_i + \mathbf{t}_i. \tag{5}$$

We solve this nonlinear least-squares problem with Levenberg-Marquardt [27]. For robust estimation we use RANSAC: We repeatedly choose a random observation set, estimate $(\mathbf{l}, \mathbf{c}_j, \lambda_{ij})$, and select the estimate with the smallest residual.

Initialization: Equation (5) is non-convex and thus affected by the initialization. To find a good initial guess, we relax our problem into a convex one as follows.

In the near light case, the objective can be written analogous to Eq. (1) as $(\mathbf{c}_j - \bar{\mathbf{s}}_{ij}) \times (\mathbf{l}_i - \bar{\mathbf{s}}_{ij}) = \mathbf{0}$ and (using $\mathbf{l}_i = \mathbf{R}_i^\top \mathbf{l} - \mathbf{R}_i^\top \mathbf{t}_i$) rewritten as

$$(\mathbf{c}_j - \bar{\mathbf{s}}_{ij}) \times (\mathbf{R}_i^\top \mathbf{l} - \mathbf{R}_i^\top \mathbf{t}_i - \bar{\mathbf{s}}_{ij}) = \mathbf{0}. \tag{6}$$

With $\mathbf{c}_j = [c_{j,x}, c_{j,y}, c_{j,z}]^\top$, $\bar{\mathbf{s}}_{ij} = [s_x, s_y, 0]^\top$, $\mathbf{R}_i^\top = \begin{bmatrix} r_0 & r_1 & r_2 \\ r_3 & r_4 & r_5 \\ r_6 & r_7 & r_8 \end{bmatrix}$, $\mathbf{l} = [l_x, l_y, l_z]^\top$, and $-\mathbf{R}_i^\top \mathbf{t}_i = [t_x, t_y, t_z]^\top$, we obtain the following equation system:

$$\underbrace{\begin{bmatrix} r_6 s_y & -r_6 s_x & r_3 s_x - r_0 s_y \\ r_7 s_y & -r_7 s_x & r_4 s_x - r_1 s_y \\ r_8 s_y & -r_8 s_x & r_5 s_x - r_2 s_y \\ 0 & t_z & s_y - t_y \\ -t_z & 0 & -s_x + t_x \\ -s_y + t_y & s_x - t_x & 0 \\ 0 & r_6 & -r_3 \\ -r_6 & 0 & r_0 \\ r_3 & -r_0 & 0 \\ 0 & r_7 & -r_4 \\ -r_7 & 0 & r_1 \\ r_4 & -r_1 & 0 \\ 0 & r_8 & -r_5 \\ -r_8 & 0 & r_2 \\ r_5 & -r_2 & 0 \end{bmatrix}^\top}_{\mathbf{A}_{ij}} \underbrace{\begin{bmatrix} l_x \\ l_y \\ l_z \\ c_{j,x} \\ c_{j,y} \\ c_{j,z} \\ l_x c_{j,x} \\ l_x c_{j,y} \\ l_x c_{j,z} \\ l_y c_{j,x} \\ l_y c_{j,y} \\ l_y c_{j,z} \\ l_z c_{j,x} \\ l_z c_{j,y} \\ l_z c_{j,z} \end{bmatrix}}_{\boldsymbol{\theta}_j} = \underbrace{\begin{bmatrix} -s_y t_z \\ s_x t_z \\ s_y t_x - s_x t_y \end{bmatrix}}_{\mathbf{b}_{ij}}. \tag{7}$$

For distant light the objective is written analogous to Eq. (3) (using $\mathbf{l}_i = \mathbf{R}_i^\top \mathbf{l}$):

$$(\mathbf{c}_j - \bar{\mathbf{s}}_{ij}) \times \mathbf{R}_i^\top \mathbf{l} = \mathbf{0}. \tag{8}$$

Keeping the definitions of $\mathbf{c}_j$, $\bar{\mathbf{s}}_{ij}$, and $\mathbf{R}_i^\top$ from above but setting $\mathbf{l} = [l_x, l_y, 1]^\top$ to reduce $\mathbf{l}$ to two degrees of freedom, the system becomes

$$\underbrace{\begin{bmatrix} r_6 s_y & -r_6 s_x & r_3 s_x - r_0 s_y \\ r_7 s_y & -r_7 s_x & r_4 s_x - r_1 s_y \\ 0 & r_8 & -r_5 \\ -r_8 & 0 & r_2 \\ r_5 & -r_2 & 0 \\ 0 & r_6 & -r_3 \\ -r_6 & 0 & r_0 \\ r_3 & -r_0 & 0 \\ 0 & r_7 & -r_4 \\ -r_7 & 0 & r_1 \\ r_4 & -r_1 & 0 \end{bmatrix}^\top}_{\mathbf{A}_{ij}} \underbrace{\begin{bmatrix} l_x \\ l_y \\ c_{j,x} \\ c_{j,y} \\ c_{j,z} \\ l_x c_{j,x} \\ l_x c_{j,y} \\ l_x c_{j,z} \\ l_y c_{j,x} \\ l_y c_{j,y} \\ l_y c_{j,z} \end{bmatrix}}_{\boldsymbol{\theta}_j} = \underbrace{\begin{bmatrix} -s_y r_8 \\ s_x r_8 \\ s_y r_2 - s_x r_5 \end{bmatrix}}_{\mathbf{b}_{ij}}. \tag{9}$$

To make the estimation of $\boldsymbol{\theta}_j$ robust against outliers, we use ℓ_1 minimization:

$$\boldsymbol{\theta}_j^* = \underset{\boldsymbol{\theta}_j}{\operatorname{argmin}} \left\| \mathbf{A}_{ij} \boldsymbol{\theta}_j - \mathbf{b}_{ij} \right\|_1. \tag{10}$$

After obtaining $\boldsymbol{\theta}_j^*$ we disregard the second-order variables $l_x c_{j,x}$, *etc.* – making the problem convex – and use $\mathbf{c}_j^*$ and $\mathbf{l}^*$ as initialization for minimizing Eq. (5).

Minimal Conditions for Initialization: Let N_p and N_c be the number of target poses and casters. For solving Eqs. (7) or (9) we must fulfill

$$\underbrace{3N_p N_c}_{\#\text{equations}} \geq \underbrace{12N_c+3}_{\#\text{variables}} \;\Leftrightarrow\; N_p \geq 4 + \frac{1}{N_c} \quad \text{or} \quad \underbrace{3N_p N_c}_{\#\text{equations}} \geq \underbrace{9N_c+2}_{\#\text{variables}} \;\Leftrightarrow\; N_p \geq 3 + \frac{2}{3N_c}.$$

Thus, 5 and 4 poses suffice for nearby and distant light, resp., regardless of N_c.

3.3 Implementation

To obtain our target's pose $\{[\mathbf{R}_i|\mathbf{t}_i]\}$, we print ArUco markers [28] on a piece of paper, attach it to the target (see Fig. 2, *left*), and use OpenCV 3D pose estimation [29]. Our shadow casters are off-the-shelf pins with a length of $\sim$30 mm and a head diameter of $\sim$3 mm, which is big enough to easily detect and small enough to accurately localize them. As mentioned, we can place the pins arbitrarily.

For shadow detection we developed a simple template matching scheme. For the templates we generated synthetic images of shadows consisting of a line with a circle at the end. To deal with varying projective transformations we use 12 rotation angles with 3 scalings each. We match the templates after binarizing the input image to extract shadowed regions more easily. Further we use the color of the pin heads to distinguishing between heads and head shadows.

For Eqs. (5), (7), and (9) we need to assign the same index j to all shadows $\bar{\mathbf{s}}_{ij}$ from the same caster $\mathbf{c}_j$ in different images. Normal SfM solves this correspondence problem using the appearance of feature points. We want our shadows to be very small and can therefore not alter their shape enough to make them clearly distinguishable. Instead, we track them through a video of the calibration process. To facilitate the tracking, we place the pins far apart from each other.

3.4 Estimating Multiple Lights Simultaneously

We can even calibrate multiple lights simultaneously to (a) save time by letting the user capture data for multiple lights in one video and (b) increase the estimation accuracy by constraining each caster's position by multiple lines from a light through the caster to a shadow (Fig. 5).

Above we discussed that tracking helps us find corresponding shadows from the same caster across all images. Multiple lights entail another correspondence problem: finding all shadows from the same

Fig. 5. Two lights casting two shadows per pin.

light to couple the correct shadows $\bar{\mathbf{s}}_{i,j,k}$ and lights $\mathbf{l}_{i,k}$ in our equations. To solve this we first put each shadow track *separately* into our algorithm. For each of the

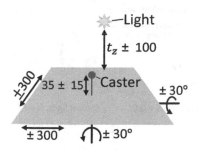

Fig. 6. Arrows show value ranges for our simulation experiments.

Table 1. Estimation error (mean of ten random trials) in a synthetic, noise-free setting.

	t_z	N_c	mean absolute/angular error of light source positions/directions
near light	500	2	6.4×10^{-14}
	500	5	9.5×10^{-14}
	500	10	5.4×10^{-14}
	1000	2	3.5×10^{-13}
	1000	5	7.0×10^{-14}
	1000	10	2.6×10^{-13}
distant light	∞	2	1.2×10^{-12} deg.
	∞	5	2.4×10^{-15} deg.
	∞	10	1.4×10^{-12} deg.

N_l lights we get N_c position estimates which vary slightly due to noise. We then cluster the $N_l \times N_c$ estimates into N_l clusters, each corresponding to one light. Finally we solve the bundle adjustment, Eq. (5), with an additional summation over all lights. We initialize Eq. (5) with the mean of the first step's N_c duplicate estimates.

This solution for the correspondence problem only requires users to provide N_l and in contrast to, *e.g.*, Powell *et al.*'s [12] ordering constraint it does not fail in certain configurations of camera, lights and target. The clustering might, however, produce wrong clusters if two lights are so close that their clusters overlap, but this may be practically irrelevant since in physics-based modeling two lights need to be far enough apart to give an information gain over one light.

Interestingly, we can even simultaneously calibrate lights whose imagery has not been captured simultaneously. This is possible since applying the board poses transforms all shadow positions – no matter whether they were captured simultaneously or not – into the same coordinate system, namely the target's.

4   Evaluation

We now assess our method's accuracy using simulation experiments (Sect. 4.1) and real-world scenes (Sect. 4.2).

4.1   Simulation

We randomly sampled board poses, caster positions and light positions (the latter only for near light conditions) from uniform distributions within the ranges shown in Fig. 6. The casters were randomly placed on a board of size 200×200. For distant light, we sampled the light direction's polar angle θ from $[0°, 45°]$.

We evaluated the absolute/angular error of estimated light positions/directions while varying the distance t_z of the light to the calibration board and the number of casters N_c. Table 1 shows that the mean error of each configuration is 14 or more orders of magnitude smaller than the scene extent,

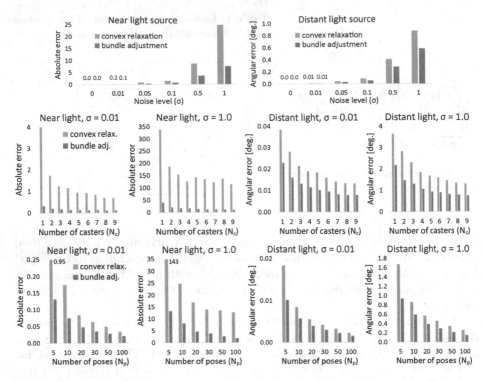

Fig. 7. Estimation error for synthetic near and distant light with Gaussian noise added to the shadow positions. Each data point is the median of 500 random trials. *Top row:* $N_p = 10$ and $N_c = 5$. The noise's standard deviation σ is on the x-axis. *Middle row:* $N_p = 5$ and N_c is on the x-axis. *Bottom row:* $N_c = 5$ and N_p is on the x-axis.

confirming that our method solves the joint estimation of light position/direction and shadow caster positions accurately in an ideal setup. In practice, light source estimates will be deteriorated by two main error sources: (1) Shadow localization and (2) the marker-based board pose estimation.

Shadow Localization Errors: To analyze the influence of shadow localization, we perturbed the shadow positions with Gaussian noise. Figure 7 shows the estimation accuracy obtained as solutions from the convex relaxation (Eq. (7) or (9)) compared to the full bundle adjustment (Eq. (5) after initialization with convex relaxation) for near and distant light in various settings. Figure 7's top row confirms that larger shadow position noise results in larger error and full bundle adjustment mitigates the error compared to solving only the convex relaxation. Increasing the number of casters or board poses makes Eqs. (10) and (5) more overconstrained and should thus reduce the error from noisy shadow locations. Figure 7's middle and bottom row confirm decreasing errors for larger N_p or N_c.

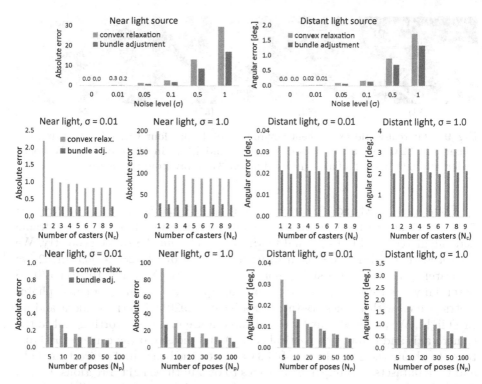

Fig. 8. Estimation error for synthetic near and distant light with Gaussian
<u>noise added to the board orientation</u> (in deg.). Each data point is the median of 500
random trials. *Top row:* $N_p = 10$ and $N_c = 5$. The noise's standard deviation σ is on
the x-axis. *Middle row:* $N_p = 5$ and N_c is on the x-axis. *Bottom row:* $N_c = 5$ and N_p
is on the x-axis.

Board Pose Estimation Errors: To simulate errors in the board pose estimation,
we performed an experiment where we added Gaussian noise to the board's
roll, pitch, and yaw. Figure 8's top row shows that the error is again higher
for stronger noise and the bundle adjustment mitigates the error of the convex
relaxation. In Fig. 8's middle and bottom row we increase the number of casters
and board poses again. Bundle adjustment and increasing the number of poses
reduce the error, but increasing the number of casters does not. However, this
is not surprising since adding constraints to our system only helps if the constraints have independent noise. Here, the noises for all shadows $\bar{\mathbf{s}}_{i,j}$ of the same
pose i stem from the same pose noise and are thus highly correlated. Therefore,
increasing the number of poses is the primary method of error reduction.

4.2   Real-World Experiments

We created 4 real-world environments, see Fig. 9. In all experiments we calibrated
the intrinsic camera parameters beforehand and removed lens distortions.

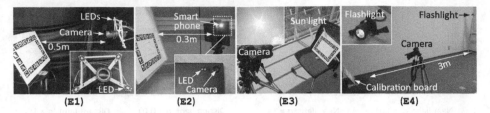

Fig. 9. Our real-world experiment environments. E1 has four LEDs fixed around the camera. In E2 we use a smartphone's camera and LED. In E3 we observe the board under sun light. E4 has a flashlight fixed about 3 m away from the board.

Environments E1 and E2 have near light, and E3 and E4 have distant light. In E1 we fixed four LEDs to positions around the camera with a 3D printed frame and calculated the LED's ground truth locations from the frame geometry. We used a FLIR FL2G-13S2C-C camera with a resolution of 1280 × 960. In E2 we separately calibrated two smartphones (Sony Xperia XZs and Huawei P9) to potentially open up the path for simple, inexpensive, end user oriented photometric stereo with phones. Both phones have a 1920 × 1080 px camera and an LED light. We assumed that LED and camera are in a plane (orthogonal to the camera axis and through the optical center) and measured the camera-LED distance to obtain the ground truth. In E3 we placed the board under direct sun light and took datasets at three different times to obtain three light directions. In E4 a flashlight was fixed about 3 m away from the board to approximate distant lighting. In both E3 and E4 we used a Canon EOS 5D Mark IV with a 35 mm single-focus lens and a resolution of 6720 × 4480 and obtained the ground truth light directions from measured shadow caster positions and hand-annotated shadow positions. In E1, E3, and E4 we used the A4-sized calibration board shown in Fig. 2. In E2, since LED and camera are close together, our normal board's pins occlude the pin shadows in the image as illustrated in Fig. 11(a). We thus used an A6-sized board with four pins with 2 mm heads and brought it close to the camera to effectively increase the baseline (see Fig. 11(b)).

Table 2. Estimation errors in our four real-world scenes.

Scene	Number of experiments	Abs./ang. light error		Abs. caster position error	
		Mean	Stdev.	Mean	Stdev.
E1	4 lights	6.4 mm	2.6 mm	1.8 mm	0.44 mm
E2	2 phones	2.5 mm	0.30 mm	1.2 mm	0.61 mm
E3	3 sun positions	1.1 deg.	0.34 deg.	2.0 mm	0.52 mm
E4	1 light	0.5 deg.	–	1.7 mm	0.51 mm

Table 2 shows the achieved estimation results. The light position errors are ~6.5 mm for E1 and ~2.5 mm for E2 (whose scene extent and target is smaller),

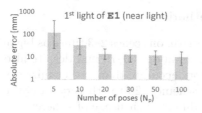 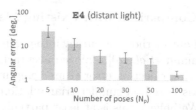

Fig. 10. Estimation error for the first light of scene **E1** and for scene **E4**. For each scene we captured 200 images, randomly picked N_p images from these, and estimated the light and caster positions. The gray bars and error bars represent median and interquartile range of 100 random iterations of this procedure.

the light direction errors are ~1°, and the caster position errors are $\le 2\,\text{mm}$. Figure 10 shows how increasing the number of board poses monotonously decreases the estimation error on two of our real-world scenes.

4.3   Estimating Multiple Lights Simultaneously

Capturing and estimating scene **E1**'s two top lights simultaneously (reliably detecting shadows of > 2 lights requires a better detector) as described in Sect. 3.4 reduces the mean light and caster position errors from 7.3 and 1.8 mm to 3.5 and 1.5 mm respectively. As mentioned, we can also jointly calibrate lights whose imagery was captured separately. For **E1** this decreases errors as shown in Table 3.

Table 3. Average estimation errors (all units in mm) in scene **E1** for 2, 3, and 4 lights captured separately and calibrated separately or simultaneously respectively.

Calibration	2 lights				3 lights				4 lights			
	Light err.		Caster err.		Light err.		Caster err.		Light err.		Caster err.	
	Mean	Stdev.	Mean	Stdev.	Mean	Stdev.	Mean	Stdev.	Mean	Stdev.	Mean	Stdev.
Separate	7.34	**1.00**	1.81	0.39	7.82	2.39	1.80	0.39	6.40	2.63	1.79	**0.44**
Simultaneous	**6.84**	1.74	**1.74**	**0.38**	**6.92**	**1.08**	**1.78**	0.39	**6.23**	**0.94**	**1.77**	0.46

Table 4. Estimation error in scene **E1** (averaged over **E1**'s 4 lights) for *Ours* and *Shen*.

Method	Mean of light error	Stdev. of light error
Ours, shadows hand-annotated	9.45 mm	1.06 mm
Ours, shadows detected	15.4 mm	7.45 mm
Shen, highlights hand-annotated	18.6 mm	5.33 mm

4.4 Comparison with Existing Method

To put our method's accuracy into perspective, on scenes 2–3 times as big as ours Ackermann *et al.* [20] achieved accuracies of about 30–70 mm despite also minimizing reprojection error (thus being more accurate than earlier mirror sphere methods based on simpler triangulation schemes [26]) with very careful execution. We believe this is at least partially due to their usage of spheres.

In this section we compare our calibration method – denoted as *Ours* – with an existing method. Because of Ackermann's achieved accuracy we ruled out spheres and compared to a reimplementation of a state-of-the-art method based on a planar mirror [4] – denoted as *Shen*. Their method observes the specular reflection of the point light in the mirror, also models the mirror with perspective projection and infers parameters similar to camera calibration. In our implementation of *Shen* we again used ArUco markers to obtain the mirrors pose and we annotated the highlight positions manually. For a fair comparison we also annotated the shadow positions for our method manually.

In both methods we observed the target while varying its pose ~500 mm away from the light source. We captured 30 poses for each method and annotated the shadows/reflections. Table 4 shows the estimation error of light source positions for *Ours* and *Shen* in scene E1. *Ours* with hand-annotated shadows as well as detected shadows outperforms *Shen* with annotated highlights.

5 Discussion

With our noise-free simulation experiments we verified that our formulation is correct and the solution method derives accurate estimates with negligible numerical errors. Thus, the solution quality is rather governed by the inaccuracy of board pose estimation and shadow detection. We showed on synthetic and real-world scenes that even with these inaccuracies our method accurately estimates light source positions/directions with measurements from a sufficient number of shadow casters and board poses, which can easily be collected by moving the proposed calibration target in front of the camera. Further, we showed that we can increase the calibration accuracy by estimating multiple lights simultaneously.

A comparison with a state-of-the-art method based on highlights on a mirror plane showed our method's superior accuracy. We believe the reason lies in our pin shadows' accurate localizability. As discussed in Sect. 2, highlights are hard to localize accurately. In contrast, our pin shadows do not "bleed" into their neighborhood and we can easily control their size through the pin head size. If higher localization accuracy is required, one can choose pins smaller than ours.

In contrast to related work, our method requires no tedious, error-prone hand annotations of, *e.g.*, sphere outlines, no precisely fabricated objects such as precise spheres, and no precise measurements of, *e.g.*, sphere positions. Our target's construction is simple, fast and cheap and most calibration steps (*e.g.*, board pose estimation and shadow detection/matching) run automatically.

The only manual interaction – moving the board and recording a video – is simple. To our knowledge no other method combines such simplicity and accuracy.

We want to add a thought on calibration target design: Ackermann [20] pointed out that narrow baseline targets (e.g., Powell's [12]) have a high light position uncertainty along the light direction. This uncertainty can be decreased by either building a big, static target such as two widely spaced spheres, or by moving the target in the scene as we do. So, again our method is strongly connected to SfM where camera movement is the key to reducing depth uncertainty.

Limitations: One limitation of our method is that it requires the camera to be able to capture sequential images (i.e., a video) for tracking the shadows to solve the shadow correspondence problem. If the casters are sufficiently far apart, a solution would be to cluster the shadows in the board coordinate system. The second limitation are scenes where light and camera are so close together that the caster occludes the image of the

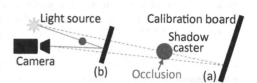

Fig. 11. With a small camera-to-light baseline the caster may occlude the shadow as seen from the camera (a). To solve this, we use a small caster, bring the board close to the camera (b) and make the board smaller so the camera can capture it fully.

shadow (see Fig. 11(a)). This occured in our smartphone environment **E2** and the solution is to effectively increase the baseline between camera and light as shown in Fig. 11(b).

Future Work: It may be possible to alleviate the occlusion problem above with a shadow detection that handles partial occlusions. Further, we want to analyze degenerate cases where our equations are rank deficient, e.g., a board with one caster being moved such that its shadow stays on the same spot. Finally, we want to solve the correspondences between shadows from multiple lights (Sect. 4.3) more mathematically principled with equations that describe the co-movement of shadows from one light and multiple casters on a moving plane.

Acknowledgments. This work was supported by JSPS KAKENHI Grant Number JP16H01732. Michael Waechter is grateful for support through a postdoctoral fellowship by the Japan Society for the Promotion of Science.

References

1. Silver, W.M.: Determining shape and reflectance using multiple images. Master's thesis, Massachusetts Institute of Technology (1980)
2. Woodham, R.J.: Photometric method for determining surface orientation from multiple images. Opt. Eng. **19**(1), 139–144 (1980)
3. Hu, B., Brown, C.M., Nelson, R.C.: The geometry of point light source from shadows. Technical report UR CSD/TR810, University of Rochester (2004)

4. Shen, H.L., Cheng, Y.: Calibrating light sources by using a planar mirror. J. Electron. Imaging **20**(1), 013002-1–013002-6 (2011)
5. Zhang, Y., Yang, Y.H.: Multiple illuminant direction detection with application to image synthesis. IEEE Trans. Pattern Anal. Mach. Intell. (PAMI) **23**(8), 915–920 (2001)
6. Wei, J.: Robust recovery of multiple light source based on local light source constant constraint. Pattern Recogn. Lett. **24**(1), 159–172 (2003)
7. Wang, Y., Samaras, D.: Estimation of multiple directional light sources for synthesis of mixed reality images. In: Proceedings of the Pacific Conference on Computer Graphics and Applications, pp. 38–47 (2002)
8. Zhou, W., Kambhamettu, C.: Estimation of illuminant direction and intensity of multiple light sources. In: Heyden, A., Sparr, G., Nielsen, M., Johansen, P. (eds.) ECCV 2002. LNCS, vol. 2353, pp. 206–220. Springer, Heidelberg (2002). https://doi.org/10.1007/3-540-47979-1_14
9. Cao, X., Shah, M.: Camera calibration and light source estimation from images with shadows. In: Proceedings of the IEEE Conference on Computer Vision and Pattern Recognition (CVPR), pp. 918–923 (2005)
10. Sato, I., Sato, Y., Ikeuchi, K.: Stability issues in recovering illumination distribution from brightness in shadows. In: Proceedings of the IEEE Conference on Computer Vision and Pattern Recognition (CVPR), pp. II-400-II-407 (2001)
11. Sato, I., Sato, Y., Ikeuchi, K.: Illumination from shadows. IEEE Trans. Pattern Anal. Mach. Intell. (PAMI) **25**(3), 290–300 (2003)
12. Powell, M.W., Sarkar, S., Goldgof, D.: A simple strategy for calibrating the geometry of light sources. IEEE Trans. Pattern Anal. Mach. Intell. (PAMI) **23**(9), 1022–1027 (2001)
13. Hara, K., Nishino, K., Ikeuchi, K.: Light source position and reflectance estimation from a single view without the distant illumination assumption. IEEE Trans. Pattern Anal. Mach. Intell. (PAMI) **27**(4), 493–505 (2005)
14. Wong, K.-Y.K., Schnieders, D., Li, S.: Recovering light directions and camera poses from a single sphere. In: Forsyth, D., Torr, P., Zisserman, A. (eds.) ECCV 2008. LNCS, vol. 5302, pp. 631–642. Springer, Heidelberg (2008). https://doi.org/10.1007/978-3-540-88682-2_48
15. Takai, T., Maki, A., Niinuma, K., Matsuyama, T.: Difference sphere: an approach to near light source estimation. Comput. Vis. Image Underst. J. (CVIU) **113**(9), 966–978 (2009)
16. Schnieders, D., Wong, K.Y.K.: Camera and light calibration from reflections on a sphere. Comput. Vis. Image Underst. J. (CVIU) **117**(10), 1536–1547 (2013)
17. Weber, M., Cipolla, R.: A practical method for estimation of point light-sources. In: Proceedings of the British Machine Vision Conference (BMVC), vol. 2, pp. 471–480 (2001)
18. Aoto, T., Taketomi, T., Sato, T., Mukaigawa, Y., Yokoya, N.: Position estimation of near point light sources using a clear hollow sphere. In: Proceedings of the International Conference on Pattern Recognition (ICPR), pp. 3721–3724 (2012)
19. Bunteong, A., Chotikakamthorn, N.: Light source estimation using feature points from specular highlights and cast shadows. Int. J. Phys. Sci. **11**(13), 168–177 (2016)
20. Ackermann, J., Fuhrmann, S., Goesele, M.: Geometric point light source calibration. In: Proceedings of Vision, Modeling, and Visualization, pp. 161–168 (2013)
21. Park, J., Sinha, S.N., Matsushita, Y., Tai, Y., Kweon, I.: Calibrating a non-isotropic near point light source using a plane. In: Proceedings of the IEEE Conference on Computer Vision and Pattern Recognition (CVPR), pp. 2267–2274 (2014)

22. Schnieders, D., Wong, K.-Y.K., Dai, Z.: Polygonal light source estimation. In: Zha, H., Taniguchi, R., Maybank, S. (eds.) ACCV 2009. LNCS, vol. 5996, pp. 96–107. Springer, Heidelberg (2010). https://doi.org/10.1007/978-3-642-12297-2_10

23. Snavely, N., Seitz, S.M., Szeliski, R.: Photo tourism: exploring photo collections in 3D. In: Proceedings of SIGGRAPH, pp. 835–846 (2006)

24. Triggs, B., McLauchlan, P.F., Hartley, R.I., Fitzgibbon, A.W.: Bundle adjustment—a modern synthesis. In: Triggs, B., Zisserman, A., Szeliski, R. (eds.) IWVA 1999. LNCS, vol. 1883, pp. 298–372. Springer, Heidelberg (2000). https:// doi.org/10.1007/3-540-44480-7_21

25. Szeliski, R.: Computer Vision: Algorithms and Applications. Springer, Heidelberg (2010). https://doi.org/10.1007/978-1-84882-935-0

26. Hartley, R.I., Sturm, P.: Triangulation. Comput. Vis. Image Underst. J. (CVIU) **68**(2), 146–157 (1997)

27. Nocedal, J., Wright, S.J.: Numerical Optimization. Springer, Heidelberg (2006). https://doi.org/10.1007/978-0-387-40065-5

28. Garrido-Jurado, S., Muñoz-Salinas, R., Madrid-Cuevas, F.J., Marín-Jiménez, M.J.: Automatic generation and detection of highly reliable fiducial markers under occlusion. Pattern Recognit. **47**(6), 2280–2292 (2014)

29. Bradski, G.: The OpenCV library. Dr. Dobb's J. Softw. Tools (2000). https:// github.com/opencv/opencv/wiki/CiteOpenCV

Programmable Triangulation Light Curtains

Jian Wang[✉], Joseph Bartels, William Whittaker,
Aswin C. Sankaranarayanan, and Srinivasa G. Narasimhan

Carnegie Mellon University, Pittsburgh, PA 15213, USA
{jianwan2,josephba,saswin}@andrew.cmu.edu, red@cmu.edu,
srinivas@cs.cmu.edu

Abstract. A vehicle on a road or a robot in the field does not need a full-featured 3D depth sensor to detect potential collisions or monitor its blind spot. Instead, it needs to only monitor if any object comes within its near proximity which is an easier task than full depth scanning. We introduce a novel device that monitors the presence of objects on a virtual shell near the device, which we refer to as a light curtain. Light curtains offer a light-weight, resource-efficient and programmable approach to proximity awareness for obstacle avoidance and navigation. They also have additional benefits in terms of improving visibility in fog as well as flexibility in handling light fall-off. Our prototype for generating light curtains works by rapidly rotating a line sensor and a line laser, in synchrony. The device is capable of generating light curtains of various shapes with a range of 20–30 m in sunlight (40 m under cloudy skies and 50 m indoors) and adapts dynamically to the demands of the task. We analyze properties of light curtains and various approaches to optimize their thickness as well as power requirements. We showcase the potential of light curtains using a range of real-world scenarios.

Keywords: Computational imaging · Proximity sensors

1 Introduction

3D sensors play an important role in the deployment of many autonomous systems including field robots and self-driving cars. However, there are many tasks for which a full-fledged 3D scanner is often unnecessary. For example, consider a robot that is maneuvering a dynamic terrain; here, while full 3D perception is important for long-term path planning, it is less useful for time-critical tasks like obstacle detection and avoidance. Similarly, in autonomous driving, collision avoidance—a task that must be continually performed—does not require full 3D perception of the scene. For such tasks, a proximity sensor with much reduced energy and computational footprint is sufficient.

Electronic supplementary material The online version of this chapter (https://doi.org/10.1007/978-3-030-01219-9_2) contains supplementary material, which is available to authorized users.

© Springer Nature Switzerland AG 2018
V. Ferrari et al. (Eds.): ECCV 2018, LNCS 11207, pp. 20–35, 2018.
https://doi.org/10.1007/978-3-030-01219-9_2

We generalize the notion of proximity sensing by proposing an optical system to detect the presence of objects that intersect a virtual shell around the system. By detecting only the objects that intersect with the virtual shell, we can solve many tasks pertaining to collision avoidance and situational awareness with little or no computational overhead. We refer to this virtual shell as a *light curtain*. We implement light curtains by triangulating an illumination plane, created by fanning out a laser, with a sensing plane of a line sensor (see Fig. 1(a)). In the absence of ambient illumination, the camera senses light only from the intersection between these two planes—which is a line in the physical world. The light curtain is then created by sweeping the illumination and sensing planes in synchrony. This idea can be interpreted as a generalization of pushbroom stereo [6] to active illumination for determining the presence of an object that intersects an arbitrary ruled surface in 3D.

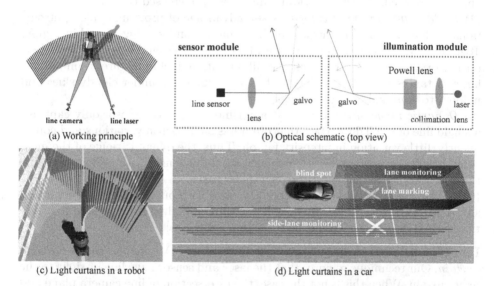

Fig. 1. We introduce the concept of a programmable triangulation light curtain—a safety device that monitors object presence in a virtual shell around the device. (a, b) This is implemented by intersecting a light plane emitted from a line laser and a plane imaged by a line scan camera. The two planes are rapidly rotated in synchrony to generate light curtains of varying shapes as demanded by the specifics of an application. (c, d) Example curtains are shown for use on a robot and a car. The device detects objects on the virtual curtains with little computational overhead, making it useful for collision detection and avoidance.

Benefits of Triangulation Light Curtains. (1) *Shape programmability*: The shape of a light curtain is programmable and can be configured dynamically to suit the demands of the immediate task. For example, light curtains can be used to determine whether a neighboring vehicle is changing lanes, whether a pedestrian is in the crosswalk, or whether there are vehicles in adjacent lanes.

Similarly, a robot might use a curtain that extrudes its planned (even curved) motion trajectory. Figure 1(c, d) shows various light curtains for use in robots and cars.

(2) *Adaptability of power and exposure*: Given an energy budget, in terms of average laser power, exposure time, and refresh rate of the light curtain, we can allocate higher power and exposure to lines in the curtain that are further away to combat inverse-square light fall-off. This is a significant advantage over traditional depth sensors that typically expend the same high power in all directions to capture a 3D point cloud of the entire volume.

(3) *Performance in scattering media*: The optical design of the light curtain shares similarities with confocal imaging [16] in that we selectively illuminate and sense a small region. When imaging in scattering media, such as fog and murky waters, this has the implicit advantage that back scattered photons are optically avoided, thereby providing images with increased contrast.

(4) *Performance in ambient light*: A key advantage of programmable light curtains is that we can concentrate the illumination and sensing to a thin region. Together with the power and exposure adaptability, this enables significantly better performance under strong ambient illumination, including direct sunlight, at large distances ($\sim$20–30 m). The performance increases under cloudy skies and indoors to $40m$ and $50m$ respectively.

(5) *Dynamic range of the sensor*: At any time instant, the sensor only captures a single line of the light curtain that often has small depth variations and consequently, little variation in intensity fall-off. Thus, the dynamic range of the measured brightness is often low. Hence, even a one-bit sensor with a programmable threshold would be ample for the envisioned tasks.

(6) *Sensor types*: Any line sensor could be used with our design including intensity sensors (CMOS, CCD, InGaAs [12]), time-of-flight (ToF) sensors (correlation, SPAD [8]), and neuromorphic sensors (DVS) [15].

Limitations of Triangulation Light Curtains. (1) *Line-of-sight to the light curtain.* Our technique requires that the laser and sensor have line-of-sight to the light curtain. When this is not the case, the intersection of line camera plane and laser sheet is inside the object and is not seen by the camera; so the technique will fail to detect objects intersecting with the light curtain. This can be resolved partially by determining if there is an object between the system and the desired curtain using a curtain whose "shape" is a sparse set of lines. (2) *Interference*: When simultaneously used, several devices can accidentally interfere with each other. This can be alleviated by using a time-of-flight sensor with different light amplitude frequencies or adding a second line camera or several line lasers as further discussed in the supplementary material. (3) *Fast motion*: Objects that move at high speeds might be able to avoid detection by crossing the light curtain in a region between two successive scans. However, the target would need to be highly maneuverable to accomplish this given our high scan rate.

2   Related Work

Safety Devices and Proximity Sensors. Devices such as "light curtains" [1], pressure-sensitive mats, and conductive rubber edges are common safeguards used in homes and factories. They are designed to stop the operation of a machine (e.g. a garage door) automatically upon detection of a nearby object. Such proximity sensing devices use many physical modalities to detect presence including capacitance, inductance, magnetism, infrared, ultrasound, Radar and LIDAR.

Depth Gating. Temporal gating [5,10] uses a combination of a pulsed laser and a camera with gated shutter, typically in the range of pico- to nano-seconds. By delaying the exposure of the camera with respect to the laser pulse, the device enables depth selection. An alternate approach relies on on-chip implementations of temporal modulated light sources and sensors [22]. Our technique can be interpreted as a specialized instance of primal-dual coding [20] where simultaneous coding is performed at the camera and projector to probe the light transport matrix associated with a scene, including implementing depth gating.

The proposed technique is inspired from existing work on robust depth scanning in presence of global and ambient light. Early work on imaging through turbid includes scanning confocal microscopy [16] and light sheet microscopy [25] which both illuminate and image the same depth with very shallow depth of focus and block out-of-focus light i.e. scattered light during image formation. Recent work for 3D measuring in scattering media have line striping-based [18] and SPAD-based [21] methods through analyzing spatial or temporal distribution of photons, respectively. An effective method for handling ambient light is concentrating the active light source's output and scanning. Gupta et al. [11] adjust the light concentration level in a structured light system adaptively according to the ambient light level. Episcan3D [19] and EpiToF [3] scan a line laser and a line sensor in synchrony such that the illumination and the sensing planes are coplanar. Finally, there are many benefits in using special functionality sensors for imaging and depth scanning; examples include the DVS sensor for structured light point scanning at high speed and dynamic range [17] as well as the short-wave infrared sensor for enhanced eye-safe property and decreased scattering [24,26]. Such sensors can be easily incorporated in our light curtains for additional robustness and capabilities.

3   Geometry of Triangulation Light Curtains

The proposed device consists of a line scan camera and a line scan laser, as shown in Fig. 1(a, b). A Powell lens fans a laser beam out into a planar sheet of light and the line camera senses light from a single plane. In the general configuration, the two planes intersect at a line in 3D and, in the absence of ambient and indirect illuminations, the sensor measures light scattered by any object on the line. By rotating both the camera and the laser at a high speed, we can sweep the intersecting line to form any ruled surface [2]. We refer to this ruled surface, on which we detect presence of objects, as the light curtain. The resulting device is programmable, in terms of its light curtain shape, and flexible, in terms of being able to vary laser power and camera exposure time to suit the demands of an application. In this section, we present the mathematical model for a light curtain as a function of the camera and laser rotation axes. Then, we describe how to estimate the camera and laser rotation angles for a particular light curtain shape and show several examples.

We consider the case where the camera and laser can each be rotated about a single fixed parallel axis (see Fig. 2). This can be easily implemented by placing two 1D galvo mirrors, one each in the front of the line sensor and the laser, respectively. Let the camera and laser rotation axes be $\mathbf{r}$. We observe that intersecting line in the curtain will also be parallel and of the form

$$\mathbf{p}_0 + u\mathbf{r},$$

where $\mathbf{p}_0$ is any 3D point on the line and $u \in (-\alpha, \alpha)$ is the offset along the axis of rotation (see Fig. 2(a, b)). Then, the light curtain $s(t, u) \subset \mathbb{R}^3$ is obtained by sweeping the intersection line such that

$$s(t, u) = \mathbf{p}(t) + u\mathbf{r},$$

where $\mathbf{p}(t) \in \mathbb{R}^3$ is a 3D path that describes the points scanned by the center pixel on the line sensor and $t \in [0, 1]$ is the parameterization of the path.

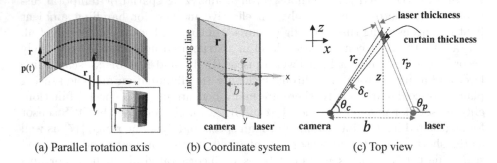

(a) Parallel rotation axis   (b) Coordinate system   (c) Top view

Fig. 2. (a) Viewing and illumination geometry of a triangulation light curtain generated by rotating the laser light plane and sensor plane about parallel axes $\mathbf{r}$. The intersection line is also parallel to the two rotation axes. (b, c) The coordinate frame and top view showing various parameters of interest. Note that changing θ_c and θ_p in synchrony generates light curtains with different shapes. (c) The finite sizes of camera pixels and finite thickness of laser sheet leads to a thick light curtain upon triangulation.

Given a light curtain $s(t, u)$, we next show how to compute the rotation angles of the camera and laser respectively. Without loss of generality, we assume that the origin of our coordinate system is at the midpoint between the centers of the line camera and the laser. We further assume that the rotation axes are aligned along the y-axis and that the 3D path can be written as $\mathbf{p}(t) = [x(t), 0, z(t)]^\top$. To achieve this light curtain, suppose that the laser rotates about its axis with an angular profile of $\theta_p(t)$, where the angle is measured counter-clockwise with respect to the x-axis. Similarly, the line sensor rotates with an angular profile of $\theta_c(t)$. Let b be the baseline between the laser and the line camera. We can derive $\theta_c(t)$ and $\theta_p(t)$ as

$$\begin{bmatrix} \theta_c(t) \\ \theta_p(t) \end{bmatrix} = \begin{bmatrix} \mathrm{atan2}(z(t), x(t) + b/2) \\ \mathrm{atan2}(z(t), x(t) - b/2) \end{bmatrix}. \tag{1}$$

Figure 1(c, d) shows different types of light curtains for use on robots and cars and Fig. 3 explains each in detail. For each curtain, we show the rendered scene with the light curtain, a 2D cross section of the curtain, and the corresponding rotation angle profiles $\theta_c(t)$ and $\theta_p(t)$, computed using (1). The first two light curtains—a cylindrical curtain for safety zone monitoring and a curved curtain for monitoring obstacles along a path—are envisioned for use on robots. The next four kinds of curtains are envisioned for use on cars: ⊓-shape lane curtain to detect proximity vehicles in front as well as those that encroach on to the lane being used (row 3), side curtain to cover blind spot zones (row 4), and a discrete sampling of neighbor lane's condition to identify presence of a vehicle in that volume (row 5). As noted in the introduction, light curtains also offer improved contrast in the presence of scattering media and hence, a curtain observing lane markings (row 6) is especially useful on foggy days.

Our proposed device can also be configured with the line sensor and laser rotating over non-parallel axes or even with each of them enjoying full rotational degree of freedom. These configurations can generate other kinds of ruled surfaces including, for example, a Möbius strip. We leave the discussion to the supplementary material. For applications that require light curtains of arbitrary shapes, we would need to use point sources and detectors; this, however, comes at the cost of large acquisition time that is required for two degrees of freedom in scanning. On the other hand, 2D imaging with a divergent source does not require any scanning but has poor energy efficiency and flexibility. In comparison, line sensors and line lasers provide a unique operating point with high acquisition speeds, high energy efficiency, and a wide range of light curtain shapes.

4   Optimizing Triangulation Light Curtains

We now quantify parameters of interest in practical light curtains—for example their thickness and signal-to-noise ratio (SNR) of measured detections—and approaches to optimize them. In particular, we are interested in minimizing thickness of the curtain as well as optimizing exposure time and laser power for improved detection accuracy when the curtain spans a large range of depths.

Thickness of Light Curtain. The light curtain produced by our device has a finite thickness due to the finite sizes of the sensor pixels and the laser illumination. Suppose that the laser plane has a thickness of Δ_L meters and each pixel has an

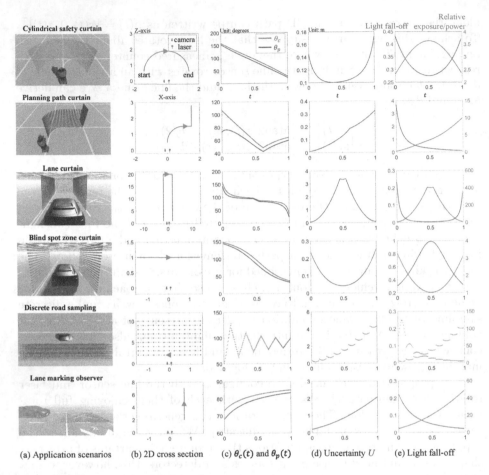

Fig. 3. Different types of light curtains used by a robot and a car. (a) Envisioned application scenarios visualized using 3D renderings. (b) 2D cross section (all units in meters) of the light curtain and placement of the camera and laser (baselines in the first two rows was 300 mm, third row was 2 m, and the remaining rows was 200 mm). The arrow on the curtain indicates the scanning direction. (c) Rotation angle profiles of camera and laser to achieve desired light curtain in each scan. (d) Thickness of the light curtain for a camera with 50 μm pixel width and focal length 6 mm. (e) Light fall-off and the corresponding adaptation of exposure/power to compensate for it.

angular extent of δ_c radians. Given a device with a baseline of length b meters and imaging a point at depth $z(t) = z$, the thickness of the light curtain is given as an area of a parallelogram shaded in Fig. 2(c), which evaluates to

$$A = \frac{r_c^2 r_p}{z} \frac{\delta_c \Delta_L}{b} \qquad (2)$$

where r_c and r_p is the distance between the intersected point and the camera and laser, respectively. We provide the derivation in the supplemental material.

Finally, given that different light curtain geometries can produce curtains of the same area, a more intuitive and meaningful metric for characterizing the thickness is the length

$$U = \frac{A}{\Delta_L} = \frac{r_c^2 r_p}{z} \frac{\delta_c}{b}. \tag{3}$$

In any given system, changing the laser thickness Δ_L requires changing the optics of the illumination module. Similarly, changing δ_c requires either changing the pixel width or the focal length of the camera. In contrast, varying the baseline provides an easier alternative to changing the thickness of the curtain that involves a single translation. This is important since different applications often have differing needs on the thickness of the curtain. A larger baseline helps in achieving very thin curtains which is important when there is a critical need to avoid false alarm. On the other hand, thick curtains that can be achieved by having a smaller baseline are important in scenarios where mis-detections, especially those arising from the discreteness of the curtain, are to be avoided.

In Fig. 3(d), we visualize the thickness of various light curtains. We set the camera's pixel width to 50 μm with a lens of focal length $f = 6$ mm, thereby giving us a value for $\delta_c = \frac{50 \mu m}{f} = 0.008$ radians. The baseline b was set to 300 mm for the first two rows, 2 m for the third row, and 200 mm for the last three rows. For example, for the lane marking observer (last row), a thickness of 2 m at the furthest point is beneficial to deal with uneven roads.

Adapting Laser Power and Exposure. Another key advantage of our light curtain device is that we can adapt the power of the laser or the exposure time for each intersecting line to compensate for light fall-off, which is inversely proportional to the square of the depth. In a traditional projector-camera system, it is common to increase the brightness of the projection to compensate for light fall-off, so that far-away scenes points can be well illuminated; however, this would imply that points close to the camera get saturated easily thereby requiring a high dynamic range camera. In contrast, our system has an additional degree of freedom where-in the laser's power and/or the camera's exposure time can be adjusted according to depth so that light fall-off is compensated to the extent possible under the device constraints and eye safety. Further, because our device only detects presence or absence of objects, in an ideal scenario where albedo is the same everywhere, the laser can send small amounts of light to just overcome the camera's readout noise or the photon noise of ambient light, and only a 1-bit camera is required. Figure 3(e) shows light fall-off and depth-adaptive exposure time or laser power for all the light curtains.

Combining with Time-of-Flight Sensors. The analysis in (3) indicates that $U \approx \frac{z^2 \delta_c}{b}$ when $r_c, r_p \approx z$ and light curtain is expected to get thicker, quadratically, with depth. Increasing baseline and other parameters of the system can only alleviate this effect in part due to the physical constraints on sensor size, laser spot thickness as well as the baseline. We show that replacing the line intensity sensor with a 1D continuous-wave time-of-flight (CW-TOF) sensor [14] alleviates the quadratic dependence of thickness with depth.

CW-TOF sensors measure phase to obtain depth. A CW-TOF sensor works by illuminating the scene with an amplitude modulated wave, typically a periodic signal of frequency f_m Hz, and measuring the phase difference between the illumination and the light received at each pixel. The phase difference ϕ and the depth d of the scene point are related as

$$\phi = \mathrm{mod}\,(f_m d/c, 2\pi)\,.$$

As a consequence, the depth resolution of a TOF sensor $\Delta d = \frac{c\Delta\phi}{f_m}$ (ignoring the phase wrapping) is constant and independent of depth. Further, the depth resolution increases with the frequency of the amplitude wave. However, TOF-based depth recovery has a phase wrapping problem due to the presence of the $\mathrm{mod}(\cdot)$ operator; this implies that the depth estimate has an ambiguity problem and this problem gets worse at higher frequencies. In contrast, traditional triangulation-based depth estimation has no ambiguity problem, but at the cost of quadratic depth uncertainty.

We can leverage the complementary strengths of traditional triangulation and CW-TOF to enable light curtains with near-constant thickness over a large range. This is achieved as follows. First, the phase and intensity of the triangulated region are measured by the CW-TOF sensor; examples of this is shown in Fig. 8(iii, iv). Second, knowing the depth of the curtain, we can calculate the appropriate phase to retain and discard pixels with phase values that are significantly different. An alternative approach to achieving this is to perform phase-based depth gating using appropriate codes at illumination and sensing [22]. The use of triangulation automatically eliminates the depth ambiguity of phase-based gating *provided* the thickness of the triangulation is smaller than half of the wavelength of the amplitude wave. With this, it is possible to create thinner light curtains over a larger depth range.

5　Hardware Prototype

Our prototype device has two modules (see Fig. 4). At the sensor end, we use an Alkeria NECTA N2K2-7 line intensity sensor with a 6 mm $f/2$ S-mount lens whose diagonal FOV is 45° and image circle has a diameter of 7 mm. The line camera has 2048 × 2 pixels with pixel size 7 μm × 7 μm; we only use the central 1000 × 2 pixels due to the lens' limited circle of illumination. The line sensor is capable of reading out 95, 057 lines/s. We fit it with an optical bandpass filter, 630 nm center wavelength and 50 nm bandwidth to suppress ambient light. For the ToF prototype, we used a Hamamatsu S11961-01CR sensor in place of the intensity sensor whose pixel size is 20 μm × 50 μm. We used a low cost 1D galvo mirror to rotate the camera's viewing angle. The 2D helper FLIR camera (shown in the middle) is used for one-time calibration of the device and visualizing the light curtains in the scene of interest by projecting the curtain to its view.

Fig. 4. Hardware prototype with components marked. The prototype implements the schematic shown in Fig. 1(b).

At the illumination side, we used a Thorlabs L638P700M 638 nm laser diode with peak power of 700 mW. The laser is collimated and then stretched into a line with a 45° Powell lens. As with the sensor side, we used a 1D galvo mirror to steer the laser sheet. The galvo mirror has dimension of 11 mm × 7 mm, and has 22.5° mechanical angle and can give the camera and laser 45° FOV since optical angle is twice the mechanical angle. It needs 500 μs to rotate 0.2° optical angle. A micro-controller (Teensy 3.2) is used to synchronize the camera, the laser and the galvos. Finally, we aligned the rotation axes to be parallel and fixed the baseline as 300 mm. The FOV is approximately 45° × 45°.

Ambient Light. The camera also measures the contribution from the ambient light illuminating the entire scene. To suppress this, we capture two images at each setting of the galvos—one with and one without the laser illumination, each with exposure of 100 μs. Subtracting the two suppresses the ambient image.

Scan Rate. Our prototype is implemented with galvo mirrors that take about 500 μs to stabilize, which limits the overall frame-rate of the device. Adding two 100 μs exposures for laser on and off, respectively, allows us to display 1400 lines per second. In our experiments, we design the curtains with 200 lines, and we sweep the entire curtain at a refresh rate of 5.6 fps. To increase the refresh rate, we can use higher-quality galvo mirrors with lower settling time, a 2D rolling shutter camera as in [19] or spatially-multiplexed line camera by digital micromirror device (DMD) [23] in the imaging side and a MEMS mirror on the laser side so that 30 fps can be easily reached.

Calibration and Eye Safety. Successful and safe deployment of light curtains require precise calibration as well as specifications of laser eye safety. Calibration is done by identifying the plane in the real world associated with each setting of laser's galvo and the line associated with each pair of camera's galvo and camera's pixel. We use a helper camera and projector to perform calibration, following steps largely adapted from prior work in calibration [7,13]. The supplemental material has detailed explanation for both calibration and laser eye safety calculations based on standards [4].

6   Results

Evaluating Programmability of Triangulation Light Curtains. Figure 5 shows the results of implementing various light curtain shapes both indoors and outdoors. When nothing "touches" the light curtain, the image is dark; when a person or other intruders touch the light curtain, it is immediately detected. The small insets show the actual images captured by the line sensor (after ambient subtraction) mosaicked for visualization. The light curtain and the detection are geometrically mapped to the 2D helper camera's view for visualization. Our prototype uses a visible spectrum (red) laser and switching to near infrared can improve performance when the visible albedo is low (e.g. dark clothing).

Light Curtains Under Sunlight. Figure 6(a) shows the detections of a white board placed at different depths (verified using a laser range finder) in bright sunlight (~100 klx). The ambient light suppression is good even at 25 m range. Under cloudy skies, the range increases to more than 40 m. Indoors, the range is approximately 50 m. These ranges assume the same refresh rate (and exposure time) for the curtains. In Fig. 6(b), we verify the accuracy of the planar curtains by sweeping a fronto-parallel curtain over a dense set of depths and visualizing the resulting detections as a depth map.

Performance Under Volumetric Scattering. When imaging in scattering media, light curtains provide images with higher contrast by suppressing backscattered light from the medium. This can be observed in Fig. 7 where we show images of an outdoor road sign under heavy smoke from a planar light curtain as well as a conventional 2D camera. The 2D camera provides images with low contrast due to volumetric scattering of the sunlight, the ambient source in the scene.

Reducing Curtain Thickness Using a TOF Sensor. We use our device with a line TOF sensor to form a fronto-parallel light curtain at a fixed depth. The results are shown in Fig. 8. Because of triangulation uncertainty, the camera could see a wide depth range as shown in (a.iii) and (b.iii). However, phase data, (a.iv) and (b.iv) helps to decrease the uncertainty as shown in (a.v) and (b.v). Note that in (b.iv), there is phase wrapping which is mitigated using triangulation.

Adapting Laser Power and Exposure. Finally, we showcase the flexibility of our device in combating light fall-off by adapting the exposure and/or the power of the laser associated with each line in the curtain. We show this using depth maps sensed by sweeping fronto-parallel curtains with various depth settings. For each pixel we assign the depth value of the planar curtain at which its intensity value

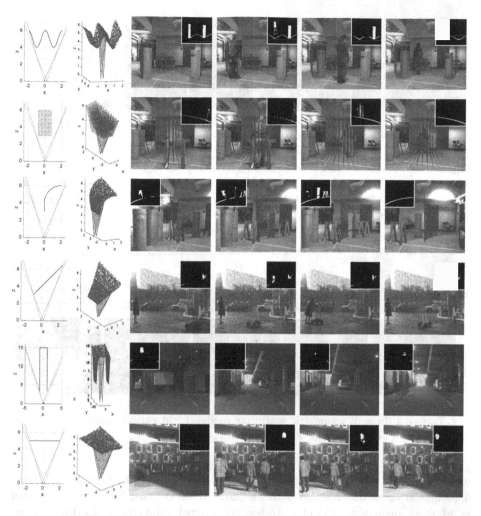

Fig. 5. Generating light curtains with different shapes. The images shown are from the 2D helper camera's view with the light curtain rendered in blue and detections rendered in green. The curtains are shown both indoors and outdoors in sunlight. The insets are images captured by the line sensor as people/objects intersect the curtains. The curtains have 200 lines with a refresh rate of 5.6 fps. The curtain in the second row detects objects by sampling a volume with a discrete set of lines. (Color figure online)

is the highest. We use an intensity map to save this highest intensity value. In Fig. 9(a), we sweep 120 depth planes in an indoor scene. We performed three strategies: two constant exposures per intersecting line and one that is depth-adaptive such that exposure is linear in depth. We show intensity map and depth map for each strategy. Notice the saturation and darkness in intensity maps with the constant exposure strategies and even brightness with the adaptive strategy. The performance of the depth-adaptive exposure is similar to that of a constant

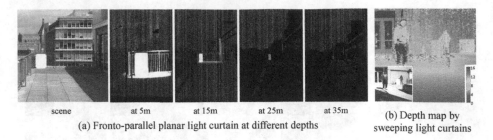

scene   at 5m   at 15m   at 25m   at 35m   (b) Depth map by

(a) Fronto-parallel planar light curtain at different depths   sweeping light curtains

Fig. 6. Performance under bright sunlight (100 klux) for two different scenes. (a) We show raw light curtain data, without post-processing, at various depths from a white board. Notice the small speck of the board visible even at 35 m. (b) We sweep the light curtain over the entire scene to generate a depth map.

Fig. 7. Seeing through volumetric scattering media. Light curtains suppress backscattered light and provide images with improved contrast.

exposure mode whose total exposure time is twice as much. Figure 9(b) shows a result on an outdoor scene with curtains at 40 depths, but here the power is adapted linearly with depth. As before, a depth-adaptive budgeting of laser power produces depth maps that are similar to those of a constant power mode with 2× the total power. Strictly speaking, depth-adaptive budgeting should be quadratic though we use a linear approximation for ease of comparison.

7   Discussion

A 3D sensor like LIDAR is often used for road scene understanding today. Let us briefly see how it is used. The large captured point cloud is registered to a pre-built or accumulated 3D map with or without the help of GPS and IMU. Then, dynamic obstacles are detected, segmented, classified using complex, computationally heavy and memory intensive deep learning approaches [9,27]. These approaches are proving to be more and more successful but perhaps all this computational machinery is not required to answer questions, such as: "Is an object cutting across into my lane?", or "Is an object in a cross-walk?".

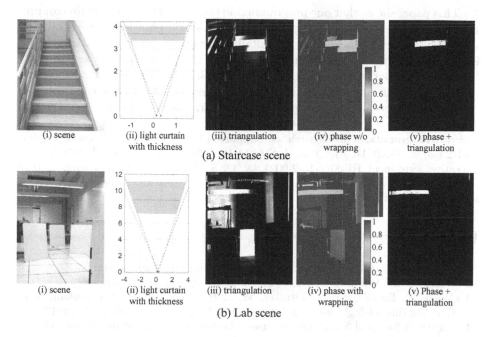

Fig. 8. Using line CW-TOF sensor. For both scenes, we show that fusing (iii) triangulation gating with (iv) phase information leads to (v) thinner light curtains without any phase wrapping ambiguity.

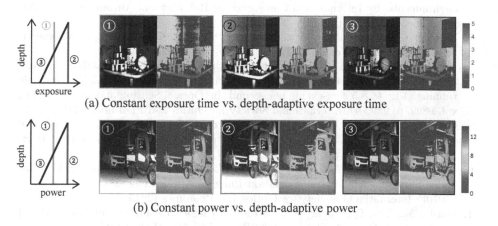

Fig. 9. We use depth adaptive budgeting of (a) exposure and (b) power to construct high-quality depth maps by sweeping a fronto-parallel curtain. In each case, we show the results of three strategies: (1) constant exposure/power at a low value, (2) constant exposure/power at a high value, and (3) depth-adaptive allocation of exposure/power such that the average matches the value used in (1). We observe that (3) achieves the same quality of depth map as (2), but using the same time/power budget as in (1).

This paper shows that our programmable triangulation light curtain can provide an alternative solution that needs little to no computational overhead, and yet has high energy efficiency and flexibility. We are by no means claiming that full 3D sensors are not useful but are asserting that light curtains are an effective addition when depths can be pre-specified. Given its inherent advantages, we believe that light curtains will be of immense use in autonomous cars, robotics safety applications and human-robot collaborative manufacturing.

Acknowledgments. This research was supported in parts by an ONR grant N00014-15-1-2358, an ONR DURIP Award N00014-16-1-2906, and DARPA REVEAL Cooperative Agreement HR0011-16-2-0021. A. C. Sankaranarayanan was supported in part by the NSF CAREER grant CCF-1652569. J. Bartels was supported by NASA fellowship NNX14AM53H.

References

1. Light curtain wikipedia. https://en.wikipedia.org/wiki/Light_curtain
2. Ruled surface Wikipedia. https://en.wikipedia.org/wiki/Ruled_surface
3. Achar, S., Bartels, J.R., Whittaker, W.L., Kutulakos, K.N., Narasimhan, S.G.: Epipolar time-of-flight imaging. ACM Trans. Graph. (TOG) **36**(4), 37 (2017)
4. American National Standards Institute: American national standard for safe use of lasers z136.1 (2014)
5. Baker, I.M., Duncan, S.S., Copley, J.W.: A low-noise laser-gated imaging system for long-range target identification. In: Defense and Security, pp. 133–144. International Society for Optics and Photonics (2004)
6. Barry, A.J., Tedrake, R.: Pushbroom stereo for high-speed navigation in cluttered environments. In: International Conference on Robotics and Automation (ICRA), pp. 3046–3052. IEEE (2015)
7. Bouguet, J.Y.: Matlab camera calibration toolbox (2000). http://www.vision.caltech.edu/bouguetj/calib_doc/
8. Burri, S., Homulle, H., Bruschini, C., Charbon, E.: LinoSPAD: a time-resolved 256× 1 CMOS SPAD line sensor system featuring 64 FPGA-based TDC channels running at up to 8.5 giga-events per second. In: Optical Sensing and Detection IV, vol. 9899, p. 98990D. International Society for Optics and Photonics (2016)
9. Geiger, A., Lenz, P., Urtasun, R.: Are we ready for autonomous driving? The KITTI vision benchmark suite. In: Conference on Computer Vision and Pattern Recognition (CVPR), pp. 3354–3361. IEEE (2012)
10. Grauer, Y., Sonn, E.: Active gated imaging for automotive safety applications. In: Video Surveillance and Transportation Imaging Applications 2015, vol. 9407, p. 94070F. International Society for Optics and Photonics (2015)
11. Gupta, M., Yin, Q., Nayar, S.K.: Structured light in sunlight. In: International Conference on Computer Vision (ICCV), pp. 545–552. IEEE (2013)
12. Hansen, M.P., Malchow, D.S.: Overview of SWIR detectors, cameras, and applications. In: Thermosense Xxx, vol. 6939, p. 69390I. International Society for Optics and Photonics (2008)
13. Lanman, D., Taubin, G.: Build your own 3D scanner: 3D photography for beginners. In: ACM SIGGRAPH 2009 Courses, p. 8. ACM (2009)
14. Li, L.: Time-of-flight camera-an introduction. Technical white paper (SLOA190B) (2014)

15. Lichtsteiner, P., Posch, C., Delbruck, T.: A 128x128 120 dB 15us latency asynchronous temporal contrast vision sensor. IEEE J. Solid State Circ. **43**(2), 566–576 (2008)
16. Marvin, M.: Microscopy apparatus, US Patent 3,013,467, 19 December 1961
17. Matsuda, N., Cossairt, O., Gupta, M.: Mc3d: motion contrast 3D scanning. In: International Conference on Computational Photography (ICCP), pp. 1–10. IEEE (2015)
18. Narasimhan, S.G., Nayar, S.K., Sun, B., Koppal, S.J.: Structured light in scattering media. In: International Conference on Computer Vision (ICCV), vol. 1, pp. 420–427. IEEE (2005)
19. O'Toole, M., Achar, S., Narasimhan, S.G., Kutulakos, K.N.: Homogeneous codes for energy-efficient illumination and imaging. ACM Trans. Graph. (ToG) **34**(4), 35 (2015)
20. O'Toole, M., Raskar, R., Kutulakos, K.N.: Primal-dual coding to probe light transport. ACM Trans. Graph. (ToG) **31**(4), 39:1–39:11 (2012)
21. Satat, G., Tancik, M., Raskar, R.: Towards photography through realistic fog. In: International Conference on Computational Photography (ICCP), pp. 1–10. IEEE (2018)
22. Tadano, R., Kumar Pediredla, A., Veeraraghavan, A.: Depth selective camera: a direct, on-chip, programmable technique for depth selectivity in photography. In: International Conference on Computer Vision (ICCV), pp. 3595–3603. IEEE (2015)
23. Wang, J., Gupta, M., Sankaranarayanan, A.C.: Lisens-a scalable architecture for video compressive sensing. In: International Conference on Computational Photography (ICCP). IEEE (2015)
24. Wang, J., Sankaranarayanan, A.C., Gupta, M., Narasimhan, S.G.: Dual structured light 3D using a 1D sensor. In: Leibe, B., Matas, J., Sebe, N., Welling, M. (eds.) ECCV 2016. LNCS, vol. 9910, pp. 383–398. Springer, Cham (2016). https://doi.org/10.1007/978-3-319-46466-4_23
25. Weber, M., Mickoleit, M., Huisken, J.: Light sheet microscopy. In: Methods in cell biology, vol. 123, pp. 193–215. Elsevier (2014)
26. Wheaton, S., Bonakdar, A., Nia, I.H., Tan, C.L., Fathipour, V., Mohseni, H.: Open architecture time of fight 3D SWIR camera operating at 150 MHz modulation frequency. Opt. Express **25**(16), 19291–19297 (2017)
27. Zhou, Y., Tuzel, O.: VoxelNet: end-to-end learning for point cloud based 3D object detection. In: Conference on Computer Vision and Pattern Recognition (CVPR) (2018)

Learning to Separate Object Sounds
by Watching Unlabeled Video

Ruohan Gao[1](✉), Rogerio Feris[2], and Kristen Grauman[3]

[1] The University of Texas at Austin, Austin, USA
{rhgao,grauman}@cs.utexas.edu
[2] IBM Research, New York, USA
rsferis@us.ibm.com
[3] Facebook AI Research, Menlo Park, USA
grauman@fb.com

Abstract. Perceiving a scene most fully requires all the senses. Yet modeling how objects look and sound is challenging: most natural scenes and events contain multiple objects, and the audio track mixes all the sound sources together. We propose to learn audio-visual object models from unlabeled video, then exploit the visual context to perform audio source separation in novel videos. Our approach relies on a deep multi-instance multi-label learning framework to disentangle the audio frequency bases that map to individual visual objects, even without observing/hearing those objects in isolation. We show how the recovered disentangled bases can be used to guide audio source separation to obtain better-separated, object-level sounds. Our work is the first to learn audio source separation from large-scale "in the wild" videos containing multiple audio sources per video. We obtain state-of-the-art results on visually-aided audio source separation and audio denoising. Our video results: http://vision.cs.utexas.edu/projects/separating_object_sounds/.

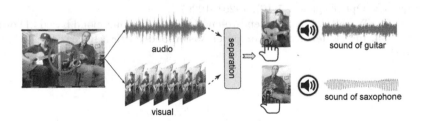

Fig. 1. Goal: learn from unlabeled video to separate object sounds

1 Introduction

Understanding scenes and events is inherently a multi-modal experience. We perceive the world by both looking and listening (and touching, smelling, and

K. Grauman—*On leave from The University of Texas at Austin.*

V. Ferrari et al. (Eds.): ECCV 2018, LNCS 11207, pp. 36–54, 2018.
https://doi.org/10.1007/978-3-030-01219-9_3

tasting). Objects generate unique sounds due to their physical properties and interactions with other objects and the environment. For example, perception of a coffee shop scene may include seeing cups, saucers, people, and tables, but also hearing the dishes clatter, the espresso machine grind, and the barista shouting an order. Human developmental learning is also inherently multi-modal, with young children quickly amassing a repertoire of objects and their sounds: dogs bark, cats mew, phones ring.

However, while recognition has made significant progress by "looking"—detecting objects, actions, or people based on their appearance—it often does not listen. Despite a long history of audio-visual video indexing [45,57,70,71,79], *objects* in video are often analyzed as if they were silent entities in silent environments. A key challenge is that in a realistic video, object sounds are observed not as separate entities, but as a *single audio channel* that mixes all their frequencies together. Audio source separation, though studied extensively in the signal processing literature [25,40,76,86], remains a difficult problem with natural data outside of lab settings. Existing methods perform best by capturing the input with multiple microphones, or else assume a clean set of single source audio examples is available for supervision (e.g., a recording of only a violin, another recording containing only a drum, etc.), both of which are very limiting prerequisites. The blind audio separation task evokes challenges similar to image segmentation—and perhaps more, since all sounds overlap in the input signal.

Our goal is to learn how different objects sound by both looking at *and* listening to unlabeled video containing multiple sounding objects. We propose an unsupervised approach to disentangle mixed audio into its component sound sources. The key insight is that observing sounds in a variety of visual contexts reveals the cues needed to isolate individual audio sources; the different visual contexts lend weak supervision for discovering the associations. For example, having experienced various instruments playing in various combinations before, then given a video with a guitar and a saxophone (Fig. 1), one can naturally anticipate what sounds could be present in the accompanying audio, and therefore better separate them. Indeed, neuroscientists report that the mismatch negativity of event-related brain potentials, which is generated bilaterally within auditory cortices, is elicited only when the visual pattern promotes the segregation of the sounds [63]. This suggests that synchronous presentation of visual stimuli should help to resolve sound ambiguity due to multiple sources, and promote either an integrated or segregated perception of the sounds.

We introduce a novel audio-visual source separation approach that realizes this intuition. Our method first leverages a large collection of unannotated videos to discover a latent sound representation for each object. Specifically, we use state-of-the-art image recognition tools to infer the objects present in each video clip, and we perform non-negative matrix factorization (NMF) on each video's audio channel to recover its set of frequency basis vectors. At this point it is unknown which audio bases go with which visible object(s). To recover the association, we construct a neural network for multi-instance multi-label learning (MIML) that maps audio bases to the distribution of detected visual objects.

From this audio basis-object association network, we extract the audio bases linked to each visual object, yielding its prototypical spectral patterns. Finally, given a novel video, we use the learned per-object audio bases to steer audio source separation.

Prior attempts at visually-aided audio source separation tackle the problem by detecting low-level correlations between the two data streams for the input video [8,12,15,27,52,61,62,64], and they experiment with somewhat controlled domains of musical instruments in concert or human speakers facing the camera. In contrast, we propose to *learn object-level sound models* from hundreds of thousands of unlabeled videos, and generalize to separate new audio-visual instances. We demonstrate results for a broad set of "in the wild" videos. While a resurgence of research on cross-modal learning from images and audio also capitalizes on synchronized audio-visual data for various tasks [3–5,47,49,59,60], they treat the audio as a single monolithic input, and thus cannot associate different sounds to different objects in the same video.

The main contributions in this paper are as follows. Firstly, we propose to enhance audio source separation in videos by "supervising" it with visual information from image recognition results[1]. Secondly, we propose a novel deep multi-instance multi-label learning framework to learn prototypical spectral patterns of different acoustic objects, and inject the learned prior into an NMF source separation framework. Thirdly, to our knowledge, we are the first to study audio source separation learned from large scale online videos. We demonstrate state-of-the-art results on visually-aided audio source separation and audio denoising.

2   Related Work

Localizing Sounds in Video Frames. The sound localization problem entails identifying which pixels or regions in a video are responsible for the recorded sound. Early work on localization explored correlating pixels with sounds using mutual information [27,37] or multi-modal embeddings like canonical correlation analysis [47], often with assumptions that a sounding object is in motion. Beyond identifying correlations for a single input video's audio and visual streams, recent work investigates learning associations from many such videos in order to localize sounding objects [4]. Such methods typically assume that there is *one* sound source, and the task is to localize the portion(s) of the visual content responsible for it. In contrast, our goal is to *separate* multiple audio sources from a monoaural signal by leveraging learned audio-visual associations.

Audio-Visual Representation Learning. Recent work shows that image and audio classification tasks can benefit from representation learning with both modalities. Given unlabeled training videos, the audio channel can be used as free self-supervision, allowing a convolutional network to learn features that tend to gravitate to objects and scenes, resulting in improved image classification [3,60].

---

[1] Our task can hence be seen as "weakly supervised", though the weak "labels" themselves are inferred from the video, not manually annotated.

Working in the opposite direction, the SoundNet approach uses image classifier predictions on unlabeled video frames to guide a learned audio representation for improved audio scene classification [5]. For applications in cross-modal retrieval or zero-shot classification, other methods aim to learn aligned representations across modalities, e.g., audio, text, and visual [6]. Related to these approaches, we share the goal of learning from unlabeled video with synchronized audio and visual channels. However, whereas they aim to improve audio or image classification, our method discovers associations in order to isolate sounds per object, with the ultimate task of audio-visual source separation.

Audio Source Separation. Audio source separation (from purely audio input) has been studied for decades in the signal processing literature. Some methods assume access to multiple microphones, which facilitates separation [20,56,82]. Others accept a single monoaural input [39,69,72,76,77] to perform "blind" separation. Popular approaches include Independent Component Analysis (ICA) [40], sparse decomposition [86], Computational Auditory Scene Analysis (CASA) [22], non-negative matrix factorization (NMF) [25,26,51,76], probabilistic latent variable models [38,68], and deep learning [36,39,66]. NMF is a traditional method that is still widely used for unsupervised source separation [31,41,44,72,75]. However, existing methods typically require supervision to get good results. Strong supervision in the form of isolated recordings of individual sound sources [69,77] is effective but difficult to secure for arbitrary sources in the wild. Alternatively, "informed" audio source separation uses special-purpose auxiliary cues to guide the process, such as a music score [35], text [50], or manual user guidance [11,19,77]. Our approach employs an existing NMF optimization [26], chosen for its efficiency, but unlike any of the above we tackle audio separation informed by automatically detected visual objects.

Audio-Visual Source Separation. The idea of guiding audio source separation using *visual* information can be traced back to [15,27], where mutual information is used to learn the joint distribution of the visual and auditory signals, then applied to isolate human speakers. Subsequent work explores audio-visual subspace analysis [62,67], NMF informed by visual motion [61,65], statistical convolutive mixture models [64], and correlating temporal onset events [8,52]. Recent work [62] attempts both localization and separation simultaneously; however, it assumes a moving object is present and only aims to decompose a video into background (assumed low-rank) and foreground sounds/pixels. Prior methods nearly always tackle videos of people speaking or playing musical instruments [8,12,15,27,52,61,62,64]—domains where salient motion signals accompany audio events (e.g., a mouth or a violin bow starts moving, a guitar string suddenly accelerates). Some studies further assume side cues from a written musical score [52], require that each sound source has a period when it alone is active [12], or use ground-truth motion captured by MoCap [61].

Whereas prior work correlates low-level visual patterns—particularly motion and onset events—with the audio channel, we propose to learn from video how different *objects* look and sound, whether or not an object moves with obvious correlation to the sounds. Our method assumes access to visual detectors, but assumes no side information about a novel test video. Furthermore, whereas existing methods analyze a single input video in isolation and are largely constrained to human speakers and instruments, our approach learns a valuable prior for audio separation from a large library of *unlabeled* videos.

Concurrent with our work, other new methods for audio-visual source separation are being explored specifically for speech [1,23,28,58] or musical instruments [84]. In contrast, we study a broader set of object-level sounds including instruments, animals, and vehicles. Moreover, our method's training data requirements are distinctly more flexible. We are the first to learn from uncurated "in the wild" videos that contain multiple objects and multiple audio sources.

Generating Sounds from Video. More distant from our work are methods that aim to *generate* sounds from a silent visual input, using recurrent networks [59, 85], conditional generative adversarial networks (C-GANs) [13], or simulators integrating physics, audio, and graphics engines [83]. Unlike any of the above, our approach learns the association between how objects look and sound in order to disentangle real audio sources; our method does not aim to synthesize sounds.

Weakly Supervised Visual Learning. Given unlabeled video, our approach learns to disentangle which sounds within a mixed audio signal go with which recognizable objects. This can be seen as a weakly supervised visual learning problem, where the "supervision" in our case consists of automatically detected visual objects. The proposed setting of weakly supervised audio-visual learning is entirely novel, but at a high level it follows the spirit of prior work leveraging weak annotations, including early "words and pictures" work [7,21], internet vision methods [9,73], training weakly supervised object (activity) detectors [2,10,14,16,78], image captioning methods [18,46], or grounding acoustic units of spoken language to image regions [32,33]. In contrast to any of these methods, our idea is to learn *sound* associations for objects from unlabeled video, and to exploit those associations for audio source separation on new videos.

3   Approach

Our approach learns what objects sound like from a batch of unlabeled, multi-sound-source videos. Given a new video, our method returns the separated audio channels and the visual objects responsible for them.

We first formalize the audio separation task and overview audio basis extraction with NMF (Sect. 3.1). Then we introduce our framework for learning audio-visual objects from unlabeled video (Sect. 3.2) and our accompanying deep multi-instance multi-label network (Sect. 3.3). Next we present an approach to use that network to associate audio bases with visual objects (Sect. 3.4). Finally, we pose audio source separation for novel videos in terms of a semi-supervised NMF approach (Sect. 3.5).

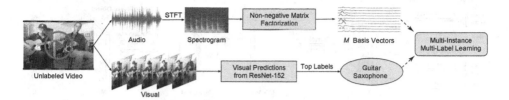

Fig. 2. Unsupervised training pipeline. For each video, we perform NMF on its audio magnitude spectrogram to get M basis vectors. An ImageNet-trained ResNet-152 network is used to make visual predictions to find the potential objects present in the video. Finally, we perform multi-instance multi-label learning to disentangle which extracted audio basis vectors go with which detected visible object(s).

3.1 Audio Basis Extraction

Single-channel audio source separation is the problem of obtaining an estimate for each of the J sources s_j from the observed linear mixture $x(t)$: $x(t) = \sum_{j=1}^{J} s_j(t)$, where $s_j(t)$ are time-discrete signals. The mixture signal can be transformed into a magnitude or power spectrogram $\mathbf{V} \in \mathbb{R}_+^{F \times N}$ consisting of F frequency bins and N short-time Fourier transform (STFT) [30] frames, which encode the change of a signal's frequency and phase content over time. We operate on the frequency domain, and use the inverse short-time Fourier transform (ISTFT) [30] to reconstruct the sources.

Non-negative matrix factorization (NMF) is often employed [25,26,51,76] to approximate the (non-negative real-valued) spectrogram matrix $\mathbf{V}$ as a product of two matrices $\mathbf{W}$ and $\mathbf{H}$:

$$\mathbf{V} \approx \tilde{\mathbf{V}} = \mathbf{WH}, \tag{1}$$

where $\mathbf{W} \in \mathbb{R}_+^{F \times M}$ and $\mathbf{H} \in \mathbb{R}_+^{M \times N}$. The number of bases M is a user-defined parameter. $\mathbf{W}$ can be interpreted as the non-negative audio spectral patterns, and $\mathbf{H}$ can be seen as the activation matrix. Specifically, each column of $\mathbf{W}$ is referred to as a *basis vector*, and each row in $\mathbf{H}$ represents the gain of the corresponding basis vector. The factorization is usually obtained by solving the following minimization problem:

$$\min_{\mathbf{W},\mathbf{H}} D(\mathbf{V}|\mathbf{WH}) \text{ subject to } \mathbf{W} \geq 0, \mathbf{H} \geq 0, \tag{2}$$

where D is a measure of divergence, e.g., we employ the Kullback-Leibler (KL) divergence.

For each unlabeled training video, we perform NMF independently on its audio magnitude spectrogram to obtain its spectral patterns $\mathbf{W}$, and throw away the activation matrix $\mathbf{H}$. M audio basis vectors are therefore extracted from each video.

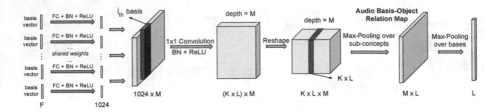

Fig. 3. Our deep multi-instance multi-label network takes a bag of M audio basis vectors for each video as input, and gives a bag-level prediction of the objects present in the audio. The visual predictions from an ImageNet-trained CNN are used as weak "labels" to train the network with unlabeled video.

3.2 Weakly-Supervised Audio-Visual Object Learning Framework

Multiple objects can appear in an unlabeled video at the same time, and similarly in the associated audio track. At this point, it is unknown which of the audio bases extracted (columns of $\mathbf{W}$) go with which visible object(s) in the visual frames. To discover the association, we devise a multi-instance multi-label learning (MIML) framework that matches audio bases with the detected objects.

As shown in Fig. 2, given an unlabeled video, we extract its visual frames and the corresponding audio track. As defined above, we perform NMF independently on the magnitude spetrogram of each audio track and obtain M basis vectors from each video. For the visual frames, we use an ImageNet pre-trained ResNet-152 network [34] to make object category predictions, and we max-pool over predictions of all frames to obtain a video-level prediction. The top labels (with class probability larger than a threshold) are used as weak "labels" for the unlabeled video. The extracted basis vectors and the visual predictions are then fed into our MIML learning framework to discover associations, as defined next.

3.3 Deep Multi-Instance Multi-Label Network

We cast the audio basis-object disentangling task as a multi-instance multi-label (MIML) learning problem. In single-label MIL [17], one has bags of instances, and a bag label indicates only that some number of the instances within it have that label. In MIML, the bag can have multiple labels, and there is ambiguity about which labels go with which instances in the bag.

We design a deep MIML network for our task. A bag of basis vectors $\mathbf{B}$ is the input to the network, and within each bag there are M basis vectors $\mathbf{B}_i$ with $i \in [1, M]$ extracted from one video. The "labels" are only available at the bag level, and come from noisy visual *predictions* of the ResNet-152 network trained for ImageNet recognition. The labels for each instance (basis vector) are unknown. We incorporate MIL into the deep network by modeling that there must be *at least one* audio basis vector from a certain object that constitutes a positive bag, so that the network can output a correct bag-level prediction that agrees with the visual prediction.

Figure 3 shows the detailed network architecture. M basis vectors are fed through a Siamese Network of M branches with shared weights. The Siamese network is designed to reduce the dimension of the audio frequency bases and learns the audio spectral patterns through a fully-connected layer (FC) followed by batch norm (BN) [42] and a rectified linear unit (ReLU). The output of all branches are stacked to form a $1024 \times M$ dimension feature map. Each slice of the feature map represents a basis vector with reduced dimension. Inspired by [24], each label is decomposed to K sub-concepts to capture latent semantic meanings. For example, for drum, the latent sub-concepts could be different types of drums, such as bongo drum, tabla, and so on. The stacked output from the Siamese network is forwarded through a 1×1 Convolution-BN-ReLU module, and then reshaped into a feature cube of dimension $K \times L \times M$, where K is the number of sub-concepts, L is the number of object categories, and M is the number of audio basis vectors. The depth of the tensor equals the number of input basis vectors, with each $K \times L$ slice corresponding to one particular basis. The activation score of the $(k, l, m)_{\text{th}}$ node in the cube represents the matching score of the k_{th} sub-concept of the l_{th} label for the m_{th} basis vector.

To get a bag-level prediction, we conduct two max-pooling operations. Max pooling in deep MIL [24,80,81] is typically used to identify the positive instances within an aggregated bag. Our first pooling is over the sub-concept dimension (K) to generate an audio basis-object relation map. The second max-pooling operates over the basis dimension (M) to produce a video-level prediction. We use the following multi-label hinge loss to train the network:

$$\mathcal{L}(A, \mathcal{V}) = \frac{1}{L} \sum_{i=1, i \neq \mathcal{V}_j}^{L} \sum_{j=1}^{|\mathcal{V}|} \max[0, 1 - (A_{\mathcal{V}_j} - A_i)], \tag{3}$$

where $A \in \mathbb{R}^L$ is the output of the MIML network, and represents the object predictions based on audio bases; $\mathcal{V}$ is the set of visual objects, namely the indices of the $|\mathcal{V}|$ objects predicted by the ImageNet-trained model. The loss function encourages the prediction scores of the correct classes to be larger than incorrect ones by a margin of 1. We find these pooling steps in our MIML formulation are valuable to learn accurately from the ambiguously "labeled" bags (i.e., the videos and their object predictions); see Supp.

3.4 Disentangling Per-Object Bases

The MIML network above learns from audio-visual associations, but does not itself disentangle them. The sounds in the audio track and objects present in the visual frames of unlabeled video are diverse and noisy (see Sect. 4.1 for details about the data we use). The audio basis vectors extracted from each video could be a component shared by multiple objects, a feature composed of them, or even completely unrelated to the predicted visual objects. The visual predictions from ResNet-152 network give approximate predictions about the objects that could be present, but are certainly not always reliable (see Fig. 5 for examples).

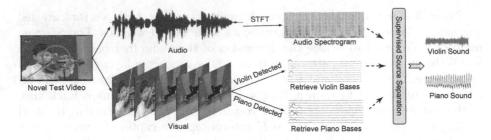

Fig. 4. Testing pipeline. Given a novel test video, we detect the objects present in the visual frames, and retrieve their learnt audio bases. The bases are collected to form a fixed basis dictionary **W** with which to guide NMF factorization of the test video's audio channel. The basis vectors and the learned activation scores from NMF are finally used to separate the sound for each detected object, respectively.

Therefore, to collect high quality representative bases for each object category, we use our trained deep MIML network as a tool. The audio basis-object relation map after the first pooling layer of the MIML network produces matching scores across all basis vectors for all object labels. We perform a dimension-wise softmax over the basis dimension (M) to normalize object matching scores to probabilities along each basis dimension. By examining the normalized map, we can discover links from bases to objects. We only collect the key bases that trigger the prediction of the correct objects (namely, the visually detected objects). Further, we only collect bases from an unlabeled video if multiple basis vectors strongly activate the correct object(s). See Supp. for details, and see Fig. 5 for examples of typical basis-object relation maps. In short, at the end of this phase, we have a set of audio bases for each visual object, discovered purely from unlabeled video and mixed single-channel audio.

3.5 Object Sound Separation for a Novel Video

Finally, we present our procedure to separate audio sources in new videos. As shown in Fig. 4, given a novel test video q, we obtain its audio magnitude spectrogram $\mathbf{V}^{(q)}$ through STFT and detect objects using the same ImageNet-trained ResNet-152 network as before. Then, we retrieve the learnt audio basis vectors for each detected object, and use them to "guide" NMF-based audio source separation. Specifically,

$$
\begin{aligned}
\mathbf{V}^{(q)} \approx \tilde{\mathbf{V}}^{(q)} &= \mathbf{W}^{(q)}\mathbf{H}^{(q)} \\
&= \left[\mathbf{W}_1^{(q)} \cdots \mathbf{W}_j^{(q)} \cdots \mathbf{W}_J^{(q)}\right]\left[\mathbf{H}_1^{(q)} \cdots \mathbf{H}_j^{(q)} \cdots \mathbf{H}_J^{(q)}\right]^T,
\end{aligned} \tag{4}
$$

where J is the number of detected objects (J potential sound sources), and $\mathbf{W}_j^{(q)}$ contains the retrieved bases corresponding to object j in input video q. In other words, we concatenate the basis vectors learnt for each detected object to construct the basis dictionary $\mathbf{W}^{(q)}$. Next, in the NMF algorithm, we hold $\mathbf{W}^{(q)}$ fixed, and only estimate activations $\mathbf{H}^{(q)}$ with multiplicative update rules. Then we obtain the spectrogram corresponding to each detected object by $\mathbf{V}_j^{(q)} = \mathbf{W}_j^{(q)} \mathbf{H}_j^{(q)}$. We reconstruct the individual (compressed) audio source signals by soft masking the mixture spectrogram:

$$\mathbb{V}_j = \frac{\mathbf{V}_j^{(q)}}{\sum_{i=1}^{J} \mathbf{V}_i^{(q)}} \mathbb{V}, \tag{5}$$

where $\mathbb{V}$ contains both magnitude and phase. Finally, we perform ISTFT on $\mathbb{V}_j$ to reconstruct the audio signals for each detected object. If a detected object does not make sound, then its estimated activation scores will be low. This phase can be seen as a self-supervised form of NMF, where the detected visual objects reveal which bases (previously discovered from unlabeled videos) are relevant to guide audio separation.

4   Experiments

We now validate our approach and compare to existing methods.

4.1   Datasets

We consider two public video datasets: AudioSet [29] and the benchmark videos from [43,53,62], which we refer to as AV-Bench.

AudioSet-Unlabeled: We use AudioSet [29] as the source of unlabeled training videos[2]. The dataset consists of short 10 s video clips that often concentrate on one event. However, our method makes no particular assumptions about using short or trimmed videos, as it learns bases in the frequency domain and pools both visual predictions and audio bases from all frames. The videos are challenging: many are of poor quality and unrelated to object sounds, such as silence, sine wave, echo, infrasound, etc. As is typical for related experimentation in the literature [4,85], we filter the dataset to those likely to display audio-visual events. In particular, we extract musical instruments, animals, and vehicles, which span a broad set of unique sound-making objects. See Supp. for a complete list of the object categories. Using the dataset's provided split, we randomly reserve some videos from the "unbalanced" split as validation data, and the rest as the training data. We use videos from the "balanced" split as test data. The final AudioSet-Unlabeled data contains 104k, 2.9k, 1k/22k, 1.2k, 0.5k/58k, 2.4k, 0.6k video clips in the train, val, test splits, for the instruments, animals, and vehicles, respectively.

AudioSet-SingleSource: To facilitate quantitative evaluation (cf. Sect. 4.4), we construct a dataset of AudioSet videos containing only a single sounding

---

[2] AudioSet offers noisy video-level audio class annotations. However, we do not use any of its label information.

object. We manually examine videos in the val/test set, and obtain 23 such videos. There are 15 musical instruments (accordion, acoustic guitar, banjo, cello, drum, electric guitar, flute, french horn, harmonica, harp, marimba, piano, saxophone, trombone, violin), 4 animals (cat, dog, chicken, frog), and 4 vehicles (car, train, plane, motorbike). Note that our method never uses these samples for training.

AV-Bench: This dataset contains the benchmark videos (Violin Yanni, Wooden Horse, and Guitar Solo) used in previous studies [43,53,62].

4.2 Implementation Details

We extract a 10 s audio clip and 10 frames (every 1s) from each video. Following common settings [3], the audio clip is resampled at 48 kHz, and converted into a magnitude spectrogram of size 2401×202 through STFT of window length 0.1s and half window overlap. We use the NMF implementation of [26] with KL divergence and the multiplicative update solver. We extract $M = 25$ basis vectors from each audio. All video frames are resized to 256×256, and 224×224 center crops are used to make visual predictions. We use all relevant ImageNet categories and group them into 23 classes by merging the posteriors of similar categories to roughly align with the AudioSet categories; see Supp. A softmax is finally performed on the video-level object prediction scores, and classes with probability greater than 0.3 are kept as weak labels for MIML training. The deep MIML network is implemented in PyTorch with $F = 2,401$, $K = 4$, $L = 25$, and $M = 25$. We report all results with these settings and did not try other values. The network is trained using Adam [48] with weight decay 10^{-5} and batch size 256. The starting learning rate is set to 0.001, and decreased by 6% every 5 epochs and trained for 300 epochs.

4.3 Baselines

We compare to several existing methods [47,55,62,72] and multiple baselines:

MFCC Unsupervised Separation [72]: This is an off-the-shelf unsupervised audio source separation method. The separated channels are first converted into Mel frequency cepstrum coefficients (MFCC), and then K-means clustering is used to group separated channels. This is an established pipeline in the literature [31,41,44,75], making it a good representative for comparison. We use the publicly available code[3].

AV-Loc [62], **JIVE** [55], **Sparse CCA** [47]: We refer to results reported in [62] for the AV-Bench dataset to compare to these methods.

AudioSet Supervised Upper-Bound: This baseline uses AudioSet ground-truth labels to train our deep MIML network. AudioSet labels are organized in an ontology and each video is labeled by many categories. We use the 23 labels

---
[3] https://github.com/interactiveaudiolab/nussl.

aligned with our subset (15 instruments, 4 animals, and 4 vehicles). This baseline serves as an upper-bound.

K-means Clustering Unsupervised Separation: We use the same number of basis vectors as our method to initialize the **W** matrix, and perform unsupervised NMF. K-means clustering is then used to group separated channels, with K equal to the number of ground-truth sources. The sound sources are separated by aggregating the channel spectrograms belonging to each cluster.

Visual Exemplar for Supervised Separation: We recognize objects in the frames, and retrieve bases from an exemplar video for each detected object class to supervise its NMF audio source separation. An exemplar video is the one that has the largest confidence score for a class among all unlabeled training videos.

Unmatched Bases for Supervised Separation: This baseline is the same as our method except that it retrieves bases of the wrong class (at random from classes absent in the visual prediction) to guide NMF audio source separation.

Gaussian Bases for Supervised Separation: We initialize the weight matrix **W** randomly using a Gaussian distribution, and then perform supervised audio source separation (with **W** fixed) as in Sect. 3.5.

4.4 Quantitative Results

Visually-Aided Audio Source Separation. For "in the wild" unlabeled videos, the ground-truth of separated audio sources never exists. Therefore, to allow quantitative evaluation, we create a test set consisting of combined single-source videos, following [8]. In particular, we take pairwise video combinations from AudioSet-SingleSource (cf. Sect. 4.1) and (1) compound their audio tracks by normalizing and mixing them and (2) compound their visual channels by max-pooling their respective object predictions. Each compound video is a test video; its reserved source audio tracks are the ground truth for evaluation of separation results.

To evaluate source separation quality, we use the widely used BSS-EVAL toolbox [74] and report the Signal to Distortion Ratio (SDR). We perform four sets of experiments: pairwise compound two videos of musical instruments (Instrument Pair), two of animals (Animal Pair), two of vehicles (Vehicle Pair), and two cross-domain videos (Cross-Domain Pair). For unsupervised clustering separation baselines, we evaluate both possible matchings and take the best results (to the baselines' advantage).

Table 1 shows the results. Our method significantly outperforms the Visual Exemplar, Unmatched, and Gaussian baselines, demonstrating the power of our learned bases. Compared with the unsupervised clustering baselines, including [72], our method achieves large gains. It also has the capability to match the separated source to acoustic objects in the video, whereas the baselines can only return ungrounded audio signals. We stress that both our method as well as the baselines use no audio-based supervision. In contrast, other state-of-the-art audio source separation methods supervise the separation process with labeled

Table 1. We pairwise mix the sounds of two single source AudioSet videos and perform audio source separation. Mean Signal to Distortion Ratio (SDR in dB, higher is better) is reported to represent the overall separation performance.

	Instrument pair	Animal pair	Vehicle pair	Cross-domain pair
Upper-bound	2.05	0.35	0.60	2.79
K-means clustering	−2.85	−3.76	−2.71	−3.32
MFCC unsupervised [72]	0.47	−0.21	−0.05	1.49
Visual exemplar	−2.41	−4.75	−2.21	−2.28
Unmatched bases	−2.12	−2.46	−1.99	−1.93
Gaussian bases	−8.74	−9.12	−7.39	−8.21
Ours	**1.83**	**0.23**	**0.49**	**2.53**

training data containing clean ground-truth sources and/or tailor separation to music/speech (e.g., [36,39,54]). Such methods are not applicable here.

Our MIML solution is fairly tolerant to imperfect visual detection. Using weak labels from the ImageNet pre-trained ResNet-152 network performs similarly to using the AudioSet ground-truth labels with about 30% of the labels corrupted. Using the true labels (Upper-Bound in Table 1) reveals the extent to which better visual models would improve results.

Visually-Aided Audio Denoising. To facilitate comparison to prior audio-visual methods (none of which report results on AudioSet), next we perform the same experiment as in [62] on visually-assisted audio denoising on AV-Bench. Following the same setup as [62], the audio signals in all videos are corrupted with white noise with the signal to noise ratio set to 0 dB. To perform audio denoising, our method retrieves bases of detected object(s) and appends the same number of randomly initialized bases as the weight matrix **W** to supervise NMF. The randomly initialized bases are intended to capture the noise signal. As in [62], we report Normalized SDR (NSDR), which measures the improvement of the SDR between the mixed noisy signal and the denoised sound.

Table 2. Visually-assisted audio denoising results on three benchmark videos, in terms of NSDR (in dB, higher is better)

	Wooden horse	Violin yanni	Guitar solo	Average
Sparse CCA (Kidron et al. [47])	4.36	5.30	5.71	5.12
JIVE (Lock et al. [55])	4.54	4.43	2.64	3.87
Audio-visual (Pu et al. [62])	8.82	5.90	**14.1**	9.61
Ours	**12.3**	**7.88**	11.4	**10.5**

Table 2 shows the results. Note that the method of [62] is tailored to separate noise from the foreground sound by exploiting the low-rank nature of background sounds. Still, our method outperforms [62] on 2 out of the 3 videos, and performs much better than the other two prior audio-visual methods [47,55]. Pu et al. [62] also exploit motion in manually segmented regions. On Guitar Solo, the hand's motion may strongly correlate with the sound, leading to their better performance.

4.5 Qualitative Results

Next we provide qualitative results to illustrate the effectiveness of MIML training and the success of audio source separation. Here we run our method on the real multi-source videos from AudioSet. They lack ground truth, but results can be manually inspected for quality (see our video[4]).

Figure 5 shows example unlabeled videos and their discovered audio basis associations. For each example, we show sample video frames, ImageNet CNN visual object predictions, as well as the corresponding audio basis-object relation map predicted by our MIML network. We also report the AudioSet audio ground truth labels, but note that they are never seen by our method. The first example (Fig. 5-a) has both piano and violin in the visual frames, which are correctly detected by the CNN. The audio also contains the sounds of both instruments, and our method appropriately activates bases for both the violin and piano. Figure 5-b shows a man playing the violin in the visual frames, but both piano and violin are strongly activated. Listening to the audio, we can hear that an out-of-view player is indeed playing the piano. This example accentuates the advantage of learning object sounds from thousands of unlabeled videos; our method has learned the correct audio bases for piano, and "hears" it even though it is off-camera in this test video. Figure 5-c/d show two examples with inaccurate visual predictions, and our model correctly activates the label of the object in the audio. Figure 5-e/f show two more examples of an animal and a vehicle, and the results are similar. These examples suggest that our MIML network has successfully learned the prototypical spectral patterns of different sounds, and is capable of associating audio bases with object categories.

Please see our **video**[4] for more results, where we use our system to detect and separate object sounds for novel "in the wild" videos.

Overall, the results are promising and constitute a noticeable step towards visually guided audio source separation for more realistic videos. Of course, our system is far from perfect. The most common failure modes by our method are when the audio characteristics of detected objects are too similar or objects are incorrectly detected (see Supp.). Though ImageNet-trained CNNs can recognize a wide array of objects, we are nonetheless constrained by its breadth. Furthermore, not all objects make sounds and not all sounds are within the camera's view. Our results above suggest that learning can be robust to such factors, yet it will be important future work to explicitly model them.

---

[4] http://vision.cs.utexas.edu/projects/separating_object_sounds/.

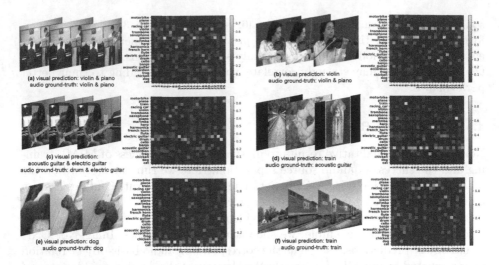

Fig. 5. In each example, we show the video frames, visual predictions, and the corresponding basis-label relation maps predicted by our MIML network. Please see our video (see footnote 4) for more examples and the corresponding audio tracks.

5   Conclusion

We presented a framework to learn object sounds from thousands of unlabeled videos. Our deep multi-instance multi-label network automatically links audio bases to object categories. Using the disentangled bases to supervise non-negative matrix factorization, our approach successfully separates object-level sounds. We demonstrate its effectiveness on diverse data and object categories. Audio source separation will continue to benefit many appealing applications, e.g., audio events indexing/remixing, audio denoising for closed captioning, or instrument equalization. In future work, we aim to explore ways to leverage scenes and ambient sounds, as well as integrate localized object detections and motion.

Acknowledgements. This research was supported in part by an IBM Faculty Award, IBM Open Collaboration Research Award, and DARPA Lifelong Learning Machines. We thank members of the UT Austin vision group and Wenguang Mao, Yuzhong Wu, Dongguang You, Xingyi Zhou and Xinying Hao for helpful input. We also gratefully acknowledge a GPU donation from Facebook.

References

1. Afouras, T., Chung, J.S., Zisserman, A.: The conversation: deep audio-visual speech enhancement. arXiv preprint arXiv:1804.04121 (2018)
2. Ali, S., Shah, M.: Human action recognition in videos using kinematic features and multiple instance learning. PAMI **32**, 288–303 (2010)
3. Arandjelovic, R., Zisserman, A.: Look, listen and learn. In: ICCV (2017)

4. Arandjelović, R., Zisserman, A.: Objects that sound. arXiv preprint arXiv:1712.06651 (2017)
5. Aytar, Y., Vondrick, C., Torralba, A.: SoundNet: learning sound representations from unlabeled video. In: NIPS (2016)
6. Aytar, Y., Vondrick, C., Torralba, A.: See, hear, and read: deep aligned representations. arXiv preprint arXiv:1706.00932 (2017)
7. Barnard, K., Duygulu, P., de Freitas, N., Blei, D., Jordan, M.: Matching words and pictures. JMLR **3**, 1107–1135 (2003)
8. Barzelay, Z., Schechner, Y.Y.: Harmony in motion. In: CVPR (2007)
9. Berg, T., et al.: Names and faces in the news. In: CVPR (2004)
10. Bilen, H., Vedaldi, A.: Weakly supervised deep detection networks. In: CVPR (2016)
11. Bryan, N.: Interactive Sound Source Separation. Ph.D. thesis, Stanford University (2014)
12. Casanovas, A.L., Monaci, G., Vandergheynst, P., Gribonval, R.: Blind audiovisual source separation based on sparse redundant representations. IEEE Trans. Multimed. **12**, 358–371 (2010)
13. Chen, L., Srivastava, S., Duan, Z., Xu, C.: Deep cross-modal audio-visual generation. In: Proceedings of the on Thematic Workshops of ACM Multimedia (2017)
14. Cinbis, R., Verbeek, J., Schmid, C.: Weakly supervised object localization with multi-fold multiple instance learning. PAMI **39**, 189–203 (2017)
15. Darrell, T., Fisher, J.W., Viola, P.: Audio-visual segmentation and the cocktail party effect. In: Tan, T., Shi, Y., Gao, W. (eds.) ICMI 2000. LNCS, vol. 1948, pp. 32–40. Springer, Heidelberg (2000). https://doi.org/10.1007/3-540-40063-X_5
16. Deselaers, T., Alexe, B., Ferrari, V.: Weakly supervised localization and learning with generic knowledge. IJCV **100**, 275–293 (2012)
17. Dietterich, T.G., Lathrop, R.H., Lozano-Pérez, T.: Solving the multiple instance problem with axis-parallel rectangles. Artif. intell. **89**, 31–71 (1997)
18. Donahue, J., et al.: Long-term recurrent convolutional networks for visual recognition and description. In: CVPR (2015)
19. Duong, N.Q., Ozerov, A., Chevallier, L., Sirot, J.: An interactive audio source separation framework based on non-negative matrix factorization. In: ICASSP (2014)
20. Duong, N.Q., Vincent, E., Gribonval, R.: Under-determined reverberant audio source separation using a full-rank spatial covariance model. IEEE Trans. Audio Speech Lang. Process. **18**, 1830–1840 (2010)
21. Duygulu, P., Barnard, K., de Freitas, J.F.G., Forsyth, D.A.: Object recognition as machine translation: learning a lexicon for a fixed image vocabulary. In: Heyden, A., Sparr, G., Nielsen, M., Johansen, P. (eds.) ECCV 2002. LNCS, vol. 2353, pp. 97–112. Springer, Heidelberg (2002). https://doi.org/10.1007/3-540-47979-1_7
22. Ellis, D.P.W.: Prediction-driven computational auditory scene analysis. Ph.D. thesis, Massachusetts Institute of Technology (1996)
23. Ephrat, A., et al.: Looking to listen at the cocktail party: a speaker-independent audio-visual model for speech separation. arXiv preprint arXiv:1804.03619 (2018)
24. Feng, J., Zhou, Z.H.: Deep MIML network. In: AAAI (2017)
25. Févotte, C., Bertin, N., Durrieu, J.L.: Nonnegative matrix factorization with the itakura-saito divergence: with application to music analysis. Neural comput. **21**, 793–830 (2009)
26. Févotte, C., Idier, J.: Algorithms for nonnegative matrix factorization with the β-divergence. Neural comput. **23**, 2421–2456 (2011)
27. Fisher III, J.W., Darrell, T., Freeman, W.T., Viola, P.A.: Learning joint statistical models for audio-visual fusion and segregation. In: NIPS (2001)

28. Gabbay, A., Shamir, A., Peleg, S.: Visual speech enhancement using noise-invariant training. arXiv preprint arXiv:1711.08789 (2017)
29. Gemmeke, J.F., et al.: Audio set: an ontology and human-labeled dataset for audio events. In: ICASSP (2017)
30. Griffin, D., Lim, J.: Signal estimation from modified short-time fourier transform. IEEE Trans. Acoust. Speech Signal Process. **32**, 236–243 (1984)
31. Guo, X., Uhlich, S., Mitsufuji, Y.: NMF-based blind source separation using a linear predictive coding error clustering criterion. In: ICASSP (2015)
32. Harwath, D., Glass, J.: Learning word-like units from joint audio-visual analysis. In: ACL (2017)
33. Harwath, D., Recasens, A., Surís, D., Chuang, G., Torralba, A., Glass, J.: Jointly discovering visual objects and spoken words from raw sensory input. arXiv preprint arXiv:1804.01452 (2018)
34. He, K., Zhang, X., Ren, S., Sun, J.: Deep residual learning for image recognition. In: CVPR (2016)
35. Hennequin, R., David, B., Badeau, R.: Score informed audio source separation using a parametric model of non-negative spectrogram. In: ICASSP (2011)
36. Hershey, J.R., Chen, Z., Le Roux, J., Watanabe, S.: Deep clustering: discriminative embeddings for segmentation and separation. In: ICASSP (2016)
37. Hershey, J.R., Movellan, J.R.: Audio vision: using audio-visual synchrony to locate sounds. In: NIPS (2000)
38. Hofmann, T.: Probabilistic latent semantic indexing. In: International ACM SIGIR Conference on Research and Development in Information Retrieval (1999)
39. Huang, P.S., Kim, M., Hasegawa-Johnson, M., Smaragdis, P.: Deep learning for monaural speech separation. In: ICASSP (2014)
40. Hyvärinen, A., Oja, E.: Independent component analysis: algorithms and applications. Neural Netw. **13**, 411–430 (2000)
41. Innami, S., Kasai, H.: NMF-based environmental sound source separation using time-variant gain features. Comput. Math. Appl. **64**, 1333–1342 (2012)
42. Ioffe, S., Szegedy, C.: Batch normalization: accelerating deep network training by reducing internal covariate shift. In: ICML (2015)
43. Izadinia, H., Saleemi, I., Shah, M.: Multimodal analysis for identification and segmentation of moving-sounding objects. IEEE Trans. Multimed. **15**, 378–390 (2013)
44. Jaiswal, R., FitzGerald, D., Barry, D., Coyle, E., Rickard, S.: Clustering NMF basis functions using shifted NMF for monaural sound source separation. In: ICASSP (2011)
45. Jhuo, I.H., Ye, G., Gao, S., Liu, D., Jiang, Y.G., Lee, D., Chang, S.F.: Discovering joint audio-visual codewords for video event detection. Machine Vis. Appl. **25**, 33–47 (2014)
46. Karpathy, A., Fei-Fei, L.: Deep visual-semantic alignments for generating image descriptions. In: CVPR (2015)
47. Kidron, E., Schechner, Y.Y., Elad, M.: Pixels that sound. In: CVPR (2005)
48. Kingma, D., Ba, J.: Adam: a method for stochastic optimization. In: ICLR (2015)
49. Korbar, B., Tran, D., Torresani, L.: Co-training of audio and video representations from self-supervised temporal synchronization. arXiv preprint arXiv:1807.00230 (2018)
50. Le Magoarou, L., Ozerov, A., Duong, N.Q.: Text-informed audio source separation. Example-based approach using non-negative matrix partial co-factorization. J. Signal Process. Syst. **79**, 117–131 (2015)
51. Lee, D.D., Seung, H.S.: Algorithms for non-negative matrix factorization. In: Advances in Neural Information Processing Systems (2001)

52. Li, B., Dinesh, K., Duan, Z., Sharma, G.: See and listen: score-informed association of sound tracks to players in chamber music performance videos. In: ICASSP (2017)
53. Li, K., Ye, J., Hua, K.A.: What's making that sound? In: ACMMM (2014)
54. Liutkus, A., Fitzgerald, D., Rafii, Z., Pardo, B., Daudet, L.: Kernel additive models for source separation. IEEE Trans. Signal Process. **62**, 4298–4310 (2014)
55. Lock, E.F., Hoadley, K.A., Marron, J.S., Nobel, A.B.: Joint and individual variation explained (JIVE) for integrated analysis of multiple data types. Ann. Appl. Stat. **7**(1), 523 (2013)
56. Nakadai, K., Hidai, K.I., Okuno, H.G., Kitano, H.: Real-time speaker localization and speech separation by audio-visual integration. In: IEEE International Conference on Robotics and Automation (2002)
57. Naphade, M., Smith, J.R., Tesic, J., Chang, S.F., Hsu, W., Kennedy, L., Hauptmann, A., Curtis, J.: Large-scale concept ontology for multimedia. IEEE Multimed. **13**, 86–91 (2006)
58. Owens, A., Efros, A.A.: Audio-visual scene analysis with self-supervised multisensory features. arXiv preprint arXiv:1804.03641 (2018)
59. Owens, A., Isola, P., McDermott, J., Torralba, A., Adelson, E.H., Freeman, W.T.: Visually indicated sounds. In: CVPR (2016)
60. Owens, A., Wu, J., McDermott, J.H., Freeman, W.T., Torralba, A.: Ambient sound provides supervision for visual learning. In: Leibe, B., Matas, J., Sebe, N., Welling, M. (eds.) ECCV 2016. LNCS, vol. 9905, pp. 801–816. Springer, Cham (2016). https://doi.org/10.1007/978-3-319-46448-0_48
61. Parekh, S., Essid, S., Ozerov, A., Duong, N.Q., Pérez, P., Richard, G.: Motion informed audio source separation. In: ICASSP (2017)
62. Pu, J., Panagakis, Y., Petridis, S., Pantic, M.: Audio-visual object localization and separation using low-rank and sparsity. In: ICASSP (2017)
63. Rahne, T., Böckmann, M., von Specht, H., Sussman, E.S.: Visual cues can modulate integration and segregation of objects in auditory scene analysis. Brain Res. **1144**, 127–135 (2007)
64. Rivet, B., Girin, L., Jutten, C.: Mixing audiovisual speech processing and blind source separation for the extraction of speech signals from convolutive mixtures. IEEE Trans. Audio Speech Lang. Process. **15**, 96–108 (2007)
65. Sedighin, F., Babaie-Zadeh, M., Rivet, B., Jutten, C.: Two multimodal approaches for single microphone source separation. In: 24th European Signal Processing Conference (2016)
66. Simpson, A.J.R., Roma, G., Plumbley, M.D.: Deep karaoke: extracting vocals from musical mixtures using a convolutional deep neural network. In: Vincent, E., Yeredor, A., Koldovský, Z., Tichavský, P. (eds.) LVA/ICA 2015. LNCS, vol. 9237, pp. 429–436. Springer, Cham (2015). https://doi.org/10.1007/978-3-319-22482-4_50
67. Smaragdis, P., Casey, M.: Audio/visual independent components. In: International Conference on Independent Component Analysis and Signal Separation (2003)
68. Smaragdis, P., Raj, B., Shashanka, M.: A probabilistic latent variable model for acoustic modeling. In: NIPS (2006)
69. Smaragdis, P., Raj, B., Shashanka, M.: Supervised and semi-supervised separation of sounds from single-channel mixtures. In: Davies, M.E., James, C.J., Abdallah, S.A., Plumbley, M.D. (eds.) ICA 2007. LNCS, vol. 4666, pp. 414–421. Springer, Heidelberg (2007). https://doi.org/10.1007/978-3-540-74494-8_52
70. Smeaton, A.F., Over, P., Kraaij, W.: Evaluation campaigns and TRECVid. In: Proceedings of the 8th ACM International Workshop on Multimedia Information Retrieval (2006)

71. Snoek, C.G., Worring, M.: Multimodal video indexing: a review of the state-of-the-art. Multimed. Tools Appl. **25**, 5–35 (2005)
72. SPIERTZ, M.: Source-filter based clustering for monaural blind source separation. In: 12th International Conference on Digital Audio Effects (2009)
73. Vijayanarasimhan, S., Grauman, K.: Keywords to visual categories: multiple-instance learning for weakly supervised object categorization. In: CVPR (2008)
74. Vincent, E., Gribonval, R., Févotte, C.: Performance measurement in blind audio source separation. IEEE Trans. Audio Speech Lang. Process. **14**, 1462–1469 (2006)
75. Virtanen, T.: Sound source separation using sparse coding with temporal continuity objective. In: International Computer Music Conference (2003)
76. Virtanen, T.: Monaural sound source separation by nonnegative matrix factorization with temporal continuity and sparseness criteria. IEEE Trans. Audio Speech Lang. Process. **15**, 1066–1074 (2007)
77. Wang, B.: Investigating single-channel audio source separation methods based on non-negative matrix factorization. In: ICA Research Network International Workshop (2006)
78. Wang, L., Xiong, Y., Lin, D., Gool, L.V.: Untrimmednets for weakly supervised action recognition and detection. In: CVPR (2017)
79. Wang, Z., et al.: Truly multi-modal YouTube-8m video classification with video, audio, and text. arXiv preprint arXiv:1706.05461 (2017)
80. Wu, J., Yu, Y., Huang, C., Yu, K.: Deep multiple instance learning for image classification and auto-annotation. In: CVPR (2015)
81. Yang, H., Zhou, J.T., Cai, J., Ong, Y.S.: MIML-FCN+: multi-instance multi-label learning via fully convolutional networks with privileged information. In: CVPR (2017)
82. Yilmaz, O., Rickard, S.: Blind separation of speech mixtures via time-frequency masking. IEEE Trans. Signal Process. **52**, 1830–1847 (2004)
83. Zhang, Z., et al.: Generative modeling of audible shapes for object perception. In: ICCV (2017)
84. Zhao, H., Gan, C., Rouditchenko, A., Vondrick, C., McDermott, J., Torralba, A.: The sound of pixels. arXiv preprint arXiv:1804.03160 (2018)
85. Zhou, Y., Wang, Z., Fang, C., Bui, T., Berg, T.L.: Visual to sound: generating natural sound for videos in the wild. arXiv preprint arXiv:1712.01393 (2017)
86. Zibulevsky, M., Pearlmutter, B.A.: Blind source separation by sparse decomposition in a signal dictionary. Neural Computat. **13**, 863–882 (2001)

Coded Two-Bucket Cameras
for Computer Vision

Mian Wei[1]([⊠]), Navid Sarhangnejad[2], Zhengfan Xia[2], Nikita Gusev[2],
Nikola Katic[2], Roman Genov[2], and Kiriakos N. Kutulakos[1]

[1] Department of Computer Science, University of Toronto, Toronto, Canada
{mianwei,kyros}@cs.toronto.edu
[2] Department of Electrical Engineering, University of Toronto, Toronto, Canada
{sarhangn,xia,nikita,roman}@ece.toronto.edu, katic.nik@gmail.com

Abstract. We introduce *coded two-bucket (C2B) imaging*, a new operating principle for computational sensors with applications in active 3D
shape estimation and coded-exposure imaging. A C2B sensor modulates
the light arriving at each pixel by controlling which of the pixel's two
"buckets" should integrate it. C2B sensors output two images per video
frame—one per bucket—and allow rapid, fully-programmable, per-pixel
control of the active bucket. Using these properties as a starting point, we
(1) develop an image formation model for these sensors, (2) couple them
with programmable light sources to acquire *illumination mosaics, i.e.*,
images of a scene under many different illumination conditions whose
pixels have been multiplexed and acquired in one shot, and (3) show
how to process illumination mosaics to acquire live disparity or normal
maps of dynamic scenes at the sensor's native resolution. We present
the first experimental demonstration of these capabilities, using a fully-
functional C2B camera prototype. Key to this unique prototype is a
novel programmable CMOS sensor that we designed from the ground
up, fabricated and turned into a working system.

1 Introduction

New camera designs—and new types of imaging sensors—have been instrumental
in driving the field of computer vision in exciting new directions. In the last
decade alone, time-of-flight cameras [1,2] have been widely adopted for vision
[3] and computational photography tasks [4–7]; event cameras [8] that support
asynchronous imaging have led to new vision techniques for high-speed motion
analysis [9] and 3D scanning [10]; high-resolution sensors with dual-pixel [11]
and assorted-pixel [12] designs are defining the state of the art for smartphone
cameras; and sensors with pixel-wise coded-exposure capabilities are starting to
appear [13,14] for compressed sensing applications [15].

Against this backdrop, we introduce a new type of computational video camera to the vision community—the *coded two-bucket (C2B) camera* (Fig. 1). The

Electronic supplementary material The online version of this chapter (https://
doi.org/10.1007/978-3-030-01219-9_4) contains supplementary material, which is
available to authorized users.

V. Ferrari et al. (Eds.): ECCV 2018, LNCS 11207, pp. 55–73, 2018.
https://doi.org/10.1007/978-3-030-01219-9_4

C2B camera is a pixel-wise coded-exposure camera that never blocks the incident light. Instead, each pixel in its sensor contains two charge-collection sites—two "buckets"—as well as a one-bit writeable memory that controls which bucket is active. The camera outputs two images per video frame—one per bucket—and performs exposure coding by rapidly controlling the active bucket of each pixel, via a programmable sequence of binary 2D patterns. Key to this unique functionality is a novel programmable CMOS sensor that we designed from the ground up, fabricated in a CMOS image sensor (CIS) process technology [16] for the first time, and turned into a working camera system.

The light efficiency and electronic per-pixel coding capabilities of C2B cameras open up a range of applications that go well beyond what is possible today. This potentially includes compressive acquisition of high-speed video [17] with optimal light efficiency; simultaneous acquisition of both epipolar-only [18] and non-epipolar video streams; fully-electronic acquisition of high-dynamic-range AC-flicker videos [19]; conferring EpiScan3D-like functionality [20] to non-rectified imaging systems; and performing many other coded-exposure imaging tasks [15, 21, 22] with a compact camera platform.

Our focus in this first paper, however, is to highlight the novel capabilities of C2B cameras for live dense one-shot 3D reconstruction: we show that from just one grayscale C2B video frame of a dynamic scene under active illumination, it is possible to reconstruct the scene's 3D snapshot (*i.e.*, per-pixel disparity or normal, plus albedo) at a resolution comparable to the sensor's pixel array. We argue that C2B cameras allow us to reduce this very difficult 3D reconstruction problem [23–28] to the potentially much easier 2D problems of image demosaicing [29, 30] and illumination multiplexing [31].

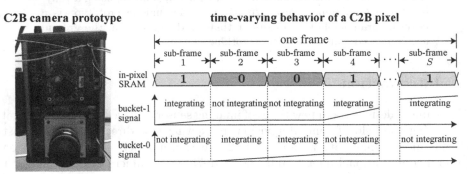

Fig. 1. *The C2B camera.* Left: Our prototype's sensor outputs video at 20 frames per second and consists of two arrays: a 244 × 160-pixel array that supports relatively slow bucket control (up to 4 sub-frames per frame) and a 35 × 48 array with much faster control (up to 120 sub-frames per frame). Right: Each frame is divided into S sub-frames during which the pixel's SRAM memory remains unchanged. A user-specified sequence of 2D binary patterns determines the SRAM's value at each pixel and sub-frame. Note that the two buckets of a pixel are never in the same state (*i.e.*, both active or both inactive) as this would degrade imaging performance—see [32] for a discussion of this and other related CMOS design issues. The light-generated charges of both buckets are read, digitized and cleared only once, at the end of each frame.

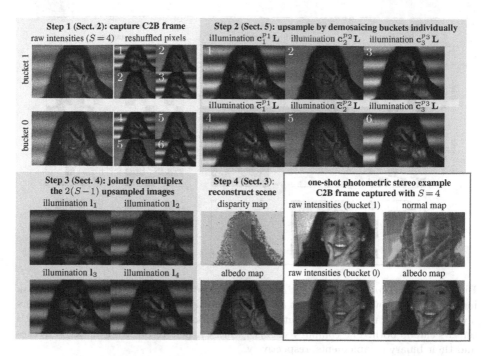

Fig. 2. *Dense one-shot reconstruction with C2B cameras.* The procedure runs in real time and is illustrated for structured-light triangulation. Please zoom in to the electronic copy to see individual pixels of the C2B frame and refer to the listed sections for notation and details. Photometric stereo is performed in an analogous way, by replacing the structured-light projector with a set of S directional light sources (a reconstruction example is shown in the lower right).

In particular, we show that C2B cameras can acquire—in one frame—images of a scene under $S \geq 3$ linearly-independent illuminations, multiplexed across the buckets of $S - 1$ neighboring pixels. We call such a frame a *two-bucket illumination mosaic*. In this setting, reconstruction at full sensor resolution involves four steps (Fig. 2): (1) control bucket activities and light sources to pack $2(S-1)$ distinct low-resolution images of the scene into one C2B frame (*i.e.*, $S-1$ images per bucket); (2) upsample these images to full resolution by demosaicing; (3) demultiplex all the upsampled images jointly, to obtain up to S linearly-independent full-resolution images; and (4) use these images to solve for shape and albedo at each pixel independently. We demonstrate the effectiveness of this procedure by recovering dense 3D shape and albedo from one shot with two of the oldest and simplest active 3D reconstruction algorithms available—multi-pattern cosine phase shifting [33,34] and photometric stereo [35].

From a hardware perspective, we build on previous attempts to fabricate sensors with C2B-like functionality [36–38], which did not rely on a CMOS image sensor process technology. More broadly, our prototype can be thought of as generalizing three families of sensors. *Programmable coded-exposure sensors* [13]

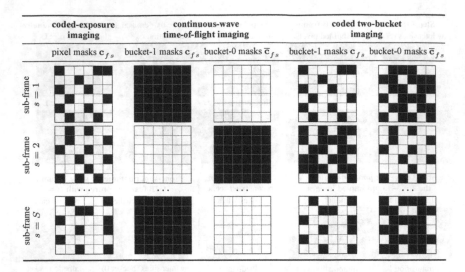

Fig. 3. *Comparison of basic sensor abilities.* Coded-exposure sensors can rapidly mask individual pixels but cannot collect all the incident light; continuous-wave ToF sensors always collect all the incident light but they cannot mask pixels individually; C2B sensors can do both. The column vectors c_{fs} and $\bar{c}_{fs}$ denote bucket-1 masks/activities and their binary complements, respectively.

allow individual pixels to be "masked" for brief periods during the exposure of a video frame (Fig. 3, left). Just like the C2B sensor, they have a writeable one-bit memory inside each pixel to control masking, but their pixels lack a second bucket so light falling onto "masked" pixels is lost. *Continuous-wave time-of-flight sensors* [1,2] can be thought of as having complementary functionality to coded-exposure sensors: their pixels have two buckets whose activity can be toggled programmatically (so no light is lost), but they have no in-pixel writeable memory. As such, the active bucket is constrained to be the same for all pixels (Fig. 3, middle). This makes programmable per-pixel coding—and acquisition of illumination mosaics in particular—impossible without specialized optics (*e.g.*, [17]). *Multi-bucket (*a.k.a., *"multi-tap")* *sensors* [39–42] have more than two buckets in each pixel but they have no writeable memory either, so per-pixel coding is not possible. In theory, an S-bucket sensor would be uniquely suited for dense one-shot reconstruction because it can acquire in each frame S full-resolution images corresponding to any set of S illuminations [43]. In practice, however, C2B sensors have several advantages: they are scalable because they can pack S linearly-independent images into one frame for any value of S—without hard-wiring this value into the pixel's CMOS design; they are much more light efficient because each extra bucket reduces the pixel's photo-sensitive region significantly for a given pixel size; and they have a broader range of applications because they enable per-pixel coding. To our knowledge, 2D sensors with more than four buckets have not been fabricated in a standard CMOS image process, and it is unclear if they could offer acceptable imaging performance.

On the conceptual side, our contributions are the following: (1) we put forth a general model for the C2B camera that opens up new directions for coded-exposure imaging with active sources; (2) we formulate its control as a novel multiplexing problem [31,44–49] in the bucket and pixel domains; (3) we draw a connection between two-bucket imaging and algorithms that operate directly on intensity ratios [50]; and (4) we provide an algorithm-independent framework for dense one-shot reconstruction that is simpler than earlier attempts [18] and is compatible with standard image processing pipelines.

Last but not least, we demonstrate all the above experimentally, on the first fully-operational C2B camera prototype.

2   Coded Two-Bucket Imaging

We begin by introducing an image formation model for C2B cameras. We consider the most general setting in this section, where a whole sequence of C2B frames may be acquired instead of just one.

C2B cameras output *two* images per video frame—one for each bucket (Fig. 2). We refer to these images as the *bucket-1 image* and *bucket-0 image*.

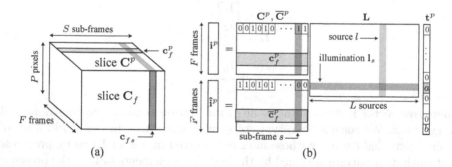

Fig. 4. (a) Structure of the code tensor $\mathbf{C}$. (b) Image formation model for pixel p. We show the transport vector $\mathbf{t}^p$ for a structured-light setting, where the contribution of ambient illumination is $\mathbf{t}^p[L] = b$, the corresponding projector pixel is l, and its albedo is $\mathbf{t}^p[l] = a$.

The Code Tensor. Programming a C2B camera amounts to specifying the time-varying contents of its pixels' memories at two different timescales: (1) at the scale of *sub-frames* within a video frame, which correspond to the updates of the in-pixel memories (Fig. 1, right), and (2) at the scale of frames within a video sequence. For a video sequence with F frames and a camera that has P pixels and supports S sub-frames, bucket activities can be represented as a three-dimensional binary tensor $\mathbf{C}$ of size $P \times F \times S$. We call $\mathbf{C}$ the *code tensor* (Fig. 4a).

We use two specific 2D "slices" of the code tensor in our analysis below, and have special notation for them. For a specific pixel p, slice $\mathbf{C}^p$ describes the activity of pixel p's buckets across all frames and sub-frames. Similarly, for a specific frame f, slice $\mathbf{C}_f$ describes the bucket activity of all pixels across all sub-frames of f:

$$
\mathbf{C}^p = \underbrace{\begin{bmatrix} \mathbf{c}_1^p \\ \mathbf{c}_2^p \\ \vdots \\ \mathbf{c}_F^p \end{bmatrix}}_{F \times S} \qquad \mathbf{C}_f = \underbrace{\begin{bmatrix} \mathbf{c}_{f1} & \mathbf{c}_{f2} & \cdots & \mathbf{c}_{fS} \end{bmatrix}}_{P \times S} , \tag{1}
$$

where $\mathbf{c}_f^p$ is an S-dimensional row vector that specifies the active bucket of pixel p in the sub-frames of frame f; and $\mathbf{c}_{f_s}$ is a P-dimensional column vector that specifies the active bucket of all pixels in sub-frame s of frame f.

The Illumination Matrix. Although C2B cameras can be used for passive imaging applications [15], we model the case where illumination is programmable at sub-frame timescales too. In particular, we represent the scene's time-varying illumination condition as an illumination matrix $\mathbf{L}$ that applies to all frames:

$$
\mathbf{L} = \underbrace{\begin{bmatrix} \mathbf{l}_1 \\ \mathbf{l}_2 \\ \vdots \\ \mathbf{l}_S \end{bmatrix}}_{S \times L} , \tag{2}
$$

where row vector $\mathbf{l}_s$ denotes the scene's illumination condition in sub-frame s of every frame. We consider two types of scene illumination in this work: a set of L directional light sources whose intensity is given by vector $\mathbf{l}_s$; and a projector that projects a pattern specified by the first $L-1$ elements of $\mathbf{l}_s$ in the presence of ambient light, which we treat as an L-th source that is "always on" (*i.e.*, element $\mathbf{l}_s[L] = 1$ for all s).

Two-Bucket Image Formation Model for Pixel p. Let $\mathbf{i}^p$ and $\hat{\mathbf{i}}^p$ be column vectors holding the intensities of pixel p's bucket 1 and bucket 0, respectively, in F frames. We model these intensities as the result of light transport from the L light sources to the pixel's two buckets (Fig. 4b):

$$
\underbrace{\begin{bmatrix} \mathbf{i}^p \\ \hat{\mathbf{i}}^p \end{bmatrix}}_{2F \times 1} = \underbrace{\begin{bmatrix} \mathbf{C}^p \\ \overline{\mathbf{C}}^p \end{bmatrix}}_{2F \times S} \underbrace{\mathbf{L}}_{S \times L} \underbrace{\mathbf{t}^p}_{L \times 1} , \tag{3}
$$

where $\overline{b}$ denotes the binary complement of matrix or vector b, $\mathbf{C}^p$ is the slice of the code tensor corresponding to p, and $\mathbf{t}^p$ is the pixel's *transport vector*.

Element $\mathbf{t}^p[l]$ of this vector describes the transport of light from source l to pixel p in the timespan of one sub-frame, across all light paths.

To gain some intuition about Eq. (3), consider the buckets' intensities in frame f:

$$\mathbf{i}^p[f] = \underbrace{\left(\mathbf{c}_f^p\,\mathbf{L}\right)}_{\substack{\text{illumination condition} \\ \text{of pixel } p,\ \text{bucket 1, frame } f}}\ \mathbf{t}^p \qquad\qquad \hat{\mathbf{i}}^p[f] = \underbrace{\left(\bar{\mathbf{c}}_f^p\,\mathbf{L}\right)}_{\substack{\text{illumination condition} \\ \text{of pixel } p,\ \text{bucket 0, frame } f}}\ \mathbf{t}^p\ . \tag{4}$$

In effect, the two buckets of pixel p can be thought of as "viewing" the scene under two potentially different illuminations given by vectors $\mathbf{c}_f^p\mathbf{L}$ and $\bar{\mathbf{c}}_f^p\mathbf{L}$, respectively. Moreover, if $\mathbf{c}_f^p$ varies from frame to frame, these illumination conditions may vary as well.

Bucket Ratios as Albedo "Quasi-Invariants". Since the two buckets of pixel p generally represent different illumination conditions, the two ratios

$$r = \frac{\mathbf{i}^p[f]}{\mathbf{i}^p[f] + \hat{\mathbf{i}}^p[f]} \quad,\quad \hat{r} = \frac{\hat{\mathbf{i}}^p[f]}{\mathbf{i}^p[f] + \hat{\mathbf{i}}^p[f]}\ , \tag{5}$$

defined by p's buckets are *illumination ratios* [50–52]. Moreover, we show in [32] that under zero-mean Gaussian image noise, these ratios are well approximated by Gaussian random variables whose means are the ideal (noiseless) ratios and whose standard deviations depend weakly on albedo. In effect, C2B cameras provide two "albedo-invariant" images per frame. We exploit this feature of C2B cameras for both shape recovery and demosaicing in Sects. 3 and 5, respectively.

2.1 Acquiring Two-Bucket Illumination Mosaics

A key feature of C2B cameras is that they offer an important alternative to multi-frame acquisition: instead of capturing F frames in sequence, they can capture a spatially-multiplexed version of them in a single C2B frame (Fig. 2). We call such a frame a *two-bucket illumination mosaic* in analogy to the RGB filter mosaics of color image sensors [12,53,54]. Unlike filter mosaics, however, which are attached to the sensor and cannot be changed, acquisition of illumination mosaics is programmable for any F.

The Bucket-1 and Bucket-0 Image Sequences. Collecting the two buckets' intensities in Eq. (4) across all frames and pixels, we define two matrices that hold all this data:

$$\mathbf{I} = \underbrace{\begin{bmatrix} \mathbf{i}^1 & \mathbf{i}^2 & \cdots & \mathbf{i}^P \end{bmatrix}}_{F \times P} \qquad\qquad \hat{\mathbf{I}} = \underbrace{\begin{bmatrix} \hat{\mathbf{i}}^1 & \hat{\mathbf{i}}^2 & \cdots & \hat{\mathbf{i}}^P \end{bmatrix}}_{F \times P}\ . \tag{6}$$

Code Tensor for Mosaic Acquisition. Formally, a two-bucket illumination mosaic is a spatial sub-sampling of the sequences $\mathbf{I}$ and $\hat{\mathbf{I}}$ in Eq. (6). Acquiring it amounts to specifying a one-frame code tensor $\widetilde{\mathbf{C}}$ that spatially multiplexes the corresponding F-frame tensor $\mathbf{C}$ in Fig. 4(a). We do this by (1) defining a regular tiling of the sensor plane and (2) specifying a correspondence $(p_i \to f_i), 1 \le i \le K$, between the K pixels in a tile and frames. The rows of $\widetilde{\mathbf{C}}$ are then defined to be

$$\widetilde{\mathbf{c}}_1^{p_i} \stackrel{\text{def}}{=} \mathbf{c}_{f_i}^{p_i} . \tag{7}$$

Mosaic Acquisition Example. The C2B frames in Fig. 2 were captured using a 2×2 pixel tile to spatially multiplex a three-frame code tensor. The tensor assigned identical illumination conditions to all pixels within a frame and different conditions across frames. Pixels within each tile were assigned to individual frames using the correspondence $\{(1,1) \to 1, (1,2) \to 2, (2,1) \to 2, (2,2) \to 3\}$.

3   Per-Pixel Estimation of Normals and Disparities

Let us now turn to the problem of normal and disparity estimation using photometric stereo and structured-light triangulation, respectively. We consider the most basic formulation of these tasks, where all computations are done independently at each pixel and the relation between observations and unknowns is expressed as a system of linear equations. These formulations should be treated merely as examples that showcase the special characteristics of two-bucket imaging; as with conventional cameras, using advanced methods to handle more general settings [55,56] is certainly possible.

From Bucket Intensities to Demultiplexed Intensities. As a starting point, we expand Eq. (3) to get a relation that involves only intensities:

$$\underbrace{\begin{bmatrix} \mathbf{i}^p \\ \hat{\mathbf{i}}^p \end{bmatrix}}_{\substack{\text{bucket measurements} \\ (2F \times 1)}} = \begin{bmatrix} \mathbf{C}^p \\ \overline{\mathbf{C}}^p \end{bmatrix} \begin{bmatrix} l_1 \mathbf{t}^p \\ \vdots \\ l_S \mathbf{t}^p \end{bmatrix} \stackrel{\text{def}}{=} \underbrace{\begin{bmatrix} \mathbf{C}^p \\ \overline{\mathbf{C}}^p \end{bmatrix}}_{\substack{\text{bucket-multiplexing} \\ \text{matrix } \mathbf{W} \\ (2F \times S)}} \underbrace{\begin{bmatrix} i_1^p \\ \vdots \\ i_S^p \end{bmatrix}}_{\substack{\text{pixel intensity under} \\ \text{illuminations } l_1, \dots, l_S \\ (S \times 1)}} . \tag{8}$$

Each scalar i_s^p in the right-hand side of Eq. (8) is the intensity that a conventional camera pixel would record if the scene's illumination condition was l_s. Therefore, Eq. (8) tells us that as far as a single pixel p is concerned, C2B cameras capture the same S measurements a conventional camera would capture for 3D reconstruction—except that these measurements are multiplexed over $2F$ bucket intensities. To retrieve them, these intensities must be demultiplexed by inverting Eq. (8):

$$\begin{bmatrix} i_1^p \\ \vdots \\ i_S^p \end{bmatrix} = (\mathbf{W}'\mathbf{W})^{-1}\mathbf{W}' \begin{bmatrix} \mathbf{i}^p \\ \hat{\mathbf{i}}^p \end{bmatrix} , \tag{9}$$

where $'$ denotes matrix transpose. This inversion is only possible if $(\mathbf{W}'\mathbf{W})^{-1}\mathbf{W}'$ is non-singular. Moreover, the signal-to-noise ratio (SNR) of the demultiplexed

Table 1. The two basic multi-image reconstruction techniques considered in this work.

	Lambertian photometric stereo	Structured-light triangulation w/ cosine patterns
Assumptions	Lambertian reflectance, non-uniform albedo; calibrated light sources; no ambient or indirect light	reflectance has non-negligible diffuse component; robustness to indirect light depends on frequency choice
Illumination vectors $\mathbf{l}_s$	each $\mathbf{l}_s$ corresponds to illumination with only source s turned on, *i.e.*, element $\mathbf{l}_s[l]$ is non-zero iff $s = l$	$\mathbf{l}_s[l] = \cos(\phi_s + \theta_l)$, where ϕ_s is phase shift of s-th pattern, θ_l is phase of projector pixel l
Vector $\mathbf{d}_s$	orientation and intensity of source s, expressed as a 3D row vector	$\mathbf{d}_s = \begin{bmatrix} \cos(\phi_s) & -\sin(\phi_s) & 1 \end{bmatrix}$
Matrix $\mathbf{D}$	matrix whose rows are the vectors $\mathbf{d}_1, \ldots \mathbf{d}_S$	matrix whose rows are the vectors $\mathbf{d}_1, \ldots \mathbf{d}_S$
Transport vector $\mathbf{t}$	$\mathbf{t}[s] = a\mathbf{d}_s\mathbf{n}$ where a is the albedo and $\mathbf{n}$ is the unit surface normal	$\mathbf{t} = \begin{bmatrix} a\mathbf{m} & b \end{bmatrix}'$, where a is albedo, b is the contribution of ambient light, and binary row vector $\mathbf{m}$ indicates the matching projector pixel, *i.e.*, $\mathbf{m}[l] = 1$ iff that pixel is l (see Fig. 4b)
Vector $\mathbf{x}$	$\mathbf{x} = \mathbf{n}$	$\mathbf{x} = \begin{bmatrix} \cos(\theta) & \sin(\theta) & \frac{b}{a} \end{bmatrix}'$ if the same cosine frequency is used for all patterns; additional frequencies contribute two unknowns each; θ is the phase of the matching projector pixel

intensities depends heavily on $\mathbf{W}$ and $\mathbf{C}^p$ (Sect. 4). Setting aside this issue for now, we consider below the task of shape recovery from already-demultiplexed intensities. For notational simplicity, we drop the pixel index p from the equations below.

Per-Pixel Constraints on 3D Shape. The relation between demultiplexed intensities and the pixel's unknowns takes exactly the same form in both photometric stereo and structured-light triangulation with cosine patterns:

$$\begin{bmatrix} i_1 \\ \vdots \\ i_S \end{bmatrix} = a\mathbf{D}\mathbf{x} + \mathbf{e}, \tag{10}$$

where $\mathbf{D}$ is known; $\mathbf{x}$ is a 3D vector that contains the pixel's shape unknowns; a is the unknown albedo; and $\mathbf{e}$ is observation noise. See Table 1 for a summary of each problem's assumptions and for the mapping of problem-specific quantities to Eq. (10).

There are (at least) three ways to turn Eq. (10) into a constraint on normals and disparities under zero-mean Gaussian noise. The resulting constraints are *not* equivalent when combining measurements from small pixel neighborhoods—as we implicitly do—because they are not equally invariant to spatial albedo variations:

1. *Direct method (DM):* treat Eq. (10) as providing S independent constraints on vector $a\mathbf{x}$ and solve for both a and $\mathbf{x}$. The advantage of this approach is that errors are Gaussian by construction; its disadvantage is that Eq. (10) depends on albedo.
2. *Ratio constraint (R):* divide individual intensities by their total sum to obtain an illumination ratio, as in Eq. (5). This yields the following constraint on $\mathbf{x}$:

$$r_l \mathbf{1Dx} = \mathbf{d}_l \mathbf{x}, \tag{11}$$

   where $r_l = i_l / \sum_k i_k$ and $\mathbf{1}$ is a row vector of all ones. The advantage here is that both r_l and Eq. (11) are approximately invariant to albedo.
3. *Cross-product constraint (CP):* instead of computing an explicit ratio from Eq. (10), eliminate a to obtain

$$i_l \mathbf{d}_k \mathbf{x} = i_k \mathbf{d}_l \mathbf{x}. \tag{12}$$

   Since Eq. (12) has intensities i_l, i_k as factors, it does implicitly depend on albedo.

Solving for the Unknowns. Both structured light and photometric stereo require at least $S \geq 3$ independent constraints for a unique solution. In the DM method, we use least-squares to solve for $a\mathbf{x}$; when using the R or CP constraints, we apply singular-value decomposition to solve for $\mathbf{x}$.

4   Code Matrices for Bucket Multiplexing

The previous section gave ways to solve for 3D shape when we have enough independent constraints per pixel. Here we consider the problem of controlling a C2B camera to actually obtain them for a pixel p. In particular, we show how to choose (1) the number of frames F, (2) the number of sub-frames per frame S, and (3) the pixel-specific slice $\mathbf{C}^p$ of the code tensor, which defines the multiplexing matrix $\mathbf{W}$ in Eq. (8).

Determining these parameters can be thought of as an instance of the *optimal multiplexing* problem [31,44–49]. This problem has been considered in numerous contexts before, as a one-to-one mapping from S desired measurements to S actual, noisy observations. In the case of coded two-bucket imaging, however, the problem is slightly different because each frame yields two measurements instead of just one.

The results below provide further insight into this particular multiplexing problem (see [32] for proofs). Observation 1 implies that even though a pixel's two buckets provide $2F$ measurements in total across F frames, at most $F+1$ of them can be independent because the multiplexing matrix $\mathbf{W}$ is rank-deficient:

Observation 1. $\operatorname{rank}\mathbf{W} \leq \min(F+1, S)$.

Intuitively, a C2B camera should not be thought of as being equivalent to two coded-exposure cameras that operate completely independently. This is because the activities of a pixel's two buckets are binary complements of each other, and thus not independent.

Corollary 1. Multiplexing S intensities requires $F \geq S - 1$ frames.

Corollary 2. The minimal configuration for fully-constrained reconstruction at a pixel p is $F = 2$ frames, $S = 3$ sub-frames per frame, and $S = 3$ linearly-independent illumination vectors of dimension $L \geq 3$. The next-highest configuration is 3 frames, 4 subframes/illumination vectors.

We now seek the optimal $(S-1) \times S$ matrix $\mathbf{C}^p$, i.e., the matrix that maximizes the SNR of the demultiplexed intensities in Eq. (9). Lemma 1 extends the lower-bound analysis of Ratner et al. [45] to obtain a lower bound on the mean-squared error (MSE) of two-bucket multiplexing [32]:

Lemma 1. For every multiplexing matrix $\mathbf{W}$, the MSE of the best unbiased linear estimator satisfies the lower bound

$$\text{MSE} = \frac{\sigma^2}{S}\operatorname{trace}\left[\left(\mathbf{W}'\mathbf{W}\right)^{-1}\right] \geq 2\sigma^2\frac{(S-1)^2+1}{(S-1)S^2} \ . \tag{13}$$

Although Lemma 1 does not provide an explicit construction, it does ensure the optimality of $\mathbf{W}$ matrices whose MSEs achieve the lower bound. We used this observation to prove the optimality of matrices derived from the standard Hadamard construction [31]:

Table 2. *Optimal matrices* $\mathbf{C}^p$ *for small S.* Note that the lower bound given by Eq. (13) is attained only for $S = 4$, i.e., for the smallest Hadamard-based construction of $\mathbf{C}^p$.

# sub-frames	$S = 3$	$S = 4$	$S = 5$	$S = 6$	$S = 7$
Eq. (13) bound for $\sigma = 1$	0.5556	0.4167	0.34	0.2889	0.2517
Optimal MSE for $\sigma = 1$	0.8333	0.4167	0.3778	0.3467	0.3210
Optimal $\mathbf{C}^p$	1 0 0	1 1 0 0	1 1 0 0 0	1 1 1 0 0 0	1 1 1 1 1 0 0
	0 1 0	1 0 1 0	1 0 1 0 0	1 1 0 0 1 0	1 1 1 0 0 0 1
		1 0 0 1	1 0 0 1 0	1 0 1 1 1 0	1 1 0 0 1 1 0
			1 0 0 0 1	1 0 1 0 1 1	1 0 1 0 1 1 0
				1 0 0 1 0 1	1 0 0 1 0 1 0
					1 0 0 0 1 0 1

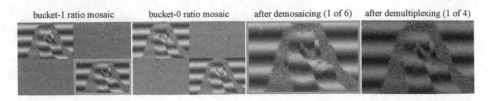

bucket-1 ratio mosaic   bucket-0 ratio mosaic   after demosaicing (1 of 6)   after demultiplexing (1 of 4)

Fig. 5. *Processing ratio mosaics.* Left to right: Intermediate results of the BRD reconstruction procedure of Sect. 5, starting from the raw C2B frame shown in Fig. 2, Step 1. In contrast to the result of Steps 2 and 3 in Fig. 2, the images above are largely unaffected by albedo variations.

Proposition 1. Let $\mathbf{C}^p = \frac{1}{2}(\widetilde{\mathbf{H}} + 1)$ where $\widetilde{\mathbf{H}}$ is derived from the $S \times S$ Hadamard matrix by removing its row of ones to create an $(S - 1) \times S$ matrix. The bucket-multiplexing matrix $\mathbf{W}$ defined by $\mathbf{C}^p$ is optimal.

The smallest S for which Proposition 1 applies are $S = 4$ and $S = 8$. Since our main goal is one-shot acquisition, optimal matrices for other small values of S are also of significant interest. To find them, we conducted a brute-force search over the space of small $(S - 1) \times S$ binary matrices to find the ones with the lowest MSE. These matrices are shown in Table 2. See Fig. 6(a), (b) and [32] for an initial empirical SNR analysis.

5 One-Shot Shape from Two-Bucket Illumination Mosaics

We use three different ways of estimating shape from a two-bucket illumination mosaic:

1. *Intensity demosaicing (ID):* treat the intensities in a mosaic tile as separate "imaging dimensions" for the purpose of demosaicing; upsample these intensities by applying either an RGB demosaicing algorithm to three of these dimensions at a time, or by using a more general assorted-pixel procedure [12,54] that takes all of them into account; demultiplex the $2F$ upsampled images using Eq. (9); and apply any of the estimation methods in Sect. 3 to the result. Fig. 2 illustrates this approach.
2. *Bucket-ratio demosaicing (BRD):* apply Eq. (5) to each pixel in the mosaic to obtain an albedo-invariant two-bucket ratio mosaic; demosaic and demultiplex them; and compute 3D shape using the ratio constraint of Sect. 3. See Fig. 5 for an example.
3. *No demosaicing (ND):* instead of upsampling, treat each mosaic tile as a "super-pixel" whose unknowns (*i.e.*, normal, disparity, *etc.*) do not vary within the tile; compute one shape estimate per tile using any of the methods of Sect. 3.

Performance Evaluation of One-Shot Photometric Stereo on Synthetic Data. Figures 6(c) and (d) analyze the effective resolution and albedo invariance of normal maps computed by several combinations of methods from Sects. 3 and 5, plus two more—*Baseline*, which applies basic photometric stereo to three full-resolution images; and *Color*, the one-shot color photometric stereo technique in [23]. To generate synthetic data, we (1) generated scenes with random spatially-varying normal maps and RGB albedo maps, (2) applied a spatial low-pass filter to albedo maps and the spherical coordinates of normal maps, (3) rendered them to create three sets of images—a grayscale C2B frame; three full-resolution grayscale images; and a Bayer color mosaic—and (4) added zero-mean Gaussian noise to each pixel, corresponding to a peak SNR of 30dB. Since all calculations except demosaicing are done per pixel, any frequency-dependent variations in performance must be due to this upsampling step. Our simulation results do match the intuition that performance should degrade for very high normal map frequencies regardless of the type of neighborhood processing. For spatial frequencies up to 0.3 the Nyquist limit, however, one-shot C2B imaging confers a substantial performance advantage. A similar evaluation for structured-light triangulation can be found in [32].

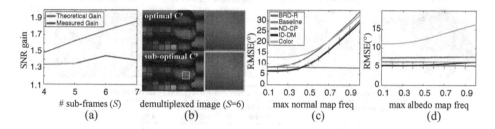

Fig. 6. (a) Optimal versus sub-optimal multiplexing. We applied bucket multiplexing to the scene shown in (b) and empirically measured the average SNR of demultiplexed images when (1) $\mathbf{C}^p$ is given by Table 2 and (2) $\mathbf{C}^p = [\mathbf{1}_{(S-1)\times(S-1)} \ \mathbf{0}]$, which is a non-degenerate and sub-optimal matrix according to its MSE using Eq. (13) ($\mathbf{1}_{(S-1)\times(S-1)}$ is the identity matrix). The ratios of these SNRs are shown in blue, suggesting that SNR gains are possible. (b) One out of S demultiplexed images obtained with each $\mathbf{C}^p$. The optimal $\mathbf{C}^p$ yielded visibly less noisy images (please zoom in to the electronic copy). (c) Angular root-mean-squared error (RMSE) of normal estimates as a function of the normal map's highest spatial frequency. Frequency 1.0 corresponds to the Nyquist limit. The highest spatial frequency of albedos was set to 0.3 the Nyquist limit. (d) Angular error as a function of the spatial frequency of the albedo map, with the maximum spatial frequency of the normal map set to 0.3 the Nyquist limit. Line colors are as indicated in (c). (Color figure online)

6   Live 3D Imaging with a C2B Camera

Experimental Conditions. Both C2B frame acquisition and scene reconstruction run at 20 Hz for all experiments, using $F = 3, S = 4$, the corresponding optimal $\mathbf{C}^p$ from Table 2, and the 2×2 mosaic tile defined in Sect. 2.1. C2B frames are always processed by the same sequence of steps—demosaicing, demultiplexing and per-pixel reconstruction. For structured light, we fit an 8 mm Schneider Cinegon $f/1.4$ lens to our camera with its aperture set to $f/2$, and use a TI LightCrafter for projecting 684×608-pixel, 24-gray-level patterns at a rate of $S \times 20$ Hz in sync with sub-frames. The stereo baseline was approximately 20 cm, the scene was 1.1–1.5 m away, and the cosine frequency was 5 for all patterns and experiments. For photometric stereo we switch to a 23mm Schneider APO-Xenoplan $f/1.4$ lens to approximate orthographic imaging conditions, and illuminate a scene 2–3 m away with four sub-frame synchronized Luxdrive 7040 Endor Star LEDs, fitted with 26.5 mm Carclo Technical Plastics lenses.

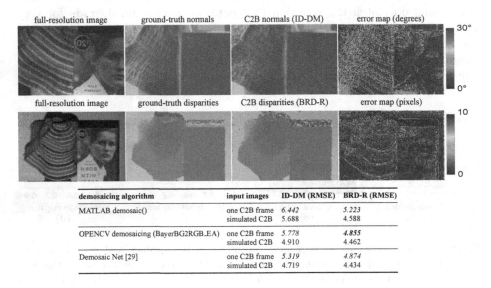

demosaicing algorithm	input images		ID-DM (RMSE)	BRD-R (RMSE)
MATLAB demosaic()	one C2B frame	*6.442*		*5.223*
	simulated C2B	5.688		4.588
OPENCV demosaicing (BayerBG2RGB_EA)	one C2B frame	*5.778*		*4.855*
	simulated C2B	4.910		4.462
Demosaic Net [29]	one C2B frame	*5.319*		*4.874*
	simulated C2B	4.719		4.434

Fig. 7. *Quantitative experiments for photometric stereo (Row 1) and structured light (Rows 2, 3). Per-pixel unit normals* **n** *are visualized by assigning to them the RGB color vector* $0.5\mathbf{n} + 0.5$.

Quantitative Experiments. Our goal was to compare the 3D accuracy of one-shot C2B imaging against that of full-resolution sequential imaging—using the exact same system and algorithms. Figure 7 shows the static scenes used for these experiments, along with example reconstructions for photometric stereo and structured light, respectively. The "ground truth," which served as our reference, was computed by averaging 1000 sequentially-captured, bucket-1 images per illumination condition and applying the same reconstruction algorithm to the lower-noise, averaged images. To further distinguish the impact of demosaicing from that of sensor-specific non-idealities, we also compute shape from a *simulated* C2B frame; to create it we spatially multiplex the S averaged images computationally in a way that simulates the operation of our C2B sensor. Row 3 of Fig. 7 shows some of these comparisons for structured light. The BRD-R

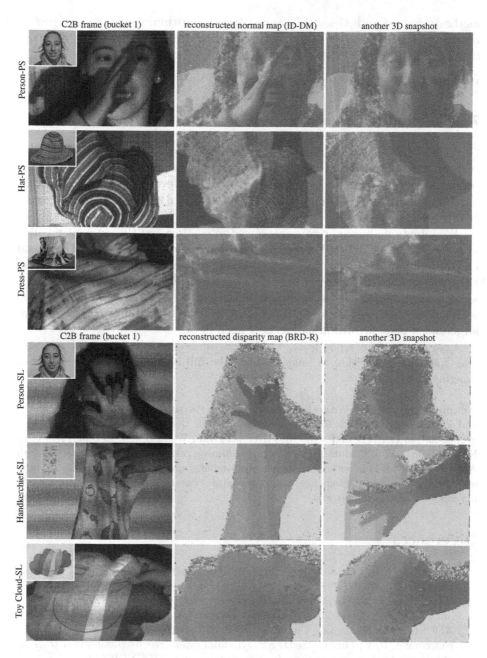

Fig. 8. *Live 3D acquisition experiments for photometric stereo (top) and structured light (bottom).* Scenes were chosen to exhibit significant albedo, color, normal and/or depth variations, as well as discontinuities. For reference, color photos of these scenes are shown as insets in Column 1. Qualitatively, reconstructions appear to be consistent with the scenes' actual 3D geometry except in regions of low albedo (*e.g.*, hair) or cast shadows. (Color figure online)

method, coupled with OpenCV's demosaicing algorithm, yields the best performance in this case, corresponding to a disparity error of 4%. See [32] for more details and additional results.

Reconstructing Dynamic Scenes. Figure 8 shows several examples.

7   Concluding Remarks

Our experiments relied on some of the very first images from a C2B sensor. Issues such as fixed-pattern noise; slight variations in gain across buckets and across pixels; and other minor non-idealities do still exist. Nevertheless, we believe that our preliminary results support the claim that 3D data are acquired at near-sensor resolution.

We intentionally used raw, unprocessed intensities and the simplest possible approaches for demosaicing and reconstruction. There is no doubt that denoised images and more advanced reconstruction algorithms could improve reconstruction performance considerably. Our use of generic RGB demosaicing software is also clearly sub-optimal, as their algorithms do not take into account the actual correlations that exist across C2B pixels. A prudent approach would be to train an assorted-pixel algorithm on precisely such data.

Last but certainly not least, we are particularly excited about C2B cameras sparking new vision techniques that take full advantage of their advanced imaging capabilities.

Acknowledgements. We gratefully acknowledge the support of the Natural Sciences and Engineering Research Council of Canada under the RGPIN, RTI and SGP programs, and of DARPA under the REVEAL program. We also wish to thank Hui Feng Ke and Gilead Wolf Posluns for FPGA programming related to the C2B sensor, Sarah Anne Kushner for help with live imaging experiments, and Michael Brown, Harel Haim and the anonymous reviewers for their many helpful comments and suggestions on earlier versions of this manuscript.

References

1. Lange, R., Seitz, P.: Solid-state time-of-flight range camera. IEEE J. Quantum Electron. **37**(3), 390–397 (2001)
2. Bamji, C.S., et al.: A 0.13 μm CMOS system-on-chip for a 512 × 424 time-of-flight image sensor with multi-frequency photo-demodulation up to 130 MHz and 2 GS/s ADC. IEEE J. Solid-State Circ. **50**(1), 303–319 (2015)
3. Newcombe, R.A., Fox, D., Seitz, S.: DynamicFusion: reconstruction and tracking of non-rigid scenes in real-time. In: Proceedings of IEEE CVPR (2015)
4. Heide, F., Hullin, M.B., Gregson, J., Heidrich, W.: Low-budget transient imaging using photonic mixer devices. In: Proceedings of ACM SIGGRAPH (2013)
5. Kadambi, A., Bhandari, A., Whyte, R., Dorrington, A., Raskar, R.: Demultiplexing illumination via low cost sensing and nanosecond coding. In: Proceedings of IEEE ICCP (2014)
6. Shrestha, S., Heide, F., Heidrich, W., Wetzstein, G.: Computational imaging with multi-camera time-of-flight systems. In: Proceedings of ACM SIGGRAPH (2016)

7. Callenberg, C., Heide, F., Wetzstein, G., Hullin, M.B.: Snapshot difference imaging using correlation time-of-flight sensors. In: Proceedings of ACM SIGGRAPH, Asia (2017)

8. Lichtsteiner, P., Posch, C., Delbruck, T.: A 128×128 120 dB 15 μs latency asynchronous temporal contrast vision sensor. IEEE J. Solid-State Circ. **43**(2), 566–576 (2008)

9. Kim, H., Leutenegger, S., Davison, A.J.: Real-time 3D reconstruction and 6-DoF tracking with an event camera. In: Leibe, B., Matas, J., Sebe, N., Welling, M. (eds.) ECCV 2016. LNCS, vol. 9910, pp. 349–364. Springer, Cham (2016). https://doi.org/10.1007/978-3-319-46466-4_21

10. Matsuda, N., Cossairt, O., Gupta, M.: MC3D: motion contrast 3D scanning. In: Proceedings of IEEE ICCP (2015)

11. Jang, J., Yoo, Y., Kim, J., Paik, J.: Sensor-based auto-focusing system using multiscale feature extraction and phase correlation matching. Sensors **15**(3), 5747–5762 (2015)

12. Yasuma, F., Mitsunaga, T., Iso, D., Nayar, S.K.: Generalized assorted pixel camera: postcapture control of resolution, dynamic range, and spectrum. IEEE-TIP **19**(9), 2241–2253 (2010)

13. Zhang, J., Etienne-Cummings, R., Chin, S., Xiong, T., Tran, T.: Compact all-CMOS spatiotemporal compressive sensing video camera with pixel-wise coded exposure. Opt. Express **24**(8), 9013–9024 (2016)

14. Sonoda, T., Nagahara, H., Endo, K., Sugiyama, Y., Taniguchi, R.: High-speed imaging using CMOS image sensor with quasi pixel-wise exposure. In: Proceedings of IEEE ICCP (2016)

15. Baraniuk, R.G., Goldstein, T., Sankaranarayanan, A.C., Studer, C., Veeraraghavan, A., Wakin, M.B.: Compressive video sensing: algorithms, architectures, and applications. IEEE Sig. Process. Mag. **34**(1), 52–66 (2017)

16. Fossum, E.R., Hondongwa, D.B.: A review of the pinned photodiode for CCD and CMOS image sensors. IEEE J. Electron Devices **2**(3), 33–43 (2014)

17. Hitomi, Y., Gu, J., Gupta, M., Mitsunaga, T., Nayar, S.K.: Video from a single coded exposure photograph using a learned over-complete dictionary. In: Proceedings of IEEE ICCV (2011)

18. O'Toole, M., Mather, J., Kutulakos, K.N.: 3D shape and indirect appearance by structured light transport. IEEE T-PAMI **38**(7), 1298–1312 (2016)

19. Sheinin, M., Schechner, Y., Kutulakos, K.N.: Computational imaging on the electric grid. In: Proceedings of IEEE CVPR (2017)

20. O'Toole, M., Achar, S., Narasimhan, S.G., Kutulakos, K.N.: Homogeneous codes for energy-efficient illumination and imaging. In: Proceedings of ACM SIGGRAPH (2015)

21. Heintzmann, R., Hanley, Q.S., Arndt-Jovin, D., Jovin, T.M.: A dual path programmable array microscope (PAM): simultaneous acquisition of conjugate and non-conjugate images. J. Microsc. **204**(2), 119–135 (2001)

22. Raskar, R., Agrawal, A., Tumblin, J.: Coded exposure photography: motion deblurring using fluttered shutter. In: Proceedings of ACM SIGGRAPH (2006)

23. Hernandez, C., Vogiatzis, G., Brostow, G.J., Stenger, B., Cipolla, R.: Non-rigid photometric stereo with colored lights. In: Proceedings of IEEE ICCV (2007)

24. Kim, H., Wilburn, B., Ben-Ezra, M.: Photometric stereo for dynamic surface orientations. In: Daniilidis, K., Maragos, P., Paragios, N. (eds.) ECCV 2010. LNCS, vol. 6311, pp. 59–72. Springer, Heidelberg (2010). https://doi.org/10.1007/978-3-642-15549-9_5

25. Fyffe, G., Yu, X., Debevec, P.: Single-shot photometric stereo by spectral multi-plexing. In: Proceedings of IEEE ICCP (2011)
26. Van der Jeught, S., Dirckx, J.J.J.: Real-time structured light profilometry: a review. Opt. Lasers Eng. **87**, 18–31 (2016)
27. Sagawa, R., Furukawa, R., Kawasaki, H.: Dense 3D reconstruction from high frame-rate video using a static grid pattern. IEEE T-PAMI **36**(9), 1733–1747 (2014)
28. Narasimhan, S.G., Koppal, S.J., Yamazaki, S.: Temporal dithering of illumination for fast active vision. In: Forsyth, D., Torr, P., Zisserman, A. (eds.) ECCV 2008. LNCS, vol. 5305, pp. 830–844. Springer, Heidelberg (2008). https://doi.org/10.1007/978-3-540-88693-8_61
29. Gharbi, M., Chaurasia, G., Paris, S., Durand, F.: Deep joint demosaicking and denoising. In: Proceedings of ACM SIGGRAPH Asia (2016)
30. Heide, F., et al.: FlexISP: a flexible camera image processing framework. In: Proceedings of ACM SIGGRAPH, Asia (2014)
31. Schechner, Y.Y., Nayar, S.K., Belhumeur, P.N.: Multiplexing for optimal lighting. IEEE T-PAMI **29**(8), 1339–1354 (2007)
32. Wei, M., Sarhangnejad, N., Xia, Z., Gusev, N., Katic, N., Genov, R., Kutulakos, K.N.: Coded two-bucket cameras for computer vision: supplemental document. In: Proceedings of ECCV (2018), also available at http://www.dgp.toronto.edu/C2B
33. Salvi, J., Fernandez, S., Pribanic, T., Llado, X.: A state of the art in structured light patterns for surface profilometry. Pattern Recogn. **43**(8), 2666–2680 (2010)
34. Salvi, J., Pages, J., Batlle, J.: Pattern codification strategies in structured light systems. Pattern Recogn. **37**(4), 827–849 (2004)
35. Woodham, R.J.: Photometric method for determining surface orientation from multiple images. Opt. Eng. **19**(1), 191139 (1980)
36. Sarhangnejad, N., Lee, H., Katic, N., O'Toole, M., Kutulakos, K.N., Genov, R.: CMOS image sensor architecture for primal-dual coding. In: International Image Sensor Workshop (2017)
37. Luo, Y., Mirabbasi, S.: Always-on CMOS image sensor pixel design for pixel-wise binary coded exposure. In: IEEE International Symposium on Circuits & Systems (2017)
38. Luo, Y., Ho, D., Mirabbasi, S.: Exposure-programmable CMOS pixel with selective charge storage and code memory for computational imaging. IEEE Trans. Circ. Syst. **65**(5), 1555–1566 (2018)
39. Wan, G., Li, X., Agranov, G., Levoy, M., Horowitz, M.: CMOS image sensors with multi-bucket pixels for computational photography. IEEE J. Solid-State Circ. **47**(4), 1031–1042 (2012)
40. Wilburn, B.S., Ben-Ezra, M.: Time interleaved exposures and multiplexed illumination. US Patent 9,100,581 (2015)
41. Wan, G., Horowitz, M., Levoy, M.: Applications of multi-bucket sensors to computational photography. Technical report, Stanford Computer Graphics Lab (2012)
42. Seo, M.W., et al.: 4.3 A programmable sub-nanosecond time-gated 4-tap lock-in pixel CMOS image sensor for real-time fluorescence lifetime imaging microscopy. In: Proceedings of IEEE ISSCC (2017)
43. Yoda, T., Nagahara, H., Taniguchi, R.I., Kagawa, K., Yasutomi, K., Kawahito, S.: The dynamic photometric stereo method using a multi-tap CMOS image sensor. Sensors **18**(3), 786 (2018)
44. Wetzstein, G., Ihrke, I., Heidrich, W.: On plenoptic multiplexing and reconstruction. Int. J. Comput. Vis. **101**(2), 384–400 (2013)
45. Ratner, N., Schechner, Y.Y., Goldberg, F.: Optimal multiplexed sensing: bounds, conditions and a graph theory link. Opt. Express **15**(25), 17072–17092 (2007)

46. Brown, C.M.: Multiplex imaging and random arrays. Ph.D. thesis, University of Chicago (1972)
47. Ratner, N., Schechner, Y.Y.: Illumination multiplexing within fundamental limits. In: Proceedings of IEEE CVPR (2007)
48. Nonoyama, M., Sakaue, F., Sato, J.: Multiplex image projection using multi-band projectors. In: IEEE Workshop on Color and Photometry in Computer Vision (2013)
49. Mitra, K., Cossairt, O.S., Veeraraghavan, A.: A framework for analysis of computational imaging systems: role of signal prior. IEEE T-PAMI Sens. Noise Multiplexing **36**(10), 1909–1921 (2014)
50. Liu, Z., Shan, Y., Zhang, Z.: Expressive expression mapping with ratio images. In: Proceedings of ACM SIGGRAPH (2001)
51. Wang, L., Yang, R., Davis, J.: BRDF invariant stereo using light transport constancy. IEEE T-PAMI **29**(9), 1616–1626 (2007)
52. Pilet, J., Strecha, C., Fua, P.: Making background subtraction robust to sudden illumination changes. In: Forsyth, D., Torr, P., Zisserman, A. (eds.) ECCV 2008. LNCS, vol. 5305, pp. 567–580. Springer, Heidelberg (2008). https://doi.org/10.1007/978-3-540-88693-8_42
53. Bayer, B.E.: Color imaging array. US Patent 3,971,065 (1976)
54. Narasimhan, S.G., Nayar, S.: Enhancing resolution along multiple imaging dimensions using assorted pixels. IEEE T-PAMI **27**(4), 518–530 (2005)
55. Queau, Y., Mecca, R., Durou, J.D., Descombes, X.: Photometric stereo with only two images: a theoretical study and numerical resolution. Image Vis. Comput. **57**, 175–191 (2017)
56. Gupta, M., Nayar, S.K.: Micro phase shifting. In: Proceedings of IEEE CVPR (2012)

Materials for Masses: SVBRDF Acquisition with a Single Mobile Phone Image

Zhengqin Li[1(✉)], Kalyan Sunkavalli[2], and Manmohan Chandraker[1]

[1] University of California, San Diego, USA
zhl378@eng.ucsd.edu
[2] Adobe Research, San Jose, USA

Abstract. We propose a material acquisition approach to recover the spatially-varying BRDF and normal map of a near-planar surface from a single image captured by a handheld mobile phone camera. Our method images the surface under arbitrary environment lighting with the flash turned on, thereby avoiding shadows while simultaneously capturing high-frequency specular highlights. We train a CNN to regress an SVBRDF and surface normals from this image. Our network is trained using a large-scale SVBRDF dataset and designed to incorporate physical insights for material estimation, including an in-network rendering layer to model appearance and a material classifier to provide additional supervision during training. We refine the results from the network using a dense CRF module whose terms are designed specifically for our task. The framework is trained end-to-end and produces high quality results for a variety of materials. We provide extensive ablation studies to evaluate our network on both synthetic and real data, while demonstrating significant improvements in comparisons with prior works.

1 Introduction

The wide variety of images around us are the outcome of interactions between lighting, shapes and materials. In recent years, the advent of convolutional neural networks (CNNs) has led to significant advances in recovering shape using just a single image [9,12]. In contrast, material estimation has not seen as much progress, which might be attributed to multiple causes. First, material properties can be more complex. Even discounting more complex global illumination effects, materials are represented by a spatially-varying bidirectional reflectance distribution function (SVBRDF), which is an unknown high-dimensional function that depends on exitant and incident lighting directions [25]. Second, while large-scale synthetic and real datasets have been collected for shape estimation

Electronic supplementary material The online version of this chapter (https://doi.org/10.1007/978-3-030-01219-9_5) contains supplementary material, which is available to authorized users.

© Springer Nature Switzerland AG 2018
V. Ferrari et al. (Eds.): ECCV 2018, LNCS 11207, pp. 74–90, 2018.
https://doi.org/10.1007/978-3-030-01219-9_5

Fig. 1. We propose a deep learning-based light-weight SVBRDF acquisition system. From a single image of a near planar surface captured with a flash-enabled mobile phone camera under arbitrary lighting, our network recovers surface normals and spatially-varying BRDF parameters – diffuse albedo and specular roughness. Rendering the estimated parameters produces an image almost identical to the input image.

[8,24], there is a lack of similar data for material estimation. Third, pixel observations in a single image contain entangled information from factors such as shape and lighting, besides material, which makes estimation ill-posed.

In this work, we present a practical material capture method that can recover an SVBRDF from a *single* image of a near-planar surface, acquired using the camera of an off-the-shelf consumer mobile phone, under unconstrained environment illumination. This is in contrast to conventional BRDF capture setups that usually require significant equipment and expense [11,21]. We address this challenge by proposing a novel CNN architecture that is specifically designed to account for the physical form of BRDFs and the interaction of light with materials, which leads to a better learning objective. We also propose to use a dataset of SVBRDFs that has been designed for perceptual accuracy of materials. This is in contrast to prior datasets that are limited to homogeneous materials, or conflate material properties with other concepts such as object categories.

We introduce a novel CNN architecture that encodes the input image into a latent representation, which is decoded into components corresponding to surface normals, diffuse texture, and specular roughness. We propose a differentiable rendering layer that recombines the estimated components with a novel lighting direction. This gives us additional supervision from images of the material rendered under arbitrary lighting directions during training; only a single image is used at test time. We also observe that coarse classification of BRDFs into material meta-categories is an easier task, so we additionally include a material classifier to constrain the latent representation. The inferred BRDF parameters from the CNN are quite accurate, but we achieve further improvement using densely-connected conditional random fields (DCRFs) with novel unary and smoothness terms that reflect the properties of the underlying microfacet BRDF model. We train the entire framework in an end-to-end manner.

Our approach – using our novel architecture and SVBRDF dataset – can outperform the state-of-art. We demonstrate that we can further improve these results by leveraging a form of acquisition control that is present on virtually every mobile phone – the camera flash. We turn on the flash of the mobile phone camera during acquisition; our images are thus captured under a combination of unknown environment illumination and the flash. The flash illumination helps further improve our reconstructions. First, it minimizes shadows caused by occlusions. Second, it allows better observation of high-frequency specular highlights, which allows better characterization of material type and more accurate estimation. Third, it provides a relatively simple setup for acquisition that eases the burden on estimation and allows the use of better post-processing techniques.

In contrast to recent works such as [2] and [1] that can reconstruct BRDFs with stochastic textures, we can handle a much larger class of materials. Also, our results, both with and without flash, are a significant improvement over the recent method of Li et al. [19] even though our trained model is more compact. Our experiments demonstrate advantages over several baselines and prior works in quantitative comparisons, while also achieving superior qualitative results. In particular, the generalization ability of our network trained on the synthetic BRDF dataset is demonstrated by strong performance on real images, acquired in the wild, in both indoor and outdoor environments, using multiple different phone cameras. Given the estimated BRDF parameters, we also demonstrate applications such as material editing and relighting of novel shapes. To summarize, we propose the following novel contributions:

- A lightweight method for high quality acquisition of SVBRDF and normal map using a single mobile phone image in an unconstrained environment.
- A physically-motivated CNN and DCRF framework for joint SVBRDF reconstruction and material classification.
- Use of a large-scale SVBRDF dataset specifically attuned to complex materials.

2   Related Work

BRDF Acquisition: The Bidirectional Reflection Distribution function (BRDF) is a 4-D function that characterizes how a surface reflects lighting from an incident direction toward an outgoing direction [25]. Alternatively, BRDFs are represented using low-dimensional parametric models [4,10,27,35]. In this work, we use a physically-based microfacet model [16] that our SVBRDF dataset uses.

Traditional methods for BRDF acquisition rely on densely sampling this 4-D space using expensive, calibrated acquisition systems [11,21,22]. Recent work has demonstrated that assuming BRDFs lie in a low-dimensional subspace allows for them to be reconstructed from a small set of measurements [26,37]. However, these measurements still to be taken under controlled settings. We assume a single image captured under largely uncontrolled settings.

Photometric stereo-based methods recover shape and BRDF from images. Some of these methods recover a homogeneous BRDF given one or both of the shape and illumination [28,31,32]. Chandraker et al. [5–7] utilize motion cues to jointly recover shape and BRDF from images under known directional illumination. Hui et al. [14] recover SVBRDFs and shape from multiple images under known illuminations. All of those methods require some form of controlled acquisition, while we estimate SVBRDFs and normal maps "in-the-wild".

Recent work has shown promising results for "in-the-wild" BRDF acquisition. Hui et al. [15] demonstrate that the collocated camera-light setup on mobile devices is sufficient to reconstruct SVBRDFs and normals. They require over 30 calibrated images, while we aim to do the same with a single image. Aittala et al. [2] propose using a flash and no-flash image pair to reconstruct *stochastic* SVBRDFs and normals using an optimization-based scheme. Our method can handle a larger class of materials and is orders of magnitude faster.

Deep Learning-Based Material Estimation: Inspired by the success of deep learning for a variety of vision and graphics tasks, recent work has considered CNN-based material recognition and estimation. Bell et al. [3] train a material parsing network using crowd-sourced labeled data. However, their material recongition is driven more by object context, rather than appearance. Liu et al. [20] demonstrate image-based material editing using a network trained to recover homogenous BRDFs. Methods have been proposed to decompose images into their intrinsic image components which are an intermediate representation for material and shape [23, 33, 34]. Rematas et al. [29] train a CNN to reconstruct the reflectance map – a convolution of the BRDF with the illumination – from a single image of a shape from a known class. In subsequent work, they disentangle the reflectance map into the BRDF and illumination [13]. Neither of these methods handle SVBRDFs, nor do they recover fine surface normal details. Kim et al. [17] reconstruct a homogeneous BRDF by training a network to aggregate multi-view observations of an object of known shape.

Similar to us, Aittala et al. [1] and Li et al. [19] reconstruct SVBRDFs and surface normals from a single image of a near-planar surface. Aittala et al. use a neural style transfer-based optimization approach to iteratively estimate BRDF parameters, however, they can only handle stationary textures and there is no correspondence between the input image and the reconstructed BRDF [1]. Li et al. use supervised learning to train a CNN to predict SVBRDF and normals from a single image captured under environment illumination [19]. Their training set is small, which necessitates a self-augmentation method to generate training samples from unlabeled real data. Further, they train a different set of networks for each parameter (diffuse texture, normals, specular albedo and roughness) and each material type (wood, metal, plastic). We demonstrate that by using our novel CNN architecture, supervised training on a high-quality dataset and acquisition under flash illumination, we are able to (a) reconstruct all these parameters with a single network, (b) learn a latent representation that also enables material recognition and editing, (c) obtain results that are significantly better qualitatively and quantitatively.

3   Acquisition Setup and SVBRDF Dataset

In this section, we describe the setup for single image SVBRDF acquisition and the dataset we use for learning.

Setup. Our goal is to reconstruct the spatially-varying BRDF of a near planar surface from a single image captured by a mobile phone with the flash turned on for illumination. We assume that the z-axis of the camera is approximately perpendicular to the planar surface (we explicitly evaluate against this assumption in our experiments). For most mobile devices, the position of the flash light is usually very close to the position of the camera, which provides us a univariate sampling of a isotropic BRDF [15]. We argue that by imaging with a collocated camera and point light, we can have additional constraints that yield better BRDF reconstructions compared to acquisition under just environment illumination.

Our surface appearance is represented by a microfacet parametric BRDF model [16]. Let $\mathbf{d}_i$, $\mathbf{n}_i$, r_i be the diffuse color, normal and roughness, respectively, at pixel i. Our BRDF model is defined as:

$$\rho(\mathbf{d}_i, \mathbf{n}_i, r_i) = \mathbf{d}_i + \frac{D(\mathbf{h}_i, r_i)F(\mathbf{v}_i, \mathbf{h}_i)G(\mathbf{l}_i, \mathbf{v}_i, \mathbf{h}_i, r_i)}{4(\mathbf{n}_i \cdot \mathbf{l}_i)(\mathbf{n}_i \cdot \mathbf{v}_i)} \tag{1}$$

where $\mathbf{v}_i$ and $\mathbf{l}_i$ are the view and light directions and $\mathbf{h}_i$ is the half angle vector. Given an observed image $I(\mathbf{d}_i, \mathbf{n}_i, r_i, \mathbf{L})$, captured under unknown illumination $\mathbf{L}$, we wish to recover the parameters $\mathbf{d}_i$, $\mathbf{n}_i$ and r_i for each pixel i in the image. Please refer to the supplementary material for more details on the BRDF model.

Dataset. We train our network on the Adobe Stock 3D Material dataset[1], which contains 688 materials with high resolution (4096×4096) spatially-varying BRDFs. Part of the dataset is created by artists while others are captured using a scanner. We use 588 materials for training and 100 materials for testing. For data augmentation, we randomly crop 12, 8, 4, 2, 1 image patches of size 512, 1024, 2048, 3072, 4096. We resize the image patches to a size of 256×256 for processing by our network. We flip patches along x and y axes and rotate them in increments of $45°$. Thus, for each material type, we have 270 image patches.[2] We randomly scale the diffuse color, normal and roughness for each image patch to prevent the network from overfitting and memorizing the materials. We manually segment the dataset into 8 materials types. The distribution is shown in Table 1, with an example visualization of each material type in Fig. 2. More details on rendering the dataset are in supplementary material.

4   Network Design for SVBRDF Estimation

In this section, we describe the components of our CNN designed for single-image SVBRDF estimation. The overall architecture is illustrated in Fig. 3.

---

[1] https://stock.adobe.com/3d-assets.
[2] The total number of image patches for each material can be computed as $(12 + 8 + 4 + 2 + 1) \times (1 + 2 + 7) = 270$.

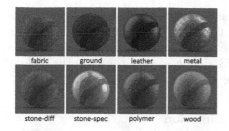

Fig. 2. Examples of our material types.

Table 1. Distribution of materials in our training and test sets.

Materials	Train	Test	Materials	Train	Test
Fabric	165	29	Polymer	33	6
Ground	23	4	Stone-diff	177	30
Leather	10	2	Stone-spec	38	6
Metal	82	13	Wood	60	10

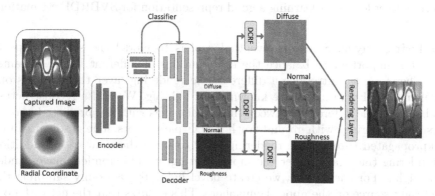

Fig. 3. Our network for SVBRDF estimation consists of an encoder, three decoder blocks with skip links to retrieve SVBRDF components, a rendering layer and a material classifier, followed by a DCRF for refinement (not visualized). See Sect. 4 for how our architectural choices are influenced by the problem structure of SVBRDF estimation and supplementary material for the hyperparameter details.

4.1 Considerations for Network Architecture

Single-image SVBRDF estimation is an ill-posed problem. Thus, we adopt a data-driven approach with a custom-designed CNN that reflects physical intuitions.

Our basic network architecture consists of a single encoder and three decoders which reconstruct the three spatially-varying BRDF parameters: diffuse color d_i, normals n_i and roughness r_i. The intuition behind using a single encoder is that different BRDF parameters are correlated, thus, representations learned for one should be useful to infer the others, which allows significant reduction in the size of the network. The input to the network is an RGB image, augmented with the pixel coordinates as a fourth channel. We add the pixel coordinates since the distribution of light intensities is closely related to the location of pixels, for instance, the center of the image will usually be much brighter. Since CNNs are spatially invariant, we need the extra signal to let the network learn to behave differently for pixels at different locations. Skip links are added to connect the encoder and decoders to preserve details of BRDF parameters.

Another important consideration is that in order to model global effects over whole images like light intensity fall-off or large areas of specular highlights, it is necessary for the network to have a large receptive field. To this end, our encoder network has seven convolutional layers of stride 2, so that the receptive field of every output pixel covers the entire image.

4.2 Loss Functions for SVBRDF Estimation

For each BRDF parameter, we have an L2 loss for direct supervision. We now describe other losses for learning a good representation for SVBRDF estimation.

Rendering Layer. Since our eventual goal is to model the surface appearance, it is important to balance the contributions of different BRDF parameters. Therefore, we introduce a differentiable rendering layer that renders our BRDF model (Eq. 1) under the known input lighting. We add a reconstruction loss based on the difference between these renderings with the predicted parameters and renderings with ground-truth BRDF parameters. The gradient can be backpropagated through the rendering layer to train the network. In addition to rendering the image under the input lighting, we also render images under *novel* lights. For each batch, we create novel lights by randomly sampling the point light source on the upper hemisphere. This ensures that the network does not overfit to collocated illumination and is able to reproduce appearance under other light conditions. The final loss function for the encoder-decoder part of our network is:

$$\mathcal{L} = \lambda_d \mathcal{L}_d + \lambda_n \mathcal{L}_n + \lambda_r \mathcal{L}_r + \lambda_{rec} \mathcal{L}_{rec}, \tag{2}$$

where $\mathcal{L}_d$, $\mathcal{L}_n$, $\mathcal{L}_r$ and $\mathcal{L}_{rec}$ are the L2 losses for diffuse, normal, roughness and rendered image predictions, respectively. Here, λ's are positive coefficients to balance the contributions of various terms, which are set to 1 in our experiments.

Since we train on near planar surfaces, the majority of the normal directions are flat. Table 2 shows the normal distributions in our dataset. To prevent the network from over-smoothing the normals, we group the normal directions into different bins and for each bin we assign a different weight when computing the L2 error. This balance various normal directions in the loss function.

Material Classification. The distribution of BRDF parameters is closely related to the surface material type. However, training separate networks for different material types similar to [19] is expensive. Also the size of the network grows linearly with the number of material types, which limits utility. Instead, we propose a split-merge network with very little computational overhead.

Given the highest level of features extracted by the encoder, we send the feature to a classifier to predict its material type. Then we evaluate the BRDF parameters for each material type and use the classification results as (the output of softmax layer) weights. This averages the prediction from different material types to obtain the final BRDF reconstruction results. Suppose we have N channels for BRDF parameters and K material types. To output the BRDF

Table 2. The θ distribution of the normal vector in the dataset, where θ is the angle between normal vector and z axis. To avoid the network from over-smoothing the normal map, we group normal vectors into three bins according to θ. With probability P_i for bin i, its weight is $W_i = 0.7 + 1/10P_i$.

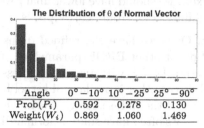

Angle	$0° - 10°$	$10° - 25°$	$25° - 90°$
Prob(P_i)	0.592	0.278	0.130
Weight(W_i)	0.869	1.060	1.469

reconstruction for each type of material, we only modify the last convolutional layer of the decoder so that the output channel will be $K \times N$ instead of N. In practice, we set K to be 8, as shown in Table 1.

The classifier is trained together with the encoder and decoder from scratch, with the weights of each label set to be inversely proportional to the number of examples in Table 1 to balance different material types in the loss function. The overall loss function of our network with the classifier is

$$\mathcal{L} = \lambda_d \mathcal{L}_d + \lambda_n \mathcal{L}_n + \lambda_r \mathcal{L}_r + \lambda_{rec} \mathcal{L}_{rec} + \lambda_{cls} \mathcal{L}_{cls}, \tag{3}$$

where $\mathcal{L}_{cls}$ is cross entropy loss and $\lambda_{cls} = 0.0005$ to limit the gradient magnitude.

4.3   Designing DCRFs for Refinement

The prediction of our base network is quite reasonable. However, accuracy may further be enhanced by post-processing through a DCRF (trained end-to-end).

Diffuse Color Refinement. For diffuse prediction, when capturing the image of specular materials, parts of the surface might be saturated by specular highlight. This can sometimes lead to artifacts in the diffuse color prediction since the network has to hallucinate the diffuse color from nearby pixels. To remove such artifacts, we incorporate a densely connected continuous conditional random field (DCRF) [30] to smooth the diffuse color prediction. Let $\hat{\mathbf{d}}_i$ be the diffuse color prediction of network at pixel i, $\mathbf{p}_i$ be its position and $\bar{\mathbf{I}}_i$ is the normalized diffuse RGB color of the input image. We use the normalized color of the input image to remove the influence of light intensity when measuring the similarity between two pixels. The energy function of the dense connected CRF that is minimized over $\{\mathbf{d}_i\}$ for diffuse prediction is defined as:

$$\sum_{i=1}^{N} \alpha_i^d (\mathbf{d}_i - \hat{\mathbf{d}}_i)^2 + \sum_{i,j}^{N} (\mathbf{d}_i - \mathbf{d}_j)^2 \Big(\beta_1^d \kappa_1(\mathbf{p}_i; \mathbf{p}_j) + \beta_2^d \kappa_2(\mathbf{p}_i, \bar{\mathbf{I}}_i; \mathbf{p}_j, \bar{\mathbf{I}}_j) + \beta_3^d \kappa_3(\mathbf{p}_i, \hat{\mathbf{d}}_i; \mathbf{p}_j, \hat{\mathbf{d}}_j) \Big). \tag{4}$$

Here κ_i are Gaussian smoothing kernels, while α_i^d and $\{\beta_i^d\}$ are coefficients to balance the contribution of unary and smoothness terms. Notice that we have a spatially varying α_i^d to allow different unary weights for different pixels. The intuition is that artifacts usually occur near the center of images with specular highlights. For those pixels, we should have lower unary weights so that the CRF learns to predict their diffuse color from nearby pixels.

Normal Refinement. Once we have the refined diffuse color, we can use it to improve the prediction of other BRDF parameters. To reduce the noise in normal prediction, we use a DCRF with two smoothness kernels. One is based on the pixel position while the other is a bilateral kernel based on the position of the pixel and the gradient of the diffuse color. The intuition is that pixels with similar diffuse color gradients often have similar normal directions. Let $\hat{\mathbf{n}}_i$ be the normal predicted by the network. The energy function for normal prediction is defined as

$$\min_{\{\mathbf{n}_i\}} : \sum_{i=1}^{N} \alpha^n (\mathbf{n}_i - \hat{\mathbf{n}}_i)^2 + \sum_{i,j}^{N} (\mathbf{n}_i - \mathbf{n}_j)^2 \left(\beta_1^n \kappa_1(\mathbf{p}_i; \mathbf{p}_j) + \beta_2^n \kappa_2(\mathbf{p}_i, \Delta \mathbf{d}_i; \mathbf{p}_j, \Delta \mathbf{d}_j) \right) \quad (5)$$

Roughness Refinement. Since we use a collocated light source to illuminate the material, once we have the normal and diffuse color predictions, we can use them to estimate the roughness term by either grid search or using a gradient-based method. However, since the microfacet BRDF model is not convex nor monotonic with respect to the roughness term, there is no guarantee that we can find a global minimum. Also, due to noise from the normal and diffuse predictions, as well as environment lighting, it is difficult to get an accurate roughness prediction using optimization alone, especially when the glossiness in the image is not apparent. Therefore, we propose to combine the output of the network and the optimization method to get a more accurate roughness prediction. We use a DCRF with two unary terms, $\hat{r}_i$ and $\tilde{r}_i$, given by the network prediction and the coarse-to-fine grid search method of [15], respectively:

$$\min_{\{r_i\}} : \sum_{i=1}^{N} \alpha_{i0}^r (r_i - \hat{r}_i)^2 + \alpha_{i1}^r (r_i - \tilde{r}_i)^2 + \sum_{i,j}^{N} (r_i - r_j)^2 \left(\beta_0 \kappa_0(\mathbf{p}_i; \mathbf{p}_j) + \beta_1 \kappa_1(\mathbf{p}_i, \mathbf{d}_i; \mathbf{p}_j, \mathbf{d}_j) \right) \quad (6)$$

All DCRF coefficients are learned in an end-to-end manner using [36]. Here, we have a different set of DCRF parameters for each material type to increase model capacity. During both training and testing, the classifier output is used to average the parameters from different material types, to determine the DCRF parameters. More implementation details are in supplementary material.

5 Experiments

In this section, we demonstrate our method and compare it to baselines on a wide range of synthetic and real data.

Rendering Synthetic Training Dataset. To create our synthetic data, we apply the SVBRDFs on planar surfaces and render them using a GPU based renderer [19] with the BRDF importance sampling suggested in [16]. We choose a camera field of view of 43.35° to mimic typical mobile phone cameras. To better model real-world lighting conditions, we render images under a combination of a dominant point light (flash) and an environment map. We use the 49 environment maps used in [19], with random rotations. We sample the light source position from a Gaussian distribution centered at the camera to make the inference robust to differences in real-world mobile phones. We render linear images, though clamped to $(0, 1)$ to mimic cameras with insufficient dynamic range. However, we still wish to reconstruct the full dynamic range of the SVBRDF parameters. To aid in this, we can render HDR images using in-our network rendering layer and compute reconstruction error w.r.t HDR ground truth images. In practice, this leads to unstable gradients in training; we mitigate this by applying a gamma of 2.2 and minor clamping to $(0, 1.5)$ when computing the image reconstruction loss. We find that this, in combination with our L2 losses on the SVBRDF parameters, allows us to hallucinate details from saturated images.

Training Details. We use Adam optimizer [18] to train our network. We set $\beta_1 = 0.5$ when training the encoder and decoders and $\beta_1 = 0.9$ when training the classifier. The initial learning rate is set to be 10^{-4} for the encoder, 2×10^{-4} for the three decoders and 2×10^{-5} for the classifier. We cut down the learning rate by half in every two epochs. Since we find that the diffuse color and normal direction contribute much more to the final appearance, we first train their encoder-decoders for 15 epochs, then we fix the encoder and train the roughness decoder separately for 8 epochs. Next, we fix the network and train the parameters for the DCRFs, using Adam optimizer to update their coefficients (Fig. 4).

5.1   Results on Synthetic Data

Qualitative Results. Figure 1 shows results of our network on our synthetic test dataset. We can observe that spatially varying surface normals, diffuse albedo and roughness are recovered at high quality, which allows relighting under novel light source directions that are very different from the input. To further demonstrate our BRDF reconstruction quality, in Fig. 5, we show relighting results under different environment maps and point lights at oblique angles. Note that our relighting results closely match the ground truth even under different lighting conditions; this indicates the accuracy of our reconstructions.

We next perform quantitative ablation studies to evaluate various components of our network design and study comparisons to prior work.

Effects of Material Classifier and DCRF: The ablation study summarized in Table 3 shows that adding the material classifier reduces the L2 error for SVBRDF and normal estimation, as well as rendering error. This validates the intuition that the network can exploit the correlation between BRDF parameters and material type to produce better estimates. We also observe that training the classifier together with the BRDF reconstruction network results in a material classification error of 73.65%, which significantly improves over just our pure

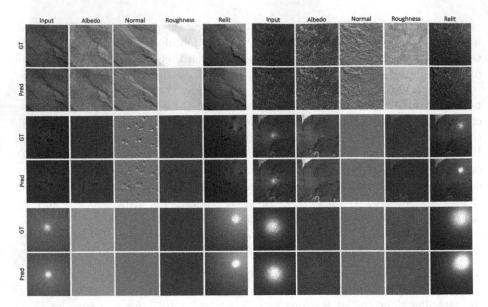

Fig. 4. BRDF reconstruction results from our full method (`clsCRF-pt` in Table 3) on the test set. We compare the ground truth parameters with our reconstructions as well as renderings of these parameters under novel lighting. The accuracy of our renderings indicates the accuracy of our method.

material classification network that achieves 54.96%. This indicates that features trained for BRDF estimation are also useful for material recognition. In our experiments, incorporating the classifier without using its output to fuse BRDF reconstruction results does not improve BRDF estimation. Figure 6 shows the reconstruction result on a sample where the classifier and the DCRF qualitatively improve the BRDF estimation, especially for the diffuse albedo.

Effect of Acquisition Under Point Illumination. Next we evaluate the effect of using point illumination during acquisition. For this, we train and test two variants of our full network – one on images rendered under only environment illumination (-`env`) and another on images illuminated by a point light besides environment illumination (-`pt`). Results are in Table 4 with qualitative visualizations in Figure 6. The model from [19] in Table 4, which is trained for

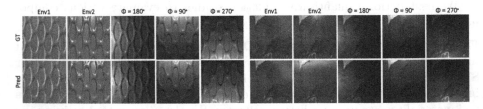

Fig. 5. Materials estimated with our method and rendered under two environment lights and three point lights (placed on a unit sphere at $\theta = 50°$ and various ϕ angles).

Table 3. Left to right: basic encoder-decoder, adding material classifier, adding DCRF and a pure material classifier. −pt indicates training and testing with dominant point and environment lighting.

Method	basic-pt	cls-pt	clsCRF-pt	clsOnly-pt
Albedo (e^{-3})	7.78	7.58	**7.42**	
Normal (e^{-2})	1.55	1.52	**1.50**	
Rough (e^{-2})	8.75	8.55	**8.53**	
Classify (%)		**73.65**	**73.65**	54.96

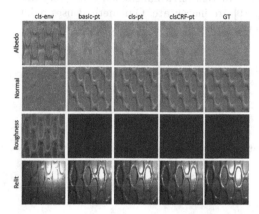

Fig. 6. Qualitative comparison of BRDF reconstruction results of different variants of our network. The notation is the same as Table 3 and −**env** represents environment illumination.

Table 4. BRDF reconstruction accuracy for different material types in our test set. Albedo-N is normalized diffuse albedo as in [19], that is, the average norm of each pixel will be 0.5.

		Albedo-N (e^{-4})	Normals (e^{-3})	Rough (e^{-2})
[19]	Metal	91.8	27.2	–
	Wood	35.9	11.2	–
	Plastic	12.5	17.6	–
	Total	56.1	19.7	–
cls-env	Metal	54.9	25.2	13.4
	Wood	13.7	11.1	19.5
	Plastic	7.96	14.2	25.3
	Total	30.9	18.1	18.0
cls-pt	Metal	21.7	15.1	4.06
	Wood	3.53	8.75	4.40
	Plastic	1.64	9.10	7.24
	Total	11.3	11.7	4.83

environment lighting, performs slightly worse than our environment lighting network cls-env. But our network trained and evaluated on point and environment lighting, cls-pt, easily outperforms both. We argue this is because a collocated point light creates more consistent illumination across training and test images, while also capturing higher frequency information. Figure 7 illustrates this: the appearance of the same material under different environment lighting can significantly vary and the network has to be invariant to this, limiting reconstruction quality.

Relative Effects of Flash and Environment Light Intensities. In Fig. 8, we train and test on a range of relative flash intensities. Note that as relative flash intensity decreases, errors increase, which justifies our use of flash light. Using flash and no-flash pairs can help remove environment lighting, but needs alignment of two images, which limits applicability.

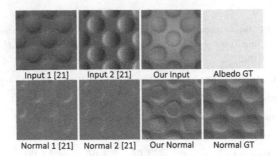

Fig. 7. The first two inputs rendered under different environment maps are very different. Thus, the normals recovered using [19] are inaccurate. Our method uses point illumination (third input) which alleviates the problem, and produces better normals.

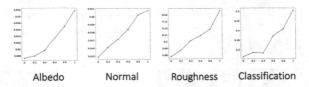

Fig. 8. SVBRDF estimation errors for relative intensities of environment against point light ranging from 0 to 0.8.

5.2   Results on Real Data

Acquisition Setup. To verify the generalizabity of our method to real data, we show results on real images captured with different mobile devices in both indoor and outdoor environments. We capture linear RAW images (with potentially clipped highlights) with the flash enabled, using the Adobe Lightroom Mobile app. The mobile phones were hand-held and the optical axis of the camera was only approximately perpendicular to the surfaces (see Fig. 1).

Qualitative Results with Different Mobile Phones. Figure 9 presents SVBRDF and normal estimation results for real images captured with three different mobile devices: Huawei P9, Google Tango and iPhone 6s. We observe that even with a single image, our network successfully predicts the SVBRDF and normals, with images rendered using the predicted parameters appear very similar to the input. Also, the exact same network generalizes well to different mobile devices, which shows that our data augmentation successfully helps the network factor out variations across devices. For some materials with specular highlights, the network can hallucinate information lost due to saturation. The network can also reconstruct reasonable normals even for complex instances.

A Failure Case. In Fig. 10, we show a failure case. Here, the material is misclassified as metal which causes the specular highlight in the center of image to be over-suppressed. In future work, we may address this with more robust material classification, potentially exploiting datasets like [3].

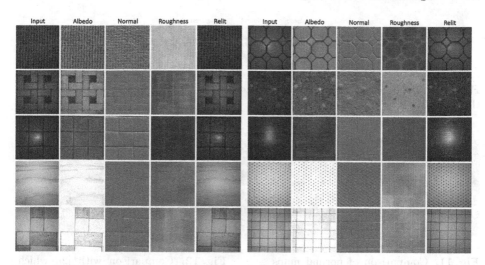

Fig. 9. BRDF reconstruction results on real data. We tried different mobile devices to capture raw images using the Adobe LightRoom Mobile app. The input images in were captured using a Huawei P9 (first three rows), Google Tango (fourth row) and iPhone 6s (fifth row), all with a handheld mobile phone where the z-axis of camera was only approximately perpendicular to the sample surface.

5.3   Further Comparisons with Prior Works

Comparison with Two-Shot BRDF Method [2]. The two-shot method of [2] can only handle images with stationary texture while our method can reconstruct arbitrarily varying SVBRDFs. For a meaningful comparison, in Fig. 12, we compare our method with [2] on a rendered stationary texture. We can see that even for this restrictive material type, the normal maps reconstructed by the two methods are quite similar, but the diffuse map reconstructed by our method is closer to ground truth. While [2] takes about 6 h to reconstruct a patch of size 192×192, our method requires 2.4 s. The aligned flash and no-flash pair for [2] is not trivial to acquire (especially on mobile cameras with effects like rolling shutter), making our single image BRDF estimation more practical.

Comparison of Normals with Environment Light and Photometric Stereo. In Fig. 11, we compare our normal map and the results from (a) [19] (from a single captured under environment lighting) and (b) photometric stereo [14]. We observe that the normals reconstructed by our method are of higher quality than [19], with details comparable or sharper than photometric stereo.

The **supplementary material** provides more information, including: details of data augmentation and continuous DCRF, error distributions of BRDF, distribution of material categories, material editing and relighted images and further qualitative results on synthetic and real data.

Fig. 10. A failure case, due to incorrect material classification into *metal*, which causes the specularity to be over-smoothed.

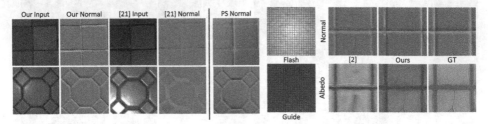

Fig. 11. Comparison of normal maps using our method and [19], with photometric stereo as reference. Even with a lightweight acquisition system, our network predicts high quality normal maps.

Fig. 12. Comparison with [2], which requires two images, assumes stationary textures and takes over 6 h (with GPU acceleration), yet our result is more accurate.

6   Discussion

We have proposed a framework for acquiring spatially-varying BRDF using a single mobile phone image. Our solution uses a convolutional neural network whose architecture is specifically designed to reflect various physical insights into the problem of BRDF estimation. We propose to use a dataset that is larger and better-suited to material estimation as compared to prior ones, as well as simple acquisition settings that are nevertheless effective for SVBRDF estimation. Our network generalizes very well to real data, obtaining high-quality results in unconstrained test environments. A key goal for our work is to take accurate material estimation from expensive and controlled lab setups, into the hands of non-expert users with consumer devices, thereby opening the doors to new applications. Our future work will take the next step of acquiring SVBRDF with unknown shapes, as well as study the role of semantic priors.

Acknowledgements. Z. Li and M. Chandraker are supported by NSF CAREER 1751365 and gratefully acknowledge funding from Adobe, BASF, Cognex and Snap. This work was partially done during Z. Li's summer internship at Adobe.

References

1. Aittala, M., Aila, T., Lehtinen, J.: Reflectance modeling by neural texture synthesis. ACM Trans. Graph. (TOG) **35**(4), 65 (2016)

2. Aittala, M., Weyrich, T., Lehtinen, J., et al.: Two-shot SVBRDF capture for stationary materials. ACM Trans. Graph. **34**(4), 110:1–110:13 (2015)
3. Bell, S., Upchurch, P., Snavely, N., Bala, K.: Material recognition in the wild with the materials in context database. In: Computer Vision and Pattern Recognition (CVPR) (2015)
4. Blinn, J.F., Newell, M.E.: Texture and reflection in computer generated images. Commun. ACM **19**(10), 542–547 (1976)
5. Chandraker, M.: On shape and material recovery from motion. In: Fleet, D., Pajdla, T., Schiele, B., Tuytelaars, T. (eds.) ECCV 2014. LNCS, vol. 8695, pp. 202–217. Springer, Cham (2014). https://doi.org/10.1007/978-3-319-10584-0_14
6. Chandraker, M.: What camera motion reveals about shape with unknown BRDF. In: Proceedings of the IEEE Conference on Computer Vision and Pattern Recognition, pp. 2171–2178 (2014)
7. Chandraker, M.: The information available to a moving observer on shape with unknown, isotropic BRDFs. IEEE Trans. Pattern Anal. Mach. Intell. **38**(7), 1283–1297 (2016)
8. Chang, A.X., et al.: Shapenet: an information-rich 3D model repository. arXiv preprint arXiv:1512.03012 (2015)
9. Choy, C.B., Xu, D., Gwak, J.Y., Chen, K., Savarese, S.: 3D-R2N2: a unified approach for single and multi-view 3D object reconstruction. In: Leibe, B., Matas, J., Sebe, N., Welling, M. (eds.) ECCV 2016. LNCS, vol. 9912, pp. 628–644. Springer, Cham (2016). https://doi.org/10.1007/978-3-319-46484-8_38
10. Cook, R.L., Torrance, K.E.: A reflectance model for computer graphics. ACM Trans. Graph. (TOG) **1**(1), 7–24 (1982)
11. Debevec, P., Hawkins, T., Tchou, C., Duiker, H.P., Sarokin, W., Sagar, M.: Acquiring the reflectance field of a human face. In: Proceedings of the 27th Annual Conference on Computer Graphics and Interactive Techniques, pp. 145–156. ACM Press/Addison-Wesley Publishing Co. (2000)
12. Eigen, D., Fergus, R.: Predicting depth, surface normals and semantic labels with a common multi-scale convolutional architecture. In: Proceedings of the IEEE International Conference on Computer Vision, pp. 2650–2658 (2015)
13. Georgoulis, S., Rematas, K., Ritschel, T., Fritz, M., Van Gool, L., Tuytelaars, T.: Delight-net: decomposing reflectance maps into specular materials and natural illumination. arXiv preprint arXiv:1603.08240 (2016)
14. Hui, Z., Sankaranarayanan, A.C.: A dictionary-based approach for estimating shape and spatially-varying reflectance. In: International Conference on Computational Photography (ICCP) (2015)
15. Hui, Z., Sunkavalli, K., Lee, J.Y., Hadap, S., Wang, J., Sankaranarayanan, A.C.: Reflectance capture using univariate sampling of BRDFs. In: IEEE International Conference on Computer Vision (ICCV) (2017)
16. Karis, B., Games, E.: Real shading in unreal engine 4. SIGGRAPH 2013 Crourse:c. Physically Based Shading Theory Practice (2013)
17. Kim, K., Gu, J., Tyree, S., Molchanov, P., Nießner, M., Kautz, J.: A lightweight approach for on-the-fly reflectance estimation. arXiv preprint arXiv:1705.07162 (2017)
18. Kingma, D., Ba, J.: Adam: a method for stochastic optimization. arXiv preprint arXiv:1412.6980 (2014)
19. Li, X., Dong, Y., Peers, P., Tong, X.: Modeling surface appearance from a single photograph using self-augmented convolutional neural networks. ACM Trans. Graph. **36**(4), 1–11 (2017). https://doi.org/10.1145/3072959.3073641

20. Liu, G., Ceylan, D., Yumer, E., Yang, J., Lien, J.M.: Material editing using a physically based rendering network. In: ICCV (2017)
21. Marschner, S.R., Westin, S.H., Lafortune, E.P., Torrance, K.E., Greenberg, D.P.: Image-based BRDF measurement including human skin. In: Lischinski, D., Larson, G.W. (eds.) Rendering Techniques 1999. EUROGRAPH, pp. 131–144. Springer, Vienna (1999). https://doi.org/10.1007/978-3-7091-6809-7_13
22. Matusik, W., Pfister, H., Brand, M., McMillan, L.: A data-driven reflectance model. ACM Trans. Graph. (TOG) 22(3), 759–769 (2003)
23. Narihira, T., Maire, M., Yu, S.X.: Direct intrinsics: Learning albedo-shading decomposition by convolutional regression. In: Proceedings of the IEEE International Conference on Computer Vision, p. 2992 (2015)
24. Silberman, N., Hoiem, D., Kohli, P., Fergus, R.: Indoor segmentation and support inference from RGBD images. In: Fitzgibbon, A., Lazebnik, S., Perona, P., Sato, Y., Schmid, C. (eds.) ECCV 2012. LNCS, vol. 7576, pp. 746–760. Springer, Heidelberg (2012). https://doi.org/10.1007/978-3-642-33715-4_54
25. Nicodemus, F.E.: Directional reflectance and emissivity of an opaque surface. Appl. Opt. 4(7), 767–775 (1965)
26. Nielsen, J.B., Jensen, H.W., Ramamoorthi, R.: On optimal, minimal BRDF sampling for reflectance acquisition. ACM Trans. Graph. (TOG) 34(6), 186 (2015)
27. Oren, M., Nayar, S.K.: Generalization of the Lambertian model and implications for machine vision. Int. J. Comput. Vis. (IJCV) 14(3), 227–251 (1995)
28. Oxholm, G., Nishino, K.: Shape and reflectance estimation in the wild. IEEE Trans. Pattern Anal. Mach. Intell. (TPAMI) 38(2), 376–389 (2016)
29. Rematas, K., Ritschel, T., Fritz, M., Gavves, E., Tuytelaars, T.: Deep reflectance maps. In: Proceedings of the IEEE Conference on Computer Vision and Pattern Recognition, pp. 4508–4516 (2016)
30. Ristovski, K., Radosavljevic, V., Vucetic, S., Obradovic, Z.: Continuous conditional random fields for efficient regression in large fully connected graphs. In: AAAI (2013)
31. Romeiro, F., Vasilyev, Y., Zickler, T.: Passive reflectometry. In: Forsyth, D., Torr, P., Zisserman, A. (eds.) ECCV 2008. LNCS, vol. 5305, pp. 859–872. Springer, Heidelberg (2008). https://doi.org/10.1007/978-3-540-88693-8_63
32. Romeiro, F., Zickler, T.: Blind reflectometry. In: Daniilidis, K., Maragos, P., Paragios, N. (eds.) ECCV 2010. LNCS, vol. 6311, pp. 45–58. Springer, Heidelberg (2010). https://doi.org/10.1007/978-3-642-15549-9_4
33. Shelhamer, E., Barron, J.T., Darrell, T.: Scene intrinsics and depth from a single image. In: Proceedings of the IEEE International Conference on Computer Vision Workshops, pp. 37–44 (2015)
34. Shi, J., Dong, Y., Su, H., Yu, S.X.: Learning non-Lambertian object intrinsics across shapenet categories. arXiv preprint arXiv:1612.08510 (2016)
35. Ward, G.J.: Measuring and modeling anisotropic reflection. In: ACM Transactions on Graphics (TOG), vol. 26 no. 2, pp. 265–272 (1992)
36. Xu, D., Ricci, E., Ouyang, W., Wang, X., Sebe, N.: Multi-scale continuous CRFs as sequential deep networks for monocular depth estimation. arXiv preprint arXiv:1704.02157 (2017)
37. Xu, Z., Nielsen, J.B., Yu, J., Jensen, H.W., Ramamoorthi, R.: Minimal BRDF sampling for two-shot near-field reflectance acquisition. ACM Trans. Graph. (TOG) 35(6), 188 (2016)

Poster Session

Video Object Segmentation with Joint Re-identification and Attention-Aware Mask Propagation

Xiaoxiao Li[1]([⊠]) [iD] and Chen Change Loy[2] [iD]

[1] Department of Information Engineering, The Chinese University of Hong Kong,
Hong Kong, China
lx015@ie.cuhk.edu.hk
[2] Nanyang Technological University, Singapore, Singapore
ccloy@ieee.org

Abstract. The problem of video object segmentation can become extremely challenging when multiple instances co-exist. While each instance may exhibit large scale and pose variations, the problem is compounded when instances occlude each other causing failures in tracking. In this study, we formulate a deep recurrent network that is capable of segmenting and tracking objects in video simultaneously by their temporal continuity, yet able to re-identify them when they re-appear after a prolonged occlusion. We combine temporal propagation and re-identification functionalities into a single framework that can be trained end-to-end. In particular, we present a re-identification module with template expansion to retrieve missing objects despite their large appearance changes. In addition, we contribute an attention-based recurrent mask propagation approach that is robust to distractors not belonging to the target segment. Our approach achieves a new state-of-the-art $\mathcal{G}$-mean of 68.2 on the challenging DAVIS 2017 benchmark (test-dev set), outperforming the winning solution. Project Page: http://mmlab.ie.cuhk.edu.hk/projects/DyeNet/.

1 Introduction

Video object segmentation aims at segmenting foreground instance object(s) from the background region in a video sequence. Typically, ground-truth masks are assumed to be given in the first frame. The goal is to begin with these masks and track them in the remaining sequence. This paradigm is sometimes known as semi-supervised video object segmentation [3,24,27]. A notable and challenging benchmark for this task is 2017 DAVIS Challenge [28]. An example of a sequence is shown in Fig. 1. The DAVIS dataset presents real-world challenges that need to be solved from two key aspects. First, there are multiple instances in a video. It is very likely that they will occlude each other causing partial or even full obstruction of a target instance. Second, instances typically experience substantial variations in both scale and pose across frames.

© Springer Nature Switzerland AG 2018
V. Ferrari et al. (Eds.): ECCV 2018, LNCS 11207, pp. 93–110, 2018.
https://doi.org/10.1007/978-3-030-01219-9_6

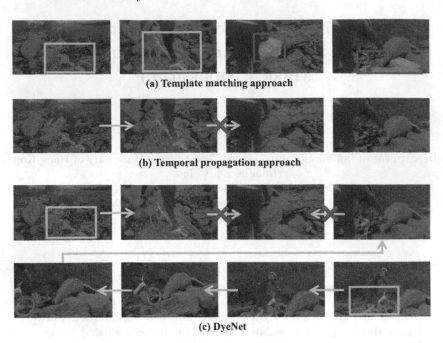

(a) Template matching approach

(b) Temporal propagation approach

(c) DyeNet

Fig. 1. We focus on the bicycle in this example. (a) Shows the result of template matching approach, which is affected by large scale and pose variations. As shown in (b), temporal propagation is incapable of handling occlusion. The proposed DyeNet joints them into a unified framework, first retrieves high confidence starting points and then propagates their masks bidirectionally to address those issues. The result of DyeNet is visualized in (c). Best viewed in color.

To address the occlusion problem, notable studies such as [3,39] adapt generic semantic segmentation deep model to the task of specific object segmentation. These methods follow a notion reminiscent of the template matching based methods that are widely used in visual tracking task [2,33]. Often, a fixed set of templates such as the masks of target objects in the first frame are used for matching targets. This paradigm fails in some challenging cases in DAVIS (see Fig. 1(a)), as using a fixed set of templates cannot sufficiently cover large scale and pose variations. To mitigate the variations in both scale and pose across frames, existing studies [15,16,26,32,34,35] exploit temporal information to maintain continuity of individual segmented regions across frames. On unconstrained videos with severe occlusions, such as that shown in Fig. 1(b), approaches based on temporal continuity are prone to errors since there is no mechanism to re-identify a target when it reappears after missing in a few video frames. In addition, these approaches may fail to track instances in the presence of distractors such as cluttered backgrounds or segments from other objects during temporal propagation.

Solving video object segmentation with multiple instances requires template matching for coping with occlusion and temporal propagation for ensuring temporal continuity. In this study, we bring both approaches into a single unified network. Our network hinges on two main modules, namely a re-identification (Re-ID) module and a recurrent mask propagation (Re-MP) module. The Re-ID module helps to establish confident starting points in non-successive frames and retrieve missing segments caused by occlusions. Based on the segments provided by the Re-ID module, the Re-MP module propagates their masks bidirectionally by a recurrent neural network to the entire video. The process of conducting Re-ID followed by Re-MP may be imagined as dyeing a fabric with multiple color dots (*i.e.*, choosing starting points with re-identification) and the color disperses from these dots (*i.e.*, propagation). Drawing from this analogy, we name our network as *DyeNet*.

There are a few methods [17,21] that improve video object segmentation through both temporal propagation and re-identification. Our approach differs by offering a unified network that allows both tasks to be optimized in an end-to-end network. In addition, unlike existing studies, the Re-ID and Re-MP steps are conducted in an iterative manner. This allows us to identify confidently predicted mask in each iteration and expand the template set. With a dynamic expansion of template set, our Re-ID module can better retrieve missing objects that reappear with different poses and scales. In addition, the Re-MP module is specially designed with attention mechanism to disregard distractors such as background objects or segments from other objects during mask propagation. As shown in Fig. 1(c), DyeNet is capable of segmenting multiple instances across a video with high accuracy through Re-ID and Re-MP. We provide a more detailed discussion against [17,21] in the related work section.

Our **contributions** are summarized as follows. (1) We propose a novel approach that joints template matching and temporal propagation into a unified deep neural network for addressing video object segmentation with multiple instances. The network can be trained end-to-end. It does not require online training (*i.e.*, fine-tune using the masks of the first frame) to do well but can achieve better results with online training. (2) We present an effective template expansion approach to better retrieve missing targets that reappear with different poses and scales. (3) We present a new attention-based recurrent mask propagation module that is more resilient to distractors.

We use the challenging DAVIS 2017 dataset [28] as our key benchmark. The winner of this challenge [21] achieves a global mean (Region Jaccard and Boundary F measure) of 66.1 on the test-dev partition. Our method obtains a global mean of 68.2 on this partition. Without online training, DyeNet can still achieve a competitive $\mathcal{G}$-mean of 62.5 while the speed is an order of magnitude faster. Our method also achieves state-of-the-art results on DAVIS 2016 [27], SegTrack$_{v2}$ [19] and YouTubeObjects [29] datasets.

2   Related Work

Image Segmentation. The goal of semi-supervised video object segmentation is different to semantic image segmentation [4,20,23,40,41] and instance segmentation [8–10,22] that perform pixel-wise class labeling. In video object segmentation, the class type is always assumed to be undefined. Thus, the challenge lies in performing accurate object-agnostic mask propagation. Our network leverages semantic image segmentation task to learn generic representation that encompasses semantic level information. The representation learned is strong, allowing our model to be applied in a dataset-agnostic manner, *i.e.*, it is not trained with any first frame annotation of each video in the target dataset as training/tuning set, but it can also be optionally fine-tuned and adapted into the targeted video domain as practiced in [16] to obtain better results. We will examine both possibilities in the experimental section.

Visual Tracking. While semi-supervised video object segmentation can be seen as a pixel-level tracking task, video object segmentation differs in its more challenging nature in terms of object scale variation across video frames and inter-object scale differences. In addition, the pose of objects is relatively stable in the tracking datasets, and there are few prolonged occlusions. Importantly, the problem differs in that conventional tracking tasks only need bounding box level tracking results, and concern about causality (*i.e.*, tracker does not use any future frames for estimation). In contrast, semi-supervised video object segmentation expects precise pixel-level tracking results, and typically does not assume causality.

Video Object Segmentation. Prior to the prevalence of deep learning, most approaches to semantic video segmentation are graph based [7,18,25,37]. Contemporary methods are mostly based on deep learning. A useful technique reminiscent of template matching is commonly applied. In particular, templates are typically formed by the ground-truth masks in the first frame. For instance, Caelles *et al.* [3] adapt a generic semantic image segmentation network to the templates for each testing video individually. Yoon *et al.* [39] distinguish the foreground objects based on the pixel-level similarity between candidates and templates, which is measured by a matching deep network. Another useful technique is to exploit temporal continuity for establishing spatiotemporal correlation. Tsai *et al.* [32] estimate object segmentation and optical flow synergistically using an iterative scheme. Jampani *et al.* [15] propagate structured information through a video sequence by a bilateral network that performs learnable bilateral filtering operations cross video frames. Perazzi *et al.* [26] and Jang *et al.* [34] estimate the segmentation mask of the current frame by using the mask from the previous frame as a guidance.

Differences Against Existing Methods that Combine Template Matching and Temporal Continuity. There are a few studies that combine the merits of the two aforementioned techniques. Khoreva *et al.* [16] show that a training set closer to the target domain is more effective. They improve [3] by synthesizing more training data from the first frame of testing videos and employ mask

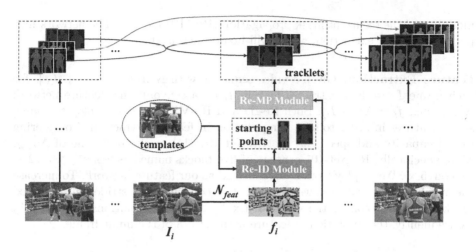

Fig. 2. The pipeline of DyeNet. The network hinges on two main modules, namely a re-identification (Re-ID) module and a recurrent mask propagation (Re-MP) module. Best viewed in color.

propagation during the inference. Instance Re-Identification Flow (IRIF) [17] divides foreground objects into human and non-human object instances, and then apply person re-identification network [36] to retrieve missing human during mask propagation. For non-human object instances, IRIF degenerates to a conventional mask propagation method. Our method differs to these studies in that we do not synthesize training data from the first frames and do not explicitly divide foreground objects into human and non-human object instances.

Li *et al.* [21] adapt person re-identification approach [36] to a generic object re-identification model and employ a two-stream mask propagation model [26]. Their method (VS-ReID) achieved the highest performance in the 2017 DAVIS Challenge [21], however, its shortcomings are also obvious: (1) VS-ReID only uses the masks of target objects in the first frame as templates. It is thus more susceptible to pose variations. (2) Their method is much slower compared to ours due to its redundant feature extraction steps and less efficient inference method. Specifically, the inference of VS-ReID takes ~3 s per frame on DAVIS dataset. The speed is 7 times slower than DyeNet. (3) VS-ReID does not have any attention mechanism in its mask propagation. Its robustness to distractors and background clutters is thus inferior to DyeNet. (4) VS-ReID cannot perform end-to-end training. By contrast, DyeNet performs joint learning of re-identification and temporal propagation.

3   Methodology

We provide an overview of the proposed approach. Figure 2 depicts the architecture of DyeNet. It consists of two modules, namely the re-identification (Re-ID) module and the recurrent mask propagation (Re-MP) module. The network first performs feature extraction, which will be detailed next.

Feature Extraction. Given a video sequence with N frames $\{I_1, \ldots, I_N\}$, for each frame I_i, we first extract a feature f_i by a convolutional feature network $\mathcal{N}_{feat}$, i.e., $f_i = \mathcal{N}_{feat}(I_i)$. Both Re-ID and Re-MP modules employ the same set of features in order to save computation in feature extraction. Considering model capacity and speed, we use ResNet-101 [11] as the backbone of $\mathcal{N}_{feat}$. More specifically, ResNet-101 consists of five blocks named as 'conv1', 'conv2_x' to 'conv5_x'. We employ 'conv1' to 'conv4_x' as our feature network. To increase the resolution of features, we decrease the convolutional strides in 'conv4_x' block and replace convolutions in 'conv4_x' by dilated convolutions similar to [4]. Consequently, the resolution of feature maps is 1/8 of the input frame.

Iterative Inference with Template Expansion. After feature extraction, DyeNet runs Re-ID and Re-MP in an iterative manner to obtain segmentation masks of all instances across the whole video sequence. We assume the availability of masks given in the first frame and use them as templates. This is the standard protocol of the benchmarks considered in Sect. 4.

In the first iteration, the Re-ID module generates a set of masks from object proposals and compares them with templates. Masks with a high similarity to templates are chosen as the starting points for Re-MP. Subsequently, Re-MP propagates each selected mask (*i.e.*, starting point) bidirectionally, and generates a sequence of segmentation masks, which we call tracklet. After Re-MP, we can additionally consider post-processing steps to link the tracklets. In subsequent iterations, DyeNet chooses confidently predicted masks to expand the template set and reapplies Re-ID and Re-MP. Template expansion avoids heavy reliance on the masks provided by the first frame, which may not capture sufficient pose variations of targets.

Note that we do not expect to retrieve all the masks of target objects in a given sequence. In the first iteration, it is sufficient to obtain several high-quality starting points for the mask propagation step. After each iteration of DyeNet, we select predictions with high confidence to augment the template set. In practice, the first iteration can retrieve nearly 25% masks as starting points on DAVIS 2017 dataset. After three iterations, this rate will increase to 33%. In this work, DyeNet stops the iterative process when no more high-confident masks can be found by the Re-ID module. Next, we present the Re-ID and Re-MP modules.

3.1   Re-identification

We introduce the Re-ID module to search for targets in the video sequences. The module has several unique features that allow it to retrieve a missing object that reappears in different scales and poses. First, as discussed previously, we expand the template set in every iteration we apply Re-ID and Re-MP. Template expansion enriches the template set for more robust matching. Second, we employ the

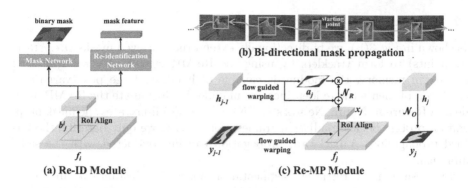

(b) Bi-directional mask propagation

(a) Re-ID Module   **(c) Re-MP Module**

Fig. 3. (a) The network architecture of the re-identification (Re-ID) module. (b) Illustration of bi-direction mask propagation. (c) The network architecture of the recurrent mask propagation (Re-MP) module. Best viewed in color.

object proposal method to estimate the location of target objects. Since these proposals are generated based on anchors of various sizes, which cover objects of various scales, the Re-ID module can handle large scale variations.

Figure 3(a) illustrates the Re-ID module. For the i-th frame, besides the feature f_i, the Re-ID module also requires the object proposals $\{b_1^i, \ldots, b_M^i\}$ as input where M indicates the number of proposal bounding boxes on this frame. We employ a Region Proposal Network (RPN) [30] to propose candidate object bounding boxes on every frame. For convenience, our RPN is trained separately from DyeNet, but their backbone networks are shareable. For each candidate bounding box b_j^i, we first extract its feature from f_i, and resize the feature into a fixed size $m \times m$ (e.g., 28×28) by RoIAlign [10], which is an improved form of RoIPool that removes harsh quantization. The extracted features are fed into two shallow sub-networks. The first sub-network is a mask network that predicts a $m \times m$ binary mask that represents the segmentation mask of the main instance in candidate bounding box b_j^i. The second sub-network is a re-identification network that projects the extracted features into an L2-normalized 256-dimensional subspace to obtain the mask features. The templates are also projected onto the same subspace for feature extraction.

By computing the cosine similarities between the mask and template features, we can measure the similarity between candidate bounding boxes and templates. If a candidate bounding box is sufficiently similar to any template, that is, the cosine similarity is larger than a threshold ρ_{reid}, we will keep its mask as a starting point for mask propagation. In practice, we set ρ_{reid} with a high value to establish high-quality starting points for our next step.

We employ 'conv5_x' block of ResNet-101 as the backbone of the sub-networks. However, some modifications are necessary to adapt them to the respective tasks. In particular, we decrease the convolutional strides in the mask network to capture more details of prediction. For the re-identification network, we keep the original strides and append a global average pooling layer and a fully connected layer to project the features into the target subspace.

3.2 Recurrent Mask Propagation

As shown in Fig. 3(b), we bi-directionally extend the retrieved masks (*i.e.*, starting points) to form tracklets by using the Re-MP module. By incorporating short-term memory, the module is capable of handling large pose variations, which complements the re-identification module. We formulate the Re-MP module as a Recurrent Neural Network (RNN). Figure 3(c) illustrates the mask propagation process between adjacent frames. For brevity, we only describe the forward propagation. A backward propagation can be conducted with the same approach.

Suppose $\hat{y}$ is a retrieved segmentation mask for instance k in the i-th frame, and we have propagated $\hat{y}$ from i-th frame to $(j-1)$-th frame, $\{y_{i+1}, y_{i+2}, \ldots, y_{j-1}\}$ is the sequence of binary masks that we obtain. We now aim to predict y_j, *i.e.*, the mask for instance k in the j-th frame. In a RNN framework, the prediction of y_j can be solved as

$$h_j = \mathcal{N}_R(h_{(j-1)\to j}, x_j), \tag{1}$$

$$y_j = \mathcal{N}_O(h_j), \tag{2}$$

where $\mathcal{N}_R$ and $\mathcal{N}_O$ are the recurrent function and output function, respectively.

We first explain Eq. (1). We begin with estimating the location, *i.e.*, the bounding box, of instance k in the j-th frame from y_{j-1} by flow guided warping. More specifically, we use FlowNet 2.0 [13] to extract the optical flow $F_{(j-1)\to j}$ between $(j-1)$-th and j-th frames. Other flow estimation methods [12,31] are applicable too. The binary mask y_{j-1} is warped to $y_{(j-1)\to j}$ according to $F_{(j-1)\to j}$ by a bilinear warping function. After that, we obtain the bounding box of $y_{(j-1)\to j}$ as the location of instance k in the j-th frame. Similar to the Re-ID module, we extract the feature map according to this bounding box from f_j by RoIAlign operation. The feature of this bounding box is denoted as x_j. The historical information of instance k from i-th frame to $(j-1)$-th frame is expressed by a hidden state or memory $h_{j-1} \in \mathbb{R}^{m\times m\times d}$, where $m \times m$ denotes the feature size and d represents the number of channels. We warp h_{j-1} to $h_{(j-1)\to j}$ by optical flow for spatial consistency. With both x_j and $h_{(j-1)\to j}$ we can estimate h_j by Eq. (1). Similar to the mask network described in Sect. 3.1, we employ 'conv5_x' block of ResNet-101 as our recurrent function $\mathcal{N}_R$. The mask for the instance k in the j-th frame, y_j, can then be obtained by using the output function in Eq. (2). The output function $\mathcal{N}_O$ is modeled by three convolutional layers.

Region Attention. The quality of propagation to obtain y_j relies on how accurate the model in capturing the shape of target instance. In many cases, a bounding box may contain distractors that can jeopardize the quality of mask propagated. As shown in Fig. 4(a), if we directly generate y_j from h_j, a model is likely to be confused by distractors that appear in the bounding box. To overcome this issue, we leverage the attention mechanism to filter out potentially noisy regions. It is worth pointing out that attention mechanism has been used

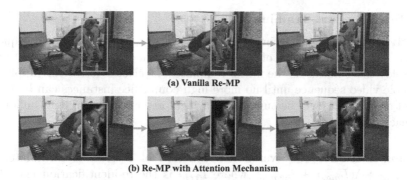

(a) Vanilla Re-MP

(b) Re-MP with Attention Mechanism

Fig. 4. Region attention in mask propagation.

in various computer vision tasks [1, 38] but not mask propagation. Our work presents the first attempt to incorporate attention mechanism in mask propagation.

Specifically, given the warped hidden state $h_{(j-1) \to j}$, we first feed it into a single convolutional layer and then a softmax function, to generate the attention distribution $a_j \in \mathbb{R}^{m \times m \times 1}$ over the bounding box. Figure 4(b) shows the attention distributions we learned. Then we multiply the current hidden state h_j by a_j across all channels to focus on the regions we interested. And the mask y_j is generated from enhanced h_j by using Eq. (2). As shown in Fig. 4, the Re-MP module concentrates on the tracked object thanks to the attention mechanism. The mask propagation of an object aborts when its size is too small, indicating a high possibility of occlusion. Finally, $\hat{y}$ is extended to a tracklet $\{y_{k1}, \ldots, y_{i+1}, \hat{y}, y_{i+1}, \ldots, y_{k2}\}$ after the forward and backward propagation. This process is applied to all the starting points to generate a set of tracklets. However, in some cases, different starting points may produce the same tracklet, which leads to redundant computation. To speed up the algorithm, we sort all starting points descendingly by their cosine similarities against templates. We extend the starting points according to the sorted order. If a starting point's mask highly overlaps with a mask in existing tracklets, we skip this starting point. This step does not affect the results; on the contrary, it greatly accelerates the inference speed.

Linking the Tracklets. The previous mask propagation step generates potentially segmented tracklets. We introduce a greedy approach to link those tracklets into consistent mask tubes. It sorts all tracklets descendingly by cosine similarities between their respective starting point and templates. Given the sorted order, tracklets with the highest similarities are assigned to the respective templates. The method then examines the remaining tracklets in turn. A tracklet is merged with a tracklet of higher order if there is no contradiction between them. In practice, this simple mechanism works well. We will investigate other plausible linking approaches (*e.g.*, conditional random field) in the future.

3.3 Inference and Training

Iterative Inference. During inference, we are given a video sequence $\{I_1, \ldots, I_N\}$, and the masks of target objects in the first frame. As mentioned, we employ those masks as the initial templates. DyeNet is iteratively applied to the whole video sequence until no more high confidence instances can be found. The set of templates will be augmented by the predictions with high confidences after each iteration.

Training Details. The overall loss function of DyeNet is formulated as: $L = L_{reid} + \lambda(L_{mask} + L_{remp})$, where L_{reid} is the re-identification loss of re-identification network in Sec. 3.1, which follows Online Instance Matching (OIM) loss in [36]. L_{mask} and L_{remp} indicate the pixel-wise segmentation losses of the mask network in Sect. 3.1 and recurrent mask propagation module in Sect. 3.2. The overall loss is a linear combination of those three losses, where λ is a weight that balances the scale of those lose terms. Following [16,21], the feature network is pre-trained by the semantic segmentation task. The DyeNet is then jointly trained on the DAVIS training sets using 24k iterations. We fix a mini-batch size of 32 images (from 8 videos, 4 frames for each video), momentum 0.9 and weight decay of 5^{-4}. The initial learning rate is 10^{-3} and dropped by a factor of 10 after every 8k iterations.

4 Experiments

Datasets. To demonstrate the effectiveness and generalization ability of DyeNet, we evaluate our method on DAVIS 2016 [27], DAVIS 2017 [28], SegTrack$_{v2}$ [19] and You-TubeObjects [29] datasets. DAVIS 2016 (DAVIS$_{16}$) dataset contains 50 high-quality video sequences (3455 frames) with all frames annotated with pixel-wise object masks. Since DAVIS$_{16}$ focuses on single-object video segmentation, each video has only one foreground object. There are 30 training and 20 validation videos. DAVIS 2017 (DAVIS$_{17}$) supplements the training and validation sets of DAVIS$_{16}$ with 30 and 10 high-quality video sequences, respectively. It also introduces another 30 development test videos and 30 challenge testing videos, which makes DAVIS$_{17}$ three times larger than its predecessor. Besides that, DAVIS$_{17}$ re-annotates all video sequences with multiple objects. All of these differences make it more challenging than DAVIS$_{16}$. SegTrack$_{v2}$ dataset contains 14 low resolution video sequences (947 frames) with 24 generic foreground objects. For YouTubeObjects [29] dataset, we consider a subset of 126 videos with around 20000 frames, and the pixel-level annotation are provided by [14].

Evaluation Metric. For DAVIS$_{17}$ dataset, we follow [28] that adopts region ($\mathcal{J}$), boundary ($\mathcal{F}$) and their average ($\mathcal{G}$) measures for evaluation. To be consistent with existing studies [3,16,26,34], we use mean intersection over union (mIoU) averaged across all instances to evaluate the performance in DAVIS$_{16}$, SegTrack$_{v2}$ and YouTubeObjects.

Table 1. Ablation study on Re-MP with DAVIS$_{17}$ *val.*

	Variant	$\mathcal{J}$-mean	$\mathcal{F}$-mean	$\mathcal{G}$-mean
MSK [26]	ResNet-101	63.3	67.2	65.3
Re-MP	No attention	65.3	69.7	67.5
	Full	**67.3**	**71.0**	**69.1**

Training Modalities. In existing studies [16,26], training modalities can be divided into **offline training** and **online training**. In offline training a model is only trained on the training set without any annotations from the test set. Since the first frame annotations are provided in the testing stage, we can use them for tuning the model, namely online training. Online training can be further divided into **per-dataset** and **per-video** training. In per-dataset online training, we fine-tune a model based on all the first frame annotations from the test set, to obtain a dataset-specific model. Per-video online training adapts the model weights to each testing video, *i.e.*, there will be as many video specific models as the testing videos during the testing stage.

4.1 Ablation Study

In this section, we investigate the effectiveness of each component in DyeNet. Unless otherwise indicated we employ the *train set* of DAVIS$_{17}$ for training. All performance are reported on the *val set* of DAVIS$_{17}$. Offline training modality is used.

Effectiveness of Re-MP Module. To demonstrate the effectiveness of Re-MP module, we do not involve the Re-ID module in this experiment. Re-MP module is directly applied to extend the annotations in the first frame to form mask tubes. This variant degenerates our method to a conventional mask propagation pipeline but with an attention-aware recurrent structure. We compare Re-MP module with the state-of-the-art mask propagation method, MSK [26]. To ensure a fair comparison, we re-implement MSK to have the same backbone ResNet-101 as DyeNet. We do not use online training and any post-processing in MSK either. The re-implemented MSK achieves 78.7 $\mathcal{J}$-mean on DAVIS$_{16}$ *val set*, which is much higher than the original result 69.9 reported in [26].

As shown in Table 1, MSK achieves 65.3 $\mathcal{G}$-mean on DAVIS$_{17}$ *val set*. Unlike MSK that propagates predicted masks only, the proposed Re-MP propagates all historical information by the recurrent architecture, and RoIAlign operation allows our network to focus on foreground regions and produce high-resolution masks, which makes Re-MP outperform MSK. The Re-MP with attention mechanism is more focused on foreground regions, which further improves $\mathcal{G}$-mean by 1.6.

Figure 5 shows propagation results of different methods. In this video, a dog passes in front of a woman and another dog. MSK dyes the woman and the back

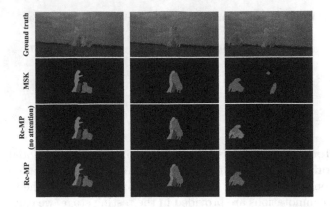

Fig. 5. Examples of mask propagation. Best viewed in color.

Table 2. Ablation study on Re-ID with DAVIS$_{17}$ *val.* The improvement of $\mathcal{G}$-mean between rows is because of template expansion.

ρ_{reid}	0.9			0.8			0.7			0.6		
	preci.	recall	$\mathcal{G}$-mean	preci.	recall	$\mathcal{G}$-mean	preci.	recall	$\mathcal{G}$-mean	preci.	recall	$\mathcal{G}$-mean
Iter. 1	97.0	16.0	72.3	87.1	22.2	73.2	78.9	26.2	73.2	76.5	29.2	73.4
Iter. 2	90.3	29.3	73.3	75.6	32.5	73.7	68.9	33.5	**74.1**	65.5	34.1	74.0
Iter. 3$^+$	90.7	30.1	73.6	74.6	32.6	73.7	68.8	33.5	**74.1**	65.3	34.2	73.9

dog with the instance id of the front dog. The plain Re-MP does not dye other instances, but it is still confused during the crossing and assigns the front dog with two instance ids. Thanks to the attention mechanism, our full Re-MP is not distracted by other instances. Due to occlusion, the masks of other instances are lost, and they will be retrieved by the Re-ID module in the complete DyeNet.

Effectiveness of Re-ID Module with Template Expansion. In DyeNet, we employ the Re-ID module to search for target objects in the video sequence. By choosing an appropriate similarity threshold ρ_{reid}, we can establish high-quality starting points for the Re-MP module. The threshold ρ_{reid} controls the trade-off between precision and recall of retrieved objects. Table 2 lists the precision and recall of retrieved starting points in each iteration as ρ_{reid} varies, and corresponding overall performance. Tracklets are linked by greedy algorithm in this experiment.

Overall, the $\mathcal{G}$-mean is increased after each iteration due to the template expansion. When ρ_{reid} decreases, more instances are retrieved in the first iteration, which leads to high recall and $\mathcal{G}$-mean. It also produces some imprecise starting points and further affects the quality of templates in subsequent iterations, so the increase of performance between each iteration is limited. In contrast, Re-ID module with high ρ_{reid} is stricter. As the template set expands, it can still achieve satisfying recall rate gradually. In practice, the iterative process stops in about three rounds. Due to our greedy algorithm, the overall

Table 3. Ablation study of each module in DyeNet with DAVIS$_{17}$ *test-dev*.

	Variant	$\mathcal{J}$-mean	$\mathcal{F}$-mean	$\mathcal{G}$-mean	$\Delta\mathcal{G}$-mean
MSK [26]	ResNet-101	50.9	52.6	51.7	–
Re-MP	No attention	55.4	60.5	58.0	+6.2
	Full	59.1	62.8	61.0	+9.2
+Re-ID		**65.8**	**70.5**	**68.2**	+7.2
Offline	Offline only	60.2	64.8	62.5	−5.6

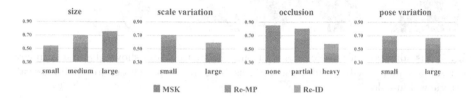

Fig. 6. Stage-wise performance increment according to specific attributes. Best viewed in color.

performance is less sensitive to ρ_{reid}. When $\rho_{reid} = 0.7$, DyeNet achieves the best $\mathcal{G}$-mean. This value is used in all the following experiments.

Effectiveness of Each Component in DyeNet. Table 3 summarizes how performance gets improved by adding each component step-by-step into our DyeNet on the *test-dev set* of DAVIS$_{17}$. Our re-implemented MSK is chosen as the baseline. All models in this experiment are first offline trained on the *train* and *val set*, and then per-dataset online trained on the *test-dev set*.

Compared with MSK, our Re-MP module with attention mechanism significantly improves $\mathcal{G}$-mean by 9.2. The full DyeNet that contains both Re-ID and Re-MP modules achieves 68.2 by using greedy algorithm to link the tracklets. More remarkably, without online training, our DyeNet achieves a competitive $\mathcal{G}$-mean of 62.5.

To further investigate the contribution of each module in DyeNet, we categorize instances in *test-dev set* by specific attributes, including:

- **Size:** Instances are categorized into 'small', 'medium', and 'large' according to their size in the first frames' annotations.
- **Scale Variation:** The area ratio among any pair of bounding boxes enclosing the target object is smaller than 0.5. The bounding boxes are obtained from our best prediction.
- **Occlusion:** An object is not, partially, or heavily occluded.
- **Pose Variation:** Noticeable pose variation, due to object motion or relative camera-object rotation.

We choose the best version of DyeNet in Table 3, and visualize its stage-wise performance according to specific attributes in Fig. 6. We find that object's size and

Fig. 7. Visualization of DyeNet's prediction. The first column shows the first frame of each video sequence with ground truth masks. The frames are chosen at equal interval. Best viewed in color.

occlusion are most important factors that affect the performance, and scale variation has more influence on the performance than pose variation. By inspecting closer, we observe that our Re-MP module can well track those small objects, which is the shortcoming of conventional mask propagation methods. It also avoids the distraction from other objects in partial occlusion cases. Complementary to Re-MP, Re-ID module retrieves missing instances due to heavy occlusions, greatly improves the performance in heavy occlusion cases. Even with large pose variations, template expansion ensures Re-ID works well.

4.2 Benchmark

In this section, we compare our DyeNet with other existing methods and show that it can achieve the state-of-the-art performance on standard benchmarks, including $DAVIS_{16}$, $DAVIS_{17}$, $SegTrack_{v2}$ and YouTubeObjects datasets. In this section, DyeNet is tested on a single scale without any post-processing. Table 4 lists the $\mathcal{J}$, $\mathcal{F}$ and $\mathcal{G}$-means on $DAVIS_{17}$ *test-dev*. Approaches with ensemble are marked with [†]. DyeNet is trained on *train* and *val sets* of $DAVIS_{17}$ and achieves a competitive $\mathcal{G}$-mean of 62.5. It further improves $\mathcal{G}$-mean to 68.2 through online fine-tuning, which is the best-performing method on $DAVIS_{17}$ benchmark.

To show the generalization ability and transferability of DyeNet, we next evaluate DyeNet on three other benchmarks, $DAVIS_{16}$, $SegTrack_{v2}$ and YouTubeObjects, which contain diverse videos. For $DAVIS_{16}$, DyeNet is trained on its *train set*. Since there is no video for offline training in $SegTrack_{v2}$ and YouTubeObjects, we directly employ the model of $DAVIS_{17}$ as their offline model. As summarized in Table 5, offline DyeNet obtains promising performance, and after online fine-tuning, our model achieves state-of-the-art performance on all three datasets. Note that although the videos in $SegTrack_{v2}$ and YouTubeObjects are very different from videos in $DAVIS_{17}$, DyeNet trained on $DAVIS_{17}$ still gains outstanding performance on those datasets without any fine-tuning, which

Table 4. Results on DAVIS$_{17}$ *test-dev*.

| | Online training | | $\mathcal{J}$-mean | $\mathcal{F}$-mean | $\mathcal{G}$-mean |
	dataset	video			
OnAVOS†[34]	√	√	53.4	59.6	56.5
LucidTracker [16]	√	√	60.1	68.3	64.2
VS-ReID [21]	√	×	64.4	67.8	66.1
LucidTracker†[16]	√	√	63.4	69.9	66.6
DyeNet (offline)	×	×	60.2	64.8	62.5
DyeNet	√	×	**65.8**	**70.5**	**68.2**

Table 5. Results (mIoU) across three datasets.

| | Online training | | DAVIS$_{16}$ | SegTrack$_{v2}$ | YoutbObjs |
	Dataset	Video			
VPN [15]	×	×	75.0	-	-
SegFlow [5]	√	√	76.1	-	-
OSVOS [3]	√	√	79.8	65.4	72.5
MSK [26]	√	√	80.3	70.3	72.6
LucidTracker [16]	√	√	84.8	77.6	76.2
OnAVOS [34]	√	√	85.7	-	77.4
DyeNet (offline)	×	×	84.7	**78.3**	74.9
DyeNet	√	×	**86.2**	**78.7**	**79.6**

shows its great generalization ability and transferability to diverse videos. We also find that our offline predictions on YouTubeObjects are even better than most ground-truth annotations, and performance losses are mainly caused by annotation bias. In Fig. 7, we demonstrate some examples of DyeNet's predictions.

Speed Analysis. Most of existing methods require online training with post-processing to achieve a competitive performance. Because of those time consuming processes, their speed of inference is slow. For example, the full OnAVOS [34] takes roughly 13 seconds per frame to achieve 85.7 mIoU on DAVIS$_{16}$ *val set*. LucidTracker [16] that achieves 84.8 mIoU requires 40k iterations per-dataset, 2k per-video online training and post-processing [6]. Our offline DyeNet is capable of obtaining similar performance (84.7 mIoU) at 2.4 FPS on a single Titan Xp GPU. After 2k per-dataset online training, our DyeNet achieves 86.2 mIoU, and the corresponding running time is 0.43 FPS.

5   Conclusion

We have presented DyeNet, which joints re-identification and attention-based recurrent temporal propagation into a unified framework to address challenging video object segmentation with multiple instances. This is the first end-to-end framework for this problem with a few compelling components. First, to cope with pose variations of targets, we relaxed the reliance of template set in the first frame by performing template expansion in our iterative algorithm. Second, to achieve robust video segmentation against distractors and background clutters, we proposed attention mechanism for recurrent temporal propagation. DyeNet does not require online training to obtain competitive accuracies at a faster speed than many existing methods. With online training, DyeNet achieves state-of-the-art performance on a wide range of standard benchmarks (including DAVIS, SegTrack$_{v2}$ and YouTubeObjects).

Acknowledgement. This work is supported by SenseTime Group Limited and the General Research Fund sponsored by the Research Grants Council of the Hong Kong SAR (CUHK 14241716, 14224316. 14209217).

References

1. Ba, J., Mnih, V., Kavukcuoglu, K.: Multiple object recognition with visual attention. In: ICLR (2015)
2. Bolme, D.S., Beveridge, J.R., Draper, B.A., Lui, Y.M.: Visual object tracking using adaptive correlation filters. In: CVPR (2010)
3. Caelles, S., Maninis, K.K., Pont-Tuset, J., Leal-Taixé, L., Cremers, D., Van Gool, L.: One-shot video object segmentation. In: CVPR (2017)
4. Chen, L.C., Papandreou, G., Kokkinos, I., Murphy, K., Yuille, A.L.: Semantic image segmentation with deep convolutional nets and fully connected CRFs. In: ICLR (2015)
5. Cheng, J., Tsai, Y.H., Wang, S., Yang, M.H.: SegFlow: joint learning for video object segmentation and optical flow. In: ICCV (2017)
6. Felzenszwalb, P.F., Huttenlocher, D.P.: Efficient belief propagation for early vision. IJCV **70**(1), 41–54 (2006)
7. Grundmann, M., Kwatra, V., Han, M., Essa, I.: Efficient hierarchical graph-based video segmentation. In: CVPR (2010)
8. Hariharan, B., Arbeláez, P., Girshick, R., Malik, J.: Simultaneous detection and segmentation. In: Fleet, D., Pajdla, T., Schiele, B., Tuytelaars, T. (eds.) ECCV 2014. LNCS, vol. 8695, pp. 297–312. Springer, Cham (2014). https://doi.org/10. 1007/978-3-319-10584-0_20
9. Hariharan, B., Arbeláez, P., Girshick, R., Malik, J.: Hypercolumns for object segmentation and fine-grained localization. In: CVPR (2015)
10. He, K., Gkioxari, G., Dollár, P., Girshick, R.: Mask R-CNN. In: ICCV (2017)
11. He, K., Zhang, X., Ren, S., Sun, J.: Deep residual learning for image recognition. In: CVPR (2016)
12. Hui, T.W., Tang, X., Loy, C.C.: LiteFlowNet: a lightweight convolutional neural network for optical flow estimation. In: CVPR (2018)

13. Ilg, E., Mayer, N., Saikia, T., Keuper, M., Dosovitskiy, A., Brox, T.: FlowNet 2.0: evolution of optical flow estimation with deep networks. In: CVPR (2017)
14. Jain, S.D., Grauman, K.: Supervoxel-consistent foreground propagation in video. In: Fleet, D., Pajdla, T., Schiele, B., Tuytelaars, T. (eds.) ECCV 2014. LNCS, vol. 8692, pp. 656–671. Springer, Cham (2014). https://doi.org/10.1007/978-3-319-10593-2_43
15. Jampani, V., Gadde, R., Gehler, P.V.: Video propagation networks. In: CVPR (2017)
16. Khoreva, A., Benenson, R., Ilg, E., Brox, T., Schiele, B.: Lucid data dreaming for object tracking. In: CVPRW (2017)
17. Le, T.N., et al.: Instance re-identification flow for video object segmentation. In: CVPRW (2017)
18. Lee, Y.J., Kim, J., Grauman, K.: Key-segments for video object segmentation. In: ICCV (2011)
19. Li, F., Kim, T., Humayun, A., Tsai, D., Rehg, J.M.: Video segmentation by tracking many figure-ground segments. In: ICCV (2013)
20. Li, X., Liu, Z., Luo, P., Loy, C.C., Tang, X.: Not all pixels are equal: difficulty-aware semantic segmentation via deep layer cascade. In: CVPR (2017)
21. Li, X., et al.: Video object segmentation with re-identification. In: CVPRW (2017)
22. Li, Y., Qi, H., Dai, J., Ji, X., Wei, Y.: Fully convolutional instance-aware semantic segmentation. In: CVPR (2017)
23. Liu, Z., Li, X., Luo, P., Loy, C.C., Tang, X.: Deep learning Markov random field for semantic segmentation. TPAMI 40, 1814–1828 (2017)
24. Märki, N., Perazzi, F., Wang, O., Sorkine-Hornung, A.: Bilateral space video segmentation. In: CVPR (2016)
25. Papazoglou, A., Ferrari, V.: Fast object segmentation in unconstrained video. In: ICCV (2013)
26. Perazzi, F., Khoreva, A., Benenson, R., Schiele, B., Sorkine-Hornung, A.: Learning video object segmentation from static images. In: CVPR (2017)
27. Perazzi, F., Pont-Tuset, J., McWilliams, B., Van Gool, L., Gross, M., Sorkine-Hornung, A.: A benchmark dataset and evaluation methodology for video object segmentation. In: CVPR (2016)
28. Pont-Tuset, J., Perazzi, F., Caelles, S., Arbeláez, P., Sorkine-Hornung, A., Van Gool, L.: The 2017 Davis challenge on video object segmentation. arXiv:1704.00675 (2017)
29. Prest, A., Leistner, C., Civera, J., Schmid, C., Ferrari, V.: Learning object class detectors from weakly annotated video. In: CVPR (2012)
30. Ren, S., He, K., Girshick, R., Sun, J.: Faster R-CNN: towards real-time object detection with region proposal networks. In: NIPS (2015)
31. Sun, D., Yang, X., Liu, M.Y., Kautz, J.: PWC-Net: CNNs for optical flow using pyramid, warping, and cost volume. In: CVPR (2018)
32. Tsai, Y.H., Yang, M.H., Black, M.J.: Video segmentation via object flow. In: CVPR (2016)
33. Valmadre, J., Bertinetto, L., Henriques, J.F., Vedaldi, A., Torr, P.H.: End-to-end representation learning for correlation filter based tracking (2017)
34. Voigtlaender, P., Leibe, B.: Online adaptation of convolutional neural networks for video object segmentation. In: BMVC (2017)
35. Xiao, F., Jae Lee, Y.: Track and segment: an iterative unsupervised approach for video object proposals. In: CVPR (2016)
36. Xiao, T., Li, S., Wang, B., Lin, L., Wang, X.: Joint detection and identification feature learning for person search. In: CVPR (2017)

37. Xu, C., Xiong, C., Corso, J.J.: Streaming hierarchical video segmentation. In: Fitzgibbon, A., Lazebnik, S., Perona, P., Sato, Y., Schmid, C. (eds.) ECCV 2012. LNCS, vol. 7577, pp. 626–639. Springer, Heidelberg (2012). https://doi.org/10.1007/978-3-642-33783-3_45
38. Yang, Z., He, X., Gao, J., Deng, L., Smola, A.: Stacked attention networks for image question answering. In: CVPR (2016)
39. Yoon, J.S., Rameau, F., Kim, J., Lee, S., Shin, S., Kweon, I.S.: Pixel-level matching for video object segmentation using convolutional neural networks. In: CVPR (2017)
40. Zhao, H., Shi, J., Qi, X., Wang, X., Jia, J.: Pyramid scene parsing network. In: CVPR (2017)
41. Zheng, S., et al.: Conditional random fields as recurrent neural networks. In: ICCV (2015)

Spatio-Temporal Transformer Network for Video Restoration

Tae Hyun Kim[1,2(✉)], Mehdi S. M. Sajjadi[1,3], Michael Hirsch[1,4],
and Bernhard Schölkopf[1]

[1] Max Planck Institute for Intelligent Systems, Tübingen, Germany
{tkim,msajjadi,bs}@tue.mpg.de
[2] Hanyang University, Seoul, Republic of Korea
[3] Max Planck ETH Center for Learning Systems, Tübingen, Germany
[4] Amazon Research, Tübingen, Germany
hirsch@amazon.com

Abstract. State-of-the-art video restoration methods integrate optical flow estimation networks to utilize temporal information. However, these networks typically consider only a pair of consecutive frames and hence are not capable of capturing long-range temporal dependencies and fall short of establishing correspondences across several timesteps. To alleviate these problems, we propose a novel Spatio-temporal Transformer Network (STTN) which handles multiple frames at once and thereby manages to mitigate the common nuisance of occlusions in optical flow estimation. Our proposed STTN comprises a module that estimates optical flow in both space and time and a resampling layer that selectively warps target frames using the estimated flow. In our experiments, we demonstrate the efficiency of the proposed network and show state-of-the-art restoration results in video super-resolution and video deblurring.

Keywords: Spatio-temporal transformer network
Spatio-temporal flow · Spatio-temporal sampler
Video super-resolution · Video deblurring

1 Introduction

Motion estimation via dense optical flow is a crucial component in video processing including restoration tasks such as video super-resolution and video deblurring. While traditional approaches try to register consecutive frames within a video sequence through energy minimization [1–3], more recent works [4–8] have demonstrated that convolutional neural networks (CNNs) enable accurate, fast and reliable optical flow estimation by end-to-end deep learning.

The success and applicability of CNNs in optical flow estimation has been made possible through the availability of large amounts of data. State-of-the-art

---

M. Hirsch—The scientific idea and a preliminary version of the code were developed at the MPI prior to joining Amazon.

ⓒ Springer Nature Switzerland AG 2018
V. Ferrari et al. (Eds.): ECCV 2018, LNCS 11207, pp. 111–127, 2018.
https://doi.org/10.1007/978-3-030-01219-9_7

approaches [4–6] are based on supervised learning and require labeled data with ground truth optical flow. However, as such networks are trained on synthetic datasets with known ground truth [9,10], their generalization to real-world data remains challenging due to the intrinsic differences between training and test data and the limited variability of synthetic imagery [8].

To circumvent the need for labeled training data with ground truth optical flow, recent work [7,11,12] has promoted unsupervised learning by introducing resampling layers that are differentiable and allow end-to-end training. Such a resampling layer would warp an image to a reference frame according to the estimated optical flow, such that the measured pixel-wise distance in image rather than optical flow space can be used as a training objective.

In this paper, we build on these ideas and propose a task-specific end-to-end unsupervised approach for *Spatio-temporal Flow* estimation which is dense optical flow that selectively captures long-range temporal dependencies by allowing for several consecutive frames as network input. To this end, we extend the Spatial Transformer Network [13] to a *Spatio-temporal Transformer Network* (STTN) which is able to establish dense pixel correspondences across space and time. We show that reasoning over several consecutive frames and choosing one of them per pixel location helps mitigate the commonly known problem of occlusions in optical flow estimation. A further advantage of our approach is that it can be trained in an unsupervised fashion and thus renders the availability of large labeled data unnecessary. When used in conjunction with a video restoration network tailored for a specific task, we obtain a substantial performance gain with minimal computational overhead. We demonstrate the effectiveness of our proposed STTN for the challenging tasks of video super-resolution and video deblurring, and improve upon the state-of-the-art by a substantial margin. In summary, we make the following contributions:

- We introduce a spatio-temporal flow estimation network which selectively captures long-range temporal dependencies without a large computational overhead and which alleviates the occlusion problem in conventional optical flow estimation.
- We present a spatio-temporal sampler which enables spatio-temporal manipulation of the input data by using the estimated spatio-temporal flow.
- We show promising results on challenging video restoration tasks such as video super-resolution and deblurring by simply placing the proposed network on top of the state-of-the-art methods.

2 Related Work

2.1 Optical Flow Estimation

Many computer vision tasks such as tracking, 3D reconstruction, and video restoration rely on accurate optical flow and as a result, flow estimation techniques have been widely studied. Traditional optical flow estimation methods are based on energy optimization, and minimize the proposed energy models with various optical flow constraints. These generative models focus on studying better prior models [14–17] and more accurate likelihood models [18–20], and these approaches perform well on the Middlebury optical flow dataset [21] where motion displacements are relatively small. With the release of more challenging datasets beyond the experimental Middlebury dataset, such as the MPI Sintel [22] and KITTI [23] datasets, more robust algorithms to handle large displacements have been studied [24–27].

As it has recently become possible to generate large synthetic flow datasets [4], deep learning based flow estimation approaches are being actively studied. In particular, Dosovitskiy *et al.* [4] propose FlowNet, the first neural approach which directly renders optical flow from two consecutive images. As FlowNet is fully convolutional, it can be trained in an end-to-end manner and exhibits real-time performance. In follow-up studies, Ilg *et al.* [5] extend FlowNet and improve flow accuracy by passing flow through a stacked architecture which includes multiple sub-networks specialized for both small and large displacements, and Ranjan *et al.* [6] propose a faster network which can handle large displacements by embedding the traditional coarse-to-fine approach into the flow estimation network.

However, as it is difficult to collect large amounts of labeled flow datasets for real scenes, there are some works that train the flow estimation networks in an unsupervised manner. Ren *et al.* [7] introduce an unsupervised learning method for flow networks which minimizes the traditional energy function with a data term based on photometric consistency coupled with a smoothness term. Meister *et al.* [8] improve the flow accuracy by training the network with robust census transform which is more reliable at occluded regions. As there is a considerable difference between synthetic flow datasets and the real-world videos used in our restoration tasks, these unsupervised learning methods which train flow networks on datasets of real scenes are more closely related to our work than supervised learning methods.

2.2 Video Restoration

Video Super-Resolution. Since spatial alignment is a key element for high-quality video super-resolution, many conventional methods seek to find correspondences among adjacent frames by optimizing energy models for the enhancement task [1,3,28]. Moreover, learning-based state-of-the-art video super-resolution methods are also composed of an alignment mechanism and a super-resolution network. After aligning several previous and future frames to the current frame, all frames are fed into a super-resolution network which then combines the information from several views. This method is often applied in a sliding window over the video [29–33]. While older methods use classical approaches for the alignment [29], recent approaches employ neural networks for this task as well. While Caballero *et al.* [30] warp frames using a dense optical flow estimation network before feeding the result to a super-resolution network, Makansi *et al.* [31] combine warping and mapping to high-resolution space into a single step. Although using a larger number of previous and future frames leads to higher-quality results, the computational overhead of aligning several frames rises linearly with the number of inputs, limiting the amount of information that can be combined into a single output frame. A recent approach by Sajjadi et al. [34] therefore uses a frame-recurrent architecture that reuses the previous output frame for the next frame which leads to higher efficiency and quality compared to sliding-window approaches. However, for higher efficiency, only a single previous frame is fed into the network for the next iteration, leading to suboptimal results in case of occlusions.

Video Deblurring. Early approaches to remove blur in video frames are based on image deblurring techniques which remove uniform blurs caused by translational camera shake. Cai et al. [35] and Zhang et al. [36] study sparsity characteristics of the latent sharp frames and the blur kernels to restore the uniformly blurred images. For the next step, to remove non-uniform blurs caused by rotational camera shake, several methods tackle the simultaneous registration and restoration problems [37–40]. In contrast, Wulff and Black [41] propose a method which jointly segments and restores the differently blurred foreground and background regions by object and ego motions, and Kim et al. [2,42] propose methods which remove spatially varying blurs without relying on accurate segmentation results by parameterizing the blur kernel using optical flow [43].

As large motion blur datasets become available [42,44–46], several deep learning approaches have been proposed to restore the video frames. First, Shuochen et al. [45] propose a deep neural network taking a stack of neighboring blurry frames as input. As these frames are aligned with the reference frame, the proposed network can easily exploit multiple frames and reconstruct sharp images. Recently, Wieschollek et al. [46] introduce a recurrent neural network which can handle an arbitrary number of temporal inputs as well as arbitrary spatial input sizes. Unlike all of the previous deblurring methods which require significant time to restore a video frame, Kim et al. [47] propose a fast online video deblurring method by efficiently increasing the receptive field of the network without adding a computational overhead to handle large motion blurs. Moreover, by training the network to enforce temporal smoothness, their method achieves state-of-the-art results with near real-time performance.

3   Proposed Method

Spatial transformer networks (STN) proposed by Jaderberg et al. [13] that enable generic warping of the feature maps are widely used in numerous vision applications. In particular for video restoration tasks, many deep learning approaches are based on variants of STN to estimate optical flow between adjacent frames and to align the target frames onto the reference frame [30–32,34]. However, the STN only allows spatial manipulation of the input data. To handle multiple video frames at each time step, one needs to employ STN multiple times which is a severe limitation when applied in real-time settings.

We therefore introduce a novel spatio-temporal transformer network (STTN) which efficiently enables spatio-temporal warping of the input data and alleviates

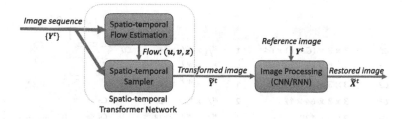

Fig. 1. Our spatio-temporal transformer network is composed of a flow estimation network which calculates spatio-temporal flow and a sampler which selectively transforms the multiple target frames to the reference. An image processing network follows for the video restoration task.

the limitations of the conventional STN without a large computational overhead. In Fig. 1, the overall structure of our proposed STTN which is composed of a spatio-temporal flow estimation network and a spatio-temporal sampler is illustrated. In the following sections, we describe the details of each component.

3.1 Spatio-Temporal Flow Estimation Network

Traditional model-based approaches solve optical flow estimation and video restoration problems jointly [1–3,28], and recent learning-based approaches estimate the optical flow by using off-the-shelf methods [29,45] or by employing sub-networks to estimate flow [30,31,34].

However, all of these previous methods estimate optical flow between two consecutive frames (reference and target frames), and thus it is required to calculate flow N times to handle N target frames for each time step. Moreover, as shown in Fig. 3, conventional flow estimation networks are unreliable where correspondences are not well established (e.g., occlusion and illumination change).

To overcome these limitations, we propose a new spatio-temporal flow estimation network which takes a sequence of multiple neighboring frames $\{\mathbf{Y}^t\} \in \mathbb{R}^{H \times W \times C \times T}$ as input where H, W, C, and T denote the height, width, number of channels and number of input frames, and outputs a normalized three-dimensional spatio-temporal flow $(\mathbf{u}, \mathbf{v}, \mathbf{z}) \in [-1, 1]^{H \times W \times 3}$. Notably, the height and width of the output flow can be different from those of input depending on applications. Therefore, our spatio-temporal network can handle multiple frames very efficiently at a single time step, and it becomes more robust to occlusions and illumination changes since there are *multiple* matching candidates from multiple target frames, unlike conventional works which consider only one target frame.

The detailed configuration of the proposed U-net [48] like spatio-temporal flow estimation network is shown in Fig. 2. All convolutional layers are performed with 3×3 filters and are followed by batch normalization [49] and ReLu except for the last convolutional layer which is followed by *tanh* to output a normalized flow. As our flow estimation network is fully convolutional, it can be used to handle frames of arbitrary (spatial) size at inference time once trained.

Layer	Filter size	Stride	Output shape
C0	$3 \times 3 \times (C \times T) \times 64$	1	$H/_1 \times W/_1 \times 64$
C1	$3 \times 3 \times 64 \times 64$	1	$H/_1 \times W/_1 \times 64$
C2	$3 \times 3 \times 64 \times 64$	1	$H/_1 \times W/_1 \times 64$
C3	$3 \times 3 \times 64 \times 128$	2	$H/_2 \times W/_2 \times 128$
C4	$3 \times 3 \times 128 \times 128$	1	$H/_2 \times W/_2 \times 128$
C5	$3 \times 3 \times 128 \times 256$	2	$H/_4 \times W/_4 \times 256$
C6	$3 \times 3 \times 256 \times 256$	1	$H/_4 \times W/_4 \times 256$
Upscaling	nearest neighbor, 2x	-	$H/_2 \times W/_2 \times 256$
C7+C4	$3 \times 3 \times 256 \times 128$	1	$H/_2 \times W/_2 \times 128$
C8	$3 \times 3 \times 128 \times 128$	1	$H/_2 \times W/_2 \times 128$
Upscaling	nearest neighbor, 2x	-	$H/_1 \times W/_1 \times 128$
C9+C2	$3 \times 3 \times 128 \times 64$	1	$H/_1 \times W/_1 \times 64$
C10	$3 \times 3 \times 64 \times 64$	1	$H/_1 \times W/_1 \times 64$
C11	$3 \times 3 \times 64 \times 3$	1	$H/_1 \times W/_1 \times 3$

Input : $\{Y^t\}$

C0
C1
C2
C3
C4
C5
C6
Upscaling
C7
C8
Upscaling
C9
C10
C11

Output: (u, v, z)

Fig. 2. Our fully convolutional spatio-temporal flow estimation network takes multiple frames as input $(H \times W \times C \times T)$ and renders a spatio-temporal flow $(H \times W \times 3)$ as output.

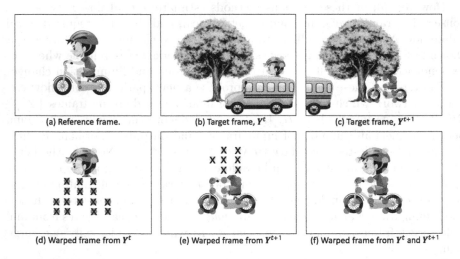

(a) Reference frame. (b) Target frame, Y^t (c) Target frame, Y^{t+1}

(d) Warped frame from Y^t (e) Warped frame from Y^{t+1} (f) Warped frame from Y^t and Y^{t+1}

Fig. 3. Spatial transformer network vs. spatio-temporal transformer network. Conventional spatial transformer networks require to be employed multiple times to extract information separately as in (d) and (e), and they are unreliable in areas of occlusions. In contrast, the proposed spatio-temporal transformer can exploit multiple frames at the same time and find a single best match among multiple target frames.

3.2   Differentiable Spatio-Temporal Sampler

To synthesize a new image aligned with the reference frame by selectively warping the multiple target frames using the spatio-temporal flow in Sect. 3.1, a new
sampler which performs sampling in three-dimensional spatio-temporal space
is required. In this paper, we propose a spatio-temporal sampler by naturally
extending the conventional spatial sampling module from two-dimensional to
three-dimensional space. Our spatio-temporal sampler interpolates intensity values from multiple target frames as:

$$\tilde{\mathbf{Y}}^t_{(x,y)} = \sum_n^W \sum_m^H \sum_{i \in \Delta} \mathbf{Y}^{t+i}_{(n,m)} \cdot \delta(\mathbf{u}_{(x,y)}, \mathbf{v}_{(x,y)}, \mathbf{z}_{(x,y)}), \tag{1}$$

where $\tilde{\mathbf{Y}}_{(x,y)}$ denotes the interpolated pixel value at location (x, y) and $\mathbf{Y}^{t+i}_{(n,m)}$ is
the intensity value of $\mathbf{Y}^{t+i}$ at a pixel location (n, m) with temporal shift $i \in \Delta$.
For example, we can define a sliding window of the form $\Delta = \{-2, \dots, 3\}$.
The function δ defines an interpolation method using the spatio-temporal flow
$(\mathbf{u}, \mathbf{v}, \mathbf{z})$. Any function δ whose sub-gradient is defined could be used for sampling
as introduced in [13]. Here, we employ trilinear interpolation for δ in our video
restoration tasks. It is given by

$$\tilde{\mathbf{Y}}^t_{(x,y)} = \sum_n^W \sum_m^H \sum_{i \in \Delta} \mathbf{Y}^{t+i}_{(n,m)} \cdot \max(0, 1 - |x + \mathbf{u}_{(x,y)} - n|)$$
$$\cdot \max(0, 1 - |y + \mathbf{v}_{(x,y)} - m|) \cdot \max(0, 1 - |\mathbf{z}_{(x,y)} - (t + i)|). \tag{2}$$

Note that the unnormalized version of spatio-temporal flow $(\mathbf{u}, \mathbf{v}, \mathbf{z})$ is used
in (2), that is, $\mathbf{u}_{(x,y)}$ and $\mathbf{v}_{(x,y)}$ denote the horizontal and vertical motion displacements, and $\mathbf{z}_{(x,y)}$ is mapped to a real value close to a target frame index
which is favored to be matched at (x, y).

Similarly to the bilinear spatial sampling procedure in [13], our trilinear sampling mechanism in three-dimensional space is also differentiable. The gradient
with respect to our spatio-temporal flow is derived as follows:

$$\frac{\partial \tilde{\mathbf{Y}}^t_{(x,y)}}{\partial \mathbf{z}_{(x,y)}} = \sum_n^W \sum_m^H \sum_{i \in \Delta} \mathbf{Y}^{t+i}_{(n,m)} \cdot \max(0, 1 - |x + \mathbf{u}_{(x,y)} - n|)$$
$$\cdot \max(0, 1 - |y + \mathbf{v}_{(x,y)} - m|) \cdot \begin{cases} 0, & \text{if } |\mathbf{z}_{(x,y)} - (t + i)| \geq 1 \\ 1, & \text{if } \mathbf{z}_{(x,y)} \leq t + i \\ -1, & \text{otherwise} \end{cases} \tag{3}$$

Note that the gradients for $\frac{\partial \tilde{\mathbf{Y}}^t_{(x,y)}}{\partial \mathbf{u}_{(x,y)}}$ and $\frac{\partial \tilde{\mathbf{Y}}^t_{(x,y)}}{\partial \mathbf{v}_{(x,y)}}$ can be derived similarly. More
generally, our spatio-temporal transformer can take a set of feature maps U^t as

input rather than images $\mathbf{Y}^t$. The gradient with respect to $\boldsymbol{U}^t$ is then given as:

$$\frac{\partial \tilde{\mathbf{Y}}^t_{(x,y)}}{\partial \mathbf{U}^t_{(n,m)}} = \sum_n^W \sum_m^H \sum_{i \in \Delta} \max(0, 1 - |x + \mathbf{u}_{(x,y)} - n|) \tag{4}$$
$$\cdot \max(0, 1 - |y + \mathbf{v}_{(x,y)} - m|) \cdot \max(0, 1 - |\mathbf{z}_{(x,y)} - (t + i)|).$$

This means that the proposed spatio-temporal sampler allows the loss gradients to backpropagate readily into the input frames or feature maps.

3.3 Spatio-Temporal Transformer Network

Our spatio-tempral flow estimation network which handles multiple different frames at the same time can replace multiple usages of optical flow estimation modules in conventional approaches [30,31,45] with much less computational effort. Moreover, our spatio-temporal sampling mechanism can also be also processed very efficiently with modern GPUs. Additionally, as the proposed network can find a better corresponding point from several frames in spatio-temporal space rather than the conventional STN approach which estimates the matching point in a single target frame. This leads to a network which is much more robust against outliers as a result of occlusion or illumination changes.

Our spatio-temporal transformer network directly extends the spatial transformer network [13] into three-dimensional space. Because of this, many characteristics of the previous spatial transformer network can be generalized in the proposed network. First, our spatio-temporal transformer network can be easily trained in an end-to-end manner as loss gradients can flow backwards through both the sampler and the flow estimation network, and it can be placed in any location of the conventional networks to selectively transform or merge multiple feature maps efficiently. As a result, the proposed module can be used in numerous applications apart from our video restoration tasks. Second, unlike the spatial transformer which enables to upscale and downscale the feature maps only in the two-dimensional spatial domain, our spatio-temporal transformer allows to change shapes not only in the spatial domain but also in temporal space. Next, as suggested in [13], our network can also be added multiple times at increasing depths of a network or in parallel to handle multiple objects at different time steps while the spatial transformer network can handle multiple objects only at a single time step.

Unsupervised Spatio-Temporal Flow Learning. Recent learning-based optical flow estimation methods are trained on large synthetic datasets such as Flyinging Chairs [4] and the MPI Sintel dataset [22]. However, to the best of our knowledge, there is no available dataset which can be used to train our spatio-temporal flow estimation network directly, and it is not straightforward to utilize optical flow datasets to train the proposed network. Therefore, we train our network in an unsupervised manner. Particularly, for our video restoration applications, we propose a loss to train our flow estimation network by constraining the synthesized image from our spatio-temporal sampler as:

$$L_{flow} = \|\tilde{\mathbf{Y}}^t - \mathbf{X}^t\|^2, \tag{5}$$

where $\mathbf{X}^t$ denotes the ground truth frame corresponding to the reference frame at time step t.

4   Experiments

In this section, we demonstrate the power and versatility of our STTN and show how state-of-the-art image and video restoration networks can be further improved with the simple addition of the proposed spatio-temporal transformer.

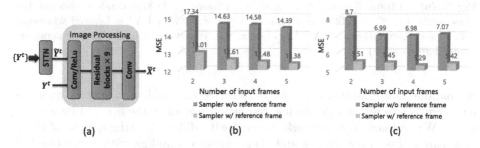

Fig. 4. Image reconstruction performance is evaluated on super-resolution and deblurring datasets for a varying number of frames. (a) Video restoration network with STTN. (b) Reconstruction loss on video super-resolution dataset. (c) Reconstruction loss on video deblurring dataset.

4.1   Ablation Study

To evaluate the warping performance of the spatio-temporal transformer network, we trained the approach using video datasets with various settings of the hyperparameters (e.g., the number of target frames). As shown in Fig. 4(a), we use a video restoration network with STTN, and the image processing module which is composed of convolutional layers and residual blocks as used in [34,44,50]. The network is trained by jointly minimizing L_{flow} in (5) and MSE between the latent and ground truth images, and we compare the warped (synthesized) and ground truth frames.

First, we train the network using a super-resolution dataset. Since no standard high-resolution video super-resolution dataset is available, we have collected a set of high-quality youtube videos and extracted 120k UHD frames to train the networks. As a next step, we have generated low-resolution video frames by

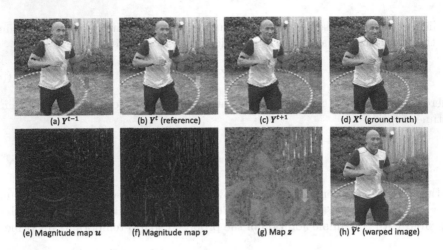

Fig. 5. (a)–(c) Input frames. (d) Ground truth frame. (e–f) Magnitude of motion displacements. (g) $\mathbf{Y}^{t-1}$ is favored whenever $0 \leq \mathbf{z} < 0.33$, and $\mathbf{Y}^t$ is favored whenever $0.33 \leq \mathbf{z} < 0.66$. Otherwise, $\mathbf{Y}^{t+1}$ is chosen. (h) Transformed image by our sampler. (Color figure online)

downscaling the clean video frames by a factor of 4 and subsequently quantizing them before we upscale the low-resolution frames to the original image size again. We evaluate eight networks trained with different settings: Four of them take two to five input frames and then perform sampling with the estimated flow and target frames. The other four networks also take two to five frames as network input, but run the sampler with the reference frame as well as target frames, that is, the reference frame is also considered as a target frame. Similarly, we also compare different networks trained on video deblurring datasets [45]. In Fig. 4(b)–(c), the quality of the warped frame $\tilde{\mathbf{Y}}^t$ is evaluated in terms of reconstruction error (i.e., L_{flow}). Overall, the networks tend to give better results with more inputs, though the gain in performance slowly saturates as we add more frames. Moreover, we observe that the reconstruction error is significantly reduced by considering the reference frame as a target, since it can then render the reference frame itself where correspondences are not available. Therefore, we consider the reference frame as a target in our network for subsequent experiments. In Fig. 5(e)–(h), our flow maps and the transformed images are visualized. As expected, the occluded background regions by the moving hula hoop ring, indicated by colored arrows, are mainly mapped by the reference frame itself.

4.2 Video Super-Resolution

We further integrate our network into state-of-the-art super-resolution networks and provide comparisons to demonstrate the performance of our network.

Comparison with VDSR [51]. Kim *et al.* proposed VDSR in Fig. 6(a) which raised the bar for single image super-resolution [51]. We show how VDSR can

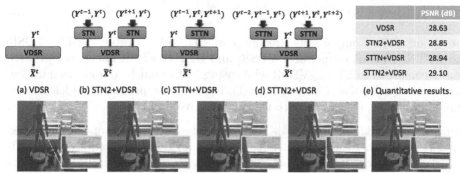

(a) VDSR   (b) STN2+VDSR   (c) STTN+VDSR   (d) STTN2+VDSR   (e) Quantitative results.

	PSNR (dB)
VDSR	28.63
STN2+VDSR	28.85
STTN+VDSR	28.94
STTN2+VDSR	29.10

(f) Qualitative comparisons. Left to right: Low resolution input (bicubic, x4), VDSR, STN2+VDSR, STTN+VDSR, STTN2+VDSR

Fig. 6. Comparisons with VDSR [51].

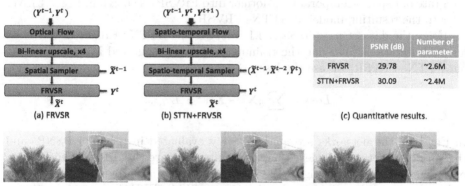

(a) FRVSR   (b) STTN+FRVSR   (c) Quantitative results.

	PSNR (dB)	Number of parameter
FRVSR	29.78	~2.6M
STTN+FRVSR	30.09	~2.4M

(d) Left to right: Two consecutive low resolution frames (bicubic, x4), results by FRVSR, results by STTN+FRVSR

Fig. 7. Comparisons with FRVSR [34]. In (b), $\hat{\mathbf{Y}}^t$ denotes the bilinearly upscaled (x4) version of the reference frame $\mathbf{Y}^t$.

be naturally improved and extended to handle multiple video frames using our spatio-temporal transformer network.

In our experiments, STN2+VDSR in Fig. 6(b) refers to the conventional model which integrates two spatial transformer networks to calculate bidirectional optical flow as in [30,31]. Our STTN+VDSR in Fig. 6(c) has one spatio-temporal transformer, and similarly to STN2+VDSR, two spatio-temporal transformer networks are placed in our STTN2+VDSR model in Fig. 6(d). Note that for fair comparisons, we modify our spatio-temporal flow estimation network in Fig. 2 to calculate optical flow (output shape: $H \times W \times 3 \rightarrow H \times W \times 2$), and use the flow in STN2+VDSR. All these networks are trained on the video super-resolution dataset used in Sect. 4.1 using the ADAM optimizer (learning rate 10^{-4}). We used 256×256 patches with a minibatch size of 8, and the networks are trained for 300k iterations. Moreover, STN2+VDSR, STTN+VDSR and STTN2+VDSR were trained by minimizing the loss

$$Loss = \|\tilde{\mathbf{X}}^t - \mathbf{X}^t\|^2 + L_{flow}, \tag{6}$$

and quantitative comparisons are given in Fig. 6(e). Notably, STTN+VDSR and STTN2+VDSR outperform VDSR, and STTN+VDSR shows competitive results compared to STN2+VDSR while using half as much computation in flow estimation. Qualitative results in Fig. 6(f) show that the proposed models restore thin edges better, consistent with the quantitative results.

Comparison with FRVSR [34]. To improve the performance of previous video super-resolution networks which do not utilize previously computed results, Sajjadi *et al.* [34] propose FRVSR which is based on a recurrent architecture, outperforming previous state-of-the-art methods. However, FRVSR only utilizes a single previously restored frame as shown in Fig. 7(a) as utilizing several frames would be computationally expensive. To handle multiple frames efficiently, we integrate our spatio-temporal transformer into FRVSR as shown in Fig. 7(b). We refer to the resulting model as STTN+FRVSR.

Using the dataset used in Sect. 4.1, FRVSR and STTN+FRVSR are trained for 500k iterations following the training procedure suggested by [34]. To train our STTN+FRVSR, we use the loss

$$Loss = \sum_t \|\tilde{\mathbf{X}}^t - \mathbf{X}^t\|^2 + L_{flow}. \tag{7}$$

In Fig. 7(c), the networks are quantitatively evaluated in terms of PSNR, and the proposed network achieves better results compared to FRVSR with fewer parameters. Moreover, in Fig. 7(d), visual comparisons are provided when there is a shot change between two consecutive frames. While FRVSR produces artifacts by propagating wrong details from the previous frame after the shot change, our STTN+FRVSR renders better result since STTN+FRVSR can use the reference frame itself for synthesizing $\tilde{\mathbf{Y}}^t$.

4.3   Video Deblurring

To further show the versatility of STTN, we also embed our network into stat-of-the-art video deblurring networks and provide comparison results.

Comparison with DVD [45]. The deep video deblurring (DVD) network proposed by Shuochen *et al.* [45] removes spatially varying motion blurs in video frames. More specifically, as shown in Fig. 8(a), DVD takes a stack of five adjacent frames as network input (one reference and four target frames) and then aligns the target frames with the reference frame using an off-the-shelf optical flow method [52]. It thus requires optical flow calculations four times at each time step, slowing down the method. To reduce the computation time in flow calculation and to further improve the deblurring performance, we propose two different models on top of DVD.

First, our STTN+DVD model in Fig. 8(b) calculates spatio-temporal flow and synthesizes a selectively transformed image from five consecutive frames.

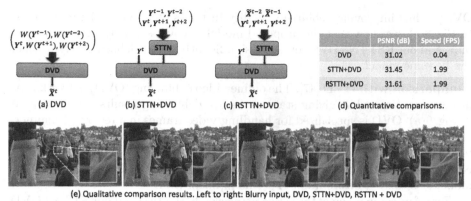

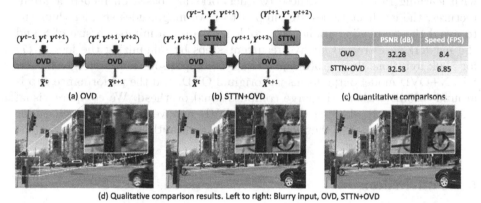

Fig. 8. Comparisons with DVD [45]. A function W in (a) warps the target frame to the reference frame.

Fig. 9. Comparisons with OVD [47].

Next, the DVD network takes both the synthesized image and the reference frame as input. Our RSTTN+DVD model in Fig. 8(c) also takes five frames at each time step, but two of them are previously restored sharp frames ($\tilde{X}^{t-2}$, $\tilde{X}^{t-1}$). RSTTN+DVD is thus a kind of recurrent network, but does not require additional resources when compared to STTN+DVD. As it is difficult to estimate flow using off-the-shelf flow estimation methods in a recurrent model, it is not straightforward to find a natural extension of DVD to the recurrent architecture. For training, we use the dataset from [45] and the same optimizer (ADAM) using a constant learning rate (10^{-4}). The networks are trained with cropped patches (128×128) as suggested in [45], where the size of the minibatch is 8. For 700k iterations, STTN+DVD minimizes the loss in (6), and RSTTN+DVD optimizes the loss in (7) for five recurrent steps. As shown by the quantitative comparison results given in Fig. 8(d), the proposed STTN+DVD and RSTTN+DVD were able to restore two HD (1280×720) frames per second (i.e., 50 times faster than

DVD), while improving deblurring quality in terms of PSNR by large margins. In Fig. 8(e), we show that the proposed model removes spatially varying motion blur, and our RSTTN+DVD renders a significantly better deblurring result than the baseline model.

Comparison with OVD [47]. The online video deblurring (OVD) network runs in near real-time while giving state-of-the-art deblurring results. As illustrated in Fig. 9(a), OVD is specialized for handling video frames in a recurrent manner. Nevertheless, our STTN+OVD, with a spatio-temporal transformer placed on top of OVD as shown in 9(b), was able to further improve the deblurring quality. Note that since adding future frames plays a key role in OVD, our STTN+OVD model also takes a future frame $\mathbf{Y}^{t+1}$ as input of OVD.

For a fair comparison of these two networks, both OVD and our STTN+OVD networks are trained under the same conditions. We use 128×128 patches extracted from the video deblurring dataset [45] and use the ADAM optimizer with learning rate 10^{-4}. As these two networks are based on recurrent architectures, the gradient values are clipped to have magnitudes smaller than one to avoid the "exploding gradients" problem. We use a minibatch size of 8 and the networks are trained for five recurrent steps by minimizing the loss in (7) for 500k iterations. In Fig. 9(c), quantitative comparison results are given. Our STTN+OVD model outperforms the original OVD, and the performance gap is around 0.25dB without the large computational overhead. We compare visual results in Fig. 9(d), showing that STTN+DVD removes spatially varying blur at the occluded region of the moving bicycle significantly better than OVD, the current state-of-the-art.

5   Conclusions

We have proposed a novel spatio-temporal transformer network (STTN) which generalizes the spatial transformer network [13] while at the same time alleviating some of its limitations. Our STTN is composed of a spatio-temporal flow estimation module which calculates spatio-temporal flow in three dimensions from multiple image frames (or feature maps), and a spatio-temporal sampler which interpolates multiple inputs in spatio-temporal space. This way, the proposed model efficiently mitigates the problems of conventional flow estimation networks which suffer from unmatched regions, by exploiting multiple inputs at the same time rather than using a single target input. The superiority of the proposed model is demonstrated in a number of video restoration tasks, and we achieve state-of-the-art performance by simply adding the proposed module on top of conventional networks.

References

1. Liu, C., Sun, D.: A Bayesian approach to adaptive video super resolution. In: Proceedings of the IEEE Conference on Computer Vision and Pattern Recognition (CVPR) (2011)

2. Kim, T.H., Lee, K.M.: Generalized video deblurring for dynamic scenes. In: Proceedings of the IEEE Conference on Computer Vision and Pattern Recognition (CVPR) (2015)
3. Zhao, W.Y., Sawhney, H.S.: Is super-resolution with optical flow feasible? In: Heyden, A., Sparr, G., Nielsen, M., Johansen, P. (eds.) ECCV 2002. LNCS, vol. 2350, pp. 599–613. Springer, Heidelberg (2002). https://doi.org/10.1007/3-540-47969-4_40
4. Dosovitskiy, A., et al.: FlowNet: learning optical flow with convolutional networks. In: Proceedings of the IEEE International Conference on Computer Vision (ICCV) (2015)
5. Ilg, E., Mayer, N., Saikia, T., Keuper, M., Dosovitskiy, A., Brox, T.: FlowNet 2.0: evolution of optical flow estimation with deep networks. In: Proceedings of the IEEE Conference on Computer Vision and Pattern Recognition (CVPR) (2017)
6. Ranjan, A., Black, M.J.: Optical flow estimation using a spatial pyramid network. In: Proceedings of the IEEE Conference on Computer Vision and Pattern Recognition (CVPR) (2017)
7. Ren, Z., Yan, J., Ni, B., Liu, B., Yang, X., Zha, H.: Unsupervised deep learning for optical flow estimation. In: Association for the Advancement of Artificial Intelligence (AAAI) (2017)
8. Meister, S., Hur, J., Roth, S.: UnFlow: unsupervised learning of optical flow with a bidirectional census loss. In: AAAI (2017)
9. Dosovitskiy, A., Springenberg, J.T., Brox, T.: Learning to generate chairs with convolutional neural networks. In: Proceedings of the IEEE Conference on Computer Vision and Pattern Recognition (CVPR) (2015)
10. Mayer, N., et al.: A large dataset to train convolutional networks for disparity, optical flow, and scene flow estimation. In: Proceedings of the IEEE Conference on Computer Vision and Pattern Recognition (CVPR) (2016)
11. Ahmadi, A., Patras, I.: Unsupervised convolutional neural networks for motion estimation. In: IEEE International Conference on Image Processing (ICIP) (2016)
12. Yu, J.J., Harley, A.W., Derpanis, K.G.: Back to basics: unsupervised learning of optical flow via brightness constancy and motion smoothness. In: Hua, G., Jégou, H. (eds.) ECCV 2016. LNCS, vol. 9915, pp. 3–10. Springer, Cham (2016). https://doi.org/10.1007/978-3-319-49409-8_1
13. Jaderberg, M., Simonyan, K., Zisserman, A., Kavukcuoglu, K.: Spatial transformer networks. In: Advances in Neural Information Processing Systems (NIPS) (2015)
14. Zimmer, H., Bruhn, A., Weickert, J.: Optic flow in harmony. Int. J. Comput. Vis. (IJCV) **93**(3), 368–388 (2011)
15. Werlberger, M., Pock, T., Bischof, H.: Motion estimation with non-local total variation regularization. In: Proceedings of the IEEE Conference on Computer Vision and Pattern Recognition (CVPR) (2010)
16. Lee, K.J., Kwon, D., Yun, I.D., Lee, S.U.: Optical flow estimation with adaptive convolution Kernel prior on discrete framework. In: Proceedings of the IEEE Conference on Computer Vision and Pattern Recognition (CVPR) (2010)
17. Sun, D., Roth, S., Black, M.J.: Secrets of optical flow estimation and their principles. In: Proceedings of the IEEE Conference on Computer Vision and Pattern Recognition (CVPR) (2010)
18. Xu, L., Jia, J., Matsushita, Y.: Motion detail preserving optical flow estimation. IEEE Trans. Pattern Anal. Mach. Intell. (PAMI) **34**(9), 1744–1757 (2012)
19. Kim, T.H., Lee, H.S., Lee, K.M.: Optical flow via locally adaptive fusion of complementary data costs. In: Proceedings of the IEEE International Conference on Computer Vision (ICCV) (2013)

20. Volz, S., Bruhn, A., Valgaerts, L., Zimmer, H.: Modeling temporal coherence for optical flow. In: Proceedings of the IEEE International Conference on Computer Vision (ICCV) (2011)
21. Baker, S., Scharstein, D., Lewis, J., Roth, S., Black, M.J., Szeliski, R.: A database and evaluation methodology for optical flow. Int. J.Comput. Vis. (IJCV) **92**(1), 1–31 (2011)
22. Butler, D.J., Wulff, J., Stanley, G.B., Black, M.J.: A naturalistic open source movie for optical flow evaluation. In: Fitzgibbon, A., Lazebnik, S., Perona, P., Sato, Y., Schmid, C. (eds.) ECCV 2012. LNCS, vol. 7577, pp. 611–625. Springer, Heidelberg (2012). https://doi.org/10.1007/978-3-642-33783-3_44
23. Geiger, A., Lenz, P., Urtasun, R.: Are we ready for autonomous driving? The KITTI vision benchmark suite. In: Proceedings of the IEEE Conference on Computer Vision and Pattern Recognition (CVPR) (2012)
24. Xu, J., Ranftl, R., Koltun, V.: Accurate optical flow via direct cost volume processing. In: Proceedings of the IEEE Conference on Computer Vision and Pattern Recognition (CVPR) (2017)
25. Güney, F., Geiger, A.: Deep discrete flow. In: Lai, S.-H., Lepetit, V., Nishino, K., Sato, Y. (eds.) ACCV 2016. LNCS, vol. 10114, pp. 207–224. Springer, Cham (2017). https://doi.org/10.1007/978-3-319-54190-7_13
26. Revaud, J., Weinzaepfel, P., Harchaoui, Z., Schmid, C.: Deepmatching: hierarchical deformable dense matching. Int. J. Comput. Vis. (IJCV) **120**(3), 300–323 (2016)
27. Bailer, C., Taetz, B., Stricker, D.: Flow fields: dense correspondence fields for highly accurate large displacement optical flow estimation. In: Proceedings of the IEEE International Conference on Computer Vision (ICCV) (2015)
28. Mitzel, D., Pock, T., Schoenemann, T., Cremers, D.: Video super resolution using duality based TV-L^1 optical flow. In: Denzler, J., Notni, G., Süße, H. (eds.) DAGM 2009. LNCS, vol. 5748, pp. 432–441. Springer, Heidelberg (2009). https://doi.org/10.1007/978-3-642-03798-6_44
29. Kappeler, A., Yoo, S., Dai, Q., Katsaggelos, A.K.: Video super-resolution with convolutional neural networks. IEEE Trans. Comput. Imaging **2**(2), 109–122 (2016)
30. Caballero, J., Ledig, C., Aitken, A., Acosta, A., Totz, J.: Real-time video super-resolution with spatio-temporal networks and motion compensation. In: Proceedings of the IEEE Conference on Computer Vision and Pattern Recognition (CVPR) (2017)
31. Makansi, O., Ilg, E., Brox, T.: End-to-end learning of video super-resolution with motion compensation. In: Proceedings of the German Conference on Pattern Recognition (GCPR) (2017)
32. Tao, X., Gao, H., Liao, R., Wang, J., Jia, J.: Detail-revealing deep video super-resolution. In: Proceedings of the IEEE International Conference on Computer Vision (ICCV) (2017)
33. Liu, D., et al.: Robust video super-resolution with learned temporal dynamics. In: Proceedings of the IEEE Conference on Computer Vision and Pattern Recognition (CVPR) (2017)
34. Sajjadi, M.S.M., Vemulapalli, R., Brown, M.: Frame-recurrent video super-resolution. In: Proceedings of the IEEE Conference on Computer Vision and Pattern Recognition (CVPR) (2018)
35. Cai, J.F., Ji, H., Liu, C., Shen, Z.: Blind motion deblurring using multiple images. J. Comput. Phys. **228**(14), 5057–5071 (2009)
36. Zhang, H., Wipf, D., Zhang, Y.: Multi-image blind deblurring using a coupled adaptive sparse prior. In: Proceedings of the IEEE Conference on Computer Vision and Pattern Recognition (CVPR) (2013)

37. Cho, S., Cho, H., Tai, Y.W., Lee, S.: Registration based non-uniform motion deblurring. Comput. Graph. Forum **31**(7), 2183–2192 (2012)
38. Zhang, H., Carin, L.: Multi-shot imaging: joint alignment, deblurring and resolution-enhancement. In: Proceedings of the IEEE Conference on Computer Vision and Pattern Recognition (CVPR) (2014)
39. Zhang, H., Yang, J.: Intra-frame deblurring by leveraging inter-frame camera motion. In: Proceedings of the IEEE Conference on Computer Vision and Pattern Recognition (CVPR) (2015)
40. Li, Y., Kang, S.B., Joshi, N., Seitz, S.M., Huttenlocher, D.P.: Generating sharp panoramas from motion-blurred videos. In: Proceedings of the IEEE Conference on Computer Vision and Pattern Recognition (CVPR) (2010)
41. Wulff, J., Black, M.J.: Modeling blurred video with layers. In: Fleet, D., Pajdla, T., Schiele, B., Tuytelaars, T. (eds.) ECCV 2014. LNCS, vol. 8694, pp. 236–252. Springer, Cham (2014). https://doi.org/10.1007/978-3-319-10599-4_16
42. Kim, T.H., Nah, S., Lee, K.M.: Dynamic video deblurring using a locally adaptive linear blur model. IEEE Transactions on Pattern Analysis and Machine Intelligence (PAMI) (2018)
43. Kim, T.H., Lee, K.M.: Segmentation-free dynamic scene deblurring. In: Proceedings of the IEEE Conference on Computer Vision and Pattern Recognition (CVPR) (2014)
44. Nah, S., Kim, T.H., Lee, K.M.: Deep multi-scale convolutional neural network for dynamic scene deblurring. In: Proceedings of the IEEE Conference on Computer Vision and Pattern Recognition (CVPR) (2017)
45. Su, S., Delbracio, M., Wang, J., Sapiro, G., Heidrich, W., Wang, O.: Deep video deblurring. In: Proceedings of the IEEE Conference on Computer Vision and Pattern Recognition (CVPR) (2017)
46. Wieschollek, P., Hirsch, M., Schölkopf, B., Lensch, H.P.: Learning blind motion deblurring. In: Proceedings of the IEEE International Conference on Computer Vision (ICCV) (2017)
47. Kim, T.H., Lee, K.M., Schölkopf, B., Hirsch, M.: Online video deblurring via dynamic temporal blending network. In: Proceedings of the IEEE International Conference on Computer Vision (ICCV) (2017)
48. Ronneberger, O., Fischer, P., Brox, T.: U-Net: convolutional networks for biomedical image segmentation. In: Navab, N., Hornegger, J., Wells, W.M., Frangi, A.F. (eds.) MICCAI 2015. LNCS, vol. 9351, pp. 234–241. Springer, Cham (2015). https://doi.org/10.1007/978-3-319-24574-4_28
49. Ioffe, S., Szegedy, C.: Batch normalization: accelerating deep network training by reducing internal covariate shift. In: International Conference on Machine Learning (2015)
50. Sajjadi, M.S.M., Schölkopf, B., Hirsch, M.: EnhanceNet: single image super-resolution through automated texture synthesis. In: Proceedings of the IEEE International Conference on Computer Vision (ICCV) (2017)
51. Kim, J., Kwon Lee, J., Mu Lee, K.: Accurate image super-resolution using very deep convolutional networks. In: Proceedings of the IEEE Conference on Computer Vision and Pattern Recognition (CVPR) (2016)
52. Pérez, J.S., Meinhardt-Llopis, E., Facciolo, G.: TV-L1 optical flow estimation. Image Process. On Line (IPOL) **3**, 137–150 (2013)

Dense Pose Transfer

Natalia Neverova[1]([⊠]), Rıza Alp Güler[2], and Iasonas Kokkinos[1]

[1] Facebook AI Research, Paris, France
{nneverova,iasonask}@fb.com
[2] INRIA-CentraleSupélec, Paris, France
riza.guler@inria.fr

Abstract. In this work we integrate ideas from surface-based modeling with neural synthesis: we propose a combination of surface-based pose estimation and deep generative models that allows us to perform accurate pose transfer, i.e. synthesize a new image of a person based on a single image of that person and the image of a pose donor. We use a dense pose estimation system that maps pixels from both images to a common surface-based coordinate system, allowing the two images to be brought in correspondence with each other. We inpaint and refine the source image intensities in the surface coordinate system, prior to warping them onto the target pose. These predictions are fused with those of a convolutional predictive module through a neural synthesis module allowing for training the whole pipeline jointly end-to-end, optimizing a combination of adversarial and perceptual losses. We show that dense pose estimation is a substantially more powerful conditioning input than landmark-, or mask-based alternatives, and report systematic improvements over state of the art generators on DeepFashion and MVC datasets.

1 Introduction

Deep models have recently shown remarkable success in tasks such as face [2], human [3–5], or scene generation [6,7], collectively known as "neural synthesis". This opens countless possibilities in computer graphics applications, including cinematography, gaming and virtual reality settings. At the same time, the potential malevolent use of this technology raises new research problems, including the detection of forged images or videos [8], which in turn requires training forgery detection algorithms with multiple realistic samples. In addition, synthetically generated images have been successfully exploited for data augmentation and training deep learning frameworks for relevant recognition tasks [9].

In most applications, the relevance of a generative model to the task directly relates to the amount of control that one can exert on the generation process.

Electronic supplementary material The online version of this chapter (https://doi.org/10.1007/978-3-030-01219-9_8) contains supplementary material, which is available to authorized users.

© Springer Nature Switzerland AG 2018
V. Ferrari et al. (Eds.): ECCV 2018, LNCS 11207, pp. 128–143, 2018.
https://doi.org/10.1007/978-3-030-01219-9_8

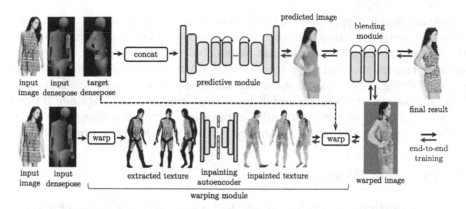

Fig. 1. Overview of our pose transfer pipeline: given an input image and a target pose we use DensePose [1] to drive the generation process. This is achieved through the complementary streams of (a) a data-driven predictive module, and (b) a surface-based module that warps the texture to UV-coordinates, interpolates on the surface, and warps back to the target image. A blending module combines the complementary merits of these two streams in a single end-to-end trainable framework.

Recent works have shown the possibility of adjusting image synthesis by controlling categorical attributes [3,10], low-dimensional parameters [11], or layout constraints indicated by a conditioning input [3–7,12]. In this work we aspire to obtain a stronger hold of the image synthesis process by relying on surface-based object representations, similar to the ones used in graphics engines.

Our work is focused on the human body, where surface-based image understanding has been most recently unlocked [1,13–18]. We build on the recently introduced SMPL model [13] and the DensePose system [1], which taken together allow us to interpret an image of a person in terms of a full-fledged surface model, getting us closer to the goal of performing *inverse graphics*.

In this work we close the loop and perform image generation by rendering the same person in a new pose through surface-based neural synthesis. The target pose is indicated by the image of a 'pose donor', i.e. another person that guides the image synthesis. The DensePose system is used to associate the new photo with the common surface coordinates and copy the appearance predicted there.

The purely geometry-based synthesis process is on its own insufficient for realistic image generation: its performance can be compromised by inaccuracies of the DensePose system as well as by self-occlusions of the body surface in at least one of the two images. We account for occlusions by introducing an inpainting network that operates in the surface coordinate system and combine its predictions with the outputs of a more traditional feedforward conditional synthesis module. These predictions are obtained independently and compounded by a refinement module that is trained so as to optimize a combination of reconstruction, perceptual and adversarial losses.

We experiment on the DeepFashion [19] and MVC [20] datasets and show that we can obtain results that are quantitatively better than the latest state-of-the-art. Apart from the specific problem of pose transfer, the proposed combination of neural synthesis with surface-based representations can also be promising for the broader problems of virtual and augmented reality: the generation process is more transparent and easy to connect with the physical world, thanks to the underlying surface-based representation. In the more immediate future, the task of pose transfer can be useful for dataset augmentation, training forgery detectors, as well as texture transfer applications like those showcased by [1], without however requiring the acquisition of a surface-level texture map.

2   Previous Works

Deep generative models have originally been studied as a means of unsupervised feature learning [21–24]; however, based on the increasing realism of neural synthesis models [2,6,7,25] such models can now be considered as components in computer graphics applications such as content manipulation [7].

Loss functions used to train such networks largely determine the realism of the resulting outputs. Standard reconstruction losses, such as ℓ_1 or ℓ_2 norms typically result in blurry results, but at the same time enhance stability [12]. Realism can be enforced by using an adapted discriminator loss trained in tandem with a generator in Generative Adversarial Network (GAN) architectures [23] to ensure that the generated and observed samples are indistinguishable. However, this training can often be unstable, calling for more robust variants such as the squared loss of [26], WGAN and its variants [27] or multi-scale discriminators as in [7]. An alternative solution is the perceptual loss used in [28,29] replacing the optimization-based style transfer of [25] with feedforward processing. This was recently shown in [6] to deliver substantially more accurate scene synthesis results than [12], while compelling results were obtained more recently by combining this loss with a GAN-style discriminator [7].

Person and clothing synthesis has been addressed in a growing body of recently works [3–5,30]. All of these works assist the image generation task through domain, person-specific knowledge, which gives both better quality results, and a more controllable image generation pipeline.

Conditional neural synthesis of humans has been shown in [4,5] to provide a strong handle on the output of the generative process. A controllable surface-based model of the human body is used in [3] to drive the generation of persons wearing clothes with controllable color combinations. The generated images are demonstrably realistic, but the pose is determined by controlling a surface based model, which can be limiting if one wants e.g. to render a source human based on a target video. A different approach is taken in the pose transfer work of [4], where a sparse set of landmarks detected in the target image are used as a conditioning input to a generative model. The authors show that pose can be generated with increased accuracy, but often losing texture properties of the source images, such as cloth color or texture properties. In the work of [31] multi-view supervision is used to train a two-stage system that can generate images from multiple views. In more recent work [5] the authors show that introducing a correspondence component in a GAN architecture allows for substantially more accurate pose transfer.

Image inpainting helps estimate the body appearance on occluded body regions. Generative models are able to fill-in information that is labelled as occluded, either by accounting for the occlusion pattern during training [32], or by optimizing a score function that indicates the quality of an image, such as the negative of a GAN discriminator loss [33]. The work of [33] inpaints arbitrarily occluded faces by minimizing the discriminator loss of a GAN trained with fully-observed face patches. In the realm of face analysis impressive results have been generated recently by works that operate in the UV coordinate system of the face surface, aiming at photorealistic face inpainting [34], and pose-invariant identification [35]. Even though we address a similar problem, the lack of access to full UV recordings (as in [34,35]) poses an additional challenge.

3 Dense Pose Transfer

We develop our approach to pose transfer around the *DensePose* estimation system [1] to associate every human pixel with its coordinates on a surface-based parameterization of the human body in an efficient, bottom-up manner. We exploit the DensePose outputs in two complementary ways, corresponding to the *predictive module* and the *warping module*, as shown in Fig. 1. The warping module uses DensePose surface correspondence and inpainting to generate a new view of the person, while the predictive module is a generic, *black-box*, generative model conditioned on the DensePose outputs for the input and the target.

These modules corresponding to two parallel streams have complementary merits: the *predictive module* successfully exploits the dense conditioning output to generate plausible images for familiar poses, delivering superior results to those obtained from sparse, landmark-based conditioning; at the same time, it cannot generalize to new poses, or transfer texture details. By contrast, the *warping module* can preserve high-quality details and textures, allows us to perform inpainting in a uniform, canonical coordinate system, and generalizes for free for a broad variety of body movements. However, its body-, rather than clothing-centered construction does not take into account hair, hanging clothes, and accessories. The best of both worlds is obtained by feeding the outputs of these two blocks into a *blending module* trained to fuse and refine their predictions using a combination of reconstruction, adversarial, and perceptual losses in an end-to-end trainable framework.

The DensePose module is common to both streams and delivers dense correspondences between an image and a surface-based model of the human body. It does so by firstly assigning every pixel to one of 24 predetermined surface parts, and then regressing the part-specific surface coordinates of every pixel. The results of this system are encoded in three output channels, comprising the part label and part-specific UV surface coordinates. This system is trained discriminatively and provides a simple, feed-forward module for dense correspondence from an image to the human body surface. We omit further details, since we rely on the system of [1] with minor implementation differences described in Sect. 4.

Having outlined the overall architecture of our system, in Sects. 3.1 and 3.3 we present in some more detail our components, and then turn in Sect. 3.4 to the loss functions used in their training. A thorough description of architecture details is left to the supplemental material. We start by presenting the architecture of the predictive stream, and then turn to the surface-based stream, corresponding to the upper and lower rows of Fig. 1, respectively.

3.1 Predictive Stream

The predictive module is a conditional generative model that exploits the Dense-Pose system results for pose transfer. Existing conditional models indicate the target pose in the form of heat-maps from keypoint detectors [4], or part segmentations [3]. Here we condition on the concatenation of the input image and DensePose results for the input and target images, resulting in an input of dimension 256 × 256 × 9. This provides conditioning that is both global (part-classification), and point-level (continuous coordinates), allowing the remaining network to exploit a richer source of information.

The remaining architecture includes an encoder followed by a stack of residual blocks and a decoder at the end, along the lines of [28]. In more detail, this network comprises (a) a cascade of three convolutional layers that encode the 256 × 256 × 9 input into 64 × 64 × 256 activations, (b) a set of six residual blocks with 3 × 3 × 256 × 256 kernels, (c) a cascade of two deconvolutional and one convolutional layer that deliver an output of the same spatial resolution as the input. All intermediate convolutional layers have 3×3 filters and are followed by instance normalization [36] and ReLU activation. The last layer has tanh non-linearity and no normalization.

3.2 Warping Stream

Our warping module performs pose transfer by performing explicit texture mapping between the input and the target image on the common surface UV-system. The core of this component is a Spatial Transformer Network (STN) [37] that warps according to DensePose the image observations to the UV-coordinate system of each surface part; we use a grid with 256 × 256 UV points for each of the 24 surface parts, and perform scattered interpolation to handle the continuous values of the regressed UV coordinates. The inverse mapping from UV to the output image space is performed by a second STN with a bilinear kernel. As shown in Fig. 3, a direct implementation of this module would often deliver poor results: the part of the surface that is visible on the source image is typically small, and can often be entirely non-overlapping with the part of the body that is visible on the target image. This is only exacerbated by DensePose failures or systematic errors around the part seams. These problems motivate the use of an inpainting network within the warping module, as detailed below.

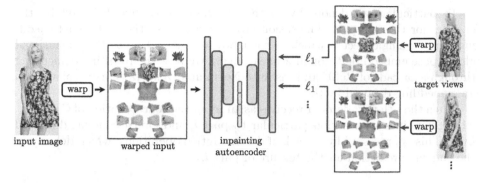

Fig. 2. Supervision signals for pose transfer on the warping stream: the input image on the left is warped to intrinsic surface coordinates through a spatial transformer network driven by DensePose. From this input, the inpainting autoencoder has to predict the appearance of the same person from different viewpoints, when also warped to intrinsic coordinates. The loss functions on the right penalize the reconstruction only on the observed parts of the texture map. This form of multi-view supervision acts like a surrogate for the (unavailable) appearance of the person on the full body surface.

Inpainting Autoencoder. This model allows us to extrapolate the body appearance from the surface nodes populated by the STN to the remainder of the surface. Our setup requires a different approach to the one of other deep inpainting methods [33], because we never observe the full surface texture during training. We handle the partially-observed nature of our training signal by using a reconstruction loss that only penalizes the observed part of the UV map, and lets the network freely *guess* the remaining domain of the signal. In particular, we use a masked ℓ_1 loss on the difference between the autoencoder predictions and the target signals, where the masks indicate the visibility of the target signal.

We observed that by its own this does not urge the network to inpaint successfully; results substantially improve when we accompany every input with multiple supervision signals, as shown in Fig. 2, corresponding to UV-wrapped shots of the same person at different poses. This fills up a larger portion of the UV-space and forces the inpainting network to predict over the whole texture domain. As shown in Fig. 3, the inpainting process allows us to obtain a uniformly observed surface, which captures the appearance of skin and tight clothes, but does not account for hair, skirts, or apparel, since these are not accommodated by DensePose's surface model.

Our inpainting network is comprised of N autoencoders, corresponding to the decomposition of the body surface into N parts used in the original DensePose system [1]. This is based on the observation that appearance properties are non-stationary over the body surface. Propagation of the context-based information from visible to invisible parts that are entirely occluded at the present view is achieved through a fusion mechanism that operates at the level of latent representations delivered by the individual encoders, and injects global pose context in the individual encoding through a concatenation operation.

In particular, we denote by $\mathcal{E}_i$ the individual encoding delivered by the encoder for the i-th part. The fusion layer concatenates these obtained encodings into a single vector which is then down-projected to a 256-dimensional global pose embedding through a linear layer. We pass the resulting embedding through a cascade of ReLU and Instance-Norm units and transform it again into an embedding denoted by $\mathcal{G}$.

Then the i-th part decoder receives as an input the concatenation of $\mathcal{G}$ with $\mathcal{E}_i$, which combines information particular to part i, and global context, delivered by $\mathcal{G}$. This is processed by a stack of deconvolution operations, which delivers in the end the prediction for the texture of part i.

3.3 Blending Module

The blending module's objective is to combine the complementary strengths of the two streams to deliver a single fused result, that will be 'polished' as measured by the losses used for training. As such it no longer involves an encoder or decoder unit, but rather only contains two convolutional and three residual blocks that aim at combining the predictions and refining their results.

In our framework, both predictive and warping modules are first pretrained separately and then finetuned jointly during blending. The final refined output is obtained by learning a residual term added to the output of the predictive stream. The blending module takes an input consisting of the outputs of the predictive and the warping modules combined with the target dense pose.

3.4 Loss Functions

As shown in Fig. 1, the training set for our network comes in the form of pairs of input and target images, x, y respectively, both of which are of the same person-clothing, but in different poses. Denoting by $\hat{y} = G(x)$ the network's prediction, the difference between $\hat{y}, y$ can be measured through a multitude of loss terms, that penalize different forms of deviation. We present them below for completeness and ablate their impact in practice in Sect. 4.

Reconstruction Loss. To penalize reconstruction errors we use the common ℓ_1 distance between the two signals: $\|\hat{y} - y\|_1$. On its own, this delivers blurry results but is important for retaining the overall intensity levels.

Perceptual Loss. As in Chen and Koltun [6], we use a VGG19 network pretrained for classification [38] as a feature extractor for both $\hat{y}, y$ and penalize the ℓ_2 distance of the respective intermediate feature activations Φ^v at 5 different network layers $v = 1, \ldots, N$:

$$\mathcal{L}_{\mathrm{p}}(y, \hat{y}) = \sum_{v=1}^{N} \|\Phi^v(y) - \Phi^v(\hat{y})\|_2. \tag{1}$$

This loss penalizes differences in low- mid- and high-level feature statistics, captured by the respective network filters.

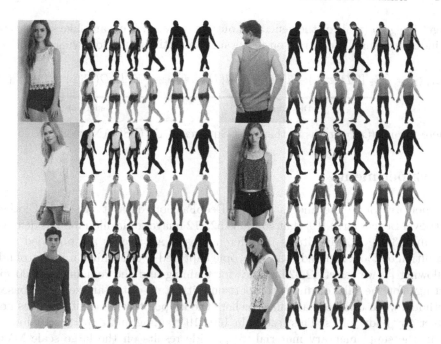

Fig. 3. Warping module results. For each sample, the top row shows interpolated textures obtained from DensePose predictions and projected on the surface of the 3D body model. The bottom row shows the same textures after inpainting in the UV space.

Style Loss. As in [28], we use the Gram matrix criterion of [25] as an objective for training a feedforward network. We first compute the Gram matrix of neuron activations delivered by the VGG network Φ at layer v for an image $\boldsymbol{x}$:

$$\mathcal{G}^v(\boldsymbol{x})_{c,c'} = \sum_{h,w} \Phi_c^v(\boldsymbol{x})[h,w]\Phi_{c'}^v(\boldsymbol{x})[h,w] \tag{2}$$

where h and w are horizontal and vertical pixel coordinates and c and c' are feature maps of layer v. The style loss is given by the sum of Frobenius norms for the difference between the per-layer Gram matrices $\mathcal{G}^v$ of the two inputs:

$$\mathcal{L}_{\text{style}}(\boldsymbol{y},\hat{\boldsymbol{y}}) = \sum_{v=1}^{B} \|\mathcal{G}^v(\boldsymbol{y}) - \mathcal{G}^v(\hat{\boldsymbol{y}})\|_F. \tag{3}$$

Adversarial Loss. We use adversarial training to penalize any detectable differences between the generated and real samples. Since global structural properties are largely settled thanks to DensePose conditioning, we opt for the patch-GAN [12] discriminator, which operates locally and picks up differences between texture patterns. The discriminator [7,12] takes as an input $\boldsymbol{z}$, a combination of the source image and the DensePose results on the target image, and either the target image y (real) or the generated output (fake) $\hat{y}$. We want fake samples to be indistinguishable from real ones – as such we optimize the following objective:

$$L_{\text{GAN}} = \underbrace{\frac{1}{2}\mathbb{E}_z\left[l(D(z,y)-1)\right] + \frac{1}{2}\mathbb{E}_z\left[l(D(z,\hat{y}))\right]}_{\text{Discriminator}} + \underbrace{\frac{1}{2}\mathbb{E}_z\left[l(D(G(z)-1))\right]}_{\text{Generator}}, \quad (4)$$

where we use $l(x) = x^2$ as in the Least Squares GAN (LSGAN) work of [26].

4   Experiments

We perform our experiments on the DeepFashion dataset (In-shop Clothes Retrieval Benchmark) [19] that contains 52,712 images of fashion models demonstrating 13,029 clothing items in different poses. All images are provided at a resolution of 256×256 and contain people captured over a uniform background. Following [5] we select 12,029 clothes for training and the remaining 1,000 for testing. For the sake of direct comparison with state-of-the-art keypoint-based methods, we also remove all images where the keypoint detector of [39] does not detect any body joints. This results in 140,110 training and 8,670 test pairs.

In the supplementary material we provide results on the large scale MVC dataset [20] that consists of 161,260 images of resolution 1920×2240 crawled from several online shopping websites and showing front, back, left, and right views for each clothing item.

4.1   Implementation Details

DensePose Estimator. We use a fully convolutional network (FCN) similar to the one used as a teacher network in [1]. The FCN is a ResNet-101 trained on cropped person instances from the COCO-DensePose dataset. The output consists of 2D fields representing body segments (I) and $\{U, V\}$ coordinates in coordinate spaces aligned with each of the semantic parts of the 3D model.

Training Parameters. We train the network and its submodules with Adam optimizer with initial learning rate $2 \cdot 10^{-4}$ and $\beta_1 = 0.5$, $\beta_2 = 0.999$ (no weight decay). For speed, we pretrain the predictive module and the inpainting module separately and then train the blending network while finetuning the whole combined architecture end-to-end; DensePose network parameters remain fixed. In all experiments, the batch size is set to 8 and training proceeds for 40 epochs. The balancing weights λ between different losses in the blending step (described in Sect. 3.4) are set empirically to $\lambda_{\ell_1} = 1$, $\lambda_p = 0.5$, $\lambda_{\text{style}} = 5 \cdot 10^5$, $\lambda_{\text{GAN}} = 0.1$.

4.2   Evaluation Metrics

As of today, there exists no general criterion allowing for adequate evaluation of the generated image quality from the perspective of both structural fidelity and

Table 1. Quantitative comparison with the state-of-the-art methods on the DeepFashion dataset [19] according to the Structural Similarity (SSIM) [40], Inception Score (IS) [41] and detection score (DS) [5] metrics. Our *best structure* model corresponds to the ℓ_1 loss, the *highest realism* model corresponds to the style loss training (see the text and Table 4). Our *balanced* model is trained using the full combination of losses.

Model	SSIM	IS	DS
Disentangled [42]	0.614	3.29	–
VariGAN [31]	0.620	3.03	–
G1+G2+D [4]	0.762	3.09	–
DSC [5]	0.761	3.39	0.966
Ours (best structure)	**0.796**	3.17	0.971
Ours (highest realism)	0.777	**3.67**	0.969
Ours (balanced)	0.785	3.61	0.971

photorealism. We therefore adopt a number of separate structural and perceptual metrics widely used in the community and report our joint performance on them.

Structure. The geometry of the generations is evaluated using the perception-correlated *Structural Similarity* metric (SSIM) [40]. We also exploit its multi-scale variant MS-SSIM [43] to estimate the geometry of our predictions at a number of levels, from body structure to fine clothing textures.

Image Realism. Following previous works, we provide the values of *Inception scores (IS)* [41]. However, as repeatedly noted in the literature, this metric is of limited relevance to the problem of within-class object generation, and we do not wish to draw strong conclusions from it. We have empirically observed its instability and high variance with respect to the perceived quality of generations and structural similarity. We also note that the ground truth images from the DeepFashion dataset have an average IS of 3.9, which indicates low degree of realism of this data according to the IS metric (for comparison, IS of CIFAR-10 is 11.2 [41] with best image generation methods achieving IS of 8.8 [2]).

In addition, we perform additional evaluation using *detection scores (DS)* [5] reflecting the similarity of the generations to the *person* class. Detection scores correspond to the maximum of confidence of the PASCAL-trained SSD detector [44] in the person class taken over all detected bounding boxes.

4.3 Comparison with the State-of-the-Art

We first compare the performance of our framework to a number of recent methods proposed for the task of *keypoint guided* image generation or multi-view synthesis. Table 1 shows a significant advantage of our pipeline in terms of structural fidelity of obtained predictions. This holds for the whole range of tested network configurations and training setups (see Table 4). In terms of perceptual quality expressed through IS, the output generations of our models are of higher

source   target   DSC [4]   ours   source   target   DSC [4]   ours

Fig. 4. Qualitative comparison with the state-of-the-art Deformable GAN (DSC) method of [5]. Each group shows the input, the target image, DSC predictions [5], predictions obtained with our full model. We observe that even though our cloth texture is occasionally not as sharp, we better retain face, gender, and skin color information.

quality or directly comparable with the existing works. Some qualitative results of our method (corresponding to the *balanced* model in Table 1) and the best performing state-of-the-art approach [5] are shown in Fig. 4.

We have also performed a user study on Amazon Mechanical Turk, following the protocol of [5]: we show 55 real and 55 generated images in a random order to 30 users for one second. As the experiment of [5] was done with the help of fellow researchers and not AMT users, we perform an additional evaluation of images generated by [5] for consistency, using the official public implementation. We perform three evaluations, shown in Table 1: *Realism* asks users if the image is real or fake. *Anatomy* asks if a real, or generated image is anatomically plausible. *Pose* shows a pair of a target and a generated image and asks if they are in the same pose. The results (correctness, in %) indicate that generations of [5] have higher degree of perceived realism, but our generations show improved pose fidelity and higher probability of overall anatomical plausibility.

4.4 Effectiveness of Different Body Representations

In order to clearly measure the effectiveness of the DensePose-based conditioning, we first compare to the performance of the 'black box', predictive module when used in combination with more traditional body representations, such as background/foreground masks, body part segmentation maps or body landmarks.

Fig. 5. Typical failures of keypoint-based pose transfer (top) in comparison with Dense-Pose conditioning (bottom) indicate disappearance of limbs, discontinuities, collapse of 3D geometry of the body into a single plane and confusion in ordering in depth.

Table 2. On effectiveness of different body representations as a ground for pose transfer. The DensePose representation results in the highest structural quality.

Model	SSIM	MS-SSIM	IS
Foreground mask	0.747	0.710	3.04
Body part segmentation	0.776	0.791	3.22
Body keypoints	0.762	0.774	3.09
DensePose $\{I, U, V\}$	**0.792**	**0.821**	3.09
DensePose $\{$one-hot $I, U, V\}$	0.782	0.799	3.32

As a segmentation map we take the index component of DensePose and use it to form a one-hot encoding of each pixel into a set of class specific binary masks. Accordingly, as a background/foreground mask, we simply take all pixels with positive DensePose segmentation indices. Finally, following [5] we use [39] to obtain body keypoints and one-hot encode them.

In each case, we train the predictive module by concatenating the source image with a corresponding representation of the source and the target poses which results in 4 input planes for the mask, 27 for segmentation maps and 21 for the keypoints.

The corresponding results shown in Table 2 demonstrate a clear advantage of fine-grained dense conditioning over the sparse, keypoint-based, or coarse, segmentation-based, representations.

Complementing these quantitative results, typical failure cases of keypoint-based frameworks are demonstrated in Fig. 5. We observe that these shortcomings are largely fixed by switching to the DensePose-based conditioning.

4.5   Ablation Study on Architectural Choices

Table 3 shows the contribution of each of the predictive module, warping module, and inpainting autoencoding blocks in the final model performance. For these experiments, we use only the reconstruction loss $\mathcal{L}_{\ell_1}$, factoring out fluctuations in the performance due to instabilities of GAN training. As expected, including the warping branch in the generation pipeline results in better performance, which is further improved by including the inpainting in the UV space. Qualitatively, exploiting the inpainted representation has two advantages over the direct warping of the partially observed texture from the source pose to the target pose: first, it serves as an additional prior for the fusion pipeline, and, second, it also prevents the blending network from generating clearly visible sharp artifacts that otherwise appear on the boarders of partially observed segments of textures.

Table 3. Contribution of each of the functional blocks of the framework

Model	SSIM	MS-SSIM	IS
Predictive module only	0.792	0.821	3.09
Predictive + blending (=self-refinement)	0.793	0.821	3.10
Predictive + warping + blending	0.789	0.814	3.12
Predictive + warping + inpainting + blending (full)	**0.796**	**0.823**	**3.17**

4.6   Ablation Study on Supervision Objectives

In Table 4 we analyze the role of each of the considered terms in the composite loss function used at the final stage of the training, while providing indicative results in Fig. 6.

The perceptual loss $\mathcal{L}_p$ is most correlated with the image structure and least correlated with the perceived realism, probably due to introduced textural artifacts. At the same time, the style loss $\mathcal{L}_{style}$ produces sharp and correctly textured patterns while hallucinating edges over uniform regions. Finally, adversarial training with the loss $\mathcal{L}_{GAN}$ tends to prioritize visual plausibility but often disregarding structural information in the input. This justifies the use of all these complimentary supervision criteria in conjunction, as indicated in the last entry of Table 4.

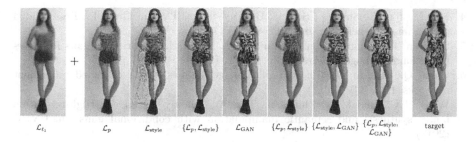

$\mathcal{L}_{\ell_1}$ $\mathcal{L}_p$ $\mathcal{L}_{\text{style}}$ $\{\mathcal{L}_p, \mathcal{L}_{\text{style}}\}$ $\mathcal{L}_{\text{GAN}}$ $\{\mathcal{L}_p, \mathcal{L}_{\text{style}}\}$ $\{\mathcal{L}_{\text{style}}, \mathcal{L}_{\text{GAN}}\}$ $\{\mathcal{L}_p, \mathcal{L}_{\text{style}}, \mathcal{L}_{\text{GAN}}\}$ target

Fig. 6. Effects of training with different loss terms and their weighted combinations.

Table 4. Comparison of different loss terms used at the final stage of the training. The perceptual loss is best correlated with the structure, and the style loss with IS. The combined model provides an optimal balance between the extreme solutions.

Model	SSIM	MS-SSIM	IS
$\{\mathcal{L}_{\ell_1}\}$	**0.796**	**0.823**	3.17
$\{\mathcal{L}_{\ell_1}, \mathcal{L}_p\}$	0.791	0.822	3.26
$\{\mathcal{L}_{\ell_1}, \mathcal{L}_{\text{style}}\}$	0.777	0.815	**3.67**
$\{\mathcal{L}_{\ell_1}, \mathcal{L}_p, \mathcal{L}_{\text{style}}\}$	0.784	0.820	3.41
$\{\mathcal{L}_{\ell_1}, \mathcal{L}_{\text{GAN}}\}$	0.771	0.807	3.39
$\{\mathcal{L}_{\ell_1}, \mathcal{L}_p, \mathcal{L}_{\text{GAN}}\}$	0.789	0.820	3.33
$\{\mathcal{L}_{\ell_1}, \mathcal{L}_{\text{style}}, \mathcal{L}_{\text{GAN}}\}$	0.787	0.820	3.32
$\{\mathcal{L}_{\ell_1}, \mathcal{L}_p, \mathcal{L}_{\text{style}}, \mathcal{L}_{\text{GAN}}\}$	**0.785**	**0.807**	**3.61**

5   Conclusion

In this work we have introduced a two-stream architecture for pose transfer that exploits the power of dense human pose estimation. We have shown that dense pose estimation is a clearly superior conditioning signal for data-driven human pose estimation, and also facilitates the formulation of the pose transfer problem in its natural, body-surface parameterization through inpainting. In future work we intend to further pursue the potential of this method for photorealistic image synthesis [2,6] as well as the treatment of more categories.

References

1. Guler, R.A., Neverova, N., Kokkinos, I.: Densepose: dense human pose estimation in the wild. In: CVPR (2018)
2. Karras, T., Aila, T., Samuli, L., Lehtinen, J.: Progressive growing of gans for improved quality, stability, and variation. In: ICLR (2018)
3. Lassner, C., Pons-Moll, G., Gehler, P.V.: A generative model of people in clothing. In: ICCV (2017)

4. Ma, L., Jia, X., Sun, Q., Schiele, B., Tuytelaars, T., Van Gool, L.: Pose guided person image generation. In: NIPS (2017)
5. Siarohin, A., Sangineto, E., Lathuiliere, S., Sebe, N.: Deformable gans for pose-based human image generation. In: CVPR (2018)
6. Chen, Q., Koltun, V.: Photographic image synthesis with cascaded refinement networks. In: ICCV (2017)
7. Wang, T.C., Liu, M.Y., Zhu, J.Y., Tao, A., Jan, K., Bryan, C.: High-resolution image synthesis and semantic manipulation with conditional gans. In: CVPR (2018)
8. Rossler, A., Cozzolino, D., Verdoliva, L., Riess, C., Thies, J., Niener, M.: Faceforensics: a large-scale video dataset for forgery detection in human faces. arXiv:1803.09179v1 (2018)
9. Shrivastava, A., Pfister, T., Tuzel, O., Susskind, J., Weng, W., Webb, R.: Learning from simulated and unsupervised images through adversarial training. In: CVPR (2017)
10. Lample, G., Zeghidour, N., Usunier, N., Bordes, A., Denoyer, L., Ranzato, M.: Fader networks: manipulating images by sliding attributes. In: NIPS (2017)
11. Shu, Z., Yumer, E., Hadap, S., Sunkavalli, K., Shechtman, E., Samaras, D.: Neural face editing with intrinsic image disentangling. In: CVPR (2017)
12. Isola, P., Zhu, J., Zhou, T., Efros, A.A.: Image-to-image translation with conditional adversarial networks. In: CVPR (2017)
13. Loper, M., Mahmood, N., Romero, J., Pons-Moll, G., Black, M.J.: SMPL: a skinned multi-person linear model. ACM Trans. Graph. 34(6), 248:1–248:16 (2015). (Proc. SIGGRAPH Asia)
14. Bogo, F., Kanazawa, A., Lassner, C., Gehler, P., Romero, J., Black, M.J.: Keep It SMPL: automatic estimation of 3D human pose and shape from a single image. In: Leibe, B., Matas, J., Sebe, N., Welling, M. (eds.) ECCV 2016. LNCS, vol. 9909, pp. 561–578. Springer, Cham (2016). https://doi.org/10.1007/978-3-319-46454-1_34
15. Lassner, C., Romero, J., Kiefel, M., Bogo, F., Black, M.J., Gehler, P.V.: Unite the people: closing the loop between 3D and 2D human representations. In: ICCV (2017)
16. Varol, G., et al.: Learning from synthetic humans. In: CVPR (2017)
17. Kanazawa, A., Black, M.J., Jacobs, D.W., Malik, J.: End-to-end recovery of human shape and pose. In: CVPR (2018)
18. Guler, R.A., Trigeorgis, G., Antonakos, E., Snape, P., Zafeiriou, S., Kokkinos, I.: Densereg: fully convolutional dense shape regression in-the-wild. In: CVPR (2017)
19. Liu, Z., Luo, P., Qiu, S., Wang, X., Tang, X.: Deepfashion: powering robust clothes recognition and retrieval with rich annotations. In: CVPR (2016)
20. Liu, K.H., Chen, T.Y., Chen, C.S.: A dataset for view-invariant clothing retrieval and attribute prediction. In: ICMR (2016)
21. Hinton, G.E., Salakhutdinov, R.R.: Reducing the dimensionality of data with neural networks. Science 313(5786), 504–507 (2006)
22. Kingma, D.P., Welling, M.: Auto-encoding variational bayes. In: ICLR (2014)
23. Goodfellow, I., et al.: Generative adversarial nets. In: NIPS (2014)
24. Radford, A., Metz, L., Chintala, S.: Unsupervised representation learning with deep convolutional generative adversarial networks. In: ICLR (2016)
25. Gatys, L.A., Ecker, A.S., Bethge, M.: A neural algorithm of artistic style. In: CVPR (2016)
26. Mao, X., Li, Q., Xie, H., Lau, R.Y., Wang, Z., Smolley, S.P.: Least squares generative adversarial networks. In: ICCV (2017)

27. Arjovsky, M., Chintala, S., Bottou, L.: Wasserstein generative adversarial networks. In: ICML (2017)
28. Johnson, J., Alahi, A., Fei-Fei, L.: Perceptual losses for real-time style transfer and super-resolution. In: Leibe, B., Matas, J., Sebe, N., Welling, M. (eds.) ECCV 2016. LNCS, vol. 9906, pp. 694–711. Springer, Cham (2016). https://doi.org/10.1007/978-3-319-46475-6_43
29. Ulyanov, D., Lebedev, V., Vedaldi, A., Lempitsky, V.: Texture networks: feed-forward synthesis of textures and stylized images. In: ICML (2016)
30. Zhu, S., Fidler, S., Urtasun, R., Lin, D., Loy, C.C.: Be your own prada: fashion synthesis with structural coherence. In: ICCV (2017)
31. Zhao, B., Wu, X., Cheng, Z.Q., Liu, H., Feng, J.: Multi-view image generation from a single-view. In: ACM on Multimedia Conference (2018)
32. Pathak, D., Krähenbühl, P., Donahue, J., Darrell, T., Efros, A.A.: Context encoders: feature learning by inpainting. In: CVPR (2016)
33. Yeh, R.A., Chen, C., Lim, T., Hasegawa-Johnson, M., Do, M.N.: Semantic image inpainting with perceptual and contextual losses. In: CVPR (2017)
34. Saito, S., Wei, L., Hu, L., Nagano, K., Li, H.: Photorealistic facial texture inference using deep neural networks. In: CVPR (2017)
35. Deng, J., Cheng, S., Xue, N., Zhou, Y., Zafeiriou, S.: UV-GAN: adversarial facial UV map completion for pose-invariant face recognition. In: CVPR (2018)
36. Ulyanov, D., Vedaldi, A., Lempitsky, V.: Improved texture networks: maximizing quality and diversity in feed-forward stylization and texture synthesis. In: CVPR (2017)
37. Jaderberg, M., Simonyan, K., Zisserman, A., Kavukcuoglu, K.: Spatial transformer networks. In: NIPS (2015)
38. Simonyan, K., Zisserman, A.: Very deep convolutional networks for large-scale image recognition. In: ICLR (2015)
39. Cao, Z., Simon, T., Wei, S., Sheikh, Y.: Realtime multiperson 2D pose estimation using part affinity fields. In: CVPR (2017)
40. Wang, Z., Bovik, A.C., Sheikh, H.R., Simoncelli, E.P.: Image quality assessment: from error visibility to structural similarity. In: TIP (2004)
41. Salimans, T., Goodfellow, I., Zaremba, W., Cheung, V., Radford, A., Chen, X.: Improved techniques for training gans. In: NIPS (2016)
42. Ma, L., Sun, Q., Georgoulis, S., Van Gool, L., Schiele, B., Fritz, M.: Disentangled person image generation. In: CVPR (2018)
43. Wang, Z., Simoncelli, E.P., Bovik, A.C.: Multi-scale structural similarity for image quality assessment. In: ACSSC (2003)
44. Liu, W., et al.: SSD: Single shot multibox detector. In: Leibe, B., Matas, J., Sebe, N., Welling, M. (eds.) ECCV 2016. LNCS, vol. 9905, pp. 21–37. Springer, Cham (2016). https://doi.org/10.1007/978-3-319-46448-0_2

Memory Aware Synapses:
Learning What (not) to Forget

Rahaf Aljundi[1]([✉]), Francesca Babiloni[1], Mohamed Elhoseiny[2],
Marcus Rohrbach[2], and Tinne Tuytelaars[1]

[1] KU Leuven, ESAT-PSI, imec, Leuven, Belgium
Rahaf.aljundi@esat.kuleuven.be
[2] Facebook AI Research, Menlo Park, USA

Abstract. Humans can learn in a continuous manner. Old rarely utilized knowledge can be overwritten by new incoming information while important, frequently used knowledge is prevented from being erased. In artificial learning systems, lifelong learning so far has focused mainly on accumulating knowledge over tasks and overcoming catastrophic forgetting. In this paper, we argue that, given the limited model capacity and the unlimited new information to be learned, knowledge has to be preserved or erased selectively. Inspired by neuroplasticity, we propose a novel approach for lifelong learning, coined Memory Aware Synapses (MAS). It computes the importance of the parameters of a neural network in an unsupervised and online manner. Given a new sample which is fed to the network, MAS accumulates an importance measure for each parameter of the network, based on how sensitive the predicted output function is to a change in this parameter. When learning a new task, changes to important parameters can then be penalized, effectively preventing important knowledge related to previous tasks from being overwritten. Further, we show an interesting connection between a local version of our method and Hebb's rule, which is a model for the learning process in the brain. We test our method on a sequence of object recognition tasks and on the challenging problem of learning an embedding for predicting <subject, predicate, object> triplets. We show state-of-the-art performance and, for the first time, the ability to adapt the importance of the parameters based on unlabeled data towards what the network needs (not) to forget, which may vary depending on test conditions.

1 Introduction

The real and digital world around us evolves continuously. Each day millions of images with new tags appear on social media. Every minute hundreds of hours of video are uploaded on Youtube. This new content contains new topics and trends that may be very different from what one has seen before - think e.g. of new

Electronic supplementary material The online version of this chapter (https://doi.org/10.1007/978-3-030-01219-9_9) contains supplementary material, which is available to authorized users.

© Springer Nature Switzerland AG 2018
V. Ferrari et al. (Eds.): ECCV 2018, LNCS 11207, pp. 144–161, 2018.
https://doi.org/10.1007/978-3-030-01219-9_9

Fig. 1. Our continuous learning setup. As common in the LLL literature, tasks are learned in sequence, one after the other. If, in between learning tasks, the agent is active and performs the learned tasks, we can use these unlabeled samples to update importance weights for the model parameters. Data that appears frequently, will have a bigger contribution. This way, the agent learns what is important and should not be forgotten.

emerging news topics, fashion trends, social media hypes or technical evolutions. Consequently, to keep up to speed, our learning systems should be able to evolve as well.

Yet the dominating paradigm to date, using supervised learning, ignores this issue. It learns a given task using an existing set of training examples. Once the training is finished, the trained model is frozen and deployed. From then on, new incoming data is processed without any further adaptation or customization of the model. Soon, the model becomes outdated. In that case, the training process has to be repeated, using both the previous and new data, and with an extended set of category labels. In a world like ours, such a practice becomes intractable when moving to real scenarios such as those mentioned earlier, where the data is streaming, might be disappearing after a given period of time or even can't be stored at all due to storage constraints or privacy issues.

In this setting, lifelong learning (LLL) [24,35,37] comes as a natural solution. LLL studies continual learning across tasks and data, tackling one task at a time, without storing data from previous tasks. The goal is to accumulate knowledge across tasks (typically via model sharing), resulting in a single model that performs well on all the learned tasks. The question then is how to overcome catastrophic forgetting [8,9,20] of the old knowledge when starting a new learning process using the same model.

So far, LLL methods have mostly (albeit not exclusively) been applied to relatively short sequences – often consisting of no more than two tasks (e.g. [16, 17,28]), and using relatively large networks with plenty of capacity (e.g. [1,6,33]). However, in a true LLL setting with a never-ending list of tasks, the capacity of the model sooner or later reaches its limits and compromises need to be made. Instead of aiming for no forgetting at all, figuring out what can possibly be forgotten becomes at least as important. In particular, exploiting context-specific test conditions may pay off in this case. Consider for instance a surveillance camera. Depending on how or where it is mounted, it always captures images under particular viewing conditions. Knowing how to cope with other conditions is no longer relevant and can be forgotten, freeing capacity for other tasks. This calls for a LLL method that can learn what (not) to forget using unlabeled test data. We illustrate this setup in Fig. 1.

Such adaptation and memory organization is what we also observe in biological neurosystems. Our ability to preserve what we have learned before is largely dependent on how frequent we make use of it. Skills that we practice often, appear to be unforgettable, unlike those that we have not used for a long time. Remarkably, this flexibility and adaptation occur in the absence of any form of supervision. According to Hebbian theory [10], the process at the basis of this phenomenon is the strengthening of synapses connecting neurons that fire synchronously, compared to those connecting neurons with unrelated firing behavior.

In this work, we propose a new method for LLL, coined *Memory Aware Synapses*, or MAS for short, inspired by the model of Hebbian learning in biological systems. Unlike previous works, *our LLL method can learn what parts of the model are important using unlabelled data*. This allows for adaptation to specific test conditions and continuous updating of importance weights. This is achieved by estimating importance weights for the network parameters without relying on the loss, but by looking at the sensitivity of the output function instead. This way, our method not only avoids the need for labeled data, but importantly it also avoids complications due to the loss being in a local minimum, resulting in gradients being close to zero. This makes our method not only more versatile, but also simpler, more memory-efficient, and, as it turns out, more effective in learning what not to forget, compared to other model-based LLL approaches.

Contributions of this paper are threefold: *First*, we propose a new LLL method *Memory Aware Synapses* (MAS). It estimates importance weights for all the network parameters in an unsupervised and online manner, allowing adaptation to unlabeled data, e.g.in the actual test environment. *Second*, we show how a local variant of MAS is linked to the Hebbian learning scheme. *Third*, we achieve better performance than state-of-the-art, both when using the standard LLL setup and when adapting to specific test conditions, both for object recognition and for predicting <subject, predicate, object> triplets, where an embedding is used instead of a softmax output.

In the following we discuss related work in Sect. 2 and give some background information in Sect. 3. Section 4 describes our method and its connection with Hebbian learning. Experimental results are given in Sect. 5 and Sect. 6 concludes the paper.

2   Related Work

While lifelong learning has been studied since a long time in different domains (e.g.robotics [37] or machine learning [30]) and touches upon the broader fields of meta-learning [7] and learning-to-learn [2], we focus in this section on more recent work in the context of computer vision mainly.

Table 1. LLL desired characteristics and the compliance of methods, that treat forgetting without storing the data, to these characteristics.

Method	Type	Constant memory	Problem agnostic	On pre-trained	Unlabeled data	Adaptive
LwF [17]	Data	✓	X	✓	n/a	X
EBLL [28]	Data	X	X	X	n/a	X
EWC [12]	Model	✓	✓	✓	X	X
IMM [16]	Model	X	✓	✓	X	X
SI [39]	Model	✓	✓	X	X	X
MAS (our)	Model	✓	✓	✓	✓	✓

The main challenge in LLL is to adapt the learned model continually to new tasks, be it from a similar or a different environment [25]. However, looking at existing LLL solutions, we observe that none of them satisfies all the characteristics one would expect or desire from a lifelong learning approach (see Table 1). First, its memory should be constant w.r.t. the number of tasks, to avoid a gradual increase in memory consumption over time. not be limited to a specific setting (e.g. only classification). We refer to this as problem agnostic. Third, given a pretrained model, it should be able to build on top of it and add new tasks. Fourth, being able to learn from unlabeled data would increase the method applicability to cases where original training data no longer exists. Finally, as argued above, within a fixed capacity network, being able to adapt what not to forget to a specific user setting would leave more free capacity for future tasks. In light of these properties, we discuss recently proposed methods. They can be divided into two main approaches: data-based and model-based approaches. Here, we don't consider LLL methods that require storing samples, such as [18,29].

Data-Based Approaches. [1,17,28,34] use data from the new task to approximate the performance of the previous tasks. This works best if the data distribution mismatch between tasks is limited. Data based approaches are mainly designed for a classification scenario and overall, the need of these approaches to have a preprocessing step before each new task, to record the targets for the previous tasks is an additional limitation.

Model-Based Approaches. [6,12,16,39], like our method, focus on the parameters of the network instead of depending on the task data. Most similar to our work are [12,39]. Like them, we estimate an importance weight for each model parameter and add a regularizer when training a new task that penalizes any changes to important parameters. The difference lies in the way the importance weights are computed. In the *Elastic Weight Consolidation* work [12], this is done based on an approximation of the diagonal of the Fisher information matrix. In the *Synaptic Intelligence* work [39], importance weights are computed during training in an online manner. To this end, they record how much the loss would change due to a change in a specific parameter and accumulate this information over the training trajectory. However, also this method has some drawbacks: (1) Relying on the weight changes in a batch gradient descent might overestimate the importance of the weights, as noted by the authors. (2) When starting from a pretrained network, as in most practical computer vision applications, some weights might be used without big changes. As a result, their importance will be underestimated. (3) The computation of the importance is done during training and fixed later. In contrast, we believe the importance of the weights should be able to adapt to the test data where the system is applied to. In contrast to the above two methods, we propose to look at the sensitivity of the learned function, rather than the loss. This simplifies the setup considerably since, unlike the loss, the learned function is not in a local minimum, so complications with gradients being close to zero are avoided.

In this work, we propose a model-based method that computes the importance of the network parameters not only in an online manner but also adaptive to the data that the network is tested on in an unsupervised manner. While previous works [26,31] adapt the learning system at prediction time in a transductive setting, our goal here is to build a continual system that can adapt the importance of the weights to what the system needs to remember. Our method requires a constant amount of memory and enjoys the main desired characteristics of lifelong learning we listed above while achieving state-of-the-art performance.

3   Background

Standard LLL Setup. Before introducing our method, we briefly remind the reader of the standard LLL setup, as used, e.g., in [1,16,17,28,39]. It focuses on image classification and consists of a sequence of disjoint *tasks*, which are learned one after the other. Tasks may correspond to different datasets, or different splits of a dataset, without overlap in category labels. The assumption of this setup is that, when training a task, only the data related to that task is accessible. Ideally, newer tasks can benefit from the representations learned by older tasks (forward transfer). Yet in practice, the biggest challenge is to avoid catastrophic forgetting of the old tasks' knowledge (i.e., forgetting how to perform the old tasks well). This is a far more challenging setup than joint learning, as typically used in the multitask learning literature, where all tasks are trained simultaneously.

Notations. We train a single, shared neural network over a sequence of tasks. The parameters $\{\theta_{ij}\}$ of the model are the weights of the connections between pairs of neurons n_i and n_j in two consecutive layers[1]. As in other model-based approaches, our goal is then to compute an importance value Ω_{ij} for each parameter θ_{ij}, indicating its importance with respect to the previous tasks. In a learning sequence, we receive a sequence of tasks $\{T_n\}$ to be learned, each with its training data $(X_n, \hat{Y}_n)$, with X_n the input data and $\hat{Y}_n$ the corresponding ground truth output data (labels). Each task comes with a task-specific loss L_n, that will be combined with an extra loss term to avoid forgetting. When the training procedure converges to a local minimum, the model has learned an approximation F of the true function $\bar{F}$. F maps a new input X to the outputs $Y_1, ..., Y_n$ for tasks $T_1...T_n$ learned so far.

4   Our Approach

In the following, we introduce our approach. Like other model-based approaches [12,39], we estimate an importance weight for each parameter in the network. Yet in our case, these importance weights approximate the *sensitivity of the learned function* to a parameter change rather than a measure of

---

[1] In convolutional layers, parameters are shared by multiple pairs of neurons. For the sake of clarity, yet without loss of generality, we focus here on fully connected layers.

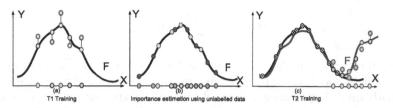

Fig. 2. [12,39] estimate the parameters importance based on the loss, comparing the network output (light blue) with the ground truth labels (green) using training data (in yellow) (a). In contrast, we estimate the parameters importance, after convergence, based on the sensitivity of the learned function to their changes (b). This allows using additional unlabeled data points (in orange). When learning a new task, changes to important parameters are penalized, the function is preserved over the domain densely sampled in (b), while adjusting not important parameters to ensure good performance on the new task (c). (Color figure online)

the (inverse of) parameter uncertainty, as in [12], or the sensitivity of the loss to a parameter change, as in [39] (see Fig. 2). As it does not depend on the ground truth labels, our approach allows computing the importance using any available data (unlabeled) which in turn allows for an adaptation to user-specific settings. In a learning sequence, we start with task T_1, training the model to minimize the task loss L_1 on the training data $(X_1, \hat{Y}_1)$ – or simply using a pretrained model for that task.

4.1 Estimating Parameter Importance

After convergence, the model has learned an approximation F of the true function $\bar{F}$. F maps the input X_1 to the output Y_1. This mapping F is the target we want to preserve while learning additional tasks. To this end, we measure how sensitive the function F output is to changes in the network parameters. For a given data point x_k, the output of the network is $F(x_k; \theta)$. A small perturbation $\delta = \{\delta_{ij}\}$ in the parameters $\theta = \{\theta_{ij}\}$ results in a change in the function output that can be approximated by:

$$F(x_k; \theta + \delta) - F(x_k; \theta) \approx \sum_{i,j} g_{ij}(x_k)\delta_{ij} \tag{1}$$

where $g_{ij}(x_k) = \frac{\partial(F(x_k;\theta))}{\partial\theta_{ij}}$ is the gradient of the learned function with respect to the parameter θ_{ij} evaluated at the data point x_k and δ_{ij} is the change in parameter θ_{ij}. Our goal is to preserve the prediction of the network (the learned function) at each observed data point and prevent changes to parameters that are important for this prediction.

Based on Eq. 1 and assuming a small constant change δ_{ij}, we can measure the importance of a parameter by the magnitude of the gradient g_{ij}, i.e. how much does a small perturbation to that parameter change the output of the learned function for data point x_k. We then accumulate the gradients over the given data points to obtain importance weight Ω_{ij} for parameter θ_{ij}:

$$\Omega_{ij} = \frac{1}{N} \sum_{k=1}^{N} \| g_{ij}(x_k) \| \tag{2}$$

This equation can be updated in an online fashion whenever a new data point is fed to the network. N is the total number of data points at a given phase. Parameters with small importance weights do not affect the output much, and can, therefore, be changed to minimize the loss for subsequent tasks, while parameters with large weights should ideally be left unchanged.

When the output function F is multi-dimensional, as is the case for most neural networks, Eq. 2 involves computing the gradients for each output, which requires as many backward passes as the dimensionality of the output. As a more efficient alternative, we propose to use the gradients of the squared ℓ_2 norm of the learned function output[2], i.e., $g_{ij}(x_k) = \frac{\partial[\ell_2^2(F(x_k;\theta))]}{\partial \theta_{ij}}$. The importance of the parameters is then measured by the sensitivity of the squared ℓ_2 norm of the function output to their changes. This way, we get one scalar value for each sample instead of a vector output. Hence, we only need to compute one backward pass and can use the resulting gradients for estimating the parameters importance. Using our method, for regions in the input space that are sampled densely, the function will be preserved and catastrophic forgetting is avoided. However, parameters not affecting those regions will be given low importance weights, and can be used to optimize the function for other tasks, affecting the function over other regions of the input space.

4.2   Learning a New Task

When a new task T_n needs to be learned, we have in addition to the new task loss $L_n(\theta)$, a regularizer that penalizes changes to parameters that are deemed important for previous tasks:

$$L(\theta) = L_n(\theta) + \lambda \sum_{i,j} \Omega_{ij}(\theta_{ij} - \theta_{ij}^*)^2 \tag{3}$$

with λ a hyperparameter for the regularizer and θ_{ij}^* the "old" network parameters (as determined by the optimization for the previous task in the sequence, T_{n-1}). As such we allow the new task to change parameters that are not important for the previous task (low Ω_{ij}). The important parameters (high Ω_{ij}) can also be reused, via model sharing, but with a penalty when changing them.

Finally, the importance matrix Ω is to be updated after training a new task, by accumulating over the previously computed Ω. Since we don't use the loss function, Ω can be computed on any available data considered most representative for test conditions, be it on the last training epoch, during the validation phase or at test time. In the experimental Sect. 5, we show how this allows our method to adapt and specialize to any set, be it from the training or from the test.

---

[2] We square the ℓ_2 norm as it simplifies the math and the link with the Hebbian method, see Sect. 4.3.

4.3   Connection to Hebbian Learning

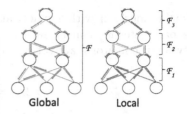

In this section, we propose a local version of our method, by applying it to a single layer of the network rather than to the network as a whole. Next, we show an interesting connection between this local version and Hebbian learning [10].

A Local Version of Our Method. Instead of considering the function F that is learned by the network as a whole, we decompose it in a sequence of functions F_l each corresponding to one layer of the network, i.e., $F(x) = F_L(F_{L-1}(...(F_1(x))))$, with L the total number of layers. By locally preserving the output of each layer given its input, we can preserve the global function F. This is further illustrated in Fig. 3. Note how "local" and "global" in this context relate to the number of layers over which the gradients are computed.

Fig. 3. Gradients flow for computing the importance weight. Local considers the gradients of each layer independently.

We use y_i^k to denote the activation of neuron n_i for a given input x_k. Analogous to the procedure followed previously, we consider the squared ℓ_2 norm of each layer after the activation function. An infinitesimal change $\delta_l = \{\delta_{ij}\}$ in the parameters $\theta_l = \{\theta_{ij}\}$ of layer l results in a change to the squared ℓ_2 norm of the local function F_l for a given input to that layer $y^k = \{y_i^k\} = F_{l-1}(...(F_1(x_k)))$ given by:

$$\ell_2^2(F_l(y^k; \theta_l + \delta_l)) - \ell_2^2(F_l(y^k; \theta_l)) \approx \sum_{i,j} g_{ij}(x_k)\delta_{ij} \qquad (4)$$

where $g_{ij}(x_k) = \frac{\partial[\ell_2^2(F_l(y^k;\theta_l))]}{\partial \theta_{ij}}$. In the case of a ReLU activation function, it can be shown that (see supplemental material):

$$g_{ij}(x_k) = 2 * y_i^k * y_j^k \qquad (5)$$

Again we consider the accumulation of the gradients evaluated at different data points $\{x_k\}$ as a measure for the importance of the parameter θ_{ij}:

$$\Omega_{ij} = \frac{1}{N} \sum_{k=1}^N g_{ij}(x_k) = 2 * \frac{1}{N} \sum_{k=1}^N y_i^k * y_j^k \qquad (6)$$

Link with Hebbian Theory. In neuroscience, Hebbian learning theory [10] provides an explanation for the phenomenon of synaptic plasticity. It postulates that "cells that fire together, wire together": the synapses (connections) between neurons that fire synchronously for a given input are strengthened over time to maintain and possibly improve the corresponding outputs. Here we reconsider this theory from the perspective of an artificial neural network after it has been trained successfully with backpropagation. Following Hebb's rule, parameters connecting neurons that often fire together (high activations for both, i.e. highly correlated outputs) are more important for the given task than those that fire asynchronously or with low activations. As such, the importance weight Ω_{ij} for the parameter θ_{ij} can be measured purely locally in terms of the correlation between the neurons' activations, i.e.

$$\Omega_{ij} = \frac{1}{N} \sum_{k=1}^{N} y_i^k * y_j^k \tag{7}$$

The similarity with Eq. 6 is striking. We can conclude that applying Hebb's rule to measure the importance of the parameters in a neural network can be seen as a local variant of our method that considers only one layer at a time instead of the global function learned by the network. Since only the relative importance weights really matter, the scale factor 2 can be ignored.

4.4 Discussion

Our global and local methods both have the advantage of computing the importance of the parameters on any given data point without the need to access the labels or the condition of being computed while training the model. The global version needs to compute the gradients of the output function while the local variant (Hebbian based) can be computed locally by multiplying the input with the output of the connecting neurons. *Our proposed method (both the local and global version) resembles an implicit memory included for each parameter of the network. We, therefore, refer to it as Memory Aware Synapses.* It keeps updating its value based on the activations of the network when applied to new data points. It can adapt and specialize to a given subset of data points rather than preserving every functionality in the network. Further, the method can be added after the network is trained. It can be applied on top of any pretrained network and compute the importance on any set of data without the need to have the labels. This is an important criterion that differentiates our work from methods that rely on the loss function to compute the importance of the parameters.

5 Experiments

We start by comparing our method to different existing LLL methods in the standard sequential learning setup of object recognition tasks. We further analyze the behavior and some design choices of our method. Next, we move to the more challenging problem of continual learning of <subject, predicate, object> triplets in an embedding space (Sect. 5.2).

5.1 Object Recognition

We follow the standard setup commonly used in computer vision to evaluate LLL methods [1, 17, 28]. It consists of a sequence of supervised classification tasks each from a particular dataset. Note that this assumes having different classification layers for each task (different "heads") that remain unshared. Moreover, an oracle is used at test time to decide on the task (i.e., which classification layer to use).

Compared Methods.

- *Finetuning* (`FineTune`). After learning the first task and when receiving a new task to learn, the parameters of the network are finetuned on the new task data. This baseline is expected to suffer from forgetting the old tasks while being advantageous for the new task.
- *Learning without Forgetting* [17] (`LwF`). Given a new task data, the method records the probabilities obtained from the previous tasks heads and uses them as targets when learning a new task in a surrogate loss function. To further control the forgetting, the method relies on first training the new task head while freezing the shared parameters as a warmup phase and then training all the parameters until convergence.
- *Encoder Based Lifelong Learning* [28] (`EBLL`) builds on LwF and learns a shallow encoder on the features of each task. A penalty on the changes to the encoded features accompanied with the distillation loss is applied to reduce the forgetting of the previous tasks. Similar to LwF, a warmup phase is used before the actual training phase.
- *Incremental Moment Matching* [16] (`IMM`). A new task is learned with an L2 penalty equally applied to the changes to the shared parameters. At the end of the sequence, the obtained models are merged through a first or second moment matching. In our experiments, mean `IMM` gives better results on the two tasks experiments while mode `IMM` wins on the longer sequence. Thus, we report the best alternative in each experiment.
- *Elastic Weight Consolidation* [12] (`EWC`). It is the first work that suggests regularizing the network parameters while learning a new task using as importance measure the diagonal of the Fisher information matrix. EWC uses individual penalty for each previous task, however, to make it computationally feasible we apply a single penalty as pointed out by [11]. Hence, we use a running sum of the Fishers in the 8 tasks sequence.
- *Synaptic Intelligence* [39] (`SI`). This method shows state-of-the-art performance and comes closest to our approach. It estimates the importance weights in an online manner while training for a new task. Similar to `EWC` and our method changes to parameters important for previous tasks are penalized during training of later tasks.
- *Memory Aware Synapses* (`MAS`). Unless stated otherwise, we use the global version of our method and with the importance weights estimated only on training data. We use a regularization parameter λ of 1; note that no tuning of λ was performed as we assume no access to previous task data.

Experimental Setup. We use the AlexNet [15] architecture pretrained on Imagenet [32] from [14][3]. All the training of the different tasks have been done with

---

[3] We use the pretrained model available in Pytorch. Note that it differs slightly from other implementations used e.g. in [17].

Table 2. Classification accuracy (%), drop in first task (%) for various sequences of 2 tasks using the object recognition setup.

Method	Birds → Scenes		Scenes → Birds		Flower → Birds		Flower → Scenes	
FineTune	45.20 (−8.0)	**57.8**	49.7 (−9.3)	**52.8**	64.87 (−13.2)	**53.8**	70.17 (−7.9)	57.31
LwF [17]	51.65 (−2.0)	55.59	55.89 (−3.1)	49.46	73.97 (−4.1)	53.64	76.20 (−1.9	58.05
EBLL [28]	52.79 (−0.8)	55.67	56.34 (−2.7)	49.41	75.45 (−2.6)	50.51	76.20 (−1.9)	**58.35**
IMM [16]	51.51 (−2.1)	52.62	54.76 (−4.2)	52.20	75.68 (−2.4)	48.32	76.28 (−1.8)	55.64
EWC [12]	52.19 (−1.4)	55.74	**58.28 (−0.8)**	49.65	76.46 (−1.6)	50.7	77.0 (−1.1)	57.53
SI [39]	52.64 (−1.0)	55.89	57.46 (−1.5)	49.70	75.19 (−2.9)	51.20	76.61 (−1.5)	57.53
MAS (ours)	**53.24 (−0.4)**	55.0	57.61 (−1.4)	49.62	**77.33 (−0.7)**	50.39	**77.24 (−0.8)**	57.38

stochastic gradient descent for 100 epochs and a batch size of 200 using the same learning rate as in [1]. Performance is measured in terms of classification accuracy.

Two Tasks Experiments. We first consider sequences of two tasks based on three datasets: MIT *Scenes* [27] for indoor scene classification (5,360 samples), Caltech-UCSD *Birds* [38] for fine-grained bird classification (5,994 samples), and Oxford *Flowers* [23] for fine-grained flower classification (2,040 samples). We consider: Scene → Birds, Birds→ Scenes, Flower→Scenes and Flower→ Birds, as used previously in [1,17,28]. We didn't consider Imagenet as a task in the sequence as this would require retraining the network from scratch to get the importance weights for SI. As shown in Table 2, FineTune clearly suffers from catastrophic forgetting with a drop in performance from 8% to 13%. All the considered methods manage to reduce the forgetting over fine-tuning significantly while having performance close to fine-tuning on the new task. On average, our method method achieves the lowest forgetting rates (around 1%) while performance on the new task is almost similar (0–3% lower).

Local vs. Global MAS on Training/Test Data. Next we analyze the performance of our method when preserving the global function learned by the network after each task (MAS) and its local Hebbian-inspired variant described in Sect. 4.3 (1-MAS). We also evaluate our methods, MAS and 1-MAS, when using unlabeled test data and/or labeled training data. Table 3 shows, independent from the set used for computing the importance of the weights, for both 1-MAS and MAS the preservation of the previous task and the performance on the current task are quite similar. This illustrates our method ability to estimate the parameters importance of a given task given any set of points, without the need for labeled data. Further, computing the gradients locally at each layer for 1-MAS allows for faster computations but less accurate estimations. As such, 1-MAS shows an average forgetting of 3% compared to 1% by MAS.

ℓ_2^2 **vs. Vector Output.** We explained in Sect. 4 that considering the gradients of the learned function to estimate the parameters importance would require as many backward passes as the length of the output vector. To avoid this

Table 3. Classification accuracies (%) for the object recognition setup - comparison between using Train and Test data (unlabeled) to compute the parameter importance Ω_{ij}.

Method	Ω_{ij} Computed on	Birds → scenes		Scenes → birds		Flower → bird		Flower → scenes	
MAS	Train	53.24 (−0.4)	55.0	57.61 (−1.4)	49.62	77.33 (−0.7)	50.39	77.24 (−0.8)	57.38
MAS	Test	53.43 (−0.2)	55.07	57.31 (−1.7)	49.01	77.62 (−0.5)	50.29	77.45 (−0.6)	57.45
MAS	Train + test	53.29 (−0.3)	56.04	57.83 (−1.2)	49.56	77.52 (−0.6)	49.70	77.54 (−0.5)	57.39
1-MAS	Train	51.36 (−2.3)	55.67	56.79 (−2.2)	49.86	73.96 (−4.1)	50.5	76.20 (−1.9)	56.68
1-MAS	Test	51.62 (−2.0)	53.95	55.74 (−3.3)	50.43	74.48 (−3.6)	50.32	76.56 (−1.5)	57.83
1-MAS	Train + test	52.15 (−1.5)	54.40	56.79 (−2.2)	48.92	73.73 (−4.3)	50.5	76.41 (−1.7)	57.91

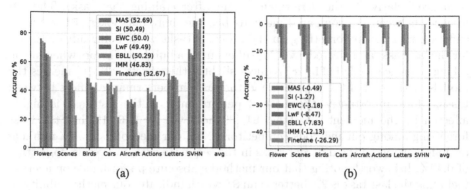

(a)   (b)

Fig. 5. (a) performance on each task, in accuracy, at the end of 8 tasks object recognition sequence. (b) drop in each task relative to the performance achieved after training each task.

complexity, we suggest using the square of the ℓ_2 norm of the function to get a scalar output. We run two experiments, Flower→Scenes and Flower→ Birds once with computing the gradients with respect to the vector output and once with respect to the ℓ_2^2 norm. We observe no significant difference on forgetting over 3 random trials where we get a mean, over 6 numbers, of $0.51\% \pm 0.18$ for the drop on the first task in the vector output case compared to $0.50\% \pm 0.19$ for the ℓ_2^2 norm case. No significant difference is observed on the second task either. As such, using ℓ_2^2 is n times faster (where n is the length of the output vector) without loss in performance.

Longer Sequence

While the two tasks setup gives a detailed look at the average expected forgetting when learning a new task, it remains easy. Thus, we next consider a sequence of 8 tasks.

To do so, we add five more datasets: Stanford Cars [13] for fine-grained car classification; FGVC-Aircraft [19] for fine-grained aircraft

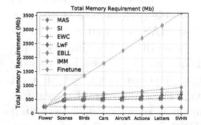

Fig. 4. Overall memory requirement for each method at each step of the sequence.

classification; VOC `Actions`, the human action classification subset of the VOC challenge 2012 [5]; `Letters`, the Chars74K dataset [3] for character recognition in natural images; and the Google Street View House Numbers SVHN dataset [22] for digit recognition.

Those datasets were also used in [1]. We run the different methods on the following sequence: Flower→Scenes→Birds→Cars→Aircraft→Actions→Letters →SVHN.

While Fig. 5a shows the performance on each task at the end of the sequence, 5a shows the observed forgetting on each task at the end of the sequence (relative to the performance right after training that task). The differences between the compared methods become more outspoken. `Finetuning` suffers from a severe forgetting on the previous tasks while being advantageous for the last task, as expected. `LwF` [17] suffers from a buildup of errors when facing a long sequence while `EBLL` [28] reduces slightly this effect. `IMM` [16] merges the models at the end of the sequence and the drop in performance differs between tasks. More importantly, the method performance on the last task is highly affected by the moment matching. `SI` [39] followed by `EWC` [12] has the least forgetting among our methods competitors. `MAS`, our method, shows a minimal or no forgetting on the different tasks in the sequence with an average forgetting of 0.49%. It is worth noting that our method's absolute performance on average including the last task is 2% better than `SI` which indicates our method ability to accurately estimate the importance weights and the new tasks to adjust accordingly. Apart from evaluating forgetting, we analyze the memory requirements of each of the compared methods. Figure 4 illustrates the memory usage of each method at each learning step in the sequence. After `Finetune` that doesn't treat forgetting, our method has the least amount of memory consumption. Note that `IMM` grows linearly in storage, but at inference time it only uses the obtained model. More details on memory requirements and absolute performances, in numbers, achieved by each method can be found in the supplemental material.

Sensitivity to the Hyper Parameter. Our method needs one extra hyper parameter, λ, that weights the penalty on the parameters changes as shown in Eq. 3.

λ is a trade-off between the allowed forgetting and the new task loss. We set λ to the largest value that allows an acceptable performance on the new task. For MAS, we used $\lambda = 1$ in all object recognition experiments while for SI[39] and EWC[12] we had to vary λ. Figure 6 shows the effect of λ on the avg. performance and the avg. forgetting in a sequence of 5 permuted MNIST tasks with a 2 layer percep-

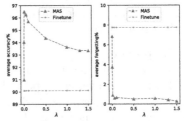

Fig. 6. Avg. performance, left, and avg. forgetting, right, on permuted mnist sequence.

tron (512 units). We see the sensitivity around $\lambda = 1$ is very low with low forgetting, although further improvements could be achieved.

Adaptation Test. As we have previously explained, MAS has the ability to adapt the importance weights to a specific subset that has been encountered at test time in an unsupervised and online manner. To test this claim, we have selected one class from the Flower dataset, Krishna Kamal flower. We learn the 8 tasks sequence as above while assuming Krishna Kamal as the only encountered class. Hence, importance weights are computed on that subset only. At the end of the sequence, we observe a minimal forgetting on that subset of 2% compared to 8% forgetting on the Flower dataset as a whole. We also observe higher accuracies on later tasks as only changes to important parameters for that class are penalized, leaving more free capacity for remaining tasks (e.g. accuracy of 84% on the last task, instead of 69% without adaptation). We repeat the experiment with two other classes and obtain similar results. This clearly indicates our method ability to adapt to user specific settings and to learn what (not) to forget.

5.2 Facts Learning

Next, we move to a more challenging setup where all the layers of the network are shared, including the last layer. Instead of learning a classifier, we learn an embedding space. For this setup, we pick the problem of Fact Learning from natural images [4]. For example, a fact could be "person eating pizza". We design different experimental settings to show the ability of our method to learn what (not) to forget.

Experimental Setup. We use the 6DS mid scale dataset presented in [4]. It consists of 28, 624 images, divided equally in training and test samples belonging to 186 unique facts. Facts are structured into 3 units: Subject (S), Object (O) and Predicate (P). We use a CNN model based on the VGG-16 architecture [36] pretrained on ImageNet. The last fully connected layer forks in three final layers enabling the model to have three separated and structured outputs for Subject, Predicate and Object as in [4]. The loss minimizes the pairwise distance

Table 4. MAP for fact learning on the 4 tasks random split, from the 6DS dataset, at the end of the sequence.

Method	Split	Method evaluated on				
		T_1	T_2	T_3	T_4	All
Finetune	1	0.19	0.19	0.28	**0.71**	0.18
SI [39]	1	0.36	0.32	0.38	0.68	0.25
MAS (ours)	1	**0.42**	**0.37**	**0.41**	0.65	**0.29**
Finetune	2	0.20	0.27	0.18	0.66	0.18
SI [39]	2	0.37	0.39	0.38	0.46	0.24
MAS (ours)	2	**0.42**	**0.42**	**0.46**	**0.65**	**0.28**
Finetune	3	0.21	0.25	0.24	0.46	0.14
SI [39]	3	**0.30**	0.31	0.36	0.61	0.24
MAS (ours)	3	**0.30**	**0.36**	**0.38**	**0.66**	**0.27**

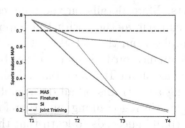

Fig. 7. MAP on the sport subset of the 6DS dataset after each task in a 4 tasks sequence. MAS managed to learn that the sport subset is important to preserve and prevents significantly the forgetting on this subset.

between the visual and the language embedding. For the language embedding, the Word2vec [21] representation of the fact units is used. To study fact learning from a lifelong perspective, we divided the dataset into tasks belonging to different groups of facts. SGD optimizer is used with a mini-batch of size 35 for 300 epochs and we use a $\lambda = 5$ for our method. For evaluation, we report the fact to image retrieval scenario. We follow the evaluation protocol proposed in [4] and report the mean average precision (MAP). For each task, we consider retrieving the images belonging to facts from this task only. We also report the mean average precision on the whole dataset which differs from the average of the performance achieved on each task. More details can be found in the supplemental materials. We focus on the comparison between the local 1-MAS and global MAS variants of our method and SI [39], the best performing method among the different competitors as shown in Fig. 5a.

Four Tasks Experiments. We consider a sequence of 4 tasks obtained from randomly splitting the facts of the same dataset into 4 groups. Table 4 presents the achieved performance on each set of the 4 tasks at the end of the learned sequence based on 3 different random splits. Similar to previous experiments, Finetune is only advantageous on the last task while drastically suffering on the previous tasks. However, here, our method differentiates itself clearly, showing 6% better MAP on the first two tasks compared to SI. Overall, MAS achieves a MAP of 0.29 compared to 0.25 by SI and only 0.18 by Finetune. When MAS importance weights are computed on both training and test data, a further improvement is achieved with 0.30 overall performance. This highlights our method ability to benefit from extra unlabeled data to further enhance the importance estimation.

Adaptation Test. Finally we want to test the ability of our method in learning not to forget a specific subset of a task. When learning a new task, we care about the performance on that specific set more than the rest. For that reason, we clustered the dataset into 4 disjoint groups of facts, representing 4 tasks, and then selected a specialized subset of T_1, namely 7 facts of person playing sports. More details on the split can be found in the supplemental material. We run our method with the importance parameters computed only over the examples from this set along the 4 tasks sequence. Figure 7 shows the achieved performance on this sport subset by each method at each step of the learning sequence. Joint Training (black dashed) is shown as reference. It violates the LLL setting as it trains on all data jointly. Note that SI can only learn importance weights during training, and therefore cannot adapt to a particular subset. Our MAS (pink) succeeds to learn that this set is important to preserve and achieves a performance of 0.50 at the end of the sequence, while the performance of finetuning and SI on this set was close to 0.20.

6   Conclusion

In this paper, we argued that, given a limited model capacity and unlimited evolving tasks, it is not possible to preserve all the previous knowledge. Instead, agents should learn what (not) to forget. Forgetting should relate to the rate at which a specific piece of knowledge is used. This is similar to how biological systems are learning. In the absence of error signals, synapses connecting biological neurons strengthen or weaken based on the concurrence of the connected neurons activations. In this work and inspired by the synaptic plasticity, we proposed a method that is able to learn the importance of network parameters from the input data that the system is active on, in an unsupervised manner. We showed that a local variant of our method can be seen as an application of Hebb's rule in learning the importance of parameters. We first tested our method on a sequence of object recognition problems in a traditional LLL setting. We then moved to a more challenging test case where we learn facts from images in a continuous manner. We showed (i) the ability of our method to better learn the importance of the parameters using training data, test data or both; (ii) state-of-the-art performance on all the designed experiments and (iii) the ability of our method to adapt the importance of the parameters towards a frequent set of data. We believe that this is a step forward in developing systems that can always learn and adapt in a flexible manner.

Acknowledgment. The first author's PhD is funded by an FWO scholarship.

References

1. Aljundi, R., Chakravarty, P., Tuytelaars, T.: Expert gate: lifelong learning with a network of experts. In: IEEE Conference on Computer Vision and Pattern Recognition (CVPR) (2017)
2. Andrychowicz, M., et al.: Learning to learn by gradient descent by gradient descent. In: Lee, D.D., Sugiyama, M., Luxburg, U.V., Guyon, I., Garnett, R. (eds.) Advances in Neural Information Processing Systems 29, pp. 3981–3989. Curran Associates, Inc. (2016)
3. de Campos, T.E., Babu, B.R., Varma, M.: Character recognition in natural images. In: Proceedings of the International Conference on Computer Vision Theory and Applications, Lisbon, Portugal, February 2009
4. Elhoseiny, M., Cohen, S., Chang, W., Price, B.L., Elgammal, A.M.: Sherlock: scalable fact learning in images. In: AAAI, pp. 4016–4024 (2017)
5. Everingham, M., Van Gool, L., Williams, C.K.I., Winn, J., Zisserman, A.: The PASCAL Visual Object Classes Challenge 2012 (VOC2012) Results (2012). http://www.pascal-network.org/challenges/VOC/voc2012/workshop/index.html
6. Fernando, C., et al.: PathNet: evolution channels gradient descent in super neural networks. arXiv preprint arXiv:1701.08734 (2017)
7. Finn, C., Abbeel, P., Levine, S.: Model-agnostic meta-learning for fast adaptation of deep networks. In: Proceedings of the International Conference on Machine Learning (ICML) (2017)
8. French, R.M.: Catastrophic forgetting in connectionist networks. Trends Cogn. Sci. **3**(4), 128–135 (1999)
9. Goodfellow, I.J., Mirza, M., Xiao, D., Courville, A., Bengio, Y.: An empirical investigation of catastrophic forgetting in gradient-based neural networks. In: ICLR 2014 (2014)

10. Hebb, D.: The organization of behavior 1949. New York Wiely **2**, 8 (2002)
11. Huszár, F.: Note on the quadratic penalties in elastic weight consolidation. In: Proceedings of the National Academy of Sciences (2018). https://doi.org/10.1073/pnas.1717042115. http://www.pnas.org/content/early/2018/02/16/1717042115
12. Kirkpatrick, J., et al.: Overcoming catastrophic forgetting in neural networks. arXiv preprint arXiv:1612.00796 (2016)
13. Krause, J., Stark, M., Deng, J., Fei-Fei, L.: 3D object representations for fine-grained categorization. In: Proceedings of the IEEE International Conference on Computer Vision Workshops, pp. 554–561 (2013)
14. Krizhevsky, A.: One weird trick for parallelizing convolutional neural networks. arXiv preprint arXiv:1404.5997 (2014)
15. Krizhevsky, A., Sutskever, I., Hinton, G.E.: Imagenet classification with deep convolutional neural networks. In: Pereira, F., Burges, C.J.C., Bottou, L., Weinberger, K.Q. (eds.) Advances in Neural Information Processing Systems 25, pp. 1097–1105. Curran Associates, Inc. (2012)
16. Lee, S.W., Kim, J.H., Jun, J., Ha, J.W., Zhang, B.T.: Overcoming catastrophic forgetting by incremental moment matching. In: Advances in Neural Information Processing Systems, pp. 4652–4662 (2017)
17. Li, Z., Hoiem, D.: Learning without forgetting. In: Leibe, B., Matas, J., Sebe, N., Welling, M. (eds.) ECCV 2016. LNCS, vol. 9908, pp. 614–629. Springer, Cham (2016). https://doi.org/10.1007/978-3-319-46493-0_37
18. Lopez-Paz, D., Ranzato, M.: Gradient episodic memory for continual learning. In: Advances in Neural Information Processing Systems, pp. 6470–6479 (2017)
19. Maji, S., Kannala, J., Rahtu, E., Blaschko, M., Vedaldi, A.: Fine-grained visual classification of aircraft. Technical report (2013)
20. McCloskey, M., Cohen, N.J.: Catastrophic interference in connectionist networks: the sequential learning problem. Psychol. Learn. Motiv. **24**, 109–165 (1989)
21. Mikolov, T., Chen, K., Corrado, G., Dean, J.: Efficient estimation of word representations in vector space. arXiv preprint arXiv:1301.3781 (2013)
22. Netzer, Y., Wang, T., Coates, A., Bissacco, A., Wu, B., Ng, A.Y.: Reading digits in natural images with unsupervised feature learning (2011)
23. Nilsback, M.E., Zisserman, A.: Automated flower classification over a large number of classes. In: Proceedings of the Indian Conference on Computer Vision, Graphics and Image Processing, December 2008
24. Pentina, A., Lampert, C.H.: Lifelong learning with non-iid tasks. In: Cortes, C., Lawrence, N.D., Lee, D.D., Sugiyama, M., Garnett, R. (eds.) Advances in Neural Information Processing Systems 28, pp. 1540–1548 (2015)
25. Pentina, A., Lampert, C.H.: Lifelong learning with non-iid tasks. In: Advances in Neural Information Processing Systems, pp. 1540–1548 (2015)
26. Quadrianto, N., Petterson, J., Smola, A.J.: Distribution matching for transduction. In: Advances in Neural Information Processing Systems, pp. 1500–1508 (2009)
27. Quattoni, A., Torralba, A.: Recognizing indoor scenes. In: IEEE Conference on Computer Vision and Pattern Recognition (CVPR), pp. 413–420. IEEE (2009)
28. Rannen, A., Aljundi, R., Blaschko, M.B., Tuytelaars, T.: Encoder based lifelong learning. In: Proceedings of the IEEE Conference on Computer Vision and Pattern Recognition, pp. 1320–1328 (2017)
29. Rebuffi, S.A., Kolesnikov, A., Sperl, G., Lampert, C.H.: iCaRL: incremental classifier and representation learning. In: IEEE Conference on Computer Vision and Pattern Recognition (CVPR), July 2017
30. Ring, M.B.: Child: a first step towards continual learning. Mach. Learn. **28**(1), 77–104 (1997)

31. Royer, A., Lampert, C.H.: Classifier adaptation at prediction time. In: Proceedings of the IEEE Conference on Computer Vision and Pattern Recognition, pp. 1401–1409 (2015)
32. Russakovsky, O.: ImageNet large scale visual recognition challenge. Int. J. Comput. Vis. (IJCV) **115**(3), 211–252 (2015). https://doi.org/10.1007/s11263-015-0816-y
33. Rusu, A.A., et al.: Progressive neural networks. arXiv preprint arXiv:1606.04671 (2016)
34. Shmelkov, K., Schmid, C., Alahari, K.: Incremental learning of object detectors without catastrophic forgetting. In: The IEEE International Conference on Computer Vision (ICCV) (2017)
35. Silver, D.L., Yang, Q., Li, L.: Lifelong machine learning systems: beyond learning algorithms. In: AAAI Spring Symposium: Lifelong Machine Learning, pp. 49–55. Citeseer (2013)
36. Simonyan, K., Zisserman, A.: Very deep convolutional networks for large-scale image recognition. arXiv preprint arXiv:1409.1556 (2014)
37. Thrun, S., Mitchell, T.M.: Lifelong robot learning. Robot. Auton. Syst. **15**(1–2), 25–46 (1995)
38. Welinder, P., et al.: Caltech-UCSD Birds 200. Technical report CNS-TR-2010-001, California Institute of Technology (2010)
39. Zenke, F., Poole, B., Ganguli, S.: Improved multitask learning through synaptic intelligence. In: Proceedings of the International Conference on Machine Learning (ICML) (2017)

Multi-view to Novel View: Synthesizing Novel Views With Self-learned Confidence

Shao-Hua Sun[1]([✉]), Minyoung Huh[2], Yuan-Hong Liao[3], Ning Zhang[4], and Joseph J. Lim[1]

[1] University of Southern California, Los Angeles, USA
shaohuas@usc.edu
[2] Carnegie Mellon University, Pittsburgh, USA
[3] National Tsing Hua University, Hsinchu, Taiwan
[4] Snap Inc., Venice, USA

Abstract. In this paper, we address the task of multi-view novel view synthesis, where we are interested in synthesizing a target image with an arbitrary camera pose from given source images. We propose an end-to-end trainable framework that learns to exploit multiple viewpoints to synthesize a novel view without any 3D supervision. Specifically, our model consists of a flow prediction module and a pixel generation module to directly leverage information presented in source views as well as hallucinate missing pixels from statistical priors. To merge the predictions produced by the two modules given multi-view source images, we introduce a self-learned confidence aggregation mechanism. We evaluate our model on images rendered from 3D object models as well as real and synthesized scenes. We demonstrate that our model is able to achieve state-of-the-art results as well as progressively improve its predictions when more source images are available.

Keywords: Novel view synthesis · Multi-view novel view synthesis

1 Introduction

With countless encounters of scenes and objects , humans learn to build a mental understanding of 3D objects and scenes just from 2D cross-sections, which in turn, allows us to imagine an unseen view with little effort. This is only possible because humans can integrate their statistical understanding of the world with the presented information. With more and more concrete prior information (e.g.

Code is available on our website https://shaohua0116.github.io/Multiview2 Novelview.

Electronic supplementary material The online version of this chapter (https://doi.org/10.1007/978-3-030-01219-9_10) contains supplementary material, which is available to authorized users.

V. Ferrari et al. (Eds.): ECCV 2018, LNCS 11207, pp. 162–178, 2018.
https://doi.org/10.1007/978-3-030-01219-9_10

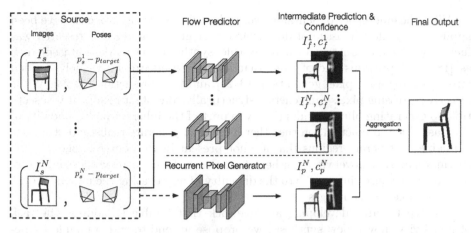

Fig. 1. Overview of our proposed network architecture. Given a set of N source images with different viewpoints and a target pose (on the left), *Flow Predictor* learns to predict a dense flow field to move the pixels presented in a source image to produce a target image for each source image. *Recurrent Pixel Generator* is trained to directly synthesize a target image given a set of source images. The two modules are trained to predict per-pixel confidence maps associated to their predictions. The final prediction is obtained by aggregating the $N + 1$ predictions with self-learned confidence maps.

more viewpoints, shape understanding etc.), humans learn to consolidate all the information to predict with more confidence. This ability allows humans to make an amodal completion from just the presented data. In computer vision, these approaches are isolated and tackled separately, and the fusion of data is less well understood. Hence, we would like to develop an approach that not only learns to utilize what is given but also incorporate its 3D statistical understanding.

The task of synthesizing a novel view given an image or a set of images is known as *novel view synthesis*. The practical applications of it range from but not limited to: computer vision, computer graphics, and virtual reality. Systems that perform on cross-view image inputs, such as action recognition [1–3] and 3D reconstruction [4–7], can leverage synthesized scenes to boost existing performance when the number of available views is limited. Furthermore, novel view synthesis can be used jointly on 3D Editing of 2D Photos [8–10] as well as rendering virtual reality environments using a history of frames [11,12].

In this paper, we are interested in the task of *novel view synthesis* when multiple source images are given. Given a target camera pose and an arbitrary number of source images and their camera poses, our goal is to develop a model that can synthesize a target image and progressively improve its predictions. To address this task, a great amount of effort have been expended in geometry-based methods [13–17] aiming to directly estimate the underlying 3D structures by exploiting the knowledge of geometry. These methods, while successful with abundant source data, are unable to recover the desired target viewpoint with only a handful of images due to the inherent ambiguity of 3D structures.

With the emergence of neural networks, learning-based approaches have been applied to tackle this issue of data sparsity. A great part of this research was fueled by the introduction of a large-scale synthetic 3D model datasets such as [18]. The previous line of work that uses learning can be vaguely divided into two categories: pixel generation [19–21] and flow prediction [22,23]. While directly regressing pixels can generate structurally consistent results, it is susceptible to generating blurry results largely in part of the inherent multi-modality of this task. Flow prediction, on the other hand, can generate realistic texture but is unable to generate regions that are not present in the source image(s). Furthermore, most of novel view synthesis frameworks focuses on synthesizing views from a single source image due to the difficulty of aggregating the understanding from multiple source images.

To step towards developing a framework that is able to address the task of multi-view novel view synthesis, we propose an end-to-end trainable framework (shown in Fig. 1) composed of two modules. The flow predictor estimates flow fields to move the pixels from a source view to a target view; the recurrent pixel generator, augmented with an internal memory, iteratively synthesizes and refines a target view when a new source view is given. We propose a self-confidence aggregation mechanism to integrate multiple intermediate predictions produced by the two modules to yield results that are both realistic and structurally consistent.

We compare our model against state-of-the-art methods on a variety of datasets such as 3D-object models as well as real and synthetic scenes. Our main contributions are as follows: we propose a hybrid framework which combines the strengths of two main lines of novel view synthesis methods and achieves significant improvement compared to existing work. We then demonstrate the flexibility of our method; we show that our model is able to synthesize views from a single source image as well as improve its predictions when additional source views are available. Furthermore, our model can be adapted to scenes rather than synthetic object data as it does not require 3D supervision.

2   Related Works

Geometry-Based View Synthesis. A great amount of efforts have been dedicated to explicitly modeling the underlying 3D structure of both scenes and objects   [13–16]. While appealing and accurate results are guaranteed when multiple source images are available, this line of work is fundamentally not able to deal with sparse inputs. Aiming to address this issue, a deep learning approach is proposed in [24] focusing on the multi-view stereo problem by regressing directly to output pixel values. On the other hand, [25] explicitly utilizes learned dense correspondences to predict the image in the middle view of a pair of source images. The above-mentioned methods are limited to synthesizing a middle view among source images and the number of source images is fixed; in contrast, our proposed framework focuses on arbitrary target views and is able to learn from source images vary in length.

Learning Dense Visual Correspondence. Discovering dense correspondences among images has been studied in [26–29] with a wide range of applications including depth estimation, optical flow prediction, image alignment, image retrieval, etc. Fundamentally differing from this task, novel view synthesis requires the ability to hallucinate pixels of the target image which are missing from source images.

Image Generation. A tremendous success in conditional image generation has been made with deep generative models. Given the style, viewpoint, and color of an object, the method proposed in [30] is able to render realistic results. However, their method is not able to generalize to novel objects or poses which are tackled in our proposed framework. Huang *et al.* [31] addressed the problem of synthesizing a frontal view face from a single side-view face image. The proposed model is specifically designed for face images. In contrast, our proposed framework is able to synthesize both scenes and objects.

Image-to-Image Translation. The task of translating an image from a domain to another domain, known as image-to-image translation has recently received a significant amount of attention [32–35]. One can consider the task of novel view synthesis as an image-to-image translation problem where the target and source domains are defined by the camera poses. Not only are the view synthesis systems required to understand the representation of domain specifications *e.g.* camera poses, but also the numbers of source and target domains are possibly infinitely many due to the continuous representations of camera poses. Moreover, novel view synthesis requires the understanding of geometry while the task of image-to-image translation often only focuses on texture transfer.

3D Voxel/Point Cloud Prediction. Explicitly reconstructing 3D geometry has been intensively addressed in a multi-view setting, such as SfM and SLAM [13–16], in which we are interested in the case where plenty of images captured from different viewing angles are available. Recently, empowered by large-scale repositories of 3D CAD models such as ShapeNet [18], predicting 3D representations such as voxels and 3D point clouds from 2D views has achieved encouraging results [6, 7]. By contrast, we are interested in synthesizing views instead of 3D representations of objects. Our approach requires no 3D supervision nor explicit 3D model.

Novel View Synthesis. [19, 20] propose to directly generate pixels of a target view, while [22] re-casts the task of novel view synthesis as predicting dense flow fields that map the pixels in the source view to the target view, but it is not able to hallucinate the pixels which are missing from source view. [23] predicts a flow to move the pixels from the source to the target view, followed by an image completion network. There are three key differences between our work and [23]. First, [23] requires 3D supervision which limits the method to only objects; on the other hand, our model requires no 3D supervision and therefore is able to synthesize scenes. Second, we address the task where the source images vary in length while [23] focuses on a single source image. Third, we design our model to predict a flow and hallucinate pixels independently, which enables our framework to take advantage of both modules to produce structural consistent shape and sharper appearance. This design also makes our model end-to-end trainable. Instead, [23] considers it as a sequential process where the pixel generation network is only considered as a refinement network.

3   Approach

When synthesizing a novel view from multi-view input, we want our model to (1) directly reuse information from the source as well as hallucinate missing information; (2) progressively improve its prediction as more information is available. To put this idea into practice, we design a flexible neural network framework that progressively improves its prediction as more input information is presented. To put (1) into practice, we design our framework to be a two-stream model that consists of a flow predictor and a pixel generator (shown in Fig. 1). The flow predictor learns to reuse the pixels presented in source images, while the pixel generator learns to hallucinate pixels. To take advantage of the strengths of both the modules as well as achieve (2), we aggregate intermediate predictions using a self-learned confidence aggregation mechanism.

3.1   Overview and Notations

Our goal is to synthesize a target image I_{target} given a target camera pose p_{target} and N (image, camera-pose) pairs $(I_s^1, p_s^1), (I_s^2, p_s^2)..., (I_s^N, p_s^N)$. We either use a one-hot vector to represent discrete camera-pose, or a 6DoF vector for continuous camera pose. We denote the flow predictor as $\mathcal{F}(\cdot)$, and denote the pixel generator as $\mathcal{P}(\cdot)$. We put a subscript f and p for predictions made by $\mathcal{F}(\cdot)$ and $\mathcal{P}(\cdot)$, respectively. Given t-th source image I_s^t and its corresponding pose p_s^t, the flow predictor generates a prediction $I_f^t, c_f^t = \mathcal{F}(p_{target}, I_s^t, p_s^t)$, where I_f^t is a predicted target image and c_f^t is the corresponding confidence map. The flow predictor independently produces N predictions from N source images since it learns to estimate the relative pixel movements from source viewpoint to the target viewpoint. The pixel generator, on the other hand, is designed as a recurrent model, which outputs a prediction $I_p^t, c_p^t = \mathcal{P}(p_{target}, I_s^1, p_s^1, ..., I_s^t, p_s^t)$ given t source images. I_p^t is the predicted target image and c_p^t is the corresponding confidence map. The final prediction $\hat{I}_{target}$ is generated by aggregating the $N+1$ predictions (N from the flow module and 1 from the pixel module).

3.2   Flow Predictor

Inspired by [22], we design a flow module that learns to predict dense flow fields. The output indicates the pixel displacement from the source image to the target image. Given t-th source image I_s^t, the model first predicts 2D dense flow fields from the original image in x and y-axis by $(x_t, y_t) = \mathcal{G}(I_s^t, p_s^t, p_{target})$. This flow field is then used to sample from the original image by $I_f^t = \mathcal{T}(x_t, y_t, I_s^t)$, where I_f^t denotes the predicted target image given I_s^t. Here $\mathcal{G}(\cdot)$ predicts the flow, and $\mathcal{T}(\cdot)$ bilinearly samples from the source image. This differentiable bilinear sampling layer was originally proposed by [36]. We optimize the flow predictor by minimizing the following equation:

$$\mathcal{L}_F = \frac{1}{N} \sum_{t=0}^{N} ||I_{target} - I_f^t||_1, \tag{1}$$

We use an encoder-decoder architecture with residual blocks and skip connections. The architecture details are left in the supplementary section. The encoder of this model takes a source image as well as its associated pose, where a pose vector is spatially tiled and concatenated to the source image channel-wise. The decoder upsamples the features to match the dimension of the input image. We empirically find that this architecture outperforms the architecture originally proposed in [22]. This comparisons can be found in Sect. 4.3.

3.3 Pixel Generator

The flow predictor is able to yield a visually appealing result when the source pose and the target pose are close – i.e. when the target is well represented by the source. Yet, it is not capable of generating pixels beyond the source pixels. Therefore, it is only natural to rely on the prior understanding of the underlying 3D structure.

The architecture of this module is very similar to our flow module. It is an encoder-decoder style network with an internal memory using Convolutional Long-Short Term Memory (ConvLSTM) [37], which is able to progressively improve its prediction with varying input lengths. Note that the ConvLSTMs are used only in the bottleneck layers and the mathematical formulation is left in the supplementary section. The pixel generator is trained to minimize the following equation:

$$\mathcal{L}_P = \frac{1}{N} \sum_{t=0}^{N} ||I_{target} - I_p^t||_1, \tag{2}$$

where I_p^t denotes a predicted target image by $I_p^t, c_p^t = \mathcal{P}(p_{target}, I_s^1, p_s^1, ..., I_s^t, p_s^t)$. To enforce our model to generate sharp images, we also incorporate an adversarial loss into our objective. We utilize the formulation proposed in [38], where an additional discriminator is trained to optimize:

$$\mathcal{L}_D = \mathbb{E}[(1 - D(I_{target}))^2] + \mathbb{E}[\frac{1}{N} \sum_{t=0}^{N}(D(I_p^t))^2]. \tag{3}$$

With the pixel generator minimizing the following additional loss:

$$\mathcal{L}_G = \mathbb{E}[\frac{1}{N} \sum_{t=0}^{N}(1 - D(I_p^t))^2]. \tag{4}$$

The final objective for the pixel module can be compactly represented as: $\mathcal{L}_P + \lambda \mathcal{L}_G$, where λ denotes the weight of the adversarial loss. The details of the discriminator architecture and GAN training can be found in the supplementary section.

3.4 Self-learned Confidence Aggregation

The flow module is able to produce visually realistic images by reusing the pixels from source images; however, synthesized images are often incomplete due to possible occlusions or pixels missing from source images. On the other hand, the pixel module is trained to directly hallucinate the target image and is able to produce structurally consistent results, their appearance is usually blurry due to the inherent ambiguity of minimizing a regression loss. Our key insight is to alleviate the disadvantages of the two modules by aggregating the advantages of both information. Inspired by the recent flourish of *Bayesian deep learning* [39,40], where we are interested in modeling *uncertainty* of neural networks, we propose to train networks to predict *confidence*.

Specifically, we want an algorithm that is able to produce a per-pixel confidence map associated with its predictions. We formulate this confidence prediction objective as:

$$\mathcal{L}_C = \frac{1}{HW} \sum_{x,y} ||I_{target} - \hat{I}||^{\circ 2} \circ \frac{c}{\sum_{x,y} ||c||_2}, \tag{5}$$

where $\hat{I}$ is the predicted target image (either from flow or pixel module), and c is the estimated confidence map with a size of H by W. $||\cdot||^{\circ 2}$ is an element-wise square operator, $\circ$ is the Hadamard product. To minimize this objective, the models have to learn to put more weight on pixels where they are confident and less on regions it is not. Each module is augmented with an additional output layer to predict the confidence map. The confidence maps are optimized via the objective described in Eq. 5.

We normalize the predicted confidences maps by applying a *Softmax* across $N + 1$ confidence maps. The normalized confidence maps, denoted as $\hat{c}$, can then be used to aggregate the predictions: $\hat{I}_{target} = I_p^N \odot \hat{c}_p^N + \sum_{i=0}^N I_f^i \odot \hat{c}_f^i$. To iterate, $\hat{I}_{target}$ denotes the final aggregated image, I_p^N denotes the last output of the recurrent pixel generator, and I_f^i denotes the output of the flow predictor given the i-th source image. The reconstruction loss on the aggregated prediction is $\mathcal{L}_A = ||I_{target} - \hat{I}_{target}||_1$. The final objective of the full model is:

$$\min \beta\mathcal{L}_A + \overbrace{\mathcal{L}_F + \alpha_f\mathcal{L}_C}^{\text{Flow Prediction}} + \overbrace{\mathcal{L}_P + \lambda\mathcal{L}_G + \alpha_p\mathcal{L}_C}^{\text{Pixel Prediction}} \tag{6}$$

where α_f, α_p, are weights for confidence map predictions and β is the weight for the global confidence scale. The effectiveness and the gradual improvement of using confidence maps are demonstrated in Sect. 4. The architecture and training details can be found in Supplemental Material.

4 Experiments

We evaluate our model in multi-view and single-view settings on ShapeNet [18] objects, real-world scenes (KITTI Visual Odometry Dataset [41]), and synthesized scenes (Synthia dataset [42]). We benchmark against a pixel generation

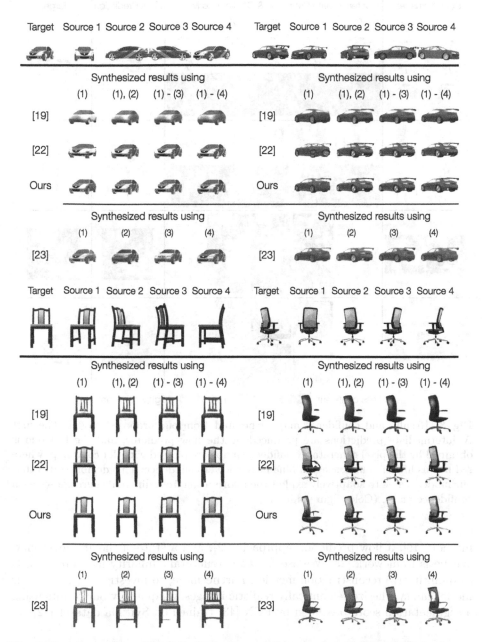

Fig. 2. Results on ShapeNet [18]. The proposed framework typically synthesized cars and chairs with correct shapes and realistic appearance. [19] generates structurally coherent but blurry images. [22] produces realistic results but suffers from distortions and missing pixels. [23] outperforms both [19] and [22] while sometimes produces unrealistic results.

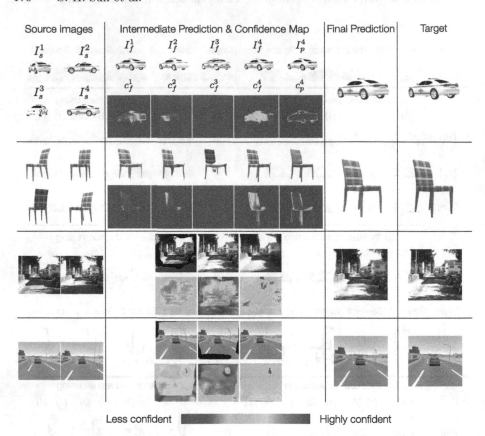

Fig. 3. Results and confidence maps generated from our proposed model. The first N intermediate predictions are produced by the flow predictor, and the last one is obtained by the pixel generator. Confidence maps are plotted with Jet colormap, where red means higher confidence and blue means lower confidence. This demonstrates that our model is able to adaptively exploit the information from different source poses with confidence maps. (Color figure online)

method [19], a flow prediction approach [22], and a state-of-the-art novel view synthesis framework [23]. We use L_1, and structural similarity measure (SSIM) as quantitative reconstruction metrics. Furthermore, to investigate whether our model can synthesize semantically realistic images, we quantify our results using a segmentation score predicted by FCN [43] trained on Synthia dataset [42].

4.1 Novel View Synthesis for Objects

We train and test the proposed model on ShapeNet [18], where ground truth views of arbitrary camera poses are available.

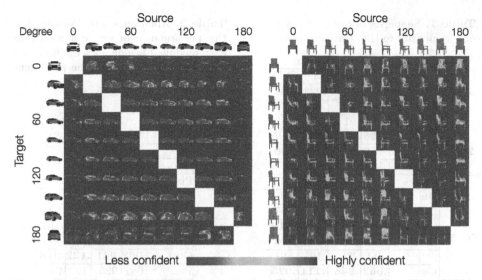

Fig. 4. Visualization of the predicted confidence maps for car and chair model. Each entry represents a predicted confidence map for a given source image and target pose. The confidence is represented using the jet-colormap, where red indicates highly confident, and blue indicating the otherwise. (Color figure online)

Data Setup. We render images of 3D models from the car category and the chair category. For each model, we render images with the dimension of 256×256 for a total of 54 viewpoints, which corresponds to 18 azimuth angles (sampled in the range $[0, 340]$ with 20-degree increments) and the elevations of 0, 10, and 20.

The pose of each image is represented as a concatenation of two one-hot vectors: an 18 element vector indicating the azimuth angle and a 3 element vector indicating the elevation. We use the same training and testing splits used in [22,23] (80% of models for training and the rest 20% for testing). Each training/testing tuple is constructed by sampling a target pose as well as N source poses and their corresponding images $\langle I_{target}, p_t, I_s^1, p_s^1, .., I_s^N, p_s^N \rangle$. We randomly sample 20,000 tuples to create the testing split. N is set to 4 for this experiment.

Results. The quantitative results are shown in Table 1 while the qualitative results can be found in Fig. 2. The results demonstrate that our proposed model is able to reliably synthesize target images when single or multiple source images are available. Our model outperforms the three methods on both L_1 distance and SSIM. The pixel generation method [19] is capable of producing well-structured shapes but not appealing texture, while the flow prediction method [22] preserves realistic texture but is not able to hallucinate pixels missing from source. While the results produced by [23] are mostly satisfactory, when the flow module fails, the synthesized images generated by the refinement network usually either do not stay true to the source image – likely due to the adversarial loss – and is

Table 1. ShapeNet objects: we compare our framework to [19], [22], and [23].

Views	Methods	Car		Chair	
		L_1	SSIM	L_1	SSIM
1	[19]	.139	.875	.223	.882
	[22]	.148	.877	.229	.871
	[23]	.119	.913	.202	.889
	Ours	**.098**	**.923**	**.181**	**.895**
2	[19]	.124	.883	.209	.890
	[22]	.107	.901	.207	.881
	Ours	**.078**	**.935**	**.141**	**.911**
3	[19]	.116	.887	.197	.898
	[22]	.089	.915	.188	.887
	Ours	**.068**	**.941**	**.122**	**.919**
4	[19]	.112	.890	.192	.900
	[22]	.081	.924	.165	.891
	Ours	**.062**	**.946**	**.111**	**.925**

Table 2. Ablation study. We compare the performance of our full model to each module. Flow denotes the flow predictor and Pixel denotes the pixel generator.

Views	Methods	Car		Chair	
		L_1	SSIM	L_1	SSIM
1	Pixel	.111	.911	.187	.892
	Flow	.119	.916	.208	.883
	Ours	**.098**	**.923**	**.181**	**.895**
2	Pixel	.095	.919	.148	.907
	Flow	.097	.927	.180	.890
	Ours	**.078**	**.935**	**.141**	**.911**
3	Pixel	.087	.923	.130	.915
	Flow	.086	.933	.164	.895
	Ours	**.068**	**.941**	**.122**	**.919**
4	Pixel	.082	.925	.119	.919
	Flow	.079	.938	.152	.900
	Oracle	.070	.941	.112	.923
	Ours	**.062**	**.946**	**.111**	**.925**

hugely distorted. Typically, our proposed framework is able to synthesize structurally consistent and realistic results by aggregating intermediate predictions with confidence maps.

We observe that the quality of the synthesized images of both cars and chairs improve as the number of source images increases. However, the marginal gain decreases as the number of source images increases. This aligns with our intuition that each additional view contributes less new information since two random views are very likely to overlap with each other. Confidence maps and intermediate predictions shown in Fig. 3 demonstrate that our model learns to adaptively exploit predictions produced by both of the two modules from multiple source images.

Learn to Predict Visibility Maps Without 3D Supervision. [23] trains the model to predict visibility maps, indicating which parts in a target image are visible from the source view. This requires prior 3D knowledge as it needs 3D coordinate and surface normal to produce ground truth visibility maps as supervision. With the predicted visibility maps, one is able to re-cast the remaining synthesis problem as image completion problem. On the other hand, as demonstrated in Fig. 4, our model learns to predict confidence maps which share a similar concept of visibility maps without any 3D supervision. Specifically, our model is implicitly forced to comprehend which target pixels are presented in source images by learning to optimize the losses introduced in the proposed self-learned confidence aggregation mechanism. This is especially important in real life application where 3D supervision is most likely not available – allowing our model to be trained on not only objects but also scenes.

4.2 Novel View Synthesis for Scenes

While most of the existing novel view synthesis approaches only focus on ShapeNet, we are also interested in generalizing our proposed model to *scenes*, where 3D supervision is not available and training category-dependent models is not trivial. To this end, we train and test our framework on both real (KITTI Visual Odometry Dataset [41]) and synthetic (Synthia Dataset [42]) scenes.

KITTI. The dataset [41] was originally proposed for SLAM evaluation. It contains frame sequences captured by a car traveling through urban city scenes with their camera poses. We use 11 sequences extracted from the dataset, whose ground truth camera poses are available, On average each sequence contains around two thousand frames. We use 80% frames for training and the rest of 20% for testing. We center-crop each frame to form an image with a dimension of 256×256. We convert each transformation matrix to its 6DoF representation (a translation vector and Euler angles) as a pose representation. We follow [22] to construct the training and testing set. We restrict the source frame and the target frame to be separated by at most 10 frames. To create the testing split, we randomly sample $20,000$ tuples. N is set to 2 for scene experiments.

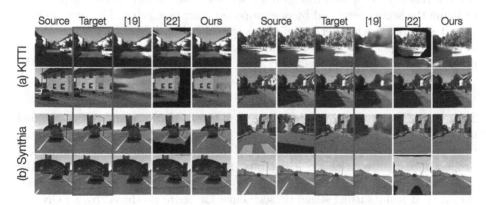

Fig. 5. Synthesized scenes on KITTI [41] and Synthia [42] datasets. Our framework typically produces structurally consistent and realistic results. Note that [22] struggles with distortions and missing pixels, and [19] is unable to generate sharp results.

Synthia. The data was originally proposed for semantic segmentation in urban scenarios. Similar to [41], it contains realistic synthetic frame sequences captured by a driving car in a virtual world with their camera poses. We use sequences from all four seasons to train our model. We follow the same preprocessing procedures as KITTI to create the training and testing tuples.

Table 3. Scenes: we compare our framework to [19] and [22] on KITTI and Synthia.

Views	Methods	KITTI		Synthia	
		L_1	SSIM	L_1	SSIM
1	[19]	.295	.505	.175	.612
	[22]	.418	.504	.221	.636
	Ours	**.203**	**.626**	**.141**	**.697**
2	[19]	.283	.511	.172	.615
	[22]	.259	.626	.154	.702
	Ours	**.163**	**.691**	**.118**	**.737**

Table 4. Ablation study. We compare the performance of our full model to each module. Flow denotes the flow predictor and Pixel denotes the pixel generator.

Views	Methods	KITTI		Synthia	
		L_1	SSIM	L_1	SSIM
1	Pixel	.259	.505	.183	.622
	Flow	.397	.539	.211	.652
	Ours	**.203**	**.626**	**.141**	**.697**
2	Pixel	.234	.525	.168	.628
	Flow	.249	.656	.149	.720
	Oracle	.199	.658	.140	.718
	Ours	**.163**	**.691**	**.118**	**.737**

Results. As shown in Table 3, our proposed framework outperforms the two methods. Qualitative comparisons are shown in Fig. 5. Both [19] and [22] learn to infer the relative camera movements and synthesized scene accordingly. However, [19] hugely suffers from blurriness due to the uncertainty, while [22] is not able to produce satisfactory results when a camera pose changes drastically. Typically, our proposed framework is able to synthesize structurally consistent and realistic results. Also, the proposed framework does not suffer from the missing pixels by utilizing the scenes rendered by our proposed pixel generator. The two modules learn to leverage each others strength, as shown in Fig. 3. We observed that none of the models perform well when some uncertainties are not able to be resolved purely based on source images and their pose. For instance, they include the speed of other driving cars, the lighting condition change, etc.

Semantic Evaluation Metrics. Although the L_1 distance and SSIM are good metrics to measure the distance between a pair of images in the pixel domain, they often fail to capture the semantics of the generated images. Isola *et al.* [32] proposed to utilize a metric, similar to *inception score* [44], to measure the semantic quality of the synthesized images. Inspired by this, we evaluate our synthesized results using semantic segmentation score produced by a FCN [43] model trained on image semantic segmentation. We obtained the pretrained segmentation model trained on PASCAL VOC dataset [45] and then fine-tuned it on the sequences extracted from Synthia dataset [42] with the same training and testing split used in our view synthesis task. The FCN scores are shown in Table. 5 and the qualitative results are shown in Fig. 6.

4.3   Ablation Study

To investigate how different blocks of the framework affect the final outcomes, we conduct ablation studies on all the datasets. The qualitative results including

Target   [19]   [22]   Ours

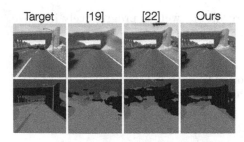

Fig. 6. Synthia FCN-results for the scenes synthesized by [19], [22], and our framework. The results produced by our framework yield better segmentation maps.

Table 5. FCN-scores for different methods. The scores are evaluated by FCN-32 pretrained on PASCAL VOC and fine-tuned on Synthia dataset. The scores are estimated on synthesized scenes produced by [19], [22] and our proposed framework with one input view.

Methods	Per-pixel acc.	Per-class acc.	IOU
[19]	0.630	0.469	0.211
[22]	0.789	0.69	0.427
Ours	**0.803**	**0.695**	**0.441**
Ground truth	0.868	0.783	0.586

intermediate predictions by the two modules can be found in Fig. 3. The quantitative results can be found in Tables 2 and 4, where *Flow* denotes aggregated predictions made by the flow predictor with its predicted confidence maps *e.g.* $\sum_{i=0}^{N} I_f^i \odot \hat{c}_f^i$, where $\hat{c}$ is softmaxed across only $c_f^1, ..., c_f^N$. Note that this does not use the image synthesized by the pixel generator. *Pixel* denotes the last results produced by the pixel generator, *e.g.* I_p^N.

One could argue that our model just learns to pick the best intermediate prediction. Hence, to investigate whether our model actually learns a meaningful self-confidence aggregation by comparing against an oracle. We quantify the best intermediate result from all $2N$ intermediate predictions produced by both modules. We denote this as the *Oracle* intermediate performance, *e.g.* $\min ||I_{target} - \hat{I}||_1 \quad \forall \hat{I} \in \{I_f^1, I_p^1, ..., I_f^N, I_p^N\}$.

We observed that our full model outperforms each module and the oracle. Also, our flow module with a fully convolutional architecture and residual blocks outperforms [22]. Our method is able to alleviate the issue of severe distortions reported in [22]. Our proposed recurrent pixel generator not only outperforms [19] but also show greater improvement (car: 26%, chair: 36%, KITTI: 10%, Synthia: 8%) when more source images are available compared to [19] (car: 19%, chair: 14%, KITTI: 4%, Synthia: 2%), which demonstrates the effectiveness of the recurrent pixel generator.

5   Conclusion

In this paper, we present an end-to-end trainable framework that is capable of synthesizing a novel view from multiple source views without utilizing 3D supervision. Specifically, we propose a two-stream model that integrates the strengths of the two main lines of existing view synthesis techniques: pixel generation and flow prediction. To adaptively merge the predictions produced by the two modules given multiple source images, we introduce a self-learned confidence aggregation mechanism. We evaluate our model on images rendered from 3D object models as well as real and synthesized scenes. We demonstrate that our model is able to achieve state-of-the-art results as well as progressively improve its predictions when more source images are available.

Acknowledgments. This project was supported by SKT. The research of Shao-Hua Sun and Minyoung Huh were partially supported by Snap Inc. The authors are grateful to Youngwoon Lee and Hyeonwoo Noh for helpful discussions about this work.

References

1. Poppe, R.: A survey on vision-based human action recognition. Image Vis. Comput. **28**, 976–990 (2010)
2. Gavrila, D.M., Davis, L.S.: 3-D model-based tracking of humans in action: a multi-view approach. In: Computer Vision and Pattern Recognition (CVPR) (1996)
3. Junejo, I.N., Dexter, E., Laptev, I., Pérez, P.: Cross-view action recognition from temporal self-similarities. In: Forsyth, D., Torr, P., Zisserman, A. (eds.) ECCV 2008. LNCS, vol. 5303, pp. 293–306. Springer, Heidelberg (2008). https://doi.org/10.1007/978-3-540-88688-4_22
4. Seitz, S.M., Curless, B., Diebel, J., Scharstein, D., Szeliski, R.: A comparison and evaluation of multi-view stereo reconstruction algorithms. In: Computer Vision and Pattern Recognition (CVPR) (2006)
5. Furukawa, Y., Ponce, J.: Accurate, dense, and robust multiview stereopsis. IEEE Trans. Pattern Anal. Mach. Intell. **32**(8), 1362–1376 (2010)
6. Choy, C.B., Xu, D., Gwak, J.Y., Chen, K., Savarese, S.: 3D-R2N2: a unified approach for single and multi-view 3D object reconstruction. In: Leibe, B., Matas, J., Sebe, N., Welling, M. (eds.) ECCV 2016. LNCS, vol. 9912, pp. 628–644. Springer, Cham (2016). https://doi.org/10.1007/978-3-319-46484-8_38
7. Fan, H., Su, H., Guibas, L.: A point set generation network for 3D object reconstruction from a single image. In: Conference on Computer Vision and Pattern Recognition (CVPR) (2017)
8. Remondino, F., El-Hakim, S.: Image-based 3D modelling: a review. Photogramm. Rec. **21**, 269–291 (2006)
9. Zwicker, M., Pauly, M., Knoll, O., Gross, M.: Pointshop 3D: an interactive system for point-based surface editing. In: ACM Transactions on Graphics (TOG) (2002)
10. Seitz, S.M., Dyer, C.R.: View morphing. In: Special Interest Group on GRAPHics and Interactive Techniques (SIGGRAPH) (1996)
11. Chen, S.E.: Quicktime VR: an image-based approach to virtual environment navigation. In: Special Interest Group on GRAPHics and Interactive Techniques (SIGGRAPH) (1995)
12. Szeliski, R., Shum, H.Y.: Creating full view panoramic image mosaics and environment maps. In: Special Interest Group on GRAPHics and Interactive Techniques (SIGGRAPH) (1997)
13. Forsyth, D., Ponce, J.: Computer Vision: A Modern Approach. Pearson, London (2011)
14. Sturm, P., Triggs, B.: A factorization based algorithm for multi-image projective structure and motion. In: Buxton, B., Cipolla, R. (eds.) ECCV 1996. LNCS, vol. 1065, pp. 709–720. Springer, Heidelberg (1996). https://doi.org/10.1007/3-540-61123-1_183
15. Montemerlo, M., Thrun, S., Koller, D., Wegbreit, B., et al.: FastSLAM: a factored solution to the simultaneous localization and mapping problem. In: AAAI/IAAI (2002)

16. Durrant-Whyte, H., Bailey, T.: Simultaneous localization and mapping: part I. IEEE Robot. Autom. Mag. **13**, 99–110 (2006)
17. Debevec, P.E., Taylor, C.J., Malik, J.: Modeling and rendering architecture from photographs: a hybrid geometry-and image-based approach. In: Proceedings of the 23rd Annual Conference on Computer Graphics and Interactive Techniques (1996)
18. Chang, A.X., et al.: Shapenet: an information-rich 3D model repository. Technical report arXiv:1512.03012 [cs.GR] (2015)
19. Tatarchenko, M., Dosovitskiy, A., Brox, T.: Single-view to multi-view: reconstructing unseen views with a convolutional network. CoRR abs/1511.06702 (2015)
20. Yang, J., Reed, S.E., Yang, M.H., Lee, H.: Weakly-supervised disentangling with recurrent transformations for 3D view synthesis. In: Advances in Neural Information Processing Systems, pp. 1099–1107 (2015)
21. Rematas, K., Nguyen, C.H., Ritschel, T., Fritz, M., Tuytelaars, T.: Novel views of objects from a single image. IEEE Trans. Pattern Anal. Mach. Intell. **38**, 1576–1590 (2017)
22. Zhou, T., Tulsiani, S., Sun, W., Malik, J., Efros, A.A.: View synthesis by appearance flow. In: Leibe, B., Matas, J., Sebe, N., Welling, M. (eds.) ECCV 2016. LNCS, vol. 9908, pp. 286–301. Springer, Cham (2016). https://doi.org/10.1007/978-3-319-46493-0_18
23. Park, E., Yang, J., Yumer, E., Ceylan, D., Berg, A.C.: Transformation-grounded image generation network for novel 3D view synthesis. In: CVPR (2017)
24. Flynn, J., Neulander, I., Philbin, J., Snavely, N.: Deepstereo: learning to predict new views from the world's imagery. In: Computer Vision and Pattern Recognition (CVPR) (2016)
25. Ji, D., Kwon, J., McFarland, M., Savarese, S.: Deep view morphing. In: Computer Vision and Pattern Recognition (CVPR) (2017)
26. Zhou, T., Krahenbuhl, P., Aubry, M., Huang, Q., Efros, A.A.: Learning dense correspondence via 3D-guided cycle consistency. In: Computer Vision and Pattern Recognition (CVPR) (2016)
27. Godard, C., Mac Aodha, O., Brostow, G.J.: Unsupervised monocular depth estimation with left-right consistency. In: Computer Vision and Pattern Recognition (CVPR) (2017)
28. Ren, Z., Yan, J., Ni, B., Liu, B., Yang, X., Zha, H.: Unsupervised deep learning for optical flow estimation. In: AAAI, pp. 1495–1501 (2017)
29. Liu, C., Yuen, J., Torralba, A., Sivic, J., Freeman, W.T.: SIFT flow: dense correspondence across different scenes. In: Forsyth, D., Torr, P., Zisserman, A. (eds.) ECCV 2008. LNCS, vol. 5304, pp. 28–42. Springer, Heidelberg (2008). https://doi.org/10.1007/978-3-540-88690-7_3
30. Dosovitskiy, A., Springenberg, J.T., Tatarchenko, M., Brox, T.: Learning to generate chairs, tables and cars with convolutional networks. IEEE Trans. Pattern Anal. Mach. Intell. (PAMI) **39**, 692–705 (2017)
31. Huang, R., Zhang, S., Li, T., He, R.: Beyond face rotation: global and local perception gan for photorealistic and identity preserving frontal view synthesis. arXiv preprint arXiv:1704.04086 (2017)
32. Isola, P., Zhu, J.Y., Zhou, T., Efros, A.A.: Image-to-image translation with conditional adversarial networks. arXiv preprint arXiv:1611.07004 (2016)
33. Zhu, J.Y., Park, T., Isola, P., Efros, A.A.: Unpaired image-to-image translation using cycle-consistent adversarial networks. arXiv preprint arXiv:1703.10593 (2017)
34. Liu, M.Y., Breuel, T., Kautz, J.: Unsupervised image-to-image translation networks. arXiv preprint arXiv:1703.00848 (2017)

35. Kim, T., Cha, M., Kim, H., Lee, J., Kim, J.: Learning to discover cross-domain relations with generative adversarial networks. arXiv preprint arXiv:1703.05192 (2017)
36. Jaderberg, M., Simonyan, K., Zisserman, A., et al.: Spatial transformer networks. In: Advances in Neural Information Processing Systems (NIPS) (2015)
37. Xingjian, S., Chen, Z., Wang, H., Yeung, D.Y., Wong, W.k., Woo, W.C.: Convolutional LSTM network: a machine learning approach for precipitation nowcasting. In: Advances in Neural Information Processing Systems, pp. 802–810 (2015)
38. Mao, X., Li, Q., Xie, H., Lau, R.Y., Wang, Z., Smolley, S.P.: Least squares generative adversarial networks. In: ICCV (2017)
39. Gal, Y., Ghahramani, Z.: Dropout as a Bayesian approximation: representing model uncertainty in deep learning. In: International Conference on Machine Learning (2016)
40. Kendall, A., Gal, Y.: What uncertainties do we need in Bayesian deep learning for computer vision? In: Advances in Neural Information Processing Systems (2017)
41. Geiger, A., Lenz, P., Urtasun, R.: Are we ready for autonomous driving? The KITTI vision benchmark suite. In: Conference on Computer Vision and Pattern Recognition (CVPR) (2012)
42. Ros, G., Sellart, L., Materzynska, J., Vazquez, D., Lopez, A.M.: The synthia dataset: a large collection of synthetic images for semantic segmentation of urban scenes. In: Computer Vision and Pattern Recognition (CVPR) (2016)
43. Long, J., Shelhamer, E., Darrell, T.: Fully convolutional networks for semantic segmentation. In: Proceedings of the IEEE Conference on Computer Vision and Pattern Recognition, pp. 3431–3440 (2015)
44. Salimans, T., Goodfellow, I., Zaremba, W., Cheung, V., Radford, A., Chen, X.: Improved techniques for training gans. In: Advances in Neural Information Processing Systems, pp. 2234–2242 (2016)
45. Everingham, M., Eslami, S.M.A., Van Gool, L., Williams, C.K.I., Winn, J., Zisserman, A.: The Pascal visual object classes challenge: a retrospective. Int. J. Comput. Vis. **111**, 98–136 (2015)

Multimodal Unsupervised Image-to-Image Translation

Xun Huang[1]([⊠]), Ming-Yu Liu[2], Serge Belongie[1], and Jan Kautz[2]

[1] Cornell University, Ithaca, USA
xh258@cornell.edu
[2] NVIDIA, Santa Clara, USA

Abstract. Unsupervised image-to-image translation is an important and challenging problem in computer vision. Given an image in the source domain, the goal is to learn the conditional distribution of corresponding images in the target domain, without seeing any examples of corresponding image pairs. While this conditional distribution is inherently multimodal, existing approaches make an overly simplified assumption, modeling it as a deterministic one-to-one mapping. As a result, they fail to generate diverse outputs from a given source domain image. To address this limitation, we propose a Multimodal Unsupervised Image-to-image Translation (MUNIT) framework. We assume that the image representation can be decomposed into a content code that is domain-invariant, and a style code that captures domain-specific properties. To translate an image to another domain, we recombine its content code with a random style code sampled from the style space of the target domain. We analyze the proposed framework and establish several theoretical results. Extensive experiments with comparisons to state-of-the-art approaches further demonstrate the advantage of the proposed framework. Moreover, our framework allows users to control the style of translation outputs by providing an example style image. Code and pretrained models are available at https://github.com/nvlabs/MUNIT.

Keywords: GANs · Image-to-image translation · Style transfer

1 Introduction

Many problems in computer vision aim at translating images from one domain to another, including super-resolution [1], colorization [2], inpainting [3], attribute transfer [4], and style transfer [5]. This cross-domain image-to-image translation setting has therefore received significant attention [6–25]. When the dataset contains paired examples, this problem can be approached by a conditional generative model [6] or a simple regression model [13]. In this work, we focus on the much more challenging setting when such supervision is unavailable.

Electronic supplementary material The online version of this chapter (https:// doi.org/10.1007/978-3-030-01219-9_11) contains supplementary material, which is available to authorized users.

© Springer Nature Switzerland AG 2018
V. Ferrari et al. (Eds.): ECCV 2018, LNCS 11207, pp. 179–196, 2018.
https://doi.org/10.1007/978-3-030-01219-9_11

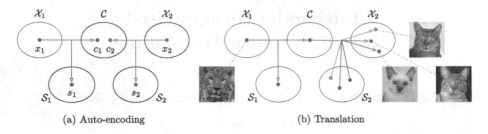

(a) Auto-encoding   (b) Translation

Fig. 1. An illustration of our method. (a) Images in each domain $\mathcal{X}_i$ are encoded to a shared content space $\mathcal{C}$ and a domain-specific style space $\mathcal{S}_i$. Each encoder has an inverse decoder omitted from this figure. (b) To translate an image in $\mathcal{X}_1$ (*e.g.*, a leopard) to $\mathcal{X}_2$ (*e.g.*, domestic cats), we recombine the content code of the input with a random style code in the target style space. Different style codes lead to different outputs.

In many scenarios, the cross-domain mapping of interest is multimodal. For example, a winter scene could have many possible appearances during summer due to weather, timing, lighting, etc. Unfortunately, existing techniques usually assume a deterministic [8–10] or unimodal [15] mapping. As a result, they fail to capture the full distribution of possible outputs. Even if the model is made stochastic by injecting noise, the network usually learns to ignore it [6,26].

In this paper, we propose a principled framework for the Multimodal UNsupervised Image-to-image Translation (MUNIT) problem. As shown in Fig. 1(a), our framework makes several assumptions. We first assume that the latent space of images can be decomposed into a content space and a style space. We further assume that images in different domains share a common content space but not the style space. To translate an image to the target domain, we recombine its content code with a random style code in the target style space (Fig. 1(b)). The content code encodes the information that should be preserved during translation, while the style code represents remaining variations that are not contained in the input image. By sampling different style codes, our model is able to produce diverse and multimodal outputs. Extensive experiments demonstrate the effectiveness of our method in modeling multimodal output distributions and its superior image quality compared with state-of-the-art approaches. Moreover, the decomposition of content and style spaces allows our framework to perform example-guided image translation, in which the style of the translation outputs are controlled by a user-provided example image in the target domain.

2   Related Works

Generative Adversarial Networks (GANs). The GAN framework [27] has achieved impressive results in image generation. In GAN training, a generator is trained to fool a discriminator which in turn tries to distinguish between generated samples and real samples. Various improvements to GANs have been proposed, such as multi-stage generation [28–33], better training objectives [34–39], and combination with auto-encoders [40–44]. In this work, we employ GANs to align the distribution of translated images with real images in the target domain.

Image-to-Image Translation. Isola *et al.* [6] propose the first unified framework for image-to-image translation based on conditional GANs, which has been extended to generating high-resolution images by Wang *et al.* [20]. Recent studies have also attempted to learn image translation without supervision. This problem is inherently ill-posed and requires additional constraints. Some works enforce the translation to preserve certain properties of the source domain data, such as pixel values [21], pixel gradients [22], semantic features [10], class labels [22], or pairwise sample distances [16]. Another popular constraint is the cycle consistency loss [7–9]. It enforces that if we translate an image to the target domain and back, we should obtain the original image. In addition, Liu *et al.* [15] propose the UNIT framework, which assumes a shared latent space such that corresponding images in two domains are mapped to the same latent code.

A significant limitation of most existing image-to-image translation methods is the lack of diversity in the translated outputs. To tackle this problem, some works propose to simultaneously generate multiple outputs given the same input and encourage them to be different [13,45,46]. Still, these methods can only generate a discrete number of outputs. Zhu *et al.* [11] propose a Bicycle-GAN that can model continuous and multimodal distributions. However, all the aforementioned methods require pair supervision, while our method does not. A couple of concurrent works also recognize this limitation and propose extensions of CycleGAN/UNIT for multimodal mapping [47]/[48].

Our problem has some connections with multi-domain image-to-image translation [19,49,50]. Specifically, when we know how many modes each domain has and the mode each sample belongs to, it is possible to treat each mode as a separate domain and use multi-domain image-to-image translation techniques to learn a mapping between each pair of modes, thus achieving multimodal translation. However, in general we do not assume such information is available. Also, our stochastic model can represent continuous output distributions, while [19,49,50] still use a deterministic model for each pair of domains.

Style Transfer. Style transfer aims at modifying the style of an image while preserving its content, which is closely related to image-to-image translation. Here, we make a distinction between example-guided style transfer, in which the target style comes from a single example, and collection style transfer, in which the target style is defined by a collection of images. Classical style transfer approaches [5,51–56] typically tackle the former problem, whereas image-to-image translation methods have been demonstrated to perform well in the latter [8]. We will show that our model is able to address both problems, thanks to its disentangled representation of content and style.

Learning Disentangled Representations. Our work draws inspiration from recent works on disentangled representation learning. For example, InfoGAN [57] and β-VAE [58] have been proposed to learn disentangled representations without supervision. Some other works [59–66] focus on disentangling content from style. Although it is difficult to define content/style and different works use different definitions, we refer to "content" as the underling spatial structure and "style" as the rendering of the structure. In our setting, we have two domains that share the same content distribution but have different style distributions.

3   Multimodal Unsupervised Image-to-Image Translation

Assumptions. Let $x_1 \in \mathcal{X}_1$ and $x_2 \in \mathcal{X}_2$ be images from two different image domains. In the unsupervised image-to-image translation setting, we are given samples drawn from two marginal distributions $p(x_1)$ and $p(x_2)$, without access to the joint distribution $p(x_1, x_2)$. Our goal is to estimate the two conditionals $p(x_2|x_1)$ and $p(x_1|x_2)$ with learned image-to-image translation models $p(x_{1 \to 2}|x_1)$ and $p(x_{2 \to 1}|x_2)$, where $x_{1 \to 2}$ is a sample produced by translating x_1 to $\mathcal{X}_2$ (similar for $x_{2 \to 1}$). In general, $p(x_2|x_1)$ and $p(x_1|x_2)$ are complex and multimodal distributions, in which case a deterministic translation model does not work well.

To tackle this problem, we make a *partially shared latent space assumption.* Specifically, we assume that each image $x_i \in \mathcal{X}_i$ is generated from a content latent code $c \in \mathcal{C}$ that is shared by both domains, and a style latent code $s_i \in \mathcal{S}_i$ that is specific to the individual domain. In other words, a pair of corresponding images (x_1, x_2) from the joint distribution is generated by $x_1 = G_1^*(c, s_1)$ and $x_2 = G_2^*(c, s_2)$, where c, s_1, s_2 are from some prior distributions and G_1^*, G_2^* are the underlying generators. We further assume that G_1^* and G_2^* are deterministic functions and have their inverse encoders $E_1^* = (G_1^*)^{-1}$ and $E_2^* = (G_2^*)^{-1}$. Our goal is to learn the underlying generator and encoder functions with neural networks. Note that although the encoders and decoders are deterministic, $p(x_2|x_1)$ is a continuous distribution due to the dependency of s_2.

Our assumption is closely related to the shared latent space assumption proposed in UNIT [15]. While UNIT assumes a fully shared latent space, we postulate that only part of the latent space (the content) can be shared across domains whereas the other part (the style) is domain specific, which is a more reasonable assumption when the cross-domain mapping is *many-to-many.*

Model. Figure 2 shows an overview of our model and its learning process. Similar to Liu *et al.* [15], our translation model consists of an encoder E_i and a decoder G_i for each domain $\mathcal{X}_i$ ($i = 1, 2$). As shown in Fig. 2(a), the latent code of each autoencoder is factorized into a content code c_i and a style code s_i, where $(c_i, s_i) = (E_i^c(x_i), E_i^s(x_i)) = E_i(x_i)$. Image-to-image translation is performed by swapping encoder-decoder pairs, as illustrated in Fig. 2(b). For example, to translate an image $x_1 \in \mathcal{X}_1$ to $\mathcal{X}_2$, we first extract its content latent code $c_1 = E_1^c(x_1)$ and randomly draw a style latent code s_2 from the prior distribution $q(s_2) \sim \mathcal{N}(0, \mathbf{I})$. We then use G_2 to produce the final output image $x_{1 \to 2} = G_2(c_1, s_2)$. We note that although the prior distribution is unimodal, the output image distribution can be multimodal thanks to the nonlinearity of the decoder.

Our loss function comprises a *bidirectional reconstruction loss* that ensures the encoders and decoders are inverses, and an *adversarial loss* that matches the distribution of translated images to the image distribution in the target domain.

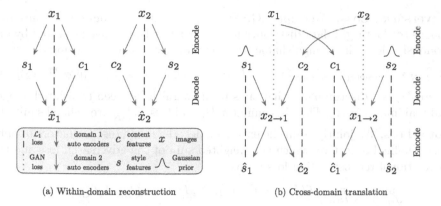

(a) Within-domain reconstruction   (b) Cross-domain translation

Fig. 2. Model overview. Our image-to-image translation model consists of two auto-encoders (denoted by red and blue arrows respectively), one for each domain. The latent code of each auto-encoder is composed of a content code c and a style code s. We train the model with adversarial objectives (dotted lines) that ensure the translated images to be indistinguishable from real images in the target domain, as well as bidirectional reconstruction objectives (dashed lines) that reconstruct both images and latent codes. (Color figure online)

Bidirectional Reconstruction Loss. To learn pairs of encoder and decoder that are inverses of each other, we use objective functions that encourage reconstruction in both image $\rightarrow$ latent $\rightarrow$ image and latent $\rightarrow$ image $\rightarrow$ latent directions:

- **Image Reconstruction.** Given an image sampled from the data distribution, we should be able to reconstruct it after encoding and decoding.

$$\mathcal{L}_{\text{recon}}^{x_1} = \mathbb{E}_{x_1 \sim p(x_1)}[\|G_1(E_1^c(x_1), E_1^s(x_1)) - x_1\|_1] \tag{1}$$

- **Latent Reconstruction.** Given a latent code (style and content) sampled from the latent distribution at translation time, we should be able to reconstruct it after decoding and encoding.

$$\mathcal{L}_{\text{recon}}^{c_1} = \mathbb{E}_{c_1 \sim p(c_1), s_2 \sim q(s_2)}[\|E_2^c(G_2(c_1, s_2)) - c_1\|_1] \tag{2}$$
$$\mathcal{L}_{\text{recon}}^{s_2} = \mathbb{E}_{c_1 \sim p(c_1), s_2 \sim q(s_2)}[\|E_2^s(G_2(c_1, s_2)) - s_2\|_1] \tag{3}$$

where $q(s_2)$ is the prior $\mathcal{N}(0, \mathbf{I})$, $p(c_1)$ is given by $c_1 = E_1^c(x_1)$ and $x_1 \sim p(x_1)$.

We note the other loss terms $\mathcal{L}_{\text{recon}}^{x_2}$, $\mathcal{L}_{\text{recon}}^{c_2}$, and $\mathcal{L}_{\text{recon}}^{s_1}$ are defined in a similar manner. We use $\mathcal{L}_1$ reconstruction loss as it encourages sharp output images.

The style reconstruction loss $\mathcal{L}_{\text{recon}}^{s_i}$ is reminiscent of the latent reconstruction loss used in the prior works [11, 31, 44, 57]. It has the effect on encouraging diverse outputs given different style codes. The content reconstruction loss $\mathcal{L}_{\text{recon}}^{c_i}$ encourages the translated image to preserve semantic content of the input image.

Adversarial Loss. We employ GANs to match the distribution of translated images to the target data distribution. In other words, images generated by our model should be indistinguishable from real images in the target domain.

$$\mathcal{L}_{\text{GAN}}^{x_2} = \mathbb{E}_{c_1 \sim p(c_1), s_2 \sim q(s_2)}[\log(1 - D_2(G_2(c_1, s_2)))] + \mathbb{E}_{x_2 \sim p(x_2)}[\log D_2(x_2)] \quad (4)$$

where D_2 is a discriminator that tries to distinguish between translated images and real images in $\mathcal{X}_2$. The discriminator D_1 and loss $\mathcal{L}_{\text{GAN}}^{x_1}$ are defined similarly.

Total Loss. We jointly train the encoders, decoders, and discriminators to optimize the final objective, which is a weighted sum of the adversarial loss and the bidirectional reconstruction loss terms.

$$\min_{E_1, E_2, G_1, G_2} \max_{D_1, D_2} \mathcal{L}(E_1, E_2, G_1, G_2, D_1, D_2) = \mathcal{L}_{\text{GAN}}^{x_1} + \mathcal{L}_{\text{GAN}}^{x_2}$$
$$+ \lambda_x(\mathcal{L}_{\text{recon}}^{x_1} + \mathcal{L}_{\text{recon}}^{x_2}) + \lambda_c(\mathcal{L}_{\text{recon}}^{c_1} + \mathcal{L}_{\text{recon}}^{c_2}) + \lambda_s(\mathcal{L}_{\text{recon}}^{s_1} + \mathcal{L}_{\text{recon}}^{s_2}) \quad (5)$$

where λ_x, λ_c, λ_s are weights that control the importance of reconstruction terms.

4   Theoretical Analysis

We now establish some theoretical properties of our framework. Specifically, we show that minimizing the proposed loss function leads to (1) matching of latent distributions during encoding and generation, (2) matching of two joint image distributions induced by our framework, and (3) enforcing a weak form of cycle consistency constraint. All the proofs are given in the supplementary material.

First, we note that the total loss in Eq. (5) is minimized when the translated distribution matches the data distribution and the encoder-decoder are inverses.

Proposition 1. *Suppose there exists E_1^*, E_2^*, G_1^*, G_2^* such that: (1) $E_1^* = (G_1^*)^{-1}$ and $E_2^* = (G_2^*)^{-1}$, and (2) $p(x_{1\to2}) = p(x_2)$ and $p(x_{2\to1}) = p(x_1)$. Then E_1^*, E_2^*, G_1^*, G_2^* minimizes $\mathcal{L}(E_1, E_2, G_1, G_2) = \max_{D_1, D_2} \mathcal{L}(E_1, E_2, G_1, G_2, D_1, D_2)$ (Eq. (5)).*

Latent Distribution Matching. For image generation, existing works on combining auto-encoders and GANs need to match the encoded latent distribution with the latent distribution the decoder receives at generation time, using either KLD loss [15,40] or adversarial loss [17,42] in the latent space. The auto-encoder training would not help GAN training if the decoder received a very different latent distribution during generation. Although our loss function does not contain terms that explicitly encourage the match of latent distributions, it has the effect of matching them implicitly.

Proposition 2. *When optimality is reached, we have:*

$$p(c_1) = p(c_2), \; p(s_1) = q(s_1), \; p(s_2) = q(s_2)$$

The above proposition shows that at optimality, the encoded style distributions match their Gaussian priors. Also, the encoded content distribution matches the distribution at generation time, which is just the encoded distribution from the other domain. This suggests that the content space becomes domain-invariant.

Joint Distribution Matching. Our model learns two conditional distributions $p(x_{1\rightarrow2}|x_1)$ and $p(x_{2\rightarrow1}|x_2)$, which, together with the data distributions, define two joint distributions $p(x_1, x_{1\rightarrow2})$ and $p(x_{2\rightarrow1}, x_2)$. Since both of them are designed to approximate the same underlying joint distribution $p(x_1, x_2)$, it is desirable that they are consistent with each other, i.e., $p(x_1, x_{1\rightarrow2}) = p(x_{2\rightarrow1}, x_2)$.

Joint distribution matching provides an important constraint for unsupervised image-to-image translation and is behind the success of many recent methods. Here, we show our model matches the joint distributions at optimality.

Proposition 3. *When optimality is reached, we have* $p(x_1, x_{1\rightarrow2}) = p(x_{2\rightarrow1}, x_2)$.

Style-Augmented Cycle Consistency. Joint distribution matching can be realized via cycle consistency constraint [8], assuming deterministic translation models and matched marginals [43,67,68]. However, we note that this constraint is too strong for multimodal image translation. In fact, we prove in the supplementary material that the translation model will degenerate to a deterministic function if cycle consistency is enforced. In the following proposition, we show that our framework admits a weaker form of cycle consistency, termed as style-augmented cycle consistency, between the image–style joint spaces, which is more suited for multimodal image translation.

Proposition 4. *Denote* $h_1 = (x_1, s_2) \in \mathcal{H}_1$ *and* $h_2 = (x_2, s_1) \in \mathcal{H}_2$. h_1, h_2 *are points in the joint spaces of image and style. Our model defines a deterministic mapping* $F_{1\rightarrow2}$ *from* $\mathcal{H}_1$ *to* $\mathcal{H}_2$ *(and vice versa) by* $F_{1\rightarrow2}(h_1) = F_{1\rightarrow2}(x_1, s_2) \triangleq (G_2(E_1^c(x_1), s_2), E_1^s(x_1))$. *When optimality is achieved, we have* $F_{1\rightarrow2} = F_{2\rightarrow1}^{-1}$.

Intuitively, style-augmented cycle consistency implies that if we translate an image to the target domain and translate it back *using the original style*, we should obtain the original image. Note that we do not use any explicit loss terms to enforce style-augmented cycle consistency, but it is implied by the proposed bidirectional reconstruction loss.

5   Experiments

5.1   Implementation Details

Figure 3 shows the architecture of our auto-encoder. It consists of a content encoder, a style encoder, and a joint decoder. More detailed information and hyperparameters are given in the supplementary material. We will provide an open-source implementation in PyTorch [69].

Content Encoder. Our content encoder consists of several strided convolutional layers to downsample the input and several residual blocks [70] to further process it. All the convolutional layers are followed by Instance Normalization (IN) [71].

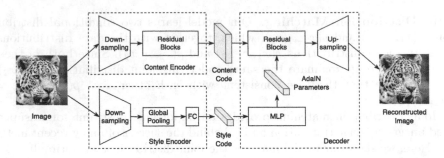

Fig. 3. Our auto-encoder architecture. The content encoder consists of several strided convolutional layers followed by residual blocks. The style encoder contains several strided convolutional layers followed by a global average pooling layer and a fully connected layer. The decoder uses a MLP to produce a set of AdaIN [54] parameters from the style code. The content code is then processed by residual blocks with AdaIN layers, and finally decoded to the image space by upsampling and convolutional layers.

Style Encoder. The style encoder includes several strided convolutional layers, followed by a global average pooling layer and a fully connected (FC) layer. We do not use IN layers in the style encoder, since IN removes the original feature mean and variance that represent important style information [54].

Decoder. Our decoder reconstructs the input image from its content and style code. It processes the content code by a set of residual blocks and finally produces the reconstructed image by several upsampling and convolutional layers. Inspired by recent works that use affine transformation parameters in normalization layers to represent styles [54,72–74], we equip the residual blocks with Adaptive Instance Normalization (AdaIN) [54] layers whose parameters are dynamically generated by a multilayer perceptron (MLP) from the style code.

$$\text{AdaIN}(z, \gamma, \beta) = \gamma \left(\frac{z - \mu(z)}{\sigma(z)} \right) + \beta \tag{6}$$

where z is the activation of the previous convolutional layer, μ and σ are channel-wise mean and standard deviation, γ and β are parameters generated by the MLP. Note that the affine parameters are produced by a learned network, instead of computed from statistics of a pretrained network as in Huang *et al.* [54].

Discriminator. We use the LSGAN objective proposed by Mao *et al.* [38]. We employ multi-scale discriminators proposed by Wang *et al.* [20] to guide the generators to produce both realistic details and correct global structure.

Domain-Invariant Perceptual Loss. The perceptual loss, often computed as a distance in the VGG [75] feature space between the output and the reference image, has been shown to benefit image-to-image translation when paired supervision is available [13,20]. In the unsupervised setting, however, we do not have a reference image in the target domain. We propose a modified version of perceptual loss that is more domain-invariant, so that we can use the input image as the reference. Specifically, before computing the distance, we perform Instance Normalization [71] (without affine transformations) on the VGG features in order to remove the original feature mean and variance, which contains much domain-specific information [54,76]. We find it accelerates training on high-resolution ($\geq 512 \times 512$) datasets and thus employ it on those datasets.

5.2 Evaluation Metrics

Human Preference. To compare the realism and faithfulness of translation outputs generated by different methods, we perform human perceptual study on Amazon Mechanical Turk (AMT). Similar to Wang *et al.* [20], the workers are given an input image and two translation outputs from different methods. They are then given unlimited time to select which translation output looks more accurate. For each comparison, we randomly generate 500 questions and each question is answered by 5 different workers.

LPIPS Distance. To measure translation diversity, we compute the average LPIPS distance [77] between pairs of randomly-sampled translation outputs from the same input as in Zhu *et al.* [11]. LPIPS is given by a weighted $\mathcal{L}_2$ distance between deep features of images. It has been demonstrated to correlate well with human perceptual similarity [77]. Following Zhu *et al.* [11], we use 100 input images and sample 19 output pairs per input, which amounts to 1900 pairs in total. We use the ImageNet-pretrained AlexNet [78] as the deep feature extractor.

(Conditional) Inception Score. The Inception Score (IS) [34] is a popular metric for image generation tasks. We propose a modified version called Conditional Inception Score (CIS), which is more suited for evaluating multimodal image translation. When we know the number of modes in $\mathcal{X}_2$ as well as the ground truth mode each sample belongs to, we can train a classifier $p(y_2|x_2)$ to classify an image x_2 into its mode y_2. Conditioned on a single input image x_1, the translation samples $x_{1\to2}$ should be mode-covering (thus $p(y_2|x_1) = \int p(y|x_{1\to2})p(x_{1\to2}|x_1)\,dx_{1\to2}$ should have high entropy) and each individual sample should belong to a specific mode (thus $p(y_2|x_{1\to2})$ should have low entropy). Combing these two requirements we get:

$$\text{CIS} = \mathbb{E}_{x_1 \sim p(x_1)}[\mathbb{E}_{x_{1\to2} \sim p(x_{2\to1}|x_1)}[\text{KL}(p(y_2|x_{1\to2})||p(y_2|x_1))]] \qquad (7)$$

To compute the (unconditional) IS, $p(y_2|x_1)$ is replaced with the unconditional class probability $p(y_2) = \iint p(y|x_{1\to2})p(x_{1\to2}|x_1)p(x_1)\,dx_1\,dx_{1\to2}$.

$$\text{IS} = \mathbb{E}_{x_1 \sim p(x_1)}[\mathbb{E}_{x_{1\to2} \sim p(x_{2\to1}|x_1)}[\text{KL}(p(y_2|x_{1\to2})||p(y_2))]] \qquad (8)$$

To obtain a high CIS/IS score, a model needs to generate samples that are both high-quality and diverse. While IS measures diversity of all output images, CIS measures diversity of outputs conditioned on a single input image. A model that deterministically generates a single output given an input image will receive a zero CIS score, though it might still get a high score under IS. We use the Inception-v3 [79] fine-tuned on our specific datasets as the classifier and estimate Eqs. (7) and (8) using 100 input images and 100 samples per input.

5.3 Baselines

UNIT [15]. The UNIT model consists of two VAE-GANs with a fully shared latent space. The stochasticity of the translation comes from the Gaussian encoders as well as the dropout layers in the VAEs.

CycleGAN [8]. CycleGAN consists of two residual translation networks trained with adversarial loss and cycle reconstruction loss. We use Dropout during both training and testing to encourage diversity, as suggested in Isola *et al.* [6].

CycleGAN* [8] **with Noise.** To test whether we can generate multimodal outputs within the CycleGAN framework, we additionally inject noise vectors to both translation networks. We use the U-net architecture [11] with noise added to input, since we find the noise vectors are ignored by the residual architecture in CycleGAN [8]. Dropout is also utilized during both training and testing.

BicycleGAN [11]. BicycleGAN is the only existing image-to-image translation model we are aware of that can generate continuous and multimodal output distributions. However, it requires paired training data. We compare our model with BicycleGAN when the dataset contains pair information.

5.4 Datasets

Edges ↔ Shoes/Handbags. We use the datasets provided by Isola *et al.* [6], Yu *et al.* [80], and Zhu *et al.* [81], which contain images of shoes and handbags with edge maps generated by HED [82]. We train one model for edges ↔ shoes and another for edges ↔ handbags without using paired information.

Animal Image Translation. We collect images from 3 categories/domains, including house cats, big cats, and dogs. Each domain contains 4 modes which are fine-grained categories belonging to the same parent category. Note that the modes of the images are not known during learning the translation model. We learn a separate model for each pair of domains.

Street Scene Images. We experiment with two street scene translation tasks:

– **Synthetic ↔ Real.** We perform translation between synthetic images in the SYNTHIA dataset [83] and real-world images in the Cityscape dataset [84]. For the SYNTHIA dataset, we use the SYNTHIA-Seqs subset which contains images in different seasons, weather, and illumination conditions.
– **Summer ↔ Winter.** We use the dataset from Liu et al. [15], which contains summer and winter street images extracted from real-world driving videos.

Yosemite Summer ↔ Winter (HD). We collect a new high-resolution dataset containing 3253 summer photos and 2385 winter photos of Yosemite. The images are downsampled such that the shortest side of each image is 1024 pixels.

| Input & GT | UNIT | CycleGAN | CycleGAN* with noise | MUNIT w/o $\mathcal{L}_{\text{recon}}^{x}$ | MUNIT w/o $\mathcal{L}_{\text{recon}}^{c}$ | MUNIT w/o $\mathcal{L}_{\text{recon}}^{s}$ | MUNIT (ours) | Bicycle-GAN |

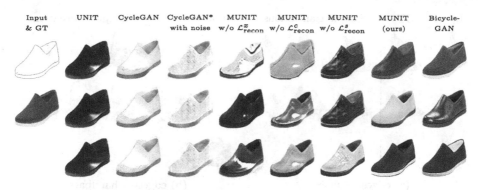

Fig. 4. Qualitative comparison on edges → shoes. The first column shows the input and ground truth output. Each following column shows 3 random outputs from a method.

Table 1. Quantitative evaluation on edges → shoes/handbags. The diversity score is the average LPIPS distance [77]. The quality score is the human preference score, the percentage a method is preferred over MUNIT. For both metrics, the higher the better.

	Edges → shoes		Edges → handbags	
	Quality	Diversity	Quality	Diversity
UNIT [15]	37.4%	0.011	37.3%	0.023
CycleGAN [8]	36.0%	0.010	40.8%	0.012
CycleGAN* [8] with noise	29.5%	0.016	45.1%	0.011
MUNIT w/o $\mathcal{L}_{\text{recon}}^{x}$	6.0%	0.213	29.0%	0.191
MUNIT w/o $\mathcal{L}_{\text{recon}}^{c}$	20.7%	0.172	9.3%	0.185
MUNIT w/o $\mathcal{L}_{\text{recon}}^{s}$	28.6%	0.070	24.6%	0.139
MUNIT	50.0%	0.109	50.0%	0.175
BicycleGAN [11]†	56.7%	0.104	51.2%	0.140
Real data	N/A	0.293	N/A	0.371

† Trained with paired supervision.

5.5 Results

First, we qualitatively compare MUNIT with the four baselines above, and three variants of MUNIT that ablate $\mathcal{L}_{\text{recon}}^{x}$, $\mathcal{L}_{\text{recon}}^{c}$, $\mathcal{L}_{\text{recon}}^{s}$ respectively. Figure 4 shows example results on edges → shoes. Both UNIT and CycleGAN (with or without noise) fail to generate diverse outputs, despite the injected randomness. Without $\mathcal{L}_{\text{recon}}^{x}$ or $\mathcal{L}_{\text{recon}}^{c}$, the image quality of MUNIT is unsatisfactory. Without $\mathcal{L}_{\text{recon}}^{s}$, the model suffers from partial mode collapse, with many outputs being almost identical (*e.g.*, the first two rows). Our full model produces images that are both diverse and realistic, similar to BicycleGAN but does not need supervision.

The qualitative observations above are confirmed by quantitative evaluations. We use human preference to measure quality and LPIPS distance to evaluate diversity, as described in Sect. 5.2. We conduct this experiment on the task of edges → shoes/handbags. As shown in Table 1, UNIT and CycleGAN produce

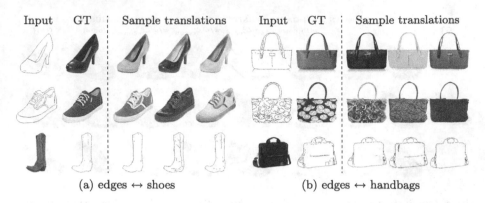

(a) edges ↔ shoes   (b) edges ↔ handbags

Fig. 5. Example results of (a) edges ↔ shoes and (b) edges ↔ handbags.

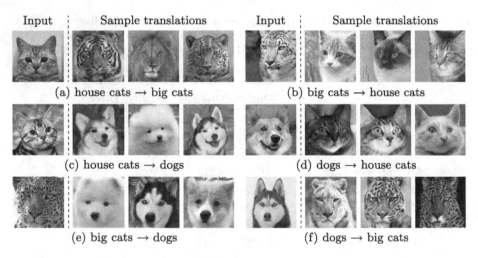

(a) house cats → big cats   (b) big cats → house cats

(c) house cats → dogs   (d) dogs → house cats

(e) big cats → dogs   (f) dogs → big cats

Fig. 6. Example results of animal image translation.

very little diversity according to LPIPS distance. Removing $\mathcal{L}^x_{\text{recon}}$ or $\mathcal{L}^c_{\text{recon}}$ from MUNIT leads to significantly worse quality. Without $\mathcal{L}^s_{\text{recon}}$, both quality and diversity deteriorate. The full model obtains quality and diversity comparable to the fully supervised BicycleGAN, and significantly better than all unsupervised baselines. In Fig. 5, we show more example results on edges ↔ shoes/handbags.

We proceed to perform experiments on the animal image translation dataset. As shown in Fig. 6, our model successfully translate one kind of animal to another. Given an input image, the translation outputs cover multiple modes, *i.e.*, multiple fine-grained animal categories in the target domain. The shape of an animal has undergone significant transformations, but the pose is overall preserved. As shown in Table 2, our model obtains the highest scores according to both CIS and IS. In particular, the baselines all obtain a very low CIS, indicating their failure to generate multimodal outputs from a given input. As the IS has been shown to correlate well to image quality [34], the higher IS of our method suggests that it also generates images of high quality than baseline approaches.

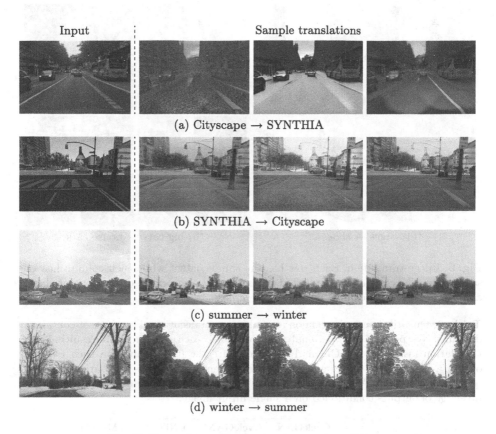

Input   Sample translations

(a) Cityscape → SYNTHIA

(b) SYNTHIA → Cityscape

(c) summer → winter

(d) winter → summer

Fig. 7. Example results on street scene translations.

Input   Sample translations

(a) Yosemite summer → winter

(b) Yosemite winter → summer

Fig. 8. Example results on Yosemite summer ↔ winter (HD resolution).

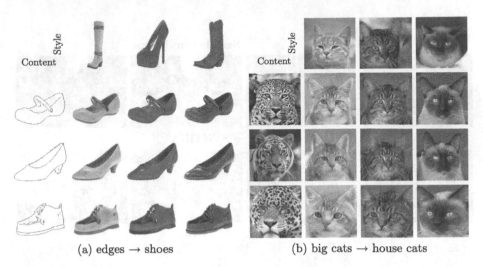

(a) edges → shoes   (b) big cats → house cats

Fig. 9. Image translation. Each row has the same content while each column has the same style. The color of the generated shoes and the appearance of the generated cats can be specified by providing example style images.

Table 2. Quantitative evaluation on animal image translation. This dataset contains 3 domains. We perform bidirectional translation for each domain pair, resulting in 6 translation tasks. We use CIS and IS to measure the performance on each task. To obtain a high CIS/IS score, a model needs to generate samples that are both high-quality and diverse. While IS measures diversity of all output images, CIS measures diversity of outputs conditioned on a single input image.

	CycleGAN		CycleGAN* with noise		UNIT		MUNIT	
	CIS	IS	CIS	IS	CIS	IS	CIS	IS
house cats → big cats	0.078	0.795	0.034	0.701	0.096	0.666	0.911	0.923
big cats → house cats	0.109	0.887	0.124	0.848	0.164	0.817	0.956	0.954
house cats → dogs	0.044	0.895	0.070	0.901	0.045	0.827	1.231	1.255
dogs → house cats	0.121	0.921	0.137	0.978	0.193	0.982	1.035	1.034
big cats → dogs	0.058	0.762	0.019	0.589	0.094	0.910	1.205	1.233
dogs → big cats	0.047	0.620	0.022	0.558	0.096	0.754	0.897	0.901
Average	0.076	0.813	0.068	0.762	0.115	0.826	1.039	1.050

Figure 7 shows results on street scene datasets. Our model is able to generate SYNTHIA images with diverse renderings (*e.g.*, rainy, snowy, sunset) from a given Cityscape image, and generate Cityscape images with different lighting, shadow, and road textures from a given SYNTHIA image. Similarly, it generates winter images with different amount of snow from a given summer image, and summer images with different amount of leafs from a given winter image. Figure 8 shows example results of summer ↔ winter transfer on the high-resolution Yosemite dataset. Our algorithm generates output images with different lighting.

Example-Guided Image Translation. Instead of sampling the style code from the prior, it is also possible to extract the style code from a reference image. Specifically, given a content image $x_1 \in \mathcal{X}_1$ and a style image $x_2 \in \mathcal{X}_2$, our model produces an image $x_{1 \to 2}$ that recombines the content of the former and the style latter by $x_{1 \to 2} = G_2(E_1^c(x_1), E_2^s(x_2))$. Examples are shown in Fig. 9.

6 Conclusions

We presented a framework for multimodal unsupervised image-to-image translation. Our model achieves quality and diversity superior to existing unsupervised methods and comparable to state-of-the-art supervised approach.

References

1. Dong, C., Loy, C.C., He, K., Tang, X.: Learning a deep convolutional network for image super-resolution. In: Fleet, D., Pajdla, T., Schiele, B., Tuytelaars, T. (eds.) ECCV 2014. LNCS, vol. 8692, pp. 184–199. Springer, Cham (2014). https://doi.org/10.1007/978-3-319-10593-2_13
2. Zhang, R., Isola, P., Efros, A.A.: Colorful image colorization. In: Leibe, B., Matas, J., Sebe, N., Welling, M. (eds.) ECCV 2016. LNCS, vol. 9907, pp. 649–666. Springer, Cham (2016). https://doi.org/10.1007/978-3-319-46487-9_40
3. Pathak, D., Krahenbuhl, P., Donahue, J., Darrell, T., Efros, A.A.: Context encoders: feature learning by inpainting. In: CVPR (2016)
4. Laffont, P.Y., Ren, Z., Tao, X., Qian, C., Hays, J.: Transient attributes for high-level understanding and editing of outdoor scenes. TOG **34**, 149 (2014)
5. Gatys, L.A., Ecker, A.S., Bethge, M.: Image style transfer using convolutional neural networks. In: CVPR (2016)
6. Isola, P., Zhu, J.Y., Zhou, T., Efros, A.A.: Image-to-image translation with conditional adversarial networks. In: CVPR (2017)
7. Yi, Z., Zhang, H., Tan, P., Gong, M.: DualGAN: unsupervised dual learning for image-to-image translation. In: ICCV (2017)
8. Zhu, J.Y., Park, T., Isola, P., Efros, A.A.: Unpaired image-to-image translation using cycle-consistent adversarial networks. In: ICCV (2017)
9. Kim, T., Cha, M., Kim, H., Lee, J., Kim, J.: Learning to discover cross-domain relations with generative adversarial networks. In: ICML (2017)
10. Taigman, Y., Polyak, A., Wolf, L.: Unsupervised cross-domain image generation. In: ICLR (2017)
11. Zhu, J.Y., Zhang, R., Pathak, D., Darrell, T., Efros, A.A., Wang, O., Shechtman, E.: Toward multimodal image-to-image translation. In: NIPS (2017)
12. Liu, M.Y., Tuzel, O.: Coupled generative adversarial networks. In: NIPS (2016)
13. Chen, Q., Koltun, V.: Photographic image synthesis with cascaded refinement networks. In: ICCV (2017)
14. Liang, X., Zhang, H., Xing, E.P.: Generative semantic manipulation with contrasting GAN. arXiv preprint arXiv:1708.00315 (2017)
15. Liu, M.Y., Breuel, T., Kautz, J.: Unsupervised image-to-image translation networks. In: NIPS (2017)
16. Benaim, S., Wolf, L.: One-sided unsupervised domain mapping. In: NIPS (2017)
17. Royer, A., et al.: XGAN: unsupervised image-to-image translation for many-to-many mappings. arXiv preprint arXiv:1711.05139 (2017)

18. Gan, Z., et al.: Triangle generative adversarial networks. In: NIPS, pp. 5253–5262 (2017)
19. Choi, Y., Choi, M., Kim, M., Ha, J.W., Kim, S., Choo, J.: StarGAN: unified generative adversarial networks for multi-domain image-to-image translation. In: CVPR (2018)
20. Wang, T.C., Liu, M.Y., Zhu, J.Y., Tao, A., Kautz, J., Catanzaro, B.: High-resolution image synthesis and semantic manipulation with conditional GANs. In: CVPR (2018)
21. Shrivastava, A., Pfister, T., Tuzel, O., Susskind, J., Wang, W., Webb, R.: Learning from simulated and unsupervised images through adversarial training. In: CVPR (2017)
22. Bousmalis, K., Silberman, N., Dohan, D., Erhan, D., Krishnan, D.: Unsupervised pixel-level domain adaptation with generative adversarial networks. In: CVPR (2017)
23. Wolf, L., Taigman, Y., Polyak, A.: Unsupervised creation of parameterized avatars. In: ICCV (2017)
24. Tau, T.G., Wolf, L., Tau, S.B.: The role of minimal complexity functions in unsupervised learning of semantic mappings. In: ICLR (2018)
25. Hoshen, Y., Wolf, L.: Identifying analogies across domains. In: ICLR (2018)
26. Mathieu, M., Couprie, C., LeCun, Y.: Deep multi-scale video prediction beyond mean square error. In: ICLR (2016)
27. Goodfellow, I., et al.: Generative adversarial nets. In: NIPS (2014)
28. Denton, E.L., Chintala, S., Fergus, R.: Deep generative image models using a Laplacian pyramid of adversarial networks. In: NIPS (2015)
29. Wang, X., Gupta, A.: Generative image modeling using style and structure adversarial networks. In: Leibe, B., Matas, J., Sebe, N., Welling, M. (eds.) ECCV 2016. LNCS, vol. 9908, pp. 318–335. Springer, Cham (2016). https://doi.org/10.1007/978-3-319-46493-0_20
30. Yang, J., Kannan, A., Batra, D., Parikh, D.: LR-GAN: layered recursive generative adversarial networks for image generation. In: ICLR (2017)
31. Huang, X., Li, Y., Poursaeed, O., Hopcroft, J., Belongie, S.: Stacked generative adversarial networks. In: CVPR (2017)
32. Zhang, H., et al.: StackGAN: text to photo-realistic image synthesis with stacked generative adversarial networks. In: ICCV (2017)
33. Karras, T., Aila, T., Laine, S., Lehtinen, J.: Progressive growing of GANs for improved quality, stability, and variation. In: ICLR (2018)
34. Salimans, T., Goodfellow, I., Zaremba, W., Cheung, V., Radford, A., Chen, X.: Improved techniques for training GANs. In: NIPS (2016)
35. Zhao, J., Mathieu, M., LeCun, Y.: Energy-based generative adversarial network. In: ICLR (2017)
36. Arjovsky, M., Chintala, S., Bottou, L.: Wasserstein generative adversarial networks. In: ICML (2017)
37. Berthelot, D., Schumm, T., Metz, L.: BEGAN: boundary equilibrium generative adversarial networks. arXiv preprint arXiv:1703.10717 (2017)
38. Mao, X., Li, Q., Xie, H., Lau, Y.R., Wang, Z., Smolley, S.P.: Least squares generative adversarial networks. In: ICCV (2017)
39. Tolstikhin, I., Bousquet, O., Gelly, S., Schoelkopf, B.: Wasserstein auto-encoders. In: ICLR (2018)
40. Larsen, A.B.L., Sønderby, S.K., Larochelle, H., Winther, O.: Autoencoding beyond pixels using a learned similarity metric. In: ICML (2016)

41. Dosovitskiy, A., Brox, T.: Generating images with perceptual similarity metrics based on deep networks. In: NIPS (2016)
42. Rosca, M., Lakshminarayanan, B., Warde-Farley, D., Mohamed, S.: Variational approaches for auto-encoding generative adversarial networks. arXiv preprint arXiv:1706.04987 (2017)
43. Li, C., et al.: Alice: towards understanding adversarial learning for joint distribution matching. In: NIPS (2017)
44. Srivastava, A., Valkoz, L., Russell, C., Gutmann, M.U., Sutton, C.: VEEGAN: reducing mode collapse in gans using implicit variational learning. In: NIPS (2017)
45. Ghosh, A., Kulharia, V., Namboodiri, V., Torr, P.H., Dokania, P.K.: Multi-agent diverse generative adversarial networks. arXiv preprint arXiv:1704.02906 (2017)
46. Bansal, A., Sheikh, Y., Ramanan, D.: PixeLNN: example-based image synthesis. In: ICLR (2018)
47. Almahairi, A., Rajeswar, S., Sordoni, A., Bachman, P., Courville, A.: Augmented cycleGAN: learning many-to-many mappings from unpaired data. arXiv preprint arXiv:1802.10151 (2018)
48. Lee, H.Y., Tseng, H.Y., Huang, J.B., Singh, M.K., Yang, M.H.: Diverse image-to-image translation via disentangled representation. In: Ferrari, V. (ed.) ECCV 2018, Part I. LNCS, vol. 11207, pp. 36–52. Springer, Cham (2018). https://doi.org/10.1007/978-3-030-01219-9_Z
49. Anoosheh, A., Agustsson, E., Timofte, R., Van Gool, L.: ComboGAN: unrestrained scalability for image domain translation. arXiv preprint arXiv:1712.06909 (2017)
50. Hui, L., Li, X., Chen, J., He, H., Yang, J., et al.: Unsupervised multi-domain image translation with domain-specific encoders/decoders. arXiv preprint arXiv:1712.02050 (2017)
51. Hertzmann, A., Jacobs, C.E., Oliver, N., Curless, B., Salesin, D.H.: Image analogies. In: SIGGRAPH (2001)
52. Li, C., Wand, M.: Combining markov random fields and convolutional neural networks for image synthesis. In: CVPR (2016)
53. Johnson, J., Alahi, A., Fei-Fei, L.: Perceptual losses for real-time style transfer and super-resolution. In: Leibe, B., Matas, J., Sebe, N., Welling, M. (eds.) ECCV 2016. LNCS, vol. 9906, pp. 694–711. Springer, Cham (2016). https://doi.org/10.1007/978-3-319-46475-6_43
54. Huang, X., Belongie, S.: Arbitrary style transfer in real-time with adaptive instance normalization. In: ICCV (2017)
55. Li, Y., Fang, C., Yang, J., Wang, Z., Lu, X., Yang, M.H.: Universal style transfer via feature transforms. In: NIPS, pp. 385–395 (2017)
56. Li, Y., Liu, M.Y., Li, X., Yang, M.H., Kautz, J.: A closed-form solution to photorealistic image stylization. In: Ferrari, V., et al. (eds.) ECCV 2018, Part III. LNCS, vol. 11207, pp. 469–486. Springer, Cham (2018). https://doi.org/10.1007/978-3-030-01219-9_Z
57. Chen, X., Duan, Y., Houthooft, R., Schulman, J., Sutskever, I., Abbeel, P.: InfoGAN: interpretable representation learning by information maximizing generative adversarial nets. In: NIPS (2016)
58. Higgins, I., et al.: beta-VAE: learning basic visual concepts with a constrained variational framework. In: ICLR (2017)
59. Tenenbaum, J.B., Freeman, W.T.: Separating style and content. In: NIPS (1997)
60. Bousmalis, K., Trigeorgis, G., Silberman, N., Krishnan, D., Erhan, D.: Domain separation networks. In: NIPS (2016)
61. Villegas, R., Yang, J., Hong, S., Lin, X., Lee, H.: Decomposing motion and content for natural video sequence prediction. In: ICLR (2017)

62. Mathieu, M.F., Zhao, J.J., Zhao, J., Ramesh, A., Sprechmann, P., LeCun, Y.: Disentangling factors of variation in deep representation using adversarial training. In: NIPS (2016)
63. Denton, E.L., et al.: Unsupervised learning of disentangled representations from video. In: NIPS (2017)
64. Tulyakov, S., Liu, M.Y., Yang, X., Kautz, J.: MocoGAN: decomposing motion and content for video generation. In: CVPR (2018)
65. Donahue, C., Balsubramani, A., McAuley, J., Lipton, Z.C.: Semantically decomposing the latent spaces of generative adversarial networks. In: ICLR (2018)
66. Shen, T., Lei, T., Barzilay, R., Jaakkola, T.: Style transfer from non-parallel text by cross-alignment. In: Advances in Neural Information Processing Systems, pp. 6833–6844 (2017)
67. Donahue, J., Krähenbühl, P., Darrell, T.: Adversarial feature learning. In: ICLR (2017)
68. Dumoulin, V., et al.: Adversarially learned inference. In: ICLR (2017)
69. Automatic differentiation in PyTorch. In: NIPS Autodiff Workshop (2017)
70. He, K., Zhang, X., Ren, S., Sun, J.: Deep residual learning for image recognition. In: CVPR (2016)
71. Ulyanov, D., Vedaldi, A., Lempitsky, V.: Improved texture networks: maximizing quality and diversity in feed-forward stylization and texture synthesis. In: CVPR (2017)
72. Dumoulin, V., Shlens, J., Kudlur, M.: A learned representation for artistic style. In: ICLR (2017)
73. Wang, H., Liang, X., Zhang, H., Yeung, D.Y., Xing, E.P.: ZM-Net: real-time zero-shot image manipulation network. arXiv preprint arXiv:1703.07255 (2017)
74. Ghiasi, G., Lee, H., Kudlur, M., Dumoulin, V., Shlens, J.: Exploring the structure of a real-time, arbitrary neural artistic stylization network. In: BMVC (2017)
75. Simonyan, K., Zisserman, A.: Very deep convolutional networks for large-scale image recognition. In: ICLR (2015)
76. Li, Y., Wang, N., Shi, J., Liu, J., Hou, X.: Revisiting batch normalization for practical domain adaptation. arXiv preprint arXiv:1603.04779 (2016)
77. Zhang, R., Isola, P., Efros, A.A., Shechtman, E., Wang, O.: The unreasonable effectiveness of deep features as a perceptual metric. In: CVPR (2018)
78. Krizhevsky, A., Sutskever, I., Hinton, G.E.: ImageNet classification with deep convolutional neural networks. In: Advances in neural information processing systems (2012)
79. Szegedy, C., Vanhoucke, V., Ioffe, S., Shlens, J., Wojna, Z.: Rethinking the inception architecture for computer vision. In: CVPR (2016)
80. Yu, A., Grauman, K.: Fine-grained visual comparisons with local learning. In: CVPR (2014)
81. Zhu, J.-Y., Krähenbühl, P., Shechtman, E., Efros, A.A.: Generative visual manipulation on the natural image manifold. In: Leibe, B., Matas, J., Sebe, N., Welling, M. (eds.) ECCV 2016. LNCS, vol. 9909, pp. 597–613. Springer, Cham (2016). https://doi.org/10.1007/978-3-319-46454-1_36
82. Xie, S., Tu, Z.: Holistically-nested edge detection. In: ICCV (2015)
83. Ros, G., Sellart, L., Materzynska, J., Vazquez, D., Lopez, A.M.: The synthia dataset: a large collection of synthetic images for semantic segmentation of urban scenes. In: CVPR (2016)
84. Cordts, M., et al.: The cityscapes dataset for semantic urban scene understanding. In: CVPR (2016)

Deeply Learned Compositional Models for Human Pose Estimation

Wei Tang, Pei Yu, and Ying Wu[✉]

Northwestern University, 2145 Sheridan Road, Evanston, IL 60208, USA
{wtt450,pyi980,yingwu}@eecs.northwestern.edu

Abstract. Compositional models represent patterns with hierarchies of meaningful parts and subparts. Their ability to characterize high-order relationships among body parts helps resolve low-level ambiguities in human pose estimation (HPE). However, prior compositional models make unrealistic assumptions on subpart-part relationships, making them incapable to characterize complex compositional patterns. Moreover, state spaces of their higher-level parts can be exponentially large, complicating both inference and learning. To address these issues, this paper introduces a novel framework, termed as Deeply Learned Compositional Model (DLCM), for HPE. It exploits deep neural networks to learn the compositionality of human bodies. This results in a novel network with a hierarchical compositional architecture and bottom-up/top-down inference stages. In addition, we propose a novel bone-based part representation. It not only compactly encodes orientations, scales and shapes of parts, but also avoids their potentially large state spaces. With significantly lower complexities, our approach outperforms state-of-the-art methods on three benchmark datasets.

1 Introduction

Human pose estimation (HPE) means to locate body parts from input images. It serves as a fundamental tool for several practical applications such as action recognition, human-computer interaction and video surveillance [1]. The most recent HPE systems have adopted convolutional neural networks (CNNs) [2–4] as their backbones and yielded drastic improvements on standard benchmarks [5–9]. However, they are still prone to fail when there exist ambiguities caused by overlapping parts, nearby persons and clutter backgrounds, *e.g.*, Fig. 1.

One promising way to tackle these difficulties is to exploit the compositionality [10,11] of human bodies. It means to represent a whole body as a hierarchy of parts and subparts, which satisfy some articulation constraints. This kind of hierarchical structure enables us to capture high-order relationships among parts and characterize an exponential number of plausible poses [12]. Based

Electronic supplementary material The online version of this chapter (https://doi.org/10.1007/978-3-030-01219-9_12) contains supplementary material, which is available to authorized users.

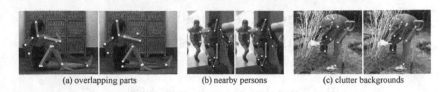

(a) overlapping parts   (b) nearby persons   (c) clutter backgrounds

Fig. 1. Pairs of pose predictions obtained by an eight-stack hourglass network [5] (left) and our approach (right). Some wrong part localizations are highlighted by green ellipses. By exploiting compositionality of human bodies, our approach is able to reduce low-level ambiguities in pose estimations. See Fig. 8 for more examples (Color figure online)

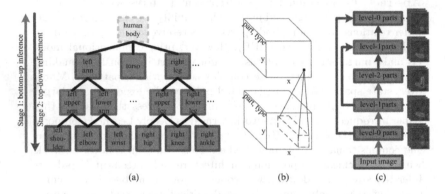

Fig. 2. (a) A typical compositional model of a human body. The pose is estimated via two stages: bottom-up inference followed by top-down refinement. (b) Each tensor represents score maps of several parts. An SLIS function aggregates information from input score maps on a spatially local support to predict output score maps. (c) Overview of our deeply learned compositional model. The orange and green arrows respectively denote SLIS functions modeled by CNNs in bottom-up and top-down stages. The colored rectangles on the left side denote predicted score maps of parts at different semantic levels while the heat maps on the right side represent their corresponding ground truth in the training phase (Color figure online)

on this principle, compositional models[1] [13,14] infer poses via two stages, as illustrated in Fig. 2(a). In the bottom-up stage, states of higher-level parts are recursively predicted from states of their child parts. In the top-down stage, states of lower-level parts are refined by their parents' states updated one step earlier. Such global adjustments enable pose estimations to optimally meet the relational constraints and thus reduce low-level image ambiguities. In the last decade, compositional models have been adopted in several HPE systems [12,15–19] and shown superior performances over their flat counterparts.

However, there are problems with existing compositional models designed for HPE [12,15–19]. First, they often assume a Gaussian distribution on the subpart-part displacement with the subpart's anchor position being its mean. While

---

[1] We focus on multilevel compositional models in this paper.

simplifying both their inference and learning [20], this assumption generally does not hold in real scenarios, *e.g.*, distributions of joints visualized in [21–23]. Thus, we argue it is incapable to characterize the complex compositional relationships among body parts. Second, a set of discrete *type* variables are often used to model the compatibility among parts. They not only include the orientation and scale of a part but also span semantic classes (a straight versus bended arm). As the distinct types of a part can be as many as the different combinations of all its children's types, state spaces for higher-level parts can be exponentially large. This makes both computation and storage demanding. Third, when the compositional structure has loops, approximate inference algorithms must be used. As a result, both the learning and testing will be adversely affected.

To address these issues, this paper introduces a novel framework, termed as Deeply Learned Compositional Model (DLCM), for HPE. We first show each bottom-up/top-down inference step of general compositional models is indeed an instantiation of a generalized process we call *spatially local information summarization* (SLIS). As shown in Fig. 2(b), it aggregates information from input score maps[2] on a spatially local support to predict output score maps. In this paper, we exploit CNNs to model this process due to their capability to approximate inference functions via spatially local connections. As a result, DLCMs can learn more sophisticated and realistic compositional patterns within human bodies. To avoid potentially large state spaces, we propose to use state variables to only denote locations and embed the type information into score maps. Specially, we use bone segments to represent a part and supervise its score map in the training phase. This novel representation not only compactly encodes the orientation, scale and shape of a part, but also reduces both computation and space complexities. Figure 2(c) provides an overview of a DLCM. We evaluate the proposed approach on three HPE benchmarks. With significantly less parameters and lower computational complexities, it outperforms state-of-the-art methods.

In summary, the novelty of this paper is as follows:

- To the best of our knowledge, this is the first attempt to explicitly learn the hierarchical compositionality of visual patterns via deep neural networks. As a result, DLCMs are capable to characterize the complex and realistic compositional relationships among body parts.
- We propose a novel part representation. It encodes the orientation, scale and shape of each part compactly and avoids their potentially large state spaces.
- Compared with prior deep neural networks, *e.g.*, CNNs, designed for HPE, our model has a hierarchical compositional structure and bottom-up/top-down inference stages across multiple semantic levels. We show in the experiments that the compositional nature of DLCMs helps them resolve the ambiguities that appear in bottom-up pose predictions.

---

[2] Each entry of a score map evaluates the goodness of a part being at a certain state, *e.g.*, location and type.

2   Related Work

Compositional Models. Compositionality has been studied in several lines of vision research [13,14,24,25] and exploited in tasks like HPE [12,15–19,26], semantic segmentation [27] and object detection [28]. However, prior compositional models adopt simple and unrealistic relational modeling, *e.g.*, pairwise potentials based on Gaussian distributions. They are incapable to model complex compositional patterns. Our approach attempts to address this difficulty by learning the compositional relationships among body parts via the powerful CNNs. In addition, we exploit a novel part representation to compactly encode the scale, orientation and shape of each part and avoid their potentially large state spaces.

CNN-Based HPE. All state-of-the-art HPE systems take CNNs as their main building block [5–7,9,29]. Newell *et al.* [5] introduce a novel *hourglass* module to process and consolidate features across all scales to best capture the various spatial relationships associated with the body. Yang *et al.* [7] combine CNNs and the expressive deformable mixture of parts [30] to enforce the spatial and appearance consistency among body parts. Hu and Ramanan [29] unroll the inference process of hierarchical rectified Gaussians as bidirectional architectures that also reason with top-down feedback. Instead of predicting body joint positions directly, Sun *et al.* [31] regress the coordinate shifts between joint pairs to encode their interactions. It is worth noting that none of these methods decomposes entities as hierarchies of meaningful and reusable parts or infers across different semantic levels. Our approach differs from them in that: (1) It has a hierarchical compositional network architecture; (2) CNNs are used to learn the compositional relationships among body parts; (3) Its inference consists of both bottom-up and top-down stages across multiple semantic levels; (4) It exploits a novel part representation to supervise the training of CNNs.

Bone-Based Part Representations. Some prior works [32,33] use heat maps of limbs between each pair of adjacent joints as supervisions of deep neural networks. Their motivation is that modeling pairs of joints helps capture additional body constraints and correlations. Different with them, our bone-based part representation has (1) a hierarchical compositional structure and (2) multiple semantic levels. It is designed to (1) tightly encode the scale, orientation and shape of a part, (2) avoid exponentially large state spaces for higher-level parts and (3) guide CNNs to learn the compositionality of human bodies.

3   Our Approach

We first make a brief introduction to general compositional models (Sect. 3.1). Their inference steps are generalized as SLIS functions and modeled with CNNs (Sect. 3.2). We then describe our novel bone-based part representation (Sect. 3.3). Finally, the deeply learned compositional models are detailed in Sect. 3.4.

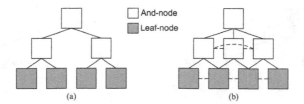

Fig. 3. Example compositional models (a) without and (b) with part sharing and higher-order cliques

3.1 Compositional Models

A compositional model is defined on a hierarchical graph, as shown in Fig. 3. It is characterized by a 4-tuple $(\mathcal{V}, \mathcal{E}, \phi^{and}, \phi^{leaf})$, which specifies its graph structure $(\mathcal{V}, \mathcal{E})$ and potential functions $(\phi^{and}, \phi^{leaf})$. We consider two types of nodes[3]: $\mathcal{V} = \mathcal{V}^{and} \cup \mathcal{V}^{leaf}$. And-nodes $\mathcal{V}^{and}$ model the composition of subparts into higher-level parts. Leaf nodes $\mathcal{V}^{leaf}$ model primitives, $i.e.$, the lowest-level parts. We call And-nodes at the highest level as root nodes. $\mathcal{E}$ denotes graph edges. In this section, we first illustrate our idea using the basic compositional model shown in Fig. 3(a), which does not share parts and considers only pairwise relationships, and then extend it to the general one, as shown in Fig. 3(b).

A state variable w_u is associated to each node/part $u \in \mathcal{V}$. For HPE, it can be the position p_u and type t_u of this part: $w_u = \{p_u, t_u\}$. As a motivating example, Yang and Ramanan [30] use types to represent orientations, scales and semantic classes (a straight versus bended arm) of parts.

Let Ω denote the set of all state variables in the model. The probability distribution over Ω is of the following Gibbs form:

$$p(\Omega|\mathbf{I}) = \frac{1}{Z} \exp\{-E(\Omega, \mathbf{I})\} \tag{1}$$

where $\mathbf{I}$ is the input image, $E(\Omega, \mathbf{I})$ is the energy and Z is the partition function. For convenience, we use a score function $S(\Omega)$, defined as the negative energy, to specify the model and omit $\mathbf{I}$. Without part sharing and higher-order potentials, it can be written as:

$$S(\Omega) \equiv -E(\Omega, \mathbf{I}) = \sum_{u \in \mathcal{V}^{leaf}} \phi_u^{leaf}(w_u, \mathbf{I}) + \sum_{u \in \mathcal{V}^{and}} \sum_{v \in ch(u)} \phi_{u,v}^{and}(w_u, w_v) \tag{2}$$

where $ch(u)$ denotes the set of children of node u. The two terms are potential functions corresponding to Leaf and nodes, respectively. The first term acts like a detector: it determines how likely the primitive modeled by Leaf-node u is present at location p_u and of type t_u. The second term models the state compatibility between a subpart v and its parent u.

---

[3] We do not need Or-nodes [13,14] here as part variations have been explicitly modeled by the state variables of And-nodes.

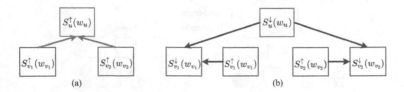

(a)   (b)

Fig. 4. Illustration of input-output relationships between child and parent score maps in the compositional inference. In this example, node u has two children v_1 and v_2. (a) In the bottom-up stage, the score map of a higher-level part is a function of its children's score maps. (b) In the top-down stage, the score map of a lower-level part is refined by its parent's score map updated one step earlier

Thanks to the tree structure, the optimal states Ω^* for an input image $\mathbf{I}$ can be computed efficiently via dynamic programming. We call this process the *compositional inference*. It is consisted of two stages. In the bottom-up stage, the maximum score, *i.e.*, $\max_\Omega S(\Omega)$, can be calculated recursively as:

$$\text{(Leaf) } S_u^\uparrow(w_u) = \phi_u^{leaf}(w_u, \mathbf{I}) \tag{3}$$

$$\text{(And) } S_u^\uparrow(w_u) = \sum_{v \in ch(u)} \max_{w_v}[\phi_{u,v}^{and}(w_u, w_v) + S_v^\uparrow(w_v)] \tag{4}$$

where $S_u^\uparrow(w_u)$ is the maximum score of the subgraph formed by node u and all its descendants, with root node u taking state w_u, and is computed recursively by Eq. (4), with boundary conditions provided by Eq. (3). The recursion begins from the Leaf-level and goes up until root nodes are reached. As a function, $S_u^\uparrow(w_u)$ assigns each possible state of part u a score. It can also be considered as a tensor/map, each entry of which is indexed by the part's state and valued by the corresponding score. Thus, we also call $S_u^\uparrow(w_u)$ the *score map* of part u.

In the top-down stage, we recursively invert Eq. (4) to obtain the optimal states of child nodes that yield the maximum score:

$$\text{(Root)} \quad w_u^* = \text{argmax}_{w_u} S_u^\downarrow(w_u) \equiv \text{argmax}_{w_u} S_u^\uparrow(w_u) \tag{5}$$

$$\text{(Non-root)} \quad w_v^* = \text{argmax}_{w_v} S_v^\downarrow(w_v) \equiv \text{argmax}_{w_v}[\phi_{u,v}^{and}(w_u^*, w_v) + S_v^\uparrow(w_v)] \tag{6}$$

where node u in Eq. (6) is the unique parent of node v, *i.e.*, $\{u\} = pa(v)$, $S_u^\uparrow(w_u)$ and $S_v^\uparrow(w_v)$ are acquired from the bottom-up stage, $S_u^\downarrow(w_u)$ and $S_v^\downarrow(w_v)$ are respectively refined score maps of nodes u and v. Specially, w_u^* and w_v^* are respectively optimal states of parts u and v, and are computed recursively by Eq. (6), with boundary conditions provided by Eq. (5). The recursion begins from root nodes and goes down until the Leaf-level is reached.

3.2   Spatially Local Information Summarization

From Eq. (6), $S_v^\downarrow(w_v)$ for non-root nodes is defined as:

$$S_v^\downarrow(w_v) = \phi_{u,v}^{and}(w_u^*, w_v) + S_v^\uparrow(w_v) \tag{7}$$

(a)   (b)

Fig. 5. (a) Illustration of the SLIS function in the compositional inference. Each cube denotes a score map corresponding to a part or subpart. Each entry in the output/right score map is obtained by aggregating information from the input/left score maps on a local spatial support. (b) Illustration of bone-based part representations. First row: the right lower arm, right upper arm, right arm and left arm of a person. Second row: right or left legs of different persons

where $\{u\} = pa(v)$, $w_u^* = \mathrm{argmax}_{w_u} S_u^\downarrow(w_u)$. We can write the bottom-up (BU) and top-down (TD) recursive equations, *i.e.*, Eqs. (4) and (7), together as

$$\text{(BU)} \quad S_u^\uparrow(w_u) = \sum_{v \in ch(u)} \max_{w_v}[\phi_{u,v}^{and}(w_u, w_v) + S_v^\uparrow(w_v)] \qquad (8)$$

$$\text{(TD)} \quad S_v^\downarrow(w_v) = \sum_{w_u} \phi_{u,v}^{and}(w_u, w_v)\bar{S}_u^\downarrow(w_u) + S_v^\uparrow(w_v) \qquad (9)$$

where $\bar{S}_u^\downarrow(w_u)$ is the hard-thresholded version of $S_u^\downarrow(w_u)$: $\bar{S}_u^\downarrow(w_u)$ equals to 1 if $w_u = w_u^*$ and 0 otherwise. As illustrated in Fig. 4, these two equations intuitively demonstrate how score maps are *propagated* upwards and downwards in the inference process, which finally gives us the globally optimal states, *i.e.*, Ω^*, of the compositional model.

In both equations, there exist summation and/or maximization operations over state variables, *e.g.*, $\sum_{v \in ch(u)} \max_{w_v}$ and $\sum_{w_u}$, as well as between score maps. They can be considered as average and maximum poolings. In the literature of statistical learning [34], pooling means to combine features in a way that preserves task-related information while removing irrelevant details, leads to more compact representations, and better robustness to noise and clutter. In the compositional inference, score maps of some parts are combined to get relevant information about the states of other related parts. This analogy leads us to think of Eqs. (8) and (9) as different kinds of *information summarization.*

Since child and parent parts should not be far apart in practice, it is unnecessary to search them within the whole image [14,35,36]. Thus, it is reasonable to constrain their relative displacements to be within a small range: $p_v - p_u \in \mathbb{D}_{uv}$, *e.g.*, $\mathbb{D}_{uv} = [-50, 50] \times [-50, 50]$. For compositional models, this constraint can be enforced by setting $\phi_{u,v}^{and}(w_u, w_v) = 0$ if $p_v - p_u \notin \mathbb{D}_{uv}$. Consequently, for each entry of the score maps on the LHS of Eqs. (8) and (9), only information within a *local spatial region* is summarized on the RHS, as the mapping shown in Fig. 5(a). Note this mapping is also *location-invariant* because the spatial compatibility between parts u and v with types t_u and t_v only depends on their relative locations and is unrelated to their global coordinates in the image space.

Our analysis indicates both recursive equations can be considered as different instantiations of a more generalized process, which aggregates information on a local spatial support and is location-invariant. We call this process *spatially local information summarization* (SLIS) and illustrate it in Fig. 5(a). In the bottom-up stage, the score map of a higher-level part $S_u^\uparrow(w_u)$ is an SLIS function of their children's score maps $\{S_v^\uparrow(w_v)\}_{v \in ch(u)}$. In the top-down stage, the score map of a lower-level part $S_v^\downarrow(w_v)$ is an SLIS function of its parent's score map $S_u^\downarrow(w_u)$ as well as its own score map estimated in the bottom-up stage $S_v^\uparrow(w_v)$.

Model SLIS Functions with CNNs. In this paper, we exploit CNNs to model our SLIS functions for two reasons. First, CNNs aggregate information on a local spatial support using location-invariant parameters. Second, CNNs are known for their capability to approximate inference functions. By learning them from data, we expect the SLIS functions are capable to infer the sophisticated compositional relationships within *real* human bodies. Specifically, we replace Eqs. (8) and (9) with:

$$(BU) \quad S_u^\uparrow(w_u) = \mathbf{c}_u^\uparrow\left(\{S_v^\uparrow(w_v)\}_{v \in ch(u)}; \Theta_u^\uparrow\right) \tag{10}$$

$$(TD) \quad S_v^\downarrow(w_v) = \mathbf{c}_v^\downarrow\left(S_u^\downarrow(w_u), S_v^\uparrow(w_v); \Theta_v^\downarrow\right) \tag{11}$$

where $\mathbf{c}_u^\uparrow$ and $\mathbf{c}_v^\downarrow$ are CNN mappings with $\Theta_u^\uparrow$ and $\Theta_v^\downarrow$ being their respective collections of convolutional kernels. Since the bottom-up and top-down SLIS functions are different, their corresponding kernels should also be different.

Part Sharing and Higher-Order Potentials. We now consider a more general compositional model, as shown in Fig. 3(b). With part sharing and higher-order potentials, the score function is

$$S(\Omega) = \sum_{u \in \mathcal{V}^{leaf}} \phi_u^{leaf}(w_u, \mathbf{I}) + \sum_{u \in \mathcal{V}^{and}} \phi_u^{and}(w_u, \{w_v\}_{v \in ch(u)}) \tag{12}$$

where $\phi_u^{and}(w_u, \{w_v\}_{v \in ch(u)})$ denotes the higher-order potential function measuring the state compatibility among part u and its child parts $\{v : v \in ch(u)\}$.

Due to the existence of loops and child sharing, states of all parts at one level should be estimated/refined jointly from all parts at a lower/higher level. By exploiting the update rules of dynamic programming [25], similar derivations (available in the supplementary material) indicate that we can approximate the SLIS functions as follows:

$$(BU) \quad \{S_u^\uparrow(w_u)\}_{u \in \mathcal{V}^L} = \mathbf{c}_L^\uparrow\left(\{S_v^\uparrow(w_v)\}_{v \in \mathcal{V}^{L-1}}; \Theta_L^\uparrow\right) \tag{13}$$

$$(TD) \quad \{S_v^\downarrow(w_v)\}_{v \in \mathcal{V}^{L-1}} = \mathbf{c}_{L-1}^\downarrow\left(\{S_u^\downarrow(w_u)\}_{u \in \mathcal{V}^L}, \{S_v^\uparrow(w_v)\}_{v \in \mathcal{V}^{L-1}}; \Theta_{L-1}^\downarrow\right) \tag{14}$$

where L indexes the semantic level, $\mathcal{V}^L$ denotes the set of nodes at the Lth level, $\Theta_L^\uparrow$ and $\Theta_{L-1}^\downarrow$ are convolutional kernels. In the bottom-up stage, score maps at a higher level are jointly estimated from all score maps at one level lower. In the top-down stage, score maps at a lower level are jointly refined by all score maps at one level higher as well as their initial estimations in the bottom-up stage.

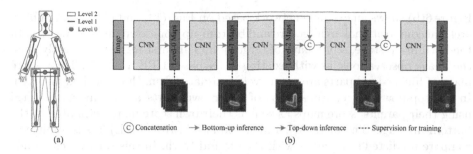

Fig. 6. (a) The compositional structure of a human body used in our experiments. It has three semantic levels, which include 16, 12 and 6 parts, respectively. Assume all the children sharing a common parent are linked to each other. (b) Network architecture of the proposed DLCM. *Maps* in the rectangles are short for score maps

3.3 Bone-Based Part Representation

Another problem with existing compositional models is that the type space for higher-level parts are potentially large. For example, if we have N types for both the left lower leg and left upper leg, there can be $O(N^2)$ types for the whole left leg and $O(N^4)$ types for the composition of left and right legs. As a result, the type dimensions of score maps $S_u^\uparrow(w_u)$ and $S_u^\downarrow(w_u)$ would be very high, which makes both storage and computation demanding. To address this issue, we propose to embed the type information into score maps and use state variables to only denote locations. As shown in Fig. 5(b), we represent each part with its *bones*, which are generated by putting Gaussian kernels along the part segments. They are then taken as the ground truth of score maps $S_u^\uparrow(w_u)$ and $S_u^\downarrow(w_u)$ when training neural networks. Specifically, for each point on the line segments of a part, we generate a heat map with a 2D Gaussian (std=1 pixel) centered at it. Then, a single heat map is formed by taking the maximum value from these heat maps at each position.

Our novel part representation has several advantages. First, score maps are now 2-D matrices with no type dimension instead of 3-D tensors. This reduces space and computation complexities in score map predictions. Second, the bones compactly encode orientations, scales and shapes of parts, as shown in Fig. 5(b). We no longer need to discretize them via clustering [12,15–19,26]. One weakness of this representation is that the ends of parts are indistinguishable. To solve this problem, we augment score maps of higher-level parts with score maps of their ends[4]. In this way, all important information of parts can be retained.

3.4 Deeply Learned Compositional Model (DLCM)

Motivated by the reasoning above, our Deeply Learned Compositional Model (DLCM) exploits CNNs to learn the compositionality of human bodies for HPE.

---

[4] In practice, we find repeated ends can be removed without deteriorating performance.

Figure 6(b) shows an example network based on Eqs. (13) and (14). It has a hierarchical compositional architecture and bottom-up/top-down inference stages. In the bottom-up stage, score maps of target joints are first regressed directly from the image observations, as with existing CNN-based HPE methods. Then, score maps of higher-level parts are recursively estimated from those of their children. In the top-down stage, score maps of lower-level parts are recursively refined using their parents' score maps as well as their own score maps estimated in the bottom-up stage. Similar as [37], a Mean Squared Error (MSE) loss is applied to compare predicted score maps with the ground truth. In this way, we can guide the network to learn the compositional relationships among body parts. Some examples of score maps predicted by our DLCM in the bottom-up and top-down stages can be found in Fig. 8(a).

4   Experiments

4.1   Implementation Details

The proposed DLCM is a general framework and can be instantiated with any compositional body structures and CNN modules. In the experiments, we use a similar compositional structure as that in [12] but include higher-order cliques and part sharing. As shown in Fig. 6(a), it has three semantic levels, which include 16, 12 and 6 parts, respectively. Assume all children sharing a common parent are linked to each other. The whole human body is not included here since it has negligible effect on overall performances, while complicating the model.

For two reasons, we exploit the hourglass module [5] to instantiate the CNN blocks in Fig. 6(b). First, the hourglass module extends the fully convolutional network [38] by processing and consolidating features across multiple scales. This enables it to capture the various spatial relationships associated with the input score maps. Second, the eight-stack hourglass network [5], formed by sequentially stacking eight hourglass modules, has achieved state-of-the-art results on several HPE benchmarks. It serves as a suitable baseline to test the effectiveness of the proposed approach. To instantiate a DLCM with three semantic levels, we need five hourglass modules, i.e., the five CNN blocks in Fig. 6(b). Newell et al. [5] add the intermediate features used to predict part score maps back to these predictions via skip connections before they are fed into the next hourglass. We follow this design in our implementation and find it helps reduce overfitting.

Our approach is evaluated on three HPE benchmark datasets of increasing difficulties: FLIC [39], Leeds Sports Poses (LSP) [40] and MPII Human Pose [21]. The FLIC dataset is composed of 5003 images (3987 for training, 1016 for testing) taken from films. The images are annotated on the upper body with most figures facing the camera. The extended LSP dataset consists of 11k training images and 1k testing images from sports activities. As a common practice [6,9,41], we train the network by including the MPII training samples. A few joint annotations in the LSP dataset are on the wrong side. We manually correct them. The MPII dataset consists of around 25k images with 40k annotated samples (28k for training, 11k for testing). The images cover a wide range of everyday human

Table 1. Comparisons of PCK@0.2 scores on the FLIC testing set

	Elbow	Wrist	Total
Tompson *et al.* [42]	93.1	89.0	91.05
Chen & Yuille [43]	95.3	92.4	93.9
Wei *et al.* [6]	97.6	95.0	96.3
Newell *et al.* [5]	99.0	97.0	98.0
Ours (3-level DLCM)	**99.5**	**98.5**	**99.0**

Table 2. Comparisons of PCK@0.2 scores on the LSP testing set

	Head	Shoulder	Elbow	Wrist	Hip	Knee	Ankle	Total
Bulat & Tzimiropoulos [8]	97.2	92.1	88.1	85.2	92.2	91.4	88.7	90.7
Insafutdinov *et al.* [44]	97.4	92.7	87.5	84.4	91.5	89.9	87.2	90.1
Lifshitz *et al.* [45]	96.8	89.0	82.7	79.1	90.9	86.0	82.5	86.7
Yu *et al.* [46]	87.2	88.2	82.4	76.3	91.4	85.8	78.7	84.3
Chu *et al.* [9]	98.1	93.7	89.3	86.9	93.4	94.0	92.5	92.6
Chen *et al.* [47]	**98.5**	94.0	89.8	87.5	93.9	94.1	93.0	93.1
Sun *et al.* [48]	97.9	93.6	89.0	85.8	92.9	91.2	90.5	91.6
Yang *et al.* [49]	98.3	94.5	92.2	88.9	94.4	95.0	93.7	93.9
Ours (3-level DLCM)	98.3	**95.9**	**93.5**	**90.7**	**95.0**	**96.6**	**95.7**	**95.1**

activities and a great variety of full-body poses. Following [5,42], 3k samples are taken as a validation set to tune the hyper-parameters.

Each input image is cropped around the target person according to the annotated body position and scale. They are then resized to 256×256 pixels. Data augmentation based on affine transformation [48,50] is used to reduce overfitting. We implement DLCMs[5] using Torch [51] and optimize them via RMSProp [52] with batch size 16. The learning rate is initialized as 2.5×10^{-4} and then dropped by a factor of 10 after the validation accuracy plateaus. In the testing phase, we run both the original input and a flipped version of a six-scale image pyramid through the network and average the estimated score maps together [49]. The final prediction is the maximum activating location of the score map for a given joint predicted by the last CNN module.

4.2 Evaluation

Metrics. Following previous work, we use the Percentage of Correct Keypoints (PCK) [21] as the evaluation metric. It calculates the percentage of detections that fall within a normalized distance of the ground truth. For LSP and FLIC, the distance is normalized by the torso size, and for MPII, by a fraction of the head size (referred to as PCKh).

---

[5] http://www.ece.northwestern.edu/~wtt450/project/ECCV18_DLCM.html.

Table 3. Comparisons of PCKh@0.5 scores on the MPII testing set

	Head	Shoulder	Elbow	Wrist	Hip	Knee	Ankle	Total
Bulat & Tzimiropoulos [8]	97.9	95.1	89.9	85.3	89.4	85.7	81.7	89.7
Gkioxary et al. [53]	96.2	93.1	86.7	82.1	85.2	81.4	74.1	86.1
Insafutdinov et al. [44]	96.8	95.2	89.3	84.4	88.4	83.4	78.0	88.5
Lifshitz et al. [45]	97.8	93.3	85.7	80.4	85.3	76.6	70.2	85.0
Belagiannis et al. [33]	97.7	95.0	88.2	83.0	87.9	82.6	78.4	88.1
Sun et al. [31]	97.5	94.3	87.0	81.2	86.5	78.5	75.4	86.4
Sun et al. [48]	98.1	96.2	91.2	87.2	89.8	87.4	84.1	91.0
Yang et al. [49]	**98.5**	96.7	92.5	**88.7**	91.1	88.6	86.0	92.0
Newell et al. [5]	98.2	96.3	91.2	87.1	90.1	87.4	83.6	90.9
Ours (3-level DLCM)	98.4	**96.9**	**92.6**	**88.7**	**91.8**	**89.4**	**86.2**	**92.3**

Table 4. Comparisons of parameter and operation numbers

	#parameters	#operations (GFLOPS)
Yang et al. [49] (state-of-the-art)	26.9M	45.9
Newell et al. [5]	23.7M	41.2
Ours (3-level DLCM)	**15.5M**	**33.6**

Accuracies. Tables 1, 2 and 3 respectively compare the performances of our 3-level DLCM and the most recent state-of-the-art HPE methods on FLIC, LSP and MPII datasets. Our approach clearly outperforms the eight-stack hourglass network [5], especially on some challenging joints. On the FLIC dataset, it achieves 1.5% improvement on *wrist* and halves the overall error rate (from 2% to 1%). On the MPII dataset, it achieves 2.6%, 2.0%, 1.7%, 1.6% and 1.4% improvements on *ankle*, *knee*, *hip*, *wrist* and *elbow*, respectively. On all three datasets, our approach achieves superior performance to the state-of-the-art methods.

Complexities. Table 4 compares the complexities of our 3-level DLCM with the eight-stack hourglass network [5] as well as the current state-of-the-art method [49]. Obviously, using only five hourglass modules instead of eight [5,49], our model has significantly less parameters and lower computational complexities. Specially, the prior top-performing method [49] on the benchmarks has 74% more parameters and needs 37% more GFLOPS.

Summary. From Tables 1, 2, 3 and 4, we can see that with significantly less parameters and lower computational complexities, the proposed approach has an overall superior performance to the state-of-the-art methods.

4.3   Component Analysis

We analyze the effectiveness of each component in DLCMs on MPII validation set. Mean PCKh@0.5 over hard joints, *i.e.*, ankle, knee, hip, wrist and elbow, is

Fig. 7. (a) Component analysis on MPII validation set. See Sect. 4.3 for details. (b) Qualitative results obtained by our approach on the MPII (top row) and LSP (bottom row) testing sets

used as the evaluation metric. A DLCM with two semantic levels is taken as the basic model. Model (i), $i \in \{1, 2, 3, 4, 5\}$, denotes one of the five variants of the basic model shown in Fig. 7(a).

To see the importance of compositional architectures, we successively remove the top-down lateral connections and compositional part supervisions, which leads to Model (1) and Model (2). Figure 7(a) indicates that both variants, especially the second one, perform worse than the basic model.

In Model (3), we replace bone-based part representations in the basic model with conventional part representations, $i.e.$, cubes in Fig. 5(a). Following [12], we use K-means to cluster each of the 12 higher-level parts into N types. Since a part sample is assigned to one type, only 1 of its N score map channels is nonzero (with a Gaussian centered at the part location). We have tested $N = 15$ [12] and $N = 30$ and reported the better result. As shown in Fig. 7(a), the novel bone-based part representation significantly outperforms the conventional one.

Finally, we explore whether using more semantic levels in a DLCM can boost its performance. Model (4) is what we have used in Sect. 4.2. Model (5) has 4 semantic levels. The highest-level part is the whole human body. Its ground truth *bone* map is the composition (location-wise maximum) of its children's *bone* maps. Figure 7(a) shows that the 3-level DLCM performs much better than the 2-level model. However, with 38% more parameters and 27% more GFLOPS, the 4-level DLCM only marginally outperforms the 3-level model.

4.4 Qualitative Results

Figure 7(b) displays some pose estimation results obtained by our approach. Figure 8(a) visualizes some score maps obtained by our method in the bottom-up (BU) and top-down (TD) inference stages. The evolution of these score maps demonstrates how the learned compositionality helps resolve the low-level ambiguities that appear in high-level pose estimations. The uncertain bottom-up estimations of the left ankle, right ankle and right elbow respectively in the first, second and fifth examples are resolved by the first-level compositions. In some more challenging cases, one level of composition is not enough to resolve the

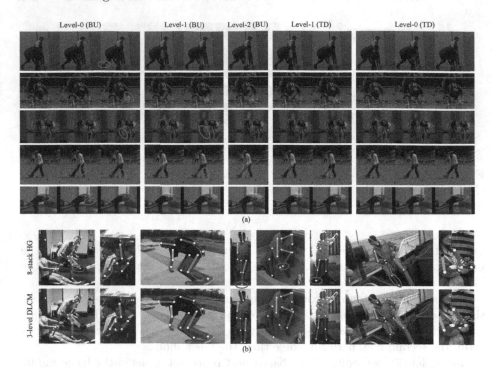

Fig. 8. (a) Score maps obtained by our method on some unseen images in the bottom-up (BU) and top-down (TD) inference stages. The five columns correspond to the five inference steps in Fig. 6(b). Due to space limit, only score maps corresponding to one of the six level-2 parts are displayed for the example at each row. From top to bottom, the level-2 parts are left leg, right leg, left arm, left leg and right arm, respectively. Within each sub-figure, parts of the same level are ordered by their distances to the body center. (b) Some examples showing that a 3-level DLCM (bottom row) is able to resolve the ambiguities that appear in bottom-up pose predictions of an 8-stack hourglass network (top row). Wrong part localizations are highlighted by green ellipses (Color figure online)

ambiguities, *e.g.*, the bottom-up predictions of the left lower arm in the third example and the left lower leg in the fourth example. Thanks to the hierarchical compositionality, their uncertainties can be reduced by the higher-level relational models. Figure 8(b) shows that our DLCM can resolve the ambiguities that appear in bottom-up pose predictions of an 8-stack hourglass network.

5   Conclusion

This paper exploits deep neural networks to learn the complex compositional patterns within human bodies for pose estimation. We also propose a novel bone-based part representation to avoid potentially large state spaces for higher-level parts. Experiments demonstrate the effectiveness and efficiency of our approach.

Acknowledgement. This work was supported in part by National Science Foundation grant IIS-1217302, IIS-1619078, and the Army Research Office ARO W911NF-16-1-0138.

References

1. Sarafianos, N., Boteanu, B., Ionescu, B., Kakadiaris, I.A.: 3D human pose estimation: a review of the literature and analysis of covariates. Comput. Vis. Image Underst. **152**, 1–20 (2016)
2. Fukushima, K., Miyake, S.: Neocognitron: a self-organizing neural network model for a mechanism of visual pattern recognition. In: Amari, S., Arbib, M.A. (eds.) Competition and Cooperation in Neural Nets, pp. 267–285. Springer, Heidelberg (1982). https://doi.org/10.1007/978-3-642-46466-9_18
3. LeCun, Y., Bottou, L., Bengio, Y., Haffner, P.: Gradient-based learning applied to document recognition. Proc. IEEE **86**(11), 2278–2324 (1998)
4. LeCun, Y., Bengio, Y., Hinton, G.: Deep learning. Nature **521**(7553), 436 (2015)
5. Newell, A., Yang, K., Deng, J.: Stacked hourglass networks for human pose estimation. In: Leibe, B., Matas, J., Sebe, N., Welling, M. (eds.) ECCV 2016. LNCS, vol. 9912, pp. 483–499. Springer, Cham (2016). https://doi.org/10.1007/978-3-319-46484-8_29
6. Wei, S.E., Ramakrishna, V., Kanade, T., Sheikh, Y.: Convolutional pose machines. In: IEEE Conference on Computer Vision and Pattern Recognition, pp. 4724–4732 (2016)
7. Yang, W., Ouyang, W., Li, H., Wang, X.: End-to-end learning of deformable mixture of parts and deep convolutional neural networks for human pose estimation. In: IEEE Conference on Computer Vision and Pattern Recognition, pp. 3073–3082 (2016)
8. Bulat, A., Tzimiropoulos, G.: Human pose estimation via convolutional part heatmap regression. In: Leibe, B., Matas, J., Sebe, N., Welling, M. (eds.) ECCV 2016. LNCS, vol. 9911, pp. 717–732. Springer, Cham (2016). https://doi.org/10.1007/978-3-319-46478-7_44
9. Chu, X., Yang, W., Ouyang, W., Ma, C., Yuille, A.L., Wang, X.: Multi-context attention for human pose estimation. In: IEEE Conference on Computer Vision and Pattern Recognition (CVPR), pp. 5669–5678 (2017)
10. Geman, S., Potter, D.F., Chi, Z.: Composition systems. Q. Appl. Math. **60**(4), 707–736 (2002)
11. Bienenstock, E., Geman, S., Potter, D.: Compositionality, MDL priors, and object recognition. In: Advances in Neural Information Processing Systems, pp. 838–844 (1997)
12. Tian, Y., Zitnick, C.L., Narasimhan, S.G.: Exploring the spatial hierarchy of mixture models for human pose estimation. In: Fitzgibbon, A., Lazebnik, S., Perona, P., Sato, Y., Schmid, C. (eds.) ECCV 2012. LNCS, vol. 7576, pp. 256–269. Springer, Heidelberg (2012). https://doi.org/10.1007/978-3-642-33715-4_19
13. Zhu, S.C., Mumford, D., et al.: A Stochastic Grammar of Images, vol. 2. Now Publishers, Inc., Hanover (2007). https://dl.acm.org/citation.cfm?id=1315337
14. Zhu, L.L., Chen, Y., Yuille, A.: Recursive compositional models for vision: description and review of recent work. J. Math. Imaging Vis. **41**(1–2), 122 (2011)
15. Wang, Y., Tran, D., Liao, Z.: Learning hierarchical poselets for human parsing. In: IEEE Conference on Computer Vision and Pattern Recognition, pp. 1705–1712 (2011)

16. Rothrock, B., Park, S., Zhu, S.C.: Integrating grammar and segmentation for human pose estimation. In: IEEE Conference on Computer Vision and Pattern Recognition, pp. 3214–3221 (2013)
17. Sun, M., Savarese, S.: Articulated part-based model for joint object detection and pose estimation. In: IEEE International Conference on Computer Vision, pp. 723–730 (2011)
18. Park, S., Zhu, S.C.: Attributed grammars for joint estimation of human attributes, part and pose. In: IEEE International Conference on Computer Vision, pp. 2372–2380 (2015)
19. Park, S., Nie, B.X., Zhu, S.C.: Attribute and-or grammar for joint parsing of human pose, parts and attributes. IEEE Trans. Pattern Anal. Mach. Intell. **40**(7), 1555–1569 (2018)
20. Felzenszwalb, P.F., Huttenlocher, D.P.: Distance transforms of sampled functions. Theory Comput. **8**(1), 415–428 (2012)
21. Andriluka, M., Pishchulin, L., Gehler, P., Schiele, B.: 2D human pose estimation: new benchmark and state of the art analysis. In: IEEE Conference on Computer Vision and Pattern Recognition, pp. 3686–3693 (2014)
22. Johnson, S., Everingham, M.: Learning effective human pose estimation from inaccurate annotation. In: IEEE Conference on Computer Vision and Pattern Recognition, pp. 1465–1472 (2011)
23. Tran, D., Forsyth, D.: Improved human parsing with a full relational model. In: Daniilidis, K., Maragos, P., Paragios, N. (eds.) ECCV 2010. LNCS, vol. 6314, pp. 227–240. Springer, Heidelberg (2010). https://doi.org/10.1007/978-3-642-15561-1_17
24. Jin, Y., Geman, S.: Context and hierarchy in a probabilistic image model. In: IEEE Conference on Computer Vision and Pattern Recognition, pp. 2145–2152 (2006)
25. Tang, W., Yu, P., Zhou, J., Wu, Y.: Towards a unified compositional model for visual pattern modeling. In: IEEE International Conference on Computer Vision, pp. 2803–2812 (2017)
26. Duan, K., Batra, D., Crandall, D.J.: A multi-layer composite model for human pose estimation. In: British Machine Vision Conference (2012)
27. Wang, J., Yuille, A.L.: Semantic part segmentation using compositional model combining shape and appearance. In: IEEE Conference on Computer Vision and Pattern Recognition, pp. 1788–1797 (2015)
28. Zhu, L., Chen, Y., Torralba, A., Freeman, W., Yuille, A.: Part and appearance sharing: recursive compositional models for multi-view. In: IEEE Conference on Computer Vision and Pattern Recognition, pp. 1919–1926 (2010)
29. Hu, P., Ramanan, D.: Bottom-up and top-down reasoning with hierarchical rectified Gaussians. In: IEEE Conference on Computer Vision and Pattern Recognition, pp. 5600–5609 (2016)
30. Yang, Y., Ramanan, D.: Articulated pose estimation with flexible mixtures-of-parts. In: IEEE Conference o Computer Vision and Pattern Recognitionn, pp. 1385–1392 (2011)
31. Sun, X., Shang, J., Liang, S., Wei, Y.: Compositional human pose regression. In: IEEE International Conference on Computer Vision, pp. 2621–2630 (2017)
32. Ai, B., Zhou, Y., Yu, Y., Du, S.: Human pose estimation using deep structure guided learning. In: IEEE Winter Conference on Applications of Computer Vision, pp. 1224–1231 (2017)
33. Belagiannis, V., Zisserman, A.: Recurrent human pose estimation. In: IEEE International Conference on Automatic Face Gesture Recognition, pp. 468–475 (2017)

34. Boureau, Y.L., Ponce, J., LeCun, Y.: A theoretical analysis of feature pooling in visual recognition. In: International Conference on Machine Learning, pp. 111–118 (2010)
35. Wan, L., Eigen, D., Fergus, R.: End-to-end integration of a convolution network, deformable parts model and non-maximum suppression. In: IEEE Conference on Computer Vision and Pattern Recognition, pp. 851–859 (2015)
36. Felzenszwalb, P.F., Girshick, R.B., McAllester, D., Ramanan, D.: Object detection with discriminatively trained part-based models. IEEE Trans. Pattern Anal. Mach. Intell. **32**(9), 1627–1645 (2010)
37. Tompson, J.J., Jain, A., LeCun, Y., Bregler, C.: Joint training of a convolutional network and a graphical model for human pose estimation. In: Advances in Neural Information Processing Systems, pp. 1799–1807 (2014)
38. Long, J., Shelhamer, E., Darrell, T.: Fully convolutional networks for semantic segmentation. In: IEEE Conference on Computer Vision and Pattern Recognition, pp. 3431–3440 (2015)
39. Sapp, B., Taskar, B.: MODEC: multimodal decomposable models for human pose estimation. In: IEEE Conference on Computer Vision and Pattern Recognition, pp. 3674–3681 (2013)
40. Johnson, S., Everingham, M.: Clustered pose and nonlinear appearance models for human pose estimation. In: British Machine Vision Conference (2010)
41. Pishchulin, L., et al.: DeepCut: joint subset partition and labeling for multi person pose estimation. In: IEEE Conference on Computer Vision and Pattern Recognition, pp. 4929–4937 (2016)
42. Tompson, J., Goroshin, R., Jain, A., LeCun, Y., Bregler, C.: Efficient object localization using convolutional networks. In: IEEE Conference on Computer Vision and Pattern Recognition, pp. 648–656 (2015)
43. Chen, X., Yuille, A.L.: Articulated pose estimation by a graphical model with image dependent pairwise relations. In: Advances in Neural Information Processing Systems, pp. 1736–1744 (2014)
44. Insafutdinov, E., Pishchulin, L., Andres, B., Andriluka, M., Schiele, B.: DeeperCut: a deeper, stronger, and faster multi-person pose estimation model. In: Leibe, B., Matas, J., Sebe, N., Welling, M. (eds.) ECCV 2016. LNCS, vol. 9910, pp. 34–50. Springer, Cham (2016). https://doi.org/10.1007/978-3-319-46466-4_3
45. Lifshitz, I., Fetaya, E., Ullman, S.: Human pose estimation using deep consensus voting. In: Leibe, B., Matas, J., Sebe, N., Welling, M. (eds.) ECCV 2016. LNCS, vol. 9906, pp. 246–260. Springer, Cham (2016). https://doi.org/10.1007/978-3-319-46475-6_16
46. Yu, X., Zhou, F., Chandraker, M.: Deep deformation network for object landmark localization. In: Leibe, B., Matas, J., Sebe, N., Welling, M. (eds.) ECCV 2016. LNCS, vol. 9909, pp. 52–70. Springer, Cham (2016). https://doi.org/10.1007/978-3-319-46454-1_4
47. Chen, Y., Shen, C., Wei, X.S., Liu, L., Yang, J.: Adversarial PoseNet: a structure-aware convolutional network for human pose estimation. In: IEEE International Conference on Computer Vision, pp. 1221–1230 (2017)
48. Sun, K., Lan, C., Xing, J., Zeng, W., Liu, D., Wang, J.: Human pose estimation using global and local normalization. In: IEEE International Conference on Computer Vision, pp. 5600–5608 (2017)
49. Yang, W., Li, S., Ouyang, W., Li, H., Wang, X.: Learning feature pyramids for human pose estimation. In: The IEEE International Conference on Computer Vision, pp. 1290–1299 (2017)

50. Forsyth, D.A., Ponce, J.: Computer Vision: A Modern Approach. Prentice Hall Professional Technical Reference, Upper Saddle River (2002)
51. Collobert, R., Kavukcuoglu, K., Farabet, C.: Torch7: a Matlab-like environment for machine learning. In: NIPS Workshop (2011)
52. Tieleman, T., Hinton, G.: Lecture 6.5-rmsprop: divide the gradient by a running average of its recent magnitude. COURSERA: Neural networks for machine learning 4(2), 26–31 (2012)
53. Gkioxari, G., Toshev, A., Jaitly, N.: Chained predictions using convolutional neural networks. In: Leibe, B., Matas, J., Sebe, N., Welling, M. (eds.) ECCV 2016. LNCS, vol. 9908, pp. 728–743. Springer, Cham (2016). https://doi.org/10.1007/978-3-319-46493-0_44

Unsupervised Video Object Segmentation with Motion-Based Bilateral Networks

Siyang Li[1,2]([⊠]) [iD], Bryan Seybold[2] [iD], Alexey Vorobyov[2], Xuejing Lei[1] [iD],
and C.-C. Jay Kuo[1] [iD]

[1] University of Southern California, Los Angeles, USA
{siyangl,xuejing}@usc.edu, cckuo@sipi.usc.edu
[2] Google AI Perception, Mountain View, USA
{seybold,vorobya}@google.com

Abstract. In this work, we study the unsupervised video object segmentation problem where moving objects are segmented without prior knowledge of these objects. First, we propose a motion-based bilateral network to estimate the background based on the motion pattern of non-object regions. The bilateral network reduces false positive regions by accurately identifying background objects. Then, we integrate the background estimate from the bilateral network with instance embeddings into a graph, which allows multiple frame reasoning with graph edges linking pixels from different frames. We classify graph nodes by defining and minimizing a cost function, and segment the video frames based on the node labels. The proposed method outperforms previous state-of-the-art unsupervised video object segmentation methods against the DAVIS 2016 and the FBMS-59 datasets.

Keywords: Video object segmentation · Bilateral networks
Instance embeddings

1 Introduction

The goal of video object segmentation (VOS) is tracking moving objects with accurate masks. It serves as an important pre-processing step in video understanding. The mask of the target object can assist many vision tasks, such as action recognition and visual effects. There are two VOS scenarios depending on whether the tracked target is indicated or not. The former is called *semi-supervised* VOS while the latter is called *unsupervised* VOS or primary object segmentation. The moving objects being tracked and the remaining regions are referred to as *foreground* and *background*, respectively.

We focus on the unsupervised scenario in this work. Since the target objects are unknown, many unsupervised VOS methods rely on motion cues, i.e., optical

Electronic supplementary material The online version of this chapter (https://doi.org/10.1007/978-3-030-01219-9_13) contains supplementary material, which is available to authorized users.

© Springer Nature Switzerland AG 2018
V. Ferrari et al. (Eds.): ECCV 2018, LNCS 11207, pp. 215–231, 2018.
https://doi.org/10.1007/978-3-030-01219-9_13

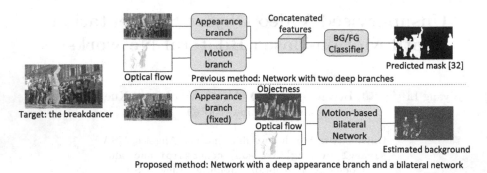

Fig. 1. Compare the proposed method with the dual-branch network in [32]. Instead of training a deep motion branch to generate motion features, we propose a light bilateral network based on motion and objectness, which identifies the background by finding regions that have similar motion patterns with low-objectness regions

flow [2,15], to find the objects to be tracked. A commonly used architecture is a dual-branch convolutional neural network [5,16,32], consisting of an appearance branch and a motion branch, which take the RGB frames and optical flow as their input, respectively, as shown at the top of Fig. 1. Although the network is jointly trained with appearance and motion, it may not be able to build the correspondence between foreground and motion patterns. For example, if all cars move in the training data, cars will always be labeled as foreground. The network may map car's appearance to foreground directly while ignoring the motion pattern. Then, static cars may become false positives in inference.

In this work, we aim at building the correspondence between motion patterns and foreground/background directly. A motion-based bilateral network (BNN) for background estimation is proposed to integrate the appearance information (i.e., objectness) and optical flow, as shown at the bottom of Fig. 1. More specifically, the bilateral network is trained to model the motion patterns based on optical flow in the non-object region (inferred by the objectness map from the appearance branch) and identify regions with similar motion patterns. It is worthwhile to point out that bilateral networks have previously been used to propagate masks temporally in [17], but in the proposed method, bilateral networks are adopted to extend the background region spatially from non-object regions to static objects. Then, to leverage the inter-frame similarity, a graph composed of pixels from consecutive frames is constructed, with the similarity defined based on the instance embeddings [9]. Because pixel-wise graph inference can be time-consuming [34], we build the graph on a reduced set of pixels and later propagate the labels to remaining pixels (Fig. 2). According to the experimental results, incorporating information from multiple frames leads to better segmentation results.

We tested the proposed method on the DAVIS 2016 dataset [29] and the FBMS-59 dataset [27]. The experimental results demonstrate superior performance over previous state-of-the-art methods. The contribution includes: (1)

proposing a trainable bilateral network to estimate background based on motion cues and objectness; (2) efficient multi-frame reasoning via graph cut of a reduced set of points seeded across objects; and (3) achieving state-of-the-art results on the DAVIS 2016 and the FBMS-59 datasets with intersection-over-union (IoU) scores of 80.4% and 73.9%, and outperforms previous best results by 1.9% and 2.0%, respectively.

2   Related Work

Unsupervised Video Object Segmentation. Prior to the popularity of deep convolutional neural networks (CNN), some methods used a Gaussian Mixture Model (GMM) and optical flow to build an appearance model and a motion model, respectively [22]. Graph cut is a commonly used technique that integrates the appearance/motion model with temporal/spatial smoothness by optimizing a cost function [28,34]. It is important to formulate the problem in a way so that it can be solved efficiently, e.g. [26]. The proposed method also uses graph cut to jointly optimize a cost function, but we formulate the graph cut over a subset of diverse seed points and rely on deep embeddings from CNNs to better model the similarity between pixels. Later, CNNs, including fully convolutional networks (FCN) that were initially developed for image segmentation [25], were adopted to segment the moving objects in videos. A common approach is training an FCN to generate a binary mask for each frame [3]. A dual branch CNN is used in [5,16,32]. It takes in a frame and its optical flow (or two consecutive frames) to generate appearance and motion features. These features are combined in a later stage and finally the network produces a binary mask. MP [31] relies on optical flow solely to produce the motion-salient regions. Due to the lack of guidance from object masks, it therefore also identifies "moving stuff" such as waves. A common challenge for VOS is the lack of densely annotated videos. FSEG [16] proposes to generate masks from weakly labeled data (bounding boxes). IET [24] transfers the instance embeddings learned from static images and uses heuristics to identify representative embeddings of the moving objects. SfMNet [35] learns object models and motion patterns without mask annotations by differentiable rendering.

Semi-supervised Video Object Segmentation. As mentioned above, for semi-supervised VOS, the object masks for the first frame (or more) are provided, which allow building an accurate appearance model. One common framework for semi-supervised VOS is mask propagation [17,21], where the predicted mask of the previous frame and the new RGB frame are input to the network. The propagation process can be viewed as a modification of the previous frame mask. Another framework for semi-supervised VOS is binary mask prediction conditioned on the user-input frames [3,5,36], which usually requires online fine-tuning for optimal performance. That is, during inference, the network weights are updated by further training on the provided mask. Online fine-tuning is expensive in terms of both runtime and memory, as each query sequence has a unique model stored. Therefore, these approaches do not scale well. Graph cut is also used for semi-supervised VOS [19,26]. BVS [26] samples a regular grid in the bilateral space and conducts graph cut on the grid vertices. CTN [19] uses a CNN to identify confident foreground and background regions based on the provided masks and optical flow. Then a graph is built, taking the color and motion similarity into consideration. PLM [37] compares the deep features of pixels from later frames with the first-frame pixels and determines the foreground probability. It also demands online fine-tuning for optimal performance.

Image Segmentation. Semantic image segmentation and object instance segmentation are two important problems in computer vision and attract a lot attention recently [4,9–11,13,14,25,38]. One popular architecture for image segmentation is the fully convolutional neural network (FCN), which predict a label for each pixel [4,25]. In semantic segmentation, the goal is to assign a semantic category label to each pixel. Building VOS approaches upon the semantic segmentation network has a natural limitation: object instances from the same category cannot be distinguished. Since we may need to track one moving instance from multiple static instances of the same category (e.g. a moving car out from parked cars) in VOS, we rely on instance segmentation networks [6,9], where different instances are distinguishable. In [9], an embedding vector is generated for each pixel and the distance between embedding vectors encode the probability of two pixels belonging to the same instance. IET [24] transfers these embeddings without further fine-tuning on video datasets and choose representative embeddings for foreground and background heuristically for each frame. Then the segmentation is done on each frame individually, so the masks are not temporally smooth enough. In this proposed method, we build a graph of sampled pixels from multiple frames and rely on the embeddings to measure the similarity along the time dimension.

3   Method

The proposed method is explained in detail in this section. An overview is depicted in Fig. 2. It contains three modules: (1) background estimation with a motion-based bilateral network, (2) classification of sampled pixels with graph cut, and (3) frame segmentation by propagating labels of sampled pixels.

3.1   Motion-Based Bilateral Networks for Background Estimation

Motion cues are essential to the solution of the unsupervised VOS problem. In MP [31], a binary segmentation neural network uses the optical flow vector as the input and produces a motion saliency map. Due to the camera motion, flow patterns do not always correspond to moving objects. Consider the following two scenarios: (1) an object with the leftward motion and a static camera, and (2) an object with the rightward motion and a camera following the object. The latter is viewed as left-moving background with a static object. The flow patterns are flipped for the two scenarios yet both expect high motion saliency on objects. In

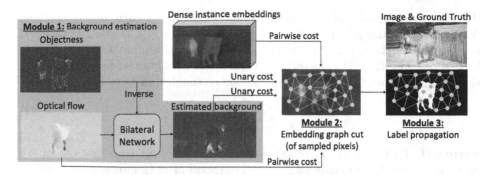

Fig. 2. An overview of the proposed method that consists of three modules. The background is estimated from the inverse objectness map and the optical flow through a bilateral network (BNN) in Module 1, which is enclosed in light blue. Then, an embedding graph that contains sampled pixels (marked by dots) from a set of consecutive frames as vertices is constructed. The unary cost is defined based on the objectness and the estimated background from the BNN. The pairwise cost is from instance embedding and optical flow similarity. All vertices are classified in Module 2 by optimizing the total cost, where magenta and yellow dots denote the foreground and background vertices, respectively. Finally, the graph vertex labels are propagated to all remaining pixels based on embedding similarity in Module 3. Best viewed in color

other words, it is confusing for the network to find motion-salient objects solely relying on optical flow.

To address this problem, we integrate optical flow with objectness scores to estimate the background, which includes static objects and non-objects (also known as *stuff* [12]). Given an objectness map output from a segmentation network [9], we can locate stuff regions by thresholding the objectness map. The optical flow in those regions can model the motion patterns of background (due to the camera motion). By identifying regions of similar motion, we can associate static objects with the background. In other words, background is expanded from stuff regions to include static objects. Inspired by temporal propagation in semi-supervised VOS with the bilateral space [17,26], we solve this background expansion problem with a bilateral network (BNN) [18], i.e. generalized bilateral filtering by replacing default Gaussian filters [1,33] with learnable ones.

Bilateral Filtering. We briefly review the bilateral filtering below and refer to [1,18] for more details. Bilateral filtering is implemented by four steps: (1) constructing a bilateral grid, (2) splatting the features of input samples to the high-dimensional bilateral grid, (3) convolution on the high-dimensional grid, and (4) slicing the filtered features on grid back to samples of interest. Let d and $\mathbf{f}_q \in \mathbb{R}^d$ denote the dimension of the bilateral space and the position vector of sample q in the bilateral space, respectively. In addition, let $s_I(i)$, $s_V(v)$ and $s_O(o)$ denote the feature of an input sample i, a vertex v of the bilateral grid, and an output sample o. We explain the case with the feature being a scalar below, but the process can be generalized to vector features (e.g., for image denoising, the feature is the 3-D color components) by repeating for each feature channel. A bilateral filtering process with $d = 2$ is illustrated in Fig. 3. The 2-D bilateral grid partitions the space into rectangles, and the position of each vertex v can be described by $\mathbf{f}_v \in \mathbb{R}^d$. The feature on the vertex is obtained by accumulating the features of input samples in its neighbor rectangles, in form of

$$s_V(v) = \sum_{i \in \Omega(v)} w(\mathbf{f}_v, \mathbf{f}_i) s_I(i), \tag{1}$$

where $w(\mathbf{f}_v, \mathbf{f}_i)$ is the weight function that defines the influence from sample i on vertex v and $\Omega(v)$ stands for the neighborhood of v. Commonly used weight functions $w(\cdot, \cdot)$ include multilinear interpolation and the nearest neighbor indicator. Afterwards, filters, $c(\cdot)$, are applied to the splatted feature on the grid, as shown in the center figure of Fig. 3:

$$s_V'(v) = \sum_m s_V(v - m) c(m), \tag{2}$$

where $s_V'(v)$ is the filtered feature on vertex v. Finally, the filtered features on vertices are *sliced* to an output sample, o, given its position $\mathbf{f}_o$, as shown in the right figure of Fig. 3. Mathematically, the feature of sample o is obtained by

$$s_O(o) = \sum_{v \in \Omega(o)} w(\mathbf{f}_o, \mathbf{f}_v) s_V'(v), \tag{3}$$

where $\Omega(o)$ represents the set of surrounding vertices, with a set size of 2^d. The weight function $w(\cdot, \cdot)$ is identical with the one in Eq. (1).

The filter $c(\cdot)$ in Eq. (2) is Gaussian in traditional bilateral filtering. It is generalized to learnable filters in [18], which can be trained by minimizing a loss defined between $s_O(o)$ and the target feature of o. The learnable filters compose the bilateral networks (BNN) [17].

Motion-Based Bilateral Networks. A commonly used bilateral space is composed by color components (e.g., RGB) and location indices (x, y), so the 5-D position vector can be written as $\mathbf{f} = (r, g, b, x, y)^T$. For videos, the timestep, t, is often taken as an additional dimension, yielding $\mathbf{f} = (r, g, b, x, y, t)^T$ [17,26].

In the proposed method, we expand static regions spatially based on motion. Therefore, we have $\mathbf{f} = (dx, dy, x, y)^T$, where $(dx, dy)^T$ denotes the optical flow vector. We do not expand the static region temporally because optical flows on consecutive frames are not necessarily aligned. We build a regular grid of size $(G_{flow}, G_{flow}, G_{loc}, G_{loc})$ in this 4-D bilateral space. To obtain a set of input samples for splatting, we locate the stuff pixels by thresholding the objectness map. This set of stuff pixels is the initial background, denoted by $\mathcal{B}^{init}$. We use the inverted objectness score as the feature to be splatted from an input pixel,

$$s_I(i) = 1 - p^{\mathrm{Obj}}(i), i \in \mathcal{B}^{init}. \tag{4}$$

The inverted objectness score can be viewed as a soft vote for the background and the splatting process by Eq. (1) is to accumulate the background votes on

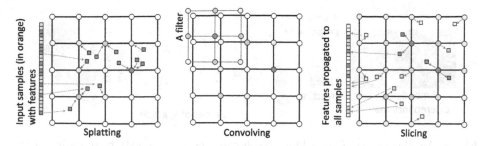

Fig. 3. Illustration of a fast bilateral filtering pipeline with a bilateral space of dimension $d = 2$: (1) **splatting** (left): the available features from input samples (orange squares) are accumulated on the bilateral grid; (2) **convolving** (center): the accumulated features on vertices are filtered and propagated to neighbors; and (3) **slicing** (right): the feature of any sample with a known position in the bilateral space can be obtained by interpolation from its surrounding vertices

the vertices of the bilateral grid. After that, a 4-D filter is applied to propagate the votes to neighboring vertices. Finally, by slicing, the propagated votes are forwarded to the remaining pixels on the same frame, based on their optical flow and spatial locations.

To train the BNN, we clip the negative background votes by ReLU and apply the tanh function to convert the clipped votes to background probability,

$$p_{\text{bnn}}^{\text{BG}}(j) = \frac{1 - \exp\{-2 \times ReLU[s_O(j)]\}}{1 + \exp\{-2 \times ReLU[s_O(j)]\}}, \tag{5}$$

and the training loss is the cross entropy between $p_{\text{bnn}}^{\text{BG}}$ and the inverted ground truth mask,

$$\mathcal{L} = -\sum_j [1 - y(j)] \ln p_{\text{bnn}}^{\text{BG}}(j) + y(j) \ln[1 - p_{\text{bnn}}^{\text{BG}}(j)], \tag{6}$$

where $y(j) \in \{0, 1\}$ is the ground truth, with 0 and 1 representing background and foreground, respectively.

3.2 Embedding Graph Cut

Because optical flow computation is imperfect, the estimated background is not a suitable final segmentation. For example, the static parts of non-rigid objects will receive high background scores from the BNN, resulting in false negatives. To achieve more accurate masks, we integrate the predicted background region with the pixel-wise instance embeddings from [9]. The embedding is a representation vector of a pixel, and the Euclidean distance between two embeddings measures the (dis-)similarity between pixels. Here the similarity is defined as the probability of two pixels belonging to the same object instance. Mathematically, the similarity score of two pixels, i and j, is expressed as

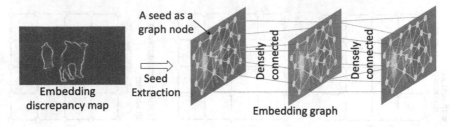

Fig. 4. An illustration of embedding graph construction. We extract seeds based on the embedding discrepancy map, which become graph nodes. Edges connect nodes that are spatial neighbors or from consecutive frames (see texts for the definition of spatial neighbors). Best viewed in color

$$R(i,j) = \frac{2}{1 + \exp(\|\mathbf{e}_i - \mathbf{e}_j\|_2^2)}, \tag{7}$$

where $\mathbf{e}_i$ is the instance embedding vector for pixel i. The instance embeddings are explicitly trained to encode the similarity by minimizing the cross entropy between $R(i,j)$ and the ground truth identical instance indicator in [9].

Given that the instance embeddings describing pixel similarity, the objectness score and background score from the BNN, we adopt the graph cut method to classify pixels by minimizing a cost function. Graph cut has been used previously to solve VOS over either pixel-level graphs [34] or superpixel-level graphs [28]. The former is time consuming considering the number of pixels in a video while the latter is prone to superpixel error. In BVS [26], the graph cut was conducted on a 6-D bilateral grid (composed by color, spatial and temporal positions). However, it is not realistic to build a grid graph in the bilateral space with high dimensional instance embeddings and locations since the splatting/slicing process would be time-consuming and the resulting grid would be sparse.

In the proposed method, we still construct a graph with pixels as vertices. To save computation, the graph is built from a small subset of pixels that are approximately evenly distributed in the spatial space and located at stable points of the instance embedding map. These sampled pixels are called "seeds" and labeled via cost minimization. Then, their labels are propagated to all pixels, which will be explained later.

Building an embedding graph. As aforementioned, building a pixel-level graph leads to time-consuming graph cut. To reduce computation load, we follow the seed extraction process in [24] to find a set of pixels with representative embeddings on every frame. To classify the seeds on frame t, we build a graph based on seeds from frames $(t-1)$ to $(t+1)$, i.e., a temporal window of length 3 centered at t. Using a different temporal window that covers frame t is also possible, as studied in Sect. 4.4. We denote the seed set by $\mathcal{V}$. The next step is to link seeds with edges in the graph. Given the seeds on a frame, we identify the closest seed to every pixel, and we link the seeds with a graph edge if two neighboring pixels are closest to different seeds. These edges are called *spatial* *edges.* For seeds from consecutive frames, they are densely linked to yield *temporal edges.* Other seed pairs are not connected. The graph edges are denoted by $\mathcal{E}$. An illustration of the embedding graph of seeds is displayed in Fig. 4.

Graph Cut. A cut of the embedding graph is obtained by minimizing the following cost function:

$$L = \sum_{i \in \mathcal{V}} \phi(i) + \lambda \sum_{(i,j) \in \mathcal{E}} [l(i) \neq l(j)]\theta(i,j), \tag{8}$$

where $l(i) \in \{0,1\}$ is the assigned label to pixel i, $\phi(\cdot)$ is the unary cost, and $\theta(\cdot,\cdot)$ is the pairwise cost. The unary cost is given by

$$\phi(i) = [1 - l(i)]\phi^{BG}(i) + l(i)\phi^{FG}(i), \tag{9}$$

where $\phi^{BG}(i)$ and $\phi^{FG}(i)$ are the costs for node i to be labeled as background and foreground, respectively. For background cost, we utilize the background probability from Eq. (5). For foreground cost, it is defined by the objectness score, $p^{\text{Obj}}(i)$, obtained by the segmentation network [9]:

$$\phi^{BG}(i) = -\ln p_{\text{bnn}}^{BG}(i); \tag{10}$$

$$\phi^{FG}(i) = -\ln p^{\text{Obj}}(i). \tag{11}$$

The pairwise cost encourages similar nodes being assigned to the same category, reducing errors from static parts of non-rigid objects. We consider both instance similarity via embeddings $\mathbf{e}_i$ and the motion similarity via optical flow $\mathbf{m}_i = [dx_i, dy_i]^T$. Specifically, $\theta(i,j)$ is given by

$$\theta(i,j) = \exp(-\frac{\|\mathbf{e}_i - \mathbf{e}_j\|_2^2}{\sigma_e^2}) + \delta(t_i, t_j)\alpha \exp(-\frac{\|\mathbf{m}_i - \mathbf{m}_j\|_2^2}{\sigma_m^2}), \tag{12}$$

where σ_e and σ_m are the standard deviation of the Gaussian kernels, α is the importance of the motion similarity relative to the embedding similarity and t_i is the frame index. If seeds i and j are from different frames, the motion similarity term is ignored as reflected by the dirac delta term, $\delta(t_i, t_j)$, since their optical flow may not be aligned. Although instance embeddings are trained on images, they are shown to be stable over consecutive frames in [24]. Thus, they are applicable to measure the similarity across frames. Our studies in Sect. 4.4 show that considering this inter-frame similarity is beneficial and ignoring temporal edges leads to inferior performance.

3.3   Label Propagation

After graph cut, the final step is to propagate the label from seeds to remaining pixels. Given an arbitrary pixel, i, with its temporal-spatial location denoted by $(x_i, y_i, t_i)^T$, we can identify its neighboring seeds on frame t_i by finding its spatially closest seed and the spatial neighbors of that seed in the graph. Besides

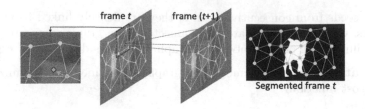

Fig. 5. Given an arbitrary pixel (marked by the diamond), its surrounding nodes (in red circles) are identified from the current frame, the previous frame (omitted here) and the following frame. The label of the node with the shortest embedding distance is assigned to the pixel. Best viewed in color

seeds on frame t_i, we also include the neighboring seeds for the pixels located at $(x_i, y_i, t_i - 1)^T$ and $(x_i, y_i, t_i + 1)^T$, i.e., pixels with the same spatial location in the previous frame and the following frame, as shown in Fig. 5. The neighboring seed set for pixel i is denoted by $\mathcal{N}(i)$. Among the seeds in $\mathcal{N}(i)$, the one with the shortest embedding distance to i is found via

$$n = \arg \min_{m \in \mathcal{N}(i)} ||\mathbf{e}_i - \mathbf{e}_m||_2^2. \tag{13}$$

The label of seed n is assigned to pixel i. We estimate the probability that pixel i is foreground from the shortest embedding distance to the nodes labeled as foreground and background in $\mathcal{N}(i)$, denoted by $d_{FG}(i)$ and $d_{BG}(i)$, respectively. The foreground probability is defined by

$$p^{FG}(i) = \frac{\exp[-d_{FG}^2(i)]}{\exp[-d_{FG}^2(i)] + \exp[-d_{BG}^2(i)]}. \tag{14}$$

Note that if the nodes in $\mathcal{N}(i)$ are all foreground (or background), then $p^{FG}(i)$ is defined to be 1 (or 0). Because the resolution of the dense embedding map is lower than the original video, we upsample the probability map using the multi-linear interpolation to the original resolution and further refine it with a dense conditional random field (CRF) [23].

4   Experiments

4.1   Datasets and Evaluation Metrics

The proposed method is evaluated on the DAVIS 2016 dataset [29] and the Freiburg-Berkeley Motion Segmentation 59 (FBMS-59) dataset [27]. The latter has multiple moving objects labeled separately. By following [31], [24], we convert the annotation to binary masks by grouping individual object masks.

DAVIS 2016. The DAVIS 2016 dataset [29] contains 50 densely annotated video sequences with high resolution. It is partitioned into two splits, *train* and *val*, with 30 and 20 sequences, respectively. Some videos from this dataset are challenging due to motion blur, occlusion and object deformation. The evaluation metrics include region similarity, boundary accuracy and temporal stability, proposed in [29]. The region similarity, denoted by $\mathcal{J}$, is defined as the intersection over union (IoU) between the annotation and the predicted mask. To measure the boundary accuracy, denoted by $\mathcal{F}$, the annotation boundary and the predicted mask boundary are compared and the F-score (the harmonic mean of precision and recall) is computed. The temporal stability, $\mathcal{T}$, measures the deformation needed to transform from one frame to its succeeding frame, and higher deformation means less smooth masks over time. This metric is applied to a subset of sequences in DAVIS 2016 as described in [29].

FBMS-59. 59 video sequences are collected in the FBMS-59 dataset [27]. In contrast to DAVIS, this dataset is sparsely annotated, with masks of 720 frames provided. We test the proposed method on the *test* split, containing 30 sequences. Apart from the aforementioned region IoU ($\mathcal{J}$), we also use the F-score protocol from [27] for this dataset, being consistent with previous methods.

4.2 Implementation

We train the bilateral network on the DAVIS 2016 *train* split. For each frame, the 4-D bilateral space position vector (dx, dy, x, y) of pixels is normalized within each frame and then input to the BNN. Theoretically, the learnable filters can be any 4-D tensor, but practically, to reduce the number of parameters of the network, the BNN is composed of four cascaded 1-D filters, one for each dimension. To train the BNN, we set the batch size to 64 and use a learning rate of 0.0001, with a total of $10k$ steps. Data augmentation is done by random sampling $M = 50k$ pixels in the low objectness region ($p^{\mathrm{Obj}} < 0.001$) for splatting. During inference, we pick the M pixels with the lowest objectness score. The objectness score used for the BNN is from [9] and the optical flow is computed by a re-implementation of FlowNet2.0 [15]. For embedding graph cut, we use the instance embeddings from [9], where the training is conducted on the Pascal dataset [7]. We do not further fine-tune on any video dataset. The hyperparameters are determined by cross validation: the pairwise cost weight, λ is 0.1; the variance for instance embeddings and optical flow in Eq. (12), $\sigma_e^2 = 1$ and $\sigma_m^2 = 10$. The weight of the motion similarity relative to embedding similarity, α, is set to 1.

4.3 Performance Comparison

DAVIS 2016. The results on DAVIS 2016 are displayed in Table 1. The proposed method outperforms other methods under the unsupervised scenario in terms of $\mathcal{J}$ Mean and $\mathcal{F}$ Mean, with an improvement of 1.9% and 3.0% over the second best method, IET [24]. Note that for $\mathcal{J}$ Mean, our method even achieves slightly better results than some recent semi-supervised methods, OSVOS [3] and MSK [21]. In terms of temporal stability, our method is the second best

Fig. 6. Qualitative segmentation results from DAVIS 2016 *val* split. The four sequences feature motion blur, occlusion, large object appearance change, and static objects in background, respectively

Table 1. The results on the *val* split of DAVIS 2016 dataset [29]. The proposed method outperforms other unsupervised methods in terms of $\mathcal{J}/\mathcal{F}$ Mean, and is even better than some semi-supervised methods. For the temporal stability ($\mathcal{T}$), our method is the second best. The $\mathcal{J}$ value of each sequence is provided in the supplementary material

	Semi-supervised			Unsupervised						
	OAVOS [36]	OSVOS [3]	MSK [21]	SFL [5]	LVO [32]	MP [31]	FSEG [16]	ARP [22]	IET [24]	Ours
$\mathcal{J}$ Mean ↑	**86.1**	79.8	79.7	67.4	75.9	70.0	70.7	76.2	78.6	**80.4**
$\mathcal{J}$ Recall ↑	**96.1**	93.6	93.1	81.4	89.1	85.0	83.5	91.1	-	**93.2**
$\mathcal{J}$ Decay ↓	5.2	14.9	8.9	6.2	**0.0**	1.3	1.5	7.0	-	4.8
$\mathcal{F}$ Mean ↑	84.9	80.6	75.4	66.7	72.1	65.9	65.3	70.6	76.1	**78.5**
$\mathcal{F}$ Recall ↑	89.7	**92.6**	87.1	77.1	83.4	79.2	73.8	83.5	-	**88.6**
$\mathcal{F}$ Decay ↓	5.8	15.0	9.0	5.1	**1.3**	2.5	1.8	7.9	-	4.4
$\mathcal{T}$ Mean ↓	**19.0**	37.8	21.8	28.2	**26.5**	57.2	32.8	39.3	-	27.8

in the unsupervised category: 1.3% worse than the most stable method, LVO [32]. We provide some visualized results in Fig. 6 and more can be found in the supplementary material.

FBMS-59. The proposed method is evaluated on the *test* split of the FBMS-59 dataset, which has 30 sequences. The results are listed in Table 2. Our method outperforms the second best method, IET [24], in the $\mathcal{J}$ Mean and the F-score by 2% and 0.4%, respectively. We provide visualized segmentation results for the FBMS-59 dataset in the supplementary material.

4.4   Analysis of Module Contributions

Motion-Based BNNs. A video clip can be segmented by directly thresholding the background probability $p_{\text{bnn}}^{\text{BG}}$ in Eq. (5). That is, a pixel is foreground if

$p_{\text{bnn}}^{\text{BG}} < T_{\text{bnn}}$ and we set $T_{\text{bnn}} = 0.5$. This serves as the first baseline and is denoted by "BNN". Since optical flow is error-prone, raw results from the motion-based BNN are not satisfactory, especially when there are unstable stuff regions, e.g., waves. The second baseline is obtained by adaptively thresholding $p_{\text{bnn}}^{\text{BG}}$ by the objectness score p^{Obj}. Namely, a pixel belongs to foreground if $p_{\text{bnn}}^{\text{BG}} < p^{\text{Obj}}$, which effectively eliminates false positives in unstable stuff regions. This baseline is referred as "Obj-BNN". It combines the motion and objectness signals without utilizing the instance embedding or graph cut (also equivalent to assigning label to pixels based on the unary potentials only).

Table 2. Performance comparison on the *test* split of the FBMS-59 dataset [27]

Method	NLC [8]	CUT [20]	FST [28]	CVOS [30]	LVO [32]	MP [31]	ARP [22]	IET [24]	Ours
$\mathcal{J}$ Mean	44.5	-	55.5	-	-	-	59.8	71.9	**73.9**
F-score	-	76.8	69.2	74.9	77.8	77.5	-	82.8	**83.2**

Adding objectness boosts the performance of "BNN" by 20.9%, as shown in Table 3. The motion-based BNN with objectness achieves better results than previous methods using dual-branch CNNs [5,16,32][1], in terms of $\mathcal{J}$ Mean on the *val* split of DAVIS 2016.

The Embedding Graph. The embedding graph can be constructed in multiple ways depending on how the pairwise cost is defined and how graph nodes are linked in Table 4. Without the graph cut, the results match the "Obj-BNN" baseline in Table 3. We present $\mathcal{J}$ Mean results with (77.6) and without (74.7) the CRF refinement. We then constructed the embedding graph without temporal edges. Three options for pairwise cost in Eq. (12) were tested: considering the similarity in embedding space only (row 2), the similarity in motion only (row 3), and both (row 4). We then explored adding different temporal dependencies to the full intra-frame model. We connected seeds in consecutive frames sparsely (row 5): for a seed pair from consecutive frames, we check the seed regions formed by the pixels closest to a seed. If their corresponding seed regions spatially overlap by at least one pixel, they are connected by a temporal edge. We also connected seeds in consecutive frames densely (row 6). The variants of embedding graph cut are evaluated by the $\mathcal{J}$ Mean of the final segmentation with seed labels propagated to all pixels. Best performance is observed with both embedding and motion similarities considered and dense temporal edges.

Online Processing. The capability to process videos online, where results are generated for frames within a fixed latency, is a desirable feature. Using only preceding frames[2] produces the shortest latency and is causal. To process the t-th frame online, the embedding graph is built within a frame window, using

---

[1] Note that [5] is not as comparable as [16] and [32]. Its motion branch does not take in explicitly computed optical flow but two consecutive frames instead.

[2] We allow accessing frame $(t + 1)$ for optical flow computation for frame t.

Table 3. Performance comparison between results of the motion-based BNN and other dual-branch methods on DAVIS 2016 *val* split (*without* CRF refinement)

Method	SFL [5]	LVO [32]	FSEG [16]	BNN	Obj-BNN
$\mathcal{J}$ Mean	67.4	70.1	70.7	53.8	**74.7**
$\mathcal{F}$ Mean	66.7	-	65.9	50.1	**70.9**

Table 4. Performance comparison of different pairwise costs and seed linking schemes. Motion similarity and dense temporal edges help to achieve better performance

	Similarity		Temporal edges		Metrics	
Variant	Embed.	Motion	Sparse	Dense	$\mathcal{J}$ Mean	$\mathcal{J}$ Mean (+CRF)
Obj-BNN					74.7	77.6
Similarity	✓				74.3	78.0
features for		✓			74.8	77.5
pairwise cost	✓	✓			75.7	78.9
Inter-frame	✓	✓	✓		76.2	79.8
seed linking	✓	✓		✓	77.3	80.4

Table 5. Building the embedding graph with different sets of consecutive frames for online and offline processing. Under the online scenario, we consider a temporal window of length $(W+1)$ ending at frame t. For offline processing, a window of length $(2W+1)$ centered at t is used. For label propagation, using seeds from the previous, the current and the following frames gives the optimal results. This group of variants is evaluated on DAVIS 2016 *val* set with $\mathcal{J}$ Mean (without CRF) as the metric. Causal variants (i.e., for online processing) are marked by a star ("*")

	Causal graph window				Acausal graph window		
Frames for label prop.	$W=0$	$W=1$	$W=5$	$W=10$	$W=1$	$W=5$	$W=10$
Current	75.3*	76.8*	76.9*	76.9*	77.0	76.9	76.8
+Previous	75.4*	77.0*	77.0*	77.1*	77.2	77.0	77.0
+Following	75.7	77.3	77.2	77.3	77.3	77.2	77.2

seeds from frames $(t-W)$ to t for the causal case and $(t-W)$ to $(t+W)$ for the acausal case. As shown in Table 5, building the embedding graph with only the current and previous frames does not affect the performance much. Note that $W=0$ eliminates temporal edges and gives the appropriately lower results matching Table 4. We also explore which frames are used for propagating labels from seeds to pixels in Eq. (13): in the top row, only the current frame is used to propagate labels; in the middle row, labels are propagated to pixels from seeds in the current and previous frames; in the bottom row, labels are propagated from the current, previous, and following frames. In the acausal case, we found that $W = 1$ gave the best performance, with seeds from the previous and the following frames included for label propagation.

5 Conclusions

A motion-based bilateral network (BNN) is proposed to reduce the false positives from static but semantically similar objects for the VOS problem in this paper. Based on optical flow and objectness scores, a BNN identifies regions with motion patterns similar to those of non-object regions, which help classify static objects as background. The estimated background obtained by the BNN is further integrated with instance embeddings for multi-frame reasoning. The integration is done by graph cut, and to improve its efficiency, we build a graph consisting of a set of sampled pixels called seeds. Finally, frames are segmented by propagating the label of seeds to remaining pixels. It is shown by experiments that the proposed method achieves the state-of-the-art performance in several benchmarking datasets.

References

1. Adams, A., Baek, J., Davis, M.A.: Fast high-dimensional filtering using the permutohedral lattice. In: Computer Graphics Forum, vol. 29, pp. 753–762. Wiley Online Library (2010)
2. Brox, T., Malik, J.: Large displacement optical flow: descriptor matching in variational motion estimation. IEEE Trans. Pattern Anal. Mach. Intell. **33**(3), 500–513 (2011)
3. Caelles, S., Maninis, K.K., Pont-Tuset, J., Leal-Taixé, L., Cremers, D., Van Gool, L.: One-shot video object segmentation. In: CVPR 2017. IEEE (2017)
4. Chen, L.C., Papandreou, G., Kokkinos, I., Murphy, K., L. Yuille, A.: DeepLab: semantic image segmentation with deep convolutional nets, atrous convolution, and fully connected CRFs. IEEE Trans. Pattern Anal. Mach. Intell. (2016)
5. Cheng, J., Tsai, Y.H., Wang, S., Yang, M.H.: SegFlow: joint learning for video object segmentation and optical flow. In: The IEEE International Conference on Computer Vision (ICCV) (2017)
6. De Brabandere, B., Neven, D., Van Gool, L.: Semantic instance segmentation with a discriminative loss function. In: IEEE Conference on Computer Vision and Pattern Recognition Workshop (CVPRW) (2017)
7. Everingham, M., Van Gool, L., Williams, C.K., Winn, J., Zisserman, A.: The PASCAL visual object classes (VOC) challenge. Int. J. Comput. Vis. (IJCV) **88**(2), 303–338 (2010)
8. Faktor, A., Irani, M.: Video segmentation by non-local consensus voting. In: BMVC, vol. 2, p. 8 (2014)
9. Fathi, A., et al.: Semantic instance segmentation via deep metric learning. arXiv preprint arXiv:1703.10277 (2017)
10. He, K., Gkioxari, G., Dollár, P., Girshick, R.: Mask R-CNN. In: 2017 IEEE International Conference on Computer Vision (ICCV), pp. 2980–2988. IEEE (2017)
11. He, Y., Chiu, W.C., Keuper, M., Fritz, M.: STD2P: RGBD semantic segmentation using spatio-temporal data-driven pooling. In: IEEE Conference on Computer Vision and Pattern Recognition (CVPR) (2017)

12. Heitz, G., Koller, D.: Learning spatial context: using stuff to find things. In: Forsyth, D., Torr, P., Zisserman, A. (eds.) ECCV 2008. LNCS, vol. 5302, pp. 30–43. Springer, Heidelberg (2008). https://doi.org/10.1007/978-3-540-88682-2_4

13. Huang, Q., Xia, C., Li, S., Wang, Y., Song, Y., Kuo, C.C.J.: Unsupervised clustering guided semantic segmentation. In: IEEE Winter Conference on Applications of Computer Vision (WACV) (2018)

14. Huang, Q., et al.: Semantic segmentation with reverse attention. In: British Machine Vision Conference (2017)

15. Ilg, E., Mayer, N., Saikia, T., Keuper, M., Dosovitskiy, A., Brox, T.: FlowNet 2.0: evolution of optical flow estimation with deep networks. In: IEEE Conference on Computer Vision and Pattern Recognition (CVPR), vol. 2 (2017)

16. Jain, S.D., Xiong, B., Grauman, K.: FusionSeg: learning to combine motion and appearance for fully automatic segmentation of generic objects in videos. In: Proceedings of the IEEE Conference on Computer Vision and Pattern Recognition (2017)

17. Jampani, V., Gadde, R., Gehler, P.V.: Video propagation networks. In: IEEE Conference on Computer Vision and Pattern Recognition, vol. 2 (2017)

18. Jampani, V., Kiefel, M., Gehler, P.V.: Learning sparse high dimensional filters: Image filtering, dense CRFs and bilateral neural networks. In: Proceedings of the IEEE Conference on Computer Vision and Pattern Recognition, pp. 4452–4461 (2016)

19. Jang, W.D., Kim, C.S.: Online video object segmentation via convolutional trident network. In: Proceedings of the IEEE Conference on Computer Vision and Pattern Recognition, pp. 5849–5858 (2017)

20. Keuper, M., Andres, B., Brox, T.: Motion trajectory segmentation via minimum cost multicuts. In: Proceedings of the IEEE International Conference on Computer Vision, pp. 3271–3279 (2015)

21. Khoreva, A., Perazzi, F., Benenson, R., Schiele, B., Sorkine-Hornung, A.: Learning video object segmentation from static images. In: Proceedings of the IEEE Conference on Computer Vision and Pattern Recognition (2017)

22. Koh, Y.J., Kim, C.S.: Primary object segmentation in videos based on region augmentation and reduction. In: Proceedings of the IEEE Conference on Computer Vision and Pattern Recognition (2017)

23. Krähenbühl, P., Koltun, V.: Efficient inference in fully connected CRFs with Gaussian edge potentials. In: Advances in Neural Information Processing Systems, pp. 109–117 (2011)

24. Li, S., Seybold, B., Vorobyov, A., Fathi, A., Huang, Q., Kuo, C.C.J.: Instance embedding transfer to unsupervised video object segmentation. In: Proceedings of the IEEE Conference on Computer Vision and Pattern Recognition (2018)

25. Long, J., Shelhamer, E., Darrell, T.: Fully convolutional networks for semantic segmentation. In: Proceedings of the IEEE Conference on Computer Vision and Pattern Recognition, pp. 3431–3440 (2015)

26. Märki, N., Perazzi, F., Wang, O., Sorkine-Hornung, A.: Bilateral space video segmentation. In: Proceedings of the IEEE Conference on Computer Vision and Pattern Recognition, pp. 743–751 (2016)

27. Ochs, P., Malik, J., Brox, T.: Segmentation of moving objects by long term video analysis. IEEE Trans. Pattern Anal. Mach. Intell. **36**(6), 1187–1200 (2014)

28. Papazoglou, A., Ferrari, V.: Fast object segmentation in unconstrained video. In: Proceedings of the IEEE International Conference on Computer Vision, pp. 1777–1784 (2013)

29. Perazzi, F., Pont-Tuset, J., McWilliams, B., Van Gool, L., Gross, M., Sorkine-Hornung, A.: A benchmark dataset and evaluation methodology for video object segmentation. In: Proceedings of the IEEE Conference on Computer Vision and Pattern Recognition (2016)
30. Taylor, B., Karasev, V., Soatto, S.: Causal video object segmentation from persistence of occlusions. In: Proceedings of the IEEE Conference on Computer Vision and Pattern Recognition, pp. 4268–4276 (2015)
31. Tokmakov, P., Alahari, K., Schmid, C.: Learning motion patterns in videos. In: Proceedings of the IEEE Conference on Computer Vision and Pattern Recognition (2017)
32. Tokmakov, P., Alahari, K., Schmid, C.: Learning video object segmentation with visual memory. In: Proceedings of the IEEE International Conference on Computer Vision (2017)
33. Tomasi, C., Manduchi, R.: Bilateral filtering for gray and color images. In: 1998 Sixth International Conference on Computer Vision, pp. 839–846. IEEE (1998)
34. Tsai, Y.H., Yang, M.H., Black, M.J.: Video segmentation via object flow. In: Proceedings of the IEEE Conference on Computer Vision and Pattern Recognition, pp. 3899–3908 (2016)
35. Vijayanarasimhan, S., Ricco, S., Schmid, C., Sukthankar, R., Fragkiadaki, K.: SfM-Net: learning of structure and motion from video. arXiv preprint arXiv:1704.07804 (2017)
36. Voigtlaender, P., Leibe, B.: Online adaptation of convolutional neural networks for video object segmentation. In: British Machine Vision Conference (2017)
37. Yoon, J.S., Rameau, F., Kim, J., Lee, S., Shin, S., Kweon, I.S.: Pixel-level matching for video object segmentation using convolutional neural networks. In: 2017 IEEE International Conference on Computer Vision (ICCV), pp. 2186–2195. IEEE (2017)
38. Zhao, H., Shi, J., Qi, X., Wang, X., Jia, J.: Pyramid scene parsing network. In: IEEE Conference on Computer Vision and Pattern Recognition (CVPR), pp. 2881–2890 (2017)

Monocular Depth Estimation with Affinity, Vertical Pooling, and Label Enhancement

Yukang Gan[1,2(✉)], Xiangyu Xu[1,3], Wenxiu Sun[1], and Liang Lin[1,2]

[1] SenseTime, Beijing, China
{ganyukang,xuxiangyu,sunwenxiu}@sensetime.com,linliang@ieee.org
[2] Sun Yat-sen University, Guangzhou, China
[3] Tsinghua University, Beijing, China

Abstract. Significant progress has been made in monocular depth estimation with Convolutional Neural Networks (CNNs). While absolute features, such as edges and textures, could be effectively extracted, the depth constraint of neighboring pixels, namely relative features, has been mostly ignored by recent CNN-based methods. To overcome this limitation, we explicitly model the relationships of different image locations with an affinity layer and combine absolute and relative features in an end-to-end network. In addition, we consider prior knowledge that major depth changes lie in the vertical direction, and thus, it is beneficial to capture long-range vertical features for refined depth estimation. In the proposed algorithm we introduce vertical pooling to aggregate image features vertically to improve the depth accuracy. Furthermore, since the Lidar depth ground truth is quite sparse, we enhance the depth labels by generating high-quality dense depth maps with off-the-shelf stereo matching method taking left-right image pairs as input. We also integrate multi-scale structure in our network to obtain global understanding of the image depth and exploit residual learning to help depth refinement. We demonstrate that the proposed algorithm performs favorably against state-of-the-art methods both qualitatively and quantitatively on the KITTI driving dataset.

Keywords: Monocular depth · Affinity · Vertical aggregation

1 Introduction

Depth estimation from images is a basic problem in computer vision, which has been widely applied in robotics, self-driving cars, scene understanding and 3D reconstruction. However, most works on 3D vision focus on the scenes with multiple observations, such as multiple viewpoints [22] and image sequences from videos [14], which are not always accessible in real cases. Therefore, monocular

---

Y. Gan and X. Xu—These two authors contribute equally to this study.

© Springer Nature Switzerland AG 2018
V. Ferrari et al. (Eds.): ECCV 2018, LNCS 11207, pp. 232–247, 2018.
https://doi.org/10.1007/978-3-030-01219-9_14

depth estimation has become a natural choice to overcome this problem, and substantial improvement has been made in this area with the rapid development of deep learning in recent years.

Specifically, most of the state-of-the-art methods [7,12,16] rely on Convolutional Neural Networks (CNNs) which learn a group of convolution kernels to extract local features for monocular depth estimation. The learned depth feature for each pixel is calculated within the receptive filed of the network. It is an absolute cue for depth inference which represents the appearance of the image patch centered at the pixel, such as edges and textures. While these absolute features for each image location from convolution layer are quite effective in existing algorithms, it ignores the depth constraint between neighboring pixels.

Intuitively, neighboring image locations with similar appearances should have close depth, while the ones with different appearances are more likely to have quite large depth changes. Therefore, the relationship between different pixels, namely affinities, are very important features for depth estimation which have been mostly ignored by deep learning-based monocular depth algorithms. These affinities are different with the absolute features which are directly extracted with convolution operations. They are relative features which describes the similarities between the appearances of different image locations. And explicitly considering these relative features could potentially help the depth map inference.

In fact, affinities have been widely used in image processing methods, such as bilateral filter [25] which takes the spatial distance and color intensity difference as relative feature for edge-preserving filtering. More related to our work, affinities have also been used to estimate depth in a Conditional Random Field (CRF) framework [23], where the relative depth features are modeled as the differences between the gradient histograms computed from two neighboring patches. And the aforementioned depth constraint of neighboring pixels is enforced by the pairwise potential in the CRF.

Different with these methods, we learn to extract the relative features in neural network by introducing a simple yet effective affinity layer. In this layer, we define the affinity between a pair of pixels as the correlation of their absolute features. Thus, the relative feature from the affinity layer for one pixel is a vector composed of the correlation values with its surrounding pixels. By integrating the affinity layer into CNNs, we can seamlessly combine learned absolute and relative features for depth estimation in a fully end-to-end model. Since only the relationship between nearby pixels is important for depth inference, the proposed operation is conducted within a local region. In the proposed method, we only use the affinity operation at the lowest feature scale to reduce computational load.

Except for the constraint between neighboring pixels, we also consider another important observation in depth estimation that there are more depth changes in the vertical direction than in the horizontal [3]. In other words, objects tend to get further from the bottom to the top in many images. For example, in driving scenes, a road stretching vertically ahead in the picture often gets further away from the camera. Thus, to capture the local information in the vertical

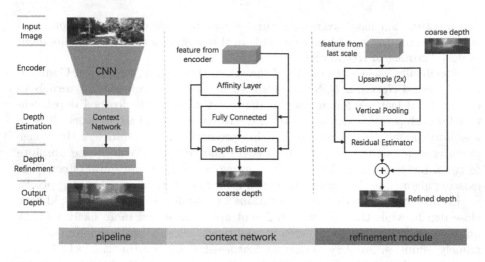

Fig. 1. An overview of the proposed network. The network is composed of a deep CNN for encoding image input, a context network for estimating coarse depth, and a multi-scale refinement module to predict more accurate depth. The context network adopts affinity and fully-connected layers to capture neighboring and global context information, respectively. The refinement module upsamples the coarse depth gradually by learning residual maps with features from previous scale and vertical pooling.

direction could potentially help refined depth estimation which motivates us to integrate vertical feature pooling in the proposed neural network.

To further improve the depth estimation results, we enhance the sparse depth ground truth from Lidar by exploiting the left-right image pairs. Different from previous methods which use photometric loss [9,16] to learn disparities which are inversely proportional to image depth, we adopt an off-the-shelf stereo matching method to predict dense depth from the image pairs and then use the predicted high-quality dense results as auxiliary labels to assist the training process.

We conduct comprehensive evaluations on the KITTI driving dataset and show that the proposed algorithm performs favorably against state-of-the-art methods both qualitatively and quantitatively. Our contributions could be summarized as follows.

- We propose a neighboring affinity layer to extract relative features for depth estimation.
- We propose to use vertical pooling to aggregate local feature to capture long-range vertical information.
- We use stereo matching network to generate high-quality depth predictions from left-right image pairs to assist the sparse Lidar depth ground truth.
- In addition, we adopt a multi-scale architecture to obtain global context and learn residual maps for better depth estimation.

2   Related Work

2.1   Supervised Depth Estimation

Supervised approaches take one single RBG image as input and use measured depth maps from RGB-D cameras or laser scanners as ground-truth for training. Saxena et al. [23] propose a learning-based approach to predict the depth map as a function of the input image. They adopt Markov Random Field (MRF) that incorporates multi-scale hand-crafted texture features to model both depths at individual points as well as the relation between depths at different points. [23] is later extended to a patch-based model known as Make3D [24] which first uses MRF to predict plane parameters of the over-segmented patches and then estimates the 3D location and orientation of these planes. We also model the relation between depths at different points. But instead of relying on hand-crafted features, we integrate a correlation operation into deep neural networks to obtain more robust and general representation.

Deep learning achieves promising results on many applications [3,12,28,29]. Many recent works [6,7,27] utilize the powerful Convolutional Neural Networks (CNN) to learn image features for monocular depth estimation. Eigen et al. [6,7] employ multi-scale deep network to predict depth from single image. They first predict a coarse global depth map based on the entire image and then refine the coarse prediction using a stacked neural network. In this paper, we also adopt multi-scale strategy to perform depth estimation. But we only predict depth map at the coarsest level and learn to predict residuals afterwards which helps refine the estimation. Li et al. [18] also use a DCNN model to learn the mapping from image patches to depth values at the super-pixel level. A hierarchical CRF is then used to refine the estimated super-pixel depth to the pixel level. Furthermore, there are several supervised approaches that adopt different techniques such as depth transfer from example images [15,21], incorporating semantic information [17,20], and formulating depth estimation as pixel-wise classification task [2].

2.2   Unsupervised Depth Estimation

Recently, several works attempt to train monocular depth prediction model in an unsupervised way which does not require ground truth depth at training time. Garg et al. [9] propose an encoder-decoder architecture which is trained for single image depth estimation on an image alignment loss. This method only requires a pair of images, source and target, at training time. To obtain the image alignment loss, the target image is warped to reconstruct the source image using the predicted depth. Godard et al. [12] extend [9] by enforcing consistency between the disparities produced relative to both the left and right images. Besides image reconstruction loss, this method also adopts appearance matching loss, disparity smooth loss and left-right consistency loss to produce more accurate disparity maps. Xie et al. [26] propose a novel approach which tries to synthesized the right view when given the left view. Instead of directly regressing disparity values, they produce probability maps for different disparity level. A selection layer is then utilized to render the right view using these probability maps and the given left view. The whole pipeline is also trained on a image reconstruction loss. Unlike the above methods that are trained using stereo images, Zhou *et al.* [30] propose to train an unsupervised learning framework on unstructured video sequences. They adopt a depth CNN and a pose CNN to estimate monocular depth and camera motion simultaneously. The nearby views are warped to the target view using the computed depth and pose to calculate the image alignment loss. Instead of using view synthesis as the supervisory signal, we employ a powerful stereo matching approach [22] to predict dense depth map from the stereo images. The predicted dense depth map, together with the sparse velodyne data, are used as ground truth during our training.

2.3   Semi-/Weakly Supervised Depth Estimation

Only few works fall in the line of research in semi- and weakly supervised training of single image depth prediction. Chen *et al.* [3] present a new approach that learns to predict depth map in unconstrained scenes using annotations of relative depth. But the annotations of relative depth only provides indirect information on continuous depth values. More recently, Kuznietsov *et al.* [16] propose to train a semi-supervise model using both sparse ground truth and unsupervised cues. They use ground truth measurement to solve the ambiguity of unsupervised cues and thus do not require coarse-to-fine image alignment loss during training.

2.4   Feature Correlations

Other works have attempted to explore correlations in feature maps in the context of classification [5,8,19]. Lin et al. [19] utilize bilinear CNNs to model local pairwise feature interactions. While the final representation of a full bilinear pooling is very high-dimensional, Gao et al. [8] reduce the feature dimensionality via two compact bilinear pooling. In order to capture higher order interactions of features, Cui et al. [5] proposed a kernel pooling scheme and combine it with CNNs. Instead of adopting bilinear models to obtain discriminative features, we propose to model feature relationships between neighboring image patches to provide more information for depth inference.

3   Method

An overview of our framework is shown in Fig. 1. The proposed network adopts an encoder-decoder architecture, where the input image is first transformed and encoded as absolute feature maps by a deep CNN feature extractor. Then a context network is used to capture both neighboring and global context information with the absolute features. Specifically, we propose an affinity layer to model relative features within a local region of each pixel. By combining the absolute and relative features with a fully-connected layer, we obtain global features which

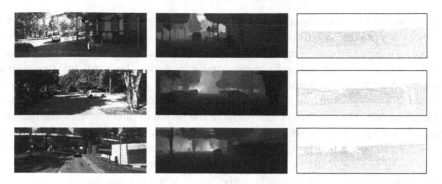

Fig. 2. Examples of the enhanced dense depth maps generated by a stereo matching model [22]. We use these depth maps as complementary data to the sparse ground truth depth maps. The left column contains RGB images, while the middle and right column show the enhanced depth maps and sparse ground truth, respectively.

indicates the global layout and properties of the image. The global features of the fully-connected layer, the absolute features from the deep encoder, and the relative features are fed into our depth estimator, a multi-layer CNN, to generate an initial coarse estimate of the image depth. In the meanwhile, we also take these features as initial input of the following multi-scale refinement modules. The refinement network at each scale is composed of a proposed vertical pooling layer which aggregates local depth information vertically, and a residual estimator which learns residual map for refining the coarse depth estimation from the last scale. Both the features from previous scale and the proposed vertical pooling layer are used in the residual estimator.

3.1 Affinity Layer

While the relationships between neighboring pixels, namely affinities, are very important cues for inferring depth, they cannot be explicitly represented in a vanilla CNN model. To overcome this limitation, we propose an affinity layer to learn these cues and combine absolute and relative features for superior depth estimation.

For concise and effective formulation, we define the affinity as the correlation between the absolute features of two image pixels. Since the absolute features represents the local appearance of image locations, such as edges and textures, the correlation operation could effectively model the appearance similarities between these pixels. Mathematically, this operation could be formulated as:

$$\mathbf{v}(\mathbf{x})_{m,n} = \mathbf{f}(\mathbf{x}) \cdot \mathbf{f}(\mathbf{x} + (m,n)]); \; m,n \in [-k,k] \tag{1}$$

where $\mathbf{v}(\mathbf{x}) \in R^{(2k+1) \times (2k+1)}$ represents the affinities of location $\mathbf{x}$ calculated in a squared local region of size $(2k+1) \times (2k+1)$. $\mathbf{f}(\mathbf{x})$ is the absolute feature vector from the convolutional feature extractor layer at location $\mathbf{x}$. In fact, we can reshape $\mathbf{v}(\mathbf{x})$ into a 1-dimensional vector of size $1 \times (2k+1)^2$, and the relative features of a input image become $(2k+1)^2$ feature maps which could be fed into the following estimation and refinement layers. Suppose the input feature map is of size $w \times h \times c$ where w, h and c are the width, height and channels, respectively. $w \times h \times c \times (2k+1)^2$ multiplications are needed for computing the relative feature which is computationally heavy. To remedy the problem of the square complexity of the affinity operation, we only perform this layer on the lowest feature scale (in the context network in Fig. 1) to reduce the computational load. The proposed affinity layer is integrated in the CNN model and works complementarily with the absolute features, which significantly helps depth estimation.

3.2 Task Specific Vertical Pooling

Depth distribution in real world scenarios has a special kind of pattern that the majority of depth changes lies in the vertical direction. *e.g.* The road often stretches to the far side alone the vertical direction. The faraway objects, such as sky and mountains, are more likely to be located at the top of a landscape picture. Recognizing this kind of patterns can provide useful information for accurate single image depth estimation. However, due to the lack of supervision and huge parameters space, normal operations in deep neural network such as convolution and pooling with squared filters may not be effective in finding such patterns. Furthermore, a relative large squared pooling layer aggregates too much unnecessary information from horizontal locations while it is more efficient to consider vertical features only.

In this paper, we propose to obtain the local context in vertical direction through vertical pooling layer. The vertical pooling layer uses average pooling with kernels of size $H \times 1$ and outputs feature maps of equal size with the input features. Multiple vertical pooling layers with different kernel heights are used in our network to handle feature maps across different scales. Specifically, we use four kernels of size 5×1, 7×1, 11×1 and 11×1 to process feature maps of scale $S/8$, $S/4$, $S/2$ and S, where S denotes the resolution of input images. More detailed analysis of vertically aggregating depth information are presented in Sect. 4.5.

3.3 Multi-scale Learning

As shown in Fig. 1, our model predicts a coarse depth map through a context network. Besides exploiting local context using operations mentioned in the preview sections, we follow [7] to take advantage of fully connected layers to integrate a global understanding of the full scene into our network. The output feature maps of the encoder and the self-correlation layer are taken as input of the fully connected layer. The output feature vector of fully connected layer is then reshaped to produce the final output feature map which is at the 1/8-resolution compared to the input image.

Given the coarse depth map, our model learns to refine the coarse depth by adopting the residual learning scheme propose by He *et al.* [13]. The refinement module first up-sample the input feature map by factor of 2. A residual estimator then learns to predict the corresponding residual signal based on the up-sampled feature, the local context feature and the long skip connected low level feature. Without the need to predict absolute depth values, the refinement module can focus on learning residual that helps produce accurate depth maps. Such learning strategy can lead to smaller network and better convergence. Several refinement modules are employed in our model to produce residuals across multiple scales. The refinement process can be formulated as:

$$d_s = UP\{d_{s+1}\} + r_s \qquad 0 \leq s \leq S \qquad (2)$$

where d_s and r_s denote depth and residual maps that are downsampled by a factor of 2^s from full resolution size. $UP\{\cdot\}$ denotes $2\times$ upsample operation. We supervise the estimated depth map across $S + 1$ scales. Ablation study in Sect. 4.5 demonstrates that incorporating residual learning can lead to more accurate depth maps compared to direct learning strategy.

3.4 Loss Function

Ground Truth Enhancement. The ground truth depth maps obtained from Lidar sensor are too sparse (only 5% pixels are valid) to provide enough supervisory signal for training a deep model. In order to produce high quality, dense depth maps, we enhance the sparse ground truth with dense depth maps predicted by a stereo matching approach [22]. We use both the dense depth maps and the sparse velodyne data as ground truth at training time. Some samples of predicted depth maps are shown in Fig. 2.

Training Loss. The enhanced dense depth maps produced by stereo matching model are not accurate enough compared to ground truth depth maps. The error between predicted and ground truth depth maps is shown in Table 1. We use a weighted sum L2 loss to suppress the noise contained in the enhanced dense depth maps:

$$Loss = \sum_{i \in \Lambda} \|pred_i - gt_i\|_2^2 + \alpha * \sum_{i \in \Omega} \|pred_i - gt_i\|_2^2 \qquad (3)$$

where $pred_i$ and gt_i denote the predicted depth and ground truth depth at i_{th} pixel. Λ denotes a collection of pixels where sparse ground truth values are valid. Ω denotes a collection of pixels where sparse ground truth values are invalid and values from enhance depth maps are used as ground truth. α is set to 0.3 in all the experiments.

4   Experiments

We show the main results in this section and present more evaluations in the supplementary material.

Table 1. Quantitative results of our method and approaches reported in the literature on the test set of the KITTI Raw dataset used by Eigen *et al.* [7] for different caps on ground-truth and/or predicted depth. Enhanced depth denotes the depth maps generated by [22]. Best results shown in bold.

Approach	Cap	ARD	SRD	RMSE	RMSE(log)	$\delta < 1.25$	$\delta < 1.25^2$	$\delta < 1.25^3$
		Lower is better				Higher is better		
Eigen *et al.* [7]	0–80 m	0.215	1.515	7.156	0.270	0.692	0.899	0.967
Liu *et al.* [21]	0–80 m	0.217	1.841	6.986	0.289	0.647	0.882	0.961
Zhou *et al.* [30]	0–80 m	0.183	1.595	6.709	0.270	0.734	0.902	0.959
Godard *et al.* [12]	0–80 m	0.114	0.898	4.935	0.206	0.861	0.949	0.976
Kuznietsov *et al.* [16]	0–80 m	0.113	0.741	4.621	0.189	0.862	0.960	**0.986**
Ours	0–80 m	**0.098**	**0.666**	**3.933**	**0.173**	**0.890**	**0.964**	0.985
Enhanced depth	0–80 m	0.025	0.075	1.723	0.049	0.994	0.998	0.999
Zhou *et al.* [30]	1–50 m	0.190	1.436	4.975	0.258	0.735	0.915	0.968
Garg *et al.* [9]	1–50 m	0.169	1.080	5.104	0.273	0.740	0.904	0.962
Godard *et al.* [12]	1–50 m	0.108	0.657	3.729	0.194	0.873	0.954	0.979
Kuznietsov *et al.* [16]	1–50 m	0.108	0.595	3.518	0.179	0.875	0.964	**0.988**
Ours	1–50 m	**0.094**	**0.552**	**3.133**	**0.165**	**0.898**	**0.967**	0.986

4.1 Dataset

We evaluate our approach on the publicly available KITTI dataset [10], which is a widely-used dataset in the field of single image depth estimation. The dataset contains over 93 thousand semi-dense depth maps with corresponding Lidar scans and RGB images. All the images in this dataset are taken from a driving car in an urban scenario, with a typical image resolution being 1242×375. In order to perform fair comparisons with existing work, we adopt the split scheme proposed by Eigen *et al.* [7] which splits the total 56 scenes from raw KITTI dataset into 28 for training and 28 for testing. Specifically, we use 22,600 images for training and the rest for validation. The evaluation is performed on the test split of 697 images. We also adopt the KITTI split provided by KITTI stereo 2015, which provides 200 high quality disparity images from 28 scenes. We use the 30,159 images from the remaining scenes as training set. While the 200 disparity images provides more depth information than the sparse, reprojected velodyne laser data, they have CAD modes inserted in place of moving cars. We evaluate our model on these high quality disparity images to obtain more convincing demonstrations.

4.2 Implementation Details

We implement our method using the publicly available TensorFlow [1] framework. The whole model is an hour-glass structure in which Resnet50 is utilized as the encoder. We trained our model from scratch for 80 epochs, with a batch size of 8 using the Adam method with $\beta_1 = 0.9, \beta_2 = 0.999$ and $\epsilon = 10^{-8}$. The learning rate is initialized as 10^{-4} and exponentially decayed by 10 every 30 epochs during training. All the parameters in our model are initialized based on xavier algorithm [11]. It costs about 7G of GPU memory and 50 h to train our model on a single NVIDIA GeForce GTX TITAN X GPU with 12 GB memory. The average training time for each image is less than 100 ms and it takes less than 70 ms to test one image.

Data augmentation is also conducted during training process. The input image is flipped with a probability of 0.5. We randomly crop the original image into size of $2h \times h$ to retain image ratio, where h is the height of the original image. The input image is obtained by resizing the cropped image to a resolution of 512×256. We also performed random brightness for color augmentation, with 50% chance, by sampling from a uniform distribution in the range of [0.5, 2.0].

4.3   Evaluation Metrics

We evaluate the performance of our approach in monocular depth prediction using the velodyne ground truth data on the test images. We follow the depth evaluation metrics used by Eigen *et al.* [7]:

ARD: $\frac{1}{|T|} \sum_{y \in T} |y - y^*|/y^*$ **RMSE:** $\sqrt{\frac{1}{|T|} \sum_{y \in T} \|y - y^*\|^2}$

SRD: $\frac{1}{|T|} \sum_{y \in T} \|y - y^*\|^2/y^*$ **RMSE(log):** $\sqrt{\frac{1}{|T|} \sum_{y \in T} \|log y - log y^*\|^2}$

Threshold: % of y_i s.t. $max(\frac{y_i}{y^*}, \frac{y^*}{y_i}) = \delta < thr$

where T denotes a collection of pixels where the ground truth values are valid. y^* denotes the ground truth value.

4.4   Comparisons with State-of-the-Art Methods

Table 1 shows the quantitative comparisons between our model and other state-of-the-art methods in monocular depth estimation. It can be observed that our method achieves best performances for all evaluation metrics at both 80 m and 50 m caps, except for the accuracy at $\delta < 1.25^3$ where we obtain comparable results with Kuznietsov *et al.* [16] at cap of 80 m (0.985 *vs* 0.986) and 50 m (0.986 *vs* 0.988). Specifically, our method reduces the RMSE metric by 20.3% compared with Godard *et al.* [12] and 14.9% compared with Kuznietsov *et al.* [16] at the cap of 80 m. Furthermore, our model obtain accuracy of 89.0% and 89.8% at $\delta < 1.25^2$ metric at the cap of 80 m and 50 m, outperforming Kuznietsov *et al.* [16] by 2.8% and 2.4% respectively.

To further evaluate the performance of our approach, we train a variant model on the training set of the official KITTI split and perform evaluation on the KITTI 2015 stereo training set which contains 200 high quality disparity images. We convert these disparity images into depth maps for evaluation using the camera parameters provided by KITTI dataset. The result is shown in Table 3. It can be observed that our method outperforms [12] by a large margin and

Table 2. Quantitative results of different variants of our method on the test set of the KITTI Raw dataset used by Eigen *et al.* [7] without capping the ground-truth. Baseline[†] denotes the baseline model that is trained using velodyne data and stereo images. Baseline[‡] denotes the baseline model that is trained using velodyne data and predicted dense depth maps. Ours[§] denotes a variant of our model which utilizes squared average pooling layers. Ours[¶] denotes a variant of our model which utilizes horizontal pooling layers. Legend: **R:** only predict depth map at the coarsest level and learn to predict residual for refinement afterwards. **A:** include affinity learning operation. **V:** use vertical pooling layer to obtain task specific context. **G:** include global context.

Method	R	A	V	G	ARD	SRD	RMSE	RMSE (log)	$\delta < 1.25$	$\delta < 1.25^2$	$\delta < 1.25^3$
					Lower is better				Higher is better		
Baseline[†]					0.120	0.757	4.734	0.202	0.856	0.953	0.972
Baseline[‡]					0.117	0.748	4.620	0.191	0.861	0.958	0.978
Ours	✓				0.115	0.740	4.514	0.189	0.865	0.958	0.980
	✓	✓			0.106	0.696	4.231	0.178	0.882	0.960	0.982
Ours[¶]	✓	✓			0.104	0.694	4.141	0.179	0.882	0.961	0.982
Ours[§]	✓	✓			0.102	0.683	4.132	0.177	0.884	0.962	0.982
Ours	✓	✓	✓		0.102	0.674	4.027	0.174	0.889	0.962	0.982
	✓	✓	✓	✓	**0.098**	**0.667**	**3.934**	**0.173**	**0.890**	**0.963**	**0.984**

Table 3. Comparisons of our method and two different approaches. Results on the KITTI 2015 stereo 200 training set images [10]. Best results shown in bold.

Approach	ARD	SRD	RMSE	RMSE(log)	$\delta < 1.25$	$\delta < 1.25^2$	$\delta < 1.25^3$
	Lower is better				Higher is better		
[12] with Deep3Ds [26]	0.151	1.312	6.344	0.239	0.781	0.931	0.976
Godard *et al.* [12]	0.097	0.896	5.093	0.176	0.879	0.962	0.986
Ours	**0.079**	**0.500**	**3.522**	**0.137**	**0.918**	**0.978**	**0.989**
Godard *et al.* [12] stereo	0.068	0.835	4.392	0.146	0.942	0.978	0.989

achieves close results with the variant model of Godard *et al.* [12] which is trained and tested with two input images.

We provide qualitative comparisons in Fig. 3 which shows that our results are visually more accurate than the compared methods. Some qualitative results on Cityscape dataset [4] and Make3D dataset [24] are shown in Fig. 5, which are estimated by our model that is trained only on KITTI dataset. The high quality results show that our model can generalize well on unseen scenes. The comparisons performed above well demonstrate the superiority of our approach in predicting accurate depth map from single images. More qualitative results on KITTI dataset are shown in Fig. 4.

4.5   Ablation Study

In this subsection, we show effectiveness and necessity of each component in our proposed model and also demonstrate the effectiveness of the network design.

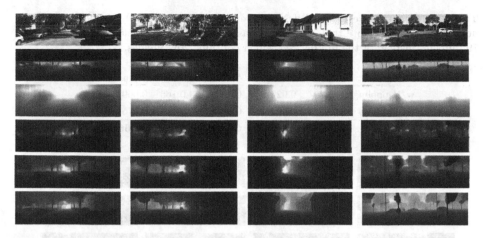

Fig. 3. Qualitative results on the test set of the KITTI Raw dataset used by Eigen *et al.* [7]. From top to bottom, the images are input, ground truth, results of Eigen *et al.* [7], results of Garg *et al.* [9], results of Godard *et al.* [12] and results of our method, respectively. Sparse ground truth have been interpolated for better visualization.

Supervisory Signal: To validate the effectiveness of using predicted dense depth maps as ground truth at training time. We compare our baseline model (denoted as Baseline‡) with a variant (denoted as Baseline†) which is trained using image alignment loss. Results are shown in the first two rows of Table 2. It can be easily observed that Baseline‡ achieves better results than Baseline† on all the metrics. This may due to the well known fact that stereo depth reconstruction based on image matching is an ill-pose problem. Training on a image alignment loss may provide inaccurate supervisory signal. On the contrary, the dense depth maps used in our method are more accurate and more robust against the ambiguity, since they are produced by a powerful stereo matching model [22] which is well designed and trained on massive data for the task of depth reconstruction. Thus, the superior result, together with the above analysis, well validate that utilizing predicted depth maps as ground truth can provide more useful supervisory signal.

Residual Learning *vs* Direct Learning: The baseline model of our approach (denoted as Baseline‡) is implemented using direct learning strategy which learns to output the depth map directly instead of the residual depth map. Note that the baseline model represents our network without any of the components R, A, V, G in Table 2. As shown in Table 2, the baseline model achieves 0.117 at ARD metric and 4.620 at RMSE metric. In order to compare residual learning strategy with direct learning strategy, we replace direct learning with residual learning in Baseline‡ and keep other settings identical to obtain a variant model with residual learning strategy. The performance of this variant model is shown in the third row of Table 2, which outperforms Baseline‡ with slight improvements on all the metrics. This may due the reason that residual learning can

Table 4. Quantitative results on NYU Depth v2 dataset(part). H-pooling denotes horizontal pooling. Note that our model was trained on the labeled training set with 795 images instead of the full dataset which contains 20K images.

Method	$\delta < 1.25$	$\delta < 1.25^2$	$\delta < 1.25^3$	rel	log_{10}	rms
w/H-pooling	0.747	0.929	0.977	0.165	0.069	0.652
w/o affinity	0.732	0.920	0.972	0.179	0.075	0.694
Ours	**0.756**	**0.934**	**0.980**	**0.158**	**0.066**	**0.631**

Fig. 4. More qualitative results on KITTI test splits.

focus on modeling the highly non-linear residuals while direct learning needs to predict absolute depth values. Moreover, residual learning also helps alleviate the problem of over-fitting [13].

Pooling Methods: To validate the idea that incorporating local context through pooling layers helps boost the performance of depth estimation, we implement three variant models that use vertical pooling layers, horizontal pooling layers (denoted as Ours¶) and squared average pooling layers (denoted as Ours§). Note that we also use multiple average pooling layers with kernels of different sizes to handle multi-scale feature maps. Specifically, we use four squared average pooling layers in Ours§ whose kernel sizes are set to $5{\times}5$, $7{\times}7$, $11{\times}11$ and 11×11 respectively. The results are shown in the middle three lines of Table 2. As one can see, by adopting squared average pooling layers, the model achieves slightly better results where SRD metric is reduced from 0.696 to 0.683 while RMSE metric is reduced from 4.231 to 4.132. The improvement demonstrates the effectiveness of exploiting local context through pooling layers. Similar improvements can be observed by integrating horizontal pooling layers. Furthermore, by replacing squared average polling layers with vertical pooling layers, our model obtains better results with more significant improvements. The further improvement proves that vertical pooling is able to model the local context more effectively compared to squared average pooling and horizontal pooling. This may due to the reason that squared average pooling combines both the depth distribution alone the horizontal and vertical direction which might introduce noise and redundant information.

Contribution of Each Component: To discover the vital elements in our proposed method, we conduct ablation study by gradually integrating each com-

Fig. 5. Qualitative results on Make3D dataset [24] (left two columns) and Cityscape dataset [4] (right two columns).

ponent into our model. The results are shown in Table 2. Besides the improvements brought by residual learning and vertical pooling modules which have been analyzed in the above comparisons, integrating affinity layer can result in major improvements on all the metrics. This proves that affinity layer is the key component of our proposed approach and thus well validate the insight that explicitly considering relative features between neighboring patches can help the monocular depth estimation. Moreover, integrating fully connected layers to exploit global context information further boosts the performance of our model. It can be seen from the last row of Table 2 that accuracy at $\delta < 1.25^3$ is further improved to 0.984. This shows that some challenge outliers can be predicted more accurately given the global context information.

We conduct more experiments to evaluate the proposed components on the NYUv2 dataset in Table 4. The Results further prove that affinity layer and vertical pooling both play an important role in improving the estimation performance, which also shows that proposed method generalizes well to the NYUv2 dataset.

5   Conclusions

In this work, we propose a novel affinity layer to model the relationship between neighboring pixels, and integrate this layer into CNN to combine absolute and relative features for depth estimation. In addition, we exploit the prior knowledge that vertical information potentially helps depth inference and develop vertical pooling to aggregate local features. Furthermore, we enhance the original sparse depth labels by using stereo matching network to generate high-quality depth predictions from left-right image pairs to assist the training process. We also adopt a multi-scale architecture with residual learning for improved depth estimation. The proposed method performs favorably against the state-of-the-art monocular depth algorithms both qualitatively and quantitatively. In future work, we will investigate more about the generalization abilities of the affinity layer and vertical pooling for indoor scenes. It will also be interesting to explore more detailed geometry relations and semantic segmentation information for more robust depth estimation.

References

1. Abadi, M., et al.: TensorFlow: a system for large-scale machine learning. In: OSDI, vol. 16, pp. 265–283 (2016)
2. Cao, Y., Wu, Z., Shen, C.: Estimating depth from monocular images as classification using deep fully convolutional residual networks. IEEE Trans. Circuits Syst. Video Technol. (2017)
3. Chen, W., Fu, Z., Yang, D., Deng, J.: Single-image depth perception in the wild. In: Advances in Neural Information Processing Systems, pp. 730–738 (2016)
4. Cordts, M., et al.: The cityscapes dataset for semantic urban scene understanding. In: Proceedings of the IEEE Conference on Computer Vision and Pattern Recognition, pp. 3213–3223 (2016)
5. Cui, Y., Zhou, F., Wang, J., Liu, X., Lin, Y., Belongie, S.J.: Kernel pooling for convolutional neural networks. In: CVPR, vol. 1, p. 7 (2017)
6. Eigen, D., Fergus, R.: Predicting depth, surface normals and semantic labels with a common multi-scale convolutional architecture. In: Proceedings of the IEEE International Conference on Computer Vision, pp. 2650–2658 (2015)
7. Eigen, D., Puhrsch, C., Fergus, R.: Depth map prediction from a single image using a multi-scale deep network. In: Advances in Neural Information Processing Systems, pp. 2366–2374 (2014)
8. Gao, Y., Beijbom, O., Zhang, N., Darrell, T.: Compact bilinear pooling. In: Proceedings of the IEEE Conference on Computer Vision and Pattern Recognition, pp. 317–326 (2016)
9. Garg, R., B.G., V.K., Carneiro, G., Reid, I.: Unsupervised CNN for single view depth estimation: geometry to the rescue. In: Leibe, B., Matas, J., Sebe, N., Welling, M. (eds.) ECCV 2016. LNCS, vol. 9912, pp. 740–756. Springer, Cham (2016). https://doi.org/10.1007/978-3-319-46484-8_45
10. Geiger, A., Lenz, P., Urtasun, R.: Are we ready for autonomous driving? The KITTI vision benchmark suite. In: 2012 IEEE Conference on Computer Vision and Pattern Recognition (CVPR), pp. 3354–3361. IEEE (2012)
11. Glorot, X., Bengio, Y.: Understanding the difficulty of training deep feedforward neural networks. In: AISTATS, vol. 9, pp. 249–256 (2010)
12. Godard, C., Mac Aodha, O., Brostow, G.J.: Unsupervised monocular depth estimation with left-right consistency. In: CVPR, vol. 2, p. 7 (2017)
13. He, K., Zhang, X., Ren, S., Sun, J.: Deep residual learning for image recognition. In: Proceedings of the IEEE Conference on Computer Vision and Pattern Recognition, pp. 770–778 (2016)
14. Karsch, K., Liu, C., Kang, S.B.: Depth extraction from video using non-parametric sampling. In: Fitzgibbon, A., Lazebnik, S., Perona, P., Sato, Y., Schmid, C. (eds.) ECCV 2012. LNCS, vol. 7576, pp. 775–788. Springer, Heidelberg (2012). https://doi.org/10.1007/978-3-642-33715-4_56
15. Konrad, J., Wang, M., Ishwar, P.: 2D-to-3D image conversion by learning depth from examples. In: 2012 IEEE Computer Society Conference on Computer Vision and Pattern Recognition Workshops (CVPRW), pp. 16–22. IEEE (2012)
16. Kuznietsov, Y., Stückler, J., Leibe, B.: Semi-supervised deep learning for monocular depth map prediction. In: Proceedings of the IEEE Conference on Computer Vision and Pattern Recognition, pp. 6647–6655 (2017)
17. Ladicky, L., Shi, J., Pollefeys, M.: Pulling things out of perspective. In: Proceedings of the IEEE Conference on Computer Vision and Pattern Recognition, pp. 89–96 (2014)

18. Li, B., Shen, C., Dai, Y., van den Hengel, A., He, M.: Depth and surface normal estimation from monocular images using regression on deep features and hierarchical CRFs. In: Proceedings of the IEEE Conference on Computer Vision and Pattern Recognition, pp. 1119–1127 (2015)

19. Lin, T.Y., RoyChowdhury, A., Maji, S.: Bilinear CNN models for fine-grained visual recognition. In: Proceedings of the IEEE International Conference on Computer Vision, pp. 1449–1457 (2015)

20. Liu, B., Gould, S., Koller, D.: Single image depth estimation from predicted semantic labels. In: 2010 IEEE Conference on Computer Vision and Pattern Recognition (CVPR), pp. 1253–1260. IEEE (2010)

21. Liu, M., Salzmann, M., He, X.: Discrete-continuous depth estimation from a single image. In: 2014 IEEE Conference on Computer Vision and Pattern Recognition (CVPR), pp. 716–723. IEEE (2014)

22. Pang, J., Sun, W., Ren, J., Yang, C., Yan, Q.: Cascade residual learning: a two-stage convolutional neural network for stereo matching. In: International Conference on Computer Vision-Workshop on Geometry Meets Deep Learning, ICCVW 2017, vol. 3 (2017)

23. Saxena, A., Chung, S.H., Ng, A.Y.: Learning depth from single monocular images. In: Advances in Neural Information Processing Systems, pp. 1161–1168 (2006)

24. Saxena, A., Sun, M., Ng, A.Y.: Make3D: learning 3D scene structure from a single still image. IEEE Trans. Pattern Anal. Mach. Intell. **31**(5), 824–840 (2009)

25. Tomasi, C., Manduchi, R.: Bilateral filtering for gray and color images. In: Sixth International Conference on Computer Vision, pp. 839–846. IEEE (1998)

26. Xie, J., Girshick, R., Farhadi, A.: Deep3D: fully automatic 2D-to-3D video conversion with deep convolutional neural networks. In: Leibe, B., Matas, J., Sebe, N., Welling, M. (eds.) ECCV 2016. LNCS, vol. 9908, pp. 842–857. Springer, Cham (2016). https://doi.org/10.1007/978-3-319-46493-0_51

27. Xu, D., Ricci, E., Ouyang, W., Wang, X., Sebe, N.: Multi-scale continuous CRFs as sequential deep networks for monocular depth estimation. In: Proceedings of CVPR, vol. 1 (2017)

28. Xu, X., Pan, J., Zhang, Y.J., Yang, M.H.: Motion blur kernel estimation via deep learning. TIP **27**, 194–205 (2018)

29. Xu, X., Sun, D., Pan, J., Zhang, Y., Pfister, H., Yang, M.H.: Learning to super-resolve blurry face and text images. In: ICCV (2017)

30. Zhou, T., Brown, M., Snavely, N., Lowe, D.G.: Unsupervised learning of depth and ego-motion from video. In: CVPR, vol. 2, p. 7 (2017)

ML-LocNet: Improving Object Localization with Multi-view Learning Network

Xiaopeng Zhang[1] , Yang Yang[2], and Jiashi Feng[1(✉)]

[1] National University of Singapore, Singapore, Singapore
{elezxi,elefjia}@nus.edu.sg
[2] University of Electronic Science and Technology of China, Chengdu, China
dlyyang@gmail.com

Abstract. This paper addresses Weakly Supervised Object Localization (WSOL) with only image-level supervision. We propose a **M**ulti-view **L**earning **Loc**alization **Net**work (ML-LocNet) by incorporating multi-view learning into a two-phase WSOL model. The multi-view learning would benefit localization due to the *complementary* relationships among the learned features from different views and the *consensus* property among the mined instances from each view. In the first phase, the representation is augmented by integrating features learned from multiple views, and in the second phase, the model performs multi-view co-training to enhance localization performance of one view with the help of instances mined from other views, which thus effectively avoids early fitting. ML-LocNet can be easily combined with existing WSOL models to further improve the localization accuracy. Its effectiveness has been proved experimentally. Notably, it achieves 68.6% CorLoc and 49.7% mAP on PASCAL VOC 2007, surpassing the state-of-the-arts by a large margin.

Keywords: Weakly supervised learning · Object localization
Multi-view learning · Object instance mining

1 Introduction

In this paper, we tackle object localization under a weakly supervised paradigm, where *only image-level labels* indicating the presence of an object are available for training. Current Weakly Supervised Object Localization (WSOL) methods [7,15,17,26] usually model the missing object locations as latent variables, and follow a two-phase learning procedure to infer the object locations. The first phase generates object candidates for latent variable initialization, and the second phase refines the candidates to optimize the localization model. Among these optimization strategies, a typical solution is to alternate between model re-training and object re-localization, which shares a similar spirit with Multiple Instance Learning (MIL) [5,17,26]. Nevertheless, such optimization is non-convex and easy to get stuck in local minima if the latent variables are not

© Springer Nature Switzerland AG 2018
V. Ferrari et al. (Eds.): ECCV 2018, LNCS 11207, pp. 248–263, 2018.
https://doi.org/10.1007/978-3-030-01219-9_15

properly initialized. As a result, they suffer limited performance, which is far below that of their fully supervised counterparts [13,20,23].

In this paper, we propose a Multi-view Learning Localization Network (ML-LocNet) by incorporating multi-view learning into a two-phase WSOL model. Our approach is motivated by the favorable properties in multi-view learning. In particular, there exist *complementary* relationships among the learned features from different views. Combining these features is beneficial to accurately describe the target regions. Besides, through co-training localization models from multiple views, different object instances would be mined, and such differences could be exploited to mitigate the over-fitting issue. In order to approach *consensus* of multi-view co-training, the detectors from multiple views would become increasingly similar as the co-training process proceeds, until the performance cannot be further improved.

Our proposed ML-LocNet is able to consistently improve the localization accuracy during each phase by exploiting the two properties of multi-view learning. To enable multi-view representation, we intentionally branch the network into several streams with different transforms, such that each stream can be treated as one view over the input. For the first phase, ML-LocNet augments the feature representation by concatenating features learned from multiple views. Benefiting from the complementary property, each view may contain knowledge that other views do not have, and combining them is beneficial to accurately describe the target regions. For the second phase, we propose a multi-view co-training algorithm which simultaneously trains multiple localization models from multiple views. The models are optimized by mining object instances on some views, and training the corresponding detectors on other views. In this way, ML-LocNet avoids overfitting the initial instances and is able to learn more general models. The two-phase learning procedure produces a powerful localization framework. On benchmark dataset PASCAL VOC 2007, we achieve 68.6% localization and 49.7% detection accuracy under weakly supervised paradigm, surpassing the-state-of-the-arts by a large margin.

It is interesting to compare our multi-view learning strategy with multi-fold MIL [5], a variant of MIL. Multi-fold MIL is reminiscent of K-fold cross validation, which proceeds by dividing the training images into K disjoint folds, and re-localize the objects in each fold images using a detector trained from images in the other folds. In this way, Multi-fold MIL avoids convergence to poor local optima. However, such cross validation method reduces the amount of effective training data, and significantly increases the complexity since we need to train K models during each iteration. As a result, it is impractical to apply multi-fold MIL to train deep networks. Instead of dividing the training data, we construct different views of the same image, which avoids overfitting the initial samples without sacrificing the amount of training data, and makes the training on deep networks tractable by sharing features over the lower layers.

Our method is also loosely related with model ensemble, a simple way to improve the performance of deep networks. Model ensemble aims at training different models on the same data and then averaging their predictions. However, making predictions using model ensemble is cumbersome and computationally expensive. Instead of training different models, we improve the performance by training models on different views. Our model can be treated as a kind of model ensemble which shares representation at the lower layers and formulates a multi-task learning by training multiple models simultaneously. In this manner, we are able to compress the knowledge in an ensemble into a single model which does not increase the complexity during training and test stages.

To sum up, we make following contributions. First, we propose an ML-LocNet model, which exploits the *complementary* and *consensus* properties of multiple views, to consistently improve the localization accuracy in WSOL. Second, ML-LocNet is independent of the backbone architecture and can be easily combined with existing WSOL models [1,15,17,26] to further improve the localization accuracy. Using the WSDDN [1] and Fast-RCNN [13] as backbone architectures, we achieve 68.6% localization CorLoc and 49.7% detection mAP on PASCAL VOC 2007 benchmark, which surpasses the state-of-the-arts by a large margin.

2   Related Work

2.1   Weakly Supervised Localization

Most related works formulate WSOL as Multiple Instance Learning (MIL) [9], in which labels are assigned to bags (a group of instances) rather than an individual instance. These methods typically alternate between learning a discriminative representation of the object and selecting the object samples in positive images based on this representation [5,21,27]. However, MIL is sensitive to initialization and easy to get stuck in a local minimum. To solve this issue, many works focus on improving the initialization. Song *et al.* [25] proposed a constrained submodular algorithm to identify an initial set of image windows and part configurations that are likely to contain the target object. Wang *et al.* [28] proposed to discover the latent objects/parts via probabilistic latent semantic analysis on the windows of positive samples. Li *et al.* [18] combined the activations of CNN with the association rule mining technique to discover representative mid-level visual patterns.

Another line of works tries to perform weakly supervised localization in an end-to-end manner. Oquab *et al.* [22] proposed a weakly supervised object localization method by explicitly searching over candidate object locations at different scales during training. Zhou *et al.* [29] leveraged a simple global average pooling to aggregate class-specific activations, which can effectively localize the discriminative parts. Zhu *et al.* [30] incorporated a soft proposal module into a CNN to guide the network to focus on the discriminative visual evidence. However, these works are all based on aggregating pixel-level confidences for image-level classification, which tend to focus on the discriminative details and fail to distinguish multiple objects from the same category. Differently, Bilen [1] *et al.* proposed a WSDDN model, which aggregates region-level scores for image-level loss and conveniently enables detection based on the region scores. Based on WSDDN model, some works exploits context information [16] and MIL refinement [26]

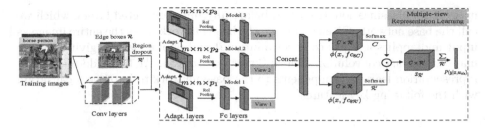

Fig. 1. Illustration of the ML-LocNet architecture during the first phase learning. The network is branched into three views with different convolutional parameters, and these views are concatenated for final feature representation

to further improve the localization. Nevertheless, these methods also cannot get out of being trapped in discriminative parts.

2.2 Multi-view Learning

Multi-view learning is a classical semi-supervised learning algorithm, which represents examples using different feature sets or different views. By taking advantage of the consensus and complementary principles of multiple view representations, learning models from multi-views will lead to an improvement in learning. Blum *et al.* [2] first proposed the multi-view learning strategy and applied it to the web document classification. Feng *et al.* [12] tackled the image annotating problem by combining multi-view co-training and active learning. Considering the complementary characteristic of different kinds of visual features, such as color and texture features, Chen *et al.* [4] introduced a co-training algorithm to conduct relevance feedback in content-based image retrieval.

3 ML-LocNet: Architecture and Training

In this section we introduce the proposed ML-LocNet with multi-view learning strategy. The model learning consists of two phases. In the first phase, we augment region representation with multi-view feature concatenation, and mine object instances with image-level supervision. In the second phase, we develop a multi-view co-training algorithm to refine the localization model with the mined instances from the first phase. In both phases, we adapt three views for implementation. The two phase procedures will be elaborated as follows.

3.1 Phase One: Multi-view Representation Learning

In the first phase, the localization network aims at mining high quality object instances with only image-level labels. As shown in Fig. 1, the model is based on a feed-forward convolutional network that aggregates region scores for computing classification loss. The early network layers are based on a pretrained network for classification, truncated before any fully connected layers, which we call the base network. Given an image, the base network takes the entire image as input and applies a sequence of convolutional and pooling layers, giving feature maps at the last convolutional block (known as *conv5*). We then add multi-view representation learning components to the base network to improve localization with the following key features:

Multi-view Features. To enable the multi-view feature representation learning, we divide the base network into three branches, with each branch representing one view. We intentionally design different convolutional parameters for different views to ensure the diversity. In particular, we add a convolutional block to each view, which we refer to as the view adaptation block, and follow the fully connected layers with different parameters. Formally, for a feature layer of size $m \times n$ with p_I channels, the view adaptation block is a $3 \times 3 \times p_I \times p_O$ small kernel which produces an output feature map with size $m \times n \times p_O$. The channel p_O is configured to be compatible with the first fully connected layer of that view. Then each view is followed by an ROI pooling layer [13] which projects region proposals $\mathcal{R}$ on the image to the feature maps and produces fixed length vectors $\phi_i(x, \mathcal{R})$, $i = 1, 2, 3$. The features among different views are weightedly combined to form the final representation $\phi(x, \mathcal{R}) = [\alpha_1 \phi_1(x, \mathcal{R}) \ \alpha_2 \phi_2(x, \mathcal{R}) \ \alpha_3 \phi_3(x, \mathcal{R})]$, where α_i ($i = 1, 2, 3$) is the weight factor that balances each view, and is automatically learned by the network.

Two-Stream Network. In the first phase learning, the only supervision is the image-level labels. We need to combine the region-level features with image-level classification. To this end, we employ the two-stream architecture of WSDDN [1], which explicitly computes image-level classification loss via aggregating region proposal scores. Formally, given an image x with region proposal $\mathcal{R}$ and image-level label $y \in \{1, -1\}^C$, where $y_c = 1$ ($y_c = -1$) indicates the presence (absence) of an object class c. The concatenated output $\phi(x, \mathcal{R})$ is branched into two data streams fc_{8C} and fc_{8R} to obtain the category specific scores. Denote the output of fc_{8C} and fc_{8R} layer as $\phi(x, fc_{8C})$ and $\phi(x, fc_{8R})$, respectively, which is of size $C \times |\mathcal{R}|$. Here, C represents the number of categories and $|\mathcal{R}|$ denotes the number of regions. The score of region r corresponding to class c is the dot product of $\phi(x, fc_{8C})$ and $\phi(x, fc_{8R})$, normalized at different dimensions:

$$x_{cr} = \frac{e^{\phi^{cr}(x, fc_{8C})}}{\sum_{i=1}^{C} e^{\phi^{ir}(x, fc_{8C})}} \cdot * \frac{e^{\phi^{cr}(x, fc_{8R})}}{\sum_{j=1}^{|\mathcal{R}|} e^{\phi^{cj}(x, fc_{8R})}}. \tag{1}$$

Thus we obtain the region score x_{cr} representing the probability of region r belonging to category c. Based on x_{cr}, the probability output y w.r.t. category c is defined as the sum of region-level scores $\phi^c(x, w_{cls}) = \sum_{j=1}^{|\mathcal{R}|} x_{cj}$, where w_{cls} denotes the non-linear mapping from input x to classification output. This network is trained by back-propagating a binary log loss, denoted as

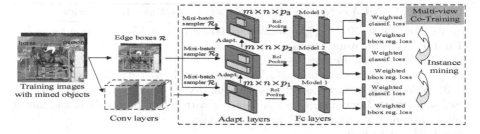

Fig. 2. Illustration of the ML-LocNet architecture during the second phase learning. Given the mined object instances, we refine the localization network via a multi-view co-training strategy. The network performs a multi-task learning procedure and is optimized via iteratively mining new object instances among views

$$L_{cls}(x, y) = \sum_{i=1}^{C} \log(y_i(\phi^i(x, w_{cls}) - 1/2) + 1/2), \qquad (2)$$

Region Dropout. The two-stream network employs a softmax operator to normalize scores of different regions (r.f. Eq. (1)), and is able to pick out the one that contains the most salient region. However, since the network is trained with classification loss, the high-score regions tend to focus on object parts instead of the whole object. As a result, the network would quickly converge to local minima due to overfitting a few region proposals. To solve this issue, we introduce a simple region dropout strategy to avoid overfitting. During forward propagation, we perform random dropout on region proposals $\mathcal{R}$, and only pass part of regions $\mathcal{R}'$ to the ROI pooling layers. The advantages of using region dropout are two-folds. First, the network is able to pick up different combinations of regions, which can be treated as some sort of data augmentation and effectively avoid network overfitting. Second, fewer regions at the fully connected layers can efficiently reduce computation and accelerate the training process.

3.2 Phase Two: Multi-view Co-training

In the first phase localization, the network is trained by image-level loss, which inevitably focuses on object parts or groups of multiple objects from the same category. To solve this issue, we introduce a multi-view instance refinement procedure, which trains the network with instance-level loss, and refines the network via a multi-view co-training strategy. The principle is that among the mined object instances, the majority of them are reliable. We hope to transfer the successful localization to those failure ones via a multi-view co-training strategy. The second phase learning is based on the fast-RCNN [13] framework, but with the following adjustments to improve the localization performance.

Initial Object Instances. The first phase learning returns a series of region scores representing their probabilities containing target objects. Since the top

---

Algorithm 1. ML-LocNet for Weakly Supervised Object Localization

---

Input: Training set $\mathcal{D} = \{x_i\}_{i=1}^N$ with image labels $Y = \{y_i\}_{i=1}^N$, iteration times K;

   First Phase Learning: Given an image x with region proposals $\mathcal{R}$:

     1) Perform *region dropout* $\mathcal{R} \rightarrow \mathcal{R}'$;

     2) Obtain *multi-view features* $\phi(x, \mathcal{R}') = [\alpha_1\phi_1(x, \mathcal{R}')\ \alpha_2\phi_2(x, \mathcal{R}')\ \alpha_3\phi_3(x, \mathcal{R}')]$;

     3) Train initial localization network with multi-view features $\phi(x, \mathcal{R}')$;

   Second Phase Learning: Given an image x with region proposals $\mathcal{R}$ and mined object instances x^o, initialize $x^{o_i} = x_o$ for each view V_i:

   for iter $k = 1$ to K **do**

     1) Perform *random mini-batch sampling* $\mathcal{R} \rightarrow \mathcal{R}_i$ for view V_i;

     2) *Training* localization model M_k with current object instances x^{o_i} for view V_i;

     3) *Relocalize* object instances for view V_i with trained model on views $\{V \setminus V_i\}$;

   end for

Output: Localization model M_K.

---

scored region easily focuses on object parts, we do not over-optimistically consider the top scored region to be accurate enough. Instead, we consider them to be accurate enough as soft voters. To be specific, given a training image containing class c, we compute its object heat map H^c, which collectively returns the confidence that pixel p lies in an object, *i.e.*, $H^c(p) = \sum_r x_{cr} D_r(p)/Z$, where $D_r(p) = 1$ when the r-th region contains pixel p, and Z is a normalization constant such that $\max H^c(p) = 1$. We binarize the heat map H^c with threshold T (set as 0.5), and choose the tightest bounding box that encloses the largest connect component as the mined object instance.

Multi-view Co-training. Due to lack of object annotations, the mined object instances inevitably include false positive samples. Current approaches [17,26] simply treat these noisy pseudo annotations as ground truths, which are suboptimal and easy to overfit the bad initial seeds. This issue is especially critical for a deep network due to its high fitting capacity. To overcome this issue, we propose a multi-view co-training strategy which aims at mining object instances on some views, while training the localization model on other view. In this way, we are able to effectively avoid overfitting the initial seeds.

The essence of the multi-view co-training module is to design multiple views and ensure the diversity of multi-view outputs. To this end, firstly we intentionally construct different views with different convolutional parameters, which is similar with the first phase learning. The difference is that instead of concatenating multi-view features to enhance representation, we independently model the outputs of each view with instance-level loss, and formulate the network training as a multi-task learning procedure. Secondly, we introduce random mini-batch sampling for each view, such that different views can see different positive and negative samples during the same forward propagation. The above two designs ensure the diversity among views not only in network structure but also in training samples, and we hope that different views are endowed with different localization capacities. For instance mining, the mean localized outputs of any two views are used for the mined object instance of the rest view during the next training. Based on the consensus principle of multiple-view co-training, the localization models from multiple views will become increasingly similar as the co-training process proceeds, until the performance cannot be further improved.

Weighted Loss. Due to the varying complexity of images, the mined object instances cannot be all reliable. It is suboptimal to treat all these instances equally important. Therefore, we penalize the network outputs with weighted loss, considering the reliability of the mined instances. Formally, let x_c^o be the relocalized object with label $y_c^o = 1$, and $\phi^c(x_c^o, w_{loc}^k)$ be the localization score returned by network M^k, where w_{loc}^k is the network parameter of M^k. The weighted classification loss w.r.t. x_c^o in the next retraining step is defined as

$$L_{cls}(x_c^o, y_c^o, M_{k+1}) = -\phi^c(x_c^o, w_{loc}^k) \log \phi^c(x_c^o, w_{loc}^{k+1}). \tag{3}$$

We employ the weighted loss on both classification and bounding box regression branches, as shown in Fig. 2. The whole algorithm of two-phase learning is summarized in Algorithm 1.

4 Experiments

We evaluate ML-LocNet for weakly supervised localization and detection, providing extensive design evaluation and making comparison with state-of-the-arts.

4.1 Experimental Setup

Datasets and Evaluation Metrics. We evaluate our approach on three widely used detection benchmarks: (1) PASCAL VOC 2007 [11], containing totally 9,963 images of 20 object classes, of which 5,011 images are included in *trainval* and the rest 4,952 in *test*; (2) PASCAL VOC 2012 [10] that is an extended version of PASCAL VOC 2007 and contains 11,540 images for *trainval* and 10,991 images for *test*; (3) Microsoft COCO 2014 [19], a large scale dataset that contains over 135k images spanning 80 categories, of which around 80k images are used for *train* and around 40k for *val*. For PASCAL VOC datasets, We choose the *trainval* split for training, and the *test* split for test, while for MS COCO, we choose the *train* split for training, and the *val* split for test. For performance evaluation, two kinds of measurements are used: (1) CorLoc [6] evaluated on the training set; (2) the VOC protocol which measures detection performance with average precision (AP) on the test set.

Models. We choose three models to evaluate our approach: (1) VGG-CNN-F [3], denoted as model **S**, meaning "small"; (2) VGG-CNN-M [3], denoted as model **M**, for "medium"; (3) VGG-VD [24] (the 16-layer model), denoted as model **L**, meaning "large". The base network is initialized from each pretrained model, truncated before any fully connected layers, while the multi-view module is initialized from the fully connected layers of three models. Our model contains three different views, which nearly triples the network parameters. For efficiency, we reduce the parameters on the fully connected $fc6$ and $fc7$ layers via a truncated SVD decomposition [13]. Specifically, each fc layer with parameters $W \in d \times 4096$ (d is the dimension of input features) is decomposed into two sub-layers fc-1 and fc-2, with weights $W_1 \in d \times 1024$ and $W_2 \in 1024 \times 4096$. We copy the parameters of the reduced fully connected layers to each view for network initialization. This leads to roughly the same amount of parameters for model **M** ($1.6\times$ for model **S**, and $0.75\times$ for model **L**).

Implementation Details. We choose edge boxes [31] to generate $|\mathcal{R}| \approx 2500$ region proposals per image on average. For VOC dataset, we choose *five-scales* with $s = \{384, 512, 640, 768, 896\}$ for training and testing, while for COCO dataset, we only use a *single scale* with $s = 640$. We denote the length of its shortest side as the scale s of an image, and cap the longest side at 1500 pixels to avoid exceeding GPU memory. In the first phase learning, we randomly drop half regions of an image during each forward propagation. The training epoch is 20, with a learning rate of 10^{-5} for the first 10 epoches and reduced to 10^{-6} for the last 10 epoches. In the second phase learning, following [13], we regard all proposals that have IoU ≥ 0.5 with the mined objects as positive, and the proposals that have IoU $\in [0.1, 0.5)$ are treated as hard negative samples. The mini-batch sampling is constructed from $N = 2$ images with a mini-batch size of $\mathcal{R}_i = 128$. The training epoch is 16, with a learning rate of 10^{-4} for the first 8 epoches and reduced by a factor of 10 for the last 8 epoches. During multi-view co-training, the iteration times K is set as $K = 3$. The mean outputs of the multi-views are used for performance evaluation.

4.2   Design Evaluation

We conduct experiments to understand how ML-LocNet works, as well as to evaluate the necessity of multi-view designs. Without loss of generality, all experiments in this section are based on VOC 2007 with model **S**.

Model Analysis. We first conduct experiments with different configurations to reveal how each component affects the performance. The localization results are shown in Table 1. From the table we make the following observations:

Multi-view Learning is Crucial. Multi-view learning is able to consistently improve the localization accuracy during both phase learning. For the first phase, multi-view feature concatenation brings up to 4.6% (52.5% → 57.1%) improvement, which demonstrates that features from multiple views are complementary and are beneficial to accurately describing image regions; For the second phase, Multi-view co-training algorithm brings another 3.7% (57.9% → 61.6%) improvement. We find that simply training fast-RCNN alike models in the second phase brings negligible gain (57.9% → 58.2%), since the network is easy

Table 1. Effects of various design choices during two phase learning

	Phase one			Phase two			
Multi-views?		✓	✓		✓	✓	✓
Region Dropout?			✓				
Random Mini-batch Sampling?						✓	✓
Weighted Loss?							✓
PASCAL VOC 2007 CorLoc (%)	52.5	57.1	**57.9**	58.2	61.6	62.8	**63.7**

to focus on the initial seeds. By introducing multi-view co-training mechanism, instances are mined from some views but used for training for other view, thus the network can effectively avoid overfitting.

Region Dropout Makes the Model Training Faster and Better. Region dropout improves accuracy by 0.8% (57.1% → 57.9%), since it selects different regions of an image for classification loss, and can be treated as data augmentation. Another advantage is that the training is faster due to a reduced number of region proposals feeded to the fully connected layers.

Random Mini-Batch Sampling is Helpful. Introducing random mini-batch sampling helps improve the localization accuracy, with a gain of 1.2% (61.6% → 62.8%). This is achieved by increasing the diversity among views, such that different views can exchange localization knowledge to boost the model.

Weighted Loss Helps. Introducing weighted loss brings about another 0.9% performance gain. This demonstrates that considering the confidence of the mined object instances is able to avoid focusing on the less reliable instances and help boost the performance.

Why Using Different Multi-view Learning Strategies in Two Phases?
In our two phase learning, the multi-view strategy is implemented in two different ways. One question is that why bother to train models with different strategies, and is it possible to simply choose the same one, *i.e.,* training both networks with multiple losses as in Fig. 2? We tried this setting, and trained the network in Fig. 1 with losses from multiple views, but the localization performance is limited, with only 54.6%, 3.3% lower than the concatenation method. The possible reason is that the losses from multiple views are hard to optimize with only image-level supervision, since the object instances are mined implicitly from the intermediate layers. Instead, enhancing feature representation is an effective method and is relatively easier to be optimized.

Does Performance Improvement Come from Multi-view Learning?
The essence of ML-LocNet is to design multiple views and introduce several modules to ensure the view diversity. It is in doubt that does the performance improvement really come from the diversity of multiple views, or is it the

Fig. 3. Localization visualization on VOC 2007 *trainval* split. The top row shows localizations before (red) and after (green) multi-view co-training. The bottom row shows the localizations of multiple views during training (Color figure online)

increased parameters (the model is 1.6× larger with multi-view design) that help? To validate this issue, we initialize different views with the same parameters (fully connected layers of model **S**), and without conducting model compression. As a result, the network is nearly 2× larger than ML-LocNet. Then we replace ML-LocNet with the above designed network during each phase learning, respectively. For the first phase, the localization performance drops from 57.9% to 56.2%, while for the second phase, it drops rapidly, from 63.7% to 58.9%. The results demonstrate that the multi-view mechanism is especially important for the second phase learning. As an illustration, Fig. 3 shows the localization results before and after the second phase learning (top row), together with the intermediate localization of multiple views (bottom row). It can be seen that multi-view co-training is effective to refine the localization by exchanging knowledge from the diversified views.

4.3   Results and Comparisons

PASCAL VOC 2007. This is a widely used dataset for weakly supervised localization and detection, and we conduct detailed comparisons on this dataset.

CorLoc Evaluation. Table 2 shows the localization results on PASCAL VOC 2007 *trainval* split in terms of CorLoc [6]. Our method achieves an accuracy of 63.7% with model **S**, which is 8.1% better than previous best result [8] (55.6%) using the same model, and even outperforms the-state-of-the-art [26] (60.6%) that using deeper model. Replacing with model **L**, we achieve a CorLoc of 67.0%, 6.4% better than the best-performing result. Finally, using the mean outputs of three models, we train another model based on model **L**, which we refer to as ML-LocNet-**L**+. We obtain an accuracy of 68.6%, which is 4.3% higher than [26] (64.3%) using the same training strategy. Note that ML-LocNet-**L**+ is based on the outputs of a single model, which is different from model ensemble that combines the outputs of multiple models during test stages. Another advantage is that our best results are based on a reduced fully connected layers, and the network scale is only 0.75× as the original model **L** used in previous works.

Table 2. Localization precision (%) comparisons on PASCAL VOC 2007 *trainval* split

method	aer	bik	brd	boa	btl	bus	car	cat	cha	cow	tbl	dog	hrs	mbk	prs	plt	shp	sfa	trn	tv	mAP
WSDDN[1]	65.1	58.8	58.5	33.1	39.8	68.3	60.2	59.6	34.8	64.5	30.5	43.0	56.8	82.4	25.5	41.6	61.5	55.9	65.9	63.7	53.5
ODGA-S[8]	83.5	70.9	65.4	42.4	39.0	63.9	80.8	58.6	30.2	69.5	24.8	51.0	66.2	78.4	25.2	48.7	66.6	26.7	63.3	55.9	55.6
DSD[15]	72.7	55.3	53.0	27.8	35.2	68.6	81.9	60.7	11.6	71.6	29.7	54.0	64.3	88.2	22.2	53.7	72.2	52.6	68.9	75.5	56.1
ConLocNet[7]	83.9	72.8	64.5	44.1	40.1	65.7	82.5	58.9	33.7	72.5	25.6	53.7	67.4	77.4	26.8	49.1	68.1	27.9	64.5	55.7	56.7
ODGA[8]	85.5	75.0	66.9	47.5	43.6	67.4	83.6	61.7	36.8	75.1	29.8	55.9	70.4	80.6	29.0	52.9	71.0	31.2	66.9	58.1	59.4
OICR[26]	81.7	80.4	48.7	49.5	32.8	81.7	85.4	40.1	40.6	79.5	35.7	33.7	60.5	88.8	21.8	57.9	76.3	59.9	75.3	81.4	60.6
ML-LocNet-S	76.9	78.2	65.8	39.8	45.9	78.0	85.1	57.0	16.9	70.9	68.5	56.5	77.0	90.6	47.4	52.2	65.6	60.7	75.5	65.2	63.7
ML-LocNet-M	78.0	78.5	66.2	43.2	51.5	76.5	86.8	65.7	34.9	69.5	59.7	55.1	79.5	88.1	40.3	58.3	71.5	64.0	77.0	61.6	65.3
ML-LocNet-L	78.6	82.3	68.2	42.0	53.3	78.5	88.5	70.3	36.4	70.2	60.5	58.0	80.5	88.2	38.8	59.2	75.0	69.0	78.2	64.5	**67.0**
OICR-L+[26]	81.7	80.4	48.7	49.5	32.8	81.7	85.4	40.1	40.6	79.5	35.7	33.7	60.5	88.8	21.8	57.9	76.3	59.9	75.3	81.4	64.3
ML-LocNet-L+	81.7	82.9	68.7	44.4	53.9	80.3	88.9	70.5	32.6	74.0	62.7	61.7	81.4	91.6	46.0	60.6	75.2	69.2	78.7	65.8	**68.6**

Table 3. Detection precision (%) comparisons on PASCAL VOC 2007 *test* split

method	aer	bik	brd	boa	btl	bus	car	cat	cha	cow	tbl	dog	hrs	mbk	prs	plt	shp	sfa	trn	tv	mAP
WSDDN[1]	39.4	50.1	31.5	16.3	12.6	64.5	42.8	42.6	10.1	35.7	24.9	38.2	34.4	55.6	9.4	14.7	30.2	40.7	54.7	46.9	34.8
ConLocNet[7]	57.1	52.0	31.5	7.6	11.5	55.0	53.1	34.1	1.7	33.1	49.2	42.0	47.3	56.6	15.3	12.8	24.8	48.9	44.4	47.8	36.3
ODGA-S [8]	45.7	58.1	37.2	24.8	19	64.8	53.7	35.2	9.7	44.8	22.6	33.7	50.4	57.8	15.9	21.7	40.8	48.2	55.4	45.8	39.3
OICR[26]	58.0	62.4	31.1	19.4	13.0	65.1	62.2	28.4	24.8	44.7	30.6	25.3	37.8	65.5	15.7	24.1	41.7	46.9	64.3	62.6	41.2
DSD[15]	52.2	47.1	35.0	26.7	15.4	61.3	66.0	54.3	3.0	53.6	24.7	43.6	48.4	65.8	6.6	18.8	51.9	43.6	53.6	62.4	41.7
ODGA[8]	50.9	61.2	40.5	31.4	21.1	71.6	58.1	42.9	11.7	46.4	30.7	44.5	48.3	64.9	16.8	24.8	47.1	55.7	61.7	55.8	44.3
ML-LocNet-S	57.0	64.0	42.6	22.1	17.9	59.3	64.0	39.5	2.2	47.6	55.0	38.9	66.4	68.1	30.6	23.5	43.2	44.1	55.4	46.3	44.4
ML-LocNet-M	57.2	64.6	44.5	26.3	21.1	65.7	67.1	56.4	16.1	51.7	50.5	37.2	64.2	69.4	24.5	25.4	51.9	51.3	56.9	42.2	47.2
ML-LocNet-L	59.3	68.9	45.7	29.0	24.5	64.8	68.4	59.3	18.6	49.1	50.2	43.1	65.8	70.2	19.9	24.3	48.1	54.2	62.8	41.8	**48.4**
OICR-L+[26]	65.5	67.2	47.2	21.6	22.1	68.0	68.5	35.9	5.7	63.1	49.5	30.3	64.7	66.1	13.0	25.6	50.0	57.1	60.2	59.0	47.0
ML-LocNet-L+	60.8	70.6	47.8	30.2	24.8	64.9	68.4	57.9	11.0	51.3	55.5	48.1	68.7	69.5	28.3	25.2	51.3	56.5	60.0	43.1	**49.7**
Fast-RCNN[13]	74.5	78.3	69.2	53.2	36.6	77.3	78.2	82.0	40.7	72.7	67.9	79.6	79.2	73.0	69.0	30.1	65.4	70.2	75.8	65.8	66.9

Table 4. Localization precision (%) comparisons on PASCAL VOC 2012 *trainval* split

method	aer	bik	brd	boa	btl	bus	car	cat	cha	cow	tbl	dog	hrs	mbk	prs	plt	shp	sfa	trn	tv	mAP
ConLocNet[7]	78.3	70.8	52.5	34.7	36.6	80.0	58.7	38.6	27.7	71.2	32.3	48.7	76.2	77.4	16.0	48.4	69.9	47.5	66.9	62.9	54.8
DSD[15]	82.4	68.1	54.5	38.9	35.9	84.7	73.1	64.8	17.1	78.3	22.5	57.0	70.8	86.6	18.7	49.7	80.7	45.3	70.1	77.3	58.8
OICR[26]	86.2	84.2	68.7	55.4	46.5	82.8	74.9	32.2	46.7	82.8	42.9	41.0	68.1	89.6	9.2	53.9	81.0	52.9	59.5	83.2	62.1
ML-LocNet-L	87.0	84.8	69.8	47.1	58.9	88.8	77.0	47.3	41.7	79.9	30.3	62.1	83.2	91.4	33.5	63.6	76.9	60.4	72.6	70.3	**66.3**
OICR-L+[26]	89.3	86.3	75.2	57.9	53.5	84.0	79.5	35.2	47.2	87.4	43.4	43.8	77.0	91.0	10.4	60.7	86.8	55.7	62.0	84.7	65.6
ML-LocNet-L+	88.1	85.5	71.2	49.4	57.4	90.7	77.6	53.5	42.6	79.6	34.1	69.1	81.7	91.9	35.4	64.6	79.3	64.3	79.3	69.6	**68.2**

Table 5. Detection precision (%) comparisons on PASCAL VOC 2012 *test* split

method	aer	bik	brd	boa	btl	bus	car	cat	cha	cow	tbl	dog	hrs	mbk	prs	plt	shp	sfa	trn	tv	mAP
ConLocNet[7]	64.0	54.9	36.4	8.1	12.6	53.1	40.5	28.4	6.6	35.3	34.4	49.1	42.6	62.4	19.8	15.2	27.0	33.1	33.0	50.0	35.3
DSD[15]	60.8	54.2	34.1	14.9	13.1	54.3	53.4	58.6	3.7	53.1	8.3	43.4	49.8	69.2	4.1	17.5	43.8	25.6	55.0	50.1	38.3
OICR[26]	67.7	61.2	41.5	25.6	22.2	54.6	49.7	25.4	19.9	47.0	18.1	26.0	38.9	67.7	2.0	22.6	41.1	34.3	37.9	55.3	37.9
ML-LocNet-L	68.1	63.3	43.7	19.9	26.5	61.1	53.0	36.7	14.8	45.8	11.9	46.1	58.4	73.4	16.8	26.9	42.5	35.3	54.5	45.4	**42.2**
OICR-L+[26]	71.4	69.4	55.1	29.8	28.1	55.0	57.9	24.4	17.2	59.1	21.8	26.6	57.8	71.3	1.0	23.1	52.7	37.5	33.5	56.6	42.5
ML-LocNet-L+	53.9	60.4	40.4	23.3	18.7	58.7	63.3	52.5	13.3	49.1	46.8	33.5	61.0	65.8	21.3	22.9	46.8	48.1	52.6	40.4	**43.6**

AP Evaluation. Table 3 shows the detection performance on VOC 2007 *test* split. Just using model **S**, our method achieves an accuracy of 44.4%, 5.1% higher than the best-performing method [8] (39.3%) using model **S**. When switching to model **L**, the detection accuracy increases to 48.4%, which is about 4.1% better than the best-performing result [8] (44.3%). Using the mean localization outputs for model initialization, we obtain a detection accuracy as high as 49.7%, and is

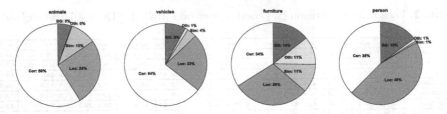

Fig. 4. Detection error analysis [14] of ML-LocNet on VOC 2007 *test* split. The detections are categorized as correct (Cor), false positive due to poor localization (Loc), confusion with similar categories (Sim), with others (Oth), and with background (BG)

Fig. 5. Example detections on PASCAL VOC 2007 (top row) and MS COCO 2014 (bottom row). The successful detections (IoU ≥ 0.5) are marked with green bounding boxes, and the failed ones are marked with red. We show all detections with scores ≥0.7 and use nms to remove duplicate detections (Color figure online)

2.7% better than [26] (47.0%) using the same training mechanism. This is a promising result considering the challenge of this task.

Error Analysis. To analysis the detection performance of our model in more details, we use the analysis tool from [14] to diagnose the detector errors. Figure 4 shows the error analysis on VOC 2007 *test* split with model **L+** (49.7% mAP). The classes are categorized into four categories, *animals*, *vehicles*, *furniture*, and *person*. Our method achieves promising results on categories *animals* and *vehicles*, but it does not work well on detecting *furniture* and *person*. This is mainly because *furniture* are usually in cluttered scenes, thus very hard to pick out for model training, and the error distribution is scattered. While for *person*, the majority of errors come from inaccurate localization (blue regions). As an illustration, we show some detection results in Fig. 5. The correct detections are marked with green bounding boxes, while the failed ones are marked with red. Our detectors are able to successfully detect objects in images with relatively simple background, and is fine for vehicles even in complex images. However, detections are easy to fail in complex scenes for other categories, and are often focus on object parts, or grouping multiple objects from the same class.

Comparing with Fully Supervised Fast-RCNN. It is interesting to compare our weakly supervised detections with the fast-RCNN [13] method, which makes use of ground truth bounding boxes for training. As shown in Table 3, the perfor-

Table 6. Localization and detection precision comparisons on MS COCO 2014

Methods	CorLoc(%)	mAP (%)
WSDDN [1]	26.1	11.5
WCCN [7]	-	12.3
ODGA [8]	-	12.8
ML-LocNet-S	**34.7**	**16.2**

mance of ML-LocNet is around 17% lower than fast-RCNN. However, for vehicles such as *bicycle* and *motorbike*, the performance approaches the fully supervised one (70.6% vs 78.3% for *bicycle* and 70.2% vs 73.0% for *motorbike*). This implies that it is possible to train corresponding detection models on these classes without requiring object annotations. However, for classes such as *chair* and *person*, the performance gap is still large. It remains a further research direction to correctly localize these objects for detection model training.

PASCAL VOC 2012. We choose the same settings as in VOC 2007 experiments, and evaluate the performance on VOC 2012. Tables 4 and 5 show the localization and detection results, respectively. We see the same performance trend as we observed on VOC 2007. For localization, ML-LocNet achieves an accuracy of 66.3% with model **L**, 4.2% point better than previous best result [26] (62.1%). The accuracy improves to 68.2% with ML-LocNet-**L+** model. For detection, the result is 42.2% with model **L**, 3.9% more accurate than [15] (38.3%). The result can be further improved to 43.6% with ML-LocNet-**L+** model.

MS COCO 2014. To further validate the ML-LocNet model, we evaluate the performance on a much larger dataset MS COCO 2014. Comparing with PASCAL VOC 2012, MS COCO is more challenging: it includes more images (135k vs 22k), more categories (80 vs 20), more complex scenes (7.7 instances per image vs 2.3 instances per image, in average), and more images with smaller objects. As far as we know, few works have reported results on MS COCO under weakly supervised paradigm. Table 6 shows the localization and detection results with model **S**. On this challenging dataset, we obtain 34.7% localization accuracy, improving the baseline WSDDN [1] by 8.6%. For detection, the result is 16.2%, which is 3.4% better than [8] (12.8%). Figure 5 shows some detection results on this dataset. Although objects are usually within more complex scenes, our model is still able to successfully detect rigid objects such as *book* and *refrigerator*.

5 Conclusions

This paper proposed a multi-view learning strategy to improve the localization accuracy in WSOL. Our method incorporates multi-view learning into a two-phase WSOL model, and is able to consistently improve the localization for both phases. In the first phase, we augment feature representation by concatenating features learned from multiple views, which is effective in describing image regions. In the second phase, we develop a multi-view co-training algorithm to refine the localization models. The models are optimized by iteratively mining new object instances among different views, thus effectually avoiding overfitting the initial seeds. Our method can be easily combined with other techniques to further improve the performance. Experiments conducted on PASCAL VOC and MS COCO benchmarks demonstrate the effectiveness of the proposed approach.

Acknowledgements. The work was supported in part to Jiashi Feng by NUS IDS R-263-000-C67-646, ECRA R-263-000-C87-133 and MOE Tier-II R-263-000-D17-112, in part to Yang Yang by NSFC under Project 61572108.

References

1. Bilen, H., Vedaldi, A.: Weakly supervised deep detection networks. In: CVPR, pp. 2846–2854 (2016)
2. Blum, A., Mitchell, T.: Combining labeled and unlabeled data with co-training. In: Computational Learning Theory, pp. 92–100. ACM (1998)
3. Chatfield, K., Simonyan, K., Vedaldi, A., Zisserman, A.: Return of the devil in the details: delving deep into convolutional nets. In: BMVC (2014)
4. Cheng, J., Wang, K.: Active learning for image retrieval with Co-SVM. Pattern Recogn. **40**(1), 330–334 (2007)
5. Cinbis, R.G., Verbeek, J., Schmid, C.: Multi-fold mil training for weakly supervised object localization. In: CVPR, pp. 2409–2416 (2014)
6. Deselaers, T., Alexe, B., Ferrari, V.: Weakly supervised localization and learning with generic knowledge. IJCV **100**(3), 275–293 (2012)
7. Diba, A., Sharma, V., Pazandeh, A., Pirsiavash, H., Van Gool, L.: Weakly supervised cascaded convolutional networks. In: CVPR, pp. 914–922 (2017)
8. Diba, A., Sharma, V., Stiefelhagen, R., Van Gool, L.: Object discovery by generative adversarial & ranking networks. arXiv preprint arXiv:1711.08174 (2017)
9. Dietterich, T.G., Lathrop, R.H., Lozano-Pérez, T.: Solving the multiple instance problem with axis-parallel rectangles. Artifi. Intell. **89**(1), 31–71 (1997)
10. Everingham, M., Eslami, S.A., Van Gool, L., Williams, C.K., Winn, J., Zisserman, A.: The PASCAL visual object classes challenge: a retrospective. IJCV **111**(1), 98–136 (2015)
11. Everingham, M., Van Gool, L., Williams, C.K., Winn, J., Zisserman, A.: The pascal visual object classes (VOC) challenge. IJCV **88**(2), 303–338 (2010)
12. Feng, H., Shi, R., Chua, T.S.: A bootstrapping framework for annotating and retrieving www images. In: ACM Multimedia, pp. 960–967. ACM (2004)
13. Girshick, R.: Fast R-CNN. In: ICCV, pp. 1440–1448 (2015)
14. Hoiem, D., Chodpathumwan, Y., Dai, Q.: Diagnosing error in object detectors. In: Fitzgibbon, A., Lazebnik, S., Perona, P., Sato, Y., Schmid, C. (eds.) ECCV 2012. LNCS, vol. 7574, pp. 340–353. Springer, Heidelberg (2012). https://doi.org/10.1007/978-3-642-33712-3_25
15. Jie, Z., Wei, Y., Jin, X., Feng, J., Liu, W.: Deep self-taught learning for weakly supervised object localization. In: CVPR (2017)

16. Kantorov, V., Oquab, M., Cho, M., Laptev, I.: ContextLocNet: context-aware deep network models for weakly supervised localization. In: Leibe, B., Matas, J., Sebe, N., Welling, M. (eds.) ECCV 2016. LNCS, vol. 9909, pp. 350–365. Springer, Cham (2016). https://doi.org/10.1007/978-3-319-46454-1_22

17. Li, D., Huang, J.B., Li, Y., Wang, S., Yang, M.H.: Weakly supervised object localization with progressive domain adaptation. In: CVPR, pp. 3512–3520 (2016)

18. Li, Y., Liu, L., Shen, C., Van Den Hengel, A.: Mining mid-level visual patterns with deep CNN activations. IJCV **121**(3), 344–364 (2017)

19. Lin, T.-Y., et al.: Microsoft COCO: common objects in context. In: Fleet, D., Pajdla, T., Schiele, B., Tuytelaars, T. (eds.) ECCV 2014. LNCS, vol. 8693, pp. 740–755. Springer, Cham (2014). https://doi.org/10.1007/978-3-319-10602-1_48

20. Liu, W., et al.: SSD: single shot multibox detector. In: Leibe, B., Matas, J., Sebe, N., Welling, M. (eds.) ECCV 2016. LNCS, vol. 9905, pp. 21–37. Springer, Cham (2016). https://doi.org/10.1007/978-3-319-46448-0_2

21. Nguyen, M.H., Torresani, L., de la Torre, F., Rother, C.: Weakly supervised discriminative localization and classification: a joint learning process. In: Proceedings of International Conference on Computer Vision, pp. 1925–1932 (2009)

22. Oquab, M., Bottou, L., Laptev, I., Sivic, J.: Is object localization for free? - weakly-supervised learning with convolutional neural networks. In: CVPR, pp. 685–694 (2015)

23. Redmon, J., Divvala, S., Girshick, R., Farhadi, A.: You only look once: unified, real-time object detection. In: CVPR, pp. 779–788 (2016)

24. Simonyan, K., Zisserman, A.: Very deep convolutional networks for large-scale image recognition. CoRR abs/1409.1556 (2014)

25. Song, H.O., Lee, Y.J., Jegelka, S., Darrell, T.: Weakly-supervised discovery of visual pattern configurations. In: NIPS, pp. 1637–1645 (2014)

26. Tang, P., Wang, X., Bai, X., Liu, W.: Multiple instance detection network with online instance classifier refinement. In: CVPR, July 2017

27. Vijayanarasimhan, S., Grauman, K.: Keywords to visual categories: multiple-instance learning for weakly supervised object categorization. In: CVPR, pp. 1–8. IEEE (2008)

28. Wang, C., Ren, W., Huang, K., Tan, T.: Weakly supervised object localization with latent category learning. In: Fleet, D., Pajdla, T., Schiele, B., Tuytelaars, T. (eds.) ECCV 2014. LNCS, vol. 8694, pp. 431–445. Springer, Cham (2014). https://doi.org/10.1007/978-3-319-10599-4_28

29. Zhou, B., Khosla, A., Lapedriza, A., Oliva, A., Torralba, A.: Learning deep features for discriminative localization. In: CVPR, pp. 2921–2929. IEEE (2016)

30. Zhu, Y., Zhou, Y., Ye, Q., Qiu, Q., Jiao, J.: Soft proposal networks for weakly supervised object localization. arXiv preprint arXiv:1709.01829 (2017)

31. Zitnick, C.L., Dollár, P.: Edge boxes: locating object proposals from edges. In: Fleet, D., Pajdla, T., Schiele, B., Tuytelaars, T. (eds.) ECCV 2014. LNCS, vol. 8693, pp. 391–405. Springer, Cham (2014). https://doi.org/10.1007/978-3-319-10602-1_26

Diagnosing Error in Temporal Action Detectors

Humam Alwassel[✉], Fabian Caba Heilbron, Victor Escorcia,
and Bernard Ghanem

King Abdullah University of Science and Technology (KAUST),
Thuwal, Saudi Arabia
{humam.alwassel,fabian.caba,victor.escorcia,
bernard.ghanem}@kaust.edu.sa,
http://www.humamalwassel.com/publication/detad/

Abstract. Despite the recent progress in video understanding and the continuous rate of improvement in temporal action localization throughout the years, it is still unclear how far (or close?) we are to solving the problem. To this end, we introduce a new diagnostic tool to analyze the performance of temporal action detectors in videos and compare different methods beyond a single scalar metric. We exemplify the use of our tool by analyzing the performance of the top rewarded entries in the latest ActivityNet action localization challenge. Our analysis shows that the most impactful areas to work on are: strategies to better handle temporal context around the instances, improving the robustness w.r.t. the instance absolute and relative size, and strategies to reduce the localization errors. Moreover, our experimental analysis finds the lack of agreement among annotator is not a major roadblock to attain progress in the field. Our diagnostic tool is publicly available to keep fueling the minds of other researchers with additional insights about their algorithms.

Keywords: Temporal action detection · Error analysis
Diagnosis tool · Action localization

1 Introduction

We are in the *Renaissance* period of video understanding. Encouraged by the advances in the image domain through representation learning [14,17,23], large scale datasets have emerged over the last couple of years to challenge existing ideas and enrich our understanding of visual streams [4,15,16,19,21,22,28,37].

The first three authors contributed equally to this work. Authors ordering was determined using Python's random.shuffle() seeded with the authors' birthday dates.

Electronic supplementary material The online version of this chapter (https://doi.org/10.1007/978-3-030-01219-9_16) contains supplementary material, which is available to authorized users.

V. Ferrari et al. (Eds.): ECCV 2018, LNCS 11207, pp. 264–280, 2018.
https://doi.org/10.1007/978-3-030-01219-9_16

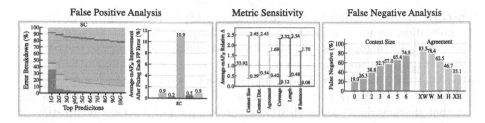

Fig. 1. Illustration of the three types of analyses that our diagnostic tool provides for action localization algorithms. Left: We analyze the false positive error sources and their impact on the performance. Middle: We investigate the localization metric sensitivity to different characteristics of the ground truth instances. Right: We inspect the influence of ground truth instance characteristics on the miss detection rate.

Recent work has already shown novel algorithms [41] and disproved misconceptions associated with underrated 3D representations for video data [7]. However, we are still awaiting the breakthrough that allows us to temporally localize the occurrence of actions in long untrimmed videos [13, 19]. In this paper, we propose to step back and analyze the recent progress on the temporal action localization as a means to fuel the next generation with the right directions to pursue.

Currently, researchers have appealing intuitions to tackle video action localization problem [1, 10, 34, 45], they are equipped with large datasets to validate their hypothesis [4, 5, 19], and they have access to appropriate computational power. Undoubtedly, these aspects helped materialize an increasing performance throughout the years [3, 13, 45]. Yet, such improvements are not enough to describe the whole picture. For example, we are still not able to answer the following questions: How close are we to achieve our goal of delimiting the start and end of actions? What makes an algorithm more effective than another? What makes an action hard to localize? Is the uncertainty of the temporal boundaries impeding the development of new algorithms? Inspired by similar studies in other areas [18, 30, 36, 44], we take a deep look at the problem beyond a single scalar metric and perform a quantitative analysis that: (i) informs us about the kind of errors a given algorithm makes, and measures the impact of fixing them; (ii) describes which action characteristics impact the performance of a given algorithm the most; and (iii) gives insights into the action characteristics a proposed solution struggles to retrieve. Figure 1 shows a brief glimpse of our diagnostic analysis applied to a state-of-the-art method on ActivityNet version 1.3 [4, 26].

Relation to Existing Studies. The seminal work of Hoiem *et al.* showcased the relevance of diagnosing the failure modes of object detectors in still images [18]. Inspired by this work, [11, 19, 27, 30–32, 36, 44] provided insightful analysis of algorithms for multiple localization tasks such as human pose estimation, object detection at large-scale and multi-label action classification, in still images in most of the cases. In contrast with them, our work contributes to the understanding of temporal action localization in untrimmed videos.

Object Detection and Human Pose Estimation. [18] pioneered the categorization of localization errors as a mean to get more insights about the performance of object detection algorithms. [30,44] extended the diagnostic tools to the context of human pose estimation showing the relevance of this approach to quantitatively identify the failure modes and to recommend ways to improve existing algorithms for body parts localization. In a similar spirit, our work is the first that characterizes the localization errors for temporal action localization in videos.

Multi-label Action Classification. Sigurdsson *et al.* [36] provides an insightful diagnosis of algorithms and relevant directions needed for understanding actions in videos. [36] studies the influence of different attributes, such as verbs, objects, human poses, and the interactions between actions in the scope of video action recognition. Most of the study is centered around action classification at the frame level or the entire video and is carried on relatively short streams of 30 seconds on average. Our work contributes with an orthogonal perspective to this study, performing an in-depth analysis of the problem of delimiting temporal boundaries for actions in long videos.

Contributions. Our contributions in this paper are threefold. (i) We collect additional annotation data for action context and temporal agreement in ActivityNet. We use the collected data to categorize the ground truth instances into six action characteristics: context size, context distance, agreement, coverage, length, and the number of instances (Sect. 3). (ii) We investigate and classify the most relevant error types to temporal action localization (Sect. 4). (iii) We provide a complete analysis tool (annotations, software, and techniques) that facilitates detailed and insightful investigation of action detectors performance. We exemplify the use and capabilities of our diagnosis tool on the top four action detectors in the recent ActivityNet 2017 challenge (Sects. 5–7).

2   Preliminaries

Evaluation Framework. We use the ActivityNet dataset v1.3 [4] as a test bed for our diagnostic analysis of the progress in temporal action localization in videos. The choice of this dataset obeys multiple reasons, (i) it is a large scale dataset of 20K videos with an average length of four minutes; (ii) it consists of a diverse set of human actions ranging from household activities, such as *washing dishes*, to sports activities, like *beach volleyball*. This allow us to make conclusions about a diverse type of actions; (iii) it is an active non-saturated benchmark with a held-out test set and an additional validation set, ensuring good machine learning practices and limiting over-fitting risk; (iv) it provides an open-source evaluation framework and runs an annual competition, which safeguards good progress on the community. Additionally, we extend our analysis to the widely used THUMOS14 dataset [20] in the *supplementary material.* In this way, we cover the most relevant benchmarks used to dictate the progress in this area.

The action localization problem measures the trade-off that an algorithm consistently retrieves the occurrence of true action instances, from different classes,

Table 1. Localization performance as measured by average-mAP and average-mAP$_N$ on ActivityNet [4]. We show the two metrics for all predictions and for the top-10G predictions, where G is the number of ground truth instances. Using average-mAP$_N$ gives slightly higher values. Notably, limiting the number of predictions to the top-10G gives performance values similar to those when considering all predictions.

Method	Average-mAP (%)		Average-mAP$_N$ (%)	
	All	top-10G	All	top-10G
SC	33.42	32.99	33.92	33.45
CES	31.87	31.83	32.24	32.20
IC	31.84	31.70	32.14	32.00
BU	16.75	16.52	17.26	17.02

without increasing the numbers of spurious predictions. This task is evaluated by measuring the precision and recall of the algorithms. The metric used to trade-off precision and recall for retrieving the segments of a particular action is the Average Precision (AP), which corresponds to an interpolated area under the precision-recall curve [11]. To evaluate the contribution of multiple action classes, the AP is computed independently for each category and averaged to form the mean AP (mAP). Given the continuous nature of the problem, a prediction segment is considered a true positive if its temporal Intersection over Union (tIoU) with a ground truth segment meets a given threshold. To account for the varied diversity of action duration, the public evaluation framework employs the average-mAP, which is the mean of all mAP values computed with tIoU thresholds between 0.5 and 0.95 (inclusive) with a step size of 0.05.

To establish a middle ground between multiple algorithms that is robust to variations of ratio between true and false positives across multiple classes, we employ the normalized mean AP [18]. In this way, we can compare the average-mAP between uneven subsets of ground truth instances, *e.g.* when the number of instances of a given category doubles the number of instances of another category for a given detection rate. We compute the normalized mAP (mAP$_N$) in terms of the normalized precision $P_N(c) = \frac{R(c) \cdot N}{R(c) \cdot N + F(c)}$, where c is the confidence level, $R(c)$ is the recall of positive samples with confidence at least c, $F(c)$ is the false positive rate for predictions with confidence at least c, and N is a constant number. We report average-mAP$_N$ as the action localization metric, and set N to the average number of ground truth segments per class.

Algorithms. We exemplify the use of our diagnostic tool by studying the four rewarded approaches in the latest action localization task in the ActivityNet challenge [13] (Table 1 summarizes the methods' performances). Interestingly, all the methods tackled the problem in a two-stage fashion, using a proposal method [2,6,9,12,34] followed by a classification scheme [38–40]. However, there are subtle design differences which are relevant to highlight.

SC [26]. It was the winner of the latest action localization challenge with a margin of 2% average-mAP. The key ingredient for its success relies on improving the action proposals stage. To this end, this work re-formulates the fully convolutional action detection network SSAD [25] as a class-agnostic detector. The detector generates a dense grid of segments with multiple durations, but only those near the occurrence of an instance receive a high score. In addition to the multi-scale proposal network, this work refines proposals' boundaries based on the outputs of the TAG grouping approach [42]. Finally, the classification stage is performed at the video level independently of the proposal stage results.

CES [13,45]. This work achieved the runner-up entry in the challenge [13], and held the state-of-the-art approach on THUMOS14 at that time. It employs a temporal grouping heuristic for generating actions proposals [42] from dense actioness predictions. The proposals are classified and refined in a subsequent stage by the SSN network [45]. Most of its effort involves enhancing the SSN network to a diverse set of actions. SSN applies a temporal pyramid pooling around the region spanned by a proposal segment, and then it classifies the segment by balancing the information inside the segment and the context information around it. This work found consistent improvement in the validation set through the use of deeper architecture and fine tuning on the larger Kinetics dataset [22].

IC [13]. This approach ranks third by employing a similar strategy to the CES submission. Its main distinction relies on using a sliding window-based proposal scheme as well as employing human pose estimation to influence the classification decisions of the SSN network [45].

BU [43]. It was awarded the challenge most innovative solution. This work extended the Faster RCNN architecture [29] to the problem of temporal action localization. It designed a temporal proposal network coupled with a multi-layer fully connected network for action classification and boundary refinement. In comparison with the top-ranked submissions that exploit optical flow or human pose estimation, this work relies solely on RGB streams to learn a temporal representation via 3D convolutions pretrained on Sports-1M dataset [21].

3   Dataset Characterization

Our first goal is to describe datasets with inherent characteristics such as coverage, length, and the number of instances. Moreover, we are interested in augmenting the dataset with two additional characteristics, temporal context and temporal boundary agreement, which we argue are critical for understanding the current status of action localization. Let's play some games to motivate our selection (Jump to Fig. 2). The first game, *guess-the-action*, consists of watching a series of frames to guess what action happens next. The second game, *let-us-agree*, asks you to pick the instant when a given action ends. We invite you to play the game and check your answers afterwards in the footnote[1]. We relate

---

[1] (1) The action that happens is *Bungee Jumping*. (2) There is not a unanimous answer for this game. 67% of our lab colleagues picked frame B as the correct answer.

the first game with whether an action instance has temporal context or not. If an action instance is in temporal context, the player should be able to exploit semantic information such as objects, scenes, or motions to guess what action happens either before or after. The second game explores how humans agree on defining temporal boundaries of an action instance. Surprisingly, this toy example reveals that defining an action's temporal boundaries is hard. Intrigued, we decided two conduct two formal online user studies with the aim of quantifying the amount of temporal context and temporal boundaries agreement for temporal action localization. In this section, we first present the online user studies that allow us to augment ActivityNet v1.3 with the temporal context and temporal boundaries agreement attributes. Then, we provide a detailed definition of each action characteristics studied in this work.

 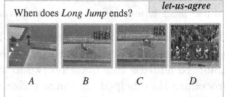

Fig. 2. Left: *guess-the-action* game. In this game you have to guess what action (one out of three options) could happen in the context of the depicted video clip. Right: *let-us-agree* game. Here, the goal is to pick the frame that best represents when the action *Long Jump* ends. To check your answers read the footnote 1.

3.1 Online User Studies

User Study I: Temporal Context of Actions. Our goal is to quantify the amount of temporal context around an action instance. To that end, we conduct an online user study that resembles the *guess-the-action* game described earlier. We choose Amazon Mechanical Turk as a test bed to hold the user study. Each participant's task is to watch a 5-second video clip and pick, from a given list, all the human actions that they believe could happen in the context of the video clip. We revisit our definition of temporal context, which describes that an action instance is in temporal context if semantic information *around* the instance helps a person to guess the action class of such instance. Thus, we investigate the temporal context of an instance by sampling six non-overlapping 5-second clips around the action's temporal boundaries. We present each user with three different candidate classes, one of the options is the correct action class, and the other two options are either similar or dissimilar class to the ground truth class. Following the findings of [3], we use objects and scene information to form sets of similar and dissimilar actions. Given that multiple selections are allowed, we consider an answer as correct if the participant chooses the correct action only, or if they pick the correct action and the option that is similar to it. If a temporal segment allows the participant to guess the action, we call that segment a *context glimpse*.

Our study involved 53 Amazon Mechanical Turk workers (Turkers), who spent a median time of 21 seconds to complete a single task. In total, we submitted a total of 30K tasks to cover the existing instances of ActivityNet. Interestingly, Turkers were able to correctly guess the action in 90.8% of the tasks. While that result can be interpreted as a signal of dataset bias towards action-centric videos, it also suggests that action localization methods would require temporal reasoning to provide accurate predictions in such scenario. For instance, most probably you used information about scene (bridge, river) and objects (elastic cord, helmet) to predict the *Bungee Jumping* answering when playing *guess-the-action*. However, such high-level information did not help you to provide the ending time of *Long Jump* in the *let-us-agree* game. In short, for each ActivityNet temporal instance, we conducted 6 temporal context experiments, which we use later when defining action characteristics.

User Study II: Finding Temporal Boundaries of Actions. After playing *let-us-agree*, the question naturally arises, can we precisely localize actions in time? To address this question, we followed [36] and designed an instance-wise procedure that helped us characterize the level of human agreement achieved after annotating temporal bounds of a given action.

We relied on 168 Turkers to *re-annotate* temporal boundaries of actions from ActivityNet. The median time to complete the task was three minutes. The task consisted in defining the boundaries of an already spotted action. Additionally, we asked the participants to annotate each temporal boundary *individually*. For each action instance, we collected three new annotations from different Turkers. We measure agreement as the median of the pairwise tIoU between all the four annotations (the original annotation and the three newly collected ones). As a result, Turkers exhibited an agreement score of 64.1% over the whole dataset. The obtained results suggests that it is hard to agree, even for humans, about the temporal boundaries of actions, which matches with previously reported conclusions [36]. In summary, we collected three additional annotations for each action instance from ActivityNet, enabling future discussions about the effect of ambiguous boundaries on action detectors.

3.2 Definitions of Action Characteristics

We annotate each instance of the ActivityNet v1.3 dataset with six different characteristics: context size, context distance, agreement, coverage, length, and number of instances. Here, we define these characteristic and discuss their distribution (Fig. 3).

Context Size. We use the collected data from User Study I to characterize the amount of temporal context around an instance. We define context size as the number of *context glimpses* associated with an instance. Thus, values of context size range from 0 to 6. Interestingly, we find that only 6.9% of instances do

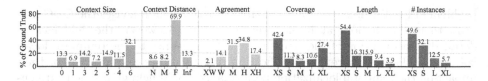

Fig. 3. Distribution of instance per action characteristic. We report the percentage of ground truth instances belonging to each characteristic bucket.

not have temporal context. Additionally, many instances have large temporal context, *e.g.* 58.4% of instances have more than 3 context glimpses.

Context Distance. We use the results from User Study I to characterize the furthest distance away from the instance where a *context glimpse* exists. We define four types of context distance: Inf, which indicates that no temporal context exists; Far (F); Middle (M); Near (N). Notably, We see that most instances (69.9%) have *context glimpses* far away.

Agreement. Our goal is to characterize an instance based on how difficult it is to agree on its temporal boundaries. To this end, we exploit the data collected from User Study II. We measure agreement as the median tIoU between all annotation pairs for an instance. We form five groups based on agreement score (median tIoU): Extra Weak (XW: $(0, 0.2]$), Weak (W: $(0.2, 0.4])$), Mid (M: $(0.4, 0.6]$), High (H: $(0.6, 0.8]$), and Extra High (XH: $(0.8, 1.0]$). We discover that a relatively small number of instances have extremely weak agreement (2.1%). On the other hand, most of the dataset (83.8% of instances) exhibit at least Mid agreement.

Coverage. To measure coverage, we normalize the length of the instance by the duration of the video. We categorize coverage values into five buckets: Extra Small (XS: $(0, 0.2]$), Small (S: $(0.2, 0.4]$), Medium (M: $(0.4, 0.6]$), Large (L: $(0.6, 0.8]$), and Extra Large (XL: $(0.8, 1.0]$). Interestingly, Extra Small and Extra Large instances compose most of the dataset with 42.4% and 27.4% of instances assigned to each bucket, respectively.

Length. We measure length as the instance duration in seconds. We create five different length groups: Extra Small (XS: $(0, 30]$), Small (S: $(30, 60]$), Medium (M: $(60, 120]$), Long (L: $(120, 180]$), and Extra Long (XL: > 180). We find that more than half (54.4%) of the instances are small. We also observe that the instance count gradually decrease with length size.

Number of Instances (# Instances). We assign each instance the total count of instances (from the same class) in its video. We create four categories for this characteristic: Extra Small (XS: 1); Small (S: $[2, 4]$); Medium (M: $[5, 8]$); Large (L: > 8). We find half of the dataset contains a single instance per video.

4 Categorization of Temporal Localization Errors

When designing new methods, researchers in the field often identify an error source current algorithms fail to fully address. For example, [33] identifies the problem of localization errors at high tIoU thresholds and devises the CDC network to predict actions at frame-level granularity. However, the field lacks a detailed categorization of the errors of specific relevance to the temporal localization problem. A thorough classification of error types and analysis of their impact on the temporal localization performance would help guide the next generation of localization algorithms to focus on the most significant errors. To this end, we propose in this section a taxonomy of the errors relevant to action localization, and we analyze the impact of these errors in Sects. 5 and 7.

Let $\mathcal{G}$ be the set of ground truth instances such that an instance $g^{(k)} = (g_l^{(k)}, g_t^{(k)})$ consists of a label $g_l^{(k)}$ and temporal bounds $g_t^{(k)}$. Let $\mathcal{P}$ be the set of prediction segments such that a prediction $p^{(i)} = (p_s^{(i)}, p_l^{(i)}, p_t^{(i)})$ consists of a score $p_s^{(i)}$, a label $p_l^{(i)}$, and a temporal extent $p_t^{(i)}$. A prediction $p^{(i)}$ is a **True Positive (TP)** if and only if $\exists g^{(k)} \in \mathcal{G}$ such that $p^{(i)}$ is the highest scoring prediction with $tIoU(g_t^{(k)}, p_t^{(i)}) \geq \alpha$ and $p_l^{(i)} = g_l^{(k)}$, where α is the tIoU threshold. Otherwise, the prediction is a **False Positive (FP)**. Suppose that $p^{(i)}$ is an FP prediction and $g^{(k)}$ is the ground truth instance with the highest tIoU with $p^{(i)}$. We classify this FP prediction into five categories (see Fig. 4).

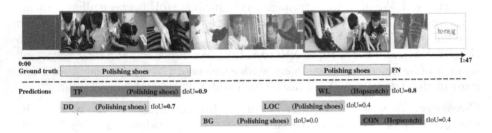

Fig. 4. Illustration of the most relevant action localization errors (Sect. 4). Predictions with bold tIoU values meet the tIoU threshold (0.55 in this example). The left action instance is correctly matched, while the right instance is miss detected (false negative). Each prediction shows a case that exhibit one of the error types we categorize.

Double Detection Error (DD). A prediction that satisfies the tIoU threshold with a ground truth instance with the correct label, however, the ground truth instance is already matched with another prediction of a higher score. We identify this error due to the nature of the ActivityNet evaluation framework, which measures performance at high tIoU thresholds and penalizes double detections.

$$tIoU(g_t^{(k)}, p_t^{(i)}) \geq \alpha, \ g_l^{(k)} = p_l^{(i)}; \exists p^{(j)} \in \mathcal{P}, tIoU(g_t^{(k)}, p_t^{(j)}) \geq \alpha, \ p_s^{(j)} \geq p_s^{(i)} \quad (1)$$

Wrong Label Error (WL). A prediction that meets the tIoU threshold but incorrectly predicts the label of the ground truth instance. The source of this error is often a weakness in the action classification module.

$$tIoU(g_t^{(k)}, p_t^{(i)}) \geq \alpha \text{ and } g_l^{(k)} \neq p_l^{(i)} \quad (2)$$

Localization Error (LOC). A prediction with the correct label that has a minimum 0.1 tIoU and fails to meet the α tIoU threshold with the ground truth instance. The source of this error is typically a weakness in the localization module and/or the temporal feature representation.

$$0.1 \leq tIoU(g_t^{(k)}, p_t^{(i)}) < \alpha \text{ and } g_l^{(k)} = p_l^{(i)} \tag{3}$$

Confusion Error (CON). A prediction of the wrong label that has a minimum 0.1 tIoU but does not meet the α tIoU threshold with the ground truth instance. This error is due to a combination of the same error sources in WL and LOC.

$$0.1 \leq tIoU(g_t^{(k)}, p_t^{(i)}) < \alpha \text{ and } g_l^{(k)} \neq p_l^{(i)} \tag{4}$$

Background Error (BG). A prediction that does not meet a minimum 0.1 tIoU with any ground truth instance. This error could arise in large percentages due to a weakness in the prediction scoring scheme.

$$tIoU(g_t^{(k)}, p_t^{(i)}) < 0.1 \tag{5}$$

Another error source of relevance to our analysis is the miss detection of ground truth instances, *i.e.* **False Negative (FN)**. In Sect. 7, we analyze why some type of instances are typically miss detected by current algorithms.

5   False Positive Analysis

In this section, we take the four state-of-the-art methods (SC, CES, IC, and BU) as an example to showcase our FP analysis procedure. First, we introduce the concept of a *False Positive Profile*, the mechanism we employ to dissect a method's FP errors. Then, we present insights gathered from the methods' FP profiles. Finally, we investigate each error type's impact on the average-mAP$_N$.

False Positive Profile. The computation of average-mAP$_N$ relies inherently on the ranking of predictions. Thus, it is important to take the prediction score into account when analyzing FP errors. Thus, we execute our analysis on the error profile of the top-10G predictions, where G is the number of ground truth instances. We pick the top predictions in a per-class manner, *i.e.* we select the top-10G_j predictions form class j, where G_j is the number of instances in class j. Moreover, to see the trend of each error type, we split the top-10G predictions into ten equal splits and investigate the breakdown of the five FP error types (defined in Sect. 4) in each split. The collection of these error breakdowns allow us to model the error rate of each type as a function of the prediction score. This intuitively allows us to examine the behaviors of the different detector components such as the classifier and scoring function.

We choose to focus on the top-10G predictions instead of all predictions for the following four reasons: (i) 10G is sufficiently large to show trends in error types; (ii) Current state-of-the-art methods exhibit an extremely low normalized

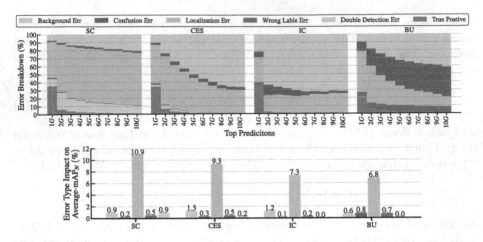

Fig. 5. Top: The false positive profiles of the four methods. Each profile demonstrates the FP error breakdown in the top-10G predictions. Bottom: The impact of error types on the average-mAP$_N$, *i.e.* the improvement gained from removing all predictions that cause each type of error. The *Localization Error* (pink bar) has the most impact. (Color figure online)

precision ($<0.05P_N$) beyond this large number of predictions. An error analysis at such low precision point is not insightful as predictions' quality degrades and the background errors dominate; (iii) The average-mAP$_N$ for the top-10G is very close to the performance of all predictions (Table 1); and (iv) It is easier to compare the FP profiles of multiple methods on the same number of predictions.

What can FP Profiles Tell Us? Figure 5 (Top) shows the four methods' FP profiles. The top-G predictions in all methods contain the majority of TP. SC is the best in terms of background error rate, while IC is the worst since the majority of its predictions beyond the top-G are background errors. This indicates a shortcoming in IC's scoring scheme. On the other hand, SC has a relatively high double detection error rate. We attribute this to the fact that SC is purely a proposal method (*i.e.* it is optimized for a high recall) combined with a video-level classifier that is independent of the proposal generation. However, this double detection rate can be fixed by applying a stricter *non-maximum-suppression* (NMS). Notably, errors due to incorrect labels (*i.e.* wrong label and confusion errors) are relatively small for the top three methods. This signals the strength of these methods' classifiers. At the same time, we can see a high wrong label and confusion errors for BU, indicating a weakness in BU's classifier.

FP Categories Impact on the Average-mAP$_N$. The insights we get from the FP profile help us to identify problems in algorithms, however, they do not tell us which problem we should prioritize fixing. In order to address this, we quantify the impact of an error type by measuring the average-mAP$_N$ after fixing that error, *i.e.* we calculate the metric after removing all predictions causing the given error type. Figure 5 (Bottom) shows the impact of the five errors on the performance of the four methods. Fixing localization errors gives a significant boost to average-mAP$_N$, while fixing other error types provides limited improvements. This is a compelling evidence that localization error is the most significant error to tackle and that the research field should focus on addressing this error in order to advance detection algorithms.

6 Average-mAP$_N$ Sensitivity

Typically, researchers design localization algorithms to tackle certain action characteristics. For example, multiple works have tried to capture the temporal context along the video [8,12,24,35,45] as a proxy for the localization of the actions. Indeed, the recent SSN architecture, presented in this study as CES, is the latest successful work in this school of thought. In this case, the architecture not only describes each segment proposal, as typically done by template based methods, but it also represents the adjacent segments around to influence the instances localization. Although, these ideas are well motivated, it is unclear if changes in performance with respect to a single metric actually corresponds to representative changes on instances with the characteristics of interest. In that sense, another important component in the diagnosis of localization algorithms is the analysis of AP variation with respect to the actions characteristics.

Figure 6 (Left) shows CES's performance variations over all the action characteristics described in Sect. 3. Each bar represents the performance after dropping all the instances that do not exhibit a particular characteristic, and the dash bar represents the performance of the method over all the instances in the dataset. In contrast with the analysis of FP profiles (Sect. 5), all four methods exhibit similar variation trends across multiple action characteristics. Refer to the *supplementary material* for the other methods' sensitivity figures.

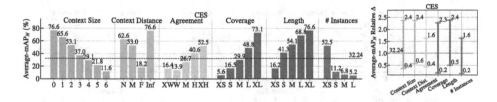

Fig. 6. Left: The detailed sensitivity CES's average-mAP$_N$ to action characteristics. The dashed line is the overall performance. Each bar measures the average-mAP$_N$ on a subset of ActivityNet for which a particular action characteristic holds. Right: The sensitivity profile summarizing the left figure. The difference between the max and min average-mAP$_N$ represents the sensitivity, while the difference between the max and the overall average-mAP$_N$ denotes the impact of the characteristic.

Among the interesting patterns to highlight, we find instances where humans tend to agree more on the starting and end of the action translates to gains in performance (H-XH agreement in the figure), while the opposite behavior shows a drop in performance. This correlation is a bit surprising considering that the models are not trained with multiple annotations per instance. Unfortunately, we do not find any concluding evidence to explain this interesting correlation besides the nature of the instances or the bias of the dataset. Similarly, instances where an action occurs naturally surrounded by enough temporal evidence that reinforces its presence are associated with drops in performance (context size of 5–6 in the figure). We argue that this is due to the presence of similar actions around the instances which creates a confusion and impedes precise boundaries positioning around the instance. In terms of coverage and instance length, the results are intuitive and easy to interpret. Short instances, either absolute in time or in relationship to the video length, tend to be more difficult to detect. This could be a consequence of the coarse temporal structure used by the algorithms to accumulate temporal evidence across the video.

Figure 6 (Right) summarizes, in a sensitivity profile, the variations in CES's average-mAP_N for each characteristic group, as well as the potential impact of improving the robustness. According to our study, all the methods exhibit a similar trend, they are more sensitive to variations in the temporal context, coverage, and length compared to variations in the agreement and number of instances. Based on experiments with ideal classifiers, [36] hypothesizes the temporal agreement between annotators is not a major roadblock for action localization. Interestingly, our diagnostic analysis shows the first experimental evidence corroborating this hypothesis. Considering the small positive and negative impacts of these instances, efforts to improve in this area must be validated carefully such that improvements do not come from more common and easier cases. Our analysis also justifies researchers' focus on designing algorithms that exploit temporal context for localization. Three out of the four models studied here would benefit the most by improving the contextual reasoning along the temporal scale.

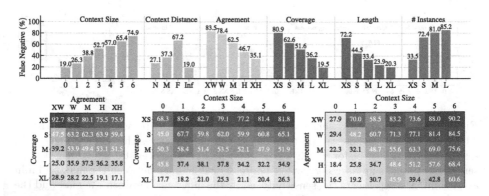

Fig. 7. Average false negative rate across algorithms for each characteristic (Top) and three pairs of characteristics (Bottom). We observe characteristics such as XS coverage and XW agreement are hard to detect individually and when paired with others. Differently, instances with XL coverage and XH agreement are relatively easy.

7   False Negative Analysis

So far, we have only considered the types of FP errors introduced by the detections algorithms, and the characteristics of the actions that introduce more variations in the performance. On the other hand, it is insightful to study what makes an action instance difficult to detect, even at minuscule confidence threshold. Towards this end, we compute the percentage of missed detections instances for each algorithm and group them according to the action characteristics defined in Sect. 3. For this purpose, we consider that an action instance is miss detected if we do not find a matching detection at a precision level higher than $0.05P_N$. Figure 7 (Top) summarizes our findings. In the interest of saving space, we average the results across multiple algorithms (refer to the *supplementary material* for the results of each algorithm by itself). The first observation that we can grasp from the results is its inverse relationship with the sensitivity profiles shown in Fig. 6. For example, the drops in performance we observed for instances with extremely weak agreement, low coverage, short length, or high temporal context size match the evidence that the algorithms struggle to retrieve such instances. On the other hand, we can appreciate that algorithms are struggling to find multiple instances per videos. Note how the amount of missed detections increase more than double due to the presence of another instance in the video. This is definitely an area where methods should focus on to mitigate the negative impact in performance. For context distance, the pattern is intuitive given that the increase in cumulative size of the *context glimpses* correlates with the spread of context and confusion in time. Thus, the chance of delimiting the start and end of the instance get worse.

Finally, we also find some interesting patterns in the FN rate at the intersection between two groups of characteristics. Figure 7 (Bottom) compactly summarizes those in a similar fashion. It is interesting how particular pairwise combinations such as low coverage (XS) - large context size (6), extremely weak agreement (XW) - large context size (6), and low coverage (XS) - extremely weak agreement (XW) are very difficult to detect, even when some are well represented in the dataset. Similarly, we find pairs involving high agreement (XH), small context (0), and high coverage (XL) relatively easy to detect. Finally, we find some interesting contours in the pairwise interactions, *e.g.* the percentage of FN diffuses in the matrix of agreement v.s. context size as we move from the top right corner to the bottom left in a non-smooth way.

8   Discussion and Conclusion

We introduced a novel diagnostic tool for temporal action localization and demoed its application by analyzing four approaches in the latest ActivityNet action localization challenge. We showed how our proposed methodology helps detection methods not only to identify their primary sources of FP errors but also to reason about their miss detections. We provided a detailed categorization of FP errors, which is tailored for action localization specifically. Using this categorization, we later defined our proposed *False Positive Profile* analysis. We found that the FP profile varies across methods. Some of the techniques exhibited shortcomings in their scoring function, while others showed weaknesses in their action classifier. We also investigated the impact of each error type, finding that *all* detectors are strongly hurt by localization errors. We conducted an extensive dataset characterization, which empowered us with a deeper understanding of what makes an action instance harder to localize. We introduced and collected six new action characteristics for the ActivityNet dataset, namely, context size, context distance, agreement, coverage, length, and the number of instances. We measured methods' sensitivities to these action characteristics. We observed all methods are very sensitive to temporal context. Also, we showed that temporal agreement between annotators is not a significant barrier towards improving action localization. For future work, we plan to explore new metrics for action localization that incorporate the inherent ambiguity of temporal action boundaries. In our *supplementary material*, we present a preliminary study that exploits the newly collected temporal annotations to ease the strict performance computation current evaluation frameworks use. With the release of our diagnostic tool, we aim to empower the temporal action localization community with a more in-depth understanding of their methods' failure modes. Most importantly, we hope that our work inspires the development of innovative models that tackle the current flaws of contemporary action localization approaches.

Acknowledgments. This publication is based upon work supported by the King Abdullah University of Science and Technology (KAUST) Office of Sponsored Research (OSR) under Award No. OSR-CRG2017-3405.

References

1. Alwassel, H., Caba Heilbron, F., Ghanem, B.: Action search: spotting actions in videos and its application to temporal action localization. In: Ferrari, V. (ed.) ECCV 2018, Part IX. LNCS, vol. 11213, pp. 253–269. Springer, Cham (2018). https://doi.org/10.1007/978-3-030-01240-3_16
2. Buch, S., Escorcia, V., Shen, C., Ghanem, B., Niebles, J.C.: SST: single-stream temporal action proposals. In: IEEE Conference on Computer Vision and Pattern Recognition, CVPR 2017, pp. 6373–6382 (2017)
3. Caba Heilbron, F., Barrios, W., Escorcia, V., Ghanem, B.: SCC: semantic context cascade for efficient action detection. In: CVPR (2017)
4. Caba Heilbron, F., Escorcia, V., Ghanem, B., Niebles, J.C.: ActivityNet: a large-scale video benchmark for human activity understanding. In: CVPR 2015, pp. 961–970 (2015)
5. Caba Heilbron, F., Lee, J.Y., Jin, H., Ghanem, B.: What do I annotate next? An empirical study of active learning for action localization. In: Ferrari, V., et al. (eds.) ECCV 2018, Part XI. LNCS, vol. 11215, pp. 212–229. Springer, Cham (2018). https://doi.org/10.1007/978-3-030-01252-6_13
6. Caba Heilbron, F., Niebles, J.C., Ghanem, B.: Fast temporal activity proposals for efficient detection of human actions in untrimmed videos. In: IEEE Conference on Computer Vision and Pattern Recognition, CVPR 2016, pp. 1914–1923 (2016)
7. Carreira, J., Zisserman, A.: Quo vadis, action recognition? A new model and the kinetics dataset. In: 2017 IEEE Conference on Computer Vision and Pattern Recognition, CVPR 2017, Honolulu, HI, USA, 21–26 July, 2017, pp. 4724–4733 (2017)

8. Dai, X., Singh, B., Zhang, G., Davis, L.S., Chen, Y.Q.: Temporal context network for activity localization in videos. In: ICCV, pp. 5727–5736 (2017)
9. Escorcia, V., Caba Heilbron, F., Niebles, J.C., Ghanem, B.: DAPs: deep action proposals for action understanding. In: Leibe, B., Matas, J., Sebe, N., Welling, M. (eds.) ECCV 2016. LNCS, vol. 9907, pp. 768–784. Springer, Cham (2016). https://doi.org/10.1007/978-3-319-46487-9_47
10. Escorcia, V., Dao, C.D., Jain, M., Ghanem, B., Snoek, C.: Guess where? Actor-supervision for spatiotemporal action localization. CoRR abs/1804.01824 (2018)
11. Everingham, M., Eslami, S.M.A., Gool, L.J.V., Williams, C.K.I., Winn, J.M., Zisserman, A.: The PASCAL visual object classes challenge: a retrospective. Int. J. Comput. Vis. IJCV **111**(1), 98–136 (2015)
12. Gao, J., Yang, Z., Sun, C., Chen, K., Nevatia, R.: Turn tap: temporal unit regression network for temporal action proposals. In: ICCV (2017)
13. Ghanem, B., et al.: ActivityNet challenge 2017 summary. CoRR abs/1710.08011 (2017)
14. Girshick, R.B., Donahue, J., Darrell, T., Malik, J.: Region-based convolutional networks for accurate object detection and segmentation. IEEE Trans. Pattern Anal. Mach. Intell. **38**(1), 142–158 (2016)
15. Goyal, R., et al.: The "something something" video database for learning and evaluating visual common sense. In: IEEE International Conference on Computer Vision, ICCV 2017, Venice, Italy, 22–29 October 2017, pp. 5843–5851 (2017). https://doi.org/10.1109/ICCV.2017.622
16. Gu, C., et al.: AVA: a video dataset of spatio-temporally localized atomic visual actions. In: IEEE Conference on Computer Vision and Pattern Recognition, CVPR 2018 (2018)
17. He, K., Zhang, X., Ren, S., Sun, J.: Deep residual learning for image recognition. In: 2016 IEEE Conference on Computer Vision and Pattern Recognition, CVPR 2016, Las Vegas, NV, USA, 27–30 June 2016, pp. 770–778 (2016). https://doi.org/10.1109/CVPR.2016.90
18. Hoiem, D., Chodpathumwan, Y., Dai, Q.: Diagnosing error in object detectors. In: Fitzgibbon, A., Lazebnik, S., Perona, P., Sato, Y., Schmid, C. (eds.) ECCV 2012. LNCS, vol. 7574, pp. 340–353. Springer, Heidelberg (2012). https://doi.org/10.1007/978-3-642-33712-3_25
19. Idrees, H., et al.: The THUMOS challenge on action recognition for videos "in the wild". Comput. Vis. Image Underst. **155**, 1–23 (2017)
20. Jiang, Y.G., et al.: THUMOS challenge: action recognition with a large number of classes (2014). http://crcv.ucf.edu/THUMOS14/
21. Karpathy, A., Toderici, G., Shetty, S., Leung, T., Sukthankar, R., Fei-Fei, L.: Large-scale video classification with convolutional neural networks. In: CVPR (2014)
22. Kay, W., et al.: The kinetics human action video dataset. CoRR abs/1705.06950 (2017)
23. Krizhevsky, A., Sutskever, I., Hinton, G.E.: ImageNet classification with deep convolutional neural networks. In: Pereira, F., Burges, C.J.C., Bottou, L., Weinberger, K.Q. (eds.) Advances in Neural Information Processing Systems 25, pp. 1097–1105. Curran Associates, Inc. (2012)
24. Laptev, I., Marszałek, M., Schmid, C., Rozenfeld, B.: Learning realistic human actions from movies. In: IEEE Conference on Computer Vision and Pattern Recognition (2008)
25. Lin, T., Zhao, X., Shou, Z.: Single shot temporal action detection. In: ACM on Multimedia Conference, MM 2017 (2017)

26. Lin, T., Zhao, X., Shou, Z.: Temporal convolution based action proposal: submission to ActivityNet 2017. CoRR abs/1707.06750 (2017)
27. Moltisanti, D., Wray, M., Mayol-Cuevas, W.W., Damen, D.: Trespassing the boundaries: labeling temporal bounds for object interactions in egocentric video. In: IEEE International Conference on Computer Vision, ICCV 2017, Venice, Italy, 22–29 October 2017, pp. 2905–2913 (2017)
28. Monfort, M., et al.: Moments in time dataset: one million videos for event understanding
29. Ren, S., He, K., Girshick, R., Sun, J.: Faster R-CNN: towards real-time object detection with region proposal networks. In: Advances in Neural Information Processing Systems (NIPS) (2015)
30. Ronchi, M.R., Perona, P.: Benchmarking and error diagnosis in multi-instance pose estimation. In: ICCV 2017, pp. 369–378 (2017)
31. Russakovsky, O., Deng, J., Huang, Z., Berg, A.C., Li, F.: Detecting avocados to zucchinis: what have we done, and where are we going? ICCV 2013, pp. 2064–2071 (2013)
32. Russakovsky, O., et al.: Imagenet large scale visual recognition challenge. Int. J. Comput. Vis. IJCV **115**(3), 211–252 (2015)
33. Shou, Z., Chan, J., Zareian, A., Miyazawa, K., Chang, S.F.: CDC: convolutional-de-convolutional networks for precise temporal action localization in untrimmed videos. In: CVPR (2017)
34. Shou, Z., Wang, D., Chang, S.F.: Temporal action localization in untrimmed videos via multi-stage CNNs. In: CVPR (2016)
35. Sigurdsson, G.A., Divvala, S., Farhadi, A., Gupta, A.: Asynchronous temporal fields for action recognition. In: The IEEE Conference on Computer Vision and Pattern Recognition (CVPR) (2017)
36. Sigurdsson, G.A., Russakovsky, O., Gupta, A.: What actions are needed for understanding human actions in videos? In: ICCV 2017, pp. 2156–2165 (2017)
37. Sigurdsson, G.A., Varol, G., Wang, X., Farhadi, A., Laptev, I., Gupta, A.: Hollywood in homes: crowdsourcing data collection for activity understanding. In: Leibe, B., Matas, J., Sebe, N., Welling, M. (eds.) ECCV 2016. LNCS, vol. 9905, pp. 510–526. Springer, Cham (2016). https://doi.org/10.1007/978-3-319-46448-0_31
38. Simonyan, K., Zisserman, A.: Two-stream convolutional networks for action recognition in videos. In: NIPS (2014)
39. Tran, D., Bourdev, L.D., Fergus, R., Torresani, L., Paluri, M.: Learning spatiotemporal features with 3D convolutional networks. In: ICCV (2015)
40. Wang, L., et al.: Temporal segment networks: towards good practices for deep action recognition. In: Leibe, B., Matas, J., Sebe, N., Welling, M. (eds.) ECCV 2016. LNCS, vol. 9912, pp. 20–36. Springer, Cham (2016). https://doi.org/10.1007/978-3-319-46484-8_2
41. Wang, X., Girshick, R.B., Gupta, A., He, K.: Non-local neural networks. CoRR abs/1711.07971 (2017)
42. Xiong, Y., Zhao, Y., Wang, L., Lin, D., Tang, X.: A pursuit of temporal accuracy in general activity detection. CoRR abs/1703.02716 (2017)
43. Xu, H., Das, A., Saenko, K.: R-C3D: region convolutional 3D network for temporal activity detection. In: ICCV (2017)
44. Zhang, S., Benenson, R., Omran, M., Hosang, J.H., Schiele, B.: How far are we from solving pedestrian detection? In: CVPR 2016, pp. 1259–1267 (2016)
45. Zhao, Y., Xiong, Y., Wang, L., Wu, Z., Tang, X., Lin, D.: Temporal action detection with structured segment networks. In: ICCV 2017, October 2017

Improved Structure from Motion Using Fiducial Marker Matching

Joseph DeGol[1]([✉]), Timothy Bretl[1], and Derek Hoiem[1,2]

[1] University of Illinois, Urbana-Champaign, USA
{degol2,tbretl,dhoiem}@illinois.edu
[2] Reconstruct Inc., Champaign, USA
derek.hoiem@reconstructinc.com

Abstract. In this paper, we present an incremental structure from motion (SfM) algorithm that significantly outperforms existing algorithms when fiducial markers are present in the scene, and that matches the performance of existing algorithms when no markers are present. Our algorithm uses markers to limit potential incorrect image matches, change the order in which images are added to the reconstruction, and enforce new bundle adjustment constraints. To validate our algorithm, we introduce a new dataset with 16 image collections of large indoor scenes with challenging characteristics (e.g., blank hallways, glass façades, brick walls) and with markers placed throughout. We show that our algorithm produces complete, accurate reconstructions on all 16 image collections, most of which cause other algorithms to fail. Further, by selectively masking fiducial markers, we show that the presence of even a small number of markers can improve the results of our algorithm.

Keywords: Structure from motion · SFM · Fiducial markers
3D reconstruction · Simultaneous localization and mapping · SLAM

1 Introduction

Fiducial markers are often claimed to be useful for 3D reconstruction [1–7]. Markers provide highly detectable and identifiable features that 3D reconstruction can use to overcome challenging scene characteristics such as low-texture surfaces (e.g., blank walls), reflective surfaces (e.g., windows), and repetitive patterns (e.g., columns and door frames). Figure 1 shows an example of a dataset with exactly these challenging characteristics. Figure 1 also shows that approaches that treat markers as texture, only use them as additional tracks, or rely on them exclusively perform no better or even worse than if markers were ignored.

In this paper, we present an incremental structure from motion (SfM) algorithm that significantly outperforms these other approaches when markers are

Electronic supplementary material The online version of this chapter (https://doi.org/10.1007/978-3-030-01219-9_17) contains supplementary material, which is available to authorized users.

Fig. 1. We introduce a new dataset of unordered image collections of challenging indoor scenes with markers placed throughout (example images along top row). We process the data using OpenSfM [8] with (a) markers ignored, (b) markers used as texture, and (c) markers used as additional tracks; with (d) MarkerMapper [9], which uses markers exclusively; and with (e) our approach, which uses markers to limit image matches, dictate resectioning order, and constrain bundle adjustment. Clearly, our method (e) outperforms the others. Moreover, the other approaches often perform worse than ignoring the markers, highlighting the importance of our method.

present in the scene. We exploit that markers can be identified with very low false positive rates (e.g. AprilTag2 with 36h11 markers has a false positive rate of 0.000044% [2]) to create a reliable marker match graph that guides image matching and resectioning. We encode constraints on marker size, shape, and planarity in bundle adjustment to further improve results. Importantly, our approach benefits from any detected markers without sacrificing performance when markers are not detected, and can benefit from even a small number of markers.

To evaluate our method, we introduce a new dataset with 16 image collections of indoor scenes. The scenes present challenging circumstances for SfM (e.g. blank hallways, reflective glass facades, and repetitive brick walls). Each indoor scene has tens to hundreds (depending on scene size) of markers placed approximately uniformly throughout. We test our system and several cutting edge benchmarks on this data and show that our system performs favorably. We also selectively mask markers and show that performance gracefully degrades towards markerless SfM as the number of markers in the scene decreases.

In summary, the **contributions** of this paper are: (1) an SfM algorithm that uses both fiducial markers (when available) and interest point features for improved results; (2) a large, challenging dataset of indoor scenes with markers placed throughout; and (3) experiments showing the effectiveness of our approach, even when only a small number of markers are visible.

2 Related Work

Incremental SfM: Early works by Schaffalitzky and Zisserman [10] and Snavely et al. [11] establish the pipeline for feature extraction, matching, and incremental SfM for unordered image collections. Focus then turns to large image collections with work by Agarwal et al. [12] and Frahm et al. [13] who use appearance based clustering to limit potential image matches; enabling reconstructions of

Fig. 2. Example images from the Neunert et al. [16] dataset: desk (top left), dataset1 (top right), cube (bottom left), and pavilion (bottom right). Experiments in Sect. 5 show that our method and current SfM methods perform well on this data, motivating our new dataset that offers new challenges and better distinguishes between approaches.

Rome from thousands of internet photos. Work by Wu [14] shows that preemptive feature matching and well timed global bundle adjustments can maintain high accuracy while reducing the runtime of SfM to roughly $\mathcal{O}(n)$. Recently, several new SfM algorithms are available including COLMAP [15] by Schönberger and Frahm and OpenSfM [8] by Mapillary. These impressive works provide the baseline for the work in this paper.

3D Reconstruction Using Fiducial Markers: Early works using markers for 3D reconstruction focus on tracking the markers in simultaneous localization and mapping (SLAM) systems. Work by Klopschitz and Schmalstieg [17] tracks both feature points and marker matches in video frames to estimate the camera pose and triangulate the marker positions in 3D. Lim and Lee [18] and Yamada et al. [19] add an extended kalman filter (EKF) for estimating robot camera pose and marker positions in 3D. Neunert et al. [16] integrates IMU measurements into the EKF-SLAM system to improve pose estimates during marker tracking. Feng et al. [20] proposes an incremental SfM approach to marker based 3D reconstruction. They use markers to create an initial reconstruction, add new images using marker matches, and add constraints to bundle adjustment to enforce the square shape and planarity of markers. The work of Muñoz-Salinas et al. [9] introduces MarkerMapper. MarkerMapper overcomes the pose ambiguity problem [21] with planar marker pose estimation to create an initial proposal of 3D camera and marker locations and refines the proposal using global bundle adjustment. Only MarkerMapper [9] and Feng et al. [20] pursue 3D reconstruction from unordered image collections. However, neither method uses both image features and marker detections for 3D reconstruction. Experiments in Sect. 5 show that both image features and marker detections can be used together to achieve the best results, and, when few or no markers are available, our system performs no worse than non-marker based SfM.

Datasets: Datasets for testing marker based 3D reconstruction are limited. Only the dataset of Neunert et al. [16] is publicly available. Figure 2 provides snapshots from the four video sequences of this dataset. With only four sequences (two of which are of very small environments with only 1–3 markers), this dataset is no longer challenging for the current state of the art (e.g. in Sect. 5, we process this data with our method and other current SfM approaches, and all perform well).

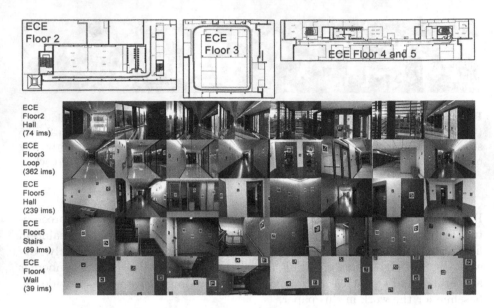

Fig. 3. The top diagrams are floor plans of ECE. The paths for image collection are superimposed in red, green, and magenta. These colors correspond to the image set name and example images. For example, *ECE Floor5 Stairs* is shown in the *ECE Floor4 and 5* floor plan as a magenta line and the name with example images is also magenta. (Color figure online)

Our new dataset (Sect. 3) consists of 16 new image collections in environments with challenging characteristics for SfM (e.g. many low-texture walls and reflective glass). We hope our dataset will offer new challenges for future work on SfM both with and without marker assistance.

3   Indoor Image Collections with Fiducial Markers

We introduce 16 new unordered image sets for evaluating structure from motion for scenes containing fiducial markers. Each set is from one of three buildings: ECE, CEE, or MUF. Figures 3 and 4 provide floor plans for the sections of these buildings that are used to collect this data. Paths are drawn on each floor plan and the colors of the paths match the respective image sets in the figures (e.g. the green path on Floor 4 and 5 of ECE matches the ECE Floor5 Hall image set). For each set, fiducial markers are placed around the scene with enough density to see at least one in every image (and images are captured to satisfy this also). All images are captured with an iPhone7 camera and have a resolution of 4032 × 3024 pixels.

There are seven image sets not shown in the figures. That is because they are either combinations or subsets of the shown sets. Specifically, *ECE Floor5* includes all the images of *ECE Floor5 Hall* and *ECE Floor5 Stairs*. *ECE Floor3*

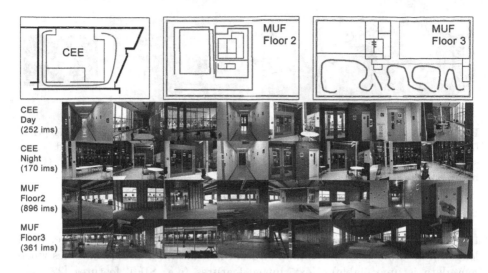

Fig. 4. The top diagrams are floor plans for CEE and MUF. The paths for image collection are superimposed in red. Image set names and example images are shown. (Color figure online)

Loop includes all the images of *ECE Floor3 Loop CW* and *ECE Floor 3 CCW*. *CEE Day* includes all the images of *CEE Day CW* and *CEE Day CCW* (plus some extra images). The nice thing about collecting data in this way is that we can test progressively larger datasets that present different circumstances that may make the image set easier or more difficult. For example, the results in Sect. 5 show that *ECE Floor3 Loop CW* and *ECE Floor3 Loop CCW* are typically more difficult than putting them together into *ECE Floor 3 Loop*. This is most likely because of the additional overlap between images since all locations are now seen more often from more viewing directions.

We use ECE, CEE, and MUF because they are large indoor scenes with characteristics that are challenging for SfM (as shown in Sect. 5). Specifically, ECE has long plain hallways, large glass walls separating conference rooms, large exterior windows, and the hallways form a loop. CEE has a two-floor glass facade and repetitive brick walls. MUF is currently under construction and has large open spaces and limited texture. See supplementary material for more examples.

4   Improving SfM with Markers

Figure 5 diagrams our marker assisted incremental SfM algorithm. The blue boxes represent the components of our algorithm that are different from typical state of the art incremental SfM approaches: detecting markers, filtering image pairs, resectioning images, and marker constraints for bundle adjustment.

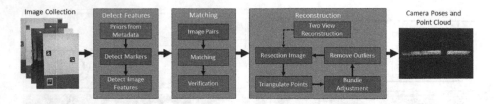

Fig. 5. This diagram depicts the typical incremental SfM approach: extracting priors from metadata (e.g. focal length), detecting features, matching features, and reconstruction. The blue boxes are the areas we added or changed in our method. (Color figure online)

4.1 Incremental SfM Overview

Incremental SfM takes a collection of images as input. For each image, focal length (and other priors) is estimated from metadata (or using heuristics when metadata is unavailable). Next, image features (e.g. SIFT features [22]) are extracted from each image. These image features are matched across image pairs. Matching is attempted between the set of all images pairs or a subset of the image pairs selected based on filtering criteria (e.g. GPS locations [13], Vocab Tree [12]). A fundamental matrix is estimated from the feature matches to filter bad matches and verify that each image pair is a good match.

After matching, reconstruction begins. Feature matches in two images are used to create an initial 3D reconstruction (pose of the two images with triangulated 3D points). Then, one at a time, a new image is added to the reconstruction (resectioning). This image is typically chosen based on the number of feature matches this image shares with the already reconstructed images. These shared feature matches are used to estimate the pose of this new camera and triangulate new 3D points. Bundle adjustment then optimizes all camera poses and 3D point positions to minimize reprojection error. Lastly, outlier points are removed. Resectioning is repeated to add all images to the reconstruction. The final output is a point cloud and set of camera poses, one for each image that is successfully resectioned.

4.2 Detect Markers

We run a square marker detection algorithm on each input image. The images are processed in parallel. Image name, marker id, corner locations, and corner pixel colors are saved for each detection.

4.3 Marker Informed Image Pairs

Prior to matching and verification, we create a set of image pairs that potentially match. We only attempt matching on the image pairs in this set. One approach is to add all possible image pairs; however, this greatly increases matching time and can lead to bad image matches that cause errors in the reconstruction. We

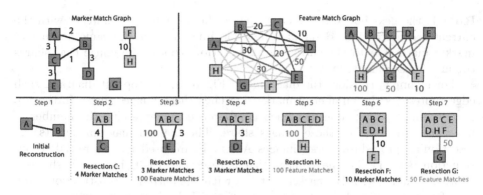

Fig. 6. The top left diagram depicts images as lettered boxes with edges representing the number of matched markers between image pairs. The top middle and top right diagrams depict the number of common feature matches between images. The bottom diagram depicts the resectioning order of images A to G based on two rules: (1) add the image that shares the most marker matches with the reconstruction; (2) break ties using most shared feature matches.

apply three rules to use marker detections to dictate which images are added. **Rule 1:** we add an image pair if the same marker (at least one) is detected in both images. **Rule 2:** if an image does not share a detected marker with any other image, we add all possible pairs that contain that image. **Rule 3:** if the set of all added pairs do not form one connected component, we connect separate components by adding pairs for each image in the separate component to each image not in the separate component.

As an example, consider the top left diagram in Fig. 6. Each lettered box represents an image, and each numbered edge represents the number of marker matches those images share. Applying rule 1, we add the following possible image pairs (A, B), (A, C), (B, C), (B, D), (C, E), and (F, H). No pair is added that includes G, so based on rule 2, we add (G, A), (G, B), ..., (G, H). Lastly, since (F, H) is a separate component (rule 3), we add (F, A), (F, B), ..., (F, E) and (H, A), (H, B), ..., (H, E). We show in the results that this strategy can greatly speed up processing and eliminate many bad image matches. Note that other filtering approaches (e.g. Vocab Tree [12]) can be used in conjunction with our approach to add or filter image pairs.

4.4   Marker Informed Resectioning

Resectioning is the process of adding a new image to the existing reconstruction. The order in which images are added is important because poorly registered images can propagate errors that result in failure. One approach is to choose the image to resection that shares the most feature matches with the images in the reconstruction. This approach works well when image features are distinct and plentiful; however, for the challenging scenes we are targeting, failure can occur. Instead, we apply two rules to use marker detections to dictate resectioning order.

Rule 1: the next image to resection shares the most marker matches with the current reconstruction. **Rule 2:** if multiple images share the same number of marker matches with the current reconstruction, choose the image that shares the most feature matches.

For example, consider the diagrams in Fig. 6. In the top left diagram, each edge represents the number of marker matches those images share. In the top middle and top right diagram, each numbered edge represents the number of image feature matches those images share. The bottom diagram depicts the resectioning procedure. First, images A and B are used for the initial reconstruction (step 1). The next image that is resectioned is C because it shares 4 (3 with A and 1 with B) marker matches with the current reconstruction (step 2). After that, image E is added because E and D both share 3 marker matches with the reconstruction, but E shares 100 feature matches and D only shares 60 (step 3). Image D is then added (step 4). No remaining images share marker matches with the current reconstruction, so image H is added based on shared image feature matches (step 5). F is added next (step 6) because it now shares marker matches with the reconstruction (because H was added). Lastly, G is added (step 7).

4.5   Marker Constraints for Bundle Adjustment

In bundle adjustment, we solve for camera poses P and 3D points X that optimize the following:

$$\min_{P,X} \left[w_R E_R \left(P, X \right) + w_S E_S \left(V \right) + w_O E_O \left(V \right) \right] . \tag{1}$$

V is the set of vectors formed between neighboring 3D corners on each marker (i.e. there are four vectors for each marker detection). w_R, w_S, and w_O are weights. Reprojection error [23] is

$$E_R \left(P, X \right) = \sum_{i=1}^{C} \sum_{j=1}^{N} L \left(x_{ij}, P_i \left(X^j \right) \right) \tag{2}$$

where C is the number of cameras, N is the number of 3D points (both marker and feature points), L is a loss function, x_{ij} is the 2D location in image i of 3D point X^j, and P_i is the projection function of camera i. Similar to [20], we also include error terms for marker scale (E_S, Eq. 3) and marker orthogonality (E_O, Eq. 4).

Marker Scale: The distance between marker corners in the reconstruction should match the known marker size. We define this error as $E_S \left(V \right) =$

$$\sum_{i=1}^{T} \left(\left\| V_{12}^i \right\|_2 - S \right)^2 + \left(\left\| V_{23}^i \right\|_2 - S \right)^2 + \left(\left\| V_{34}^i \right\|_2 - S \right)^2 + \left(\left\| V_{41}^i \right\|_2 - S \right)^2 \tag{3}$$

where V_{NM}^i is the 3D vector from the 3D point of corner N to the 3D point of corner M on marker i, T is the number of markers, and S is the marker size.

Marker Orthogonality: Adjacent sides of the marker should be perpendicular. We define this error as $E_O(\boldsymbol{V}) =$

$$\sum_{i=1}^{T} \left(\boldsymbol{V}_{12}^{i} \cdot \boldsymbol{V}_{23}^{i}\right)^2 + \left(\boldsymbol{V}_{23}^{i} \cdot \boldsymbol{V}_{34}^{i}\right)^2 + \left(\boldsymbol{V}_{34}^{i} \cdot \boldsymbol{V}_{41}^{i}\right)^2 + \left(\boldsymbol{V}_{41}^{i} \cdot \boldsymbol{V}_{12}^{i}\right)^2 \qquad (4)$$

where $\boldsymbol{V}_{NM}^{i}$ is the 3D vector from the 3D point of corner N to the 3D point of corner M on marker i, and T is the number of markers.

4.6 Implementation Details

We implement our approach on top of OpenSfM v0.1.0 [8]. We use default parameters, which work well for unordered image collections. We use AprilTag2 [2] to detect markers. For all experiments, we use a soft L1 loss for L; cost weights of $w_R = 62500$, $w_S = 100$, and $w_O = 100$; and marker size $S = 0.21$ m. In principal, our approach works with any square marker detector and can be integrated with any incremental or global [24,25] (except resectioning) SfM method.

5 Results

We process our new dataset using: (1) OpenSfM [8], an open source state of the art SfM algorithm that is actively used and maintained by Mapillary [26]; (2) OpenSfM, but with all feature points on markers masked; (3) MarkerMapper [9], a state of the art algorithm for marker based SfM; (4) OpenSfM with the four marker corners used as tracks in reconstruction; and (5) our method. Table 1 provides quantitative results on the number of images localized, number of points, and reprojection errors. Failure reconstructions are denoted by a "-". Figures 7 and 8 provide qualitative results of the 3D reconstructions. The green pyramids are the camera locations. The floor plans in Figs. 3 and 4 provide guidelines for how each reconstruction should look (e.g. ECE Floor3 Loop should be a rectangle). Because of the challenging nature of these datasets, the algorithms often fail or have large, noticeable mistakes; therefore, we focus more on the qualitative results because they illustrate the improvements clearly.

We also process the Neunert et al. [16] dataset. Since it is video data, we subsample the frames by a factor of 5 to simulate an unordered image collection. All OpenSfM methods and our method successfully reconstruct all image sets. MarkerMapper has trouble with this dataset because there are few (often only one) markers in each image. Reconstruction and timing results are shown in Tables 1 and 2 respectively. Qualitative results are in the supplementary material.

We do an ablation study with marker informed matching (Sect. 4.3) and marker informed resectioning (Sect. 4.4). For each dataset and method we calculate the percent of images localized. The average percentages of localized images are 98% (our full method), 68% (no marker informed resectioning), 50% (no marker informed matching), and 42% (OpenSfM with markers masked — the next best method). These percentages show that both marker informed matching

Table 1. Reconstruction results for OpenSfM [8], OpenSfM with markers masked (denoted by [8]*), MarkerMapper [9], OpenSfM with marker tracks (denoted by MT), and our method. Failure reconstructions (Figs. 7 and 8) are blank because the numbers can be misleading (e.g. all cameras localized to one spot). Our method achieves similar or better results for number of registered images and points for all reconstructions.

	# Images	# Registered					# Points					Avg. Rep. Error [px]				
		[8]	[8]*	[9]	MT	Ours	[8]	[8]*	[9]	MT	Ours	[8]	[8]*	[9]	MT	Ours
ECE F2 Hall	74	-	70	-	-	71	-	15.9K	-	-	16.4K	-	3.1	-	-	2.8
ECE F3 Loop CCW	192	-	-	190	-	191	-	-	808	-	61K	-	-	200.8	-	2.8
ECE F3 Loop CW	170	-	-	166	-	170	-	-	736	-	58K	-	-	358.1	-	2.7
ECE F3 Loop	362	-	-	356	-	360	-	-	920	-	105K	-	-	324.0	-	2.8
ECE F5 Hall	239	230	230	213	223	231	50K	45K	736	47K	63K	2.8	2.7	141.0	2.7	2.7
ECE F5 Stairs	89	52	51	-	45	89	20K	20K	-	14K	43K	1.9	1.7	-	1.9	1.8
ECE F5	328	313	315	-	-	327	79K	73K	-	-	109K	2.3	2.3	-	-	2.3
ECE F4 Wall	39	21	18	39	18	39	13K	9K	204	9K	28K	1.1	1.1	25.8	1.2	1.2
CEE Day CW	63	55	52	-	52	62	24K	20K	-	28K	30K	1.6	1.6	-	1.6	1.6
CEE Day CCW	120	65	116	-	116	119	30K	52K	-	56K	64K	1.6	1.5	-	1.6	1.5
CEE Day	252	-	251	238	103	246	-	89K	768	398	104K	-	1.7	204.8	0.2	1.8
CEE Night CW	96	96	96	96	-	96	48K	44K	548	-	51K	1.7	1.6	164.0	-	1.7
CEE Night CCW	79	-	-	79	-	77	-	-	580	-	40K	-	-	116.6	-	1.5
CEE Night	170	-	166	170	-	170	-	61K	760	-	77K	-	1.6	181.4	-	1.6
MUF F2	896	883	514	-	885	882	224K	133K	-	151K	251K	2.5	2.5	-	2.1	2.9
MUF F3	361	343	-	-	324	358	84K	-	-	55K	89K	2.8	-	-	2.4	2.8
cube [16]	327	327	327	-	327	327	99K	101K	-	100K	99K	0.8	0.8	-	0.8	0.8
dataset1 [16]	91	91	91	3	91	91	31K	30K	8	31K	33K	0.9	0.9	0.6	0.9	0.8
pavilion [16]	585	585	585	-	585	583	178K	168K	-	186K	178K	0.8	0.7	-	0.7	0.7
table [16]	80	80	49	38	80	80	7K	5K	12	7K	6K	0.9	1.0	0.3	0.9	1.0

and resectioning are useful individually, but most effective when used together. We also test our method without marker scale (E_S, Eq. 3) and orthogonality (E_O, Eq. 4) constraints and find that they provide little to no gain, sometimes making the results worse. See supplementary material for more details about the ablation study.

All experiments use an Intel Xeon E5-2620 V4 2.1 GHz 16 cores (32 virtual cores) processor with 128 GB of RAM. No graphics card is used.

Using Markers as Texture Often Makes Reconstructions Worse. Masking the markers shows how OpenSfM performs if the scenes have no markers. Comparing column 1 (OpenSfM) and column 2 (OpenSfM with masked markers) in Figs. 7 and 8, shows that masking the markers often produces better results. For example, *ECE Floor2 Hall* should have an "L" shape, which OpenSfM with masked markers achieves, but OpenSfM does not. Other examples where masking markers is clearly better are *ECE Floor3 Loop CW*, *ECE Floor5 Stairs*, *CEE Day CCW*, *CEE Day*, and *CEE Night*.

Marker texture does not always produce bad results (e.g. *MUF Floor3*), but marker texture can cause bad feature matches because the appearance is similar between the markers (i.e. black and white squares). This reinforces the need for our approach which takes advantage of visible markers to improve results.

Using Marker Detections as Tracks Has Little Effect. Comparing column 4 (OpenSfM with marker tracks) to columns 1 and 2 (OpenSfM with and without markers masked) of Figs. 3 and 4 shows that the marker tracks rarely improve

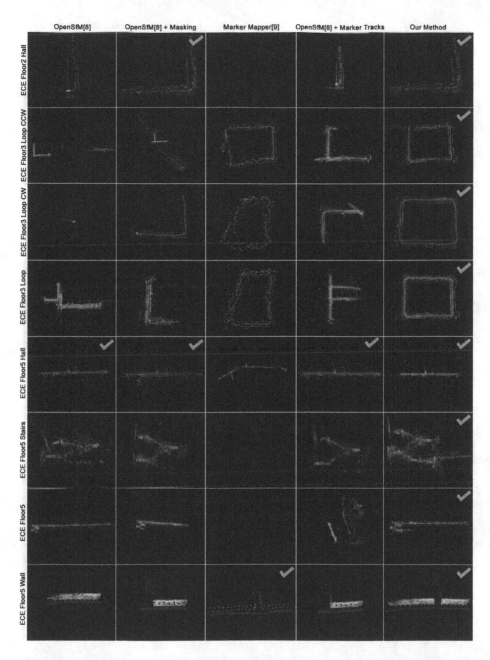

Fig. 7. Reconstructions for OpenSfM, OpenSfM with markers masked, MarkerMapper, OpenSfM with marker tracks, and our method on the ECE image collections. Using the markers as texture often produces worse results (e.g. *ECE Floor2 Hall, ECE Floor3 Loop CW, ECE Floor3 Loop,* and *ECE Floor5 Stairs*). Our method produces complete reconstructions that are as good or better than the other methods for all image collections. The best results are denoted by a green check mark. (Color figure online)

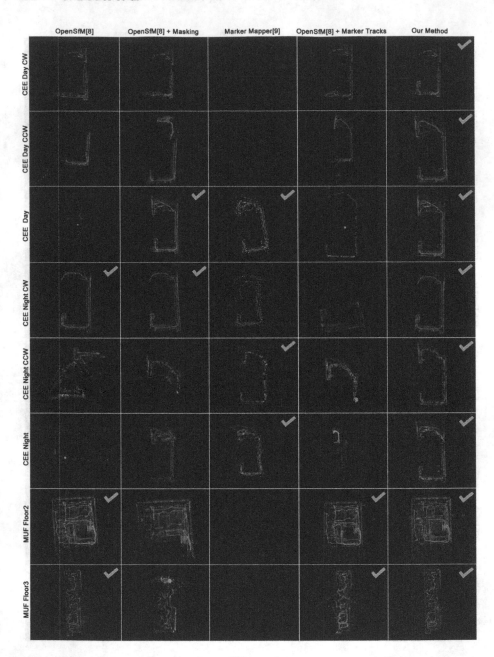

Fig. 8. Reconstructions for OpenSfM, OpenSfM with markers masked, MarkerMapper, OpenSfM with marker tracks, and our method on the CEE and MUF image collections. Again, using the markers as texture often produces worse results (e.g. *CEE Day CCW*, *CEE Day*, and *CEE Night*). Our method produces complete reconstructions that are as good or better than the other methods for all image collections. The best results are denoted by a green check mark. (Color figure online)

Table 2. Reconstruction timings for OpenSfM [8], OpenSfM with markers masked (denoted by [8]*), MarkerMapper [9], OpenSfM with marker tracks (denoted by MT), and our method. Using the markers to limit possible image pairs decreases the matching time significantly. Also, because more images are resectioned, the reconstruction time increases. Overall, our method produces better reconstructions in a shorter time.

	# Images	Marker Detection [s]				Matching [s]				Reconstruction [s]				
		[8]	[8]*	MT	Ours	[8]	[8]*	MT	Ours	[8]	[8]*	[9]	MT	Ours
ECE F2	74	0	14	14	14	215	186	223	73	331	222	-	363	277
ECE F3 Loop CCW	192	0	32	32	32	1356	1160	1398	293	3433	2766	85	2282	3097
ECE F3 Loop CW	170	0	30	30	30	1071	888	1152	273	2797	2084	83	2430	2367
ECE F3 Loop	362	0	59	59	59	4568	3820	4675	876	9944	5082	195	9239	9704
ECE F5 Hall	239	0	40	40	40	1955	1650	1974	296	2810	2363	80	2774	3061
ECE F5 Stairs	89	0	16	16	16	307	258	317	55	425	278	-	347	658
ECE F5	328	0	57	57	57	3787	3195	3945	372	6341	5083	-	7268	5513
ECE F4 Wall	39	0	9	9	9	61	46	47	8	133	46	22	63	263
CEE Day CW	63	0	11	11	11	160	126	171	49	336	216	-	489	382
CEE Day CCW	120	0	21	21	21	535	437	570	139	1011	1377	-	2305	1809
CEE Day	252	0	41	41	41	2373	1919	2567	440	7137	5205	148	4102	4987
CEE Night CW	96	0	16	16	16	358	278	380	99	1083	793	25	1136	1010
CEE Night CCW	79	0	14	14	14	247	193	70	69	425	418	32	917	654
CEE Night	170	0	30	30	30	1093	873	1154	216	3232	2251	93	3287	2984
MUF F2	896	0	158	158	158	31180	25613	35844	5596	72055	40958	-	66095	60542
MUF F3	361	0	64	64	64	5094	4302	5205	758	8977	6903	-	5017	9090
cube [16]	327	0	6	6	6	3473	2724	2776	423	4066	5232	-	4244	4134
dataset1 [16]	91	0	1	1	1	351	305	304	207	847	593	1	619	595
pavilion [16]	585	0	7	7	7	9103	9239	9219	2100	22908	15931	-	21903	22594
table [16]	80	0	1	1	1	64	60	63	65	113	188	2	205	191

the reconstructions and sometimes make them worse (e.g. *ECE Floor5* and *CEE Night*). We suspect this is because the localization of the marker corners can be less accurate (e.g. off by 3–5 pixels [3]) than image features.

Our Approach Succeeds Where Others Fail. From Figs. 7 and 8, we see that our method produces a successful reconstruction for every image set. We also see that our method produces better results than the other methods on the challenging sets. Most notable are *ECE Floor3 Loop CW*, *ECE Floor3 Loop*, and *CEE Day CCW* because all other methods fail or have significant mistakes. For *ECE Floor5 stairs*, *ECE Floor5*, and *CEE Day CW*, other methods produce reasonable results, but our approach is more complete.

Our Approach Succeeds Where Others Succeed. There are several image sets where all (or most) of the methods produce successful reconstructions (e.g. *ECE Floor5 Hall* and *CEE Night CW*). In these cases, our method also produces nice reconstructions. This is important because our algorithm improves on the challenging image sets without sacrificing accuracy on the easier image sets.

Using Markers Improves Reconstruction Time. Table 2 provides the run times for marker detection, matching, and reconstruction for all image sets. Timings for other parts of SfM are not included since they do not change between methods. Also, only the total run time of MarkerMapper is reported because it does not follow the same pipeline as the others. One main thing to note is that using markers to limit pairs for image matching can decrease run times significantly (e.g. for *MUF Floor2*, our method took 5596 seconds and the other OpenSfM approaches took 5–6 times longer). Time is added to detect markers in each image, but it is typically negligible compared to the time saved in matching. Another interesting point is that reconstruction time often increases. This is because more images are able to be registered with our method.

Few Marker Detections Still Improves Reconstructions. Figure 9 demonstrates how marker density effects the reconstructions. In particular, the left six images show how the reconstruction of *ECE Floor3 Loop CCW* improves as the marker density increases. Here AMD stands for average marker detections per image (e.g. AMD $= 0.0$ means there are no markers detected, and AMD $= 6.0$ means that there were an average of 6 markers detected per image).

The plot in Fig. 9 shows how the percent of localized images increases as the AMD increases for seven datasets. These datasets were chosen because our method achieves clear improvements over the other methods. The trend line is plotted in black. We see from this plot that markers help even when AMD is less than 1 (sometimes even 100% of the images are localized). As AMD increases, the number of localized images increases towards 100%. Placing enough markers for an AMD of 6 will likely produce accurate, complete reconstructions with 90+% of images localized. However, markers are most useful in areas with challenging conditions for SfM, so placing more markers in these challenging areas and fewer (or zero) markers in easier areas can help our method achieve accurate, complete reconstructions with drastically fewer total marker detections.

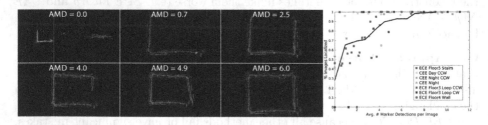

Fig. 9. The left six images show how the reconstruction of *ECE Floor3 Loop CCW* improves as marker density increases. Here AMD means average marker detections per image. The right image shows the percent of images localized as the AMD increases. Each color represents a different dataset. The trend line is shown in black. As the AMD increases, the percent of localized images increased to 100%. (Color figure online)

6   Conclusion

We present an incremental SfM method that significantly outperforms existing methods when fiducial markers are detected in the scene. We introduce a new dataset with 16 image collections of indoor scenes with square markers placed throughout. We use the unique marker IDs to improve image matching and resectioning order and show that these improvements greatly improve reconstruction results when compared to other methods. Lastly, we show that even a small number of visible markers often improves reconstruction results.

Acknowledgement. This work is supported by NSF Grant CMMI-1446765 and the DoD National Defense Science and Engineering Graduate Fellowship (NDSEG). Thank you also to Reconstruct for computational resources that enabled this research and Daniel Yuan, Jae Yong Lee, and Shreya Jagarlamudi for help with data collection.

References

1. Birdal, T., Dobryden, I., Ilic, S.: X-tag: a fiducial tag for flexible and accurate bundle adjustment. In: 2016 Fourth International Conference on 3D Vision (3DV), pp. 556–564, October 2016
2. Wang, J., Olson, E.: AprilTag 2: efficient and robust fiducial detection. In: Proceedings of the IEEE/RSJ International Conference on Intelligent Robots and Systems (IROS), October 2016
3. DeGol, J., Bretl, T., Hoiem, D.: ChromaTag: a colored marker and fast detection algorithm. In: ICCV (2017)
4. Garrido-Jurado, S., noz Salinas, R.M., Madrid-Cuevas, F., Marín-Jiménez, M.: Automatic generation and detection of highly reliable fiducial markers under occlusion. Pattern Recogn. **47**(6), 2280–2292 (2014)
5. Fiala, M.: Designing highly reliable fiducial markers. IEEE Trans. Pattern Anal. Mach. Intell. **32**(7), 1317–1324 (2010)
6. Bergamasco, F., Albarelli, A., Cosmo, L., Rodola, E., Torsello, A.: An accurate and robust artificial marker based on cyclic codes. IEEE Trans. Pattern Anal. Mach. Intell. **PP**(99), 1 (2016)
7. Calvet, L., Gurdjos, P., Griwodz, C., Gasparini, S.: Detection and accurate localization of circular fiducials under highly challenging conditions. In: The IEEE Conference on Computer Vision and Pattern Recognition (CVPR), June 2016
8. OpenSfM. https://github.com/mapillary/opensfm
9. Muoz-Salinas, R., Marn-Jimenez, M.J., Yeguas-Bolivar, E., Medina-Carnicer, R.: Mapping and localization from planar markers. Pattern Recogn. **73**, 158–171 (2018)
10. Schaffalitzky, F., Zisserman, A.: Multi-view matching for unordered image sets, or "How Do I Organize My Holiday Snaps?". In: Heyden, A., Sparr, G., Nielsen, M., Johansen, P. (eds.) ECCV 2002. LNCS, vol. 2350, pp. 414–431. Springer, Heidelberg (2002). https://doi.org/10.1007/3-540-47969-4_28
11. Snavely, N., Seitz, S.M., Szeliski, R.: Photo tourism: exploring photo collections in 3D. In: Proceedings of ACM SIGGRAPH (2006)
12. Agarwal, S., Snavely, N., Simon, I., Seitz, S.M., Szeliski, R.: Building Rome in a day. In: IEEE 12th International Conference on Computer Vision, pp. 72–79, September 2009
13. Frahm, J.-M., et al.: Building Rome on a cloudless day. In: Daniilidis, K., Maragos, P., Paragios, N. (eds.) ECCV 2010. LNCS, vol. 6314, pp. 368–381. Springer, Heidelberg (2010). https://doi.org/10.1007/978-3-642-15561-1_27
14. Wu, C.: Towards linear-time incremental structure from motion. In: 2013 International Conference on 3D Vision - 3DV 2013 (2013)
15. Schönberger, J.L., Frahm, J.M.: Structure-from-motion revisited. In: IEEE Conference on Computer Vision and Pattern Recognition (CVPR) (2016)

16. Neunert, M., Bloesch, M., Buchli, J.: An open source, fiducial based, visual-inertial motion capture system. In: 2016 19th International Conference on Information Fusion (FUSION) (2016)
17. Klopschitz, M., Schmalstieg, D.: Automatic reconstruction of wide-area fiducial marker models. In: 2007 6th IEEE and ACM International Symposium on Mixed and Augmented Reality (2007)
18. Lim, H., Lee, Y.S.: Real-time single camera slam using fiducial markers. In: 2009 ICCAS-SICE (2009)
19. Yamada, T., Yairi, T., Bener, S.H., Machida, K.: A study on slam for indoor blimp with visual markers. In: ICCAS-SICE 2009, pp. 647–652 (2009)
20. Feng, C., Kamat, V., Menassa, C.C.: Marker-assisted structure from motion for 3D environment modeling and object pose estimation. In: Construction Research Congress (2016)
21. Schweighofer, G., Pinz, A.: Robust pose estimation from a planar target. IEEE Trans. Pattern Anal. Mach. Intell. **28**(12), 2024–2030 (2006)
22. Lowe, D.G.: Distinctive image features from scale-invariant keypoints. Int. J. Comput. Vis. **60**(2), 91–110 (2004)
23. Hartley, R.I., Zisserman, A.: Multiple View Geometry in Computer Vision, 2nd edn. Cambridge University Press, Cambridge (2004). ISBN 0521540518
24. Moulon, P., Monasse, P., Marlet, R., et al.: OpenMVG. An open multiple view geometry library. https://github.com/openMVG/openMVG
25. Moulon, P., Monasse, P., Marlet, R.: Global fusion of relative motions for robust, accurate and scalable structure from motion. In: 2013 IEEE International Conference on Computer Vision (2013)
26. Mapillary. https://www.mapillary.com/

Unsupervised Domain Adaptation for Semantic Segmentation via Class-Balanced Self-training

Yang Zou[1](✉), Zhiding Yu[2], B. V. K. Vijaya Kumar[1], and Jinsong Wang[3]

[1] Carnegie Mellon University, Pittsburgh, PA 15213, USA
yzou2@andrew.cmu.edu, kumar@ece.cmu.edu
[2] NVIDIA, Santa Clara, CA 95051, USA
zhidingy@nvidia.com
[3] General Motors R & D, Warren, MI 48092, USA
jinsong.wang@gm.com

Abstract. Recent deep networks achieved state of the art performance on a variety of semantic segmentation tasks. Despite such progress, these models often face challenges in real world "wild tasks" where large difference between labeled training/source data and unseen test/target data exists. In particular, such difference is often referred to as "domain gap", and could cause significantly decreased performance which cannot be easily remedied by further increasing the representation power. Unsupervised domain adaptation (UDA) seeks to overcome such problem without target domain labels. In this paper, we propose a novel UDA framework based on an iterative self-training (ST) procedure, where the problem is formulated as latent variable loss minimization, and can be solved by alternatively generating pseudo labels on target data and re-training the model with these labels. On top of ST, we also propose a novel class-balanced self-training (CBST) framework to avoid the gradual dominance of large classes on pseudo-label generation, and introduce spatial priors to refine generated labels. Comprehensive experiments show that the proposed methods achieve state of the art semantic segmentation performance under multiple major UDA settings.

1 Introduction

Semantic segmentation is a core computer vision task where one aims to densely assign labels to each pixel in the input image. In the past decade, significant amount of effort has been devoted to this area [1,5,6,9,10,13,20,38,39,44,45], leading to considerable progress with the recent advance of deep representation learning [15,19,31]. The competition on major open benchmark datasets [10]

Y. Zou and Z. Yu—Equal contribution.

Electronic supplementary material The online version of this chapter (https://doi.org/10.1007/978-3-030-01219-9_18) contains supplementary material, which is available to authorized users.

© Springer Nature Switzerland AG 2018
V. Ferrari et al. (Eds.): ECCV 2018, LNCS 11207, pp. 297–313, 2018.
https://doi.org/10.1007/978-3-030-01219-9_18

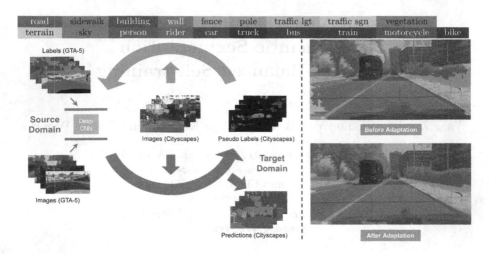

Fig. 1. Illustration of the proposed itertive self-training framework for unsupervised domain adaptation. Left: algorithm workflow. Right figure: semantic segmentation results on Cityscapes before and after adaptation.

have resulted in a number of more powerful models that tend to overfit to the benchmark data. While the boundaries of benchmark performance have been pushed to new limits, these models often encounter challenges in practical applications such as autonomous driving, where one needs ubiquitous good performance of the perception module. This is because benchmark datasets are usually biased to specific environments, while the testing scenario may encounter large domain differences caused by a number of factors, including change of geological position, illumination, camera, weather condition, etc. In this case, even the performance of a powerful model often drops dramatically, and such issue can not be easily remediated by further building up the model power [9,16,17].

A natural idea to improve network's generalization ability is to collect and annotate data covering more diverse scenes. However, densely annotating image is time-consuming and labor-intensive. For example, each Cityscapes image on average takes about 90 min to annotate [10]. To overcome the limitation, efforts were made to efficiently generate densely annotated images from rendered scenes, such as the Grand Theft Auto V (GTA5) [24] and SYNTHIA [26]. However, the large appearance gap across simulated/real domains significantly degrades the performance of synthetically trained models.

In light of the above issues, in this paper we focus on the challenging problem of unsupervised domain adaptation for semantic segmentation, aiming to unsupervisedly adapt a segmentation model trained on a labeled source domain to a target domain without knowing target labels. Recently, unsupervised domain adaptation has been widely explored for classification and detection tasks. There is a predominant trend to use adversarial training based methods for matching the distributions of both source and target features [3,9,12,17,29]. In particular, these methods aim to minimize a domain adversarial loss to reduce both the global and class-wise discrepancy between source and target feature distributions, while retaining good performance on source domain task by minimizing the task-specific loss.

Adversarial training based domain adaptation methods have recently achieved great success. However, in this work we show that similar or even better adaptation performance can be achieved by taking an alternative way without using adversarial training. Rather than trying to adapt by confusing the domain discriminator, our method kind of unifies the feature space alignment and the task itself together under a single, unified loss, which is given in Sect. 4. Under the single unified loss, we incorporate both the global and class-wise feature alignment as parts of our unified task, instead of considering feature matching and classification task separately.

Traditional self-training methods with handcrafted features is a common semi-supervised learning method that can learn better decision boundary for source and target data. Usually these approaches do not consider feature distribution matching. But combined with CNN, self-training becomes a powerful domain adaptation method that can not only learn better decision boundary, but also find a feature space of matched source and target distribution. In essence, the feature learning in self-training guided by softmax cross-entropy loss not only encourages global closeness of source and target features but also the class-wise feature alignment. The CNN based self-training methods share the same goal of adversarial training based global and class-wise feature alignment methods [9,17], but it try to solve domain adaption by a simpler and more elegant way.

The area of self-training based domain adaptation for semantic segmentation is underdevelopment. We propose a typical CNN based self-training (ST) framework for domain adaptation in semantic segmentation of which workflow is shown in Fig. 1, taking adapting from GTA5 → Cityscapes as an example. ST is carried out by alternately generating a set of pseudo-labels corresponding to large selection scores (i.e., softmax probability) in target domain, and then fine tuning network based on these pseudo-labels and labeled source data. It should be mentioned that ST assumes that target samples with larger prediction probability have better prediction accuracy.

The visual (e.g., appearance, scale, etc.) domain gap between source and target domains are usually different between classes. This can result in different difficulty degree for the network to learn transferable knowledge for each class. For instance, different countries may have different construction views and plants, but traffic lights and vehicles are similar. So it's harder for the source pre-trained models to learn transferable knowledge for construction and plants than for traffic lights and vehicles. Moreover, the imbalanced class distribution of source domain, and difference between source distribution and target distribution can also cause different degree of difficulty in transferring knowledge among different classes. This causes different prediction confidence levels for various classes in target domain. Since ST selects pseudo-labels with large confidence, it tends to be biased towards easy-to-transfer classes ignoring other classes and have inferior adaptation performance.

In summary, we focus on self-training based adaptation methods for semantic segmentation in this work. Our contributions are as follows.

- Building on deep nets, we introduce a self-training (ST) with self-paced learning adaptation framework for segmentation. We formulate it as a loss minimization problem in the form of mixed integer nonlinear program, which can be solved in an end-to-end way. Both domain-invariant features and classifier are expected be learned.
- To solve the class imbalance problem of pseudo-labels in ST, we propose a novel class-balanced self-training (CBST) adaptation for semantic segmentation. The proposed CBST utilizes confidence scores normalized classwise to select and generate pseudo-labels with balanced class distribution.
- Moreover, we observe that a traffic scene has its own spatial structure and introduce the concept of spatial priors (SP). We incorporate spatial priors into proposed self-training leading to class-balanced self-training with spatial priors (CBST-SP). The probability scores weighted by spatial priors are used for pseudo-label generation metric.
- We comprehensively evaluate our approaches in adapting large-scale rendered image dataset SYNTHIA/GTA5, to real image dataset, Cityscapes, and achieve state-of-the-art performance, outperforming other methods by a large margin. Also we test our methods in cross city adaptation settings, Cityscapes to NTHU dataset, and achieve state-of-the-art performance.

2   Related Works

The revolution of deep learning inspired broad interest in deep neural network based semantic segmentation. Long et al. [20] proposed a fully convolutional network for pixel-level classification. Recently several researchers proposed powerful segmentation nets, such as ResNet-38, PSPNet, etc. [38,39,44].

Unsupervised domain adaptation has been widely investigated in computer vision primarily for classification and detection tasks. In the era of deep neural network, the main adaption idea is to learn domain invariant features by minimizing difference between source and target feature distributions in an end-to-end way [11,12,14,21,32,35,37]. Among them, several methods utilize Maximum Mean Discrepancy (MMD) and its kernel variants to achieve the goal of feature distribution difference minimization. Recently there is an increasing interest in utilizing adversarial learning based methods to reduce the gap between source and target domains [14,21,36,37].

Another important strategy for unsupervised domain adaptation is based on self-training [4,47], which has many applications in vision and natural language processing [22,25,40,47]. Tang et al. [33] proposed a self-paced adaptation to shift object detection model from images to videos by learning labeled source samples and target data with pseudo-labels in an easy-to-hard way. Chen et al. [7] proposed a adaptation framework by slowly adapting its training set from the source to the target domain, using ideas from co-training. Bekker [2] et al. tackle the noisy labels problem.

As pointed out in [43], approaches addressing classification do not translate well to the semantic segmentation problem. So recently domain adaptation for semantic segmentation has emerged as a hot topic. Several researchers have focused on utilizing adversarial learning to minimize the domain gap of feature spaces. [9,17] proposed pixel level adversarial domain adaptation methods to reduce domain gap in feature spaces. Based on the domain adversarial training, [28] introduced a critic network detecting samples near the boundary and a generator that can generate discriminative features for target domain. [43] proposed a curriculum adaption method to regularize the predicted label distribution in the target domain to follow label distributions in source domain. Another possible direction to solve the domain adaptation problem is to utilize style transfer technique to stylize annotated source domain images as target domain images. Following this idea, based on the style transfer network Cycle-GAN [16,46] proposed a cycle-consistent adaptation framework combining the cycle-consistent loss with adversarial loss to minimize both pixel level and feature level domain gap.

3   Preliminaries

3.1   Fine-Tuning for Supervised Domain Adaptation

If the labels for the same task in both source and target are available, possibly the most direct way to perform domain adaptation is supervised fine-tuning the model on both domains. For semantic segmentation nets with softmax output, the adaptation problem can be formulated as minimizing the following loss function:

$$\min_{\mathbf{w}} \mathcal{L}_S(\mathbf{w}) = -\sum_{s=1}^{S}\sum_{n=1}^{N} \mathbf{y}_{s,n}^{\top} \log(\mathbf{p}_n(\mathbf{w}, \mathbf{I}_s)) - \sum_{t=1}^{T}\sum_{n=1}^{N} \mathbf{y}_{t,n}^{\top} \log(\mathbf{p}_n(\mathbf{w}, \mathbf{I}_t)) \qquad (1)$$

where $\mathbf{I}_s$ denotes the image in source domain indexed by $s = 1, 2, ..., S$, $\mathbf{y}_{s,n}$ the ground truth label for the n-th pixel ($n = 1, 2, ..., N$) in I_s, and $\mathbf{w}$ contains the network weights. $\mathbf{p}_n(\mathbf{w}, \mathbf{I}_s)$ is the softmax output containing the class probabilities at pixel n. Similar definitions apply for $\mathbf{I}_t$, $\mathbf{y}_{t,n}$ and $\mathbf{p}_n(\mathbf{w}, \mathbf{I}_t)$.

3.2   Self-training for Unsupervised Domain Adaptation

In the case of unsupervised domain adaptation, the target ground truth labels are not available. An alternate way to fine-tune the segmentation model is to consider the target labels as hidden variables that can be learned. Accordingly, the problem can be formulated as follows:

$$\min_{\mathbf{w}, \hat{\mathbf{y}}} \mathcal{L}_U(\mathbf{w}, \hat{\mathbf{y}}) = -\sum_{s=1}^{S}\sum_{n=1}^{N} \mathbf{y}_{s,n}^{\top} \log(\mathbf{p}_n(\mathbf{w}, \mathbf{I}_s)) - \sum_{t=1}^{T}\sum_{n=1}^{N} \hat{\mathbf{y}}_{t,n}^{\top} \log(\mathbf{p}_n(\mathbf{w}, \mathbf{I}_t))$$

$$s.t. \; \hat{\mathbf{y}}_{t,n} \in \{\mathbf{e}^{(i)} | \mathbf{e}^{(i)} \in \mathbb{R}^C\}, \forall t, n \qquad (2)$$

where $\hat{y}$ indicates the set of target labels, C is the number of classes, and $\mathbf{e}^{(i)}$ a one-hot vector. By minimizing the loss in Eq. (2) with respect to $\hat{y}$, the optimized $\hat{y}$ should approximate the underlying true target ground truth. Domain adaptation can then be performed similarly to Eq. (1). We call $\hat{y}$ "pseudo-labels", and regard such training strategy as self-training.

4 Proposed Methods

4.1 Self-training (ST) with Self-paced Learning

Jointly learning the model and optimizing pseudo-labels on unlabeled data is naturally difficult as it is not possible to completely guarantee the correctness of the generated pseudo-labels. A better strategy is to follow an "easy-to-hard" scheme via self-paced curriculum learning, where one seeks to generate pseudo-labels from the most confident predictions and hope they are mostly correct. Once the model is updated and better adapted to the target domain, the scheme then explores the remaining pseudo-labels with less confidence. To incorporate curriculum learning, we consider the following revised self-training formulation:

$$
\min_{\mathbf{w},\hat{\mathbf{y}}} \mathcal{L}_{ST}(\mathbf{w},\hat{\mathbf{y}}) = -\sum_{s=1}^{S}\sum_{n=1}^{N} \mathbf{y}_{s,n}^{\top} \log(\mathbf{p}_n(\mathbf{w},\mathbf{I}_s))
$$

$$
-\sum_{t=1}^{T}\sum_{n=1}^{N} \left[\hat{\mathbf{y}}_{t,n}^{\top} \log(\mathbf{p}_n(\mathbf{w},\mathbf{I}_t)) + k|\hat{\mathbf{y}}_{t,n}|_1 \right] \tag{3}
$$

$$
s.t.\ \hat{\mathbf{y}}_{t,n} \in \{\{\mathbf{e}^{(i)}|\mathbf{e}^{(i)} \in \mathbb{R}^C\} \cup \mathbf{0}\}, \forall t,n
$$

$$
k > 0
$$

where assigning $\mathbf{y}_{s,n}$ as $\mathbf{0}$ leads to ignoring this pseudo-label in model training, and the L_1 regularization serves as a negative sparse promoting term to prevent the trivial solution of ignoring all pseudo-labels. k is a hyperparameter controlling the amount of ignored pseudo-labels. A larger k encourages the selection of more pseudo-labels for model training. To minimize the loss in Eq. (3), we take the following alternative block coordinate descent algorithm:

- (a) Fix (initialize) $\mathbf{w}$ and minimize the loss in Eq. 3 with respect to $\hat{y}_{t,n}$.
- (b) Fix $\hat{y}_{t,n}$ and optimize the objective in Eq. 3 with respect to $\mathbf{w}$.

We call one step of (a) followed by one step of (b) as one **round**. In this work, we propose a self-training algorithm where step (a) and step (b) are alternately repeated for multiple rounds. Intuitively, step (a) selects a certain portion of most confident pseudo-labels from the target domain, while step (b) trains the network model given the pseudo-labels selected in step (a). Figure 1 illustrates the proposed algorithm flow in the domain adaptation example of GTA5 $\rightarrow$ Cityscapes.

Solving step (b) leads to network learning with stochastic gradient descent. However, solving step (a) requires a nonlinear integer programming given the optimization over discrete variables. Given $k > 0$, step (a) can be rewritten as:

$$\min_{\hat{\mathbf{y}}} - \sum_{t=1}^{T} \sum_{n=1}^{N} \left[\sum_{c=1}^{C} \hat{y}_{t,n}^{(c)} \log(p_n(c|\mathbf{w}, \mathbf{I}_t)) + k|\hat{\mathbf{y}}_{t,n}|_1 \right]$$
$$\text{s.t. } \hat{\mathbf{y}}_{t,n} = \left[\hat{y}_{t,n}^{(1)}, ..., \hat{y}_{t,n}^{(C)} \right] \in \{ \{ \mathbf{e}^{(i)} | \mathbf{e}^{(i)} \in \mathbb{R}^C \} \cup \mathbf{0} \}, \forall \, t, n$$
$$k > 0 \tag{4}$$

Since $\hat{\mathbf{y}}_{t,n}$ is required to be either a discrete one-hot vector or a zero vector, the pseudo-label configuration can be optimized via the following solver:

$$\hat{y}_{t,n}^{(c)*} = \begin{cases} 1, \text{ if } c = \arg\max_{c} p_n(c|\mathbf{w}, \mathbf{I}_t), \\ \qquad p_n(c|\mathbf{w}, \mathbf{I}_t) > \exp(-k) \\ 0, \text{ otherwise} \end{cases} \tag{5}$$

Unlike traditional self-training adaptation with handcrafted features that learn a domain-invariant classifier, CNN based self-training can learn not only domain-invariant classifier but also domain-invariant features. The softmax loss implicitly tries to reduce the domain difference in feature space. In addition, the self-training also has the missing value (pseudo-label) problem, similar to EM algorithm. The proposed alternate optimization method can learn the weights of models without prior observation of target domain labels.

One may note that the proposed framework is similar to [33] and several other related works. However, the proposed method presents a more generalized model for self-training and self-paced learning, in the sense that pseudo-label generation is unified with curriculum learning under a single learning framework. More importantly, in terms of the specific application, the above self-training framework sheds light on a relatively new direction for adapting semantic segmentation models. We will show that self-training based methods lead to considerably better or competitive performance compared to many current state of the art methods that are predominantly based on adversarial training.

4.2   Class-Balanced Self-training (CBST)

As mentioned in Sect. 1, the difference in visual domain gap and class distribution can cause different domain-transfer difficulty among classes, resulting in relatively higher prediction confidence scores for easy-to-transfer classes in target domain. Since ST generates pseudo-labels corresponding to large confidence, an issue comes out that model tends to be biased towards these initially well-transferred classes and ignore other hard classes along the training process. Thus it is difficult for ST to perform well in multi-class segmentation adaptation problem. To overcome this issue, we propose the following class-balanced self-training framework where class-wise confidence levels are normalized:

$$\min_{\mathbf{w},\hat{\mathbf{y}}} \mathcal{L}_{CB}(\mathbf{w},\hat{\mathbf{y}}) = -\sum_{s=1}^{S}\sum_{n=1}^{N} \mathbf{y}_{s,n}^{\top} \log(\mathbf{p}_n(\mathbf{w},\mathbf{I}_s))$$

$$-\sum_{t=1}^{T}\sum_{n=1}^{N}\sum_{c=1}^{C} [\hat{y}_{t,n}^{(c)}\log(p_n(c|\mathbf{w},\mathbf{I}_t)) + k_c\hat{y}_{t,n}^{(c)}] \qquad (6)$$

$$s.t. \ \hat{\mathbf{y}}_{t,n} = [\hat{y}_{t,n}^{(1)},...,\hat{y}_{t,n}^{(C)}] \in \{\{\mathbf{e}^{(i)}|\mathbf{e}^{(i)} \in \mathbb{R}^C\} \cup \mathbf{0}\}, \forall t,n$$

$$k_c > 0, \forall c$$

where each k_c is a separate parameter determining the proportion of selected pseudo-labels in class c. As one may observe, it is the difference between k_c that introduces different levels of class-wise bias for pseudo-label selection, and addresses the issue of inter-class balance.

The optimization flow of class-balanced self-training is the same as in Eq. (3) except for pseudo-label generation. Again, we can rewrite the step of pseudo-label optimization as:

$$\min_{\hat{\mathbf{y}}} -\sum_{t=1}^{T}\sum_{n=1}^{N}\sum_{c=1}^{C} [\hat{y}_{t,n}^{(c)}\log(p_n(c|\mathbf{w},\mathbf{I}_t)) + k_c\hat{y}_{t,n}^{(c)}]$$

$$s.t. \ \hat{\mathbf{y}}_{t,n} = [\hat{y}_{t,n}^{(1)},...,\hat{y}_{t,n}^{(C)}] \in \{\{\mathbf{e}|\mathbf{e} \in \mathbb{R}^C\} \cup \mathbf{0}\}, \forall \ t,n \qquad (7)$$

$$k_c > 0, \forall \ c$$

Note that the loss function in Eq. (7) can not be trivially minimized by the solver of Eq. (3). Instead, optimizing Eq. (7) requires the following class-balanced solver:

$$\hat{y}_{t,n}^{(c)*} = \begin{cases} 1, \textbf{ if } c = \arg\max_{c} \dfrac{p_n(c|\mathbf{w},\mathbf{I}_t)}{\exp(-k_c)}, \\ \qquad \dfrac{p_n(c|\mathbf{w},\mathbf{I}_t)}{\exp(-k_c)} > 1 \\ 0, \text{ otherwise} \end{cases} \qquad (8)$$

From Eq. (8), one can see that pseudo-label generation in Eq. (6) is no longer dependent on the output $p_n(c|\mathbf{w},\mathbf{I}_t)$, but hinges on the normalized output $\frac{p_n(c|\mathbf{w},\mathbf{I}_t)}{\exp(-k_c)}$. Pseudo-label assignment using this normalized output owns the benefit of balancing towards the class with relatively low score but having high within-class confidence. As a result, k_c should be set in a way that $\exp(-k_c)$ encodes the response strength of each class to balance different classes. In addition, for CBST, the pseudo-label of any pixel is only filtered when all the balanced responses are smaller than 1. There could also be multiple classes with $\frac{p_n(c|\mathbf{w},\mathbf{I}_t)}{\exp(-k_c)} > 1$. In this case, the class with the maximum balanced response is selected.

4.3   Self-paced Learning Policy Design

Determination of k in ST. From previous sections, we know that k plays a key role in filtering out pseudo-labels with probabilities smaller than k. To control the proportion of selected pseudo-labels in each round, we set k based on the following strategy:

We take the maximum output probability at each pixel, and sort such probabilities across all pixel locations and all target images in descending order. We then set k such that $\exp(-k)$ equals the probability ranked at $\text{round}(p * T * N)$, where p is a proportion number between $[0, 1]$. In this case, pseudo-label optimization produces $p \times 100\%$ most confident pseudo-labels for network training. The above policy can be summarized in Algorithm 1.

Algorithm 1. Determination of k in ST

    Input   : Neural network $P(\mathbf{w})$, all target images $\mathbf{I}_t$, portion p of selected
                         pseudo-labels
    Output: k
1 **for** $t=1$ to T **do**
2 | $\mathrm{P}_{\mathbf{I}_t} = \mathrm{P}(\mathbf{w},\mathbf{I}_t)$
3 | $\mathrm{MP}_{\mathbf{I}_t} = \max(\mathrm{P}_{\mathbf{I}_t},\text{axis}=0)$
4 | $\mathrm{M} = [\mathrm{M}, \text{matrix\_to\_vector}(\mathrm{MP}_{\mathbf{I}_t})]$
5 **end**
6 $\mathrm{M} = \text{sort}(\mathrm{M},\text{order}=\text{descending})$
7 $\text{len}_{th} = \text{length}(\mathrm{M}) \times \mathrm{p}$
8 $\mathrm{k} = \text{-log}(\mathrm{M}[\text{len}_{th}])$
9 **return** k

We design the self-paced learning policy such that more pseudo-labels are incorporated for each additional round. In particular, we start p from 20%, and empirically add 5% to p in each additional round of pseudo-label generation. The maximum portion is set to be 50%.

Determination of k_c in CBST. The policy of k_c in CBST is similarly defined. Although CBST seemingly introduce much more parameters than ST, we propose a strategy to easily determine k_c, and effectively encode the class-wise confidence levels.

Note that Algorithm 2 determines k_c by ranking the class c probabilities on all pixels predicted as class c, and setting k_c such that $\exp(-k_c)$ equals to the probability ranked at $\text{round}(p * N_c)$, where N_c indicates the number of pixels predicted as class c. Such a strategy basically takes the probability ranked at $p \times 100\%$ separately from each class as a reference for both thresholding and confidence normalization. The proportion variable p and its increasing policy is defined exactly the same to ST.

4.4   Incorporating Spatial Priors

For adapting models in the case of street scenes, we could take advantage of the spatial prior knowledge. Traffic scenes have common structures. For example, sky is not likely to appear at the bottom and road is not likely to appear at the top. If the image views in source domain and target domain are similar, we believe this knowledge can help to adapt source model. Thus we introduce spatial priors, similar to [30], by counting the class frequencies in the source domain, followed by smoothing with a 70×70 Gaussian kernel. In particular, we use $q_n(c)$ to indicate the frequency of class c at pixel n. Upon obtaining the class frequencies, we also normalize them by requiring $\sum_{i=1}^{N} q_n(c) = 1$. Figure 2 shows the heat map of spatial priors, calculated from GTA5 dataset, where yellow color indicates higher energy and blue color indicates lower energy.

To incorporate spatial priors into proposed CBST, we multiply the softmax output with the spatial priors, and consider the resulting potential as selection metric in pseudo-label generation:

$$\min_{\mathbf{w},\hat{\mathbf{y}}} \mathcal{L}_{SP}(\mathbf{w},\hat{\mathbf{y}}) = -\sum_{s=1}^{S}\sum_{n=1}^{N} \mathbf{y}_{s,n}^{\top} \log(\mathbf{p}_n(\mathbf{w},\mathbf{I}_s))$$

$$-\sum_{t=1}^{T}\sum_{n=1}^{N}\sum_{c=1}^{C} [\hat{y}_{t,n}^{(c)} \log(q_n(c)p_n(c|\mathbf{w},\mathbf{I}_t)) + k_c\hat{y}_{t,n}^{(c)}] \quad (9)$$

$$s.t. \ \hat{\mathbf{y}}_{t,n} \in \{\{\mathbf{e}|\mathbf{e} \in \mathbb{R}^C\} \cup \mathbf{0}\}, \forall t, n$$

$$k_c > 0, \forall c$$

Algorithm 2. Determination of k_c in CBST

Input : Neural network $f(\mathbf{w})$, all target images $\mathbf{I}_t$, portion p of selected pseudo-labels

Output: $\mathbf{k}_c$

1 **for** $t=1$ *to* T **do**
2 $\quad$ $P_{\mathbf{I}_t} = P(\mathbf{w},\mathbf{I}_t)$
3 $\quad$ $LP_{\mathbf{I}_t} = \text{argmax}(P,\text{axis}=0)$
4 $\quad$ $MP_{\mathbf{I}_t} = \text{max}(P,\text{axis}=0)$
5 $\quad$ **for** $c=1$ *to* C **do**
6 $\quad\quad$ $MP_{c,\mathbf{I}_t} = MP_{\mathbf{I}_t}(LP_{\mathbf{I}_t} == c)$
7 $\quad\quad$ $M_c = [M_c, \text{matrix\_to\_vector}(MP_{c,\mathbf{I}_t})]$
8 $\quad$ **end**
9 **end**
10 **for** $c=1$ *to* C **do**
11 $\quad$ $M_c = \text{sort}(M_c,\text{order}=\text{descending})$
12 $\quad$ $len_{c,th} = \text{length}(M_c) \times p$
13 $\quad$ $k_c = -\log(M_c[len_{c,th}])$
14 **end**
15 **return** $\mathbf{k}_c$

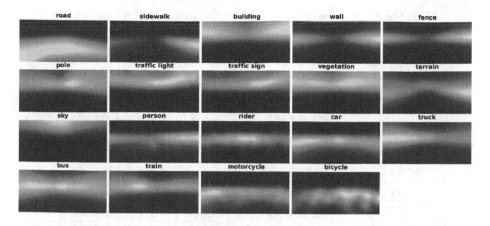

Fig. 2. Spatial priors on GTA5

We denote the above algorithm as CBST-SP. The workflow and self-paced learning policy are identical to CBST, except that the potential $q_n(c)p_n(c|\mathbf{w}, \mathbf{I}_t)$ is used to replace $p_n(c|\mathbf{w}, \mathbf{I}_t)$ in CBST. It should be noted that incorporating the spatial prior does not change network training, since $q_n(c)$ can be taken out of $\log(\cdot)$ as constants.

5 Numerical Experiments

In this section, we provide a comprehensive evaluation of proposed methods by performing experiments on three benchmark datasets. We firstly consider a cross-city adaptation case of shifting from Cityscapes to NTHU dataset [9]. Following [9], we choose the training set of Cityscapes as source. The NTHU dataset contains 400 $1,024 \times 2,048$ from 4 different cities: Rome, Rio, Tokyo and Taipei. Also we consider two challenging problems: from SYNTHIA [26] to Cityscapes [10] and from GTA5 [24] to Cityscapes. We use SYNTHIA-RAND-CITYSCAPES subset including labeled 9,400 760×1280 images. GTA5 dataset includes annotated 24,966 $1,052 \times 1,914$ images captured from the GTA5. The validation set of Cityscapes is treated as target domain.

Implementation Details. We use FCN8s-VGG16 [20] as our base network in SYNTHIA to Cityscapes and GTA5 to Cityscapes to give fair comparison with other methods utilizing the same base net. Further we boost our methods' performance via a better model ResNet-38 [39]. In the cross-city setting, we show state-of-the-art performance via CBST with ResNet-38. The networks were pretrained on ImageNet [27]. SGD has been used to train all the models by MXNET [8]. We use NVIDIA Titan Xp. In the CBST and CBST-SP experiments of GTA5 to Cityscapes and Cityscapes to NTHU, we use a hard sample mining strategy which mines the least prediction classes according to target prediction

Table 1. Experimental results for Cityscapes → NTHU dataset

City	Method	Road	SW	Build	TL	TS	Veg.	Sky	PR	Rider	Car	Bus	Motor	Bike	Mean
	Source Dilation-Frontend [9]	77.7	21.9	83.5	0.1	10.7	78.9	88.1	21.6	10.0	67.2	30.4	6.1	0.6	38.2
	GCAA [9]	79.5	29.3	84.5	0.0	22.2	80.6	82.8	29.5	13.0	71.7	37.5	25.9	1.0	42.9
Rome	DeepLab-v2 [34]	83.9	34.3	87.7	13.0	41.9	84.6	92.5	37.7	22.4	80.8	38.1	39.1	5.3	50.9
	MAA [34]	83.9	34.2	88.3	**18.8**	40.2	**86.2**	**93.1**	47.8	21.7	80.9	**47.8**	48.3	8.6	**53.8**
	Source Resnet-38	86.0	21.4	81.5	14.3	47.4	82.9	59.8	30.8	20.9	83.1	20.2	40.0	5.6	45.7
	ST	85.9	20.2	84.3	15.0	46.4	84.9	73.5	**48.5**	21.6	84.6	17.6	46.2	6.7	48.9
	CBST	**87.1**	**43.9**	**89.7**	14.8	**47.7**	85.4	90.3	45.4	**26.6**	**85.4**	20.5	**49.8**	**10.3**	53.6
	Source Dilation-Frontend [9]	69.0	31.8	77.0	4.7	3.7	71.8	80.8	38.2	8.0	61.2	38.9	11.5	3.4	38.5
	GCAA [9]	74.2	43.9	79.0	2.4	7.5	77.8	69.5	39.3	10.3	67.9	**41.2**	27.9	10.9	42.5
Rio	DeepLab-v2 [34]	76.6	47.3	82.5	12.6	22.5	77.9	86.5	43.0	19.8	74.5	36.8	29.4	16.7	48.2
	MAA [34]	76.2	44.7	84.6	9.3	25.5	**81.8**	**87.3**	55.3	**32.7**	74.3	28.9	**43.0**	**27.6**	51.6
	Source Resnet-38	80.6	36.0	81.8	**21.0**	33.1	79.0	64.7	36.0	21.0	73.1	33.6	22.5	7.8	45.4
	ST	80.1	41.4	83.8	19.1	**39.1**	80.8	71.2	**56.3**	27.7	**79.9**	32.7	36.4	12.2	50.8
	CBST	**84.3**	**55.2**	**85.4**	19.6	30.1	80.5	77.9	55.2	28.6	79.7	33.2	37.6	11.5	**52.2**
	Source Dilation-Frontend [9]	81.2	26.7	71.7	8.7	5.6	73.2	75.7	39.3	14.9	57.6	19.0	1.6	33.8	39.2
	GCAA [9]	83.4	**35.4**	72.8	12.3	12.7	77.4	64.3	42.7	21.5	64.1	**20.8**	8.9	40.3	42.8
Tokyo	DeepLab-v2 [34]	83.4	35.4	72.8	12.3	12.7	77.4	64.3	42.7	21.5	64.1	20.8	8.9	40.3	42.8
	MAA [34]	81.5	26.0	77.8	**17.8**	26.8	82.7	**90.9**	55.8	**38.0**	72.1	4.2	24.5	**50.8**	**49.9**
	Source Resnet-38	83.8	26.4	73.0	6.5	27.0	80.5	46.6	35.6	22.8	71.3	4.2	10.5	36.1	40.3
	ST	83.1	27.7	74.8	7.1	29.4	**84.4**	48.5	**57.2**	23.3	**73.3**	3.3	22.7	45.8	44.6
	CBST	**85.2**	33.6	**80.4**	8.3	**31.1**	83.9	78.2	53.2	28.9	72.7	4.4	**27.0**	47.0	48.8
	Source Dilation-Frontend [9]	77.2	20.9	76.0	5.9	4.3	60.3	81.4	10.9	11.0	54.9	32.6	15.3	5.2	35.1
	GCAA [9]	78.6	28.6	80.0	13.1	7.6	68.2	82.1	16.8	9.4	60.4	34.0	26.5	9.9	39.6
Taipei	DeepLab-v2 [34]	78.6	28.6	80.0	13.1	7.6	68.2	82.1	16.8	9.4	60.4	34.0	26.5	9.9	39.6
	MAA [34]	81.7	29.5	**85.2**	26.4	15.6	**76.7**	**91.7**	31.0	12.5	71.5	**41.1**	47.3	27.7	49.1
	Source Resnet-38	84.9	26.0	80.1	8.3	**28.0**	73.9	54.4	18.9	26.8	71.6	26.0	48.2	14.7	43.2
	ST	83.1	23.5	78.2	9.6	25.4	74.8	35.9	**33.2**	27.3	75.2	32.3	52.2	28.8	44.6
	CBST	**86.1**	**35.2**	84.2	15.0	22.2	75.6	74.9	22.7	**33.1**	**78.0**	37.6	**58.0**	**30.9**	**50.3**

portions. The mining classes are the worst 5 classes and top priority are given to classes whose portions are smaller than 0.1%. Other more details are provided in supplementary document.

5.1 Small Shift: Cross City Adaptation

NTHU dataset contains 13 classes shared with Cityscapes. We follow the same protocol as [9] to use a 10-fold cross validation. The IoU (Intersection-over-Union) of each class and the mIoU (mean IoU) are reported. Table 1 shows the results. Our CBST achieves superior or competitive performance compared with state-of-the-art.

5.2 Large Shift: Synthetic to Real Adaptation

From SYNTHIA to Cityscapes. We follow the same evaluation protocol as other works [17,43], we choose 16 common classes between SYNTHIA and CITYSCAPES as our valid labels. There is another setting only considering 13 classes excluding wall, fence and pole [34].

Table 2 reports the results. mIoU* is the mean IoU of 13 classes, excluding the classes with *. With FCN8s-VGG16 as base model, our CBST provides competitive performance compared with other methods. Equipped with a better base net ResNet-38, CBST achieves the superior performance outperforming

Table 2. Experimental results for SYNTHIA → Cityscapes

Method	Base Net	Road	SW	Build	Wall*	Fence*	Pole*	TL	TS	Veg.	Sky	PR	Rider	Car	Bus	Motor	Bike	mIoU	mIoU*
Source only [17]	Dilation-Frontend	6.4	17.7	29.7	1.2	0.0	15.1	0.0	7.2	30.3	66.8	51.1	1.5	47.3	3.9	0.1	0.0	17.4	20.2
FCN wild [17]	[41]	11.5	19.6	30.8	4.4	0.0	20.3	0.1	11.7	42.3	68.7	51.2	3.8	54.0	3.2	0.2	0.6	20.2	22.1
Source only [43]	FCN8s-VGG16	5.6	11.2	59.6	8.0	0.5	21.5	8.0	5.3	72.4	75.6	35.1	9.0	23.6	4.5	0.5	18.0	22.0	27.6
Curr. DA [43]	[20]	65.2	26.1	74.9	0.1	0.5	10.7	3.5	3.0	76.1	70.6	47.1	8.2	43.2	20.7	0.7	13.1	29.0	34.8
Source only	FCN8s-VGG16	24.1	19.1	68.5	0.9	0.3	16.4	5.7	10.8	75.2	76.3	43.2	15.2	26.7	15.0	5.9	8.5	25.7	30.3
GAN DA	[20]	79.1	31.1	77.1	3.0	0.2	22.8	6.6	15.2	77.4	78.9	47.0	14.8	67.5	16.3	6.9	13.0	34.8	40.8
Source only	DeepLab-v2 [34]	55.6	23.8	74.6	–	–	–	6.1	12.1	74.8	79.0	55.3	19.1	39.6	23.3	13.7	25.0	–	38.6
MAA	[34]	**84.3**	**42.7**	**77.5**	–	–	4.7	7.0	77.9	82.5	54.3	21.0	72.3	**32.2**	18.9	32.3	–	46.7
Source only	FCN8s-VGG16	17.2	19.7	47.3	1.1	0.0	19.1	3.0	9.1	71.8	78.3	37.6	4.7	42.2	9.0	0.1	0.9	22.6	26.2
ST	[20]	0.2	14.5	53.8	1.6	0.0	18.9	0.9	7.8	72.2	80.3	48.1	6.3	67.7	4.7	0.2	4.5	23.9	27.8
CBST		69.6	28.7	69.5	12.1	0.1	25.4	11.9	13.6	82.0	81.9	49.1	14.5	66.0	6.6	3.7	32.4	35.4	36.1
Source only	ResNet-38	32.6	21.5	46.5	4.8	0.1	26.5	14.8	13.1	70.8	60.3	56.6	3.5	74.1	20.4	8.9	13.1	29.2	33.6
ST	[39]	38.2	19.6	70.2	3.9	0.0	31.9	17.6	17.2	82.4	68.3	63.1	5.3	78.4	11.2	0.8	7.5	32.2	36.9
CBST		53.6	23.7	75.0	**12.5**	0.3	**36.4**	**23.5**	**26.3**	**84.8**	74.7	**67.2**	17.5	**84.5**	28.4	15.2	**55.8**	**42.5**	**48.4**

Table 3. Experimental results for GTA5 → Cityscapes

Method	Base Net	Road	SW	Build	Wall	Fence	Pole	TL	TS	Veg.	Terrain	Sky	PR	Rider	Car	Truck	Bus	Train	Motor	Bike	mIoU
Source only [17]	Dilation-Frontend	31.9	18.9	47.7	7.4	3.1	16.0	10.4	1.0	76.5	13.0	58.9	36.0	1.0	67.1	9.5	3.7	0.0	0.0	0.0	21.2
FCN wild [17]	[41]	70.4	32.4	62.1	14.9	5.4	10.9	14.2	2.7	79.2	21.3	64.6	44.1	4.2	70.4	8.0	7.3	0.0	3.5	0.0	27.1
Source only [43]	FCN8s-VGG16	18.1	6.8	64.1	7.3	8.7	21.0	14.9	16.8	45.9	2.4	64.4	41.6	17.5	55.3	8.4	5.0	6.9	4.3	13.8	22.3
Curr. DA [43]	[20]	74.9	22.0	71.7	6.0	11.9	8.4	16.3	11.1	75.7	13.3	66.5	38.0	9.3	55.2	18.8	18.9	0.0	16.8	16.6	28.9
Source only [16]	FCN8s-VGG16	26.0	14.9	65.1	5.5	12.9	8.9	6.0	2.5	70.0	2.9	47.0	24.5	0.0	40.0	12.1	1.5	0.0	0.0	0.0	17.9
CyCADA [16]	[20]	85.2	37.2	76.5	21.8	15.0	23.8	22.9	21.5	80.5	31.3	60.7	50.5	9.0	76.9	17.1	28.2	4.5	9.8	0.0	35.4
Source only [16]	Dilated ResNet-26	42.7	26.3	51.7	5.5	6.8	13.8	23.6	6.9	75.5	11.5	36.8	49.3	0.9	46.7	3.4	5.0	0.0	5.0	1.4	21.7
CyCADA [16]	[42]	79.1	33.1	77.9	23.4	17.3	32.1	33.3	31.8	81.5	26.7	69.0	62.8	14.7	74.5	20.9	25.6	6.9	18.8	20.4	39.5
Source only [28]	ResNet-50	64.5	24.9	73.7	14.8	2.5	18.0	15.9	0	74.9	16.4	72.0	42.3	0.0	39.5	8.6	13.4	0.0	0.0	0.0	25.3
ADR [28]	[15]	87.8	15.6	77.4	20.6	9.7	19.0	19.9	7.7	82.0	31.5	74.3	43.5	9.0	77.8	17.5	27.7	1.8	9.7	0.0	33.3
Source only [23]	DenseNet	67.3	23.1	69.4	13.9	14.4	21.6	19.2	12.4	78.7	24.5	74.8	49.3	3.7	54.1	8.7	5.3	2.6	6.2	1.9	29.0
I2I Adapt [23]	[18]	85.8	37.5	80.2	23.3	16.1	23.0	14.5	9.8	79.2	**36.5**	**76.4**	53.4	7.4	82.8	19.1	15.7	2.8	13.4	1.7	35.7
Source only [34]	DeepLab-v2	75.8	16.8	77.2	12.5	21.0	25.5	30.1	20.1	81.3	24.6	70.3	53.8	26.4	49.9	17.2	25.9	6.5	25.3	36.0	36.6
MAA [34]	[18]	86.5	36.0	**79.9**	23.4	23.3	23.9	35.2	14.8	83.4	33.3	75.6	58.5	27.6	73.7	32.5	35.4	3.9	30.1	28.1	42.4
Source only	FCN8s-VGG16	64.0	22.1	68.6	13.3	8.7	19.9	15.5	5.9	74.9	13.4	37.0	37.7	10.3	48.2	6.1	1.2	1.8	10.8	2.9	24.3
ST	[17]	83.8	17.4	72.1	14.3	2.9	16.5	16.0	6.8	81.4	24.2	47.2	40.7	7.6	71.7	10.2	7.6	0.5	11.1	0.9	28.1
CBST		66.7	26.8	73.7	14.8	9.5	28.3	25.9	10.1	75.5	15.7	51.6	47.2	6.2	71.9	3.7	2.2	5.4	18.9	32.4	30.9
CBST-SP		**90.4**	50.8	72.0	18.3	9.5	27.2	28.6	14.1	82.4	25.1	70.8	42.6	14.5	76.9	5.9	12.5	1.2	14.0	28.6	36.1
Source only	ResNet-38	70.0	23.7	67.8	15.4	18.1	40.2	41.9	25.3	78.8	11.7	31.4	**62.9**	**29.8**	60.1	21.5	26.8	7.7	28.1	12.0	35.4
ST	[39]	90.1	56.8	77.9	28.5	23.0	41.5	45.2	39.6	84.8	26.4	49.2	59.0	27.4	82.3	39.7	45.6	**20.9**	**34.8**	**46.2**	41.5
CBST		86.8	46.7	76.9	26.3	**24.8**	42.0	46.0	38.6	80.7	15.7	48.0	57.3	27.9	78.2	24.5	49.6	17.7	25.5	45.1	45.2
CBST-SP		88.0	56.2	77.0	27.4	22.4	40.7	47.3	**40.9**	82.4	21.6	60.3	50.2	20.4	**83.8**	35.0	**51.0**	15.2	20.6	37.0	46.2
CBST-SP+MST		89.6	**58.9**	78.5	**33.0**	22.3	**41.4**	**48.2**	39.2	**83.6**	24.3	65.4	49.3	20.2	83.3	**39.0**	48.6	12.5	20.3	35.3	**47.0**

state-of-the-art by 1.7. Compared with ST, CBST with either FCN8s-VGG16 or ResNet-38 achieves better performance for mIoU and IoU of these initially not well-transfered classes, such as wall, rider, motorcycle and bike. The appearance of fence in SYNTHIA (car barriers) is extremely different from the fence in Cityscapes (pedestrian barriors) and it's very hard for the model to learn transferable knowledge for fence from SYNTHIA to Cityscapes. Figure 3 gives the visualization segmentation results in Cityscapes.

From GTA5 to Cityscapes. Table 3 gives experimental results of the shared 19 classes. For the results with FCN8s-VGG16 as base model, the performance of ST demonstrates that the adapted model can be easily biased towards initial easy-to-transfer classes. However, the CBST not only achieves better mIoU than ST, but also better IoU for these initial hard-to-transfer classes. Moreover, since images from GTA5 and Cityscapes have similar view structure, we evaluate our proposed CBST-SP, achieving mIoU 36.1, which is better than the results using powerful base models, ResNet-50 [28] and DenseNet [23]. Equipped with a powerful model ResNet-38, our method get a much better score 46.2, outper-

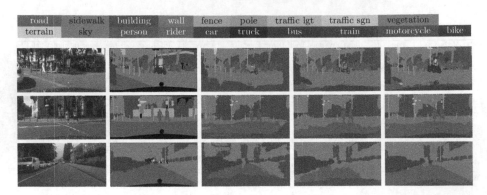

Fig. 3. Adaptation results on SYNTHIA → Cityscapes. Rows correspond to predictions for sample images in Cityscapes. Columns correspond to original images, ground truth, and results of source ResNet-38, ST, CBST

Fig. 4. Adaptation results on GTA5 → Cityscapes. Rows correspond to predictions for sample images in Cityscapes. Columns correspond to original images, ground truth, and results of source ResNet-38, ST, CBST and CBST-SP

forming other methods by a large margin. The multi-scale testing (0.5,0.75,1.0) boosts the mIoU to 47.0. Figure 4 gives the visualization segmentation results in Cityscapes.

6   Conclusions

In this paper, we proposed a deep neural network based self-training (ST) framework for unsupervised domain adaptation in the context of semantic segmentation. The ST is formulated as a loss minimization problem allowing learning of domain-invariant features and classifier in an end-to-end way. A class-balanced self-training (CBST) is introduced to overcome the imbalance issue of transferring difficulty among classes via generating pseudo-labels with balanced class distribution. Moreover, if there is a small domain difference in image view, we could incorporate spatial priors (SP) into CBST, resulting in CBST-SP. We experimentally demonstrate that our proposed methods achieve superior results outperforming other state-of-the-art methods by a large margin. We empirically show our proposed methods is compatible with adversarial domain adaptation methods.

References

1. http://data-bdd.berkeley.edu/
2. Bekker, A.J., Goldberger, J.: Training deep neural-networks based on unreliable labels. In: 2016 IEEE International Conference on Acoustics, Speech and Signal Processing (ICASSP), pp. 2682–2686. IEEE (2016)
3. Bousmalis, K., Trigeorgis, G., Silberman, N., Krishnan, D., Erhan, D.: Domain separation networks. In: Advances in Neural Information Processing Systems, pp. 343–351 (2016)
4. Chapelle, O., Scholkopf, B., Zien, A.: Semi-supervised learning. IEEE Trans. Neural Netw. 20(3), 542–542 (2009). (Chapelle, O. et al. (eds.) 2006) [book reviews]
5. Chen, L.C., Papandreou, G., Kokkinos, I., Murphy, K., Yuille, A.L.: DeepLab: semantic image segmentation with deep convolutional nets, atrous convolution, and fully connected CRFs. arXiv preprint arXiv:1606.00915 (2016)
6. Chen, L.C., Papandreou, G., Schroff, F., Adam, H.: Rethinking atrous convolution for semantic image segmentation. arXiv preprint arXiv:1706.05587 (2017)
7. Chen, M., Weinberger, K.Q., Blitzer, J.: Co-training for domain adaptation. In: Advances in Neural Information Processing Systems, pp. 2456–2464 (2011)
8. Chen, T., et al.: MXNet: a flexible and efficient machine learning library for heterogeneous distributed systems. arXiv preprint arXiv:1512.01274 (2015)
9. Chen, Y.H., Chen, W.Y., Chen, Y.T., Tsai, B.C., Frank Wang, Y.C., Sun, M.: No more discrimination: cross city adaptation of road scene segmenters. In: The IEEE International Conference on Computer Vision (ICCV), October 2017
10. Cordts, M., et al.: The cityscapes dataset for semantic urban scene understanding. In: Proceedings of the IEEE Conference on Computer Vision and Pattern Recognition, pp. 3213–3223 (2016)
11. Ganin, Y., Lempitsky, V.: Unsupervised domain adaptation by backpropagation. In: International Conference on Machine Learning, pp. 1180–1189 (2015)
12. Ganin, Y., et al.: Domain-adversarial training of neural networks. J. Mach. Learn. Res. 17(59), 1–35 (2016)
13. Geiger, A., Lenz, P., Urtasun, R.: Are we ready for autonomous driving? The KITTI vision benchmark suite. In: 2012 IEEE Conference on Computer Vision and Pattern Recognition (CVPR), pp. 3354–3361. IEEE (2012)
14. Gretton, A., Smola, A., Huang, J., Schmittfull, M., Borgwardt, K., Schölkopf, B.: Covariate shift and local learning by distribution matching, pp. 131–160. MIT Press, Cambridge (2009)
15. He, K., Zhang, X., Ren, S., Sun, J.: Deep residual learning for image recognition. In: Proceedings of the IEEE Conference on Computer Vision and Pattern Recognition, pp. 770–778 (2016)
16. Hoffman, J., et al.: CyCADA: cycle-consistent adversarial domain adaptation. arXiv preprint arXiv:1711.03213 (2017)
17. Hoffman, J., Wang, D., Yu, F., Darrell, T.: FCNs in the wild: pixel-level adversarial and constraint-based adaptation. arXiv preprint arXiv:1612.02649 (2016)
18. Huang, G., Liu, Z.: Densely connected convolutional networks
19. Krizhevsky, A., Sutskever, I., Hinton, G.E.: ImageNet classification with deep convolutional neural networks. In: Advances in Neural Information Processing Systems (2012)

20. Long, J., Shelhamer, E., Darrell, T.: Fully convolutional networks for semantic segmentation. In: Proceedings of the IEEE Conference on Computer Vision and Pattern Recognition, pp. 3431–3440 (2015)
21. Long, M., Cao, Y., Wang, J., Jordan, M.: Learning transferable features with deep adaptation networks. In: International Conference on Machine Learning, pp. 97–105 (2015)
22. Maeireizo, B., Litman, D., Hwa, R.: Co-training for predicting emotions with spoken dialogue data. In: Proceedings of the ACL 2004 on Interactive Poster and Demonstration Sessions, p. 28. Association for Computational Linguistics (2004)
23. Murez, Z., Kolouri, S., Kriegman, D., Ramamoorthi, R., Kim, K.: Image to image translation for domain adaptation. arXiv preprint arXiv:1712.00479 (2017)
24. Richter, S.R., Vineet, V., Roth, S., Koltun, V.: Playing for data: ground truth from computer games. In: Leibe, B., Matas, J., Sebe, N., Welling, M. (eds.) ECCV 2016. LNCS, vol. 9906, pp. 102–118. Springer, Cham (2016). https://doi.org/10.1007/978-3-319-46475-6_7
25. Riloff, E., Wiebe, J., Wilson, T.: Learning subjective nouns using extraction pattern bootstrapping. In: Proceedings of the Seventh Conference on Natural Language Learning at HLT-NAACL 2003, vol. 4, pp. 25–32. Association for Computational Linguistics (2003)
26. Ros, G., Sellart, L., Materzynska, J., Vazquez, D., Lopez, A.M.: The SYNTHIA dataset: a large collection of synthetic images for semantic segmentation of urban scenes. In: Proceedings of the IEEE Conference on Computer Vision and Pattern Recognition, pp. 3234–3243 (2016)
27. Russakovsky, O., et al.: Imagenet large scale visual recognition challenge. Int. J. Comput. Vis. **115**(3), 211–252 (2015)
28. Saito, K., Ushiku, Y., Harada, T., Saenko, K.: Adversarial dropout regularization. arXiv preprint arXiv:1711.01575 (2017)
29. Sankaranarayanan, S., Balaji, Y., Jain, A., Lim, S.N., Chellappa, R.: Unsupervised domain adaptation for semantic segmentation with gans. arXiv preprint arXiv:1711.06969 (2017)
30. Silberman, N., Fergus, R.: Indoor scene segmentation using a structured light sensor. In: 2011 IEEE International Conference on Computer Vision Workshops (ICCV Workshops), pp. 601–608. IEEE (2011)
31. Simonyan, K., Zisserman, A.: Very deep convolutional networks for large-scale image recognition. In: International Conference on Learning Representations (2015)
32. Sun, B., Saenko, K.: Deep CORAL: correlation alignment for deep domain adaptation. In: Hua, G., Jégou, H. (eds.) ECCV 2016. LNCS, vol. 9915, pp. 443–450. Springer, Cham (2016). https://doi.org/10.1007/978-3-319-49409-8_35
33. Tang, K., Ramanathan, V., Fei-Fei, L., Koller, D.: Shifting weights: adapting object detectors from image to video. In: Advances in Neural Information Processing Systems, pp. 638–646 (2012)
34. Tsai, Y.H., Hung, W.C., Schulter, S., Sohn, K., Yang, M.H., Chandraker, M.: Learning to adapt structured output space for semantic segmentation. arXiv preprint arXiv:1802.10349 (2018)
35. Tzeng, E., Hoffman, J., Darrell, T., Saenko, K.: Simultaneous deep transfer across domains and tasks. In: Proceedings of the IEEE International Conference on Computer Vision, pp. 4068–4076 (2015)
36. Tzeng, E., Hoffman, J., Darrell, T., Saenko, K.: Adversarial discriminative domain adaptation. In: Computer Vision and Pattern Recognition (CVPR) (2017)

37. Tzeng, E., Hoffman, J., Zhang, N., Saenko, K., Darrell, T.: Deep domain confusion: maximizing for domain invariance. arXiv preprint arXiv:1412.3474 (2014)
38. Wang, P., et al.: Understanding convolution for semantic segmentation. arXiv preprint arXiv:1702.08502 (2017)
39. Wu, Z., Shen, C., van den Hengel, A.: Wider or deeper: revisiting the ResNet model for visual recognition. arXiv preprint arXiv:1611.10080 (2016)
40. Yarowsky, D.: Unsupervised word sense disambiguation rivaling supervised methods. In: Proceedings of the 33rd Annual Meeting on Association for Computational Linguistics, pp. 189–196. Association for Computational Linguistics (1995)
41. Yu, F., Koltun, V.: Multi-scale context aggregation by dilated convolutions. arXiv preprint arXiv:1511.07122 (2015)
42. Yu, F., Koltun, V., Funkhouser, T.: Dilated residual networks. In: Computer Vision and Pattern Recognition, vol. 1 (2017)
43. Zhang, Y., David, P., Gong, B.: Curriculum domain adaptation for semantic segmentation of urban scenes. In: The IEEE International Conference on Computer Vision (ICCV), October 2017
44. Zhao, H., Shi, J., Qi, X., Wang, X., Jia, J.: Pyramid scene parsing network. In: The IEEE Conference on Computer Vision and Pattern Recognition (CVPR), July 2017
45. Zhou, B., Zhao, H., Puig, X., Fidler, S., Barriuso, A., Torralba, A.: Semantic understanding of scenes through the ADE20K dataset. arXiv preprint arXiv:1608.05442 (2016)
46. Zhu, J.Y., Park, T., Isola, P., Efros, A.A.: Unpaired image-to-image translation using cycle-consistent adversarial networks
47. Zhu, X.: Semi-supervised learning literature survey (2005)

Towards Human-Level License Plate Recognition

Jiafan Zhuang⬛, Saihui Hou⬛, Zilei Wang⁽✉⁾⬛, and Zheng-Jun Zha⬛

University of Science and Technology of China, Hefei, China
{jfzhuang,saihui}@mail.ustc.edu.cn, {zlwang,zhazj}@ustc.edu.cn

Abstract. License plate recognition (LPR) is a fundamental component of various intelligent transport systems, which is always expected to be accurate and efficient enough. In this paper, we propose a novel LPR framework consisting of semantic segmentation and character counting, towards achieving human-level performance. Benefiting from innovative structure, our method can recognize a whole license plate once rather than conducting character detection or sliding window followed by per-character recognition. Moreover, our method can achieve higher recognition accuracy due to more effectively exploiting global information and avoiding sensitive character detection, and is time-saving due to eliminating one-by-one character recognition. Finally, we experimentally verify the effectiveness of the proposed method on two public datasets (AOLP and Media Lab) and our License Plate Dataset. The results demonstrate our method significantly outperforms the previous state-of-the-art methods, and achieves the accuracies of more than 99% for almost all settings.

Keywords: License Plate Recognition (LPR)
Semantic segmentation · Convolutional Neural Networks (CNN)
Character counting

1 Introduction

License plate recognition (LPR) from images as a fundamental component is vitally important for various intelligent transport systems (ITS), such as security control of restricted areas [9,28] and traffic safety enforcement [16,33], as the license plate is generally used as the identification of a vehicle. So the LPR algorithm is always required to be accurate and efficient enough for facilitating the deployment and application in terminal equipments or transport systems. On the other hand, LPR in complex scenes that the vehicle images may be highly deformed or blurred is probably the main consideration in many real-world applications. For instance, the suspect vehicles are the mainly concerned targets that need to extract the structured information in the safety surveillance, while other normal ones can be completely ignored. But the acquired images for such vehicles are usually harder to analyze. Therefore, developing accurate and robust LPR is essential, especially for complex scenes.

© Springer Nature Switzerland AG 2018
V. Ferrari et al. (Eds.): ECCV 2018, LNCS 11207, pp. 314–329, 2018.
https://doi.org/10.1007/978-3-030-01219-9_19

LPR needs to handle the diverse illuminance conditions, image blurring, defacing, and vehicle deformation [1,2,10,26,31]. The existing works can be roughly divided into two broad categories: traditional methods consisting of character detection and recognition, and recent sequential methods. The first type of methods are intuitive which first detect all characters in a license plate and then independently recognize the detected characters. In practice, the methods are too sensitive to the environmental factors and consequently error-prone [11]. Thus they are applicable only to the restricted scenarios with fixed conditions, e.g., parking entrances. The sequential methods [6,7,21,32] are proposed in recent years, which first conduct sliding window to extract the sequential features of a license plate, and then recognize the license plate from the extracted features by a CNN or RNN model. Relatively, these methods can produce better recognition performance, but it is not enough to meet the requirements of real systems. Meanwhile, too many calls to deep learning models make these methods time-consuming, leading to low computational efficiency.

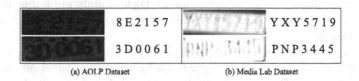

(a) AOLP Dataset   (b) Media Lab Dataset

Fig. 1. Some example results recognized by our proposed method. The images are from two public datasets: AOLP and Media Lab

In this paper, we propose a novel LPR framework with aims of simultaneously improving the recognition accuracy and computational efficiency. It consists of two key components: semantic segmentation and character counting. Owing to such an innovative structure, our approach is robust to various image quality, and Fig. 1 provides some example results of our method. To our knowledge, this work is the first attempt to adopt advanced semantic segmentation in LPR. Indeed, our proposed method can achieve outstanding recognition accuracy benefiting from the following facts. First, semantic segmentation directly processes an entire license plate image rather than subimages of individual characters, which helps to exploit more information from both global and local contexts. Second, we conduct the pixel-level recognition instead of character recognition in previous works, which can endure a small part of pixels to be misclassified without causing a failure of LPR. Third, our method does not require very precise character detection since semantic segmentation has completed the recognition function, but which is exactly one of the main obstacles in the traditional methods. On the other hand, our proposed method possesses higher computational efficiency because semantic segmentation once recognizes all pixels of an input image and only several times (far less than the number of characters in a license plate) of calls to the CNN model are needed in the subsequent counting procedure.

We experimentally evaluate the proposed method on two public license plate datasets (AOLP and Media Lab) and our own License Plate Dataset, which all are built using the images from real scenes and cover many difficult conditions. The results on public datasets consistently demonstrate that our method is greatly superior to the previous state-of-the-art methods. And for most of settings, a recognition accuracy of more than 99% is achieved, which implies that our method is applicable to real-world systems, even for complex scenes. Furthermore, we also conduct error study by analyzing all failure samples produced by our method. It is observed that these samples are extremely difficult to recognize accurately, and most of them is very confusing even for human being. This indicates that the performance of our proposed method is very close to the human level.

2   Related Work

Before the explosion of deep learning, almost all traditional LPR methods [3,11] adopt a similar process flow, *i.e.*, character detection followed by separately character recognition. The differences among them mainly are minor implementation details. Here we briefly review the related works on character detection and recognition.

Character detection is to detect each character in a license plate image with a bounding box. Most of existing algorithms for character detection can be simply divided into two families. The first one is based on Connected Component Analysis (CCA) [2,15]. After removing image noise and eroding the connecting area of neighboring characters in the binarized license plate image, CCA is performed to obtain all connected areas and each of them is regard as a character. The second family relies on the projection methods [12,13,18,34,35]. Different from the first one, they project the binary image horizontally to obtain the top and bottom boundary, and then vertically to segment each character.

Character recognition is to recognize each candidate extracted by character detection. Various methods have been proposed for this task. [13,15,26,34] are based on the template matching that measures the similarity between the character and templates. These methods are computationally costly and easily affected by interference. The feature based methods use more discriminate features, *e.g.*, hand-crafted feature [18,35], and a specific classifier, *e.g.*, probabilistic neural network (PNN) [2], HMM [12], and MLP neural network [27]. [14,15] extract the LBP features and adopt a linear discriminant analysis (LDA) as classifier. With the arrival of deep learning, character recognition in the LPR task is usually implemented by a CNN network [25].

Recently, the advancement of deep learning techniques brings new ideas to find a solution without character detection. A typical method uses a sliding window way to extract sequential features of license plate, and then infers the character sequence by feeding the extracted features into a classification model. Here the models for feature extraction include sweep OCR [7], CNN [21], and FCN [32]. The inference models include HMM [7], RNN with LSTM [21], and customized NMS algorithm [32]. Benefiting from the elimination of character detection, these methods can achieve better recognition performance, which indeed are the state-of-the-art. However, these methods need to repeatedly apply the character classifier many times, leading to low computational efficiency. Moreover, the methods conduct the character recognition on a small patch of the license plate image, which is easily influenced by interference in complex scenes. A related work [29] utilizes single-histogram approach to perform pixel-wise prediction to identify the character regions, followed by the street name recognition with template matching.

In this work, we propose a novel LPR framework. Unlike the existing works, we adopt semantic segmentation to recognize a whole license plate followed by character counting. Our framework avoids the sensitive character detection and meanwhile utilizes global information of a license plate image. Besides, our method is computationally efficient without a sliding window profile.

3   Our Method

3.1   Overview

Our purpose in this work is to invent an accurate and efficient license plate recognition (LPR) method by overcoming the drawbacks of previous works. To this end, we particularly introduce the semantic segmentation technique as the main component since it can directly process a whole license plate image. Here the input refers to the cropped subimages from raw images that only contain the license plate content with little background, which in practice is easily accomplished by applying some handy detection methods [12,13,18,34,35]. We illustrate the proposed LPR framework in Fig. 2, which consists of two key modules: semantic segmentation and counting refinement.

Semantic segmentation is used to produce the semantic map of the input license plate image with the same size, whose value represents the character class of corresponding pixel. We then operate on the produced semantic maps to obtain the character sequence of a license plate. Compared with the character recognition in traditional methods, semantic segmentation can exploit more information in addition to the advantage of high computational efficiency, as the entire input image is fed once and both the global and local information from different network layers are fused. In this module, we conduct pre-processing on the input images and character sequence inference on the resulting maps besides semantic segmentation. Here the pre-processing is to make the images suitable for semantic segmentation, and only a simple projection is adopted in our implementation. As for the character sequence inference, an initial recognition result would be produced from the semantic map.

In the resulting semantic segmentation maps, we cannot distinguish the successive characters of the same type. To handle such situations, a counting refinement module is proposed to append to the semantic segmentation module in this work, which is used to predict the number of successive characters. In theory, the times to conduct the character counting for a license plate is at most half of the total number of characters. Thus this procedure is statistically time-saving, which together with semantic segmentation makes our method very efficient compared to the previous methods based on deep learning. Finally, we would obtain the character sequence of an input license plate.

From Fig. 2, we can observe the following features of the proposed LPR framework. First, we adopt the pixel-wise recognition to replace the character recognition in the traditional methods. Such replacement eliminates the character detection that is sensitive to imaging conditions and would deteriorate the overall performance of LPR, and meantime improves the robustness to image interference as the wrong prediction on a small proportion of pixels almost has no effect on the final results. Second, our framework processes a whole license plate once and avoids time-costly sliding window in the previous works, which thus is more efficient. Third, our proposed framework is flexible and upgradeable, in which each module can be assigned a different model. Thus one application can be equipped with the appropriate models by considering the actual demands in accuracy and efficiency. Next we will elaborate on the details of two key modules.

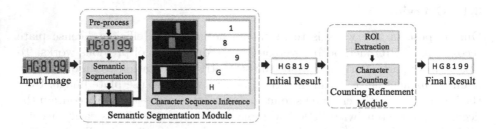

Fig. 2. Illustration of our proposed LPR framework. The framework consists of two key modules: semantic segmentation and counting refinement. The semantic segmentation module is to produce the semantic map and initial character sequence, which includes pre-processing, semantic segmentation, and character sequence inference. The counting refinement module is to generate the final character sequence through counting characters. Best viewed in color

3.2   Semantic Segmentation Module

The semantic segmentation module is functionally to produce a semantic map and initial character sequence for an input license plate image. Here the semantic map has the same size as the input. In particular, we first pre-process the input image to make it more suitable for semantic segmentation, and then infer the initial character sequence by analyzing the semantic map. For pre-processing, we first find the character boundary by horizontally and vertically projection analysis, and then crop the main body of license plate image as the input. For semantic segmentation, we adopt a modified DeeplabV2 ResNet-101 model and put our focuses on the data preparation. For character sequence inference, we expect that the obtained initial character sequence are robust enough even when the segmentation results are not good with wrong predictions on some pixels.

Segmentation Groundtruth. In the LPR scenario, the results of semantic segmentation are essentially used to produce the character sequences, which is a bit different from the usage in traditional segmentation tasks aiming to precisely predict the semantic label of each pixel. Thus we propose to adopt a relatively simple segmentation ground truth for each license plate in this work.

Considering the difficulty of labeling all pixels, we particularly use the wrapped bounding box of each character as its segmentation ground truth, instead of a subtle mask representing the character contour. All pixels in the bounding box are labeled the class of corresponding character, and other pixels not belonging to any character are labeled the background class. Figure 3 illustrates the ground truth generation of a license plate by an example. Obviously, the box-level annotation is more labor-saving than the pixel-level annotation, which benefits the proposed framework more operable than other semantic segmentation tasks.

Moreover, learning the bounding boxes of characters is more robust for LPR due to containing more pixels, unlike the prediction of character contours that is prone to be broken due to the thinness of labeled area. Consequently, some wrong prediction over a few pixels has almost no negative effect on the overall results in our method. On the other hand, the proposed segmentation groundtruth also makes the subsequent analysis of character sequence easier as a bigger semantic area has lower complication.

Fig. 3. Illustration of box-level label for a license plate image. The sample is from the AOLP dataset. Here different colors denote different character classes. The pixels not belonging to any character box are labeled as the background class (black). Best viewed in color

Semantic Segmentation Model. Here we mainly consider the semantic segmentation models based on deep learning due to their achieved state-of-the-art performance. In theory, any advanced semantic segmentation model can be used in the proposed LPR framework, such as Fully Convolution Network (FCN) [24], DeepLabv2 [8], and SegNet [5]. In our implementation, a modified version of DeepLabv2 ResNet-101 is particularly adopted, as shown in Fig. 4, whose performance has proven by evaluation to be good enough for LPR.

Here we simplify the original DeepLabv2 ResNet-101 model to boost the computational efficiency. The original model performs multi-scale process to obtain more accurate segmentation results, which essentially is to fuse the hierarchical global information. In the LPR task, however, the semantic areas of different characters have lower correlation. Meanwhile, our proposed analysis method is robust to wrong prediction on a few pixels. Thus in this work we only reserve

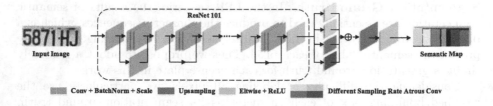

Fig. 4. The modified DeepLabv2 ResNet-101 model. The network mainly includes the ResNet-101 for feature extraction, atrous spatial pyramid pooling (ASPP), and upsampling layers. Best viewed in color

the original resolution branch and remove other auxiliary branches. Actually, we conduct the comparative analysis between the simplified version and the original DeepLabv2 ResNet-101 by experiments. The results show that the modified one performs faster without involving an accuracy decrease on the final LPR results. Specifically, with the fixed configuration (GeForce GTX 1080Ti), our version achieves 38 FPS, while the original DeepLabv2 only has 13 FPS.

Model Pre-training. Semantic Segmentation usually requires a massive collection of training samples to achieve accurate prediction. But the existing license plate datasets are commonly small in scale and cannot afford such data requirements. To address this issue, we propose to pre-train the model and then fine-tune it using the samples in a specific dataset. For pre-training, we use the synthetic images of license plate in this work since the data scale is extensible and the ground truth is easily obtained that can be concurrently generated in the synthesis process.

Here we propose to synthesize the license plate images by the combination of different characters. Specifically, we first set a base dataset containing many license plate images, in which various images with different illumination, color, blurring, and viewpoint need be embodied for each character. In our implementation, a subset of our own License Plate Dataset in Sect. 4.4 is particularly employed. Then we sample substantial character images by cropping from the license plate images, which form the materials of data synthesis. The cropping operation is natural since we use a bounding box to annotate each character. Finally, we synthesize plenty of license plate images by replacing one character region in a license plate image with another character image. To generate balanced samples, we randomly choose the base license plate image and character to be replaced, and use the images of different character to yield multiple samples. Here the character image for a given type is selected by measuring the style similarity between the base image and character image.

Following this way, we finally produce 60,000 synthetic license plate images together with their groundtruth segmentation for model training. Figure 5 provides some samples. It can be seen that the synthetic images are very similar to the real ones, which are hard to be distinguished even by human beings. In particular, we also utilize t-SNE, a strong tool for feature visualization, to reveal the data distribution. The results show that the synthesis dataset presents the similar distribution to our Chinese dataset.

Fig. 5. Samples of synthetic license plate images. All of them are produced using a random strategy. Here the first character to denote the province is masked for each license plate due to the privacy. Best viewed in color

Character Sequence Inference. After obtaining the semantic map of a license plate, we can infer an initial character sequence, which actually represents the label sequence of semantic area along the horizontal direction. Formally, we firstly transform the semantic map L into C class-specific binary map L'_c with a switch function, where $c \in (1, C)$ and C is the number of character classes.

$$L'_c(x, y) = \begin{cases} 1, & L(x,y) = c \\ 0, & L(x,y) \neq c \end{cases}$$

For a binary map L'_c, we remove the noisy regions of small areas. Then we conduct Connected Component Analysis (CCA) on L'_c to generate the character areas $\{A_{ci}\}$, where A_{ci} denotes the ith area in L'_c.

The wrong prediction of semantic segmentation may make the inference confused and unreasonable. In this work, we propose the following method to improve the robustness. Specifically, we check the Intersection-over-Union (IOU) between the current character area and all previous areas separately. If the IOU exceeds a threshold T_f ($T_f = 0.5$ in our implementation), these two character areas are considered to be overlapped. Such case in theory is unreasonable since the characters in a license plate are always arranged separately. We extract the conflicting areas as ROIs, and then apply a classifier (e.g., Inception-v3 model [30]) to determine the final character class. This situation happens occasional in practice, but the proposed method is proven important to correct the hard samples.

3.3 Counting Refinement Module

The counting refinement is used to produce the final character sequence from the raw license plate image, semantic map, and initial character sequence. The main procedures are illustrated in Fig. 6. In our LPR framework, it is difficult for semantic segmentation to accurately distinguish the successive character instances of the same class, since the neighboring characters in a license plate are very close to each other and the background region to separate them is too thin for precise recognition. Consequently, multiple characters of the same class are probably regarded as one character in the initial character sequence. To address this issue, we propose to count the characters for such regions.

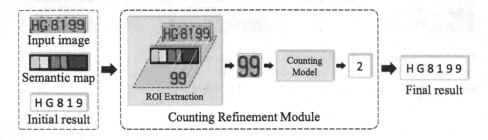

Fig. 6. Illustration of Counting Refinement Module. Our counting refinement module extracts the character region of interests and then applies a classifier to predict the character count. Best viewed in color

Object counting [4,20] is one of typical visual tasks which aims to obtain the number of specific objects in a given image ROI. In this work, we crop the image regions containing multiple characters of the same class according to the semantic segmentation results as the inputs of the counting model. Considering the application scenario of LPR, the number of characters in a license plate is always limited and even fixed (e.g., 7). Thus we formulate the character counting into a classification problem instead of the regression problem in previous works [23]. Note that the label in this task denotes the number of characters rather than the character class in traditional image classification. Then, we can directly employ some sophisticated classification networks. In this work, AlexNet [19] is particularly adopted due to its high computational efficiency.

In practice, it is observed that the characters '1' and '7' are often misclassified due to their simple contours. Through analysis, it is seen that resizing the input images, which may contain different number of characters in a large range, makes the similar characters harder to distinguish. To handle this issue, we particularly utilize the fact that the region label has been recognized by semantic segmentation. To be specific, we add one white line on the middle of "1" images and two white lines on the middle of "7" images to enhance their appearance difference. This small trick can effectively increase the counting performance.

4   Experiment

In this section, we experimentally evaluate the proposed LPR method. Here three challenging license plate datasets are used, *i.e.*, AOLP [14], Media Lab [3], and our own dataset (Chinese License Plate Dataset). For performance metrics, we adopt the recognition accuracy of whole license plate, which is different from the character classification since the recognition result of a license plate would be considered false as long as one of characters is wrongly predicted. For each public dataset, we provide the performance comparison with state-of-the-art methods.

4.1 Implementation Details

All of our models are implemented in Caffe [17], and trained/tested on a Tesla K80 GPU. We use a mini-batch of the size 16 at training time. We adopt the Inception-v3 [30] as the character classification model, and AlexNet [19] as the character counting model. Throughout the experiments, the license plate images are resized to 50×160, whose aspect ratio is close to that of physical license plates. For each dataset, the semantic segmentation model is pre-trained on our synthetic license plate images, and then fine-tuned using specific images provided by the dataset. To prevent overfitting, we adopt the common data augmentation strategies, such as noising, blurring, rotation, and color jittering. The semantic segmentation model and character counting model are trained separately. Detailed training protocols are listed in Table 1.

Table 1. Training protocols for semantic segmentation and character counting.

	base_lr	batchsize	lr_policy	gamma	step	max_iter
Semantic segmentation	10^{-4}	20	multistep	0.1	$[30k, 50k]$	$60k$
Character counting	10^{-2}	512	multistep	0.1	$[3k, 5k]$	$10k$

4.2 AOLP Dataset

The application-oriented license plate benchmark database (AOLP) collects 1874 images of Taiwan license plates, which is the largest public license plate dataset to our knowledge. The dataset is divided into three subsets according to the usage scenarios, including access control (AC), law enforcement (LE), and road patrol (RP). Specifically, there are 681 images in AC, 582 images in LE, and 611 images in RP. The images in these subsets present different appearance characteristics (*e.g.*, perspective), and thus it is challenging to accurately recognize every license plate. We compare our proposed method with state-of-the-art methods, including Deep FCN [32], LSTMs [21], and Hsu [15].

In the experiment, we use the same training/test split as in LSTMs [21], *i.e.*, two subsets are used for training and the remaining one is for test. We conduct three experiments with different subset for test, and then calculate the recognition accuracies on three subsets and their average accuracy. Table 2 provides the results, where AC/LE/RP denotes the corresponding subset is used for test.

From the results in Table 2, it can be seen that our proposed LPR method achieves the best performance with the accuracies of more than 99% on all subsets. Besides, it is well demonstrated that our method is robust as the images

Table 2. Recognition accuracies on AOLP Dataset. Our proposed method achieves the accuracies of more than 99% in all subsets

	AC (%)	LE (%)	RP (%)	Avg (%)
Hsu [15]	88.50	86.60	85.70	86.93
LSTMs [21]	94.85	94.19	88.38	92.47
DeepFCN [32]	97.90	97.60	98.20	97.90
Our method	**99.41**	**99.31**	**99.02**	**99.25**

in different AOLP subsets are highly varying in appearance. In particular, our method outperforms Hsu [15] by a 12.32% accuracy improvement, which is mainly due to the elimination of character detection. Compared with LSTMs [21] and Deep FCN [32], which adopt a sliding window profile, our method is still superior with an accuracy gain of 6.78% and 1.35%, which experimentally indicates the advantages of the proposed semantic segmentation.

In the above experiment, the recognition performance is evaluated using the subset split. However, high appearance variance in different subsets certainly will decrease the accuracy. To more fully explore the potential of our method, we conduct another experiment using a homogeneous split. Specifically, we evenly divide each subset into three parts with a random strategy. Then we collect two parts of each subset to form the training set and the remaining images are for test. Consequently, three new test subsets are built for performance evaluation, which contain 625, 625, and 624 images, respectively. Table 3 gives the experimental results for the settings. As expected, our method achieves higher recognition accuracies (up to 99.79% for average, *i.e.*, only 4 plates are failed).

Table 3. Recognition accuracies of our method with new settings on AOLP Dataset

	Set1 (%)	Set2 (%)	Set3 (%)	Avg (%)
Our method	**99.84**	**99.68**	**99.84**	**99.79**

4.3   Media Lab Dataset

NTUA Media Lab dataset consists of 706 Greek license plate images, which covers normal condition and some difficult conditions, *e.g.*, blocking by shadows and extreme illumination. It is divided into a normal subset with 427 samples and a difficult subset with 279 samples. We take Anagnostopoulos [2] and Siyu Zhu [35] as our baselines as they are the state-of-the-art methods on this dataset.

The dataset does not provide the data split for training and test. For fair comparison, we use the images in the normal subset as the test data to evaluate the performance, just like the baseline methods. In our experiment, specifically, we evenly divide the normal subset into four parts with a random strategy. We then conduct four experiments, in each of which three parts with the difficult subset are used for training and the rest one is for test. Table 4 gives the experimental results on Media Lab Dataset. It can be seen that our method outperforms the baselines with an accuracy improvement of more than 10%, which again indicates the superiority of the proposed framework. The average accuracy of 97.89% means that only 9 license plates are failed in total.

Table 4. Recognition accuracy on Media Lab Dataset.

	Set1(%)	Set2(%)	Set3(%)	Set4(%)	Avg(%)
Anagnostopoulos [2]	-	-	-	-	86.00
Zhu [35]	-	-	-	-	87.33
Our method	97.14	98.13	98.10	98.18	**97.89**

In addition, we perform another statistical analysis on the AOLP and Media Lab datasets to demonstrate the robustness of our algorithm to the predictions of semantic segmentation. As shown in Table 5, the license plates can be recognized correctly even when the semantic segmentation module produces imperfect results in pixels.

Table 5. Statistics on *the proportion of **W**rongly **P**redicted **P**ixels by the semantic segmentation model in the character regions that are finally recognized correctly (denoted as WPP).* The first three columns shows the *Max, Min, Mean WPP* in all the samples, while the last three columns are averaged on the Top-K *(K=5%, 10%, 20%)* samples sorted by the *WPP* in a descending order.

	Max	Min	Mean	Top 5%	Top 10%	Top 20%
AOLP	38.04%	0.41%	9.21%	24.10%	21.39%	18.32%
Media Lab	35.98%	0.86%	5.53%	16.69%	13.17%	10.46%

4.4   Chinese License Plate Dataset

Finally, we evaluate the proposed method on our own dataset, a Chinese License Plate dataset. The dataset is built by collecting the images from the traffic surveillance cameras, where the license plate images are obtained by applying the SSD [22] detector to raw images. Compared with the public license plate datasets, our dataset is much larger and contains 5057 license plate images. Particularly, the dataset covers diverse conditions, *e.g.*, high varying illumination, motion blurring, and low resolution. Some example images in our dataset are shown in Fig. 7. According to the specification of Chinese license plates, each license plate image in the datasets contains a sequence of 7 characters. In particular, there are totally $(m + 34)$ character classes, including 10 digits, 24 English letters ('O' and 'I' are excluded), and m Chinese characters[1].

Fig. 7. Example images in Chinese License Plate Dataset. It can be seen that the images present high varying appearance, including illumination, blurring, color, etc. Here the first character is masked due to the privacy. Best viewed in color

In our experiments, we randomly split the dataset into two subsets with 4057 images for training and 1000 images for test. Note that the data used for image synthesis are all from the training set. On this dataset, our proposed method achieves a outstanding recognition accuracy of 99.7%. That is, only three license plates in the test set are failed. In addition, our method achieves real-time performance in the computational efficiency (more than 25 FPS on a Nvidia Titan X GPU).

4.5   Error Study

In this section, we conduct an error study to more intuitively demonstrate the performance achieved by our proposed method. In particular, two public datasets, *i.e.*, AOLP and Media Lab, are both used and all failed samples in the above experiments are analyzed. To be specific, the results of 4 failed samples on AOLP and 9 failed samples on Media Lab are provided, as shown in Fig. 8. Here we list the raw images, generated semantic maps, ground truth, predicted character sequence, and cause of failure.

From Fig. 8, it can be observed that the failure is mainly caused by the poor quality of raw images. For example, the failure that "8" in the first row is recognized as "B" is due to the severely tilt and blurring of license plate, which even cannot be right recognized by a human being. Other failed samples have similar reasons. Overall, the probable causes of failure include image blurring, blocking patches, and severe interference. For these extremely hard samples, our method can still recognize most of characters correctly. Considering the failure cases in error study, we think the performance of our proposed LPR method is very close to the human level.

---

[1] In the current version of our dataset, $m = 3$ is used due to the limitation of image acquisition.

Image	Segmentation	Ground Truth	Predicted	Cause of Failure
AOLP Dataset				
6B-7733		687733	6B7733	blurry condition semantic segmentation mistake
 0750-J0		0750J0	D750J0	'0' is blocked semantic segmentation mistake
 7250-FK		7250EK	7250FK	'E' is incomplete semantic segmentation mistake
 0750-J0		0750J0	D750J0	'0' is blocked character classifier mistake
Media Lab Dataset				
 M1B6822		M1B6822	M1B692	extremely blurry condition
 M010312		M010312	H016312	extremely blurry condition
 B183886		B183886	B1B3886	blurry condition semantic segmentation mistake
 M1A-2326		M1A2326	M1A2328	'6' is blocked semantic segmentation mistake
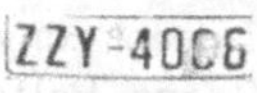 ZZY-4006		ZZY4006	ZZY4066	'0' is blocked semantic segmentation mistake
 NE-G027		NEG027	NE6027	'G' is distorted character classifier mistake
 YBB-7795		YBB7799	YBB7795	'9' is blocked semantic segmentation mistake
 YYX-4317		YYX4317	YNX4317	blurry condition semantic segmentation mistake
 YKZ-5790		YXZ5790	YKZ5790	'X' is distorted character classifier mistake

Fig. 8. Error study on AOLP Dataset and Media Lab Dataset. Here the processing component causing failure (semantic segmentation or character classifier) is also provided for each sample. Best viewed in color

5 Conclusion

In this paper, we proposed a novel license plate recognition framework, which not only achieves outstanding recognition performance but also has high computational efficiency. In particular, our proposed framework introduces the semantic segmentation technique followed by a counting refinement module to accomplish the recognition of a whole license plate. The experimental results on benchmark datasets demonstrate that our method consistently outperforms previous state-of-the-art methods with a remarkable accuracy improvement. In particular, the error study indicates that the performance of our proposed method is very close to the human level, which makes our method applicable to real systems even for complex scenes. In the future works, we plan to add more components into the proposed framework to support more types of license plates.

Acknowledgment. This work is supported partially by the NSFC under Grant 61673362, Youth Innovation Promotion Association CAS, and the Fundamental Research Funds for the Central Universities.

References

1. Adorni, G., Bergenti, F., Cagnoni, S.: Vehicle license plate recognition by means of cellular automata. In: IV (1998)
2. Anagnostopoulos, C.N.E., Anagnostopoulos, I.E., Loumos, V., Kayafas, E.: A license plate-recognition algorithm for intelligent transportation system applications. IEEE Trans. Intell. Transp. Syst. **7**(3), 377–392 (2006)
3. Anagnostopoulos, C.N.E., Anagnostopoulos, I.E., Psoroulas, I.D., Loumos, V., Kayafas, E.: License plate recognition from still images and video sequences: a survey. IEEE Trans. Intell. Transp. Syst. **9**(3), 377–391 (2008)
4. Arteta, C., Lempitsky, V., Noble, J.A., Zisserman, A.: Interactive object counting. In: Fleet, D., Pajdla, T., Schiele, B., Tuytelaars, T. (eds.) ECCV 2014. LNCS, vol. 8691, pp. 504–518. Springer, Cham (2014). https://doi.org/10.1007/978-3-319-10578-9_33
5. Badrinarayanan, V., Kendall, A., Cipolla, R.: SegNet: a deep convolutional encoder-decoder architecture for image segmentation. IEEE Trans. Pattern Anal. Mach. Intell. **39**(12), 2481–2495 (2017)
6. Bulan, O., Kozitsky, V., Ramesh, P., Shreve, M.: Segmentation-and annotation-free license plate recognition with deep localization and failure identification. IEEE Trans. Intell. Transp. Syst. **18**(9), 2351–2363 (2017)
7. Cheang, T.K., Chong, Y.S., Tay, Y.H.: Segmentation-free vehicle license plate recognition using convnet-RNN. arXiv preprint arXiv:1701.06439 (2017)
8. Chen, L.C., Papandreou, G., Kokkinos, I., Murphy, K., Yuille, A.L.: DeepLab: semantic image segmentation with deep convolutional nets, atrous convolution, and fully connected CRFs. IEEE Trans. Pattern Anal. Mach. Intell. **40**(4), 834–848 (2018)
9. Cherng, S., Fang, C.Y., Chen, C.P., Chen, S.W.: Critical motion detection of nearby moving vehicles in a vision-based driver-assistance system. IEEE Tran. Intell. Transp. Syst. **10**(1), 70–82 (2009)
10. Davies, P., Emmott, N., Ayland, N.: License plate recognition technology for toll violation enforcement. In: Image Analysis for Transport Applications (1990)
11. Du, S., Ibrahim, M., Shehata, M., Badawy, W.: Automatic license plate recognition (ALPR): a state-of-the-art review. IEEE Trans. Circuits Syst. Video Technol. **23**(2), 311–325 (2013)
12. Duan, T.D., Du, T.H., Phuoc, T.V., Hoang, N.V.: Building an automatic vehicle license plate recognition system. In: RIVF (2005)
13. Hegt, H.A., De La Haye, R.J., Khan, N.A.: A high performance license plate recognition system (1998)
14. Hsu, G.S., Alexandra, P., Chen, J.C., Yeh, F., Chen, M.H.: License plate recognition for categorized applications. In: ICVES (2011)
15. Hsu, G.S., Chen, J.C., Chung, Y.Z.: Application-oriented license plate recognition. IEEE Trans. Veh. Technol. **62**(2), 552–561 (2013)
16. Huang, Y.S., Weng, Y.S., Zhou, M.: Critical scenarios and their identification in parallel railroad level crossing traffic control systems. IEEE Trans. Intell. Transp. Syst. **11**(4), 968–977 (2010)

17. Jia, Y., et al.: Caffe: convolutional architecture for fast feature embedding. In: ACM MM (2014)
18. Kim, K.K., Kim, K., Kim, J., Kim, H.J.: Learning-based approach for license plate recognition. In: Neural Networks for Signal Processing (2000)
19. Krizhevsky, A., Sutskever, I., Hinton, G.E.: ImageNet classification with deep convolutional neural networks. In: NIPS (2012)
20. Lempitsky, V., Zisserman, A.: Learning to count objects in images. In: NIPS (2010)
21. Li, H., Shen, C.: Reading car license plates using deep convolutional neural networks and LSTMs. arXiv preprint arXiv:1601.05610 (2016)
22. Liu, W., et al.: SSD: single shot MultiBox detector. In: Leibe, B., Matas, J., Sebe, N., Welling, M. (eds.) ECCV 2016. LNCS, vol. 9905, pp. 21–37. Springer, Cham (2016). https://doi.org/10.1007/978-3-319-46448-0_2
23. Liu, X., Wang, Z., Feng, J., Xi, H.: Highway vehicle counting in compressed domain. In: CVPR (2016)
24. Long, J., Shelhamer, E., Darrell, T.: Fully convolutional networks for semantic segmentation. In: CVPR (2015)
25. Masood, S.Z., Shu, G., Dehghan, A., Ortiz, E.G.: License plate detection and recognition using deeply learned convolutional neural networks. arXiv preprint arXiv:1703.07330 (2017)
26. Naito, T., Tsukada, T., Yamada, K., Kozuka, K., Yamamoto, S.: Robust license-plate recognition method for passing vehicles under outside environment. IEEE Trans. Veh. Technol. 49(6), 2309–2319 (2000)
27. Nijhuis, J., et al.: Car license plate recognition with neural networks and fuzzy logic (1995)
28. Omitaomu, O.A., Ganguly, A.R., Patton, B.W., Protopopescu, V.A.: Anomaly detection in radiation sensor data with application to transportation security. IEEE Trans. Intell. Transp. Syst. 10(2), 324–334 (2009)
29. Parizi, S.N., Targhi, A.T., Aghazadeh, O., Eklundh, J.O.: Reading street signs using a generic structured object detection and signature recognition approach. In: VISAPP (2009)
30. Szegedy, C., Vanhoucke, V., Ioffe, S., Shlens, J., Wojna, Z.: Rethinking the inception architecture for computer vision. In: CVPR (2016)
31. Wang, F., Man, L., Wang, B., Xiao, Y., Pan, W., Lu, X.: Fuzzy-based algorithm for color recognition of license plates. Pattern Recogn. Lett. 29(7), 1007–1020 (2008)
32. Wu, Y., Li, J.: License plate recognition using deep FCN. In: Sun, F., Liu, H., Hu, D. (eds.) ICCSIP 2016. CCIS, vol. 710, pp. 225–234. Springer, Singapore (2017). https://doi.org/10.1007/978-981-10-5230-9_25
33. Yamaguchi, K., Nagaya, Y., Ueda, K., Nemoto, H., Nakagawa, M.: A method for identifying specific vehicles using template matching (1999)
34. Yu, M., Kim, Y.D.: An approach to Korean license plate recognition based on vertical edge matching (2000)
35. Zhu, S., Dianat, S., Mestha, L.K.: End-to-end system of license plate localization and recognition. JEI 24(2), 023020 (2015)

Zoom-Net: Mining Deep Feature Interactions for Visual Relationship Recognition

Guojun Yin[1,2], Lu Sheng[2], Bin Liu[1], Nenghai Yu[1], Xiaogang Wang[2], Jing Shao[3]([✉]), and Chen Change Loy[4]

[1] Key Laboratory of Electromagnetic Space Information,
University of Science and Technology of China,
The Chinese Academy of Sciences, Hefei, China
gjyin@mail.ustc.edu.cn, {flowice,ynh}@ustc.edu.cn
[2] The Chinese University of Hong Kong, Shatin, China
{lsheng,xgwang}@ee.cuhk.edu.hk
[3] SenseTime Research, Beijing, China
shaojing@sensetime.com
[4] Nanyang Technological University, Singapore, Singapore
ccloy@ieee.org

Abstract. Recognizing visual relationships ⟨subject-predicate-object⟩ among any pair of localized objects is pivotal for image understanding. Previous studies have shown remarkable progress in exploiting linguistic priors or external textual information to improve the performance. In this work, we investigate an orthogonal perspective based on feature interactions. We show that by encouraging deep message propagation and interactions between local object features and global predicate features, one can achieve compelling performance in recognizing complex relationships without using any linguistic priors. To this end, we present two new pooling cells to encourage feature interactions: (i) Contrastive ROI Pooling Cell, which has a unique deROI pooling that inversely pools local object features to the corresponding area of global predicate features. (ii) Pyramid ROI Pooling Cell, which broadcasts global predicate features to reinforce local object features. The two cells constitute a *Spatiality-Context-Appearance Module (SCA-M)*, which can be further stacked consecutively to form our final *Zoom-Net*. We further shed light on how one could resolve ambiguous and noisy object and predicate annotations by Intra-Hierarchical trees (IH-tree). Extensive experiments conducted on Visual Genome dataset demonstrate the effectiveness of our feature-oriented approach compared to state-of-the-art methods (Acc@1 11.42% from 8.16%) that depend on explicit modeling of linguistic interactions. We further show that SCA-M can be incorporated seamlessly into existing approaches to improve the performance by a large margin.

© Springer Nature Switzerland AG 2018
V. Ferrari et al. (Eds.): ECCV 2018, LNCS 11207, pp. 330–347, 2018.
https://doi.org/10.1007/978-3-030-01219-9_20

1   Introduction

Visual relationship recognition [22,30,38] aims at interpreting rich interactions between a pair of localized objects, *i.e.*, performing tuple recognition in the form of ⟨*subject-predicate-object*⟩ as shown in Fig. 1(a). The fundamental challenge of this task is to recognize various vaguely defined relationships given diverse spatial layouts of objects and complex inter-object interactions. To complement visual-based recognition, a promising approach is to adopt a linguistic model and learn relationships between object and predicate labels from the language. This strategy has been shown effective by many existing methods [6,26,30,47–49]. These language-based methods either apply statistical inference to the tuple label set, establish a linguistic graph as the prior, or mine linguistic knowledge from external billion-scale textual data (*e.g.*, Wikipedia).

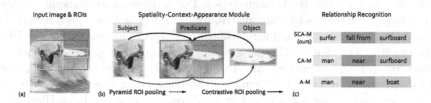

Fig. 1. Given an image '*surfer fall from surfboard*' and its region-of-interests (ROI) in (a), traditional methods without mining contextual interactions between object (subject) and predicate (*e.g.*, Appearance Module (A-M)) or ignoring spatial information (*e.g.*, Context-Appearance Module (CA-M)) may fail in relationship recognition, as shown in the two bottom rows of (c). The proposed Spatiality-Context-Appearance Module (SCA-M) in (b) permits global inter-object interaction and sharing of spatiality-aware contextual information, thus leading to a better recognition performance.

In this paper, we explore a novel perspective beyond the linguistic-based paradigm. In particular, contemporary approaches typically recognize the tuple ⟨*subject-predicate-object*⟩ via separate convolutional neural network (CNN) branches. We believe that by enhancing message sharing and feature interactions among these branches, the participating objects and their visual relationship can be better recognized. To this end, we formulate a new spatiality-aware contextual feature learning model, named as **Zoom-Net**. Differing from previous studies that learn appearance and spatial features separately, Zoom-Net propagates spatiality-aware object features to interact with the predicate features and broadcasts predicate features to reinforce the features of subject and object.

The core of Zoom-Net is a **Spatiality-Context-Appearance Module**, abbreviated as **SCA-M**. It consists of two novel pooling cells that permit deep feature interactions between objects and predicates, as shown in Fig. 1(b). The first cell, *Contrastive ROI Pooling Cell*, facilitates predicate feature learning by inversely pooling object/subject features to a matching spatial context of predicate features via a unique deROI pooling. This allows all subject and object to fall on the same spatial 'palette' for spatiality-aware feature learning. The second cell is called *Pyramid ROI Pooling Cell*. It helps object/subject feature learning through broadcasting the predicate features to the corresponding object's/subject's spatial area. Zoom-Net stacks multiple SCA-Ms consecutively in an end-to-end network that allows multi-scale bidirectional message passing among subject, predicate and object. As shown in Fig. 1(c), the message sharing and feature interaction not only help recognize individual objects more accurately but also facilitate the learning of inter-object relation.

Another contribution of our work is an effective strategy of mitigating ambiguity and imbalanced data distribution in ⟨*subject-predicate-object*⟩ annotations. Specifically, we conduct our main experiments on the challenging Visual Genome (VG) dataset [22], which consists of over 5,319 object categories, 1,957 predicates, and 421,697 relationship types. The large-scale ambiguous categories and extremely imbalanced data distribution in VG dataset prevent previous methods from predicting reliable relationships despite they succeed in the Visual Relationship Detection (VRD) dataset [30] with only 100 object categories, 70 predicates and 6,672 relationships. To alleviate the ambiguity and imbalanced data distribution in VG, we reformulate the conventional one-hot classification as a n-hot multi-class hierarchical recognition via a novel Intra-Hierarchical trees (IH-trees) for each label set in the tuple ⟨*subject-predicate-object*⟩.

Contributions. Our contributions are summarized as follows:

(1) *A general feature learning module that permits feature interactions* - We introduce a novel SCA-M to mining intrinsic interactions between low-level spatial information and high-level semantical appearance features simultaneously. By stacking multiple SCA-Ms into a Zoom-Net, we achieve compelling results on VG dataset thanks to the multi-scale bidirectional message passing among subject, predicate and object.

(2) *Multi-class Intra-Hierarchical tree* - To mitigate label ambiguity in large-scale datasets, we reformulate the visual relationship recognition problem to a multi-label recognition problem. The recognizability is enhanced by introducing an Intra-Hierarchical tree (IH-tree) for the object and predicate categories, respectively. We show that IH-tree can benefit other existing methods as well.

(3) *Large-scale relationship recognition* - Extensive experiments demonstrate the respective effectiveness of the proposed SCA-M and IH-tree, as well as their combination on the challenging large-scale VG dataset.

It is noteworthy that the proposed method differs significantly from previous works as Zoom-Net neither models explicit nor implicit label-level interactions between ⟨*subject-predicate-object*⟩. We show that feature-level interactions alone, which is enabled by SCA-M, can achieve state-of-the-art performance. We further demonstrate that previous state-of-the-arts [26] that are based on label-level interaction can benefit from the proposed SCA-M and IH-trees.

2   Related Work

Contextual Learning. Contextual information has been employed in various tasks [1,13,15,25,34,40,42], *e.g.*, object detection, segmentation, and retrieval. For example, the visual features captured from a bank of object detectors are combined with global features in [5,24]. For both detection and segmentation, learning feature representations from a global view rather than the located object itself has been proven effective in [3,23,32]. Contextual feature learning for visual relationship recognition is little explored in previous works.

Class Hierarchy. In previous studies [8,9,11,17,33], class hierarchy that encodes diverse label relations or structures is used to improve performances on classification and retrieval. For instance, Deng *et al.* [11] improve large-scale visual recognition of object categories by forming a semantic hierarchy that consists of many levels of abstraction. While object categories can be clustered easily by their semantic similarity given the clean and explicit labels of objects, building a semantic hierarchy for visual relationship recognition can be more challenging due to noisy and ambiguous labels. Moreover, the semantic similarity between some phrases and prepositions such as *walking on a* versus *walks near the* is not directly measurable. In our paper, we employ the part-of-speech tagger toolkit to extract and normalize the keywords of these labels, *e.g. walk*, *on* and *near*.

Visual Relationship. Recognizing visual relationship [38] has been shown beneficial to various tasks, including action recogntion [7,15], pose estimation [12], recognition and object detection [4,36], and scene graph generation [27,44]. Most recent works [6,18,27–30,35,45,48,50] focus on measuring linguistic relations with textual priors or language models. The linguistic relations have been explored for object recognition [9,31,43], object detection [37], retrieval [39], and caption generation [16,20,21]. Yu *et al.* [46] employ billions of external textual data to distill useful knowledge for triplet ⟨*subject-predicate-object*⟩ learning. These methods do not fully explore the potential of feature learning and feature-level message sharing for the problem of visual relationship recognition. Li *et al.* [26] propose a message passing strategy to encourage feature sharing between features extracted from ⟨*subject-predicate-object*⟩. However, the network does not capture the relative location of different objects thus it cannot capture valid contextual information between subject, predicate and object.

3   Zoom-Net: Mining Deep Feature Interactions

We propose an end-to-end visual relationship recognition model that is capable of mining feature-level interactions. This is beyond just measuring the interactions among the triplet labels with additional linguistic priors, as what previous studies considered.

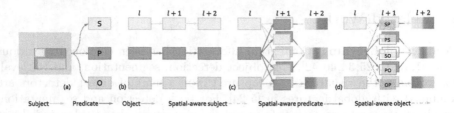

Fig. 2. (a) Given the ROI-pooled features of subject (S), predicate (P) and object (O) from an input image, (b) An Appearance module (A-M) separately processes these features without any message passing, (c) a Context-Appearance module (CA-M) attempts to capture contextual information by directly fusing pairwise features. The proposed SCA-M in (d) integrates the local and global contextual information in a spatiality-aware manner. The SP/PS/SO/PO/OP features are combined by channel-wise concatenation. For instance, SP feature is the result of combining subject and predicate features.

3.1 Appearance, Context and Spatiality

As shown in Fig. 2(a), given the ROI-pooled features of the subject, predicate and object, we consider a question: how to learn good features for both object (subject) and predicate? We investigate three plausible modules as follows.

Appearance Module. This module focuses on the intra-dependencies within each ROI, *i.e.*, the features of the subject, predicate and object branches are learned independently without any message passing. We term this network structure as Appearance Module (A-M), as shown in Fig. 2(a). No contextual and spatial information can be derived from such a module.

Context-Appearance Module. The Context-Appearance Module (CA-M) [26] directly fuses pairwise features among three branches, in which subject/object features absorb the contextual information from the predicate features, and predicate features also receive messages from both subject/object features, as shown in Fig. 2(b). Nonetheless, these features are concatenated regardless of their relative spatial layout in the original image. The incompatibility of scale and spatiality makes the fused features less optimal in capturing the required spatial and contextual information.

Spatiality-Context-Appearance Module. The spatial configuration, *e.g.*, the relative positions and sizes of subject and object, is not sufficiently represented in CA-M. To address this issue, we propose a Spatiality-Context-Appearance module (**SCA-M**) as shown in Fig. 2(c). It consists of two novel spatiality-aware feature alignment cells (*i.e.*, *Contrast ROI Pooling* and *Pyramid ROI Pooling*) for message passing between different branches. In comparison to CA-M, the proposed SCA-M reformulates the local and global

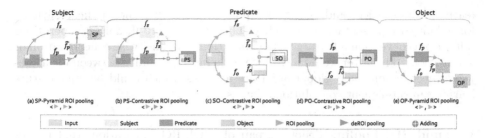

Fig. 3. The Spatiality-Context-Appearance Module (SCA-M) hinges on two components: (i) Contrastive ROI pooling (b–d), denoted as $\langle$ROI, deROI$\rangle$, which propagates spatiality-aware features $\hat{f}_s, \hat{f}_o$ from *subject* and *object* into the spatial 'palette' of *predicate* features f_p, and (ii) Pyramid ROI pooling (a,e), $\langle$ROI, ROI$\rangle$, which broadcasts the global *predicate* features $\hat{f}_p$ to local features f_s, f_o in *subject* and *object* branches.

information integration in a spatiality-aware manner, leading to superior capability in capturing spatial and contextual relationships between the features of $\langle$*subject-predicate-object*$\rangle$.

3.2 Spatiality-Context-Appearance Module (SCA-M)

We denote the respective regions of interest (ROIs) of the subject, predicate and object as $\mathcal{R}_s$, $\mathcal{R}_p$, and $\mathcal{R}_o$, where $\mathcal{R}_p$ is the union bounding box that tightly covers both the subject and object. The ROI-pooled features for these three ROIs are $\mathbf{f}_t, t \in \{s, p, o\}$, respectively. In this section, we present the details of SCA-M. In particular, we discuss how Contrastive ROI Pooling and Pyramid ROI Pooling cells, the two elements in SCA-M, permit deep feature interactions between objects and predicates.

Contrastive ROI Pooling denotes a pair of $\langle$ROI, deROI$\rangle$ operations that the object[1] features $\mathbf{f}_o$ are at first ROI pooled for extracting normalized local features, and then these features are deROI pooled back to the spatial palette of the predicate feature $\mathbf{f}_p$, so as to generate a spatiality-aware object feature $\hat{\mathbf{f}}_o$ with the same size as the predicate feature, as shown in Fig. 3(b) marked by the purple triangle. Note that the remaining region outside the relative object ROI in $\hat{\mathbf{f}}_o$ is set to 0. The spatiality-resumed local feature $\hat{\mathbf{f}}_o$ can thus influence the respective regions in the global feature map $\mathbf{f}_p$. In practice, the proposed deROI pooling can be considered as an inverse operation of the traditional ROI pooling (green triangle in Fig. 3), which is analogous to the top-down deconvolution versus the bottom-up convolution.

There are three Contrastive ROI pooling cells presented in the SCA-M module to integrate the feature pairs *subject-predicate*, *subject-object* and *predicate-object*, as shown in Fig. 3(b–d). Followed by several convolutional layers, the

---

[1] Subject and object refer to the same concept, thus we only take object as the example for illustration.

features from subject and object are spatially fused into the predicate feature for enhanced representation capability. The proposed ⟨ROI, deROI⟩ operations differ from conventional feature fusion operations (channel-wise concatenation or summation). The latter would introduce scale incompatibility between local subject/object features and global predicate features, which could hamper feature learning in subsequent convolutional layers.

Pyramid ROI Pooling denotes a pair of ⟨ROI, ROI⟩ operations that broadcasts the global predicate features to local features in the subject and object branches, as shown in Fig. 3(a) and (e). Specifically, with the help of ROI pooling unit, we first ROI-pool the features of predicate from the input region $\tilde{\mathcal{R}}$, which convey global contextual information of the region. Next, we perform a second ROI pooling on predicate features with the subject/object ROIs to further mine the contextual information from the global predicate feature region. The Pyramid ROI pooling thus provides multi-scale contexts to facilitate subject/object feature learning.

3.3 Zoom-Net: Stacked SCA-M

By stacking multiple SCA-Ms, the proposed **Zoom-Net** is capable of capturing multi-scale feature interactions with dynamic contextual and spatial information aggregation. It enables a reliable recognition of the visual relationship triplet ⟨s-p-o⟩, where the predicate p indicates the relationships (e.g., spatiality, preposition, action and etc.) between a pair of localized subject s and object o.

As visualized in Fig. 4, we use a shared feature extractor with convolutional layers until `conv3_3` to encode appearance features of different object categories.

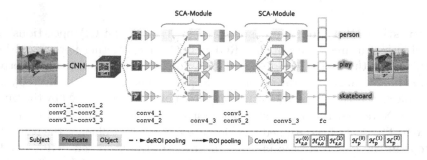

Fig. 4. The architecture of Zoom-Net. The subject (in light yellow), predicate (in red) and object (in dark yellow) share the same feature extraction procedure in the lower layers, and are then ROI-pooled into three branches. Following each branch of pooled feature maps is two convolutional layers to learn appearance features which are then fed into two stacked SCA-Ms to further fuse multi-scale spatiality-aware contextual information across different branches. Three classifiers with intra-hierarchy structures are applied to the features obtained from each branch for visual relationship recognition. (Color figure online)

By indicating the regions of interests (ROIs) for subject, predicate and object, the associated features are ROI-pooled to the same spatial size and respectively fed into three branches. The features in three branches are at first independently fed into two convolutional layers (the conv4_1 and conv4_2 layers in VGG-16) for a further abstraction of their *appearance* features. Then these features are put into the first SCA-M to fuse *spatiality*-aware *contextual* information across different branches. After receiving the interaction-augmented subject, predicate and object features from the first SCA-M, $\mathcal{M}^1_{SCA}$, we continue to convolve these features with another two appearance abstraction layers (mimicking the structures of conv5_1 and conv5_2 layers in VGG-16) and then forward them to the second SCA-M, $\mathcal{M}^2_{SCA}$. After this module, the multi-scale interaction-augmented features in each branch are fed into three fully connected layers fc_s, fc_p and fc_o to classify subject, predicate and object, respectively.

4   Hierarchical Relational Classification

To thoroughly evaluate the proposed Zoom-Net, we adopt the Visual Genome (VG) dataset[2] [22] for its large scale and diverse relationships. Our goal is to understand the a much broader scope of relationships with a total number of 421,697 relationship types, in comparison to the VRD dataset [30] that focuses on only 6,672 relationships. Recognizing relationships in VG is a non-trivial task due to several reasons:

(1) *Variety* - There are a total of 5,319 object categories and 1,957 predicates, tens times than those available in the VRD dataset.
(2) *Ambiguity* - Some object categories share a similar appearance, and multiple predicates refer to the same relationship.
(3) *Imbalance* - We observe long tail distributions both for objects and predicates.

To circumvent the aforementioned challenges, existing studies typically simplify the problem by manually removing a considerable portion of the data by frequency filtering or cleaning [6,26,46,47]. Nevertheless, infrequent labels like "old man" and "white shirt" contain common attributes like "man" and "shirt" and are unreasonable to be pruned. Moreover, the flat label structure assumed by these methods is limited to describe the label space of the VG dataset with ambiguous and noisy labels.

To overcome the aforementioned issues, we propose a solution by establishing two Intra-Hierarchical trees (IH-tree) for measuring intra-class correlation within object[3] and predicate, respectively. IH-tree builds a hierarchy of concepts that systematically groups rare, noisy and ambiguous labels together with those clearly defined labels. Unlike existing works that regularize relationships across

---

[2] Extremely rare labels (fewer than 10 samples) were pruned for a valid evaluation.
[3] Subject and object refer to the same term in this paper, thus we only take the object as the example for illustration.

the triplet $\langle s\text{-}p\text{-}o \rangle$ by external linguistic priors, we only consider the intra-class correlation to independently regularize the occurrences of the object and predicate labels. During end-to-end training, the network employs the weighted Intra-Hierarchical losses for visual relationship recognition as $\mathcal{L} = \alpha \mathcal{L}_s + \beta \mathcal{L}_p + \gamma \mathcal{L}_o$, where hyper-parameters α, β, γ balance the losses with respect to subject $\mathcal{L}_s$, predicate $\mathcal{L}_p$ and object $\mathcal{L}_o$. $\alpha = \beta = \gamma = 1$ in our experiments. We introduce IH-tree and the losses next.

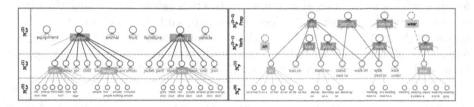

Fig. 5. An illustration of Intra-Hierarchical Tree. Both IH-trees for object (left) and predicate (right) start from the base layer $\mathcal{H}_{s,p,o}^{(0)}$ to a purified layer $\mathcal{H}_{s,p,o}^{(1)}$ but have a different construction in the third layer. The $\mathcal{H}_o^{(2)}$ clusters similar semantic concepts from $\mathcal{H}_o^{(1)}$, while the $\mathcal{H}_p^{(2)}$ separately cluster verb and preposition words from $\mathcal{H}_p^{(1)}$.

4.1   Intra-Hierarchical Tree $\mathcal{H}_o$ for Object

We build an IH-tree, $\mathcal{H}_o$, for object with a depth of three, where the base layer $\mathcal{H}_o^{(0)}$ consists of the raw object categories.

(1) $\mathcal{H}_o^{(0)} \to \mathcal{H}_o^{(1)}$: $\mathcal{H}_o^{(1)}$ is extracted from $\mathcal{H}_o^{(0)}$ by pruning noisy labels with the same concept but different descriptive attributes or in different singular and plural forms. We employ the part-of-speech tagger toolkit from NLTK [2] and NLTK Lemmatizer to filter and normalize the noun keyword, e.g., "man" from "old man", "bald man" and "men".

(2) $\mathcal{H}_o^{(1)} \to \mathcal{H}_o^{(2)}$: We observe that some labels have a close semantic correlation. As shown in the left panel of Fig. 5, labels with similar semantic concepts such as "shirt" and "jacket" are hyponyms of "clothing" and need to be distinguished from other semantic concepts like "animal" and "vehicle". Therefore, we cluster labels in $\mathcal{H}_o^{(1)}$ to the third level $\mathcal{H}_o^{(2)}$ by semantical similarities computed by Leacock-Chodorow distance [40] from NLTK. We find that a threshold of 0.65 is well-suited for splitting semantic concepts.

The output of the subject/object branch is a concatenation of three independent `softmax` activated vectors corresponded to three hierarchical levels in the IH-tree. The loss $\mathcal{L}_s$ ($\mathcal{L}_o$) is thus a summation of three independent `softmax` losses with respect to these levels, encouraging the intra-level mutual label exclusion and inter-level label dependency.

4.2   Intra-Hierarchical Tree $\mathcal{H}_p$ for Predicate

The predicate IH-tree also has three hierarchy levels. Different from the object IR-tree that only handles nouns, the predicate categories include various part-of-speech types, *e.g.*, verb (action) and preposition (spatial position). Even a single predicate label may contain multiple types, *e.g.*, "are standing on" and "walking next to a".

(1) $\mathcal{H}_p^{(0)} \rightarrow \mathcal{H}_p^{(1)}$: Similar to $\mathcal{H}_o^{(1)}$, $\mathcal{H}_p^{(1)}$ is constructed aiming at extracting and normalizing keywords from predicates. We retain the keywords and normalize tenses with respective to three main part-of-speech types, *i.e.*, verb, preposition and adjective, and abandon other pointless and ambiguous words. As shown in the right panel of Fig. 5, "wears a", "wearing a yellow" and "wearing a pink" are mapped to the same keyword "wear".

(2) $\mathcal{H}_p^{(1)} \rightarrow \mathcal{H}_p^{(2)}$: Different part-of-speech types own particular characteristics with various context representations, and hence a separate hierarchical structure for the verb (action) and preposition (spatial) is indispensable for better depiction. To this end, we construct $\mathcal{H}_p^{(2)}$ for verb and preposition label independently, *i.e.*, $\mathcal{H}_p^{(2-1)}$ for action information and $\mathcal{H}_p^{(2-2)}$ for spatial configuration. There are two cases in $\mathcal{H}_p^{(1)}$: (a) the label is in the form of phrase that consists of both verb and preposition (*e.g.* "stand on" and "walk next to") and (b) the label is a single word (*e.g.*, "on" and "wear"). For the first case, $\mathcal{H}_p^{(2-1)}$ extracts the verb words from the two phrases while $\mathcal{H}_p^{(2-2)}$ extracts the preposition words. It thus causes that a label might be simultaneously clustered into different partitions of $\mathcal{H}_p^{(2)}$. If the label is a single word, it would be normally clustered into the corresponding part-of-speech but remained the same in the opposite part-of-speech, as shown with the dotted line in the right panel of Fig. 5. The loss $\mathcal{L}_p$ is constructed similarly to that for the object.

5   Experiments on Visual Genome (VG) Dataset

Dataset. We evaluate our method on the Visual Genome (VG) dataset (version 1.2). Each image is annotated with a triplet $\langle subject\text{-}predicate\text{-}object \rangle$, where the subjects and objects are annotated with labels and bounding boxes while the predicates only have labels. We randomly split the VG dataset into training and testing set with a ratio of 8 : 2. Note that both sets are guaranteed to have positive and negative samples from each object or predicate category. The details of data preprocessing and the source code will be released.

Evaluation Metrics. (1) *Acc@N*. We adopt the *Accuracy* score as the major evaluation metric in our experiments. The metric is commonly used in traditional classification tasks. Specifically, we report the values of both Acc@1 and Acc@5 for *subject, predicate, object* and *relationship*, where the accuracy of *relationship* is calculated as the averaged accuracies of *subject, predicate* and *object*.

(2) *Rec@N*. Following [30], we use *Recall* as another metric so as to handle incomplete annotations. Rec@N computes the ratio of the correct relationship instance that is covered in the top N predictions per image. We report Rec@50 and Rec@100 in our experiments. For a fair comparison, we follow [30] to evaluate Rec@N on three tasks, *i.e.*, *predicate recognition* where both the labels and bounding boxes of the subject and object are given; *phrase recognition* that takes a triplet as a union bounding box and predicts the triple labels; *relationship recognition*, which also outputs triple labels but evaluates separate bounding boxes of subject and object. The recall performance is relative to the number of *predicate* per *subject-object* pair to be evaluated, *i.e.*, top k predictions. In the experiments on VG dataset, we adopt top $k = 100$ for evaluation.

Training Details. We use VGG16 [41] pre-trained on ImageNet [10] as the network backbone. The newly introduced layers are randomly initialized. We set the base learning rate as 0.001 and fix the parameters from conv1_1 to conv3_3. The implementations are based on Caffe [19], and the networks are optimized via SGD. The conventional feature fusion operations are implemented by channel-wise concatenation in SCA-M cells here.

5.1   Ablation Study

SCA-Module. The advantage of Zoom-Net lies in its unique capability of learning spatiality-aware contextual information through the SCA-M. To demonstrate the benefits of learning visual features with spatial-oriented and context-aided cues, we compare the recognition performance of Zoom-Net with a set of variants achieved by removing each individual cue step by step, *i.e.*, the SCA-M without stacked structure, the CA-M that disregard the spatial layouts, and the vanilla A-M that does not perform message passing (see Sect. 3.1). Their accuracy and recall scores are reported in Table 1.

In comparison to the vanilla A-M, both the CA-M and SCA-M obtain a significant improvement suggesting the importance of contextual information to individual subject, predicate, and object classification and their relationship recognition. Note that contemporary CNNs have already shown a remarkable performance on subject and object classification, *i.e.*, it is not hard to recognize object via individual appearance information, and thus the gap (4.96%) of subject is smaller than that of predicate (12.25%) between A-M and SCA-M on Top-1 accuracy. Not surprisingly, since the key inherent problem of relationship recognition is to learning the interactions between subject and object, the proposed SCA-M module exhibit a strong performance, thanks to its capability in capturing correlation between spatiality and semantic appearance cues among different object. Its effectiveness can also be observed from qualitative comparisons in Fig. 6(a).

Intra-Hierarchical Tree. We use the two auxiliary levels of hierarchical labels $\mathcal{H}^{(1)}$ and $\mathcal{H}^{(2)}$ to facilitate the prediction of the raw ground truth labels $\mathcal{H}^{(0)}$ for

Table 1. Recognition performances (Acc@N and Rec@N) of Zoom-Net on VG dataset compared with (i) three variants of SCA module, and (ii) Zoom-Net discarding IH-trees. The best results are indicated in bold.

Metrics		@N	Zoom-Net	SCA-M	CA-M	A-M	Zoom-Net w/o $\mathcal{H}^{(1,2)}$	Zoom-Net w/o $\mathcal{H}^{(2)}$
Acc.	Subject	1	**38.94**	37.48	34.84	32.52	36.52	37.88
		5	**65.70**	64.09	61.59	58.28	62.63	63.97
	Predicate	1	**48.73**	48.14	46.81	35.89	47.18	48.26
		5	**77.64**	76.97	75.55	67.05	76.43	77.18
	Object	1	**45.09**	44.13	42.66	41.39	42.52	43.67
		5	**71.69**	70.64	69.55	67.99	69.33	70.35
	Relationship	1	**11.42**	10.51	9.46	6.39	9.92	10.76
		5	**22.80**	21.31	19.70	14.06	20.44	22.08
Rec.	Predicate	50	**67.25**	66.54	65.07	53.94	65.84	66.73
		100	**77.51**	76.92	75.45	66.53	76.30	77.16
	Relationship	50	**19.97**	18.60	17.14	12.23	17.78	18.92
		100	**25.07**	23.51	21.63	15.86	22.53	23.88
	Phrase	50	**20.84**	19.55	18.12	13.05	18.65	19.78
		100	**26.16**	24.70	22.85	16.92	23.62	24.96

the subject, predicate and object, respectively. Here we show that by involving hierarchical structures to semantically cluster ambiguous and noisy labels, the recognition performance *w.r.t.* the raw labels of the subject, predicate, object as well as their relationships are all boosted, as shown in Table 1. Discarding one of two levels in IH-tree clearly hamper the performance, *i.e.*, Zoom-Net without IH-tree experiences a drop of around 1%–4% on different metrics. It reveals that intra-hierarchy structures do provide beneficial information to improve the recognition robustness. Besides, Fig. 6(b) shows the Top-5 triple relationship prediction results of Zoom-Net with and without IH-trees. The novel design of the hierarchical label structure help resolves data ambiguity for both on object and predicate. For example, thanks to the hierarchy level $\mathcal{H}^{(1)}$ introduced in Sect. 4, the predicates related to "wear" (*e.g.*, "wearing" and "wears") can be ranked in top predictions. Another example shows the contribution of $\mathcal{H}^{(2)}$ designed for semantic label clustering, *e.g.* "sitting in", which is grouped in the same cluster of the ground truth "in", also appears in top ranking results.

5.2   Comparison with State-of-the-Art Methods

We summarize the comparative results on VG in Table 2 with two recent state of the arts [6,26]. For a fair comparison, we implement both methods with the VGG-16 as the network backbone. The proposed Zoom-Net significantly outperforms these methods, quantitatively and qualitatively. Qualitative results are

Table 2. Recognition performances (Acc@N and Rec@N) of Zoom-Net on VG dataset compared with the state-of-the-art methods. Results in bold font are the best by a single model, while the underlined results indicate the best performance of a combined model that incorporates the proposed modules into other state-of-the-art architectures.

Metrics		@N	Zoom-Net	DR-Net [6]	ViP [26]	ViP+SCA -M	ViP+IH -tree	ViP+SCA-M +IH-tree
Acc.	Subject	1	**38.94**	30.10	31.10	*37.13*	*34.36*	*38.78*
		5	**65.70**	55.46	57.33	*63.61*	*61.03*	*65.69*
	Predicate	1	**48.73**	44.14	45.17	*48.40*	*46.54*	*49.07*
		5	**77.64**	71.67	74.26	*77.28*	*75.30*	*78.07*
	Object	1	**45.09**	37.91	39.18	*43.09*	*43.18*	*44.96*
		5	**71.69**	64.30	65.68	*69.93*	*69.48*	*71.58*
	Relationship	1	**11.42**	6.69	8.16	*10.65*	*9.97*	*11.79*
		5	**22.80**	13.11	17.01	*21.63*	*20.40*	*23.28*
Rec.	Predicate	50	**67.25**	62.05	63.44	*66.87*	*64.80*	*67.63*
		100	**77.51**	71.96	74.15	*77.22*	*75.29*	*77.89*
	Relationship	50	**19.97**	12.56	14.78	*18.73*	*17.76*	*20.41*
		100	**25.07**	16.06	18.85	*23.67*	*22.35*	*25.55*
	Phrase	50	**20.84**	13.51	15.70	*19.61*	*18.72*	*21.31*
		100	**26.16**	17.23	19.96	*24.70*	*23.50*	*26.66*

shown in the first row of Fig. 6(c). DR-Net [6] exploits binary dual masks as the spatial configuration in feature learning and therefore loses the critical interaction between visual context and spatial information. ViP [26] focuses on learning label interaction by proposing a phrase-guided message passing structure. Additionally, the method tries to capture contextual information by passing messages across triple branches before ROI pooling and thus fail to explore in-depth spatiality-aware feature representations.

Transferable SCA-M Module and IH-Tree. We further demonstrate the effectiveness of the proposed SCA-M module in capturing spatiality, context and appearance visual cues, and IH-trees for resolving ambiguous annotations, by plugging them into architectures of existing works. Here, we take the network of ViP [26] as the backbone for its end-to-end training scheme and state-of-the-art results (Table 2). We compare three configurations, *i.e.*, *ViP+SCA-M*, *ViP+IH-tree* and *ViP+SCA-M+IH-tree*. For a fair comparison, the ViP is modified by replacing the targeted components with SCA-M or IH-tree with other components fixed. As shown in Table 2, the performance of ViP is improved by a considerable margin on all evaluation metrics after applying our SCA-M (*i.e. ViP+SCA-M*). The results again suggest the superiority of the proposed spatiality-aware feature representations to that of ViP. Note that the overall performance by adding both stacked SCA module and IH-tree (*i.e., ViP+SCA-M+IH-tree*) surpasses that of ViP itself. The ViP designs a phrase-guided message passing structure to learn textual connections among ⟨*subject-predicate-object*⟩ at label-level. On the contrary, we concentrate

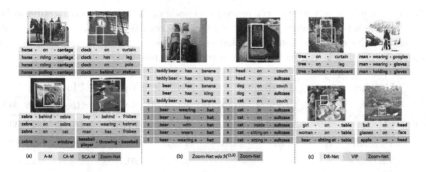

Fig. 6. Qualitative results on VG dataset. (a) Comparison results with the variants of different module configurations. (b) Results by discarding IH-trees. (c) Comparison between Zoom-Net with state-of-the-art methods. (a) and (c) show Top-1 prediction results while (b) provides Top-5 results for each method. The ground truth are in bold.

more on capturing contextual connections among ⟨*subject-predicate-object*⟩ at feature-level. Therefore, it's not surprising that a combination of these two aspects can provide a better result.

6   Comparisons on Visual Relationship Dataset (VRD)

Settings. We further quantitatively compare the performance of the proposed method with previous state of the arts on the Visual Relationship Dataset (VRD) [30]. The following comparisons keep the same settings as the prior arts. Since VRD has a clean annotation, we fine-tune the construction of IH-tree by removing the $\mathcal{H}_o^{(1)}$ and $\mathcal{H}_p^{(1)}$, which aim at reducing data ambiguity and noise in VG (details in Sect. 4). For a fair comparison, object proposals are generated by RPN [14] here and we use triplet NMS to remove redundant triplet candidates following the setting in [26] due to its excellent performance.

Evaluation Metrics. We follow [6,46] to report Recall@50 and Recall@100 when $k = 70$. The IoU between the predicted bounding boxes and the ground truth is required above 0.5 here. In addition, some previous works used $k = 1$ for evaluation and thus we report our results with $k = 1$ as well to compare these previous methods under the same conditions.

Results. The results listed in Table 3 show that the proposed Zoom-Net outperforms the state-of-the-art methods by significant gains on almost all the evaluation metrics[4]. In comparison to previous state-of-the-art approaches, Zoom-

---

[4] Note that Yu *et al.* [46] take external Wikipedia data with around 4 billion and 450 million sentences to distill linguistic knowledge for modeling the tuple correlation from label-aspect. It's not surprising to achieve a superior performance. In this experiment, we only compare with the results [46] without knowledge distillation.

Table 3. Comparisons with the referenced methods on VRD dataset. Results in bold indicate the best performance while the underlined results represent the next best. * marks the results of LK without knowledge distillation. ** marks the results of LK with knowledge distillation including large-scale external Wikipedia data.

k	Methods	Predicate		Relationship		Phrase	
		Rec@50	Rec@100	Rec@50	Rec@100	Rec@50	Rec@100
$k = 1$	LP [30]	47.87	47.87	13.86	14.70	16.17	17.03
	VTransE [47]	44.76	44.76	14.07	15.20	19.42	22.42
	VRL [29]	-	-	18.19	20.79	21.37	22.60
	PPRFCN [48]	47.43	47.43	14.41	15.72	19.62	23.15
	SA-Full [35]	50.40	50.40	14.90	16.10	16.70	18.10
	LK [46]*	47.50	47.50	16.57	17.69	19.15	19.98
	LK [46]**	<u>55.16</u>	<u>55.16</u>	<u>19.17</u>	21.34	23.14	24.03
	ViP [26]	-	-	17.32	20.01	22.78	27.91
	CAI [49]	53.59	53.59	15.63	17.39	17.60	19.24
	Zoom-Net	50.69	50.69	18.92	<u>21.41</u>	<u>24.82</u>	<u>28.09</u>
	CAI + SCA-M	**55.98**	**55.98**	**19.54**	**22.39**	**25.21**	**28.89**
$k = 70$	LK [46]*	74.98	86.97	20.12	<u>28.94</u>	22.59	25.54
	LK [46]**	<u>85.64</u>	**94.65**	**22.68**	**31.89**	26.32	29.43
	DR-Net [6]	80.78	81.90	17.73	20.88	19.93	23.45
	Zoom-Net	84.25	90.59	21.37	27.30	<u>29.05</u>	<u>37.34</u>
	CAI + SCA-M	**89.03**	<u>94.56</u>	<u>22.34</u>	28.52	**29.64**	**38.39**

Net improves the recall of predicate prediction by 3.47% Rec@50 and 3.62% Rec@100 when $k = 70$. Besides, the Rec@50 on relationship and phrase prediction tasks are increased by 1.25% and 6.46%, respectively. Note that the result of *predicate* ($k = 1$) only achieves comparable performance with some prior arts [29, 35, 46, 49] since these methods use the groundtruth of *subject* and *object* and only predict *predicate* while our method predicts *subject, predicate, object* together.

Among all prior arts designed without external data, CAI [49] has achieved the best performance on predicate prediction (53.59% Rec@50) by designing a context-aware interaction recognition framework to encode the labels into semantic space. To demonstrate the effectiveness and robustness of the proposed SCA-M in feature representation, we replace the visual feature representation in CAI [49] with our SCA-M (*i.e. CAI + SCA-M*). The performance improvements are significant as shown in Table 3 due to the better visual feature learned, *e.g.*, predicate Rec@50 is increased by 2.39% compared to [49]. In addition, with neither language priors, linguistic models nor external textual data, the proposed method can still achieve the state-of-the-art performance on most of the evaluation metrics, thanks to its superior feature representations.

7 Conclusion

We have presented an innovative framework Zoom-Net for visual relationship recognition, concentrating on feature learning with a novel Spatiality-Context-Appearance module (SCA-M). The unique design of SCA-M, which contains the proposed Contrastive ROI Pooling and Pyramid ROI Pooling Cells, benefits the learning of spatiality-aware contextual feature representation. We further designed the Intra-Hierarchical tree (IH-tree) to model intra-class correlations for handling ambiguous and noisy labels. Zoom-Net achieves the state-of-the-art performance on both VG and VRD datasets. We demonstrated the superiority and transferability of each component of Zoom-Net. It is interesting to explore the notion of feature interactions in other applications such as image retrieval and image caption generation.

Acknowledgment. This work is supported in part by the National Natural Science Foundation of China (Grant No. 61371192), the Key Laboratory Foundation of the Chinese Academy of Sciences (CXJJ-17S044) and the Fundamental Research Funds for the Central Universities (WK2100330002, WK3480000005), in part by SenseTime Group Limited, the General Research Fund sponsored by the Research Grants Council of Hong Kong (Nos. 14213616, 14206114, 14205615, 14203015, 14239816, 419412, 14207-814, 14208417, 14202217, 14209217), the Hong Kong Innovation and Technology Support Program (No. ITS/121/15FX).

References

1. Alexe, B., Heess, N., Teh, Y.W., Ferrari, V.: Searching for objects driven by context. In: NIPS (2012)
2. Bird, S., Klein, E., Loper, E.: Natural Language Processing with Python: Analyzing Text with the Natural Language Toolkit. O'Reilly Media Inc., Newton (2009)
3. Carreira, J., Li, F., Sminchisescu, C.: Object recognition by sequential figure-ground ranking. IJCV **98**, 243–262 (2012)
4. Chen, X., Shrivastava, A., Gupta, A.: Neil: Extracting visual knowledge from web data. In: ICCV (2013)
5. Choi, M.J., Lim, J.J., Torralba, A., Willsky, A.S.: Exploiting hierarchical context on a large database of object categories. In: CVPR (2010)
6. Dai, B., Zhang, Y., Lin, D.: Detecting visual relationships with deep relational networks. In: CVPR (2017)
7. Delaitre, V., Sivic, J., Laptev, I.: Learning person-object interactions for action recognition in still images. In: NIPS (2011)
8. Deng, J., Berg, A.C., Fei-Fei, L.: Hierarchical semantic indexing for large scale image retrieval. In: CVPR, pp. 785–792. IEEE (2011)
9. Deng, J., et al.: Large-scale object classification using label relation graphs. In: Fleet, D., Pajdla, T., Schiele, B., Tuytelaars, T. (eds.) ECCV 2014. LNCS, vol. 8689, pp. 48–64. Springer, Cham (2014). https://doi.org/10.1007/978-3-319-10590-1_4
10. Deng, J., Dong, W., Socher, R., Li, L.J., Li, K., Li, F.F.: ImageNet: a large-scale hierarchical image database. In: CVPR (2009)

11. Deng, J., Krause, J., Berg, A.C., Li, F.F.: Hedging your bets: optimizing accuracy-specificity trade-offs in large scale visual recognition. In: CVPR, pp. 3450–3457. IEEE, June 2012

12. Desai, C., Ramanan, D.: Detecting actions, poses, and objects with relational phraselets. In: Fitzgibbon, A., Lazebnik, S., Perona, P., Sato, Y., Schmid, C. (eds.) ECCV 2012. LNCS, vol. 7575, pp. 158–172. Springer, Heidelberg (2012). https://doi.org/10.1007/978-3-642-33765-9_12

13. Desai, C., Ramanan, D., Fowlkes, C.C.: Discriminative models for multi-class object layout. IJCV **95**, 1–12 (2011)

14. Girshick, R.: Fast R-CNN. In: ICCV (2015)

15. Gkioxari, G., Girshick, R., Malik, J.: Contextual action recognition with R* CNN. In: ICCV (2015)

16. Guadarrama, S., et al.: YouTube2Text: recognizing and describing arbitrary activities using semantic hierarchies and zero-shot recognition. In: ICCV (2013)

17. Hu, H., Zhou, G.T., Deng, Z., Liao, Z., Mori, G.: Learning structured inference neural networks with label relations. In: CVPR, pp. 2960–2968 (2016)

18. Hu, R., Rohrbach, M., Andreas, J., Darrell, T., Saenko, K.: Modeling relationships in referential expressions with compositional modular networks. In: CVPR (2017)

19. Jia, Y., et al.: Caffe: convolutional architecture for fast feature embedding. In: ACM MM (2014)

20. Karpathy, A., Joulin, A., Li, F.F.: Deep fragment embeddings for bidirectional image sentence mapping. In: NIPS (2014)

21. Karpathy, A., Li, F.F.: Deep visual-semantic alignments for generating image descriptions. In: CVPR (2015)

22. Krishna, R., et al.: Visual genome: connecting language and vision using crowd-sourced dense image annotations. IJCV **123**, 32–73 (2017)

23. Li, C., Parikh, D., Chen, T.: Extracting adaptive contextual cues from unlabeled regions. In: ICCV (2011)

24. Li, L.J., Su, H., Fei-Fei, L., Xing, E.P.: Object bank: a high-level image representation for scene classification & semantic feature sparsification. In: NIPS (2010)

25. Li, Y., Huang, C., Loy, C.C., Tang, X.: Human attribute recognition by deep hierarchical contexts. In: Leibe, B., Matas, J., Sebe, N., Welling, M. (eds.) ECCV 2016. LNCS, vol. 9910, pp. 684–700. Springer, Cham (2016). https://doi.org/10.1007/978-3-319-46466-4_41

26. Li, Y., Ouyang, W., Wang, X., Tang, X.: ViP-CNN: Visual phrase guided convolutional neural network. In: CVPR (2017)

27. Li, Y., Ouyang, W., Zhou, B., Wang, K., Wang, X.: Scene graph generation from objects, phrases and region captions. In: ICCV (2017)

28. Liang, X., Hu, Z., Zhang, H., Gan, C., Xing, E.P.: Recurrent topic-transition GAN for visual paragraph generation. In: ICCV (2017)

29. Liang, X., Lee, L., Xing, E.P.: Deep variation-structured reinforcement learning for visual relationship and attribute detection. In: CVPR (2017)

30. Lu, C., Krishna, R., Bernstein, M., Fei-Fei, L.: Visual relationship detection with language priors. In: Leibe, B., Matas, J., Sebe, N., Welling, M. (eds.) ECCV 2016. LNCS, vol. 9905, pp. 852–869. Springer, Cham (2016). https://doi.org/10.1007/978-3-319-46448-0_51

31. Marszalek, M., Schmid, C.: Semantic hierarchies for visual object recognition. In: CVPR (2007)

32. Mottaghi, R., et al.: The role of context for object detection and semantic segmentation in the wild. In: CVPR (2014)

33. Ordonez, V., Deng, J., Choi, Y., Berg, A.C., Berg, T.L.: From large scale image categorization to entry-level categories. In: ICCV, pp. 2768–2775. IEEE (2013)

34. Park, D., Ramanan, D., Fowlkes, C.: Multiresolution models for object detection. In: Daniilidis, K., Maragos, P., Paragios, N. (eds.) ECCV 2010. LNCS, vol. 6314, pp. 241–254. Springer, Heidelberg (2010). https://doi.org/10.1007/978-3-642-15561-1_18

35. Peyre, J., Laptev, I., Schmid, C., Sivic, J.: Weakly-supervised learning of visual relations. In: ICCV (2017)

36. Rabinovich, A., Vedaldi, A., Galleguillos, C., Wiewiora, E., Belongie, S.: Objects in context. In: ICCV (2007)

37. Redmon, J., Farhadi, A.: Yolo9000: Better, faster, stronger. In: CVPR (2017)

38. Sadeghi, M.A., Farhadi, A.: Recognition using visual phrases. In: CVPR (2011)

39. Schuster, S., Krishna, R., Chang, A., Fei-Fei, L., Manning, C.D.: Generating semantically precise scene graphs from textual descriptions for improved image retrieval. In: Proceedings of the Fourth Workshop on Vision and Language (2015)

40. Seco, N., Veale, T., Hayes, J.: An intrinsic information content metric for semantic similarity in WordNet. In: Proceedings of the 16th European Conference on Artificial Intelligence (2004)

41. Simonyan, K., Zisserman, A.: Very deep convolutional networks for large-scale image recognition. In: arXiv preprint (2014)

42. Torralba, A., Murphy, K.P., Freeman, W.T.: Using the forest to see the trees: exploiting context for visual object detection and localization. Commun. ACM **53**, 107–114 (2010)

43. Wang, J., Markert, K., Everingham, M.: Learning models for object recognition from natural language descriptions. In: BMVC (2009)

44. Xu, D., Zhu, Y., Choy, C.B., Fei-Fei, L.: Scene graph generation by iterative message passing. In: CVPR (2017)

45. Yatskar, M., Zettlemoyer, L., Farhadi, A.: Situation recognition: visual semantic role labeling for image understanding. In: CVPR (2016)

46. Yu, R., Li, A., Morariu, V.I., Davis, L.S.: Visual relationship detection with internal and external linguistic knowledge distillation. In: ICCV (2017)

47. Zhang, H., Kyaw, Z., Chang, S.F., Chua, T.S.: Visual translation embedding network for visual relation detection. In: CVPR (2017)

48. Zhang, H., Kyaw, Z., Yu, J., Chang, S.F.: PPR-FCN: weakly supervised visual relation detection via parallel pairwise R-FCN. In: ICCV (2017)

49. Zhuang, B., Liu, L., Shen, C., Reid, I.: Towards context-aware interaction recognition for visual relationship detection. In: ICCV (2017)

50. Zhuang, B., Wu, Q., Shen, C., Reid, I., van den Hengel, A.: Care about you: towards large-scale human-centric visual relationship detection. In: arXiv preprint (2017)

Quantized Densely Connected U-Nets for Efficient Landmark Localization

Zhiqiang Tang[1]([✉]), Xi Peng[2], Shijie Geng[1], Lingfei Wu[3], Shaoting Zhang[4], and Dimitris Metaxas[1]

[1] Rutgers University, New Brunswick, USA
{zt53,sg1309,dnm}@rutgers.edu
[2] Binghamton University, Binghamton, USA
xpeng@binghamton.edu
[3] IBM T. J. Watson, Yorktown Heights, USA
lwu@email.wm.edu
[4] SenseTime, Beijing, China
zhangshaoting@sensetime.com

Abstract. In this paper, we propose quantized densely connected U-Nets for efficient visual landmark localization. The idea is that features of the same semantic meanings are globally reused across the stacked U-Nets. This dense connectivity largely improves the information flow, yielding improved localization accuracy. However, a vanilla dense design would suffer from critical efficiency issue in both training and testing. To solve this problem, we first propose order-K dense connectivity to trim off long-distance shortcuts; then, we use a memory-efficient implementation to significantly boost the training efficiency and investigate an iterative refinement that may slice the model size in half. Finally, to reduce the memory consumption and high precision operations both in training and testing, we further quantize weights, inputs, and gradients of our localization network to low bit-width numbers. We validate our approach in two tasks: human pose estimation and face alignment. The results show that our approach achieves state-of-the-art localization accuracy, but using ~70% fewer parameters, ~98% less model size and saving ~32× training memory compared with other benchmark localizers.

1 Introduction

Locating visual landmarks, such as human body joints [37] and facial key points [41], is an important yet challenging problem. The stacked U-Nets, *e.g.* hourglasses (HGs) [23], are widely used in landmark localization. Generally speaking, their success can be attributed to design patterns: (1) within each U-Net, connect the top-down and bottom-up feature blocks to encourage gradient flow; and (2) stack multiple U-Nets in a cascade to refine prediction stage by stage.

However, the shortcut connection exists only "locally" inside each U-Net [32]. There is no "global" connection across U-Nets except the cascade. Blocks

© Springer Nature Switzerland AG 2018
V. Ferrari et al. (Eds.): ECCV 2018, LNCS 11207, pp. 348–364, 2018.
https://doi.org/10.1007/978-3-030-01219-9_21

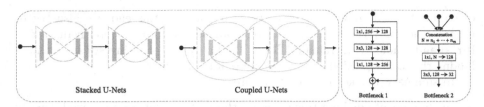

Fig. 1. Illustration of stacked U-Nets and DU-Net. Stacked U-Nets has skip connections only within each U-Net. In contrast, DU-Net also connects blocks with the same semantic meanings across different U-Nets. The feature reuse could significantly reduce the size of bottleneck in each block, as shown in the right figure. Consequently, with the same number of U-Nets, DU-Net has only 30% parameters of stacked U-Nets.

in different U-Nets cannot share features, which may impede the information flow and lead to redundant parameters.

We propose densely connected U-Nets (DU-Net) to address this issue. The key idea is to directly connect blocks of the same semantic meanings, *i.e.* having the same resolution in either top-down or bottom-up context, from any U-Net to all subsequent U-Nets. Please refer to Fig. 1 for an illustration. The dense connectivity is similar to DenseNet [14] but generalizing the design philosophy from feature to semantic level. It encourages information flow as well as feature reuse "globally" across the stacked U-Nets, yielding improved localization accuracy.

Yet there are critical issues in designing DU-Net: (1) The number of parameters would have a quadratic growth since n stacked U-Nets could generate $O(n^2)$ connections. (2) A naive implementation may allocate new memory for every connection, making the training highly expensive and limiting the maximum depth of DU-Nets.

Our solution to those efficiency issues is threefold. **First**, instead of connecting all stacked U-Nets, we only connect a U-Net to its K successors. We name it as the *order-K* connectivity, which aims to balance the fitting accuracy and parameter efficiency by cutting off long-distance connections. **Second**, we employ a memory-efficient implementation in training. The key idea is to reuse a pre-allocated memory so all connected blocks could share the same memory. Compared with the naive implementation, this strategy makes it possible to train a very deep DU-Net (actually, 2× deeper). **Third**, to further improve the efficiency, we investigate an iterative design that may reduce the model size to one half. More specifically, the output of the first pass of the DU-Net is used as the input of the second pass, where detection or regression loss is applied as supervision.

Besides shrinking the number of network parameters, we also study to further quantize each parameter. This motivates from the ubiquitous mobile applications. Although current mobile devices could carry models of dozens of MBs, deploying such networks requires high-end GPUs. However, quantized models could be accelerated by some specifically designed low-cost hardwares. Beyond only deploying models on mobile devices [18], training deep neural networks on distributed mobile devices emerges recently [22]. To this end, we also try to quantize not only the model parameters but also its inputs (intermediate features) and gradients in training. This is the first attempt to investigate training landmark localizers using quantized inputs and gradients.

In summary, our key contributions are:

- To the best of our knowledge, we are the first to propose quantized densely connected U-Nets for visual landmark localization, which largely improves the information flow and feature reuse at the semantic level.
- We propose the *order-K* connectivity to balance accuracy and efficiency. It decreases the growth of model size from quadratic to linear by removing trivial connections.
- Very deep U-Nets can be trained using a memory-efficient implementation, where pre-allocated memory is reused by all connected blocks.
- We further investigate an iterative refinement that may cut down half of the model size, by forwarding DU-Net twice using either detection or regression supervision.
- Different from previous efforts of quantizing only the model parameters, we are the first to quantize their inputs and gradients for better training efficiency on landmark localization tasks. By choosing appropriate quantization bit-widths for weights, inputs and gradients, quantized DU-Net achieves ∼32× memory saving with comparable performance to the-state-of-art approaches.
- Exhaustive experiments are performed to validate DU-Net in different aspects. In both human pose estimation and face alignment, DU-Net demonstrates comparable localization accuracy and use ∼2% model size compared with state-of-the-art methods.

2   Related Work

In this section, we review the recent developments on designing convolutional network architectures, quantizing the neural networks, human pose estimation and facial landmark localization.

Network Architecture. The identity mappings make it possible to train very deep ResNet [12]. The popular stacked U-Nets [23] are designed based on the residual modules. More recently, the DenseNet [14] outperforms the ResNet in the image classification task, benefitting from its dense connections. We would like to use the dense connectivity into multiple U-Nets.

Network Quantization. Training deep neural networks usually consumes a large amount of computational resources, which makes it hard to deploy on mobile devices. Recently, network quantization approaches [9,19,31,40,47] offer an efficient solution to reduce the size of network through cutting down high precision operations and operands. In the recent binarized convolutional landmark localizer (BCLL) [5] architecture, XNOR-Net [31] was utilized for network binarization. However, BCLL only quantizes weights for inference and bring in real-value scaling factors. Due to its high precision demand in training, it cannot save training memory and improve training efficiency. To this end, we explore to quantize our DU-Net in training and inference simultaneously.

Human Pose Estimation. Starting from the DeepPose [37], CNNs based approaches [3,4,6,15,20,28,39,46] become the mainstream in human pose estimation and prediction. Recently, the architecture of stacked hourglasses [23] has obviously beaten all the previous ones in terms of usability and accuracy. Therefore, all recent state-of-the-art methods [7,8,26,42] build on its architecture. They replace the residual modules with more sophisticated ones, add graphical models to get better inference, or use an additional network to provide adversarial supervisions or do adversarial data augmentation [26]. In contrast, we design a simple yet very effective connectivity pattern for stacked U-Nets.

Facial Landmark Localization. Similarly, CNNs have largely reshaped the field of facial landmark localization. Traditional methods could be easily outperformed by the CNNs based [21,24,25,44,45]. In the recent Menpo Facial Landmark Localization Challenge [43], stacked hourglasses [23] achieves state-of-the-art performance. The proposed *order-K* connected U-Nets could produce even better results but with much fewer parameters.

3 Our Method

In this section, we first introduce the DU-Net after recapping the stacked U-Nets [23]. Then we present the *order-K* connectivity to improve its parameter efficiency, an efficient implementation to reduce its training memory, and an iterative refinement to make it more parameter efficient. Finally, network quantization is utilized to further reduce training memory and model size.

3.1 DU-Net

A U-Net contains top-down, bottom-up blocks and skip connections between them. Suppose multiple U-Nets are stacked together, for the ℓth top-down and bottom-up blocks in the nth U-Net, we use $f_\ell^n(\cdot)$ and $g_\ell^n(\cdot)$ to denote their non-linear transformations. Their outputs are represented by $\mathbf{x}_\ell^n$ and $\mathbf{y}_\ell^n$. $f_\ell^n(\cdot)$ and $g_\ell^n(\cdot)$ comprise operations of Convolution (Conv), Batch Normalization (BN) [16], rectified linear units (ReLU) [11], and pooling.

Stacked U-Nets. The feature transitions at the ℓth top-down and bottom-up blocks of the nth U-Net are:

$$\mathbf{x}_\ell^n = f_\ell^n(\mathbf{x}_{\ell-1}^n), \mathbf{y}_\ell^n = g_\ell^n(\mathbf{y}_{\ell-1}^n + \mathbf{x}_\ell^n). \tag{1}$$

The skip connections only exist locally within each U-Net, which may restrict that information flows across U-Nets.

DU-Net. To make information flow efficiently across stacked U-Nets, we propose a global connectivity pattern. Blocks at the same locations of different

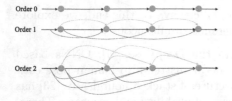

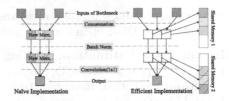

Fig. 2. Illustration of *order-K* connectivity. For simplicity, each dot represents one U-Net. The red and blue lines are the shortcut connections of inside semantic blocks and outside inputs. *Order-*0 connectivity (**Top**) strings U-Nets together only by their inputs and outputs, i.e. stacked U-Nets. *Order-*1 connectivity (**Middle**) has shortcut connections for adjacent U-Nets. Similarly, *order-*2 connectivity (**Bottom**) has shortcut connections for 3 nearby U-Nets.

Fig. 3. Illustration of memory efficient implementation. It is for the Concat-BN-ReLU-Conv(1 × 1) in each bottleneck structure. ReLU is not shown since it is an inplace operation with no memory request. The efficient implementation pre-allocates fixed memory space to store the concatenated and normalized features of connected blocks. In contrast, the naive implementation always allocates new memories for them, causing high memory consumption.

U-Nets have direct connections. Hence, we refer to this densely connected U-Nets architecture as *DU-Net*. Figure 1 gives an illustration. Mathematically, the feature transitions at the ℓth top-down and bottom-up blocks of the nth U-Net can be formulated as:

$$\mathbf{x}_\ell^n = f_\ell^n([\mathbf{x}_{\ell-1}^n, \mathbf{X}_\ell^{n-1}]), \mathbf{y}_\ell^n = g_\ell^n([\mathbf{y}_{\ell-1}^n, \mathbf{x}_\ell^n, \mathbf{Y}_\ell^{n-1}]), \tag{2}$$

where $\mathbf{X}_\ell^{n-1} = \mathbf{x}_\ell^0, \mathbf{x}_\ell^1, \cdots, \mathbf{x}_\ell^{n-1}$ are the outputs of the ℓth top-down blocks in all preceding U-Nets. Similarly, $\mathbf{Y}_\ell^{n-1} = \mathbf{y}_\ell^0, \mathbf{y}_\ell^1, \cdots, \mathbf{y}_\ell^{n-1}$ represent the outputs from the ℓth bottom-up blocks. $[\cdots]$ denotes the feature concatenation, which could make information flow more efficiently than the summation operation in Eq. 1.

According to Eq. 2, a block receives features not only from connected blocks in the current U-Net but also the output features of the same semantic blocks from all its preceding U-Nets. Note that this semantic level dense connectivity is a generalization of the dense connectivity in DenseNet [14] that connects layers only within each block.

3.2   Order-K Connectivity

In the above formulation of DU-Net, we connect blocks with the same semantic meanings across all U-Nets. The connections would have quadratic growth depthwise. To make DU-Net parameter efficient, we propose to cut off some trivial connections. For compensation, we add an intermediate supervision at the end of each U-Net. The intermediate supervisions, as the skip connections, could also alleviate the gradient vanish problem. Mathematically, the features $\mathbf{X}_\ell^{n-1}$ and $\mathbf{Y}_\ell^{n-1}$ in Eq. 2 turns into

$$\mathbf{X}_\ell^{n-1} = \mathbf{x}_\ell^{n-k}, \cdots, \mathbf{x}_\ell^{n-1}, \tag{3}$$
$$\mathbf{Y}_\ell^{n-1} = \mathbf{y}_\ell^{n-k}, \cdots, \mathbf{y}_\ell^{n-1}, \tag{4}$$

where $0 \leq k \leq n$ represents how many preceding nearby U-Nets connect with the current one. $k = n$ or $k = 0$ would result in the stacked U-Nets or fully densely connected U-Nets. A medium order could reduce the growth of DU-Net parameters from quadratic to linear. Therefore, it largely improves the parameter efficiency of DU-Net and could make DU-Net grow several times deeper.

The proposed *order-K* connection has similar philosophy as the Variable Order Markov (VOM) models [2]. Each U-Net can be viewed as a state in the Markov model. The current U-Net depends on a fixed number of preceding nearby U-Nets, instead of preceding either only one or all U-Nets. In this way, the long-range connections are cut off. Figure 2 illustrates connections of three different orders. In Fig. 2, the connections above the central axes follow VOM patterns of *order*-0, *order*-1 and *order*-2 whereas the central axes together with connections below them follow VOM patterns of *order*-1, *order*-2 and *order*-3.

Dense connectivity is a special case of *order-K* connectivity on the limit of K. For small K, *order-K* connectivity is much more parameter efficient. But fewer connections may affect the prediction accuracy of very deep DU-Net. To make DU-Net have both high parameter efficiency and prediction accuracy, we propose to use *order-K* connectivity in conjunction with intermediate supervisions. In contrast, DenseNet [14] has only one supervision at the end. Thus, it cannot effectively take advantage of *order-K* connectivity.

3.3 Memory Efficient Implementation

Benefitting from the *order-K* connectivity, our DU-Net is quite parameter efficient. However, a naive implementation would prevent from training very deep DU-Net, since every connection would make a copy of input features. To reduce the training memory, we follow the efficient implementation [29]. More specifically, concatenation operations of the same semantic blocks in all U-Nets share a memory allocation and their subsequent batch norm operations share another memory allocation. Suppose a DU-Net includes N U-Nets each of which has L top-down blocks and L bottom-up blocks. We need to pre-allocate two memory space for each of $2L$ semantic blocks. For the ℓth top-down blocks, the concatenated features $[\mathbf{x}_{\ell-1}^1, \mathbf{X}_\ell^0], \cdots, [\mathbf{x}_{\ell-1}^{N-1}, \mathbf{X}_\ell^{N-2}]$ share the same memory space. Similarly, the concatenated features $[\mathbf{y}_{\ell-1}^0, \mathbf{x}_\ell^0], [\mathbf{y}_{\ell-1}^1, \mathbf{x}_\ell^1, \mathbf{Y}_\ell^0], \cdots, [\mathbf{y}_{\ell-1}^{N-1}, \mathbf{x}_\ell^{N-1}, \mathbf{Y}_\ell^{N-2}]$ in the ℓth bottom-up blocks share the same memory space.

In one shared memory allocation, later produced features would overlay the former features. Thus, the concatenations and their subsequent batch norm operations require to be re-computed in backward phase. Figure 3 illustrates naive and efficient implementations.

3.4 Iterative Refinement

In order to further improve the parameter efficiency of DU-Net, we consider an iterative refinement. It uses only half of a DU-Net but may achieve comparable performance. In the iterative refinement, a DU-Net has two forward passes. In the first pass, we concatenate the inputs of the first and last U-Nets and merge them in a small dense block. Then the refined input is fed forward in the DU-Net again. Better output is expected because of the refined input.

In this iterative pipeline, the DU-Net has two groups of supervisions in the first and second iterations. Both the detection and regression supervisions [4] are already used in the landmark detection tasks. However, there is no investigation how they compare with each other. To this end, we could try different combinations of detection and regression supervisions for two iterations. Our comparison could give some guidance for future research.

3.5 Network Quantization

We aim at cutting down high precision operations and parameters both in training and inference stages of DU-Net. The bit-width of weights can be reduced to one or two bits through sign function or symmetrical threshold, whereas the layerwise gradients and inputs are quantized with linear mapping. In previous XNOR-Net [31], a scaling factor was introduced to approximate the real-value weight. However, calculating these float factor costs additional computational resources. To further decrease memory usage and model size, we try to remove the scaling factor and follow WAGE [40] to quantize dataflow during training. More specifically, weights are binarized to -1 and 1 by the following equation:

$$q(x) = sign(clip(x, -1, 1)) \tag{5}$$

or ternarized to $-1, 0$ and -1 by the a positive threshold δ as [19] presented, where $\delta \approx \frac{0.7}{n} \sum_{i=1}^{n} |w_i|$ provided that w_i is initialized by Gaussian distributions. The dataflows, i.e. gradients and inputs, are quantized to k-bit values by the following linear mapping function:

$$q(x, k) = clip(\sigma(k) \cdot round(x\sigma(k)) - 1 + \sigma(k), 1 - \sigma(k)) \tag{6}$$

Here, the unit distance σ is calculated by $\sigma(k) = \frac{1}{2^k - 1}$. In the following experiments, we explore different combinations of bit-widths to balance performance and memory consumption.

4 Experiments

In this section, we first demonstrate the effectiveness of DU-Net through its comparison with the stacked U-Nets. Then we explore the relation between the prediction accuracy and *order-K* connectivity. After that, we evaluate the iterative refinement to halve DU-Net parameters. Finally, we test the network quantization. Different combinations of bit-widths to find appropriate ones which balance accuracy, model size and memory consumption. The general comparisons are given at last. Some qualitative results are shown in Fig. 6.

Network. The input resolution is normalized to 256×256. Before the DU-Net, a Conv(7×7) filter with stride 2 and a max pooling would produce 128 features with resolution 64×64. Hence, the maximum resolution of DU-Net is 64×64. Each block in DU-Net has a bottleneck structure as shown on the right side of Fig. 1. At the beginning of each bottleneck, features from different connections are concatenated and stored in a shared memory. Then the concatenated features are compressed by the Conv(1×1) to 128 features. At last, the Conv(3×3) further produces 32 new features. The batch norm and ReLU are used before the convolutions.

Training. We implement the DU-Net using the PyTorch. The DU-Net is trained by the optimizer RMSprop. When training human pose estimators, the initial learning rate is 2.5×10^{-4} which is decayed to 5×10^{-5} after 100 epochs. The whole training takes 200 epochs. The facial landmark localizers are easier to train. Also starting from 2.5×10^{-4}, its learning rate is divided by 5, 2 and 2 at epoch 30, 60 and 90 respectively. The above settings remain the same for quantized DU-Net. In order to match the pace of dataflow, we set the same bitwidth for gradients and inputs. We quantize dataflows and parameters all over the DU-Net except the first and last convolutional layers, since localization is a fine-grained task requires high precision of heatmaps.

Human Pose Datasets. We use two benchmark human pose estimation datasets: MPII Human Pose [1] and Leeds Sports Pose (LSP) [17]. The **MPII** is collected from YouTube videos with a broad range of human activities. It has 25K images and 40K annotated persons, which are split into a training set of 29K and a test set of 11K. Following [35], 3K samples are chosen from the training set as validation set. Each person has 16 labeled joints. The **LSP** dataset contains images from many sport scenes. Its extended version has 11K training samples and 1K testing samples. Each person in LSP has 14 labeled joints. Since there are usually multiple people in one image, we crop around each person and resize it to 256×256. We also use scaling ($0.75-1.25$), rotation ($\pm 30°$) and random flip to augment the data.

Facial Landmark Datasets. The experiments of the facial lanmark localization are conducted on the composite of HELEN, AFW, LFPW and IBUG which are re-annotated in the 300-W challenge [33]. Each face has 68 landmarks. Following [48] and [21], we use the training images of HELEN, LFPW and all images of AFW, totally 3148 images, as the training set. The testing is done on the common subset (testing images of HELEN and LFPW), challenge subset (all images from IBUG) and their union. We use the provided bounding boxes from the 300-W challenge to crop faces. The same augmentations of scaling and rotation as in human pose estimation are applied.

Metric. We use the standard metrics in both human pose estimation and face alignment. Specifically, Percentage of Correct Keypoints (PCK) is used to evaluate approaches for human pose estimation. And the normalized mean error

Table 1. *Order*-1 DU-Net *v.s.* stacked U-Nets on MPII validation set measured by PCKh(%) and parameter number. *Order*-1 DU-Net achieves comparable performance as stacked U-Nets. But it has only about 30% parameters of stacked U-Nets. The feature reuse across U-Nets make each U-Net become light-weighted.

Method	PCKh	# Parameters	Parameter ratio
Stacked U-Nets(16)	-	50.5M	100%
DU-Net(16)	89.9	15.9M	31.5%
Stacked U-Nets(8)	89.3	25.5M	100%
DU-Net(8)	89.5	7.9M	31.0%
Stacked U-Nets(4)	88.3	12.9M	100%
DU-Net(4)	88.2	3.9M	30.2%

Table 2. NME(%) on 300-W using *Order*-1 DU-Net(4) with iterative refinement, detection and regression supervisions. The top two and bottom three rows are non-iterative and iterative results. Iterative refinement could lower localization errors. Besides, the regression supervision outperforms the detection supervision.

Method	Easy subset	Hard subset	Full set	# Para.
Detection only	3.63	5.60	4.01	3.9M
Regression only	2.91	5.12	3.34	3.9M
Detection Detection	3.52	5.59	3.93	4.1M
Detection Regression	2.95	5.12	3.37	4.1M
Regression Regression	2.87	4.97	3.28	4.1M

(NME) is employed to measure the performance of localizing facial landmarks. Following the convention of 300-W challenge, we use the inter-ocular distance to normalize mean error. For network quantization, we propose the balance index (BI) to examine the trade-off between performance and efficiency.

4.1   DU-Net *vs* Stacked U-Nets

To demonstrate the advantages of DU-Net, we first compare it with traditional stacked U-Nets. This experiment is done on the MPII validation set. All DU-Nets use the *order*-1 connectivity and intermediate supervisions. Table 1 shows three pairs of comparisons with 4, 8 and 16 U-Nets. Both their PCKh and number of convolution parameters are reported. We could observe that, with the same number of U-Nets, DU-Net could obtain comparable or even better accuracy. More importantly, the number of parameters in DU-Net is decreased by about 70% of that in stacked U-Nets. The feature reuse across U-Nets make each U-Net in DU-Net become light-weighted. Besides, the high parameter efficiency makes it possible to train 16 *order*-1 connected U-Nets in a 12G GPU with batch size 16. In contrast, training 16 stacked U-Nets is infeasible. Thus, *order*-1 together with intermediate supervisions could make DU-Net obtain accurate prediction as well as high parameter efficiency, compared with stacked U-Nets.

4.2   Evaluation of *Order-K* Connectivity

The proposed *order-K* connectivity is key to improve the parameter efficiency of DU-Net. In this experiment, we investigate how the PCKh and convolution parameter number change along with the order value. Figure 4 gives the results from MPII validation set. The left and right figures show results of DU-Net with 8 and 16 U-Nets. It is clear that the convolution parameter number increases

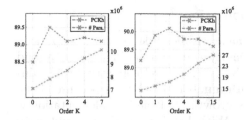

Fig. 4. Relation of PCKh(%), # parameters and *order-K* connectivity on MPII validation set. The parameter number of DU-Net grows approximately linearly with the order of connectivity. However, the PCKh first increases and then decreases. A small order 1 or 2 would be a good balance for prediction accuracy and parameter efficiency.

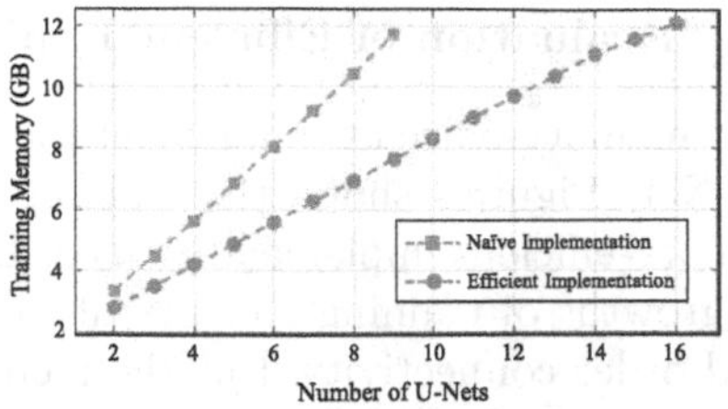

Fig. 5. Naive implementation *v.s.* memory-efficient implementation. The *order*-1 connectivity, batch size 16 and a 12 GB GPU are used. The naive implementation can only support 9 U-Nets at most. In contrast, the memory-efficient implementation allows to train 16 U-Nets, which nearly doubles the depth of DU-Net.

Table 3. *Order*-1 DU-Net(8) *v.s.* *order*-7 DU-Net(8), measured by training and validation PCKhs(%) on MPII. *Order*-7 DU-Net(8) overfits the training set a little bit. Its validation PCKh is lower at last, though it always has higher training PCKh.

Table 4. Iterative *order*-1 DU-Net(4) *v.s.* non-iterative *order*-1 DU-Net(8) on 300-W measured by NME(%). Iterative DU-Net(4), with few additional parameters on DU-Net(4), achieves comparable performance as DU-Net(8). Thus, the iterative refinement has the potential to halve parameters of DU-Net but still maintain comparable performance.

Epoch	1	50	100	150
PCKh on training set				
Order-1 DU-Net(8)	20.3	83.2	87.7	91.7
Order-7 DU-Net(8)	**25.2**	**84.7**	**89.3**	**93.1**
PCKh on validation set				
Order-1 DU-Net(8)	29.4	82.8	**85.7**	**87.1**
Order-7 DU-Net(8)	**36.6**	84.0	85.1	86.7

Method	Easy subset	Hard subset	Full set	# Parameters
DU-Net(4)	2.91	5.12	3.34	3.9M
Iter. DU-Net(4)	2.87	4.97	3.28	4.1M
DU-Net(8)	2.82	5.07	3.26	7.9M

as the order becomes larger. However, the left and right PCKh curves have a similar shape of first increasing and then decreasing. *Order*-1 connectivity is always better than *order*-0.

However, very dense connections may not be a good choice, which is kind of counter-intuitive. This is because the intermediate supervisions already provide additional gradients. Too dense connections make gradients accumulate too much, causing the overfitting of training set. Further evidence of overfitting is shown in Table 3. The *order*-7 connectivity has the higher training PCKh the *order*-1 in all training epochs. But its validation PCKh is a little lower in the last training epochs. Thus, small orders are recommended in DU-Net.

4.3   Evaluation of Efficient Implementation

The memory-efficient implementation makes it possible to train very deep DU-Net. Figure 5 shows the training memory consumption of both naive and memory-efficient implementations of DU-Net with order-1 connectivity. The linear growths of training memory along with number of U-Nets is because of the fixed order connectivity. But the memory growth of efficient implementation is much slower than that of the naive one. With batch size 16, we could train a DU-Net with 16 U-Nets in 12 GB GPU. Under the same setting, the naive implementation could accept only 9 U-Nets.

4.4   Evaluation of Iterative Refinement

The iterative refinement is designed to make DU-Net more parameter efficient. First, experiments are done on the 300-W dataset using DU-Net(4). Results are shown in Table 2. For both detection and regression supervisions, adding an iteration could lower the localization errors, demonstrating effectiveness of the iterative refinement. Meanwhile, the model parameters only increase 0.2M, making DU-Net even more parameter efficient. Besides, the regression supervision outperforms the detection one no matter in the iterative or non-iterative setting, making it a better choice for landmark localization.

Further, we compare iterative DU-Net(4) with non-iterative DU-Net(8). Table 4 gives the comparison. We could find that, the iterative DU-Net(4) could obtain comparable NME as DU-Net(8). However, DU-Net(8) has double parameters of DU-Net(4) whereas iterative DU-Net(4) increases only 0.2M additional parameters on DU-Net(4).

4.5   Evaluation of Network Quantization

Through network quantization, high precision operations and parameters can be efficiently represented by a few discrete values. In order to find appropriate choices of bit-widths, we try a series of bit-width combinations on the 300-W dataset based on *order*-1 DU-Net(4). The performance and balance ability of these combinations on several methods are shown in Table 5, where DU-Net(4) is DU-Net with 4 blocks, BW and TW respectively represents binarized weight and ternarized weight without α, BW-α is binarized weight with float scaling factor α, the suffix QIG means quantized inputs and gradients.

For mobile devices with limited computational resources, slightly performance drop is tolerable provided that corresponding large efficiency enhancement. For the evaluation purpose, we propose a balance index (BI) to better examine the trade-off between performance and efficiency:

$$BI = NME^2 \cdot TM \cdot MS \qquad (7)$$

where TM and MS is respectively short for training memory and model size compression ratios to the original network without quantization. The square of

Table 5. Performance and balance ability of different combinations of bit-width values on the 300-W dataset measured by NME(%), all quantized networks are based on *order*-1 DU-Net(4). BW and TW is short for binarized and ternarized weight, α represents float scaling factor, QIG is short for quantized inputs and gradients. Bit_I, Bit_W, Bit_G represents the bit-width of inputs, weights, gradients respectively. Training memory and model size is represented by the compression ratio to the original DU-Net(4). Balance index is calculated by Eq. 7. Comparable error rate could be achieved by binarized the model parameters. Further quantizing the inputs and gradients could substantially reduce the training memory with some increase of detection error. The balance index is a indicator for balancing the quantization and accuracy.

Method	Bit_I	Bit_W	Bit_G	NME (%) Full set	NME (%) Easy set	NME (%) Hard set	Training Memory	Model Size	Balance Index
DU-Net(4)	32	32	32	3.38	2.95	5.13	1.00	1.00	11.4
BW-QIG	6	1	6	5.93	5.10	9.34	0.17	0.03	0.18
BW-QIG	8	1	8	4.30	3.67	6.86	0.25	0.03	**0.14**
BW-α-QIG	8	1	8	4.47	3.75	7.40	0.25	0.03	0.15
BW	32	1	32	3.75	3.20	5.99	1.00	0.03	0.42
BW-α	32	1	32	**3.58**	3.12	5.45	1.00	0.03	0.38
TW	32	2	32	3.73	3.21	5.85	1.00	0.06	0.83
TW-QIG	6	2	6	4.27	3.70	6.59	0.17	0.06	0.19
TW-QIG	8	2	8	4.13	3.55	6.50	0.25	0.06	0.26

NME is calculated in the above formula to emphasize the prior importance of performance. For BI, the smaller the value, the better the ability of balance.

According to Table 5, BW-QIG(818) could achieve the best balance between performance and model efficiency among all the combinations. BW-QIG(818) could reduce more than 4× training memory and 32× model size while reach a better performance than TSR [21]. Besides, BW-α-QIG(818), BW-QIG(616) and TW-QIG(626) also have small balance index. Among all the combinations, the binarized network with scaling factor α, i.e. BW-α gets the closest error to the original network DU-Net(4).

For BW-α-QIG(818), the performance is not better than BW-QIG(818). This is mainly because that BW-α is heavily rely on the parameter α. However, the quantization of dataflow could reduce the approximation ability of α. TW and

Table 6. Comparison of convolution parameter number (Million) and model size (Megabyte) with state-of-the-art methods. DU-Net(16) has 27%-62% parameters of other methods. Its binarized version DU-Net-BW-α(16) has less than **2%** model size.

Method	Yang *et al.* [42]	Wei *et al.* [39]	Bulat *et al.* [4]	Chu *et al.* [8]	Newell *et al.* [23]	DU-Net(16)	*Order*-1 DU-Net-BW-α(16)
# Parameters	28.0M	29.7M	58.1M	58.1M	25.5M	**15.9M**	**15.9M**
Model size	110.2 MB	116.9 MB	228.7 MB	228.7 MB	100.5 MB	62.6 MB	**2.0 MB**

Fig. 6. Qualitative results of human pose estimation and facial landmark localization. DU-Net could handle a wide range of human poses, even with occlusions. It could also detect accurate facial landmarks with various head poses and expressions.

Table 7. PCKh(%) comparison on MPII test sets. *Order*-1 DU-Net could achieve comparable performance as state-of-the-art methods. More importantly, DU-Net-BW-α(16) has at least ~**30%** parameters and at most ~**2%** model size.

Method	Head	Sho.	Elb.	Wri.	Hip	Knee	Ank.	Mean
Pishchulin *et al.* ICCV'13 [27]	74.3	49.0	40.8	34.1	36.5	34.4	35.2	44.1
Tompson *et al.* NIPS'14 [36]	95.8	90.3	80.5	74.3	77.6	69.7	62.8	79.6
Carreira *et al.* CVPR'16 [6]	95.7	91.7	81.7	72.4	82.8	73.2	66.4	81.3
Tompson *et al.* CVPR'15 [35]	96.1	91.9	83.9	77.8	80.9	72.3	64.8	82.0
Hu *et al.* CVPR'16 [13]	95.0	91.6	83.0	76.6	81.9	74.5	69.5	82.4
Pishchulin *et al.* CVPR'16 [28]	94.1	90.2	83.4	77.3	82.6	75.7	68.6	82.4
Lifshitz *et al.* ECCV'16 [20]	97.8	93.3	85.7	80.4	85.3	76.6	70.2	85.0
Gkioxary *et al.* ECCV'16 [10]	96.2	93.1	86.7	82.1	85.2	81.4	74.1	86.1
Rafi *et al.* BMVC'16 [30]	97.2	93.9	86.4	81.3	86.8	80.6	73.4	86.3
Belagiannis *et al.* FG'17 [3]	97.7	95.0	88.2	83.0	87.9	82.6	78.4	88.1
Insafutdinov *et al.* ECCV'16 [15]	96.8	95.2	89.3	84.4	88.4	83.4	78.0	88.5
Wei *et al.* CVPR'16 [39]	97.8	95.0	88.7	84.0	88.4	82.8	79.4	88.5
Bulat *et al.* ECCV'16 [4]	97.9	95.1	89.9	85.3	89.4	85.7	81.7	89.7
Newell *et al.* ECCV'16 [23]	98.2	96.3	91.2	87.1	90.1	87.4	83.6	90.9
Chu *et al.* CVPR'17 [8]	**98.5**	96.3	91.9	**88.1**	**90.6**	**88.0**	**85.0**	**91.5**
Order-1 DU-Net(16)	97.4	**96.4**	**92.1**	87.7	90.2	87.7	84.3	91.2
Order-1 DU-Net-BW-α(16)	97.6	96.4	91.7	87.3	90.4	87.3	83.8	91.0

TW-QIG usually gets better results than BW and BW-QIG, since they have more choices in terms of weight value. The above results proves the effectiveness of network quantization, yet a correct combination of bit-widths is a crucial factor.

4.6 Comparison with State-of-the-art Methods

Human Pose Estimation. Tables 7 and 9 show comparisons of human pose estimation on MPII and LSP test sets. The *order*-1 DU-Net-BW-α(16) achieves

Table 8. NME(%) comparison with state-of-the-art facial landmark localization methods on 300-W dataset. DU-Net-BW-α refers to the DU-Net with binarized weights and scaling factor α The binarized DU-Net obtains comparable performance with state-of-the-art method [23]. But it has $\sim$**50**$\times$ smaller model size.

Method	CFAN [44]	Deep Reg [34]	CFSS [48]	TCDCN [45]	MDM [38]	TSR [21]	HGs(4) [23]	Order-1 DU-Net(8)	Order-1 DU-Net(8)-BW-α
Easy subset	5.50	4.51	4.73	4.80	4.83	4.36	2.90	**2.82**	3.00
Hard subset	16.78	13.80	9.98	8.60	10.14	7.56	5.15	**5.07**	5.36
Full set	7.69	6.31	5.76	5.54	5.88	4.99	3.35	**3.26**	3.46

comparable state-of-the-art performances. In contrast, as shown in Table 6, it has only 27%–62% parameters and less than 2% model size of other recent state-of-the-art methods. The DU-Net is concise and simple. Other state-of-the-art methods use stacked U-Nets with either sophisticated modules [42], graphical models [8] or adversarial networks [7].

Facial Landmark Localization. The DU-Net is also compared with other state-of-the-art facial landmark localization methods on 300-W. Please refer to Table 8. We uses a smaller network *order*-1 DU-Net(8) than that in human pose estimation, since localizing the facial landmarks is easier. The *order*-1 DU-Net-BW-α(8) gets comparable errors state-of-the-art method [23]. However, *order*-1 DU-Net-BW-α(8) has only $\sim$2% model size.

Table 9. PCK(%) comparison on LSP test set. The *Order*-1 DU-Net could also obtain comparable state-of-the-art performance. But DU-Net-BW-α(16) has at most $\sim$**70%** fewer parameters and $\sim$**50**$\times$ smaller model size than other state-of-the-art methods.

Method	Head	Sho.	Elb.	Wri.	Hip	Knee	Ank.	Mean
Belagiannis *et al.* FG'17 [3]	95.2	89.0	81.5	77.0	83.7	87.0	82.8	85.2
Lifshitz *et al.* ECCV'16 [20]	96.8	89.0	82.7	79.1	90.9	86.0	82.5	86.7
Pishchulin *et al.* CVPR'16 [28]	97.0	91.0	83.8	78.1	91.0	86.7	82.0	87.1
Insafutdinov *et al.* ECCV'16 [15]	97.4	92.7	87.5	84.4	91.5	89.9	87.2	90.1
Wei *et al.* CVPR'16 [39]	97.8	92.5	87.0	83.9	91.5	90.8	89.9	90.5
Bulat *et al.* ECCV'16 [4]	97.2	92.1	88.1	85.2	92.2	91.4	88.7	90.7
Chu *et al.* CVPR'17 [8]	98.1	93.7	89.3	86.9	93.4	94.0	92.5	92.6
Newell *et al.* ECCV'16 [23]	**98.2**	94.0	91.2	87.2	93.5	**94.5**	92.6	93.0
Yang *et al.* ICCV'17 [42]	**98.3**	94.5	92.2	88.9	**94.4**	95.0	93.7	93.9
Order-1 DU-Net(16)	97.5	**95.0**	**92.5**	**90.1**	93.7	**95.2**	94.2	**94.0**
Order-1 DU-Net-BW-α(16)	97.8	94.3	91.8	89.3	93.1	94.9	**94.4**	93.6

5 Conclusion

We have generalized the dense connectivity into the stacked U-Nets, resulting in a novel, simple and effective DU-Net. It connects blocks with the same semantic meanings in different U-Nets. *Order-K* connectivity is proposed to improve its parameter efficiency. An iterative refinement is also introduced make it more parameter efficient. It could halve a DU-Net but achieves comparable accuracy. Through network quantization, the training memory consumption and model size can further be reduced simultaneously. Experiments on both human pose estimation and face alignment show that DU-Net could achieve state-of-the-art performances but with only ∼30% parameters and ∼2% model size.

Acknowledgment. This work is partly supported by the Air Force Office of Scientific Research (AFOSR) under the Dynamic Data-Driven Application Systems Program, NSF 1763523, 1747778, 1733843 and 1703883 Awards.

References

1. Andriluka, M., Pishchulin, L., Gehler, P., Schiele, B.: 2D human pose estimation: New benchmark and state of the art analysis. In: CVPR (2014)
2. Begleiter, R., El-Yaniv, R., Yona, G.: On prediction using variable order Markov models. J. Artif. Res. **22**, 385–421 (2004)
3. Belagiann., V., Zisserman, A.: Recurrent human pose estimation. In: FG (2017)
4. Bulat, A., Tzimiropoulos, G.: Human pose estimation via convolutional part heatmap regression. In: Leibe, B., Matas, J., Sebe, N., Welling, M. (eds.) ECCV 2016. LNCS, vol. 9911, pp. 717–732. Springer, Cham (2016). https://doi.org/10.1007/978-3-319-46478-7_44
5. Bulat, A., Tzimiropoulos, G.: Binarized convolutional landmark localizers for human pose estimation and face alignment with limited resources. In: ICCV (2017)
6. Carreira, J., Agrawal, P., Fragkiadaki, K., Malik, J.: Human pose estimation with iterative error feedback. In: CVPR (2016)
7. Chen, Y., Shen, C., Wei, X.S., Liu, L., Yang, J.: Adversarial posenet: A structure-aware convolutional network for human pose estimation. In: ICCV (2017)
8. Chu, X., Yang, W., Ouyang, W., Ma, C., Yuille, A., Wang, X.: Multi-context attention for human pose estimation. In: CVPR (2016)
9. Courbariaux, M., Hubara, I., Soudry, D., El-Yaniv, R., Bengio, Y.: Binarized neural networks: training deep neural networks with weights and activations constrained to +1 or −1. arXiv (2016)
10. Gkioxari, G., Toshev, A., Jaitly, N.: Chained predictions using convolutional neural networks. In: Leibe, B., Matas, J., Sebe, N., Welling, M. (eds.) ECCV 2016. LNCS, vol. 9908, pp. 728–743. Springer, Cham (2016). https://doi.org/10.1007/978-3-319-46493-0_44
11. Glorot, X., Bordes, A., Bengio, Y.: Deep sparse rectifier neural networks. In: AISTAT (2011)
12. He, K., Zhang, X., Ren, S., Sun, J.: Deep residual learning for image recognition. In: CVPR (2016)
13. Hu, P., Ramanan, D.: Bottom-up and top-down reasoning with hierarchical rectified Gaussians. In: CVPR (2016)

14. Huang, G., Liu, Z., Weinberger, K.Q., van der Maaten, L.: Densely connected convolutional networks. In: CVPR (2017)
15. Insafutdinov, E., Pishchulin, L., Andres, B., Andriluka, M., Schiele, B.: DeeperCut: a deeper, stronger, and faster multi-person pose estimation model. In: Leibe, B., Matas, J., Sebe, N., Welling, M. (eds.) ECCV 2016. LNCS, vol. 9910, pp. 34–50. Springer, Cham (2016). https://doi.org/10.1007/978-3-319-46466-4_3
16. Ioffe, S., Szegedy, C.: Batch normalization: accelerating deep network training by reducing internal covariate shift. In: ICML (2015)
17. Johnson, S., Everingham, M.: Clustered pose and nonlinear appearance models for human pose estimation. In: BMVC (2010)
18. Li, D., Wang, X., Kong, D.: DeepRebirth: accelerating deep neural network execution on mobile devices. AAAI (2018)
19. Li, F., Zhang, B., Liu, B.: Ternary weight networks. arXiv (2016)
20. Lifshitz, I., Fetaya, E., Ullman, S.: Human pose estimation using deep consensus voting. In: Leibe, B., Matas, J., Sebe, N., Welling, M. (eds.) ECCV 2016. LNCS, vol. 9906, pp. 246–260. Springer, Cham (2016). https://doi.org/10.1007/978-3-319-46475-6_16
21. Lv, J., Shao, X., Xing, J., Cheng, C., Zhou, X.: A deep regression architecture with two-stage re-initialization for high performance facial landmark detection. In: CVPR (2017)
22. McMahan, H.B., Moore, E., Ramage, D., Hampson, S., et al.: Communication-efficient learning of deep networks from decentralized data. arXiv (2016)
23. Newell, A., Yang, K., Deng, J.: Stacked hourglass networks for human pose estimation. In: Leibe, B., Matas, J., Sebe, N., Welling, M. (eds.) ECCV 2016. LNCS, vol. 9912, pp. 483–499. Springer, Cham (2016). https://doi.org/10.1007/978-3-319-46484-8_29
24. Peng, X., Feris, R.S., Wang, X., Metaxas, D.N.: A recurrent encoder-decoder network for sequential face alignment. In: Leibe, B., Matas, J., Sebe, N., Welling, M. (eds.) ECCV 2016. LNCS, vol. 9905, pp. 38–56. Springer, Cham (2016). https://doi.org/10.1007/978-3-319-46448-0_3
25. Peng, X., Feris, R.S., Wang, X., Metaxas, D.N.: RED-Net: a recurrent encoder-decoder network for video-based face alignment. IJCV (2018)
26. Peng, X., Tang, Z., Yang, F., Feris, R.S., Metaxas, D.: Jointly optimize data augmentation and network training: adversarial data augmentation in human pose estimation. In: CVPR (2018)
27. Pishchulin, L., Andriluka, M., Gehler, P., Schiele, B.: Strong appearance and expressive spatial models for human pose estimation. In: ICCV (2013)
28. Pishchulin, L., et al.: DeepCut: joint subset partition and labeling for multi person pose estimation. In: CVPR (2016)
29. Pleiss, G., Chen, D., Huang, G., Li, T., van der Maaten, L., Weinberger, K.Q.: Memory-efficient implementation of DenseNets. arXiv (2017)
30. Rafi, U., Leibe, B., Gall, J., Kostrikov, I.: An efficient convolutional network for human pose estimation. In: BMVC (2016)
31. Rastegari, M., Ordonez, V., Redmon, J., Farhadi, A.: XNOR-Net: ImageNet classification using binary convolutional neural networks. In: Leibe, B., Matas, J., Sebe, N., Welling, M. (eds.) ECCV 2016. LNCS, vol. 9908, pp. 525–542. Springer, Cham (2016). https://doi.org/10.1007/978-3-319-46493-0_32
32. Ronneberger, O., Fischer, P., Brox, T.: U-Net: convolutional networks for biomedical image segmentation. In: Navab, N., Hornegger, J., Wells, W.M., Frangi, A.F. (eds.) MICCAI 2015. LNCS, vol. 9351, pp. 234–241. Springer, Cham (2015). https://doi.org/10.1007/978-3-319-24574-4_28

33. Sagonas, C., Tzimiropoulos, G., Zafeiriou, S., Pantic, M.: 300 faces in-the-wild challenge: the first facial landmark localization challenge. In: ICCVW (2013)
34. Shi, B., Bai, X., Liu, W., Wang, J.: Deep regression for face alignment. arXiv (2014)
35. Tompson, J., Goroshin, R., Jain, A., LeCun, Y., Bregler, C.: Efficient object localization using convolutional networks. In: CVPR (2015)
36. Tompson, J.J., Jain, A., LeCun, Y., Bregler, C.: Joint training of a convolutional network and a graphical model for human pose estimation. In: NIPS (2014)
37. Toshev, A., Szegedy, C.: DeepPose: human pose estimation via deep neural networks. In: CVPR (2014)
38. Trigeorgis, G., Snape, P., Nicolaou, M.A., Antonakos, E., Zafeiriou, S.: Mnemonic descent method: a recurrent process applied for end-to-end face alignment. In: CVPR (2016)
39. Wei, S.E., Ramakrishna, V., Kanade, T., Sheikh, Y.: Convolutional pose machines. In: CVPR (2016)
40. Wu, S., Li, G., Chen, F., Shi, L.: Training and inference with integers in deep neural networks. In: ICLR (2018)
41. Xiong, X., De la Torre, F.: Supervised descent method and its applications to face alignment. In: CVPR (2013)
42. Yang, W., Li, S., Ouyang, W., Li, H., Wang, X.: Learning feature pyramids for human pose estimation. In: ICCV (2017)
43. Zafeiriou, S., Trigeorgis, G., Chrysos, G., Deng, J., Shen, J.: The Menpo facial landmark localisation challenge: a step towards the solution. In: CVPRW (2017)
44. Zhang, J., Shan, S., Kan, M., Chen, X.: Coarse-to-fine auto-encoder networks (CFAN) for real-time face alignment. In: Fleet, D., Pajdla, T., Schiele, B., Tuytelaars, T. (eds.) ECCV 2014. LNCS, vol. 8690, pp. 1–16. Springer, Cham (2014). https://doi.org/10.1007/978-3-319-10605-2_1
45. Zhang, Z., Luo, P., Loy, C.C., Tang, X.: Facial landmark detection by deep multi-task learning. In: Fleet, D., Pajdla, T., Schiele, B., Tuytelaars, T. (eds.) ECCV 2014. LNCS, vol. 8694, pp. 94–108. Springer, Cham (2014). https://doi.org/10.1007/978-3-319-10599-4_7
46. Zhao, L., Peng, X., Tian, Y., Kapadia, M., Metaxas, D.: Learning to forecast and refine residual motion for image-to-video generation. In: ECCV (2018)
47. Zhou, S., Wu, Y., Ni, Z., Zhou, X., Wen, H., Zou, Y.: DoReFa-Net: training low bitwidth convolutional neural networks with low bitwidth gradients. arXiv (2016)
48. Zhu, S., Li, C., Change Loy, C., Tang, X.: Face alignment by coarse-to-fine shape searching. In: CVPR (2015)

Grassmann Pooling as Compact Homogeneous Bilinear Pooling for Fine-Grained Visual Classification

Xing Wei[1], Yue Zhang[1], Yihong Gong[1(✉)], Jiawei Zhang[2], and Nanning Zheng[1]

[1] Institute of Artificial Intelligence and Robotics,
Xi'an Jiaotong University, Xi'an, China
ygong@mail.xjtu.edu.cn
[2] SenseTime Research, Shenzhen, China

Abstract. Designing discriminative and invariant features is the key to visual recognition. Recently, the bilinear pooled feature matrix of Convolutional Neural Network (CNN) has shown to achieve state-of-the-art performance on a range of fine-grained visual recognition tasks. The bilinear feature matrix collects second-order statistics and is closely related to the covariance matrix descriptor. However, the bilinear feature could suffer from the visual burstiness phenomenon similar to other visual representations such as VLAD and Fisher Vector. The reason is that the bilinear feature matrix is sensitive to the magnitudes and correlations of local CNN feature elements which can be measured by its singular values. On the other hand, the singular vectors are more invariant and reasonable to be adopted as the feature representation. Motivated by this point, we advocate an alternative pooling method which transforms the CNN feature matrix to an orthonormal matrix consists of its principal singular vectors. Geometrically, such orthonormal matrix lies on the Grassmann manifold, a Riemannian manifold whose points represent subspaces of the Euclidean space. Similarity measurement of images reduces to comparing the principal angles between these "homogeneous" subspaces and thus is independent of the magnitudes and correlations of local CNN activations. In particular, we demonstrate that the projection distance on the Grassmann manifold deduces a bilinear feature mapping without explicitly computing the bilinear feature matrix, which enables a very compact feature and classifier representation. Experimental results show that our method achieves an excellent balance of model complexity and accuracy on a variety of fine-grained image classification datasets.

Keywords: Fine-grained visual classification
Bilinear pooling · Singular Value Decomposition · Grassmann manifold
Visual burstiness

1 Introduction

Visual recognition problems mainly have two challenges: between-class similarity and within-class variance. Thus, designing discriminative and invariant features

© Springer Nature Switzerland AG 2018
V. Ferrari et al. (Eds.): ECCV 2018, LNCS 11207, pp. 365–380, 2018.
https://doi.org/10.1007/978-3-030-01219-9_22

is the key to visual recognition [1–6]. The fine-grained image classification aims to recognize subordinate categories of some base categories, such as different models of cars [7,8], species of birds [9], variants of aircraft [10], kinds of foods [11], *etc.* Compared to general image classification, fine-grained classification is even more challenging since that visual differences between distinct fine-grained categories could be very small and subtle.

An approach to deal with such challenges is to incorporate strong supervision, for example, part-level and attribute annotations [12–14]. These methods first learn to detect semantic parts of the target object and then model the features of the local part for classification. Methods with strong supervision have shown to improve the fine-grained recognition accuracy significantly. However, annotating object parts is obviously much more expensive than assigning class labels. To avoid dependency on strong supervision, some have proposed to use the attention models [15–17] for unsupervised discovery of discriminative parts. Another promising approach is to absorb the effectiveness of training with web-scale datasets [18–20] via active learning.

Recently, a very simple method named bilinear pooling [21] has achieved state-of-the-art performance on a range of fine-grained classification benchmarks. The bilinear pooling method learns two separate CNNs whose outputs are multiplied using the outer product at each location and then summed to obtain a holistic representation of an image. The bilinear pooled matrix captures second-order statistics which is closely related to the covariance matrix descriptor [22].

A major drawback of the bilinear pooling is that the pooled feature is very high-dimensional. Thus the research line of this topic has focused on reducing the model complexity, both for the feature descriptor and classifier [23–25]. On the other hand, little attention has been paid to address the burstiness problem [26], where the feature elements may have large variances within the same class that adversely disturb the similarity measurement. Actually, bilinear pooling [21] and its variants [23–25] perform element-wise signed square root normalization to compensate for burstiness, taking the idea from other feature representations [26–28]. However, there is little analysis on how the bursts come into being in this framework.

Another approach [29] applies matrix power normalization where the singular values of the bilinear feature matrix are element-wise square rooted. Such normalization has shown to improve the performance of the bilinear feature. In fact, this idea is partially consistent with our opinion. We argue that the singular values are sensitive to the burstiness of visual elements while the singular vectors are more robust and reasonable to be considered as invariant features for recognition.

We thus advocate an alternative pooling method which transforms the CNN feature matrix to an orthonormal matrix consists of its principal singular vectors. Geometrically, such orthonormal matrix lies on the Grassmann manifold [30], a Riemannian manifold whose points represent subspaces of the Euclidean space. Similarity measurement of images reduces to comparing the principal angles between these "homogeneous" subspaces and thus is independent of the magnitudes and correlations of local CNN activations. Specifically, we show that the projection distance [31,32] of the Grassmann manifold deduces a bilinear feature mapping without explicitly computing the bilinear feature matrix, which leads to a very compact feature representation. Moreover, we also propose a Grassmann classifier that enjoys the same compact form which remarkably decreases the parameter size of the classifier. Finally, we propose a Grassmann projection approach in order to reduce the number of feature maps to compress our model further. Our previous work [33] adopts a triplet network to deal with the task of local patch matching. In this work, we focus on the basic image classification problem and analysis the connections to the bilinear pooling method in depth.

2   Related Work

Tenenbaum and Freeman [34] first introduced the bilinear model to separate style and content. Thereafter, second-order models have been studied in several computer vision problems, such as object detection [22], semantic segmentation [35], fine-grained classification [21], visual question answering [36], *etc.* Other feature representations have also been explored for visual recognition. The Bag-of-Words (BoW) framework [2,3] used vector quantization for hard visual words assignment. While sparse coding [4,5] improved by linear encoding with the sparse constraint. VLAD [37] and Fisher Vector [28] incorporated second-order information in the descriptors beyond linear encoding. The key issue to a feature representation is its discriminative and invariant power. Particularly, the burstiness problem has drawn much attention from various feature representations.

2.1   Bilinear Pooling and Variants

In this section, we briefly review several related bilinear pooling methods. The bilinear pooling [21] calculates second-order statistics of local features over the whole image to form a holistic representation for recognition. An obvious disadvantage of the original bilinear pooling is that pooled feature is very high-dimensional. To address this problem, Gao *et al.* [23] proposed two approximate methods via Random Maclaurin [38] and Tensor Sketch [39] to obtain compact bilinear representations. The compact models typically reduce the dimensionality up to 90% without losing noticeable classification accuracies. While the compact approximations reduce feature dimension remarkably, they ignore the matrix structure of the pooled feature matrix but vectorize it and apply a linear classifier. Kong *et al.* [24] proposed to maintain the matrix structure and learn a low-rank bilinear classifier. The resulting classifier can be evaluated without explicitly computing the bilinear feature matrix which allows a large reduction on the parameter size. Li *et al.* [25] proposed a similar idea to model pairwise feature interaction by performing a quadratic transformation with the low-rank constraint. They also proposed a regularization method to reduce the risk of over-fitting for the bilinear pooling. Lin and Maji [29] explored several matrix normalizations to increase the performance over the original bilinear feature.

Elegant Tern   Baklava

Hummer SUV 2000   Hawk T1
(a) Illumination and appearance changes   (b) Repeated structures

Fig. 1. In general, visual burstiness corresponds to the problem that the feature representation is not invariant enough where the feature elements have large variances within the same class. The problem can be caused by (a) large illumination and appearance changes and (b) correlated elements such as repeated structures

They found that the matrix power normalization outperforms several alternative schemes such as the matrix logarithm normalization.

2.2 On the Burstiness of Visual Representation

The phenomenon of burstiness of visual elements was first explored in the BoW setting [26]: a given visual element appears many times in an image such that it can strongly affect the similarity measurement between two images since the contribution of other essential elements is substantially decreased. *Generally speaking, burstiness corresponds to the problem that the feature descriptor is not invariant enough where the feature elements may have large variances within the same class.* The problem can be caused by large illumination and appearance variations and correlated elements such as repeated structures, see Fig. 1 for some examples. Visual burstiness has found widespread and important in many visual representations, from local patch descriptors to global image features.

Root-SIFT. Root-SIFT [40] transforms the original SIFT descriptor [1] by first L_1 normalizing the SIFT vector and then square rooting each element. It is shown that performing the scalar product in Root-SIFT space is equivalent to computing the Hellinger kernel in the original space. Because SIFT calculates the histogram of gradients, the effect of the Root-SIFT mapping can actually reduce the dominance of large gradient values and increase the importance of smaller but meaningful gradients.

Bag-of-Words (BoW). The BoW representation is obtained by quantizing the local descriptors into the visual words, resulting in frequency vectors. As noted by Jgou *et al.* [26], BoW can be very unbalanced caused by several high-frequent elements, usually as repeated patterns. This problem can be alleviated by discounting large values by element-wise square rooting the BoW vectors and re-normalizing them.

VLAD and Fisher Vector. In a similar manner, VLAD and Fisher Vector are signed square root normalized [28,37]. To further suppress bursts, another kind of normalization termed intra-normalization was proposed in [27], where the sum of residuals is L_2 normalized within each VLAD block.

Bilinear Pooling. Similar to previous methods, the bilinear pooling method and its variants [21,23,24] also find that proper feature normalization provides a non-trivial improvement on performance. They consistently apply signed square root and L_2 normalization on the bilinear features. Another approach [29] compares several matrix based normalizations and find that matrix power normalization can improve the classification accuracy remarkably.

3 Grassmann Pooling as Compact Homogeneous Bilinear Pooling

To compute the bilinear feature matrix for an image, we first extract dense local image features by feeding it into a CNN. We take the output at a specific convolution layer, and form it as a matrix $\mathbf{A} \in \mathbb{R}^{c \times hw}$ where each row $i \in [0, c]$ represents the i'th feature map stacked to a 1D vector, and each column $j \in [0, hw]$ corresponds to a spatial location. The number, height, and width of feature maps are denoted by c, h, and w, respectively. Thus the symmetric form of bilinear pooling can be written in matrix notation by $\mathbf{B} = \mathbf{A}\mathbf{A}^T$.

3.1 Grassmann Pooling via Singular Value Decomposition

A major disadvantage of the bilinear pooling is that the produced feature is of high dimensionality. In the original bilinear pooling method [21], the pooled feature is reshaped into a vector $\mathbf{z} = vec(\mathbf{A}\mathbf{A}^T) \in \mathbb{R}^{c^2}$. Consider the VGG network which has $c = 512$ feature maps at the last convolution layer. Thus the dimensionality of the bilinear feature pooled at this layer is 2^{18}. Furthermore, if $c > hw$, thus $\mathbf{B} = \mathbf{A}\mathbf{A}^T$ is rank deficient. These reasons motivate us to find a more compact form of the bilinear feature matrix. To achieve this goal, we resort to Singular Value Decomposition (SVD) for low-rank matrix approximation. Before describing the pooling method, we first introduce two simple Lemmas.

Lemma 1. Let $\mathbf{A} = \sum_{i=1}^{c} \sigma_i \mathbf{u}_i \mathbf{v}_i^T$ be the SVD of $\mathbf{A}$ and $\sigma_1 \geq \sigma_2 \geq \cdots \geq \sigma_c$. For $k \in \{1, 2, \ldots, c\}$, let $\mathbf{A}_k = \sum_{i=1}^{k} \sigma_i \mathbf{u}_i \mathbf{v}_i^T$ be the sum truncated after k terms, thus $\mathbf{A}_k$ has rank k. We have, for any matrix $\mathbf{X}$ of rank at most k, $\|\mathbf{A} - \mathbf{A}_k\|_F \leq \|\mathbf{A} - \mathbf{X}\|_F$, where $\|\cdot\|_F$ is the Frobenius norm.

Lemma 2. Let $\mathbf{A} = \sum_{i=1}^{c} \sigma_i \mathbf{u}_i \mathbf{v}_i^T$ be the SVD of $\mathbf{A}$, if $\mathbf{B} = \mathbf{A}\mathbf{A}^T$, then

$$\mathbf{B} = \left(\sum_i \sigma_i \mathbf{u}_i \mathbf{v}_i^T\right)\left(\sum_j \sigma_j \mathbf{u}_j \mathbf{v}_j^T\right)^T = \sum_i \sum_j \sigma_i \sigma_j \mathbf{u}_i \mathbf{v}_i^T \mathbf{v}_j \mathbf{u}_j^T = \sum_i \sigma_i^2 \mathbf{u}_i \mathbf{u}_i^T \tag{1}$$

Lemma 1 shows that $\mathbf{A}_k$ is the best rank k approximation to $\mathbf{A}$ when error is measured by the Frobenius norm. Thus we can use SVD to find a low-rank approximation of the bilinear feature matrix without losing much accuracy. Lemma 2 gives two important information. First, the bilinear feature matrix $\mathbf{B}$ has the same singular vectors as the original feature matrix $\mathbf{A}$, and there is a one-to-one mapping between their singular values. So instead of approximating the bilinear feature matrix $\mathbf{B}$, we can just compute the SVD on the raw feature matrix $\mathbf{A}$, which could reduce computation complexity when $c > hw$. Second, the singular values of $\mathbf{B}$ change quadratically compared to those of $\mathbf{A}$. We argue that such phenomenon makes the bilinear feature matrix much more sensitive to the magnitudes and correlations of local CNN activations, which may cause the burstiness problem [26]. Consider that the original feature matrix $\mathbf{A}$ has a large singular value, thus it will be amplified dramatically in $\mathbf{B}$ and dominate the similarity measurement. To address this problem, we suggest the following pooling method.

Definition 1 *(Grassmann/Subspace Pooling). Let $\mathbf{A} \in \mathbb{R}^{c \times hw}$ be the feature maps at a specific convolution layer and $\mathbf{A} = \sum_{i=1}^{c} \sigma_i \mathbf{u}_i \mathbf{v}_i^T$ be the SVD, the Grassmann pooling or subspace pooling [33] reads: $g_k(\mathbf{A}) = \mathbf{U}_k = [\mathbf{u}_1|\mathbf{u}_2|\cdots|\mathbf{u}_k]$.*

That is, the pooling method transforms the CNN feature matrix $\mathbf{A}$ to an orthonormal matrix consists of its k principal left singular vectors. In geometry, the pooled CNN features obtained in this manner are k-dimensional linear subspaces of the c-dimensional Euclidean space, which lie on the (c, k) Grassmann manifold [30], denoted by $\mathcal{G}_c^k$. Now the bilinear feature matrix becomes $\mathbf{B}' = \mathbf{U}_k \mathbf{U}_k^T$. When inserted into a CNN and trained in an end-to-end fasion, this pooling method leads the model to learn only structural features which are independent of the magnitudes and correlations of visual elements. Please note that though singular values do not appear in this formulation, it does not mean that we think singular values are completely useless and discard all the information carried by them. Actually this representation can be understood as $\mathbf{B}' = \sum_{i=1}^{c} \sigma_i' \mathbf{u}_i \mathbf{v}_i^T$, where $\sigma_i' = 1$ for $i \in \{1, ..., k\}$ and $\sigma_i' = 0$ for $i \in \{k+1, ..., c\}$. We name bilinear pooling of the orthonormal matrix obtained in this manner as *homogeneous bilinear pooling*. Moreover, our method is also compact since $k < c$.

Figure 2 illustrates the differences of conventional bilinear pooling [21,24], bilinear pooling with matrix power normalization [29] and our compact homogeneous bilinear pooling. Our pooling method has mainly two advantages. On the one hand, for large singular values that correspond to the major feature structures, our pooling method does not cause the burstiness problem since they are flattened to be ones. On the other hand, singular vectors correspond to the small singular values are often trivial structures or even noises, therefore are discarded by this representation which significantly reduces the feature size. Furthermore, we shall explain later it is even unnecessary to compute the homogenous bilinear feature matrix $\mathbf{B}' = \mathbf{U}_k \mathbf{U}_k^T \in \mathbb{R}^{c \times c}$ explicitly, but directly using the more

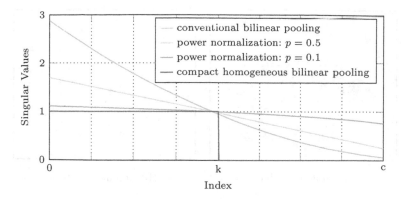

Fig. 2. A comparison of conventional bilinear pooling, bilinear pooling with matrix power normalization and our compact homogeneous bilinear pooling. Conventional bilinear pooling methods [21,24] keep the whole spectrum and do not apply normalization on the singular values. Thus their feature matrices could suffer from the burstiness problem. The matrix power normalization [29] is proposed to handle this problem better. However, when the exponent p is approaching to zero, all the singular values are close to ones. Thus many trivial structures corresponding to the small singular values are amplified excessively. On the contrary, our compact homogeneous bilinear pooling adopts binary singular values, and its feature is compact which only contains the major feature structures corresponding to the large singular values and does not cause the burstiness problem

compact form $\mathbf{U}_k \in \mathbb{R}^{c \times k}$, where $k \ll c$ in practice[1]. The significance of this property resides in two respects. (1) For retrieval based or distributed applications which require features to be stored in a database, the storage can be substantially decreased. (2) For classification problems, especially when the numbers of categories is large, it can significantly reduce the parameter size of classifiers. Before explaining how to avoid the computation of bilinear feature matrix, we first make more analyses on the singular values and singular vectors.

3.2 Understanding Singular Values and Singular Vectors

To better understand the motivation of our pooling method, it is important to show some properties of singular values and singular vectors, respectively. We first consider two toy examples for analysis and then give some visualizations on a real dataset.

Toy Examples. We consider two toy examples that mimic the burstiness phenomenon displayed in Fig. 1 in a simplified way. This allows us to analyze the behaviors of singular values and singular vectors in a closed-form.

---

[1] For the rest of this paper, we use $\mathbf{U}$ instead of $\mathbf{U}_k$ for simplicity, and thereafter, the subscript will represent different examples, *e.g.*, $\mathbf{U}_1$ and $\mathbf{U}_2$.

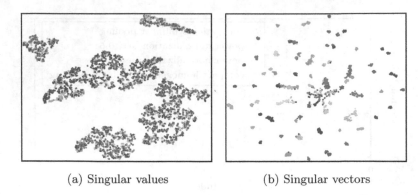

(a) Singular values   (b) Singular vectors

Fig. 3. Visualizing singular values and singular vectors as feature descriptors using t-SNE [41] using the original bilinear pooling method. (a) The singular values can be influenced by the magnitudes and correlations of local CNN feature elements, and they are wide-spread and mixed with different classes. (b) In contrast, the distributions of singular vectors are much more compact and easier to distinguished from each class

1. Linear illumination transform: $\mathbf{B} = (s\mathbf{A})(s\mathbf{A})^T = s^2\mathbf{A}\mathbf{A}^T = \sum_i s^2\sigma_i^2\mathbf{u}_i\mathbf{u}_i^T$. For a linear illumination transform when $\mathbf{A}$ is scaled by a scalar s, the singular values of $\mathbf{B}$ are scaled by s^2.

2. Repeated structures: $\mathbf{B} = [\mathbf{A}|\mathbf{A}][\mathbf{A}|\mathbf{A}]^T = 2\mathbf{A}\mathbf{A}^T = \sum_i 2\sigma_i^2\mathbf{u}_i\mathbf{u}_i^T$. Consider that two duplicated feature matrix $\mathbf{A}$ generated by a CNN are concatenated together, thus the singular values of $\mathbf{B}$ are multiplied by a factor of 2.

As we can see from the two examples, singular values can actually reflect the magnitudes of the matrix and correlations on elements and could even be more sensitive to these factors when performing the bilinear pooling. On the other hand, singular vectors are more robust than singular values. They have unit norms, reflect only structural information and thus we believe should be more reasonable to consider as invariant features for recognition. Of course, real cases are much more complex than the toy examples where the illumination changes and correlations may not occur globally. Nevertheless, such examples show that how to pool CNN features in a more robust manner.

Real Cases. We also make several visualizations on a real dataset. Specifically, we use the fine-grained aircraft dataset [10] as a testbed. We train the original bilinear pooling model on this dataset and extract the feature matrices of all the images in the test set. We then perform SVD on each feature matrix and get the singular values and singular vectors, respectively. We take $vec(\mathbf{U}\mathbf{U}^T)$ and $[\sigma_1, \sigma_2, \ldots]$ as two kinds of features and use the t-SNE [41] method to visualize them. As we can see from Fig. 3(a), the singular values for each class spread widely and are mixed with different classes. On the contrary, the distributions of singular vectors are much more compact and easier to distinguish from each class as shown in Fig. 3(b).

3.3 Learning Grassmann Classifiers

The Grassmann pooling method described in Sect. 3.1 maps each feature matrix to a subspace lies on the Grassmann manifold. The similarity measurement of images reduces to comparing the principal angles between these subspaces. For two points $\mathbf{U}_1$ and $\mathbf{U}_2$ on the $\mathcal{G}_c^k$ manifold, a popular distance measurement is the projection distance [31,32] defined by $d_P(\mathbf{U}_1, \mathbf{U}_2) = k - \left\|\mathbf{U}_1^T\mathbf{U}_2\right\|_F^2$. Interestingly, we show that the projection distance deduces a bilinear feature mapping without explicitly computing the bilinear feature matrix, which leads to a very compact feature representation. Moreover, we can also train a Grassmann classifier that enjoys the same compact form thus the number of parameters of the classifier can be substantially reduced.

Lemma 3. *The projection distance deduces an implicit bilinear mapping of* $\mathbf{B}_1' = \mathbf{U}_1\mathbf{U}_1^T$ *and* $\mathbf{B}_2' = \mathbf{U}_2\mathbf{U}_2^T$:

$$
\begin{aligned}
d_P(\mathbf{U}_1, \mathbf{U}_2) &= k - \left\|\mathbf{U}_1^T\mathbf{U}_2\right\|_F^2 \\
&= \frac{1}{2}tr(\mathbf{U}_1\mathbf{U}_1^T) + \frac{1}{2}tr(\mathbf{U}_2\mathbf{U}_2^T) - tr(\mathbf{U}_1\mathbf{U}_1^T\mathbf{U}_2\mathbf{U}_2^T) \\
&= \frac{1}{2}tr(\mathbf{U}_1\mathbf{U}_1^T\mathbf{U}_1\mathbf{U}_1^T + \mathbf{U}_2\mathbf{U}_2^T\mathbf{U}_2\mathbf{U}_2^T - 2\mathbf{U}_1\mathbf{U}_1^T\mathbf{U}_2\mathbf{U}_2^T) \\
&= \frac{1}{2}\left\|\mathbf{U}_1\mathbf{U}_1^T - \mathbf{U}_2\mathbf{U}_2^T\right\|_F^2
\end{aligned}
\tag{2}
$$

Equation (2) indicates a valid similarity measurement between $\mathbf{U}_1$ and $\mathbf{U}_2$: $\left\|\mathbf{U}_1^T\mathbf{U}_2\right\|_F^2$, and we use this formula to define our classifier. For a K-way classification problem, we aim to learn K classifiers $\mathbf{W}_i \in \mathcal{G}_c^k, i \in [1, K]$. In particular, given an feature matrix $\mathbf{U} \in \mathcal{G}_c^k$, we compute a similarity score for each classifier by $\left\|\mathbf{W}_i^T\mathbf{U}\right\|_F^2$ and assign a label to the class which has the largest response. This formulation has a similar form to the bilinear SVM classifier defined in [24] but different in their meanings. The bilinear SVM [24] decomposes a classifier $\mathbf{W}_i \in \mathbb{R}^{c \times c}, rank(\mathbf{W}_i) = r, \mathbf{W}_i = \mathbf{W}_i^T$ into two parts:

$$
\mathbf{W}_i = \mathbf{U}_i\mathbf{\Sigma}_i\mathbf{U}_i^T = \mathbf{U}_{i+}\mathbf{\Sigma}_{i+}\mathbf{U}_{i+}^T - \mathbf{U}_{i-}|\mathbf{\Sigma}_{i-}|\mathbf{U}_{i-}^T = \hat{\mathbf{U}}_{i+}\hat{\mathbf{U}}_{i+}^T - \hat{\mathbf{U}}_{i-}\hat{\mathbf{U}}_{i-}^T \tag{3}
$$

The two parts are further relaxed to lie on the Euclidean space, *i.e.*, $\hat{\mathbf{U}}_{i-}$ and $\hat{\mathbf{U}}_{i+} \in \mathbb{R}^{c \times r/2}$. For an input feature matrix $\mathbf{X} \in \mathbb{R}^{c \times hw}$, the classification score is defined as $\|\hat{\mathbf{U}}_{i+}^T\mathbf{X}\|_F^2 - \|\hat{\mathbf{U}}_{i-}^T\mathbf{X}\|_F^2$. On the contrary, our method is exactly derived from the projection distance on the Grassmann manifold.

To learn a Grassmann classifier $\mathbf{W}_i \in \mathcal{G}_c^k$, we first initialize a random matrix $\mathbf{M}_i \in \mathbb{R}^{c \times k}$ and then perform SVD on $\mathbf{M}_i$, assigning the left singular vectors to $\mathbf{W}_i$. Thus we train the classifiers end-to-end using the error back-propagation training method. Another better initialization of $\mathbf{W}_i$ is assigning each classifier to the center of its feature cluster. Specifically, for each class in the training set, the center is calculated by first summing all the features $\sum_j \mathbf{U}_j\mathbf{U}_j^T$, and then taking the singular vectors. We find that the later initialization facilitates CNN training and needs fewer epochs to convergence.

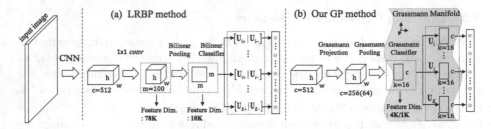

Fig. 4. Our GP method compares to the LRBP method [24]. Our GP mainly differs from LRBP in two respects: (1) pooling: GP transforms CNN features to the compact Grassmann manifold while LRBP uses the conventional (or does not explicitly compute) bilinear feature matrix. This directly matters on the feature dimension: 1K/4K vs. 10K/78K. (2) classifier: the Classifier of GP is exactly derived from the projection distance of the Grassmann manifold; while for LRBP, it is derived from the bilinear SVM and is further approximated in the Euclidean space

3.4 Learning a Grassmann Projection for Model Compression

Typically, reducing the number of feature maps in CNN is performed by a 1×1 *conv* layer, setting a smaller number of the output feature maps. Mathematically, for a spatial location crosses all the channels of the feature maps, noted by a vector $\mathbf{x} \in \mathbb{R}^c$. The 1×1 *conv* layer learns a weight matrix $\mathbf{M} \in \mathbb{R}^{c \times c'}$ and gives the output $\mathbf{y} = \mathbf{M}^T \mathbf{x} \in \mathbb{R}^{c'}$ at each spatial location. This operation is equivalent to applying weighted sums along the channels of feature maps, and thus the outputs are linear combinations of the inputs. However, there may be correlations on these linear combinations such that the output feature maps are degenerate in terms of diversity.

To address this problem, we propose to learn c' ($c' < c$) orthonormal bases $\mathbf{W} \in \mathcal{G}_c^{c'}$ for dimension reduction. This approach is inspired by PCA which performs dimension reduction by mapping data using their principal orthonormal directions. The main difference between PCA and our method is that the proposed approach is supervised and trained end-to-end. To train the orthonormal directions, we first initialize a matrix $\mathbf{M}$, and set $\mathbf{W}$ to the left singular vectors of $\mathbf{M}$, similar to training the Grassmann classifiers. We will show in the experiment section that this dimension reduction approach performs favourably against the 1×1 *conv* operation.

The overall pipeline of our approach and a comparison with the LRBP method [24] is illustrated in Fig. 4. Our method relies on SVD in several respects. The SVD operation is differentiable, thus the whole pipeline can be trained end-to-end using the standard back-propagation training procedure. However, computing the gradients with respect to SVD for back-propagation is non-trivial. Previously, Ionescu *et al.* [42] have explored such matrix back-propagation in CNN which is also adopted in this work. We refer readers to [42] for the details of derivation.

4   Experimental Evaluation

In this section, we first provide details about the implementation of our method. We then compare our approach to several baselines on four widely used fine-grained classification benchmarks.

4.1   Implementation

We implement our method using the PyTorch library. We remove the fully connected layer of the original backbone network, and add our dimension reduction layer, pooling layer and classification layer. The stochastic gradient descent (SGD) optimization is used to train our model. We use an initial learning rate of 0.1 which linearly decreases to 0, weight decay of 0.0001 and momentum of 0.9. We perform random horizontal flipping as data augmentation for training. At the testing stage, we pass the original image and its horizontal flip to the CNN independently and use their average as the final classification score.

4.2   Baseline Methods

We now describe several baseline methods which we compare our approach with. To make a fair comparison, we choose the VGG-16 [43] network pre-trained on ImageNet as the backbone model which is the same as all the related bilinear methods. All the methods use the same K-way softmax loss function except for the low-rank bilinear pooling, which was specifically designed to incorporate a low-rank hinge loss [24].

Fully Connected layers (FC) [43]: This is the original VGG-16 network pre-trained on ImageNet. The last fully connected layer of VGG-16 is replaced with a randomly initialized K-way classification layer and then fine-tuned on each fine-grained classification dataset. Since VGG-16 requires a fixed input image size of 224×224, all input images are resized to this resolution for this method.

Full Bilinear Pooling (FBP) [21]: The full bilinear pooling is applied over the *conv5_3* feature maps, which is the best-performed B-CNN [D, D] in [21]. Before the final classification layer, an element-wise square root normalization and L_2 normalization layer is added as suggested in [21].

Compact Bilinear Pooling (CBP-RM and CBP-TS) [23]: We compare two compact methods proposed in [23] using Random Maclaurin [38] and Tensor Sketch [39]. The element-wise signed square root normalization and L_2 normalization are also used as the full bilinear model. The projection dimension is set to $d = 8192$, which is shown to be sufficient to achieve competitive performance as full bilinear pooling.

Low-Rank Bilinear Pooling (LRBP) [24]: This is the compression method using the bilinear SVM classifier. Following the original paper, the projection dimension is set to $m = 100$ and its rank $r = 8$. The dimensionality reduction

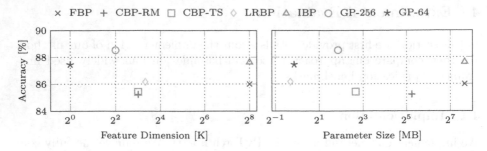

Fig. 5. A comparison of feature dimension/parameter size and accuracy for bilinear pooling methods. Accuracy is the average classification accuracy of the four datasets

layer is initialized using PCA on the feature maps of training set, and a scaled square root is applied with a factor of 2×10^5 over the $conv5\_3$ feature maps.

Improved Bilinear Pooling (IBP) [29]: This corresponds to the bilinear pooling with matrix square root normalization. Following the original paper, after fine-tuning the last layer is replaced by K one-vs-rest linear SVMs for classification.

4.3 Analysis of Model Complexity

In this section, we study the model and computational complexity for each method. For our Grassmann Pooling (GP) method, we use two different numbers of feature channels $c_1 = 256$ and $c_2 = 64$ (GP-256 and GP-64) and set $k = 16$ which is enough to achieve near maximum accuracy.

Table 1 provides a comprehensive comparison with respect to the feature dimension, the computational complexity for generating features and classification scores, and the parameter sizes of feature extractor (after the last convolution layer) and classifiers. For the CBP method, $d = 8192$ is used to achieve the best performance as reported in [23]. And for the LRBP method, $m = 100$ and $r = 8$ is enough to achieve similar or better performance than CBP. From Table 1 we can see that CBP-TS, LRBP, and our GP are most competitive with respect to model complexity. The feature dimension and parameter size are significantly smaller than FBP and IBP.

4.4 Performance Comparison on Benchmarks

We compare our method with related bilinear methods on four widely used fine-grained classification datasets, CUB Bird-200 [9], Stanford Car [7], Aircraft [10] and Food-101 [11]. All the datasets provide a fixed train and test split. We train our models only using the fine-grained class labels without any part or bounding box annotation provided by the datasets. The images are resized to 448×448 of all the datasets except for Food-101, which are resized to 224×224.

Table 1. A comparison of different bilinear pooling methods in terms of dimensionality, number of parameters, and computational complexity. The bilinear features are computed over feature maps of dimension $c \times h \times w$ for a K-way classification problem. For the VGG-16 [43] network on an input image of size 448×448, we have $c = 512$ and $h = w = 28$. FBP [21] and IBP [29] generate a full bilinear map which has a very high dimensionality. The CBP [23]: RM and TS use the polynomial kernel approximation, generating a feature vector of dimension d. Typically, the two methods can achieve near-maximum performance with $d = 8192$. LRBP [24] uses reduced feature dimension $m = 100$ and a low-rank classifier $r = 8$ to compress the bilinear model. We test two configurations of our method, setting $k = 16$ and $c_1 = 256, c_2 = 64$, respectively. Numbers in brackets indicate typical values when bilinear pooling is applied after the last convolutional layer of VGG-16 model over the CUB Bird-200 dataset [9] where $K = 200$. Model size only counts the parameters after the last convolutional layer

	Feature Dim.	Feature Comp.	Classifier Comp.	Feature Param.	Classifier Param.
FBP [21]	c^2 [256K]	$O(hwc^2)$	$O(Kc^2)$	0	Kc^2 [K·1 MB]
CBP-RM [23]	d [8K]	$O(hwcd)$	$O(Kd)$	$2cd$ [40 MB]	Kd [K·32 KB]
CBP-TS [23]	d [8K]	$O(hw(c + d \log d))$	$O(Kd)$	$2c$ [4 KB]	Kd [K·32 KB]
LRBP [24]	m^2 [10K]	$O(hwmc + hwm^2)$	$O(Krm^2)$	cm [200 KB]	Krm [K·3 KB]
IBP [29]	c^2 [256K]	$O(hwc^2 + c^3)$	$O(Kc^2)$	0	Kc^2 [K·1 MB]
Our GP-256	kc_1 [4K]	$O(hwcc_1 + c_1^3)$	$O(Kkc_1)$	cc_1 [512 KB]	Kkc_1 [K·16 KB]
Our GP-64	kc_2 [1K]	$O(hwcc_2 + c_2^3)$	$O(Kkc_2)$	cc_2 [128 KB]	Kkc_2 [K·4 KB]

Table 2. Fine-grained image classification benchmark results. We compare our method with a fully connected network of VGG-16 [43], original bilinear pooling [21], Random Maclaurin and Tensor Sketch of the compact bilinear pooling [23], low-rank bilinear pooling [24], factorized bilinear pooling [25] and improved bilinear pooling [29] on four fine-grained classification datasets. We also list the feature dimension and parameter size for each method

	Bird [9]	Car [7]	Aircraft [10]	Food [11]	Feature Dim	Parameters
FC [43]	70.4	76.8	74.1	80.9	4K	3 MB
FBP [21]	84.1	90.6	86.9	82.4	256K	200 MB
CBP-RM [23]	83.9	90.5	84.3	82.2	8K	38 MB
CBP-TS [23]	84.0	91.2	84.1	82.4	8K	6.3 MB
LRBP [24]	84.2	90.9	87.3	82.3	10K	0.8 MB
IBP [29]	85.8	92.0	88.5	84.2	256K	200 MB
Our GP-256	**85.8**	**92.8**	**89.8**	**85.7**	4K	3.6 MB
Our GP-64	85.4	91.7	88.1	84.6	1K	0.9 MB

As can be seen from Table 2, all the bilinear pooling methods outperform the basic VGG-16 model a significant margin, especially for our GP-256 method which has the same feature dimension. The feature dimension of GP-256 is 64 times smaller than those of FBP and IBP with improved performance. LRBP has the smallest model among the baseline methods, while GP-64 outperforms it both in terms of accuracy and feature dimension with similar model size. The

Table 3. A comparison of dimension reduction methods. We compare our Grassmann projection approach with a 1×1 *conv* layer for reducing the number of feature maps. The results are reported using the proposed pooling method with $k = 16$ on the Aircraft [10] dataset. Values in the bracket are the numbers of feature maps and $1\times$ indicates the original VGG-16 model which has 512 feature maps

	$1\times[512]$	$2\times[256]$	$4\times[128]$	$8\times[64]$
1×1 *conv*	89.8	89.2	88.5	87.7
Our method		89.8	88.9	88.1

feature dimension of our GP-64 is only 10% of that of LRBP. An illustration of model size vs. classification accuracy for the bilinear pooling methods is displayed in Fig. 5.

We also compare our Grassmann projection approach with the conventional 1×1 *conv* operation for dimension reduction. As can be seen from Table 3, the proposed Grassmann projection approach generally performs better than the 1×1 *conv*. It can reduce the number of feature maps by a factor of 2 of the original VGG-16 model, without losing noticeable classification accuracy.

5 Conclusions

This paper presents detailed analysis on the burstiness problem of the bilinear feature representation. We show that the bilinear feature matrix is sensitive to the magnitudes and correlations of local CNN feature elements which can be measured by its singular values. Thus we advocate an alternative pooling method that does not suffer from such a problem. Another advantage of our method is that it avoids to explicitly computing the bilinear feature matrix, which not only leads to a compact feature representation but also enables to train compact classifiers. Our method achieves an excellent balance of model complexity and accuracy on a variety of benchmarks for fine-grained image classification.

Acknowledgements. This work was supported by the National Basic Research Program of China (Grant No. 2015CB351705), and the State Key Program of National Natural Science Foundation of China (Grant No. 61332018).

References

1. Lowe, D.G.: Distinctive image features from scale-invariant keypoints. IJCV **60**(2), 91–110 (2004)
2. Leung, T., Malik, J.: Representing and recognizing the visual appearance of materials using three-dimensional textons. IJCV **43**(1), 29–44 (2001)
3. Lazebnik, S., Schmid, C., Ponce, J.: Beyond bags of features: spatial pyramid matching for recognizing natural scene categories. In: CVPR, pp. 2169–2178 (2006)
4. Yang, J., Yu, K., Gong, Y., Huang, T.: Linear spatial pyramid matching using sparse coding for image classification. In: CVPR, pp. 1794–1801 (2009)

5. Wang, J., Yang, J., Yu, K., Lv, F., Huang, T., Gong, Y.: Locality-constrained linear coding for image classification. In: CVPR, pp. 3360–3367 (2010)
6. Krizhevsky, A., Sutskever, I., Hinton, G.E.: ImageNet classification with deep convolutional neural networks. In: NIPS, pp. 1097–1105 (2012)
7. Krause, J., Stark, M., Deng, J., Fei-Fei, L.: 3D object representations for fine-grained categorization. In: 4th International IEEE Workshop on 3D Representation and Recognition (3dRR) (2013)
8. Yang, L., Luo, P., Change Loy, C., Tang, X.: A large-scale car dataset for fine-grained categorization and verification. In: CVPR (2015)
9. Wah, C., Branson, S., Welinder, P., Perona, P., Belongie, S.: The Caltech-UCSD birds-200-2011 dataset (2011)
10. Maji, S., Rahtu, E., Kannala, J., Blaschko, M., Vedaldi, A.: Fine-grained visual classification of aircraft. arXiv preprint arXiv:1306.5151 (2013)
11. Bossard, L., Guillaumin, M., Van Gool, L.: Food-101 – mining discriminative components with random forests. In: Fleet, D., Pajdla, T., Schiele, B., Tuytelaars, T. (eds.) ECCV 2014. LNCS, vol. 8694, pp. 446–461. Springer, Cham (2014). https://doi.org/10.1007/978-3-319-10599-4_29
12. Zhang, N., Donahue, J., Girshick, R., Darrell, T.: Part-based R-CNNs for fine-grained category detection. In: Fleet, D., Pajdla, T., Schiele, B., Tuytelaars, T. (eds.) ECCV 2014. LNCS, vol. 8689, pp. 834–849. Springer, Cham (2014). https://doi.org/10.1007/978-3-319-10590-1_54
13. Zhang, X., Zhou, F., Lin, Y., Zhang, S.: Embedding label structures for fine-grained feature representation. In: CVPR (2016)
14. Huang, S., Xu, Z., Tao, D., Zhang, Y.: Part-stacked CNN for fine-grained visual categorization. In: CVPR (2016)
15. Jaderberg, M., Simonyan, K., Zisserman, A., et al.: Spatial transformer networks. In: NIPS, pp. 2017–2025 (2015)
16. Xiao, T., Xu, Y., Yang, K., Zhang, J., Peng, Y., Zhang, Z.: The application of two-level attention models in deep convolutional neural network for fine-grained image classification. In: CVPR (2015)
17. Zheng, H., Fu, J., Mei, T., Luo, J.: Learning multi-attention convolutional neural network for fine-grained image recognition. In: ICCV (2017)
18. Krause, J., et al.: The unreasonable effectiveness of noisy data for fine-grained recognition. In: Leibe, B., Matas, J., Sebe, N., Welling, M. (eds.) ECCV 2016. LNCS, vol. 9907, pp. 301–320. Springer, Cham (2016). https://doi.org/10.1007/978-3-319-46487-9_19
19. Xu, Z., Huang, S., Zhang, Y., Tao, D.: Augmenting strong supervision using web data for fine-grained categorization. In: ICCV (2015)
20. Cui, Y., Zhou, F., Lin, Y., Belongie, S.: Fine-grained categorization and dataset bootstrapping using deep metric learning with humans in the loop. In: CVPR (2016)
21. Lin, T.Y., RoyChowdhury, A., Maji, S.: Bilinear CNN models for fine-grained visual recognition. In: ICCV (2015)
22. Tuzel, O., Porikli, F., Meer, P.: Region covariance: a fast descriptor for detection and classification. In: Leonardis, A., Bischof, H., Pinz, A. (eds.) ECCV 2006. LNCS, vol. 3952, pp. 589–600. Springer, Heidelberg (2006). https://doi.org/10.1007/11744047_45
23. Gao, Y., Beijbom, O., Zhang, N., Darrell, T.: Compact bilinear pooling. In: CVPR (2016)
24. Kong, S., Fowlkes, C.: Low-rank bilinear pooling for fine-grained classification. In: CVPR (2017)

25. Li, Y., Wang, N., Liu, J., Hou, X.: Factorized bilinear models for image recognition. In: ICCV (2017)
26. Jégou, H., Douze, M., Schmid, C.: On the burstiness of visual elements. In: CVPR, pp. 1169–1176 (2009)
27. Arandjelovic, R., Zisserman, A.: All about VLAD. In: CVPR (2013)
28. Jegou, H., Perronnin, F., Douze, M., Sánchez, J., Perez, P., Schmid, C.: Aggregating local image descriptors into compact codes. IEEE TPAMI **34**(9), 1704–1716 (2012)
29. Lin, T.Y., Maji, S.: Improved bilinear pooling with CNNs. In: BMVC (2017)
30. Turaga, P., Veeraraghavan, A., Chellappa, R.: Statistical analysis on Stiefel and Grassmann manifolds with applications in computer vision. In: CVPR, pp. 1–8 (2008)
31. Hamm, J., Lee, D.D.: Grassmann discriminant analysis: a unifying view on subspace-based learning. In: ICML (2008)
32. Jayasumana, S., Hartley, R., Salzmann, M., Li, H., Harandi, M.: Kernel methods on Riemannian manifolds with Gaussian RBF kernels. IEEE TPAMI **37**(12), 2464–2477 (2015)
33. Wei, X., Zhang, Y., Gong, Y., Zheng, N.: Kernelized subspace pooling for deep local descriptors. In: CVPR (2018)
34. Tenenbaum, J.B., Freeman, W.T.: Separating style and content. In: NIPS, pp. 662–668 (1997)
35. Carreira, J., Caseiro, R., Batista, J., Sminchisescu, C.: Semantic segmentation with second-order pooling. In: Fitzgibbon, A., Lazebnik, S., Perona, P., Sato, Y., Schmid, C. (eds.) ECCV 2012. LNCS, vol. 7578, pp. 430–443. Springer, Heidelberg (2012). https://doi.org/10.1007/978-3-642-33786-4_32
36. Fukui, A., Park, D.H., Yang, D., Rohrbach, A., Darrell, T., Rohrbach, M.: Multimodal compact bilinear pooling for visual question answering and visual grounding. arXiv preprint arXiv:1606.01847 (2016)
37. Jégou, H., Chum, O.: Negative evidences and co-occurences in image retrieval: the benefit of PCA and whitening. In: Fitzgibbon, A., Lazebnik, S., Perona, P., Sato, Y., Schmid, C. (eds.) ECCV 2012. LNCS, pp. 774–787. Springer, Heidelberg (2012). https://doi.org/10.1007/978-3-642-33709-3_55
38. Kar, P., Karnick, H.: Random feature maps for dot product kernels. In: Artificial Intelligence and Statistics, pp. 583–591 (2012)
39. Pham, N., Pagh, R.: Fast and scalable polynomial kernels via explicit feature maps. In: ACM SIGKDD, pp. 239–247 (2013)
40. Arandjelović, R., Zisserman, A.: Three things everyone should know to improve object retrieval. In: CVPR, pp. 2911–2918 (2012)
41. Maaten, L., Hinton, G.: Visualizing data using t-SNE. JMLR **9**, 2579–2605 (2008)
42. Ionescu, C., Vantzos, O., Sminchisescu, C.: Matrix backpropagation for deep networks with structured layers. In: ICCV (2015)
43. Simonyan, K., Zisserman, A.: Very deep convolutional networks for large-scale image recognition. arXiv preprint arXiv:1409.1556 (2014)

CGIntrinsics: Better Intrinsic Image Decomposition Through Physically-Based Rendering

Zhengqi Li$^{(\boxtimes)}$ and Noah Snavely

Department of Computer Science & Cornell Tech,
Cornell University, Ithaca, USA
zl548@cs.cornell.edu

Abstract. Intrinsic image decomposition is a challenging, long-standing computer vision problem for which ground truth data is very difficult to acquire. We explore the use of synthetic data for training CNN-based intrinsic image decomposition models, then applying these learned models to real-world images. To that end, we present CGINTRINSICS, a new, large-scale dataset of physically-based rendered images of scenes with full ground truth decompositions. The rendering process we use is carefully designed to yield high-quality, realistic images, which we find to be crucial for this problem domain. We also propose a new end-to-end training method that learns better decompositions by leveraging CGIN-TRINSICS, and optionally IIW and SAW, two recent datasets of sparse annotations on real-world images. Surprisingly, we find that a decomposition network trained solely on our synthetic data outperforms the state-of-the-art on both IIW and SAW, and performance improves even further when IIW and SAW data is added during training. Our work demonstrates the suprising effectiveness of carefully-rendered synthetic data for the intrinsic images task.

1 Introduction

Intrinsic images is a classic vision problem involving decomposing an input image I into a product of reflectance (albedo) and shading images $R \cdot S$. Recent years have seen remarkable progress on this problem, but it remains challenging due to its ill-posedness. An attractive proposition has been to replace traditional hand-crafted priors with learned, CNN-based models. For such learning methods data is key, but collecting ground truth data for intrinsic images is extremely difficult, especially for images of real-world scenes.

One way to generate large amounts of training data for intrinsic images is to render synthetic scenes. However, existing synthetic datasets are limited to images of single objects [1,2] (e.g., via ShapeNet [3]) or images of CG animation

Electronic supplementary material The online version of this chapter (https://doi.org/10.1007/978-3-030-01219-9_23) contains supplementary material, which is available to authorized users.

© Springer Nature Switzerland AG 2018
V. Ferrari et al. (Eds.): ECCV 2018, LNCS 11207, pp. 381–399, 2018.
https://doi.org/10.1007/978-3-030-01219-9_23

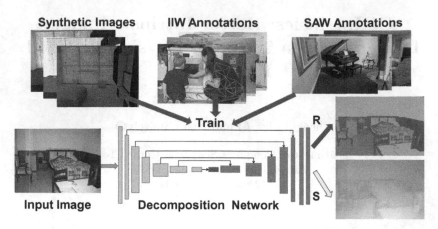

Fig. 1. Overview and network architecture. Our work integrates physically-based rendered images from our CGINTRINSICS dataset and reflectance/shading annotations from IIW and SAW in order to train a better intrinsic decomposition network.

that utilize simplified, unrealistic illumination (e.g., via Sintel [4]). An alternative is to collect ground truth for real images using crowdsourcing, as in the Intrinsic Images in the Wild (IIW) and Shading Annotations in the Wild (SAW) datasets [5,6]. However, the annotations in such datasets are sparse and difficult to collect accurately at scale.

Inspired by recent efforts to use synthetic images of scenes as training data for indoor and outdoor scene understanding [7–10], we present the first large-scale scene-level intrinsic images dataset based on high-quality physically-based rendering, which we call CGINTRINSICS (CGI). CGI consists of over 20,000 images of indoor scenes, based on the SUNCG dataset [11]. Our aim with CGI is to help drive significant progress towards solving the intrinsic images problem for Internet photos of real-world scenes. We find that high-quality physically-based rendering is essential for our task. While SUNCG provides physically-based scene renderings [12], our experiments show that the details of how images are rendered are of critical importance, and certain choices can lead to massive improvements in how well CNNs trained for intrinsic images on synthetic data generalize to real data.

We also propose a new partially supervised learning method for training a CNN to directly predict reflectance and shading, by combining ground truth from CGI and sparse annotations from IIW/SAW. Through evaluations on IIW and SAW, we find that, surprisingly, decomposition networks trained solely on CGI can achieve state-of-the-art performance on both datasets. Combined training using both CGI and IIW/SAW leads to even better performance. Finally, we find that CGI generalizes better than existing datasets by evaluating on MIT Intrinsic Images, a very different, object-centric, dataset.

2   Related Work

Optimization-Based Methods. The classical approach to intrinsic images is to integrate various priors (smoothness, reflectance sparseness, etc.) into an optimization framework [5, 13–17]. However, for images of real-world scenes, such hand-crafted prior assumptions are difficult to craft and are often violated. Several recent methods seek to improve decomposition quality by integrating surface normals or depths from RGB-D cameras [18–20] into the optimization process. However, these methods assume depth maps are available during optimization, preventing them from being used for a wide range of consumer photos.

Learning-Based Methods. Learning methods for intrinsic images have recently been explored as an alternative to models with hand-crafted priors, or a way to set the parameters of such models automatically. Barron and Malik [21] learn parameters of a model that utilizes sophisticated priors on reflectance, shape and illumination. This approach works on images of objects (such as in the MIT dataset), but does not generalize to real world scenes. More recently, CNN-based methods have been deployed, including work that regresses directly to the output decomposition based on various training datasets, such as Sintel [22,23], MIT intrinsics and ShapeNet [1,2]. Shu *et al.* [24] also propose a CNN-based method specifically for the domain of facial images, where ground truth geometry can be obtained through model fitting. However, as we show in the evaluation section, the networks trained on such prior datasets perform poorly on images of real-world scenes.

Two recent datasets are based on images of real-world scenes. Intrinsic Images in the Wild (IIW) [5] and Shading Annotations in the Wild (SAW) [6] consist of sparse, crowd-sourced reflectance and shading annotations on real indoor images. Subsequently, several papers train CNN-based classifiers on these sparse annotations and use the classifier outputs as priors to guide decomposition [6, 25–27]. However, we find these annotations alone are insufficient to train a direct regression approach, likely because they are sparse and are derived from just a few thousand images. Finally, very recent work has explored the use of time-lapse imagery as training data for intrinsic images [28], although this provides a very indirect source of supervision.

Synthetic Datasets for Real Scenes. Synthetic data has recently been utilized to improve predictions on real-world images across a range of problems. For instance, [7,10] created a large-scale dataset and benchmark based on video games for the purpose of autonomous driving, and [29,30] use synthetic imagery to form small benchmarks for intrinsic images. SUNCG [12] is a recent, large-scale synthetic dataset for indoor scene understanding. However, many of the images in the PBRS database of physically-based renderings derived from SUNCG have low signal-to-noise ratio (SNR) and non-realistic sensor properties. We show that higher quality renderings yield much better training data for intrinsic images.

3   CGINTRINSICS Dataset

To create our CGINTRINSICS (CGI) dataset, we started from the SUNCG dataset [11], which contains over 45,000 3D models of indoor scenes. We first considered the PBRS dataset of physically-based renderings of scenes from SUNCG [12]. For each scene, PBRS samples cameras from good viewpoints, and uses the physically-based Mitsuba renderer [31] to generate realistic images under reasonably realistic lighting (including a mix of indoor and outdoor illumination sources), with global illumination. Using such an approach, we can also generate ground truth data for intrinsic images by rendering a standard RGB image I, then asking the renderer to produce a reflectance map R from the same viewpoint, and finally dividing to get the shading image $S = I/R$. Examples of such ground truth decompositions are shown in Fig. 2. Note that we automatically mask out light sources (including illumination from windows looking outside) when creating the decomposition, and do not consider those pixels when training the network.

However, we found that the PBRS renderings are not ideal for use in training real-world intrinsic image decomposition networks. In fact, certain details in how images are rendered have a dramatic impact on learning performance:

Rendering Quality. Mitsuba and other high-quality renderers support a range of rendering algorithms, including various flavors of path tracing methods that sample many light paths for each output pixel. In PBRS, the authors note that bidirectional path tracing works well but is very slow, and opt for Metropolis Light Transport (MLT) with a sample rate of 512 samples per pixel [12]. In

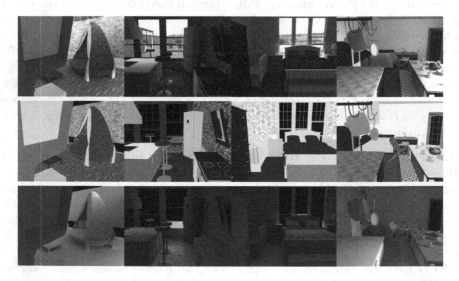

Fig. 2. Visualization of ground truth from our CGINTRINSICS dataset. Top row: rendered RGB images. Middle: ground truth reflectance. Bottom: ground truth shading. Note that light sources are masked out when creating the ground truth decomposition.

contrast, for our purposes we found that bidirectional path tracing (BDPT) with very large numbers of samples per pixel was the only algorithm that gave consistently good results for rendering SUNCG images. Comparisons between selected renderings from PBRS and our new CGI images are shown in Fig. 3. Note the significantly decreased noise in our renderings.

This extra quality comes at a cost. We find that using BDPT with 8,192 samples per pixel yields acceptable quality for most images. This increases the render time per image significantly, from a reported 31 s [12], to approximately 30 min[1]. One reason for the need for large numbers of samples is that SUNCG scenes are often challenging from a rendering perspective—the illumination is often indirect, coming from open doorways or constrained in other ways by geometry. However, rendering is highly parallelizable, and over the course of about six months we rendered over ten thousand images on a cluster of about 10 machines.

Fig. 3. Visual comparisons between our CGI and the original SUNCG dataset. Top row: images from SUNCG/PBRS. Bottom row: images from our CGI dataset. The images in our dataset have higher SNR and are more realistic.

Tone Mapping from HDR to LDR. We found that another critical factor in image generation is how rendered images are tone mapped. Renderers like Mitsuba generally produce high dynamic range (HDR) outputs that encode raw, linear radiance estimates for each pixel. In contrast, real photos are usually low dynamic range. The process that takes an HDR input and produces an LDR output is called *tone mapping*, and in real cameras the analogous operations are the auto-exposure, gamma correction, etc., that yield a well-exposed, high-contrast photograph. PBRS uses the tone mapping method of Reinhard *et al.* [33], which is inspired by photographers such as Ansel Adams, but which can produce images that are very different in character from those of consumer

---

[1] While high, this is still a fair ways off of reported render times for animated films. For instance, each frame of Pixar's *Monsters University* took a reported 29 hours to render [32].

cameras. We find that a simpler tone mapping method produces more natural-looking results. Again, Fig. 3 shows comparisons between PBRS renderings and our own. Note how the color and illumination features, such as shadows, are better captured in our renderings (we noticed that shadows often disappear with the Reinhard tone mapper).

In particular, to tone map a linear HDR radiance image I_{HDR}, we find the 90th percentile intensity value r_{90}, then compute the image $I_{LDR} = \alpha I_{HDR}^{\gamma}$, where $\gamma = \frac{1}{2.2}$ is a standard gamma correction factor, and α is computed such that r_{90} maps to the value 0.8. The final image is then clipped to the range $[0, 1]$. This mapping ensures that at most 10% of the image pixels (and usually many fewer) are saturated after tone mapping, and tends to result in natural-looking LDR images.

Table 1. Comparisons of existing intrinsic image datasets with our CGINTRINSICS dataset. PB indicates physically-based rendering and non-PB indicates non-physically-based rendering.

Dataset	Size	Setting	Rendered/real	Illumination	GT type
MPI Sintel [34]	890	Animation	non-PB	Spatial-varying	Full
MIT intrinsics [35]	110	Object	Real	Single global	Full
ShapeNet [2]	2M+	Object	PB	Single global	Full
IIW [5]	5230	Scene	Real	Spatial-varying	Sparse
SAW [6]	6677	Scene	Real	Spatial-varying	Sparse
CGINTRINSICS	20,000+	Scene	PB	Spatial-varying	Full

Using the above rendering approach, we re-rendered ~20,000 images from PBRS. We also integrated 152 realistic renderings from [30] into our dataset. Table 1 compares our CGI dataset to prior intrinsic image datasets. Sintel is a dataset created for an animated film, and does not utilize physical-based rendering. Other datasets, such as ShapeNet and MIT, are object-centered, whereas CGI focuses on images of indoor scenes, which have more sophisticated structure and illumination (cast shadows, spatial-varying lighting, etc). Compared to IIW and SAW, which include images of real scenes, CGI has full ground truth and and is much more easily collected at scale.

4   Learning Cross-Dataset Intrinsics

In this section, we describe how we use CGINTRINSICS to jointly train an intrinsic decomposition network end-to-end, incorporating additional sparse annotations from IIW and SAW. Our full training loss considers training data from each dataset:

$$\mathcal{L} = \mathcal{L}_{CGI} + \lambda_{IIW}\mathcal{L}_{IIW} + \lambda_{SAW}\mathcal{L}_{SAW}. \tag{1}$$

where $\mathcal{L}_{\mathsf{CGI}}$, $\mathcal{L}_{\mathsf{IIW}}$, and $\mathcal{L}_{\mathsf{SAW}}$ are the losses we use for training from the CGI, IIW, and SAW datasets respectively. The most direct way to train would be to simply incorporate supervision from each dataset. In the case of CGI, this supervision consists of full ground truth. For IIW and SAW, this supervision takes the form of sparse annotations for each image, as illustrated in Fig. 1. However, in addition to supervision, we found that incorporating smoothness priors into the loss also improves performance. Our full loss functions thus incorporate a number of terms:

$$\mathcal{L}_{\mathsf{CGI}} = \mathcal{L}_{\mathsf{sup}} + \lambda_{\mathsf{ord}}\mathcal{L}_{\mathsf{ord}} + \lambda_{\mathsf{rec}}\mathcal{L}_{\mathsf{reconstruct}} \tag{2}$$

$$\mathcal{L}_{\mathsf{IIW}} = \lambda_{\mathsf{ord}}\mathcal{L}_{\mathsf{ord}} + \lambda_{\mathsf{rs}}\mathcal{L}_{\mathsf{rsmooth}} + \lambda_{\mathsf{ss}}\mathcal{L}_{\mathsf{ssmooth}} + \mathcal{L}_{\mathsf{reconstruct}} \tag{3}$$

$$\mathcal{L}_{\mathsf{SAW}} = \lambda_{\mathsf{S/NS}}\mathcal{L}_{\mathsf{S/NS}} + \lambda_{\mathsf{rs}}\mathcal{L}_{\mathsf{rsmooth}} + \lambda_{\mathsf{ss}}\mathcal{L}_{\mathsf{ssmooth}} + \mathcal{L}_{\mathsf{reconstruct}} \tag{4}$$

We now describe each term in detail.

4.1   Supervised Losses

CGIntrinsics-Supervised Loss. Since the images in our CGI dataset are equipped with a full ground truth decomposition, the learning problem for this dataset can be formulated as a direct regression problem from input image I to output images R and S. However, because the decomposition is only up to an unknown scale factor, we use a scale-invariant supervised loss, $\mathcal{L}_{\mathsf{siMSE}}$ (for "scale-invariant mean-squared-error"). In addition, we add a gradient domain multi-scale matching term $\mathcal{L}_{\mathsf{grad}}$. For each training image in CGI, our supervised loss is defined as $\mathcal{L}_{\mathsf{sup}} = \mathcal{L}_{\mathsf{siMSE}} + \mathcal{L}_{\mathsf{grad}}$, where

$$\mathcal{L}_{\mathsf{siMSE}} = \frac{1}{N}\sum_{i=1}^{N}(R_i^* - c_r R_i)^2 + (S_i^* - c_s S_i)^2 \tag{5}$$

$$\mathcal{L}_{\mathsf{grad}} = \sum_{l=1}^{L}\frac{1}{N_l}\sum_{i=1}^{N_l}\left\|\nabla R_{l,i}^* - c_r\nabla R_{l,i}\right\|_1 + \left\|\nabla S_{l,i}^* - c_s\nabla S_{l,i}\right\|_1. \tag{6}$$

$R_{l,i}$ ($R_{l,i}^*$) and $S_{l,i}$ ($S_{l,i}^*$) denote reflectance prediction (resp. ground truth) and shading prediction (resp. ground truth) respectively, at pixel i and scale l of an image pyramid. N_l is the number of valid pixels at scale l and $N = N_1$ is the number of valid pixels at the original image scale. The scale factors c_r and c_s are computed via least squares.

In addition to the scale-invariance of $\mathcal{L}_{\mathsf{siMSE}}$, another important aspect is that we compute the MSE in the linear intensity domain, as opposed to the all-pairs pixel comparisons in the log domain used in [22]. In the log domain, pairs of pixels with large absolute log-difference tend to dominate the loss. As we show in our evaluation, computing $\mathcal{L}_{\mathsf{siMSE}}$ in the linear domain significantly improves performance.

Finally, the multi-scale gradient matching term $\mathcal{L}_{\mathsf{grad}}$ encourages decompositions to be piecewise smooth with sharp discontinuities.

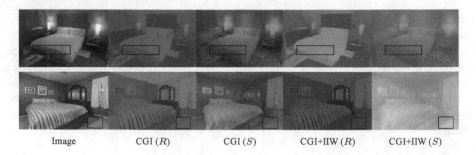

Image   CGI (R)   CGI (S)   CGI+IIW (R)   CGI+IIW (S)

Fig. 4. Examples of predictions with and without IIW training data. Adding real IIW data can qualitatively improve reflectance and shading predictions. Note for instance how the quilt highlighted in first row has a more uniform reflectance after incorporating IIW data, and similarly for the floor highlighted in the second row.

Ordinal Reflectance Loss. IIW provides sparse *ordinal* reflectance judgments between pairs of points (e.g., "point i has brighter reflectance than point j"). We introduce a loss based on this ordinal supervision. For a given IIW training image and predicted reflectance R, we accumulate losses for each pair of annotated pixels (i, j) in that image: $\mathcal{L}_{\text{ord}}(R) = \sum_{(i,j)} e_{i,j}(R)$, where

$$
e_{i,j}(R) = \begin{cases} w_{i,j}(\log R_i - \log R_j)^2, & r_{i,j} = 0 \\ w_{i,j} \left(\max(0, m - \log R_i + \log R_j)\right)^2, & r_{i,j} = +1 \\ w_{i,j} \left(\max(0, m - \log R_j + \log R_i)\right)^2, & r_{i,j} = -1 \end{cases} \tag{7}
$$

and $r_{i,j}$ is the ordinal relation from IIW, indicating whether point i is darker (-1), j is darker $(+1)$, or they have equal reflectance (0). $w_{i,j}$ is the confidence of the annotation, provided by IIW. Example predictions with and without IIW data are shown in Fig. 4.

We also found that adding a similar ordinal term derived from CGI data can improve reflectance predictions. For each image in CGI, we over-segment it using superpixel segmentation [36]. Then in each training iteration, we randomly choose one pixel from every segmented region, and for each pair of chosen pixels, we evaluate $\mathcal{L}_{\text{ord}}$ similar to Eq. 7, with $w_{i,j} = 1$ and the ordinal relation derived from the ground truth reflectance.

SAW Shading Loss. The SAW dataset provides images containing annotations of smooth (S) shading regions and non-smooth (NS) shading points, as depicted in Fig. 1. These annotations can be further divided into three types: regions of constant shading, shadow boundaries, and depth/normal discontinuities.

We integrate all three types of annotations into our supervised SAW loss $\mathcal{L}_{\text{S/NS}}$. For each constant shading region (with N_c pixels), we compute a loss $\mathcal{L}_{\text{constant-shading}}$ encouraging the variance of the predicted shading in the region to be zero:

Image   CGI (R)   CGI (S)   CGI+SAW (R)   CGI+SAW (S)

Fig. 5. Examples of predictions with and without SAW training data. Adding SAW training data can qualitatively improve reflectance and shading predictions. Note the pictures/TV highlighted in the decompositions in the first row, and the improved assignment of texture to the reflectance channel for the paintings and sofa in the second row.

$$\mathcal{L}_{\text{constant}-\text{shading}} = \frac{1}{N_c} \sum_{i=1}^{N_c} (\log S_i)^2 - \frac{1}{N_c^2} \left(\sum_{i=1}^{N_c} \log S_i \right)^2. \tag{8}$$

SAW also provides individual point annotations at cast shadow boundaries. As noted in [6], these points are not localized precisely on shadow boundaries, and so we apply a morphological dilation with a radius of 5 pixels to the set of marked points before using them in training. This results in shadow boundary regions. We find that most shadow boundary annotations lie in regions of constant reflectance, which implies that for all pair of shading pixels within a small neighborhood, their log difference should be approximately equal to the log difference of the image intensity. This is equivalent to encouraging the variance of $\log S_i - \log I_i$ within this small region to be 0 [37]. Hence, we define the loss for each shadow boundary region (with N_{sd}) pixels as:

$$\mathcal{L}_{\text{shadow}} = \frac{1}{N_{\text{sd}}} \sum_{i=1}^{N_{\text{sd}}} (\log S_i - \log I_i)^2 - \frac{1}{N_{\text{sd}}^2} \left(\sum_{i=1}^{N_{\text{sd}}} (\log S_i - \log I_i) \right)^2 \tag{9}$$

Finally, SAW provides depth/normal discontinuities, which are also usually shading discontinuities. However, since we cannot derive the actual shading change for such discontinuities, we simply mask out such regions in our shading smoothness term $\mathcal{L}_{\text{ssmooth}}$ (Eq. 11), i.e., we do not penalize shading changes in such regions. As above, we first dilate these annotated regions before use in training. Examples predictions before/after adding SAW data into our training are shown in Fig. 5.

4.2   Smoothness Losses

To further constrain the decompositions for real images in IIW/SAW, following classical intrinsic image algorithms we add reflectance smoothness $\mathcal{L}_{\text{rsmooth}}$

and shading smoothness $\mathcal{L}_{\text{ssmooth}}$ terms. For reflectance, we use a multi-scale ℓ_1 smoothness term to encourage reflectance predictions to be piecewise constant:

$$\mathcal{L}_{\text{rsmooth}} = \sum_{l=1}^{L} \frac{1}{N_l l} \sum_{i=1}^{N_l} \sum_{j \in \mathcal{N}(l,i)} v_{l,i,j} \|\log R_{l,i} - \log R_{l,j}\|_1 \tag{10}$$

where $\mathcal{N}(l,i)$ denotes the 8-connected neighborhood of the pixel at position i and scale l. The reflectance weight $v_{l,i,j} = \exp\left(-\frac{1}{2}(\mathbf{f}_{l,i} - \mathbf{f}_{l,j})^T \Sigma^{-1}(\mathbf{f}_{l,i} - \mathbf{f}_{l,j})\right)$, and the feature vector $\mathbf{f}_{l,i}$ is defined as $[\ \mathbf{p}_{l,i}, I_{l,i}, c_{l,i}^1, c_{l,i}^2\ ]$, where $\mathbf{p}_{l,i}$ and $I_{l,i}$ are the spatial position and image intensity respectively, and $c_{l,i}^1$ and $c_{l,i}^2$ are the first two elements of chromaticity. Σ is a covariance matrix defining the distance between two feature vectors.

We also include a densely-connected ℓ_2 shading smoothness term, which can be evaluated in linear time in the number of pixels N using bilateral embeddings [28,38]:

$$\mathcal{L}_{\text{ssmooth}} = \frac{1}{2N} \sum_{i}^{N} \sum_{j}^{N} \hat{W}_{i,j} \left(\log S_i - \log S_j\right)^2 \approx \frac{1}{N} \mathbf{s}^\top (I - N_b S_b^\top \bar{B}_b S_b N_b)\mathbf{s} \tag{11}$$

where $\hat{W}$ is a bistochastic weight matrix derived from W and $W_{i,j} = \exp\left(-\frac{1}{2}\|\frac{\mathbf{p}_i - \mathbf{p}_j}{\sigma_p}\|_2^2\right)$. We refer readers to [28,38] for a detailed derivation. As shown in our experiments, adding such smoothness terms to real data can yield better generalization.

4.3 Reconstruction Loss

Finally, for each training image in each dataset, we add a loss expressing the constraint that the reflectance and shading should reconstruct the original image:

$$\mathcal{L}_{\text{reconstruct}} = \frac{1}{N} \sum_{i=1}^{N} \left(I_i - R_i S_i\right)^2. \tag{12}$$

4.4 Network Architecture

Our network architecture is illustrated in Fig. 1. We use a variant of the "U-Net" architecture [28,39]. Our network has one encoder and two decoders with skip connections. The two decoders output log reflectance and log shading, respectively. Each layer of the encoder mainly consists of a 4×4 stride-2 convolutional layer followed by batch normalization [40] and leaky ReLu [41]. For the two decoders, each layer is composed of a 4×4 deconvolutional layer followed by batch normalization and ReLu, and a 1×1 convolutional layer is appended to the final layer of each decoder.

Table 2. Numerical results on the IIW test set. Lower is better for WHDR. The table is split into two subtables for space (prior methods are shown in the left subtable, and our results are shown on the right). The "Training set" column specifies the training data used by each learning-based method: "−" indicates an optimization-based method. IIW(O) indicates original IIW annotations and IIW(A) indicates augmented IIW comparisons. "All" indicates CGI+IIW(A)+SAW. * indicates that CNN predictions are post-processed with a guided filter [45].

Method	Training set	WHDR	Method	Training set	WHDR
Retinex-Color [35]	-	26.9%	Ours (log, $\mathcal{L}_{\text{siMSE}}$)	CGI	22.7%
Garces *et al.* [17]	-	24.8%	Ours (w/o $\mathcal{L}_{\text{grad}}$)	CGI	19.7%
Zhao *et al.* [14]	-	23.8%	Ours (w/o $\mathcal{L}_{\text{ord}}$)	CGI	19.9%
Bell *et al.* [5]	-	20.6%	Ours (w/o $\mathcal{L}_{\text{rsmooth}}$)	All	16.1%
			Ours	SUNCG	26.1%
Zhou *et al.* [25]	IIW	19.9%			
			Ours	CGI	17.8%
Bi *et al.* [44]	-	17.7%	Ours*	CGI	17.1%
Nestmeyer *et al.* [45]	IIW	19.5%	Ours	CGI+IIW(O)	17.5%
Nestmeyer *et al.* [45]*	IIW	17.7%	Ours	CGI+IIW(A)	16.2%
DI [22]	Sintel	37.3%	Ours	All	**15.5%**
Shi *et al.* [2]	ShapeNet	59.4%	Ours*	All	**14.8%**

5   Evaluation

We conduct experiments on two datasets of real world scenes, IIW [5] and SAW [6] (using test data unseen during training) and compare our method with several state-of-the-art intrinsic images algorithms. Additionally, we also evaluate the generalization of our CGI dataset by evaluating it on the MIT Intrinsic Images benchmark [35].

Network Training Details. We implement our method in PyTorch [42]. For all three datasets, we perform data augmentation through random flips, resizing, and crops. For all evaluations, we train our network from scratch using the Adam [43] optimizer, with initial learning rate 0.0005 and mini-batch size 16. We refer readers to the supplementary material for the detailed hyperparameter settings.

5.1   Evaluation on IIW

We follow the train/test split for IIW provided by [27], also used in [25]. We also conduct several ablation studies using different loss configurations. Quantitative comparisons of Weighted Human Disagreement Rate (WHDR) between our method and other optimization- and learning-based methods are shown in Table 2.

Comparing direct CNN predictions, our CGI-trained model is significantly better than the best learning-based method [45], and similar to [44], even though [45] was directly trained on IIW. Additionally, running the post-processing

Table 3. Quantitative results on the SAW test set. Higher is better for AP%. The second column is described in Table 2. The third and fourth columns show performance on the unweighted SAW benchmark and our more challenging gradient-weighted benchmark, respectively.

Method	Training set	AP% (unweighted)	AP% (challenge)
Retinex-Color [35]	-	91.93	85.26
Garces *et al.* [17]	-	96.89	92.39
Zhao *et al.* [14]	-	97.11	89.72
Bell *et al.* [5]	-	97.37	92.18
Zhou *et al.* [25]	IIW	96.24	86.34
Nestmeyer *et al.* [45]	IIW	97.26	89.94
Nestmeyer *et al.* [45]*	IIW	96.85	88.64
DI [22]	Sintel+MIT	95.04	86.08
Shi *et al.* [2]	ShapeNet	86.62	81.30
Ours (log, $\mathcal{L}_{\mathrm{siMSE}}$)	CGI	97.73	93.03
Ours (w/o $\mathcal{L}_{\mathrm{grad}}$)	CGI	98.15	93.74
Ours (w/o $\mathcal{L}_{\mathrm{ssmooth}}$)	CGI+IIW(A)+SAW	98.60	94.87
Ours	SUNCG	96.56	87.09
Ours	CGI	98.43	94.08
Ours	CGI+IIW(A)	98.56	94.69
Ours	CGI+IIW(A)+SAW	**98.78**	**96.57**

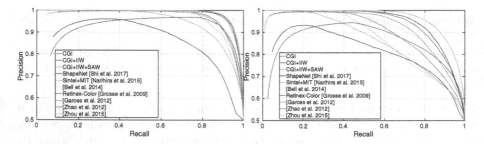

Fig. 6. Precision-Recall (PR) curve for shading images on the SAW test set. Left: PR curves generated using the unweighted SAW error metric of [28]. Right: curves generated using our more challenging gradient-weighted metric.

from [45] on the results of the CGI-trained model achieves a further performance boost. Table 2 also shows that models trained on SUNCG (i.e., PBRS), Sintel, MIT Intrinsics, or ShapeNet generalize poorly to IIW likely due to the lower quality of training data (SUNCG/PBRS), or the larger domain gap with respect to images of real-world scenes, compared to CGI. The comparison to SUNCG suggests the key importance of our rendering decisions.

We also evaluate networks trained jointly using CGI and real imagery from IIW. As in [25], we augment the pairwise IIW judgments by globally exploiting their transitivity and symmetry. The right part of Table 2 demonstrates that including IIW training data leads to further improvements in performance, as does also including SAW training data. Table 2 also shows various ablations on variants of our method, such as evaluating losses in the log domain and removing terms from the loss functions. Finally, we test a network trained on *only* IIW/SAW data (and not CGI), or trained on CGI and fine-tuned on IIW/SAW. Although such a network achieves ∼19% WHDR, we find that the decompositions are qualitatively unsatisfactory. The sparsity of the training data causes these networks to produce degenerate decompositions, especially for shading images.

5.2   Evaluation on SAW

To evaluate our shading predictions, we test our models on the SAW [6] test set, utilizing the error metric introduced in [28]. We also propose a new, more challenging error metric for SAW evaluation. In particular, we found that many of the constant-shading regions annotated in SAW also have smooth image intensity (e.g., textureless walls), making their shading easy to predict. Our proposed metric downweights such regions as follows. For each annotated region of constant shading, we compute the average image gradient magnitude over the region. During evaluation, when we add the pixels belonging to a region of constant shading into the confusion matrices, we multiply the number of pixels by this average gradient. This proposed metric leads to more distinguishable performance differences between methods, because regions with rich textures will contribute more to the error compared to the unweighted metric.

Figure 6 and Table 3 show precision-recall (PR) curves and average precision (AP) on the SAW test set with both unweighted [28] and our proposed challenge error metrics. As with IIW, networks trained solely on our CGI data can achieve state-of-the-art performance, even *without* using SAW training data. Adding real IIW data improves the AP in term of both error metrics. Finally, the last column of Table 3 shows that integrating SAW training data can significantly improve the performance on shading predictions, suggesting the effectiveness of our proposed losses for SAW sparse annotations.

Note that the previous state-of-the-art algorithms on IIW (e.g., Zhou *et al.* [25] and Nestmeyer *et al.* [45]) tend to overfit to reflectance, hurting the accuracy of shading predictions. This is especially evident in terms of our proposed challenge error metric. In contrast, our method achieves state-of-the-art results on *both* reflectance and shading predictions, in terms of all error metrics. Note that models trained on the original SUNCG, Sintel, MIT intrinsics or ShapeNet datasets perform poorly on the SAW test set, indicating the much improved generalization to real scenes of our CGI dataset.

Qualitative Results on IIW/SAW. Figure 7 shows qualitative comparisons between our network trained on all three datasets, and two other state-of-the-art intrinsic images algorithms (Bell *et al.* [5] and Zhou *et al.* [25]), on images from the IIW/SAW test sets. In general, our decompositions show significant

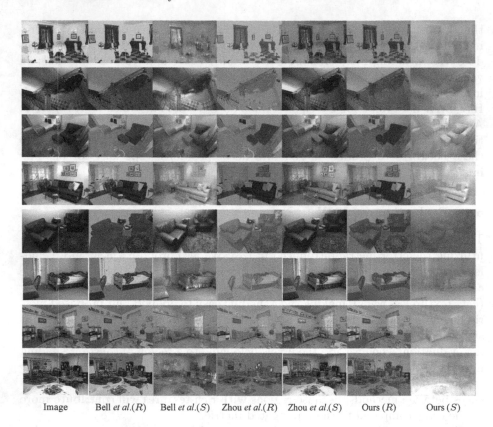

| Image | Bell *et al.*(R) | Bell *et al.*(S) | Zhou *et al.*(R) | Zhou *et al.*(S) | Ours (R) | Ours (S) |

Fig. 7. Qualitative comparisons on the IIW/SAW test sets. Our predictions show significant improvements compared to state-of-the-art algorithms (Bell *et al.* [5] and Zhou *et al.* [25]). In particular, our predicted shading channels include significantly less surface texture in several challenging settings.

improvements. In particular, our network is better at avoiding attributing surface texture to the shading channel (for instance, the checkerboard patterns evident in the first two rows, and the complex textures in the last four rows) while still predicting accurate reflectance (such as the mini-sofa in the images of third row). In contrast, the other two methods often fail to handle such difficult settings. In particular, [25] tends to overfit to reflectance predictions, and their shading estimates strongly resemble the original image intensity. However, our method still makes mistakes, such as the non-uniform reflectance prediction for the chair in the fifth row, as well as residual textures and shadows in the shading and reflectance channels.

5.3 Evaluation on MIT Intrinsic Images

For the sake of completeness, we also test the ability of our CGI-trained networks to generalize to the MIT Intrinsic Images dataset [35]. In contrast to IIW/SAW,

Table 4. Quantitative Results on MIT intrinsics testset. For all error metrics, lower is better. The second column shows the dataset used for training. * indicates models fine-tuned on MIT.

Method	Training set	MSE		LMSE		DSSIM	
		Refl.	Shading	Refl.	Shading	Refl.	Shading
SIRFS [21]	MIT	**0.0147**	**0.0083**	0.0416	**0.0168**	**0.1238**	**0.0985**
DI [22]	Sintel+MIT	0.0277	0.0154	0.0585	0.0295	0.1526	0.1328
Shi *et al.* [2]	ShapeNet	0.0468	0.0194	0.0752	0.0318	0.1825	0.1667
Shi *et al.* [2]*	ShapeNet+MIT	0.0278	0.0126	0.0503	0.0240	0.1465	0.1200
Ours	CGI	0.0221	0.0186	0.0349	0.0259	0.1739	0.1652
Ours*	CGI +MIT	0.0167	0.0127	**0.0319**	0.0211	0.1287	0.1376

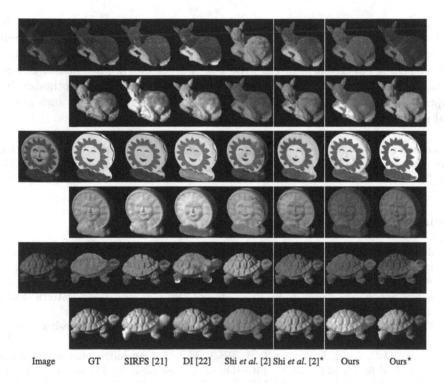

Image   GT   SIRFS [21]   DI [22]   Shi *et al.* [2] Shi *et al.* [2]*   Ours   Ours*

Fig. 8. Qualitative comparisons on MIT intrinsics testset. Odd rows: reflectance predictions. Even rows: shading predictions. * are the predictions fine-tuned on MIT.

the MIT dataset contains 20 real objects with 11 different illumination conditions. We follow the same train/test split as Barron *et al.* [21], and, as in the work of Shi *et al.* [2], we directly apply our CGI trained networks to MIT testset, and additionally test fine-tuning them on the MIT training set.

We compare our models with several state-of-the-art learning-based methods using the same error metrics as [2]. Table 4 shows quantitative comparisons and

Fig. 8 shows qualitative results. Both show that our CGI-trained model yields better performance compared to ShapeNet-trained networks both qualitatively and quantitatively, even though like MIT, ShapeNet consists of images of rendered objects, while our dataset contains images of scenes. Moreover, our CGI-pretrained model also performs better than networks pretrained on ShapeNet and Sintel. These results further demonstrate the improved generalization ability of our CGI dataset compared to existing datasets. Note that SIRFS still achieves the best results, but as described in [2,22], their methods are designed specifically for single objects and generalize poorly to real scenes.

6   Conclusion

We presented a new synthetic dataset for learning intrinsic images, and an end-to-end learning approach that learns better intrinsic image decompositions by leveraging datasets with different types of labels. Our evaluations illustrate the surprising effectiveness of our synthetic dataset on Internet photos of real-world scenes. We find that the details of rendering matter, and hypothesize that improved physically-based rendering may benefit other vision tasks, such as normal prediction and semantic segmentation [12].

Acknowledgments. We thank Jingguang Zhou for his help with data generation. This work was funded by the National Science Foundation through grant IIS-1149393, and by a grant from Schmidt Sciences.

References

1. Janner, M., Wu, J., Kulkarni, T., Yildirim, I., Tenenbaum, J.B.: Self-supervised intrinsic image decomposition. In: Neural Information Processing Systems (2017)
2. Shi, J., Dong, Y., Su, H., Yu, S.X.: Learning non-Lambertian object intrinsics across ShapeNet categories. In: Proceedings Computer Vision and Pattern Recognition (CVPR), pp. 5844–5853 (2017)
3. Chang, A.X., et al.: ShapeNet: an information-rich 3D model repository. arXiv preprint arXiv:1512.03012 (2015)
4. Butler, D.J., Wulff, J., Stanley, G.B., Black, M.J.: A naturalistic open source movie for optical flow evaluation. In: Fitzgibbon, A., Lazebnik, S., Perona, P., Sato, Y., Schmid, C. (eds.) ECCV 2012. LNCS, vol. 7577, pp. 611–625. Springer, Heidelberg (2012). https://doi.org/10.1007/978-3-642-33783-3_44
5. Bell, S., Bala, K., Snavely, N.: Intrinsic images in the wild. ACM Trans. Graph. **33**(4), 159 (2014)
6. Kovacs, B., Bell, S., Snavely, N., Bala, K.: Shading annotations in the wild. In: Proceedings of the Computer Vision and Pattern Recognition (CVPR), pp. 850–859 (2017)
7. Richter, S.R., Vineet, V., Roth, S., Koltun, V.: Playing for data: ground truth from computer games. In: Leibe, B., Matas, J., Sebe, N., Welling, M. (eds.) ECCV 2016. LNCS, vol. 9906, pp. 102–118. Springer, Cham (2016). https://doi.org/10.1007/978-3-319-46475-6_7

8. Ros, G., Sellart, L., Materzynska, J., Vazquez, D., Lopez, A.M.: The SYNTHIA dataset: a large collection of synthetic images for semantic segmentation of urban scenes. In: Proceedings of the Computer Vision and Pattern Recognition (CVPR), pp. 3234–3243 (2016)

9. Gaidon, A., Wang, Q., Cabon, Y., Vig, E.: Virtual worlds as proxy for multi-object tracking analysis. In: Proceedings of the Computer Vision and Pattern Recognition (CVPR), pp. 4340–4349 (2016)

10. Richter, S.R., Hayder, Z., Koltun, V.: Playing for benchmarks. In: Proceedings of the International Conference on Computer Vision (ICCV), pp. 2232–2241 (2017)

11. Song, S., Yu, F., Zeng, A., Chang, A.X., Savva, M., Funkhouser, T.: Semantic scene completion from a single depth image. In: Proceedings Computer Vision and Pattern Recognition (CVPR), pp. 190–198 (2017)

12. Zhang, Y., et al.: Physically-based rendering for indoor scene understanding using convolutional neural networks. In: Proceedings of the Computer Vision and Pattern Recognition (CVPR), pp. 5057–5065 (2017)

13. Land, E.H., McCann, J.J.: Lightness and retinex theory. Josa 61(1), 1–11 (1971)

14. Zhao, Q., Tan, P., Dai, Q., Shen, L., Wu, E., Lin, S.: A closed-form solution to retinex with nonlocal texture constraints. Trans. Pattern Anal. Mach. Intell. 34(7), 1437–1444 (2012)

15. Rother, C., Kiefel, M., Zhang, L., Schölkopf, B., Gehler, P.V.: Recovering intrinsic images with a global sparsity prior on reflectance. In: Neural Information Processing Systems, pp. 765–773 (2011)

16. Shen, L., Yeo, C.: Intrinsic images decomposition using a local and global sparse representation of reflectance. In: Proceedings Computer Vision and Pattern Recognition (CVPR), pp. 697–704 (2011)

17. Garces, E., Munoz, A., Lopez-Moreno, J., Gutierrez, D.: Intrinsic images by clustering. In: Computer Graphics Forum (Proceedings of the EGSR 2012), vol. 31, no. 4 (2012)

18. Chen, Q., Koltun, V.: A simple model for intrinsic image decomposition with depth cues. In: Proceedings Computer Vision and Pattern Recognition (CVPR), pp. 241–248 (2013)

19. Barron, J.T., Malik, J.: Intrinsic scene properties from a single RGB-D image. In: Proceedings of the Computer Vision and Pattern Recognition (CVPR), pp. 17–24 (2013)

20. Jeon, J., Cho, S., Tong, X., Lee, S.: Intrinsic image decomposition using structure-texture separation and surface normals. In: Fleet, D., Pajdla, T., Schiele, B., Tuytelaars, T. (eds.) ECCV 2014. LNCS, vol. 8695, pp. 218–233. Springer, Cham (2014). https://doi.org/10.1007/978-3-319-10584-0_15

21. Barron, J.T., Malik, J.: Shape, illumination, and reflectance from shading. Trans. Pattern Anal. Mach. Intell. 37(8), 1670–1687 (2015)

22. Narihira, T., Maire, M., Yu, S.X.: Direct intrinsics: learning albedo-shading decomposition by convolutional regression. In: Proceedings International Conference on Computer Vision (ICCV), pp. 2992–2992 (2015)

23. Kim, S., Park, K., Sohn, K., Lin, S.: Unified depth prediction and intrinsic image decomposition from a single image via joint convolutional neural fields. In: Leibe, B., Matas, J., Sebe, N., Welling, M. (eds.) ECCV 2016. LNCS, vol. 9912, pp. 143–159. Springer, Cham (2016). https://doi.org/10.1007/978-3-319-46484-8_9

24. Shu, Z., Yumer, E., Hadap, S., Sunkavalli, K., Shechtman, E., Samaras, D.: Neural face editing with intrinsic image disentangling. In: Proceedings of the Computer Vision and Pattern Recognition (CVPR), pp. 5444–5453 (2017)

25. Zhou, T., Krahenbuhl, P., Efros, A.A.: Learning data-driven reflectance priors for intrinsic image decomposition. In: Proceedings of the International Conference on Computer Vision (ICCV), pp. 3469–3477 (2015)
26. Zoran, D., Isola, P., Krishnan, D., Freeman, W.T.: Learning ordinal relationships for mid-level vision. In: Proceedings of the International Conference on Computer Vision (ICCV), pp. 388–396 (2015)
27. Narihira, T., Maire, M., Yu, S.X.: Learning lightness from human judgement on relative reflectance. In: Proceedings of the Computer Vision and Pattern Recognition (CVPR), pp. 2965–2973 (2015)
28. Li, Z., Snavely, N.: Learning intrinsic image decomposition from watching the world. In: Proceedings of the Computer Vision and Pattern Recognition (CVPR) (2018)
29. Beigpour, S., et al.: Intrinsic image evaluation on synthetic complex scenes. In: International Conference on Image Processing (2013)
30. Bonneel, N., Kovacs, B., Paris, S., Bala, K.: Intrinsic decompositions for image editing. In: Computer Graphics Forum (Eurographics State of the Art Reports 2017), vol. 36, no. 2 (2017)
31. Jakob, W.: Mitsuba renderer (2010). http://www.mitsuba-renderer.org
32. Takahashi, D.: How Pixar made Monsters University, its latest technological marvel (2013). https://venturebeat.com/2013/04/24/the-making-of-pixars-latest-technological-marvel-monsters-university/
33. Reinhard, E., Stark, M., Shirley, P., Ferwerda, J.: Photographic tone reproduction for digital images. ACM Trans. Graph. SIGGRAPH **21**, 267–276 (2002)
34. Butler, D.J., Wulff, J., Stanley, G.B., Black, M.J.: A naturalistic open source movie for optical flow evaluation. In: Fitzgibbon, A., Lazebnik, S., Perona, P., Sato, Y., Schmid, C. (eds.) ECCV 2012. LNCS, vol. 7577, pp. 611–625. Springer, Heidelberg (2012). https://doi.org/10.1007/978-3-642-33783-3_44
35. Grosse, R., Johnson, M.K., Adelson, E.H., Freeman, W.T.: Ground truth dataset and baseline evaluations for intrinsic image algorithms. In: Proceedings of the International Conference on Computer Vision (ICCV) (2009)
36. Achanta, R., Shaji, A., Smith, K., Lucchi, A., Fua, P., Süsstrunk, S.: SLIC superpixels compared to state-of-the-art superpixel methods. Trans. Pattern Anal. Mach. Intell. **34**(11), 2274–2282 (2012)
37. Eigen, D., Puhrsch, C., Fergus, R.: Depth map prediction from a single image using a multi-scale deep network. In: Neural Information Processing Systems, pp. 2366–2374 (2014)
38. Barron, J.T., Adams, A., Shih, Y., Hernández, C.: Fast bilateral-space stereo for synthetic defocus. In: Proceedings of the Computer Vision and Pattern Recognition (CVPR), pp. 4466–4474 (2015)
39. Isola, P., Zhu, J.Y., Zhou, T., Efros, A.A.: Image-to-image translation with conditional adversarial networks. In: Proceedings of the Computer Vision and Pattern Recognition (CVPR), pp. 6967–5976 (2017)
40. Ioffe, S., Szegedy, C.: Batch normalization: accelerating deep network training by reducing internal covariate shift. In: Proceedings of the International Conference on Machine Learning, pp. 448–456 (2015)
41. He, K., Zhang, X., Ren, S., Sun, J.: Delving deep into rectifiers: surpassing human-level performance on ImageNet classification. In: Proceedings of the International Conference on Computer Vision (ICCV) (2015)
42. Pytorch (2016). http://pytorch.org
43. Kingma, D.P., Ba, J.: Adam: A method for stochastic optimization. CoRR abs/1412.6980 (2014)

44. Bi, S., Han, X., Yu, Y.: An $l1$ image transform for edge-preserving smoothing and scene-level intrinsic decomposition. ACM Trans. Graph. **34**, 78:1–78:12 (2015)
45. Nestmeyer, T., Gehler, P.V.: Reflectance adaptive filtering improves intrinsic image estimation. In: Proceedings of the Computer Vision and Pattern Recognition (CVPR) (2017)

Simultaneous Edge Alignment
and Learning

Zhiding Yu[1]([✉]), Weiyang Liu[3], Yang Zou[2], Chen Feng[4],
Srikumar Ramalingam[5], B. V. K. Vijaya Kumar[2], and Jan Kautz[1]

[1] NVIDIA, Santa Clara, USA
{zhidingy,jkautz}@nvidia.com
[2] Carnegie Mellon University, Pittsburgh, USA
yzou2@andrew.cmu.edu, kumar@ece.cmu.edu
[3] Georgia Institute of Technology, Atlanta, Georgia
wyliu@gatech.edu
[4] New York University, New York City, USA
cfeng@nyu.edu
[5] University of Utah, Salt Lake City, USA
srikumar@cs.utah.edu

Abstract. Edge detection is among the most fundamental vision problems for its role in perceptual grouping and its wide applications. Recent advances in representation learning have led to considerable improvements in this area. Many state of the art edge detection models are learned with fully convolutional networks (FCNs). However, FCN-based edge learning tends to be vulnerable to misaligned labels due to the delicate structure of edges. While such problem was considered in evaluation benchmarks, similar issue has not been explicitly addressed in general edge learning. In this paper, we show that label misalignment can cause considerably degraded edge learning quality, and address this issue by proposing a simultaneous edge alignment and learning framework. To this end, we formulate a probabilistic model where edge alignment is treated as latent variable optimization, and is learned end-to-end during network training. Experiments show several applications of this work, including improved edge detection with state of the art performance, and automatic refinement of noisy annotations.

1 Introduction

Over the past decades, edge detection played a significant role in computer vision. Early edge detection methods often formulate the task as a low-level or mid-level grouping problem where Gestalt laws and perceptual grouping play considerable roles in algorithm design [7,16,23,44]. Latter works start to consider learning edges in a data-driven way, by looking into the statistics of features near boundaries [1,2,12,13,25,31,34,39]. More recently, advances in deep representation

Electronic supplementary material The online version of this chapter (https://doi.org/10.1007/978-3-030-01219-9_24) contains supplementary material, which is available to authorized users.

V. Ferrari et al. (Eds.): ECCV 2018, LNCS 11207, pp. 400–417, 2018.
https://doi.org/10.1007/978-3-030-01219-9_24

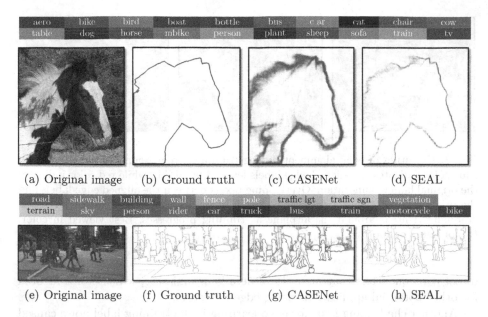

| aero | bike | bird | boat | bottle | bus | c ar | cat | chair | cow |
| table | dog | horse | mbike | person | plant | sheep | sofa | train | tv |

(a) Original image   (b) Ground truth   (c) CASENet   (d) SEAL

| road | sidewalk | building | wall | fence | pole | traffic lgt | traffic sgn | vegetation |
| terrain | sky | person | rider | car | truck | bus | train | motorcycle | bike |

(e) Original image   (f) Ground truth   (g) CASENet   (h) SEAL

Fig. 1. Examples of edges predicted by different methods on SBD (a-d) and Cityscapes (e–h). "CASENet" indicates the original CASENet from [52]. "SEAL" indicates the proposed framework trained with CASENet backbone. Best viewed in color. (Color figure online)

learning [18,26,43] have further led to significant improvements on edge detection, pushing the boundaries of state of the art performance [3,20,24,49,50] to new levels. The associated tasks also expended from the conventional binary edge detection problems to the recent more challenging category-aware edge detection problems [4,17,22,38,52]. As a result of such advancement, a wide variety of other vision problems have enjoyed the benefits of reliable edge detectors. Examples of these applications include, but are not limited to (semantic) segmentation [1,4,5,9,51], object proposal generation [4,50,53], object detection [29], depth estimation [19,32], and 3D vision [21,33,42], etc.

With the strong representation abilities of deep networks and the dense labeling nature of edge detection, many state of the art edge detectors are based on FCNs. Despite the underlying resemblance to other dense labeling tasks, edge learning problems face some typical challenges and issues. First, in light of the highly imbalanced amounts of positive samples (edge pixels) and negative samples (non-edge pixels), using reweighted losses where positive samples are weighted higher has become a predominant choice in recent deep edge learning frameworks [22,24,30,49,52]. While such a strategy to some extent renders better learning behaviors[1], it also induces thicker detected edges as well as more false positives. An example of this issue is illustrated in Figs. 1(c) and (g), where the edge mapspredicted by CASENet [52] contains thick object boundaries. A

---

[1] E.g., more stabled training, and more balanced prediction towards smaller classes.

Fig. 2. Evolution of edge alignment during training (progression from left to right). Blue color indicates the aligned edge labels learned by SEAL, while red color indicates the original human annotation. Overlapping pixels between the aligned edge labels and the original annotation are color-coded to be blue. Note how the aligned edge labels gradually tightens around the airplane as training progresses. Best viewed in color. (Color figure online)

direct consequence is that many local details are missing, which is not favored for other potential applications using edge detectors.

Another challenging issue for edge learning is the training label noise caused by inevitable misalignment during annotation. Unlike segmentation, edge learning is generally more vulnerable to such noise due to the fact that edge structures by nature are much more delicate than regions. Even slight misalignment can lead to significant proportion of mismatches between ground truth and prediction. In order to predict sharp edges, a model should learn to distinguish the few true edge pixels while suppressing edge responses near them. This already presents a considerable challenge to the model as non-edge pixels near edges are likely to be hard negatives with similar features, while the presence of misalignment further causes significant confusion by continuously sending false positives during training. The problem is further aggravated under reweighted losses, where predicting more false positives near the edge is be an effective way to decrease the loss due to the significant higher weights of positive samples.

Unfortunately, completely eliminating misalignment during annotation is almost impossible given the limit of human precision and the diminishing gain of annotation quality from additional efforts as a result. For datasets such as Cityscapes [11] where high quality labels are generated by professional annotators, misalignment can still be frequently observed. For datasets with crowdsourcing annotations where quality control presents another challenge, the issue can become even more severe. Our proposed solution is an end-to-end framework towards Simultaneous Edge Alignment and Learning (SEAL). In particular, we formulate the problem with a probabilistic model, treating edge labels as latent variables to be jointly learned during training. We show that the optimization of latent edge labels can be transformed into a bipartite graph min-cost assignment problem, and present an end-to-end learning framework towards model training. Figure 2 shows some examples where the model gradually learns how to align noisy edge labels to more accurate positions along with edge learning.

Contrary to the widely believed intuition that reweighted loss benefits edge learning problems, an interesting and counter-intuitive observation made in this paper is that (regular) sigmoid cross-entropy loss works surprisingly well under the proposed framework despite the extremely imbalanced distribution. The underlying reason is that edge alignment significantly reduces the training confusion by increasing the purity of positive edge samples. Without edge alignment, on the other hand, the presence of label noise together with imbalanced distribution makes the model more difficult to correctly learn positive classes. As a result of the increased label quality and the benefit of better negative suppression using unweighted loss, our proposed framework produces state of the art detection performance with high quality sharp edges (see Figs. 1(d) and (h)).

2   Related Work

2.1   Boundary Map Correspondence

Our work is partly motivated by the early work of boundary evaluation using precision-recall and F-measure [34]. To address misalignment between prediction and human ground truth, [34] proposed to compute a one-to-one correspondence for the subset of matchable edge pixels from both domains by solving a min-cost assignment problem. However, [34] only considers the alignment between fixed boundary maps, while our work addresses a more complicated learning problem where edge alignment becomes part of the optimization with learnable inputs.

2.2   Mask Refinement via Energy Minimization

Yang et al. [50] proposed to use dense-CRF to refine object mask and contour. Despite the similar goal, our method differs from [50] in that: 1. The refinement framework in [50] is a separate preprocessing step, while our work jointly learns refinement with the model in an end-to-end fashion. 2. The CRF model in [50] only utilizes low-level features, while our model considers both low-level and high-level information via a deep network. 3. The refinement framework in [50] is segmentation-based, while our framework directly targets edge refinement.

2.3   Object Contour and Mask Learning

A series of works [8,37,40] seek to learn object contours/masks in a supervised fashion. Deep active contour [40] uses learned CNN features to steer contour evolution given the input of an initialized contour. Polygon-RNN [8] introduced a semi-automatic approach for object mask annotation, by learning to extract polygons given input bounding boxes. DeepMask [37] proposed an object proposal generation method to output class-agnostic segmentation masks. These methods require accurate ground truth for contour/mask learning, while this work only assumes noisy ground truths and seek to refine them automatically.

2.4 Noisy Label Learning

Our work can be broadly viewed as a structured noisy label learning framework where we leverage abundant structural priors to correct label noise. Existing noisy label learning literatures have proposed directed graphical models [48], conditional random fields (CRF) [45], neural networks [46,47], robust losses [35] and knowledge graph [27] to model and correct image-level noisy labels. Alternatively, our work considers pixel-level labels instead of image-level ones.

2.5 Virtual Evidence in Bayesian Networks

Our work also shares similarity with virtual evidence [6,28,36], where the uncertainty of an observation is modeled by a distribution rather than a single value. In our problem, noisy labels can be regarded as uncertain observations which give conditional prior distributions over different configurations of aligned labels.

3   A Probabilistic View Towards Edge Learning

In many classification problems, training of the models can be formulated as maximizing the following likelihood function with respect to the parameters:

$$\max_{\mathbf{W}} \mathcal{L}(\mathbf{W}) = P(\mathbf{y}|\mathbf{x}; \mathbf{W}), \tag{1}$$

where $\mathbf{y}$, $\mathbf{x}$ and $\mathbf{W}$ indicate respectively training labels, observed inputs and model parameters. Depending on how the conditional probability is parameterized, the above likelihood function may correspond to different types of models. For example, a generalized linear model function leads to the well known logistic regression. If the parameterization is formed as a layered representation, the model may turn into CNNs or multilayer perceptrons. One may observe that many traditional supervised edge learning models can also be regarded as special cases under the above probabilistic framework. Here, we are mostly concerned with edge detection using fully convolutional neural networks. In this case, the variable $\mathbf{y}$ indicates the set of edge prediction configurations at every pixel, while $\mathbf{x}$ and $\mathbf{W}$ denote the input image and the network parameters, respectively.

4   Simultaneous Edge Alignment and Learning

To introduce the ability of correcting edge labels during training, we consider the following model. Instead of treating the observed annotation $\mathbf{y}$ as the fitting target, we assume there is an underlying ground truth $\hat{\mathbf{y}}$ that is more accurate than $\mathbf{y}$. Our goal is to treat $\hat{\mathbf{y}}$ as a latent variable to be jointly estimated during learning, which leads to the following likelihood maximization problem:

$$\max_{\hat{\mathbf{y}}, \mathbf{W}} \mathcal{L}(\hat{\mathbf{y}}, \mathbf{W}) = P(\mathbf{y}, \hat{\mathbf{y}}|\mathbf{x}; \mathbf{W}) = P(\mathbf{y}|\hat{\mathbf{y}})P(\hat{\mathbf{y}}|\mathbf{x}; \mathbf{W}), \tag{2}$$

where $\hat{\mathbf{y}}$ indicates the underlying true ground truth. The former part $P(\mathbf{y}|\hat{\mathbf{y}})$ can be regarded as an edge prior probabilistic model of an annotator generating labels given the observed ground truths, while the latter part $P(\hat{\mathbf{y}}|\mathbf{x}; \mathbf{W})$ is the standard likelihood of the prediction model.

4.1   Multilabel Edge Learning

Consider the multilabel edge learning setting where one assumes that $\mathbf{y}$ does not need to be mutually exclusive at each pixel. In other words, any pixel may correspond to the edges of multiple classes. The likelihood can be decomposed to a set of class-wise joint probabilities assuming the inter-class independence:

$$\mathcal{L}(\hat{\mathbf{y}}, \mathbf{W}) = \prod_k P(\mathbf{y}^k|\hat{\mathbf{y}}^k)P(\hat{\mathbf{y}}^k|\mathbf{x}; \mathbf{W}), \tag{3}$$

where $\mathbf{y}^k \in \{0,1\}^N$ indicates the set of binary labels corresponding to the k-th class. A typical multilabel edge learning example which alsoassumes inter-class independence is CASENet [52]. In addition, binary edge detection methods such as HED [49] can be viewed as special cases of multilabel edge learning.

4.2   Edge Prior Model

Solving Eq. (2) is not easy given the additional huge search space of $\hat{\mathbf{y}}$. Fortunately, there is some prior knowledge one could leverage to effectively regularize $\hat{\mathbf{y}}$. One of the most important prior is that $\hat{\mathbf{y}}^k$ should not be too different from $\mathbf{y}^k$. In addition, we assume that edge pixels in $\mathbf{y}^k$ is generated from those in $\hat{\mathbf{y}}^k$ through an one-to-one assignment process, which indicates $|\mathbf{y}^k| = |\hat{\mathbf{y}}^k|$. In other words, let $y_{\mathbf{q}}^k$ denote the label of class k at pixel $\mathbf{q}$, and similarly for $\hat{y}_{\mathbf{p}}^k$, there exists a set of one-to-one correspondences between edge pixels in $\hat{\mathbf{y}}^k$ and $\mathbf{y}^k$:

$$\mathcal{M}(\mathbf{y}^k, \hat{\mathbf{y}}^k) = \{m(\cdot)|\forall \mathbf{u}, \mathbf{v} \in \{\mathbf{q}|y_{\mathbf{q}}^k = 1\} : \hat{y}_{m(\mathbf{u})}^k = 1,$$
$$\hat{y}_{m(\mathbf{v})}^k = 1, \mathbf{u} \neq \mathbf{v} \Rightarrow m(\mathbf{u}) \neq m(\mathbf{v})\}, \tag{4}$$

where each $m(\cdot)$ is associated with a finite set of pairs:

$$m(\cdot) \sim E_m = \{(\mathbf{p}, \mathbf{q})|\hat{y}_{\mathbf{p}}, y_{\mathbf{q}} = 1, m(\mathbf{q}) = \mathbf{p}\}. \tag{5}$$

The edge prior therefore can be modeled as a product of Gaussian similarities maximized over all possible correspondences:

$$P(\mathbf{y}^k|\hat{\mathbf{y}}^k) \propto \sup_{m \in \mathcal{M}(\mathbf{y}^k, \hat{\mathbf{y}}^k)} \prod_{(\mathbf{p}, \mathbf{q}) \in E_m} \exp\left(-\frac{\|\mathbf{p} - \mathbf{q}\|^2}{2\sigma^2}\right)$$
$$= \exp\left(-\inf_{m \in \mathcal{M}(\mathbf{y}^k, \hat{\mathbf{y}}^k)} \sum_{(\mathbf{p}, \mathbf{q}) \in E_m} \frac{\|\mathbf{p} - \mathbf{q}\|^2}{2\sigma^2}\right), \tag{6}$$

where σ is the bandwidth that controls the sensitivity to misalignment. The misalignment is quantified by measuring the lowest possible sum of squared distances between pairwise pixels, which is determined by the tightest correspondence.

4.3   Network Likelihood Model

We now consider the likelihood of the prediction model, where we assume that the class-wise joint probability can be decomposed to a set of pixel-wise probabilities modeled by bernoulli distributions with binary configurations:

$$P(\hat{\mathbf{y}}^k|\mathbf{x}; \mathbf{W}) = \prod_{\mathbf{p}} P(\hat{y_{\mathbf{p}}}^k|\mathbf{x}; \mathbf{W}) = \prod_{\mathbf{p}} h_k(\mathbf{p}|\mathbf{x}; \mathbf{W})^{\hat{y}_{\mathbf{p}}^k}(1 - h_k(\mathbf{p}|\mathbf{x}; \mathbf{W}))^{(1-\hat{y}_{\mathbf{p}}^k)},$$

(7)

where $\mathbf{p}$ is the pixel location index, and h_k is the hypothesis function indicating the probability of the k-th class. We consider the prediction model as FCNs with k sigmoid outputs. As a result, the hypothesis function in Eq. (7) becomes the sigmoid function, which will be denoted as $\sigma(\cdot)$ in the rest part of this section.

4.4   Learning

Taking Eqs. (6) and (7) into Eq. (3), and taking log of the likelihood, we have:

$$\log \mathcal{L}(\hat{\mathbf{y}}, \mathbf{W}) = \sum_{k} \Big\{ - \inf_{m \in \mathcal{M}(\mathbf{y}^k, \hat{\mathbf{y}}^k)} \sum_{(\mathbf{p},\mathbf{q}) \in E_m} \frac{\|\mathbf{p} - \mathbf{q}\|^2}{2\sigma^2}$$
$$+ \sum_{\mathbf{p}} \Big[\hat{y}_{\mathbf{p}}^k \log \sigma_k(\mathbf{p}|\mathbf{x}; \mathbf{W}) + (1 - \hat{y}_{\mathbf{p}}^k) \log(1 - \sigma_k(\mathbf{p}|\mathbf{x}; \mathbf{W})) \Big] \Big\},$$

(8)

where the second part is the widely used sigmoid cross-entropy loss. Accordingly, learning the model requires solving the constrained optimization:

$$\min_{\hat{\mathbf{y}}, \mathbf{W}} - \log \mathcal{L}(\hat{\mathbf{y}}, \mathbf{W})$$
$$\text{s.t. } |\hat{\mathbf{y}}^k| = |\mathbf{y}^k|, \forall k$$

(9)

Given a training set, we take an alternative optimization strategy where $\mathbf{W}$ is updated with $\hat{\mathbf{y}}$ fixed, and vice versa. When $\hat{\mathbf{y}}$ is fixed, the optimization becomes:

$$\min_{\mathbf{W}} \sum_{k} \sum_{\mathbf{p}} - \Big[\hat{y}_{\mathbf{p}}^k \log \sigma_k(\mathbf{p}|\mathbf{x}; \mathbf{W}) + (1 - \hat{y}_{\mathbf{p}}^k) \log(1 - \sigma_k(\mathbf{p}|\mathbf{x}; \mathbf{W})) \Big], \quad (10)$$

which is the typical network training with the aligned edge labels and can be solved with standard gradient descent. When $\mathbf{W}$ is fixed, the optimization can be modeled as a constrained discrete optimization problem for each class:

$$\min_{\hat{\mathbf{y}}^k} \inf_{m \in \mathcal{M}(\mathbf{y}^k, \hat{\mathbf{y}}^k)} \sum_{(\mathbf{p},\mathbf{q}) \in E_m} \frac{\|\mathbf{p} - \mathbf{q}\|^2}{2\sigma^2}$$
$$- \sum_{\mathbf{p}} \Big[\hat{y}_{\mathbf{p}}^k \log \sigma_k(\mathbf{p}) + (1 - \hat{y}_{\mathbf{p}}^k) \log(1 - \sigma_k(\mathbf{p})) \Big]$$

(11)

$$\text{s.t. } |\hat{\mathbf{y}}^k| = |\mathbf{y}^k|$$

where $\sigma(\mathbf{p})$ denotes $\sigma(\mathbf{p}|\mathbf{x}; \mathbf{W})$ for short. Solving the above optimization is seemingly difficult, since one would need to enumerate all possible configurations of $\hat{\mathbf{y}}^k$ satisfying $|\hat{\mathbf{y}}^k| = |\mathbf{y}^k|$ and evaluate the associated cost. It turns out, however, that the above optimization can be elegantly transformed to a bipartite graph assignment problem with available solvers. We first have the following definition:

Definition 1. *Let* $\hat{\mathbf{Y}} = \{\hat{\mathbf{y}} || \hat{\mathbf{y}}| = |\mathbf{y}|\}$, *a mapping space* $\mathbf{M}$ *is the space consisting all possible one-to-one mappings:*

$$\mathbf{M} = \{m | m \in \mathcal{M}(\mathbf{y}, \hat{\mathbf{y}}), \hat{\mathbf{y}} \in \hat{\mathbf{Y}}\}$$

Definition 2. *A label realization is a function which maps a correspondence to the corresponding label given:*

$$f_L : \mathbf{Y} \times \mathbf{M} \mapsto \hat{\mathbf{Y}}$$
$$f_L(\mathbf{y}, m) = \hat{\mathbf{y}}$$

Lemma 1. *The mapping* $f_L(\cdot)$ *is surjective.*

Remark. Lemma 1 shows that a certain label configuration $\hat{\mathbf{y}}$ may correspond to multiple underlying mappings. This is obviously true since there could be multiple ways in which pixels in $\mathbf{y}$ are assigned to the $\hat{\mathbf{y}}$.

Lemma 2. *Under the constraint* $|\hat{\mathbf{y}}| = |\mathbf{y}|$, *if:*

$$\hat{\mathbf{y}}^* = \arg\min_{\hat{\mathbf{y}}} - \sum_{\mathbf{p}} \left[\hat{y}_{\mathbf{p}} \log \sigma(\mathbf{p}) + (1 - \hat{y}_{\mathbf{p}}) \log(1 - \sigma(\mathbf{p})) \right]$$

$$m^* = \arg\min_{m \in \mathbf{M}} \sum_{(\mathbf{p}, \mathbf{q}) \in E_m} \left[\log(1 - \sigma(\mathbf{p})) - \log \sigma(\mathbf{p}) \right]$$

then $f_L(\mathbf{y}, m^*) = \hat{\mathbf{y}}^*$.

Proof. Suppose in the beginning all pixels in $\hat{\mathbf{y}}$ are 0. The corresponding loss therefore is:

$$\mathcal{C}_N(\mathbf{0}) = - \sum_{\mathbf{p}} \log(1 - \sigma(\mathbf{p}))$$

Flipping $y_{\mathbf{p}}$ to 1 will accordingly introduce a cost $\log(1 - \sigma(\mathbf{p})) - \log \sigma(\mathbf{p})$ at pixel $\mathbf{p}$. As a result, we have:

$$\mathcal{C}_N(\hat{\mathbf{y}}) = \mathcal{C}_N(\mathbf{0}) + \sum_{\mathbf{p} \in \{\mathbf{p} | \hat{y}_{\mathbf{p}} = 1\}} \left[\log(1 - \sigma(\mathbf{p})) - \log \sigma(\mathbf{p}) \right]$$

In addition, Lemma 1 states that the mapping $f_L(\cdot)$ is surjective, which incites that the mapping search space $\mathbf{M}$ exactly covers $\hat{\mathbf{Y}}$. Thus the top optimization problem in Lemma 2 can be transformed into the bottom problem.

Lemma 2 motivates us to reformulate the optimization in Eq. (11) by alternatively looking to the following problem:

$$\min_{m \in M} \sum_{(\mathbf{p},\mathbf{q}) \in E_m} \left[\frac{\|\mathbf{p} - \mathbf{q}\|^2}{2\sigma^2} + \log(1 - \sigma(\mathbf{p})) - \log \sigma(\mathbf{p}) \right] \tag{12}$$

Equation (12) is a typical minimum cost bipartite assignment problem which can be solved by standard solvers, where the cost of each assignment pair $(\mathbf{p}, \mathbf{q})$ is associated with the weight of a bipartite graphos edge. Following [34], we formulate a sparse assignment problem and use the Goldbergos CSA package, which is the best known algorithms for min-cost sparse assignment [10,15]. Upon obtaining the mapping, one can recover $\hat{\mathbf{y}}$ through label realization.

However, solving Eq. (12) assumes an underlying relaxation where the search space contains m which may not follow the infimum requirement in Eq. (11). In other words, it may be possible that the minimization problem in Eq. (12) is an approximation to Eq. (11). The following theorem, however, proves the optimality of Eq. (12):

Theorem 1. *Given a solver that minimizes Eq. (12), the solution is also a minimizer of the problem in Eq. (11).*

Proof. We use contradiction to prove Theorem 1. Suppose there exists a solution of (12) where:

$$f_L(\mathbf{y}, m^*) = \hat{\mathbf{y}}, \ m^* \neq \arg\min_{m \in \mathcal{M}(\mathbf{y}^k, \hat{\mathbf{y}}^k)} \sum_{(\mathbf{p},\mathbf{q}) \in E_m} \frac{\|\mathbf{p} - \mathbf{q}\|^2}{2\sigma^2}$$

There must exist another mapping m' which satisfies:

$$f_L(\mathbf{y}, m') = \hat{\mathbf{y}}, \ \sum_{(\mathbf{p},\mathbf{q}) \in E_{m'}} \frac{\|\mathbf{p} - \mathbf{q}\|^2}{2\sigma^2} < \sum_{(\mathbf{p},\mathbf{q}) \in E_{m^*}} \frac{\|\mathbf{p} - \mathbf{q}\|^2}{2\sigma^2}$$

Since $f_L(\mathbf{y}, m') = f_L(\mathbf{y}, m^*) = \hat{\mathbf{y}}$, substituting m' to (12) leads to an even lower cost, which contradicts to the assumption that m^* is the minimizer of (12).

In practice, we follow the mini-batch SGD optimization, where $\hat{\mathbf{y}}$ of each image and $\mathbf{W}$ are both updated once in every batch. To begin with, $\hat{\mathbf{y}}$ is initialized as $\mathbf{y}$ for every image in the first batch. Basically, the optimization can be written as a loss layer in a network, and is fully compatible with end-to-end training.

4.5   Inference

We now consider the inference problem given a trained model. Ideally, the inference problem of the model trained by Eq. (2) would be the following:

$$\hat{\mathbf{y}}^* = \arg\max_{\hat{\mathbf{y}}} P(\mathbf{y}|\hat{\mathbf{y}})P(\hat{\mathbf{y}}|\mathbf{x}; \mathbf{W}) \tag{13}$$

(a) Isotropic Gaussian   (b) B.G.+MRF   (c) Illustration

Fig. 3. Examples of edge alignment using different priors and graphical illustration.

However, in cases where $\mathbf{y}$ is not available during testing. we can alternatively look into the second part of (2) which is the model learned under $\hat{\mathbf{y}}$:

$$\hat{\mathbf{y}}^* = \arg\max_{\hat{\mathbf{y}}} P(\hat{\mathbf{y}}|\mathbf{x}; \mathbf{W}) \tag{14}$$

Both cases can find real applications. In particular, (14) corresponds to general edge prediction, whereas (13) corresponds to refining noisy edge labels in a dataset. In the latter case, $\mathbf{y}$ is available and the inferred $\hat{\mathbf{y}}$ is used to output the refined label. In the experiment, we will show examples of both applications.

5   Biased Gaussian Kernel and Markov Prior

The task of SEAL turns out not easy, as it tends to generate artifacts upon having cluttered background. A major reason causing this failure is the fragmented aligned labels, as shown in Fig. 3(a). This is not surprising since we assume an isotropic Gaussian kernel, where labels tend to break and shift along the edges towards easy locations. In light of this issue, we assume that the edge prior follows a biased Gaussian (B.G.), with the long axis of the kernel perpendicular to local boundary tangent. Accordingly, such model encourages alignment perpendicular to edge tangents while suppressing shifts along them.

Another direction is to consider the Markov properties of edges. Good edge labels should be relatively continuous, and nearby alignment vectors should be similar. Taking these into consideration, we can model the edge prior as:

$$P(\mathbf{y}|\hat{\mathbf{y}}) \propto \sup_{m \in \mathcal{M}(\mathbf{y}, \hat{\mathbf{y}})} \prod_{(\mathbf{p}, \mathbf{q}) \in E_m} \exp(-\mathbf{m}_{\mathbf{q}}^\top \Sigma_{\mathbf{q}} \mathbf{m}_{\mathbf{q}}) \prod_{\substack{(\mathbf{u}, \mathbf{v}) \in E_m, \\ \mathbf{v} \in \mathcal{N}(\mathbf{q})}} \exp(-\lambda \|\mathbf{m}_{\mathbf{q}} - \mathbf{m}_{\mathbf{v}}\|^2) \tag{15}$$

where λ controls the strength of the smoothness. $\mathcal{N}(\mathbf{q})$ is the neighborhood of $\mathbf{q}$ defined by the geodesic distance along the edge. $\mathbf{m}_{\mathbf{q}} = \mathbf{p} - \mathbf{q}$, and $\mathbf{m}_{\mathbf{v}} = \mathbf{u} - \mathbf{v}$. An example of the improved alignment and a graphical illustration are shown in Figs. 3(b) and (c). In addition, the precision matrix $\Sigma_{\mathbf{q}}$ is defined as:

$$\Sigma_{\mathbf{q}} = \begin{bmatrix} \dfrac{\cos(\theta_{\mathbf{q}})^2}{2\sigma_x^2} + \dfrac{\sin(\theta_{\mathbf{q}})^2}{2\sigma_y^2} & \dfrac{\sin(2\theta_{\mathbf{q}})}{4\sigma_y^2} - \dfrac{\sin(2\theta_{\mathbf{q}})}{4*\sigma_x^2} \\ \dfrac{\sin(2\theta_{\mathbf{q}})}{4\sigma_y^2} - \dfrac{\sin(2\theta_{\mathbf{q}})}{4\sigma_x^2} & \dfrac{\sin(\theta_{\mathbf{q}})^2}{2\sigma_x^2} + \dfrac{\cos(\theta_{\mathbf{q}})^2}{2\sigma_y^2} \end{bmatrix}$$

where $\theta_\mathbf{q}$ is the angle between edge tangent and the positive x-axis, and σ_y corresponds to the kernel bandwidth perpendicular to the edge tangent. With the new prior, the alignment optimization becomes the following problem:

$$
\begin{aligned}
\min_{m\in\mathbf{M}}\ \mathcal{C}(m) &= \mathcal{C}_{Unary}(m) + \mathcal{C}_{Pair}(m) \\
&= \sum_{(\mathbf{p},\mathbf{q})\in E_m}\left[\mathbf{m}_\mathbf{q}^\top\mathbf{\Sigma}_\mathbf{q}\mathbf{m}_\mathbf{q} + \log((1-\sigma(\mathbf{p}))/\sigma(\mathbf{p}))\right] \\
&+ \lambda \sum_{(\mathbf{p},\mathbf{q})\in E_m}\sum_{\substack{(\mathbf{u},\mathbf{v})\in E_m,\\ \mathbf{v}\in\mathcal{N}(\mathbf{q})}}\|\mathbf{m}_\mathbf{q}-\mathbf{m}_\mathbf{v}\|^2
\end{aligned}
\tag{16}
$$

Note that Theorem 1 still holds for (16). However, solving (16) becomes more difficult as pairwise dependencies are included. As a result, standard assignment solvers can not be directly applied, and we alternatively decouple $\mathcal{C}_{Pair}$ as:

$$
\mathcal{C}_{Pair}(m, m') = \sum_{(\mathbf{p},\mathbf{q})\in E_m}\sum_{\substack{(\mathbf{u},\mathbf{v})\in E_{m'},\\ \mathbf{v}\in\mathcal{N}(\mathbf{q})}}\|\mathbf{m}_\mathbf{q}-\mathbf{m}_\mathbf{v}\|^2
\tag{17}
$$

and take the iterated conditional mode like iterative approximation where the alignment of neighboring pixels are taken from the alignment in previous round:

Initialize: $m^{(0)} = \arg\min_{m\in\mathbf{M}} \mathcal{C}_{Unary}(m)$

Assign: $m^{(t+1)} = \arg\min_{m\in\mathbf{M}} \mathcal{C}_{Unary}(m) + \mathcal{C}_{Pair}(m, m^{(t)})$

Update: $\mathcal{C}_{Pair}(m, m^{(t)}) \rightarrow \mathcal{C}_{Pair}(m, m^{(t+1)})$

where the **Assign** and **Update** steps are repeated multiple times. The algorithm converges very fast in practice. Usually two or even one **Assign** is sufficient.

6   Experimental Results

In this section, we comprehensively test the performance of SEAL on category-ware semantic edge detection, where the detector not only needs to localize object edges, but also classify to a predefined set of semantic classes.

6.1   Backbone Network

In order to guarantee fair comparison across different methods, a fixed backbone network is needed for controlled evaluation. We choose CASENet [52] since it is the current state of the art on our task. For additional implementation details such as choice of hyperparameters, please refer to the supplementary material.

Table 1. Results on the SBD test set. MF scores are measured by %.

Metric	Method	aero	bike	bird	boat	bottle	bus	car	cat	chair	cow	table	dog	horse	mbike	person	plant	sheep	sofa	train	tv	mean
MF (Thin)	CASENet	83.6	75.3	82.3	63.1	70.5	83.5	76.5	82.6	56.8	76.3	47.5	80.8	80.9	75.6	80.7	54.1	77.7	52.3	77.9	68.0	72.3
	CASENet-S	**84.5**	**76.5**	**83.7**	**65.3**	71.3	**83.9**	**78.3**	84.5	**58.8**	76.8	50.8	81.9	**82.3**	**77.2**	82.7	**55.9**	78.1	54.0	**79.5**	69.4	**73.8**
	CASENet-C	83.9	71.1	82.5	62.6	71.0	82.2	76.8	83.4	56.5	**76.9**	49.2	81.0	81.1	75.4	81.4	54.0	**78.5**	53.3	77.1	67.0	72.2
	SEAL	**84.5**	**76.5**	**83.7**	64.9	**71.7**	83.8	78.1	**85.0**	**58.8**	76.6	**50.9**	**82.4**	82.2	77.1	**83.0**	55.1	78.4	**54.4**	79.3	**69.6**	**73.8**
MF (Raw)	CASENet	71.8	60.2	72.6	49.5	59.3	73.3	65.2	70.8	51.9	64.9	41.2	67.9	72.5	64.1	71.2	44.0	71.7	45.7	65.4	55.8	62.0
	CASENet-S	75.8	65.0	78.4	56.2	64.7	76.4	71.8	75.2	55.2	68.7	45.8	72.8	77.0	68.1	76.5	47.1	75.5	49.0	70.2	60.6	66.5
	CASENet-C	80.4	67.1	79.9	57.9	65.9	77.6	72.6	79.2	53.5	72.7	45.5	76.7	79.4	71.2	78.3	**50.8**	77.6	50.7	71.6	61.6	68.5
	SEAL	**81.1**	**69.6**	**81.7**	**60.6**	**68.0**	**80.5**	**75.1**	**80.7**	**57.0**	**73.1**	**48.1**	**78.2**	**80.3**	**72.1**	**79.8**	50.0	**78.2**	**51.8**	**74.6**	**65.0**	**70.3**

6.2 Evaluation Benchmarks

We follow [17] to evaluate edges with class-wise precision recall curves. However, the benchmarks of our work differ from [17] by imposing considerably stricter rules. In particular: 1. We consider non-suppressed edges inside an object as false positives, while [17] ignores these pixels. 2. We accumulate false positives on any image, while the benchmark code from [17] only accumulates false positives of a certain class on images containing that class. Our benchmark can also be regarded as a multiclass extension of the BSDS benchmark [34].

Both [17] and [34] by default thin the prediction before matching. We propose to match the raw predictions with unthinned ground truths whose width is kept the same as training labels. The benchmark therefore also considers the local quality of predictions. We refer to this mode as "Raw" and the previous conventional mode as "Thin". Similar to [34], both settings use maximum F-Measure (MF) at optimal dataset scale (ODS) to evaluate the performance.

Another difference between the problem settings of our work and [17] is that we consider edges between any two instances as positive, even though the instances may belong to the same class. This differs from [17] where such edges are ignored. Our motivation on making such changes is two fold: 1. We believe instance-sensitive edges are important and it makes better sense to distinguish these locations. 2. The instance-sensitive setting may better benefit other potential applications where instances need to be distinguished.

6.3 Experiment on the SBD Dataset

The Semantic Boundary Dataset (SBD) [17] contains 11355 images from the trainval set of PASCAL VOC2011 [14], with 8498 images divided as training set and 2857 images as test set. The dataset contains both category-level and instance-level semantic segmentation annotations, with semantic classes defined following the 20 class definitions in PASCAL VOC.

Table 2. Results on the SBD test set (re-annotated). MF scores are measured by %.

Metric	Method	aero	bike	bird	boat	bottle	bus	car	cat	chair	cow	table	dog	horse	mbike	person	plant	sheep	sofa	train	tv	mean
MF (Thin)	CASENet	74.5	59.7	73.4	48.0	67.1	78.6	67.3	76.2	47.5	69.7	36.2	75.7	72.7	61.3	74.8	42.6	71.8	48.9	71.7	54.9	63.6
	CASENet-S	75.9	62.4	75.5	52.0	66.7	79.7	**71.0**	79.0	**50.1**	70.0	39.8	77.2	74.5	65.0	77.0	47.3	72.7	51.5	72.9	57.3	65.9
	CASENet-C	**78.4**	60.9	74.9	49.7	64.4	75.8	67.2	77.1	48.2	71.2	40.9	76.1	72.9	64.5	75.9	**51.4**	71.3	51.6	68.6	55.4	64.8
	SEAL	78.0	**65.8**	**76.6**	**52.4**	**68.6**	**80.0**	70.4	**79.4**	50.0	**72.8**	**41.4**	**78.1**	**75.0**	**65.5**	**78.5**	49.4	**73.3**	**52.2**	**73.9**	**58.1**	**67.0**
MF (Raw)	CASENet	65.8	51.5	65.0	43.1	57.5	68.1	58.2	66.0	45.4	59.8	32.9	64.2	65.8	52.6	65.7	40.9	65.0	42.9	61.4	47.8	56.0
	CASENet-S	68.9	55.8	70.9	47.4	62.0	71.5	64.7	71.2	48.0	64.8	37.3	69.1	68.9	58.2	70.2	44.3	68.7	46.1	65.8	52.5	60.3
	CASENet-C	**75.4**	57.7	73.0	48.7	62.1	72.2	64.4	74.3	46.8	68.8	38.8	73.4	71.4	**62.2**	72.1	**50.3**	69.8	48.4	66.1	53.0	62.4
	SEAL	75.3	**60.5**	**75.1**	**51.2**	65.4	**76.1**	**67.9**	**75.9**	49.7	**69.5**	39.9	**74.8**	**72.7**	62.1	**74.2**	48.4	**72.3**	49.3	**70.6**	**56.7**	**64.4**

Parameter Analysis. We set $\sigma_x = 1$ and $\sigma_y > \sigma_x$ to favor alignment perpendicular to edge tangents. Details on the validation of σ_y and λ are in supplementary.

Results on SBD Test Set. We compare SEAL with CASENet, CASENet trained with regular sigmoid cross-entropy loss (CASENet-S), and CASENet-S trained on labels refined by dense-CRF following [50] (CASENet-C), with the results visualized in Fig. 5 and quantified in Table 1. Results show that SEAL is on par with CASENet-S under "Thin" setting, while significantly outperforms all other baselines when edge sharpness is taken into account.

Results on Re-annotated SBD Test Set. A closer analysis shows that SEAL actually outperforms CASENet-S considerably under the "Thin" setting. The original SBD labels turns out to be noisy, which can influence the validity of evaluation. We re-annotated more than 1000 images on SBD test set using LabelMe [41], and report evaluation using these high-quality labels in Table 2. Results indicates that SEAL outperforms CASENet-S in both settings.

Results of SBD GT Refinement. We output the SEAL aligned labels and compare against both dense-CRF and original annotation. We match the aligned labels with re-annotated labels by varying the tolerance threshold and generating F-Measure scores. Figure 4 shows that SEAL indeed can improve the label quality, while dense-CRF performs even worse than original labels. In fact, the result of CASENet-C also indicates the decreased model performance.

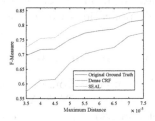

Fig. 4. MF vs. tolerance.

Non-Instance-Insensitive (non-IS) Mode. We also train/evaluate under non-IS mode, with the evaluation using re-annotated SBD labels. Table 3 shows that the scores have high correlation with IS mode.

Table 3. Non-IS results.

Mode	CNet	CNet-S	CNet-C	SEAL
Thin	63.6	66.4	64.7	**66.9**
Raw	56.1	60.6	62.1	**64.6**

Table 4. Results on SBD test following the same benchmark and ground truths as [52].

Method	aero	bike	bird	boat	bottle	bus	car	cat	chair	cow	table	dog	horse	mbike	person	plant	sheep	sofa	train	tv	mean
[52]	83.3	76.0	80.7	63.4	69.2	81.3	74.9	83.2	54.3	74.8	46.4	80.3	80.2	76.6	80.8	53.3	77.2	50.1	75.9	66.8	71.4
SEAL	**84.9**	**78.6**	**84.6**	**66.2**	**71.3**	**83.0**	**76.5**	**87.2**	**57.6**	**77.5**	**53.0**	**83.5**	**82.2**	**78.3**	**85.1**	**58.7**	**78.9**	**53.1**	**77.7**	**69.7**	**74.4**

Table 5. Results on the Cityscapes dataset. MF scores are measured by %.

Metric	Method	road	sidewalk	building	wall	fence	pole	t-light	t-sign	veg	terrain	sky	person	rider	car	truck	bus	train	motor	bike	mean
MF (Thin)	CASENet	86.2	74.9	74.5	47.6	**46.5**	72.8	70.0	73.3	79.3	57.0	86.5	80.4	66.8	88.3	49.3	64.6	**47.8**	**55.8**	71.9	68.1
	CASENet-S	**87.6**	77.1	**75.9**	**48.7**	46.2	**75.5**	**71.4**	75.3	80.6	59.7	86.8	81.4	68.1	**89.2**	**50.7**	**68.0**	42.5	54.6	72.7	**69.1**
	SEAL	**87.6**	**77.5**	**75.9**	47.6	46.3	**75.5**	71.2	**75.4**	**80.9**	**60.1**	**87.4**	**81.5**	**68.9**	88.9	50.2	67.8	44.1	52.7	**73.0**	**69.1**
MF (Raw)	CASENet	66.8	64.6	66.8	39.4	40.6	71.7	64.2	65.1	71.1	50.2	80.3	73.1	58.6	77.0	42.0	53.2	39.1	46.1	62.2	59.6
	CASENet-S	79.2	70.8	70.4	42.5	42.4	73.9	66.7	68.2	74.6	54.6	82.5	75.7	61.5	82.7	46.0	59.7	39.1	47.0	64.8	63.3
	SEAL	**84.4**	**73.5**	**72.7**	**43.4**	**43.2**	**76.1**	**68.5**	**69.8**	**77.2**	**57.5**	**85.3**	**77.6**	**63.6**	**84.9**	**48.6**	**61.9**	**41.2**	**49.0**	**66.7**	**65.5**

Comparison with State of the Art. Although proposing different evaluation criteria, we still follow [52] by training SEAL with instance-insensitive labels and evaluating with the same benchmark and ground truths. Results in Table 4 show that this work outperforms previous state of the art by a significant margin.

6.4 Experiment on the Cityscapes Dataset

Results on Validation Set. The Cityscapes dataset contains 2975 training images and 500 images as validation set. Following [52], we train SEAL on the training set and test on the validation set, with the results visualized in Fig. 6 and quantified in Table 5. Again, SEAL overall outperforms all comparing baselines.

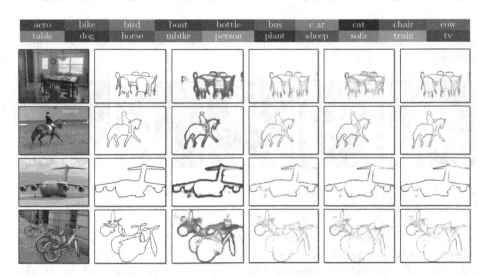

Fig. 5. Qualitative comparison among ground truth, CASENet, CASENet-S, CASENet-C, and SEAL (ordering from left to right). Best viewed in color. (Color figure online)

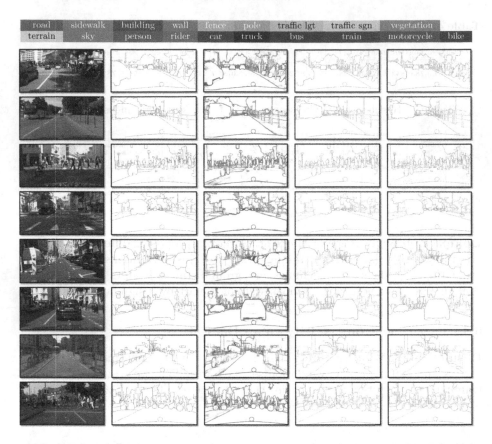

road	sidewalk	building	wall	fence	pole	traffic lgt	traffic sgn	vegetation
terrain	sky	person	rider	car	truck	bus	train	motorcycle	bike

Fig. 6. Qualitative comparison among ground truth, CASENet, CASENet-S, and SEAL (ordering from left to right in the figure). Best viewed in color. (Color figure online)

Fig. 7. Edge alignment on Cityscapes. Color coding follows Fig. 2. Best viewed in color. (Color figure online)

Alignment Visualization. We show that misalignment can still be found on Cityscapes. Figure 7 shows misaligned labels and the corrections made by SEAL.

7 Concluding Remarks

In this paper, we proposed SEAL: an end-to-end learning framework for joint edge alignment and learning. Our work considers a novel pixel-level noisy label learning problem, levering structured priors to address an open issue in edge learning. Extensive experiments demonstrate that the proposed framework is able to correct noisy labels and generate sharp edges with better quality.

References

1. Arbeláez, P., Maire, M., Fowlkes, C., Malik, J.: Contour detection and hierarchical image segmentation. IEEE Trans. PAMI **33**(5), 898–916 (2011)
2. Arbeláez, P., Pont-Tuset, J., Barron, J., Marques, F., Malik, J.: Multiscale combinatorial grouping. In: CVPR (2014)
3. Bertasius, G., Shi, J., Torresani, L.: Deepedge: a multiscale bifurcated deep network for top-down contour detection. In: CVPR (2015)
4. Bertasius, G., Shi, J., Torresani, L.: High-for-low, low-for-high: efficient boundary detection from deep object features and its applications to high-level vision. In: ICCV (2015)
5. Bertasius, G., Shi, J., Torresani, L.: Semantic segmentation with boundary neural fields. In: CVPR (2016)
6. Bilmes, J.: On virtual evidence and soft evidence in Bayesian networks. Technical report (2004)
7. Canny, J.: A computational approach to edge detection. IEEE Trans. PAMI **6**, 679–698 (1986)
8. Castrejón, L., Kundu, K., Urtasun, R., Fidler, S.: Annotating object instances with a polygon-RNN. In: CVPR (2017)
9. Chen, L.C., Barron, J.T., Papandreou, G., Murphy, K., Yuille, A.L.: Semantic image segmentation with task-specific edge detection using CNNS and a discriminatively trained domain transform. In: CVPR (2016)
10. Cherkassky, B.V., Goldberg, A.V.: On implementing push-relabel method for the maximum flow problem. In: Balas, E., Clausen, J. (eds.) IPCO 1995. LNCS, vol. 920, pp. 157–171. Springer, Heidelberg (1995). https://doi.org/10.1007/3-540-59408-6_49
11. Cordts, M., et al.: The Cityscapes dataset for semantic urban scene understanding. In: CVPR (2016)
12. Dollar, P., Tu, Z., Belongie, S.: Supervised learning of edges and object boundaries. In: CVPR (2006)
13. Dollár, P., Zitnick, C.L.: Fast edge detection using structured forests. IEEE Trans. PAMI **37**(8), 1558–1570 (2015)
14. Everingham, M., Van Gool, L., Williams, C.K.I., Winn, J., Zisserman, A.: The PASCAL visual object classes challenge 2011 (VOC2011) results. http://www.pascal-network.org/challenges/VOC/voc2011/workshop/index.html
15. Goldberg, A.V., Kennedy, R.: An efficient cost scaling algorithm for the assignment problem. SIAM J. Discrete Math. (1993)
16. Hancock, E.R., Kittler, J.: Edge-labeling using dictionary-based relaxation. IEEE Trans. PAMI **12**(2), 165–181 (1990)
17. Hariharan, B., Arbeláez, P., Bourdev, L., Maji, S., Malik, J.: Semantic contours from inverse detectors. In: ICCV (2011)

18. He, K., Zhang, X., Ren, S., Sun, J.: Deep residual learning for image recognition. In: CVPR (2016)
19. Hoiem, D., Efros, A.A., Hebert, M.: Geometric context from a single image. In: ICCV (2005)
20. Hwang, J., Liu, T.L.: Pixel-wise deep learning for contour detection. In: ICLR (2015)
21. Karsch, K., Liao, Z., Rock, J., Barron, J.T., Hoiem, D.: Boundary cues for 3D object shape recovery. In: CVPR (2013)
22. Khoreva, A., Benenson, R., Omran, M., Hein, M., Schiele, B.: Weakly supervised object boundaries. In: CVPR (2016)
23. Kittler, J.: On the accuracy of the sobel edge detector. Image Vis. Comput. $\mathbf{1}(1)$, 37–42 (1983)
24. Kokkinos, I.: Pushing the boundaries of boundary detection using deep learning (2016)
25. Konishi, S., Yuille, A.L., Coughlan, J.M., Zhu, S.C.: Statistical edge detection: learning and evaluating edge cues. IEEE Trans. PAMI $\mathbf{25}(1)$, 57–74 (2003)
26. Krizhevsky, A., Sutskever, I., Hinton, G.E.: ImageNet classification with deep convolutional neural networks. In: NIPS (2012)
27. Li, Y., Yang, J., Song, Y., Cao, L., Luo, J., Li, L.J.: Learning from noisy labels with distillation. In: CVPR (2017)
28. Liao, L., Choudhury, T., Fox, D., Kautz, H.A.: Training conditional random fields using virtual evidence boosting. In: IJCAI (2007)
29. Lim, J., Zitnick, C., Dollar, P.: Sketch tokens: a learned mid-level representation for contour and object detection. In: CVPR (2013)
30. Liu, Y., Cheng, M.M., Hu, X., Wang, K., Bai, X.: Richer convolutional features for edge detection. In: CVPR (2017)
31. Maire, M., Yu, S.X., Perona, P.: Reconstructive sparse code transfer for contour detection and semantic labeling. In: Cremers, D., Reid, I., Saito, H., Yang, M.-H. (eds.) ACCV 2014. LNCS, vol. 9006, pp. 273–287. Springer, Cham (2015). https://doi.org/10.1007/978-3-319-16817-3_18
32. Malik, J.: Interpreting line drawings of curved objects. Int. J. Comput. Vis. $\mathbf{1}(1)$, 73–103 (1987)
33. Malik, J., Maydan, D.: Recovering three-dimensional shape from a single image of curved objects. IEEE Trans. PAMI $\mathbf{11}(6)$, 555–566 (1989)
34. Martin, D.R., Fowlkes, C.C., Malik, J.: Learning to detect natural image boundaries using local brightness, color, and texture cues. IEEE Trans. PAMI $\mathbf{26}(5)$, 530–549 (2004)
35. Patrini, G., Rozza, A., Menon, A.K., Nock, R., Qu, L.: Making deep neural networks robust to label noise: a loss correction approach. In: CVPR (2017)
36. Pearl, J.: Probabilistic reasoning in intelligent systems: networks of plausible inference (1988)
37. Pinheiro, P.O., Collobert, R., Dollár, P.: Learning to segment object candidates. In: NIPS (2015)
38. Prasad, M., Zisserman, A., Fitzgibbon, A., Kumar, M.P., Torr, P.H.S.: Learning class-specific edges for object detection and segmentation. In: Kalra, P.K., Peleg, S. (eds.) ICVGIP 2006. LNCS, vol. 4338, pp. 94–105. Springer, Heidelberg (2006). https://doi.org/10.1007/11949619_9
39. Ren, X., Fowlkes, C.C., Malik, J.: Learning probabilistic models for contour completion in natural images. Int. J. Comput. Vis. $\mathbf{77}(1$–$3)$, 47–63 (2008)
40. Rupprecht, C., Huaroc, E., Baust, M., Navab, N.: Deep active contours. arXiv preprint arXiv:1607.05074 (2016)

41. Russell, B.C., Torralba, A., Murphy, K.P., Freeman, W.T.: Labelme: a database and web-based tool for image annotation. IJCV **77**(1–3), 157–173 (2008)
42. Shan, Q., Curless, B., Furukawa, Y., Hernandez, C., Seitz, S.: Occluding contours for multi-view stereo. In: CVPR (2014)
43. Simonyan, K., Zisserman, A.: Very deep convolutional networks for large-scale image recognition. In: ICLR (2015)
44. Sugihara, K.: Machine Interpretation of Line Drawings. MIT Press, Wiley (1986)
45. Vahdat, A.: Toward robustness against label noise in training deep discriminative neural networks. In: NIPS (2017)
46. Veit, A., Alldrin, N., Chechik, G., Krasin, I., Gupta, A., Belongie, S.: Learning from noisy large-scale datasets with minimal supervision. In: CVPR (2017)
47. Wang, Y., et al.: Iterative learning with open-set noisy labels. In: CVPR (2018)
48. Xiao, T., Xia, T., Yang, Y., Huang, C., Wang, X.: Learning from massive noisy labeled data for image classification. In: CVPR (2015)
49. Xie, S., Tu, Z.: Holistically-nested edge detection. In: ICCV (2015)
50. Yang, J., Price, B., Cohen, S., Lee, H., Yang, M.H.: Object contour detection with a fully convolutional encoder-decoder network. In: CVPR (2016)
51. Yu, Z., Liu, W., Liu, W., Peng, X., Hui, Z., Kumar, B.V.: Generalized transitive distance with minimum spanning random forest. In: IJCAI (2015)
52. Yu, Z., Feng, C., Liu, M.Y., Ramalingam, S.: CaseNet: deep category-aware semantic edge detection. In: CVPR (2017)
53. Zitnick, C.L., Dollár, P.: Edge boxes: locating object proposals from edges. In: Fleet, D., Pajdla, T., Schiele, B., Tuytelaars, T. (eds.) ECCV 2014. LNCS, vol. 8693, pp. 391–405. Springer, Cham (2014). https://doi.org/10.1007/978-3-319-10602-1_26

ICNet for Real-Time Semantic Segmentation on High-Resolution Images

Hengshuang Zhao[1]([✉]), Xiaojuan Qi[1], Xiaoyong Shen[2], Jianping Shi[3],
and Jiaya Jia[1,2]

[1] The Chinese University of Hong Kong, Shatin, Hong Kong
{hszhao,xjqi,leojia}@cse.cuhk.edu.hk
[2] Tencent Youtu Lab, Shenzhen, China
dylanshen@tencent.com
[3] SenseTime Research, Beijing, China
shijianping@sensetime.com

Abstract. We focus on the challenging task of real-time semantic segmentation in this paper. It finds many practical applications and yet is with fundamental difficulty of reducing a large portion of computation for pixel-wise label inference. We propose an image cascade network (ICNet) that incorporates multi-resolution branches under proper label guidance to address this challenge. We provide in-depth analysis of our framework and introduce the cascade feature fusion unit to quickly achieve high-quality segmentation. Our system yields real-time inference on a single GPU card with decent quality results evaluated on challenging datasets like Cityscapes, CamVid and COCO-Stuff.

Keywords: Real-time · High-resolution · Semantic segmentation

1 Introduction

Semantic image segmentation is a fundamental task in computer vision. It predicts dense labels for all pixels in the image, and is regarded as a very important task that can help deep understanding of scene, objects, and human. Development of recent deep *convolutional neural networks* (CNNs) makes remarkable progress on semantic segmentation [1–6]. The effectiveness of these networks largely depends on the sophisticated model design regarding depth and width, which has to involve many operations and parameters.

CNN-based semantic segmentation mainly exploits *fully convolutional networks* (FCNs). It is common wisdom now that increase of result accuracy almost means more operations, especially for pixel-level prediction tasks like semantic segmentation. To illustrate it, we show in Fig. 1(a) the accuracy and inference time of different frameworks on Cityscapes [7] dataset.

Electronic supplementary material The online version of this chapter (https://doi.org/10.1007/978-3-030-01219-9_25) contains supplementary material, which is available to authorized users.

V. Ferrari et al. (Eds.): ECCV 2018, LNCS 11207, pp. 418–434, 2018.
https://doi.org/10.1007/978-3-030-01219-9_25

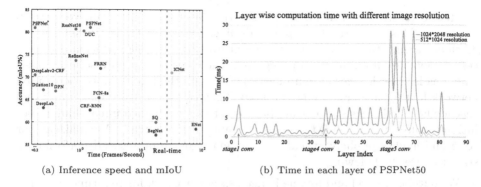

(a) Inference speed and mIoU

(b) Time in each layer of PSPNet50

Fig. 1. (a): Inference speed and mIoU performance on Cityscapes [7] test set. Methods involved are PSPNet [5], ResNet38 [6], DUC [10], RefineNet [11], FRRN [12], DeepLabv2-CRF [13], Dilation10 [14], DPN [15], FCN-8s [1], DeepLab [2], CRF-RNN [16], SQ [9], ENet [8], SegNet [3], and our ICNet. (b): Time spent on PSPNet50 with dilation 8 for two input images. Roughly running time is proportional to the pixel number and kernel number. (Blue ones are tested with downsampled images. Inference speed is reported with single network forward while accuracy of several mIoU aimed approaches (like PSPNet*) may contain testing tricks like multi-scale and flipping, resulting much more time. See supplementary material for detailed information.) (Color figure online)

Status of Fast Semantic Segmentation. Contrary to the extraordinary development of high-quality semantic segmentation, research along the line to make semantic segmentation run *fast* while not sacrificing too much quality is left behind. We note actually this line of work is similarly important since it can inspire or enable many practical tasks in, for example, automatic driving, robotic interaction, online video processing, and even mobile computing where running time becomes a critical factor to evaluate system performance.

Our experiments show that high-accuracy methods of ResNet38 [6] and PSPNet [5] take around 1 second to predict a 1024 × 2048 high-resolution image on one Nvidia TitanX GPU card during testing. These methods fall into the area illustrated in Fig. 1(a) with high accuracy and low speed. Recent fast semantic segmentation methods of ENet [8] and SQ [9], contrarily, take quite different positions in the plot. The speed is much accelerated; but accuracy drops, where the final mIoUs are lower than 60%. These methods are located in the lower right phase in the figure.

Our Focus and Contributions. In this paper, we focus on building a practically fast semantic segmentation system with decent prediction accuracy. Our method is the first in its kind to locate in the top-right area shown in Fig. 1(a) and is one of the only two available real-time approaches. It achieves decent trade-off between efficiency and accuracy.

Different from previous architectures, we make comprehensive consideration on the two factors of speed and accuracy that are seemingly contracting. We first make in-depth analysis of time budget in semantic segmentation frameworks and conduct extensive experiments to demonstrate insufficiency of intuitive speedup strategies. This motivates development of *image cascade network* (ICNet), a high efficiency segmentation system with decent quality. It exploits efficiency of processing low-resolution images and high inference quality of high-resolution ones. The idea is to let low-resolution images go through the full semantic perception network first for a coarse prediction map. Then cascade feature fusion unit and cascade label guidance strategy are proposed to integrate medium and high resolution features, which refine the coarse semantic map gradually. We make all our code and models publicly available[1]. Our main contributions and performance statistics are the following.

- We develop a novel and unique image cascade network for real-time semantic segmentation, it utilizes semantic information in low resolution along with details from high-resolution images efficiently.
- The developed cascade feature fusion unit together with cascade label guidance can recover and refine segmentation prediction progressively with a low computation cost.
- Our ICNet achieves 5× speedup of inference time, and reduces memory consumption by 5× times. It can run at high resolution 1024 × 2048 in speed of 30 fps while accomplishing high-quality results. It yields real-time inference on various datasets including Cityscapes [7], CamVid [17] and COCO-Stuff [18].

2 Related Work

Traditional semantic segmentation methods [19] adopt handcrafted feature to learn the representation. Recently, CNN based methods largely improve the performance.

High Quality Semantic Segmentation. FCN [1] is the pioneer work to replace the last fully-connected layers in classification with convolution layers. DeepLab [2,13] and [14] used dilated convolution to enlarge the receptive field for dense labeling. Encoder-decoder structures [3,4] can combine the high-level semantic information from later layers with the spatial information from earlier ones. Multi-scale feature ensembles are also used in [20–22]. In [2,15,16], conditional random fields (CRF) or Markov random fields (MRF) were used to model spatial relationship. Zhao *et al.* [5] used pyramid pooling to aggregate global and local context information. Wu *et al.* [6] adopted a wider network to boost performance. In [11], a multi-path refinement network combined multi-scale image features. These methods are effective, but preclude real-time inference.

High Efficiency Semantic Segmentation. In object detection, speed became one important factor in system design [23,24]. Recent Yolo [25,26] and SSD [27] are representative solutions. In contrast, high speed inference in semantic segmentation is under-explored. ENet [8] and [28] are lightweight networks. These methods greatly raise efficiency with notably sacrificed accuracy.

---

[1] https://github.com/hszhao/ICNet.

Video Semantic Segmentation. Videos contain redundant information in frames, which can be utilized to reduce computation. Recent Clockwork [29] reuses feature maps given stable video input. Deep feature flow [30] is based on a small-scale optical flow network to propagate features from key frames to others. FSO [31] performs structured prediction with dense CRF applied on optimized features to get temporal consistent predictions. NetWarp [32] utilizes optical flow of adjacent frames to warp internal features across time space in video sequences. We note when a good-accuracy fast image semantic-segmentation framework comes into existence, video segmentation will also be benefited.

3   Image Cascade Network

We start by analyzing computation time budget of different components on the high performance segmentation framework PSPNet [5] with experimental statistics. Then we introduce the *image cascade network* (ICNet) as illustrated in Fig. 2, along with the cascade feature fusion unit and cascade label guidance, for fast semantic segmentation.

3.1   Speed Analysis

In convolution, the transformation function Φ is applied to input feature map $V \in \mathbb{R}^{c \times h \times w}$ to obtain the output map $U \in \mathbb{R}^{c' \times h' \times w'}$, where c, h and w denote features channel, height and width respectively. The transformation operation $\Phi : V \to U$ is achieved by applying c' number of 3D kernels $K \in \mathbb{R}^{c \times k \times k}$ where $k \times k$ (e.g, 3×3) is kernel spatial size. Thus the total number of operations $O(\Phi)$ in convolution layer is $c' c k^2 h' w'$. The spatial size of the output map h' and w' are highly related to the input, controlled by parameter stride s as $h' = h/s, w' = w/s$, making

$$O(\Phi) \approx c' c k^2 h w / s^2. \tag{1}$$

The computation complexity is associated with feature map resolution (e.g., h, w, s), number of kernels and network width (e.g., c, c'). Figure 1(b) shows the time cost of two resolution images in PSPNet50. Blue curve corresponds to high-resolution input with size 1024×2048 and green curve is for image with resolution 512×1024. Computation increases squarely regarding image resolution. For either curve, feature maps in stage4 and stage5 are with the same spatial resolution, i.e., $1/8$ of the original input; but the computation in stage5 is four times heavier than that in stage4. It is because convolutional layers in stage5 double the number of kernels c together with input channel c'.

3.2   Network Architecture

According to above time budget analysis, we adopt intuitive speedup strategies in experiments to be detailed in Sect. 5, including downsampling input, shrinking feature maps and conducting model compression. The corresponding results

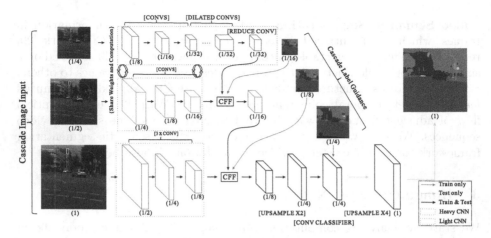

Fig. 2. Network architecture of ICNet. 'CFF' stands for cascade feature fusion detailed in Sect. 3.3. Numbers in parentheses are feature map size ratios to the full-resolution input. Operations are highlighted in brackets. The final ×4 upsampling in the bottom branch is only used during testing.

show that it is very difficult to keep a good balance between inference accuracy and speed. The intuitive strategies are effective to reduce running time, while they yield very coarse prediction maps. Directly feeding high-resolution images into a network is unbearable in computation.

Our proposed system *image cascade network* (ICNet) does not simply choose either way. Instead it takes cascade image inputs (i.e., low-, medium- and high-resolution images), adopts cascade feature fusion unit (Sect. 3.3) and is trained with cascade label guidance (Sect. 3.4). The new architecture is illustrated in Fig. 2. The input image with full resolution (e.g., 1024 × 2048 in Cityscapes [7]) is downsampled by factors of 2 and 4, forming cascade input to medium- and high-resolution branches.

Segmenting the high-resolution input with classical frameworks like FCN directly is time consuming. To overcome this shortcoming, we get semantic extraction using low-resolution input as shown in top branch of Fig. 2. A 1/4 sized image is fed into PSPNet with downsampling rate 8, resulting in a 1/32-resolution feature map. To get high quality segmentation, medium and high resolution branches (middle and bottom parts in Fig. 2) help recover and refine the coarse prediction. Though some details are missing and blurry boundaries are generated in the top branch, it already harvests most semantic parts. Thus we can safely limit the number of parameters in both middle and bottom branches. Light weighted CNNs (green dotted box) are adopted in higher resolution branches; different-branch output feature maps are fused by cascade-feature-fusion unit (Sect. 3.3) and trained with cascade label guidance (Sect. 3.4).

Although the top branch is based on a full segmentation backbone, the input resolution is low, resulting in limited computation. Even for PSPNet with 50+ layers, inference time and memory are 18 ms and 0.6 GB for the large images in Cityscapes. Because weights and computation (in 17 layers) can be shared between low- and medium-branches, only 6ms is spent to construct the fusion map. Bottom branch has even less layers. Although the resolution is high, inference only takes 9 ms. Details of the architecture are presented in the supplementary file. With all these three branches, our ICNet becomes a very efficient and memory friendly architecture that can achieve good-quality segmentation.

3.3   Cascade Feature Fusion

To combine cascade features from different-resolution inputs, we propose a cascade feature fusion (CFF) unit as shown in Fig. 3. The input to this unit contains three components: two feature maps F_1 and F_2 with sizes $C_1 \times H_1 \times W_1$ and $C_2 \times H_2 \times W_2$ respectively, and a ground-truth label with resolution $1 \times H_2 \times W_2$. F_2 is with doubled spatial size of F_1.

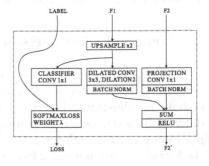

Fig. 3. Cascade feature fusion.

We first apply upsampling rate 2 on F_1 through bilinear interpolation, yielding the same spatial size as F_2. Then a dilated convolution layer with kernel size $C_3 \times 3 \times 3$ and dilation 2 is applied to refine the upsampled features. The resulting feature is with size $C_3 \times H_2 \times W_2$. This dilated convolution combines feature information from several originally neighboring pixels. Compared with deconvolution, upsampling followed by dilated convolution only needs small kernels, to harvest the same receptive field. To keep the same receptive field, deconvolution needs larger kernel sizes than upsampling with dilated convolution (i.e., 7×7 vs. 3×3), which causes more computation.

For feature F_2, a projection convolution with kernel size $C_3 \times 1 \times 1$ is utilized to project F_2 so that it has the same number of channels as the output of F_1. Then two batch normalization layers are used to normalize these two processed features as shown in Fig. 3. Followed by an element-wise 'sum' layer and a 'ReLU' layer, we obtain the fused feature F_2' as $C_3 \times H_2 \times W_2$. To enhance learning of F_1, we use an auxiliary label guidance on the upsampled feature of F_1.

3.4   Cascade Label Guidance

To enhance the learning procedure in each branch, we adopt a cascade label guidance strategy. It utilizes different-scale (e.g., 1/16, 1/8, and 1/4) ground-truth labels to guide the learning stage of low, medium and high resolution input. Given $\mathcal{T}$ branches (i.e., $\mathcal{T} = 3$) and $\mathcal{N}$ categories. In branch t, the predicted feature map $\mathcal{F}^t$ has spatial size $\mathcal{Y}_t \times \mathcal{X}_t$. The value at position (n, y, x) is $\mathcal{F}^t_{n,y,x}$. The corresponding ground truth label for 2D position (y, x) is $\hat{n}$. To train ICNet, we append weighted softmax cross entropy loss in each branch with related loss weight λ_t. Thus we minimize the loss function $\mathcal{L}$ defined as

$$\mathcal{L} = -\sum_{t=1}^{\mathcal{T}} \lambda_t \frac{1}{\mathcal{Y}_t \mathcal{X}_t} \sum_{y=1}^{\mathcal{Y}_t} \sum_{x=1}^{\mathcal{X}_t} \log \frac{e^{\mathcal{F}^t_{\hat{n},y,x}}}{\sum_{n=1}^{\mathcal{N}} e^{\mathcal{F}^t_{n,y,x}}}. \tag{2}$$

In the testing phase, the low and medium guidance operations are simply abandoned, where only high-resolution branch is retained. This strategy makes gradient optimization smoother for easy training. With more powerful learning ability in each branch, the final prediction map is not dominated by any single branch.

4   Structure Comparison and Analysis

Now we illustrate the difference of ICNet from existing cascade architectures for semantic segmentation. Typical structures in previous semantic segmentation systems are illustrated in Fig. 4. Our proposed ICNet (Fig. 4(d)) is by nature different from others. Previous frameworks are all with relatively intensive computation given the high-resolution input. While in our cascade structure, only the lowest-resolution input is fed into the heavy CNN with much reduced computation to get the coarse semantic prediction. The higher-res inputs are designed to recover and refine the prediction progressively regarding blurred boundaries and missing details. Thus they are processed by light-weighted CNNs. Newly introduced cascade-feature-fusion unit and cascade label guidance strategy integrate medium and high resolution features to refine the coarse semantic map gradually. In this special design, ICNet achieves high-efficiency inference with reasonable-quality segmentation results.

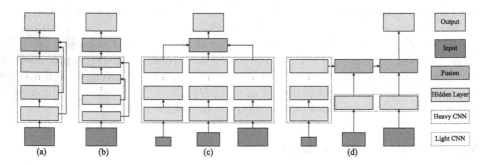

Fig. 4. Comparison of semantic segmentation frameworks. (a) Intermediate skip connection used by FCN [1] and Hypercolumns [21]. (b) Encoder-decoder structure incorporated in SegNet [3], DeconvNet [4], UNet [33], ENet [8], and step-wise reconstruction & refinement from LRR [34] and RefineNet [11]. (c) Multi-scale prediction ensemble adopted by DeepLab-MSC [2] and PSPNet-MSC [5]. (d) Our ICNet architecture.

5   Experimental Evaluation

Our method is effective for high resolution images. We evaluate the architecture on three challenging datasets, including urban-scene understanding dataset Cityscapes [7] with image resolution 1024×2048, CamVid [17] with image resolution 720×960 and stuff understanding dataset COCO-Stuff [18] with image resolution up to 640×640. There is a notable difference between COCO-Stuff and object/scene segmentation datasets of VOC2012 [35] and ADE20K [36]. In the latter two sets, most images are of low resolution (e.g., 300×500), which can already be processed quickly. While in COCO-Stuff, most images are larger, making it more difficult to achieve real-time performance.

In the following, we first show intuitive speedup strategies and their drawbacks, then reveal our improvement with quantitative and visual analysis.

5.1   Implementation Details

We conduct experiments based on platform Caffe [37]. All experiments are on a workstation with Maxwell TitanX GPU cards under CUDA 7.5 and CUDNN V5. Our testing uses only one card. To measure the forward inference time, we use the time measure tool 'Caffe time' and set the repeating iteration number to 100 to eliminate accidental errors during testing. All the parameters in batch normalization layers are merged into the neighboring front convolution layers.

For the training hyper-parameters, the mini-batch size is set to 16. The base learning rate is 0.01 and the 'poly' learning rate policy is adopted with power 0.9, together with the maximum iteration number set to 30K for Cityscapes, 10K for CamVid and 30K for COCO-Stuff. Momentum is 0.9 and weight decay is 0.0001. Data augmentation contains random mirror and rand resizing between 0.5 and 2. The auxiliary loss weights are empirically set to 0.4 for λ_1 and λ_2, 1 for λ_3 in Eq. 2, as adopted in [5]. For evaluation, both *mean of class-wise intersection over union* (mIoU) and *network forward time* (Time) are used.

5.2   Cityscapes

We first apply our framework to the recent urban scene understanding dataset Cityscapes [7]. This dataset contains high-resolution 1024×2048 images, which make it a big challenge for fast semantic segmentation. It contains 5,000 finely annotated images split into training, validation and testing sets with 2,975, 500, and 1,525 images respectively. The dense annotation contains 30 common classes of road, person, car, etc. 19 of them are used in training and testing.

Intuitive Speedup. According to the time complexity shown in Eq. (1), we do intuitive speedup in three aspects, namely downsampling input, downsampling feature, and model compression.

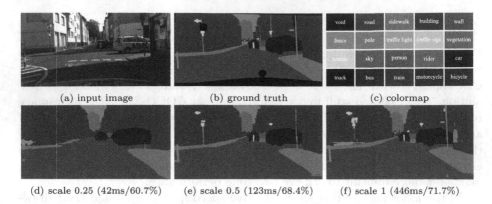

(a) input image   (b) ground truth   (c) colormap

(d) scale 0.25 (42ms/60.7%)   (e) scale 0.5 (123ms/68.4%)   (f) scale 1 (446ms/71.7%)

Fig. 5. Downsampling input: prediction of PSPNet50 on the validation set of Cityscapes. Values in the parentheses are the inference time and mIoU.

Table 1. Left: Downsampling feature with factors 8, 16 and 32. Right: model compression with kernel keeping rates 1, 0.5 and 0.25.

Downsample Size	8	16	32
mIoU (%)	71.7	70.2	67.1
Time (ms)	446	177	131

Kernel Keeping Rates	1	0.5	0.25
mIoU (%)	71.7	67.9	59.4
Time (ms)	446	170	72

Downsampling Input. Image resolution is the most critical factor that affects running speed as analyzed in Sect. 3.1. A simple approach is to use the small-resolution image as input. We test downsampling the image with ratios 1/2 and 1/4, and feeding the resulting images into PSPNet50. We directly upsample prediction results to the original size. This approach empirically has several drawbacks as illustrated in Fig. 5. With scaling ratio 0.25, although the inference time is reduced by a large margin, the prediction map is very coarse, missing many small but important details compared to the higher resolution prediction. With scaling ratio 0.5, the prediction recovers more information compared to the 0.25 case. Unfortunately, the person and traffic light far from the camera are still missing and object boundaries are blurred. To make things worse, the running time is still too long for a real-time system.

Downsampling Feature. Besides directly downsampling the input image, another simple choice is to scale down the feature map by a large ratio in the inference process. FCN [1] downsampled it for 32 times and DeepLab [2] did that for 8 times. We test PSPNet50 with downsampling ratios of 1:8, 1:16 and 1:32 and show results in the left of Table 1. A smaller feature map can yield faster inference at the cost of sacrificing prediction accuracy. The lost information is mostly detail contained in low-level layers. Also, even with the smallest resulting feature map under ratio 1:32, the system still takes 131ms in inference.

Table 2. Performance of ICNet with different branches on validation set of Citysapes. The baseline method is PSPNet50 compressed to a half. 'sub4', 'sub24' and 'sub124' represent predictions in low-, medium-, and high-resolution branches respectively.

Items	Baseline	sub4	sub24	sub124
mIoU (%)	67.9	59.6	66.5	**67.7**
Time (ms)	170	18	25	33
Frame (fps)	5.9	55.6	40	**30.3**
Speedup	1×	9.4×	6.8×	**5.2×**
Memory (GB)	9.2	0.6	1.1	1.6
Memory save	1×	15.3×	8.4×	**5.8×**

Table 3. Effectiveness of cascade feature fusion unit (CFF) and cascade label guidance (CLG). 'DC3', 'DC5' and 'DC7' denote replacing 'bilinear upsampling + dilated convolution' with deconvolution operation with kernels 3×3, 5×5 and 7×7 respectively.

DC3	DC5	DC7	CFF	CLG	mIoU (%)	Time (ms)
✓				✓	66.7	31
	✓			✓	66.7	34
		✓		✓	68.0	38
			✓	✓	**67.7**	**33**
			✓		66.8	33

Model Compression. Apart from the above two strategies, another natural way to reduce network complexity is to trim kernels in each layer. Compressing models becomes an active research topic in recent years due to the high demand. The solutions [38–41] can make a complicated network reduce to a lighter one under user-controlled accuracy reduction. We adopt recent effective classification model compression strategy presented in [41] on our segmentation models. For each filter, we first calculate the sum of kernel ℓ_1-norm. Then we sort these sum results in a descending order and keep only the most significant ones. Disappointingly, this strategy also does not meet our requirement given the compressed models listed in the right of Table 1. Even by keeping only a quarter of kernels, the inference time is still too long. Meanwhile the corresponding mIoU is intolerably low – it already cannot produce reasonable segmentation for many applications.

Cascade Branches. We do ablation study on cascade branches, the results are shown in Table 2. Our baseline is the half-compressed PSPNet50, 170 ms inference time is yielded with mIoU reducing to 67.9%. They indicate that model compression has almost no chance to achieve real-time performance under the condition of keeping decent segmentation quality. Based on this baseline, we test our ICNet on different branches. To show the effectiveness of the proposed

Table 4. Predicted mIoU and inference time on Cityscapes test set with image resolution 1024×2048. 'DR' stands for image downsampling ratio during testing (e.g, DR = 4 represents testing at resolution 256×512). Methods trained using both fine and coarse data are marked with '†'.

Method	DR	mIoU (%)	Time (ms)	Frame (fps)
SegNet [3]	4	57.0	60	16.7
ENet [8]	2	58.3	13	76.9
SQ [9]	No	59.8	60	16.7
CRF-RNN [16]	2	62.5	700	1.4
DeepLab [2]	2	63.1	4000	0.25
FCN-8S [1]	No	65.3	500	2
Dilation10 [14]	No	67.1	4000	0.25
FRRN [12]	2	71.8	469	2.1
PSPNet[a] [5]	No	81.2	1288	0.78
ICNet	No	**69.5**	**33**	**30.3**
ICNet†	No	**70.6**	**33**	**30.3**

[a]Single network forward costs 1288 ms (with TitanX Maxwell, 680 ms for Pascal) while mIoU aimed testing for boosting performance (81.2% mIoU) costs 51.0 s

cascade framework, we denote the outputs of low-, medium- and high-resolution branches as 'sub4', 'sub24' and 'sub124', where the numbers stand for the information used. The setting 'sub4' only uses the top branch with the low-resolution input. 'sub24' and 'sub124' respectively contain top two and all three branches.

We test these three settings on the validation set of Cityscapes and list the results in Table 2. With just the low-resolution input branch, although running time is short, the result quality drops to 59.6%. Using two and three branches, we increase mIoU to 66.5% and 67.7% respectively. The running time only increases by 7ms and 8ms. Note our segmentation quality nearly stays the same as the baseline, and yet is 5.2× times faster. The memory consumption is significantly reduced by 5.8×.

Cascade Structure. We also do ablation study on cascade feature fusion unit and cascade label guidance. The results are shown in Table 3. Compared to the deconvolution layer with 3×3 and 5×5 kernels, with similar inference efficiency, cascade feature fusion unit gets higher mIoU performance. Compared to deconvolution layer with a larger kernel with size 7×7, the mIoU performance is close, while cascade feature fusion unit yields faster processing speed. Without the cascade label guidance, the performance drops a lot as shown in the last row.

Methods Comparison. We finally list mIoU performance and inference time of our proposed ICNet on the test set of Cityscapes. It is trained on training and

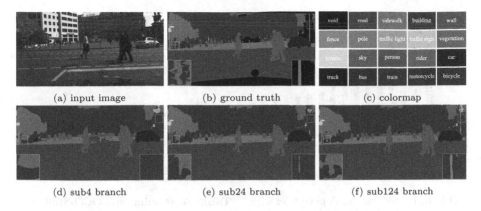

Fig. 6. Visual prediction improvement of ICNet in each branch on Cityscapes dataset.

validation sets of Cityscapes for 90K iterations. Results are included in Table 4. The reported mIoUs and running time of other methods are shown in the official Cityscapes leadboard. For fairness, we do not include methods without reporting running time. Many of these methods may have adopted time-consuming multi-scale testing for the best result quality.

Our ICNet yields mIoU 69.5%. It is even quantitatively better than several methods that do not care about speed. It is about 10 points higher than ENet [8] and SQ [9]. Training with both fine and coarse data boosts mIoU performance to 70.6%. ICNet is a 30 fps method on 1024×2048 resolution images using only one TitanX GPU card. Video example can be accessed through link[2].

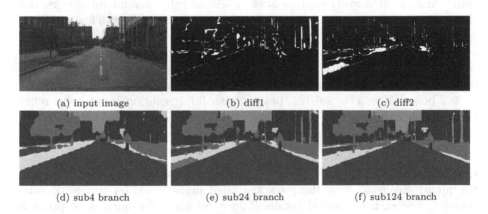

Fig. 7. Visual prediction improvement of ICNet. White regions in 'diff1' and 'diff2' denote prediction difference between 'sub24' and 'sub4', and between 'sub124' and 'sub24' respectively. (Color figure online)

---

[2] https://youtu.be/qWl9idsCuLQ.

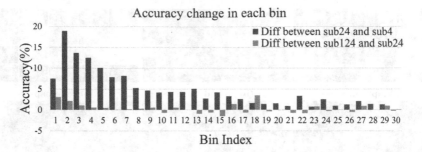

Fig. 8. Quantitative analysis of accuracy change in connected components.

Table 5. Results on CamVid test set with time reported on resolution 720 × 960.

Method	mIoU (%)	Time (ms)	Frame fps
SegNet [3]	46.4	217	4.6
DPN [15]	60.1	830	1.2
DeepLab [2]	61.6	203	4.9
Dilation8 [14]	65.3	227	4.4
PSPNet50 [5]	69.1	185	5.4
ICNet	**67.1**	**36**	**27.8**

Table 6. Results on COCO-Stuff test set with time reported on resolution 640 × 640.

Method	mIoU (%)	Time (ms)	Frame fps
FCN [1]	22.7	169	5.9
DeepLab [2]	26.9	124	8.1
PSPNet50 [5]	32.6	151	6.6
ICNet	**29.1**	**28**	**35.7**

Visual Improvement Figures 6 and 7 show the visual results of ICNet on Cityscapes. With proposed gradual feature fusion steps and cascade label guidance structure, we produce decent prediction results. Intriguingly, output of the 'sub4' branch can already capture most of semantically meaningful objects. But the prediction is coarse due to the low-resolution input. It misses a few small-size important regions, such as poles and traffic signs.

With the help of medium-resolution information, many of these regions are re-estimated and recovered as shown in the 'sub24' branch. It is noticeable that objects far from the camera, such as a few persons, are still missing with blurry object boundaries. The 'sub124' branch with full-resolution input helps refine these details – the output of this branch is undoubted the best. It manifests that our different-resolution information is properly made use of in this framework.

Quantitative Analysis. To further understand accuracy gain in each branch, we quantitatively analyze the predicted label maps based on connected components. For each connected region R_i, we calculate the number of pixels it contains, denoted as S_i. Then we count the number of pixels correctly predicted in the corresponding map as s_i. The predicted region accuracy p_i in R_i is thus s_i/S_i. According to the region size S_i, we project these regions onto a histogram $\mathcal{H}$ with interval $\mathcal{K}$ and average all related region accuracy p_i as the value of current bin.

In experiments, we set bin size of the histogram as 30 and interval K as 3,000. It thus covers region size S_i between 1 to 90K. We ignore regions with size exceeding 90K. Figure 8 shows the accuracy change in each bin. The blue histogram stands for the difference between 'sub24' and 'sub4' while the green histogram shows the difference between 'sub124' and 'sub24'. For both histograms, the large difference is mainly on the front bins with small region sizes. This manifests that small region objects like traffic light and pole can be well improved in our framework. The front changes are large positives, proving that 'sub24' can restore much information on small objects on top of 'sub4'. 'sub124' is also very useful compared to 'sub24'.

5.3 CamVid

CamVid [17] dataset contains images extracted from high resolution video sequences with resolution up to 720 × 960. For easy comparison with prior work, we adopt the split of Sturgess et al. [42], which partitions the dataset into 367, 100, and 233 images for training, validation and testing respectively. 11 semantic classes are used for evaluation.

The testing results are listed in Table 5, our base-model is no compressed PSPNet50. ICNet gets much faster inference speed than other methods on this high resolution, reaching the real-time speed of 27.8 fps, 5.7 times faster than the second one and 5.1 times faster compared to the basic model. Apart from high efficiency, it also accomplishes high quality segmentation. Visual results are provided in the supplementary material.

5.4 COCO-Stuff

COCO-Stuff [18] is a recently labeled dataset based on MS-COCO [43] for stuff segmentation in context. We evaluate ICNet following the split in [18] that 9 K images are used for training and another 1 K for testing. This dataset is much more complex for multiple categories – up to 182 classes are used for evaluation, including 91 thing and 91 stuff classes.

Table 6 shows the testing results. ICNet still performs satisfyingly regarding common thing and stuff understanding. It is more efficient and accurate than modern segmentation frameworks, such as FCN and DeepLab. Compared to our baseline model, it achieves 5.4 times speedup. Visual predictions are provided in the supplementary material.

6 Conclusion

We have proposed a real-time semantic segmentation system ICNet. It incorporates effective strategies to accelerate network inference speed without sacrificing much performance. The major contributions include the new framework for saving operations in multiple resolutions and the powerful fusion unit.

We believe the optimal balance of speed and accuracy makes our system important since it can benefit many other tasks that require fast scene and object segmentation. It greatly enhances the practicality of semantic segmentation in other disciplines.

References

1. Long, J., Shelhamer, E., Darrell, T.: Fully convolutional networks for semantic segmentation. In: CVPR (2015)
2. Chen, L., Papandreou, G., Kokkinos, I., Murphy, K., Yuille, A.L.: Semantic image segmentation with deep convolutional nets and fully connected CRFs. In: ICLR (2015)
3. Badrinarayanan, V., Kendall, A., Cipolla, R.: SegNet: a deep convolutional encoder-decoder architecture for image segmentation. arXiv:1511.00561 (2015)
4. Noh, H., Hong, S., Han, B.: Learning deconvolution network for semantic segmentation. In: ICCV (2015)
5. Zhao, H., Shi, J., Qi, X., Wang, X., Jia, J.: Pyramid scene parsing network. In: CVPR (2017)
6. Wu, Z., Shen, C., van den Hengel, A.: Wider or deeper: revisiting the ResNet model for visual recognition. arXiv:1611.10080 (2016)
7. Cordts, M., et al.: The cityscapes dataset for semantic urban scene understanding. In: CVPR (2016)
8. Paszke, A., Chaurasia, A., Kim, S., Culurciello, E.: ENet: a deep neural network architecture for real-time semantic segmentation. arXiv:1606.02147 (2016)
9. Treml, M., et al.: Speeding up semantic segmentation for autonomous driving. In: NIPS Workshop (2016)
10. Wang, P., et al.: Understanding convolution for semantic segmentation. arXiv:1702.08502 (2017)
11. Lin, G., Milan, A., Shen, C., Reid, I.D.: RefineNet: multi-path refinement networks for high-resolution semantic segmentation. In: CVPR (2017)
12. Pohlen, T., Hermans, A., Mathias, M., Leibe, B.: Full-resolution residual networks for semantic segmentation in street scenes. In: CVPR (2017)
13. Chen, L., Papandreou, G., Kokkinos, I., Murphy, K., Yuille, A.L.: DeepLab: semantic image segmentation with deep convolutional nets, atrous convolution, and fully connected CRFs. arXiv:1606.00915 (2016)
14. Yu, F., Koltun, V.: Multi-scale context aggregation by dilated convolutions. In: ICLR (2016)
15. Liu, Z., Li, X., Luo, P., Loy, C.C., Tang, X.: Semantic image segmentation via deep parsing network. In: ICCV (2015)
16. Zheng, S., et al.: Conditional random fields as recurrent neural networks. In: ICCV (2015)
17. Brostow, G.J., Fauqueur, J., Cipolla, R.: Semantic object classes in video: a high-definition ground truth database. Pattern Recognit. Lett. **30**, 88–97 (2009)
18. Caesar, H., Uijlings, J., Ferrari, V.: Coco-stuff: thing and stuff classes in context. arXiv:1612.03716 (2016)
19. Liu, C., Yuen, J., Torralba, A.: Nonparametric scene parsing via label transfer. TPAMI **33**, 2368–2382 (2011)
20. Chen, L., Yang, Y., Wang, J., Xu, W., Yuille, A.L.: Attention to scale: scale-aware semantic image segmentation. In: CVPR (2016)

21. Hariharan, B., Arbeláez, P.A., Girshick, R.B., Malik, J.: Hypercolumns for object segmentation and fine-grained localization. In: CVPR (2015)
22. Xia, F., Wang, P., Chen, L.-C., Yuille, A.L.: Zoom better to see clearer: human and object parsing with hierarchical auto-zoom net. In: Leibe, B., Matas, J., Sebe, N., Welling, M. (eds.) ECCV 2016. LNCS, vol. 9909, pp. 648–663. Springer, Cham (2016). https://doi.org/10.1007/978-3-319-46454-1_39
23. Girshick, R.: Fast R-CNN. In: ICCV (2015)
24. Ren, S., He, K., Girshick, R., Sun, J.: Faster R-CNN: towards real-time object detection with region proposal networks. In: NIPS. (2015)
25. Redmon, J., Divvala, S.K., Girshick, R.B., Farhadi, A.: You only look once: unified, real-time object detection. In: CVPR (2016)
26. Redmon, J., Farhadi, A.: YOLO9000: better, faster, stronger. In: CVPR (2017)
27. Liu, W., et al.: SSD: single shot multibox detector. In: Leibe, B., Matas, J., Sebe, N., Welling, M. (eds.) ECCV 2016. LNCS, vol. 9905, pp. 21–37. Springer, Cham (2016). https://doi.org/10.1007/978-3-319-46448-0_2
28. Romera, E., Alvarez, J.M., Bergasa, L.M., Arroyo, R.: Efficient ConvNet for real-time semantic segmentation. In: Intelligent Vehicles Symposium (IV) (2017)
29. Shelhamer, E., Rakelly, K., Hoffman, J., Darrell, T.: Clockwork convnets for video semantic segmentation. In: Hua, G., Jégou, H. (eds.) ECCV 2016. LNCS, vol. 9915, pp. 852–868. Springer, Cham (2016). https://doi.org/10.1007/978-3-319-49409-8_69
30. Zhu, X., Xiong, Y., Dai, J., Yuan, L., Wei, Y.: Deep feature flow for video recognition. In: CVPR (2017)
31. Kundu, A., Vineet, V., Koltun, V.: Feature space optimization for semantic video segmentation. In: CVPR (2016)
32. Gadde, R., Jampani, V., Gehler, P.V.: Semantic video CNNs through representation warping. In: ICCV (2017)
33. Ronneberger, O., Fischer, P., Brox, T.: U-net: convolutional networks for biomedical image segmentation. In: Navab, N., Hornegger, J., Wells, W.M., Frangi, A.F. (eds.) MICCAI 2015. LNCS, vol. 9351, pp. 234–241. Springer, Cham (2015). https://doi.org/10.1007/978-3-319-24574-4_28
34. Ghiasi, G., Fowlkes, C.C.: Laplacian pyramid reconstruction and refinement for semantic segmentation. In: Leibe, B., Matas, J., Sebe, N., Welling, M. (eds.) ECCV 2016. LNCS, vol. 9907, pp. 519–534. Springer, Cham (2016). https://doi.org/10.1007/978-3-319-46487-9_32
35. Everingham, M., Gool, L.J.V., Williams, C.K.I., Winn, J.M., Zisserman, A.: The pascal visual object classes VOC challenge. IJCV **88**, 303–338 (2010)
36. Zhou, B., Zhao, H., Puig, X., Fidler, S., Barriuso, A., Torralba, A.: Semantic understanding of scenes through the ADE20K dataset. arXiv:1608.05442 (2016)
37. Jia, Y., et al.: Caffe: convolutional architecture for fast feature embedding. In: ACM MM (2014)
38. Iandola, F.N., Moskewicz, M.W., Ashraf, K., Han, S., Dally, W.J., Keutzer, K.: SqueezeNet: AlexNet-level accuracy with 50x fewer parameters and <1mb model size. arXiv:1602.07360 (2016)
39. Han, S., Mao, H., Dally, W.J.: Deep compression: compressing deep neural network with pruning, trained quantization and Huffman coding. In: ICLR (2016)
40. Han, S., et al.: DSD: regularizing deep neural networks with dense-sparse-dense training flow. In: ICLR (2017)
41. Li, H., Kadav, A., Durdanovic, I., Samet, H., Graf, H.P.: Pruning filters for efficient convnets. In: ICLR (2017)

42. Sturgess, P., Alahari, K., Ladicky, L., Torr, P.H.: Combining appearance and structure from motion features for road scene understanding. In: BMVC (2009)
43. Lin, T.-Y.: Microsoft COCO: common objects in context. In: Fleet, D., Pajdla, T., Schiele, B., Tuytelaars, T. (eds.) ECCV 2014. LNCS, vol. 8693, pp. 740–755. Springer, Cham (2014). https://doi.org/10.1007/978-3-319-10602-1_48

Part-Activated Deep Reinforcement Learning for Action Prediction

Lei Chen[1], Jiwen Lu[2(✉)], Zhanjie Song[1], and Jie Zhou[2]

[1] Tianjin University, Tianjin, China
{chen_lei,zhanjiesong}@tju.edu.cn
[2] Tsinghua University, Beijing, China
{lujiwen,jzhou}@tsinghua.edu.cn

Abstract. In this paper, we propose a part-activated deep reinforcement learning (PA-DRL) method for action prediction. Most existing methods for action prediction utilize the evolution of whole frames to model actions, which cannot avoid the noise of the current action, especially in the early prediction. Moreover, the loss of structural information of human body diminishes the capacity of features to describe actions. To address this, we design the PA-DRL to exploit the structure of the human body by extracting skeleton proposals under a deep reinforcement learning framework. Specifically, we extract features from different parts of the human body individually and activate the action-related parts in features to enhance the representation. Our method not only exploits the structure information of the human body, but also considers the saliency part for expressing actions. We evaluate our method on three popular action prediction datasets: UT-Interaction, BIT-Interaction and UCF101. Our experimental results demonstrate that our method achieves the performance with state-of-the-arts.

Keywords: Action prediction · Deep reinforcement learning Skeleton · Part model

1 Introduction

Human activity analysis has aroused much attention in computer vision due to its broad prospects of applications [8,17,19,29,36]. As an important branch of human activity analysis, predicting the activity of humans presents importance in a number of real-world applications, such as video detection [43], abnormal behavior detection [7,40] and robot interaction [36]. In spite of the enormous amount of works conducted in this area [21,25,26], this task is still challenging due to the fundamental challenges inherent in the problem like the large variance among the activities and huge spatiotemporal scale variation. Recognizing the action in the full length video is too luxury to wait for the whole video completed [44]. For example, predicting the falling down of human can save the person as early as possible. Different from action recognition [4,5,34,35,41,42,46,47],

© Springer Nature Switzerland AG 2018
V. Ferrari et al. (Eds.): ECCV 2018, LNCS 11207, pp. 435–451, 2018.
https://doi.org/10.1007/978-3-030-01219-9_26

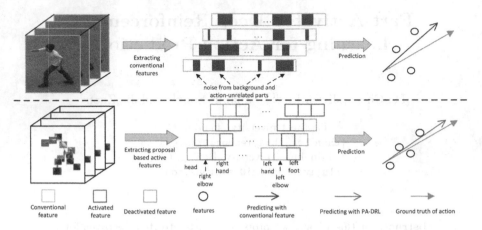

Fig. 1. The advantage of PA-DRL in representing the evolution of the action. Top: the features are extracted by the conventional methods with noise, which disturbs the action prediction. The gray parts in the feature are noise which are introduced by feature extraction and push the features far away from the evolution direction of the actual actions. Bottom: our method is to purify the feature from noise with considering the structure of the human body. Moreover, we activate the action-related parts for action prediction to pull the feature of frames to the direction of action evolution. (Best viewed in color)

action prediction aims to take full advantage of the partially observed video for predicting the action as early as possible. Action prediction [31] is defined as the inference of the ongoing activities of humans just with observing the partial videos or sequences, when the action has not been completed.

It is challenging to model the process of the partially observed action in both spatial and temporal domain for predicting the ongoing actions [16]. The majority of the existing action prediction works can be mainly divided into two categories: exploiting reliable features with template matching [2,20,44] and developing classification models [14,16,31,33]. Approaches in the first category aim to design a template-based model for the prediction. However, these templates are easily affected by the outliers and perform poorly when actors present large pose variations. Methods in the second category focus on discovering temporal characteristics of human actions, because the confidence of prediction increases with more frames gradually observed. However, most existing methods extract holistic features of frames to exploit the temporal information, which ignores the essential structural information of the human body. The challenge of action prediction is that the useful information of predicting actions is very limited, but the redundant information has strong ability of disturbing the prediction. The top of Fig. 1 shows that the conventional features extracting from the whole frame captures the noise, which disturbs the action prediction.

To address the above limitations, we present a part-activated deep reinforcement learning method for action prediction. The bottom of Fig. 1 shows the main process of activating the action-related parts. Based on the structural information of the human body by skeleton proposals, we activate the action-related parts of human body and deactivate the noise parts by deep reinforcement learning. Depending on the skeleton of the human body, our method extracts features in the region proposals which are decided by the joints of skeleton. Then we concatenate the features in order to keep the structural information of the body. For different actions, our method attends the action-related parts of features. Our proposed method learns a part-activated policy for activating and deactivating the parts of features with the deep reinforcement learning. Experimental results on three benchmarks demonstrate the effectiveness of our proposed approach.

2 Related Work

Action Prediction: Simply modeling action prediction as an ensemble of action classification is non-optimal. Conventional action recognition methods hold the assumption that the temporal information of an activity is complete, while only partial temporal information of an action is observed in action prediction. Most existing methods for action prediction can be divided into two categories: exploiting reliable features and developing classification models. For the first category, most existing methods design a template for action prediction. For example, Ryoo [31] proposed the integral bag-of-words (IBoW) and dynamic bag-of-words (DBoW) approaches for action prediction. The action model of every progress level is computed by averaging features of a particular progress level with the same category. The model suffers from the difficulty with the situation that the videos of the same action have a large variation in the spatial domain and it is sensitive to the outliers. Lan *et al.* [20] exploited templates at multiple levels of granularities in a hierarchical representation, which can capture and compare human movements at different context levels. For the second category, methods focus on exploiting the temporal information of human actions. For example, Cao *et al.* [2] designed an action prediction model with sparse coding to learn the features and reconstructed the testing partial videos with the bases extracted from the training activities. In their model, they addressed the problem of the intra-class action variations with bases from long-short segments. Kong *et al.* [16] proposed a multiple temporal scale support vector machine (MTSSVM) for action prediction and they took full advantage of the evolution of segments. Ma *et al.* [24] proposed a hybrid Siamese network with three branches to jointly learn both the future label and the starting time. They found that using more frames yielded high prediction performance. However, most existing methods try to capture the temporal information through the duration of partially observed actions, which ignore the importance of structural information of the human body for action representation.

Deep Reinforcement Learning: Recently, the field of reinforcement learning resurrects with the strong support from deep learning [13,18,45]. Deep reinforcement learning effectively learns the better policy than the supervised way for challenge tasks [22] and it can be divided into two main architectures:

Q-network and policy gradient. Deep reinforcement learning technique is introduced to optimize the sequential model with delayed reward [23] and performs very promising results in a series of problems. For example, Mnih *et al.* [28] achieved the human-level performance in the Atari game with their proposed deep Q-networks. Goodrich *et al.* [6] designed an architecture with 32 actions to shift the focal point and reward the agent when finding the goal. Caicedo *et al.* [1] defined a transformations set for the bounding box as the action of agent and rewarded the agent when the bounding box moves close to the ground-truth with iterations. More recently, deep reinforcement learning has been applied in many computer vision tasks [9–11,27,38]. For example, Krull *et al.* [18] applied a policy gradient approach to the object pose estimation problem. Kong *et al.* [13] proposed a novel multi-agent Q-learning solution that facilitates learnable inter-agent communication with gated cross connections between the Q-networks. Ren *et al.* [30] presented a novel decision-making framework for image captioning utilizing a policy network and a value network. However, little progress has been made in reinforcement learning for activity analysis, especially in action prediction. In this work, we develop a part-activated deep reinforcement learning model to learn the policy of activating the attention parts of the human body for predicting the unfinished actions.

3   Approach

In this section, we first show the pipeline of our part-activated deep reinforcement learning (PA-DRL) method for action prediction. Then we describe our proposed skeletal proposal for extracting features of actions. Lastly, we detail the method of our part-activated deep reinforcement learning method.

Figure 2 shows the pipeline of our action prediction architecture and we first utilize the skeleton extracted by [3] to extract proposal. To take advantage of the information of the partial sequence, we provide the proposal for extracting the action features. To predict the action effectively, we design a two-step architecture to activate the original features extracted from the frames of videos.

- We extract those features in local patches of skeleton proposals which are decided by the joints of the skeleton. The extracted features contain action-related information and are used as the candidates for part-activating. Then we concatenate the features from the same frame in the order of the skeleton to keep the structural information of human body.
- We active the most related parts in features by learning the part-activated strategy with deep reinforcement learning. The activated parts of consequent frames enhance the action-related information in both spatial and temporal domain, which reduces the distance between the predicting action and the actual action in feature space.

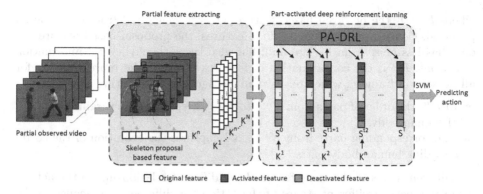

Fig. 2. The pipeline of our PA-DRL. The aim of our PA-DRL is to predict the ongoing actions based on the frames at the beginning of the action. The input are partially observed videos and sequences. We extract the skeleton proposal based features from every frame. Then our PA-DRL activates action-related parts of features frame by frame with deep reinforcement learning. The activated parts of features capture the action-related information, which are used for predicting the actions.

3.1   Partial Feature Extraction

To solve the problem for the lack of apparent information of the skeleton, we use the skeleton as a proposal to select a local patch around the joint points. We extract apparent features in the local patches to provide spatial information for the structure of human body. The local patch extracted by joints of skeleton in our architecture is denoted as the skeleton proposal. The skeleton proposal carries two parts of information:

- The patches are extracted from images and contain the apparent information around the joints.
- The concatenating order of features keeps the structural information of human body.

All patches in the skeleton proposal are decided by the skeleton joints and the order of the concatenated feature keeps the structure of skeleton.

We define the operation of concatenating the features as $\Gamma(\cdot)$. We propose our skeleton proposal for video-based action prediction. Thus the input of our method are videos and sequences. For a video, the number of observed frames is defined as N. In every frame, the index of persons are indicated as p and the total number of people is P. The skeletons of people are defined by their indexes $\{S_1, S_2, ..., S_p, ..., S_P\}$. We assume that the skeleton has E joints that can be represented as $\{J_{S_p,1}, J_{S_p,2}, ..., J_{S_p,e}, ..., J_{S_p,E}\}$. Then we extract features based on joints of the skeleton, which is denoted by $F_{J_{p,e}}^n$. To keep the structure of skeleton, we concatenate the features in the order from 1 to E for one person. $U = P \times E$ represents the total number of parts in the state. For the nth frame, we formulate the concatenation of features as follows:

$$K^n = \Gamma_{p \in P}(\Gamma_{e \in E}(F_{J_{p,e}}^n)) = \Gamma_{u \in U}(F_{J_u}^n), \tag{1}$$

where $F^n_{J_{p,e}}$ is the proposal based feature which is generated from the skeleton proposal. Comparing with the original features, the proposal-based feature not only has less noise from background, but also keeps the structural information of actions. K^n is the concatenation of features denoting the representation for all persons in frame n, which has two advantages on representing the video:

- In K^n, the order of parts from $F^n_{J_{1,1}}$ to $F^n_{J_{P,E}}$ keeps the structural information of human body.
- The corresponding parts from K^1 to K^n captures the evolution of the corresponding human body parts.

Different parts in the same feature have different relationship to the action. The same part in different stages of the action has different significance in the whole action. For example, during the action of *boxing*, most of the joints of skeleton are moving. The joints at elbows and hands are positive for understanding the action of *boxing*. But the joints on feet disturb the representation of features. To address the problem of the noise from the unrelated parts for actions, we propose a part-activated deep reinforcement learning method to select the saliency parts of features on the human body.

3.2   Part-Activated Deep Reinforcement Learning

For action prediction, we use the partially observed videos to recognize the action. The number of observed frames is much less than the whole video. Our aim is to predict the ongoing action as early as possible. With a few frames at the beginning of the action, it is very essential to take fully advantage of action-related parts and to reduce interference of noise. We propose part-activated deep reinforcement learning method (PA-DRL) to active the action-related parts. The architecture of our method is based on the actor-critic. For every frame, there exists not "ground-truth" of action-related part. However, our PA-DRL is to learn the policy of activating the action-related parts only with the label of the action. Based on the deep reinforcement learning, PA-DRL makes a series of decisions to get the holistic optimal result for activating the action-related parts.

Figure 3 shows the part-activated process of our method with observed frames. As shown in this figure, the red points represent the activated parts in the feature. With the starting frames of the action, the noise pushes the features away from the actual action in feature space, which makes the predicting evolutionary direction (yellow arrow) away from the actual evolutionary direction (black line of dashes). PA-DRL deactivates the parts with lager distance and pull features close to the actual action. The green points are the action-unrelated parts in features and are deactivated by our PA-DRL. The part-activated features predict a new evolutionary direction to represent the action, which is close to the actual action. PA-DRL deactivates some parts of the feature and changes the prediction result with deep reinforcement learning.

Problem Settings: To activate and deactivate parts in the feature, we have to confirm the relationship between parts and the action. However, it is hard to

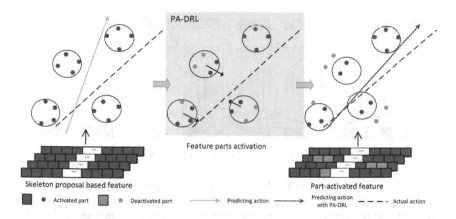

Fig. 3. The PA-DRL for feature parts activation. The red points represent the activated parts in corresponding features. The large black circle represents the whole feature which is decided by the all activated parts in the feature. The black circles from left to right reflect the temporal evolution of the action. Yellow arrow is the predicting evolutionary direction of the action. Black dashed line is the actual evolutionary direction of the action. (Color figure online)

obtain all labels of activation and deactivation for every part in skeleton proposal based features. Different from conventional supervised deep learning methods, our PA-DRL aims to learn the policy for activating the action-related parts and deactivate the noise without labels of all parts. Based on the deep reinforcement leaning, our PA-DRL has three important elements: state, action and reward. To distinguish the action in the prediction task and the action in the learning architecture, we use *action* for the action in the learning architecture instead.

We define the *action* space Λ with two types of action for every part of state S_w^t. We denote the *action* $a_{u,w}^t \in \Lambda$ for the part $\beta_{u,w}^t$. Two types of *action* in action space Λ are activation and deactivation. For $\beta_{u,w}^t$, the *action* of activation can be represented by a vector of 1 with the same dimension of $\beta_{u,w}^t$. Similarly, the *action* deactivation can be represented by a vector of 0. Then we represent concatenated *action* A_w^t for state S_w^t as follows:

$$A_w^t = [a_{1,w}^t, ..., a_{U,w}^t], a_{u,w}^t \in \{1^b, 0^b\}, \tag{2}$$

where b is the dimension of feature $\beta_{u,w}^t$.

We define the state of our policy as S_w^t, where $w \in W$ is the index of videos and $t \in T_w$ is the iteration of learning process. T_w is the terminal step of video w. The original state S_w^0 equals the skeleton proposal based feature K^0. During the learning process, the state S_w changes with the iteration t. S_w^t denotes the activated feature at the tth iteration for the wth video. Thus we formulate the state S_w^t as follows:

$$S_w^t = \Gamma_{u \in U} \left(\beta_{u,w}^t \right), \tag{3}$$

where $\beta_{u,w}^t$ is the uth part of state S_w after the tth iteration.

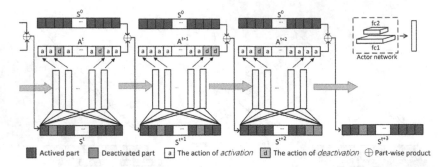

| ■ Actived part ■ Deactivated part | a | The action of *activation* | d | The action of *deactivation* ⊕ Part-wise product |

Fig. 4. State transformation in PA-DRL. The activated part is the corresponding part of original state. The deactivated part is the original part multiplying by 0. The deactivated part can be reactivated by adding the corresponding original part. We define a part-wise product to generate the new state. The new state S^{t+1} is computed by the part-wise product of the last state S^t and corresponding *action* A^t.

We define the step reward for *action* A_w^t as $r(A_w^t)$. The predicting label of state S_w^t is η_w^t. The label of ground truth for the corresponding frame is ϵ_w. If η_w^t equals to ϵ_w, the *action* A_w^{t-1} is positive for prediction and will receive a positive reward by the policy. If the category of action is correctly predicted in continuous iterations, we decide a reward of $|r(A_w^{t-1})| + 1$ for the *action*. Otherwise, we give the negative reward for the continuous wrong predictions with $-|r(A_w^{t-1})| - 1$. At iteration t, we formulate the step reward $r(A_w^t)$ as follows:

$$r(A_w^t) = \Theta(\eta_w^t, \epsilon_w) \times (|r(A_w^{t-1})| + 1), \tag{4}$$

where $\Theta(\cdot)$ is characteristic function which equals 1 if prediction is correct and equals 0 else. Based on the step reward, we define the final reward function as $R(w)$. After the terminal iteration, we feedback the series *actions* A_w with the final reward $R(w)$. When the state stops at the terminal iteration S_w^T, the final reward $R(w)$ is the average value of all step rewards of every iteration. We represent final reward $R(w)$ for the video w as:

$$R(w) = \frac{1}{T} \sum_{t \in T} r(A_w^t). \tag{5}$$

The final reward is used for updating the model at the terminal step of one training sample.

State Transformation: Figure 4 shows the state transformation of PA-DRL. We denote the actor network as Π_θ, which is parameterized by θ. We formulate the state transformation from state S_w^{t-1} to S_w^t as follows:

$$A_w^{t-1} = \Pi_\theta(S_w^{t-1}), \tag{6}$$

$$S_w^t = S_w^0 \odot A_w^{t-1}, \tag{7}$$

where S_w^0 is the state of original skeleton proposal feature and $\odot$ is element-wise product. The *action* A_w^{t-1} implements on the original state S_w^0 to activate and deactivate the parts of features. We prefer to compute the element wise product of A_w^{t-1} and S_w^0. The reason is that the *action* A_w^{t-1} cannot reactivate the part of S_w^{t-1} which is already deactivated in the previous iterations. The information of the part is lost and cannot be recovered in the following iterations. After several iterations, the state of S_w^T has the possibility to form a vector of all zeros, which cannot represent the action.

To stop the iteration softly, we set the condition of terminal iteration. For the training process, we count the number of continuously correct predictions as σ. When σ is larger than the stop value λ, the iteration stops. For the testing process, we count the number of continuously consistent predictions as σ. The condition of termination is the same as that in training. The last *action* of frame n is the initial *action* of frame $n+1$. Because the adjacent two frames are similar, which makes the *action* similar. We use the constraint of continuity on the *action* to reflect the continuity of frames.

3.3 Implement Details

We first utilized the skeleton which was extracted with [3] as the proposal for extracting the features of the human body. The number of parts extracted by [3] is 14 and we uniformly used 28 parts (14×2) per frame, where we trained one actor network for each part. For every frame, we selected region proposals at joints of skeleton. The center of region was the joint of skeleton and the size of region was 20×20 pixels. At every joint, we extracted of the spatial feature with pre-trained model of VGG-16. The feature size of one patch was 1000. The extracted 14 features of one person were concatenated into a vector and then the features of different persons were concatenated. The generated feature was used as the input of our actor network. Our actor network consisted of two fully convolution layer $fc1$ and $fc2$. The $fc1$ layer had 128 units and the $fc2$ layer had 2 units. The layer of $fc1$ and $fc2$ were activated by the $relu(\cdot)$ function. We separately trained 28 actor networks with the same input and the output of every network referred to the *action* corresponding to the part. The critic part of our reinforcement learning was linear-SVM. The stop value λ was set as 5. The max value in training process and testing process were both set as 10. We used Adam [12] as the optimizer in training and set the learning rate as 10^{-4}. The discount factor γ was set as 0.99.

4 Experiments and Results

4.1 Datasets

We evaluated PA-DRL on the UT-Interaction #1, the UT-Interaction #2 [32], the BIT-Interaction dataset [15] and UCF101 dataset [37].

UTI #1 and UTI #2 Datasets: The two sets of the UT-Interaction dataset contain videos of continuous actions of 6 classes: shake-hands, point, hug, push, kick and punch. Each video contains at least one execution per interaction, providing 8 executions of human activities per video on average. Both sets have 60 video clips with 10 videos per action class. Backgrounds in the Set #2 are more complex than those in the Set #1.

BIT-Interaction Dataset: The BIT-Interaction dataset has a list of 23 interactive phrases based on 17 attributes for all the videos. Videos are captured in realistic scenes with cluttered background. People in each interaction class behave totally different and thus have diverse motion attributes. This dataset consists of 8 classes of human interactions (bow, boxing, handshake, high-five, hug, kick, pat, and push), with 50 videos per class.

UCF101 Dataset: UCF101 action recognition dataset has collected from YouTube, where the videos are realistic without constraint. The total categories of dataset are 101 and all videos are divided into 25 groups with 101 action categories. There are 13320 videos in all 101 categories.

4.2 Experimental Settings

In the training process, we trained the model by feeding one sample each round. We fixed the parameters of the linear-SVM in the process of training with each video. The model updated with the final reward by using (5) and calculated the reward with (4) in every iteration. In the training process, we terminated the iterative updating of each video when predicted labels were the same as the ground truth or the iteration number reached the max value. The parameters of network in our model updated after the iterative updating of each video was terminated. In the testing process, PA-DRL outputted the final feature for one video when predicted labels did not change in continuous 3 iterations or the iteration number reached the max value. On UT-Interaction datasets, we followed the experimental settings in [32] and utilized 10-fold leave-one-sequence-out to measure the performance of our proposal based PA-DRL on both the UTI #1 and the UTI #2. For every round, we measured the performance 10 times while changing the test set iteratively, finding the average performance. Every time, we utilized 6 videos in one of 10 folds as the testing set and used the other 54 videos as the training set. On BIT-Interaction dataset, we followed the settings in [15]. With randomly choosing 272 videos, we trained the model and utilized the remaining 128 videos for testing. On UCF101 dataset, we followed the split scheme proposed in [37]. We used the first 15 groups for training, the next 3 groups for cross-validation and the remaining 7 groups for testing.

4.3 Results and Analysis

We first compared our PA-DRL method with thirteen state-of-the-art action prediction methods, including SVM [31], Bayesian [31], IBOW [31], DBOW [31], SC [2], MSSC [2], Lan *et al.* [20], MTSSVM [16], AAC [44], MMAPM [14], C3D [39], Lai *et al.* [19] and Deep SCN [17]. We employed the results of these compared methods provided by the original authors. Table 1 illustrates the accuracy of PA-DRL compared with several state-of-the-art methods for action prediction. The

Table 1. The accuracy (%) of different methods on the UTI #1, the UTI #2.

Methods	UTI Set #1		UTI Set #2	
	OR = 0.5	OR = 1.0	OR = 0.5	OR = 1.0
SVM [31]	25.3	69.2	27.2	69.2
Bayesian [31]	20.9	78.0	21.8	50.7
IBoW [31]	65.0	81.7	45.7	59.3
DBoW [31]	70.0	85.0	51.2	65.3
SC [2]	70.0	76.7	68.5	80.0
MSSC [2]	70.0	83.3	71.0	81.5
Lan et al. [20]	83.1	88.4	78.3	82.0
MTSSVM [16]	78.3	95.0	74.3	87.3
AAC [44]	88.3	95.0	75.6	63.9
MMAPM [14]	78.3	95.0	75.0	87.3
PA-DRL	**91.7**	**96.7**	**83.3**	**91.7**

Table 2. The accuracy (%) of different methods on the BIT and UCF101 datasets.

Methods	BIT dataset		UCF101	
	OR = 0.5	OR = 1.0	OR = 0.5	OR = 1.0
IBoW [31]	49.2	43.0	74.6	76.0
DBoW [31]	46.9	53.1	53.2	53.2
MSSC [2]	48.4	68.0	62.6	61.9
MTSSVM [16]	60.0	76.6	82.3	82.5
Lai et al. [19]	79.4	85.3	-	-
Deep SCN [17]	78.1	90.6	85.5	86.7
C3D [39]	57.8	69.6	80.0	82.4
PA-DRL	**85.9**	**91.4**	**87.3**	**87.7**

comparisons were taken on UTI, BIT and UCF101 dataset at $OR = 0.5$ and $OR = 1.0$ separately. The OR indicates the observation ratio.

Comparisons with the State-of-the-Arts: From Tables 1 and 2, we clearly see that PA-DRL achieves the performance of the state-of-the-art on three datasets. For the difference of three sets, we compared the results in three sets individually. On the UTI #1, the performance of our PA-DRL reached 91.7% and 96.7% at $OR = 0.5$ and $OR = 1.0$. At $OR = 0.5$, comparing with the AAC, our PA-DRL improved 3%. For the other approaches, our PA-DRL outperformed at least 3.5%. The result of our method demonstrated that our PA-DRL has the strong ability of representing at the half observation of actions on this set. Although our PA-DRL achieved the similar performance at $OR = 1.0$, we obviously outperformed than other methods on half observed videos.

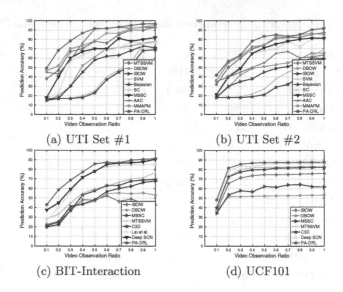

(a) UTI Set #1　　　　　　(b) UTI Set #2

(c) BIT-Interaction　　　　　(d) UCF101

Fig. 5. The accuracy curve of prediction. The observation ratio changes from 0.1 to 1.0. The comparisons are presented on UTI #1, UTI #2, BIT and UCF101 dataset.

The categories of actions in UTI #2 are the same as that of the UTI #1, but the variations of background in UTI #2 are larger, which makes it more difficult to predict the actions. Depending on the UTI #2 in Table 1, our PA-DRL achieved the best performance comparing with other methods. At $OR = 0.5$, PA-DRL raised 7.7% than AAC and improved 5% comparing with Lan *et al.* [20]. The large variation of background made the prediction difficult. Nevertheless, our proposed method performed best by extracting features from skeleton proposal, especially when the video was observed with a half.

The BIT dataset has more categories of actions and is more complex than the sets of the UTI. Nevertheless, we achieved the state-of-the-art with the accuracy of 85.9% and 91.4%. The complexity of actions reduced the predicting precision of other approaches. But for PA-DRL, the variance of actions would not change the order of joints on the skeleton, which could minimize the impact of complexity. Our PA-DRL outperformed Lai *et al.* [19] and Deep SCN [17], which are the leading approaches on BIT dataset. Because PA-DRL enhanced the action-related parts in features and made these parts much more attentional to the original features. The enhanced features highlighted the discriminative information and achieved PA-DRL to outperformed other methods.

UCF101 dataset is a dataset of action recognition, which is much larger than the previous two dataset and has collected from realistic videos. The complexity of actions makes the prediction more difficult. However, at $OR = 0.5$, PA-DRL outperformed 1.8% than Deep SCN [17], which obtained the state-of-the-art results on UCF101 for action prediction. Comparing with the action recognition method, C3D [39], PA-DRL raised the accuracy with 7.3%. The significant gap with demonstrated that when the action was observed incompletely, the method for full length action recognition had difficult to predict the action. While PA-DRL successfully predicted the actions on the incomplete action videos.

Figure 5 illustrates the comparisons between PA-DRL and other approaches on three datasets. In this figure, the horizontal axis of the figure corresponds to the observation ratio, and the vertical axis represents the average prediction accuracy. Our PA-DRL outperformed the other methods on the BIT dataset.

From Fig. 5(a), we see that the prediction curve of PA-DRL increased rapidly from $OR = 0.3$ to $OR = 0.5$, and became stable since $OR = 0.7$. The methods of the SVM [31] and the Bayesian [31] relayed on the complete information of actions and achieved a good performance at $OR = 0.9$. The method of MTSSVM [16] quickly increased at low observation ratio, especially at $OR = 0.3$. But our PA-DRL outperformed the MTSSVM since $OR = 0.4$. Comparing with the method of MMAPM [14], our PA-DRL obtained a better performance at $OR = 0.5$ and $OR = 0.7$ and reached the comparable results with the MMAPM. The result demonstrates that our proposed PA-DRL has the strong ability for representing the full length actions.

From Fig. 5(b), we see that our proposed method performed the best at $OR = 0.5$ and $OR = 1.0$. The repaid increasing from $OR = 0.3$ and $OR = 0.5$ indicated that our method effectively captured the evolution of actions with the increasing of observation ratio. The MTSSVM is benefited from using histogram features of both local and global information in temporal domain. The MMAPM used the multi-temporal scale to model the ongoing actions. However, our PA-DRL just used the global information with temporal pooling. The comparable results demonstrates that our PA-DRL exploited the structural information of the human body effectively and enhanced the discriminative power of features.

From Fig. 5(c), we see that the prediction of PA-DRL performed the state-of-the-art on the BIT dataset. The Lai *et al.* [19] and Deep SCN [17] are leading approaches on the BIT dataset, which do not mine the structural information of human. However, our PA-DRL achieved a higher performance with exploiting the structural information and mining the saliency information of human. The high performance with little observation of the whole video indicated that our PA-DRL could predict the activity at the early stage.

From Fig. 5(d), PA-DRL performed an accuracy with 81.5% even at $OR = 0.2$, which the observed video was just the beginning of actions. By activating the action-related parts, PA-DRL precisely predicted the direction of action evolution with a few frames of the beginning part of videos. Comparing with C3D, PA-DRL performed well with observation ratio higher than 0.6. Because the method failed to reduce the disturbance of action-unrelated parts in features. PA-DRL enhanced the action-related parts and made the predicted direction of the action evolution close to the actual direction.

Analysis of Different Components: To analyze the effectiveness of PA-DRL, we took the experiments comparing PA-DRL with skeleton feature without local patch feature and skeleton proposal based feature without deep reinforcement learning (DRL). Table 3 illustrates the results. In our experiments, skeleton

Table 3. The accuracy (%) of action prediction with different settings for PA-DRL on the UTI #1, the UTI #2 and BIT dataset.

Different settings	Dataset	OR = 0.5	OR = 1.0
Skeleton feature without local patch feature	UTI #1	69.9	73.3
Skeleton proposal based feature without RL	UTI #1	76.7	91.7
PA-DRL	UTI #1	91.7	96.7
Skeleton feature without local patch feature	UTI #2	66.7	70.0
Skeleton proposal based feature without RL	UTI #2	70.0	86.7
PA-DRL	UTI #2	83.3	91.7
Skeleton feature without local patch feature	BIT	62.3	75.7
Skeleton proposal based feature without RL	BIT	68.6	87.5
PA-DRL	BIT	85.9	91.4

feature without local patch feature denoted that the feature used for predicting action was the just the skeleton feature, which was composed of the position of skeleton joints. Skeleton proposal based feature without DRL utilized the feature of local patch around skeleton joints without activating process.

As can be seen in Table 3, PA-DRL effectively exploited the relationship between the part in feature and actions and used the action-related parts to predict the direction of action evolution. The setting of using skeleton feature obtained the worst performance on three sets, which indicated that without using the apparent information could substantially decrease the precision of prediction. The performance of skeleton proposal based feature was higher than that of skeleton feature, which indicated that the structural information and apparent information were complementary for representing actions. The comparisons between skeleton proposal based feature and PA-DRL showed that there was a significant gap. The improvement demonstrated that the action-unrelated parts in the feature limited the representation ability, while our PA-DRL effectively exploited the relationship between feature and actions for representation.

From $OR = 0.5$, we see that the observed video did not contain the sufficient information of the action. Treating all parts of the feature equally reduced the ability of action-related parts to represent the action and relatively generated the disturbance by the noise. PA-DRL selected the action-related parts to inhibit the influence of noise and performed a significant improvement. At $OR = 1.0$, the feature with the complete information of the action reduced the disturbance of noise, which made the skeleton proposal based feature achieve a good performance. However, PA-DRL still outperformed skeleton proposal based feature by precisely predicting the direction of action evolution.

5   Conclusion

In this paper, we have proposed a part-activated deep reinforcement learning (PA-DRL) method for action prediction. The aim of our proposed PA-DRL is to learn the policy of activating action-related parts. Our PA-DRL exploits the structural information through extracting features by the skeleton proposal and mines the related information of human body for the ongoing actions. Experimental results on UTI, BIT and UCF101 dataset have been presented to demonstrate the effectiveness of the propose method for action prediction.

Acknowledgment. This work was supported in part by the National Key Research and Development Program of China under Grant 2017YFA0700802, in part by the National Natural Science Foundation of China under Grant 61672306, Grant U1713214, Grant 61572271, Grant 91746107, in part by the Shenzhen Fundamental Research Fund (Subject Arrangement) under Grant JCYJ20170412170602564 and in part by the Natural Science Foundation of Tianjin under Grant 16JCYBJC15900.

References

1. Caicedo, J.C., Lazebnik, S.: Active object localization with deep reinforcement learning. In: ICCV, pp. 2488–2496 (2015)
2. Cao, Y., et al.: Recognize human activities from partially observed videos. In: CVPR, pp. 2658–2665 (2013)
3. Cao, Z., Simon, T., Wei, S.E., Sheikh, Y.: Realtime multi-person 2D pose estimation using part affinity fields. In: CVPR, pp. 7291–7299 (2017)
4. Carreira, J., Zisserman, A.: Quo Vadis, action recognition? A new model and the kinetics dataset. In: CVPR, pp. 6299–6308 (2017)
5. Du, Y., Wang, W., Wang, L.: Hierarchical recurrent neural network for skeleton based action recognition. In: CVPR, pp. 1110–1118 (2015)
6. Goodrich, B., Arel, I.: Reinforcement learning based visual attention with application to face detection. In: CVPRW, pp. 19–24 (2012)
7. Hinami, R., Mei, T., Satoh, S.: Joint detection and recounting of abnormal events by learning deep generic knowledge. In: ICCV, pp. 3619–3627 (2017)
8. Hu, J.-F., Zheng, W.-S., Ma, L., Wang, G., Lai, J.: Real-time RGB-D activity prediction by soft regression. In: Leibe, B., Matas, J., Sebe, N., Welling, M. (eds.) ECCV 2016. LNCS, vol. 9905, pp. 280–296. Springer, Cham (2016). https://doi. org/10.1007/978-3-319-46448-0_17
9. Huang, C., Lucey, S., Ramanan, D.: Learning policies for adaptive tracking with deep feature cascades. In: ICCV, pp. 105–114 (2017)
10. Jie, Z., Liang, X., Feng, J., Jin, X., Lu, W., Yan, S.: Tree-structured reinforcement learning for sequential object localization. In: NIPS, pp. 127–135 (2016)
11. Karayev, S., Baumgartner, T., Fritz, M., Darrell, T.: Timely object recognition. In: NIPS, pp. 890–898 (2012)
12. Kingma, D.P., Ba, J.: Adam: a method for stochastic optimization. In: ICLR (2015)
13. Kong, X., Xin, B., Wang, Y., Hua, G.: Collaborative deep reinforcement learning for joint object search. In: CVPR, pp. 1695–1704 (2017)
14. Kong, Y., Fu, Y.: Max-margin action prediction machine. TPAMI **38**(9), 1844–1858 (2016)

15. Kong, Y., Jia, Y., Fu, Y.: Learning human interaction by interactive phrases. In: Fitzgibbon, A., Lazebnik, S., Perona, P., Sato, Y., Schmid, C. (eds.) ECCV 2012. LNCS, vol. 7572, pp. 300–313. Springer, Heidelberg (2012). https://doi.org/10.1007/978-3-642-33718-5_22

16. Kong, Y., Kit, D., Fu, Y.: A discriminative model with multiple temporal scales for action prediction. In: Fleet, D., Pajdla, T., Schiele, B., Tuytelaars, T. (eds.) ECCV 2014. LNCS, vol. 8693, pp. 596–611. Springer, Cham (2014). https://doi.org/10.1007/978-3-319-10602-1_39

17. Kong, Y., Tao, Z., Fu, Y.: Deep sequential context networks for action prediction. In: CVPR, pp. 1473–1481 (2017)

18. Krull, A., Brachmann, E., Nowozin, S., Michel, F., Shotton, J., Rother, C.: Poseagent: budget-constrained 6D object pose estimation via reinforcement learning. In: CVPR, pp. 6702–6710 (2017)

19. Lai, S., Zheng, W.S., Hu, J.F., Zhang, J.: Global-local temporal saliency action prediction. TIP **27**, 2272–2285 (2017)

20. Lan, T., Chen, T.-C., Savarese, S.: A hierarchical representation for future action prediction. In: Fleet, D., Pajdla, T., Schiele, B., Tuytelaars, T. (eds.) ECCV 2014. LNCS, vol. 8691, pp. 689–704. Springer, Cham (2014). https://doi.org/10.1007/978-3-319-10578-9_45

21. Liang, X., Lee, L., Dai, W., Xing, E.P.: Dual motion GAN for future-flow embedded video prediction. In: ICCV (2017)

22. Liang, X., Lee, L., Xing, E.P.: Deep variation-structured reinforcement learning for visual relationship and attribute detection. In: CVPR, pp. 848–857 (2017)

23. Littman, M.L.: Reinforcement learning improves behaviour from evaluative feedback. Nature **521**(7553), 445–451 (2015)

24. Ma, S., Sigal, L., Sclaroff, S.: Learning activity progression in LSTMs for activity detection and early detection. In: CVPR, pp. 1942–1950 (2016)

25. Mahmud, T., Hasan, M., Roy-Chowdhury, A.K.: Joint prediction of activity labels and starting times in untrimmed videos. In: ICCV, pp. 5773–5782 (2017)

26. Martinez, J., Black, M.J., Romero, J.: On human motion prediction using recurrent neural networks. In: CVPR, pp. 2891–2900 (2017)

27. Mathe, S., Pirinen, A., Sminchisescu, C.: Reinforcement learning for visual object detection. In: CVPR, pp. 2894–2902 (2016)

28. Mnih, V., et al.: Human-level control through deep reinforcement learning. Nature **518**(7540), 529–533 (2015)

29. Qi, S., Huang, S., Wei, P., Zhu, S.C.: Predicting human activities using stochastic grammar. In: ICCV, pp. 1164–1172 (2017)

30. Ren, Z., Wang, X., Zhang, N., Lv, X., Li, L.J.: Deep reinforcement learning-based image captioning with embedding reward. In: CVPR, pp. 290–298 (2017)

31. Ryoo, M.S.: Human activity prediction: early recognition of ongoing activities from streaming videos. In: ICCV, pp. 1036–1043 (2011)

32. Ryoo, M.S., Aggarwal, J.: UT-interaction dataset, ICPR contest on semantic description of human activities (SDHA). In: ICPR, vol. 2, p. 4 (2010)

33. Ryoo, M.S., Matthies, L.: First-person activity recognition: what are they doing to me? In: CVPR, pp. 2730–2737 (2013)

34. Shi, Q., Cheng, L., Wang, L., Smola, A.: Human action segmentation and recognition using discriminative semi-markov models. IJCV **93**(1), 22–32 (2011)

35. Simonyan, K., Zisserman, A.: Two-stream convolutional networks for action recognition in videos. In: NIPS, pp. 568–576 (2014)

36. Singh, G., Saha, S., Sapienza, M., Torr, P.H.S., Cuzzolin, F.: Online real-time multiple spatiotemporal action localisation and prediction. In: ICCV, pp. 3637–3646 (2017)
37. Soomro, K., Zamir, A.R., Shah, M.: UCF101: a dataset of 101 human actions classes from videos in the wild. arXiv preprint arXiv:1212.0402 (2012)
38. Supancic III, J.S., Ramanan, D.: Tracking as online decision-making: learning a policy from streaming videos with reinforcement learning. In: ICCV, pp. 322–331 (2017)
39. Tran, D., Bourdev, L., Fergus, R., Torresani, L., Paluri, M.: Learning spatiotemporal features with 3D convolutional networks. In: ICCV, pp. 4489–4497 (2015)
40. Tudor Ionescu, R., Smeureanu, S., Alexe, B., Popescu, M.: Unmasking the abnormal events in video. In: ICCV, pp. 2895–2903 (2017)
41. Wang, J., Liu, Z., Wu, Y., Yuan, J.: Mining actionlet ensemble for action recognition with depth cameras. In: CVPR, pp. 1290–1297 (2012)
42. Wang, L., Xiong, Y., Lin, D., Van Gool, L.: Untrimmednets for weakly supervised action recognition and detection. In: CVPR, pp. 4325–4334 (2017)
43. Wei, S.E., Ramakrishna, V., Kanade, T., Sheikh, Y.: Convolutional pose machines. In: CVPR, pp. 4724–4732 (2016)
44. Xu, Z., Qing, L., Miao, J.: Activity auto-completion: predicting human activities from partial videos. In: ICCV, pp. 3191–3199 (2015)
45. Yoo, Y., Yun, S., Choi, J., Yun, K., Choi, J.Y.: Action-decision networks for visual tracking with deep reinforcement learning. In: CVPR, pp. 2711–2720 (2017)
46. Zaki, H.F.M., Shafait, F., Mian, A.: Modeling sub-event dynamics in first-person action recognition. In: CVPR, pp. 7253–7262 (2017)
47. Zhuang, B., Liu, L., Shen, C., Reid, I.: Towards context-aware interaction recognition for visual relationship detection. In: ICCV, pp. 589–598 (2017)

Lifelong Learning via Progressive Distillation and Retrospection

Saihui Hou[1]([✉]) [iD], Xinyu Pan[2] [iD], Chen Change Loy[3] [iD], Zilei Wang[1] [iD], and Dahua Lin[2] [iD]

[1] Department of Automation, University of Science and Technology of China, Hefei, China
saihui@mail.ustc.edu.cn
[2] Department of Information Engineering, The Chinese University of Hong Kong, Hong Kong, China
[3] Nanyang Technological University, Singapore, Singapore

Abstract. Lifelong learning aims at adapting a learned model to new tasks while retaining the knowledge gained earlier. A key challenge for lifelong learning is how to strike a balance between the *preservation* on old tasks and the *adaptation* to a new one within a given model. Approaches that combine both objectives in training have been explored in previous works. Yet the performance still suffers from considerable degradation in a long sequence of tasks. In this work, we propose a novel approach to lifelong learning, which tries to seek a better balance between *preservation* and *adaptation* via two techniques: *Distillation* and *Retrospection*. Specifically, the target model adapts to the new task by knowledge distillation from an intermediate expert, while the previous knowledge is more effectively preserved by caching a small subset of data for old tasks. The combination of *Distillation* and *Retrospection* leads to a more gentle learning curve for the target model, and extensive experiments demonstrate that our approach can bring consistent improvements on both old and new tasks (Project page: http://mmlab.ie.cuhk.edu.hk/projects/lifelong/).

Keywords: Lifelong learning · Knowledge distillation · Retrospection

1 Introduction

Lifelong learning aims at adapting a learned model to new tasks while retaining the knowledge acquired in the past. With the wide adoption of computer vision in real-world applications, there is an increasing demand for learning systems that

---

S. Hou, X. Pan—Indicates joint first authorship.

Electronic supplementary material The online version of this chapter (https://doi.org/10.1007/978-3-030-01219-9_27) contains supplementary material, which is available to authorized users.

© Springer Nature Switzerland AG 2018
V. Ferrari et al. (Eds.): ECCV 2018, LNCS 11207, pp. 452–467, 2018.
https://doi.org/10.1007/978-3-030-01219-9_27

are able to carry out lifelong learning over a series of tasks in a continual fashion. For example, a real-world object classification system is often required to be upgraded constantly by absorbing the knowledge from fresh domains. Directly repeating the training process with both previous and new data is often infeasible, due to various issues such as computation cost, storage budget, and privacy. For lifelong learning, a key challenge is to overcome the risk of catastrophic forgetting [9], namely a learned model usually suffers from accuracy degradation on old tasks when it adapts to a new one.

In this work, we focus on incremental multi-task object categorization in the context of deep learning. Here we assume that the classification tasks for different domains arrive in a sequential manner and a single model is required to perform well on all presented tasks at the end of each training stage. This setting serves as a reasonable starting point for further generalization. Some classical methods can be applied to the setting but with significant drawbacks. Specifically, (a) *Feature Extraction* [7] is suboptimal for a new task with the feature extractor frozen; (b) *Finetuning* [8], which adapts the whole network to new data, leads to a dramatic performance drop on old tasks; (c) *Joint Training* [4] brings the excessive demand for data storage and increasing training cost.

To overcome these drawbacks, various methods have been proposed and can be roughly divided into two categories. The first one [3,12,15,20,21] is based on knowledge distillation [10] and uses a modified cross-entropy loss to maintain the performance on old tasks. These methods have been proven to be effective, however, the performance drops when the target model is exposed to a sequence of tasks drawn from different distributions. The second one [2,13,27] focuses on the model itself and tries to identify the importance of parameters for old tasks, which is used as the guidance for adaptation to the new task. However, it is difficult to design a metric to weight all the parameters such that the performance on old tasks can be preserved very well, especially in a long sequence of tasks.

In this work, we propose a novel approach for lifelong learning on visual tasks, by drawing wisdom from human learning. When a student studies at school, he needs to gradually learn the knowledge of various courses without forgetting those previously learned. It is usually more efficient for him to learn the knowledge from a great teacher than directly from a book or by repeatedly doing exercises. Besides, he has to review those that have been learned early from time to time in order to not forget. Motivated by these observations, an approach consisting of two techniques, *Distillation* and *Retrospection*, is proposed with the aims of striking a better balance between the performance preservation on old tasks and the adaptation to a new task.

Distillation provides a novel way to adapt to a new task, which is the abbreviation of our algorithm named *Adaptation by Distillation*. Instead of directly finetuning on new data, we first train an *Expert CNN* dedicated to the new task and then uses it as an *advisor* to guide the adaptation of target model, via knowledge distillation [10]. Whereas previous works [15,20] that utilize knowledge distillation for lifelong learning primarily focus on preserving the knowledge obtained in the past, we find that the distillation-based learning from an

Expert CNN, which offers soft supervision, leads to a more gentle learning curve for adaptation to the new task. As a result, the target model can adapt more smoothly, thus achieving better performance on the new task as well as old tasks. *Retrospection* allows the target model to revisit the previous data from time to time, which emulates how we human beings try not to forget. It differs from *Joint Training* [4] where the data for all tasks are completely available. Instead, *Retrospection* requires only a small fraction of previous data to be reserved. Our study shows that even a very small subset of data from the past can help remarkably preserve the performance on earlier tasks, without incurring significant cost on computation and storage.

In summary, our contributions of this work mainly lie in three aspects: (1) We propose a new algorithm named *Adaptation by Distillation* for multi-task lifelong learning, which is expected to become a better practice to train a single model for a long sequence of tasks. (2) We explore the new setting in multi-task lifelong learning with a small subset of old data available and show that *Retrospection* is greatly helpful for the performance preservation on old tasks. (3) Extensive experiments demonstrate that *Distillation+Retrospection* can bring consistent improvements over the baselines and outperform *Learning without Forgetting* [15] by a large margin. For example, on ImageNet which comes as the first task in the five-task scenario, the final accuracy by *Distillation+Retrospection* exceeds the baseline [15] by more than 6%.

2   Related Work

Our method is built on the insights of multiple earlier works, not only for lifelong learning but also for other visual tasks. In the section, we summarize the most related ones to our work, which are comprised of the following three parts.

Multi-task Learning. The goal of multi-task lifelong learning is to train a single model which can predict well on multiple tasks, with the data for different tasks provided sequentially. It is at the intersection of multi-task learning and lifelong learning. Standard multi-task learning [4] is equivalent to *Joint Training* described in Sect. 1. The initial objective is to make use of the knowledge across different tasks (*i.e.*, so-called inductive bias [17]) to improve the accuracy on each individual task, which has the benefit of relaxing the number of required samples per task. However, the main drawback of this standard practice for lifelong learning is that it requires all the data for different tasks available. In this work, we first validate the effectiveness of *Distillation* without accessing the data for old tasks. And then we further explore the setting with *Retrospection*, *i.e.*, a small subset of data is reserved for old tasks.

Knowledge Distillation. Knowledge distillation is proposed by Hinton *et al.* [10], where knowledge is transferred from a large network or a network assembly to a small network for efficient deployment. The small network is trained using a modified cross-entropy loss (denoted by KD-Loss), which encourages the responses of the original and new network to be similar. This method is widely used to produce a network of different structure that approximates the original one, *e.g.*, Romero *et al.* [22] transfer to a deeper and thinner network for network compression, Chen *et al.* [5] generate a deeper and wider network for fast hyper-parameter exploration. For lifelong learning, Li *et al.* [15] propose an algorithm called *Learning without Forgetting* and first introduce knowledge distillation to preserve the performance on old tasks. KD-Loss [10] is adopted to mimic the output of the original network in the adaptation to a new task. Our work is also based on knowledge distillation [10]. The significant differences between our work and [15] lie in the learning for the new task. In our algorithm, the target model adapts to a new task by distilling the knowledge from an intermediate *Expert CNN*, which can facilitate the learning on the new task and is also beneficial to preserve the performance on old tasks. Besides, Tzeng *et al.* [24] dealing with domain adaptation use knowledge distillation to help the training on a new domain. However, the soft labels in [24] come from the model trained on a well-labeled source domain, and they do not need to consider maintaining the performance on the source domain. While in our algorithm, the soft labels are obtained by fine-tuning an *Expert CNN* on new data ignoring the constraint of preserving the performance on old tasks.

Lifelong Learning Based on Knowledge Distillation. As stated in Sect. 1, recent works on lifelong learning can be roughly divided into two categories, one of which is based on knowledge distillation. Besides *Learning without Forgetting* [15], here we discuss other works of this category [3,12,20,21]. Aljundi *et al.* [3] propose to train multiple networks on different tasks and take an auto-encoder to choose a network for each test sample, where the algorithm in [15] is adopted when the task relatedness is high. Rannen *et al.* [20] also introduce an auto-encoder but the goal is to help preserve the crucial features for old tasks. Jung *et al.* [12] propose to approximate the features of the original network for old tasks rather than the output of the last layer. The focuses of these works, especially [12,20], are to more effectively preserve the performance for old tasks, while the accuracy on the new task is comparable or a little inferior to the baseline [15]. Differently, our algorithm can simultaneously improve the performance on both old and new tasks, and the *Distillation*-based learning for a new task as well as the *Retrospection* on old data can also be integrated with these methods. Besides, Rebuffi *et al.* [21] deal with multi-class lifelong learning. The main difference between multi-class and multi-task lifelong learning lies in the prediction step: a multi-class learner has to train a unified classifier that predicts correctly any of the observed class, while a multi-task learner can make use of multiple classifiers, each of which is evaluated only on the data from its own domain. In this work, we focus on multi-task lifelong learning. Rebuffi *et al.* [21] also keep some data for old classes, while we first explore the setting with a small subset of old data available in the multi-task scenario and get some different observations, which will be provided in Sect. 4.

3   Distillation and Retrospection

The approach proposed in this work is illustrated in Fig. 1. The framework consists of two key components: *Distillation* and *Retrospection*. It deals with multi-task lifelong learning aiming at training a single Convolutional Neural Network (CNN) that can perform reasonably well on a variety of classification tasks. The training data and ground truth for each task are presented to the model in a sequential manner. In each phase, the model evolves to a new task without accessing all the data for old tasks. The input to our algorithm is an *Original CNN* that contains the feature extractor F and task-specific classifiers T_o for old tasks. The network learns to adapt to a new task by distilling the knowledge from an intermediate *Expert CNN*. The output is the updated feature extractor F^* and task-specific classifiers T_o^* for old tasks as well as a task-specific classifier T_n^* for the new task. In the following, we will first review *Learning without Forgetting* [15] as background. Then we will elaborate how *Distillation* works to facilitate the learning on the new task and simultaneously benefit the performance preservation on old tasks. Finally, we will introduce *Retrospection*, *i.e.*, a small subset of data is reserved for old tasks.

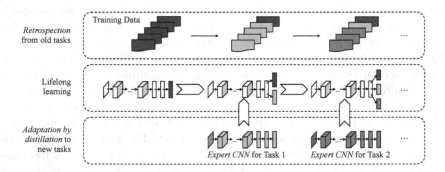

Fig. 1. Illustration of *Distillation* and *Retrospection*. The model learns the knowledge on a new task through the *Distillation* from an *Expert CNN*. *Retrospection* allows the model to revisit a small subset of data for old tasks.

3.1   Background

Learning without Forgetting (LwF) [15] is a representative method for multi-task lifelong learning. It first introduces knowledge distillation [10] for lifelong learning to preserve the performance on old tasks. The loss function for adapting the model to a new task is the sum of two terms: L_{new}^F for the new task and L_{old}^F for the old task[1].

---

[1] The regularization terms are omitted for simplicity.

Specifically, in the context of image classification, L_{new}^F is the standard cross-entropy loss [14,23]:

$$L_{\text{new}}^F(X_{\text{n}}, Y_{\text{n}}) = -\frac{1}{|N_{\text{n}}|} \sum_{i=1}^{|N_{\text{n}}|} \sum_{k=1}^{K_{\text{n}}} y_{\text{n}}^{ik} \cdot \log\left(p_{\text{n}}^{ik}\right), \tag{1}$$

where $X_{\text{n}}/Y_{\text{n}}$ are the training data and ground truth for the new task, N_{n} is a batch of samples drawn from X_{n}, K_{n} is the number of classes for the new task, y_{n}^i is the one-hot ground truth labels of the i-th sample, p_{n}^i is the corresponding softmax output. The loss encourages the predictions of target model for the new task to match the one-hot labels.

L_{old}^F is the knowledge distillation loss (KD-Loss). In order to compute it, the output of *Original CNN* for the old task denoted by $\widehat{Y}_{\text{o}}$ is first computed and recorded before the training starts. It is worth noting that, since the data for the old task is not available [15], $\widehat{Y}_{\text{o}}$ is computed on new data. For image classification, $\widehat{Y}_{\text{o}}$ is the set of label probabilities, *i.e.*soft labels. Then, L_{old}^F is computed as follows in the training:

$$L_{\text{old}}^F(X_{\text{n}}, \widehat{Y}_{\text{o}}) = -\frac{1}{|N_{\text{n}}|} \sum_{i=1}^{|N_{\text{n}}|} \sum_{k=1}^{K_{\text{o}}} \hat{y}_{\text{o}}^{(ik)'} \cdot \log\left(p_{\text{o}}^{(ik)'}\right), \tag{2}$$

where K_{o} is the number of classes for the old task, $\hat{y}_{\text{o}}^{(i)'}$ and $p_{\text{o}}^{(i)'}$ are the modified versions of recorded soft labels by *Original CNN* and current network predictions for the old task:

$$\hat{y}_{\text{o}}^{(ik)'} = \frac{\left(\hat{y}_{\text{o}}^{(ik)}\right)^{1/\gamma_{\text{o}}}}{\sum_j \left(\hat{y}_{\text{o}}^{(ij)}\right)^{1/\gamma_{\text{o}}}}, \ p_{\text{o}}^{(ik)'} = \frac{\left(p_{\text{o}}^{(ik)}\right)^{1/\gamma_{\text{o}}}}{\sum_j \left(p_{\text{o}}^{(ij)}\right)^{1/\gamma_{\text{o}}}}, \tag{3}$$

where γ_{o} is usually set to be greater than 1 which increases the weights of small values. L_{old}^F moves towards performance preservation by encouraging the current predictions for the old task to match the soft labels by *Original CNN*, though the predictions and soft labels are both computed on new data. When there are multiple old tasks, the loss in Eq. (2) is computed for each old task and then the sum of them is used for L_{old}^F.

There exist some limitations in *LwF*. First, for preserving the performance on old tasks, the target model adapts to a new task with the constraint of mimicking the output of *Original CNN* as much as possible. Though sometimes this constraint provides useful regularization to the cases with rare new samples, it is also likely to hinder the adaptation to the new task. Second, the performance on old tasks degrades a lot when the model is exposed to a long sequence of tasks for different domains [3] since the loss for old tasks is computed on the new coming data which is likely to be drawn from a significantly different distribution compared to the previous data.

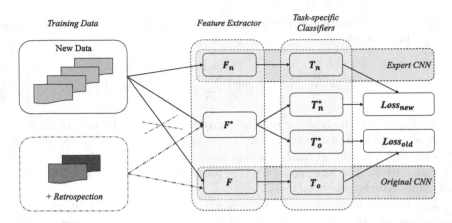

Fig. 2. Illustration of network structures for *Distillation+Retrospection*. The structures with or without *Retrospection* are the same, while the differences lie in the composition of training data and the computation of loss for old tasks. The responses of *Expert CNN* as well as *Original CNN* can be recorded before training, both of which do not bring additional GPU memory consumption. When adapting the original model to the new task, only weights of F^*, T_o^*, T_n^* are *not fixed*.

3.2   Distillation

Distillation is the abbreviation of our algorithm named *Adaptation by Distillation*, which is motivated to facilitate the adaptation to a new task while preserving the performance on old tasks. The network structures are depicted in Fig. 2. The main differences between *Distillation* and *LwF* lie in the learning on the new task. In our algorithm, the target model adapts to a new task through knowledge distillation instead of directly training on new data. The steps for *Distillation* are described below.

First, an *Expert CNN* is trained purely on the new task. The loss function has only one term for image classification, *i.e.*, the cross-entropy loss as in Eq. (1). The resulting *Expert CNN* is skilled at discriminating new data so that it theoretically provides an upper bound for the performance on the new task. Second, the responses of *Expert CNN* for new data denoted by $\widehat{Y}_n$ are computed and recorded, which are used as the supervision for learning on the new task in the next step.

Finally, it comes to adapting to the new task without catastrophic forgetting. Knowledge distillation [10] is not only used to preserve the performance on old tasks, but also utilized for the adaptation to the new task. The loss function is also composed of two terms for the old and the new task respectively. The one for the old task is a type of KD-Loss computed as in Eq. (2), while the other for the new task is another KD-Loss instead of cross-entropy loss, which is computed as follows:

$$L_{\text{new}}^{D}(X_n, \widehat{Y}_n) = -\frac{1}{|N_n|} \sum_{i=1}^{|N_n|} \sum_{k=1}^{K_n} \hat{y}_n^{(ik)'} \cdot \log\left(p_n^{(ik)'}\right), \tag{4}$$

where $X_n/\widehat{Y}_n$ are the new training data and the soft labels output by *Expert CNN*, N_n is the batch drawn from X_n, K_n is the number of classes for the new task, $\hat{y}_n^{(i)'}$ and $p_n^{(i)'}$ are the modified versions of recorded soft labels by *Expert CNN* and current network predictions for the new task:

$$\hat{y}_n^{(ik)'} = \frac{\left(\hat{y}_n^{(ik)}\right)^{1/\gamma_n}}{\sum_j \left(\hat{y}_n^{(ij)}\right)^{1/\gamma_n}}, \quad p_n^{(ik)'} = \frac{\left(p_n^{(ik)}\right)^{1/\gamma_n}}{\sum_j \left(p_n^{(ij)}\right)^{1/\gamma_n}}, \tag{5}$$

where γ_n is also set to be greater than 1 to enhance the contribution of small values. In other words, the learning of the new task is based on the knowledge distillation from *Expert CNN*. In the training, the one-hot labels of new data are replaced by the soft labels output by *Expert CNN*, which can enforce the relationship among classes [24] and thus facilitate the learning on the new task. Besides, *Distillation* is also beneficial for the performance preservation on old tasks since it is easier for *Original CNN* to match the output on new data to a soft distribution (*i.e.* soft labels by *Expert CNN*) instead of a very peaked one (*i.e.* one-hot labels).

3.3   Retrospection

Retrospection means that a small fraction of data for old tasks is reserved for lifelong learning. Though additional memory space is required, we find that a rather small subset of data for old tasks is enough to offer great help for performance preservation, especially with a long sequence of tasks for different domains, such as Scenes, Birds, Flowers and Aircrafts.

In comparison to *LwF*, the loss for the old task with *Retrospection* is computed in a different way:

$$L_{\text{old}}^{R}(X_o, \widehat{Y}_o) = -\frac{1}{|N_o|} \sum_{i=1}^{|N_o|} \sum_{k=1}^{K_o} \hat{y}_o^{(ik)'} \cdot \log\left(p_o^{(ik)'}\right), \tag{6}$$

where X_o is a small subset of data for the old task, Y_o is the recorded responses by *Original CNN*, N_o is a batch of samples drawn from X_o. Besides, $\hat{y}_o^{(i)'}$ and $p_o^{(ik)'}$ are the modified versions of recorded responses by *Original CNN* and current network predictions for the old task, which are computed as in Eq. (3).

Note that, with *Retrospection*, the loss for the old task (L_{old}^{R}) as well as the responses of *Original CNN* ($\widehat{Y}_o$) is computed on the reserved small subset of data for the old task instead of new data. In the cases of more than one old tasks, the loss above is computed for each old task with the data from its own domain, and then L_{old}^{R} is computed as the sum of them in order to preserve the performance on these tasks.

3.4 Summary

In our approach consisting of *Distillation* and *Retrospection*, the loss function for lifelong learning is also composed of two terms for the old task and the new one respectively. Compared to *LwF*, *Distillation* adopts a type of KD-Loss instead of cross-entropy loss for the new task, while *Retrospection* updates the loss for the old task by computing it on the reserved small subset of data rather than on new data. In the final version of our approach, *i.e.*, *Distillation+Retrospection*, the loss function is the sum of L_{new}^D in Eq. (4) for the new task and L_{old}^R in Eq. (6) for the old task, which can help outperform *LwF* by a large margin on each individual task. Besides, *Distillation* is superior to *LwF* with or without *Retrospection*. *Retrospection* can also be integrated with *LwF* to significantly improve the performance on old tasks, which is also helpful for the new task.

4 Experiments

4.1 Settings

Experiments are conducted on a variety of classification tasks, including ImageNet [6], Scenes [19], Birds [26], Flowers [18] and Aircrafts [16]. We consider the sets of two and five tasks coming in a sequential manner.

Datasets. The statistics of the datasets evaluated in this work, which are also used in [3,15,20], are summarized in Table 1. For ImageNet [19], the evaluation is done on its validation set.

Table 1. The statistics of the datasets used in this work.

Task	Datasets	#Category	#Training	#Test
ImageNet	ILSVRC-2012 [19]	1000	1,281,167	50,000
Birds	CUB-200-2011 [26]	200	5994	5794
Flowers	Oxford Flowers [18]	102	2040	6149
Scenes	MIT Scenes [19]	67	5360	1340
Aircrafts	FGVC-Aircrafts [16]	100	6667	3333

Implementation Details. All models are implemented with Caffe [11] and trained on Titan-X GPUs. AlexNet [14] is adopted as the backbone network due to its simplicity and efficient deployment, which is widely used in the literature for lifelong learning [2,3,12,15,20,27]. The feature extractor F consists of the five convolutional layers and the first two fully connected layers, while the task-specific classifiers T_o/T_n refer to the last fully connected layer. The standard practice described in [1] is applied to train the *Expert CNN*. As for the adaptation to the new task without catastrophic forgetting, it is conducted with the loss to mimic the output of *Original CNN* and we follow the similar practice. Stochastic gradient descent (SGD) is used for the optimization. The initial learning rate is set to 0.001 and scaled to its 1/10 three times until convergence. The training images (resized to 256×256) are randomly flipped and cropped as input, and no other data augmentation is used. The inference is done with a single center crop of test images. All the results are reported as the top-1 accuracy of percentage.

For other hyper-parameters, the batch sizes for N_o/N_n are set to 128, and the temperatures for KD-Loss, *i.e.*, γ_o/γ_n, are set to 2. The loss weights for different tasks are set to 1, which turns out to be a reasonable choice in our implementation. For *Retrospection*, given that we deal with the cases that multiple tasks come in various sequences, the number of classes for old tasks rises at different rates. To enable a fair comparison, we choose to reserve five images for each class instead of a fixed budget for all classes. These images are randomly selected, and the strategy for *Retrospection* will be further discussed in Sect. 4.3.

Baselines. In order to validate the effectiveness of *Distillation* (denoted by D) and *Retrospection* (denoted by R), we compare our method to several baselines listed as follows:

(a) *Feature Extraction* [7]: as described in Sect. 1, it provides the reference performance for the first task.
(b) *Finetuning* [8]: as described in Sect. 1, it provides the reference performance for the last task.
(c) *Learning without Forgetting(LwF)* [15]: as described in Sect. 3.1, a representative method for multi-task lifelong learning.
(d) *Distillation*: as described in Sect. 3.2, *Adaptation by Distillation* without accessing the data for old tasks.
(e) *LwF+Retrospection*: the method to integrate *Retrospection* with *LwF*, L_{old}^R in Eq. (6) is adopted as the loss for old tasks instead of L_{old}^F in Eq. (2).
(f) *Distillation+Retrospection*: the final version of our approach, as described in Sects. 3.2 and 3.3, *Adaptation by Distillation* with a small subset of data reserved for old tasks.

Besides, the method from [20], denoted by *Encoder-based-LwF*, which is orthogonal to our approach, will be separately discussed and compared.

Table 2. Classification accuracy (%) for two-task scenario starting from ImageNet. *Feature Extraction* provides the reference performance for the first task while *Finetuning* provides the reference for the second one. D for *Distillation*, and R for *Retrospection*.

	ImageNet → Birds		ImageNet→ Flowers		ImageNet → Scenes	
Feature Extraction	57.44 (ref)	50.12 (−7.07)	57.44 (ref)	83.10 (−3.99)	57.44 (ref)	60.22 (−2.61)
Finetuning	43.20 (−14.25)	57.19 (ref)	48.45 (−8.99)	87.09 (ref)	46.61 (−10.84)	62.84 (ref)
LwF [15]	54.49 (−2.95)	57.45 (+0.26)	55.77 (−1.67)	85.87 (−1.22)	55.01 (−2.43)	64.03 (+1.19)
D (ours)	55.34 (−2.11)	58.21 (+1.02)	55.95 (−1.49)	86.19 (−0.89)	55.65 (−1.79)	64.70 (+1.87)
LwF+R	55.61 (−1.83)	57.79 (+0.60)	56.48 (−0.96)	86.53 (−0.55)	55.71 (−1.73)	64.70 (+1.87)
D+R (ours)	55.85 (−1.59)	59.55 (+2.36)	56.53 (−0.92)	87.02 (−0.07)	56.02 (−1.43)	65.00 (+2.16)

Table 3. Classification accuracy (%) for two-task scenario starting from Flowers. *Feature Extraction* provides the reference performance for the first task while *Finetuning* provides the reference for the second one. *D* for *Distillation*, and *R* for *Retrospection*.

	Flowers → Birds		Flowers → Scenes		Flowers → Aircrafts	
Feature Extraction	87.09 (ref)	48.29 (−8.72)	87.09 (ref)	57.09 (−5.07)	87.09 (ref)	40.98 (−26.13)
Finetuning	72.97 (−14.12)	57.02 (ref)	72.97 (−14.12)	62.16 (ref)	70.88 (−16.20)	67.12 (ref)
LwF [15]	85.08 (−2.00)	54.55 (−2.46)	84.86 (−2.23)	61.87 (−0.30)	81.69 (−5.40)	66.10 (−1.02)
D (ours)	85.30 (−1.79)	56.64 (−0.38)	85.36 (−1.72)	62.31 (+0.15)	82.14 (−4.94)	67.57 (+0.45)
LwF+R	85.15 (−1.93)	56.79 (−0.22)	85.31 (−1.77)	62.54 (+0.37)	85.07 (−2.02)	66.88 (−0.24)
D+R (ours)	**85.38 (−1.71)**	**58.16 (+1.14)**	**85.73 (−1.35)**	**64.03 (+1.87)**	**85.57 (−1.51)**	**68.38 (+1.26)**

4.2   Performance Comparison

Two-Task Scenario. Tables 2 and 3 show the performance comparison in the two-task scenario. The experiments in Table 2 start from ImageNet, while those in Table 3 start from the smaller Flowers. In Table 3, ImageNet is not considered as a task in the sequence but used to pretrain the model for preventing training from scratch on small datasets.

From the results in Tables 2 and 3, we observe that, either with or without *Retrospection*, *Distillation* outperforms *LwF* on each individual task. It demonstrates that adapting to the new task by knowledge distillation can facilitate the learning on the new task and simultaneously benefit the performance preservation on the old task. In some cases, *e.g.*, ImageNet → Birds, the performance of *Distillation* on the new task is superior to the reference provided by *Finetuning*. As far as we can observe, one reason is due to the regularization caused by mimicking the output of *Original CNN* as suggested in [15]. Another reason is that soft labels for the new task can not only enforce the relationship among classes [24] but also reduce the overfitting on new data, thus making the resulting model generalize better.

Besides, we respectively evaluate the effect of *Retrospection* on *LwF* and *Distillation*. The results indicate that a small subset of old data is beneficial for the performance preservation on the old task and also helpful for the learning on the new task.

Five-Task Scenario. Table 4 displays the final accuracy by different methods in five-task scenario. *LwF* is treated as a strong baseline here. It can be seen that *Distillation* also works reasonably well with a longer sequence of tasks, and achieves superior (or at least comparable) performance to *LwF* on each individual task either with or without *Retrospection*. For a thorough comparison, we also illustrate the degradation of accuracy on ImageNet as the number of tasks grows in Fig. 3, where the curve of *Distillation+Retrospection* goes down in the slowest rate. *Retrospection* further demonstrates its effectiveness for the performance preservation on old tasks. It is noteworthy that, with the help of *Retrospection*, on ImageNet which comes as the first task, the final accuracy with

Table 4. Classification accuracy (%) for five-task scenario. The results are reported at the end of the last training stage. *LwF* is treated as the baseline here. *D* for *Distillation*, and *R* for *Retrospection*.

	Imagenet → Scenes → Birds → Flowers → Aircrafts					
	Imagenet	Scenes	Birds	Flowers	Aircrafts	Average
LwF [15]	44.20 (ref)	55.90 (ref)	52.22 (ref)	81.64 (ref)	65.80 (ref)	59.95 (ref)
D (ours)	46.15 (+1.95)	55.67 (-0.22)	53.17 (+0.95)	82.37 (+0.73)	66.79 (+0.99)	60.83 (+0.88)
LwF+R	49.70 (+5.49)	59.25 (+3.36)	56.45 (+4.22)	85.49 (+3.85)	66.82 (+1.02)	63.54 (+3.59)
D+R(ours)	**50.58 (+6.38)**	**60.52 (+4.63)**	**56.84 (+4.62)**	**86.00 (+4.36)**	**68.41 (+2.61)**	**64.47 (+4.52)**
	Imagenet → Birds → Flowers → Aircrafts → Scenes					
	Imagenet	Birds	Flowers	Aircrafts	Scenes	Average
LwF [15]	43.37 (ref)	52.26 (ref)	79.91 (ref)	63.25 (ref)	60.82 (ref)	59.92 (ref)
D (ours)	45.94 (+2.57)	51.90 (-0.36)	81.21 (+1.30)	64.30 (+1.05)	60.90 (+0.07)	60.85 (+0.93)
LwF+R	50.05 (+6.67)	55.60 (+3.34)	85.12 (+5.20)	66.43 (+3.18)	62.39 (+1.57)	63.92 (+3.99)
D+R(ours)	**50.84 (+7.47)**	**57.05 (+4.79)**	**85.72 (+5.81)**	**67.42 (+4.17)**	**62.91 (+2.09)**	**64.79 (+4.87)**
	Imagenet → Flowers → Aircrafts → Scenes → Birds					
	Imagenet	Flowers	Aircrafts	Scenes	Birds	Average
LwF [15]	44.49 (ref)	77.50 (ref)	61.57 (ref)	60.30 (ref)	56.02 (ref)	59.98 (ref)
D (ours)	46.37 (+1.88)	79.25 (+1.74)	62.47 (+0.90)	60.00 (-0.30)	57.22 (+1.21)	61.06 (+1.08)
LwF+R	50.26 (+5.77)	84.48 (+6.98)	65.38 (+3.81)	62.31 (+2.01)	57.54 (+1.52)	63.99 (+4.02)
D+R(ours)	**50.76 (+6.26)**	**85.07 (+7.56)**	**65.83 (+4.26)**	**62.54 (+2.24)**	**59.52 (+3.50)**	**64.74 (+4.76)**

our method outperforms that with *LwF* by more than 6% in all three cases of five-task scenario shown in Table 4.

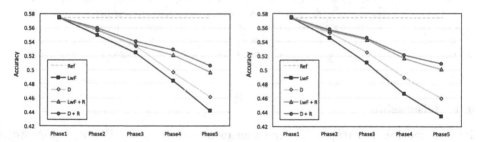

(a) Imagenet→Scenes→Birds→Flowers→Aircrafts. (b) Imagenet→Birds→Flowers→Aircrafts→Scenes.

Fig. 3. Accuracy degradation on ImageNet in five-task scenario. D for *Distillation*, and R for *Retrospection*.

Comparison with *Encoder-Based-LwF*. In Table 5, we compare *Distillation* to an orthogonal method denoted by *Encoder-based-LwF* [20]. It builds on the top of *LwF* and adds an auto-encoder for each old task, which aims at preserving the crucial features for old tasks at the cost of slightly increasing the model size.

We first carry on the experiments following the settings in [20], *i.e.*, the data for old tasks is not available[2]. The gain brought by *Encoder-based-LwF* compared to *LwF* is mainly for the old tasks and the performance on the latest task is comparable or a little inferior. In the sequence of five-task scenario shown in Table 5, *Distillation* is inferior to *Encoder-based-LwF* in the first two tasks but superior in the last three tasks, resulting in the comparable average performance. Moreover, the auto-encoder introduced by [20] can also be integrated with *Distillation*, which can further improve the accuracy.

Then the experiments are further conducted with *Retrospection*, *i.e.*, a small subset of data is reserved for old tasks. The results are shown in the bottom half of Table 5. With an auto-encoder [20] incorporated for each old task, *Retrospection* is still much useful for performance preservation compared to those without revisiting the data for old tasks. Besides, the combination of *Distillation+Retrospection* and the auto-encoder [20] leads to the best result.

Table 5. Classification accuracy (%) for comparison with *Encoder-based-LwF*. The reference performances are respectively given by *LwF* and *LwF+R*. D for *Distillation*, R for *Retrospection*, and *Encoder* for the approach in [20].

| | Imagenet → Scenes → Birds → Flowers → Aircrafts | | | | | |
	Imagenet	Scenes	Birds	Flowers	Aircrafts	Average
LwF [15]	44.20 (ref)	55.90 (ref)	52.22 (ref)	81.64 (ref)	65.80 (ref)	59.95 (ref)
LwF+Encoder [20]	46.35 (+2.14)	58.43 (+2.54)	52.95 (+0.72)	82.03 (+0.39)	64.75 (−1.05)	60.90 (+0.95)
D (ours)	46.15 (+1.95)	55.67 (−0.22)	53.17 (+0.95)	82.37 (+0.73)	66.79 (+0.99)	60.83 (+0.88)
D+Encoder (ours)	47.61 (+3.40)	57.76 (+1.86)	53.71 (+1.48)	82.56 (+0.93)	66.43 (+0.63)	**61.61 (+1.66)**
LwF+R	49.70 (ref)	59.25 (ref)	56.45 (ref)	85.49 (ref)	66.82 (ref)	63.54 (ref)
LwF+Encoder+R	50.47 (+0.77)	60.00 (+0.75)	56.45 (ref)	85.23 (−0.26)	66.46 (−0.36)	63.72 (+0.18)
D+R (ours)	50.58 (+0.89)	60.52 (+1.27)	56.84 (+0.40)	86.00 (+0.50)	68.41 (+1.59)	64.47 (+0.93)
D+Encoder+R (ours)	51.21 (+1.51)	61.49 (+2.24)	57.22 (+0.78)	86.04 (+0.55)	68.20 (+1.38)	**64.83 (+1.29)**

4.3   Discussion

Retrospection Strategy. In our experimental settings for *Retrospection*, we randomly select five images per class for old tasks, and the results with different random seeds are consistent. Here we further conduct an ablation study to investigate the number of images per class reserved for old tasks and the sampling strategy. Imagenet → Birds and Flowers → Birds are taken as the benchmarks. The results are obtained by *Distillation+Retrospection*. The performance on the old task is adopted as the criterion here.

As shown in Fig. 4, the performance on the old task rises as the number of stored images per class increases. Conserving five images per class for old

---

[2] The results with *Encoder-based-LwF* in Table 5 are from our re-implementation, which basically agree with those in [20]. The models in [20] are implemented with MatConvnet [25] and the data augmentation is adopted when recording the output of *Original CNN*. Besides the case of five-task scenario, we also take the experiments in the two-task scenario, which are provided in the supplementary material.

tasks is a reasonable trade-off between performance and memory consumption. As for the sampling strategy, in addition to random selection, here we attempt another sampling strategy. Specifically, a class center is first computed for each class by averaging the features of all samples belonging to this class, and then the images close to the class center are selected for *Retrospection*. The results in Fig. 4 indicate that this strategy does not show significant superiority to random selection. It is worth further exploration to develop more effective strategies for *Retrospection, e.g.*, to discover the number of images for each class adaptively.

Computation Cost. The computation cost introduced by *Distillation* compared to *LwF* [15] lies in two aspects: training *Expert CNN* on the new task and then recording its output, neither of which is cumbersome. The target model size is not increased at all. As for *Retrospection*, it requires additional memory space to store the data of old tasks. Nevertheless, our study shows that a small subset of old data can greatly benefit the performance preservation on old tasks, especially in a long sequence of tasks for different domains. For example, in the first case of five-task scenario shown in Table 4, the top-1 accuracy on ImageNet with *LwF+Retrospection* outperforms that with *LwF* by 5.49%, while the 5000 images reserved for ImageNet is less than 1/240 of the total training set.

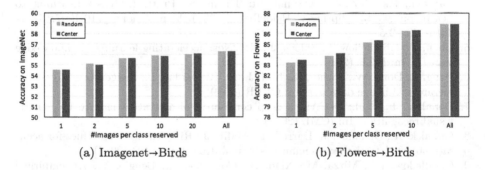

(a) Imagenet→Birds   (b) Flowers→Birds

Fig. 4. Ablation study on *Retrospection* strategy. Random for random selection, and Center for selecting images close to the class center. The accuracy on the old task increases with the increasing number of images reserved for each class. Choosing images close to the class center is not significantly superior to random selection.

5   Conclusion

This work proposes a novel approach, consisting of *Distillation* and *Retrospection*, for multi-task lifelong learning, which strikes a better balance on the performance preservation on old tasks and the adaptation to a new task. *Adaptation by Distillation* from an intermediate *Expert CNN* can not only facilitate the learning on the new task but also is beneficial for preserving the performance on old tasks. *Retrospection* is proposed to cache a small subset of data for old tasks, which proves to be greatly helpful for the performance preservation, especially in long sequences of tasks drawn from different distributions. The combination of *Distillation* and *Retrospection* outperforms *LwF* by a large margin, and bring consistent improvements to both old and new tasks.

Acknowledgment. This work is partially supported by the NSFC under Grant 61673362, Youth Innovation Promotion Association CAS, and the Fundamental Research Funds for the Central Universities. This work is also partially supported by the Big Data Collaboration Research grant from SenseTime Group (CUHK Agreement No. TS1610626), the General Research Fund (GRF) of Hong Kong (No. 14236516, 14241716, 14224316, 14209217).

References

1. http://nbviewer.jupyter.org/github/BVLC/caffe/blob/master/examples/02-fine-tuning.ipynb
2. Aljundi, R., Babiloni, F., Elhoseiny, M., Rohrbach, M., Tuytelaars, T.: Memory aware synapses: learning what (not) to forget. arXiv preprint arXiv:1711.09601 (2017)
3. Aljundi, R., Chakravarty, P., Tuytelaars, T.: Expert gate: lifelong learning with a network of experts. In: CVPR (2017)
4. Caruana, R.: Multitask learning. In: Thrun, S., Pratt, L. (eds.) Learning to Learn, pp. 95–133. Springer, Heidelberg (1998). https://doi.org/10.1007/978-1-4615-5529-2_5
5. Chen, T., Goodfellow, I., Shlens, J.: Net2Net: accelerating learning via knowledge transfer. In: ICLR (2016)
6. Deng, J., Dong, W., Socher, R., Li, L.J., Li, K., Fei-Fei, L.: Imagenet: a large-scale hierarchical image database. In: CVPR (2009)
7. Donahue, J., et al.: DeCAF: a deep convolutional activation feature for generic visual recognition. In: ICML (2014)
8. Girshick, R., Donahue, J., Darrell, T., Malik, J.: Rich feature hierarchies for accurate object detection and semantic segmentation. In: CVPR (2014)
9. Goodfellow, I.J., Mirza, M., Xiao, D., Courville, A., Bengio, Y.: An empirical investigation of catastrophic forgetting in gradient-based neural networks. arXiv preprint arXiv:1312.6211 (2013)
10. Hinton, G., Vinyals, O., Dean, J.: Distilling the knowledge in a neural network. arXiv preprint arXiv:1503.02531 (2015)
11. Jia, Y., et al.: Caffe: convolutional architecture for fast feature embedding. arXiv preprint arXiv:1408.5093 (2014)
12. Jung, H., Ju, J., Jung, M., Kim, J.: Less-forgetful learning for domain expansion in deep neural networks. In: AAAI (2018)
13. Kirkpatrick, J., et al.: Overcoming catastrophic forgetting in neural networks. Proc. Natl. Acad. Sci. **114**(13), 3521–3526 (2017)
14. Krizhevsky, A., Sutskever, I., Hinton, G.E.: Imagenet classification with deep convolutional neural networks. In: NIPS (2012)
15. Li, Z., Hoiem, D.: Learning without forgetting. IEEE Trans. Pattern Anal. Mach. Intell., 1 (2018)
16. Maji, S., Kannala, J., Rahtu, E., Blaschko, M., Vedaldi, A.: Fine-grained visual classification of aircraft. Technical report (2013)

17. Mitchell, T.M.: The need for biases in learning generalizations. Department of Computer Science, Laboratory for Computer Science Research, Rutgers University, New Jersey (1980)
18. Nilsback, M.E., Zisserman, A.: Automated flower classification over a large number of classes. In: Proceedings of the Indian Conference on Computer Vision, Graphics and Image Processing (2008)
19. Quattoni, A., Torralba, A.: Recognizing indoor scenes. In: CVPR (2009)
20. Rannen Ep Triki, A., Aljundi, R., Blaschko, M., Tuytelaars, T.: Encoder based lifelong learning. In: ICCV (2017)
21. Rebuffi, S.A., Kolesnikov, A., Lampert, C.H.: iCaRL: incremental classifier and representation learning. In: CVPR (2017)
22. Romero, A., Ballas, N., Kahou, S.E., Chassang, A., Gatta, C., Bengio, Y.: Fitnets: hints for thin deep nets. In: ICLR (2015)
23. Simonyan, K., Zisserman, A.: Very deep convolutional networks for large-scale image recognition. arXiv preprint arXiv:1409.1556 (2014)
24. Tzeng, E., Hoffman, J., Darrell, T., Saenko, K.: Simultaneous deep transfer across domains and tasks. In: ICCV (2015)
25. Vedaldi, A., Lenc, K.: MatConvNet - convolutional neural networks for MATLAB. In: ACM Multimedia (2015)
26. Wah, C., Branson, S., Welinder, P., Perona, P., Belongie, S.: The Caltech-UCSD birds-200-2011 dataset. Technical report CNS-TR-2011-001, California Institute of Technology (2011)
27. Zenke, F., Poole, B., Ganguli, S.: Continual learning through synaptic intelligence. In: ICML (2017)

A Closed-Form Solution to Photorealistic Image Stylization

Yijun Li[1](✉), Ming-Yu Liu[2], Xueting Li[1], Ming-Hsuan Yang[1,2], and Jan Kautz[2]

[1] University of California, Merced, Merced, USA
{yli62,xli75,mhyang}@ucmerced.edu
[2] NVIDIA, Santa Clara, USA
{mingyul,jkautz}@nvidia.com

Abstract. Photorealistic image stylization concerns transferring style of a reference photo to a content photo with the constraint that the stylized photo should remain photorealistic. While several photorealistic image stylization methods exist, they tend to generate spatially inconsistent stylizations with noticeable artifacts. In this paper, we propose a method to address these issues. The proposed method consists of a stylization step and a smoothing step. While the stylization step transfers the style of the reference photo to the content photo, the smoothing step ensures spatially consistent stylizations. Each of the steps has a closed-form solution and can be computed efficiently. We conduct extensive experimental validations. The results show that the proposed method generates photorealistic stylization outputs that are more preferred by human subjects as compared to those by the competing methods while running much faster. Source code and additional results are available at https://github.com/NVIDIA/FastPhotoStyle.

Keywords: Image stylization · Photorealism · Closed-form solution

1 Introduction

Photorealistic image stylization aims at changing style of a photo to that of a reference photo. For a faithful stylization, content of the photo should remain the same. Furthermore, the output photo should look like a real photo as it were captured by a camera. Figure 1 shows two photorealistic image stylization examples. In one example, we transfer a summery photo to a snowy one, while in the other, we transfer a day-time photo to a night-time photo.

Classical photorealistic stylization methods are mostly based on color/tone matching [1–4] and are often limited to specific scenarios (e.g., seasons [5] and headshot portraits [6]). Recently, Gatys et al. [7,8] show that the correlations between deep features encode the visual style of an image and propose an optimization-based method, the neural style transfer algorithm, for image stylization. While the method shows impressive performance for *artistic* stylization

© Springer Nature Switzerland AG 2018
V. Ferrari et al. (Eds.): ECCV 2018, LNCS 11207, pp. 468–483, 2018.
https://doi.org/10.1007/978-3-030-01219-9_28

(a) Style   (b) Content   (c) Gatys et al. [8] (d) Luan et al. [9]   (e) Ours

Fig. 1. Given a style photo (a) and a content photo (b), photorealistic image stylization aims at transferring style of the style photo to the content photo as shown in (c), (d) and (e). Comparing with existing methods [8,9], the output photos computed by our method are stylized more consistently and with fewer artifacts. Moreover, our method runs an order of magnitude faster.

(converting images to paintings), it often introduces structural artifacts and distortions when applied to photorealistic image stylization as shown in Fig. 1(c). In a follow-up work, Luan et al. [9] propose adding a regularization term to the optimization objective function of the neural style transfer algorithm for avoiding distortions in the stylization output. However, this often results in inconsistent stylizations in semantically uniform regions as shown in Fig. 1(d). To address the issues, we propose a photorealistic image stylization method.

Our method consists of a stylization step and a smoothing step. Both have a closed-form solution[1] and can be computed efficiently. The stylization step is based on the whitening and coloring transform (WCT) [10], which stylizes images via feature projections. The WCT was designed for *artistic* stylization. Similar to the neural style transfer algorithm, it suffers from structural artifacts when applied to photorealistic image stylization. Our WCT-based stylization step resolves the issue by utilizing a novel network design for feature transform. The WCT-based stylization step alone may generate spatially inconsistent stylizations. We resolve this issue by the proposed smoothing step, which is based on a manifold ranking algorithm. We conduct extensive experimental validation with comparison to the state-of-the-art methods. User study results show that our method generates outputs with better stylization effects and fewer artifacts.

2   Related Work

Existing stylization methods can be classified into two categories: global and local. Global methods [1,2,11] achieve stylization through matching the means and variances of pixel colors [1] or their histograms [2]. Local methods [5,6,12–14] stylize images through finding dense correspondences between the content and

---

[1] A closed-form solution means that the solution can be obtained in a fixed finite number of operations, including convolutions, max-pooling, whitening, etc.

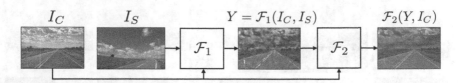

Fig. 2. Our photorealistic image stylization method consists of two closed-form steps: $\mathcal{F}_1$ and $\mathcal{F}_2$. While $\mathcal{F}_1$ maps I_C to an intermediate image carrying the style of I_S, $\mathcal{F}_2$ removes noticeable artifacts, which produces a photorealistic output.

style photos based on either low-level or high-level features. These approaches are slow in practice. Also, they are often developed for specific scenarios (e.g., day-time or season change).

Gatys et al. [7,8] propose the neural style transfer algorithm for *artistic* stylization. The major step in the algorithm is to solve an optimization problem of matching the Gram matrices of deep features extracted from the content and style photos. A number of methods have been developed [10,15–21] to further improve its stylization performance and speed. However, these methods do not aim for preserving photorealism (see Fig. 1(c)). Post-processing techniques [22, 23] have been proposed to refine these results by matching the gradients between the input and output photos.

Photorealistic image stylization is related to the image-to-image translation problem [24–31] where the goal is to learn to translate an image from one domain to another. However, photorealistic image stylization does not require a training dataset of content and style images for learning the translation function. Photorealistic image stylization can be considered as a special kind of image-to-image translation. Not only can it be used to translate a photo to a different domain (e.g., form day to night-time) but also transfer style (e.g., extent of darkness) of a specific reference image to the content image.

Closest to our work is the method of Luan et al. [9]. It improves photorealism of stylization outputs computed by the neural style transfer algorithm [7,8] by incorporating a new loss term to the optimization objective, which has the effect of better preserving local structures in the content photo. However, it often generates inconsistent stylization with noticeable artifacts (Fig. 1(d)). Moreover, the method is computationally expensive. Our proposed algorithm aims at efficient and effective photorealistic image stylization. We demonstrate that it performs favorably against Luan et al. [9] in terms of both quality and speed.

3   Photorealistic Image Stylization

Our photorealistic image stylization algorithm consists of two steps as illustrated in Fig. 2. The first step is a stylization transform $\mathcal{F}_1$ called PhotoWCT. Given a style photo I_S, $\mathcal{F}_1$ transfer the style of I_S to the content photo I_C while minimizing structural artifacts in the output image. Although $\mathcal{F}_1$ can faithfully stylize I_C, it often generates inconsistent stylizations in semantically similar regions.

Therefore, we use a photorealistic smoothing function $\mathcal{F}_2$, to eliminate these artifacts. Our whole algorithm can be written as a two-step mapping function:

$$\mathcal{F}_2\Big(\mathcal{F}_1\big(I_C, I_S\big), I_C\Big), \tag{1}$$

In the following, we discuss the stylization and smoothing steps in details.

3.1 Stylization

The PhotoWCT is based on the WCT [10]. It utilizes a novel network design for achieving photorealistic image stylization. We briefly review the WCT below.

WCT. The WCT [10] formulates stylization as an image reconstruction problem with feature projections. To utilize WCT, an auto-encoder for general image reconstruction is first trained. Specifically, it uses the VGG-19 model [32] as the encoder $\mathcal{E}$ (weights are kept fixed) and trains a decoder $\mathcal{D}$ for reconstructing the input image. The decoder is symmetrical to the encoder and uses upsampling layers (pink blocks in Fig. 3(a)) to enlarge the spatial resolutions of the feature maps. Once the auto-encoder is trained, a pair of projection functions are inserted at the network bottleneck to perform stylization through the whitening (P_C) and coloring (P_S) transforms. The key idea behind the WCT is to directly match feature correlations of the content image to those of the style image via the two projections. Specifically, given a pair of content image I_C and style image I_S, the WCT first extracts their vectorised VGG features $H_C = \mathcal{E}(I_C)$ and $H_S = \mathcal{E}(I_S)$, and then transform the content feature H_C via

$$H_{CS} = P_S P_C H_C, \tag{2}$$

where $P_C = E_C \Lambda_C^{-\frac{1}{2}} E_C^\top$, and $P_S = E_S \Lambda_S^{\frac{1}{2}} E_S^\top$. Here Λ_C and Λ_S are the diagonal matrices with the eigenvalues of the covariance matrix $H_C H_C^\top$ and $H_S H_S^\top$ respectively. The matrices E_C and E_S are the corresponding orthonormal matrices of the eigenvectors, respectively. After the transformation, the correlations of transformed features match those of the style features, i.e., $H_{CS} H_{CS}^\top = H_S H_S^\top$. Finally, the stylized image is obtained by directly feeding the transformed feature map into the decoder: $Y = \mathcal{D}(H_{CS})$. For better stylization performance, Li et al. [10] use a multi-level stylization strategy, which performs the WCT on the VGG features at different layers.

The WCT performs well for artistic image stylization. However it generates structural artifacts (e.g., distortions on object boundaries) for photorealistic image stylization (Fig. 4(c)). The proposed PhotoWCT is designed to suppress these structural artifacts.

PhotoWCT. Our PhotoWCT design is motivated by the observation that the max-pooling operation in the WCT reduces spatial information in feature maps. Simply upsampling feature maps in the decoder fails to recover detailed structures of the input image. That is, we need to pass the lost spatial information to the decoder to facilitate reconstructing these fine details. Inspired by the success

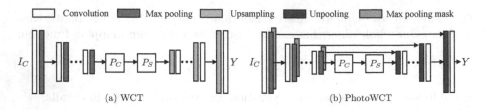

Fig. 3. The PhotoWCT and WCT share the same encoder architecture and projection steps. In the PhotoWCT, we replace the upsampling layers (pink) with unpooling layers (green). Note that the unpooling layer is used together with the pooling mask (yellow) which records *where* carries the *maximum* over each max pooling region in the corresponding pooling layer [33]. (Color figure online)

of the unpooling layer [33–35] in preserving spatial information, the PhotoWCT replaces the upsampling layers in the WCT with unpooling layers. The PhotoWCT function is formulated as

$$Y = \mathcal{F}_1(I_C, I_S) = \overline{\mathcal{D}}(P_S P_C H_C),$$ (3)

where $\overline{\mathcal{D}}$ is the decoder, which contains unpooling layers and is trained for image reconstruction. Figure 3 illustrates the network architecture difference between the WCT and the proposed PhotoWCT.

Figure 4(c) and (d) compare the stylization results of the WCT and PhotoWCT. As highlighted in close-ups, the straight lines along the building boundary in the content image becomes zigzagged in the WCT stylization result but remains straight in the PhotoWCT result. The PhotoWCT-stylized image has much fewer structural artifacts. We also perform a user study in the experiment section to quantitatively verify that the PhotoWCT generally leads to better stylization effects than the WCT.

3.2 Photorealistic Smoothing

The PhotoWCT-stylized result (Fig. 4(d)) still looks less like a photo since semantically similar regions are often stylized inconsistently. As shown in Fig. 4, when applying the PhotoWCT to stylize the day-time photo using the night-time photo, the stylized sky region would be more photorealistic if it were uniformly dark blue instead of partly dark and partly light blue. It is based on this observation, we employ the pixel affinities in the content photo to smooth the PhotoWCT-stylized result.

We aim to achieve two goals in the smoothing step. First, pixels with similar content in a local neighborhood should be stylized similarly. Second, the output should not deviate significantly from the PhotoWCT result in order to maintain the global stylization effects. We first represent all pixels as nodes in a graph and define an affinity matrix $W = \{w_{ij}\} \in \mathbb{R}^{N \times N}$ (N is the number of pixels) to describe pixel similarities. We define a smoothness term and a fitting term that model these two goals in the following optimization problem:

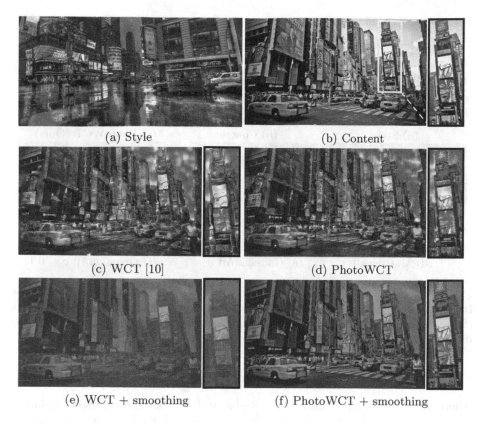

Fig. 4. The stylization output generated by the PhotoWCT better preserves local structures in the content images, which is important for the image smoothing step as shown in (e) and (f). (Color figure online)

$$\operatorname*{argmin}_{r} \frac{1}{2} \left(\sum_{i,j=1}^{N} w_{ij} \| \frac{r_i}{\sqrt{d_{ii}}} - \frac{r_j}{\sqrt{d_{jj}}} \|^2 + \lambda \sum_{i=1}^{N} \| r_i - y_i \|^2 \right), \qquad (4)$$

where y_i is the pixel color in the PhotoWCT-stylized result Y and r_i is the pixel color in the desired smoothed output R. The variable $d_{ii} = \sum_j w_{ij}$ is the diagonal element in the degree matrix D of W, i.e., $D = \operatorname{diag}\{d_{11}, d_{22}, ..., d_{NN}\}$. In (4), λ controls the balance of the two terms.

Our formulation is motivated by the graph-based ranking algorithms [36,37]. In the ranking algorithms, Y is a binary input where each element indicates if a specific item is a query ($y_i = 1$ if y_i is a query and $y_i = 0$ otherwise). The optimal solution R is the ranking values of all the items based on their pairwise affinities. In our method, we set Y as the PhotoWCT-stylized result. The optimal solution R is the smoothed version of Y based on the pairwise pixel affinities, which encourages consistent stylization within semantically similar regions. The above optimization problem is a simple quadratic problem with a closed-form solution, which is given by

(a) Style   (b) Content   (c) PhotoWCT (Ours)

(d) MattingAff   (e) GaussianAff $\sigma = 1$ (f) GaussianAff $\sigma = 0.1$

Fig. 5. Smoothing with different affinities. To refine the PhotoWCT result in (c), it is hard to find an optimal σ for the Gaussian Affinity that performs globally well as shown in (e)–(f). In contrast, using the Matting Affinity can simultaneously smooth different regions well as shown in (d).

$$R^* = (1 - \alpha)(I - \alpha S)^{-1}Y, \tag{5}$$

where I is the identity matrix, $\alpha = \frac{1}{1+\lambda}$ and S is the normalized Laplacian matrix computed from I_C, i.e., $S = D^{-\frac{1}{2}}WD^{-\frac{1}{2}} \in \mathbb{R}^{N \times N}$. As the constructed graph is often sparsely connected (i.e., most elements in W are zero), the inverse operation in (5) can be computed efficiently. With the closed-form solution, the smoothing step can be written as a function mapping given by:

$$R^* = \mathcal{F}_2(Y, I_C) = (1 - \alpha)(I - \alpha S)^{-1}Y. \tag{6}$$

Affinity. The affinity matrix W is computed using the content photo based on an 8-connected image graph assumption. While several choices of affinity metrics exist, a popular one is to define the affinity (denoted as GaussianAff) as $w_{ij} = e^{-\|I_i - I_j\|^2/\sigma^2}$ where I_i, I_j are the RGB values of adjacent pixels i, j and σ is a global scaling hyper-parameter [38]. However, it is difficult to determine the σ value in practice. It often results in either over-smoothing the entire photo (Fig. 5(e)) or stylizing the photo inconsistently (Fig. 5(f)). To avoid selecting one global scaling hyper-parameter, we resort to the matting affinity [39, 40] (denoted as MattingAff) where the affinity between two pixels is based on means and variances of pixels in a local window. Figure 5(d) shows that the matting affinity is able to simultaneously smooth different regions well.

WCT Plus Smoothing. We note that the smoothing step can also remove structural artifacts in the WCT as shown in Fig. 4(e). However, it leads to unsatisfactory stylization. The main reason is that the content photo and the WCT result are severely misaligned due to spatial distortions. For example, a stylized pixel of the building in the WCT result may correspond to a pixel of the sky in the content photo. Consequently this causes wrong queries in Y for the smoothing step. This shows why we need to use the PhotoWCT to remove distortions first. Figure 4(f) shows that the combination of PhotoWCT and smoothing leads to better photorealism while still maintaining faithful stylization.

4 Experiments

In the section, we will first discuss the implementation details. We will then present visual and user study evaluation results. Finally, we will analyze various design choices and run-time of the proposed algorithm.

Implementation Details. We use the layers from $conv1\_1$ to $conv4\_1$ in the VGG-19 network [32] for the encoder $\mathcal{E}$. The encoder weights are given by ImageNet-pretrained weights. The decoder $\overline{\mathcal{D}}$ is the inverse of the encoder. We train the decoder by minimizing the sum of the L_2 reconstruction loss and perceptual loss [17] using the Microsoft COCO dataset [41]. We adopt the multi-level stylization strategy proposed in the WCT [10] where we apply the PhotoWCT to VGG features in different layers.

Similar to the state-of-the-art methods [9,42], our algorithm can leverage semantic label maps for obtaining better stylization results when they are available. When performing PhotoWCT stylization, for each semantic label, we compute a pair of projection matrices P_C and P_S using the features from the image regions with the same label in the content and style photos, respectively. The pair is then used to stylize these image regions. With a semantic label map, content and style matching can be performed more accurately. We note that the proposed algorithm does not need precise semantic label maps for obtaining good stylization results. Finally, we also use the efficient filtering step described in Luan et al. [9] for post-processing.

Visual Comparison. We compare the proposed algorithm to two categories of stylization algorithms: photorealistic and artistic. The evaluated photorealistic stylization algorithms include Reinhard et al. [1], Pitié et al. [2], and Luan et al. [9]. Both Reinhard et al. [1] and Pitié et al. [2] represent classical techniques that are based on color statistics matching, while Luan et al. [9] is based on neural style transfer [8]. On the other hand, the set of evaluated artistic stylization algorithms include Gatys et al. [8], Huang et al. [21], and the WCT [10]. They all utilize deep networks.

Figure 6 shows visual results of the evaluated photorealistic stylization algorithms. Overall, the images generated by the proposed algorithm exhibit better stylization effects. While both Reinhard et al. [1] and Pitié et al. [2] change colors of the content photos, they fail to transfer the style. We argue that photorealistic stylization cannot be purely achieved via color transfer. It requires adding new patterns that represent the style photo to the content photo. For example, in the third example of Fig. 6 (bottom), our algorithm not only changes the color of

Fig. 6. Visual comparisons with photorealistic stylization methods. In addition to color transfer, our method also synthesizes patterns in the style photos (e.g., the dark cloud in the top example, the snow at the bottom example).

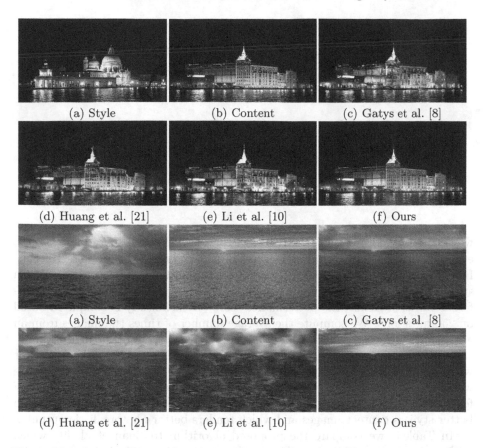

Fig. 7. Visual comparison with artistic stylization algorithms. Note the structural distortions on object boundaries (e.g., building) and detailed edges (e.g., sea, cloud) generated by the competing stylization methods.

ground regions to white but also synthesizes the snow patterns as they appear in the style photo. The method of Luan et al. [9] achieves good stylization effects at first glance. However, a closer look reveals that the generated photos contain noticeable artifacts, e.g., the irregular brightness on buildings and trees. Several semantically similar regions are stylized inconsistently.

Figure 7 shows the visual comparison between the proposed algorithm and artistic stylization algorithms. Although the other evaluated algorithms are able to transfer the style well, they render noticeable structural artifacts and inconsistent stylizations across the images. In contrast, our method produces more photorealistic results.

User Studies. We resort to user studies for performance evaluation since photorealistic image stylization is a highly subjective task. Our benchmark dataset consists of a set of 25 content–style pairs provided by Luan et al. [9]. We use the Amazon Mechanical Turk (AMT) platform for evaluation. In each question,

Table 1. User preference: proposed vs. Luan et al. and proposed vs. Pitié et al.

	Luan et al. [9]/proposed	Pitié et al. [2]/proposed
Better stylization	36.9%/**63.1%**	44.8%/**55.2%**
Fewer artifacts	26.5%/**73.5%**	48.8%/**51.2%**

Table 2. User preference: proposed versus *artistic* stylization algorithms.

	Gatys et al. [8]	Huang et al. [21]	Li et al. [10]	proposed
Better stylization	19.2%	8.4%	16.0%	**56.4%**
Fewer artifacts	21.6%	6.0%	6.8%	**65.6%**

we show the AMT workers a content–style pair and the stylized results from the evaluated algorithms displayed in random order. The AMT workers (lifetime Human Intelligent Task approval rate greater than 98%) are asked to select a stylized result based on the instructions. Each question is answered by 10 different workers. Hence, the performance score for each study is computed based on 250 questions. We compute the average number of times the images from an algorithm is selected, which is used as the preference score of the algorithm.

We conduct two user studies. In one study, we ask the AMT workers to select which stylized photo better carries the target style. In the other study, we ask the workers to select which stylized photo looks more like a real photo (containing fewer artifacts). Through the studies, we would like to answer which algorithm better stylizes content images and which renders better photorealistic outputs.

In Table 1, we compare the proposed algorithm to Luan et al. [9], which is the current state-of-the-art. The results show that 63.1% of the users prefer the stylization results generated by our algorithm and 73.5% regard our output photos as more photorealistic. We also compare our algorithm to the classical algorithm of Pitié et al. [2]. From Table 1, our results are as photorealistic as those computed by the classical algorithm (which simply performs color matching), and 55.2% of the users consider our stylization results better.

Table 2 compares our algorithm with the artistic stylization algorithms for user preference scores. We find our algorithm achieves a score of 56.4% and 65.6% for the stylization effect and photorealism, which are significantly better than the other algorithms. The artistic stylization algorithms do not perform well since they are not designed for the photorealistic stylization task.

WCT Versus PhotoWCT. We compare the proposed algorithm with a variant where the PhotoWCT step is replaced by the WCT [10]. Again, we conduct two user studies on stylization effects and photorealism as described earlier. The result shows that the proposed algorithm is favored over its variant for better stylization 83.6% of the times and favored for better photorealism 83.2% of the times.

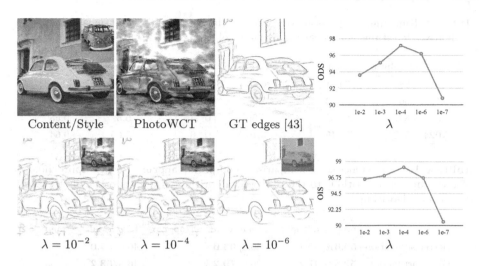

Fig. 8. Visualization of effects of using different λ values in the photorealistic smoothing step. We show the edge maps of different stylization results (inset) at bottom and compare them with the edge map of the content in terms of the ODS and OIS metric (rightmost).

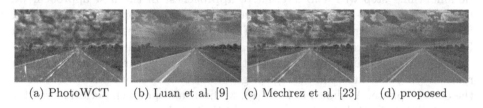

(a) PhotoWCT   (b) Luan et al. [9]   (c) Mechrez et al. [23]   (d) proposed

Fig. 9. Comparison between using our photorealistic smoothing step and other refinement methods (b)–(d)

Sensitivity Analysis on λ. In the photorealistic smoothing step, the λ balances between the smoothness term and fitting term in (4). A smaller λ renders smoother results, while a larger λ renders results that are more faithful to the queries (the PhotoWCT result). Figure 8 shows results of using different λ values. In general, decreasing λ helps remove artifacts and hence improves photorealism. However, if λ is too small, the output image tends to be over-smoothed. In order to find the optimal λ, we perform a grid search. We use the similarity between the boundary maps extracted from stylized and original content photos as the criteria since object boundaries should remain the same despite the stylization [44]. We employ the HED method [43] for boundary detection and use two standard boundary detection metrics: ODS and OIS. A higher ODS or OIS score means a stylized photo better preserves the content in the original photo. The average scores over the benchmark dataset are shown on the rightmost of Fig. 8. Based on the results, we use $\lambda = 10^{-4}$ in all the experiments.

Table 3. Run-time comparison. We compute the average run time (in seconds) of the evaluated algorithms across various image resolutions.

Image resolution	Luan et al. [9]	proposed	PhotoWCT	smoothing	approx
256 × 128	79.61	0.96	0.40	0.56	0.41
512 × 256	186.52	2.95	0.42	2.53	0.47
768 × 384	380.82	7.05	0.53	6.52	0.55
1024 × 512	650.45	13.16	0.56	12.60	0.64

Table 4. User preference score comparison: comparing `approx` (the fast approximation of the proposed algorithm) to the proposed algorithm as well as other photorealistic stylization algorithms.

	proposed/approx	Luan et al. [9]/approx	Pitié et al. [2]/approx
Better stylization	**59.6%**/40.4	36.4/**63.6%**	46.0/**54.0%**
Fewer artifacts	**52.8%**/47.2	20.8/**79.2%**	46.8/**53.2%**

Alternative Smoothing Techniques. In Fig. 9, we compare our photorealistic smoothing step with two alternative approaches. In the first approach, we use the PhotoWCT-stylized photo as the initial solution for solving the second optimization problem in the method of Luan et al. [9]. The result is shown in Fig. 9(b). This approach leads to noticeable artifacts as the road color is distorted. In the second approach, we use the method of Mechrez et al. [23], which refines stylized results by matching the gradients in the output photo to those in the content photo. As shown in Fig. 9(c), we find this approach performs well for removing structural distortions on boundaries but does not remove visual artifacts. In contrast, our method (Fig. 9(d)) generates more photorealistic results with an efficient closed-form solution.

Run-Time. In Table 3, we compare the run-time of the proposed algorithm to that of the state-of-the-art [9]. We note that while our algorithm has a closed-form solution, Luan et al. [9] rely on non-convex optimization. To stylize a photo, Luan et al. [9] solve two non-convex optimization problems sequentially where the solution to the first optimization problem is used as an initial solution to solve the second optimization problem. We report the total run-time required for obtaining the final stylization results. We resize the content images in the benchmark dataset to different sizes and report the average run-time for each image size. The experiment is conducted on a PC with an NVIDIA Titan X Pascal GPU. To stylize images of 1024 × 512 resolution, our algorithm takes 13.16 s, which is 49 times faster than 650.45 s achieved by Luan et al. [9].

In Table 3, we also report the run-time of each step in our algorithm. We find the smoothing step takes most of the computation time, since it involves inverting the sparse matrix W in (5) using the LU decomposition. By employing efficient LU-decomposition algorithms developed for large sparse matrices, the complexity can be roughly determined by the number of non-zero entries in the matrices

Content/Style   Reinhard et al. [1]   Pitié et al. [2]   Luan et al. [9]   Ours

Fig. 10. Failure case. Both the proposed and other photorealistic stylization algorithms fail to transfer the flower patterns to the pot.

only. In our case, since each pixel is only connected to its neighbors (e.g., 3×3 window), the number of non-zero values in W grows linearly with the image size.

For further speed-up, we can approximate the smoothing step using guided image filtering [45], which can smooth the PhotoWCT output based on the content photo. We will refer to this version of our algorithm `approx`. Although approximating the smoothing step with guided image filtering results in slightly degraded performance as comparing to the original algorithm, it leads to a large speed gain as shown in Table 3. To stylize images of 1024×512 resolution, `approx` only takes 0.64 s, which is 1,016 times faster than 650.45 s achieved by Luan et al. [9]. To quantify the performance degradation due to the approximation, we conduct additional user studies comparing the proposed algorithm and its approximation. We use the same evaluation protocol as described above. The results are shown in Table 4. In general, the stylization results rendered by `approx` are less preferred by the users as compared to those generated by the full algorithm. However, the results from `approx` are still preferred over other methods in terms of both stylization effects and photorealism.

Failure Case. Figure 10 shows a failure case where the proposed method fails to transfer the flower patterns in the style photo to the content photo. Similar limitations also apply to the other photorealistic stylization methods [1,2,9]. Since the proposed method uses the pixel affinity of the content in the photorealistic smoothing step, it favors a stylization output with smooth color transition on the pot surface as in the input photo.

5   Conclusions

We presented a novel fast photorealistic image stylization method. It consists of a stylization step and a photorealistic smoothing step. Both steps have efficient closed-form solutions. Experimental results show that our algorithm generates stylization outputs that are much more preferred by human subject as compared to those by the state-of-the-art, while running much faster.

References

1. Reinhard, E., Ashikhmin, M., Gooch, B., Shirley, P.: Color transfer between images. IEEE Comput. Graph. Appl. **21**(5), 34–41 (2001)
2. Pitié, F., Kokaram, A.C., Dahyot, R.: N-dimensional probability density function transfer and its application to color transfer. In: ICCV (2005)
3. Sunkavalli, K., Johnson, M.K., Matusik, W., Pfister, H.: Multi-scale image harmonization. ACM Trans. Graph. **29**(4), 125 (2010)
4. Bae, S., Paris, S., Durand, F.: Two-scale tone management for photographic look. ACM Trans. Graph. **25**(3), 637–645 (2006)
5. Laffont, P.Y., Ren, Z., Tao, X., Qian, C., Hays, J.: Transient attributes for high-level understanding and editing of outdoor scenes. ACM Trans. Graph. **33**(4), 149 (2014)
6. Shih, Y., Paris, S., Barnes, C., Freeman, W.T., Durand, F.: Style transfer for headshot portraits. In: SIGGRAPH (2014)
7. Gatys, L.A., Ecker, A.S., Bethge, M.: Texture synthesis using convolutional neural networks. In: NIPS (2015)
8. Gatys, L.A., Ecker, A.S., Bethge, M.: Image style transfer using convolutional neural networks. In: CVPR (2016)
9. Luan, F., Paris, S., Shechtman, E., Bala, K.: Deep photo style transfer. In: CVPR (2017)
10. Li, Y., Fang, C., Yang, J., Wang, Z., Lu, X., Yang, M.H.: Universal style transfer via feature transforms. In: NIPS (2017)
11. Freedman, D., Kisilev, P.: Object-to-object color transfer: optimal flows and SMSP transformations. In: CVPR (2010)
12. Shih, Y., Paris, S., Durand, F., Freeman, W.T.: Data-driven hallucination of different times of day from a single outdoor photo. In: SIGGRAPH (2013)
13. Wu, F., Dong, W., Kong, Y., Mei, X., Paul, J.C., Zhang, X.: Content-based colour transfer. In: Computer Graphics Forum, vol. 32, pp. 190–203 (2013)
14. Tsai, Y.H., Shen, X., Lin, Z., Sunkavalli, K., Yang, M.H.: Sky is not the limit: semantic-aware sky replacement. ACM Trans. Graph. **35**(4), 149 (2016)
15. Li, C., Wand, M.: Combining Markov random fields and convolutional neural networks for image synthesis. In: CVPR (2016)
16. Ulyanov, D., Lebedev, V., Vedaldi, A., Lempitsky, V.: Texture networks: feed-forward synthesis of textures and stylized images. In: ICML (2016)
17. Johnson, J., Alahi, A., Fei-Fei, L.: Perceptual losses for real-time style transfer and super-resolution. In: Leibe, B., Matas, J., Sebe, N., Welling, M. (eds.) ECCV 2016. LNCS, vol. 9906, pp. 694–711. Springer, Cham (2016). https://doi.org/10.1007/978-3-319-46475-6_43
18. Li, Y., Fang, C., Yang, J., Wang, Z., Lu, X., Yang, M.H.: Diversified texture synthesis with feed-forward networks. In: CVPR (2017)
19. Dumoulin, V., Shlens, J., Kudlur, M.: A learned representation for artistic style. In: ICLR (2017)
20. Ghiasi, G., Lee, H., Kudlur, M., Dumoulin, V., Shlens, J.: Exploring the structure of a real-time, arbitrary neural artistic stylization network. In: BMVC (2017)
21. Huang, X., Belongie, S.: Arbitrary style transfer in real-time with adaptive instance normalization. In: ICCV (2017)
22. Li, S., Xu, X., Nie, L., Chua, T.S.: Laplacian-steered neural style transfer. In: ACM MM (2017)

23. Mechrez, R., Shechtman, E., Zelnik-Manor, L.: Photorealistic style transfer with screened Poisson equation. In: BMVC (2017)
24. Isola, P., Zhu, J.Y., Zhou, T., Efros, A.A.: Image-to-image translation with conditional adversarial networks. In: CVPR (2017)
25. Wang, T.C., Liu, M.Y., Zhu, J.Y., Tao, A., Kautz, J., Catanzaro, B.: High-resolution image synthesis and semantic manipulation with conditional GANs. In: CVPR (2018)
26. Liu, M.Y., Tuzel, O.: Coupled generative adversarial networks. In: NIPS (2016)
27. Taigman, Y., Polyak, A., Wolf, L.: Unsupervised cross-domain image generation. In: ICLR (2017)
28. Shrivastava, A., Pfister, T., Tuzel, O., Susskind, J., Wang, W., Webb, R.: Learning from simulated and unsupervised images through adversarial training. In: CVPR (2017)
29. Liu, M.Y., Breuel, T., Kautz, J.: Unsupervised image-to-image translation networks. In: NIPS (2017)
30. Zhu, J.Y., Park, T., Isola, P., Efros, A.A.: Unpaired image-to-image translation using cycle-consistent adversarial networks. In: ICCV (2017)
31. Huang, X., Liu, M.Y., Belongie, S., Kautz, J.: Multimodal unsupervised image-to-image translation. In: ECCV (2018)
32. Simonyan, K., Zisserman, A.: Very deep convolutional networks for large-scale image recognition. In: ICLR (2015)
33. Zhao, J., Mathieu, M., Goroshin, R., LeCun, Y.: Stacked what-where auto-encoders. In: ICLR Workshop (2016)
34. Zeiler, M.D., Fergus, R.: Visualizing and understanding convolutional networks. In: Fleet, D., Pajdla, T., Schiele, B., Tuytelaars, T. (eds.) ECCV 2014. LNCS, vol. 8689, pp. 818–833. Springer, Cham (2014). https://doi.org/10.1007/978-3-319-10590-1_53
35. Noh, H., Hong, S., Han, B.: Learning deconvolution network for semantic segmentation. In: ICCV (2015)
36. Zhou, D., Weston, J., Gretton, A., Bousquet, O., Schölkopf, B.: Ranking on data manifolds. In: NIPS (2004)
37. Yang, C., Zhang, L., Lu, H., Ruan, X., Yang, M.H.: Saliency detection via graph-based manifold ranking. In: CVPR (2013)
38. Shi, J., Malik, J.: Normalized cuts and image segmentation. PAMI 22(8), 888–905 (2000)
39. Levin, A., Lischinski, D., Weiss, Y.: A closed-form solution to natural image matting. PAMI 30(2), 228–242 (2008)
40. Zelnik-Manor, L., Perona, P.: Self-tuning spectral clustering. In: NIPS (2005)
41. Lin, T.-Y., et al.: Microsoft COCO: common objects in context. In: Fleet, D., Pajdla, T., Schiele, B., Tuytelaars, T. (eds.) ECCV 2014. LNCS, vol. 8693, pp. 740–755. Springer, Cham (2014). https://doi.org/10.1007/978-3-319-10602-1_48
42. Gatys, L.A., Ecker, A.S., Bethge, M., Hertzmann, A., Shechtman, E.: Controlling perceptual factors in neural style transfer. In: CVPR (2017)
43. Xie, S., Tu, Z.: Holistically-nested edge detection. In: ICCV (2015)
44. Cutzu, F., Hammoud, R., Leykin, A.: Estimating the photorealism of images: distinguishing paintings from photographs. In: CVPR (2003)
45. He, K., Sun, J., Tang, X.: Guided image filtering. PAMI 35(6), 1397–1409 (2013)

Visual Tracking via Spatially Aligned Correlation Filters Network

Mengdan Zhang[1]([✉]), Qiang Wang[1], Junliang Xing[1], Jin Gao[1], Peixi Peng[1], Weiming Hu[1], and Steve Maybank[2]

[1] CAS Center for Excellence in Brain Science and Intelligence Technology, National Laboratory of Pattern Recognition, Institute of Automation, Chinese Academy of Sciences, University of Chinese Academy of Sciences, Beijing, China
{mengdan.zhang,qiang.wang,jin.gao,wmhu}@nlpr.ia.ac.cn, pxpeng@pku.edu.cn
[2] Birkbeck College, University of London, London, UK
sjmaybank@dcs.bbk.ac.uk

Abstract. Correlation filters based trackers rely on a periodic assumption of the search sample to efficiently distinguish the target from the background. This assumption however yields undesired boundary effects and restricts aspect ratios of search samples. To handle these issues, an end-to-end deep architecture is proposed to incorporate geometric transformations into a correlation filters based network. This architecture introduces a novel spatial alignment module, which provides continuous feedback for transforming the target from the border to the center with a normalized aspect ratio. It enables correlation filters to work on well-aligned samples for better tracking. The whole architecture not only learns a generic relationship between object geometric transformations and object appearances, but also learns robust representations coupled to correlation filters in case of various geometric transformations. This lightweight architecture permits real-time speed. Experiments show our tracker effectively handles boundary effects and aspect ratio variations, achieving state-of-the-art tracking results on recent benchmarks.

Keywords: Visual tracking · Spatial transformer network
Deep learning · Correlation filters network

1 Introduction

Generic visual tracking aims to estimate the trajectory of a target in a video, given only its initial location. It has been widely applied, for example to

---

M. Zhang and Q. Wang—Contributed equally to this work.

Electronic supplementary material The online version of this chapter (https://doi.org/10.1007/978-3-030-01219-9_29) contains supplementary material, which is available to authorized users.

Fig. 1. Example videos (*Gymnastic3*, *Fish3* and *Pedestrian1*) in VOT2015 benchmark. General correlation filters (CF) based trackers such as DCFNet [33] and SRDCF [9] suffer performance decline in case of aspect ratio variations. DCFNet fails in case of fast motions because of the boundary effect.

video surveillance [1,13], and event recognition [27]. Visual tracking is challenging because the tracking scene contains complex motion patterns such as in-plane/out-of-plane rotation, deformation, and camera motion. A tracker has limited online samples with which to learn to adapt to these motion patterns.

The visual tracking of translating objects has been successfully tackled by recent correlation filters (CF) based approaches [10,18]. In these approaches, a circular window is moved over the search sample, leading to a dense and accurate estimation of the object translation. This circular sliding window operation assumes a periodic extension of the search sample, which enables efficient detection using the Fast Fourier transform, it however yields undesired boundary effects and restricts the aspect ratio of the search sample. Therefore, in cases of fast motions, rotations, and deformations which are common in practice, the performance of CF based trackers often drops significantly. As shown in Fig. 1, aspect ratio variation occurs frequently in the videos *Gymnastic3* and *Fish3*, and fast motion occurs frequently in the video *Pedestrian1*. Translation based CF trackers often fail on these challenging scenarios.

To address the above issues, spatially regularized CF based trackers [6,7,9,11] introduce a spatial regularization component within the CF to ensure that a CF tracker can work on a large image region effectively and can thus handle fast motions by reducing the boundary effect. The major disadvantage of these methods is that the regularized objective function is costly to optimize, even in the Fourier domain. CF with limited boundaries (CFLB) [16] and background-aware CF (BACF) [15] propose to exploit a masking matrix to allow search samples larger than the filter. However, BACF does not have a closed-form solution, which makes it difficult to be integrated into a deep neural network to boost the tracking performance. Many CF based trackers [8,15,16,26,44] ignore the aspect ratio variation, and the scale variation is handled by searching on several scale layers or learning a scale CF. Recently, the IBCCF tracker [25] addresses aspect ratio variation by integrating 1D Boundary and 2D Center CFs where boundary and center filters are enforced by a nearly orthogonal regularization term. However, this integration has a high computation cost, which rules out real-time applications.

In this paper, we propose a novel end-to-end learnable spatially aligned CF based network to handle complex motion patterns of the target. A spatial alignment module (SAM) is incorporated into a differentiable CF based network to provide spatial alignment capabilities and reduce the CF's search space of the object motion. To be specific, conditioned on the consecutive frame regions (former target region and latter search region), SAM performs translation, aspect ratio variation and cropping on the search frame. This allows the network not only to select a region of an image that is most relevant to the target, but also to transform this region to a canonical pose to simplify the localization and recognition in the following CF layer. Once the CF layer obtains the transformed image from the SAM, it generates a Gaussian response map reflecting the object's position, scale and aspect ratio. Therefore, to generate this kind of the Gaussian response, our feature learning coupled to the CF layer is restricted to be positively adaptive to object geometric variations, which further boosts the capability of our network to handle complex object motion patterns. It should be noted that both the SAM and the CF layer can be trained with the standard back-propagation algorithm, allowing for end-to-end training of the whole tracking network on the ILSVRC2015 [12] dataset. After the whole network training on ILSVRC2015, both the SAM and the cascade CF tracking are learned in a data driven manner to be robust to general transformations existed in the training sample pairs.

In the online tracking process, the weights from the feature extraction layers and the SAM are frozen, while the coefficients of the CF layer are updated continuously to learn video-specific tracking cues. The SAM brings our tracker's attention to the target area according to its knowledge of various motion patterns learnt off-line and guides our CF to estimate the object motion more adaptively and accurately. Moreover, the light-weight network architecture and the fast calculation of the CF layer allow efficient tracking at a real-time speed. We conduct experiments on large benchmarks [22,41,42], and the results demonstrate that our algorithm performs competitively against state-of-the-art methods.

To sum up, the contributions of this work are three folds:

- We introduce a differentiable SAM in CF based tracking to address the challenging issues including boundary effects and aspect ratio variations in the previous CF based trackers, enabling better learnability for complex object motion patterns.
- We propose to learn discriminative convolutional features coupled to the spatially aligned CF to generate a Gaussian response map reflecting object's position, scale and aspect ratio, which allows accurate object localization.
- The proposed deep architecture for spatially aligned CF tracking is trained off-line from end to end. The spatial alignment and the CF based localization

are conducted in a mutual reinforced way, which ensures an accurate motion estimation inferred from the consistently optimized network. Our network also permits real-time tracking.

2   Related Work

Correlation Filter Based Trackers. The CF based trackers [8,26] are very popular due to their promising performance and computational efficiency. Since Bolme et al. [3] introduced the CF into the visual tracking field, several extensions have been proposed to improve the tracking performance. The examples include kernelized correlation filters [18,36], multiple dimensional features [10], context learning [15,28], scale estimation [8,26], re-detection [30], short-term and long-term memory [20], spatial regularization [9] and deep learning based CFs [6,29,32,38]. In this paper, we demonstrate that feature extraction, spatial alignment, CF based appearance modeling can be integrated into one network for end-to-end prediction and optimization, so that motion patterns of the object such as fast motions and aspect ratio variations are handled well by the CF based trackers.

Deep Learning Based Trackers. Recent works based on online deep learning trackers have shown high performance [31,35,40]. Despite the high performances, these trackers require frequent fine-tuning to adapt to object appearance changes. This fine-tuning is slow and prohibits real-time tracking. Furthermore, Siamese networks have received growing attention due to its two stream identical structure. These include tracking by object verification [37], tracking by correlation [2] and tracking by location axis prediction [17]. Although our spatial alignment module has a similar network architecture as [17], it permits back-propagation and is learnt with the CF in a mutual reinforced way. It provides the CF with an approximately aligned target to simplify the localization and recognition conducted in the CF layer. The CF layer is updated online to refine the alignment provided by the spatial alignment module for tracking accuracy. Moreover, to avoid over-fitting the network to tracking datasets, we train our network on ILSVRC2015 dataset instead of the ALOV300++ dataset.

Spatial Transformer Network. The spatial transformer network (STN) [21] has demonstrated excellent performances in selecting regions of interests automatically. It is used in face detection [4] to map the detected facial landmarks to their canonical positions to better normalize the face patterns. Dominant human proposals are extracted by STN in regional multi-person pose estimation [14]. For the first time, we introduce an STN into visual tracking. In order to well fit the characteristic of visual tracking, we modify a general STN from a single-input module to a two-stream module. Therefore, our two-stream module is called a spatial alignment module, which transforms the target object more purposefully for visual tracking.

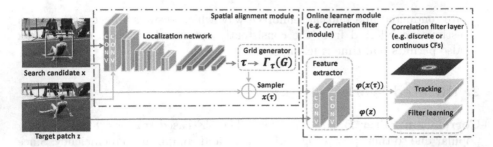

Fig. 2. Pipeline of our algorithm. Note that the red bounding box in the search patch **x** represents the initial candidate target position and the yellow one represents the aligned position provided by our SAM. Our SAM is generic and the CF module can be replaced by other online tracking learners. (Color figure online)

3 Spatially Aligned Correlation Filters Network

3.1 Overview

The architecture of the proposed spatially aligned CF based network (SACFNet) is shown in Fig. 2 to handle complex motion patterns of the target. It contains two components: a novel spatial alignment module (SAM) and a correlation filter (CF) module. The SAM contains a localization network, a grid generator and a sampler. The CF module contains a feature extractor and a CF based appearance modeling and tracking layer. The SAM brings the target into a CF's attention in the form of a canonical pose (centralized with the fixed scale and aspect ratio). Since this module is differentiable, the spatial alignment and CF based localization are optimized in a mutual reinforced way, which ensures accurate motion estimations inferred from the consistently optimized network.

Denote a training sample as **x** which contains a target object drifting away from the center of this sample with different scale and aspect ratio from the canonical one. Let τ° be the expected transformation according to which the target object in **x** can be transformed to the center with the canonical scale and aspect ratio. In this paper, we just consider the object translations, scale and aspect ratio variations. Thus, τ° has four parameters including translations and scales along the horizontal and vertical axes, denoted $\tau^\circ = \{dx, dy, dsx, dsy\}$. $\mathbf{y}(\tau^\circ)$ is a canonical Gaussian correlation response based on the expected transformation τ°. $\{\varphi^l(\cdot)\}_{l=1}^D$ denotes the D-dimensional representations obtained from the feature extractor coupled to the CF layer. The multi-channel CF is denoted as $\{\mathbf{w}^l\}_{l=1}^D$. Then, learning an SACFNet in the spatial domain is formulated by minimizing the objective function:

$$\epsilon(\theta_1, \theta_2) = \frac{1}{2}\|\sum_{l=1}^D \mathbf{w}_{\theta_2}^l \star \varphi_{\theta_2}^l(\mathbf{x}(\tau_{\theta_1})) - \mathbf{y}(\tau^\circ)\|_2^2 + \lambda \sum_{l=1}^D \|\mathbf{w}_{\theta_2}^l\|_2^2, \tag{1}$$

$$\text{s.t.} \quad \mathbf{x}(\tau_{\theta_1}) = \mathbf{x} \circ \tau_{\theta_1}, \mathbf{y}(\tau^\circ) = \mathbf{y} \circ \tau^\circ,$$

where $\star$ denotes a circular correlation operator, $\circ$ denotes that the image is transformed according to the transformation parameters via the grid generator and the sampler as in STN [21] and the constant $\lambda \geq 0$ is the weight of the regularization term. Note that $\mathbf{y}$ is the Gaussian correlation response whose mean, variance and magnitude are related to the object position, scale and aspect ratio in the sample $\mathbf{x}$. We learn parameters of the SAM denoted as θ_1 to generate an estimate of the object transformation denoted as τ_{θ_1}. This estimate τ_{θ_1} is expected to be equal to the true transformation τ°. At the same time, we learn parameters of the feature extractor θ_2 to generate $\{\varphi^l(\cdot)\}_{l=1}^{D}$ and $\{\mathbf{w}^l\}_{l=1}^{D}$.

We find that it is difficult to directly learn these two twisted parameters in Eq. (1). Traditional image alignment algorithms such as [34,43] usually learn parameters of image transformations and object appearance models using the iterative optimization strategy. Therefore, in the training stage of out network, for a easy convergence, we divide the off-line training process of SACFNet into three steps: (1) pre-training the SAM, (2) boosting the feature learning in the CF module based on the pre-trained SAM, and (3) end-to-end fine-tuning for a global optimization. In the tracking stage, object localization is carried out directly with one pass based on our pre-learnt deep neural network. No network fine-tuning is carried out in the tracking stage. More details will be shown in the following three subsections.

3.2 Spatial Alignment Module

Because the parameters are twisted together in the optimization problem in Eq. (1), it is straightforward to first fix the feature extractor θ_2 and learn the SAM based on the subproblem:

$$\epsilon_1(\theta_1) = \frac{1}{2}\|\sum_{l=1}^{D} \mathbf{w}^l \star \varphi^l(\mathbf{x}(\tau_{\theta_1})) - \mathbf{y}(\tau^{\circ})\|_2^2, \tag{2}$$

$$\text{s.t.} \quad \mathbf{x}(\tau_{\theta_1}) = \mathbf{x} \circ \tau_{\theta_1}, \mathbf{y}(\tau^{\circ}) = \mathbf{y} \circ \tau^{\circ}.$$

Because in the beginning of the training process of the SACFNet, parameters in the feature extractor θ_2 are randomly initialized. Thus, the corresponding correlation filter $\{\mathbf{w}^l\}_{l=1}^{D}$ has a poor tracking performance. It can not provide a reliable supervision to the SAM, which affects the quality of the learning process of this module. Meanwhile, since 3D object movements such as deformations and out-of-plane rotations usually occur in visual tracking, learning 2D transformations based on the image matching loss as in Eq. (3) has limitations to handle 3D movements and has a large modeling error:

$$\epsilon_1(\theta_1) = \|\mathbf{x}(\tau_{\theta_1}) - \mathbf{x}(\tau^{\circ})\|_2. \tag{3}$$

Therefore, our SAM focuses on regressing the target bounding boxes to integrally contain the target instead of a detailed image matching:

$$\epsilon_1(\theta_1) = \|\tau_{\theta_1} - \tau^{\circ}\|_1. \tag{4}$$

2D affine transform is sufficient to model the target global transform and this loss is also exploited in GOTURN [17]. Compared to the particle filtering based tracking methods [24,31] which generate transformed sample candidates based on the random sampling on a Gaussian distribution, our SAM learns to directly estimate the correct transform and generate a sample containing the centralized object with the proper scale and aspect ratio.

Network Architecture. We exploit a two-stream (Siamese) architecture for the localization network of the SAM to estimate the target transformation. The target patch in the preceding frame $t-1$ and the search patch in the consecutive frame t are fed into this module as inputs. In this way, the object in the search patch is not only brought into attention, but also aligned with the object in the target patch, which is more favorable for visual tracking. Each stream contains the first five convolutional layers of the CaffeNet [23]. Features from two streams are then combined and fed into following three fully connected layers, which finally output the transformation parameters. Specifically, the number of feature channels in each fully connected layer is set to 4096 and the number of the transformation parameters is set to 4. The predicted transformation parameters are used to create a sampling grid to select a target region from the whole image, namely the grid generator and sampler in STN [21]. In this stage, the selected target region is not exploited for the optimization in Eq. (4).

3.3 Feature Learning for Correlation Filters

After the first stage training of the SAM, we freeze this module and carry out feature learning coupled to the CF layer:

$$\epsilon_2(\theta_2) = \frac{1}{2}\|\sum_{l=1}^{D}\mathbf{w}_{\theta_2}^l \star \varphi_{\theta_2}^l(\mathbf{x}(\tau_{\theta_1^\diamond})) - \mathbf{y}(\tau_{\theta_1^\diamond})\|_2^2 + \lambda\sum_{l=1}^{D}\|\mathbf{w}_{\theta_2}^l\|_2^2, \tag{5}$$

$$\text{s.t.} \quad \mathbf{x}(\tau_{\theta_1^\diamond}) = \mathbf{x} \circ \tau_{\theta_1^\diamond}, \mathbf{y}(\tau_{\theta_1^\diamond}) = \mathbf{y} \circ \tau_{\theta_1^\diamond},$$

where the transformation $\tau_{\theta_1^\diamond}$ is estimated by the pre-trained SAM. Notably, $\mathbf{y}(\tau_{\theta_1^\diamond})$ is a Gaussian response in the joint scale-displacement space corresponding to the augmented sample $\mathbf{x}(\tau_{\theta_1^\diamond})$. Compared to the canonical Gaussian response $\mathbf{y}(\tau^\diamond)$, its center $\mu(\tau_{\theta_1^\diamond})$, variance $\Sigma(\tau_{\theta_1^\diamond})$ and magnitude changes according to the Euclidean distance between the object state (position, scale and aspect ratio) in $\mathbf{x}(\tau_{\theta_1^\diamond})$ and the object state in the canonical image patch. The object in the canonical image patch is centralized with the fixed scale and aspect ratio. Therefore, compared to a general CFNet [33,38] whose training samples contain objects with a canonical pose and the Gaussian response is unique, our CF based appearance modeling considers object motion variations and is context-aware.

Network Architecture. Similar to [33], our CF module consists two branches: a filter learning branch and a tracking branch. Both branches exploit the same feature extractor which contains two convolutional layers with kernels whose sizes are $3 \times 3 \times 3 \times 96$ and $3 \times 3 \times 96 \times 32$. Specifically, a target patch $\mathbf{z}$ is fed into the filter learning branch to learn the parameters in the CF layer:

$$\hat{\mathbf{w}}_{\theta_2}^l = \frac{\hat{\mathbf{y}}^* \odot \hat{\varphi}_{\theta_2}^l(\mathbf{z})}{\sum_{k=1}^{D} \hat{\varphi}_{\theta_2}^k(\mathbf{z}) \odot (\hat{\varphi}_{\theta_2}^k(\mathbf{z}))^* + \lambda}, \tag{6}$$

where $\hat{\mathbf{y}}$ denotes the discrete Fourier transform of $\mathbf{y}$, i.e., $\mathcal{F}(\mathbf{y})$, $\mathbf{y}^*$ represents the complex conjugate of $\mathbf{y}$, and $\odot$ denotes the Hadamard product. Note that for CF based appearance modeling, the object in the target patch $\mathbf{z}$ is centralized with the fixed scale and aspect ratio. Thus, its corresponding response $\mathbf{y}$ has a canonical form. The other tracking branch works on a search patch selected by the SAM from the whole image. The correlation response between the learnt CF in Eq. (6) and this search patch is calculated in the CF layer. Then, the CF module is trained by minimizing the difference between this real correlation response $g_{\theta_2}(\mathbf{x}(\tau_{\theta_1^\circ}))$ and the expected Gaussian-shaped response $\mathbf{y}(\tau_{\theta_1^\circ})$:

$$\epsilon_2(\theta_2) = \|g_{\theta_2}(\mathbf{x}(\tau_{\theta_1^\circ})) - \mathbf{y}(\tau_{\theta_1^\circ})\|_2^2 + \gamma\|\theta_2\|_2^2, \tag{7}$$

$$g_{\theta_2}(\mathbf{x}(\tau_{\theta_1^\circ})) = \mathcal{F}^{-1}(\sum_{l=1}^{D} \hat{\mathbf{w}}_{\theta_2}^{l*} \odot \hat{\varphi}_{\theta_2}^l(\mathbf{x}(\tau_{\theta_1^\circ}))), \tag{8}$$

where the constant $\gamma \geq 0$ is the relative weight of the regularization term. Therefore, effective feature learning is achieved by training the CF module under the guidance of the SAM.

The training process of the CF module is explained as follows. For explanation clarity, we omit the subscript θ_2 in the following equations. Since the operations in the forward pass only contain Hadamard product and division, we can calculate the derivative per-element:

$$\frac{\partial \epsilon_2}{\partial \hat{g}_{uv}^*(\mathbf{x}(\tau_{\theta_1^\circ}))} = \left(\mathcal{F}\left(\frac{\partial \epsilon_2}{\partial g(\mathbf{x}(\tau_{\theta_1^\circ}))}\right)\right)_{uv}. \tag{9}$$

For the back-propagation of the tracking branch,

$$\frac{\partial \epsilon_2}{\partial (\hat{\varphi}_{uv}^l(\mathbf{x}(\tau_{\theta_1^\circ})))^*} = \frac{\partial \epsilon_2}{\partial \hat{g}_{uv}^*(\mathbf{x}(\tau_{\theta_1^\circ}))}(\hat{\mathbf{w}}_{uv}^l), \tag{10}$$

$$\frac{\partial \epsilon_2}{\partial \varphi^l(\mathbf{x}(\tau_{\theta_1^\circ}))} = \mathcal{F}^{-1}\left(\frac{\partial \epsilon_2}{\partial (\hat{\varphi}^l(\mathbf{x}(\tau_{\theta_1^\circ})))^*}\right). \tag{11}$$

For the back-propagation of the filter learning branch, we treat $\hat{\varphi}_{uv}^l(\mathbf{z})$ and $(\hat{\varphi}_{uv}^l(\mathbf{z}))^*$ as independent variables.

$$\frac{\partial \epsilon_2}{\partial \hat{\varphi}_{uv}^l(\mathbf{z})} = \frac{\partial \epsilon_2}{\partial \hat{g}_{uv}^*(\mathbf{x}(\tau_{\theta_1^\circ}))} \Gamma_1, \tag{12}$$

$$\Gamma_1 = \frac{(\hat{\varphi}_{uv}^l(\mathbf{x}(\tau_{\theta_1^\circ})))^* \hat{\mathbf{y}}_{uv}^*(\tau_{\theta_1^\circ}) - \hat{g}_{uv}^*(\mathbf{x}(\tau_{\theta_1^\circ}))(\hat{\varphi}_{uv}^l(\mathbf{z}))^*}{\sum_{k=1}^{D} \hat{\varphi}_{uv}^k(\mathbf{z})(\hat{\varphi}_{uv}^k(\mathbf{z}))^* + \lambda}, \tag{13}$$

$$\frac{\partial \epsilon_2}{\partial (\hat{\varphi}_{uv}^l(\mathbf{z}))^*} = \frac{\partial \epsilon_2}{\partial \hat{g}_{uv}^*(\mathbf{x}(\tau_{\theta_1^\circ}))} \Gamma_2, \tag{14}$$

$$\varGamma_2 = \frac{-\hat{g}_{uv}^*(\mathbf{x}(\tau_{\theta_1^\diamond}))\hat{\varphi}_{uv}^l(\mathbf{z})}{\sum_{k=1}^D \hat{\varphi}_{uv}^k(\mathbf{z})(\hat{\varphi}_{uv}^k(\mathbf{z}))^* + \lambda}, \tag{15}$$

$$\frac{\partial \epsilon_2}{\partial \varphi^l(\mathbf{z})} = \mathcal{F}^{-1}\left(\frac{\partial \epsilon_2}{\partial(\hat{\varphi}^l(\mathbf{z}))^*} + \left(\frac{\partial \epsilon_2}{\partial \hat{\varphi}^l(\mathbf{z})}\right)^*\right). \tag{16}$$

3.4   Model Training and Online Tracking

Model Training. We design a three-step procedure to train the proposed deep architecture for visual tracking: (1) pre-training the SAM (Sect. 3.2), (2) pre-training the CF module based on the pre-trained SAM (Sect. 3.3), and (3) fine-tuning the whole network to make the spatial alignment and the CF based localization optimized in a mutual reinforced way:

$$\epsilon(\theta_1, \theta_2) = \frac{1}{2}\|\sum_{l=1}^D \mathbf{w}_{\theta_2}^l \star \varphi_{\theta_2}^l(\mathbf{x}(\tau_{\theta_1})) - \mathbf{y}(\tau^\diamond)\|_2^2 + \lambda \sum_{l=1}^D \|\mathbf{w}_{\theta_2}^l\|_2^2 + \|\tau_{\theta_1} - \tau^\diamond\|_1, \tag{17}$$

$$\text{s.t.}\quad \mathbf{x}(\tau_{\theta_1}) = \mathbf{x} \circ \tau_{\theta_1}, \mathbf{y}(\tau^\diamond) = \mathbf{y} \circ \tau^\diamond,$$

We maintain the loss from Eq. (4) for a better convergence as many STN based methods have done [4]. All the training stages are carried out on the ILSVRC2015 dataset, because it contains different scenes and objects from the canonical tracking benchmarks. A deep model can be safely trained on it without the risk of over-fitting to the domain of tracking videos. Pairs of search and target patches are extracted from this video dataset. Specifically, a target patch is generated for each frame by cropping an image region from an object bounding box. For each search patch, we randomly sample a set of source patches from the consecutive frame. The source patches are generated by randomly perturbing the bounding box to mimic motion changes (*e.g.*, translations, scale and aspect ratio variations) between frames. We follow the practice in GOTURN, assuming that the motion between frames follows a Laplace distribution.

Online Tracking. In the online tracking process, the feature extractor and the SAM are frozen. The CF layer is updated following the common practice in CF based trackers:

$$\hat{\mathbf{w}}_t^l = (1 - \alpha) \cdot \hat{\mathbf{w}}_{t-1}^l + \alpha \cdot \hat{\mathbf{w}}^l, \tag{18}$$

where $\alpha = 0.01$ is the update rate. The computation cost of this online adaptation strategy is cheap compared to online network fine-tuning, and it is effective for a CF to adapt to object appearance changes quickly. When a new frame comes, we extract a search patch from the center location predicted in the previous frame. The SAM works on this patch and the target patch from the previous frame, and provides an initial estimation of object translation, scale and aspect ratio. The grid generator and sampler extract an aligned image patch in this new frame. For a more accurate scale estimation, based on this aligned image patch, we extract another two image patches using the scale factors

$\{a^s | a = 1.0275, s = \{-1, 1\}\}$ similarly to [33] for fine-grained alignment. These image patches are fed into the CF module for object localization. The final target scale is estimated based on the scale factors and the transformation parameters from the SAM.

Issue of General Object Movements. SAM is motivated to solve issues of the fixed target aspect ratio and the boundary effect in CF based appearance modeling and tracking. As the learning of general transformations such as deformations and out-of-plane rotations is very difficult even with accurate sample annotations, it is thus infeasible in the tracking problem to learn all these transformations in a single model without sample annotations. Nevertheless, our algorithm can well handle general transformations: (1) SAM focuses on regressing the target bounding boxes to integrally contain the target instead of a detailed target matching as explained in Sect. 3.2. SAM is trained in a data driven manner to be robust to deformations and out-of-plane rotations existed in the training sample pairs; and (2) the following processing step of cascade CF tracking is also very robust to these transformations owning to its data driven learning. As the objective of visual tracking is to estimate the target bounding boxes, we find our current design of SAM is effective and provide more accurate object locations than its counterparts.

4   Experiments

4.1   Experimental Setups

Implementation Details. Because our SAM is generic, apart from the canonical CF formulation, it is straightforward to introduce SAM into other online learners. Thus, in our experiments, we provide two versions of our SACFNet: (1) $\text{SACF}^{(D)}$ exploits a canonical discrete CF module as explained in Sect. 3.3; (2) $\text{SACF}^{(C)}$ exploits a continuous CF module which is same as ECO[1]. In the pre-training process of the SAM, we extract a target patch of 2^2 times the size of the target bounding box and then resize it to 227×227. The parameters of the convolutional layers are frozen and taken from the CaffeNet. We train three fully connected layers where the learning rate is $1e{-}5$, and the batch size is 50. In the pre-training process of the CF module, following the canonical CF setting, the padding size is 2 and the input size of the feature extractor is 125×125. The regularization weight λ is set to $1e{-}4$ and the Gaussian spatial bandwidth is set to 0.1. We train this CF module with a learning rate exponentially decaying from $1e{-}4$ to $1e{-}5$ and a batch size of 32. In the end-to-end training process, the two modules are learnt in a mutual reinforce manner with a learning rate of $1e{-}5$ and a batch size of 32. Our experiments are performed with the MatConvNet toolbox [39] on a PC with an i7 3.4 GHz CPU and a GeForce GTX Titan Black GPU. The mean speed of $\text{SACF}^{(D)}$ on OTB2015 dataset is 23 frames per second.

---

[1] https://github.com/martin-danelljan/ECO.

Benchmark Datasets and Evaluation Metrics. OTB [41,42] is a standard benchmark which contains 100 fully annotated targets with 11 different attributes. We follow the protocol of OTB and report results based on success plots and precision plots. The success plots show the percentage of frames in which the overlap score exceeds a threshold. In these plots, the trackers are ranked using the area under the curve (AUC) displayed in the legend. The precision plots show the percentage of frames where the center location error is below a threshold. A threshold of 20 pixels is exploited to rank trackers. The VOT dataset [22] comprises 60 videos showing various objects in challenging backgrounds. Trackers are evaluated in terms of accuracy and robustness. The accuracy score is based on the overlap with ground truth, while the robustness is determined by the failure rate. We use the expected average overlap (EAO) measure to analyze the overall tracking performance.

4.2 Ablation Studies

Our $SACF^{(D)}$ is learnt off-line in three steps as discussed in Sect. 3.4. In this section, we conduct ablation analysis on three datasets to validate the effectiveness of the proposed training steps, as shown in Table 1.

First, our SAM learned in the first training step is compared with GOTURN to show the effect of the training dataset and the tracking performance. SAM has a lower tracking performance than GOTURN on VOT2015 and OTB2013, because the annotations of bounding boxes in ILSVRC2015 are quite looser than ALOV300++ which is the training dataset of GOTURN, and there are video overlaps between ALOV300++ and VOT2015/OTB2013/OTB2015. The loose annotations make SAM tend to contain the whole object as shown in the video *Gymnastic3* in Fig. 1, and provide a coarse prediction which requires further precise localization from the CF module. Both SAM and GOTURN suffer easy tracking drifts because of the error accumulation and perform poorly on OTB2015 dataset which has a lower overlap ratio of videos with ALOV300++. Therefore, it is very difficult to precisely learn complex geometric transformations under a single supervision of the regression loss in Eq. (4).

Second, to verify the superiority of the training strategy in the second step, our CF module which is trained in the second step under the guidance of the SAM (denoted by CF-Aug) is compared with its baseline namely DCFNet tracker. Specifically, CF-Aug and DCFNet have the same tracking process and differ in the training strategy. In the training stage, the input search patch of CF-Aug outputted by SAM contains a target drifting from the center with the aspect ratio variation. It is expected to generate a Gaussian response whose center, variance, and magnitude vary correspondingly. Contrastively, DCFNet works on a canonical search patch and generates a canonical response. As shown in Table 1, with data augmentation and the appearance modeling related to object scale and aspect ratio variations, our learnt CF-Aug performs favorably against DCFNet. Third, the integration of the SAM and the CF-Aug learned from the second training step is named $SACF^{(D)}$-iter1. In the tracking process, this tracker exploits the SAM to first coarsely localize the target to reduce a CF's search

Table 1. An illustration of the effectiveness of each training stage on VOT2015, OTB2013, and OTB2015. Red, blue and green fonts indicate the 1st, 2nd, and 3rd performance respectively.

Stage	Tracker	VOT2015 A	VOT2015 R	VOT2015 EAO	OTB2013 AUC	OTB2015 AUC
1	GOTURN [17]	0.48	2.02	0.203	0.457	0.115
	SAM	0.43	3.24	0.158	0.297	0.132
2	DCFNet [33]	0.53	1.68	0.217	0.622	0.580
	CF-Aug	0.55	1.67	0.225	0.628	0.600
	SAM-DCFNet	0.52	1.19	0.280	0.639	0.610
	SACF$^{(D)}$-iter1	0.52	1.16	0.287	0.648	0.612
3	SACF$^{(D)}$	0.51	1.00	0.324	0.664	0.633
-	ECO [6]	0.57	1.29	0.326	0.709	0.688
-	SACF$^{(C)}$	0.57	1.07	0.343	0.713	0.693

space and then achieves the fine-grained localization based on a CF. The direct combination of SAM and DCFNet is named SAM-DCFNet. Because CF-aug is learnt coupled to SAM, SACF$^{(D)}$-iter1 shows a better performance.

Moreover, the effectiveness of the end-to-end fine-tuning is evaluated by comparing the fine-tuned SACF$^{(D)}$ in the third training step and SACF$^{(D)}$-iter1. SACF$^{(D)}$ outperforms SACF$^{(D)}$-iter1 on all three benchmark datasets because the SAM and the CF module are learnt in a reinforced way. Conclusively, SAM estimates the global transform of a target in two consecutive frames and thus provides a coarse target localization. Only based on coarse estimations, background noise is gradually introduced into the target template leading to tracking drifts. CFs work well in local fine-grained search spaces of translations and scales, but cannot well handle aspect ratio variations and large motions, suffering tracking misalignment and drifts. By combining two complementary components, the target template exploited by SAM is more precise and the search space of CFs can be narrowed to local refinement. SACF$^{(D)}$ is superior to SAM and CF-Aug on three datasets. SACF$^{(C)}$ also outperforms baseline ECO as shown in Table 1 and Fig. 5. Note that because object annotations in VOT benchmarks change aspect ratios more frequently than in the OTB benchmarks, SACF$^{(C)}$ obtains more significant improvements in VOT benchmarks. The results also prove the generalization capability of our SAM. Especially, according to the robustness measure in VOT2015, the incorporation of a SAM does not degrade the robustness of SACF$^{(D)}$ and SACF$^{(C)}$.

4.3   Comparisons with the State-of-the-Arts

OTB Dataset. We compare our two versions of SACFNet (SACF$^{(D)}$ and SACF$^{(C)}$) against recent state-of-the-art trackers including BACF [15], ECO [6], SINT_flow [37], STAPLE_CA (CACF) [28], CFNet [38], ACFN [5], IBCCF [25], SiamFC_3s [2], SAMF [26], SRDCF [9], and CNN-SVM [19]. Figure 3 illustrates precision and success plots on OTB2013 and OTB2015.

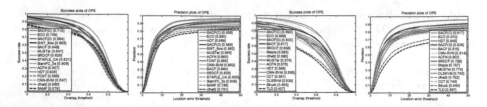

Fig. 3. Success plots and precision plots showing a comparison with recent state-of-the-art methods on OTB2013 and OTB2015.

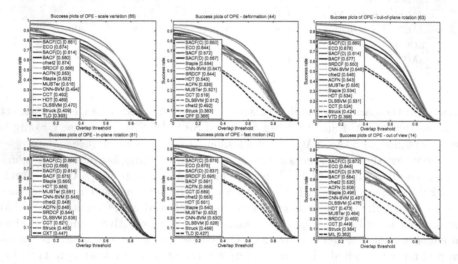

Fig. 4. Attribute-based analysis on the OTB2015 dataset.

From Fig. 3 we can draw three conclusions. First, $SACF^{(D)}$ outperforms most CF based trackers with a scale estimation (*e.g.*, SiamFC_3s and SAMF). $SACF^{(D)}$ is superior to IBCCF (AUC scores of 0.660 and 0.630 on OTB2013 and OTB2015) which considers the aspect ratio variation issue, and is more efficient than IBCCF. $SACF^{(D)}$ significantly outperforms ACFN, although ACFN introduces an attentional CF network to handle the target drift, blurriness, occlusion, scale changes, and flexible aspect ratio. $SACF^{(C)}$ also outperforms ECO benefiting from the consideration of object aspect ratio variations. Conclusively, SACFNet provides an effective and efficient way to tackle issues of the object scale and aspect ratio variations.

Second, $SACF^{(D)}$ provides a competitive tracking performance against BACF and SRDCF which solve the boundary effect problem. In contrast to SINT_flow where the Siamese tracking network and the optical flow method are isolated to each other, our SAM and CF module cooperate with each other and are learnt in a mutual reinforced way. Conclusively, compared to recent CF based trackers designed for handling boundary effects and Siamese network based trackers con-

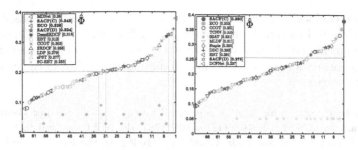

Fig. 5. EAO ranking with trackers in VOT2015 (left) and VOT2016 (right).

sidering object motions, $SACF^{(D)}$ provides a new strategy to benefit from the motion information while reducing boundary effects.

Third, $SACF^{(D)}$ outperforms traditional CFs based trackers (*e.g.*, CFNet, STAPLE_CA and HDT) and Siamese network based trackers (*e.g.*, SINT_flow, SiamFC_3s) on both datasets. Our feature learning coupled to the CF layer and the guidance of the SAM enhance the performance of a CF based tracker. Moreover, benefited from the integration of a CF layer, compared to other Siamese networks, our $SACF^{(D)}$ can online update the object appearance modeling efficiently without fine-tuning the network.

Attribute Based Analysis Related to Object Complex Motions. $SACF^{(D)}$ is evaluated on attributes to show its capability of tackling issues of aspect ratio variation and boundary effects on OTB2015 dataset, as shown in Fig. 4. Specifically, in cases of scale variation, deformation, and in-plane/out-of-plane rotation, the target scale and aspect ratio changes. In cases of fast motion and out-of-view, the boundary effects degrades tracking performance easily. We copy the AUC scores of IBCCF from its paper (scale variation: 0.610, occlusion: 0.600, out-of-plane rotation: 0.597, in-plane rotation: 0.589). $SACF^{(D)}$ is superior to IBCCF in all these cases related to the aspect ratio variation. $SACF^{(D)}$ outperforms its baseline tracker CFNet by large margins in cases of all the attributes. Our SAM learns useful motion patterns from the external dataset and simplify the localization and recognition in the following CF module.

VOT Dataset. We show the comparative results on VOT dataset in Fig. 5. $SACF^{(D)}$ and $SACF^{(C)}$ significantly exceed the VOT2015 *published sota bound* (grey line) and outperforms C-COT [11], DeepSRDCF [7] and EBT [45]. $SACF^{(C)}$ ranks first in VOT2016 dataset and outperforms ECO. The experimental results show the effectiveness of feature learning and the SAM.

5   Conclusion

We propose a novel visual tracking network that tackles the issues of boundary effects and aspect ratio variations in CF based trackers. The proposed deep architecture enables feature learning, spatial alignment and CF based appearance modeling to be carried out simultaneously from end-to-end. Therefore, the spatial alignment and CF based localization are conducted in a mutual reinforced way, which ensures an accurate motion estimation inferred from the consistently optimized network.

Acknowledgements. This work is supported by the Natural Science Foundation of China (Grant No. 61751212, 61472421, 61602478), the NSFC-general technology collaborative Fund for basic re-search (Grant No. U1636218), the Key Research Program of Frontier Sciences, CAS, Grant No. QYZDJ-SSW-JSC040, and the CAS External cooperation key project.

References

1. Andriluka, M., Roth, S., Schiele, B.: People-tracking-by-detection and people-detection-by-tracking. In: Proceedings of IEEE Conference on Computer Vision and Pattern Recognition, pp. 1–8 (2008)
2. Bertinetto, L., Valmadre, J., Henriques, J.F., Vedaldi, A., Torr, P.H.S.: Fully-convolutional siamese networks for object tracking. In: Hua, G., Jégou, H. (eds.) ECCV 2016. LNCS, vol. 9914, pp. 850–865. Springer, Cham (2016). https://doi.org/10.1007/978-3-319-48881-3_56
3. Bolme, D., Beveridge, J., Draper, B., Lui, Y.: Visual object tracking using adaptive correlation filters. In: Proceedings of IEEE Conference on Computer Vision and Pattern Recognition, pp. 2544–2550 (2010)
4. Chen, D., Hua, G., Wen, F., Sun, J.: Supervised transformer network for efficient face detection. In: Leibe, B., Matas, J., Sebe, N., Welling, M. (eds.) ECCV 2016. LNCS, vol. 9909, pp. 122–138. Springer, Cham (2016). https://doi.org/10.1007/978-3-319-46454-1_8
5. Choi, J., Chang, H., Yun, S., Fischer, T., Demiris, Y., Choi, J.: Attentional correlation filter network for adaptive visual tracking, pp. 4828–4837 (2017)
6. Danelljan, M., Bhat, G., Khan, F., Felsberg, M.: ECO: efficient convolution operators for tracking. In: Proceedings of IEEE Conference on Computer Vision and Pattern Recognition, pp. 6931–6939 (2017)
7. Danelljan, M., Häger, G., Khan, F., Felsberg, M.: Convolutional features for correlation filter based visual tracking. In: Proceedings of IEEE International Conference on Computer Vision Workshops, pp. 58–66 (2015)
8. Danelljan, M., Häger, G., Khan, F., Felsberg, M.: Accurate scale estimation for robust visual tracking. In: Proceedings of British Machine Vision Conference, pp. 65.1–65.11 (2014)
9. Danelljan, M., Häger, G., Khan, F., Felsberg, M.: Learning spatially regularized correlation filters for visual tracking. In: Proceedings of IEEE International Conference on Computer Vision, pp. 4310–4318 (2015)
10. Danelljan, M., Khan, F., Felsberg, M., van de Weijer, J.: Adaptive color attributes for real-time visual tracking. In: Proceedings of IEEE Conference on Computer Vision and Pattern Recognition, pp. 1090–1097 (2014)
11. Danelljan, M., Robinson, A., Shahbaz Khan, F., Felsberg, M.: Beyond correlation filters: learning continuous convolution operators for visual tracking. In: Leibe, B., Matas, J., Sebe, N., Welling, M. (eds.) ECCV 2016. LNCS, vol. 9909, pp. 472–488. Springer, Cham (2016). https://doi.org/10.1007/978-3-319-46454-1_29

12. Deng, J., Dong, W., Socher, R., Li, L., Li, K., Li, F.: Imagenet: a large-scale hierarchical image database. In: Proceedings of IEEE Conference on Computer Vision and Pattern Recognition, pp. 248–255 (2009)

13. Emami, A., Dadgostar, F., Bigdeli, A., Lovell, B.: Role of spatiotemporal oriented energy features for robust visual tracking in video surveillance. In: Proceedings of International Conference on Advanced Video and Signal-Based Surveillance, pp. 349–354 (2012)

14. Fang, H., Xie, S., Lu, C.: RMPE: regional multi-person pose estimation. arXiv preprint arXiv:1612.00137 (2016)

15. Hamed, K., Ashton, F., Simon, L.: Learning background-aware correlation filters for visual tracking. In: Proceedings of IEEE International Conference on Computer Vision, pp. 1144–1152 (2017)

16. Hamed, K., Terence, S., Simon, L.: Correlation filters with limited boundaries. In: Proceedings of IEEE Conference on Computer Vision and Pattern Recognition, pp. 4630–4638 (2015)

17. Held, D., Thrun, S., Savarese, S.: Learning to track at 100 FPS with deep regression networks. In: Leibe, B., Matas, J., Sebe, N., Welling, M. (eds.) ECCV 2016. LNCS, vol. 9905, pp. 749–765. Springer, Cham (2016). https://doi.org/10.1007/978-3-319-46448-0_45

18. Henriques, J., Caseiro, R., Martins, P., Batista, J.: High-speed tracking with kernelized correlation filters. IEEE Trans Pattern Anal. Mach. Intell. **37**(3), 583–596 (2015)

19. Hong, S., You, T., Kwak, S., Han, B.: Online tracking by learning discriminative saliency map with convolutional neural network. In: Proceedings of International Conference on Machine Learning, pp. 597–606 (2015)

20. Hong, Z., Chen, Z., Wang, C., Mei, X., Prokhorov, D., Tao, D.: Multi-store tracker (MUSTer): a cognitive psychology inspired approach to object tracking. In: Proceedings of IEEE Conference on Computer Vision and Pattern Recognition, pp. 749–758 (2015)

21. Jaderberg, M., Simonyan, K., Zisserman, A.: Spatial transformer networks. In: Proceedings of Neural Information Processing Systems, pp. 2017–2025 (2015)

22. Kristan, M., et al.: The visual object tracking VOT2015 challenge results. In: Proceedings of IEEE International Conference on Computer Vision Workshops, pp. 1–23 (2015)

23. Krizhevsky, A., Sutskever, I., Hinton, G.: Imagenet classification with deep convolutional neural networks. In: Proceedings of Neural Information Processing Systems, pp. 1097–1105 (2012)

24. Kwon, J., Lee, K.: Visual tracking decomposition. In: Proceedings of IEEE Conference on Computer Vision and Pattern Recognition, pp. 1269–1276 (2010)

25. Li, F., Yao, Y., Li, P., Zhang, D., Zuo, W., Yang, M.: Integrating boundary and center correlation filters for visual tracking with aspect ratio variation. arXiv preprint arXiv:1710.02039 (2017)

26. Li, Y., Zhu, J.: A scale adaptive kernel correlation filter tracker with feature integration. In: Agapito, L., Bronstein, M.M., Rother, C. (eds.) ECCV 2014. LNCS, vol. 8926, pp. 254–265. Springer, Cham (2015). https://doi.org/10.1007/978-3-319-16181-5_18

27. Liu, L., Xing, J., Ai, H., Ruan, X.: Hand posture recognition using finger geometric feature. In: Proceedings of IEEE International Conference on Pattern Recognition, pp. 565–568 (2012)

28. Mueller, M., Neil, S., Bernard, G.: Context-aware correlation filter tracking. In: Proceedings of IEEE Conference on Computer Vision and Pattern Recognition, pp. 1387–1395 (2017)
29. Ma, C., Huang, J., Yang, X., Yang, M.: Hierarchical convolutional features for visual tracking. In: Proceedings of IEEE International Conference on Computer Vision, pp. 3074–3082 (2015)
30. Ma, C., Yang, X., Zhang, C., Yang, M.: Long-term correlation tracking. In: Proceedings of IEEE Conference on Computer Vision and Pattern Recognition, pp. 5388–5396 (2015)
31. Nam, H., Han, B.: Learning multi-domain convolutional neural networks for visual tracking, pp. 4293–4302 (2016)
32. Qi, Y., et al.: Hedged deep tracking. In: Proceedings of IEEE Conference on Computer Vision and Pattern Recognition, pp. 4303–4311 (2016)
33. Wang, Q., Gao, J., Xing, J., Zhang, M., Hu, W.: DCFNet: discriminant correlation filters network for visual tracking. arXiv preprint arXiv:1704.04057 (2017)
34. Song, W., Zhu, J., Li, Y., Chen, C.: Image alignment by online robust PCA via stochastic gradient descent. IEEE Trans Circuits Syst. Video Technol. **26**(7), 1241–1250 (2016)
35. Song, Y., Ma, C., Gong, L., Zhang, J., Lau, R., Yang, M.: CREST: convolutional residual learning for visual tracking, pp. 2574–2583 (2017)
36. Tang, M., Feng, J.: Multi-kernel correlation filter for visual tracking. In: Proceedings of IEEE International Conference on Computer Vision, pp. 3038–3046 (2015)
37. Tao, R., Gavves, E., Smeulders, A.: Siamese instance search for tracking. In: Proceedings of IEEE Conference on Computer Vision and Pattern Recognition, pp. 1420–1429 (2016)
38. Valmadre, J., Bertinetto, L., Henriques, J., Vedaldi, A., Torr, P.: End-to-end representation learning for correlation filter based tracking. In: Proceedings of IEEE Conference on Computer Vision and Pattern Recognition, pp. 5000–5008 (2017)
39. Vedaldi, A., Lenc, K.: MatConvNet: convolutional neural networks for Matlab. In: ACM MM (2015)
40. Wang, L., Ouyang, W., Wang, X., Lu, H.: Visual tracking with fully convolutional networks. In: Proceedings of IEEE International Conference on Computer Vision, pp. 3119–3127 (2015)
41. Wu, Y., Lim, J., Yang, M.H.: Online object tracking: a benchmark. In: Proceedings of IEEE Conference on Computer Vision and Pattern Recognition, pp. 2411–2418 (2013)
42. Wu, Y., Lim, J., Yang, M.: Object tracking benchmark. IEEE Trans. Pattern Anal. Mach. Intell. **37**(9), 1834–1848 (2015)
43. Wu, Y., Shen, B., Ling, H.: Online robust image alignment via iterative convex optimization. In: Proceedings of IEEE Conference on Computer Vision and Pattern Recognition, pp. 1808–1814 (2012)
44. Zhang, M., Xing, J., Gao, J., Hu, W.: Robust visual tracking using joint scale-spatial correlation filters. In: Proceedings of IEEE International Conference on Image Processing, pp. 1468–1472 (2015)
45. Zhu, G., Porikli, F., Li, H.: Tracking randomly moving objects on edge box proposals. arXiv preprint arXiv:1507.08085 (2015)

Online Dictionary Learning for Approximate Archetypal Analysis

Jieru Mei, Chunyu Wang$^{(\boxtimes)}$, and Wenjun Zeng

Microsoft Research Asia, Beijing, China
meijieru@gmail.com, {chnuwa,wezeng}@microsoft.com

Abstract. Archetypal analysis is an unsupervised learning approach which represents data by convex combinations of a set of archetypes. The archetypes generally correspond to the extremal points in the dataset and are learned by requiring them to be convex combinations of the training data. In spite of its nice property of interpretability, the method is slow. We propose a variant of archetypal analysis which scales gracefully to large datasets. The core idea is to decouple the binding between data and archetypes and require them to be unit normalized. Geometrically, the method learns a convex hull inside the unit sphere and represents the data by their projections on the closest surfaces of the convex hull. By minimizing the representation error, the method pushes the convex hull surfaces close to the regions of the sphere where the data reside. The vertices of the convex hull are the learned archetypes. We apply the method to human faces and poses to validate its effectiveness in the context of reconstructions and classifications.

Keywords: Archetypal analysis · Convex hull · Sparsity

1 Introduction

Unsupervised basis learning is a class of methods [8] which aims to discover the underlying low-dimensional structures of the data. They may serve different purposes depending on the specific tasks. For example, methods such as [23,32, 36] are usually used for dimension reductions. Methods such as sparse coding [17,21], non-negative matrix factorization [14] and the clustering methods [5,37] are usually used as data modeling tools.

Archetypal Analysis (AA) [4,6] is an unsupervised learning method which represents data by convex combinations of the archetypes. One distinctive property of AA is that the archetypes are convex combinations of the training data which binds the data and archetypes. There is a geometric interpretation for the

---

Electronic supplementary material The online version of this chapter (https:// doi.org/10.1007/978-3-030-01219-9_30) contains supplementary material, which is available to authorized users.

V. Ferrari et al. (Eds.): ECCV 2018, LNCS 11207, pp. 501–516, 2018.
https://doi.org/10.1007/978-3-030-01219-9_30

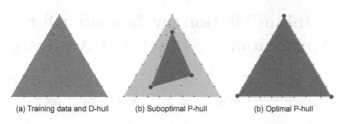

Fig. 1. Illustrations of D-hulls and P-hulls. (a) The convex combinations of training data form a convex hull called D-hull. (b) The red dots denote the archetypes. Each archetype is chosen from convex combinations of training data. So it is within the D-hull. Archetypal analysis represents data by convex combinations of archetypes which forms another hull called P-hull (c) To minimize the representation error, the P-hull should be large enough to represent all the data. (Color figure online)

method. See Fig. 1. First, convex combinations of the archetypes form a principal convex hull which we call *P-hull*. To minimize the representation error on the dataset, the P-hull should be large enough to cover as many training data as possible. Second, since each archetype is required to be chosen from the convex hull (*D-hull*) formed by convex combinations of training data, the P-hull should be within the D-hull. So archetypal analysis seeks for the largest P-hull whose vertices are within the D-hull. In general cases, the learned archetypes approximately correspond to the extremal points in the dataset.

In spite of the nice interpretability, the method has not received sufficient attention because it is slow especially when the dataset is large. To scale to large training datasets, sparse coding uses online dictionary learning [20] to iteratively update the bases, where each iteration is based on a mini-batch of data. However, this learning scheme cannot be applied to AA because of the explicit binding between the data and the archetypes. More specifically, updating the archetypes needs to recompute the coefficients with respect to *all* the training data which makes mini-batch learning meaningless.

In this work, we propose a fast variant of archetypal analysis called Decoupled Archetypal Analysis (DAA). The core idea is to decouple the binding between the data and the archetypes, thus making mini-batch based dictionary learning possible. The method first projects the data onto the unit sphere without severely distorting the data structures. Then it learns a set of archetypes on the sphere. Instead of requiring the archetypes to be within the D-hull as in the original AA method, we require them to be within the unit sphere which is a relaxation of the original requirement.

As shown in Fig. 2(b), the method learns a convex hull (triangle in the figure) *within* the sphere and represents data using their surfaces. By minimizing the representation error, DAA drives the surfaces to be close to the data. Thus the convex hull vertices are pushed towards the extremal points. The union of the surfaces resembles the P-hull in AA.

The decoupling between data and archetypes enables us to use an online algorithm (similar to [20]) to optimize the problem which scales gracefully to

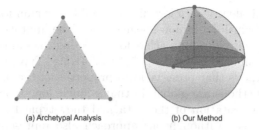

(a) Archetypal Analysis   (b) Our Method

Fig. 2. Comparisons of (a) archetypal analysis and (b) our method. The gray and red dots represent the training data and the learned archetypes, respectively. Our method first embeds the two-dimensional data to a 3D unit sphere and learns a convex hull whose surfaces are close to the data. (Color figure online)

large datasets. For example, we learn 400 archetypes from 300K human pose data using only several minutes. We present extensive experiments on realistic data sources including human faces and poses. In particular, we obtain decent performance on 3D human pose estimation and pose-based action recognition which are comparable to the state-of-the-arts.

2 Related Work

We briefly discuss the related work on unsupervised learning including sparse coding, non-negative matrix factorization and manifold learning.

2.1 Sparse Coding and Non-negative Matrix Factorization

It is natural to compare our approach to sparse coding [9, 24, 25, 33] which activates only a small number of bases when representing a datum. Sparse coding enforces that the l_1-norm of the coefficients is smaller than a threshold λ. In contrast, our method requires that the l_1-norm of the coefficients equals one. In addition, the representation is also sparse which we will discuss in more details later. Another related work is non-negative matrix factorization, which assumes the data are non-negative and learns two non-negative and rank-reduced factor matrices such that their product approximates the input data. Some variants of sparse coding such as [13] incorporate these two methods and require non-negative coefficients in addition to sparsity in order to learn additive object parts features. Our approach differs from the above approaches in that we require the data and bases to be unit normalized and enforce joint non-negative and sum-to-one constraints.

2.2 Manifold Learning

Principal Component Analysis (PCA) is a common method for representing high-dimensional data in terms of bases. It is well suited for data which lie in a linear space or equivalently on a low-dimensional linear manifold. But it is inappropriate for data which lie in non-linear spaces. The limitations of PCA motivate researchers to develop approaches for detecting low-dimensional manifold structures in high-dimensional data [1,7,12,27,31,39]. Typically these methods use projection methods that preserve local properties of the data (*e.g.*, geodesic distance). These methods are global, in that a single low dimensional structure is used in the representation of the data and they typically assume that the manifold is connected. Although our approach also represents data by bases (archetypes), it does not explicitly learn the low-dimensional data manifolds as the above approaches. Instead it learns a set of representative bases which correspond to the extremal data to best represent the dataset.

3   Revisit Archetypal Analysis

We consider a dataset $\mathbf{X} = \{\mathbf{x}_1, \cdots, \mathbf{x}_n\}$ having n training data where $\mathbf{x}_i \in \mathbb{R}^m$ is a datum. Archetypal analysis represents a datum $\mathbf{x}$ by convex combinations of archetypes $\mathbf{Z} = \{\mathbf{z}_1, \cdots, \mathbf{z}_k\}$: $\mathbf{x} = \mathbf{Z}\boldsymbol{\alpha}$ where $\boldsymbol{\alpha}$ resides in the simplex Δ_k:

$$\Delta_k \triangleq \left\{ \boldsymbol{\alpha} \in \mathbb{R}^k \text{ s.t. } \boldsymbol{\alpha} \succeq 0 \text{ and } |\boldsymbol{\alpha}|_1 = 1 \right\}. \tag{1}$$

Meanwhile each archetype $\mathbf{z}$ is required to be chosen from the convex combinations of the training data: $\mathbf{z} = \mathbf{X}\boldsymbol{\beta}$ where $\boldsymbol{\beta} \in \Delta_n$. The archetypes are learned by minimizing the representation error on the whole training dataset:

$$\min_{\mathbf{A},\mathbf{B}} \|\mathbf{X} - \mathbf{X}\mathbf{B}\mathbf{A}\|_{\mathrm{F}}^2, \quad \mathbf{A} = [\boldsymbol{\alpha}_1, \cdots, \boldsymbol{\alpha}_n], \quad \mathbf{B} = [\boldsymbol{\beta}_1, \cdots, \boldsymbol{\beta}_k]$$
$$\boldsymbol{\alpha}_i \in \Delta_k, \quad \text{for} \quad i = 1 \ldots n, \quad \boldsymbol{\beta}_j \in \Delta_n, \quad \text{for} \quad j = 1 \ldots k, \tag{2}$$

where $\mathbf{Z} = \mathbf{X}\mathbf{B}$ denotes the learned k archetypes.

It would help to give a geometric interpretation for AA which inspires our approach. There are two convex hulls which are constructed from the dataset (D-hull) and the archetypes (P-hull), respectively. See Fig. 1 for illustrations. Loosely speaking, the P-hull is within the D-hull and is optimized to have the largest overlap with the D-hull. Ideally, the P-hull is the same as the D-hull.

4   Decoupled Archetypal Analysis

We learn archetypes without requiring them to be chosen from convex combinations of data. However, if there is no constraint on the archetypes, the problem becomes ill-posed and has infinite numbers of solutions. We solve the problem by normalizing the data to lie on the unit sphere and the archetypes are within the unit sphere which can be regarded as a relaxation to the constraints in AA.

4.1 Project Data onto the Unit Sphere

We normalize each datum $\mathbf{x}_i$ such that it lies on the unit sphere: $\|\mathbf{x}_i\|_2 = 1$, $\forall i$. This is usually accomplished by directly normalizing the data: $\mathbf{x}_i \mapsto \frac{\mathbf{x}_i}{\|\mathbf{x}_i\|_2}$, or by centering and then normalizing: $\mathbf{x}_i \mapsto \frac{\mathbf{x}_i - \bar{\mathbf{x}}}{\|\mathbf{x}_i - \bar{\mathbf{x}}\|_2}$ where $\bar{\mathbf{x}}$ is the data mean $\frac{1}{n}\sum_{i=1}^{n} \mathbf{x}_i$. For many signals, little information is lost in normalization. Indeed the normalization is a common first step in many applications. We directly normalize the data in the following experiments in this paper unless stated elsewhere.

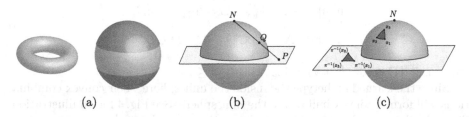

Fig. 3. (a) The torus is flattened into a band when normalized. (b) Stereographic projection from the equatorial plane into the sphere maps P to Q. (c) A triangle in the plane and the corresponding curved triangle on the sphere.

However, some structures may collapse under direct normalization. Consider, for example, the usual two-dimensional torus. Figure 3(a) shows the torus and its normalization in the sphere. The normalization flattens the torus into a band around the equator and the inner cavity is lost. To avoid data collision, we use stereographic projection to map data in $\mathbb{R}^d$ into the d dimensional sphere $\mathbb{S}^d$ in $\mathbb{R}^{d+1}$. Figure 3(b) shows stereographic projection from the equatorial plane onto the sphere, through the north pole N. The point P is mapped to the point Q, which is the intersection of the line through N, P and the unit sphere. It is worth noting that this is an invertible conformal map because it preserves angles between curves. The mapping is: $P \mapsto Q = N + \frac{2}{1+|P|^2}(P - N)$, and the inverse mapping is $Q \mapsto P = N + \frac{1}{1-Q_{d+1}}(Q - N)$, where Q_{d+1} is the $(d+1)$-th coordinate of Q. In some situations, the entire data analysis can be carried out in the normalized space rather than in the original space. But for some situations, e.g., for visualization purposes, it would help to map the learned bases back to the original space. Figure 3(c) shows an example in which the learned bases are back-projected to the original space.

4.2 Learning the Archetypes

We now describe how to learn a set of archetypes $\mathbf{D} = [\mathbf{d}_1, \cdots, \mathbf{d}_k]$ from the normalized data. We first give the formulation and then explain why the formulation can learn the archetypes. The following is the proposed formulation:

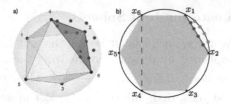

Fig. 4. Illustration of data reconstructions in 3D and 2D. The black points are the learned archetypes and the blue/cyan points are the data. (Color figure online)

$$\min_{D,C}\|X - DC\|_F^2, \quad C = [c_1, \cdots, c_n],$$
$$c_i \in \Delta_k, \quad \|x_i\|_2 = 1, \quad D \in \mathcal{C}, \tag{3}$$

where $\mathcal{C} \triangleq \{D \in \mathbb{R}^{m \times k} \text{s.t.} \forall j = 1 \ldots k, \ \|d_j\|_2^2 \le 1.\}$

Since the learned archetypes lie inside the unit sphere, their convex combinations will form a convex hull *inside* the unit sphere. See Fig. 4 for an illustration. Since the data are also normalized to lie on the unit sphere, they are guaranteed to lie *outside* the convex hull. So in the reconstruction stage, the data will be projected onto the *surfaces* of the convex hull so as to minimize the representation error. In the learning stage, to minimize the overall representation error on the whole dataset, the algorithm will push the surfaces as close to the data as possible. The union of the set of convex hull surfaces (which data are projected on) resembles the P-hull as defined in the original archetypal analysis. The convex hull vertices are the learned archetypes. In summary, directly optimizing the problem (3) will learn archetypes which approximately correspond to the extremal points in the dataset.

4.3   Represent Data by Archetypes

After learning the archetypes, we represent a datum x by convex combinations of the archetypes: $\hat{x} = Dc^*$ where

$$c^* \triangleq \arg\min_{c \in \Delta_k} \|x - Dc\|_2^2 \tag{4}$$

We would like to note that by solving the equation (4), the datum is projected to the surface of the convex hull. In ideal cases, the difference between x and the reconstructed datum $\hat{x}$ is small.

One interesting property of our method is that only the archetypes on the same surface can be activated at the same time (co-activated). For example, in Fig. 4(b), the archetypes x_4 and x_6 will never be co-activated to represent a datum. If they are co-activated, the datum would be projected into the interior of the convex hull, which is impossible. This is because projecting the datum to the interior will first cross a surface and projecting the datum to that surface achieves smaller error. So the archetypes learned using our method are automatically clustered in groups which provides a tight representation of the datasets. This is a desirable property for reconstruction and classification tasks which need strong regularization capabilities.

4.4   Geometric Comparison with Related Work

To highlight their differences to our approach, we provide geometric interpretations for sparse coding and non-negative matrix factorization. Sparse coding represents a datum by a small number of bases by constraining the l_1-norm of the coefficient vector $\|\boldsymbol{\alpha}\|_1$ to be smaller than a constant λ, which could be interpreted geometrically. We augment each basis $\mathbf{d}$ by its negative $-\mathbf{d}$ and require non-negative coefficients as shown in Fig. 5(a). Sparse coding projects a datum to a scaled convex hull (cyan in Fig. 5(a)) formed by the bases where the scale is $\|\boldsymbol{\alpha}\|_1$ which varies for different data. The variation of the scale makes it nontrivial to interpret the properties of the bases. In contrast, the scale of the convex hull for our approach is fixed to be one.

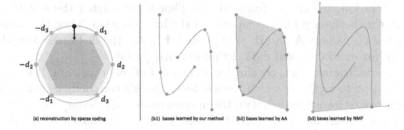

Fig. 5. Geometric interpretation of sparse coding and comparison of different methods on a naive dataset. The orange points represent the learned bases and the points within the orange area could be reconstructed without any error. (Color figure online)

We also compare different methods on a naive dataset in Fig. 5(b). Geometrically, data lie in a convex polyhedral cone and NMF aims to find the edges of the cone. Similar to archetypal analysis, this method also tends to learn a large convex hull for non-convex datasets but does not explore the local structures of the manifold. Instead, our method tends to use a mixture of small surfaces to approximate the local non-convex regions.

5   Optimization

We sketch the optimization algorithm in this section. Although the problem (3) is not convex with respect to $\mathbf{D}$ and $\mathbf{C}$, it is convex with respect to one of them with the other fixed. We propose an online learning algorithm similar to [20]. At each iteration, only a mini-batch of samples are used to update the dictionary of archetypes, endowing us with the ability to handle large-scale datasets. Similarly as [20], the sufficient statistics with respect to coefficients $\mathbf{c}_i$ are aggregated, which are used for dictionary updates.

Algorithm 1. Online dictionary learning

Require: Data $\mathbf{X}$ in $\mathbb{R}^{m \times n}$, k (number of archetypes), T (number of iterations)
1: $\mathbf{A}_0 \leftarrow 0, \mathbf{B}_0 \leftarrow 0$ (reset past information).
2: Initialize $\mathbf{D}$ in $\mathbb{R}^{m \times k}$ with random columns from $\mathbf{X}$.
3: **for** $t = 1 \rightarrow T$ **do**
4:     Sample $\mathbf{x}_t$ from $\mathbf{X}$.
5:     Compute coefficient $\mathbf{c}_t$ for $\mathbf{x}_t$ by solving equation (5)
6:     $\mathbf{A}_t \leftarrow \mathbf{A}_{t-1} + \mathbf{c}_t \mathbf{c}_t^T$.
7:     $\mathbf{B}_t \leftarrow \mathbf{B}_{t-1} + \mathbf{x}_t \mathbf{c}_t^T$.
8:     Compute dictionary $\mathbf{D}_t$ using equation (6)
9: **end for**
10: **return** $\mathbf{D}_T$

5.1   Algorithm Outline

The outline is shown in Algorithm 1. At each iteration t, we deal with one sample $\mathbf{x}_t$ (the extension to multiple samples is straightforward). Given the sample for current iteration, we first compute the coefficient by solving the equation (5) based on the dictionary $\mathbf{D}_{t-1}$ computed in the last iteration. Then the sufficient statistics of $\mathbf{c}_i$, namely $\mathbf{A}$ and $\mathbf{B}$, are updated. Finally, the dictionary is updated based on historical observed data, by minimizing $\hat{f}_t(\mathbf{D}) \triangleq \frac{1}{t} \sum_{i=1}^{t} \|\mathbf{x}_i - \mathbf{D}\mathbf{c}_i\|_2^2$, where the coefficients $\mathbf{c}_i$ are obtained at iteration i of the algorithm. It acts as an approximation to $\hat{\mathbf{c}}_i(\mathbf{D}_{t-1})$ which denotes recomputing the coefficients for all the data in previous iterations based on the update-to-date dictionary $\mathbf{D}_{t-1}$. We will describe the details for computing the coefficients and updating the dictionary in the following subsections.

5.2   Compute Coefficients

For calculating the coefficient $\mathbf{c}_t$ given current dictionary $\mathbf{D}_{t-1}$, we need to solve the following problem:

$$\mathbf{c}_t \triangleq \arg\min_{\mathbf{c} \in \Delta_k} \|\mathbf{x}_t - \mathbf{D}_{t-1}\mathbf{c}\|_2^2. \tag{5}$$

which is a least-squares optimization problem with simplicial constraint. Several approaches have been used for this kind of problem. Culter et al. [6] proposed a penalty approach. Also, fast iterative shrinkage-thresholding algorithm (FISTA) could be used. Following [4], we use an active-set algorithm, which benefits from the sparsity of the coefficient $\mathbf{c}$. It is worth noting that the coefficients obtained by the equation (5) are sparse because of the interaction of curved geometry of the sphere and the linear surfaces, which encourages using low dimensional surfaces to represent the data. The maximum number of activated archetypes is determined by the number of vertices of the surface.

5.3   Update Dictionary

We update the dictionary using the sufficient statistics $\mathbf{A}$ and $\mathbf{B}$:

$$
\begin{aligned}
\mathbf{D}_t &\triangleq \arg\min_{\mathbf{D}\in\mathcal{C}} \frac{1}{t} \sum_{i=1}^{t} \|\mathbf{x}_i - \mathbf{D}\mathbf{c}_i\|_2^2 \\
&= \arg\min_{\mathbf{D}\in\mathcal{C}} \frac{1}{t} (\mathrm{Tr}(\mathbf{D}^T \mathbf{D}\mathbf{A}_t) - 2\,\mathrm{Tr}(\mathbf{D}^T \mathbf{B}_t)).
\end{aligned}
\tag{6}
$$

Since this formula is the same as the one in [20], we utilize the same dictionary update scheme. Block-coordinate descent approach with warm restart is used, and the main advantage of it is parameter free.

We sequentially update the column $\mathbf{d}_j$, while fixing the others. Firstly, the algorithm calculates a new position $\mathbf{u}_j = \mathbf{d}_j + (1/\mathbf{A}[j,j])(\mathbf{b}_j - \mathbf{D}\mathbf{a}_j)$, where $\mathbf{b}_j$ and $\mathbf{a}_j$ are j-th column of $\mathbf{A}$ and $\mathbf{B}$ respectively. Then we project $\mathbf{u}_j$ into the unit sphere by $\mathbf{d}_j' = \mathbf{u}_j / \max(\|\mathbf{u}_j\|_2, 1)$ to satisfy the constraint $\|\mathbf{d}_j\| \leq 1$. The convergence of this convex optimization problem is guaranteed.

6   Experiments

We evaluate the proposed method from three aspects. First, we evaluate the learning speed on large-scale datasets and compare with the original archetypal analysis method [4]. Second, we experimentally demonstrate that the convex combinations of the learned archetypes accurately approximate the D-hull. In particular, the archetypes correspond to the extremal points in the dataset. Third, we give applications of using the archetypes for data modeling in the context of reconstruction and classification tasks[1].

6.1   Speed

We implement our algorithm based on Eigen [11]. For the original AA method [4], we use the fastest implementation included in the SPAMS toolbox [20]. Both approaches use Intel MKL and multi-threading. The experiments are done on a single Intel CPU of i7-5930K.

We experiment on the H3.6M dataset [16] which has about three million human poses. The dimension of a pose is 48. Following the protocol in [22], we sample about 300 K training poses and 3000 testing poses. We learn 400 archetypes from the dataset. The results are shown in Fig. 6.

First, the reconstruction error of our approach on the training dataset drops to a lower level than [4]. This is expected as the archetypes in our approach have larger flexibility because they can be anywhere in the sphere. This differs from [4] where the archetypes can only be in the D-hull. Second, our approach uses much less time than [4] to reach similar levels of reconstruction errors. In

---

[1] We give more experiment results in the supplementary files.

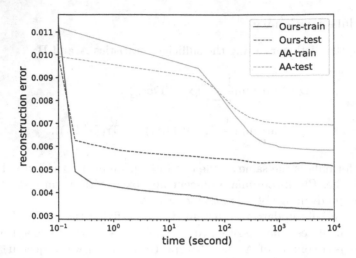

Fig. 6. Comparison of the learning speed for our approach and [4] on the H3.6M dataset. The results of our method and [4] are represented by blue and red lines, respectively. The solid line denotes the results on the training set and the dotted line denotes the results on the testing set. For [4], the points are plotted for each iteration. For our method, the points are plotted for every ten batches. (Color figure online)

particular, when the first iteration (which has to traverse *the whole* dataset once) of archetypal analysis is finished, our method has updated the dictionary for about 1700 times (around 3 epochs) and obtained a small reconstruction error. The gap will become even larger when the number of training data increases.

6.2 Interpretability

One distinctive property of archetypal analysis [4,6] is that some of the learned archetypes correspond to the extremal points in the dataset. In this case, the convex combinations of the archetypes will form a convex hull which tightly surrounds the data hull. In this section, we examine the archetypes learned on two data sources: human faces and poses.

Face Images. It is known that the imaging of an object in variable illumination conditions can be accurately approximated by convex combinations of a set of images captured at extreme illumination conditions [10]. Hence this is a good data source to visually evaluate whether the proposed approach can identify the extremal points as the AA method.

We experiment on the cropped Yale face dataset [10]. We normalize each image to have unit l_2-norm for our method. The archetypal analysis directly uses the original images. The results are shown in Fig. 7. For visualization purposes, for each archetype, we find the nearest neighbor in the face dataset and highlight that face image in a particular color. The face images with blue rectangles denote

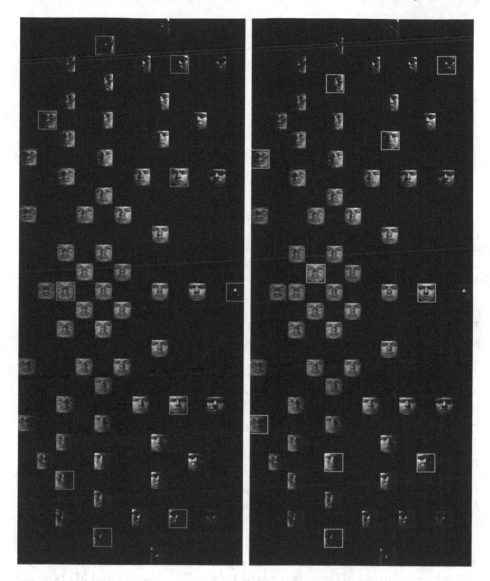

Fig. 7. This figure shows 64 images from the Yale face dataset which correspond to the same person under different lighting directions. We arrange the images according to the two axis-es of the lighting directions. The nearest neighbors of archetypes identified by our method and archetypal analysis are annotated with blue and red rectangles, respectively. (Color figure online)

the archetypes learned by our method. We also visualize the archetypes learned by AA in red rectangles. We can see that for both methods, the archetypes mostly correspond to the extremal illumination conditions, and the convex hull of the archetypes largely overlapped with the convex hull of the images, which justifies the effectiveness of our method.

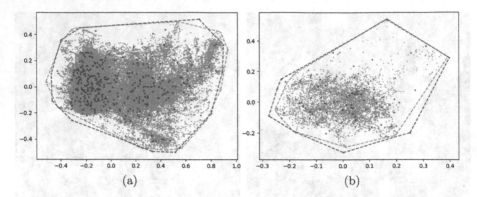

Fig. 8. Visualization of the learned archetypes on human poses. We use [36] to project the data into 2D. The data and the learned archetypes are represented by cyan and red points respectively. The convex hull of the data/archetypes is plotted using the dotted line. (a) the archetypes learned on all poses. (b) the archetypes learned on the poses of a particular action. (Color figure online)

Pose. We also experiment on the large 3D human pose dataset H3.6M. We visualize the poses and the learned archetypes by projecting them to two-dimensional space using PCA [36]. The results are shown in Fig. 8. We can see that some of the learned archetypes correspond to the extremal points in the dataset. In addition, the convex combinations of the archetypes form a convex hull which tightly surrounds the training dataset. The left and right figures show the results learned on all poses and on poses of a particular action respectively.

6.3 Applications

In this section, we use the learned archetypes as a data modeling tool for 3D human pose estimation and pose-based action recognition where strong regularization capabilities would help.

3D Pose Estimation. A 2D pose is represented by d joint locations in 2D $\mathbf{x} \in \mathbb{R}^{2d}$. Similarly, a 3D pose is denoted by $\mathbf{y} \in \mathbb{R}^{3d}$. The 2D and 3D pose are related by the camera parameters $\mathbf{M}$: $\mathbf{x} = \mathbf{M}\mathbf{y}$ [26].

The task of 3D human pose estimation is to estimate the 3D pose $\mathbf{y}$ and the camera parameters $\mathbf{M}$ from a 2D pose $\mathbf{x}$. It is usually achieved by minimizing $\|\mathbf{x} - \mathbf{M}\mathbf{y}\|_2$ which is an ill-posed problem. The authors of [26] propose to reduce the ambiguities by representing a 3D pose by a set of PCA bases $\mathbf{B}$ and seeking for the optimal coefficient for a testing 2D pose: $\mathbf{M}^*, \beta^* = \arg\min_{\mathbf{M}, \beta} \|\mathbf{x} - \mathbf{M}\mathbf{B}\beta\|_2$. The estimated 3D pose is $\hat{\mathbf{y}} = \mathbf{B}\beta^*$.

We replace the PCA bases in [26] with the archetypes learned by our approach. In particular, we learn 400 archetypes on the training set. We also compare with a related baseline which uses the bases learned by sparse coding [20]. The sparse bases are learned with the regularization factor being set as $\lambda = 1.2/\sqrt{3d}$ as suggested in [20] where $3d$ is the data dimension.

We experiment on the H3.6M dataset where the groundtruth 2D poses are assumed known. To reveal the properties of different bases (or archetypes), we calculate three metrics: (1) the projection error in 2D which is computed as $\|\mathbf{x} - \mathbf{MB}\beta^*\|$ when groundtruth camera parameters are known; the unit is pixel; (2) the mean per joint position error (MPJPE) in 3D when groundtruth camera parameters are known; the unit is mm; (3) MPJPE in 3D when camera parameters are jointly estimated.

Table 1. Pose estimation results on the H3.6M dataset. Results using estimated 2D pose are listed in parentheses for comparison with state-of-the-arts.

Method	Projection error	MPJPE	
		Known camera	Estimated camera
Chen et al. [3]	-	-	- (114.18)
Tome et al. [34]	-	-	- (88.39)
Zhou et al. [40]	-	-	- (79.90)
Sun et al. [30]	-	-	- (59.10)
Sparse coding	0.37	231.82	252.86 (276.75)
Archetypal analysis	4.13	52.56	75.93 (126.88)
Our method	3.68	50.71	76.91 (106.52)

The results are shown in Table 1. First, we can see that the projection error of sparse coding is much smaller than archetypal analysis and our method. However, the 3D pose estimation error is much larger. This is because the bases learned by sparse coding have weaker regularization properties. In other words, sparse coding doesn't provide a tight/bounded representation for the data manifold as our method. Second, the result of our method is similar to archetypal analysis. Third, the final error 106.52mm is achieved when the 2D poses are estimated by [2] and the camera parameters are jointly estimated using our method. The result is comparable to some state-of-the-arts which rely on deep networks.

Pose-Based Action Recognition. We also evaluate our approach on a classification task of pose-based action recognition. We adopt a simple nearest neighbor based classification framework. For a pose sequence, following [35], we extract a set of snippets with each being a short sequence of poses, to represent the original sequence. Then for each action class, we learn a set of archetypes based on the snippets. In the testing stage, for a pose sequence, we reconstruct its snippets using the archetypes of each class and the class which achieves the minimum average reconstruction error over all the snippets of the sequence is the predicted action class.

We experiment on the NTU RGB+D dataset [28], which is a large benchmark consisting of four million poses. The number of archetypes is set to 1024 by cross-validation. For sparse coding, the regularization factor is set to 0.1 by cross-validation. Following previous works, we report the results using two different train/test split methods: Cross-Subject (CS) and Cross-View (CV).

Table 2. Action recognition accuracy (%) on the NTU RGB+D dataset with Cross-Subject and Cross-View settings.

Method	CS	CV
LieNet [15]	61.37	66.95
PA-LSTM [28]	62.93	70.27
ST-LSTM (Tree Traversal) + Trust Gate [19]	69.20	77.70
STA-LSTM [29]	73.40	81.20
Ensemble TS-LSTM [18]	74.60	81.25
VA-LSTM [38]	**79.40**	**87.60**
Archetypal analysis	-	-
Sparse coding	64.95	77.61
Our method	68.07	80.93

The experimental results are shown in Table 2. It is not feasible to learn archetypes using [4] on such a large dataset so we don't list its results. We observe our method outperforms sparse coding by 3.12% and 3.32% in accuracy for CS and CV settings respectively, as our method learns a tighter representation than sparse coding. We also compare with the state-of-the-art methods which take advantage of deep neural networks such as [15, 18, 19, 28, 29, 38]. The recognition accuracy of our method is lower than VA-LSTM. The reason may be that our method doesn't model the motions as LSTM. However, considering that our method is simple and not tuned for the action recognition task, the results are already promising.

7   Conclusion

We present a fast variant of archetypal analysis, which not only maintains the favorable interpretability, but also scales gracefully to large datasets. It decouples the deep binding between data and archetypes, thus enables an online optimization algorithm. This formulation learns tight representations which is a favorable property for many tasks. Experiments on pose estimation and pose-based action recognition reveal its power.

References

1. Belkin, M., Niyogi, P.: Laplacian eigenmaps for dimensionality reduction and data representation. Neural Comput. **15**(6), 1373–1396 (2003)
2. Cao, Z., Simon, T., Wei, S., Sheikh, Y.: Realtime multi-person 2D pose estimation using part affinity fields. In: CVPR, pp. 1302–1310 (2017)
3. Chen, C., Ramanan, D.: 3D human pose estimation = 2D pose estimation + matching. In: CVPR, pp. 5759–5767 (2017)
4. Chen, Y., Mairal, J., Harchaoui, Z.: Fast and robust archetypal analysis for representation learning. In: CVPR, pp. 1478–1485 (2014)
5. Coates, A., Ng, A.Y.: Learning feature representations with K-means. In: Montavon, G., Orr, G.B., Müller, K.-R. (eds.) Neural Networks: Tricks of the Trade. LNCS, vol. 7700, pp. 561–580. Springer, Heidelberg (2012). https://doi.org/10.1007/978-3-642-35289-8_30
6. Cutler, A., Breiman, L.: Archetypal analysis. Technometrics **36**(4), 338–347 (1994)
7. Donoho, D.L., Grimes, C.: Hessian eigenmaps: locally linear embedding techniques for high-dimensional data. Proc. Nat. Acad. Sci. **100**(10), 5591–5596 (2003)
8. Duda, R.O., Hart, P.E., Stork, D.G.: Pattern Classification. Wiley, New York (1973)
9. Efron, B., Hastie, T., Johnstone, I., Tibshirani, R.: Least angle regression. Ann. Stat. **32**(2), 407–499 (2004)
10. Georghiades, A.S., Belhumeur, P.N., Kriegman, D.J.: From few to many: illumination cone models for face recognition under variable lighting and pose. TPAMI **23**(6), 643–660 (2001)
11. Guennebaud, G., Jacob, B., et al.: Eigen v3 (2010). http://eigen.tuxfamily.org
12. Ham, J., Lee, D.D., Mika, S., Schölkopf, B.: A kernel view of the dimensionality reduction of manifolds. In: ICML (2004)
13. Hoyer, P.O.: Non-negative sparse coding. In: Proceedings of the 12th IEEE Workshop on Neural Networks for Signal Processing, NNSP 2002, Martigny, Valais, Switzerland, 4–6 September 2002, pp. 557–565 (2002)
14. Hoyer, P.O.: Non-negative matrix factorization with sparseness constraints. J. Mach. Learn. Res. **5**, 1457–1469 (2004)
15. Huang, Z., Wan, C., Probst, T., Gool, L.V.: Deep learning on lie groups for skeleton-based action recognition. In: CVPR, pp. 1243–1252 (2017)
16. Ionescu, C., Papava, D., Olaru, V., Sminchisescu, C.: Human3.6m: large scale datasets and predictive methods for 3D human sensing in natural environments. TPAMI **36**(7), 1325–1339 (2014)
17. Lee, H., Battle, A., Raina, R., Ng, A.Y.: Efficient sparse coding algorithms. In: NIPS, pp. 801–808 (2006)
18. Lee, I., Kim, D., Kang, S., Lee, S.: Ensemble deep learning for skeleton-based action recognition using temporal sliding LSTM networks. In: ICCV, pp. 1012–1020 (2017)
19. Liu, J., Shahroudy, A., Xu, D., Wang, G.: Spatio-temporal LSTM with trust gates for 3D human action recognition. In: Leibe, B., Matas, J., Sebe, N., Welling, M. (eds.) ECCV 2016. LNCS, vol. 9907, pp. 816–833. Springer, Cham (2016). https://doi.org/10.1007/978-3-319-46487-9_50
20. Mairal, J., Bach, F.R., Ponce, J., Sapiro, G.: Online dictionary learning for sparse coding. In: ICML, pp. 689–696 (2009)
21. Mallat, S.: A Wavelet Tour of Signal Processing. Academic press, Cambridge (1999)

22. Martinez, J., Hossain, R., Romero, J., Little, J.J.: A simple yet effective baseline for 3D human pose estimation. In: ICCV, pp. 2659–2668 (2017)
23. Mika, S., Ratsch, G., Weston, J., Scholkopf, B., Mullers, K.R.: Fisher discriminant analysis with kernels. In: Proceedings of the 1999 IEEE Signal Processing Society Workshop on Neural Networks for Signal Processing IX, 1999, pp. 41–48. IEEE (1999)
24. Olshausen, B.A.: Emergence of simple-cell receptive field properties by learning a sparse code for natural images. Nature 381(6583), 607–609 (1996)
25. Osborne, M.R., Presnell, B., Turlach, B.A.: On the lasso and its dual. J. Comput. Graph. Stat. 9(2), 319–337 (2000)
26. Ramakrishna, Varun, Kanade, Takeo, Sheikh, Yaser: Reconstructing 3D human pose from 2D image landmarks. In: Fitzgibbon, Andrew, Lazebnik, Svetlana, Perona, Pietro, Sato, Yoichi, Schmid, Cordelia (eds.) ECCV 2012. LNCS, vol. 7575, pp. 573–586. Springer, Heidelberg (2012). https://doi.org/10.1007/978-3-642-33765-9_41
27. Saul, L.K., Roweis, S.T.: Think globally, fit locally: unsupervised learning of low dimensional manifolds. J. Mach. Learn. Res. 4(Jun), 119–155 (2003)
28. Shahroudy, A., Liu, J., Ng, T., Wang, G.: NTU RGB+D: a large scale dataset for 3D human activity analysis. In: CVPR, pp. 1010–1019 (2016)
29. Song, S., Lan, C., Xing, J., Zeng, W., Liu, J.: An end-to-end spatio-temporal attention model for human action recognition from skeleton data. In: AAAI, pp. 4263–4270 (2017)
30. Sun, X., Shang, J., Liang, S., Wei, Y.: Compositional human pose regression. In: ICCV, pp. 2621–2630 (2017)
31. Tenenbaum, J.B., De Silva, V., Langford, J.C.: A global geometric framework for nonlinear dimensionality reduction. Science 290(5500), 2319–2323 (2000)
32. Thompson, B.: Canonical correlation analysis. Encyclopedia of statistics in behavioral science (2005)
33. Tibshirani, R.: Regression shrinkage and selection via the lasso. J. Roy. Stat. Soc. B(Methodological), 267–288 (1996)
34. Tomè, D., Russell, C., Agapito, L.: Lifting from the deep: convolutional 3D pose estimation from a single image. In: CVPR, pp. 5689–5698 (2017)
35. Wang, C., Wang, Y., Yuille, A.L.: Mining 3D key-pose-motifs for action recognition. In: CVPR, pp. 2639–2647 (2016)
36. Wold, S., Esbensen, K., Geladi, P.: Principal component analysis. Chemometr. Intell. Lab. Syst. 2(1–3), 37–52 (1987)
37. Yu, G., Sapiro, G., Mallat, S.: Solving inverse problems with piecewise linear estimators: From Gaussian mixture models to structured sparsity. IEEE Trans. Image Process. 21(5), 2481–2499 (2012)
38. Zhang, P., Lan, C., Xing, J., Zeng, W., Xue, J., Zheng, N.: View adaptive recurrent neural networks for high performance human action recognition from skeleton data. In: ICCV, pp. 2136–2145 (2017)
39. Zhang, Z., Zha, H.: Principal manifolds and nonlinear dimensionality reduction via tangent space alignment. SIAM J. Sci. Comput. 26(1), 313–338 (2004)
40. Zhou, X., Zhu, M., Pavlakos, G., Leonardos, S., Derpanis, K.G., Daniilidis, K.: Monocap: Monocular human motion capture using a CNN coupled with a geometric prior. CoRR arXiv:abs/1701.02354 (2017)

Compositing-Aware Image Search

Hengshuang Zhao[1(✉)], Xiaohui Shen[2], Zhe Lin[3], Kalyan Sunkavalli[3],
Brian Price[3], and Jiaya Jia[1,4]

[1] The Chinese University of Hong Kong, Shatin, Hong Kong
{hszhao,leojia}@cse.cuhk.edu.hk
[2] ByteDance AI Lab, Menlo Park, USA
shenxiaohui@bytedance.com
[3] Adobe Research, San Jose, USA
{zlin,sunkaval,bprice}@adobe.com
[4] Tencent Youtu Lab, Shenzhen, China

Abstract. We present a new image search technique that, given a background image, returns compatible foreground objects for image compositing tasks. The compatibility of a foreground object and a background scene depends on various aspects such as semantics, surrounding context, geometry, style and color. However, existing image search techniques measure the similarities on only a few aspects, and may return many results that are not suitable for compositing. Moreover, the importance of each factor may vary for different object categories and image content, making it difficult to manually define the matching criteria. In this paper, we propose to learn feature representations for foreground objects and background scenes respectively, where image content and object category information are jointly encoded during training. As a result, the learned features can adaptively encode the most important compatibility factors. We project the features to a common embedding space, so that the compatibility scores can be easily measured using the cosine similarity, enabling very efficient search. We collect an evaluation set consisting of eight object categories commonly used in compositing tasks, on which we demonstrate that our approach significantly outperforms other search techniques.

1 Introduction

Image compositing is a fundamental task in photo editing and graphic design, in which foreground objects and background scenes from different sources are blended together to generate new composites. While previous work has considered the problem of rendering realistic composites [1–5] when the foreground and

---

H. Zhao—This work was partly done when H. Zhao was an intern at Adobe Research.

Electronic supplementary material The online version of this chapter (https://doi.org/10.1007/978-3-030-01219-9_31) contains supplementary material, which is available to authorized users.

V. Ferrari et al. (Eds.): ECCV 2018, LNCS 11207, pp. 517–532, 2018.
https://doi.org/10.1007/978-3-030-01219-9_31

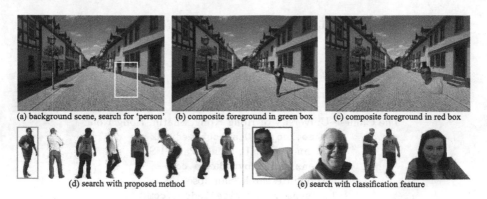

(a) background scene, search for 'person'   (b) composite foreground in green box   (c) composite foreground in red box

(d) search with proposed method   (e) search with classification feature

Fig. 1. Compositing-aware image search. Given a background image as a query, the task is to find foreground objects of a certain category that can be composited into the background at a specific location, as indicated by the rectangle. (Color figure online)

background images are given, users often find it challenging and time-consuming to find compatible foreground and background images to begin with.

Specifically, a foreground is considered compatible with the background if they *roughly match* in terms of semantics, viewpoint, style, color, etc., so that realistic composites can be generated with a reasonable amount of subsequent editing. For example in Fig. 1, a user intends to insert a person standing on the street at the location indicated by the yellow box. With the foreground in the green box, a realistic image can be rendered (Fig. 1(b)) by adjusting the color and adding a shadow. On the other hand, when given an incompatible foreground, it is practically impossible to generate a realistic composite with any editing technique (Fig. 1(c)).

The compatibility of a foreground and background pair can be determined by various aspects, whose importance may vary for different object categories and background scenes. For example, viewpoint is more important when inserting a car on the road, whereas semantic consistency might be more critical when composing a skier with snowy mountains. Existing search techniques usually only focus on one certain aspect, or manually extract features and define the matching criteria [6,7], which cannot adapt to different object categories and background scenes.

In this paper, we propose a learning based approach for compositing-aware image search. Instead of manually designing the matching criteria or hand engineering features, we learn new feature representations for foreground objects and background images respectively from a large amount of training data, which can adaptively encode the compatibility according to different foreground objects and background scenes. Specifically, we design a two-stream convolutional neural network (CNN) to learn the feature embedding from background images and foreground objects, where the object category information is encoded together with the images through multimodal compact bilinear pooling [8]. Triplets from existing datasets with segmentation mask annotations are constructed to learn a common embedding space, where the compatibility of a foreground and background image can be easily measured using the cosine similarity between their corresponding feature vectors. As a result, efficient search can be performed on huge amounts of foreground assets with existing visual search techniques such as Product Quantization [9]. To make the training more stable from large-scale yet noisy data, we further develop novel sampling algorithms to expand the triplets by finding additional similar foregrounds.

To evaluate the effectiveness of our proposed algorithm, we collected an evaluation dataset consisting of eight common foreground categories used in image compositing. Our experiments on the evaluation set show that our learned feature representations can adaptively capture the most important factors in terms of compatibility given different background images and foreground categories, and significantly outperforms other search techniques.

2   Related Work

Traditional text-based search paradigms mostly measure the semantic relevance between the text queries and the images, without considering other factors that are important for image compositing, and therefore often return many irrelevant results. Image-based search is often an alternative solution when the search criteria are hard to describe with text. Specific features describing various characteristics such as semantics and appearances [10], styles [11], and spatial layouts [12] are learned to serve different tasks. However, with no suitable foreground images available, it is often ineffective if using the background image as query due to the significant appearance gap between foreground images and background images.

Early efforts on this task such as Photo Clip Art [6] used handcrafted features to find the foreground assets according to several matching criteria such as camera orientation, lighting, resolution and local context. More recently, Tan *et al.* [7] used off-the-shelf deep CNN features to capture local surrounding context particularly for person compositing. However, these approaches lack generality as they only consider limited aspects and cannot adapt to different object categories and background scenes. Moreover, they assume the foreground objects have surrounding background context, and are therefore not feasible on those foreground images with pure background, which is very common in the images in stock sites[1,2] and preferred by users.

Zhu *et al.* [13] trained a discriminative network to estimate the realism of a composite image, which can possibly be used to select compatible foregrounds. However, in compositing tasks, the foregrounds need to be manually adjusted in the end in order to make the final image realistic, as it is very rare, if not impossible, to directly find a foreground perfectly matched with the scene. It is therefore not reliable to determine the realism of a composite image without users in the loop. It is also computationally impractical to try out every foreground

---

[1] https://shutterstock.com.
[2] https://stock.adobe.com.

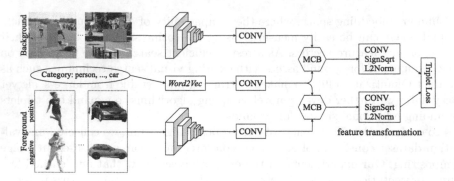

Fig. 2. Overall framework of the proposed *compositing-aware image search* (CAIS) system. A symmetric two-stream feature embedding network is utilized to extract background and foreground image features separately, in which a MCB module is introduced to incorporate category information. A feature transformation module is then performed to generate the final feature representations.

candidate from a huge number of assets. Moreover, their trained model mainly considers color compatibility due to their training procedure.

By contrast, benefiting from end-to-end feature learning, our approach is general and adaptive to different object categories and image scenes, and at the same time very efficient on large-scale foreground assets.

3   Proposed Approach

In this section, we describe the details of our proposed *compositing-aware image search* (CAIS) algorithm. Given a background image, a foreground object category, and the location in the background scene where the foreground will be composed, our task is to return foreground images of that category that are suitable for compositing. As discussed in the introduction, it is difficult to hand-design the matching criteria as the compatibility can be decided by many factors, which may vary in different background scenes and with different object categories. Therefore we aim to learn the feature embedding between the background scenes and foreground assets from a large amount of training data, so that the learned feature representations can encode rich information specifically for image compositing, and can adapt to various image content. Besides, the search algorithm should have the ability to deal with multiple foreground categories in a single framework. In this way, our designed network should be sensitive to category information.

In particular, to deal with this multiclass fine-grained ranking problem, we design a symmetric two-stream network, with each stream taking the background image or foreground object as input respectively, and generating a corresponding feature vector as output. Also, to incorporate the category information, a light weighted word feature extraction branch is added. The image and word features are then fed into a multimodal compact bilinear pooling (MCB) module [8].

MCB has proven to be an effective technique in the context of visual question answering (VQA) in fusing information from multiple modalities with negligible amount of additional parameters. Here we use it to jointly encode the category information and the image content.

During training, we encourage the feature vectors from compatible foreground and background images to be more similar than those from incompatible pairs. During testing, the learned features can be directly used to calculate the similarity in terms of compatibility for image compositing, which enables efficient large-scale image search. In the following sections, we first introduce our detailed network architecture, and then present our training and sampling strategies that are proved to be of great effectiveness.

3.1 Network Architecture

The architecture of our two-stream feature embedding network is illustrated in Fig. 2. The top stream takes the background scene as input. We use image mean values to fill the rectangle that indicates the location where the object to be inserted, so that the information regarding desired object location, size and aspect ratio can be provided to the network. Meanwhile, the bottom stream takes the foreground image with pure background (e.g., white background) as input. We focus on those pure foreground assets in our work, as they are abundant in those stock image sites and preferred by the users, and at the same time difficult to be retrieved by traditional search techniques.

The search algorithm should have the ability to deal with multiple foreground categories in a single framework. The importance of different factors in determining the compatibility may vary cross different categories. One straightforward solution is training a category-specific network for each category, or in a practically more reasonable design, learning a shared feature encoder and then branching out for each category to learn category-specific features. Nevertheless, neither solution can scale up to many categories, as the number of parameters would linearly increase with the number of class labels. To have a single compact model that can handle multiple categories at the same time, we propose to encode the category information into the foreground and background streams through multimodal compact bilinear pooling (MCB) [8]. During testing, by changing the class label we intend to search, the learned features can adapt to the most important compatibility factors with respect to the object category.

Specifically, to learn the features, we adopt the popular ResNet50 [14] (up to the 'pool5' layer) as our initial weights, after which global average pooling is performed to obtain a feature map of size $1 \times 1 \times 2048$. While the background stream and foreground stream are initialized with the same weights from ResNet50, we expect after learning they can encode different information, with the top stream focuses more on scene context, and the bottom stream learns object-oriented features. To learn the category-specific feature mapping, we use the word2vec [15] model to extract a 300 dimension vector as the input of the word encoding branch. After several convolutional layers, it is then fused with the background and foreground features in each separate MCB modules. A light weighted feature transformation module, including one convolution layer, an element-wise signed square root layer $(y = sign(x)\sqrt{|x|})$ and an instance-wise ℓ_2 normalization operation, is further appended to the network, resulting in a unit feature vector for background and foreground respectively, which encodes both the category information and image content.

3.2 Objective Function

To train the network, we construct triplets consisting of a background image as an anchor, a compatible foreground as the positive sample, and a incompatible foreground as the negative sample. We then adopt triplet loss [16] to train the proposed network and enforce the feature similarity between background anchor and positive foreground to be closer to the one between anchor and negative sample. Since the feature vectors have unit length after ℓ_2 normalization, we can easily calculate their similarity using squared ℓ_2 distance[3]. To encourage the distinguishing ability between positive and negative sample pairs, a positive margin α_i is introduced for class i. For convenience, we group feature extraction, multimodal compact bilinear pooling and ℓ_2 normalization into operation representation $\mathcal{F}$. Thus we want:

$$\|\mathcal{F}_i^b(B_i) - \mathcal{F}_i^f(F_i^p)\|_2^2 + \alpha_i < \|\mathcal{F}_i^b(B_i) - \mathcal{F}_i^f(F_i^n)\|_2^2 \tag{1}$$

where $\mathcal{F}_i^b$ and $\mathcal{F}_i^f$ are operations of category i in background and foreground streams separately. B_i and F_i^p, F_i^n stands for background image and its related positive (i.e., compatible) and negative foreground objects. In the training, we are going to minimize the following loss function $\mathcal{L}$:

$$\mathcal{L}(B_i, F_i^p, F_i^n) = max(0, \|\mathcal{F}_i^b(B_i) - \mathcal{F}_i^f(F_i^p)\|_2^2 + \alpha_i \\ - \|\mathcal{F}_i^b(B_i) - \mathcal{F}_i^f(F_i^n)\|_2^2) \tag{2}$$

3.3 Computational Efficiency

We found that our design is much more effective than sharing all the features across multiple categories, which cannot encode sufficient category-specific information, as demonstrated in Sect. 5. Our solution is also much more computationally efficient than learning separate feature representations dedicated for each category independently, and demonstrate to have very competitive results compared with those individual models. As for running time during testing, it includes feature extraction on input image (14.04 ms), MCB module encoding (0.62 ms), feature transformation (3.15 ms) and similarity calculation (4.32 ms with 100 foreground images). Moreover, Product Quantization [9] can be easily used to support real-time retrieval with millions of foreground assets.

---

[3] It is equivalent to their cosine similarity as $\|\mathbf{x} - \mathbf{y}\|^2 = 2 - 2\cos(\mathbf{x}, \mathbf{y})$.

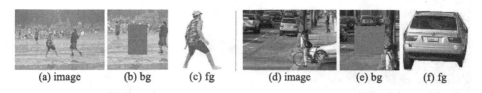

(a) image   (b) bg   (c) fg   (d) image   (e) bg   (f) fg

Fig. 3. Data preparation and augmentation. 'bg' and 'fg' denote background and foreground images respectively.

4 Training Data Acquisition

To learn a new feature representation for image compositing, it is crucial to have a large amount of training data. However, unfortunately there is no available training set specifically for the compositing-aware image search task. Collecting such a training set also seems impractical, as it is not only very time-consuming to manually label many pairs of background and foreground images, but also requires expertise in image compositing and photo editing to decide if the two are compatible. On the other hand, there are several publicly available datasets that contain object instance segmentation masks such as MS-COCO [17], PASCAL VOC 2012 [18] and ADE20K [19]. Utilizing those mask annotations, we can decompose the image into background scenes and foreground objects. Since they are generated from the exact same image, we know for sure that they are compatible, and usually more suitable than any other possible candidate pairs. Therefore, to form a triplet, we can treat the background scene of the image as the anchor, and the foreground from the same image as the positive sample, and then randomly sample a foreground from any other image as the negative sample. In this way, we can generate plenty of triplets for our feature learning.

Specifically, based on these three datasets, we select eight categories that frequently appear and are widely used in image compositing for our task: 'person', 'car', 'boat', 'dog', 'plant', 'bottle', 'chair' and 'painting'. The statistics regarding the training data are listed in the supplementary materials.

Triplet Preparation. Given an image with object masks, the process of generating background and foreground samples is illustrated in Fig. 3. During testing, the background scene image does not have the foreground in it. To mimic this situation in training, we obtain the rectangle bounding the foreground based on the mask, and fill in the rectangle with image mean values. It essentially removes the foreground object from the scene. When a user draw a bounding box to indicate the location of object insertion during testing, we can apply the same filling operation to make the training and testing input consistent. To make background images more consistent so that the training is more stable, we crop a square image from the original background, which contains as much context as possible, and place the filled rectangle as close to the image center as possible, as shown in Fig. 3(b) and (e). As for the foreground sample, we paste the

(a) semantic context   (b) shape

Fig. 4. Triplet extension. The blue ones are the original foregrounds, while the others are retrieved using (a) semantic context information and (b) shape information, respectively. (Color figure online)

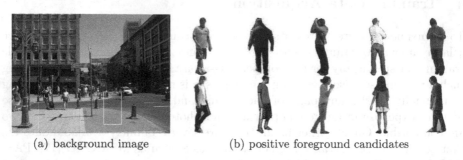

(a) background image   (b) positive foreground candidates

Fig. 5. An example background image with its labeled positive foreground candidates.

foreground in a square image with pure white background at the center location, as shown in Fig. 3(c) and (f).

By including the filled rectangle in the background image, the learned background features can respond to the location, size and aspect ratio of the object to be inserted when measuring compatibility. For example, when inserting a person on the lawn, a tall rectangle implies the user may want a standing person, while a wide rectangle may indicate a sitting person. At the same time, such constraint should not be very strict, as the rectangle drawn by the user may not be very accurate. Motivated by this, we introduce the data augmentation process to relax the size and scale constraints between paired foreground and background images to a limited extent. For background augmentation, we add random padding of the bounding box with maximum possible padding space being half of the bounding box's width and height. The new padded region is filled with mean value as well. Similarly for foreground augmentation, we add random padding and fill in the padded region with white color. For the negative foreground in the triplet, it is randomly chosen from another image with similar augmentation procedure. It would inevitably choose some foreground objects that are actually compatible with the background. However, we argue that the foreground from the same image is still more compatible, and accordingly Eq. 1 should still suffice. Moreover, as will be presented in the next section, we propose a triplet extension approach to include those foreground images as positive samples, which significantly improves the feature learning performance.

Triplet Extension. Paired foregrounds and backgrounds from the same images are easy to harvest, but they are much less than that of negative pairs (e.g., m vs. $m(m-1)$ if there are m images in a certain class). The severe imbalance in the number of training samples, coupled with the noise in negative pair sampling where some compatible foregrounds are mistreated as negative samples, makes our feature learning rather difficult. To overcome these limitations, we propose a triplet extension strategy by augmenting with more positive foreground samples. Given a foreground, we aim to find similar foregrounds using two matching criteria: semantic context and shape information.

For semantic context information, since those foreground images are generated from the ones with background scenes, we can fill in the background of those foreground images with their original background, and then extract semantic features using ResNet50 trained on image classification. Similar foreground are then retrieved by comparing the ℓ_2 distances of the extracted features. We found that such design yields much more consistent results than extracting features on the foreground images with pure background. Some sample retrieval results using the semantic context information on the 'person' category are shown in Fig. 4(a). For the shape information, we simply calculate the intersection over union (IoU) score of two foreground masks after aligning them around the mask center. Foregrounds with higher IoU scores over masks are considered more similar. Sample retrieval results using this criteria on the 'car' category are shown in Fig. 4(b).

In practice, we observed that when the objects have more rigid shapes that are more sensitive to viewpoints, shape information is more effective in finding similar foregrounds; while when the objects have more diverse appearance that may vary according to different scenes, using semantic context information produces more consistent results. Based on this observation, we choose to use shape information to augment positive foregrounds for 'bottle', 'car', 'chair' and 'painting', and adopt semantic context information to retrieve similar foregrounds for 'boat', 'dog', 'person' and 'plant'. Given a foreground and its corresponding background from the same image, we retrieve top N similar foreground images, and treat them as compatible foregrounds for the background as well. We found that such triplet extension strategy can largely increase the number of positive training pairs, and meanwhile reduces the noise in negative pair sampling. As a result, it significantly improves the feature learning, as shown in Sect. 5.

5   Experiments

Before presenting experimental results, we describe the implementation details in the following. We carry our experiments on the public platform Caffe [20]. We fix the learning rate as 0.001 for training until model achieves convergence. Momentum and weight decay are set to 0.9 and 0.0001 respectively. Batch size is set to 12 and margin in the triplet loss is set to 0.1. In triplet extension, we use top 10 retrieved foreground images as additional positive foreground samples. For model input, square background and foreground images are resized to 256×256 before being fed into their related feature extraction streams. To ease the training process, we performed two-stage feature learning: first learn the features without the MCB module, thus harvesting the common properties that can be shared across different categories like viewpoint, style and color. Once the model converges, we use the learned network as initialization, and jointly train the model with the MCB and feature transformation module, thus capturing category specific attributes for certain classes like semantics and shape.

5.1   Evaluation Set and Metric

While the image compositing task as a whole requires a lot of components including various editing and blending operations, in this paper we mainly address the first step in the task, i.e., finding compatible foreground assets given a background image. In order to make the evaluation focus on this step, we created an evaluation set composed of background images and compatible/incompatible foreground objects. Specifically, given a background image and a location where the object is going to be inserted, we insert every possible foreground candidate at that location to generate the composite, and label the foreground compatible only when it is possible to make the composite realistic with some basic image editing operations. Some labeled compatible foreground images for the background in Fig. 5(a) are shown in Fig. 5(b).

The evaluation set contains the eight object categories we selected for this task as mentioned in Sect. 4. Each category has 10 background images with various scenes. We draw a bounding box on each of the background image in appropriate position that is suitable for object insertion. For candidate foreground images, we utilize object instance masks from validation sets of MS-COCO, VOC 2012 and ADE20K. Each category has 100–400 candidate foreground objects, with 223 candidates on average. For ground truth, background images in each category has 16–140 compatible foreground candidates.

Intuitively, given a background image, a good search algorithm should rank all the compatible foregrounds higher than others. It naturally leads to adopting *Mean Average Precision* (MAP) as our evaluation metric, which is commonly used in image retrieval. We average the MAPs of all the 10 testing samples for each category to obtain category-wise MAP, and also report the mean evaluation results by averaging the results over all the categories. The MAP scores shown in the tables are all in percentage.

5.2   Ablation Study

Triplet Extension. We first perform ablation study on different triplet extension criteria. To focus more on the effects caused by triplet sampling, the study is conducted in the first-stage feature learning, i.e., when learning the shared features without MCB. Results are listed in Table 1. We can see using shape information alone in triplet extension in fact made the results worse, possibly because many irrelevant foreground images are returned for categories such as 'person' and 'dog', making the training data even noisier. With semantic context, the results are significantly improved, demonstrating the importance of triplet

Table 1. Ablation study on triplet extension criteria. 'Basic' denotes training without triplet extension. 'Semantics' and 'Shape' denote using semantic context and shape information. 'Combine' stands for our combined criteria.

Meth	boat	bottle	car	chair	dog	paint	person	plant	mean
Basic	60.66	40.84	28.72	14.18	57.74	27.44	31.69	44.79	38.26
Shape	48.80	44.96	36.37	20.73	42.62	32.48	18.65	41.89	35.81
Semantics	66.16	43.97	29.69	18.36	62.48	28.28	51.25	53.23	44.18
Combine	71.58	42.33	36.71	19.74	62.32	30.95	50.84	51.16	45.70

Table 2. Ablation study on output dimension of the MCB module.

Dim	No MCB	2048	8192	10240	20480	40960
mean mAP(%)	46.02	46.17	46.46	47.18	48.42	47.91

Table 3. Ablation study on network structures.

Method	boat	bottle	car	chair	dog	paint	person	plant	mean
Separate modules	69.65	49.71	42.93	22.57	62.00	34.72	54.75	53.17	48.69
Ours	71.04	55.00	39.84	18.97	65.45	34.09	51.14	51.83	48.42

Table 4. Comparison with other search methods. 'RealismCNN.' stands for the method in [13]. 'Shape' and 'Classification' denote searching using shape features and classification features.

Method	boat	bottle	car	chair	dog	paint	person	plant	mean
RealismCNN	46.81	49.05	15.56	08.60	50.12	27.37	21.48	37.48	32.06
Shape	46.12	39.08	34.77	11.54	44.77	26.43	15.25	43.09	32.63
Classification	63.30	**55.51**	14.93	11.03	45.90	23.96	33.48	46.10	36.78
Ours	**71.04**	55.00	**39.84**	**18.97**	**65.45**	**34.09**	**51.14**	**51.83**	**48.42**

extension. Finally, our combined strategy yields the best results, outperforming the 'Basic' method by 7.44% in absolute difference and 19.45% in relative improvement.

Network Structure. We also did the ablation study on the output dimension of the MCB module, as shown in Table 2. "No MCB" means the network without the MCB module. Therefore the network is shared across different categories, with no category information is encoded. The ones with the MCB module obtain better performance, which demonstrates the effectiveness of encoding category information and learning category-adaptive features. The performance improves when the dimension increase, and is saturated after the dimension reaches 20480. Therefore we set the dimension to be 20480 in the subsequent experiments. Also

Fig. 6. Our search results are tuned to location and aspect ratio of the bounding box.

note that training in one stage is less stable and converges poorer than the two stage solution (mean MAP 44.65% *vs.* 48.42% in two stage training).

We further investigate different network designs on feature learning in dealing with multiple object categories. As mentioned in Sect. 3, one straightforward solution to handle multiple categories is learning a shared feature encoder and then learning category-specific feature mapping for each category separately. In our implementation, we keep the shared ResNet50 backbone model, remove the MCB module, and learn an individual feature transformation module for each of the eight categories. The results are reported in Table 3. While it obtains good performance, it comes with much more parameters, and is not feasible with larger number of categories, as we need to train each separate branch for every class. Our adopted solution shown in the second row has very similar performance while being much more compact.

5.3   Comparison with Other Search Methods

We compare our proposed CAIS approach with three baseline methods: Realism-CNN [13], Shape feature and Classification feature. The rectangle drawn in the background image indicate desired size and aspect ratio by the user. Therefore we can match the drawn rectangle with the rectangle bounding the foreground object by calculating the IoU score of the two rectangles after aligning them around center position. We denote this baseline method by search with 'Shape feature'. In addition, we can also use semantic features learned through image classification, which are commonly used in image-based visual search, to retrieve foreground. For RealismCNN, we generate composite images by fitting the foreground candidates into the drawn rectangle in the background image together with Poisson blending [1], and use the realism score predicted by the Realism-CNN to rank all the candidates. The results of these three baseline search methods as well as ours are shown in Table 4. Our approach significantly outperforms all the other methods. It is 11.64% higher than the second best one in term of absolute difference and 31.65% better in terms of relative improvement.

The visual search results are shown in Fig. 9, from which we can see our method accounts for different factors and returns more compatible foreground

Fig. 7. Sample results of Poisson blending that are adopted in user study.

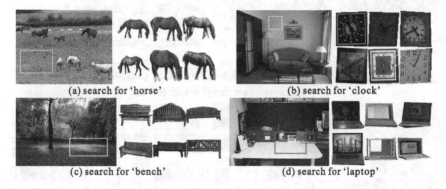

(a) search for 'horse'   (b) search for 'clock'

(c) search for 'bench'   (d) search for 'laptop'

Fig. 8. Generalization to new categories.

objects. Moreover, our learned features can consider the location and aspect ratio of user-drawn rectangles, and return suitable foregrounds accordingly, as shown in Fig. 6. More examples are in our supplementary materials.

5.4 User Study

To further evaluation the search results in terms of the compositing quality, we performed a user study to compare the composites generated by our retrieved foreground objects and the ones generated by the foregrounds that are retrieved using the classification feature, which performs best among the three baseline methods in quantitative evaluation. Poisson blending [1] is used to blend the images and reduce boundary artifacts. Some sample results are shown in Fig. 7.

We randomly selected 20 background images from our evaluation set, and use the top retrieved foreground by each method to generate the composites. In the study, the participants are asked to choose the results they think are more realistic. Overall we have 30 subjects participate the study. On average, 70.38% composites with foregrounds retrieved by the proposed method were rated more realistic than those searched by classification feature.

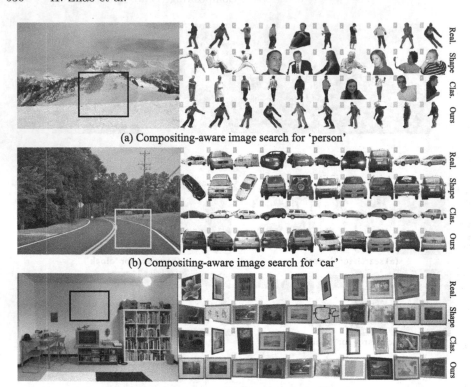

(a) Compositing-aware image search for 'person'

(b) Compositing-aware image search for 'car'

(c) Compositing-aware image search for 'painting'

Fig. 9. Visual search results. In each example, the yellow box indicates the position of foreground object to be inserted. The 1st to the 4th rows show the retrieved results using RealismCNN, shape information, classification features and our approach, respectively. The text boxes with 'green' and 'red' color in the top left corner of the foregrounds represent 'positive' and 'negative' foregrounds respectively. Our returned results contain more compatible foregrounds for image compositing. (Color figure online)

5.5   Generalization to New Categories

To further exhibit the representation ability of our learned shared feature across multiple classes, we test our method on new categories that have not been trained. The search results are illustrated in Fig. 8. Even without training on the new classes, the algorithm still works reasonably well. Interestingly, the retrieved clocks are all in rectangular shape, mostly because of the bias induced from the 'painting' category during training. Our method can easily scale up to much more categories if new training data are available, as the category information can be incorporated through the word feature branch, while the network architecture would still remain the same.

6   Concluding Remarks

In this paper, we present a general compositing-aware image search algorithm that aims on large-scale foreground assets for image compositing. Our proposed novel training and sampling strategies facilitate the feature embedding between background scenes and foreground objects, and thus enable efficient and accurate search with light online computation. We further show the learned feature representations can generalize to new categories and used for other search scenarios.

References

1. Pérez, P., Gangnet, M., Blake, A.: Poisson image editing. ACM Trans. Graph. (TOG) **22**, 313–318 (2003)
2. Sun, J., Jia, J., Tang, C.K., Shum, H.Y.: Poisson matting. ACM Trans. Graph. (TOG) **23**, 315–321 (2004)
3. Sunkavalli, K., Johnson, M.K., Matusik, W., Pfister, H.: Multi-scale image harmonization. ACM Trans. Graph. (TOG) (2010)
4. Xue, S., Agarwala, A., Dorsey, J., Rushmeier, H.: Understanding and improving the realism of image composites. ACM Trans. Graph. (TOG) (2012)
5. Tsai, Y.H., Shen, X., Lin, Z., Sunkavalli, K., Lu, X., Yang, M.H.: Deep image harmonization. In: CVPR (2017)
6. Lalonde, J.F., Hoiem, D., Efros, A.A., Rother, C., Winn, J., Criminisi, A.: Photo clip art. ACM Trans. Graph. (TOG) (2007)
7. Tan, F., Bernier, C., Cohen, B., Ordonez, V., Barnes, C.: Where and Who? Automatic semantic-aware person composition. In: WACV (2018)
8. Fukui, A., Park, D.H., Yang, D., Rohrbach, A., Darrell, T., Rohrbach, M.: Multimodal compact bilinear pooling for visual question answering and visual grounding. In: EMNLP (2016)
9. Jegou, H., Douze, M., Schmid, C.: Product quantization for nearest neighbor search. TPAMI (2011)
10. Gordo, A., Almazán, J., Revaud, J., Larlus, D.: Deep image retrieval: learning global representations for image search. In: Leibe, B., Matas, J., Sebe, N., Welling, M. (eds.) ECCV 2016. LNCS, vol. 9910, pp. 241–257. Springer, Cham (2016). https://doi.org/10.1007/978-3-319-46466-4_15
11. Collomosse, J., Bui, T., Wilber, M., Fang, C., Jin, H.: Sketching with style: visual search with sketches and aesthetic context. In: ICCV (2017)
12. Mai, L., Jin, H., Lin, Z., Fang, C., Brandt, J., Liu, F.: Spatial-semantic image search by visual feature synthesis. In: CVPR (2017)
13. Zhu, J.Y., Krähenbühl, P., Shechtman, E., Efros, A.A.: Learning a discriminative model for the perception of realism in composite images. In: ICCV (2015)
14. He, K., Zhang, X., Ren, S., Sun, J.: Deep residual learning for image recognition. In: CVPR (2016)
15. Mikolov, T., Chen, K., Corrado, G., Dean, J.: Efficient estimation of word representations in vector space. arXiv:1301.3781 (2013)
16. Schroff, F., Kalenichenko, D., Philbin, J.: FaceNet: a unified embedding for face recognition and clustering. In: CVPR (2015)

17. Lin, T.-Y., et al.: Microsoft COCO: common objects in context. In: Fleet, D., Pajdla, T., Schiele, B., Tuytelaars, T. (eds.) ECCV 2014. LNCS, vol. 8693, pp. 740–755. Springer, Cham (2014). https://doi.org/10.1007/978-3-319-10602-1_48
18. Everingham, M., Gool, L.J.V., Williams, C.K.I., Winn, J.M., Zisserman, A.: The PASCAL visual object classes VOC challenge. IJCV (2010)
19. Zhou, B., Zhao, H., Puig, X., Fidler, S., Barriuso, A., Torralba, A.: Scene parsing through ADE20K dataset. In: CVPR (2017)
20. Jia, Y., et al.: Caffe: convolutional architecture for fast feature embedding. In: ACM MM (2014)

Improving Sequential Determinantal Point Processes for Supervised Video Summarization

Aidean Sharghi[1](✉)(iD), Ali Borji[1](✉), Chengtao Li[2](✉)(iD), Tianbao Yang[3](✉)(iD), and Boqing Gong[4](✉)(iD)

[1] Center for Research in Computer Vision, University of Central Florida, Orlando, FL, USA
aidean.sharghi@gmail.com, aliborji@gmail.com
[2] Massachusetts Institute of Technology, Cambridge, MA, USA
ctli@mit.edu
[3] University of Iowa, Iowa City, IA, USA
tianbao-yang@uiowa.edu
[4] Tencent AI Lab, Seattle, WA, USA
boqinggo@outlook.com

Abstract. It is now much easier than ever before to produce videos. While the ubiquitous video data is a great source for information discovery and extraction, the computational challenges are unparalleled. Automatically summarizing the videos has become a substantial need for browsing, searching, and indexing visual content. This paper is in the vein of supervised video summarization using sequential determinantal point processes (SeqDPPs), which models diversity by a probabilistic distribution. We improve this model in two folds. In terms of learning, we propose a large-margin algorithm to address the exposure bias problem in SeqDPP. In terms of modeling, we design a new probabilistic distribution such that, when it is integrated into SeqDPP, the resulting model accepts user input about the expected length of the summary. Moreover, we also significantly extend a popular video summarization dataset by (1) more egocentric videos, (2) dense user annotations, and (3) a refined evaluation scheme. We conduct extensive experiments on this dataset (about 60 h of videos in total) and compare our approach to several competitive baselines.

1 Introduction

It is now much easier than ever before to produce videos due to ubiquitous acquisition capabilities. The videos captured by UAVs and drones, from ground surveillance, and by body-worn cameras can easily reach the scale of gigabytes per day. In 2017, it was estimated that there were at least 2.32 billion active

Electronic supplementary material The online version of this chapter (https://doi.org/10.1007/978-3-030-01219-9_32) contains supplementary material, which is available to authorized users.

V. Ferrari et al. (Eds.): ECCV 2018, LNCS 11207, pp. 533–550, 2018.
https://doi.org/10.1007/978-3-030-01219-9_32

camera phones in the world [24]. In 2015, 2.4 million GoPro body cameras were sold worldwide [13]. While the big video data is a great source for information discovery and extraction, the computational challenges are unparalleled. Automatically summarizing the videos has become a substantial need for browsing, searching, and indexing visual content.

Under the *extractive* video summarization framework, a summary is composed of important shots of the underlying video. This notion of importance, however, varies drastically from work to work in the literature. Wolf defines the importance as a function of motion cues [41]. Zhao and Xing formulate it by reconstruction errors [47]. Gygli et al. learn a mixture of *interestingness, representativeness*, and *uniformity* measures to find what is important [12]. These differences highlight the complexity of video summarization. The criteria for summarizing vastly depend on the content, styles, lengths, etc. of the video and, perhaps more importantly, users' preferences. For instance, to summarize a surveillance video, a running action might flag an important event whereas in a football match it is a normal action observed throughout the video.

To overcome those challenges, there are two broad categories of approaches in the literature. One is to constrain the problem domain to a homogeneous set of videos which share about the same characteristics (e.g., length and style) so that experts can engineer some domain-specific criteria of good summaries [26,34]. The other is to design models that can learn the criteria automatically, often from human-annotated summaries in a supervised manner [9,30,31,46]. The latter is more appealing because a learner can be trained for different settings of choice, while the former is not so scalable.

This paper is also in the vein of supervised video summarization based on determinantal point processes (DPPs) [18]. Arising from quantum physics and random matrix theories, DPP is a powerful tool to balance importance and diversity, two axiomatic properties in extractive video summarization. Indeed, a good summary must be collectively diverse in the sense that it should not have redundancy of information. Moreover, a shot selected into the summary must add value to the quality of the summary; otherwise, it is not important in the context of the summary. Thanks to the versatility of DPP and one of its extensions called SeqDPP [9] for handling sequences, they have been employed in a rich line of recent works on video summarization [30,31].

This paper makes two-pronged contribution, improving these models from the perspectives of both model flexibility and learning strategy. In terms of learning, we propose a large-margin algorithm to address the SeqDPP's exposure bias problem explained below. In terms of modeling, we design a new probabilistic block such that, when it is integrated into SeqDPP, the resulting model accepts user input about the expected length of the summary.

We first explain the exposure bias problem with the existing SeqDPP works—it is actually a mismatch issue in many sequence to sequence (seq2seq) learning methods [1,29,35,36,39]. When the model is trained by maximizing the likelihood of user annotations, the model takes as input user annotated "oracle" summaries. At the test time, however, the model generates output by searching over the output space in a greedy fashion and its intermediate conditional distributions may receive input from the previous time step that deviates from the oracle. In other words, the model is exposed to different environments in the training and testing stages, respectively. This exposure bias also results in the loss-evaluation mismatch [27] between the training phase and the inference.

To tackle these issues, we adapt the *Large-Margin* algorithm originally derived for training LSTMs [40] to the SeqDPPs. The main idea is to alleviate the exposure bias by incorporating the techniques of the test time into the objective function used for training. Meanwhile, we add to the large-margin formulation a multiplicative reward term which is related to the evaluation metrics to mitigate the loss-evaluation mismatch.

In addition to the new large-margin learning algorithm, we also improve the SeqDPP model by a novel probabilistic distribution in order to allow users to control the lengths of system-generated video summaries. To this end, we propose a generalized DPP (*G*DPP) in which an arbitrary prior distribution can be imposed over the sizes of the subsets of video shots. As a result, both vanilla DPP and k-DPP [17] can be considered as special instances of *G*DPP. Moreover, we can conveniently substitute the (conditional) DPPs in SeqDPP by *G*DPP. When a user gives an expected length of the summary, we dynamically allocate it to different segments of the video and then choose the right number of video shots from a segment.

We conduct extensive experiments to verify the improved techniques for supervised video summarization. First of all, we significantly extend the UTE dataset [19], its annotations of video summaries, and per-shot concepts [31] by another eight egocentric videos [8]. Following the protocol described in [31], we collect three user summaries for each of the hours-long videos as well as concept annotations for each video shot. We evaluate the large-margin learning algorithm on not only the proposed sequential *G*DPP but also the existing SeqDPP models.

2   Related Work and Background

We briefly review the related work in this section. Besides, we also describe the major body of DPPs and SeqDPPs. Readers are referred to [18] and [9] for more details and properties of the two versatile probability models.

Supervised Video Summarization. In recent years, data-driven learning algorithms have prevailed in a variety of computer vision problems. This is mainly because they can learn complex relations from data, especially when the underlying relations are too subtle or complex to handcraft. Video summarization is an instance of such cases. The fact that different users prefer different summaries is a strong evidence to the complexity of the problem. To overcome the impediments, one solution is to learn how to make good summaries in a supervised manner. The degree of supervision, however, is different in the literature. In [4,15,16,42], weakly supervised web image and video priors help define visual importance. Captions associated with videos are used by [22,33] to infer semantic importance. Finally, many frameworks (e.g., [9,12,30,31,46]) learn a summarizer directly from user-annotated summaries.

Sequence-to-Sequence Learning. Sequence-to-sequence (Seq2seq) modeling has been successfully employed in a vast set of applications, especially in Natural Language Processing (NLP). By the use of Recurrent Neural Networks (RNNs), impressive modeling capabilities and results are achieved in various fields such as machine translation [1] and text generation applications (e.g., for image and video captioning [38,43]).

The Seq2seq models are conveniently trained as conditional language models, maximizing the probability of observing next ground truth word conditioned on the input and target words. This translates to using merely a word-level loss (usually a simple cross-entropy over the vocabulary).

While the training procedure described above has shown to be effective in various word-generation tasks, the learned models are not used as conditional models during inference at test time. Conventionally, a greedy approach is taken to generate the output sequence. Moreover, when evaluating, the complete output sequence is compared against the gold target sequence using a sequence-level evaluation metric such as ROUGE [21] and BLEU [25].

Determinantal Point Process (DPP). A discrete DPP [14,18] defines a distribution over all the subsets of a ground set measuring the negative correlation, or repulsion, of the elements in each subset. Given a ground set $\mathcal{Y} = \{1, \ldots, N\}$, one can define $K \in \mathbb{R}^{N \times N}$, a positive semi-definite kernel matrix that represents the per-element importance as well as the pairwise similarities between the N elements. A distribution over a random subset $Y \subseteq \mathcal{Y}$ is a DPP, if for every $y \subseteq \mathcal{Y}$ the following holds:

$$P(y \subseteq Y; K) = \det(K_y) \tag{1}$$

where K_y is the squared sub-kernel of K with rows and columns indexed by the elements in y, and $\det(.)$ is the determinant function. K is referred to as the marginal kernel since one can compute the probability of any subset y being included in $\mathcal{Y}$. It is the property of the determinant that promotes diversity: in order to have a high probability $P(i, j \in Y; K) = K_{ii}K_{jj} - K_{ij}^2$, the per-element importance terms K_{ii} and K_{jj} must be high and meanwhile the pairwise similarity terms K_{ij} must be low.

To directly specify the atomic probabilities for all the subsets of $\mathcal{Y}$, Borodin and Rains derived another form of DPPs through a positive semi-definite matrix $L = K(I - K)^{-1}$ [2], where I is an identity matrix. It samples a subset $y \subseteq \mathcal{Y}$ with probability

$$P_L(Y = y; L) = \frac{\det(L_y)}{\det(L + I)}, \tag{2}$$

where the denominator $\det(L + I)$ is a normalization constant.

Sequential DPP (seqDPP). Gong et al. proposed SeqDPP [10] to preserve partial orders of the elements in the ground set. Given a long sequence $\mathcal{V}$ of elements (e.g., video shots), we divide them into T disjoint yet consecutive partitions $\bigcup_{t=1}^{T} \mathcal{V}_t = \mathcal{V}$. The elements within each partition are orderless to apply DPP and yet the orders between the partitions are observed in the following manner. At the t-th time step, SeqDPP selects a diverse subset of elements by a variable $X_t \subseteq \mathcal{V}_t$ from the corresponding partition and conditioned on the elements $x_{t-1} \subseteq \mathcal{V}_{t-1}$ selected from the previous partition. In particular, the distribution of the subset selection variable X_t is given by a conditional DPP,

$$P(X_t = x_t | X_{t-1} = x_{t-1}) := P_L(Y_t = x_t \cup x_{t-1} | x_{t-1} \subseteq Y_t; L^t) \qquad (3)$$

$$= P_L(X_t = x_t; \Omega^t) = \frac{\det \Omega_{x_t}^t}{\det(\Omega^t + I)}, \qquad (4)$$

where $P_L(Y_t; L^t)$ and $P_L(X_t; \Omega^t)$ are two L-ensemble DPPs with the ground sets $x_{t-1} \cup \mathcal{V}_t$ and $\mathcal{V}_t$, respectively—namely, the conditional DPP itself is a valid DPP over the "shrinked" ground set. The relationship between the two L-ensemble kernels L^t and Ω^t is given by [2],

$$\Omega^t = \left([(L^t + I_{\mathcal{V}_t})^{-1}]_{\mathcal{V}_t} \right)^{-1} - I, \qquad (5)$$

where $I_{\mathcal{V}_t}$ is an identity matrix of the same size as L^t except that the diagonal entries corresponding to x_{t-1} are 0's, $[\cdot]_{\mathcal{V}_t}$ is the squared submatrix of $[\cdot]$ indexed by the elements in $\mathcal{V}_t$, and the number of rows/columns of the last identity matrix I equals the size of the t-th video segment $\mathcal{V}_t$.

3   A Large-Margin Algorithm for Learning SeqDPPs

We present the main large-margin learning algorithm in this section. We first review the mismatch between the training and inference of SeqDPPs [9] and then describe the large-margin algorithm in detail.

Training and Inference of SeqDPP. For the application of supervised video summarization, SeqDPP is trained by maximizing the likelihood (MLE) of user summaries. At the test time, however, an approximate online inference is employed:

$$\hat{x}_1 = \text{argmax}_{x \in \mathcal{V}_1} P(X_1 = \hat{x}), \quad \hat{x}_2 = \text{argmax}_{x \in \mathcal{V}_2} P(X_2 = \hat{x} | X_1 = \hat{x}_1), \quad \dots \quad (6)$$

We note that, in the inference phase, a possible error at one time step (e.g., $\hat{x}_1$) propagates to the future but MLE always feeds the oracle summary to SeqDPP in the training stage (i.e., exposure bias [27]). Besides, the likelihood based objective function used in training does not necessarily correlate well with the evaluation metrics in the test stage (i.e., loss-evaluation mismatch [27]).

    The issues above are common in seq2seq learning. It has been shown that improved results can be achieved if one tackles them explicitly [5,6,27,28,32]. Motivated by these findings, we propose a large-margin algorithm for SeqDPP to mitigate the exposure bias and loss-evaluation mismatch issues in existing SeqDPP works. Our algorithm is extended from [40], which studies the large-margin principle in training recurrent neural networks. However, we are not constrained by the beam search, do not need to change the probabilistic SeqDPP model to any non-probabilistic version, and also fit a test-time evaluation metric into the large-margin formulation.

We now design a loss function as the following,

$$\mathcal{L}(\theta) = \sum_{t=1}^{T} \delta(x_{1:t-1}^* \cup \hat{x}_t, x_{1:t}^*) M(x_t^*, \hat{x}_t, x_{t-1}^*; L), \tag{7}$$

which includes two components: (1) a sequence-level cost δ which allows us to scale the loss function depending on how erroneous the test-time inference is compared to the oracle summary, and (2) a margin-sensitive loss term M which penalizes the situation when the probability of an oracle sequence fails to exceed the probability of the model-inferred ones by a margin. Denote by $\hat{x}_t$ and $\hat{x}_t^*$ the subsets selected from the t-th partition $\mathcal{V}_t$ by SeqDPP and by an "oracle" user, respectively. Let $x_{1:t}^*$ represent the oracle summary *until* time step t. The sequence-level cost $\delta(x_{1:t-1}^* \cup \hat{x}_t, x_{1:t}^*)$ can be any accuracy metric (e.g., 1-F-score) contrasting a system-generated summary with a user summary.

Assuming SeqDPP is able to choose the right subset x_{t-1}^* from partition $\mathcal{V}_{t-1}$, given the next partition $\mathcal{V}_t$, the margin-sensitive loss penalizes the situation that the model selects a different subset $\hat{x}_t$ from the oracle x_t^*,

$$M(x_t^*, \hat{x}_t, x_{t-1}^*; L) := [1 - \log P(X_t = x_t^* | x_{t-1}^*) + \log P(X_t = \hat{x}_t | x_{t-1}^*)]_+$$
$$= [1 - \log \det(L_{x_t^* \cup x_{t-1}^*}) + \log \det(L_{\hat{x}_t \cup x_{t-1}^*})]_+ \tag{8}$$

where $[\cdot]_+ = \max(\cdot, 0)$. When we use this loss term to train SeqDPP, we always assume that the correct subset $\hat{x}_{t-1} = x_{t-1}^*$ is chosen at the previous time step $t - 1$. In other words, we penalize the model step by step instead of checking the whole sequence of subsets predicted by the model. This allows more effective training because it (1) enforces the model to choose the correct subset at every time step, and (2) enables us to set the gradient weights according to how erroneous a mistake is at a time step, rather than the whole sequence of all steps, in the eyes of the evaluation metric.

Compared to MLE, it is especially appealing that the large-margin formulation flexibly takes the evaluation metric into account. As a result, it does not require SeqDPP to predict exactly the same summaries as the oracles. Instead, when the predicted and oracle summaries are equivalent (not necessarily identical) according to the evaluation metric, the model parameters are not updated.

4   Disentangling Size and Content in SeqDPP

In this section, we propose a sequential model of generalized DPPs (Seq GDPP) that accepts an arbitrary distribution over the sizes of the subsets whose content follow DPP distributions. It allows users to provide priors or constraints over the total items to be selected. We first present the generalized DPP and then describe how to use it to devise the sequential model, SeqGDPP.

4.1   Generalized DPPs (GDPPs)

Kulesza and Taskar have made an intriguing observation about the vanilla DPP: it conflates the size and content of the variable Y for selecting subsets from the ground set $\mathcal{Y}$ [17]. To see this point more clearly, we can re-write a DPP as a mixture of elementary DPPs $P_E(Y)$ [18, Lemma 2.6],

$$P_L(Y; L) = \frac{1}{\det(L + I)} \sum_{J \subseteq \mathcal{Y}} P_E(Y; J) \prod_{n \in J} \lambda_n, \tag{9}$$

$$\propto \sum_{k=0}^{N} \sum_{J \subseteq \mathcal{Y}, |J|=k} P_E(Y; J) \prod_{n \in J} \lambda_n \tag{10}$$

where the first summation is over all the possible sizes of the subsets and the second is about the particular items of each subset. Eigen-decomposing the L-ensemble kernel to $L = \sum_{n=1}^{N} \lambda_n v_n v_n^T$, the marginal kernel of the elementary DPP $P_E(Y; J)$ is $K^J = \sum_{n \in J} v_n v_n^T$—it is interesting to note that, due to this form of the marginal kernel, the elementary DPPs do not have their counterpart L-ensembles. The elementary DPP $P_E(Y; J)$ always chooses $|J|$ items from the ground set $\mathcal{Y}$, namely, $P(|Y| = |J|) = 1$.

Equation (10) indicates that, to sample from the vanilla DPP, one may sample the size of a subset from a uniform distribution followed by drawing items/content for the subset. We propose to perturb this process and explicitly impose a distribution $\pi = \{\pi_k\}_{k=0}^{N}$ over the sizes of the subsets,

$$P_G(Y; L) \propto \sum_{k=0}^{N} \pi_k \sum_{J \subseteq \mathcal{Y}, |J|=k} P(Y; J) \prod_{n \in J} \lambda_n \tag{11}$$

As a result, the generalized DPP (GDPP) $P_G(Y; L)$ entails both DPP and k-DPP [17] as special cases (when π is uniform and when π is a Dirac delta distribution, respectively), offering a larger expressive spectrum. Another interesting result is that, for a truncated uniform distribution π over the sizes of the subsets, we arrive at a DPP which selects subsets with bounded cardinality, $P(Y \mid k_1 \leq |Y| \leq k_2; L)$. Such constraint arises from real applications like document summarization, image display, and sensor placement.

Normalization. The normalization constant for GDPP is $Z_G = \sum_{J \subseteq \mathcal{Y}} \pi_{|J|} \prod_{n \in J} \lambda_n$. Details are included in the supplementary materials (Suppl.). The computation complexity of this normalization depends on the eigen-decomposition of L. With the eigenvalues λ_n, we can compute the constant Z_G in polynomial time $O(N^2)$ with some slight change to the recursive algorithm [18, Algorithm

7], which calculates all the elementary symmetric polynomials $\sum_{|J|=k} \prod_{n \in J} \lambda_n$ for $k = 0, \cdots, N$ in $O(N^2)$ time. Therefore, the overall complexity of computing the normalization constant for $GDPP$ is about the same as the complexity of normalizing an L-ensemble DPP (i.e., computing $\det(L + I)$).

Evaluation. With the normalization constant Z_G, we are ready to write out the probability of selecting a particular subset $y \subseteq \mathcal{Y}$ from the ground set by $GDPP$,

$$P_G(Y = y; L) = \frac{\pi_{|y|}}{Z_G} \det(L_y) \tag{12}$$

in which the concise form is due to the property of the elementary DPPs that $P_E(Y = y; J) = 0$ when $|y| \neq |J|$.

GDPP as a Mixture of k-DPPs. The $GDPP$ expressed above has a close connection to the k-DPPs [17]. This is not surprising due to the definition of $GDPP$ (cf. Eq. (11)). Indeed, $GDPP$ can be exactly interpreted as a mixture of $N + 1$ k-DPPs $P_k(Y = y; L), k = 0, 1, \cdots, N$,

$$P_G(Y = y; L) = \frac{\pi_{|y|} \sum_{|J|=|y|} \prod_{n \in J} \lambda_n}{Z_G} P_{|y|}(Y = y; L)$$

if **all the k-DPPs**, i.e., the mixture components, **share the same L-ensemble kernel** L as $GDPP$. If we introduce a new notation for the mixture weights, $p_k \triangleq \pi_k / Z_G \sum_{|J|=k} \prod_{n \in J} \lambda_n$, the $GDPP$ can then be written as

$$P_G(Y; L) = \sum_{k=0}^{N} p_k P_k(Y; L). \tag{13}$$

Moreover, there is no necessity to adhere to the involved expression of p_k. Under some scenarios, directly playing with p_k may significantly ease the learning process. We will build a sequential model upon the $GDPP$ of form (13) in the next section.

Exact Sampling. Following the interpretation of $GDPP$ as a weighted combination of k-DPPs, we have the following decomposition of the probability:

$$P(Y|Y \sim GDPP) = P(Y|Y \sim k - DPP)P(k|k \sim GDPP),$$

where, with a slight abuse of notation, we let $k \sim GDPP$ denote the probability of sampling a k-DPP from $GDPP$. Therefore, we can employ a two-phase sampling procedure from the $GDPP$,

- Sample k from the discrete distribution $p = \{p_i\}_{i=0}^{N}$.
- Sample Y from k-DPP.

The supplementary materials present another sampling method via a Markov chain.

4.2   A Sequential Model of GDPPs (Seq$G$DPP)

In this section, we construct a sequential model of the generalized DPPs (Seq$G$DPP) such that not only it models the temporal and diverse properties as SeqDPP does, but also allows users to specify the prior or constraint over the length of the video summary.

We partition a long video sequence $\mathcal{V}$ into T disjoint yet consecutive short segments $\bigcup_{t=1}^{T} \mathcal{V}_t = \mathcal{V}$. The main idea of Seq$G$DPP is to adaptively distribute the expected length M_0 of the video summary to different video segments over each of which a GDPP is defined. In particular, we replace the conditional DPPs in SeqDPP (cf. Eq. (4)) by GDPPs,

$$P(X_t = x_t | X_{t-1} = x_{t-1}) \tag{14}$$

$$\triangleq P_G(X_t = x_t; \Omega^t) = p^t_{|x_t|} P_{|x_t|}(X_t = x_t; \Omega^t), \tag{15}$$

where the last equality follows Eq. (13), and recall that the L-ensemble kernel Ω^t encodes the dependencies on the video frames/shots selected from the immediate past segment $x_{t-1} \subseteq \mathcal{V}_{t-1}$ (cf. Sect. 2, Eq. (5)). The discrete distribution $p^t = \{p^t_k\}$ is over all the possible sizes $\{k\}$ of the subsets at time step t.

We update p^t adaptively according to

$$p^t_k \propto \exp(-\alpha(k - \mu^t)^2), \tag{16}$$

where the mean $\mu^t \in [0, |\mathcal{V}_t|]$ is our belief about how many items should be selected from the current video segment $\mathcal{V}_t$ and the concentration factor $\alpha > 0$ tunes the confidence of the belief. When α approaches infinity, the GDPP $P_G(X_t; \Omega^t)$ degenerates to k-DPP and chooses exactly μ^t items into the video summary.

Our intuition for parameterizing the mean μ^t encompasses three pieces of information: the expected length M_0 over the overall video summary, number of items that have been selected into the summary up to the t-th time step, and the variety of the visual content in the current video segment $\mathcal{V}_t$. Specifically,

$$\mu^t \triangleq \frac{M_0 - \sum_{t'=1}^{t-1} |x_{t'}|}{T - t + 1} + w^T \phi(\mathcal{V}_t) \tag{17}$$

where the first term is the average number of items to be selected from each of the remaining video segments to make up an overall summary of length M_0, the second term $w^T \phi(\mathcal{V}_t)$ is an offset to the average number depending on the current video segment $\mathcal{V}_t$, and $\phi(\cdot)$ extracts a feature vector from the segment. We learn w from the training data—user annotated video summaries and their underlying videos. We expect that a visually homogeneous video segment gives rise to negative $w^T \phi(\mathcal{V}_t)$ such that less than the average number of items will be selected from it, and vice versa.

4.3   Learning and Inference

For the purpose of out-of-sample extension, we shall parameterize Seq$G$DPP in such a way that, at time step t, it conditions on the corresponding video segment $\mathcal{V}_t$ and the selected shots $X_{t-1} = x_{t-1}$ from the immediate previous time step. We use a simple convex combination of D base GDPPs whose kernels are predefined over the video for the parameterization. Concretely, at each time step t,

$$P(X_t|x_{t-1}, \mathcal{V}_t) = P_G(X_t; \Omega^t, \mathcal{V}_t) \triangleq \sum_{i=1}^{D} \beta_i P_G(X_t; \Omega^{t(i)}, \mathcal{V}_t)$$

$$= \sum_{k=0}^{|\mathcal{V}_t|} p_k^t \sum_{i=1}^{D} \beta_i P_k(X_t; \Omega^{t(i)}, \mathcal{V}_t) \quad (18)$$

where the L-ensemble kernels $\Omega^{t(i)}, i = 1, \cdots, D$ of the base GDPPs are derived from the corresponding kernels $L^{t(i)}$ of the conditional DPPs (Eq. (5)). We compute different Gaussian RBF kernels for $L^{t(i)}$ from the segment $\mathcal{V}_t$ and previously selected subset x_{t-1} by varying the bandwidths. The combination coefficients ($\beta_i \geq 0, \sum_i \beta_i = 1$) are learned from the training videos and summaries.

Consider a single training video $\mathcal{V} = \cup_{t=1}^{T} \mathcal{V}_t$ and its user summary $\{x_t \subseteq \mathcal{V}_t\}_{t=1}^{T}$ for the convenience of presentation. We learn Seq$G$DPP by maximizing the log-likelihood,

$$\mathcal{L} = \log \text{Seq}GDPP = \sum_{t=1}^{T} \log P(X_t = x_t | x_{t-1}, \mathcal{V}_t)$$

$$= \sum_{t=1}^{T} \log p_{|x_t|}^t + \sum_{t=1}^{T} \log \left(\sum_{i=1}^{D} \beta_i P_{|x_t|} \left(X_t = x_t; \Omega_i^{t(i)} \right) \right).$$

5   Experimental Setup and Results

In this section, we provide details on compiling an egocentric video summarization dataset, annotation process, and the employed evaluation procedure, followed by extensive comparison experiments on this dataset.

Dataset. While various video summarization datasets exist [7,11,33], we put consumer grade egocentric videos in our priority. They are often lengthy and carry a high level of redundancy, making summarization pressing need for the downstream applications. The UT Egocentric [19] dataset contains 4 videos each between 3–5 h long, covering activities such as driving, shopping, studying, etc. in uncontrolled environments. In this paper, we build our video summarization dataset by extending it with another 8 egocentric videos (on average over 6 h long each) from the social interactions dataset [8]. These videos are recorded using head-mounted cameras worn by individuals during their visits to Disney parks. Our efforts result in a dataset consisting of 12 long egocentric videos with a total duration of over 60 h.

Table 1. Some statistics about the lengths of the summaries generated by three annotators.

	User 1	User 2	User 3	Oracle
Min	79	74	45	74
Max	174	222	352	200
Avg.	105.75 ± 27.21	133.33 ± 54.04	177.92 ± 90.96	135.92 ± 45.99

User Summary Collection. We recruit three students to summarize the videos. The only instruction we give them is to operate on the 5-s video shot level. Namely, the full shot will be selected into the summary once any frame in the shot is chosen. Without any further constraints, the participants use their own preferences to summarize the videos at the granularities of their choice. Some statistics of Table 1 exhibit that the users have their own distinct preferences about the summary lengths.

Oracle Summaries. Supervised video summarization approaches are conventionally trained on one target summary per video. Having obtained 3 user summaries per video, we aggregate them into one *oracle summary* using a greedy algorithm that has been used in several previous works [9,30,31], and learn using them as the supervision. We leave the details of the greedy algorithm to the supplementary materials.

Features. We follow Zhang et al. [46] in extracting the features, i.e., using a pre-trained GoogleNet [37] to obtain the frame's pool5 activations and then aggregating them to a 1024-d feature representation for each shot of the video.

Evaluation. There has been a plethora of different metrics for evaluating the quality of video summaries including user studies [20,23], using low-level or pixel level measurements to compare system summaries with user summaries [9,15, 16,45,47], and temporal overlaps defined for two summaries [11,12,26,46]. We share the same opinion as [30,31,44] in that the evaluation of video summaries should take account of the high-level semantics the summaries convey.

To measure the quality of system summaries from the semantics perspective, Sharghi et al. [31] proposed to obtain dense shot-level concept annotations, termed as semantic vectors in which 1/0 indicates the presence/absence of a visual concept (e.g., SKY, CAR, TREE, etc.). It is straightforward to measure the similarity between two shots using the intersection-over-union (IoU) of their concept vectors. For instance, if one shot is tagged by {STREET,TREE,SUN} and the other by {LADY,CAR,STREET,TREE}, then the IoU is $2/5 = 0.4$. Having defined the similarity measure between shots, one can conveniently perform maximum weight matching on the bipartite graph, where the user and system summaries are placed on opposing sides of the graph.

Before collecting the per-shot concepts, we have to designate a good dictionary. We start with the dictionary of [31] and remove the concepts that do not

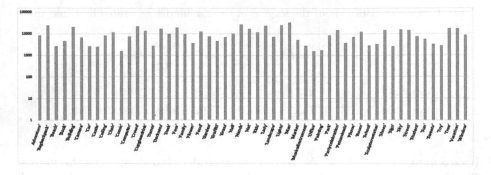

Fig. 1. Count of concept appearances in the collected annotations for the 12 videos.

appear frequently enough such as BOAT and OCEAN. Furthermore, we apply SentiBank detectors [3] (with over 1400 pre-trained classifiers) on the frames of the videos to make a list of visual concepts appearing commonly throughout the dataset. Next, by watching the videos, we select from this list the top candidates and append them into the final dictionary that includes 54 concepts (cf. Fig. 1).

Equipped with the dictionary of concepts, we uniformly sample 5 frames from each shot and ask Amazon Mechanical Turk workers to tag them with relevant concepts. The instruction here is that a concept must be selected if it appears in any of the 5 frames. We hire 3 Turkers per shot and pool their annotations by taking the union. On average, each shot is tagged with ~11 concepts. This is significantly larger than the average of 4 tags/shot in Sharghi et al. [31], resulting in more reliable assessment upon evaluation. Amazon Mechnical Turk. Figure 1 shows the total number of each visual concept appeared in our dataset.

While the metric introduced in [31] compares summaries using the high-level concepts, it allows a shot in one summary to be matched with any shot in the other without any temporal restrictions. We modify this metric by applying a temporal filter on the pairwise similarities. We use two types of filters: (1) a Π (rectangular shaped) function and (2) a Gaussian function. The Π filter sets the similarities outside of a time range to zero, hence forcing the metric to match a shot to its temporally close candidates only. The Gaussian filter on the other hand applies a decaying factor on the matches far apart.

To evaluate a summary, we compare it to all 3 user-annotated summaries and average the scores. We report the performance by varying the filters' parameters (the temporal window size and the bandwidth in the Π and Gaussian filters, respectively). In addition, we compute the Area-Under-the-Curve (AUC) of the average F1-scores in Table 2. It is worth mentioning that setting the parameters of the filters to infinity results in the same metric defined by Sharghi et al. [31].

Data Split. In order to have a comprehensive assessment of the models, we employ a leave-one-out strategy. Therefore, we run 12 sets of experiments, each time leaving one video out for testing, two for validation (to tune hyper-parameters), and the remaining 9 for training. We report the average results of the 12 rounds of experiments.

Large-Margin Training/Inference. Similar to the practices in seq2seq learning [27,40], we pre-train the models by maximizing the likelihood of user summaries using SGD. This finds a good initialization for the model, resulting in faster training process and better generalization to the test video. At the test time, we follow Eq. (6) to generate the system summary.

SeqGDPP Details. Given the features that are extracted using GoogleNet, we compute the Gaussian RBF kernels $\{L^{t(i)}\}_{i=1}^{D}$ over the video shots by varying the bandwidths $\sigma_i = 1.2^k\sigma_0$, where σ_0 is the median of all pairwise distances between the video shots. The base kernels $\{\Omega^{t(i)}\}$ for GDPPs are then computed through Eq. (5) such that they take account of the dependency between two adjacent time steps.

We also need to extract the feature vector $\phi(\mathcal{V}_t)$ to capture the variability in each video segment $\mathcal{V}_t$. In Eq. (17), we use such feature vector to help determine the mean of the distribution p over the possible subset sizes. Intuitively, larger subsets should be selected from segments with more frequent visual appearance changes. As such, we compute the standard deviation per feature dimension within the segment $\mathcal{V}_t$ for $\phi(\mathcal{V}_t)$.

There are three sets of parameters in SeqGDPP: α and w in the distribution over the subset size, and $\{\beta_i\}$ for the convex combination of some base GDPPs. We consider w and $\{\beta_i\}$ as model parameters to be learned by MLE or the large-margin algorithm and α as a hyper-parameter tuned according to the validation set.

Computational Cost Comparison. It takes about 28 s for SeqDPP to complete one epoch of the MLE training and about 4 s for SeqGDPP. The latter is faster because the kernel parameterization of SeqGDPP is less complex. The training time of either model doubles after we use the large-margin method to train it. This is not surprising because the large-margin method introduces extra cost for computing the margin. However, we find that this cost can be controlled in the following way. We first train the model (either SeqDPP or SeqGDPP) by the conventional MLE. After that, we fine-tune it by the large-margin method. By doing this, less than 10 epochs are required for the large-margin algorithm to converge.

5.1 Quantitative Results and Analyses

In this section, we report quantitative results comparing our proposed models against various baselines:

- *Uniform.* As the name suggests, we sample shots with fixed step size from the video such that the generated summary has an equal length (the same number of shots) as the oracle summary.

Table 2. Comparison results for supervised video summarization (%). The AUCs are computed by the F1-score curves drawn in Fig. 2 until the 60 s mark. The blue and red colors group the base model and its large-margin version.

	AUC_Π	$AUC_{Gaussian}$
Uniform	12.33	12.36
SubMod [12]	11.20	11.12
SuperFrames [11]	11.46	11.28
LSTM-DPP [47]	7.38	7.36
SeqDPP [9]	9.71	9.56
LM-SeqDPP	15.05	14.69
SeqGDPP	15.29	14.86
LM-SeqGDPP	**15.87**	**15.43**

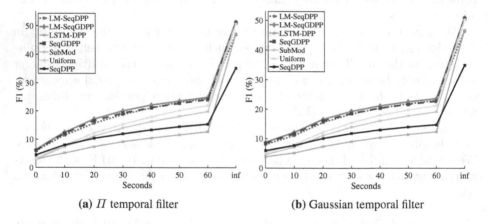

(a) Π temporal filter   (b) Gaussian temporal filter

Fig. 2. Comparison results for supervised video summarization. The X axis represents the temporal filters' parameters. In the case of the Π filter, it indicates how far apart a match can be temporally (in terms of seconds), whereas in the Gaussian filter, it is the kernel bandwidth.

- *SubMod.* Gygli et al. [12] learn a convex combination of interestingness, representativeness, and uniformity from user summaries in a supervised manner. At the test time, given the expected summary length, which is the length of the oracle summary, the model generates the summary of that length.
- *SuperFrames.* In [11], Gygli et al. first segment the video into superframes and then measure their individual importance scores. Given the scores, the subsets that achieve the highest accumulative scores are considered the desired summary. Since a shot is 5-s long in our dataset, we skip the super-frame segmentation component. We train a neural network consisting of three fully-connected layers to measure each shot's importance score, and then choose the subsets with the highest accumulated scores as the summary.

- *LSTM-DPP.* In [46], Zhang et al. exploit LSTMs to model the temporal dependency between the shots of the video, and further use DPPs to enforce diversity in selecting important shots. Similar to previous baselines, this model has access to the expected summary length at the test time.
- *SeqDPP.* This is the original framework of Gong et al. [9]. Unlike other baselines, this model determines the summary length automatically.

The comparison results are shown in Table 2 and Fig. 2. There are some interesting observations as shown below.

(1) Comparing SeqDPP and the large-margin SeqDPP (denoted by LM-SeqDPP), we observe a significant performance boost thanks to the large-margin training algorithm. As illustrated in Fig. 2, the performance gap is consistently large throughout different filter parameters. Although both SeqDPP and LM-SeqDPP determine the summary lengths automatically, we find that the latter makes summaries that resemble the oracle summaries in terms of both length and semantic information conveyed.

(2) Comparing SeqGDPP to SeqDPP, for which users cannot tune the expected length of the summary, we can see that SeqGDPP significantly outperforms SeqDPP. This is not surprising since SeqDPP does not have a mechanism to take the supplied summary length into account. As a result, the number of selected shots by SeqDPP is sometimes much less or more than the length of the user summary. Here both SeqGDPP and SeqDP are trained by MLE.

(3) The large-margin SeqGDPP (LM-SeqGDPP) performs slightly better than SeqGDPP, and it outperforms all the other methods. Nothing that both models generate summaries of the oracle lengths, the advantage of LM-SeqGDPP is soly due to that it selects the shots that better match the user summaries than SeqGDPP does.

(4) As described earlier, our refined evaluation scheme is a generalization of the bipartite matching of per-shot concepts [30]—if we set the filter parameters to infinity (hence no temporal restriction enforced by the filters), we can obtain the performance of the original metric. We can see from Fig. 2 that the relative orders of different methods remain about the same under different evaluation metrics but the refined one gives clearer and consistent margin between the methods. Hence, the AUC under the F1-score curve gives a more reliable quantitative comparison than the original metric (i.e., the rightmost points of the curves in Fig. 2).

6 Conclusion

In this work, we make twofold contribution towards improving the sequential determinantal point process (SeqDPP) models for supervised video summarization. We propose a large-margin training scheme that facilitates learning models more effectively by addressing the common problems in most seq2seq frameworks – exposure bias and loss-evaluation mismatch. Furthermore, we introduce a new probabilistic module, GDPP, which enables the resulting sequential model to accept priors about the expected summary length. Finally, we compile a large video summarization dataset consisting of 12 egocentric videos totalling over 60 h. We collecte 3 user-annotated summaries per video as well as dense concept annotations required for the evaluation. Experiments on this dataset verify the effectiveness of our large-margin training algorithm as well as the sequential GDPP model.

Acknowledgements. This work was supported in part by NSF IIS 1741431 & 1566511, gifts from Adobe, and gift GPUs from NVIDIA.

References

1. Bahdanau, D., Cho, K., Bengio, Y.: Neural machine translation by jointly learning to align and translate. arXiv preprint arXiv:1409.0473 (2014)
2. Borodin, A., Rains, E.M.: Eynard-Mehta theorem, Schur process, and their pfaffian analogs. J. Stat. Phys. **121**(3), 291–317 (2005)
3. Borth, D., Ji, R., Chen, T., Breuel, T., Chang, S.F.: Large-scale visual sentiment ontology and detectors using adjective noun pairs. In: Proceedings of the 21st ACM International Conference on Multimedia, pp. 223–232. ACM (2013)
4. Chu, W.S., Song, Y., Jaimes, A.: Video co-summarization: video summarization by visual co-occurrence. In: Proceedings of the IEEE Conference on Computer Vision and Pattern Recognition, pp. 3584–3592 (2015)
5. Collins, M., Roark, B.: Incremental parsing with the perceptron algorithm. In: Proceedings of the 42nd Annual Meeting on Association for Computational Linguistics, p. 111. Association for Computational Linguistics (2004)
6. Daumé, H., Langford, J., Marcu, D.: Search-based structured prediction. Mach. Learn. **75**(3), 297–325 (2009)
7. De Avila, S.E.F., Lopes, A.P.B., da Luz Jr., A., de Albuquerque Araújo, A.: VSUMM: a mechanism designed to produce static video summaries and a novel evaluation method. Pattern Recog. Lett. **32**(1), 56–68 (2011)
8. Fathi, A., Hodgins, J.K., Rehg, J.M.: Social interactions: a first-person perspective. In: 2012 IEEE Conference on Computer Vision and Pattern Recognition (CVPR), pp. 1226–1233. IEEE (2012)
9. Gong, B., Chao, W.L., Grauman, K., Sha, F.: Diverse sequential subset selection for supervised video summarization. In: Advances in Neural Information Processing Systems, pp. 2069–2077 (2014)
10. Gong, B., Chao, W., Grauman, K., Sha, F.: Diverse sequential subset selection for supervised video summarization. In: Advances in Neural Information Processing Systems (NIPS), pp. 2069–2077 (2014)
11. Gygli, M., Grabner, H., Riemenschneider, H., Van Gool, L.: Creating summaries from user videos. In: Fleet, D., Pajdla, T., Schiele, B., Tuytelaars, T. (eds.) ECCV 2014. LNCS, vol. 8695, pp. 505–520. Springer, Cham (2014). https://doi.org/10.1007/978-3-319-10584-0_33
12. Gygli, M., Grabner, H., Van Gool, L.: Video summarization by learning submodular mixtures of objectives. In: Proceedings of the IEEE Conference on Computer Vision and Pattern Recognition, pp. 3090–3098 (2015)
13. Hirsch, R.: Seizing the Light: A Social and Aesthetic History of Photography. Taylor & Francis, Routledge (2017)

14. Hough, J.B., Krishnapur, M., Peres, Y., Virág, B.: Determinantal processes and independence. Probab. Surv. **3**, 206–229 (2006)
15. Khosla, A., Hamid, R., Lin, C.J., Sundaresan, N.: Large-scale video summarization using web-image priors. In: Proceedings of the IEEE Conference on Computer Vision and Pattern Recognition, pp. 2698–2705 (2013)
16. Kim, G., Sigal, L., Xing, E.P.: Joint summarization of large-scale collections of web images and videos for storyline reconstruction. In: Proceedings of the IEEE Conference on Computer Vision and Pattern Recognition, pp. 4225–4232 (2014)
17. Kulesza, A., Taskar, B.: k-DPPs: fixed-size determinantal point processes. In: Proceedings of the 28th International Conference on Machine Learning (ICML), pp. 1193–1200 (2011)
18. Kulesza, A., Taskar, B.: Determinantal point processes for machine learning. Found. Trends® Mach. Learn. **5**(2–3), 123–286 (2012)
19. Lee, Y.J., Ghosh, J., Grauman, K.: Discovering important people and objects for egocentric video summarization. In: 2012 IEEE Conference on Computer Vision and Pattern Recognition (CVPR), pp. 1346–1353. IEEE (2012)
20. Lee, Y.J., Grauman, K.: Predicting important objects for egocentric video summarization. Int. J. Comput. Vis. **114**(1), 38–55 (2015)
21. Lin, C.Y.: Rouge: a package for automatic evaluation of summaries. In: Text Summarization Branches Out: Proceedings of the ACL 2004 Workshop, Barcelona, Spain, vol. 8 (2004)
22. Liu, W., Mei, T., Zhang, Y., Che, C., Luo, J.: Multi-task deep visual-semantic embedding for video thumbnail selection. In: Proceedings of the IEEE Conference on Computer Vision and Pattern Recognition, pp. 3707–3715 (2015)
23. Lu, Z., Grauman, K.: Story-driven summarization for egocentric video. In: Proceedings of the IEEE Conference on Computer Vision and Pattern Recognition, pp. 2714–2721 (2013)
24. Obile, W.: Ericsson mobility report (2016)
25. Papineni, K., Roukos, S., Ward, T., Zhu, W.J.: Bleu: a method for automatic evaluation of machine translation. In: Proceedings of the 40th Annual Meeting on Association for Computational Linguistics, pp. 311–318. Association for Computational Linguistics (2002)
26. Potapov, D., Douze, M., Harchaoui, Z., Schmid, C.: Category-specific video summarization. In: Fleet, D., Pajdla, T., Schiele, B., Tuytelaars, T. (eds.) ECCV 2014. LNCS, vol. 8694, pp. 540–555. Springer, Cham (2014). https://doi.org/10.1007/978-3-319-10599-4_35
27. Ranzato, M., Chopra, S., Auli, M., Zaremba, W.: Sequence level training with recurrent neural networks. arXiv preprint arXiv:1511.06732 (2015)
28. Ross, S., Gordon, G.J., Bagnell, D.: A reduction of imitation learning and structured prediction to no-regret online learning. In: International Conference on Artificial Intelligence and Statistics, pp. 627–635 (2011)
29. Serban, I.V., Sordoni, A., Bengio, Y., Courville, A.C., Pineau, J.: Building end-to-end dialogue systems using generative hierarchical neural network models. In: AAAI, pp. 3776–3784 (2016)
30. Sharghi, A., Gong, B., Shah, M.: Query-focused extractive video summarization. In: Leibe, B., Matas, J., Sebe, N., Welling, M. (eds.) ECCV 2016. LNCS, vol. 9912, pp. 3–19. Springer, Cham (2016). https://doi.org/10.1007/978-3-319-46484-8_1
31. Sharghi, A., Laurel, J.S., Gong, B.: Query-focused video summarization: dataset, evaluation, and a memory network based approach. arXiv preprint arXiv:1707.04960 (2017)

32. Shen, S., et al.: Minimum risk training for neural machine translation. arXiv preprint arXiv:1512.02433 (2015)
33. Song, Y., Vallmitjana, J., Stent, A., Jaimes, A.: TVSum: summarizing web videos using titles. In: Proceedings of the IEEE Conference on Computer Vision and Pattern Recognition, pp. 5179–5187 (2015)
34. Sun, M., Farhadi, A., Seitz, S.: Ranking domain-specific highlights by analyzing edited videos. In: Fleet, D., Pajdla, T., Schiele, B., Tuytelaars, T. (eds.) ECCV 2014. LNCS, vol. 8689, pp. 787–802. Springer, Cham (2014). https://doi.org/10. 1007/978-3-319-10590-1_51
35. Sutskever, I., Martens, J., Hinton, G.E.: Generating text with recurrent neural networks. In: Proceedings of the 28th International Conference on Machine Learning (ICML 2011), pp. 1017–1024 (2011)
36. Sutskever, I., Vinyals, O., Le, Q.V.: Sequence to sequence learning with neural networks. In: Advances in Neural Information Processing Systems, pp. 3104–3112 (2014)
37. Szegedy, C., et al.: Going deeper with convolutions. In: Proceedings of the IEEE Conference on Computer Vision and Pattern Recognition, pp. 1–9 (2015)
38. Venugopalan, S., Rohrbach, M., Donahue, J., Mooney, R., Darrell, T., Saenko, K.: Sequence to sequence-video to text. In: Proceedings of the IEEE International Conference on Computer Vision, pp. 4534–4542 (2015)
39. Vinyals, O., Kaiser, Ł., Koo, T., Petrov, S., Sutskever, I., Hinton, G.: Grammar as a foreign language. In: Advances in Neural Information Processing Systems, pp. 2773–2781 (2015)
40. Wiseman, S., Rush, A.M.: Sequence-to-sequence learning as beam-search optimization. arXiv preprint arXiv:1606.02960 (2016)
41. Wolf, W.: Key frame selection by motion analysis. In: 1996 IEEE International Conference on Acoustics, Speech, and Signal Processing, ICASSP 1996, vol. 2, pp. 1228–1231. IEEE (1996)
42. Xiong, B., Grauman, K.: Detecting snap points in egocentric video with a web photo prior. In: Fleet, D., Pajdla, T., Schiele, B., Tuytelaars, T. (eds.) ECCV 2014. LNCS, vol. 8693, pp. 282–298. Springer, Cham (2014). https://doi.org/10. 1007/978-3-319-10602-1_19
43. Xu, K., et al.: Show, attend and tell: neural image caption generation with visual attention. In: International Conference on Machine Learning, pp. 2048–2057 (2015)
44. Yeung, S., Fathi, A., Fei-Fei, L.: VideoSET: video summary evaluation through text. arXiv preprint arXiv:1406.5824 (2014)
45. Zhang, K., Chao, W.L., Sha, F., Grauman, K.: Summary transfer: exemplar-based subset selection for video summarization. In: Proceedings of the IEEE Conference on Computer Vision and Pattern Recognition, pp. 1059–1067 (2016)
46. Zhang, K., Chao, W.-L., Sha, F., Grauman, K.: Video summarization with long short-term memory. In: Leibe, B., Matas, J., Sebe, N., Welling, M. (eds.) ECCV 2016. LNCS, vol. 9911, pp. 766–782. Springer, Cham (2016). https://doi.org/10. 1007/978-3-319-46478-7_47
47. Zhao, B., Xing, E.P.: Quasi real-time summarization for consumer videos. In: Proceedings of the IEEE Conference on Computer Vision and Pattern Recognition, pp. 2513–2520 (2014)

Online Detection of Action Start in Untrimmed, Streaming Videos

Zheng Shou[1(✉)] ⓘ, Junting Pan[1,2], Jonathan Chan[1], Kazuyuki Miyazawa[3],
Hassan Mansour[4], Anthony Vetro[4], Xavier Giro-i-Nieto[2], and Shih-Fu Chang[1]

[1] Columbia University, New York, NY, USA
zs2262@columbia.edu
[2] Universitat Politecnica de Catalunya, Barcelona, Catalonia, Spain
[3] Mitsubishi Electric, Tokyo, Japan
[4] Mitsubishi Electric Research Laboratories, Inc., Cambridge, MA, USA

Abstract. We aim to tackle a novel task in action detection - Online
Detection of Action Start (ODAS) in untrimmed, streaming videos. The
goal of ODAS is to detect the start of an action instance, with high categorization accuracy and low detection latency. ODAS is important in
many applications such as early alert generation to allow timely security or emergency response. We propose three novel methods to specifically address the challenges in training ODAS models: (1) hard negative
samples generation based on Generative Adversarial Network (GAN) to
distinguish ambiguous background, (2) explicitly modeling the temporal consistency between data around action start and data succeeding
action start, and (3) adaptive sampling strategy to handle the scarcity
of training data. We conduct extensive experiments using THUMOS'14
and ActivityNet. We show that our proposed methods lead to significant performance gains and improve the state-of-the-art methods. An
ablation study confirms the effectiveness of each proposed method.

Keywords: Online detection · Action start
Generative Adversarial Network · Evaluation protocol

1   Introduction

In this paper, we investigate a novel task - **Online Detection of Action Start
(ODAS)** in untrimmed, streaming videos:

i. Online detection requires continuously monitoring the live video stream
in real time. When a new video frame arrives, online detection system processes it immediately, without any side information or access to the future
frames.
ii. We refer the start/onset of an action instance as its **Action Start (AS)**,
which is a time point and is associated with one action instance.

Z. Shou and J. Pan—Equal contributions.

© Springer Nature Switzerland AG 2018
V. Ferrari et al. (Eds.): ECCV 2018, LNCS 11207, pp. 551–568, 2018.
https://doi.org/10.1007/978-3-030-01219-9_33

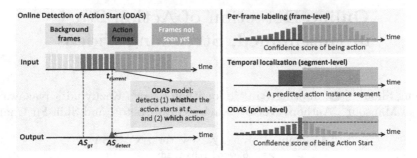

Fig. 1. Left: Illustration of the novel **Online Detection of Action Start (ODAS)** task; Right: comparisons with the conventional action detection tasks

iii. Following recent online detection works [21,23], we target **untrimmed, long, unconstrained** videos with large amounts of complex background streams. ODAS differs from prior works on early event detection such as [28,29], which targeted relatively simple videos and assumed that each video contained only one action instance and which the action class is going to happen is known beforehand. ODAS targets the more practical setting that each video can contain multiple action instances and the action class in the testing video is not known in advance.

As illustrated in Fig. 1 left, ODAS aims to detect the occurrence and class of AS as soon as the action happens. ODAS is very important in many practical application scenarios, such as early alert generation. For example, the surveillance camera monitoring system needs to detect AS and then issue an alert as soon as possible to allow timely security response; autonomous driving car needs to detect AS of accidents happening in front of it as soon as possible so that the car can slow down or change course timely to avoid collision; robot looking after walking-impaired people shall detect AS of falling as soon as possible to provide assistance before the person has fallen down already. Consequently, in each of such scenarios, it is important to detect AS timely and accurately.

As illustrated in Fig. 1 right, ODAS differs from the conventional action detection tasks. Recent online detection works [21,23] target the **per-frame labeling** task which aims to correctly classifying every frame into either the background class or certain action classes. Recent offline detection works [6,7, 12,14,15,18–20,22,26,27,40,47,50,51,53,59,70,72,73,75–77] target the **temporal localization** task which aims to predict a set of action segment instances in a long, untrimmed video. Despite lacking the need to correctly classify every frame (as in per-frame labeling) or localize the complete action segment instance (as in temporal localization), ODAS explicitly focuses on detecting AS, which is quite challenging as discussed in the next paragraph. Traditional methods for per-frame labeling and temporal localization can indeed be adapted for ODAS. But since they were originally designed to address different problems, the challenges in detecting AS have not been specifically considered and deeply investi-

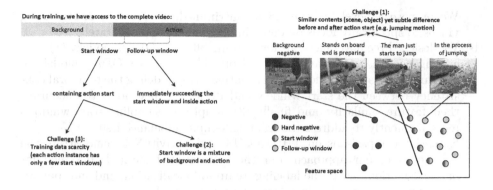

Fig. 2. We identify three challenges in training a good ODAS model

gated. Therefore, methods excelling at per-frame labeling or temporal localization might not perform well in ODAS.

In this paper, we identify three **challenges** in training a good ODAS model and accordingly propose three novel **solutions**. (Challenge 1) As the example shown in Fig. 2, it is important to learn and detect characteristics that can correctly distinguish the start window from the background, which precedes AS and may share very similar scenes but without the actual occurrence of actions. Note that we follow the state-of-the-art video classification models such as C3D [60,61], TSN [67], I3D [9] to accept short temporal sliding window as the network input. To address this challenge, we introduce an auxiliary generative network trained in an adversarial process to automatically **generate hard negative samples** during training. Although hard negative data may be rare in the training videos, our generator directly learns to model the distribution of hard negatives and thus can generate a much larger pool of hard negatives. (Challenge 2) We define the start window and its follow-up window in Fig. 2. A start window contains both action frames and background frames. Background preceding action can provide temporal contextual information but can also be confusing. Due to the shared contents (background scene and object), the feature of the start window may be closer to the preceding background window than the actual action window after the start. To remedy this issue, since the follow-up window is completely inside action, we propose to model the **temporal consistency** between the start window and its follow-up window during training. (Challenge 3) It is important to accurately classify start windows in ODAS. But each action instance only has a few training samples of start windows, and thus the number of training samples for start windows is much more scarce than others such as background windows and windows fully inside action. To address this issue, we design an **adaptive sampling** strategy to increase the percentage of start windows in each training batch. Our experiments in Sect. 6 will prove the effectiveness and necessity of each proposed method and putting three methods together results in significant performance gains.

In summary, we make three contributions in this paper:

(a) We propose a novel task ODAS in untrimmed, unconstrained, streaming videos to specifically focus on detecting AS timely and accurately.
(b) We design three novel methods for training effective ODAS models: (1) generating hard negative samples based on GAN to assist ODAS models in discriminating start windows from negatives, (2) modeling the temporal consistency between the start window and its follow-up window to encourage their feature similarity, and finally (3) adaptively sampling start windows more frequently to address the training sample unbalance issue.
(c) Extensive comparisons on THUMOS'14 and ActivityNet demonstrate the superiority of our approach over the conventional methods designed for online detection, per-frame labeling, temporal localization, and shot boundary detection in specifically solving the ODAS problem.

2   Related Works

Action Classification. Given a video clip, the goal of the classification task is to recognize the action categories contained in the whole video. Impressive progress [9,10,16,17,32,44,54,60,65–67,71] has been made to address this problem. Various network architectures have been proposed, such as 3D ConvNets, two-stream network [54,67], I3D [9], etc. Detailed review can be found in surveys [2,4,11,34,45,69].

Temporal Action Localization. Given a long, untrimmed video, temporal action localization needs to temporally localize each action instance: we not only predict its category but also detect when it starts and ends. This task has raised a lot of interest in recent [6,7,12,14,15,19,20,22,26,27,40,47,50,51,53, 59,70,72,73,75–77]. Shou et al. [51] proposed a Convolutional-De-Convolutional (CDC) network to detect precise segment boundary; Zhao et al. [77] presented the Structured Segment Network (SSN) to model the temporal structure of each action segment; Buch et al. [6] designed an end-to-end system to stream the video and detect action segments ending at the current time.

Although these methods for temporal localization were originally designed for the offline setting, some of them can be adapted to conduct temporal localization in an online manner. However, besides detecting AS, temporal localization requires detecting the Action End (AE) as well. To this end, many methods have to wait for seeing AE in order to localize the action segment as a whole so that can determine AS, resulting in high latency. Also, a good temporal localization method may excel at AE detection but perform poorly in AS detection (considering a detected segment that overlaps with the ground truth segment with IoU 0.7 and has the same AE as the ground truth). ODAS focuses on AS specifically.

Early Recognition and Detection. Similar to ODAS, early recognition and detection also aim to detect action as soon as it happens in streaming videos. Early recognition was effectively formulated as partial action classification [3,8,36–38,48,74]: the videos used in early recognition literatures are usually relatively short; during testing, they cut each video to only keep its first certain portion of the whole video, and then classify the cut video into the pre-defined action classes.

ODAS is more related to early detection. Hoai and De la Torre [28,29] made attempts to detect actions in an online manner yet under a simplified setting (e.g., one action instance per video). Huang et al. [30] worked on a scenario that the background contents are simple (i.e. the person is standing and keeping still). In this paper, like [21,23], we focus on the realistic videos that are unconstrained and contain complex backgrounds of large variety. Ma et al. [42] approached the early detection task by cutting the first certain portion of the whole testing video and then conducting temporal localization on the cut video. Hence, besides detecting AS, this work also focused on detecting whether the action ends or not.

Online Action Detection. Recent works on online action detection are very close to ODAS. De Geest et al. [23] first simulated the online action detection problem using untrimmed, realistic videos and benchmarked the existing models. Gao et al. [21] designed a training strategy to encourage a LSTM-based Reinforced Encoder-Decoder (RED) Network to make correct frame-level label predictions as early as possible. But both of them formulated online action detection as online per-frame labeling task, which requires correctly classifying every frame rather than just detecting AS. A good per-frame labeling method might not be necessarily good at detecting AS (considering a per-frame labeling method correctly classifying frames in the 30%–100% portion of each action instance but mis-classifying frames in its 0%–30% portion). Consequently, as for the applications that detecting AS is the most important task, ODAS is the best fit.

In addition, there are also works on spatio-temporally localizing actions in an online manner but also limited to short videos [55,57]. Li et al. [39] and Liu et al. [41] leveraged Kinect sensors and performed detection based on the tracked skeleton information. Vondrick et al. [63] targeted future prediction, which is a more ambitious online detection task.

Adversarial Learning. The idea of training in an adversarial process was first proposed in [24] and has been adopted in many applications [31,43,62,64,78]. Generative Adversarial Network (GAN) [24,46] consists of two networks trained simultaneously to compete with each other: a generator network G that learns to generate fake samples indistinguishable from real data and a discriminator network D which is optimized to recognize whether input data samples are real or fake. To the best of our knowledge, we are the first to explore GAN for action detection.

3   Framework

In this Section, we introduce our ODAS framework as shown in Fig. 1. We follow the state-of-the-art video classification networks like C3D [60,61], TSN [67], I3D

[9] to accept temporal sliding windows as input. In particular, we set the window length to 16 frames and use C3D as our backbone network in Sects. 3 and 4 to help illustrate technical ideas.

We outline our ODAS framework by walking through the testing pipeline. During testing, when a new frame arrives at the current time t, we immediately feed the streaming window ending at t into our network. The network output at t consists of the semantic class c_t which could be either background or action $1, \ldots, K$ (K is the total number of action classes) and the confidence score s_t. In order to detect AS, we compare the network outputs at $t-1$ and t. We generate an AS point prediction whenever the following conditions are all satisfied: (1) c_t is action; (2) $c_t \neq c_{t-1}$; (3) s_t exceeds the threshold obtained by grid search on the training set. Such an AS point prediction is associated with the time point t, the predicted class (set to c_t) and the confidence score (set to s_t).

4   Our Methods

As for training our ODAS model, the complete videos are available during training. We slide windows over time with a stride of 1 frame to first construct a set of training windows to be fed into the network. For each window, we assign its label as the action class of the last frame of the window. In this section, we propose three novel methods to improve the capability of the backbone networks at detecting action in a timely manner. We first illustrate our intuition of designing these methods and then present their formulations. We close this section by summarizing the full objective used for training.

4.1   Intuition

Adaptively Sample the Training Data. Since we want to detect actions as soon as possible, it is important for ODAS to accurately classify start windows. This is a challenging task because the start window contains various background contents, and the number of start windows is quite scarce. If we construct each training batch via randomly sampling out of all windows, the model might not see enough start windows during training in order to generalize to the testing data well. To solve this issue, we guide the ODAS model to pay more attention to start windows via adaptively sampling more start windows during each training batch. Using this strategy, the ODAS model can learn a better classification boundary to distinguish start windows against negatives more accurately.

Model the Temporal Consistency. The start window is a mixture of action frames and background frames. Therefore, in the feature space, start windows could be close to or even mixed with negatives. It is important to accurately distinguish start windows and negatives in ODAS so that the model can more timely detect action start when the video stream switches from negative to action. Since

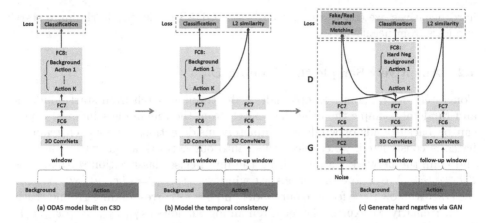

Fig. 3. The network architectures of our ODAS models built on C3D [60] and the proposed training objectives. (a) Our basic ODAS model consists of 3D ConvNets from Conv1 to Pool5 and 3 fully connected layers (FC6, FC7, FC8). We keep the same backbone network architecture as C3D while setting the number of nodes in FC8 to $K+1$, standing for K actions and background. The output of FC8 is used for calculating multi-class classification softmax loss. (b) We model the temporal consistency between the start window and its paired follow-up window by adding a temporal consistency loss term to minimize the L2 similarity computed using their FC7 activations. Two streams in this siamese network share the same parameters. (c) Further, we design a GAN-based framework to automatically generate hard negative samples to help our model more accurately distinguish actions against negatives. G is generator and D is discriminator. G accepts random noise as input and output fake Pool5 features. We add an additional class in FC8 for fake samples. All blue blocks of the same name are the same layer and share weights. More details of GAN can be found in Sect. 4.4

the follow-up windows are completely inside action, they are far away from negative data in the feature space. Thus we explicitly model the **Temporal Consistency (TC)** between each start window and its follow-up window to encourage their feature similarity. Using this training method, start windows move closer to follow-up windows and thus become more separable from negatives.

Generate Hard Negative Samples via GAN. As exampled in Fig. 2, it is important to train the ODAS model to capture the subtle differences that can serve as evidences for discriminating start windows from negatives preceding AS. Hard negatives that have subtle differences with start windows might be close to start windows in the feature space. In order to learn a better decision boundary, we aim to identify such hard negative samples in the training set during training. However, exhaustively finding such samples is time-consuming because such hard negatives are rare and may even not exist in the training data. Therefore, we propose to train a model to automatically synthesize samples that are hard to distinguish from true start windows. Equipped by these synthesized hard negatives, we can learn an even better ODAS model to discriminate start windows from negatives.

4.2   Adaptively Sample the Training Data

Concretely, we randomly sample half of the training batch from start windows and randomly sample the other half batch from the remaining windows, which can be backgrounds or windows completely inside actions. After each training batch is constructed, we can feed them into our network as shown in Fig. 3(a) and train the network via minimizing the multi-class classification softmax loss $\mathcal{L}_{\text{classification}}$. We denote the set of start windows as $p_{\text{start}} = \{(x_s, y)\}$ where x_s is the start window to be fed into our model and y is its corresponding ground truth label. Similarly, we express the set of remaining windows as $p_{\text{notstart}} = \{(x_{ns}, y)\}$. The label space of y is $1, \ldots, K+1$ where the first K classes are actions and the $K+1$-th class stands for background. Our network takes x as input and predicts a vector $\{o_1, \ldots, o_{K+1}\}$ of $K+1$ dimension. Finally we apply the softmax function to obtain the normalized probability of being class i: $P_{\text{model}}(i|x) = \frac{e^{o_i}}{\sum_{k=1}^{K+1} e^{o_k}}$. We use $\mathbb{E}[\cdot]$ to represent expectation. The classification loss is defined as:

$$\mathcal{L}_{\text{classification}} = \begin{aligned} &\mathbb{E}_{(x_s, y) \sim p_{\text{start}}} \left[-\log\left(P_{\text{model}}\left(y|x_s\right)\right)\right] \\ &+\mathbb{E}_{(x_{ns}, y) \sim p_{\text{notstart}}} \left[-\log\left(P_{\text{model}}\left(y|x_{ns}\right)\right)\right]. \end{aligned} \tag{1}$$

4.3   Model the Temporal Consistency

Formally, we denote the training set of the paired start window and follow-up window as $p_{\text{startfollowup}} = \{(x_s, x_f, y)\}$, where x_s represents the start window and x_f is its associated follow-up window and y is still the ground truth label. We model the temporal consistency via minimizing the similarity $\mathcal{L}_{\text{similarity}}$ measured by L2 distance of the feature representation between x_s and x_f:

$$\mathcal{L}_{\text{similarity}} = \mathbb{E}_{(x_s, x_f, y) \sim p_{\text{startfollowup}}} \left\| F\left(x_s\right) - F\left(x_f\right) \right\|_2^2, \tag{2}$$

where the function $F(\cdot)$ indicates extracting feature representation. As shown in Fig. 3(b), we set $F(\cdot)$ to be the output of FC7 because it is also the input to the final layer FC8 for classification. Trained with this temporal consistency loss, the features of start windows become more distinguishable from negatives, which leads to the ODAS performance improvements as shown in Sect. 6.1.

4.4   Generate Hard Negative Samples via GAN

In order to separate start windows and hard negatives which have subtle differences from start windows, we design a GAN-based framework which synthesizes hard negative samples to assist ODAS model training.

Generator (G). Since directly generating video is very challenging, we use GAN to generate features rather than raw videos. As shown in Fig. 3(c), our GAN model has a fixed 3D ConvNets (from `Conv1` to `Pool5`) to extract real `Pool5` features from raw videos and also has a G to generate fake `Pool5` features. Upper layers serve as **Discriminator (D)**, which will be explained later.

G accepts a random noise z as input and learns to capture the true distribution of real start windows. Consequently, G has the potential to generate various fake `Pool5` samples which may not exist in the real training set but may appear during testing. This enables our model to continuously explore more discriminative classification boundary in the high-level feature space. Following [46], z is a 100-dimensional vector randomly drawn from the standard normal distribution. In practice, we find that a simple G consisting of two fully connected layers `FC1` and `FC2` works well. Each fully connected layer is followed by a BatchNorm layer and a ReLU layer.

When training G, the principle is to generate **hard** negative samples that are similar to real start windows. Conventional GANs utilize a binary real/fake classifier to provide supervision signal for training G. However, this method usually encounters an instability issue. Following [49], instead of adding a binary classifier, we require G to generate fake data matching the statistics of the real data. Specifically, the feature matching objective is forcing G to match the expectation of the real features on an intermediate layer of D (we use `FC7` layer as indicated in Fig. 3(c)). Formally, we denote the feature extraction part of using the fixed 3D ConvNets as $\phi(\cdot)$ and the process from `Pool5` to `FC7` as $\psi(\cdot)$. The feature matching loss is defined as follows:

$$\mathcal{L}_{\text{matching}} = \left\| \mathbb{E}_{(x_s,y)\sim p_{\text{start}}} \left[\psi\left(\phi\left(x_s\right)\right) \right] - \mathbb{E}_{z\sim noise} \left[\psi\left(G\left(z\right)\right) \right] \right\|_2^2, \tag{3}$$

where $G(\cdot)$ denotes the generator, $p_{\text{start}} = \{(x_s, y)\}$ is the training set of start windows, x_s represents the start window, and y is the ground truth label.

Discriminator (D). The principle for designing D is that the generated samples should be still separable from real start windows despite their similarity, so that the generated samples can be regarded as hard **negatives**. As shown in Fig. 3(c) and D consists of `FC6`, `FC7`, and `FC8`. Instead of adding a binary real/fake classifier, we add an additional node in `FC8` layer to represent the hard negative class, which is the ground truth label for the generated samples. Note that this additional class is used during training only and is removed during testing.

Similarly, some previous works also replaced the binary discriminator with a multi-class classifier that has an additional class for the fake samples [13, 49, 58]. However, their motivation is mainly extending GAN to the semi-supervised setting: the unlabeled real samples could belong to any class except fake. But in this paper, we focus on generating hard negatives which should be similar to actions but dissimilar to backgrounds; meanwhile our D needs to distinguish hard negatives from not only actions but also from backgrounds.

Given a `Pool5` feature $\phi(x)$ either extracted from real data or generated by G, D accepts $\phi(x)$ as input and predicts a vector $\{o_1, \ldots, o_{K+2}\}$ which goes through a softmax function to get class probabilities: $P_D(i|\phi(x)) = \frac{e^{o_i}}{\sum_{k=1}^{K+2} e^{o_k}}$, where $i \in \{1, \ldots, K+2\}$. Regarding the real samples, we can calculate their corresponding classification loss $\mathcal{L}_{\text{real}}$ via extending $\mathcal{L}_{\text{classification}}$ defined in Eq. 1:

$$\mathcal{L}_{\text{real}} = \mathbb{E}_{(x_s,y)\sim P_{\text{start}}} \left[-\log P_D(y|\phi(x_s)) \right] \\ + \mathbb{E}_{(x_{ns},y)\sim P_{\text{notstart}}} \left[-\log P_D(y|\phi(x_{ns})) \right]. \tag{4}$$

As for the generated fake samples, the loss is:

$$\mathcal{L}_{\text{fake}} = \mathbb{E}_{z\sim noise} \left[-\log P_D(K+2|G(z)) \right], \tag{5}$$

where $K+2$ represents the hard negative class.

4.5 The Full Objective

We first pre-train the whole network via minimizing $\mathcal{L}_{\text{classification}} + \lambda \cdot \mathcal{L}_{\text{similarity}}$, which combines the classification loss (Eq. 1) and the temporal consistency loss (Eq. 2) together with the weighting parameter λ. Based on such initialization, we train G and D in an alternating manner during each iteration: **When training G**, we fix D and train G so that the full objective is $\min_G \mathcal{L}_G$. $\mathcal{L}_G$ contains only the feature matching loss (Eq. 3): $\mathcal{L}_G = \mathcal{L}_{\text{matching}}$. **When training D**, we fix G and train D so that the full objective is $\min_D \mathcal{L}_D$. $\mathcal{L}_D$ contains the classification loss for both the real and fake samples (Eqs. 4 and 5) and also the temporal consistency loss (Eq. 2): $\mathcal{L}_D = \mathcal{L}_{\text{real}} + \mathcal{L}_{\text{fake}} + \lambda \cdot \mathcal{L}_{\text{similarity}}$, where λ is the weight.

5 Evaluation

5.1 Conventional Protocols and Metrics

Hoai and De la Torre [28,29] first worked on early detection and proposed three evaluation protocols to respectively evaluate classification accuracy, detection timeliness, and localization precision. As comprehensively discussed in [23], their protocols do not suit online detection in realistic, unconstrained videos, because their protocols were designed for a simplified setting: each video contains only one action instance of interest.

Therefore, as mentioned in Sect. 2, recent online detection works [21,23] effectively worked on the per-frame labeling task and evaluated the frame-level classification mean Average Precision (mAP) or its calibrated version. In addition, temporal localization methods detect both the start and end times of each action instance and evaluate the segment-level detection mAP. As for ODAS, the performance of detecting AS can indeed affect both the frame-level mAP and the segment-level mAP. However, since the frame-level mAP is mainly used to evaluate the accuracy of classifying every frame and the segment-level mAP involves evaluating the correctness of detecting the end, both metrics are not exactly evaluating the performance in detecting action starts.

5.2   Proposed New Protocol and Metrics

In order to specifically evaluate ODAS performance, we propose a new evaluation protocol. We evaluate ODAS at the point level for each AS instance. As mentioned in Sect. 3, ODAS system outputs a rank list of detected AS points. Each AS point prediction is associated with the time point t, the predicted action class and the confidence score.

We aim to evaluate the detection accuracy and timeliness of ODAS system compared to the human annotated ground truths[1]. As for the timeliness, inspired by the segment-level mAP which measures the temporal overlap between the ground truth segment and the predicted segment, we measures the temporal offset (absolute distance) between the ground truth AS point and the predicted AS point.

We propose the **point-level AS detection mAP** to evaluate ODAS results. Each AS point prediction is counted as correct only when its action class is correct and its offset is smaller than the evaluation threshold. We evaluate the point-level AP for each action class and average over all action classes to get the point-level mAP. We do not allow duplicate detections for the same ground truth AS point.

6   Experiments

In order to simulate the ODAS setting, we employ standard benchmarks consisting of untrimmed videos to simulate the sequential arrival of video frames.

6.1   Results on THUMOS'14

Dataset. THUMOS'14 [33] involves 20 actions and videos over 20 h: 200 validation videos (3,007 action instances) and 213 test videos (3,358 action instances). These videos are untrimmed and contain at least one action instance. Each video has 16.8 action instances in average. We use the validation videos for training and use the test videos to simulate streaming videos for testing ODAS.

Metrics. We evaluate the point-level AS detection mAP at different temporal offset thresholds to compare ODAS systems under the different user tolerances or application requirements. Note that *AP depth at recall X%* means averaging the precisions at points on the P-R curve with the recall ranging from 0% to X%. The aforementioned default detection mAP is evaluated at AP depth at recall 100%. In order to look at the precision of top ranked predictions, we can evaluate detection mAP at different AP depth. At each AP depth, we average the detection mAP under different offset thresholds to obtain the average mAP.

---

[1] According to the human annotations on THUMOS'14 test set [33], people usually can form agreement on when the action starts: out of 3,358 action instances, 3,259 instances (97%) have their AS time annotations agreed by multiple human annotators. The instances with ambiguous start times are excluded during evaluation.

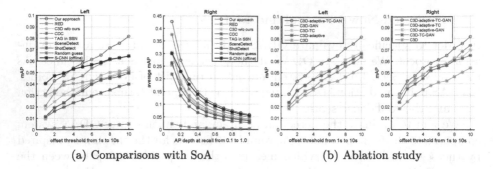

(a) Comparisons with SoA   (b) Ablation study

Fig. 4. Experimental results on THUMOS'14. (a) Comparisons with state-of-the-art methods. Left: y-axis is the point-level AS detection mAP and x-axis is varying the offset threshold. Right: y-axis is the average mAP averaged over offsets from 1 s to 10 s at AP depth at X% recall and x-axis is varying X% from 0.1 to 1. (b) Ablation study of our methods. Point-level AS detection mAP vs. offset threshold. Left: Using one of proposed training methods only. Right: removing one method out of the whole three combination

Comparisons. As for our approach, our network architecture can be found in Fig. 3. Since we build our model upon C3D [60] which has been pre-trained on Sports-1M [35], we use it to initialize models shown in Fig. 3. Since Pool5 output has 8,192 dimensions, we use 4,096 nodes for both FC1 and FC2 in G. We compare with the following baselines. (1) **Random guess**: we replace the network output scores for K actions and background mentioned in Sect. 3 via randomly splitting score 1 into $K + 1$ numbers all within $[0, 1]$. (2) C3D w/o ours: we use the C3D model which has exactly the same network architecture as our model used during testing but is trained without our proposed methods. (3) RED: Gao et al. [21] achieved the state-of-the-art performances on THUMOS'14 in online action detection task by encouraging the LSTM network to make correct frame-level predictions at the early part of a sequence. We obtained the results from the authors and evaluated based on our proposed protocol. (4) Per-frame labeling method - **CDC**: Shou et al. [51] designed a Convolutional-De-Convolutional Network to operate on the testing video in an online manner to output the per-frame classification scores, which can be used to determine AS points following the same pipeline as proposed in Sect. 3. (5) Temporal localization method - **TAG in SSN**: Zhao et al. [77] proposed an effective segment proposal method called temporal actionness grouping (TAG). Based on the actionness score sequence, TAG can be operated in an online manner to detect the start of a segment and then also detect its end. Thus TAG can be used for ODAS to generate class-agnostic AS point proposals. For fair comparisons, we determine the action score of each proposal by applying the AS classifier obtained by our best model (trained with all three methods). (6) Shot boundary detection methods [5,56,68] detect the change boundaries in the video which can be considered as AS proposals. Then we utilize our best classifier to classify each AS proposal. We employ two popular open-source shot detection methods **ShotDetect**[2] and **SceneDetect**[3] respectively for comparisons. (7) Offline detection method: **S-CNN** [50] uses the same C3D network architecture as our model but performs testing in offline.

Since the duration of action instance varies from <1 s to >20 s and thus during evaluation we vary the offset threshold from 1 s to 10 s. As shown in Fig. 4, when using the proposed training strategies specifically designed to tackle ODAS, our approach improves the C3D w/o ours baseline by a large margin. Notably, our approach is far better than **random guess** and also outperforms RED, which is a state-of-the-art method developed very recently to detect action as soon as possible. Also, our method is better than other per-frame labeling method (i.e. **CDC**) and some class-agnostic start point detection methods (i.e. **TAG in SSN, ShotDetect, SceneDetect**). Furthermore, our approach can even achieve better results under high offset thresholds than the offline **S-CNN** method.

Ablation Study of Individual Proposed Method. We conduct in-depth study on THUMOS'14 to analyze the performance gain contributed by each proposed training method. In Fig. 4(b) left, we report the results on THUMOS'14 when training with only one of our proposed methods. All approaches in the following have the same network architecture during testing: **C3D** is trained without any proposed methods; **C3D-adaptive** is trained with the adaptive sampling strategy; **C3D-TC** is trained with modeling the temporal consistency; **C3D-GAN** is trained within our proposed GAN-based framework; **C3D-adaptive-TC-GAN** combines all three proposed methods together during training and achieves the best performance. These results indicate that all three proposed methods are effective in improving the ODAS model.

In Fig. 4(b) right, we report the results on THUMOS'14 when training without one of our proposed methods. We add additional approaches of the same network architecture during testing: **C3D-TC-GAN** is trained without the adaptive sampling strategy; **C3D-adaptive-GAN** is trained without modeling the temporal consistency; **C3D-adaptive-TC** is trained without our proposed GAN-based framework. These results indicate that all three proposed methods are necessary for training a good ODAS model.

6.2 Results on ActivityNet

Dataset. ActivityNet [1,25] v1.3 involves 200 actions and untrimmed videos over 800 h: around 10K training videos (15K instances) and 5K validation videos (7.6K instances). Each video has 1.7 action instances in average. We train on the training videos and evaluate ODAS using the validation videos.

---

[2] https://github.com/johmathe/Shotdetect.
[3] https://github.com/Breakthrough/PySceneDetect.

Table 1. AS detection mAP (%) on ActivityNet when varying the offset threshold

Offset threshold (s)	10	50	100
Random guess	0.06	0.14	0.17
SceneDetect	4.71	18.93	25.84
ShotDetect	6.10	24.35	33.76
TSN w/o ours	8.18	31.39	44.15
Our approach	**8.33**	**33.08**	**46.97**

Comparisons. As for our approach, given the superior performances of TSN on ActivityNet video classification task [67], following [20], for each window of 16 frames, we use TSN to extract a feature vector of 3,072 dimensions to serve as input to our network. Our backbone network for ActivityNet consists of three fully connected layers (i.e. FC6, FC7, FC8) that are the same as these in C3D, but we train this network directly from scratch. As for G, since the dimension of fake samples here is 3,072, we set FC1 and FC2 in G to be 2,048 dimensions.

The duration of action instance varies from <1 s to >200 s in ActivityNet and thus during evaluation we vary the temporal offset from 10 s to 100 s. As shown in Table 1, **our approach** significantly outperform the baseline methods again and improves **TSN w/o ours** which indicates that it also accepts TSN features as input and has the same testing network architecture as **our approach** but is trained without our proposed methods.

6.3   Efficiency

In terms of testing speed, unlike offline detection which evaluates how many frames can be processed per second simultaneously, it is important for ODAS to evaluate the detection delay which is the time duration between the system receives a new video frame and the system outputs the prediction for this frame. Our model in Fig. 3(c) is able to respond within 0.16 s on one single Titan X GPU. Further, our method can maintain similar mAP results even when the striding distance of the input window is increased to 8 frames, thus allowing real-time implementations.

7   Conclusion and Future Works

In this paper, we have proposed a novel Online Detection of Action Start task in a practical setting involving untrimmed, unconstrained videos. Three training methods have been proposed to specifically improve the capability of ODAS models in detecting action timely and accurately. Our methods can be applied to any existing video backbone network. Extensive experiments demonstrate the effectiveness of our approach. Supplementary details can be found in [52].

Acknowledgment. We appreciate the support from Mitsubishi Electric for this project.

References

1. Activitynet challenge 2016. http://activity-net.org/challenges/2016/ (2016)
2. Aggarwal, J.K., Ryoo, M.S.: Human activity analysis: a review. ACM Comput. Surv. (2011)
3. Aliakbarian, M.S., Saleh, F., Salzmann, M., Fernando, B., Petersson, L., Andersson, L.: Encouraging LSTMs to anticipate actions very early. In: ICCV (2017)
4. Asadi-Aghbolaghi, M., et al.: A survey on deep learning based approaches for action and gesture recognition in image sequences. In: FG (2017)
5. Boreczky, J.S., Rowe, L.A.: Comparison of video shot boundary detection techniques. J. Electron. Imaging (1996)
6. Buch, S., Escorcia, V., Ghanem, B., Fei-Fei, L., Niebles, J.C.: End-to-end, single-stream temporal action detection in untrimmed videos. In: BMVC (2017)
7. Buch, S., Escorcia, V., Shen, C., Ghanem, B., Niebles, J.C.: SST: single-stream temporal action proposals. In: CVPR (2017)
8. Cao, Y., et al.: Recognize human activities from partially observed videos. In: CVPR (2013)
9. Carreira, J., Zisserman, A.: Quo vadis, action recognition? A new model and the kinetics dataset. In: CVPR (2017)
10. Chen, Y., Kalantidis, Y., Li, J., Yan, S., Feng, J.: Multi-fiber networks for video recognition. In: ECCV (2018)
11. Cheng, G., Wan, Y., Saudagar, A.N., Namuduri, K., Buckles, B.P.: Advances in human action recognition: a survey (2015). http://arxiv.org/abs/1501.05964
12. Dai, X., Singh, B., Zhang, G., Davis, L.S., Chen, Y.Q.: Temporal context network for activity localization in videos. In: ICCV (2017)
13. Dai, Z., Yang, Z., Yang, F., Cohen, W.W., Salakhutdinov, R.: Good semi-supervised learning that requires a bad GAN. In: NIPS (2017)
14. Dave, A., Russakovsky, O., Ramanan, D.: Predictive-corrective networks for action detection. In: CVPR (2017)
15. Escorcia, V., Caba Heilbron, F., Niebles, J.C., Ghanem, B.: DAPs: deep action proposals for action understanding. In: Leibe, B., Matas, J., Sebe, N., Welling, M. (eds.) ECCV 2016. LNCS, vol. 9907, pp. 768–784. Springer, Cham (2016). https://doi.org/10.1007/978-3-319-46487-9_47
16. Feichtenhofer, C., Pinz, A., Zisserman, A.: Convolutional two-stream network fusion for video action recognition. In: CVPR (2016)
17. Gan, C., Wang, N., Yang, Y., Yeung, D.Y., Hauptmann, A.G.: DevNet: a deep event network for multimedia event detection and evidence recounting. In: CVPR (2015)
18. Gao, J., Chen, K., Nevatia, R.: Ctap: Complementary temporal action proposal generation. ECCV (2018)
19. Gao, J., Sun, C., Yang, Z., Nevatia, R.: Tall: temporal activity localization via language query. In: ICCV (2017)
20. Gao, J., Yang, Z., Nevatia, R.: Cascaded boundary regression for temporal action detection. In: BMVC (2017)
21. Gao, J., Yang, Z., Nevatia, R.: Red: reinforced encoder-decoder networks for action anticipation. In: BMVC (2017)

22. Gao, J., Yang, Z., Sun, C., Chen, K., Nevatia, R.: Turn tap: temporal unit regression network for temporal action proposals. In: ICCV (2017)
23. De Geest, R., Gavves, E., Ghodrati, A., Li, Z., Snoek, C., Tuytelaars, T.: Online action detection. In: Leibe, B., Matas, J., Sebe, N., Welling, M. (eds.) ECCV 2016. LNCS, vol. 9909, pp. 269–284. Springer, Cham (2016). https://doi.org/10.1007/978-3-319-46454-1_17
24. Goodfellow, I., et al.: Generative adversarial nets. In: NIPS (2014)
25. Heilbron, F.C., Escorcia, V., Ghanem, B., Niebles, J.C.: ActivityNet: a large-scale video benchmark for human activity understanding. In: CVPR (2015)
26. Heilbron, F.C., Barrios, W., Escorcia, V., Ghanem, B.: SCC: semantic context cascade for efficient action detection. In: CVPR (2017)
27. Heilbron, F.C., Niebles, J.C., Ghanem, B.: Fast temporal activity proposals for efficient detection of human actions in untrimmed videos. In: CVPR (2016)
28. Hoai, M., De la Torre, F.: Max-margin early event detectors. In: CVPR (2012)
29. Hoai, M., De la Torre, F.: Max-margin early event detectors. In: IJCV (2014)
30. Huang, D., Yao, S., Wang, Y., De La Torre, F.: Sequential max-margin event detectors. In: Fleet, D., Pajdla, T., Schiele, B., Tuytelaars, T. (eds.) ECCV 2014. LNCS, vol. 8691, pp. 410–424. Springer, Cham (2014). https://doi.org/10.1007/978-3-319-10578-9_27
31. Isola, P., Zhu, J.Y., Zhou, T., Efros, A.A.: Image-to-image translation with conditional adversarial networks. In: CVPR (2017)
32. Jégou, H., Douze, M., Schmid, C., Pérez., P.: Aggregating local descriptors into a compact image representation. In: CVPR (2010)
33. Jiang, Y.G., et al.: THUMOS challenge: action recognition with a large number of classes (2014). http://crcv.ucf.edu/THUMOS14/
34. Kang, S.M., Wildes, R.P.: Review of action recognition and detection methods. arXiv preprint arXiv:1610.06906 (2016)
35. Karpathy, A., Toderici, G., Shetty, S., Leung, T., Sukthankar, R., Fei-Fei, L.: Large-scale video classification with convolutional neural networks. In: CVPR (2014)
36. Kong, Y., Kit, D., Fu, Y.: A discriminative model with multiple temporal scales for action prediction. In: Fleet, D., Pajdla, T., Schiele, B., Tuytelaars, T. (eds.) ECCV 2014. LNCS, vol. 8693, pp. 596–611. Springer, Cham (2014). https://doi.org/10.1007/978-3-319-10602-1_39
37. Kong, Y., Tao, Z., Fu, Y.: Deep sequential context networks for action prediction. In: CVPR (2017)
38. Lan, T., Chen, T.-C., Savarese, S.: A hierarchical representation for future action prediction. In: Fleet, D., Pajdla, T., Schiele, B., Tuytelaars, T. (eds.) ECCV 2014. LNCS, vol. 8691, pp. 689–704. Springer, Cham (2014). https://doi.org/10.1007/978-3-319-10578-9_45
39. Li, Y., Lan, C., Xing, J., Zeng, W., Yuan, C., Liu, J.: Online human action detection using joint classification-regression recurrent neural networks. In: Leibe, B., Matas, J., Sebe, N., Welling, M. (eds.) ECCV 2016. LNCS, vol. 9911, pp. 203–220. Springer, Cham (2016). https://doi.org/10.1007/978-3-319-46478-7_13
40. Lin, T., Zhao, X., Shou, Z.: Single shot temporal action detection. In: ACM MM (2017)
41. Liu, C., Li, Y., Hu, Y., Liu, J.: Online action detection and forecast via multitask deep recurrent neural networks. In: ICASSP (2017)
42. Ma, S., Sigal, L., Sclaroff, S.: Learning activity progression in LSTMs for activity detection and early detection. In: CVPR (2016)
43. Odena, A., Olah, C., Shlens, J.: Conditional image synthesis with auxiliary classifier GANs. In: ICML (2017)

44. Perronnin, F., Sánchez, J., Mensink, T.: Improving the fisher kernel for large-scale image classification. In: Daniilidis, K., Maragos, P., Paragios, N. (eds.) ECCV 2010. LNCS, vol. 6314, pp. 143–156. Springer, Heidelberg (2010). https://doi.org/10.1007/978-3-642-15561-1_11

45. Poppe, R.: A survey on vision-based human action recognition. In: Image and Vision Computing (2010)

46. Radford, A., Metz, L., Chintala, S.: Unsupervised representation learning with deep convolutional generative adversarial networks. arXiv preprint arXiv:1511.06434 (2015)

47. Richard, A., Gall, J.: Temporal action detection using a statistical language model. In: CVPR (2016)

48. Ryoo, M.S.: Human activity prediction: Early recognition of ongoing activities from streaming videos. In: ICCV (2011)

49. Salimans, T., Goodfellow, I., Zaremba, W., Cheung, V., Radford, A., Chen, X.: Improved techniques for training GANs. In: NIPS (2016)

50. Shou, Z., Wang, D., Chang, S.F.: Temporal action localization in untrimmed videos via multi-stage CNNs. In: CVPR (2016)

51. Shou, Z., Chan, J., Zareian, A., Miyazawa, K., Chang, S.F.: CDC: convolutional-de-convolutional networks for precise temporal action localization in untrimmed videos. In: CVPR (2017)

52. Shou, Z., et al.: Online detection of action start in untrimmed, streaming videos. arXiv preprint arXiv:1802.06822 (2018)

53. Sigurdsson, G.A., Divvala, S., Farhadi, A., Gupta, A.: Asynchronous temporal fields for action recognition. In: CVPR (2017)

54. Simonyan, K., Zisserman, A.: Two-stream convolutional networks for action recognition in videos. In: NIPS (2014)

55. Singh, G., Saha, S., Cuzzolin, F.: Online real time multiple spatiotemporal action localisation and prediction on a single platform. In: ICCV (2017)

56. Smeaton, A.F., Over, P., Doherty, A.R.: Video shot boundary detection: seven years of trecvid activity. Comput. Vis. Image Underst. 114, 411–418 (2010)

57. Soomro, K., Idrees, H., Shah, M.: Predicting the where and what of actors and actions through online action localization. In: CVPR (2016)

58. Springenberg, J.T.: Unsupervised and semi-supervised learning with categorical generative adversarial networks. In: ICLR (2016)

59. Sun, C., Shetty, S., Sukthankar, R., Nevatia, R.: Temporal localization of fine-grained actions in videos by domain transfer from web images. In: ACM MM (2015)

60. Tran, D., Bourdev, L., Fergus, R., Torresani, L., Paluri, M.: Learning spatiotemporal features with 3D convolutional networks. In: ICCV (2015)

61. Tran, D., Ray, J., Shou, Z., Chang, S.F., Paluri, M.: ConvNet architecture search for spatiotemporal feature learning. arXiv preprint arXiv:1708.05038 (2017)

62. Tzeng, E., Hoffman, J., Saenko, K., Darrell, T.: Adversarial discriminative domain adaptation. In: CVPR (2017)

63. Vondrick, C., Pirsiavash, H., Torralba, A.: Anticipating the future by watching unlabeled video. In: CVPR (2016)

64. Vondrick, C., Torralba, A.: Generating the future with adversarial transformers. In: CVPR (2017)

65. Wang, H., Kläser, A., Schmid, C., Liu, C.L.: Action recognition by dense trajectories. In: CVPR (2011)

66. Wang, H., Schmid, C.: Action recognition with improved trajectories. In: ICCV (2013)

67. Wang, L., et al.: Temporal segment networks: towards good practices for deep action recognition. In: Leibe, B., Matas, J., Sebe, N., Welling, M. (eds.) ECCV 2016. LNCS, vol. 9912, pp. 20–36. Springer, Cham (2016). https://doi.org/10.1007/978-3-319-46484-8_2

68. Warhade, K., Merchant, S.N., Desai, U.B.: Video Shot Boundary Detection. River Publishers, Delft (2011)

69. Weinland, D., Ronfard, R., Boyer, E.: A survey of vision-based methods for action representation, segmentation and recognition. Comput. Vis. Image Underst. **115**, 224–241 (2011)

70. Xu, H., Das, A., Saenko, K.: R-C3D: Region convolutional 3D network for temporal activity detection. In: ICCV (2017)

71. Xu, Z., Yang, Y., Hauptmann, A.G.: A discriminative CNN video representation for event detection. In: CVPR (2015)

72. Yang, Z., Gao, J., Nevatia, R.: Spatio-temporal action detection with cascade proposal and location anticipation. In: BMVC (2017)

73. Yeung, S., Russakovsky, O., Mori, G., Fei-Fei, L.: End-to-end learning of action detection from frame glimpses in videos. In: CVPR (2016)

74. Yu, G., Yuan, J., Liu, Z.: Predicting human activities using spatio-temporal structure of interest points. In: ACM MM (2012)

75. Yuan, J., Ni, B., Yang, X., Kassim, A.: Temporal action localization with pyramid of score distribution features. In: CVPR (2016)

76. Yuan, Z., Stroud, J.C., Lu, T., Deng, J.: Temporal action localization by structured maximal sums. In: CVPR (2017)

77. Zhao, Y., Xiong, Y., Wang, L., Wu, Z., Tang, X., Lin, D.: Temporal action detection with structured segment networks. In: ICCV (2017)

78. Zhu, J.Y., Park, T., Isola, P., Efros, A.A.: Unpaired image-to-image translation using cycle-consistent adversarial networks. In: ICCV (2017)

Temporal Modular Networks for Retrieving Complex Compositional Activities in Videos

Bingbin Liu[1(✉)] [iD], Serena Yeung[1,2] [iD], Edward Chou[1] [iD], De-An Huang[1] [iD], Li Fei-Fei[1,2], and Juan Carlos Niebles[1,2] [iD]

[1] Stanford University, Stanford, CA 94305, USA
bingbin@stanford.edu
[2] Google Cloud AI, Mountain View, CA 94043, USA

Abstract. A major challenge in computer vision is scaling activity understanding to the long tail of complex activities without requiring collecting large quantities of data for new actions. The task of video retrieval using natural language descriptions seeks to address this through rich, unconstrained supervision about complex activities. However, while this formulation offers hope of leveraging underlying compositional structure in activity descriptions, existing approaches typically do not explicitly model compositional reasoning. In this work, we introduce an approach for explicitly and dynamically reasoning about compositional natural language descriptions of activity in videos. We take a modular neural network approach that, given a natural language query, extracts the semantic structure to assemble a compositional neural network layout and corresponding network modules. We show that this approach is able to achieve state-of-the-art results on the DiDeMo video retrieval dataset.

Keywords: Video retrieval · Action recognition · Modular networks

1 Introduction

A fundamental goal of computer vision is understanding rich, diverse and complex activities occurring over time in a dynamic visual world. While there has been significant progress in activity recognition, it is often restricted to a constrained setting with a fixed number of action classes for each particular dataset [1,6,22,25,26,28,33,51,66]. Scaling these recognition models to the long tail of complex activities is still an open problem in this paradigm, as it requires collecting large quantities of data for new action classes and does not explicitly exploit similarity between activities.

To address this problem, a natural solution is to describe complex activity in natural language [5,7,39,44,59]. This allows for supervised labels containing rich, unconstrained information about the activity, and motivates tasks such as video retrieval [16,47,52,55]. This formulation also gives hope of leveraging

© Springer Nature Switzerland AG 2018
V. Ferrari et al. (Eds.): ECCV 2018, LNCS 11207, pp. 569–586, 2018.
https://doi.org/10.1007/978-3-030-01219-9_34

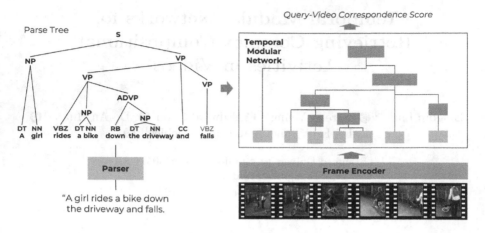

Fig. 1. Given a natural language query and video as input, Temporal Modular Networks (TMN) uses the underlying language structure of the query to dynamically assemble a corresponding modular neural network that reasons compositionally over the video to produce a query-video correspondence score.

the underlying structure in the activity description in order to reuse learned sub-concepts across activities. The approach we use endows models with an increasingly compositional structure. For example, a complex concept like "girl riding a bike down a driveway then falling" can be decomposed into two sub-events "riding" and "falling" which can be observed and learned in very different contexts (riding a bike vs. a skateboard, down a driveway vs. down a hill).

In this work, we focus on the *natural language video retrieval task*. Given an input in the form of natural language description, the goal is to retrieve the best matching video. The variety of the language descriptions and visual appearances makes it a challenging task beyond the classification of predefined action categories. Existing video retrieval methods typically learn embedding representations of language and video using recurrent neural networks [9,14,16, 61,63] or spatio-temporal convolutions [21,25,54]. While simple and effective, these approaches fail to capture, and more importantly, leverage, the inherently compositional structure of the concepts and fail to properly relate each subconcept for efficient reasoning. We posit that explicitly modeling compositional structure is key for the generalizability and scalability needed for complex video understanding.

To this end, we introduce a dynamic compositional approach for reasoning about complex natural language descriptions of activity in videos. We draw inspiration from recent successes in visual question answering using compositional models [2,3,17,18,24,58]. Given a natural language query and a video, our approach explicitly makes use of the underlying language structure of the query to dynamically (and hierarchically) assemble a corresponding modular network to reason over the video, and output the correspondence between the query and the video (Fig. 1). More specifically, we use a natural language parser to extract a structure from the description. Using this structure, we construct a hierarchical layout based on which corresponding neural network modules are assembled. Because the modules are reused across different queries, we can jointly learn the module parameters across these queries and their corresponding videos to enable efficient learning and scaling to diverse concepts.

Our contributions are as follow:

- We propose a new model called Temporal Modular Networks that explicitly uses the compositionality in natural languages for temporal reasoning in videos.
- We demonstrate that by leveraging this additional structure, our model is able to achieve state-of-the-art results on DiDeMo [16], a diverse dataset for localizing free-form queries in videos.

2   Related Work

There is a large body of work on the problem of activity recognition in videos [1, 6, 9, 21, 22, 25, 26, 35, 37, 43, 45, 51, 53, 54, 56, 57]. However, the majority of these have focused on recognizing a fixed set of activity classes with large numbers of labeled data [1, 6, 22, 25, 26, 51], which is not a practical paradigm for scaling to the large number of long-tail and complex activities. In this section, we focus the discussion on work that tackles the challenge of scaling through zero-shot, compositional, and natural language-based approaches.

Zero-Shot Action Recognition. Zero-shot approaches seek to avoid the need of training examples for every class of interest. This is related to our work as a popular approach is to use the word embedding as the representation of the class to achieve zero-shot learning [11]. A popular direction is to leverage links other than visual cues to recognize a large number of novel classes given a smaller number of known ones. [20, 29, 30] draw links between actions and objects. [65] uses attributes such as duration and dynamics for each verb, and predicts unseen verbs jointly from these attributes and semantic embedding. [41] takes a similar approach, but instead uses a bank of simpler actions to describe more complex meta-actions. Our approach is related to the zero-shot setting in the sense that it can extend to previously unseen descriptions by leveraging the language structure to compose the network, whose base module can also be seen as a zero-shot model for detecting visual concept based on the word.

Compositional Action Recognition. Methods for compositional action recognition have taken the approach of defining actions using a set of atomic actions or objects. This includes interpreting an action as a sequence of poses with a part-based model on body segments [19, 31, 34], or as composed of a set of action primitives [10, 12, 13, 64]. Compositional action recognition methods are useful specially for instructional videos, with clearly defined instruction sequences that are naturally compositional [38, 40, 42, 67]. For example, Rohrbach et al. [40] applies a hand-centric pose estimation technique to recognize fine-grained activities, using which complex cooking activities are then composed.

Compositionality Through Natural Language. A complementary way to model complex concepts is at the higher level of unconstrained natural language, which is inherently compositional. Related to action recognition, a natural setting is video retrieval [1,6,16,22,25,26,28,33,51,66]. While most of these works use recurrent neural networks for language encoding [14,61,63], more explicit compositional and hierarchical reasoning has recently been used, such as in the setting of visual question-answering in images (VQA [4]). These build off previous work relating language structure to visual scenes in images [48,49]. [60] uses a two-layer stacked attention network, and demonstrates that this hierarchical structure allows the first layer to focus on scattered objects which are then aggregated by the second layer. [32] shares a similar structure, but defines the hierarchy based on the word-phrase-sentence structure of natural languages, and calculates attention at each level independently to avoid error propagation. Xiao [58] follows a parsed language structure more closely, and adds two types of structural losses to constraint attentions at different nodes. Our work builds on these directions of using explicit compositional reasoning based on natural language, and extends to the video domain for the retrieval task.

The idea of leveraging language structure naturally points to related work in natural language processing, such as Recursive Neural Networks [49,50]. While these works have laid the foundation of tree-structured reasoning, our work differs from them in two key aspects. First, our work uses instance-dependent modules that are parameterized by specific queries, while the computation units in recursive neural networks remain the same for all instances. Second, as mentioned earlier, our work focus on the adaptation to the video domain which has remained unexplored. In particular, [49] works on semantic segmentation, and [50] learns compositionally aggregated semantic features, which are setting rather disparate from ours.

Modular Neural Networks. Recently, there have been approaches to image question-answering that model compositionality through dynamic neural network layouts. [3] proposes modular neural networks which composes reusable modules using layouts output by a natural language parser. To overcome the limitations of a fixed parser, [2] reassembles subsets of modules to obtain a list of candidate layouts, from which it selects the best one using reinforcement learning. [17] takes a step further to explore a wider layout space, while still using parser output as "expert policies" for supervised learning at the initial learning stage. Finally, [24] instead learns a program generator to predict the network layout. However, these works work on image-question answering where queries and modules have structures with limited variations, and the images often come from synthetic datasets such as CLEVR [23]). For a more realistic setting, [18] applies compositional modular networks to real-world images with free-form queries, but as a trade-off, it only uses a fixed triplet structure. In contrast, our work adapts the modular approach to the video domain, and works on video retrieval with natural language. In order to handle the diversity in natural language descriptions of complex activity, we leverage a language parser for network structure, and introduce modular network components suitable for handling diverse activity descriptions for videos. To the best of our knowledge, our work is the first to explore dynamic modular networks for free-form, language-based reasoning about videos.

3   Temporal Modular Networks

In this work, we address the natural language video retrieval task. Given an input sentence, the goal is to retrieve the best corresponding video. Our key observation is that there is an underlying structure in the natural language description that plays an essential role in the compositional understanding of the corresponding video. Based on this intuition, we propose Temporal Modular Networks (TMN), a novel framework for compositional reasoning of complex activities in videos that takes a natural language description and a video as input, and outputs scores indicating the correspondence between sub-videos and the description. Our method uses dynamically-assembled neural modular networks to explicitly model the compositional structure of diverse and complex natural language description of the activity, which is in contrast to previous work where language and visual embedding are performed in separation.

In Sect. 3.1, we first describe how we leverage natural language parsing to transform diverse descriptions into tree structures compatible with compositional reasoning. In Sect. 3.2, we then present how, for any given description, we can use these tree structures to dynamically assemble a corresponding modular neural network over the video. The assembled networks explicitly model the compositionality in natural language descriptions, and we refer to these as *Temporal Modular Networks (TMN)*. Finally, in Sect. 3.3 we explain how we jointly learn the module components of TMN given pairs of descriptions and corresponding videos.

3.1   Transforming Phrases into Compositional Structure

Given a natural language description of a complex activity, we need to first decompose this description into a compositional structure. While there exist approaches that model constrained forms of compositional activity description and structure, our goal is to enable reasoning over rich and unconstrained natural language descriptions of activity.

We therefore use a natural language parser to extract structures from arbitrary descriptions. Natural language has inherent structures in the form of word-phrase-sentence hierarchies, and natural language parsers formalize this through parse trees. In particular, we use the Stanford Parser [27], a probabilistic context-free grammar parser, to obtain grammatical relationships between words in the description and to obtain an initial parse tree with part-of-speech (POS) tags.

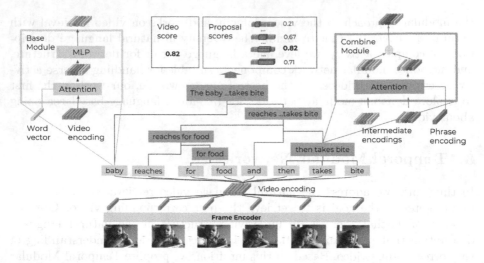

Fig. 2. Temporal modular network architecture. The compositional layout of the network is determined by structure extracted from a natural language parser (Sect. 3.1). *Base modules* (yellow) in the network reason directly over the temporal sequence of frame-level visual encodings for a video, based on node-specific word embeddings. *Combine modules* (green) combine information from child nodes, based on node-specific higher-level phrase embeddings. The output of the top-level combine module is used to produce, depending on the setting, a score corresponding to the strength of the video match with the query, or scores of temporal proposals within the video. See Sect. 3.2 for more details. (Color figure online)

The choice of a constituency parser over a dependency parser comes from the fact that a dependency parser is designed to be invariant to syntactic structure, while a constituency parser captures the syntactic structure which represents the language compositionality that we desire [48]. Sequential events, for example, is not clearly presented in a dependency parse tree. For the description "girl riding a bike then falling" which includes two sequential actions "riding" and "falling", a dependency parser would treat the second action "falling" as a dependent of the first action "riding", resulting in a misleading hierarchy, whereas a constituency parser gives a parallel structure over the two (verb) phrases.

While a parser provides an initial compositional structure, some POS tags neither represent nor relate visual concepts, such as *DT* (determiner) and *RP* (particle). We therefore discard these elements from the parse tree. We furthermore merge tags that differ in tenses or pluralities but belong to the same word class. For example, *VBZ* (verb, third-person singular present) and *VBD* (verb, past tense) are merged as *VB* (verb, base form). Table 1 specifies the POS tag mapping. After merging and discarding, the total number of POS tags appearing in a tree is reduced from 36 to 8.

Table 1. Part-of-speech (POS) tag mapping from those output by the natural language parser those in the processed compositional trees. The original POS tag(s) corresponding to each mapped tag are listed.

Mapped tag	Description	Original tag(s)
CC	Coordinating conjunction	CC
FW	Foreign word	FW
IN	Preposition or subordinating conjunction	IN
JJ	Adjective	JJ, JJR, JJS
NN	Noun	NN, NNS, NNP, NNPS, PRP
RB	Adverb	RB, RBR, RBS
TO	To	TO
VB	Verb	VB, VBD, VBG, VBN, VBP, VBZ

Then, nodes in the resulting tree can be categorized into two types: *base nodes* that correspond to single words in a description, and *combine nodes* which correspond to phrases (sequences of words) and combine its child nodes.

3.2 Dynamically Assembling Compositional Networks over Video

We have described in Sect. 3.1 how we can use natural language parsing to obtain inherent compositional structures from arbitrary descriptions of complex activities. The challenge at hand then becomes how we can use this structure to perform compositional reasoning in videos. Our key insight is that we can leverage this language structure to modularize the corresponding video understanding network for modeling the structure of the activity.

Our modular approach, which we call Temporal Modular Networks (TMN), reasons about a natural language description paired with a video with a dynamically assembled modular network. A set of neural network modules are used to represent nodes in the description's corresponding compositional tree. The complete network connects these composable modules following the tree structure (Fig. 2).

We use two types of modules, namely base modules and combine modules, corresponding respectively to the two types of nodes in the structure described in Sect. 3.1. The lower-level *base modules* reason directly over video features, while higher-level *combine modules* operate on the outputs from child modules. Intuitively, the base module is used to detect atomic visual concepts described by the words, and the combine module learns to gradually combine the visual information flowing from its child modules. Our modular design allows us to share parameters in each type of the modules. Following, we describe base and combine modules in more detail, how they operate over temporal video data, as well as how to obtain correspondence scores between queries (i.e. natural language descriptions) and parts of videos for intra-video retrieval.

Base Modules. Base modules correspond to the base nodes in a compositional tree (Fig. 2). Each base module takes as input a temporal sequence of segment-level visual encoding of a video, $M^{\text{in}} \in \mathbb{R}^{D_v \times n}$, and the word embedding $v_w \in \mathbb{R}^{D_w}$ of a single word corresponding to the module. Here D_v is the dimension of the visual encoding, D_w is the dimension of the word embedding, and n is the length of the temporal sequence. Intuitively, we would like the module to encode the semantic presence of the word in the video. The base module therefore first produces a temporal attention vector based on the word embedding and the visual encoding following [60], and then passes the temporally attended feature map through a multi-layer perceptron. The output feature map M^{out} may be of arbitrary dimension but we choose it to be the same as the input dimension, and formally compute it as:

$$
\begin{aligned}
h_{\text{att}} &= \tanh(W_v M^{\text{in}} \oplus (W_w v_w + b_w)) \in \mathbb{R}^{k \times n_{seg}} \\
a &= \text{softmax}(W_a h_{\text{att}} + b_a) \in \mathbb{R}^n \\
M^{\text{att}} &= a \odot M^{\text{in}} \in \mathbb{R}^{D_v \times n} \\
M^{\text{out}} &= \text{MLP}(M^{\text{att}}) \in \mathbb{R}^{D_v \times n}
\end{aligned}
\tag{1}
$$

Here k is the dimension of the common embedding space which the visual encoding and the word vector are mapped into, and $W_v \in \mathbb{R}^{k \times D_w}$ and $W_w \in \mathbb{R}^{k \times D_v}$ are the embedding matrices of the visual encoding and word vector, respectively. $\oplus$ denotes matrix-vector addition where the vector is added to each column of the matrix. $W_a \in \mathbb{R}^{1 \times k}$ maps h_{att} to a vector of length n, the temporal length of the sequence, which is then normalized by softmax to produce the temporal attention weights. b_w and b_a are bias terms. $\odot$ denotes matrix-vector multiplication that multiplies the i_{th} column of the matrix with the i_{th} entry of the vector. Finally, the attended feature map M^{att} is passed through a multi-layer perceptron to produce the output M^{out}.

Combine Modules. Combine modules correspond to the combine nodes of a compositional tree, whose function is to combine child feature maps to pass the information upwards in the compositional hierarchy. The flexible structure of parse-based compositional trees means that the combine module may have a variable arity (i.e. number in children). This contrasts with previous modular network approaches in settings where the arity of modules is fixed [3,24], or where the number of children is expected to be within a predefined limit [48]. To handle this, the combine modules iteratively combine adjacent child feature maps. Given a pair of child feature maps $M^a, M^b \in \mathbb{R}^{D_v \times n}$, a combine module computes an attention vector $a \in \mathbb{R}^n$ parameterized by the encoding of the module's corresponding natural language phrase, indicating desired relative weighting in combining M^a vs. M^b at each temporal segment. Formally, the output of a combine module with C children is computed iteratively as:

$$
\begin{cases}
M^{1^*} = M^1 \\
M^{c^*} = a \cdot M^{(c-1)^*} + (1-a) \cdot M^c, 1 < c < C \\
M^{\text{out}} = M^{C^*} = a \cdot M^{(C-1)^*} + (1-a) \cdot M^C
\end{cases}
\tag{2}
$$

Here M^c is the feature map of the c_{th} child, and M^{c^*} is the feature map aggregated over children 1 to c. The output feature map is the aggregated feature map from the last child, i.e. $M^{\text{out}} = M^C$. This iterative formulation allows us to handle a variable module arity.

The attention vector $a \in \mathbb{R}^n$ weighting the combination of two child feature maps $M^a, M^b \in \mathbb{R}^{D_v \times n}$ is computed from the feature maps and the combine module's corresponding phrase encoding $v_p \in \mathbb{R}^{D_p}$ as follows:

$$
\begin{aligned}
h_p &= W_p v_p + b_p \in \mathbb{R}^{D_v} \\
h_1, h_2 &= h_p^T M^a, h_p^T M^b \in \mathbb{R}^n \\
h_{\text{weight}} &= \text{softmax}([h_1, h_2], \dim = 1) \in \mathbb{R}^{n \times 2} \\
a, 1 - a &= h_{\text{weight}}^0, h_{\text{weight}}^1 \in \mathbb{R}^n
\end{aligned}
\tag{3}
$$

where $W_p \in \mathbb{R}^{D_v \times D_p}$ and $b_p \in \mathbb{R}^{D_v}$ are weight and bias terms for embedding the phrase encoding v_p to a common embedding space with the visual encoding. In practice, we use a bag-of-words representation where a phrase encoding is obtained by averaging of the word vectors in the phrase. h_1, $h_2 \in \mathbb{R}^n$ represent affinity scores between the phrase encoding and each dimension of child feature maps M^a and M^b, which are then stacked into a $\mathbb{R}^{n \times 2}$ matrix and normalized per-dimension as h_{weight}. Finally, attention vectors a and $1 - a$, taking from the two columns of h_{weight}, provide the relative weights of M^a and M^b in their combination by each temporal segment.

Query Scores. The output feature map of the highest level combine module is used to compute the correspondence scores between parts of the video and the query through two fully connected layers. The retrieval task we are addressing is the *intra-video setting*, where the goal is to localize the best matching temporal moment within a video. We therefore wish to output scores for each sub-video (temporal proposal) of variable length. Given that the input video has temporal length n, the network will first regress n correspondence scores for each temporal segment, and then combine the scores of consecutive segments to produce $\sum_{i=1}^{n} i = \frac{n(n+1)}{2}$ scores for all possible sub-videos. The sub-video with the maximum score is predicted as the best match for intra-video retrieval. Note that when combining the scores, TMN uses the sum rather than the average to avoid outputting scattered segments and to encourage longer sub-videos, which is in a similar spirit to [15] and gives a significant enhancement on rank-5 accuracy. Moreover, the scores may take negative values; thus longer sub-videos are not always more favorable. This scoring scheme can easily generalize the video retrieval task to the *inter-video setting*, where the goal is to retrieve the best matching video from a set of candidate videos. In this case, the correspondence score for a video can simply be chosen as the max score among all sub-videos.

3.3   Training

Our goal is to learn the parameters of the base and combine modules, as well as the scoring layers at the root, which can be jointly learned given pairs of natural language queries and corresponding videos. Training is performed on minibatches of query-video pairs, where one example in the minibatch is the correct pair and the remaining incorrect. In each batch, inter-video negative examples encourage the modules to distinguish between various scene semantics, while intra-video negatives encourage the modules to focus on learning temporal concepts.

The network is trained end-to-end using a ranking loss function, which is defined as

$$\mathcal{L}_{\text{rank}} = \sum_{i \in N} \max(0, s_i - s^* + b) \qquad (4)$$

where N is the set of all possible negative clips, s_i is the score of negative clip i, s^* is the predicted score of the ground truth clip, and b is a margin. While the model can also be trained using binary cross-entropy (BCE) loss, ranking loss is more effective for ous intra-video setting. For example, an inter-video negative with unrelated content should be scored lower than an intra-video negative which contains the best matching video segment but is not chosen optimal match by not being temporally tight, which is a nuance that the BCE loss fails to capture.

4   Experiments

We evaluate our approach for compositional reasoning of complex activities on the task of intra-video retrieval. Given an input natural language description, the goal is to locate the best corresponding sub-video. We posit that explicitly modeling the compositional structure is key to the success of this task. Specifically, we show that under the intra-video retrieval setting, the proposed temporal modular networks can achieve state-of-the-art results on DiDeMo dataset [16]. Here intra-video means the retrieval is within a single video, where given an input query-video pair, the network is expected to temporally locate the query within the video. We use this setting since the subjects and scene in a short (here, 25 to 30 seconds long) video are often unchanged, which ensures that the network must indeed learn to perform temporal reasoning, rather than relying on other information such as objects or scene which may contain strong priors [20,29,30], rendering the task more challenging.

4.1   Implementation Details

We represent a video by a temporal sequence of segment-level visual encoding as described in Sect. 4.2. The Stanford Parser [27] is used to obtain the initial parse trees for the compositional structure. For word vectors as part of the base module input, we use the 300-dimensional GloVe [36] vectors pretrained on Common Crawl (42 billion tokens). For the combine modules, a bag-of-words model is used to generate a fixed-size representation of the corresponding phrase. We use Adam optimizer [8] in all experiments with an initial learning rate of 5e−6 and a weight decay varying from 5e−5 to 3e−7.

4.2 Dataset

We use the DiDeMo [16] dataset which consists of 26,892 videos, each of 25 or 30 seconds and randomly selected from YFCC100M [5]. There are 33,005 video-query pairs in the training set, 4180 in the validation and 4021 in the test set. A video may appear in multiple query-video pairs with different queries matched to different sub-videos. DiDeMo is especially suitable for the intra-video setting, since it desirably offers referring expressions temporally aligned with parts of videos, as opposed to [7,39,59,62] where descriptions are at the video level.

For intra-video retrieval, each video in DiDeMo is divided into 6 segments of 5 seconds long each, and the task is to select the sub-video that best matches the query. Each sub-video contains one or more consecutive segments. In total there are 21 possible candidates for each query, corresponding to 6 single-segment sub-videos, 5 two-segment sub-videos, and so on. Performance is measured by rank-1 accuracy ($rank@1$) and rank-5 accuracy ($rank@5$) for prediction confidence, which is the percentage of examples where the best matches are ranked respectively as top 1 or among top 5, as well as segment-level mean intersection-over-union ($miou$) for temporal precision.

Quantitative Results. Table 2 shows results comparing TMN with Moment Context Network (MCN), the state-of-the-art approach introduced in [16]. For fair comparison, we use the same RGB, flow, and fused features as provided by [16]. The features are extracted from VGG [46] $fc7$ and are average-pooled over frames to produce a 4096-d vector for each segment. A video is hence represented by a temporal sequence of 6 feature vectors. We do not compare with the temporal endpoint features in [16], as these directly correspond to dataset priors and do not reflect a model's temporal reasoning capability. It can be seen that TMN outperforms MCN [16] across all modalities, with significant improvements on $rank@1$ and $rank@5$ accuracy and comparable performance on mean IoU.

In contrast to MCN which uses an LSTM for language encoding and outputs matching scores based on the distance between language and visual embedding, the explicit compositional modeling in TMN is crucial for performance gain for all types of features. Interestingly, while MCN had noticeably lower performance on RGB features, TMN is able to large bridge the performance gap to optical flow features. Since optical flow provides additional motion information over RGB, this gain highlights TMN's strong ability to perform compositional reasoning over temporal video even when features contain weaker motion information. The combination of both RGB and flow features ("fused") further boosts the performance of TMN as expected. Moreover, when the base module and combine module are sequentially applied to each word, the network functions similarly to a recurrent neural network. Therefore, the performance gain of TMN showcases the importance of an appropriate compositional structure.

Qualitative Results. One advantage of a compositional network is its interpretability. Figure 3 visualizes the hierarchical pattern in the temporal attentions

Table 2. TMN outperforms MCN using RGB, flow, and fused (RGB+flow) features. The significant gain on RGB features in particular shows TMN's ability of temporal reasoning without relying on motion information in features.

Feature	Model	Rank@1	Rank@5	mean IoU
RGB	MCN	13.10	44.82	25.13
	TMN	**18.71**	**72.97**	**30.14**
Flow	MCN	18.35	56.25	31.46
	TMN	**19.90**	**75.14**	**31.95**
Fuse	MCN	19.88	62.39	33.51
	TMN	**22.92**	**76.08**	**35.17**

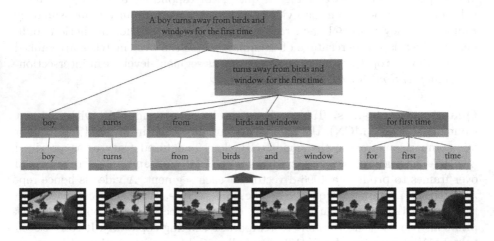

Fig. 3. Qualitative example of TMN evaluated on a query-video pair. Attention maps at base and combine nodes are visualized, where the color bars represent attention weights with darker blue indicating higher weights. Attention maps for the base nodes show the activation of a single word, while the attention map in a combine node shows how information from children are aggregated, and how the modules specifically take in the temporal quality ("for the first time") of the phrase encoding in each module.

generated by each combine module, which means the network learns to aggregate information correctly. Figure 4 provides more example outputs. It can be seen that the advantage of TMN is best pronounced for tasks that rely on the temporal dimension.

Ablation Study. We perform ablation studies to investigate the variations in module design, network structures, and loss functions:

- *Type of base modules*: We experimented with two types of base module: the *POS* setting with one base module per POS tag, and the *Single* setting where a single based module is shared across all tags. The *POS* setting may ease

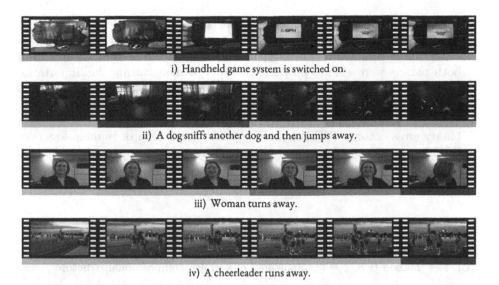

i) Handheld game system is switched on.

ii) A dog sniffs another dog and then jumps away.

iii) Woman turns away.

iv) A cheerleader runs away.

Fig. 4. Example outputs of TMN, where TMN is able to recognize temporal changes such as "*switch on*" and "*turn/run away*", as well as compositional relations such as "*then*"

the learning for TMN by making each module more specialized, whereas the *single* setting allows TMN to learn from larger amounts of data and may help capture patterns existing across POS tags. For example, a single shared module may be similarly parameterized by words with different POS tags but appearing in a similar context. Moreover, using a single module was shown to be more robust since it provides better tolerance towards the parser error, which sometimes mistakenly assigns a noun tag to a singular form verb. The *single* setting was chosen based on our experimental results.

- *Attention in combine module*: In addition to having the combine module selectively attend to different temporal segments based on the phrase encoding, we also considered max pooling as a simplified alternative to combining multiple child feature maps, where the output feature map is element-wise max pooled from all children. This is inspired by the parent-child constraint in [58], where a structure loss is used to penalize the combined feature map from deviating from the union of child feature maps, which is essentially approximating a max pool layer. Formally, the combined feature map is defined such that $\forall i \in \{1 \ldots n\}$, $j \in \{1 \ldots D_v\}$,

$$M_{i,j}^{out} = \max_{c \in C} M_{i,j}^c \qquad (5)$$

where C is the set of children and M^c is the feature map of the c_{th} child.

- *Effect of a proper compositional network structure*: We compared three network structures. The first one was without the compositional tree. Since TMN resembles a vanilla RNN when the compositional structure is taken away, the performance gap between MCN [16] and TMN corresponds to the gain of the compositional structure. The other two structures came from a dependency parser and a constituency parser. We found out that structures from both parsers were able to outperform MCN, demonstrating the importance of compositional reasoning. Further, the performance gap between the two parse structures shows the advantage of a proper structure.

- *Choice of loss function*: We trained TMN with both a ranking loss and a binary cross entropy (BCE) loss. The performance gain of ranking loss over BCE loss verifies our hypothesis that the intra-video setting poses additional requirement on temporal localization, which is better coped with relative ranking rather than absolute scores.

Table 3. Ablation study for effectiveness of TMN components: *Lines 1 & 2:* effectiveness of a compositional structure *Lines 3 & 4, 5 & 6*: advantage of ranking loss over BCE loss. *Lines 3 & 5, 4 & 6*: importance of a proper compositional structure.

#id	Model	Rank@1	Rank@5	mean IoU
1	MCN [16] (i.e. no tree structure)	19.88	62.39	33.51
2	const + max pool + rank loss	21.89	75.69	34.24
3	dep + combine attention + BCE loss	20.41	75.38	32.86
4	dep + combine attention + rank loss	21.67	75.98	33.94
5	const + combine attention + BCE loss	21.60	75.81	34.40
6	const + combine attention + rank loss	**22.92**	**76.08**	**35.17**

Table 3 shows ablation results, where *max pool* and *combine attention* analyzes the effect of attention in combine modules, *const* and *dep* refer to structures given by a constituency parser and a dependency parser respectively, and *rank loss* and *BCE loss* compare the choice of loss functions.

5   Conclusions

In this work, we introduced Temporal Modular Networks (TMN), a compositional approach for temporal reasoning in videos through dynamically assembled modular networks. We demonstrated the effectiveness of this approach on the DiDeMo dataset [16] under the intra-video retrieval setting. We believe our work is a first step that highlights the potential of using dynamic compositionality of neural networks to tackle the challenge of scaling video understanding to the large space of complex activities. Future work includes exploring richer modules that can effectively trade-off between handling diverse structure and stronger reasoning about common patterns of activity.

Acknowledgment. We would like to thank members in the Stanford Vision Lab as well as Lu Jiang, Mei Han and Jia Li from Google, for helpful discussions and support. We would also like to thank the anonymous reviewers, whose suggestions and comments have helped to improve the paper.

References

1. Abu-El-Haija, S., et al.: YouTube-8M: a large-scale video classification benchmark. arXiv preprint arXiv:1609.08675 (2016)
2. Andreas, J., Rohrbach, M., Darrell, T., Klein, D.: Learning to compose neural networks for question answering. arXiv preprint arXiv:1601.01705 (2016)
3. Andreas, J., Rohrbach, M., Darrell, T., Klein, D.: Neural module networks. In: CVPR (2016)
4. Antol, S., et al.: VQA: visual question answering. In: ICCV (2015)
5. Thomee, B., et al.: YFCC100M: the new data in multimedia research. Commun. ACM **59**(2), 64–73 (2016)
6. Caba Heilbron, F., Escorcia, V., Ghanem, B., Carlos Niebles, J.: ActivityNet: a large-scale video benchmark for human activity understanding. In: CVPR (2015)
7. Chen, D.L., Dolan, W.B.: Collecting highly parallel data for paraphrase evaluation. In: Proceedings of the 49th Annual Meeting of the Association for Computational Linguistics: Human Language Technologies, HLT 2011, vol. 1, pp. 190–200. Association for Computational Linguistics, Stroudsburg (2011). http://dl.acm.org/citation.cfm?id=2002472.2002497
8. Kingma, D.P., Ba, J.: Adam: a method for stochastic optimization. In: ICLR (2015)
9. Donahue, J., et al.: Long-term recurrent convolutional networks for visual recognition and description. In: CVPR (2015)
10. Feng, X., Perona, P.: Human action recognition by sequence of movelet codewords. In: Proceedings of First International Symposium on 3D Data Processing Visualization and Transmission, pp. 717–721 (2002). https://doi.org/10.1109/TDPVT.2002.1024148
11. Frome, A., Corrado, G.S., Shlens, J., Bengio, S., Dean, J., Mikolov, T., et al.: Devise: a deep visual-semantic embedding model. In: NIPS (2013)
12. Gaidon, A., Harchaoui, Z., Schmid, C.: Temporal localization of actions with actoms. IEEE TPAMI **35**(11), 2782–2795 (2013)
13. Gu, C., et al.: AVA: a video dataset of spatio-temporally localized atomic visual actions. CoRR abs/1705.08421 (2017). arXiv:1705.08421
14. Guadarrama, S., et al.: YouTube2Text: recognizing and describing arbitrary activities using semantic hierarchies and zero-shot recognition. In: ICCV (2013)
15. Han, W., et al.: Seq-NMS for video object detection. arXiv preprint arXiv:1602.08465 (2016)
16. Hendricks, L.A., Wang, O., Shechtman, E., Sivic, J., Darrell, T., Russell, B.C.: Localizing moments in video with natural language. In: ICCV (2017)
17. Hu, R., Andreas, J., Rohrbach, M., Darrell, T., Saenko, K.: Learning to reason: end-to-end module networks for visual question answering. In: ICCV (2017)
18. Hu, R., Rohrbach, M., Andreas, J., Darrell, T., Saenko, K.: Modeling relationships in referential expressions with compositional modular networks. In: CVPR (2017)
19. İkizler, N., Forsyth, D.A.: Searching for complex human activities with no visual examples. IJCV **80**, 337–357 (2008)
20. Jain, M., van Gemert, J.C., Mensink, T., Snoek, C.G.: Objects2action: classifying and localizing actions without any video example. In: ICCV (2015)

21. Ji, S., Xu, W., Yang, M., Yu, K.: 3D convolutional neural networks for human action recognition. TPAMI **35**(1), 221–231 (2013)
22. Jiang, Y.G., et al.: THUMOS challenge: action recognition with a large number of classes (2014). http://crcv.ucf.edu/THUMOS14/
23. Johnson, J., Hariharan, B., van der Maaten, L., Fei-Fei, L., Zitnick, C.L., Girshick, R.: CLEVR: a diagnostic dataset for compositional language and elementary visual reasoning. In: CVPR, pp. 1988–1997. IEEE (2017)
24. Johnson, J., et al.: Inferring and executing programs for visual reasoning. In: ICCV (2017)
25. Karpathy, A., Toderici, G., Shetty, S., Leung, T., Sukthankar, R., Fei-Fei, L.: Large-scale video classification with convolutional neural networks. In: CVPR (2014)
26. Kay, W., et al.: The kinetics human action video dataset. arXiv preprint arXiv:1705.06950 (2017)
27. Klein, D., Manning, C.D.: Accurate unlexicalized parsing. In: Proceedings of the 41st Annual Meeting on Association for Computational Linguistics, vol. 1, pp. 423–430. Association for Computational Linguistics (2003)
28. Kuehne, H., Jhuang, H., Garrote, E., Poggio, T., Serre, T.: HMDB: a large video database for human motion recognition. In: ICCV (2011)
29. Li, L.J., Su, H., Fei-Fei, L., Xing, E.P.: Object bank: a high-level image representation for scene classification & semantic feature sparsification. In: NIPS (2010)
30. Li, L.-J., Su, H., Lim, Y., Fei-Fei, L.: Objects as attributes for scene classification. In: Kutulakos, K.N. (ed.) ECCV 2010. LNCS, vol. 6553, pp. 57–69. Springer, Heidelberg (2012). https://doi.org/10.1007/978-3-642-35749-7_5
31. Lillo, I., Niebles, J.C., Soto, A.: Sparse composition of body poses and atomic actions for human activity recognition in RGB-D videos. Image Vis. Comput. **59**, 63–75 (2017)
32. Lu, J., Yang, J., Batra, D., Parikh, D.: Hierarchical question-image co-attention for visual question answering. In: NIPS (2016)
33. Monfort, M., et al.: Moments in time dataset: one million videos for event understanding. arXiv preprint arXiv:1801.03150 (2018)
34. Niebles, J.C., Chen, C.-W., Fei-Fei, L.: Modeling temporal structure of decomposable motion segments for activity classification. In: Daniilidis, K., Maragos, P., Paragios, N. (eds.) ECCV 2010. LNCS, vol. 6312, pp. 392–405. Springer, Heidelberg (2010). https://doi.org/10.1007/978-3-642-15552-9_29
35. Peng, X., Schmid, C.: Multi-region two-stream R-CNN for action detection. In: Leibe, B., Matas, J., Sebe, N., Welling, M. (eds.) ECCV 2016. LNCS, vol. 9908, pp. 744–759. Springer, Cham (2016). https://doi.org/10.1007/978-3-319-46493-0_45
36. Pennington, J., Socher, R., Manning, C.: GloVe: global vectors for word representation. In: EMNLP (2014)
37. Poppe, R.: A survey on vision-based human action recognition. Image Vis. Comput. **28**(6), 976–990 (2010)
38. Regneri, M., Rohrbach, M., Wetzel, D., Thater, S., Schiele, B., Pinkal, M.: Grounding action descriptions in videos. Trans. Assoc. Comput. Linguist. (2013)
39. Rohrbach, A., Torabi, A., Rohrbach, M., Tandon, N., Pal, C., Larochelle, H., Courville, A., Schiele, B.: Movie description. IJCV **123**(1), 94–120 (2017)
40. Rohrbach, M., et al.: Recognizing fine-grained and composite activities using hand-centric features and script data. IJCV **119**, 346–373 (2016)
41. Sadanand, S., Corso, J.J.: Action bank: a high-level representation of activity in video. In: CVPR (2012)
42. Schiele, B.: A database for fine grained activity detection of cooking activities. In: CVPR (2012)

43. Scovanner, P., Ali, S., Shah, M.: A 3-dimensional sift descriptor and its application to action recognition. In: Proceedings of the 15th ACM International Conference on Multimedia, MM 2007 (2007)
44. Sigurdsson, G.A., Varol, G., Wang, X., Farhadi, A., Laptev, I., Gupta, A.: Hollywood in homes: crowdsourcing data collection for activity understanding. In: Leibe, B., Matas, J., Sebe, N., Welling, M. (eds.) ECCV 2016. LNCS, vol. 9905, pp. 510–526. Springer, Cham (2016). https://doi.org/10.1007/978-3-319-46448-0_31
45. Simonyan, K., Zisserman, A.: Two-stream convolutional networks for action recognition in videos. In: NIPS (2014)
46. Simonyan, K., Zisserman, A.: Very deep convolutional networks for large-scale image recognition. ICLR (2015)
47. Sivic, J., Zisserman, A.: Video Google: a text retrieval approach to object matching in videos. In: ICCV (2003)
48. Socher, R., Karpathy, A., Le, Q.V., Manning, C.D., Ng, A.Y.: Grounded compositional semantics for finding and describing images with sentences. Trans. Assoc. Comput. Linguist. (2014)
49. Socher, R., Lin, C.C., Manning, C., Ng, A.Y.: Parsing natural scenes and natural language with recursive neural networks. In: ICML (2011)
50. Socher, R., et al.: Recursive deep models for semantic compositionality over a sentiment treebank. In: Proceedings of the 2013 Conference on Empirical Methods in Natural Language Processing (2013)
51. Soomro, K., Zamir, A.R., Shah, M.: UCF101: a dataset of 101 human actions classes from videos in the wild. arXiv preprint arXiv:1212.0402 (2012)
52. Torabi, A., Tandon, N., Sigal, L.: Learning language-visual embedding for movie understanding with natural-language. arXiv preprint arXiv:1609.08124 (2016)
53. Tran, A., Cheong, L.F.: Two-stream flow-guided convolutional attention networks for action recognition. arXiv preprint arXiv:1708.09268 (2017)
54. Tran, D., Bourdev, L.D., Fergus, R., Torresani, L., Paluri, M.: C3D: generic features for video analysis. CoRR abs/1412.0767 (2014). arXiv:1412.0767
55. Wang, H., Kläser, A., Schmid, C., Liu, C.L.: Action recognition by dense trajectories. In: CVPR (2011)
56. Wang, L., et al.: Temporal segment networks: towards good practices for deep action recognition. In: Leibe, B., Matas, J., Sebe, N., Welling, M. (eds.) ECCV 2016. LNCS, vol. 9912, pp. 20–36. Springer, Cham (2016). https://doi.org/10.1007/978-3-319-46484-8_2
57. Weinland, D., Ronfard, R., Boyer, E.: A survey of vision-based methods for action representation, segmentation and recognition. Comput. Vis. Image Underst. 115, 224–241 (2011)
58. Xiao, F., Sigal, L., Lee, Y.J.: Weakly-supervised visual grounding of phrases with linguistic structures. In: CVPR (2017)
59. Xu, J., Mei, T., Yao, T., Rui, Y.: MSR-VTT: a large video description dataset for bridging video and language. In: CVPR (2016)
60. Yang, Z., He, X., Gao, J., Deng, L., Smola, A.: Stacked attention networks for image question answering. In: CVPR (2016)
61. Yao, L., et al.: Describing videos by exploiting temporal structure. In: ICCV (2015)
62. Yeung, S., Fathi, A., Fei-Fei, L.: VideoSET: video summary evaluation through text. arXiv preprint arXiv:1406.5824 (2014)
63. Yu, H., Wang, J., Huang, Z., Yang, Y., Xu, W.: Video paragraph captioning using hierarchical recurrent neural networks. In: CVPR (2016)
64. Zacks, J.M., Tversky, B.: Event structure in perception and conception. Psychol. Bull. 127, 3–21 (2001)

65. Zellers, R., Choi, Y.: Zero-shot activity recognition with verb attribute induction. arXiv preprint arXiv:1707.09468 (2017)
66. Zhao, H., Yan, Z., Wang, H., Torresani, L., Torralba, A.: SLAC: a sparsely labeled dataset for action classification and localization. arXiv preprint arXiv:1712.09374 (2017)
67. Zhou, L., Xu, C., Corso, J.J.: ProcNets: learning to segment procedures in untrimmed and unconstrained videos. CoRR abs/1703.09788 (2017)

Meta-tracker: Fast and Robust Online Adaptation for Visual Object Trackers

Eunbyung Park[✉] and Alexander C. Berg

Department of Computer Science, University of North Carolina at Chapel Hill,
Chapel Hill, USA
{eunbyung,aberg}@cs.unc.edu

Abstract. This paper improves state-of-the-art visual object trackers that use online adaptation. Our core contribution is an offline meta-learning-based method to adjust the initial deep networks used in online adaptation-based tracking. The meta learning is driven by the goal of deep networks that can quickly be adapted to robustly model a particular target in future frames. Ideally the resulting models focus on features that are useful for future frames, and avoid overfitting to background clutter, small parts of the target, or noise. By enforcing a small number of update iterations during meta-learning, the resulting networks train significantly faster. We demonstrate this approach on top of the high performance tracking approaches: tracking-by-detection based MDNet [1] and the correlation based CREST [2]. Experimental results on standard benchmarks, OTB2015 [3] and VOT2016 [4], show that our meta-learned versions of both trackers improve speed, accuracy, and robustness.

1 Introduction

[1] Visual object tracking is a task that locates target objects precisely over a sequence of image frames given a target bounding box at the initial frame. In contrast to other object recognition tasks, such as object category classification and detection, in visual object tracking, instance-level discrimination is an important factor. For example, a target of interest could be one particular person in a crowd, or a specific product (e.g. coke can) in a broader category (e.g. soda cans). Therefore, an accurate object tracker should be capable of not only recognizing generic objects from background clutter and other categories of objects, but also discriminating a particular target among similar distractors that may be of the same category. Furthermore, the model learned during tracking should be flexible to account for appearance variations of the target due to viewpoint change, occlusion, and deformation.

---

[1] The code is available at https://github.com/silverbottlep/meta_trackers.

Electronic supplementary material The online version of this chapter (https://doi.org/10.1007/978-3-030-01219-9_35) contains supplementary material, which is available to authorized users.

© Springer Nature Switzerland AG 2018
V. Ferrari et al. (Eds.): ECCV 2018, LNCS 11207, pp. 587–604, 2018.
https://doi.org/10.1007/978-3-030-01219-9_35

One approach to these challenges is applying online adaptation. The model of the target during tracking, e.g. DCF (discriminative correlation filter) or binary classifier (the object vs backgrounds), is initialized at the first frame of a sequence, and then updated to be adapted to target appearance in subsequent frames [1,2,5–10]. With the emergence of powerful generic deep-learning representations, recent top performing trackers now leverage the best of both worlds: deep learned features and online adaptation methods. Offline-only trackers trained with deep methods have also been suggested, with promising results and high speed, but with a decrease in accuracy compared to state-of-the-art online adaptive trackers [11–13], perhaps due to difficulty finely discriminating specific instances in videos.

A common practice to combine deep learning features and online adaptation is to train a target model on top of deeply learned features, pre-trained over a large-scale dataset. These pre-trained features have proven to be a powerful and broad representation that can recognize many generic objects, enabling effective training of target models to focus on the specified target instance. Although this type of approach has shown the best results so far, there remain several important issues to be resolved.

First, very few training examples are available. We are given a single bounding box for the target in the initial frame. In subsequent frames, trackers collect additional images, but many are redundant since they are essentially the same target and background. Furthermore, recent trends towards building deep models for target appearance [1,2] make the problem more challenging since deep models are known to be vulnerable to overfitting on small datasets. As a consequence, a target model trained on top of deeply learned features sometimes suffers because it overfits to background clutter, small parts or features of the target, or noise. Many recent studies have proposed various methods to resolve these issues. Some include using a large number of positive and negative samples with aggressive regularizers [1], factorized convolution [6], spatio-residual modules [2], or incorporating contextual information [14].

Second, most state-of-the-art trackers spend a significant amount of time on the initial training stage [1,2,6]. Although many works have proposed fast training methods [6,7], this still remains a bottleneck. In many practical applications of object tracking, such as surveillance, real-time processing is required. Depending on the application, falling behind on the initial frame could mean failure on the whole task. On the other hand, an incompletely trained initial target model could affect performance on future frames, or in the worst case, result in failures on all subsequent frames. Therefore, it is highly desirable to obtain the robust target model very quickly at the initial frame.

In this work, we propose a generic and principled way of tackling these challenges. Inspired by recent meta-learning (learning to learn) studies [15–20], we seek to learn how to obtain the target model. The key idea is to train the target model in a way that generalizes well over future frames. In all previous works [1,2,5–10], the target model is trained to minimize a loss function on the current frame. Even if the model reaches an optimal solution, it does not necessarily mean it would work well for future frames. Instead, we suggest to use error signals from future frames. During the meta-training phase, we aim to find a generic initial representation and gradient directions that enable the target model to focus on features that are useful for future frames. Also, this meta-training phase helps to avoid overfitting to distractors in the current frame. In addition, by enforcing the number of update iterations during meta-training, the resulting networks train significantly faster during the initialization.

Our proposed approach can be applied to any learning based tracker with minor modifications. We select two *state-of-the-art trackers*, MDNet [1], from the classifier based tracker (tracking-by-detection) category, and CREST [2], a correlation based tracker. Experimental results show that our meta-learned version of these trackers can adapt very quickly—just one iteration—for the first frame while improving accuracy and robustness. Note that this is done even without employing some of the hand engineered training techniques, sophisticated architectural design, and hyperparameter choices of the original trackers. In short, we present an easy way to make very good trackers even better without too much effort, and demonstrate its success on two different tracking architectures, indicating potentially general applicability.

2 Related Work

Online Trackers: Many online trackers use correlation filters as the back-bone of the algorithms due to computational efficiency and discriminative power. From the early success of the MOSSE tracker [10], a large number of variations have been suggested. [7] makes it more efficient by taking advantage of circulant matrices, further improved by resolving artificial boundary issues [21,22]. Many hard cases have been tackled by using context information [14,23], short and long-term memory [24,25], and scale-estimation [26], just to name a few. Recently, deep learning features have begun to play an important role in correlation filters [1,2,5,6,8,27,28]. On the other hand, tracking-by-detection approaches typically learn a classifier to pick up the positive image patches wrapping around the target object. Pioneered by [9], many learning techniques have been suggested, e.g. multiple instance learning [29], structured output SVMs [30], online boosting [31], and model ensembles [32]. More recently, MDNet [1], with deep features and a deep classifier, achieved significantly higher accuracy.

Offline Trackers: Several recent studies have shown that we can build accurate trackers without online adaptation [11–13] due to powerful deep learning features. Siamese-style networks take a small target image patch and a large search image patch, and directly regress the target location [12] or generate a response map [11] via a correlation layer [33]. In order to consider temporal information, recurrent networks have also been explored in [34–37].

Meta-learning: This is an emerging field in machine learning and its applications. Although it is not a new concept [38–41], many recent works have shown very promising results along with deep learning success. [17,42–44] attempted to replace hand-crafted optimization algorithms with meta-learned deep networks. [16] took this idea into few shot or one shot learning problem. It aimed

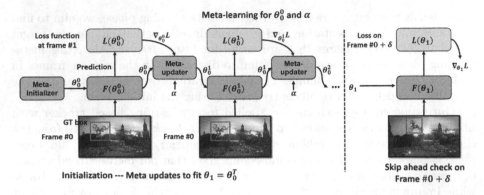

Fig. 1. Our meta-training approach for visual object tracking: a computational graph for meta-training object trackers. For each iteration, it gets the gradient with respect to the loss after the first frame, and a meta-updater updates parameters of the tracker using those gradients. For added stability and robustness a final loss is computed using a future frame to compute the gradients w.r.t parameters of meta-initializer and meta-updater. More details in Sect. 3.

to learn optimal update strategies based on how accurate a learner can classify test images with few training examples when the learner follows the strategies from the meta-learner. Instead of removing existing optimization algorithms, [15] focuses on learning initialization that are most suitable for existing algorithms. [19] further learns parameters of existing optimization algorithms along with the initialization. Unlike approaches introduced above, there also have been several studies to directly predict the model parameters without going through the optimization process [37,45,46] (Fig. 1).

3 Meta-learning for Visual Object Trackers

In this section, we explain the proposed generalizable meta-training framework for visual object trackers. The details for applying this to each tracker are found in Sect. 4.

3.1 Motivation

A typical tracking episode is as follows: The tracking model is adapted to a specified bounding box around the target in the initial frame of a sequence. Aggressive regularizers and fast optimization techniques are adopted to allow this adaptation/training to be done quickly so that the resulting model is robust to target variations and environment changes. Then, the tracking model is used to predict the target location in subsequent frames. Predicted target locations and images are then stored in the database, and the models are regularly updated with collected data according to their own strategies.

A key motivation is to incorporate these actual tracking scenarios into the meta-learning process. The eventual goal of trackers is to predict the target locations in future frames. Thus, it would be desirable to learn trackers with this eventual goal. For example, if we could look at variations in future frames, then we could build more robust target models and prevent them from overfitting to the current target appearance or background clutter. We can take a step back and observe trackers running on videos, see if the trackers generalize well, and find a reason why they become distracted and adjust the adaptation procedure accordingly.

3.2   A General Online Tracker

This formulation of online tracking is made general in order to apply to a variety of trackers. Consider the key operation in a tracker, $\hat{y} = F(x, \theta)$, that takes an input x, e.g. image patches around the target or a cropped image centered on putative target from an image I, and the tracker parameters θ and produces an estimate $\hat{y}$ of the label, e.g. a response map or a location in the frame that indicates the target position. For *initialization*, x_0 from the initial frame I_0 with specified y_0, we (approximately) solve for $\theta_1(x_0, y_0)$, or θ_1 for brevity, with respect to a loss, $L\left(F\left(x_0, \theta_1\right), y_0\right)$, measuring how well the model predicts the specified label. For *updates* during tracking, we take the parameters θ_j from frame $j - 1$ and find $\hat{y}_j = F(x_j, \theta_j)$, then find θ_{j+1} with respect to a loss. Then, we may incorporate transforming $\hat{y}_j$ into a specific estimate of the target location as well as temporal smoothing, etc. We can write the tracking process initialized with x_0 and y_0 in an initial frame and then proceeding to track and update for frames $I_1 \ldots I_n$ as Track $(\theta_1(x_0, y_0), I_1, \ldots, I_n)$ and its output as $\hat{y}_n$, an estimate of the label in the nth frame (indicating target position) and θ_{n+1}, the model parameters after the nth frame.

3.3   Meta-training Algorithm

Our meta-training approach has two goals. One is that initialization for a tracker on a sequence can be performed by starting with θ_0 and applying one or a very small number of iterations of a update function M parameterized by α. Another goal is that the resulting tracker be accurate and robust on later frames.

The gradient-descent style update function M is parameterized by α:

$$M(\theta, \nabla_\theta L; \alpha) = \theta - \alpha \odot \nabla_\theta L, \tag{1}$$

where α is the same size as the tracker parameters θ [19], L is a loss function, and $\odot$ is element-wise product. α could be a scalar value, which might be either learnable [20] or manually fixed [15]. We empirically found that having per parameter coefficients was the most effective in our settings.

Our meta-training algorithm is to find a good θ_0 and α by repeatedly sampling a video, performing initialization, applying the learned initial model to a frame slightly ahead in the sequence, and then back-propagating to update θ_0

Algorithm 1. Meta-training object trackers algorithm

Input: Randomly initialized θ_0 and α, training dataset D
Output: θ_0^* and α^*

1: **while** not converged **do**
2:     $\text{grad}_{\theta_0}, \text{grad}_\alpha = \mathbf{0}$ ▷ Initialize to zero vector
3:     **for all** $k \in \{0, \ldots, N_{\text{mini}} - 1\}$ **do**
4:         $S, j, \delta \sim p(D)$ ▷ Sample a training example
5:         $\theta_0^0 = \theta_0$
6:         **for all** $t \in \{0, \ldots, T - 1\}$ **do**
7:             $\hat{y}_j = F(x_j, \theta_0^t)$
8:             $\theta_0^{t+1} = \theta_0^t - \alpha \odot \nabla_{\theta_0^t} L(y_j, \hat{y}_j; \theta_0^t)$
9:         **end for**
10:         $\theta_1 = \theta_0^T$
11:         $\hat{y}_{j+\delta} = F(x_{j+\delta}, \theta_1)$ ▷ Apply to a future frame
12:         $\text{grad}_{\theta_0} = \text{grad}_{\theta_0} + \nabla_{\theta_0} L(y_{j+\delta}, \hat{y}_{j+\delta})$ ▷ Accumulate the gradients
13:         $\text{grad}_\alpha = \text{grad}_\alpha + \nabla_\alpha L(y_{j+\delta}, \hat{y}_{j+\delta})$
14:     **end for**
15:     $\theta_0 = \text{Optimizer}(\theta_0, \text{grad}_{\theta_0})$ ▷ Update θ_0
16:     $\alpha = \text{Optimizer}(\alpha, \text{grad}_\alpha)$ ▷ Update α
17: **end while**

---

and α. Applying the initial model to a frame slightly ahead in the sequence has two goals, the model should be robust enough to handle more than frame-to-frame variation, and if so, this should make updates during tracking fast as well if not much needs to be fixed.

After sampling a random starting frame from a random video, we perform optimization for initialization starting with $\theta_0^0 = \theta_0$ given the transformed input and output pair, (x_j, y_j). A step of optimization proceeds as

$$\theta_0^{i+1} = M(\theta_0^i, \nabla_{\theta_0^i} L(y_j, F(x_j, \theta_0^i))). \tag{2}$$

This step can be repeated up to a predefined number of times T to find, $\theta_1(x_j, y_j) = \theta_0^T$. Then, we randomly sample a future frame $I_{j+\delta}$ and evaluate the model trained on the initial frame on that future frame to produce: $\hat{y}_{j+\delta} = F(x_{j+\delta}, \theta_1)$.

The larger δ, the larger target object variations and environment changes are incorporated into training process. Now, we can compute the loss based on the future frame and trained tracker parameters. The objective function is defined as

$$\theta_0^*, \alpha^* = \underset{\theta_0, \alpha}{\text{argmin}} \, \mathbb{E}_{S,j,\delta}[L(y_{j+\delta}, \hat{y}_{j+\delta})]. \tag{3}$$

We used the ADAM [47] gradient descent algorithm to optimize. Note that θ_0 and α are fixed across different episodes in a mini-batch, but $\theta_0^1, \ldots, \theta_0^T$ are changed over every episode. To compute gradients of the objective function w.r.t θ_0 and α, it is required to compute higher-order gradients (the gradients of function of gradients). This type of computation has been exploited in recent studies [15,

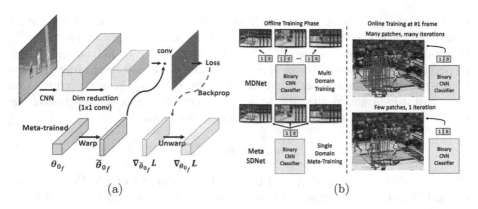

Fig. 2. (a) MetaCREST (b) MDNet vs MetaSDNet

48, 49]. We can easily compute this thanks to automatic differentiation software libraries [50]. More details are explained in Algorithm 1.

Update Rules for Subsequent Frames. Most online trackers, including the two trackers we meta-train (Sect. 4), update the target model regularly to adjust to new examples collected by itself during tracking. We could simply use meta-trained α to update the model, $\theta_j = \theta_{j-1} - \alpha \odot \nabla_{\theta_{j-1}} L$ (only one iteration presented for brevity). However, it often diverges on longer sequences or the sequences that have very small frame-to-frame variations. We believe this is mainly because we train α for fast adaptation at the initial frame, so the values of α are relatively large, which causes unstable convergence behavior (A similar phenomenon was reported in [20] albeit in a different context). Since α is stable when it teams up with θ_0, we could define the update rules for subsequent frames as $\theta_j = \theta_0 - \alpha \odot \nabla_{\theta_0} L$, as suggested in [20]. We could also combine two strategies, $\theta_j = \beta(\theta_{j-1} - \alpha \odot \nabla_{\theta_{j-1}} L) + (1 - \beta)(\theta_0 - \alpha \odot \nabla_{\theta_0} L)$. Although we could resolve unstable convergence behavior with these strategies, none of these performed better than simply searching for a single learning rate. Therefore, we find a learning rate for subsequent frames and then use existing optimization algorithms to update the models as was done in the original versions of the trackers.

4   Meta-trackers

In this section, we show how our proposed meta-learning technique can be realized in state-of-the-art trackers. We selected two different types of trackers, one from correlation based trackers, CREST [2], and one from tracking-by-detection based trackers MDNet [1].

4.1   Meta-training of Correlation Based Tracker

CREST. A typical correlation filter objective is defined as follows.

$$\underset{f}{\mathrm{argmin}} \, ||y - \Phi(x) * f||^2 + \lambda ||f||^2, \tag{4}$$

where f is the correlation filter, $*$ is the convolution operation, and Φ is a feature extractor, e.g. CNN. x is a cropped image centered on the target, and $y \in \mathbb{R}^{H \times W}$, is a gaussian shaped response map, where H and W are height and width, respectively. The cropped image is usually larger than the target object so that it can provide enough background information. Once we have the correlation filter trained, target localization at a new future frame is simply finding the coordinates (h, w) that has the maximum response value.

$$\underset{(h,w)}{\mathrm{argmax}}\, \hat{y}(h, w), \tag{5}$$

where $\hat{y} = \Phi(x_{\text{new}}) * f$, and $\hat{y}(h, w)$ represents the element of $\hat{y}$ in (h, w) coordinates. CREST used a variation of the correlation filter objective, defined as

$$\sum_{(h,w) \in P} \frac{1}{|P|} (e^{y(h,w)} |y(h, w) - \hat{y}(h, w)|)^2 + \lambda ||f||^2, \tag{6}$$

where $P = \{(h, w) \mid |y(h, w) - \hat{y}(h, w)| > 0.1\}$. This would encourage the model to focus on parts that are far from the ground truth values.

By reformulating the correlation filter as a convolutional layer, it can be effectively integrated into an CNN framework [2]. This allows us to add new modules easily, since the optimization can be nicely done with standard gradient descent in end-to-end fashion. They inserted spatio-temporal residual modules to avoid target model degradation by large appearance changes. They also devised sophisticated initialization, learning rates, and weight decay regularizers, e.g. 1000 times larger weight decay parameter on spatio-temporal residual modules. Without those bells and whistles, we aim to learn a robust single layer correlation filter via proposed meta-learning process. There are two important issues for plugging CREST tracker into proposed meta-training framework, and we present our solutions in following sections.

Meta-learning Dimensionality Reduction. CREST used PCA to reduce the number of channels of extracted CNN features, from 512 to 64. This not only reduces computational cost, but also it helps to increase robustness of the correlation filter. PCA is performed at the initial frame and learned projection matrix are used for the rest of the sequence. This becomes an issue when meta-training the correlation filter. We seek to find a global initialization of the correlation filter for the all targets from different episodes. However, PCA would change the basis for every sequences, which makes impossible to obtain a global initialization in projected feature spaces that are changing every time. We propose to learn to reduce dimensions of the features. In CREST, we can insert 1×1 convolution layer right after the feature extraction, the weights of this layer are also meta-learnable and jointly trained during the meta-learning process along with the correlation filter. θ_0 in proposed meta-training framework, therefore, consists of θ_{0_d} and θ_{0_f}, the parameters of dimensionality reduction and the correlation filter, respectively.

Canonical Size Initialization. The size of the correlation filter varies depending on the target shape and size. In order to meta-train a fixed size initialization of the correlation filter θ_{0_f}, we should resize all objects to the same size and same aspect ratio. However, it introduces distortion of the target and has been known to degrade recognition performance [51,52]. In order to fully make use of the power of the correlation filter, we propose to use canonical size initialization and its size and aspect ratio are calculated as a mean of the objects in the training dataset. Based on canonical size initialization, we warp it to the specific size taylored to the target object for each tracking episodes, $\tilde{\theta}_{0_f} = \text{Warp}(\theta_{0_f})$. We used differentiable bilinear sampling method [53] to pass through gradients all the way down to θ_{0_f}.

Putting it all together, $F(x_j, \theta)$ in our proposed meta-training framework for CREST, now takes an input a cropped image x_j from an input frame I_j, pass it through a CNN feature extractor followed by dimensionality reduction (1×1 convolution with the weight θ_{0_d}). Then, it warps the correlation filter θ_{0_f}, and finally apply warped correlation filter $\tilde{\theta}_{0_f}$ to produce a response map $\hat{y}_j$ (Fig. 2a).

4.2 Meta-training of Tracking-by-Detection Tracker

MDNet. MDNet is based on a binary CNN classifier consisting of a few of convolutional layers and fully connected layers. In the offline phase, it uses a multi-domain training technique to pre-train the classifier. At the initial frame, it randomly initializes the last fully connected layer, and trains around 30 iterations with a large number of positive and negative patches (Fig. 2b). Target locations in the subsequent frames are determined by average of bounding box regression outputs of top scoring positive patches. It collects positive and negative samples during the tracking process, and regularly updates the classifier. Multi-domain pre-training was a key factor to achieve robustness, and they used an aggressive dropout regularizer and different learning rates at different layers to further avoid overfitting to current target appearance. Without those techniques (the multi-domain training and regularizers), we aim to obtain robust and quickly adaptive classifier solely resting on the proposed meta-learning process.

Meta-training. It can be also easily pluged into the proposed meta-leraning framework. $F(x_j; \theta)$ takes as input image patches $x_j \in \mathbb{R}^{N \times D}$ from an input frame I_j (and $y_j \in \{0,1\}^N$ is the corresponding labels), where D is the size of the patches and N is the number of patches. Then, the patches go through a CNN classifier, and the loss function L is a simple cross entropy loss $- \sum_{k=1}^{N} y_j^k \log(F^k(x_j; \theta))$.

Label Shuffling. Although a large-scale video detection dataset contains rich variation of objects in videos, the number of objects and categories are limited compared to other still image datasets. This might lead a deep CNN classifier to memorize all object instances in the dataset and classify newly seen objects as backgrounds. In order to avoid this issue, we adopted the label shuffling trick, suggested in [18]. Every time we run a tracking episode, we shuffle the labels, meaning sometimes labels of positive patches become 0 instead of 1, negative patches become 1 instead of 0. This trick encourages the classifier to learn how to distinguish the target objects from background by looking at current training examples, rather than memorizing specific targets appearance.

5   Experiments

5.1   Experimental Setup

VOT2016. It contains 60 videos (same videos from VOT 2015 [54]). Trackers are automatically reinitialized once it drifts off the target: zero overlap between predicted bounding box and the ground truth. In this reset-based experiments, three primary measures have been used, (i) *accuracy*, (ii) *robustness* and (iii) *expected average overlap (EAO)*. The accuracy is defined as average overlap during successful tracking periods. The robustness is defined as how many times the trackers fail during tracking. The expected average overlap is an estimator of the average overlap a tracker is expected to attain on a large collection of short-term sequences.

OTB2015. It consists of 100 fully annotated video sequences. Unlike VOT2016, the one pass evaluation (OPE) is commonly used in OTB dataset (no restart at failures). The precision plots (based on the center location error) and the success plots (based on the bounding box overlap) are used to access the tracker performance.

Dataset for Meta-training. We used a large scale video detection dataset [55] for meta-training both trackers. It consists of 30 object categories, which is a subset of 200 categories in the object detection dataset. Since characteristics of the dataset are slightly different from the object tracking dataset, we sub-sampled the dataset. First, we picked a video frame that contains a target object whose size is not larger than 60% of the image size. Then, a training video sequence is constructed by sampling all subsequent frames from that frame until the size of the target object reaches 60%. We ended up having 718 video sequences. In addition, for the experiments on OTB2015 dataset, we also used an additional 58 sequences from object tracking datasets in VOT2013,VOT2014, and VOT2015 [4], excluding the videos included in OTB2015, following MDNet's approach [1]. These sequences were selected in the mini-batch selection stage with the probability 0.3. Similarly, we used 80 sequences from OTB2015, excluding the videos in VOT2016 for the experiments on VOT2016 dataset.

Baseline Implementations. We selected two trackers, MDNet [1] and CREST [2]. For CREST, we re-implemented our own version in python based on publicly released code written in MATLAB. We meta-trained our version. For MDNet, the authors of MDNet provide two different source codes, written in MATLAB and python, respectively. We used the latter one and called it as pyMDNet or pySDNet, depending on pre-training methods. We meta-trained pySDNet, and call it as MetaSDNet. Note that overall accuracy of pyMDNet is lower than MDNet on OTB2015 (.652 vs .678 in success rates with overlap metric). For fair comparison, we compared our MetaSDNet to pyMDNet.

Meta-training Details. In MetaSDNet, we used the first three conv layers from pre-trained vgg16 as feature extractors. During meta-training, we randomly initialized the last three fc layers, and used Adam as the optimizer with learning rate 1e–4. We only updated the last three fc layers for the first 5,000 iterations and trained all layers for the rest of iterations. The learning rate was reduced to 1e–5 after 10,000 iterations, and we trained up to 15,000 iterations. For α, we initialized to 1e–4, and also used Adam with learning rate 1e–5, then was decayed to 1e–6 after 10,000 iterations. We used mini-batch size $N_{mini} = 8$. For the meta-update iteration T, larger T gave us only small improvement, so we set to 1. For each training episode, we sample one random future frame uniformly from 1 to 10 ahead. In MetaCREST, we randomly initialized θ_0 and also used Adam with learning rate 1e–6. For α, we initialized to 1e–6, and learning rate of Adam was also set to 1e–6. $N_{mini} = 8$ and meta-training iterations was 10,000 (at 50,000 iterations, the learning rate was reduced to 1e–7). We used same hyper-parameters for both OTB2015 and VOT2016 experiments. For other hyper-parameters, we mostly followed the ones in the original trackers. For more details, the code and raw results will be released.

5.2 Experimental Results

Quantitative Evaluation. Table 1 shows quantitative results on VOT2016. In VOT2016, EAO is considered as the main metric since it consider both accuracy and robustness. Our meta-trackers, both MetaCREST and MetaSDNet, consistently improved upon their counterparts by significant margins. Note that this is the improvement without their advanced techniques, e.g. pyMDNet with specialized multi-domain training and CREST with spatio-temporal residual modules. The performances of the accuracy metric are not very different than the original trackers. Because it computes the average overlap by only taking successful tracking periods into account, we did not change other factors that might affect the accuracy in the original trackers, e.g. scale estimation. Quantitative results on OTB2015 are depicted in Fig. 3. Both of MetaSDNet and MetaCREST also improved upon their counterparts in both precision and success plots with only one iteration for initialization. Detailed results of individual sequences in both of VOT2016 and OTB2015 are presented in Appendix.

We require only one iteration at the initial frame to outperform the original trackers. We also performed the experiments with more than one iteration, but the performance gain was not significant. On the other hand, MDNet takes 30 iterations to converge at the initial frame as reported in their paper, and fewer iterations caused serious performance degradation. This confirms that getting a robust target model at the initial frame is very important for subsequent frames. For CREST, performance drop was not significant as MDNet, but it was still more than 10 iterations to reach to its maximum performance. MDNet updates the model 15 iterations for subsequent frames at every 10 frames regularly (or when it failed, meaning its score is below a predefined threshold).

Table 1. Quantitative results on VOT2016 dataset. The numbers in legends represent the number of iterations at the initial frame. EAO (expected average overlap) - 0 to 1 scale, higher is better. A (Accuracy) - 0 to 1 scale, higher is better. R (Robustness) - 0 to N, lower is better. We ran each tracker 15 times and reported averaged scores following VOT2016 convention.

	EAO	Acc	R		EAO	Acc	R
MetaCREST-01	**0.317**	**0.519**	**0.932**	MetaSDNet-01	**0.314**	0.526	**0.934**
CREST	0.283	0.514	1.083	pyMDNet-30	0.304	**0.540**	0.943
CREST-Base	0.249	0.502	1.383	pyMDNet-15	0.299	0.541	0.977
CREST-10	0.252	0.509	1.380	pyMDNet-10	0.291	0.535	0.989
CREST-05	0.262	0.510	1.298	pyMDNet-05	0.254	0.523	1.198
CREST-03	0.262	0.514	1.283	pyMDNet-03	0.184	0.488	1.703
CREST-01	0.259	0.505	1.277	pyMDNet-01	0.119	0.431	2.733

(a) The results of MetaCREST   (b) The results of MetaSDNet

Speed and Performance of the Initialization. We reported the wall clock time speed at the initial frame in Table 2, on a single TITAN-X GPU. In CREST, in addition to feature extraction, there are two more computational bottlenecks. The first is the convolution with correlation filters. Larger objects means larger filters and more computations. We reported average time across all 100 sequences. Another heavy computation comes from PCA at the initial frame. It also depends on the size of the objects. Larger objects lead to larger center cropped images, features, and more computation in PCA.

MDNet requires many positive and negative patches, and also many model update iterations to converge. A large part of the computation comes from extracting CNN features for every patch. MetaSDNet needs only a few training patches and can achieve 30x speedup (0.124 vs 3.508), while improving accuracy. If we used more compact CNNs for feature extractions, the speed could have been in the range of real-time processing. For subsequent frames in MDNet, model update time is of less concern because MDNet only updates the last 3 fully connected layers, which are relatively faster than feature extractors. The features are extracted at every frame, stored in a database, and update the model every 10 frames. Therefore, the actual computation is well distributed across every frames.

We also showed the performance of the initialization to see the effectiveness of our approach (in Table 2. We measured the performance with learned initialization. After initial training, we measure the performance on the first frame and 5 future frames to see generalizability of trackers. MetaSDNet achieved very high accuracy after only one iteration, but accuracy of pyMDNet after one iteration was barely above guessing (guessing is 50% and all negative prediction is 75% accuracy since sampling ratio was 1:3 between positive and negative samples). The effectiveness is more apparent in MetaCREST. MetaCREST-01 without any updates gave already close performance to CREST-05 after training (0.48 vs 0.45). In original CREST tracker, they train the model until it reaches a loss

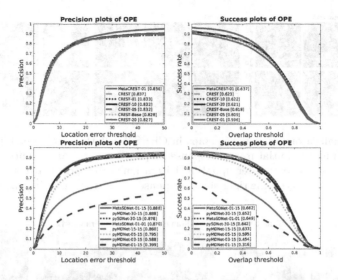

Fig. 3. Precision and success plots over 100 sequences in OTB2015 dataset with one-pass evaluation (OPE). For CREST (top row), The numbers in legends represent the number of iterations at the initial frame, and all used 2 iterations for the subsequent model updates. For MDNet experiments (bottom row), 01–15 means, 1 training iterations at the initial frame and 15 training iterations for the subsequent model updates.

Table 2. Speed and performance of the initialization: The right table shows the losses of estimated response map in MetaCREST. The left table shows the accuracy of image patches in MetaSDNet. B (Before) - the performance of the initial frame before training, A (After) - the performance of the initial frame after training, LH (Lookahead) - the performance of next 5 frames after training, Time - wall clock time to train in seconds

	B	A	LH	Time(s)		B	A	LH	Time(s)
MetaCREST-01	0.48	0.04	**0.05**	**0.090**	MetaSDNet-01	0.50	0.98	**0.97**	**0.124**
CREST-01	0.95	0.82	0.87	0.395	pyMDNet-01	0.51	0.56	0.56	0.123
CREST-03	0.95	0.62	0.75	0.424	pyMDNet-03	0.51	0.79	0.78	0.373
CREST-05	0.95	0.45	0.63	0.550	pyMDNet-05	0.51	0.84	0.84	0.656
CREST-10	0.95	0.24	0.40	0.668	pyMDNet-10	0.51	0.95	0.93	1.171
CREST-20	0.95	0.18	0.31	1.048	pyMDNet-15	0.51	0.97	**0.97**	1.819
CREST-65	0.95	0.01	0.30	1.529	pyMDNet-30	0.51	0.99	**0.98**	3.508

of 0.02, which corresponds to an average 65 iterations. However, its generalizability at future frames is limited compared to ours (.05 vs .30). Although this is not directly proportional to eventual tracking performance, we believe this is clear evidence that our meta-training algorithm based on future frames is indeed effective, as also supported by overall tracking performance.

Visualization of Response Maps. We visualized response maps in MetaCREST at the initial frame (Fig. 4). A meta-learned initialization, θ_0 should

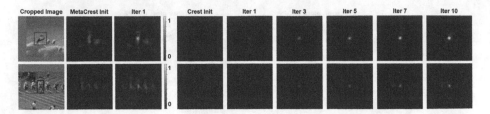

Fig. 4. Visualizations of response maps in CREST: left three columns represents the image patch at the initial frame, response map with meta-learned initial correlation filters θ_{0_f}, response map after updating 1 iteration with learned α, respectively. The rest of seven columns on the right shows response maps after updating the model up to 10 iterations.

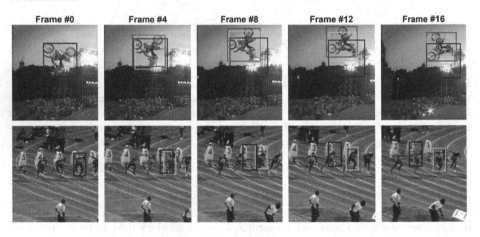

Fig. 5. Qualitative examples: tracking results at early stage of MotorRolling (top) and Bolt2 (bottom) sequences in OTB2015 dataset. Color coded boxes: ground truth (Red), MetaCREST-01 (Green) and CREST (Blue). (Color figure online)

be capable of learning generic objectness or visual saliency. At the same time, it should not be instance specific. It turns out that is the case. The second column in Fig. 4 shows response maps by applying correlation filters to the cropped image (first column) with θ_0. Without any training, it already generates high response values on some locations where there are objects. But, more importantly, there is no clear maximum. After one iteration, the maximum is clearly located at the center of the response map. In contrast to MetaCREST, CREST consumes more iterations to produce high response values on the target.

Qualitative Examples of Robust Initialization. In Fig. 5, we present some examples where MetaCrest overcomes some of the issues in the original CREST. In MotorRolling sequence (top row), CREST was distracted by a horizontal line from the forest in the background. CREST easily reached to 0.0000 loss defined in Eq. 6 at the initial frame, as opposed to 0.1255 in MetaCREST. This is a strong evidence that an optimal solution does not necessarily mean good generalizability on future frames. In contrast, MetaCREST, generalizes well to future frames, despite not finding an optimal solution at the current frame. In Bolt2 sequence (bottom row), CREST also reached to 0.0000 loss (vs 0.0534 in MetaCREST). In a similar way, a top left part in the bounding box was the distractor. MetaCREST could easily ignore the background clutter and focused on the object in the center of the bounding box.

6   Conclusion and Future Work

In this paper, we present an approach to use meta-learning to improve online trackers based on deep networks. We demonstrate this by improving two state-of-the-art trackers (CREST and MDNet). We learn to obtain a robust initial target model based on the error signals from future frames during meta-training phase. Experimental results show improvements in speed, accuracy, and robustness for both trackers. The proposed technique is general so that other trackers may benefit from it as well.

Other than target appearance modeling, which is the focus of this paper, there are many additional important factors in object tracking algorithms. For example, when or how often to update the model [56], how to manage the database [6], and how to define the search space. These considerations are sometimes more important than target appearance modeling. In future work we propose including handling of these as part of learning and meta-learning.

Acknowledgments. We thank the reviewers for their valuable feedback and acknowledge support from NSF 1452851, 1526367, 1446631.

References

1. Nam, H., Han, B.: Learning multi-domain convolutional neural networks for visual tracking. In: CVPR (2016)
2. Song, Y., Ma, C., Gong, L., Zhang, J., Lau, R., Yang, M.H.: CREST: convolutional residual learning for visual tracking. In: ICCV (2017)
3. Wu, Y., Lim, J., Yang, M.H.: Object tracking benchmark. TPAMI **37**, 1834–1848 (2015)
4. Kristan, M., Leonardis, A., Matas, J., Felsberg, M., et al.: The visual object tracking VOT2016 challenge results. In: ECCV Workshop (2016)
5. Danelljan, M., Robinson, A., Shahbaz Khan, F., Felsberg, M.: Beyond correlation filters: learning continuous convolution operators for visual tracking. In: ECCV (2016)
6. Danelljan, M., Bhat, G., Shahbaz Khan, F., Felsberg, M.: ECO: efficient convolution operators for tracking. In: CVPR (2017)
7. Henriques, J.F., Caseiro, R., Martins, P., Batista, J.: High-speed tracking with kernelized correlation filters. TPAMI (2015). https://doi.org/10.1109/TPAMI.2014.2345390
8. Ma, C., Huang, J.B., Yang, X., Yang, M.H.: Hierarchical convolutional features for visual tracking. In: ICCV (2015)

9. Kalal, Z., Mikolajczyk, K., Matas, J.: Tracking-learning-detection. TPAMI **34**, 1409 (2010)
10. Bolme, D.S., Beveridge, J.R., Draper, B.A., Lui, Y.M.: Visual object tracking using adaptive correlation filters. In: CVPR (2010)
11. Bertinetto, L., Valmadre, J., Henriques, J.F., Vedaldi, A., Torr, P.H.S.: Fully-convolutional siamese networks for object tracking. In: Hua, G., Jégou, H. (eds.) ECCV 2016. LNCS, vol. 9914, pp. 850–865. Springer, Cham (2016). https://doi.org/10.1007/978-3-319-48881-3_56
12. Held, D., Thrun, S., Savarese, S.: Learning to track at 100 FPS with deep regression networks. In: Leibe, B., Matas, J., Sebe, N., Welling, M. (eds.) ECCV 2016. LNCS, vol. 9905, pp. 749–765. Springer, Cham (2016). https://doi.org/10.1007/978-3-319-46448-0_45
13. Tao, R., Gavves, E., Smeulders, A.W.M.: Siamese instance search for tracking. In: CVPR (2016)
14. Mueller, M., Smith, N., Ghanem, B.: Context-aware correlation filter tracking. In: CVPR (2017)
15. Finn, C., Abbeel, P., Levine, S.: Model-agnostic meta-learning for fast adaptation of deep networks. In: ICML (2017)
16. Ravi, S., Larochelle, H.: Optimization as a model for few-shot learning. In: ICLR (2017)
17. Andrychowicz, M., et al.: Learning to learn by gradient descent by gradient descent. In: NIPS (2016)
18. Santoro, A., Bartunov, S., Botvinick, M., Wierstra, D., Lillicrap, T.: Meta-learning with memory-augmented neural networks. In: ICML (2016)
19. Li, Z., Zhou, F., Chen, F., Li, H.: Meta-SGD: learning to learn quickly for few shot learning. arXiv:1707.09835 (2017)
20. Al-Shedivat, M., Bansal, T., Burda, Y., Sutskever, I., Mordatch, I., Abbeel, P.: Continuous adaptation via meta-learning in nonstationary and competitive environments. In: ICLR (2018)
21. Danelljan, M., Hager, G., Khan, F.S., Felsberg, M.: Learning spatially regularized correlation filters for visual tracking. In: ICCV (2015)
22. Galoogahi, H.K., Sim, T., Lucey, S.: Correlation filters with limited boundaries. In: CVPR (2015)
23. Zhang, K., Zhang, L., Liu, Q., Zhang, D., Yang, M.-H.: Fast visual tracking via dense spatio-temporal context learning. In: Fleet, D., Pajdla, T., Schiele, B., Tuytelaars, T. (eds.) ECCV 2014. LNCS, vol. 8693, pp. 127–141. Springer, Cham (2014). https://doi.org/10.1007/978-3-319-10602-1_9
24. Ma, C., Yang, X., Zhang, C., Yang, M.H.: Long-term correlation tracking. In: CVPR (2015)
25. Hong, Z., Chen, Z., Wang, C., Mei, X., Prokhorov, D., Tao, D.: MUlti-Store Tracker (MUSTer): a cognitive psychology inspired approach to object tracking. In: CVPR (2015)
26. Danelljan, M., Hager, G., Khan, F.S., Felsberg, M.: Accurate scale estimation for robust visual tracking. In: BMVC (2014)
27. Valmadre, J., Bertinetto, L., Henriques, J.F., Vedaldi, A., Torr, P.H.S.: End-to-end representation learning for correlation filter based tracking. In: CVPR (2017)
28. Li, H., Li, Y., Porikli, F.: DeepTrack: learning discriminative feature representations by convolutional neural networks for visual tracking. In: BMVC (2014)
29. Babenko, B., Yang, M.H., Belongie, S.: Robust object tracking with online multiple instance learning. TPAMI **33**, 1619–1632 (2010)

30. Hare, S.: Struck: structured output tracking with kernels. TPAMI **38**, 2096–2109 (2015)

31. Grabner, H., Leistner, C., Bischof, H.: Semi-supervised on-line boosting for robust tracking. In: Forsyth, D., Torr, P., Zisserman, A. (eds.) ECCV 2008. LNCS, vol. 5302, pp. 234–247. Springer, Heidelberg (2008). https://doi.org/10.1007/978-3-540-88682-2_19

32. Bai, Q., Wu, Z., Sclaroff, S., Betke, M., Monnier, C.: Randomized ensemble tracking. In: ICCV (2013)

33. Fischer, P., Dosovitskiy, A., Ilg, E., Hausser, P., Hazrbas, C., Golkov, V.: FlowNet: learning optical flow with convolutional networks. In: CVPR (2015)

34. Kahou, S.E., Michalski, V., Memisevic, R.: RATM: recurrent attentive tracking model. In: CVPR Workshop (2017)

35. Gan, Q., Guo, Q., Zhang, Z., Cho, K.: First step toward model-free, anonymous object tracking with recurrent neural networks. arXiv:1511.06425 (2015)

36. Gordon, D., Farhadi, A., Fox, D.: Re3: real-time recurrent regression networks for object tracking. arXiv:1705.06368 (2017)

37. Yang, T., Chan, A.B.: Recurrent filter learning for visual tracking. In: ICCV (2017)

38. Schmidhuber, J.: Evolutionary principles in self-referential learning. Diploma thesis, Institut f. Informatik, Technical University of Munich (1987)

39. Schmidhuber, J.: Learning to control fast-weight memories: an alternative to dynamic recurrent networks. Neural Comput. **4**, 131–139 (1992)

40. Hochreiter, S., Younger, A.S., Conwell, P.R.: Learning to learn using gradient descent. In: Dorffner, G., Bischof, H., Hornik, K. (eds.) ICANN 2001. LNCS, vol. 2130, pp. 87–94. Springer, Heidelberg (2001). https://doi.org/10.1007/3-540-44668-0_13

41. Thrun, S., Pratt, L.: Learning to learn: introduction and overview. In: Thrun, S., Pratt, L. (eds.) Learning to Learn, pp. 3–17. Springer, Heidelberg (1998). https://doi.org/10.1007/978-1-4615-5529-2_1

42. Chen, Y., et al.: Learning to learn without gradient descent by gradient descent. In: ICML (2017)

43. Wichrowska, O., et al.: Learned optimizers that scale and generalize. In: ICML (2017)

44. Li, K., Malik, J.: Learning to optimize. In: ICLR (2017)

45. Bertinetto, L., Henriques, J.F., Valmadre, J., Torr, P.H.S., Vedaldi, A.: Learning feed-forward one-shot learners. In: NIPS (2016)

46. Wang, Y.-X., Hebert, M.: Learning to learn: model regression networks for easy small sample learning. In: Leibe, B., Matas, J., Sebe, N., Welling, M. (eds.) ECCV 2016. LNCS, vol. 9910, pp. 616–634. Springer, Cham (2016). https://doi.org/10.1007/978-3-319-46466-4_37

47. Kingma, D.P., Ba, J.L.: Adam: a method for stochastic optimization. In: ICLR (2015)

48. Maclaurin, D., Duvenaud, D., Adams, R.P.: Gradient-based hyperparameter optimization through reversible learning. In: ICML (2015)

49. Metz, L., Poole, B., Pfau, D., Sohl-Dickstein, J.: Unrolled generative adversarial networks. In: ICLR (2017)

50. Pytorch. http://www.pytorch.org

51. Liu, W., et al.: SSD: single shot MultiBox detector. In: ECCV (2016)

52. Ren, S., He, K., Girshick, R., Sun, J.: Faster R-CNN: towards real-time object detection with region proposal networks. In: NIPS (2016)

53. Jaderberg, M., Simonyan, K., Zisserman, A., Kavukcuoglu, K.: Spatial transformer networks. In: NIPS (2016)

54. Kristan, M., et al.: The visual object tracking VOT2014 challenge results. In: Agapito, L., Bronstein, M.M., Rother, C. (eds.) ECCV 2014. LNCS, vol. 8926, pp. 191–217. Springer, Cham (2015). https://doi.org/10.1007/978-3-319-16181-5_14
55. Russakovsky, O.: ImageNet large scale visual recognition challenge. IJCV **115**, 211–252 (2015)
56. Supancic, J., Ramanan, D.: Tracking as online decision-making: learning a policy from streaming videos with reinforcement learning. In: ICCV (2017)

Collaborative Deep Reinforcement Learning for Multi-object Tracking

Liangliang Ren[1], Jiwen Lu[1(✉)], Zifeng Wang[1], Qi Tian[2,3], and Jie Zhou[1]

[1] Tsinghua University, Beijing, China
{renll16,wangzf14}@mails.tsinghua.edu.cn, {lujiwen,jzhou}@tsinghua.edu.cn
[2] Huawei Noah'S Ark Lab, Beijing, China
qi.tian@utsa.edu
[3] University of Texas at San Antonio, San Antonio, USA

Abstract. In this paper, we propose a collaborative deep reinforcement learning (C-DRL) method for multi-object tracking. Most existing multi-object tracking methods employ the tracking-by-detection strategy which first detects objects in each frame and then associates them across different frames. However, the performance of these methods rely heavily on the detection results, which are usually unsatisfied in many real applications, especially in crowded scenes. To address this, we develop a deep prediction-decision network in our C-DRL, which simultaneously detects and predicts objects under a unified network via deep reinforcement learning. Specifically, we consider each object as an agent and track it via the prediction network, and seek the optimal tracked results by exploiting the collaborative interactions of different agents and environments via the decision network. Experimental results on the challenging MOT15 and MOT16 benchmarks are presented to show the effectiveness of our approach.

Keywords: Object tracking · Multi-object
Deep reinforcement learning

1 Introduction

Multi-object tracking (MOT) has attracted increasing interests in computer vision over the past few years, which has various practical applications in surveillance, human computer interface, robotics and advanced driving assistant systems. The goal of MOT is to estimate the trajectories of different objects and track those objects across the video. While a variety of MOT methods have been proposed in recent years [7,8,14,27,34,36,40,45–47,52], it remains a challenging problem to track multiple objects in many unconstrained environments, especially in crowded scenes. This is because occlusions between different objects and large intra-class variations usually occur in such scenarios.

Existing MOT approaches can be mainly divided into two categories, (1) offline (batch or semi-batch) [7,27,40,45,46,52] and (2) online [8,14,34,36,47].

© Springer Nature Switzerland AG 2018
V. Ferrari et al. (Eds.): ECCV 2018, LNCS 11207, pp. 605–621, 2018.
https://doi.org/10.1007/978-3-030-01219-9_36

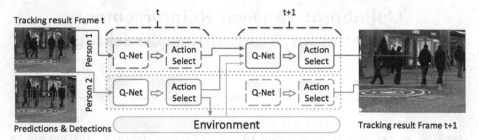

Fig. 1. The key idea of our proposed C-DRL method for multi-object tracking. Given a video and the detection results of different objects for the tth frame, we model each object as an agent and predict the location of each object for the following frames, where we seek the optimal tracked results by considering the interactions of different agents and environment via a collaborative deep reinforcement learning method. Lastly, we take actions to update agents at frame $t+1$ according to the outputs of the decision network

The key idea of offline methods is to group detections into short trajectory segments or tracklets, and then use more reliable features to connect those tracklets to full trajectories. Representative off-line methods use min-cost network flow [5,54], energy minimization [28] or generalized minimum clique graphs [52] to address the data association problem. Online MOT methods estimate the object trajectories with the detections of the current and past frames, which can be applied to real-time applications such as advanced driving assistant systems or robotics. Conventional online methods usually employ Kalman filtering [19], Particle filtering [32] or Markov decisions [47]. However, the tracking accuracy of these methods is sensitive to the occlusions and noisy detection results, such as missing detections, false detections and the non-accurate bounding boxes, which make these methods difficult to be applied for videos of crowded scenes.

In this paper, we propose a collaborative deep reinforcement learning (C-DRL) method for multi-object tracking. Figure 1 illustrates the basic idea of our proposed approach. Given a video and the detection results of different objects for the tth frame, we model each object as an agent and predict the locations of objects of the following frames by using the history trajectories and the appearance information of the $(t + 1)$th image frame. We exploit the collaborative interaction of each agent between the neighboring agents and the environment, and make decisions for each agent to update, track or delete the target object via a decision network, where the influence of occlusions between objects and noisy detection results can be well alleviated by maximizing their shared utility. Experimental results on the challenging MOT15 and MOT16 benchmarks are presented to demonstrate the efficiency of our approach.

2   Related Work

Multi-object Tracking: Most existing MOT methods can be categorized into two classes: (1) offline [7,27,40,45,46,52] and (2) online [8,14,34,36,47]. Methods in the first class group all detection results into short trajectory segments or tracklets, and connect those tracklets into full trajectories. For example, Zamir *et al.* [52] associated all detection results which incorporate both the appearance and motion information in a global manner by using generalized minimum clique graphs. Tang *et al.* [40] introduced a graph-based method that links and clusters objects hypotheses over time by solving a subgraph multicut problem. Maksai *et al.* [27] proposed an approach to track multiple objects with non-Markovian behavioral constraints. Methods in the second class estimate object trajectories with the detection results of the current and past frames. For example, Yang *et al.* [48,49] introduced an online learned CRF model by solving an energy minimization problem with nonlinear motion patterns and robust appearance constraints for multi-object tracking. Xiang *et al.* [47] formulated MOT as a decision-making problem via a Markov decision process. Choi *et al.* [7] presented an aggregated local flow descriptor to accurately measure the affinity between different detection results. Hong *et al.* [14] proposed a data-association method to exploit structural motion constraints in the presence of large camera motion. Sadeghian *et al.* [34] encoded dependencies across multiple cues over a temporal window and learned multi-cue representation to compute the similarity scores in a tracking framework. To overcome the influence of noisy detection, several methods have also been proposed. For example, Shu *et al.* [36] introduced a part-based representation under the tracking-by-detection framework to handle partial occlusions. Chu *et al.* [8] focused on learning a robust appearance model for each target by using a single object tracker. To address the occlusion and noisy detection problem, our approach uses a prediction-decision network to make decisions for online multi-object tracking.

Deep Reinforcement Learning: Deep reinforcement learning has gained significant successes in various vision applications in recent years, such as object detection [25], face recognition [33], image super-resolution [6] and object search [20]. Current deep reinforcement learning methods can be divided into two classes: deep Q learning [12,29,30,42] and policy gradient [1,37,50]. For the first class, Q-values are fitted to capture the expected return for taking a particular action at a particular state. For example, Cao *et al.* [6] proposed an attention-aware face hallucination framework with deep reinforcement learning to sequentially discover attended patches and perform facial part enhancement by fully exploiting the global interdependency of the image. Rao *et al.* [33] proposed a attention-aware deep reinforcement learning method to select key frames for video face recognition. Kong *et al.* [20] presented a collaborative deep reinforcement learning method to localize objects jointly in a few iterations. For the second class, the distribution of policies is represented explicitly and the policy is increased by updating the parameters in the gradient direction. Liu *et al.* [26] applied a policy gradient method to optimize a variety of captioning

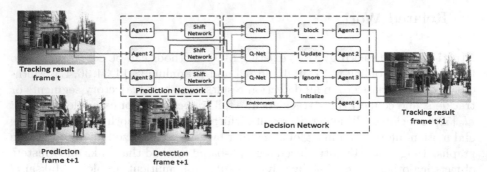

Fig. 2. The framework of the proposed C-DRL for multi-object tracking. In this figure, there are three objects at frame t. We first predict the locations of these three objects at frame $t+1$. Then we use a decision network to combine the prediction and detection results and make decisions for each agent to maximize their shared utility. For example, Agent 2 is blocked by its neighborhood (Agent 1). Agent 1 updates itself by using the nearest detection result, and Agent 3 ignores the noisy detection. We initialize Agent 4 by using the remaining detection result in the environment. Lastly we use the locations of each agent as the tracking results at frame $t+1$

metrics. Yu *et al.* [50] proposed a sequence generative adversarial nets with policy gradient. More recently, deep reinforcement learning [15,16,39,51,53] has also been employed in visual tracking. For example, Yun *et al.* [51] proposed an action-decision network to generate actions to seek the locations and sizes of the objects in a new coming frame. Supancic *et al.* [39] proposed a decision policy tracker by using reinforcement learning to decide where to look in the upcoming frames, and when to re-initialize and update its appearance model for the tracked object. However, these methods can not be applied to multi-object tracking directly since they ignore the communication between different objects. In this work, we propose a collaborative deep reinforcement learning method to exploit the interactions of different objects for multi-object tracking.

3   Approach

Figure 2 shows the framework of the proposed C-DRL method for multi-object tracking, which contains two parts, (1) a prediction network and (2) a decision network. Given a video and the detection results of different objects at frame t, we model each object as an agent and predict the locations of objects for the following frames, and seek the optimal tracked results by considering the interactions of different agents and environment via the decision network. Lastly, we take actions to update, delete or initialize agents at frame $t+1$ according to decisions. In the following subsections, we will detail the prediction network and the decision network, respectively.

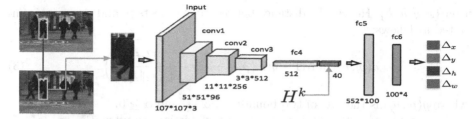

Fig. 3. The framework of the prediction network. The prediction network learns the movement of the target object given an initial location of the object, which contains three convolutional layers and three fully connected layers

3.1   Learning of the Prediction Network

Given initial locations of objects, the prediction network aims to learn the movement of objects to predict the locations of the target object. As shown in Fig. 3, the inputs to the prediction network are the raw image cropped by the initial bounding box of the next frame and history trajectories. We randomly sample bounding boxes $b \in B_{i,t}$ around the location of the object $b^*_{i,t}$ in each frame in the training videos as the training set to learn the prediction network. The prediction network takes the $(t+1)$th frame cropped by the initial location b and the history trajectories H of the last K frames for position prediction, where K is set as 10 in our work. We formulate location prediction as the following regression problem:

$$\arg \max_{\phi} J(\phi) = \sum_{i,t} \sum_{b \in B_{i,t}} g(b^*_{i,t+1}, b + \phi(I_t, b, H_t)), \tag{1}$$

where J is the optimization objective function at the top layer of the prediction network, ϕ is the parameter set of the network, $b^*_{i,t+1}$ is the ground truth of the object p_i at frame $t+1$, and $g(\cdot)$ denotes the intersection-over-union (IoU) of two bounding boxes.

$$g(b_i, b_j) = \frac{b_i \cap b_j}{b_i \cup b_j}. \tag{2}$$

3.2   Collaborative Deep Reinforcement Learning

As shown in Fig. 2, the decision network is a collaborative system which contains multiple agents and the environment. Each agent takes actions with the information from itself, the neighborhoods and the environment, where the interactions between agents and the environment are exploited by maximizing their shared utility. To make better use of such contextual information, we formulate multi-object tracking as a collaborative optimization problem.

We consider each object as an agent. Each agent p contains the trajectory $\{(x_0, y_0), (x_1, y_1), \cdots, (x_t, y_t)\}$, the appearance feature f, and the current location $\{x, y, w, h\}$. Hence, the distance between two objects p_i and p_j can be computed as follows:

$$d(p_i, p_j) = \alpha(1 - g(p_i, p_j)) + \left(1 - \frac{f_i^T f_j}{\|f_i\|_2 \|f_j\|_2}\right), \tag{3}$$

where $g(p_i, p_j)$ is the IoU of two bounding boxes, and $\alpha \geq 0$.

The environment contains the object detection results: $\mathcal{P}_t^* = \{p_1^*, p_2^*, \cdots, p_{N_t}^*\}$. The distance between the object p_i and the detection results can be computed as follows:

$$d(p_i, p_j^*) = \alpha(1 - g(p_i, p_j^*)) + \left(1 - \frac{f_i^T f_j}{\|f_i\|_2 \|f_j^*\|_2}\right). \tag{4}$$

Let I_t be the tth frame of the selected video, which contains n_t objects, $\mathcal{P}_t = \{p_1, p_2, \cdots, p_{n_t}\}$. The state at frame t, $s_t = \{\mathcal{P}_t, \mathcal{P}_t^*\}$ contains the current agents and the detection results. For the object p_i, we first use a prediction network to generate the position at frame $t + 1$. Then, we select the nearest neighborhood $p_j \in \mathcal{P}_t - \{p_i\}$ and the nearest detection result $p_k^* \in \mathcal{P}_{t+1}^*$. Subsequently, we take these three images as the input to the decision network if $d(p_j, p_i) < \tau$ and $d(p_k^*, p_i) < \tau$. If $d(p_j, p_i) \geq \tau$ or $d(p_k^*, p_i) < \tau$, we replace it with a zero image.

The object has two different status in each frame: *visible* or *invisible*. If the object is *visible*, we update the agent with the prediction or the detection result. If the detection result is reliable, we use both the detection result and the prediction result. If the detection results is not reliable, we only use the prediction result. If the object is *invisible*, the object may be blocked by other objects or disappears. If the object is blocked, we keep the appearance feature and only use the movement model to predict the location of the object for the next frame. If the object disappears, we delete the object directly. Hence, for each agent, the action set is defined as $\mathcal{A} = \{update, ignore, block, delete\}$.

For the action *update*, we use both the prediction and detection results to update the position of p_i and the appearance feature, described as below:

$$f_i = (1 - \rho)f_i + \rho f_i^*, \tag{5}$$

where ρ is the learning rate of appearance features.

We delete the detection results which are used to update agents features. For remaining detection results in the environment, we initialize an agent for each remaining result. For a false detection, the agent is also initialized, but the reward of the action $\{update, ignore, block\}$ is set to -1 while the reward of the action *delete* is set to 1. Then, the agent is deleted in the next iteration.

For the action *ignore*, the detection result is not reliable or missing, while the prediction result is more reliable. We use the prediction result to update the position of p_i.

For the action *block*, we keep the feature of p_i as the object has been blocked by other objects, and the location is updated according to the prediction result.

For the action *delete*, the object disappears, and we delete the object p_i directly.

Therefore, the rewards $r_{i,t}^*$ of each action contains two terms: $r_{i,t}$ and $r_{j,t+1}$, where $r_{i,t}$ describes its own state in the next frame, and $r_{j,t+1}$ refers to its nearest neighborhood state in the next frame. The final rewards can be computed as follows:

$$r_{i,t}^* = r_{i,t} + \beta r_{j,t+1}, \tag{6}$$

where $\beta \geq 0$ is the balance parameter.

The $r_{i,t}$ of actions {*update, ignore, block*} is defined by the IoU of the prediction location with the ground truth in the next frame. If the value of IoU is too small or the object disappears, $r_{i,t}$ is set to -1.

$$r_{i,t} = \begin{cases} 1 & \text{if } IoU \geq 0.7 \\ 0 & \text{if } 0.5 \leq IoU \leq 0.7 \\ -1 & else \end{cases}. \tag{7}$$

The $r_{i,t}$ of the action *delete* is defined by the states of objects. If the object disappears in the next frame, $r_{i,t}$ is 1, and otherwise -1.

$$r_{\text{delete}} = \begin{cases} 1 & \text{if object disappeared} \\ -1 & \text{else} \end{cases}. \tag{8}$$

We compute the Q value of $\{s_{i,t}, a_{i,t}\}$ as follows:

$$Q(s_{i,t}, a_{i,t}) = r_{i,t}^* + \gamma r_{i,t+1}^* + \gamma^2 r_{i,t+2}^* + \cdots, \tag{9}$$

where γ is the decaying parameter.

The optimization problem of the decision network is formulated as follows:

$$\arg\max_{\theta} L(\theta) = \mathbb{E}_{s,a} \log(\pi(a|s, \theta)) Q(s, a), \tag{10}$$

where θ is the parameter set of the decision network, and the policy gradient can be computed as follows:

$$\Delta_\theta L(\theta) = \mathbb{E}_{s,a} \Delta_\theta \log(\pi(a|s, \theta)) Q(s, a)$$
$$= \mathbb{E}_{s,a} \frac{Q(s, a)}{\pi(a|s, \theta)} \Delta_\theta \pi(a|s, \theta). \tag{11}$$

The gradient shows that we can increase the probability of actions which have positive Q values, and decrease the probability of actions which have negative Q values. However, in some easy scenes, the Q values of most actions are positive, while the Q values of all actions are negative in some challenging cases or at the beginning of the training stage. Hence, the policy gradient network is difficult to converge. Therefore, we use the advantage value of actions to replace the Q value, where we first compute the value of the state s as follows:

$$V(s) = \frac{\sum_a p(a|s) Q(s, a)}{\sum_a p(a|s)}. \tag{12}$$

Algorithm 1. Learning the Decision Network

Input: Training set: $\mathbf{V} = \{V_i\}$, and convergence error ϵ_1 maximal iterations number M.
Output: θ
1: Initialize θ;
2: **for all** $l = 1, 2, \ldots, M$ **do**
3:       Randomly select a video (V);
4:       Initialize agents set $\mathcal{P}$ using the detection results in 1-st frame
5:       **for all** $t = 2, 3, \ldots, I_t$ **do**
6:             **for all** $p \in \mathcal{P}$ **do**
7:                   Take actions according to the output of decision networks;
8:                   Update or delete p according to actions;
9:             **end for**
10:             Add $p_i^* \in \mathcal{P}^*$
11:       **end for**
12:       Calculate L_t according to (10);
13:       Calculate advantage value $A(s, a)$ for each agent;
14:       Update policy network θ according to (15) ;
15:       **if** $l > 1$ and $|L_t - L_{t-1}| < \epsilon_1$ **then**
16:             Go to **return**
17:       **end if**
18: **end for**
19: **return** θ

Then, the advantage value is computed as follows:

$$A(s, a) = Q(s, a) - V(s). \tag{13}$$

The final formulation of the policy gradient is defined as:

$$L(\theta) = \mathbb{E}_{s,a} \log(\pi(a|s, \theta)) A(s, a). \tag{14}$$

The parameter θ can be updated as follows:

$$\begin{aligned} \theta &= \theta + \rho \frac{L(\theta)}{\partial \theta} \\ &= \theta + \rho \mathbb{E}_{s,a} \frac{A(s, a)}{\pi(a|s, \theta)} \frac{\partial \pi(a|s, \theta)}{\partial \theta}. \end{aligned} \tag{15}$$

Algorithm 1 summarizes the detailed learning procedure of our decision network.

4   Experiments

4.1   Datasets

MOT15 [22]: It contains 11 training sequences and 11 testing sequences. For each testing sequence, we have a training set of similar conditions so that we can learn our model parameters accordingly. The most challenging sequence in MOT15 is the AVG-TownCentre in the testing sequences because its frame rate is very low, and there is no corresponding training sequence.

MOT16: It contains 7 training sequences and 7 testing sequences. Generally, MOT16 is more challenging than MOT15 because the ground truth annotations are more accurate (some hard examples are taken into account), the background settings are more complex (e.g. with moving cars or captured with a fast moving camera), and the pedestrians are more crowded so that the occlusion possibility is increased. The camera motion, camera angle and the imaging conditions vary largely among different sequences in both datasets.

4.2 Evaluation Metrics

We adopted the widely used CLEAR MOT metrics [4] including multiple object tracking precision (MOTP) and multiple object tracking accuracy (MOTA) which combine false positives (FP), false negatives (FN) and the identity switches (ID Sw) to evaluate the effectiveness of different MOT methods. We also used the metrics defined in [24] which contains the percentage of mostly tracked targets (MT, the ratio of ground-truth trajectories that is covered by a track hypothesis for at least 80% of their respective life span), the percentage of mostly lost targets (ML, the ratio of ground-truth trajectories that are covered by a track hypothesis for at most 20% of their respective life span), and the time of a trajectory is fragmented (Frag, interrupted during tracking).

4.3 Implementation Details

Decision Network: Our decision network consists of a feature extraction part and a decision-making part. We used the part of MDNet [31] which was pre-trained on ImageNet [9] to extract the feature of each object. The input size of the network is $3 \times 107 \times 107$. It consists of three consecutive convolution layer ($7 \times 7 \times 96$, $5 \times 5 \times 256$, $3 \times 3 \times 512$) and max pooling layer combos (including batch normalization layers), and finally a fully connected layer to flatten the feature to a column vector D of size 512×1. We then calculate the position feature P (of size 4×1) and concatenate D and P to a mixed feature vector W. Having predicted $agent_1$ with feature W_1, the agent which is closest to $agent_1$ in the predicted model is called $agent_2$ with feature W_2, and the counterpart $agent_1^{det}$ with feature W_1^{det} for $agent_1$ in the detection of the next frame, and finally $agent_1$ in the previous frame with feature D_1^{pre}. Having concatenated all features, we obtain the input to the decision-making network (input size: 2060×1). The structure of the network is relatively simple, we just utilized 3 fully connected layers (with dropout when training) to reduce the dimension to 4×1, which is corresponding to these four strategies.

In order to show that our network can learn to make decisions under various scenarios, we trained the decision network on all training sequences (both from MOT15 and MOT16) and then evaluate it on all the testing sequences without further processing. Here we trained the decision network on the training sequence of MOT15 and MOT16 for 10 epochs (1 epoch loops through all training sets including both MOT15 and MOT16). We optimized the network with stochastic gradient descent with weight decay at the rate of 0.0005 and momentum at the rate of 0.9. We set the learning rate 0.0002 at first 5 epochs and changed it into 0.0001 for the next 5 epochs. We applied a dynamic batch size strategy, which means that we obtain each frame and feed all objects in this frame to the network as a batch. This process best mimics the real tracking process thus is good for our network to be utilized to real tracking scenarios.

As for the reinforcement learning hyper-parameters, we firstly set balance parameter β and discount rate parameter γ to zero to simplify the training phase and let the decision network converge to a certain reward. Here the reward is 0.637. We then did grid search based on fine tuning the network. As shown in Fig. 4 that when $\gamma = 0.8$ and $\beta = 0.4$, we get maximized normalized reward (we normalize it to $[0, 1]$), so we set the hyper-parameters as above.

Prediction Network: We extracted all positive examples from the all training sequences from the datasets. In order to simulate noisy situations, we merged the information of detections and ground truth annotations, and computed the IoU of the detection bounding boxes and ground truth bounding boxes. If $IoU > 0.5$, the detection is valid and we put the detection into our dataset; otherwise, we treated the detection as a false positive and discard it. Therefore, we combined the detection and ground truth information when training the shift network. Our prediction network shares the same feature extraction part with the C-DRL network. Having obtained the feature vector D, we concatenated it with $H^{10}(x, y, h, w)$, which is the trajectory of the past 10 frames of the target. We trained the network for 20 epochs with a batch size of 20. We selected stochastic gradient descend with a learning rate of 0.002 and weight decay at the rate of 0.0005 and the momentum at the rate of 0.95. We halved the learning rate every 5 epochs. Our tracking system was implemented under the MATLAB 2015b platform with the MatConvNet [43] toolbox.

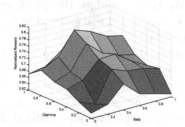

Fig. 4. The average normalized rewards versus different β and γ on the MOT15 training dataset

Table 1. Performance of our method under different inter-frame relation thresholds

THRESH	Rcll	FP	FN	IDs	MOTA	MOTAL
1	83.1	81.7	6598	481	63	64
2	83.0	83.3	6673	440	65	66
3	82.8	83.9	6742	411	65	66
4	82.5	84.6	6837	380	66	67
5	82.3	85.2	6929	359	67	68
6	82.1	85.6	7003	348	67	68
7	81.8	86.1	7142	329	67	68
8	81.4	86.4	7292	307	67	68
9	81.0	86.7	7448	293	67	68

4.4   Ablation Studies

We conducted ablation studies on MOT the SubCNN detection of MOT15 training set which was provided in [47].

Influences of the Inter-frame Relation: We changed the consecutive frame information in our network to investigate how it affects the performance. Our method automatically wipes out the agents of relatively short continuous appearing time, which has been utilized in the training stage of our C-DRL network (e.g. when an agent is lost for a certain number of frames, our method gives the command to pop it out and renews the weights in that direction). We set the threshold from 1 to 9. From Table 1, we see that when more inter-frame information is utilized, more constraints to our agents can be included, so that the noisy detection results can be well eliminated in our model. We also notice that as our FP goes up, our FN falls as well, which is a trade-off between the precision and recall. Since MOTA seems to be saturated after THRESH $\geq$ 8, setting THRESH to be 8 is a good choice for optimizing MOTA.

Influences of Decision Network: We set inter-frame threshold to 8 from the conclusion of previous part. Our original baseline (OB) is our full pipeline without modification. We replaced our decision network with vanilla Hungarian algorithm and fixed all other parameters (DN → HA). We find that the overall performance of the whole system falls drastically according to 2. Especially, the FP almost doubles and the IDs increases by an order of magnitude. Our decision network effectively wipes out false positives and id switches by conducting appropriate actions.

Influences of Prediction Network: We replaced our prediction network with velocity model method (PN → VM). We predict the position of each agent by using the trace of them. In other words, we model the instant velocity of agents by using their previous movement. According to our experiment result showed in Table 2, the performance gets worse as well. As the movement of pedestrians in MOT15 training set is relatively smooth and slow, there are rarely edge cases like turning or running. As a result, the performance is not bad. However, our original pipeline is still able to give more precise position prediction.

Influences of MDNet Feature: We replaced the MDNet part of our decision and the prediction networks with simple color histogram feature (PN → VM) and then feed them to the fully-connected layers. This time, the performance downgrade is slight, which means our reinforcement learning method is robust to different feature representations. However, more delicate and informative feature is a boost.

We could easily see the advantage of our decision network and the effectiveness of prediction network. As our decision network apparently enhances the performance by a large margin, thats the core part of our whole system.

Table 2. Ablation studies of different settings

Method	Rcll	Prcn	GT	MT	ML	FP	FN	IDs	MOTA	MOTP	MOTAL
OB	81.4	86.4	458	293	66	4995	7292	307	67.8	85.2	68.6
DN → HA	83.2	78.3	458	317	31	9042	6562	2048	54.9	84.4	60.1
PN → VM	83.1	81.7	458	317	31	7296	6620	453	63.3	84.7	64.4
MD → HIST	81.8	84.7	458	304	35	5772	7121	463	65.9	85.2	67.1

Fig. 5. Some tracking results on the MOT15 and MOT16 public detections, where the trajectory of each object has been painted from the first frame in the same color as its bounding box

4.5 Evaluations on MOT15

Comparison with State-of-the-Arts: For a fair comparison, we used the public detection results on MOT15 and MOT16. Sampled results are showed in Fig. 5. As shown in Table 3, our method outperforms most state-of-the-art trackers on MOT15 under the MOTA metric, which is one of the most important and persuasive metrics in multi-object tracking. Our method is also comparable with AMIR15 [34]. Moreover, we obtained the best FN among all online methods, which indicates that our method is able to recover detections effectively. We noticed that some methods such as LINF1 [10] can obtain relatively high performance on FP and ID Sw. However, it sacrifices lots of hard examples, which leads to a bad FN performance. Our method also outperforms all offline methods (e.g. they have access to all frames regardless of the time order so that they get far more information than an online one), which indicates that our network can well learn contextual information via the deep reinforcement learning framework.

4.6 Evaluations on MOT16

Comparison with State-of-the-Arts: As shown in Table 4, our method achieved the best MOTA result among all online MOT methods and is comparable to the best offline methods such as LMP [41] and FWT [13]. In terms of MT and ML, our method also achieves the best performance among all online methods, which indicates that our method can keep track of relatively more objects than other methods under complex environments. Since the detection

Table 3. The performance of different methods on MOT15

Mode	Method	MOTA↑	MOTP↑	FAF↓	MT(%)↑	ML(%)↓	FP↓	FN↓
Offline	LINF1 [10]	24.5	71.3	1.0	5.5	64.6	5864	40207
	LP_SSVM [44]	25.2	71.7	1.4	5.8	53.0	8369	36932
	MHT_DAM [18]	32.4	71.8	1.6	16.0	43.8	9064	32060
	NMOT [7]	33.7	**71.9**	1.3	12.2	44.0	7762	32547
	QuadMOT [38]	33.8	73.4	1.4	12.9	36.9	7898	32061
	JointMC [17]	35.6	**71.9**	1.8	**23.2**	39.3	10580	**28508**
Online	SCEA [14]	29.1	71.1	1.0	8.9	47.3	6060	36912
	MDP [47]	30.3	71.3	1.7	13.0	38.4	9717	32422
	CDA_DDALpb [2]	32.8	70.7	**0.9**	9.7	42.2	**4983**	35690
	AMIR15 [34]	**37.6**	71.7	1.4	15.8	**26.8**	7933	29397
	Ours	37.1	71.0	1.2	14.0	31.3	7036	30440

Table 4. The performance of different methods on MOT16

Mode	Method	MOTA↑	MOTP↑	FAF↓	MT(%)↑	ML(%)↓	FP↓	FN↓
Offline	TBD [11]	33.7	76.5	1.0	7.2	54.2	5804	112587
	LTTSC-CRF [21]	37.6	75.9	2.0	9.6	55.2	11969	101343
	LINF1 [10]	41.0	74.8	1.3	11.6	51.3	7896	99224
	MHT_DAM_16 [18]	45.8	76.3	1.1	16.2	43.2	6412	91758
	NOMT [7]	46.4	76.7	1.6	**18.3**	41.4	9753	87565
	NLLMPa [23]	47.6	78.5	1.0	17.0	40.4	5844	89093
	LMP [41]	**48.8**	**79.0**	1.1	18.2	40.1	6654	**86245**
Online	OVBT [3]	38.4	75.4	1.9	7.5	47.3	11517	99463
	EAMTT_pub [35]	38.8	75.1	1.4	7.9	49.1	8114	102452
	CDA_DDALv2 [2]	43.9	74.7	1.1	10.7	44.4	6450	95175
	AMIR [34]	47.2	75.8	**0.5**	14.0	41.6	**2681**	92856
	Ours	47.3	74.6	1.1	17.4	**39.9**	6375	88543

results of MOT16 are more accurate, our decision network and prediction network can learn more right behaviors and decrease the possibility of losing objects. Another observation is that our method obtains the best FN performance among all online methods, which is because our method recovers some missing objects that were missed in the detector via the decision network. Since the public detector does not cover all positive samples in MOT16, the rates of FN are naturally high for all methods. However, our method addresses this decently. We see that our method outperforms these offline methods by a large margin, which shows that the effectiveness of the decision network where collaborative interaction maximizing the utilization of contextual information is effectively exploited to enhance the generalization ability of our network. Also, our FP gets the second place among both online and offline methods, which means our method has strong ability to eliminate false positives exist in the detection results. In Fig. 6 (a) the top image shows the provided public detection results which contain

(a)   (b)

Fig. 6. (a) False positives eliminating (b) ID switch problems

multiple detections of same people. However, in the tracking result below, our method successfully eliminate those redundant detections.

Failure Cases: Figure 6(b) shows some failure examples of our method . For the first row, we could see that when people walk by each other, it is easy for them to switch their ids. For example the woman in white is initially in blue box, however the blue box moves to the man in blue in the next frames. For the second row, we could see that when occlusion lasts for long time, the reappeared person would be assigned with a new id (i.e. A bounding box with a new color in our picture). For instance, the man in white is initially in yellow box and he is hidden by another one in the second frame. When he reappears in the third frame, he is in a newly assigned yellow box. Our method has a relatively high ID switch and Frag (actually these two metrics are closely correlated) on both the MOT15 and MOT16 datasets, which indicates that our decision network is sometimes over-cautious when there are some changes on conditions. In such scenarios, our method will assign the object a new ID label. For the memory optimization, we keep the object in our model for several frames (where we set 2 in our experiments) if it got lost at a certain frame. For some videos of high sampling rates, the object lost for relatively more frames due to occlusion and this also caused ID switch as well. However, this can be relieved by saving the feature of possibly disappeared objects in our model for longer frames and training the network with more similar sequences so that the network can better utilize dynamic information. Another reason is that when two or more objects move to each other, both their position and appearance feature are extremely similar, which poses large challenges for MOT trackers.

5   Conclusion

In this paper, we have proposed a collaborative deep reinforcement learning method for multi-object tracking. Specifically, we have employed a prediction-network to estimate the location of objects in the next frame, and used deep reinforcement learning to combine the prediction results and detection results and make decisions of state updates to overcome the occlusion and the missed or false detection. Experimental results on both the challenging MOT15 and

MOT16 benchmarks are presented to show the effectiveness of our approach. How to apply our method to camera-network multi-object tracking seems to be an interesting future work.

Acknowledgement. This work was supported in part by the National Key Research and Development Program of China under Grant 2017YFA0700802, in part by the National Natural Science Foundation of China under Grant 61672306, Grant U1713214, Grant 61572271, and in part by supported by NSFC under Grant No. 61429201, in part to Dr. Qi Tian by ARO grant W911NF-15-1-0290 and Faculty Research Gift Awards by NEC Laboratories of America and Blippar.

References

1. Ammar, H.B., Eaton, E., Ruvolo, P., Taylor, M.: Online multi-task learning for policy gradient methods. In: ICML, pp. 1206–1214 (2014)
2. Bae, S.H., Yoon, K.J.: Confidence-based data association and discriminative deep appearance learning for robust online multi-object tracking. TPAMI **40**, 595–610 (2017)
3. Ban, Y., Ba, S., Alameda-Pineda, X., Horaud, R.: Tracking multiple persons based on a variational Bayesian model. In: ECCV, pp. 52–67 (2016)
4. Bernardin, K., Stiefelhagen, R.: Evaluating multiple object tracking performance: the CLEAR MOT metrics. EURASIP **2008**(1), 246309 (2008)
5. Butt, A.A., Collins, R.T.: Multi-target tracking by Lagrangian relaxation to min-cost network flow. In: CVPR, pp. 1846–1853 (2013)
6. Cao, Q., Lin, L., Shi, Y., Liang, X., Li, G.: Attention-aware face hallucination via deep reinforcement learning. In: CVPR, pp. 690–698 (2017)
7. Choi, W.: Near-online multi-target tracking with aggregated local flow descriptor. In: ICCV, pp. 3029–3037 (2015)
8. Chu, Q., Ouyang, W., Li, H., Wang, X., Liu, B., Yu, N.: Online multi-object tracking using CNN-based single object tracker with spatial-temporal attention mechanism. In: ICCV, pp. 4836–4845 (2017)
9. Deng, J., Dong, W., Socher, R., Li, L.J., Li, K., Fei-Fei, L.: ImageNet: a large-scale hierarchical image database. In: CVPR, pp. 248–255 (2009)
10. Fagot-Bouquet, L., Audigier, R., Dhome, Y., Lerasle, F.: Improving multi-frame data association with sparse representations for robust near-online multi-object tracking. In: ECCV, pp. 774–790 (2016)
11. Geiger, A., Lauer, M., Wojek, C., Stiller, C., Urtasun, R.: 3D traffic scene understanding from movable platforms. TPAMI **36**(5), 1012–1025 (2014)
12. Gu, S., Lillicrap, T., Sutskever, I., Levine, S.: Continuous deep Q-learning with model-based acceleration. In: ICML, pp. 2829–2838 (2016)
13. Henschel, R., Leal-Taixé, L., Cremers, D., Rosenhahn, B.: Improvements to Frank-Wolfe optimization for multi-detector multi-object tracking. arXiv preprint arXiv:1705.08314 (2017)
14. Hong Yoon, J., Lee, C.R., Yang, M.H., Yoon, K.J.: Online multi-object tracking via structural constraint event aggregation. In: CVPR, pp. 1392–1400 (2016)
15. Huang, C., Lucey, S., Ramanan, D.: Learning policies for adaptive tracking with deep feature cascades. In: ICCV, pp. 105–114 (2017)
16. Kamalapurkar, R., Andrews, L., Walters, P., Dixon, W.E.: Model-based reinforcement learning for infinite-horizon approximate optimal tracking. TNNLS **28**(3), 753–758 (2017)

17. Keuper, M., Tang, S., Zhongjie, Y., Andres, B., Brox, T., Schiele, B.: A multi-cut formulation for joint segmentation and tracking of multiple objects. arXiv preprint arXiv:1607.06317 (2016)
18. Kim, C., Li, F., Ciptadi, A., Rehg, J.M.: Multiple hypothesis tracking revisited. In: ICCV, pp. 4696–4704 (2015)
19. Kim, D.Y., Jeon, M.: Data fusion of radar and image measurements for multi-object tracking via Kalman filtering. Inf. Sci. **278**, 641–652 (2014)
20. Kong, X., Xin, B., Wang, Y., Hua, G.: Collaborative deep reinforcement learning for joint object search. In: CVPR, pp. 1695–1704 (2017)
21. Le, N., Heili, A., Odobez, J.-M.: Long-term time-sensitive costs for CRF-based tracking by detection. In: Hua, G., Jégou, H. (eds.) ECCV 2016. LNCS, vol. 9914, pp. 43–51. Springer, Cham (2016). https://doi.org/10.1007/978-3-319-48881-3_4
22. Leal-Taixé, L., Milan, A., Reid, I., Roth, S., Schindler, K.: MOTChallenge 2015: towards a benchmark for multi-target tracking. arXiv preprint arXiv:1504.01942 (2015)
23. Levinkov, E., et al.: Joint graph decomposition & node labeling: problem, algorithms, applications. In: CVPR, pp. 6012–6020 (2017)
24. Li, Y., Huang, C., Nevatia, R.: Learning to associate: Hybridboosted multi-target tracker for crowded scene. In: CVPR, pp. 2953–2960 (2009)
25. Liang, X., Lee, L., Xing, E.P.: Deep variation-structured reinforcement learning for visual relationship and attribute detection. arXiv preprint arXiv:1703.03054 (2017)
26. Liu, S., Zhu, Z., Ye, N., Guadarrama, S., Murphy, K.: Optimization of image description metrics using policy gradient methods. arXiv preprint arXiv:1612.00370 (2016)
27. Maksai, A., Wang, X., Fleuret, F., Fua, P.: Non-Markovian globally consistent multi-object tracking. In: ICCV, pp. 2544–2554 (2017)
28. Milan, A., Leal-Taixé, L., Reid, I., Roth, S., Schindler, K.: MOT16: a benchmark for multi-object tracking. arXiv preprint arXiv:1603.00831 (2016)
29. Mnih, V., et al.: Playing Atari with deep reinforcement learning. arXiv preprint arXiv:1312.5602 (2013)
30. Mnih, V., Kavukcuoglu, K., Silver, D., Rusu, A.A., Veness, J., Bellemare, M.G., Graves, A., Riedmiller, M., Fidjeland, A.K., Ostrovski, G., et al.: Human-level control through deep reinforcement learning. Nature **518**(7540), 529–533 (2015)
31. Nam, H., Han, B.: Learning multi-domain convolutional neural networks for visual tracking. In: CVPR, pp. 4293–4302 (2016)
32. Okuma, K., Taleghani, A., De Freitas, N., Little, J.J., Lowe, D.G.: A boosted particle filter: multitarget detection and tracking. In: ECCV, pp. 28–39 (2004)
33. Rao, Y., Lu, J., Zhou, J.: Attention-aware deep reinforcement learning for video face recognition. In: ICCV, pp. 3931–3940 (2017)
34. Sadeghian, A., Alahi, A., Savarese, S.: Tracking the untrackable: learning to track multiple cues with long-term dependencies. arXiv preprint arXiv:1701.01909 (2017)
35. Sanchez-Matilla, R., Poiesi, F., Cavallaro, A.: Multi-target tracking with strong and weak detections. In: ECCVW, vol. 5, p. 18 (2016)
36. Shu, G., Dehghan, A., Oreifej, O., Hand, E., Shah, M.: Part-based multiple-person tracking with partial occlusion handling. In: CVPR, pp. 1815–1821 (2012)
37. Silver, D., Lever, G., Heess, N., Degris, T., Wierstra, D., Riedmiller, M.: Deterministic policy gradient algorithms. In: ICML, pp. 387–395 (2014)
38. Son, J., Baek, M., Cho, M., Han, B.: Multi-object tracking with quadruplet convolutional neural networks. In: ICCV, pp. 5620–5629 (2017)

39. Supancic, III, J., Ramanan, D.: Tracking as online decision-making: learning a policy from streaming videos with reinforcement learning. In: ICCV, pp. 322–331 (2017)
40. Tang, S., Andres, B., Andriluka, M., Schiele, B.: Multi-person tracking by multicut and deep matching. In: Hua, G., Jégou, H. (eds.) ECCV 2016. LNCS, vol. 9914, pp. 100–111. Springer, Cham (2016). https://doi.org/10.1007/978-3-319-48881-3_8
41. Tang, S., Andriluka, M., Andres, B., Schiele, B.: Multiple people tracking by lifted multicut and person reidentification. In: ICCV, pp. 3539–3548 (2017)
42. Van Hasselt, H., Guez, A., Silver, D.: Deep reinforcement learning with double q-learning. In: AAAI, pp. 2094–2100 (2016)
43. Vedaldi, A., Lenc, K.: MatConvNet: convolutional neural networks for MATLAB. In: ACMMM, pp. 689–692 (2015)
44. Wang, S., Fowlkes, C.C.: Learning optimal parameters for multi-target tracking with contextual interactions. IJCV **122**(3), 484–501 (2017)
45. Wen, L., Lei, Z., Lyu, S., Li, S.Z., Yang, M.H.: Exploiting hierarchical dense structures on hypergraphs for multi-object tracking. TPAMI **38**(10), 1983–1996 (2016)
46. Wu, Z., Thangali, A., Sclaroff, S., Betke, M.: Coupling detection and data association for multiple object tracking. In: CVPR, pp. 1948–1955 (2012)
47. Xiang, Y., Alahi, A., Savarese, S.: Learning to track: online multi-object tracking by decision making. In: ICCV, pp. 4705–4713 (2015)
48. Yang, B., Nevatia, R.: Multi-target tracking by online learning of non-linear motion patterns and robust appearance models. In: CVPR, pp. 1918–1925 (2012)
49. Yang, B., Nevatia, R.: An online learned CRF model for multi-target tracking. In: CVPR, pp. 2034–2041 (2012)
50. Yu, L., Zhang, W., Wang, J., Yu, Y.: SeqGAN: sequence generative adversarial nets with policy gradient. In: AAAI, pp. 2852–2858 (2017)
51. Yun, S., Choi, J., Yoo, Y., Yun, K., Young Choi, J.: Action-decision networks for visual tracking with deep reinforcement learning. In: CVPR, pp. 2711–2720 (2017)
52. Zamir, A.R., Dehghan, A., Shah, M.: GMCP-tracker: global multi-object tracking using generalized minimum clique graphs. In: ECCV, pp. 343–356 (2012)
53. Zhang, D., Maei, H., Wang, X., Wang, Y.F.: Deep reinforcement learning for visual object tracking in videos. arXiv preprint arXiv:1701.08936 (2017)
54. Zhang, L., Li, Y., Nevatia, R.: Global data association for multi-object tracking using network flows. In: CVPR, pp. 1–8 (2008)

Multi-scale Context Intertwining
for Semantic Segmentation

Di Lin[1], Yuanfeng Ji[1], Dani Lischinski[2], Daniel Cohen-Or[1,3],
and Hui Huang[1(✉)]

[1] Shenzhen University, Shenzhen, China
`ande.lin1988@gmail.com`, `jyuanfeng8@gmail.com`, `cohenor@gmail.com`,
`hhzhiyan@gmail.com`
[2] The Hebrew University of Jerusalem, Jerusalem, Israel
`danix3d@gmail.com`
[3] Tel Aviv University, Tel Aviv, Israel

Abstract. Accurate semantic image segmentation requires the joint consideration of local appearance, semantic information, and global scene context. In today's age of pre-trained deep networks and their powerful convolutional features, state-of-the-art semantic segmentation approaches differ mostly in how they choose to combine together these different kinds of information. In this work, we propose a novel scheme for aggregating features from different scales, which we refer to as *Multi-Scale Context Intertwining* (MSCI). In contrast to previous approaches, which typically propagate information between scales in a one-directional manner, we merge pairs of feature maps in a bidirectional and recurrent fashion, via connections between two LSTM chains. By training the parameters of the LSTM units on the segmentation task, the above approach learns how to extract powerful and effective features for pixel-level semantic segmentation, which are then combined hierarchically. Furthermore, rather than using fixed information propagation routes, we subdivide images into super-pixels, and use the spatial relationship between them in order to perform image-adapted context aggregation. Our extensive evaluation on public benchmarks indicates that all of the aforementioned components of our approach increase the effectiveness of information propagation throughout the network, and significantly improve its eventual segmentation accuracy.

Keywords: Semantic segmentation · Deep learning
Convolutional neural network · Long short-term memory

1 Introduction

Semantic segmentation is a fundamental task in computer vision, whose goal is to associate a semantic object category with each pixel in an image [1–4]. Many real-world applications, e.g., autonomous driving [4], medical analysis [5], and

© Springer Nature Switzerland AG 2018
V. Ferrari et al. (Eds.): ECCV 2018, LNCS 11207, pp. 622–638, 2018.
https://doi.org/10.1007/978-3-030-01219-9_37

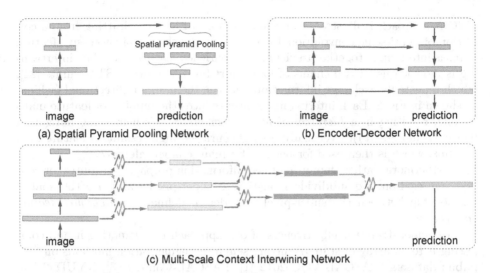

(a) Spatial Pyramid Pooling Network

(b) Encoder-Decoder Network

(c) Multi-Scale Context Interwining Network

Fig. 1. Alternative approaches for encoding multi-scale context information into segmentation features for per-pixel prediction. The spatial pyramid pooling (SPP) network (a) and the encoder-decoder (ED) network (b) propagate information across the hierarchy in a one-directional fashion. In contrast, our multi-scale context intertwining architecture (c) exchanges information between adjacent scales in a bidirectional fashion, and hierarchically combines the resulting feature maps. Figure 2 provides a more detailed illustration of the multi-stage recurrent context intertwining process.

computational photography [6], can benefit from accurate semantic segmentation that provides detailed information about the content of an image.

In recent years, we have witnessed a tremendous progress in semantic segmentation accuracy. These advances are largely driven by the power of fully convolutional networks (FCNs) [7] and their derivatives [8,9], which are pre-trained on large-scale datasets [2,10]. It has also become apparent that accounting for the semantic context leads to more accurate segmentation of individual objects [9,11–19].

The feature maps extracted by the deeper layers of a convolutional network encode higher-level semantic information and context contained in the large receptive field of each neuron. In contrast, the shallower layers encode appearance and location. State-of-the-art semantic segmentation approaches propagate coarse semantic context information back to the shallow layers, yielding richer features, and more accurate segmentations [7,9,17–21]. However, in these methods, context is typically propagated along the feature hierarchy in a one-directional manner, as illustrated in Fig. 1(a) and (b).

In this paper, we advocate the idea that more powerful features can be learned by enabling context to be exchanged between scales in a bidirectional manner. We refer to such information exchange as *context intertwining*. The intuition here is that semantics and context of adjacent scales are strongly correlated, and hence the descriptive power of the features may be significantly enhanced by such intertwining, leading to more precise semantic labeling.

Our approach is illustrated by the diagram in Fig. 1(c). Starting from a collection of multi-scale convolutional feature maps, each pair of successive feature maps is intertwined together to yield a new enriched feature map. The intertwining is modeled using two chains of long short-term memory (LSTM) units [22], which repeatedly exchange information between them, in a bidirectional fashion, as shown in Fig. 2. Each intertwining phase reduces the number of feature maps by one, resulting in a *hierarchical feature combination* scheme (the horizontal hierarchy in Fig. 1(c)). Eventually, a single enriched high-resolution feature map remains, which is then used for per-pixel semantic label inference.

Furthermore, rather than using fixed information propagation routes for context aggregation, we subdivide images into super-pixels, and use the spatial relationship between the super-pixel in order to define *image-adapted feature connections*.

We demonstrate the effectiveness of our approach by evaluating it and comparing it to an array of state-of-the-art semantic segmentation methods on four public datasets (PASCAL VOC 2012 [1], PASCAL-Context [3], NYUDv2 [23] and SUN-RGBD [24] datasets). On the PASCAL VOC 2012 validation set, we outperform the state-of-the-art (with 85.1% mean IoU). On the PASCAL VOC 2012 test set, our performance (87.0% mean IoU) is second only to the recent result of Chen et al. [25], who uses a backbone network trained on an internal JFT dataset [26–28], while our backbone network is trained on the ImageNet dataset [10].

2   Related Work

Fully convolutional networks (FCNs) [7] have proved effective for semantic image segmentation by leveraging the powerful convolutional features of classification networks [27,29,30] pre-trained on large-scale data [10,24]. The feature maps extracted by the different convolutional layers have progressively coarser spatial resolutions, and their neurons correspond to progressively larger receptive fields in the image space. Thus, the collection of feature maps of different resolutions encodes multi-scale context information. Semantic segmentation methods have been trying to exploit this multi-scale context information for accurate segmentation. In this paper, we focus on two aspects, i.e., *Feature Combination* and *Feature Connection*, which have also been explored by most of the recent works [7,9,18–20,31–33] to make better use of the image context.

Feature Combination. To capture the multi-scale context information in the segmentation features, many works combine feature maps whose neurons have different receptive fields. Various schemes for the combination of feature maps have been proposed. Spatial pyramid pooling (SPP) [34] has been successfully applied for combining different convolutional feature maps [9,18,20]. Generally, the last convolutional feature map, which is fed to the pixel-wise classifier, is equipped with an SPP (see Fig. 1(a)). But the SPP-enriched feature maps have little detailed information that is missed by the down-sampling operations of an FCN. Though the atrous convolution can preserve the resolutions of feature maps for more details, it requires a large budget of GPU storage for computation [27, 29, 30]. To save the GPU memory and improve the segmentation performance, some networks [17, 19, 21, 35] utilize an Encoder-Decoder (ED) network to gradually combine adjacent feature maps along the top-down hierarchy of a common FCN architecture, propagating the semantic information from the low-resolution feature maps to the high-resolution feature maps and using the high-resolution feature maps to recover the details of objects (see Fig. 1(b)). The latest work [25] further uses the ED network along with an atrous spatial pyramid pooling (ASPP) [20], and combines multi-resolution feature maps for information enrichment. In the ED network, each feature map of the decoder part only directly receives the information from the feature map at the same level of the encoder part. But the strongly-correlated semantic information, which is provided by the adjacent lower-resolution feature map of the encoder part, has to pass through additional intermediate layers to reach the same decoder layer, which may result in information decay.

In contrast, our approach directly combines pairs of adjacent feature maps in the deep network hierarchy. It creates new feature maps that directly receive the semantic information and context from a lower-resolution feature map and the improved spatial detail from a higher-resolution feature map. In addition, in our architecture the information exchange between feature maps is recurrent and bidirectional, enabling better feature learning. The pairwise bidirectional connections produce a second, *horizontal* hierarchy of the resulting feature maps, leading up to a full resolution context-enriched feature map (rightmost feature map in Fig. 1(c)), which is used for pixel-wise label prediction.

Feature Connection. Connections between feature maps enable the communication between neurons with different receptive field sizes, yielding new feature maps that encode multi-scale context information. Basically, FCN-based models [7–9, 17–20, 31] use separate neurons to represent the regular regions in an image. Normally, they use convolutional/pooling kernels with predefined shapes to aggregate the information of adjacent neurons, and propagate this information to the neurons of other feature maps. But traditional convolutional/pooling kernels only capture the context information in a local scale. To leverage richer context information, graphical models are integrated with FCNs [12, 13, 16]. Graphical models build dense connections between feature maps, allowing neurons to be more sensitive to the global image content that is critical for learning good segmentation features. Note that previous works use one-way connections that extract context information from the feature maps separately, which is eventually combined. Thus, the learned features at a given scale are not given the opportunity to optimally account for the multi-scale context information from all of the other scales.

In contrast to previous methods, our bidirectional connections exchange multi-scale context information to improve the learning of all features. We employ super-pixels computed based on the image structure, and use the relationship between them to define the exchange routes between neurons in different feature maps. This enables more adaptive context information propagation.

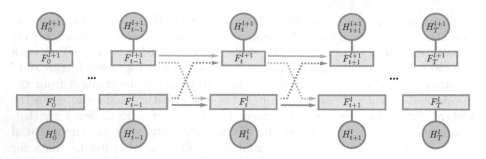

Fig. 2. Multi-scale context intertwining between two successive feature maps in the deep hierarchy. The green arrows propagate the context information from the lower-resolution feature map to the higher-resolution one. Conversely, the blue arrows forward information from the higher-resolution feature map to augment the lower-resolution one. The orange circle in each stage indicates the hidden features output by LSTMs, including the cell states and gates. (Color figure online)

Several previous works [31–33, 36] also use super-pixels to define the feature connections. And information exchange has been studied in [37, 38] for object detection. But these works do not exchange the information between feature maps of different resolutions, which is critical for semantic segmentation.

3   Multi-scale Context Intertwining

To utilize multi-scale context information, the common networks use one-way connections to combine feature maps of different resolution, following the top-down order of the network hierarchy (see Fig. 1(a) and (b)). Here, we present a multi-scale context intertwining (MSCI) architecture, where the context information can be propagated along different dimensions. The first dimension is along the vertical deep hierarchy (see Fig. 1(c)): our context intertwining scheme has connections to exchange the multi-scale context information between the adjacent feature maps. The connection is bidirectional with two different long short-term memory (LSTM) chains [22] that intertwines feature maps of different resolution in a sequence of stages. By training the LSTM units, the bidirectional connections learn to produce more powerful feature maps. The second dimension is along the horizontal hierarchy: the feature maps produced by our bidirectional connections are fed to the next phase of context intertwining, which can encode the context information memorized by our bidirectional connections into the new feature maps.

The overall MSCI architecture is illustrated in Fig. 1(c). Initially, we use the backbone FCN to compute a set $\{F^l\}$ convolutional feature maps of different resolutions, where $l = 1, ..., L$ and F^1 has the highest resolution. Figure 2 provides a more detailed view of context intertwining between two successive feature maps F^l and F^{l+1}. To exchange the context information between F^l and F^{l+1},

---

Algorithm 1. Multi-Scale Context Intertwining

1: **Input:**
   1) the number of stages T for each phase of the context intertwining;
   2) a set of convolutional feature maps $F = \{F^l\}$, where $l = 1, ..., L$;
   3) the trained parameter set $\{(P^{l \rightarrow l+1}, P^{l+1 \rightarrow l})\}$.
2: **Initialization:**
   1) a total K phases for the context intertwining, where $K = L - 1$;
   2) a set $Q = \{Q_k\}$, where $Q_0 = \{Q_0^l | Q_0^l = F^l\}$; and $Q_k = \emptyset, k = 1, ..., K$;
   3) a set of cell states $\{(C^{l \rightarrow l+1}, C^{l+1 \rightarrow l})\}$, where $C^{l \rightarrow l+1}, C^{l+1 \rightarrow l} = 0$.
3: **for** $k = 1 \rightarrow K$ **do**
4:     **for** $l = 1 \rightarrow |Q_{k-1}| - 1$ **do**
5:         $\{Q_k^l, C_T^{l \rightarrow l+1}, C_T^{l+1 \rightarrow l}\} = \mathcal{L}(Q_{k-1}^l, Q_{k-1}^{l+1}, C^{l \rightarrow l+1}, C^{l+1 \rightarrow l}, P^{l \rightarrow l+1}, P^{l+1 \rightarrow l}, T)$
6:         $Q_k = Q_k \cup \{Q_k^l\}, (C^{l \rightarrow l+1}, C^{l+1 \rightarrow l}) = (C_T^{l \rightarrow l+1}, C_T^{l+1 \rightarrow l})$
7:     **end for**
8: **end for**
9: **Output:** the segmentation feature map Q_K^1.

---

we construct a bidirectional connection $\mathcal{L}$:

$$\{Q^l, C_T^{l \rightarrow l+1}, C_T^{l+1 \rightarrow l}\} = \mathcal{L}(F^l, F^{l+1}, C^{l \rightarrow l+1}, C^{l+1 \rightarrow l}, P^{l \rightarrow l+1}, P^{l+1 \rightarrow l}, T). \quad (1)$$

The bidirectional connection $\mathcal{L}$ consists of two different LSTM chains. One chain has the parameter set $P^{l \rightarrow l+1}$. It extracts the context information from F^l and passes it to F^{l+1}. The other chain has the parameter set $P^{l+1 \rightarrow l}$ and passes context information from F^{l+1} to F^l. $C^{l \rightarrow l+1}$ and $C^{l+1 \rightarrow l}$ are the cell states of the two LSTMs, and they are initialized to zeros in the very beginning. As shown in Fig. 2, the information exchange takes place over T stages. At each stage t, information is exchanged between the feature maps F_t^l and F_t^{l+1}, yielding the maps F_{t+1}^l and F_{t+1}^{l+1}. Note that the resulting feature map F_T^l has higher resolution than F_T^{l+1}. Thus, we deconvolve the feature map F_T^{l+1} with the kernel D_f^{l+1} and add it to F_T^l to obtain a combined high-resolution feature map Q^l:

$$Q^l = F_T^l + D_f^{l+1} * F_T^{l+1}. \quad (2)$$

Note that the feature map Q^l and the cell states $C_T^{l \rightarrow l+1}$ and $C_T^{l+1 \rightarrow l}$ can be further employed to drive the next phase of context intertwining (the next level of the horizontal hierarchy). Along the LSTM chains, the feature maps contain neurons with larger receptive fields, i.e., with richer global context. Besides, the cell states of LSTMs can memorize the context information exchanged at different stages. Due to the shortcut design of the cell states [22], the local context from the early stages can be easily propagated to the last stage, encoding the multi-scale context including the local and global information to the final feature map.

The entire MSCI process is summarized in Algorithm 1. We assume the MSCI process has K phases totally. Each phase of Algorithm 1 produces new feature maps. As each pair of feature maps is intertwined, the corresponding cell states

$(C^{l \to l+1}, C^{l+1 \to l})$ are iteratively updated to provide the memorized context to assist the information exchange in the next phase. Finally, the output is the high-resolution feature map Q_K^1 that is fed to the pixel-wise classifier for segmentation. Algorithm 1 describes the feed-forward pass through the LSTMs. We remark that the LSTM parameters are reusable, and the LSTMs are trained using the standard stochastic gradient descent (SGD) algorithm with back-propagation. Below, we focus on a single context intertwining phase, and thus omit the subscript k to simplify notation.

4   Bidirectional Connection

In this section, we describe in more detail the bidirectional connections that enable mutual exchange of context information between low- and high-resolution feature maps. Our bidirectional connections are guided by the super-pixel structure of the original image, as illustrated in Fig. 3. Given an input image I, we divide it into non-overlapping super-pixels, which correspond to a set of regions $\{S_n\}$. Let F_t^l and F_t^{l+1} denote two adjacent resolution feature maps in our network, where l is the resolution level and t is the LSTM stage. The context information exchange between F_t^l and F_t^{l+1} is conducted using the regions defined by the super-pixels. Informally, at each of the two levels, for each region S_n we first aggregate the neurons whose receptive fields are centered inside S_n. Next, we sum together the aggregated features of S_n and all of its neighboring regions at one level and pass the resulting context information to the neurons of the other level that reside in region S_n. This is done in both directions, as shown in Fig. 3(a) and (b). Thus, we enrich the locally aggregated context information of each neuron with that of its counterpart in the other level, as well as with the more global context aggregated from the surrounding regions. Our results show that this significantly improves segmentation accuracy.

Formally, given the feature map F_t^l and a region S_n, we first aggregate the neurons in S_n, yielding a regional context feature $R_{n,t}^l \in \mathbb{R}^C$:

$$R_{n,t}^l = \sum_{(h,w) \in \Phi(S_n)} F_t^l(h, w), \tag{3}$$

where $\Phi(S_n)$ denotes the set of centers of the receptive fields inside the region S_n. Next, we define a more global context feature $M_{n,t}^l$, by aggregating the regional features of S_n and of its adjacent regions $\mathcal{N}(S_n)$:

$$M_{n,t}^l = \sum_{S_m \in \mathcal{N}(S_n)} R_{m,t}^l. \tag{4}$$

The above features are propagated bidirectionally between F_t^l and F_t^{l+1} using a pair of LSTM chains, as illustrated in Fig. 2. In the tth stage, an LSTM unit generates a new feature F_{t+1}^{l+1} from F_t^{l+1}, $R_{n,t}^l$, and $M_{n,t}^l$, as follows:

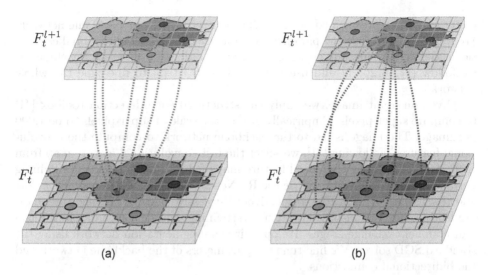

Fig. 3. Bidirectional context aggregation. The features are partitioned into different regions defined by super-pixels. We aggregate the neurons resided in the same region, and pass the information of the adjacent regions along the bidirectional connection (a) from a low-resolution feature to a high-resolution feature; and (b) from a high-resolution feature to a low-resolution feature.

$$G_{i,t}^{l \rightarrow l+1}(h,w) = \sigma(W_i^{l+1} * F_t^{l+1}(h,w) + W_{s,i}^l * R_{n,t}^l + W_{a,i}^l * M_{n,t}^l + b_i^{l+1}),$$

$$G_{f,t}^{l \rightarrow l+1}(h,w) = \sigma(W_f^{l+1} * F_t^{l+1}(h,w) + W_{s,f}^l * R_{n,t}^l + W_{a,f}^l * M_{n,t}^l + b_f^{l+1}),$$

$$G_{o,t}^{l \rightarrow l+1}(h,w) = \sigma(W_o^{l+1} * F_t^{l+1}(h,w) + W_{s,o}^l * R_{n,t}^l + W_{a,o}^l * M_{n,t}^l + b_o^{l+1}),$$

$$G_{c,t}^{l \rightarrow l+1}(h,w) = \tanh(W_c^{l+1} * F_t^{l+1}(h,w) + W_{s,c}^l * R_{n,t}^l + W_{a,c}^l * M_{n,t}^l + b_c^{l+1}),$$

$$C_{t+1}^{l \rightarrow l+1}(h,w) = G_{f,t}^{l \rightarrow l+1}(h,w) \odot C_t^{l \rightarrow l+1}(h,w) + G_{i,t}^{l \rightarrow l+1}(h,w) \odot G_{c,t}^{l \rightarrow l+1}(h,w),$$

$$A_{t+1}^{l \rightarrow l+1}(h,w) = \tanh(G_{o,t}^{l \rightarrow l+1}(h,w) \odot C_{t+1}^{l \rightarrow l+1}(h,w)),$$

$$F_{t+1}^{l+1}(h,w) = F_t^{l+1}(h,w) + A_{t+1}^{l \rightarrow l+1}(h,w), \tag{5}$$

where $(h,w) \in \Phi(S_n)$. W and b are convolutional kernels and biases. In Eq. (5), convolutions are denoted by $*$, while $\odot$ denotes the Hadamard product. Respectively, G and C represents the gate and cell state of an LSTM unit. $A_{t+1}^{l \rightarrow l+1}$ is the augmentation feature for F_t^{l+1}, and they have equal resolution. We add the augmentation feature $A_{t+1}^{l \rightarrow l+1}$ with F_t^{l+1}, producing the new feature F_{t+1}^{l+1} for the next stage. The sequence of features F_t^l is defined in the same way as above (with the l superscripts replaced by $l+1$, and vice versa).

5   Implementation Details

We use the Caffe platform [39] to implement our approach. Our approach can be based on different deep architectures [29,30,40], and we use the ResNet-152 architecture [30] pre-trained on ImageNet dataset [10] as our backbone network. We randomly initialize the parameters of our LSTM-based bidirectional connections. Before training our network for the evaluations on different benchmarks, we follow [17,18,20,25] and use the COCO dataset [2] to fine-tune the whole network.

Given an input image, we apply the structured edge detection toolbox [41] to compute super-pixels. Empirically, we set the scale of super-pixels to be 1,000 per image. The image is fed to the backbone network to compute the convolutional features. Following [31], we select the last convolutional feature map from each residual block as the initial feature maps fed into our context intertwining network. More specifically, we use the ResNet-152 network layers *res2*, *res3*, *res4* and *res5* as $\{F_0^1, F_0^2, F_0^3, F_0^4\}$, respectively. Successive pairs of these feature maps are fed into our LSTM-based context intertwining modules, each of which has 3 bidirectional exchange stages. We optimize the segmentation network using the standard SGD solver. We fine-tune the parameters of the backbone network and the bidirectional connections.

During training, we use the common flipping, cropping, scaling and rotating of the image to augment the training data. The network is fine-tuned with a learning rate of 1e−3 for 60K mini-batches. After that, we decay the learning rate to 1e−4 for the next 60K mini-batches. The size of each mini-batch is set to 12. With the trained model, we perform multi-scale testing on each image to obtain the segmentation result. That is, we rescale each testing image using five factors (i.e., $\{0.4, 0.6, 0.8, 1.0, 1.2\}$) and feed the differently scaled versions into the network to obtain predictions. The predictions are averaged to yield the final result.

6   Experiments

We evaluate our approach on four public benchmarks for semantic segmentation, which are PASCAL VOC 2012 [1], PASCAL-Context [3], NYUDv2 [23] and SUN-RGBD [24] datasets. The PASCAL VOC 2012 dataset [1] has been widely used for evaluating segmentation performance. It contains 10,582 training images along with the pixel-wise annotations for 20 object classes and the background. The PASCAL VOC 2012 dataset also provides a validation set of 1,449 images and a test set of 1,456 images. We use this dataset for the major evaluation of our network. We further use the PASCAL-Context, NYUDv2 and SUN-RGBD datasets for extensive comparisons with state-of-the-art methods. We report all the segmentation scores in terms of mean Intersection-over-Union (IoU).

Ablation Study of MSCI. Our MSCI architecture is designed to enable exchange of multi-scale context information between feature maps. It consists of recurrent bidirectional connections defined using super-pixels. Below, we report an ablation study of our approach, which examines the effect that removing various key components has on segmentation performance. The results are summarized in Table 1.

Our approach is based on LSTMs, each of which can be regarded as a special recurrent neural network (RNN) unit with a cell state for memorization. By removing the RNNs and the cell states, we effectively disable the bidirectional connection between feature maps. In this case, our model degrades to a basic FCN, and obtains the segmentation score of 77.8 that lags far behind our full MSCI model.

Table 1. Ablation experiments on the PASCAL VOC 2012 validation set. Segmentation accuracy is reported in terms of mean IoU (%).

RNN	Cell states	Super-pixels	Mean IoU
			77.8
✓		✓	84.4
✓	✓		84.3
✓	✓	✓	**85.1**

Table 2. Comparison of different feature combination strategies. Performance is evaluated on the PASCAL VOC 2012 and PASCAL-Context validation sets. Segmentation accuracy is reported in terms of mean IoU (%).

Strategy	Method	VOC 2012	CONTEXT
w/o combination	basic FCN [9]	77.8	41.2
w/o hierarchy	SPP [18]	81.1	43.6
	Encoder-Decoder [17]	81.4	44.3
	ASPP [20]	82.2	46.0
	Encoder-Decoder + ASPP [25]	82.5	47.4
w/hierarchy	MSCI	**85.1**	**50.3**

Next, we investigate the importance of the cell states. The cell states are employed by our approach to memorize the local and global context information, which enriches the final segmentation feature map. With all the cell states removed from our bidirectional connections, our approach achieves an accuracy of 84.4%, which is significantly lower than the 85.1% accuracy of our full approach.

In our approach, the super-pixels adaptively partition the features into different regions according to the image structure, which are then used for context aggregation and exchange (Fig. 3). We remove the super-pixels and interpolate the low-resolution feature maps [17,18] to match with the high-resolution maps. Thus, each neuron aggregates context from a local regular window. Compared to our full model, the performance drops to 84.3%, demonstrating the effectiveness of using super-pixels to guide context aggregation.

Feature Combination Strategies. Our approach combines in a hierarchical manner the features produced by the bidirectional connections. In Table 2, we compare our feature combination strategy to those of other networks [9,17,18,20,25]. For a fair comparison, we reproduce the compared networks by pre-training them with the ResNet-152 backbone model on the ImageNet dataset, and fine-tuning them on the COCO dataset and the PASCAL VOC 2012 training set. Without any combination of features, the backbone network FCN model achieves the score of 77.8%. Next, we compare our network to the SPP network [9,18,20] and Encoder-Decoder [17,19,21,25,35] network. For the SPP network, we chose a state-of-the-art model proposed in [18] for comparison. The ASPP network [20] is a variant of the SPP network, and it can achieve better results than the SPP network. For the Encoder-Decoder network, we select the model proposed in [17] for comparison here. We also compare our network with the latest Encoder-Decoder network with ASPP components [25]. These models combine the adjacent features that are learned with our bidirectional connections, which generally leads to 0.4–1.2 improvement in the segmentation scores, compared to the counterparts without bidirectional connections. We find that our approach performs better than other methods. In Fig. 4, we can also observe that MSCI provides better visual results than other methods.

Table 3. Comparisons with other state-of-the-art methods. The performances are evaluated on the PASCAL VOC 2012 validation set (left) and test set (right). Segmentation accuracy is reported in terms of mean IoU (%).

Val set		Test set	
Method	Mean IoU	Method	Mean IoU
Chen et al. [9]	77.6	Wang et al. [42]	83.1
Sun et al. [43]	80.6	Peng et al. [19]	83.6
Wu et al. [44]	80.8	Lin et al. [17]	84.2
Shen et al. [45]	80.9	Wu et al. [44]	84.9
Peng et al. [19]	81.0	Zhao et al. [18]	85.4
Zhao et al. [18]	81.4	Wang et al. [46]	86.3
Lin et al. [17]	82.7	Fu et al. [47]	86.6
Chen et al. [20]	82.7	Luo et al. [48]	86.8
Chen et al. [25]	84.6	Chen et al. [20]	86.9
Fu et al. [47]	84.8	Chen et al. [25]	**89.0**
MSCI	**85.1**	MSCI	88.0

Comparisons with State-of-the-Art Methods. In Table 3, we report the results of our approach on the PASCAL VOC 2012 validation set and test set, and compare with state-of-the-art methods. On the validation set (see Table 3(left)), MSCI achieves a better result than all of other methods. Specifically, given the same set of training images, it outperforms the models proposed

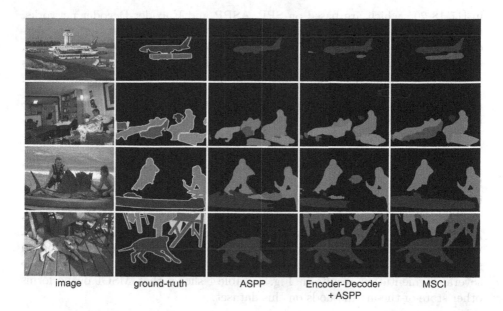

Fig. 4. The segmentation results of the ASPP model [20], Encoder-Decoder with ASPP model [25] and our MSCI. The images are taken from the PASCAL VOC 2012 validation set.

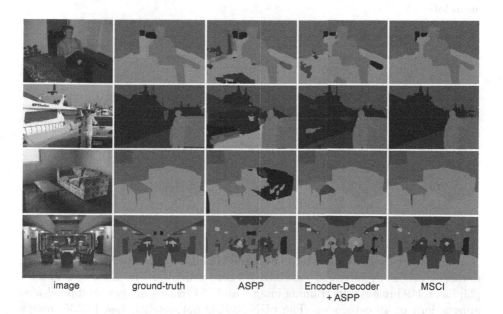

Fig. 5. The segmentation results of the ASPP model [20], Encoder-Decoder with ASPP model [25] and our MSCI. The images are scenes taken from the PASCAL-Context validation set.

in [17,18,20], which are based on SPP, ASPP and Encoder-Decoder networks, respectively. In addition, we also report our result on the test set. Our per-category results on the test set can be found on PASCAL VOC leaderboard[1]. Our result of 88.0% is second only to the score reported in [25], which leverages a stronger backbone network, trained on an internal JFT-300M dataset [26–28].

Experiments on Scene Labeling Datasets. We perform additional experiments on three scene labeling datasets, including the PASCAL-Context [3], NYUDv2 [23], and SUN-RGBD [24]. In contrast to the object-centric PASCAL VOC 2012 dataset, these scene labeling datasets provide more complex pixel-wise annotations for objects and stuff, which require segmentation networks to have a full reasoning about the scene in an image. We use these datasets to verify if our network can label the scene images well.

The PASCAL-Context dataset [3] contains 59 categories and background, providing 4,998 images for training and 5,105 images for validation. In Table 2, we already used this dataset to compare MSCI to other feature combination strategies, and found that it works well on the scene labeling task. We provide several segmentation results in Fig. 5. Table 4 shows that MSCI outperforms other state-of-the-art methods on this dataset.

Table 4. Comparison with other state-of-the-art methods. Performance is evaluated on the PASCAL-Context validation set (left), NYUDv2 validation set (middle) and the SUN-RGBD validation set (right). Segmentation accuracy is reported in terms of mean IoU (%).

CONTEXT		NYUDv2		SUN-RGBD	
Method	mIoU	Method	mIoU	Method	mIoU
Dai et al. [49]	40.5	Long et al. [7]	34.0	Chen et al. [9]	27.4
Lin et al. [15]	42.0	Eigen et al. [50]	34.1	Kendall et al. [51]	30.7
Lin et al. [16]	43.3	He et al. [52]	40.1	Long et al. [7]	35.1
Wu et al. [53]	44.5	Lin et al. [16]	40.6	Hazirbas et al. [54]	37.8
Chen et al. [9]	45.7	Zhao et al. [18]	45.2	Lin et al. [16]	42.3
Lin et al. [17]	47.3	Lin et al. [17]	47.0	Lin et al. [17]	47.3
Wu et al. [44]	48.1	Lin et al. [55]	47.7	Lin et al. [55]	48.1
MSCI	**50.3**	MSCI	**49.0**	MSCI	**50.4**

We further evaluate our method on the NYUDv2 [23] and SUN-RGBD [24] datasets, originally intended for RGB-D scene labeling. The NYUDv2 dataset [23] has 1,449 images (795 training images and 654 testing images) and pixel-wise annotations of 40 categories. The SUN-RGBD dataset [24] has 10,335 images (5,285 training images and 5,050 testing images) and pixel-wise annotations of 37 categories. Unlike the PASCAL-Context dataset, the NYUDv2 and SUN-RGBD

---

[1] http://host.robots.ox.ac.uk:8080/anonymous/F58739.html.

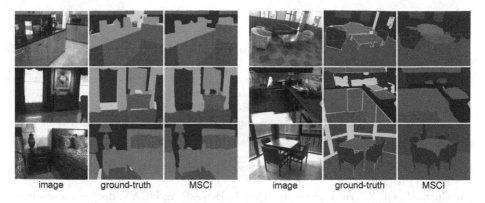

image   ground-truth   MSCI   image   ground-truth   MSCI

Fig. 6. MSCI segmentation results. The images are taken from the NYUDv2 validation set (left) and the SUN-RGBD validation set (right).

datasets consist of images of indoor scenes. We report the segmentation scores of MSCI and other state-of-the-art methods in Table 4. We note that the best previous method proposed in [55] uses the RGB and depth information jointly for segmentation, and achieves the scores of 47.7 and 48.1 on the NYUDv2 and SUN-RGBD validation sets, respectively. Even without the depth information, MSCI outperforms the previous best results. We show some of our segmentation results on the NYUDv2 and SUN-RGBD validation sets in Fig. 6.

7   Conclusions

Recent progress in semantic segmentation may be attributed to powerful deep convolutional features and the joint consideration of local and global context information. In this work, we have proposed a novel approach for connecting and combining feature maps and context from multiple scales. Our approach uses interconnected LSTM chains in order to effectively exchange information among feature maps corresponding to adjacent scales. The enriched maps are hierarchically combined to produce a high-resolution feature map for pixel-level semantic inference. We have demonstrated that our approach is effective and outperforms the state-of-the-art on several public benchmarks.

In the future, we plan to apply our MSCI approach to stronger backbone networks and more large-scale datasets for training. In addition, we aim to extend MSCI to other recognition tasks, such as object detection and 3D scene understanding.

Acknowledgments. We thank the anonymous reviewers for their constructive comments. This work was supported in part by NSFC (61702338, 61522213, 61761146002, 61861130365), 973 Program (2015CB352501), Guangdong Science and Technology Program (2015A030312015), Shenzhen Innovation Program (KQJSCX20170727101233642, JCYJ20151015151249564), and ISF-NSFC Joint Research Program (2472/17).

References

1. Everingham, M., Van Gool, L., Williams, C.K., Winn, J., Zisserman, A.: The Pascal visual object classes (VOC) challenge. IJCV **88**, 303–338 (2010)
2. Lin, T.-Y., Maire, M., Belongie, S., Hays, J., Perona, P., Ramanan, D., Dollár, P., Zitnick, C.L.: Microsoft COCO: common objects in context. In: Fleet, D., Pajdla, T., Schiele, B., Tuytelaars, T. (eds.) ECCV 2014. LNCS, vol. 8693, pp. 740–755. Springer, Cham (2014). https://doi.org/10.1007/978-3-319-10602-1_48
3. Mottaghi, R., et al.: The role of context for object detection and semantic segmentation in the wild. In: CVPR (2014)
4. Cordts, M., et al.: The Cityscapes dataset for semantic urban scene understanding. In: CVPR (2016)
5. Chen, H., Qi, X., Yu, L., Dou, Q., Qin, J., Heng, P.A.: DCAN: deep contour-aware networks for object instance segmentation from histology images. Med. Image Anal. **36**, 135–146 (2017)
6. Yoon, Y., Jeon, H.G., Yoo, D., Lee, J.Y., Kweon, I.S.: Light-field image super-resolution using convolutional neural network. IEEE Signal Process. Lett. **24**, 848–852 (2017)
7. Long, J., Shelhamer, E., Darrell, T.: Fully convolutional networks for semantic segmentation. In: CVPR (2015)
8. Noh, H., Hong, S., Han, B.: Learning deconvolution network for semantic segmentation. In: ICCV (2015)
9. Chen, L.C., Papandreou, G., Kokkinos, I., Murphy, K., Yuille, A.L.: DeepLab: semantic image segmentation with deep convolutional nets, atrous convolution, and fully connected CRFs. arXiv (2016)
10. Deng, J., Dong, W., Socher, R., Li, L.J., Li, K., Fei-Fei, L.: ImageNet: a large-scale hierarchical image database. In: CVPR (2009)
11. Hariharan, B., Arbeláez, P., Girshick, R., Malik, J.: Hypercolumns for object segmentation and fine-grained localization. In: CVPR (2015)
12. Zheng, S., et al.: Conditional random fields as recurrent neural networks. In: ICCV (2015)
13. Liu, Z., Li, X., Luo, P., Loy, C.C., Tang, X.: Semantic image segmentation via deep parsing network. In: ICCV (2015)
14. Papandreou, G., Chen, L.C., Murphy, K., Yuille, A.L.: Weakly-and semi-supervised learning of a DCNN for semantic image segmentation. arXiv preprint arXiv:1502.02734 (2015)
15. Lin, D., Dai, J., Jia, J., He, K., Sun, J.: ScribbleSup: scribble-supervised convolutional networks for semantic segmentation. In: CVPR (2016)
16. Lin, G., Shen, C., van den Hengel, A., Reid, I.: Efficient piecewise training of deep structured models for semantic segmentation. In: CVPR (2016)
17. Lin, G., Milan, A., Shen, C., Reid, I.: RefineNet: multi-path refinement networks with identity mappings for high-resolution semantic segmentation. arXiv (2016)
18. Zhao, H., Shi, J., Qi, X., Wang, X., Jia, J.: Pyramid scene parsing network. arXiv (2016)
19. Peng, C., Zhang, X., Yu, G., Luo, G., Sun, J.: Large kernel matters-improve semantic segmentation by global convolutional network. arXiv (2017)
20. Chen, L.C., Papandreou, G., Schroff, F., Adam, H.: Rethinking atrous convolution for semantic image segmentation. arXiv (2017)
21. Pohlen, T., Hermans, A., Mathias, M., Leibe, B.: Full-resolution residual networks for semantic segmentation in street scenes. In: CVPR (2017)

22. Hochreiter, S., Schmidhuber, J.: Long short-term memory. Neural Comput. **9**, 1735–1780 (1997)
23. Silberman, N., Hoiem, D., Kohli, P., Fergus, R.: Indoor segmentation and support inference from RGBD images. In: Fitzgibbon, A., Lazebnik, S., Perona, P., Sato, Y., Schmid, C. (eds.) ECCV 2012. LNCS, vol. 7576, pp. 746–760. Springer, Heidelberg (2012). https://doi.org/10.1007/978-3-642-33715-4_54
24. Song, S., Lichtenberg, S.P., Xiao, J.: SUN RGB-D: a RGB-D scene understanding benchmark suite. In: CVPR (2015)
25. Chen, L.C., Zhu, Y., Papandreou, G., Schroff, F., Adam, H.: Encoder-decoder with atrous separable convolution for semantic image segmentation. arXiv preprint arXiv:1802.02611 (2018)
26. Hinton, G., Vinyals, O., Dean, J.: Distilling the knowledge in a neural network. In: NIPS (2014)
27. Chollet, F.: Xception: deep learning with depthwise separable convolutions. In: CVPR (2017)
28. Sun, C., Shrivastava, A., Singh, S., Gupta, A.: Revisiting unreasonable effectiveness of data in deep learning era. In: ICCV (2017)
29. Krizhevsky, A., Sutskever, I., Hinton, G.E.: ImageNet classification with deep convolutional neural networks. In: NIPS (2012)
30. He, K., Zhang, X., Ren, S., Sun, J.: Deep residual learning for image recognition. In: CVPR (2016)
31. Lin, T.Y., Dollár, P., Girshick, R., He, K., Hariharan, B., Belongie, S.: Feature pyramid networks for object detection. In: CVPR (2017)
32. Liang, X., Shen, X., Feng, J., Lin, L., Yan, S.: Semantic object parsing with graph LSTM. In: Leibe, B., Matas, J., Sebe, N., Welling, M. (eds.) ECCV 2016. LNCS, vol. 9905, pp. 125–143. Springer, Cham (2016). https://doi.org/10.1007/978-3-319-46448-0_8
33. Liang, X., Shen, X., Xiang, D., Feng, J., Lin, L., Yan, S.: Semantic object parsing with local-global long short-term memory. In: CVPR, pp. 3185–3193 (2016)
34. Lazebnik, S., Schmid, C., Ponce, J.: Beyond bags of features: spatial pyramid matching for recognizing natural scene categories. In: CVPR (2006)
35. Ronneberger, O., Fischer, P., Brox, T.: U-Net: convolutional networks for biomedical image segmentation. In: MICCAI (2015)
36. Gadde, R., Jampani, V., Kiefel, M., Kappler, D., Gehler, P.V.: Superpixel convolutional networks using bilateral inceptions. In: ECCV (2016)
37. Bell, S., Lawrence Zitnick, C., Bala, K., Girshick, R.: Inside-outside net: detecting objects in context with skip pooling and recurrent neural networks. In: CVPR (2016)
38. Zeng, X.: Crafting GBD-Net for object detection. PAMI **40**, 2109–2123 (2017)
39. Jia, Y., et al.: Caffe: convolutional architecture for fast feature embedding. In: ACM International Conference on Multimedia (2014)
40. Simonyan, K., Zisserman, A.: Very deep convolutional networks for large-scale image recognition. arXiv (2014)
41. Dollár, P., Zitnick, C.L.: Structured forests for fast edge detection. In: ICCV (2013)
42. Wang, P., et al.: Understanding convolution for semantic segmentation. arXiv preprint arXiv:1702.08502 (2017)
43. Sun, H., Xie, D., Pu, S.: Mixed context networks for semantic segmentation. arXiv preprint arXiv:1610.05854 (2016)
44. Wu, Z., Shen, C., Hengel, A.v.d.: Wider or deeper: revisiting the ResNet model for visual recognition. arXiv preprint arXiv:1611.10080 (2016)

45. Shen, F., Gan, R., Yan, S., Zeng, G.: Semantic segmentation via structured patch prediction, context CRF and guidance CRF. In: CVPR (2017)
46. Wang, G., Luo, P., Lin, L., Wang, X.: Learning object interactions and descriptions for semantic image segmentation. In: CVPR (2017)
47. Fu, J., Liu, J., Wang, Y., Lu, H.: Stacked deconvolutional network for semantic segmentation. arXiv preprint arXiv:1708.04943 (2017)
48. Luo, P., Wang, G., Lin, L., Wang, X.: Deep dual learning for semantic image segmentation. In: CVPR (2017)
49. Dai, J., He, K., Sun, J.: BoxSup: exploiting bounding boxes to supervise convolutional networks for semantic segmentation. In: ICCV (2015)
50. Eigen, D., Fergus, R.: Predicting depth, surface normals and semantic labels with a common multi-scale convolutional architecture. In: ICCV (2015)
51. Kendall, A., Badrinarayanan, V., Cipolla, R.: Bayesian SegNet: model uncertainty in deep convolutional encoder-decoder architectures for scene understanding. arXiv (2015)
52. He, Y., Chiu, W.C., Keuper, M., Fritz, M.: RGBD semantic segmentation using spatio-temporal data-driven pooling. arXiv (2016)
53. Wu, Z., Shen, C., Hengel, A.V.D.: High-performance semantic segmentation using very deep fully convolutional networks. arXiv preprint arXiv:1604.04339 (2016)
54. Hazirbas, C., Ma, L., Domokos, C., Cremers, D.: FuseNet: incorporating depth into semantic segmentation via fusion-based CNN architecture. In: ACCV (2016)
55. Lin, D., Chen, G., Cohen-Or, D., Heng, P.A., Huang, H.: Cascaded feature network for semantic segmentation of RGB-D images. In: ICCV (2017)

Second-Order Democratic Aggregation

Tsung-Yu Lin[1(✉)], Subhransu Maji[1], and Piotr Koniusz[2]

[1] College of Information and Computer Sciences,
University of Massachusetts Amherst, Amherst, USA
{tsungyulin,smaji}@cs.umass.edu
[2] Data61/CSIRO, Australian National University, Canberra, Australia
piotr.koniusz@data61.csiro.au

Abstract. Aggregated second-order features extracted from deep convolutional networks have been shown to be effective for texture generation, fine-grained recognition, material classification, and scene understanding. In this paper, we study a class of orderless aggregation functions designed to minimize *interference* or equalize *contributions* in the context of second-order features and we show that they can be computed just as efficiently as their first-order counterparts and they have favorable properties over aggregation by summation. Another line of work has shown that matrix power normalization after aggregation can significantly improve the generalization of second-order representations. We show that matrix power normalization implicitly equalizes contributions during aggregation thus establishing a connection between matrix normalization techniques and prior work on minimizing interference. Based on the analysis we present γ-democratic aggregators that interpolate between sum ($\gamma = 1$) and democratic pooling ($\gamma = 0$) outperforming both on several classification tasks. Moreover, unlike power normalization, the γ-democratic aggregations can be computed in a low dimensional space by sketching that allows the use of very high-dimensional second-order features. This results in a state-of-the-art performance on several datasets.

Keywords: Second-order features · Democratic pooling
Matrix power normalization · Tensor sketching

1 Introduction

Second-order statistics have been demonstrated to improve performance of classification on images of objects, scenes and textures as well as fine-grained problems, action classification and tracking [6,15,25,30,33,34,44,52]. In the simplest form, such statistics are obtained by taking the outer product of some feature vectors and aggregating them over some region of interest which results in an autocorrelation [6,24] or covariance matrix [52]. Such a second-order image descriptor

Electronic supplementary material The online version of this chapter (https://doi.org/10.1007/978-3-030-01219-9_38) contains supplementary material, which is available to authorized users.

© Springer Nature Switzerland AG 2018
V. Ferrari et al. (Eds.): ECCV 2018, LNCS 11207, pp. 639–656, 2018.
https://doi.org/10.1007/978-3-030-01219-9_38

is then passed as a feature to train a SVM, *etc.* Several recent works obtained an increase in accuracy after switching from the first- to second-order statistics [24–26,28,32–34,59]. Further improvements were obtained by considering the impact of spectrum of such statistics on aggregation into the final representations [24–26,28,31,33,37]. For instance, analysis conducted in [24,25] concluded that decorrelating feature vectors from an image via the matrix power normalization has a positive impact on classification due to the signal whitening properties which prevent so-called *bursts* of features [19]. However, evaluating the power of matrix is a costly procedure with complexity $\mathcal{O}(d^\omega)$, where $2 < \omega < 2.376$ concerns the complexity of SVD. In recent CNN approaches [28,31,33] which perform end-to-end learning, the complexity becomes a prohibitive factor for typical $d \geq 1024$ due to a costly backpropagation step which involves SVD or solving a Lyapunov equation [33] in every iteration of the CNN fine-tuning process; thus adding several hours of computations to training. However, another line of aggregation mechanisms aim to reweight the first-order feature vectors prior to their aggregation [37] in order to balance their contributions to the final image descriptor. Such a reweighting scheme, called a democratic aggregation [21,37], is solved very efficiently by a modified Sinkhorn algorithm [23].

In this paper, we study democratic aggregation in the context of second-order feature descriptors and show that this feature descriptor has favorable properties when combined with the democratic aggregator which was applied originally to the first-order descriptors. We take a closer look at the relation between the reweighted representations and the matrix power normalization in terms of the variance of feature contributions. In addition, we propose a γ-democratic aggregation scheme which generalizes democratic aggregation and allows to interpolate between sum pooling and democratic pooling. We show that our formulation can be solved via the Sinkhorn algorithm as efficiently as approach [37] while resulting in a performance comparable to the matrix power normalization. Computationally, our approach involves Sinkhorn iterations, which requires matrix-vector multiplications, and is faster by an order of magnitude even when compared to approximate matrix power normalization via the Newton's method, which involves matrix-matrix operations [33]. Unlike the power matrix normalization, our γ-democratic aggregation can be performed via sketching [12,42] enabling the use of high-dimensional feature vectors.

To summarize, our contributions are: (i) we propose a new second-order γ-democratic aggregation, (ii) we obtain reweighting factors via the Sinkhorn algorithm which enjoys an order of magnitude speedup over the fast matrix power normalization via Newton's iterations while it achieves comparable results, (iii) we provide theoretical bounds on feature contributions in relation to the matrix power normalization, (iv) we present state-of-the-art results on several datasets by applying democratic aggregation of second-order representations with sketching.

2   Related Work

Mechanisms of aggregating first- and second-order features have been extensively studied in the context of image retrieval, texture and object recognition [6,20, 25,38,40,41,44,47,53]. In what follows, we first describe shallow approaches and non-Euclidean aggregation schemes followed by the CNN-based approaches.

Shallow Approaches. Early approaches to aggregating second-order statistics include Region Covariance Descriptors [44,53], Fisher Vector Encoding [40,41,47] and Vector of Locally Aggregated Tensors [38], to name but a few of approaches.

Region Covariance Descriptors capture co-occurrences of luminance, first- and second-order partial derivatives of images [44,53] and, in some cases, even binary patterns [46]. The main principle of these approaches is to aggregate the co-occurrences of some feature vectors into a matrix which represents an image.

Fisher Vector Encoding [40] precomputes a visual vocabulary by clustering over a set of feature vectors and captures the element-wise squared difference between each feature vector and its nearest cluster center. Subsequently, the re-normalization of the captured statistics with respect to the cluster variance and the sum aggregation are performed. Furthermore, extension [41] proposes to apply the element-wise square root to the aggregated statistics which improves the classification results. Vector of Locally Aggregated Tensors extends Fisher Vector Encoding to second-order off-diagonal feature interactions.

Non-Euclidean Distances. To take the full advantage of statistics captured by the scatter matrices, several works employ non-Euclidean distances. For positive definite matrices, geodesic distances (or their approximations) known from the Riemannian geometry are used [2,3,39]. Power-Euclidean distance [11] extends to semidefinite positive matrices. Distances such as Affine-Invariant Riemannian Metric [3,39], KL-Divergence Metric [55], Jensen-Bregman LogDet Divergence [7] and Log-Euclidean distance [2] are frequently used for comparing scatter matrices resulting from aggregation of second-order statistics. However, the above distances are notoriously difficult to backpropagate through for end-to-end learning and often computationally prohibitive [27].

Pooling Normalizations. Both first- and second-order aggregation methods often employ normalizations of pooled feature vectors. The early works on image retrieval apply the square root [19] to aggregated feature vectors to limit the impact of frequently occurring features and boost the impact of infrequent and highly informative ones (so-called notion of feature *bursts*). The roots of this approach in computer vision can be traced back to so-called generalized histogram of intersection kernel [5]. For second-order approaches, similar strategy is used by Fisher Vector Encoding [41]. The notion of *bursts* is further studied in the context of Bags-of-Words approach as well scatter matrices and tensors for which their spectra are power normalized [24–26] (so-called Eigenvalue Power Normalization or EPN for short). However, the square complexity of scatter matrices w.r.t. length of feature vectors deems them somewhat impractical in classification. A recent study [21,37] shows how to exploit second-order image-wise statistics and reweight sets of feature vectors per image at the aggregation time to obtain an informative first-order representation. So-called Democratic Aggregation (DA) and Generalized Max-Pooling (GMP) strategies are proposed whose goal is to reweight feature vectors per image prior to the sum aggregation so that interference between frequent and infrequent feature vectors is minimized. Strategies such as EPN (Matrix Power Normalization, MPN for short, is a special case of EPN), DA and GMP can be seen as ways of equalizing contributions of feature vectors into the final image descriptor and they are closely related to Zero-phase Component Analysis (ZCA) whose role is to whiten the signal representation.

Pooling and Aggregation in CNNs. The early image retrieval and recognition CNN-based approaches aggregate first-order statistics extracted from the CNN maps *e.g.*, [1,14,57]. In [14], multiple feture vectors are aggregated over multiple image regions. In [57], feature vectors are aggregated for retrieval. In [1], so-called VLAD descriptor is extended to allow end-to-end training.

More recent approaches form co-occurrence patterns from CNN feature vectors similar in spirit to Region Covariance Descriptors. In [34], the authors combine two CNN streams of feature vectors via outer product and demonstrate that such a setup is robust for the task of the fine-grained image recognition. A recent approach [49] extracts feature vectors at two separate locations in feature maps and performs an outer product to form a CNN co-occurrence layer.

Furthermore, a number of recent approaches are dedicated to performing backpropagation on the spectrum-normalized scatter matrices [17,18,28,31,33]. In [18], the authors employ the backpropagation via the SVD of matrix to implement the Log-Euclidean distance in end-to-end fashion. In [31], the authors extend Eigenvalue Power Normalization [25] to an end-to-end learning scenario which also requires to backpropagate via the SVD of matrix. Concurrently, approach [33] suggests to perform Matrix Power Normalization via the Newton's method and backpropagate w.r.t. the square root of matrix by solving a Lyapunov equation for greater numerical stability. An approach [58] phrases the matrix normalization as the problem of robust covariance estimation. Lastly, compact bilinear pooling [12] uses so-called tensor sketching [42]. Where indicated, we also make use of tensor sketching in our work.

There has been no connection made between reweighting feature vectors and its impact on the spectrum of the corresponding scatter matrix. Our work closely related to the approaches [21,37], however, introduce a mechanisms of limiting the interference in the context of second-order features. We demonstrate their superiority over the first-order inference approaches [21,37] and show that we can obtain results comparable to the matrix square root aggregation [33] with much lower computational complexity at the training and testing stages.

3   Method

Given a sequence of features $\mathcal{X} = (\mathbf{x}_1, \mathbf{x}_2, \ldots, \mathbf{x}_n)$, where $\mathbf{x}_i \in \mathbb{R}^d$, we are interested in a class of functions that compute an *orderless aggregation* of the sequence to obtain a global descriptor $\xi(\mathcal{X})$. If the descriptor is orderless, it implies that any permutation of features does not effect the global descriptor. A common approach is to encode each feature using a non-linear function $\phi(\mathbf{x})$ before aggregation via a simple symmetric function such as sum or max. For example, the global descriptor using sum pooling can be written as:

$$\xi(\mathcal{X}) = \sum_{\mathbf{x} \in \mathcal{X}} \phi(\mathbf{x}). \tag{1}$$

In this work, we investigate outer-product encoders, *i.e.* $\phi(\mathbf{x}) = \mathrm{vec}(\mathbf{x}\mathbf{x}^T)$, where $\mathbf{x}^T$ denotes the transpose and $\mathrm{vec}(\cdot)$ is the vectorization operator. Thus, if $\mathbf{x}$ is d dimensional then $\phi(\mathbf{x})$ is d^2 dimensional.

3.1   Democratic Aggregation

The democratic aggregation approach was proposed in [37] to minimize interference or equalize contributions of each element in the sequence. The contribution of a feature is measured as the similarity of the feature to the overall descriptor. In the case of sum pooling, the contribution $C(\mathbf{x})$ of a feature $\mathbf{x}$ is given by:

$$C(\mathbf{x}) = \phi(\mathbf{x})^T \sum_{\mathbf{x}' \in \mathcal{X}} \phi(\mathbf{x}'). \tag{2}$$

For sum pooling, the contributions $C(\mathbf{x})$ may not be equal for all features $\mathbf{x}$. In particular, the contribution is affected by both the norm and frequency of the feature. Democratic aggregation is a scheme that weights each feature by a scalar $\alpha(\mathbf{x})$ that depends on both $\mathbf{x}$ and the overall set of features in $\mathcal{X}$ such that the weighted aggregation $\xi(\mathcal{X})$ satisfies:

$$\alpha(\mathbf{x})\phi(\mathbf{x})^T \xi(\mathcal{X}) = \alpha(\mathbf{x})\phi(\mathbf{x})^T \sum_{\mathbf{x}' \in \mathcal{X}} \alpha(\mathbf{x}')\phi(\mathbf{x}') = C, \ \forall \mathbf{x} \in \mathcal{X}, \tag{3}$$

under the constraint that $\forall \mathbf{x} \in \mathcal{X}$, $\alpha(\mathbf{x}) > 0$. The above equation only depends on the dot product between the elements since:

$$\alpha(\mathbf{x}) \sum_{\mathbf{x}' \in \mathcal{X}} \alpha(\mathbf{x}')\phi(\mathbf{x})^T \phi(\mathbf{x}') = \alpha(\mathbf{x}) \sum_{\mathbf{x}' \in \mathcal{X}} \alpha(\mathbf{x}')k(\mathbf{x}, \mathbf{x}'), \tag{4}$$

where $k(\mathbf{x}, \mathbf{x}')$ denotes the dot product between the two vectors $\phi(\mathbf{x})$ and $\phi(\mathbf{x}')$. Following the notation in [37], if we denote $\mathbf{K}_{\mathcal{X}}$ to be the kernel matrix of the set $\mathcal{X}$, the above constraint is equivalent to finding a vector of weights $\boldsymbol{\alpha}$ such that:

$$\mathrm{diag}(\boldsymbol{\alpha})\mathbf{K}\mathrm{diag}(\boldsymbol{\alpha})\mathbf{1}_n = C\mathbf{1}_n, \tag{5}$$

Algorithm 1. Dampened Sinkhorn Algorithm

1: **procedure** SINKHORN($\mathbf{K}, \tau, \mathrm{T}$)
2:    $\boldsymbol{\alpha} \leftarrow \mathbf{1}_n$
3:    **for** $t = 1$ to T **do**
4:        $\boldsymbol{\sigma} = \text{diag}(\boldsymbol{\alpha})\mathbf{K}\text{diag}(\boldsymbol{\alpha})\mathbf{1}_n$
5:        $\boldsymbol{\alpha} \leftarrow \boldsymbol{\alpha}/\boldsymbol{\sigma}^\tau$
6:    **return** $\boldsymbol{\alpha}$

---

where diag is the diagonalization operator and $\mathbf{1}_n$ is an n dimensional vector of ones. In practice, the aggregated features $\xi(\mathcal{X})$ are ℓ_2 normalized hence the constant C does not matter and can be set to 1.

The authors [37] noted that the above equation can be efficiently solved by a dampened Sinkhorn algorithm [23]. The algorithm returns a unique solution as long as certain conditions are met, namely the entries in $\mathbf{K}$ are non-negative and the matrix is not fully decomposable. In practice, these conditions are not satisfied since the dot product between two features can be negative. A solution proposed in [37] is to compute $\boldsymbol{\alpha}$ by setting the negative entries in $\mathbf{K}$ to zero.

For completeness, the dampened Sinkhorn algorithm is included in Algorithm 1. Given n features of d dimensions, computing the kernel matrix takes $\mathcal{O}(n^2 d)$, whereas each Sinkhorn iteration takes $\mathcal{O}(n^2)$ time. In practice, 10 iterations are sufficient to find a good solution. The damping factor $\tau = 0.5$ is typically used. This slows the convergence rate but avoids oscillations and other numerical issues associated with the undampened version ($\tau = 1$).

γ-**Democratic Aggregation.** We propose a parametrized family of democratic aggregation functions that interpolate between sum pooling and fully democratic pooling. Given a parameter $0 \leq \gamma \leq 1$, the γ-democratic aggregation is obtained by solving for a vector of weights $\boldsymbol{\alpha}$ such that:

$$\text{diag}(\boldsymbol{\alpha})\mathbf{K}\text{diag}(\boldsymbol{\alpha})\mathbf{1}_n = (\mathbf{K}\mathbf{1}_n)^\gamma. \tag{6}$$

When $\gamma = 0$, this corresponds to the democratic aggregation, and when $\gamma = 1$, this corresponds to sum aggregation since $\boldsymbol{\alpha} = \mathbf{1}_n$ satisfies the above equation. The above equation can be solved by modifying the update rule for computing σ in the Sinkhorn iterations to:

$$\boldsymbol{\sigma} = \text{diag}(\boldsymbol{\alpha})\mathbf{K}\text{diag}(\boldsymbol{\alpha})\mathbf{1}_n/(\mathbf{K}\mathbf{1}_n)^\gamma, \tag{7}$$

in Algorithm 1, where/denotes element-wise division. Thus, the solution can be equally efficient for any value of γ. Intermediate values of γ allow the contributions $C(\mathbf{x})$ of each feature $\mathbf{x}$ within the set to vary and, in our experiments, we find this can lead to better results than the extremes (*i.e.*, $\gamma = 1$).

Second-Order Democratic Aggregation. In practice, features extracted using deep ConvNets can be high-dimensional. For example, an input image I is passed through layers of a ConvNet to obtain a feature map $\boldsymbol{\Phi}(I)$ of size

$W \times H \times D$. Here $d = D$ corresponds to the number of filters in the convolutional layer and $n = W \times H$ corresponds to the spatial resolution of the feature. For state-of-the-art ConvNets from which features are typically extracted, the values of n and d are comparable and in the range of a few hundred to a thousand. Thus, explicitly realizing the outer products can be expensive. Below we show several properties of democratic aggregation with outer-product encoders. Some of these properties allow aggregation in a computationally and memory efficient manner.

Proposition 1. *For outer-product encoders, the solution to the γ-democratic kernels exists for all values of γ as long as $\|\mathbf{x}\| > 0, \; \forall \mathbf{x} \in \mathcal{X}$.*

Proof. For the outer-product encoder we have:

$$k(\mathbf{x}, \mathbf{x}') = \phi(\mathbf{x})^T \phi(\mathbf{x}') = \mathrm{vec}(\mathbf{x}\mathbf{x}^T)^T \, \mathrm{vec}(\mathbf{x}'\mathbf{x}'^T) = (\mathbf{x}^T\mathbf{x}')^2 \geq 0.$$

Thus, all the entries of the kernel matrix are non-negative and the kernel matrix is strictly positive definite when $\|\mathbf{x}\| > 0, \; \forall \mathbf{x} \in \mathcal{X}$. This is a sufficient condition for the solution to exist [23]. Note that the kernel matrix of the outer product encoders is positive even when $\mathbf{x}^T\mathbf{x}' < 0$.

Proposition 2. *For outer-product encoders, the solution α to the γ-democratic kernels can be computed in $\mathcal{O}(n^2 d)$ time and $\mathcal{O}(n^2 + nd)$ space.*

Proof. The running time of the Sinkhorn algorithm is dominated by the time to compute the kernel matrix $\mathbf{K}$. Naively computing the kernel matrix for d^2 dimensional features would take $\mathcal{O}(n^2 d^2)$ time and $\mathcal{O}(n^2 + nd^2)$ space. However, since the kernel entries of the outer products are just the square of the kernel entries of the features before the encoding step, one can compute the kernel $\mathbf{K}$ by simply squaring the kernel of the raw features, which can be computed in $\mathcal{O}(n^2 d)$ time and $\mathcal{O}(n^2 + nd)$ space. Thus the weights α for the second-order features can also be computed in $\mathcal{O}(n^2 d)$ time and $\mathcal{O}(n^2 + nd)$ space.

Proposition 3. *For outer-product encoders, γ-democratic aggregation $\xi(\mathcal{X})$ can be computed with low-memory overhead using Tensor Sketching.*

Proof. Let θ be a low-dimensional embedding that approximates the inner product between two outer-products, *i.e.*,

$$\theta(\mathbf{x})^T \theta(\mathbf{x}') \sim \mathrm{vec}(\mathbf{x}\mathbf{x}^T)^T \, \mathrm{vec}(\mathbf{x}'\mathbf{x}'^T), \tag{8}$$

and $\theta(\mathbf{x}) \in \mathbb{R}^k$ with $k << d^2$. Since the γ-democratic aggregation of $\mathcal{X}$ is a linear combination of the outer-products, the overall feature $\xi(\mathcal{X})$ can be written as:

$$\xi(\mathcal{X}) = \sum_{\mathbf{x} \in \mathcal{X}} \alpha(\mathbf{x})\mathbf{x}\mathbf{x}^T \sim \sum_{\mathbf{x} \in \mathcal{X}} \alpha(\mathbf{x})\theta(\mathbf{x}). \tag{9}$$

Thus, instead of realizing the overall feature $\xi(\mathcal{X})$ of size d^2, one can use the embedding θ to obtain a feature of size k as a democratic aggregation of the approximate outer-products. One example of an approximate outer-product embedding is the Tensor Sketching (TS) approach of Pham and Pagh [42]. Tensor sketching has been used to approximate second-order sum pooling [12] resulting in an order-of-magnitude savings in space at a marginal loss in performance on classification tasks. Our experiments show that sketching also performs well in the context of democratic aggregation.

3.2   Spectral Normalization of Second-Order Representations

A different line of work [6,31,33,58] has investigated matrix functions to normalize the second-order representations obtained by sum pooling. For example, the improved bilinear pooling [33] and second-order approaches [24,25,28] construct a global representation by sum pooling of outer-products:

$$A = \sum_{x \in \mathcal{X}} xx^T. \tag{10}$$

The matrix A is subsequently normalized using matrix power function A^p with $0 < p < 1$. When $p = 1/2$, this corresponds to the matrix square-root which is defined as matrix Z such that $ZZ = A$. Matrix function can be computed using the Singular Value Decomposition (SVD). Given matrix A with a SVD given by $A = U \Lambda U^T$, where the matrix $\Lambda = \texttt{diag}(\lambda_1, \lambda_2, ..., \lambda_d)$, with $\lambda_i \geq \lambda_{i+1}$, the matrix function f can be written as $Z = f(A) = U g(\Lambda) U^T$, where g is applied to the elements in the diagonal of Λ. Thus, the matrix power can be computed as $A^p = U \Lambda^p U^T = U \texttt{diag}(\lambda_1^p, \lambda_2^p, ..., \lambda_d^p) U^T$. Such spectral normalization techniques scale the spectrum of the matrix A. The following establishes a connection between the spectral normalization techniques and democratic pooling.

Let $\hat{A}^p$ be the ℓ_2 normalized version of A^p and $r_{\max}$ and $r_{\min}$ be the maximum and minimum squared radii of the data $x \in \mathcal{X}$ defined as:

$$r_{\max} = \max_{x \in \mathcal{X}} ||x||^2, \ r_{\min} = \min_{x \in \mathcal{X}} ||x||^2. \tag{11}$$

As earlier, let $C(x)$ be the contribution of the vector x to the the aggregated representation defined as:

$$C(x) = \texttt{vec}(xx^T)^T \, \texttt{vec}(\hat{A}^p). \tag{12}$$

Proposition 4. *The following properties hold true:*

1. *The ℓ_2 norm of* $\texttt{vec}(A^p)$ *is* $\rho(A^p) = ||\texttt{vec}(A^p)|| = \left(\sum_i \lambda_i^{2p} \right)^{1/2}$.
2. $\sum_{x \in \mathcal{X}} C(x) = Trace(A^{1+p}/||A^p||) = \left(\sum_i \lambda_i^{1+p} \right) / \rho(A^p)$.
3. *The maximum value* $M = \max_{x \in \mathcal{X}} C(x) \leq r_{\max} \lambda_1^p / \rho(A^p)$.
4. *The minimum value* $m = \min_{x \in \mathcal{X}} C(x) \geq r_{\min} \lambda_d^p / \rho(A^p)$.

Proof. The proof is left in the supplementary material.

Proposition 5. *The variance σ^2 of the contributions $C(\mathbf{x})$ satisfies*

$$\sigma^2 \leq (M - \mu)(\mu - m) \leq \frac{(M - m)^2}{4} \leq \frac{r_{max}^2 \lambda_1^{2p}}{4\rho(\mathbf{A}^p)^2}, \tag{13}$$

where M and m are the maximum and minimum values defined above and μ is the mean of $C(\mathbf{x})$ given by $\sum_{\mathbf{x} \in \mathcal{X}} C(\mathbf{x})/n$ where n is the cardinality of $\mathcal{X}$. All of the above quantities can be computed from the spectrum of the matrix $\mathbf{A}$.

Proof. The proof can be obtained by a straightforward application of Popoviciu's inequality on variances [43] and a tighter variant by Bhatia and Davis [4]. The last inequality is obtained by setting $m = 0$.

The above shows that smaller values p reduce an upper-bound on the variance of the contributions thereby equalizing their contributions. The upper bound is a monotonic function of the exponent p and is minimized when $p = 0$ reducing all the spectrum to an identity matrix. This corresponds to whitening of the matrix $\mathbf{A}$. However, complete whitening often leads to poor results while intermediate values such as $p = 1/2$ can be significantly better than $p = 1$ [24,25,31,33]. In the experiments section we evaluate these bounds on deep features from real data.

Proposition 6. *For exponents $0 < p < 1$, the matrix power $\mathbf{A}^p$ may not lie in the linear span of the outer-products of the features $\mathbf{x} \in \mathcal{X}$.*

The proof of Proposition 6 is left in the supplementary material. A consequence of this is that the matrix power cannot be easily computed in the low-dimensional embedding space of outer-products encoding such as Tensor Sketch. It does however lie in the linear span of the outer-products of the eigenvectors. However, computing eigenvectors can be significantly slower than computing weighted aggregates. We describe the computation and memory trade-offs between computing the matrix powers and democratic pooling in Sect. 4.5.

4   Experiments

We analyze the behavior of matrix power normalization and γ-democratic pooling empirically on several fine-grained and texture recognition datasets. The general experiment setting and the datasets are described in Sect. 4.1. We validate the theoretical bounds on the feature contributions with real data in Sect. 4.2. We compare our models against sum-pooling baseline, matrix power normalization, and other state-of-the-art methods in Sects. 4.3 and 4.4. Finally, we include a discussion on runtime and memory consumption for various approaches and a technique to perform end-to-end fine-tuning in Sect. 4.5.

4.1 Experimental Setup

Datasets. We experiment on Caltech-UCSD Birds [56], Stanford Cars [29] and FGVC Aircrafts [35] datasets. Birds dataset contains 11,788 images which contain over 200 bird species. Stanford Cars dataset consists of 16.185 images across 196 categories and FGVC Aircrafts provides 10,000 images of 100 categories. For each dataset, we use the train and test splits provided by the benchmarks and only the corresponding category labels are used during training phase. In addition to the above fine-grained classification tasks, we also analyze the performance of various approaches on the following datasets: Describable Texture Dataset (DTD) [8], Flickr Material Dataset (FMD) [48] and MIT indoor scene dataset [45]. DTD consists of 5,640 images across 47 texture attributes. We report results averaged over the 10 splits provided by the dataset. FMD provides 1000 images from 10 different material categories. We randomly split half of images for training and the rest for testing for each category and report results across multiple splits. The MIT indoor scene dataset contains 67 indoor scene categories, each of which includes 80 images for training and 20 for testing.

Features. We aggregate the second-order features with γ-democratic pooling and matrix power normalization using VGG-16 [50] and ResNet101 [16] networks. We follow the work [34] and resize input images to 448×448 and aggregate the last convolutional layer features after ReLU activations. For the VGG-16 network architecture, this results in feature maps of size $28 \times 28 \times 512$ (before aggregation), while for the ResNet101 architecture this results in maps of size $14 \times 14 \times 2048$. For γ-democratic pooling, we run the modified Sinkhorn algorithm for 10 iterations with the power exponent $\tau = 0.5$. Fully democratic pooling [37] and sum pooling can be implemented by setting $\gamma = 0$ and $\gamma = 1$, respectively. The aggregated features are followed by element-wise signed square-root and ℓ_2 normalization. For fine-grained recognition datasets, we aggregate the VGG-16 features fine-tuned with vanilla BCNN models, while the ImageNet pretrained networks without fine-tuning are used for texture and scene datasets.

4.2 The Distribution of the Spectrum and Feature Contributions

In this section, we analyze how democratic pooling and matrix normalization effect the spectrum (set of eigenvalues) of the aggregated representation, as well as how the contributions of individual features are distributed as a function of γ for the democratic pooling and p of the matrix power normalization.

We randomly sampled 50 images from CUB and MIT indoor datasets each and plotted the spectrum (normalized to unit length) and the feature vector contributions $C(\mathbf{x})$ (Eq. (12)) in Fig. 1. In this experiment, we use the matrix power $p = 0.5$ and $\gamma = 0.5$. Figure 1(a) shows that the square root yields a flatter spectrum in comparison to the sum aggregation. Democratic aggregation distributes the energy away from the top eigenvalues but has considerably sharper spectrum in comparison to the square root. The γ-democratic pooling interpolates between sum and fully democratic pooling.

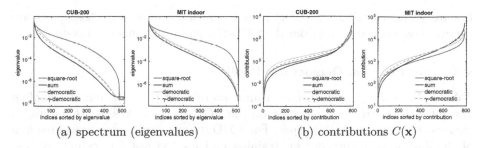

(a) spectrum (eigenvalues)   (b) contributions $C(\mathbf{x})$

Fig. 1. (a) The spectrum (eigenvalues) for various feature aggregators on CUB-200 and MIT indoor datasets. (b) The individual feature vector contributions $C(\mathbf{x})$.

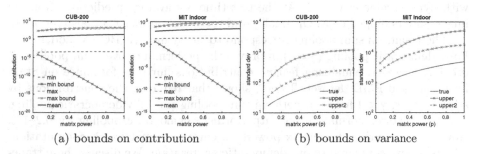

(a) bounds on contribution   (b) bounds on variance

Fig. 2. (a) The upper (red solid) and lower bounds (blue solid) on the contributions to the set similarity versus the exponent of matrix power normalization on Birds and MIT indoor datasets. Maximum and minimum values are shown in dashed lines and the the mean is shown in black solid lines. (b) The upper bounds to the variance of feature contributions $C(\mathbf{x})$. (Color figure online)

Figure 1(b) shows the contributions of each feature $\mathbf{x}$ to the aggregate for different pooling techniques (Eq. (12)). The contributions are more evenly distributed for the matrix square root in comparison to sum pooling. Democratic pooling flattens the individual contributions the most – we note that it is explicitly designed to have this effect. These two plots show that democratic aggregation and power normalization both achieve equalization of feature contributions.

Figure 2 shows the variances of the contributions $C(\mathbf{x})$ to the aggregation $\hat{\mathbf{A}}^p$ using the VGG-16 features for different values of the exponent p. Figure 2(a) shows the true minimum, maximum, mean as well as the bounds of these quantities expressed in Proposition 4. The upper bound on the maximum contribution, i.e., $r_{\max}\lambda_1^p/\rho(\mathbf{A}^p)$, is tight on both datasets, as can be seen in the overlapping red lines, while the lower bound is significantly less tight.

Figure 2(b) shows the true deviation and two different upper bounds on the variance of the contributions as expressed in Proposition 5 and Eq. (13). The tighter bound shown by the dashed red line corresponds to the version with the mean μ in Eq. (13). The plot shows that the matrix power normalization implicitly reduces the variance in feature contributions similar to equalizing the feature vector contributions $C(\mathbf{x})$ in democratic aggregation. These plots are averaged over 50 examples from the CUB-200 and MIT indoor datasets.

4.3   Effect of γ on Democratic Pooling

Table 1 shows the performance as a function of γ for the γ-democratic pooling and p for the matrix normalization on the VGG-16 network. For DTD dataset, we report results on the first split. For FMD dataset, we randomly sample half of the data in each category for training and use the rest for testing. We use the standard training and testing splits on remaining datasets. We augment the training set by flipping its images and train k one-vs-all linear SVM classifiers with hyperparameter $C = 1$. At the test time, we average predictions from an image and its flipped copy. Optimal γ and the matrix power p are also reported.

The results on sum pooling correspond to the symmetric BCNN models [33]. Fully democratic pooling ($\gamma = 0$) improves the performance over sum pooling by 0.7–1%. However, equalizing feature contributions hurts performance on Stanford Cars and FMD dataset. Table 1 shows that reducing the contributions by adjusting $0 < \gamma < 1$ helps outperform sum pooling and fully democratic pooling.

Matrix power normalization outperforms γ-democratic pooling by 0.2–1%. However, computing the matrix powers on covariance matrices is computationally expensive compared to our democratic aggregation. We discuss these trade-offs in the Sect. 4.5.

Table 1. The accuracy of aggregating second-order features w.r.t. various aggregators using fine-tuned VGG-16 on fine-grained recognition (top) and using ImageNet pretrained VGG-16 on other (bottom) datasets. From left to right, we vary γ values and compare democratic pooling, γ-democratic pooling and average pooling with the matrix power aggregation. The optimal values of γ and p are indicated in parentheses.

Dataset	γ-democratic			$\mathbf{A}^p$
	Democratic	Optimal	Sum	
	$\gamma = 0$	γ	$\gamma = 1$	
Caltech UCSD Birds	84.7	84.9 (0.5)	84.0	85.9 (0.3)
Stanford Cars	89.7	90.8 (0.5)	90.6	91.7 (0.5)
FGVC Aircrafts	86.7	86.7 (0.0)	85.7	87.6 (0.3)
DTD	72.2	72.3 (0.3)	71.2	72.9 (0.6)
FMD	82.8	84.8 (0.8)	84.6	85.0 (0.7)
MIT indoor	79.6	80.4 (0.3)	79.5	80.9 (0.6)

4.4   Democratic Pooling with Tensor Sketching

One of the main advantages of the democratic pooling approaches over matrix power normalization techniques is that the embeddings can be computed in a low-dimensional space using tensor sketching. To demonstrate this advantage, we compute the second-order democratic pooling combined with tensor sketching on 2048 dimensional ResNet-101 features. Direct construction of second-order features yields ~4M dimensional features which are impractical to manipulate on GPU/CPU. Therefore, we apply the Tensor Sketch [42] to approximate the outer product using 8192 dimensional features, which is far lower than 2048^2 of the full outer product. The features are aggregated using γ-democratic approach with $\gamma = 0.5$. We compare our method to the state of the art on MIT indoor, FMD and DTD datasets. We report the mean accuracy. For DTD and FMD, we also indicate the standard deviation over 10 splits.

Results on MIT Indoor. Table 2 reports the accuracy on MIT indoor. The baseline model approximating second-order features with tensor sketch followed by sum pooling achieves 82.8% accuracy. With democratic pooling, our model achieves state-of-the-art accuracy of 84.3% which is 1.5% more than the baseline. Moreover, Table 1 shows that we outperform the matrix power normalization using VGG-16 network by 3.4%. Note that (i) matrix power normalization is impractical for ResNet101 features, (ii) it cannot be computed by sketching due to Proposition 6. We also outperform FASON [10] by 2.6%. FASON fuses the first- and second-order features from *conv4_4* and *conv5_4* layers of the VGG-19 networks given 448×448 image size and scores 81.7% accuracy. Recent work on Spectral Features [22] achieves the same accuracy as our best model with democratic pooling. However, approach [22] uses more data augmentations (rotation, shifts, *etc.*) during training and pretrains the VGG-19 network on the large-scale Places205 dataset. In contrast, our networks are pretrained on ImageNet which arguably has a larger domain shift from the MIT indoor dataset than Places205.

Table 2. Evaluations and comparisons to the state of the art on MIT indoor dataset.

Method	Accuracy
Places-205 [54]	80.9
Deep Filter Banks [9]	81.0
Spectral Features [22]	84.3
FASON [10]	81.7
ResNet101 + TS + sum pooling (baseline)	82.8
ResNet101 + TS + γ-democratic (ours)	**84.3**

Results on FMD. Table 3 compares the accuracy on FMD dataset. Recent work on Deep filter banks [9], denoted as FV+FC+CNN, which combines fully-connected CNN features and Fisher Vector approach, scores 82.1% accuracy. In contrast to several methods, FASON uses single-scale input images (224×224) and also scores 82.1% accuracy. Our second-order democratic pooling outperforms FASON by 0.7% given the same image size. For 448×448 image size, our model scores 84.3% and outperforms other state-of-the-art approaches.

Table 3. Evaluations and comparisons to the state of the art on the FMD dataset. The middle column indicates the image size used by each method (*ms* indicates multiple scales while hyphen denotes an unknown size).

Method	Input size	Accuracy
IFV+DeCAF [8]	ms	65.5 ± 1.3
FV+FC+CNN [9]	ms	82.2 ± 1.4
LFV [51]	ms	82.1 ± 1.9
SMO Task [60]	-	82.3 ± 1.7
FASON [10]	224	82.1 ± 1.9
ResNet101 + TS + sum pooling (baseline)	448	83.7 ± 1.3
ResNet101 + TS + γ-democratic (ours)	448	**84.3** ± 1.5
ResNet101 + TS + γ-democratic (ours)	224	82.8 ± 2.5

Results on DTD. Table 4 presents our results and comparisons on DTD dataset. Deep filter banks [9], denoted as FV+FC+CNN, reports 75.5% accuracy. Combined second-order features and tensor sketching outperforms Deep filter banks by 0.3%. With second-order democratic pooling and 448 × 448 size images, our model achieves 76.2% accuracy and outperforms FV+FC+CNN 0.7%. Note that FV+FC+CNN exploits several scales of image sizes.

Table 4. Evaluations and comparisons to the state of the art on the DTD dataset. The middle column indicates the image size used by each method (*ms* indicates multiple scales while hyphen denotes an unknown size).

Method	Input size	Accuracy
LFV [51]	ms	73.8 ± 1.0
FV+FC+CNN [9]	ms	75.5 ± 0.8
FASON [10]	224	72.9 ± 0.7
ResNet101 + TS + sum pooling (baseline)	448	75.8 ± 0.7
ResNet101 + TS + γ-democratic (ours)	448	**76.2** ± 0.7
ResNet101 + TS + γ-democratic (ours)	224	73.0 ± 0.6

4.5   Discussion

While matrix power normalization achieves marginally better performance, it requires SVD which is computationally expensive and not GPU friendly *e.g.*, the CUDA BLAS cannot perform SVD for large matrices. Even in the case of matrix square root which can be approximated via Newton's iterations [33], the iterations involve matrix-matrix multiplication of $\mathcal{O}(n^3)$ complexity. In contrast, solving democratic pooling via the Sinkhorn algorithm (Algorithm 1) involves only matrix-vector multiplication which is $\mathcal{O}(n^2)$. Empirically, we find that solving Sinkhorn iterations is an order of magnitude faster than solving the matrix square root on a NVIDIA Titan X GPU. Moreover, the complexity of Sinkhorn iteration depends only on the kernel matrix – it is independent of the feature vector size. In contrast, the memory required by a covariance matrix grows with $\mathcal{O}(n^2)$ which becomes prohibitive for feature vectors greater than 512 dimensions. Second-order democratic pooling with tensor sketching yields comparable results and reduces the memory usage by two orders of magnitude over the matrix power normalization.

Although we did not report results using end-to-end training, one can easily obtain the gradients of the Sinkhorn algorithm using automatic differentiation by implementing Algorithm 1 in a library such as PyTorch or Tensorflow. Training using gradients from iterative solvers has been performed in a number of applications (*e.g.*, [13] and [36]) which suggests that it is a promising direction.

5 Conclusions

We proposed a second-order aggregation method referred to as γ-democratic pooling that interpolates between sum ($\gamma = 1$) and democratic pooling ($\gamma = 0$) and outperforms other aggregation approaches on several classification tasks. We demonstrated that our approach enjoys low computational complexity compared to the matrix square root approximations via Newton's iterations. With the use of sketching, our approach is not limited to aggregating small feature vectors which is typically the case for the matrix power normalization. The source code for the project is available at http://vis-www.cs.umass.edu/o2dp.

Acknowlegements. We acknowledge support from NSF (#1617917, #1749833) and the MassTech Collaborative grant for funding the UMass GPU cluster.

References

1. Arandjelović, R., Gronat, P., Torii, A., Pajdla, T., Sivic, J.: NetVLAD: CNN architecture for weakly supervised place recognition. In: CVPR (2016)
2. Arsigny, V., Fillard, P., Pennec, X., Ayache, N.: Log-euclidean metrics for fast and simple calculus on diffusion tensors. Magn. Reson. Med. **56**(2), 411–421 (2006)
3. Bhatia, R.: Positive Definite Matrices. Princeton University Press, Princeton (2007)
4. Bhatia, R., Davis, C.: A better bound on the variance. Am. Math. Mon. **107**(4), 353–357 (2000)
5. Boughorbel, S., Tarel, J.P., Boujemaa, N.: Generalized histogram intersection kernel for image recognition. In: ICIP (2005)
6. Carreira, J., Caseiro, R., Batista, J., Sminchisescu, C.: Semantic segmentation with second-order pooling. In: Fitzgibbon, A., Lazebnik, S., Perona, P., Sato, Y., Schmid, C. (eds.) ECCV 2012 Part VII. LNCS, vol. 7578, pp. 430–443. Springer, Heidelberg (2012). https://doi.org/10.1007/978-3-642-33786-4_32

7. Cherian, A., Sra, S., Banerjee, A., Papanikolopoulos, N.: Jensen-Bregman LogDet divergence with application to efficient similarity search for covariance matrices. TPAMI **35**(9), 2161–2174 (2013)
8. Cimpoi, M., Maji, S., Kokkinos, I., Mohamed, S., Vedaldi, A.: Describing textures in the wild. In: CVPR (2014)
9. Cimpoi, M., Maji, S., Vedaldi, A.: Deep filter banks for texture recognition and segmentation. In: CVPR (2015)
10. Dai, X., Yue-Hei Ng, J., Davis, L.S.: FASON: first and second order information fusion network for texture recognition. In: CVPR (2017)
11. Dryden, I.L., Koloydenko, A., Zhou, D.: Non-euclidean statistics for covariance matrices, with applications to diffusion tensor imaging. Ann. Appl. Stat. **3**(3), 1102–1123 (2009)
12. Gao, Y., Beijbom, O., Zhang, N., Darrell, T.: Compact bilinear pooling. In: CVPR (2016)
13. Genevay, A., Peyré, G., Cuturi, M.: Learning generative models with sinkhorn divergences (2017). arXiv preprint arXiv:1706.00292
14. Gong, Y., Wang, L., Guo, R., Lazebnik, S.: Multi-scale orderless pooling of deep convolutional activation features. In: ECCV (2014)
15. Guo, K., Ishwar, P., Konrad, J.: Action recognition from video using feature covariance matrices. Trans. Image Procss. **22**(6), 2479–2494 (2013)
16. He, K., Zhang, X., Ren, S., Sun, J.: Deep residual learning for image recognition. In: CVPR (2016)
17. Huang, Z., Gool, L.V.: A Riemannian network for SPD matrix learning. In: AAAI (2017)
18. Ionescu, C., Vantzos, O., Sminchisescu, C.: Matrix Backpropagation for deep networks with structured layers. In: ICCV (2015)
19. Jégou, H., Douze, M., Schmid, C.: On the burstiness of visual elements. In: CVPR (2009)
20. Jégou, H., Douze, M., Schmid, C., Pérez, P.: Aggregating local descriptors into a compact image representation. In: CVPR (2010)
21. Jégou, H., Zisserman, A.: Triangulation embedding and democratic aggregation for image search. In: CVPR (2014)
22. Khan, S.H., Hayat, M., Porikli, F.: Scene categorization with spectral features. In: ICCV (2017)
23. Knight, P.A.: The Sinkhorn-Knopp algorithm: convergence and applications. SIAM J. Matrix Anal. Appl. **30**(1), 261–275 (2008)
24. Koniusz, P., Yan, F., Gosselin, P., Mikolajczyk, K.: Higher-order occurrence pooling on mid- and low-level features: visual concept detection. Technical report, HAL Id: hal-00922524 (2013)
25. Koniusz, P., Yan, F., Gosselin, P., Mikolajczyk, K.: Higher-order occurrence pooling for bags-of-words: visual concept detection. PAMI **39**(2), 313–326 (2017)
26. Koniusz, P., Cherian, A., Porikli, F.: Tensor representations via kernel linearization for action recognition from 3D skeletons. In: Leibe, B., Matas, J., Sebe, N., Welling, M. (eds.) ECCV 2016 Part IV. LNCS, vol. 9908, pp. 37–53. Springer, Cham (2016). https://doi.org/10.1007/978-3-319-46493-0_3
27. Koniusz, P., Tas, Y., Zhang, H., Harandi, M., Porikli, F., Zhang, R.: Museum exhibit identification challenge for the supervised domain adaptation. In: ECCV (2018)
28. Koniusz, P., Zhang, H., Porikli, F.: A deeper look at power normalizations. In: CVPR, pp. 5774–5783 (2018)

29. Krause, J., Stark, M., Deng, J., Fei-Fei, L.: 3D object representations for fine-grained categorization. In: Workshop on 3D Representation and Recognition (3DRR) (2013)

30. Li, P., Wang, Q.: Local log-euclidean covariance matrix (L^2ECM) for image representation and its applications. In: Fitzgibbon, A., Lazebnik, S., Perona, P., Sato, Y., Schmid, C. (eds.) ECCV 2012 Part III. LNCS, vol. 7574, pp. 469–482. Springer, Heidelberg (2012). https://doi.org/10.1007/978-3-642-33712-3_34

31. Li, P., Xie, J., Wang, Q., Zuo, W.: Is second-order information helpful for large-scale visual recognition? In: ICCV (2017)

32. Lin, T.Y., RoyChowdhury, A., Maji, S.: Bilinear convolutional neural networks for fine-grained visual recognition. IEEE TPAMI **40**(6), 1309–1322 (2018)

33. Lin, T.Y., Maji, S.: Improved bilinear pooling with CNNs. In: BMVC (2017)

34. Lin, T.Y., RoyChowdhury, A., Maji, S.: Bilinear CNN models for fine-grained visual recognition. In: ICCV (2015)

35. Maji, S., Kannala, J., Rahtu, E., Blaschko, M., Vedaldi, A.: Fine-grained visual classification of aircraft (2013)

36. Mena, G., Belanger, D., Linderman, S., Snoek, J.: Learning latent permutations with Gumbel-Sinkhorn networks (2018). arXiv preprint arXiv:1802.08665

37. Murray, N., Jégou, H., Perronnin, F., Zisserman, A.: Interferences in match Kernels. IEEE TPAMI **39**(9), 1797–1810 (2017)

38. Negrel, R., Picard, D., Gosselin, P.H.: Compact tensor based image representation for similarity search. In: ICIP (2012)

39. Pennec, X., Fillard, P., Ayache, N.: A Riemannian framework for tensor computing. IJCV **66**(1), 41–66 (2006)

40. Perronnin, F., Dance, C.: Fisher kernels on visual vocabularies for image categorization. In: CVPR (2007)

41. Perronnin, F., Sánchez, J., Mensink, T.: Improving the fisher kernel for large-scale image classification. In: Daniilidis, K., Maragos, P., Paragios, N. (eds.) ECCV 2010 Part IV. LNCS, vol. 6314, pp. 143–156. Springer, Heidelberg (2010). https://doi.org/10.1007/978-3-642-15561-1_11

42. Pham, N., Pagh, R.: Fast and scalable polynomial kernels via explicit feature maps. In: KDD (2013)

43. Popoviciu, T.: Sur les équations algébriques ayant toutes leurs racines réelles. Mathematica **9**, 129–145 (1935)

44. Porikli, F., Tuzel, O.: Covariance tracker. In: CVPR (2006)

45. Quattoni, A., Torralba, A.: Recognizing indoor scenes. In: CVPR (2009)

46. Romero, A., Terán, M.Y., Gouiffès, M., Lacassagne, L.: Enhanced local binary covariance matrices for texture analysis and object tracking. In: MIRAGE (2013)

47. Sánchez, J., Perronnin, F., Mensink, T., Verbeek, J.: Image classification with the fisher vector: theory and practice. IJCV **105**(3), 222–245 (2013)

48. Sharan, L., Rosenholtz, R., Adelson, E.: Material perceprion: what can you see in a brief glance? J. Vis. **9**(8), 784 (2009)

49. Shih, Y.F., Yeh, Y.M., Lin, Y.Y., Weng, M.F., Lu, Y.C., Chuang, Y.Y.: Deep co-occurrence feature learning for visual object recognition. In: CVPR (2017)

50. Simonyan, K., Zisserman, A.: Very deep convolutional networks for large-scale image recognition. In: ICLR (2015)

51. Song, Y., Zhang, F., Li, Q., Huang, H., O'Donnell, L.J., Cai, W.: Locally-transferred fisher vectors for texture classification. In: ICCV, October 2017

52. Tuzel, O., Porikli, F., Meer, P.: Region covariance: a fast descriptor for detection and classification. In: Leonardis, A., Bischof, H., Pinz, A. (eds.) ECCV 2006 Part

II. LNCS, vol. 3952, pp. 589–600. Springer, Heidelberg (2006). https://doi.org/10. 1007/11744047_45

53. Tuzel, O., Porikli, F., Meer, P.: Pedestrian detection via classification on riemannian manifolds. IEEE TPAMI **30**(10), 1713–1727 (2008)
54. Wang, L., Guo, S., Huang, W., Qiao, Y.: Places205-VGGnet models for scene recognition. CoRR abs/1508.01667 (2015)
55. Wang, Z., Vemuri, B.C.: An affine invariant tensor dissimilarity measure and its applications to tensor-valued image segmentation. In: CVPR (2004)
56. Welinder, P., et al.: Caltech-UCSD Birds 200. Technical report. CNS-TR-2010-001. California Institute of Technology (2010)
57. Yandex, A.B., Lempitsky, V.: Aggregating local deep features for image retrieval. In: ICCV (2015)
58. Yu, K., Salzmann, M.: Second-order convolutional neural networks. abs/1703.06817 (2017)
59. Yu, K., Salzmann, M.: Statistically-motivated second-order pooling. In: ECCV (2018)
60. Zhang, Y., Ozay, M., Liu, X., Okatani, T.: Integrating deep features for material recognition. In: ICPR (2016)

Occlusion-Aware R-CNN: Detecting Pedestrians in a Crowd

Shifeng Zhang[1,2] (ID), Longyin Wen[3] (ID), Xiao Bian[3] (ID), Zhen Lei[1,2(✉)] (ID),
and Stan Z. Li[4,1,2]

[1] Center for Biometrics and Security Research, National Laboratory of Pattern Recognition, Institute of Automation, Chinese Academy of Sciences, Beijing, China
{shifeng.zhang,zlei,szli}@nlpr.ia.ac.cn
[2] University of Chinese Academy of Sciences, Beijing, China
[3] GE Global Research, Niskayuna, NY, USA
{longyin.wen,xiao.bian}@ge.com
[4] Macau University of Science and Technology, Macau, China

Abstract. Pedestrian detection in crowded scenes is a challenging problem since the pedestrians often gather together and occlude each other. In this paper, we propose a new occlusion-aware R-CNN (OR-CNN) to improve the detection accuracy in the crowd. Specifically, we design a new *aggregation loss* to enforce proposals to be close and locate compactly to the corresponding objects. Meanwhile, we use a new part occlusion-aware region of interest (PORoI) pooling unit to replace the RoI pooling layer in order to integrate the prior structure information of human body with visibility prediction into the network to handle occlusion. Our detector is trained in an end-to-end fashion, which achieves state-of-the-art results on three pedestrian detection datasets, *i.e.*, CityPersons, ETH, and INRIA, and performs on-pair with the state-of-the-arts on Caltech.

Keywords: Pedestrian detection · Occlusion-aware
Convolutional network · Structure information · Visibility prediction

1 Introduction

Pedestrian detection is an important research topic in computer vision field with various applications, such as autonomous driving, video surveillance, and robotics, which aims to predict a series of bounding boxes enclosing pedestrian instances in an image. Recent advances in object detection [10,20,27,43,57,68] are driven by the success of deep convolutional neural networks (CNNs), which uses the bounding box regression techniques to accurately localize the objects based on the deep features.

Electronic supplementary material The online version of this chapter (https://doi.org/10.1007/978-3-030-01219-9_39) contains supplementary material, which is available to authorized users.

© Springer Nature Switzerland AG 2018
V. Ferrari et al. (Eds.): ECCV 2018, LNCS 11207, pp. 657–674, 2018.
https://doi.org/10.1007/978-3-030-01219-9_39

Actually, in real life complex scenarios, occlusion is one of the most significant challenges in detecting pedestrian, especially in the crowded scenes. For example, as pointed out in [55], 48.8% annotated pedestrians are occluded by other pedestrians in the CityPersons dataset [67]. Previous methods only require each predicted bounding box to be close to its designated ground truth, without considering the relations among them. Thus, they make the detectors sensitive to the threshold of non-maximum suppression (NMS) in the crowded scenes, wherein filling with occlusions. To that end, Wang *et al.* [55] design a repulsion loss, which not only pushes each proposal to approach its designated target, but also to keep it away from the other ground truth objects and their corresponding designated proposals. However, it is difficult to control the balance between the repulsion and attraction terms in the loss function to handle the overlapping pedestrians.

In this paper, we propose a new occlusion-aware R-CNN (OR-CNN) based on the Faster R-CNN detection framework [43] to mitigate the impact of occlusion challenge. Specifically, to reduce the false detections of the adjacent overlapping pedestrians, we expect the proposals to be close and locate compactly to the corresponding objects. Thus, inspired by the herd behavior in psychology, we design a new loss function, called *aggregation loss* (AggLoss), not only to enforce proposals to be close to the corresponding objects, but also to minimize the internal region distances of proposals associated with the same objects. Meanwhile, to effectively handle partial occlusion, we propose a new part occlusion-aware region of interest (PORoI) pooling unit to replace the original RoI pooling layer in the second stage Fast R-CNN module of the detector, which integrates the prior structure information of human body with visibility prediction into the network. That is, we first partition the pedestrian region into five parts, and pool the features under each part's projection as well as the whole proposal's projection onto the feature map into fixed-length feature vectors by adaptively-sized pooling bins. After that, we use the learned sub-network to predict the visibility score of each part to combine the extracted features for pedestrian detection.

Several experiments are carried out on four pedestrian detection datasets, *i.e.*, CityPersons [67], Caltech [14], ETH [18] and INRIA [11], to demonstrate the superiority of the proposed method, especially for the crowded scenes. Notably, the proposed OR-CNN method achieves the state-of-the-art results with 11.3% MR^{-2} on the CityPersons dataset, 24.5% MR^{-2} on the ETH dataset, and 6.4% MR^{-2} on the INRIA dataset. The main contributions of this work are summarized as follows.

- We propose a new occlusion-aware R-CNN method, which uses a new designed AggLoss to enforce proposals to be close to the corresponding objects, as well as minimize the internal region distances of proposals associated with the same objects.
- We design a new PORoI pooling unit to replace the RoI pooling layer in the second Fast R-CNN module to integrate the prior structure information of human body with visibility prediction into the network.

- Several experiments are carried out on four challenging pedestrian detection datasets, *i.e.*, CityPersons [67], Caltech [14], ETH [18], and INRIA [11], to demonstrate the superiority of the proposed method.

2   Related Work

Generic Object Detection. Early generic object detectors [12,19,40,53] rely on the sliding window paradigm based on the hand-crafted features and classifiers to find the objects of interest. In recent years, with the advent of deep convolutional neural network (CNN), a new generation of more effective object detection methods based on CNN significantly improve the state-of-the-art performances, which can be roughly divided into two categories, *i.e.*, the one-stage approach and the two-stage approach. The one-stage approach [28,42] directly predicts object class label and regresses object bounding box on the pretiled anchor boxes using deep CNNs. The main advantage of the one-stage approach is its high computational efficiency. In contrast to the one-stage approach, the two-stage approach [10,27,43] always achieves top accuracy on several benchmarks, which first generates a pool of object proposals by a separated proposal generator (*e.g.*, Selective Search [52], EdgeBoxes [74], and RPN [43]), and then predicts the class label and accurate location and size of each proposal.

Pedestrian Detection. Even as one of the long-standing problems in computer vision field with an extensive literature, pedestrian detection still receives considerable interests with a wide range of applications. A common paradigm [3,13,58,59,64] to address this problem is to train a pedestrian detector that exhaustively operates on the sub-images across all locations and scales. Dalal and Triggs [11] design the histograms of oriented gradient (HOG) descriptors and support vector machine (SVM) classifier for human detection. Dollár *et al.* [12] demonstrate that using features from multiple channels can significantly improve the performance. Zhang *et al.* [66] provide a systematic analysis for the filtered channel features, and find that with the proper filter bank, filtered channel features can reach top detection quality. Paisitkriangkrai *et al.* [39] design a new features built on the basis of low-level visual features and spatial pooling, and directly optimize the partial area under the ROC curve for better performance.

Recently, pedestrian detection is dominated by the CNN-based methods (*e.g.*, [4,5,22,44,50,60]). Sermanet *et al.* [44] present an unsupervised method using the convolutional sparse coding to pre-train CNN for pedestrian detection. In [6], a complexity-aware cascaded detector is proposed for an optimal trade-off between accuracy and speed. Angelova *et al.* [1] combine the ideas of fast cascade and a deep network to detect pedestrian. Yang *et al.* [61] use scale-dependent pooling and layer-wise cascaded rejection classifiers to detect objects efficiently. Zhang *et al.* [63] present an effective pipeline for pedestrian detection via using RPN followed by boosted forests. To jointly learn pedestrian detection with the given extra features, a novel network architecture is presented in [30]. Li *et al.* [25] use multiple built-in sub-networks to adaptively detect pedestrians across scales. Brazil et al. [4] exploit weakly annotated boxes via a segmentation infusion network to achieve considerable performance gains.

However, occlusion still remains one of the most significant challenges in pedestrian detection, which increases the difficulty in pedestrian localization. Several methods [16,17,32,35,36,46,49,56,72] use part-based model to describe the pedestrian in occlusion handling, which learn a series of part detectors and design some mechanisms to fuse the part detection results to localize partially occluded pedestrians. Besides the part-based model, Leibe et al. [24] propose an implicit shape model to generate a set of pedestrian hypotheses that are further refined to obtain the visible regions. Wang et al. [54] divide the template of pedestrian into a set of blocks and conduct occlusion reasoning by estimating the visibility status of each block. Ouyang et al. [37] exploit multi-pedestrian detectors to aid single-pedestrian detectors to handle partial occlusions, especially when the pedestrians gather together and occlude each other in real-world scenarios. In [41,48], a set of occlusion patterns of pedestrians are discovered to learn a mixture of occlusion-specific detectors. Zhou et al. [73] propose to jointly learn part detectors so as to exploit part correlations and reduce the computational cost. Wang et al. [55] introduce a novel bounding box regression loss to detect pedestrians in the crowd scenes. Although numerous pedestrian detection methods are presented in literature, how to robustly detect each individual pedestrian in crowded scenarios is still one of the most critical issues for pedestrian detectors.

3 Occlusion-Aware R-CNN

Our occlusion-aware R-CNN detector follows the adaptive Faster R-CNN detection framework [67] for pedestrian detection, with the new designed aggregation loss (Sect. 3.1), and the PORoI pooling unit (Sect. 3.2). Specifically, Faster R-CNN [43] consists of two modules, i.e., the first region proposal network (RPN) module and the second Fast R-CNN module. The RPN module is designed to generate high-quality region proposals, and the Fast R-CNN module is used to classify and regress the accurate locations and sizes of objects, based on the generated proposals.

To effectively generate accurate region proposals in the first RPN module, we design the AggLoss term to enforce the proposals locate closely and compactly to the ground-truth object, which is defined as

$$\mathbb{L}_{\mathrm{rpn}}(\{p_i\}, \{t_i\}, \{p_i^*\}, \{t_i^*\}) = \mathcal{L}_{\mathrm{cls}}(\{p_i\}, \{p_i^*\}) + \alpha \cdot \mathcal{L}_{\mathrm{agg}}(\{p_i^*\}, \{t_i\}, \{t_i^*\}), \quad (1)$$

where i is the index of anchor in a mini-batch, p_i and t_i are the predicted confidence of the i-th anchor being a pedestrian and the predicted coordinates of the pedestrian, p_i^* and t_i^* are the associated ground truth class label and coordinates of the i-th anchor, α is the hyperparameters used to balance the two loss terms, $\mathcal{L}_{\mathrm{cls}}(\{p_i\}, \{p_i^*\})$ is the classification loss, and $\mathcal{L}_{\mathrm{agg}}(\{p_i^*\}, \{t_i\}, \{t_i^*\})$ is the AggLoss (see Sect. 3.1). We use the log loss to calculate the classification loss over two classes (pedestrian $p_i^* = 1$ *vs.* background $p_i^* = 0$), *i.e.*,

$$\mathcal{L}_{\text{cls}}(\{p_i\}, \{p_i^*\}) = \frac{1}{N_{\text{cls}}} \sum_i -\left(p_i^* \log p_i + (1 - p_i^*) \log (1 - p_i)\right), \qquad (2)$$

where N_{cls} is the total number of anchors in classification.

3.1   Aggregation Loss

To reduce the false detections of the adjacent overlapping pedestrians, we enforce proposals to be close and locate compactly to the corresponding ground truth objects. To that end, we design a new aggregation loss (AggLoss) for both the region proposal network (RPN) and Fast R-CNN [20] modules in the Faster R-CNN algorithm, which is a multi-task loss pushing proposals to be close to the corresponding ground truth object, while minimizing the internal region distances of proposals associated with the same objects, *i.e.*,

$$\mathcal{L}_{\text{agg}}(\{p_i^*\}, \{t_i\}, \{t_i^*\}) = \mathcal{L}_{\text{reg}}(\{p_i^*\}, \{t_i\}, \{t_i^*\}) + \beta \cdot \mathcal{L}_{\text{com}}(\{p_i^*\}, \{t_i\}, \{t_i^*\}), \quad (3)$$

where $\mathcal{L}_{\text{reg}}(\{p_i^*\}, \{t_i\}, \{t_i^*\})$ is the regression loss which requires each proposal to approach the designated ground truth, and $\mathcal{L}_{\text{com}}(\{p_i^*\}, \{t_i\}, \{t_i^*\})$ is the compactness loss which enforces proposals locate compactly to the designated ground truth object, and β is the hyper-parameters used to balance the two loss terms.

Similar to Fast R-CNN [20], we use the smooth L1 loss as the regression loss $\mathcal{L}_{\text{reg}}(\{p_i^*\}, \{t_i\}, \{t_i^*\})$ to measure the accuracy of predicted bounding boxes, *i.e.*,

$$\mathcal{L}_{\text{reg}}(\{p_i^*\}, \{t_i\}, \{t_i^*\}) = \frac{1}{N_{\text{reg}}} \sum_i p_i^* \Delta(t_i - t_i^*), \qquad (4)$$

where N_{reg} is the total number of anchors in regression, and $\Delta(t_i - t_i^*)$ is the smooth L1 loss of the predicted bounding box t_i.

The compactness term $\mathcal{L}_{\text{com}}(\{p_i^*\}, \{t_i\}, \{t_i^*\})$ is designed to consider the attractiveness among proposals associated with the same ground truth object. In this way, we can make the proposals to locate compactly around the ground truth to reduce the false detections of adjacent overlapping objects. Specifically, we set $\{\tilde{t}_1^*, \cdots, \tilde{t}_\rho^*\}$ to be the ground truth set associated with more than one anchor, and $\{\Phi_1, \cdots, \Phi_\rho\}$ to be the index sets of the associated anchors corresponding to the ground truth objects, *i.e.*, the anchors indexed by Φ_k are associated to the ground truth $\tilde{t}_k^*$, where ρ is the total number of ground-truth object associated with more than one anchor. Thus, we have $\tilde{t}_k^* \in \{t_i^*\}$, for $k = 1, \cdots, \rho$, and $\Phi_i \cap \Phi_j = \emptyset$. We use the smooth L1 loss to measure the difference between the average predictions of the anchors indexed by each set in $\{\Phi_1, \cdots, \Phi_\rho\}$ and the corresponding ground truth object, describing the compactness of predicted bounding boxes with respect to the ground truth object, *i.e.*,

$$\mathcal{L}_{\text{com}}(\{p_i^*\}, \{t_i\}, \{t_i^*\}) = \frac{1}{N_{\text{com}}} \sum_{i=1}^{\rho} \Delta(\tilde{t}_i^* - \frac{1}{|\Phi_i|} \sum_{j \in \Phi_i} t_j), \qquad (5)$$

where N_{com} is the total number of ground truth object associated with more than one anchor (*i.e.*, $N_{\text{com}} = \rho$), and $|\Phi_i|$ is the number of anchors associated with the i-th ground truth object.

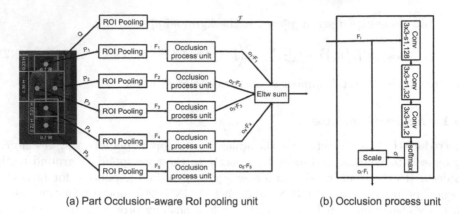

(a) Part Occlusion-aware RoI pooling unit   (b) Occlusion process unit

Fig. 1. For each proposal Q, we divide it into 5 parts $(P_1, \cdots, P_5)$ and use RoIPooling to get the features $(F_1, \cdots, F_5)$, then feed them into the occlusion process unit to predict the visibility scores $(o_1, \cdots, o_5)$. We also apply RoIPooling on Q to generate the holistic feature $\mathcal{F}$. The final features is computed as $\mathcal{F} \oplus (o_1 \cdot F_1) \oplus (o_2 \cdot F_2) \oplus (o_3 \cdot F_3) \oplus (o_4 \cdot F_4) \oplus (o_5 \cdot F_5)$ for subsequent classification and regression.

3.2 Part Occlusion-Aware RoI Pooling Unit

In real life complex scenarios, occlusion is ubiquitous challenging the accuracy of detectors, especially in crowded scenes. As indicated in [35,49,73], the part-based model is effective in handling occluded pedestrians. In contrast to the aforementioned methods, we design a new part occlusion-aware RoI pooling unit to integrate the prior structure information of human body with visibility prediction into the Fast R-CNN module of the detector, which assembles a micro neural network to estimate the part occlusion status. As shown in Fig. 1 (a), we first divide the pedestrian region into five parts with the empirical ratio in [19]. For each part, we use the RoI pooling layer [20] to pool the features into a small feature map with a fixed spatial extent of $H \times W$ (*e.g.*, 7×7).

We introduce an occlusion process unit, shown in Fig. 1 (b), to predict the visibility score of the corresponding part based on the pooled features. Specifically, the occlusion process unit is constructed by three convolutional layers followed by a softmax layer with the log loss in training. Symbolically, $c_{i,j}$ indicates the j-th part of the i-th proposal, $o_{i,j}$ represents its predicted visibility score, and $o_{i,j}^*$ is the corresponding ground truth visibility score. If half of the part $c_{i,j}$ is visible, $o_{i,j}^* = 1$, otherwise $o_{i,j}^* = 0$. Mathematically, if the intersection between $c_{i,j}$ and the visible region of ground truth object divided by the area of $c_{i,j}$ is larger than the threshold 0.5, $o_{i,j}^* = 1$, otherwise $o_{i,j}^* = 0$. That is

$$
o_{i,j}^* = \begin{cases} 1 & \dfrac{\Omega\big(U(c_{i,j}) \cap V(t_i^*)\big)}{\Omega\big(U(c_{i,j})\big)} > \theta, \\[4mm] 0 & \dfrac{\Omega\big(U(c_{i,j}) \cap V(t_i^*)\big)}{\Omega\big(U(c_{i,j})\big)} \le \theta, \end{cases} \tag{6}
$$

where $\Omega(\cdot)$ is the area computing function, $U(c_{i,j})$ is the region of $c_{i,j}$, $V(t_i^*)$ is the visible region of the ground truth object t_i^*, and $\cap$ is the intersection operation between two regions. Then, the loss function of the occlusion process unit is calculated as $\mathcal{L}_{occ}(\{t_i\}, \{t_i^*\}) = \sum_{j=1}^{5} -(o_{i,j}^* \log o_{i,j} + (1 - o_{i,j}^*) \log(1 - o_{i,j}))$.

After that, we apply the element-wise multiplication operator to multiply the pooled features of each part and the corresponding predicted visibility score to generate the final features with the dimensions $512 \times 7 \times 7$. The element-wise summation operation is further used to combine the extracted features of the five parts and the whole proposal for classification and regression in the Fast R-CNN module (see Fig. 1).

To further improve the regression accuracy, we also use AggLoss in the Fast R-CNN module, which is defined as:

$$\mathbb{L}_{frc}(\{p_i\}, \{t_i\}, \{p_i^*\}, \{t_i^*\}) = \mathcal{L}_{cls}(\{p_i\}, \{p_i^*\}) + \alpha \cdot \mathcal{L}_{agg}(\{p_i^*\}, \{t_i\}, \{t_i^*\}) \\ + \lambda \cdot \mathcal{L}_{occ}(\{t_i\}, \{t_i^*\}), \tag{7}$$

where α and λ are used to balance the three loss terms, $\mathcal{L}_{cls}(\{p_i\}, \{p_i^*\})$ and $\mathcal{L}_{agg}(\{p_i^*\}, \{t_i\}, \{t_i^*\})$ are the classification and aggregation losses, defined the same as that in the RPN module, and $\mathcal{L}_{occ}(\{t_i\}, \{t_i^*\})$ is the occlusion process loss.

4   Experiments

Several experiments are conducted on four datasets: CityPersons [67], Caltech-USA [14], ETH [18], and INRIA [11], to demonstrate the performance of the proposed OR-CNN method.

4.1   Experimental Setup

Our OR-CNN detector follows the adaptive Faster R-CNN framework [67] and uses VGG-16 [47] as the backbone network, pre-trained on the ILSVRC CLS-LOC dataset [23]. To improve the detection accuracy of pedestrians with small scale, we use the method presented in [69,70] to dense the anchor boxes with the height less than 100 pixels two times, and use the matching strategy in [71] to associate the anchors and the ground truth objects.

All the parameters in the newly added convolutional layers are randomly initialized by the "xavier" method [21]. We optimize the OR-CNN detector using the Stochastic Gradient Descent (SGD) algorithm with 0.9 momentum and 0.0005 weight decay, which is trained on 2 Titan X GPUs with the mini-batch involving 1 image per GPU. For the Citypersons dataset, we set the learning rate to 10^{-3} for the first $40k$ iterations, and decay it to 10^{-4} for another $20k$ iterations. For the Caltech-USA dataset, we train the network for $120k$ iterations with the initial learning rate 10^{-3} and decrease it by a factor of 10 after the first $80k$ iterations. All the hyperparameters α, β and λ are empirically set to 1.

Table 1. Pedestrian detection results on the CityPersons validation set. All models are trained on the training set. The scale indicates the enlarge number of original images in training and testing. MR^{-2} is used to compare the performance of detectors (lower score indicates better performance). The top three results are highlighted in red, blue and green, respectively.

Method			Scale	Backbone	*Reasonable*	*Heavy*	*Partial*	*Bare*
Adapted Faster RCNN [67]			×1	VGG-16	15.4	-	-	-
			×1.3	VGG-16	12.8	-	-	-
Repulsion Loss [55]			×1	ResNet-50	13.2	56.9	16.8	7.6
			×1.3	ResNet-50	11.6	55.3	14.8	7.0
	AggLoss	PORoI						
OR-CNN			×1	VGG-16	14.4	59.4	18.4	7.9
	√	√	×1	VGG-16	12.8	55.7	15.3	6.7
			×1.3	VGG-16	12.5	54.5	16.8	6.8
	√		×1.3	VGG-16	11.4	52.6	13.8	6.2
		√	×1.3	VGG-16	11.7	53.0	14.8	6.6
	√	√	×1.3	VGG-16	11.0	51.3	13.7	5.9

4.2 CityPersons Dataset

The CityPersons dataset [67] is built upon the semantic segmentation dataset Cityscapes [7] to provide a new dataset of interest for pedestrian detection. It is recorded across 18 different cities in Germany with 3 different seasons and various weather conditions. The dataset includes 5,000 images (2,975 for training, 500 for validation, and 1,525 for testing) with ~35,000 manually annotated persons plus ~13,000 ignore region annotations. Both the bounding boxes and visible parts of pedestrians are provided and there are approximately 7 pedestrians in average per image.

Following the evaluation protocol in CityPersons, we train our OR-CNN detector on the training set, and evaluate it on both the validation and the testing sets. The log miss rate averaged over the false positive per image (FPPI) range of $[10^{-2}, 10^0]$ (MR^{-2}) is used to measure the detection performance (lower score indicates better performance). We use the adaptive Faster R-CNN method [67] trained by ourselves as the baseline detector, which achieves 12.5 MR^{-2} on the validation set with ×1.3 scale, sightly better than the reported result (12.8 MR^{-2}) in [67].

Ablation Study on AggLoss. To demonstrate the effectiveness of AggLoss, we construct a detector, denoted as OR-CNN-A, that use AggLoss instead of the original regression loss in the baseline detector [67], and evaluate it on the validation set of CityPersons in Table 1. For a fair comparison, we use the same setting of parameters of OR-CNN-A and our OR-CNN detector in both training and testing. All of the experiments are conducted on the reasonable train/validation sets for training and testing.

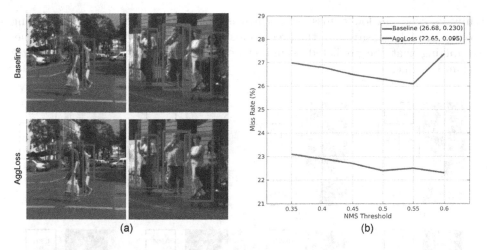

Fig. 2. (a) Visual comparisons of the predicted bounding boxes before NMS of the baseline and OR-CNN-A detectors. The predictions of OR-CNN-A locate more compactly than that of the baseline detector. (b) Results with AggLoss across various NMS thresholds at FPPI = 10^{-2}. The curve of AggLoss is smoother than that of the baseline detector, which indicates that it is less sensitive to the NMS threshold. The scores in the parentheses of the legend are the mean and variance of the miss rate on the curve.

Comparing the detection results between the baseline and OR-CNN-A in Table 1, we find that using the newly proposed AggLoss can reduce the MR^{-2} by 1.1% (*i.e.*, 11.4% MR^{-2} *vs.* 12.5% MR^{-2}) with ×1.3 scale. It is worth noting that the OR-CNN-A detector achieves 11.4% MR^{-2} with ×1.3 scale, surpassing the state-of-the-art method using Repulsion Loss [55] (11.6% MR^{-2}), which demonstrates that AggLoss is more effective than Repulsion Loss [55] for detecting the pedestrians in a crowd.

In addition, we also show some visual comparison results of the predicted bounding boxes before NMS of the baseline and OR-CNN-A detectors in Fig. 2(a). As shown in Fig. 2(a), the predictions of OR-CNN-A locate more compactly than that of the baseline detector, and there are fewer predictions of OR-CNN-A lying in between two adjacent ground-truth objects than the baseline detector. This phenomenon demonstrates that AggLoss can push the predictions lying compactly to the ground-truth objects, making the detector less sensitive to the NMS threshold with better performance in the crowd scene. To further validate this point, we also present the results with AggLoss across various NMS threshold at FPPI = 10^{-2} in Fig. 2(b). A high NMS threshold may lead to more false positives, while a low NMS threshold may lead to more false negatives. As shown in Fig. 2(b), we find that the curve of OR-CNN-A is smoother than that of baseline (*i.e.*, the variances of the miss rates are 0.095 *vs.* 0.230), which indicates that the former is less sensitive to the NMS threshold. It is worth noting that across various NMS thresholds at FPPI = 10^{-2}, the OR-CNN-A method always produces lower miss rate, which is due to the NMS operation filtering out more false positives in the predictions of OR-CNN-A than that of baseline, implying that the predicted bounding boxes of OR-CNN-A locate compactly than baseline.

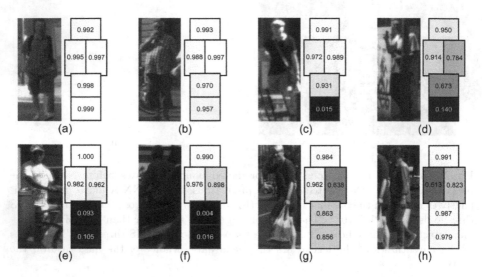

Fig. 3. Some examples of the predicted visibility scores of the pedestrian parts using the proposed PORoI pooling unit.

Ablation Study on PORoI Pooling. To validate the effectiveness of the PORoI pooling unit, we construct a detector, denoted as OR-CNN-P, that use the PORoI pooling unit instead of the RoI pooling layer in baseline [67], and evaluate it on the validation set of CityPersons in Table 1. For a fair comparison, we use the same parameter settings of OR-CNN-P and our OR-CNN detector in both training and testing. All of the ablation experiments involved CityPersons are conducted on the reasonable train/validation sets for training and testing.

As shown in Table 1, comparing to baseline, OR-CNN-P reduces 0.8% MR^{-2} with ×1.3 scale (*i.e.*, 11.7% *vs.* 12.5%), which demonstrates the effectiveness of the PORoI pooling unit in pedestrian detection. Meanwhile, we also present some qualitative results of the predictions with the visibility scores of the corresponding parts in Fig. 3. Notably, we find that the visibility scores predicted by the PORoI pooling unit are in accordance with the human visual system. As shown in Fig. 3(a) and (b), if the pedestrian is not occluded, the visibility score of each part of the pedestrian approaches 1. However, if some parts of the pedestrians are occluded by the background obstacles or other pedestrians, the scores of the corresponding parts decrease, such as the occluded thigh and calf in Fig. 3(c)–(f). Besides, if two pedestrians gather together and occlude each other, our PORoI pooling unit successfully detects the occluded human parts that can help lower the contributions of the occluded parts in pedestrian detection, see

Table 2. Pedestrian detection results of the proposed OR-CNN method and other state-of-the-art methods on the CityPersons testing set. The scale indicates the enlarge number of original images in training and testing. MR^{-2} is used to compare of the performance of detectors (lower score indicates better performance).

Method	Backbone	Scale	*Reasonable*	*Reasonable-Small*
Adapted FasterRCNN [67]	VGG-16	×1.3	12.97	37.24
Repulsion Loss [55]	ResNet-50	×1.5	11.48	15.67
OR-CNN	VGG-16	×1.3	**11.32**	**14.19**

Fig. 3(g) and (h). Notably, the detection accuracy of the OR-CNN detector can not be improved if we fix the visibility score of each part to 1 instead of using the predictions of the occlusion process unit (see Fig. 1). Thus, the occlusion process unit is the key component to detection accuracy, since it enables our PORoI pooling unit to detect the occluded parts of pedestrians, which is useful to help extract effective features for detection.

Evaluation Results. We compare the proposed OR-CNN method[1] with the state-of-the-art detectors [55,67] on both the validation and testing sets of CityPersons in Tables 1 and 2, respectively. Our OR-CNN achieves the state-of-the-art results on the validation set of CityPersons by reducing 0.6% MR^{-2} (*i.e.*, 11.0% *vs.* 11.6% of [55]) with ×1.3 scale and 0.4% MR^{-2} (*i.e.*, 12.8% *vs.* 13.2% of [55]) with ×1 scale, surpassing all published approaches [55,67], which demonstrates the superiority of the proposed method in pedestrian detection.

To demonstrate the effectiveness of OR-CNN under various occlusion levels, we follow the strategy in [55] to divide the *Reasonable* subset in the validation set (occlusion < 35%) into the *Reasonable-Partial* subset (10% < occlusion ≤ 35%), denoted as *Partial* subset, and the *Reasonable-Bare* subset (occlusion ≤ 10%), denoted as *Bare* subset. Meanwhile, we denote the annotated pedestrians with the occlusion ratio larger than 35% (that are not included in the *Reasonable* set) as *Heavy* subset. We report the results of the proposed OR-CNN method and other state-of-the-art methods [55,67] on these three subsets in Table 1. As shown in Table 1, OR-CNN outperforms the state-of-the-art methods consistently across all three subsets, *i.e.*, reduces 1.1% MR^{-2} on the *Bare* subset, 1.1% MR^{-2} on the *Partial* subset, and 4.0% MR^{-2} on the *Heavy* subset. Notably, when the occlusion becomes severely (*i.e.*, from *Bare* subset to *Heavy* subset), the performance improvement of our OR-CNN is more obvious compared to the state-of-the-art methods [55,67], which demonstrates that the AggLoss and PORoI pooling unit are extremely effective to address the occlusion challenge.

---

[1] Due to the shortage of computational resources and the memory issue, we only train OR-CNN with two kinds of input sizes, *i.e.*, ×1 and ×1.3 scale. We believe the accuracy of OR-CNN can be further improved using larger input images. Thus, we only compare the proposed method with the state-of-the-art detectors using ×1 and ×1.3 input scales.

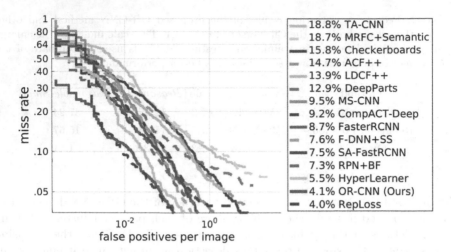

Fig. 4. Comparisons with the state-of-the-art methods on the Caltech-USA dataset. The scores in the legend are the MR^{-2} scores of the corresponding methods

In addition, we also evaluate the proposed OR-CNN method on the testing set of CityPersons [67]. Following its evaluation protocol, we submit the detection results of OR-CNN to the authors for evaluation and report the results in Table 2. The proposed OR-CNN method achieves the top accuracy with only ×1.3 scale. Although the second best detector Repulsion Loss [55] uses much bigger input images (*i.e.*, ×1.5 scale of [55] *vs.* ×1.3 scale of OR-CNN) and stronger backbone network (*i.e.*, ResNet-50 of [55] *vs.* VGG-16 of OR-CNN), it still produces 0.16% higher MR^{-2} on the *Reasonable* subset and 1.48% higher MR^{-2} on the *Reasonable-Small* subset. We believe the performance of OR-CNN can be further improved by using bigger input images and stronger backbone network.

4.3 Caltech-USA Dataset

The Caltech-USA dataset [14] is one of the most popular and challenging datasets for pedestrian detection, which comes from approximately 10 h 30 Hz VGA video recorded by a car traversing the streets in the greater Los Angeles metropolitan area. We use the new high quality annotations provided by [65] to evaluate the proposed OR-CNN method. The training and testing sets contains 42, 782 and 4, 024 frames, respectively. Following [14], the log-average miss rate over 9 points ranging from 10^{-2} to 10^{0} FPPI is used to evaluate the performance of the detectors.

We directly fine-tune the detection models pre-trained on CityPersons [67] of the proposed OR-CNN method on the training set in Caltech-USA. Similar to [55], we evaluate the OR-CNN method on the *Reasonable* subset of the Caltech-USA dataset, and compare it to other state-of-the-art methods (*e.g.*, [5, 6, 9, 15, 25, 30, 34, 49, 50, 55, 63, 66]) in Fig. 4. Notably, the *Reasonable* subset

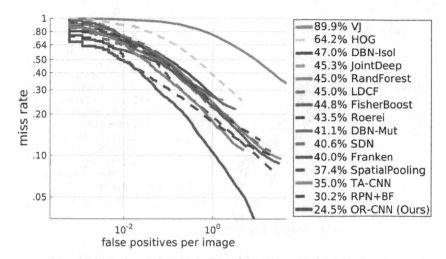

Fig. 5. Comparisons with the state-of-the-art methods on the ETH dataset. The scores in the legend are the MR^{-2} scores of the corresponding methods.

(occlusion < 35%) only includes the pedestrians with at least 50 pixels tall, which is widely used to evaluate the pedestrian detectors. As shown in Fig. 4, the OR-CNN method performs competitively with the state-of-the-art method [55] by producing 4.1% MR^{-2}.

4.4   ETH Dataset

To verify the generalization capacity of the proposed OR-CNN detector, we directly use the model trained on the CityPersons [67] dataset to detect the pedestrians in the ETH dataset [18] without fine-tuning. That is, all 1, 804 frames in three video clips of the ETH dataset [18] are used to evaluate the performance of the OR-CNN detector. We use MR^{-2} to evaluate the performance of the detectors, and compare the proposed OR-CNN method with other state-of-the-art methods (*i.e.*, [3, 11, 29, 31–33, 35, 36, 38, 39, 45, 50, 53, 63]) in Fig. 5. Our OR-CNN detector achieves the top accuracy by reducing 5.7% MR^{-2} comparing to the state-of-the-art results (*i.e.*, 24.5% of OR-CNN *vs.* 30.2% RFN-BF [63]). The results on the ETH dataset not only demonstrates the superiority of the proposed OR-CNN method in pedestrian detection, but also verifies its generalization capacity to other scenarios.

4.5   INRIA Dataset

The INRIA dataset [11] contains images of high resolution pedestrians collected mostly from holiday photos, which consists of 2, 120 images, including 1, 832 images for training and 288 images. Specifically, there are 614 positive images and 1, 218 negative images in the training set. We use the 614 positive images

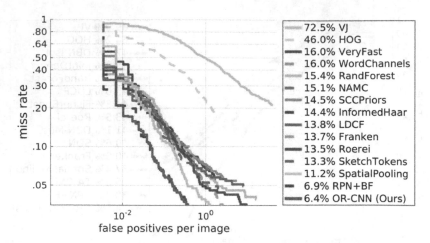

Fig. 6. Comparisons with the state-of-the-art methods on the INRIA dataset. The scores in the legend are the MR^{-2} scores of the corresponding methods.

in the training set to fine-tune our model pre-trained on CityPersons for $5k$ iterations, and test it on the 288 testing images. Figure 6 shows that our OR-CNN method achieves an MR^{-2} of 6.4%, better than the other available competitors (*i.e.*, [2, 3, 8, 11, 26, 31–33, 39, 51, 53, 62–64]), which demonstrates the effectiveness of the proposed method in pedestrian detection.

5   Conclusions

In this paper, we present a new occlusion-aware R-CNN method to improve the pedestrian detection accuracy in crowded scenes. Specifically, we design a new aggregation loss to reduce the false detections of the adjacent overlapping pedestrians, by simultaneously enforcing the proposals to be close to the associated objects, and locate compactly. Meanwhile, to effectively handle partial occlusion, we propose a new part occlusion-aware RoI pooling unit to replace the RoI pooling layer in the Fast R-CNN module of the detector, which integrates the prior structure information of human body with visibility prediction into the network to handle occlusion. Our method is trained in an end-to-end fashion and achieves the state-of-the-art accuracy on three pedestrian detection datasets, *i.e.*, CityPersons, ETH, and INRIA, and performs on-pair with the state-of-the-arts on Caltech. In the future, we plan to improve the method in two aspects. First, we would like to redesign the PORoI pooling unit to jointly estimate the location, size, and occlusion status of the object parts in the network, instead of using the empirical ratio. And then, we plan to extend the proposed method to detect other kinds of objects, *e.g.*, car, bicycle, tricycle, etc.

Acknowledgments. This work was supported by the National Key Research and Development Plan (Grant No. 2016YFC0801002), the Chinese National Natural

Science Foundation Projects #61473291, #61572501, #61502491, #61572536, the Science and Technology Development Fund of Macau (No. 0025/2018/A1, 151/2017/A, 152/2017/A), JDGrapevine Plan and AuthenMetric R&D Funds. We also thank NVIDIA for GPU donations through their academic program.

References

1. Angelova, A., Krizhevsky, A., Vanhoucke, V., Ogale, A.S., Ferguson, D.: Real-time pedestrian detection with deep network cascades. In: BMVC, pp. 32.1–32.12 (2015)
2. Benenson, R., Mathias, M., Timofte, R., Gool, L.J.V.: Pedestrian detection at 100 frames per second. In: CVPR, pp. 2903–2910 (2012)
3. Benenson, R., Mathias, M., Tuytelaars, T., Gool, L.J.V.: Seeking the strongest rigid detector. In: CVPR, pp. 3666–3673 (2013)
4. Brazil, G., Yin, X., Liu, X.: Illuminating pedestrians via simultaneous detection and segmentation. In: IEEE International Conference on Computer Vision, ICCV 2017, Venice, Italy, 22–29 October 2017, pp. 4960–4969 (2017)
5. Cai, Z., Fan, Q., Feris, R.S., Vasconcelos, N.: A unified multi-scale deep convolutional neural network for fast object detection. In: Leibe, B., Matas, J., Sebe, N., Welling, M. (eds.) ECCV 2016 Part IV. LNCS, vol. 9908, pp. 354–370. Springer, Cham (2016). https://doi.org/10.1007/978-3-319-46493-0_22
6. Cai, Z., Saberian, M.J., Vasconcelos, N.: Learning complexity-aware cascades for deep pedestrian detection. In: ICCV, pp. 3361–3369 (2015)
7. Cordts, M., et al.: The cityscapes dataset for semantic urban scene understanding. In: CVPR, pp. 3213–3223 (2016)
8. Costea, A.D., Nedevschi, S.: Word channel based multiscale pedestrian detection without image resizing and using only one classifier. In: CVPR (2014)
9. Costea, A.D., Nedevschi, S.: Semantic channels for fast pedestrian detection. In: CVPR, pp. 2360–2368 (2016)
10. Dai, J., Li, Y., He, K., Sun, J.: R-FCN: object detection via region-based fully convolutional networks. In: NIPS, pp. 379–387 (2016)
11. Dalal, N., Triggs, B.: Histograms of oriented gradients for human detection. In: CVPR, pp. 886–893 (2005)
12. Dollár, P., Appel, R., Belongie, S.J., Perona, P.: Fast feature pyramids for object detection. TPAMI **36**(8), 1532–1545 (2014)
13. Dollár, P., Tu, Z., Perona, P., Belongie, S.J.: Integral channel features. In: BMVC, pp. 1–11 (2009)
14. Dollár, P., Wojek, C., Schiele, B., Perona, P.: Pedestrian detection: an evaluation of the state of the art. TPAMI **34**(4), 743–761 (2012)
15. Du, X., El-Khamy, M., Lee, J., Davis, L.S.: Fused DNN: a deep neural network fusion approach to fast and robust pedestrian detection. In: WACV (2017)
16. Duan, G., Ai, H., Lao, S.: A structural filter approach to human detection. In: Daniilidis, K., Maragos, P., Paragios, N. (eds.) ECCV 2010 Part VI. LNCS, vol. 6316, pp. 238–251. Springer, Heidelberg (2010). https://doi.org/10.1007/978-3-642-15567-3_18
17. Enzweiler, M., Eigenstetter, A., Schiele, B., Gavrila, D.M.: Multi-cue pedestrian classification with partial occlusion handling. In: CVPR, pp. 990–997 (2010)
18. Ess, A., Leibe, B., Gool, L.J.V.: Depth and appearance for mobile scene analysis. In: ICCV, pp. 1–8 (2007)

19. Felzenszwalb, P.F., Girshick, R.B., McAllester, D.A., Ramanan, D.: Object detection with discriminatively trained part-based models. TPAMI **32**(9), 1627–1645 (2010)
20. Girshick, R.B.: Fast R-CNN. In: ICCV, pp. 1440–1448 (2015)
21. Glorot, X., Bengio, Y.: Understanding the difficulty of training deep feedforward neural networks. In: AISTATS, pp. 249–256 (2010)
22. Hosang, J.H., Omran, M., Benenson, R., Schiele, B.: Taking a deeper look at pedestrians. In: CVPR, pp. 4073–4082 (2015)
23. Krizhevsky, A., Sutskever, I., Hinton, G.E.: Imagenet classification with deep convolutional neural networks. In: NIPS, pp. 1106–1114 (2012)
24. Leibe, B., Seemann, E., Schiele, B.: Pedestrian detection in crowded scenes. In: CVPR, pp. 878–885 (2005)
25. Li, J., Liang, X., Shen, S., Xu, T., Yan, S.: Scale-aware fast R-CNN for pedestrian detection. IEEE Trans. Multimed. **20**, 985–996 (2017)
26. Lim, J.J., Zitnick, C.L., Dollár, P.: Sketch tokens: a learned mid-level representation for contour and object detection. In: CVPR, pp. 3158–3165 (2013)
27. Lin, T., Dollár, P., Girshick, R.B., He, K., Hariharan, B., Belongie, S.J.: Feature pyramid networks for object detection. In: CVPR (2017)
28. Liu, W., et al.: SSD: single shot multibox detector. In: ECCV, pp. 21–37 (2016)
29. Luo, P., Tian, Y., Wang, X., Tang, X.: Switchable deep network for pedestrian detection. In: CVPR, pp. 899–906 (2014)
30. Mao, J., Xiao, T., Jiang, Y., Cao, Z.: What can help pedestrian detection? In: CVPR, pp. 6034–6043 (2017)
31. Marín, J., Vázquez, D., López, A.M., Amores, J., Leibe, B.: Random forests of local experts for pedestrian detection. In: ICCV, pp. 2592–2599 (2013)
32. Mathias, M., Benenson, R., Timofte, R., Gool, L.J.V.: Handling occlusions with Franken-classifiers. In: ICCV, pp. 1505–1512 (2013)
33. Nam, W., Dollár, P., Han, J.H.: Local decorrelation for improved pedestrian detection. In: NIPS, pp. 424–432 (2014)
34. Ohn-Bar, E., Trivedi, M.M.: To boost or not to boost? On the limits of boosted trees for object detection. In: ICPR, pp. 3350–3355 (2016)
35. Ouyang, W., Wang, X.: A discriminative deep model for pedestrian detection with occlusion handling. In: CVPR, pp. 3258–3265 (2012)
36. Ouyang, W., Wang, X.: Joint deep learning for pedestrian detection. In: ICCV, pp. 2056–2063 (2013)
37. Ouyang, W., Wang, X.: Single-pedestrian detection aided by multi-pedestrian detection. In: CVPR, pp. 3198–3205 (2013)
38. Ouyang, W., Zeng, X., Wang, X.: Modeling mutual visibility relationship in pedestrian detection. In: CVPR, pp. 3222–3229 (2013)
39. Paisitkriangkrai, S., Shen, C., van den Hengel, A.: Strengthening the effectiveness of pedestrian detection with spatially pooled features. In: Fleet, D., Pajdla, T., Schiele, B., Tuytelaars, T. (eds.) ECCV 2014 Part IV. LNCS, vol. 8692, pp. 546–561. Springer, Cham (2014). https://doi.org/10.1007/978-3-319-10593-2_36
40. Papageorgiou, C., Poggio, T.A.: A trainable system for object detection. IJCV **38**(1), 15–33 (2000)
41. Pepik, B., Stark, M., Gehler, P.V., Schiele, B.: Occlusion patterns for object class detection. In: CVPR, pp. 3286–3293 (2013)
42. Redmon, J., Farhadi, A.: YOLO9000: better, faster, stronger. CoRR abs/1612.08242 (2016)
43. Ren, S., He, K., Girshick, R.B., Sun, J.: Faster R-CNN: towards real-time object detection with region proposal networks. TPAMI **39**(6), 1137–1149 (2017)

44. Sermanet, P., Kavukcuoglu, K., Chintala, S., LeCun, Y.: Pedestrian detection with unsupervised multi-stage feature learning. In: CVPR, pp. 3626–3633 (2013)
45. Shen, C., Wang, P., Paisitkriangkrai, S., van den Hengel, A.: Training effective node classifiers for cascade classification. IJCV 103(3), 326–347 (2013)
46. Shet, V.D., Neumann, J., Ramesh, V., Davis, L.S.: Bilattice-based logical reasoning for human detection. In: CVPR (2007)
47. Simonyan, K., Zisserman, A.: Very deep convolutional networks for large-scale image recognition. CoRR abs/1409.1556 (2014)
48. Tang, S., Andriluka, M., Schiele, B.: Detection and tracking of occluded people. In: BMVC, pp. 1–11 (2012)
49. Tian, Y., Luo, P., Wang, X., Tang, X.: Deep learning strong parts for pedestrian detection. In: ICCV, pp. 1904–1912 (2015)
50. Tian, Y., Luo, P., Wang, X., Tang, X.: Pedestrian detection aided by deep learning semantic tasks. In: CVPR, pp. 5079–5087 (2015)
51. Toca, C., Ciuc, M., Patrascu, C.: Normalized autobinomial Markov channels for pedestrian detection. In: BMVC, pp. 175.1–175.13 (2015)
52. Uijlings, J.R.R., van de Sande, K.E.A., Gevers, T., Smeulders, A.W.M.: Selective search for object recognition. IJCV 104(2), 154–171 (2013)
53. Viola, P.A., Jones, M.J.: Robust real-time face detection. IJCV 57(2), 137–154 (2004)
54. Wang, X., Han, T.X., Yan, S.: An HOG-LBP human detector with partial occlusion handling. In: ICCV, pp. 32–39 (2009)
55. Wang, X., Xiao, T., Jiang, Y., Shao, S., Sun, J., Shen, C.: Repulsion loss: detecting pedestrians in a crowd. CoRR abs/1711.07752 (2017)
56. Wu, B., Nevatia, R.: Detection of multiple, partially occluded humans in a single image by Bayesian combination of edgelet part detectors. In: ICCV (2005)
57. Xu, H., Lv, X., Wang, X., Ren, Z., Bodla, N., Chellappa, R.: Deep regionlets for object detection. CoRR abs/1712.02408 (2017)
58. Yan, J., Lei, Z., Yi, D., Li, S.Z.: Multi-pedestrian detection in crowded scenes: a global view. In: CVPR, pp. 3124–3129 (2012)
59. Yan, J., Zhang, X., Lei, Z., Liao, S., Li, S.Z.: Robust multi-resolution pedestrian detection in traffic scenes. In: CVPR, pp. 3033–3040 (2013)
60. Yang, B., Yan, J., Lei, Z., Li, S.Z.: Convolutional channel features. In: ICCV (2015)
61. Yang, F., Choi, W., Lin, Y.: Exploit all the layers: fast and accurate CNN object detector with scale dependent pooling and cascaded rejection classifiers. In: CVPR (2016)
62. Yang, Y., Wang, Z., Wu, F.: Exploring prior knowledge for pedestrian detection. In: BMVC, pp. 176.1–176.12 (2015)
63. Zhang, L., Lin, L., Liang, X., He, K.: Is faster R-CNN doing well for pedestrian detection? In: Leibe, B., Matas, J., Sebe, N., Welling, M. (eds.) ECCV 2016 Part II. LNCS, vol. 9906, pp. 443–457. Springer, Cham (2016). https://doi.org/10.1007/978-3-319-46475-6_28
64. Zhang, S., Bauckhage, C., Cremers, A.B.: Informed Haar-like features improve pedestrian detection. In: CVPR, pp. 947–954 (2014)
65. Zhang, S., Benenson, R., Omran, M., Hosang, J.H., Schiele, B.: How far are we from solving pedestrian detection? In: CVPR, pp. 1259–1267 (2016)
66. Zhang, S., Benenson, R., Schiele, B.: Filtered channel features for pedestrian detection. In: CVPR, pp. 1751–1760 (2015)
67. Zhang, S., Benenson, R., Schiele, B.: CityPersons: a diverse dataset for pedestrian detection. In: CVPR, pp. 4457–4465 (2017)

68. Zhang, S., Wen, L., Bian, X., Lei, Z., Li, S.Z.: Single-shot refinement neural network for object detection. In: CVPR (2018)
69. Zhang, S., Zhu, X., Lei, Z., Shi, H., Wang, X., Li, S.Z.: Detecting face with densely connected face proposal network. In: CCBR, pp. 3–12 (2017)
70. Zhang, S., Zhu, X., Lei, Z., Shi, H., Wang, X., Li, S.Z.: Faceboxes: a CPU real-time face detector with high accuracy. In: IJCB (2017)
71. Zhang, S., Zhu, X., Lei, Z., Shi, H., Wang, X., Li, S.Z.: S^3FD: single shot scale-invariant face detector. In: ICCV (2017)
72. Zhou, C., Yuan, J.: Learning to integrate occlusion-specific detectors for heavily occluded pedestrian detection. In: Lai, S.-H., Lepetit, V., Nishino, K., Sato, Y. (eds.) ACCV 2016 Part II. LNCS, vol. 10112, pp. 305–320. Springer, Cham (2017). https://doi.org/10.1007/978-3-319-54184-6_19
73. Zhou, C., Yuan, J.: Multi-label learning of part detectors for heavily occluded pedestrian detection. In: ICCV, pp. 3506–3515 (2017)
74. Zitnick, C.L., Dollár, P.: Edge boxes: locating object proposals from edges. In: Fleet, D., Pajdla, T., Schiele, B., Tuytelaars, T. (eds.) ECCV 2014 Part V. LNCS, vol. 8693, pp. 391–405. Springer, Cham (2014). https://doi.org/10.1007/978-3-319-10602-1_26

Seeing Deeply and Bidirectionally: A Deep Learning Approach for Single Image Reflection Removal

Jie Yang[(✉)], Dong Gong, Lingqiao Liu, and Qinfeng Shi

School of Computer Science, University of Adelaide, Adelaide, Australia
{jie.yang01,lingqiao.liu,javen.shi}@adelaide.edu.au,
edgong01@gmail.com

Abstract. Reflections often obstruct the desired scene when taking photos through glass panels. Removing unwanted reflection automatically from the photos is highly desirable. Traditional methods often impose certain priors or assumptions to target particular type(s) of reflection such as shifted double reflection, thus have difficulty to generalize to other types. Very recently a deep learning approach has been proposed. It learns a deep neural network that directly maps a reflection contaminated image to a background (target) image (*i.e.*reflection free image) in an end to end fashion, and outperforms the previous methods. We argue that, to remove reflection truly well, we should estimate the reflection and utilize it to estimate the background image. We propose a cascade deep neural network, which estimates both the background image and the reflection. This significantly improves reflection removal. In the cascade deep network, we use the estimated background image to estimate the reflection, and then use the estimated reflection to estimate the background image, facilitating our idea of seeing deeply and bidirectionally.

1 Introduction

When taking photos through windows or vitrines, reflections of the scene on the same side of the camera, often obstruct the desired scene and ruin the photos. The reflections, however, are often unavoidable due to the limitations on time and/or space. There are practical demands for image reflection removal.

To deal with the image reflection, we first assume that, without the obstruction from the reflection, we can take a clear image, $\mathbf{B} \in \mathbb{R}^{m \times n}$, and then model the reflection contaminated image $\mathbf{I} \in \mathbb{R}^{m \times n}$ as a linear combination of $\mathbf{B}$ and a reflection layer (called reflection) $\mathbf{R} \in \mathbb{R}^{m \times n}$ [1]:

$$\mathbf{I} = \alpha * \mathbf{B} + (1 - \alpha) * (\mathbf{K} \otimes \mathbf{R}), \tag{1}$$

J. Yang and D. Gong—Equal contribution.

Q. Shi—This work was supported by Australian Research Council grants DP140102270 and DP160100703.

where the real scale weight $\alpha \in (0.5, 1)$ is usually assumed as a homogeneous constant [1–3], $\otimes$ is a convolution operator and $\mathbf{K}$ usually represents a Gaussian blurring kernel corresponding a defocus effect on the reflection. Note that $\mathbf{K}$ can also be a delta function (*i.e.* no blur on $\mathbf{R}$) to represent the case where $\mathbf{B}$ and $\mathbf{R}$ are both in-focus (Fig. 1).

(a) I   (b) B   (c) I   (d) B

Fig. 1. An example of single image reflection removal. (a) and (c) are images taken in front of a glass display case, which is degenerated by the reflection. (b) and (d) are the recovered background images of the proposed reflection removal method.

Given an image $\mathbf{I}$ contaminated by reflection $\mathbf{R}$, reflection removal aims to recover the clear background image $\mathbf{B}$. This is challenging since it is highly ill-posed [4]. Some methods thus require multiple images with variations in reflection and/or background as input [1,5–8] or user assistance to label the potential area of reflection and background [4] to reduce the issue. Multiple images and reliable user guidance are often not easy to acquire, however. To make reflection removal practical, single image reflection removal has received increasing attentions [3,9,10].

Solving for $\mathbf{B}$ from a single observation $\mathbf{I}$ usually requires some priors or assumptions to distinguish reflection and background. For example, the ghosting cue [9] is used to identify a special pattern of the shifted double reflection layers from two reflection surfaces. Priors on image gradients are often used to capture the different properties of the different layers [3,11]. These methods assume the reflection $\mathbf{K} \otimes \mathbf{R}$ is highly blurry due to out-of-focus. Relying on this, recently, a deep learning based method [10] has been proposed to achieve end-to-end single image reflection removal, which utilizes strong edges to identify the background scene, and is trained on the images synthesized with highly blurry reflection layers.

These methods have achieved state-of-the-art performance on many testing examples. However, they also exhibit some limitations in practices such as over-smoothing the image, can not handle the case when the reflections do not have strong blurry or have similar brightness and structure with the background. In this paper, considering the success of the deep learning on image restoration [12–15], we propose to tackle the single image reflection removal by using a cascade deep neural network. Instead of training a network to estimate $\mathbf{B}$ alone from $\mathbf{I}$, we show that estimating not only $\mathbf{B}$, but also the reflection $\mathbf{R}$ (a seemingly unnecessary step), can significantly improve the quality of reflection removal.

Since our network is trained to reconstruct the scenes on both sides of the reflection surface (*e.g.* glass pane), and in the cascade we use $\mathbf{B}$ to estimate $\mathbf{R}$, and use $\mathbf{R}$ to estimate $\mathbf{B}$, we call our network bidirectional network (BDN).

2 Related Work

Methods Relying on Conventional Priors. Single image reflection removal is a very ill-posed problem. Previous methods rely on certain priors or additional information to handle specific kinds of scenarios.

In some cases, the objects in background layer and reflection layer are approximately in the same focal plane. Some methods exploited gradient sparsity priors to decompose background and reflection with minimal gradients and local features such as edges and corners [16,17].

In other cases, when taking pictures of objects in the background, the objects reflected from the other side are out of focus due to the different distances to the camera, which leads to the different levels of blur in background and reflection. Li and Brown [3] exploited the relative smoothness and proposed a probabilistic model to regularize the gradients of the two layers. In addition to ℓ_0 gradient sparsity prior, Arvanitopoulos *et al.* [11] proposed to impose a Laplacian data fidelity term to preserve the fine details of the original image. Wan [18] used a multi-scale Depth of Filed map to guide edge classification and used the method in [4] for layer reconstruction afterward.

To distinguish the reflection layer from the background layer, Shih *et al.* [9] studied ghosting cues, which is a specific phenomenon when the glass has a certain thickness and employed a patch-based GMM prior to model the natural image for reflection removal.

Deep Learning Based Methods. Some recent works start to employ learning based methods in reflection removal problems.

Fan *et al.* [10] proposed a deep learning based methods to recover background from the image contaminated by reflections. Similar to [3], it also relies on the assumption that the reflection layer is more blurry due to out of focus and they further argue that in some real-world cases, the bright lights contributes a lot to the generation of reflections. They proposed a data generation model to mimic such properties by performing additional operations on the reflection part. They proposed a two-stage framework to first predict an intrinsic edge map to guide the recovery of the background.

Zhang *et al.* [19] used a deep neural network with a combination of perceptual loss, adversarial loss and an exclusion loss to exploit low-level and high-level image information. Wan *et al.* [20] proposed to combine gradient inference and image reconstruction in one unified framework. They also employed perceptual loss to measure the difference between estimation and ground-truth in feature space.

Other Related Methods. Many previous works use multiple observation images as additional information for the recovery of background images. Some use pairs of images in different conditions, such as flash/non-flash [21], different focus [22]. Some use images from different viewpoints, such as video frames [1,2,5–7,23–25], through a polarizer at multiple orientations [7,26,27], *etc.* But in many real scenarios, we do not have the required multi-frame images for reflection removal. Some work requires manual labelling of edges belonging to reflections to distinguish between reflection and background [4], which is also not suitable for general applications.

3   Proposed Method

Focusing on reflection removal, we seek to learn a neural network which is able to recover a reflection-free image from an observation containing reflection obstruction. Specifically, our final goal is to learn a mapping function $\mathcal{F}(\cdot)$ to predict the background image $\widehat{\mathbf{B}} = \mathcal{F}(\mathbf{I})$ from an observed image $\mathbf{I}$. Instead of training only on the image pairs $(\mathbf{I}, \mathbf{B})$'s, we impose the ground truth reflection layers $\mathbf{R}$'s to boost the training of $\mathcal{F}(\cdot)$ by training on a set of triplets $\{(\mathbf{I}_t, \mathbf{B}_t, \mathbf{R}_t)\}_{t=1}^{N}$. Note that $\mathbf{R}_t$'s are only used in training, not in testing.

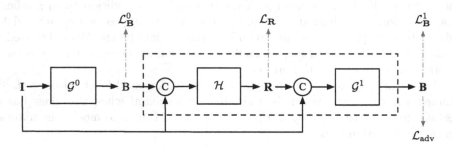

Fig. 2. Overview of our proposed BDN network architecture and the training objectives. Component C stands for tensor concatenation.

3.1   Bidirectional Estimation Model

To directly estimate $\mathbf{B}$ from a given $\mathbf{I}$ in an end-to-end manner, the straightforward idea is to let $\mathcal{F}(\cdot)$ be a neural network taking $\mathbf{I}$ as input and generating $\mathbf{B}$ as output. Our method also includes such a mapping function, and we call it *vanilla generator* $\mathcal{G}^0(\cdot)$. However, our solution further introduces two mapping networks $\mathcal{H}(\cdot)$ and $\mathcal{G}^1(\cdot)$ to estimate the reflection image and refine the background image estimation. In the following parts, we call a composition of $\mathcal{H}$ and $\mathcal{G}^1$ as the bidirectional unit since together they provide estimates for both reflection and background images based on the output of the vanilla generator. The overall structure of the proposed network is shown in Fig. 2.

Vanilla Generator. The vanilla generator takes the observation $\mathbf{I}$ as the input and generates a background image $\mathbf{B}^0$, *i.e.* $\mathbf{B}^0 = \mathcal{G}^0(\mathbf{I})$, which is the input to the following bidirectional unit.

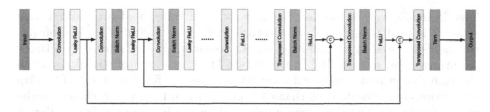

Fig. 3. The network structure of $\mathcal{G}^0$, $\mathcal{H}$ and $\mathcal{G}^1$. C stands for tensor concatenation.

Bidirectional Unit. As shown in Fig. 2, the bidirectional unit consists of two components, one for predicting the reflection image and the other for predicting the background image. The first component $\mathcal{H}(\cdot)$ in the bidirectional estimates the reflection image $\mathbf{R}$ from the observation $\mathbf{I}$ and the background estimation $\mathbf{B}^0$ from $\mathcal{G}^0$, *i.e.* $\mathbf{R} = \mathcal{H}(\mathbf{B}^0, \mathbf{I})$. After that, another background estimator $\mathcal{G}^1(\cdot)$ refines the background estimation by utilizing information from the estimation of $\mathbf{R}$ and the original observation $\mathbf{I}$. Thus, the final estimation of background image is calculated by

$$\hat{\mathbf{B}} = \mathcal{G}^1(\mathcal{H}(\mathbf{B}^0, \mathbf{I}), \mathbf{I}). \tag{2}$$

The motivation of using the above bidirectional estimation model is the mutual dependency of the estimation of reflection images and background images. Intuitively, if a good estimation of the reflection image is provided, it will be easier to estimate the background image, vice versa. Also, including the objective of recovering the reflection image provides additional supervision signals to train the network.

Bidirectional Prediction Model. Based on the above definition of $\mathcal{G}^0(\cdot)$, $\mathbf{H}(\cdot)$ and $\mathcal{G}^1(\cdot)$, we can formulate the whole bidirectional prediction model as:

$$\hat{\mathbf{B}} = \mathcal{G}^1(\mathcal{H}(\mathcal{G}^0(\mathbf{I}), \mathbf{I}), \mathbf{I}), \tag{3}$$

which only takes the observation $\mathbf{I}$ as input. The model shown in Eq. (3) approaches the mapping function $\mathcal{F}(\cdot)$ from the observation $\mathbf{I}$ to the background image $\mathbf{B}$ via a composition of $\mathcal{G}^0(\cdot)$, $\mathcal{H}(\cdot)$ and $\mathcal{G}^1(\cdot)$.

3.2 Network Structure for $\mathcal{G}^0(\cdot)$, $\mathcal{H}(\cdot)$ and $\mathcal{G}^1(\cdot)$

The proposed BDN mainly consists of three subnetworks $\mathcal{G}^0(\cdot)$, $\mathcal{H}(\cdot)$ and $\mathcal{G}^1(\cdot)$. We employ a variation of U-net [28,29] to implement $\mathcal{G}^0(\cdot)$, $\mathcal{H}(\cdot)$ and $\mathcal{G}^1(\cdot)$. All the three modules share the same network structure (except for the first convolutional layer) but not the same parameters. $\mathcal{G}^0(\cdot)$ has 14 layers, while $\mathcal{H}(\cdot)$ and $\mathcal{G}^1(\cdot)$ has 10 layer. The structure of the network structure is illustrated in Fig. 3.

The U-net employed here contains an encoder part and a decoder part. For the encoder network, all convolution layers are followed by BatchNorm layer [30] and leaky ReLU with slope 0.2, except for the first convolution, which does not have Batch-Norm. For the decoder network, each transposed convolution with stride 2 is used to upsample the feature maps by a factor of 2. The output channel is followed by a Tanh function. All convolutions are followed by a Bach-Norm layer and a leaky ReLU activation. The kernel size of the filters in all the convolution and transposed convolution layers is fixed to 4×4. The skip connections concatenate each channel from layer i to layer $n - i$ where n is the number of layers. The skip connections combine the information from different layers, specifically allowing low-level information to be shared between input and output. The use of skip connections doubles the number of input channels in the decoder network. The inputs of $\mathcal{H}(\cdot)$ and $\mathcal{G}^1(\cdot)$ are two images. We simply concatenate those two images to make the input have 6 channels rather than 3 color channels.

4   Network Training

4.1   Training Objective

The goal of our network is to learn a mapping function from $\mathbf{I}$ to $\mathbf{B}$ given training samples $\{(\mathbf{I}_t, \mathbf{B}_t, \mathbf{R}_t)\}_{t=1}^N$.

Our model consists of three mapping operations: $\mathcal{G}^0 : \mathbf{I} \to \mathbf{B}$, $\mathcal{H} : (\mathbf{I}, \mathbf{B}) \to \mathbf{R}$ and $\mathcal{G}^1 : (\mathbf{I}, \mathbf{R}) \to \mathbf{B}$. Each of the above mapping operations leads to a loss for comparing the compatibility of the estimation and the ground-truth results. In this work, we consider to minimizer the difference between the estimate and the ground truth relying on the ℓ_2-loss and the adversarial loss.

(1) ℓ_2-loss

ℓ_2-loss is widely used to measure the Euclidean distance between the estimated image and the ground-truth image. Minimizing the ℓ_2-loss favors the small mean-squared-error (MSE). Since we have three estimations from the three sub-networks in our network, three respective loss terms are defined and the summation of the three loss term will be used to train the network:

$$\mathcal{L}_2 = \mathcal{L}_{\mathbf{B}}^0 + \mathcal{L}_{\mathbf{R}} + \mathcal{L}_{\mathbf{B}}^1, \tag{4}$$

where

$$\mathcal{L}_{\mathbf{B}}^0 = \sum_{t=1}^N ||\mathcal{G}^0(\mathbf{I}_t) - \mathbf{B}_t||_2, \tag{5}$$

$$\mathcal{L}_{\mathbf{R}} = \sum_{t=1}^N ||\mathcal{H}(\mathbf{I}_t, \mathbf{B}) - \mathbf{R}_t||_2, \tag{6}$$

$$\mathcal{L}_{\mathbf{B}}^1 = \sum_{t=1}^N ||\mathcal{G}^1(\mathbf{I}_t, \mathbf{R}) - \mathbf{B}_t||_2. \tag{7}$$

In (6) and (7), the $\mathbf{B}$ and $\mathbf{R}$ can be the ground truth $\mathbf{B}_t$ or $\mathbf{R}_t$ or the estimates from previous blocks, which depends on the settings in training (See Sect. 4.2).

(2) Adversarial loss

ℓ_2-loss only calculates the pixel-wise difference between two images, which may not reflect the perceptual difference between two images. Recently, there are an increasing number of works [12,29,31–33] applying the adversarial loss [34] to provide additional supervision for training an image mapping network. The adversarial loss was originally proposed in Generative adversarial networks [34]. The idea is to iteratively train a discriminator to differentiate the ground-truth images from the images generated by a generator at the certain stage of training. Then the objective becomes to encourage the generator to generate images that can confuse the current discriminator. When applying such an adversarial loss to image processing (mapping), we treat the mapping function that maps the observations to the desired output as the generator. The discriminator in the adversarial loss implicitly leans a distribution of the natural images, as an image prior. By applying adversarial loss, the implicit image prior performs as guidance for recovering the images following the natural image distribution. To simplify the training process, we only apply this adversarial loss to the last estimation of the background image, namely, the output of $\mathcal{G}^1$. Formally, the generation function is defined as $\mathcal{F}(\mathbf{I}) = \mathcal{G}^1(\mathcal{H}(\mathbf{B}^0, \mathbf{I})$ and a discriminator $\mathcal{D}$ is trained by optimizing the following objective:

$$\mathcal{L}_{\mathcal{D}} = \sum_{t=1}^{N} \log \mathcal{D}(\mathbf{B}_t) + \sum_{t=1}^{N} \log(1 - \mathcal{D}(\mathcal{F}(\mathbf{I}_t))), \qquad (8)$$

and the adversarial loss is defined as

$$\mathcal{L}_{\mathrm{adv}} = \sum_{t=1}^{N} - \log \mathcal{D}(\mathcal{F}(\mathbf{I}_t)) \qquad (9)$$

Full Objective. Finally, we sum the ℓ_2 loss and adversarial loss as the final objective:

$$\mathcal{L} = \mathcal{L}_2 + \lambda \mathcal{L}_{\mathrm{adv}}, \qquad (10)$$

where λ is the hyper-parameter that controls the relative importance of the two objectives.

4.2 Training Strategies

Our proposed network has three cascaded modules, the vanilla generator, the reflection estimator and the refined background estimator. These components can be trained independently or jointly. In our work, we explored three ways to conduct training:

- The most straightforward way is to train the whole network end-to-end from scratch.
- Each module can also be trained independently. Specifically, we can progressively train each component until converged and then stack its output to the next component as the input. We call this training strategy as greedy training.

- We can also first train each sub-network progressively and then fine-tune the whole network, which is referred as "greedy training + fine-tuning".

In Sect. 5.1, we will present the comparison and analysis of these training strategies.

4.3 Implementation

Training Data Generation. We use the model in Eq. (1) to simulate the images with reflections. To synthesize one image, we sample two natural images from the dataset and randomly crop the images into 256×256 patches. One patch is served as background $\mathbf{B}$ and the other is used as reflection $\mathbf{R}$. A Gaussian blur kernel of standard deviation $\sigma \in [0, 2]$ is applied on the reflection patch to simulate the defocus blur may appear on the reflection layer in reality. The two patches are blended using scale weight $\alpha \in [0.6, 0.8]$. The generated dataset contains triplets of $\{(\mathbf{I}_t, \mathbf{B}_t, \mathbf{R}_t)\}_{t=1}^{N}$.

We use images from PASCAL VOC dataset [35] to generate our synthetic data. The dataset contains natural images in a variety of scenes, and it is suitable to represent the scenes where the reflection is likely to occur. We generate 50K training images from the training set of PASCAL VOC dataset, which contains 5717 images.

To compare with [10], which is the only available learning based method as far as we know, we also use the method introduced by [10] to generate another training dataset. It subtracts an adaptively computed value followed by clipping to avoid the brightness overflow when mixing two images. We use the same setting as [10] in data synthesis. The images are also from PASCAL VOC dataset and are cropped at 224×224. The training data is generated from 7643 images, and test set is generated from 850 images. We trained our network and [10] using both our training data and training data generated by the method of [10].

Training Details. We implement our model using PyTorch and train the models using Adam optimizer [36] using the default parameters $\beta_1 = 0.9$, $\beta_2 = 0.999$, and the initial learning rate is set to be 0.001. Weights are initialized using the method in [37]. The code is available at https://github.com/yangj1e/bdn-refremv.

5 Experiments

In this section, we first present comparisons of ablations of our methods to illustrate the significance of our design decisions. Then we quantitatively and qualitatively evaluate our approach on single image reflection removal against previous methods [3, 10, 11] and demonstrate state-of-the-art performance. For numerical analysis, we employed peak-signal-to-noise-ratio (PSNR) and structural similarity index (SSIM) [38] as evaluation metrics.

5.1 Ablation Studies for the Bidirectional Network

Testing Data. For ablation studies, we use a dataset synthesized from PASCAL VOC [35] validation set, which does not contain any images appeared in the training set. We generate 400 images for testing in ablation studies. The setting of testing data generation is the same as the setting in Sect. 4.3 for training data generation.

To analyze the performance of reflection removal with respect to the scale weight of the background, which reflects relative strength between background and reflection, we generate another smaller dataset. We increment the scale weight from 0.55 to 0.85, with a step size of 0.05 and generate 10 images for each scale weight.

Analysis of the Model Structure. To verify the importance of our bidirectional unit, we compare three model structures: vanilla generator $\mathcal{G}^0$, vanilla generator $\mathcal{G}^0$ + reflection estimator $\mathcal{H}$, and the full bidirectional network (*i.e.* the composition of $\mathcal{G}^0$, $\mathcal{H}$ and $\mathcal{G}^1$, which is referred as $\mathcal{G}^0 + \mathcal{H} + \mathcal{G}^1$ in the following).

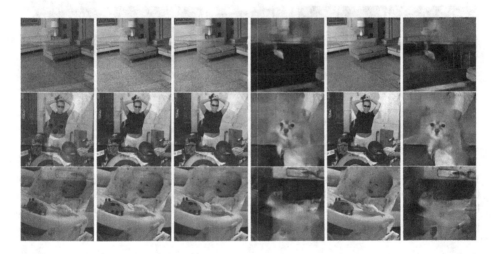

Fig. 4. Visual comparison of our ablation studies on model structure. From left to right: **I**, **B** $(\mathcal{G}^0)$, **B** $(\mathcal{G}^0 + \mathcal{H})$, **R** $(\mathcal{G}^0 + \mathcal{H})$, **B** $(\mathcal{G}^0 + \mathcal{H} + \mathcal{G}^1)$, **R** $(\mathcal{G}^0 + \mathcal{H} + \mathcal{G}^1)$. Best viewed on screen with zoom.

All networks are trained from scratch using the settings specified in Sect. 4.3. Since adding the bidirectional unit to vanilla generator will increase the depth of the network and the number of parameters, we cascade three blocks of the vanilla generator to match the depth and number of parameters of our full model. Table 1 shows that merely training a vanilla generator is not good enough to recover reflection free images. Increasing the number of layers of the vanilla generator (see Vanilla $\mathcal{G}^0$ (deep) in Table 1) to enhance the capacity of the model can slightly improve the performance, but it still underperforms our full model.

Appending a reflection estimator to vanilla generator improved the performance by regularizing the reconstruction and cascading a background estimator to form a bidirectional unit improve the performance further. Figure 4 shows several qualitative examples. It can be observed that adding background estimator improved the result of estimation the reflection layer, which enhances the recovery of background in reverse.

Ablation Study of the Objective Functions. In Table 1, we compare against ablations of our full loss. To employ adversarial loss, we need to train a discriminator network with our model. We adopt the 70×70 PatchGAN of [29] for discriminator, which only penalizes structure at the scale of patches. To train the network with GAN, we pretrain our BDN without adversarial loss first for 2 epochs, and then use the pretrained network to initialize the generator. As the evaluation metrics like PSNR is directly related to MSE, adding adversarial loss has very little improvements compared to directly optimizing ℓ_2 loss in numerical analysis, but for visual appearance, we noticed improvements in restoring the fine details of the background, as shown in Fig. 5.

Fig. 5. Visual comparison of our ablation studies on model structure on objective functions. From left to right: **I**, **B** (BDN w/o adversarial loss), **R** (BDN w/o adversarial loss), **B** (BDN with adversarial loss), **R** (BDN with adversarial loss). The upper image is synthetic and the bottom image is real. Best viewed on screen with zoom.

Analysis of Training Strategy. We compare three training strategies specified in Sect. 4.2. Progressively training each module and then stacking them together, $i.e.$BDN (greedy training + fine-tuning) in Table 1, results in poor performance. The reason is that the reflection estimator and background estimator in the bidirectional unit needs to coordinate, $e.g.$ if we train background estimator greedily using the ground truth pairs $\{(\mathbf{I}_t, \mathbf{B}_t)\}_{t=1}^{N}$, but when we stack it after the vanilla generator, the input of this module becomes $\{(\mathbf{I}_t, \widehat{\mathbf{B}}_t)\}_{t=1}^{N}$. Although finetuning from the progressively trained module improves performance and converges quickly, it underperforms end-to-end joint training from scratch, as the greedy initialization is more likely to converge to a bad local optima. For all the following experiments, we train our model from scratch, $i.e.$the three subnetworks are trained jointly.

Table 1. Quantitative comparison with ablation of our methods and with the state-of-the-art methods on 500 synthetic images with reflection generated using the method in Sect. 4.3, the best results are bold-faced.

	PSNR	SSIM
Vanilla $\mathcal{G}^0$	22.10	0.811
Vanilla $\mathcal{G}^0$ (deep)	22.16	0.817
Vanilla $\mathcal{G}^0 + \mathcal{H}$	22.30	0.813
BDN (greedy training)	20.82	0.792
BDN (greedy training + fine-tuning)	22.43	0.825
BDN (joint training, w/o adversarial loss)	23.06	0.833
BDN	**23.11**	**0.835**
Li and Brown [3]	16.46	0.745
Arvanitopoulos et al. [11]	19.18	0.760
Fan et al. [10]	19.80	0.782

5.2 Quantitative Evaluation

Comparison with the-State-of-the-Art. We perform quantitative comparison between our method and the-state-of-the-art single image reflection methods of Li and Brown [3], Arvanitopoulos et al. [11] and Fan et al. [10] using synthetic dataset. The numerical results shown in Table 1 indicates that our method outperforms the state-of-the-art.

Comparison with Learning Based Method. We specifically perform some comparisons with [10] as [10] is the only method of solving single image reflection removal problem using deep learning techniques so far. Both [10] and our method require training with synthetic data, but we use different data synthesis mechanism. To compare with [10], we train both our model and [10] using our training data as described in Sect. 4.3 and a training set generated using the algorithm in [10]. Then we evaluate trained models on the corresponding test set, and the results are shown in Table 2.

Table 2. Comparison between our method and [10]. Both models are trained and evaluated using the synthetic dataset of [10], the best results are bold-faced.

	Dataset in [10]		Our dataset	
	PSNR	SSIM	PSNR	SSIM
BDN (ours)	**20.82**	0.832	**23.11**	**0.835**
Fan et al. [10]	18.29	**0.8334**	20.03	0.790

Trained on synthetic data in [10], our model achieves comparable performance on the test set in [10] and outperforms [10] when training and testing on our synthetic dataset. Because [10] explicitly utilize edge information and removes reflection by recovering the intrinsic edge of the background image, it relies more on the assumption that the reflection layer is blurry. Therefore, when training in our dataset, which is less blurry and contains a more general form of reflections, [10] does not perform as well as it does in [10]. By contrast, our model has a stronger capacity to learn from data directly and dealing with less blurry reflections.

Learning based methods train models on synthetic data due to the lack of real labeled data. Since we choose different methods to generate training data and it is difficult to tell which data synthesis method fits the real data the best, we use SIR dataset [39] to evaluate the generational ability of our model on real data with reflections. SIR dataset [39] contains 454 triplets of images shot under various capture settings, *e.g.* glass thickness, aperture size and exposure time, to cover various types of reflections. The dataset contains three scenarios: postcards, solid objects, and wild scenes. The images in this dataset are in size 540×400 (Table 3).

Table 3. Numerical study of the learning based methods on SIR benchmark dataset [39], the best results are bold-faced.

	Postcard		Solid objects		Wild scenes	
	PSNR	SSIM	PSNR	SSIM	PSNR	SSIM
Fan *et al.* [10]	**21.0829**	0.8294	**23.5324**	**0.8843**	22.0618	0.8261
BDN (ours)	20.4076	**0.8548**	22.7076	0.8627	**22.1082**	**0.8327**

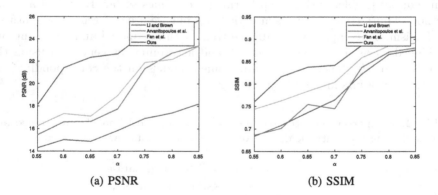

| (a) PSNR | (b) SSIM |

Fig. 6. Evaluation of PSNR and SSIM with the change of scale weight α for the background.

Sensitivity to the Reflection Level. Considering the weight α in model (1) reflects the strength of the reflection level, to study the sensitivity of the

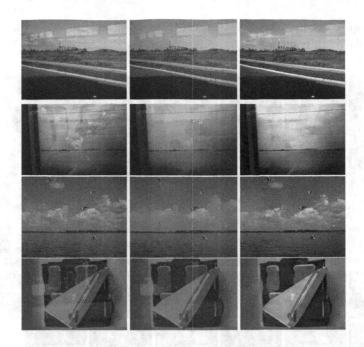

Fig. 7. Comparison with the method of Arvanitopoulos *et al.* [11] on real images. From left to right: **I**, **B** [11], **B** (ours). [11] tends to be oversmooth and our results look more natural. Best viewed on screen with zoom.

proposed method to the reflection, we conduct and experiments to evaluate the performance of different methods on the images with different α's. As shown in Fig. 6, with the scale weight of background decreases, it is increasingly difficult to separate reflection from the background. Actually when the background layer and reflection layer have similar brightness and structure, sometimes it is even painful for humans to distinguish them apart. Also, note that the range of α exceeds the range we used in data synthesis, and our methods are robust in different levels of scale weights.

5.3   Qualitative Evaluation

We compare with the previous works using real images collected from previous works [5, 10, 11] and collected from the Internet and wild scenes. Since these images have no ground truth, we can only perform the visual comparison.

Comparison with the Method Only Estimating Background. Arvanitopoulos *et al.* [11] focus on suppressing the reflections, *i.e.*they do not recover the reflection layer. Therefore, we can only show the comparison with **I** and **B** in Fig. 7. It can be seen that our method better preserves the details in the background and has fewer artifacts, while [11] tends to oversmooth the image and lose too much information details. For example, in the image of clouds, our result keeps more details of cloud than [11] and in the image of the bag, our result looks more realistic.

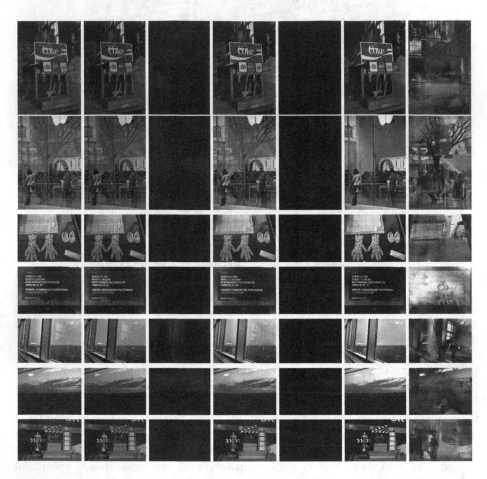

Fig. 8. Comparision of our method with the-stat-of-the-art on real images. From left to right: **I**, **B** ([3]), (**R** [3]), (**B** [10]), (**R** [10]), **B** (ours), **R** (ours). Our networks has clearer background estimation and better color recovery. Best viewed on screen with zoom.

Comparison with Methods Separating Two Layers. We compare our methods with Li and Brown [3], and Fan *et al.* [10], which generate a reflection layer along with the background layer. Although our method focuses on recovering the background rather than separating two layers, our estimation of reflection contains more meaningful information compared to previous methods by looking bidirectional. The quality of the reflection layer reconstructed helps boost our recovery of background in our case. Figure 8 shows the qualitative comparison results. Our methods outperform the state-of-the-art in recovering the

Fig. 9. An example of failure case. From left to right: **I**, **B** ([3]), **B** ([11]), **B** ([10]), **B** (ours)

clear background in real scenes with obstructive reflections. Compared to [10], our method better recovers the color of the original image. Because a portion of the light will be reflected back to the side of the background, the objects in the background usually look pale compared to the observation directly without glass. This is reflected by the scale operation when generating our training data.

In Fig. 9, we show an examples of failure case. The image, which is from [39], is taken using two postcards through a thick glass. The reflection is very strong and contains ghosting artefacts, while the background is very blurry, and the interactions between reflections have very complex structure. None of the methods works well in this case.

6 Conclusion

In this paper, we studied the single image reflection removal problem. Motivated by an idea that one can estimate the reflection and use it to boost the estimation of the background, we propose a deep neural network with a cascade structure for single image removal, which is referred as the bidirectional network (BDN). Benefiting from the powerful supervision, the proposed BDN can recover the background image effectively. Extensive experiments on synthetic data and the real-world data demonstrate that the proposed methods work well in diverse scenarios.

References

1. Xue, T., Rubinstein, M., Liu, C., Freeman, W.T.: A computational approach for obstruction-free photography. ACM Trans. Graph. **34**(4), 79 (2015)
2. Szeliski, R., Avidan, S., Anandan, P.: Layer extraction from multiple images containing reflections and transparency. In: CVPR, vol. 1, pp. 246–253. IEEE (2000)
3. Li, Y., Brown, M.S.: Single image layer separation using relative smoothness. In: CVPR, pp. 2752–2759. IEEE (2014)
4. Levin, A., Weiss, Y.: User assisted separation of reflections from a single image using a sparsity prior. IEEE Trans. PAMI **29**(9), 1647–1654 (2007)
5. Li, Y., Brown, M.S.: Exploiting reflection change for automatic reflection removal. In: ICCV, pp. 2432–2439 (2013)
6. Guo, X., Cao, X., Ma, Y.: Robust separation of reflection from multiple images. In: CVPR, pp. 2187–2194. IEEE (2014)

7. Sarel, B., Irani, M.: Separating transparent layers through layer information exchange. In: Pajdla, T., Matas, J. (eds.) ECCV 2004. LNCS, vol. 3024, pp. 328–341. Springer, Heidelberg (2004). https://doi.org/10.1007/978-3-540-24673-2_27

8. Han, B.J., Sim, J.Y.: Reflection removal using low-rank matrix completion. In: CVPR, vol. 2. IEEE (2017)

9. Shih, Y., Krishnan, D., Durand, F., Freeman, W.T.: Reflection removal using ghosting cues. In: CVPR, pp. 3193–3201. IEEE (2015)

10. Fan, Q., Yang, J., Hua, G., Chen, B., Wipf, D.P.: A generic deep architecture for single image reflection removal and image smoothing. In: ICCV, pp. 3258–3267 (2017)

11. Arvanitopoulos, N., Achanta, R., Süsstrunk, S.: Single image reflection suppression. In: CVPR, pp. 1752–1760. IEEE (2017)

12. Ledig, C., et al.: Photo-realistic single image super-resolution using a generative adversarial network. In: CVPR, vol. 2, p. 4. IEEE (2017)

13. Gong, D., et al.: From motion blur to motion flow: a deep learning solution for removing heterogeneous motion blur. In: IEEE Conference on Computer Vision and Pattern Recognition (CVPR) (2017)

14. Mao, X., Shen, C., Yang, Y.B.: Image restoration using very deep convolutional encoder-decoder networks with symmetric skip connections. In: Advances in Neural Information Processing Systems, pp. 2802–2810 (2016)

15. Gong, D., Zhang, Z., Shi, Q., Hengel, A.V.D., Shen, C., Zhang, Y.: Learning an optimizer for image deconvolution. arXiv preprint arXiv:1804.03368 (2018)

16. Levin, A., Zomet, A., Weiss, Y.: Learning to perceive transparency from the statistics of natural scenes. In: NIPS, pp. 1271–1278 (2003)

17. Levin, A., Zomet, A., Weiss, Y.: Separating reflections from a single image using local features. In: CVPR, vol. 1, pp. 306–313. IEEE (2004)

18. Wan, R., Shi, B., Hwee, T.A., Kot, A.C.: Depth of field guided reflection removal. In: ICIP, pp. 21–25. IEEE (2016)

19. Zhang, X., Ng, R., Chen, Q.: Single image reflection separation with perceptual losses. In: CVPR. IEEE (2018)

20. Wan, R., Shi, B., Duan, L.Y., Tan, A.H., Kot, A.C.: CRRN: multi-scale guided concurrent reflection removal network. In: CVPR, pp. 4777–4785. IEEE (2018)

21. Agrawal, A., Raskar, R., Nayar, S.K., Li, Y.: Removing photography artifacts using gradient projection and flash-exposure sampling. ACM Trans. Graph. **24**(3), 828–835 (2005)

22. Schechner, Y.Y., Kiryati, N., Basri, R.: Separation of transparent layers using focus. IJCV **39**(1), 25–39 (2000)

23. Gai, K., Shi, Z., Zhang, C.: Blind separation of superimposed moving images using image statistics. IEEE Trans. PAMI **34**(1), 19–32 (2012)

24. Sinha, S.N., Kopf, J., Goesele, M., Scharstein, D., Szeliski, R.: Image-based rendering for scenes with reflections. ACM Trans. Graph. **31**(4), 100–1 (2012)

25. Yang, J., Li, H., Dai, Y., Tan, R.T.: Robust optical flow estimation of double-layer images under transparency or reflection. In: CVPR, pp. 1410–1419 (2016)

26. Schechner, Y.Y., Shamir, J., Kiryati, N.: Polarization and statistical analysis of scenes containing a semireflector. JOSA A **17**(2), 276–284 (2000)

27. Kong, N., Tai, Y.W., Shin, J.S.: A physically-based approach to reflection separation: from physical modeling to constrained optimization. IEEE Trans. PAMI **36**(2), 209–221 (2014)

28. Ronneberger, O., Fischer, P., Brox, T.: U-Net: convolutional networks for biomedical image segmentation. In: Navab, N., Hornegger, J., Wells, W.M., Frangi, A.F.

(eds.) MICCAI 2015. LNCS, vol. 9351, pp. 234–241. Springer, Cham (2015). https://doi.org/10.1007/978-3-319-24574-4_28

29. Isola, P., Zhu, J.Y., Zhou, T., Efros, A.A.: Image-to-image translation with conditional adversarial networks. In: CVPR, pp. 5967–5976. IEEE (2017)

30. Ioffe, S., Szegedy, C.: Batch normalization: accelerating deep network training by reducing internal covariate shift. In: ICML, pp. 448–456 (2015)

31. Zhu, J.Y., Park, T., Isola, P., Efros, A.A.: Unpaired image-to-image translation using cycle-consistent adversarial networks. In: ICCV, pp. 2242–2251. IEEE (2017)

32. Lettry, L., Vanhoey, K., van Gool, L.: DARN: a deep adversarial residual network for intrinsic image decomposition. In: WACV, pp. 1359–1367. IEEE (2018)

33. Shrivastava, A., Pfister, T., Tuzel, O., Susskind, J., Wang, W., Webb, R.: Learning from simulated and unsupervised images through adversarial training. In: CVPR, vol. 2, p. 5. IEEE (2017)

34. Goodfellow, I., et al.: Generative adversarial nets. In: Advances in Neural Information Processing Systems, pp. 2672–2680 (2014)

35. Everingham, M., Van Gool, L., Williams, C.K., Winn, J., Zisserman, A.: The Pascal visual object classes (VOC) challenge. IJCV **88**(2), 303–338 (2010)

36. Kingma, D., Ba, J.: Adam: a method for stochastic optimization. arXiv preprint arXiv:1412.6980 (2014)

37. He, K., Zhang, X., Ren, S., Sun, J.: Delving deep into rectifiers: surpassing human-level performance on imagenet classification. In: ICCV, pp. 1026–1034 (2015)

38. Wang, Z., Bovik, A.C., Sheikh, H.R., Simoncelli, E.P.: Image quality assessment: from error visibility to structural similarity. IEEE Trans. Image Process. **13**(4), 600–612 (2004)

39. Wan, R., Shi, B., Duan, L.Y., Tan, A.H., Kot, A.C.: Benchmarking single-image reflection removal algorithms. In: ICCV, pp. 3942–3950. IEEE (2017)

Long-Term Tracking in the Wild: A Benchmark

Jack Valmadre[1]([✉]), Luca Bertinetto[1], João F. Henriques[1], Ran Tao[2], Andrea Vedaldi[1], Arnold W. M. Smeulders[2], Philip H. S. Torr[1], and Efstratios Gavves[2]

[1] University of Oxford, Oxford, UK
`jack@valmadre.net`
[2] University of Amsterdam, Amsterdam, The Netherlands

Abstract. We introduce the OxUvA dataset and benchmark for evaluating single-object tracking algorithms. Benchmarks have enabled great strides in the field of object tracking by defining standardized evaluations on large sets of diverse videos. However, these works have focused exclusively on sequences that are just tens of seconds in length and in which the target is always visible. Consequently, most researchers have designed methods tailored to this "short-term" scenario, which is poorly representative of practitioners' needs. Aiming to address this disparity, we compile a long-term, large-scale tracking dataset of sequences with average length greater than two minutes and with frequent target object disappearance. The OxUvA dataset is much larger than the object tracking datasets of recent years: it comprises 366 sequences spanning 14 h of video. We assess the performance of several algorithms, considering both the ability to locate the target and to determine whether it is present or absent. Our goal is to offer the community a large and diverse benchmark to enable the design and evaluation of tracking methods ready to be used "in the wild". The project website is oxuva.net.

1 Introduction

Visual object tracking is the task of locating an arbitrary, user-specified target in all frames of a video sequence. Traditionally, the target is specified using a rectangle in a single frame. The ability to track an arbitrary object would be useful for many applications including video analytics, surveillance, robotics, augmented reality and video editing. However, the requirement to be able to track *anything* given only a single example presents a significant challenge due to the many complex factors that affect appearance, such as out-of-plane rotation, non-rigid deformation, camera perspective, motion blur, illumination changes, occlusions and clutter.

J. Valmadre, L. Bertinetto, E. Gavves—Equal contribution.

Electronic supplementary material The online version of this chapter (https://doi.org/10.1007/978-3-030-01219-9_41) contains supplementary material, which is available to authorized users.

V. Ferrari et al. (Eds.): ECCV 2018, LNCS 11207, pp. 692–707, 2018.
https://doi.org/10.1007/978-3-030-01219-9_41

Fig. 1. Example sequences and annotations. Unlike standard benchmarks, our dataset focuses on long sequences with annotated disappearance of the target object.

Tracking benchmarks [13,14,16,21,28,34] have played a huge role in the advancement of the field, enabling the objective comparison of different techniques and driving impressive progress in recent years. However, these benchmarks have focused on the problem of "short-term tracking" according to the definition of Kristan *et al.* [13], which does not require methods to perform re-detection. This implies that the object is always present in the video frame.

This constraint was perhaps introduced with the intention of limiting the scope of the problem to facilitate progress. However, the influence of these benchmarks has been so pervasive that the large majority of modern trackers estimate a bounding box in *every frame*, implicitly assuming that the target never disappears from the scene. For most practical applications, however, it is critical to track objects through disappearance and re-appearance events, and further, to be *aware* of the presence or absence of the object.

Existing benchmarks are also *short-term* in the literal sense that the average video length does not exceed 20–30 s. Such short sequences do not accurately represent practical applications, in which videos can easily be several minutes, and possibly arbitrarily long. Little is known of which trackers are most effective in this scenario: while short-term benchmarks make a particular effort to include a variety of challenging situations, tracking in long videos may introduce unforeseen challenges. For instance, many methods use their past predictions to update an internal appearance model. While this generally improves the results in short-term tracking, the accumulation of errors over time leads to model drift [26], which may have a catastrophic effect in longer videos.

With this work, we introduce a novel single-object tracking benchmark and aim to advance the literature through several contributions:

1. Our dataset contains sequences with an average duration of 2.4 min, seven times more than OTB-100. With 14 h of video (1.5 million frames), it is also the largest tracking dataset to date.
2. We deliberately assess methods in situations where the target disappears (Fig. 1), an event that occurs in roughly half the videos of the dataset.
3. Unlike existing tracking benchmarks, we split the data into two sets: development (*dev*) and *test*. The ground-truth for the test set is only accessible via a rate-limited evaluation server. This helps avoid over-fitting hyper-parameters to the singular dataset of the benchmark, thus promoting generalization.
4. We design a new evaluation that captures the ability of a tracker to both decide the presence or absence of the object and to locate it in the image.
5. Instead of manually-annotated binary attributes, which can be subjective, we propose *continuous attributes*, which allow an in-depth study of how smoothly-varying conditions affect each tracker.
6. We evaluate and compare several representative methods from the literature that either perform well or seem particularly well-suited to the problem.

We hope this paper encourages the community to relax the strong assumptions of short-term tracking benchmarks and to develop methods that can be readily used in the many applications that present a "long-term" scenario.

2   Related Work

Large-Scale Video Datasets. There has been an increasing interest by the computer vision community in large-scale video datasets. Two notable examples are the datasets for object detection in video, ImageNet VID [25] and YouTube Bounding Boxes [23] (YTBB). ImageNet VID contains 20 classes and almost four thousand videos, with every object instance annotated in every frame. YTBB contains 23 classes and 240k videos from YouTube, with a single instance of each class annotated once per second for up to twenty seconds. YTBB specifically aims to comprise videos "in the wild" by considering only those with 100 views or less on YouTube. This was observed to be a good heuristic for selecting unedited videos of personal users. This work uses YTBB as a source from which to curate and further annotate the sequences that constitute our long-term benchmark.

Tracking Benchmarks. The practice of evaluating tracking algorithms has improved considerably in recent years. In the past, researchers were limited to evaluating tracking performance on a mere handful of sequences (*e.g.* [1, 4,19,24]). Benchmarks like ALOV [28], VOT [13] and OTB [34] underlined the importance of testing methods on a much larger set of sequences which encompasses a variety of object classes and factors of variation. To evaluate tracker performance, ALOV computes an F-score per video using a 50% intersection-over-union (IOU) criterion, then visualizes the distribution of F-scores. OTB instead reports, for a range of thresholds, the percentage of frames in which the IOU exceeds each threshold. The VOT benchmark is distinct from others in that trackers are restarted after each failure. Motivated by a correlation study, two metrics (mean IOU and number of failures) are used to quantify tracker performance, and these are jointly expressed in the Expected Average Overlap. Recently, TempleColor [16] (TC), UAV123 [21] and NUS-PRO [14] have introduced new sequences and adopted the OTB performance measures.

Differently from our work, standard benchmarks only offer sequences that are relatively short (lasting 7–30 s on average) and do not contain disappearance of the target, thus not requiring methods to perform re-detection. In the rare frames where the object is fully occluded, OTB-100 places a bounding box on top of the occluder, while UAV123 ignores the frame during evaluation.

Long-Term Tracking. To our knowledge, the first attempt in the literature to evaluate tracking algorithms on long sequences with disappearances was the *long-term detection and tracking* workshop (LTDT) [5]. Despite the fact that the number of frames in LTDT is comparable to OTB-100 [34], its modest number of sequences (five) makes it unsuitable for assessing the performance of a general purpose tracker. Tao *et al.* [31] investigated object tracking in half-hour sequences using the periodic, symmetric extension of short sequences. However, this does not necessarily capture the same level of difficulty as real videos.

Two long-term tracking datasets have been proposed in concurrent work [17, 20], both of which include sequences with labelled target absences. However, to our knowledge, neither provides a test set with secret ground-truth.

3   Long-Term Tracking Dataset

3.1   Dataset Compilation and Curation

Our aim is to collect long and realistic video sequences in which the target object can disappear and re-appear. We use the YTBB [23] *validation* set as a superset from which to select our data. YTBB contains 380k tracklets from 240k different YouTube videos, annotated at 1 Hz with either a bounding box or the absent label. Despite being an excellent starting point, the data of YTBB are not ready to be used for the purpose of evaluating methods in a long-term scenario. Several stages of manual data curation are required.

The major issue is that the tracklet duration is limited to less than 20 s. However, it often occurs that multiple tracklets in one video refer to the same object instance. We identify these tracklets and combine their annotations in order to obtain significantly longer sequences, albeit with large gaps between annotated segments. This process involves finding the videos which contain multiple tracklets of the same class, watching the video and manually specifying which (if any) refer to the same object instance. Another issue with YTBB is that the first frame of a track may not be a suitable initial example to specify the target. To remedy this issue, for each video we manually select the first annotated frame in which the bounding box alone provides a clear and sufficient definition of the target. All annotations preceding this frame are discarded. The final manual stage is to exclude sequences that are of little interest for tracking, for example those in which the target object undergoes little motion or fills most of the image in most of the frames. To ensure the quality of annotations, all manual operations have been performed by a pool of five expert annotators. Each sequence has been assessed by two annotators and included only if both agreed.

Table 1. Comparison of the proposed OxUvA long-term tracking benchmark to existing benchmarks. Our proposal presents the longest average sequence length and is the only one testing trackers against object disappearance.

	OxUvA 2018	OTB-100 2015 [34]	VOT 2017 [13]	UAV123 2016 [21]	DTB 2017 [15]	NUSi-PRO 2016 [14]	TC 2015 [16]	ALOV 2013 [28]	NfS 2017 [11]
Frames	**1.55M**	59k	21k	113k	15k	135k	60k	152k	380k
Tracks	**366**	100	60	123	70	**365**	128	314	100
... w/ absent labels	**52%**	0%	0%	0%	0%	0%	0%	0%	0%
Avg length (min)	**2.36**	0.33	0.20	0.51	0.12	0.21	0.26	0.27	0.26
Median length (min)	**1.46**	0.22	0.17	0.49	0.10	0.17	0.22	0.15	0.17
Max length (min)	**20.80**	2.15	0.83	1.71	0.35	2.8	2.15	3.32	1.44
Min length (min)	**0.50**	0.04	0.02	0.06	0.04	0.08	0.04	0.01	0.01
Avg absent labels	**2.2**	0	0	0	0	0	0	0	0
Object classes	22	16	24	9	15	8	**27**	–	–

Once this manual process was complete, we assessed the performance of a naive baseline that simply reports the initial location in every subsequent frame. We then discarded all sequences in which this trivial tracker achieves at least 50% IOU in at least 50% of the frames.

Our final dataset comprises 366 object tracks in 337 videos. These were selected from an initial pool of about 1700 candidate videos, all of which were watched by at least two expert annotators. Table 1 summarizes some interesting statistics and compares the proposed dataset against existing ones. Remarkably, the total number of frames is respectively 26 and 10 times larger than the popular OTB-100 and ALOV respectively, making our proposed dataset the largest to date. Moreover, existing benchmarks never label the target object as absent. In contrast, our proposal contains an average of 2.2 absent labels per track and at least one labelled disappearance in 52% of the tracks. Finally, the sequences we propose are much longer, exhibiting an average duration of 2.3 min.

3.2 Data Subsets and Challenges

We split our dataset of 366 tracks into *dev* and *test* sets of 200 and 166 tracks respectively. The classes in the dev and test sets are disjoint, and this split is chosen randomly. The dev set contains bear, elephant, cat, bus, knife, boat, dog and bird; the test set contains zebra, potted plant, airplane, truck, horse, cow, giraffe, person, bicycle, umbrella, motorcycle, skateboard, car and toilet. The ground-truth labels for the testing set are secret, and can only be accessed

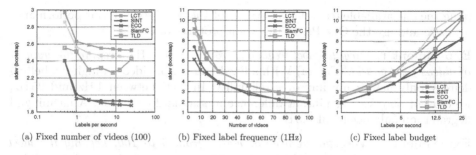

(a) Fixed number of videos (100)   (b) Fixed label frequency (1Hz)   (c) Fixed label budget

Fig. 2. Impact of annotation density and number of sequences on the evaluation reliability (higher standard deviation implies a less reliable evaluation).

through the evaluation server[1]. All results in the main paper are for the test set unless otherwise stated. A comparison between the dev and test sets can be found in the supplementary material.

Using these subsets, we further define two challenges: *constrained* and *open*. For the constrained challenge, trackers can be developed using only data from our dev set (long-term videos), from the dev classes in the original YTBB *train* set and from standard tracking benchmarks (see the website for precise rules). For the open challenge, trackers can use any public dataset except for the YTBB *validation* set, from which OxUvA is constructed. The constrained setting is closer to traditional model-free or one-shot tracking, since the object categories in the test set have not been seen before. All trackers in the constrained challenge are automatically entered into the open challenge. Note that methods using model parameters that were pre-trained for an auxiliary task are only eligible for the open challenge. The results for the constrained trackers alone are deferred to the supplementary material.

3.3 Annotation Density

Unlike most existing tracking benchmarks, in which every frame is labelled, the tracklets in YTBB are only labelled at a frequency of 1 Hz. We argue that this is sufficient for tracker evaluation since *(a)* it is unlikely that a tracker will fail and recover within one second, and *(b)* a tracking failure of less than a second would be relatively harmless in many applications. To verify this hypothesis, we investigate the results of several representative trackers on the OTB-100 [34] benchmark, varying the label frequency and number of videos in three experiments.

We study the effect of each experiment on the variance of the overall score considering the test set to be a random variable. Lower variance indicates a more reliable evaluation. Although we only have one sample from the distribution of test sets, this distribution can be approximated by repeatedly bootstrap sam-

---

[1] https://competitions.codalab.org/competitions/19529.

pling the one available test set [33]. We adopt the AUC score as our performance measure and use the One Pass Evaluation protocol of OTB-100.

Experiment 1: *Vary the label frequency from 0.5 to 25 Hz, keeping the number of videos fixed at 100.* (Fig. 2a) With a fixed number of videos, a higher labelling density only marginally improves reliability. In fact, between 1 Hz and 25 Hz, we did not observe a significant difference in standard deviation. A meaningful degradation only occurs at 0.5 Hz.

Experiment 2: *Vary the number of videos from 5 to 100, keeping the label frequency fixed at 1 Hz.* (Fig. 2b) Increasing the number of videos while keeping the frequency constant results in a steady and significant reduction in variance.

Experiment 3: *With a fixed budget of labels for the dataset, increase the label frequency by decreasing the number of videos (from 100 videos at 1 Hz to 4 videos at 25 Hz).* (Fig. 2c) A more reliable evaluation is obtained by increasing the number of videos at the expense of having fewer labels per second. Annotating *more* videos *sparsely* (at 1 Hz) leads to 4–5× smaller standard deviation than annotating *fewer* videos *densely* (at 25 Hz).

We conclude that *(a)* labelling at 1 Hz does not adversely affect the robustness of evaluation and *(b)* a large number of videos is paramount.

4   Tracker Evaluation

4.1   Evaluating Object Presence and Localization

Given an initial bounding box for the target, we require a tracker to predict either **present** or **absent** in each subsequent frame, and to estimate its location with an axis-aligned bounding box if present. This raises the question of how to evaluate a tracker's ability both to locate the target and to decide its presence.

With this intention, we introduce an analogy to binary classification. Let us equate object presence with the positive class and absence with the negative. In a frame where the object is absent, we declare a true negative (TN) if the tracker predicts **absent**, and a false positive (FP) otherwise. In a frame where the object is present, we declare a true positive (TP) if the tracker predicts **present** *and* reports the correct location, and a false negative (FN) otherwise. The location is determined to be correct if the IOU is above a threshold. Using these definitions, we can quantify tracking success using standard performance measures from classification.

However, some performance measures are inappropriate because the dataset possesses a severe class imbalance: although target disappearance is a frequent event, and occurs in roughly half of all sequences, only 4% of the actual annotations are **absent**. As a result, it would be possible to achieve high accuracy, high precision and high recall without making a single **absent** prediction. We therefore propose to evaluate trackers in terms of True Positive Rate (TPR) and True Negative Rate (TNR), which are *invariant* to class imbalance [7]. TPR gives the fraction of present objects that are reported **present** and correctly located, while TNR gives the fraction of absent objects that are reported **absent**. Note that, in contrast to typical binary classification problems, these metrics are not symmetric. While it is trivial to achieve TNR = 1 by reporting **absent** in every frame, it is only possible to achieve TPR = 1 by reporting **present** in every frame *and* successfully locating the object.

To obtain a single measure of tracking performance, we propose the geometric mean GM = $\sqrt{\text{TPR} \cdot \text{TNR}}$. This has the advantage that relative improvements in either metric are equally valuable since $\sqrt{(\alpha x)y} = \sqrt{x(\alpha y)}$.

4.2 Operating Points

In the object detection literature, it is usual to report a precision-recall curve, which plots the range of operating points that are obtained by varying a threshold on the scores of the predictions (*i.e.* to decide which are considered detections). The overall performance is then computed from multiple operating points, typically the average precision at multiple desired values of recall. Unfortunately, we cannot use the same methodology because trackers are *causal*. If we were to evaluate trackers using a range of operating points that are obtained without re-running the tracker, it may give an artificial advantage to state-less algorithms. Furthermore, if the tracker maintains an internal state, applying a threshold would cause its reported state to diverge from its internal state. Therefore, we require the tracker to output a hard decision in each frame, corresponding to a single point in TPR-TNR space.

However, even without making use of prediction scores, we can still consider a simple range of operating points. Specifically, a TPR-TNR curve is obtained by randomly flipping each **present** prediction to **absent** with probability $p \in [0, 1]$. This traces a straight line to the trivial operating point TPR = 0, TNR = 1, at which all predictions are **absent** (see Fig. 3, left). This line establishes a lower bound on the TPR of a method at a higher TNR. One tracker is said to be dominated by another if its TPR is below the lower bound of the other tracker at the same TNR.

Since most existing trackers never predict **absent**, they will have GM = TNR = 0. To enable a more informative comparison to these trackers, we instead consider the maximum geometric mean along this lower bound

$$\text{MaxGM} = \max_{0 \leq p \leq 1} \sqrt{((1 - p) \cdot \text{TPR})((1 - p) \cdot \text{TNR} + p)}. \tag{1}$$

5 Evaluated Trackers

We now explore how methods from the recent literature perform on our dataset. We limit the analysis to a selection of ten baselines which have shown strong performance or have affinity to the scenario we are considering. The baselines we select are roughly representative of three groups of methods.

- We first consider **LCT** [18], **EBT** [35] and **TLD** [10], three methods that have an affinity with long-term tracking for their design. Although based on different features and classifiers, they are each capable of locating the target anywhere in the frame, an important property when the target can disappear. This is in contrast to most methods, which search only a local neighbourhood. Unfortunately, EBT does not output the presence or absence of the object, and its source code is not available.
- As a second family, we consider methods that originate from short-term correlation filter trackers like KCF [9]. In particular, we chose recent methods which can operate in real-time and achieve high performance: **ECO-HC** [6], **BACF** [12] and **Staple** [2].
- Lastly, we consider three popular algorithms based on deep convolutional networks: **MDNet** [22] and the Siamese network-based trackers **SINT** [30] and **SiamFC** [3]. Both SINT and SiamFC only evaluate the offline-learned similarity function during tracking, whereas MDNet performs online fine-tuning. SiamFC is fully-convolutional, adopts a five-layer network and it is trained from scratch as a similarity function. SINT uses RoI pooling [8], is based on a VGG-16 [27] architecture pre-trained on ImageNet and fine-tuned on ALOV and uses bounding-box regression during tracking.

From the recent literature, TLD and LCT were the only methods that we could find with source code available that determine the presence or absence of the object. In order to have an additional method with TNR $\neq 0$, we equipped SiamFC with a simple re-detection logic similar to that described in [29]. If the maximum score of the response falls below a threshold, the tracker enters *object absent* mode. From this state, it considers a search area at a random location in each frame until the maximum score again surpasses the threshold, at which point the tracker returns to *object present* mode. Note that this implementation is method agnostic, does not require extra time for re-detection, and can be applied to any method which uses local search and produces a score in every frame. For both SiamFC and SiamFC + R we used the baseline model from the CFNet paper [32].

For all methods, we use the code and default hyper-parameters provided by the authors. None of the trackers have been trained on YTBB or tuned for our long-term dataset. However, some models have been trained on external datasets that share classes with YTBB: SINT and MDNet are initialized with networks pre-trained for image classification and SiamFC is trained on ImageNet VID.

6   Analysis

Main evaluation. Fig. 3 (left) shows the operating points of the evaluated methods in a TPR vs. TNR plot assuming overlap criterion IOU ≥ 0.5. The exact numbers are detailed in the accompanying table. Most methods are not designed to report absent predictions, therefore their operating points lie on the vertical axis (TNR $= 0$). The dashed lines represent operating points that can be obtained by randomly flipping predictions from `present` to `absent` as described

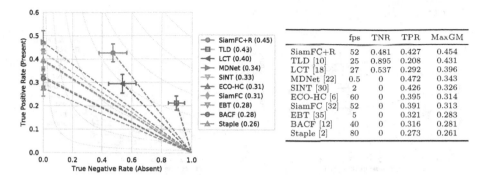

Fig. 3. Accuracy of the evaluated trackers in terms of True Positive Rate (TPR) and True Negative Rate (TNR) for IOU ≥ 0.5. The figure shows each tracker on a 2D plot (top right is best). Trackers that always report the object **present** appear on the vertical axis. The dashed lines are obtained by randomly switching predictions from **present** to **absent**. Methods are ranked by the maximum geometric mean along this line. The level sets of the geometric mean are shown in the background.

in Sect. 4.2. MDNet, SiamFC + R and TLD dominate other methods in the sense that their collective lower bounds exceed all other trackers. The following sections will investigate the results in greater depth.

To obtain error-bars, the set of videos is considered a random variable and the variance of each scalar quantity is estimated using bootstrap sampling [33] as in the earlier experiments. Naively assuming each variable to be approximately Gaussian, error-bars are plotted for the 90% confidence interval ($\pm 1.64\sigma$). This technique will be used in all following experiments.

Tracker Performance Over Time. We analyze the performance of all methods in different time ranges. Figure 4 (left) plots the TPR for frames $t \in (0, x]$ whereas Fig. 4 (right) plots the TPR for frames $t \in (x, \infty)$. With the possible exception of SINT, these plots show that the performance of all methods decays rapidly after the first minute. This seems to be most severe for methods based on online-learned linear templates and hand-crafted features (LCT, Staple, BACF and ECO-HC, to a varying degree). Although SiamFC is similar in design to SINT, its performance decays more rapidly. This may be due to architectural differences, or because SINT is initialized with parameters pre-trained for image classification, or because SINT is more restrictive in its scale-space search.

Influence of Object Disappearance. We compare the performance of the different methods on videos that contain at least one **absent** annotation to those in which every annotation is **present**. This is a heuristic for whether the object disappears in the duration of the sequence. Figure 5 (left) visualizes the relationship between the TPR for these two subsets of videos. Intuitively, the closer a method is to the diagonal $y = x$, the less its performance is affected by disappearance.

We observe that all baselines have better performance in the set of videos in which the target object never disappears. This is not surprising, as most methods

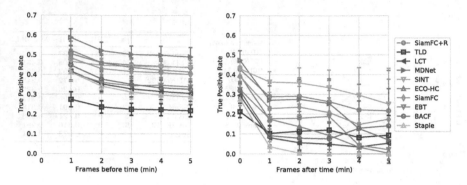

Fig. 4. Degradation of tracker performance over time. SINT seems more robust to this effect than most other methods. The variance becomes large when considering only frames beyond four minutes because there are less annotations in this region.

assume that the target object is always present. Nonetheless, TLD and SINT seem to be slightly less affected by disappearance than other methods, as they are relatively close to the diagonal.

Post-hoc Score Thresholding. Although we have stated that we do not wish to evaluate methods at multiple operating points by varying a score threshold, it is natural for a tracker to possess such an internal score, and it may be informative to inspect the result of applying this "post-hoc" threshold. Figure 5 (right) illustrates the different results obtained by sweeping the range of score thresholds. Note that this plot can only be constructed for the *dev* set, because the evaluation server for the *test* set returns a statistical summary of the results, not the validation of each individual frame.

The large gaps between the lower bound curves (dashed line) and the post-hoc curves (continuous line) show that there is a lot to be gained by simply thresholding the prediction score. Intuition might suggest that post-hoc thresholding is itself a lower bound on the performance that could be obtained by adjusting the model's internal threshold: if modifying the threshold improves the predictions, then surely it would be even better for the tracker to have made this decision internally? However, this is not necessarily the case, since changing the internal decision in one frame may have an unpredictable effect in the frames that follow. Indeed, the re-detection module of SiamFC + R hardly improves over the post-hoc threshold curve of SiamFC.

In the high-TNR region, the approaches based on offline-trained Siamese networks seem more promising than the online-trained MDNet and Staple.

7   Continuous Attributes

7.1   Definition

While measuring performance on a large set of videos is an important indicator of a tracker's overall quality, such an aggregate metric hides many subtleties

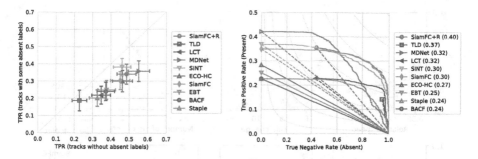

Fig. 5. *(left)* Impact of disappearances. All baselines are negatively impacted in the presence of target absences, although to a different extent. *(right)* Effect of post-hoc score thresholding (on the *dev* set) for trackers that output a score.

that differentiate trackers. For a more in-depth analysis, modern datasets usually include binary attribute annotations [13,14,16,21,28,34]. By measuring performance on a subset of videos with a particular attribute, such as "scale change" or "fast motion", one can characterize the strengths and weaknesses of a tracker.

Unfortunately, the manual annotation of binary attributes is highly subjective: how fast does the target have to move in order to be labelled "fast motion", or what is the threshold for "scale change"? Instead, we decided to measure quantities that are correlated to some informative attributes, but which can be calculated directly from bounding box annotations and meta-data. We refer to these quantities as *continuous attributes*. Each frame i where the target is present is annotated with a time instant t_i, 2D position vector p_i, and bounding box dimensions (w_i, h_i), expressed as a fraction of the image size. The continuous attributes are then defined as follows:

Size. Trackers have different strategies to search across scale, so they can be sensitive to different object sizes. The target size at each frame is defined $s_i = s(w_i, h_i) = \sqrt{w_i h_i}$. This metric was chosen because it is invariant to aspect ratio changes (*i.e.* $s(rw_i, h_i/r) = s(w_i, h_i)$). It also changes linearly when the object is re-scaled by an isotropic factor (*i.e.* $s(\sigma w_i, \sigma h_i) = \sigma s(w_i, h_i)$).

Relative Speed. Fast-moving targets can lose trackers that depend heavily on temporal smoothness. We compute the target speed relative to its size, Δ_i, with:

$$\Delta_i = \frac{1}{\sqrt{s_i s_{i-1}}} \frac{\|p_i - p_{i-1}\|_2}{t_i - t_{i-1}} \ .$$

The second factor is the instantaneous speed of the target, while the first factor normalizes it w.r.t. the object size. The normalization is needed since the object size is inversely correlated to the distance from the camera, and perspective effects result in closer (larger) objects moving more than objects further away.

Scale Change. Some targets may remain mostly at the same scale across a video, while others will vary wildly due to perspective changes. We measure the range of scale variation in a video as $S = \max_i s_i / \min_i s_i$.

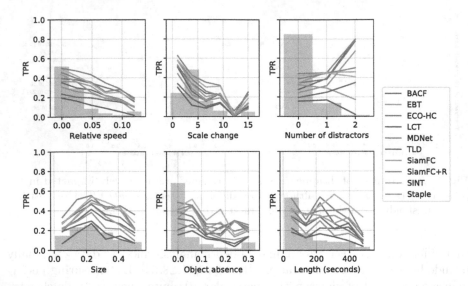

Fig. 6. True-Positive Rate (at IOU $\geq$ 0.5) of each tracker as a function of different continuous attributes. The continuous attributes are computed per frame or per video, and are then distributed into discrete bins. TPR is computed separately for the frames/videos in each bin. The shaded boxes show the fraction of frames/videos that belong to each bin. Only relative speed and size are computed per-frame, the remaining are per-video.

Object Absence. In addition to the analysis of Sect. 6, here we measure performance as a function of the fraction of frames in which the target is absent.

Distractors. Appearance-based methods can be distracted by objects that are similar to the target, *e.g.* objects of the same class. To explore this aspect, we leverage the multiple annotations per video and define the number of distractors as the number of other objects with the same class as the target.

Length. In long videos the effects of small errors are compounded over time, causing trackers to drift. We define video length as the elapsed time in seconds between the first and last annotations of the target.

While these attributes could be thresholded to yield binary attributes that are comparable to the previous benchmarks, we found that *binning* them can yield a more informative plot, especially if performance is presented together with the size of each bin, in order to indicate its reliability.

7.2   Influence of Continuous Attributes

We partition each attribute into 6 bins, except for "distractors" which takes only 3 discrete values. Figure 6 shows a histogram (shaded boxes) with the fraction of frames/videos that fall into each bin of each attribute, together with a plot indicating the performance (TPR) of each tracker over the subset corresponding to each bin. Notice how, for the points in the plots corresponding to bins with fewer videos, the variance is quite high and thus their results may be difficult to interpret. However, we can still draw several conclusions:

Relative Speed. Unsurprisingly, all trackers performing local search show degraded performance as the target moves more rapidly. Among all the methods able to consider the entire frame (TLD, LCT, EBT and SiamFC+R) the least affected by high speeds is TLD.

Scale Change. Videos where the target maintains the same size seem to be the optimal operating point for all trackers. There is a significant dip in performance around 6× variation in scale. Since this bin contains a significant fraction of the videos, there is a large opportunity for improvement by focusing on this case.

Number of Distractors. Methods do not seem to be confounded by distractors of the same class as much as one would expect. For videos with one distractor, most trackers' performances are maintained. This means that they are not simply detecting broad object categories, which was a plausible concern over the use of pre-trained deep networks. With two distractors, only EBT and LCT seem to perform significantly worse, possibly locking on distractor objects during their full-image search strategy.

Size. Most trackers seem to be well-adapted to the range of object sizes in the dataset, with a performance peak reached at 0.2 by all the methods taken into account. Unlike others, MDNet and LCT seem to maintain their performances at the largest object sizes.

Object Absence. As already noted in Sect. 6, disappearance of the target object affects all methods, which show a meaningful drop in performance when the number of frames where the object is **absent** increases from 0% to 10%. SiamFC+R, MDNet and ECO-HC seem to be less affected by larger absences.

Length. As noted in Sect. 6, probably due to the short-term nature of the benchmarks that they were calibrated for, most trackers are severely affected after only a few minutes of tracking. For example, both MDNet and ECO-HC present a large drop in performance in videos longer than three minutes. SINT, followed by MDNet, are the most obvious exceptions to this trend.

8   Conclusion

We have introduced the OxUvA long-term tracking dataset, with which it is possible to assess methods on sequences that are minutes in length and often contain disappearance of the target object. Our benchmark is the largest ever proposed in the single-object tracking community and contains more than 25× the number of frames of OTB-100. In order to afford such a vast dataset, we opt for a relatively sparse labelling of the target objects at 1 Hz. To justify this decision, we empirically show that, for the sake of reliability, a high density of labels is not important while a large number of videos is paramount.

Adapting the metrics of True Positive and True Negative Rate from classification, we design an evaluation that measures the ability of a tracker to correctly understand whether the target object is present in the frame and where it is located. We then evaluate the performance of several popular tracking methods on the 166 sequences that comprise our testing set, also considering the effect of several factors such as the object's speed and size, the sequence length, the number of distractors and the amount of occlusion. We believe that our contribution will spur the design of algorithms ready to be used in the many practical applications that require trackers able to deal with long sequences and capable of determining whether the object is present or not.

References

1. Babenko, B., Yang, M.H., Belongie, S.: Visual tracking with online multiple instance learning. In: IEEE Conference on Computer Vision and Pattern Recognition (2009)
2. Bertinetto, L., Valmadre, J., Golodetz, S., Miksik, O., Torr, P.H.S.: Staple: complementary learners for real-time tracking. In: IEEE Conference on Computer Vision and Pattern Recognition (2016)
3. Bertinetto, L., Valmadre, J., Henriques, J.F., Vedaldi, A., Torr, P.H.S.: Fully-convolutional siamese networks for object tracking. In: Hua, G., Jégou, H. (eds.) ECCV 2016. LNCS, vol. 9914, pp. 850–865. Springer, Cham (2016). https://doi.org/10.1007/978-3-319-48881-3_56
4. Breitenstein, M.D., Reichlin, F., Leibe, B., Koller-Meier, E., Van Gool, L.: Robust tracking-by-detection using a detector confidence particle filter. In: IEEE Conference on Computer Vision and Pattern Recognition (2009)
5. Camps, O., Cucchiara, R., Del Bimbo, A., Matas, J., Pernici, F., Sclaroff, S.: Long-term detection and tracking workshop (2014). http://www.micc.unifi.it/LTDT2014
6. Danelljan, M., Bhat, G., Khan, F.S., Felsberg, M.: ECO: efficient convolution operators for tracking. In: IEEE Conference on Computer Vision and Pattern Recognition (2017)
7. Fawcett, T.: An introduction to ROC analysis. Pattern Recogn. Lett. **27**(8), 861–874 (2006)
8. Girshick, R.: Fast R-CNN. In: IEEE International Conference on Computer Vision (2015)
9. Henriques, J.F., Caseiro, R., Martins, P., Batista, J.: High-speed tracking with kernelized correlation filters. IEEE Trans. Pattern Anal. Mach. Intell. **37**(3), 583–596 (2015)
10. Kalal, Z., Mikolajczyk, K., Matas, J.: Tracking-learning-detection. IEEE Trans. Pattern Anal. Mach. Intell. **34**(7), 1409–1422 (2012)
11. Kiani, H., Fagg, A., Huang, C., Ramanan, D., Lucey, S.: Need for speed: A benchmark for higher frame rate object tracking. In: IEEE International Conference on Computer Vision (2017)
12. Kiani, H., Fagg, A., Lucey, S.: Learning background-aware correlation filters for visual tracking. In: IEEE Conference on Computer Vision and Pattern Recognition (2017)
13. Kristan, M., et al.: A novel performance evaluation methodology for single-target trackers. IEEE Trans. Pattern Anal. Mach. Intell. **38**(11), 2137–2155 (2016)
14. Li, A., Lin, M., Wu, Y., Yang, M.H., Yan, S.: NUS-PRO: a new visual tracking challenge. IEEE Trans. Pattern Anal. Mach. Intell. **38**, 335–349 (2016)

15. Li, S., Yeung, D.Y.: Visual object tracking for unmanned aerial vehicles: a benchmark and new motion models. In: AAAI (2017)
16. Liang, P., Blasch, E., Ling, H.: Encoding color information for visual tracking: algorithms and benchmark. IEEE Trans. Image Process. **24**(12), 5630–5644 (2015)
17. Lukežič, A., Čehovin Zajc, L., Vojíř, T., Matas, J., Kristan, M.: Now you see me: evaluating performance in long-term visual tracking. arXiv preprint arXiv:1804.07056 (2018)
18. Ma, C., Yang, X., Zhang, C., Yang, M.H.: Long-term correlation tracking. In: IEEE Conference on Computer Vision and Pattern Recognition (2015)
19. Mei, X., Ling, H.: Robust visual tracking using ℓ_1 minimization. In: 2009 IEEE 12th International Conference on Computer Vision, pp. 1436–1443. IEEE (2009)
20. Moudgil, A., Gandhi, V.: Long-term visual object tracking benchmark. arXiv preprint arXiv:1712.01358 (2017)
21. Mueller, M., Smith, N., Ghanem, B.: A benchmark and simulator for UAV tracking. In: Leibe, B., Matas, J., Sebe, N., Welling, M. (eds.) ECCV 2016. LNCS, vol. 9905, pp. 445–461. Springer, Cham (2016). https://doi.org/10.1007/978-3-319-46448-0_27
22. Nam, H., Han, B.: Learning multi-domain convolutional neural networks for visual tracking. In: IEEE Conference on Computer Vision and Pattern Recognition (2016)
23. Real, E., Shlens, J., Mazzocchi, S., Pan, X., Vanhoucke, V.: YouTube-Bounding Boxes: a large high-precision human-annotated data set for object detection in video. In: IEEE Conference on Computer Vision and Pattern Recognition (2017)
24. Ross, D.A., Lim, J., Lin, R.S., Yang, M.H.: Incremental learning for robust visual tracking. Int. J. Comput. Vis. **77**(1–3), 125–141 (2008)
25. Russakovsky, O., et al.: ImageNet large scale visual recognition challenge. Int. J. Comput. Vis. **115**(3), 211–252 (2015)
26. Santner, J., Leistner, C., Saffari, A., Pock, T., Bischof, H.: PROST: parallel robust online simple tracking. In: IEEE Conference on Computer Vision and Pattern Recognition (2010)
27. Simonyan, K., Zisserman, A.: Very deep convolutional networks for large-scale image recognition. arXiv preprint arXiv:1409.1556 (2014)
28. Smeulders, A.W.M., Chu, D.M., Cucchiara, R., Calderara, S., Dehghan, A., Shah, M.: Visual tracking: an experimental survey. IEEE Trans. Pattern Anal. Mach. Intell. **36**(7), 1442–1468 (2014)
29. Supancic, III, J., Ramanan, D.: Tracking as online decision-making: learning a policy from streaming videos with reinforcement learning. In: IEEE International Conference on Computer Vision (2017)
30. Tao, R., Gavves, E., Smeulders, A.W.M.: Siamese instance search for tracking. In: IEEE Conference on Computer Vision and Pattern Recognition (2016)
31. Tao, R., Gavves, E., Smeulders, A.W.M.: Tracking for half an hour. arXiv preprint arXiv:1711.10217 (2017)
32. Valmadre, J., Bertinetto, L., Henriques, J.F., Vedaldi, A., Torr, P.H.S.: End-to-end representation learning for correlation filter based tracking. In: IEEE Conference on Computer Vision and Pattern Recognition (2017)
33. Wasserman, L.: All of Statistics: A Concise Course in Statistical Inference. Springer Science & Business Media, New York (2013)
34. Wu, Y., Lim, J., Yang, M.H.: Object tracking benchmark. IEEE Trans. Pattern Anal. Mach. Intell. **37**(9), 1834–1848 (2015)
35. Zhu, G., Porikli, F., Li, H.: Beyond local search: tracking objects everywhere with instance-specific proposals. In: IEEE Conference on Computer Vision and Pattern Recognition (2016)

Affinity Derivation and Graph Merge for Instance Segmentation

Yiding Liu[1]([⊠]), Siyu Yang[2], Bin Li[3], Wengang Zhou[1], Jizheng Xu[3],
Houqiang Li[1], and Yan Lu[3]

[1] Department of Electronic Engineering and Information Science,
University of Science and Technology of China, Hefei, China
liuyd123@mail.ustc.edu.cn, {zhwg,lihq}@ustc.edu.cn
[2] Beihang University, Beijing, China
yangsiyu@buaa.edu.cn
[3] Microsoft Research, Beijing, China
{libin,jzxu,yanlu}@microsoft.com

Abstract. We present an instance segmentation scheme based on pixel affinity information, which is the relationship of two pixels belonging to the same instance. In our scheme, we use two neural networks with similar structures. One predicts the pixel level semantic score and the other is designed to derive pixel affinities. Regarding pixels as the vertexes and affinities as edges, we then propose a simple yet effective graph merge algorithm to cluster pixels into instances. Experiments show that our scheme generates fine grained instance masks. With Cityscape training data, the proposed scheme achieves 27.3 AP on test set.

Keywords: Instance segmentation · Pixel affinity · Graph merge
Proposal-free

1 Introduction

With the fast development of Convolutional Neural Networks (CNN), recent years have witnessed breakthroughs in various computer vision tasks. For example, CNN based methods have surpassed humans in image classification [24]. Rapid progress has been made in the areas of object detection [14,26,43], semantic segmentation [17], and even instance segmentation [19,21].

Semantic segmentation and instance segmentation try to label every pixel in images. Instance segmentation is more challenging as it also tells which object one pixel belongs to. Basically, there are two categories of methods for instance segmentation. The first one is developed from object detection. If one already has results of object detection, i.e. a bounding box for each object, one can move one step further to refine the bounding box semantic information to generate

---

This work was done when Yiding Liu and Siyu Yang took internship at Microsoft Research Asia.

© Springer Nature Switzerland AG 2018
V. Ferrari et al. (Eds.): ECCV 2018, LNCS 11207, pp. 708–724, 2018.
https://doi.org/10.1007/978-3-030-01219-9_42

instance results. Since the results rely on the proposals from object detection, such a category can be regarded as proposal-based methods. The other one is to cluster pixels into instances based on semantic segmentation results. We refer to this category as proposal-free methods.

Recent instance segmentation methods have advanced in both directions above. Proposal-based methods are usually extensions of object detection frameworks [18,38,42]. Fully Convolutional Instance-aware Semantic Segmentation (FCIS) [33] produces position-sensitive feature maps [12] and generates masks by merging features in corresponding areas. Mask RCNN (Mask Region CNN) [23] extends Faster RCNN [44] with another branch to generate masks with different classes. Proposal-based methods produce instance-level results in the region of interest (ROI) to make the mask precise. Therefore, performance depends highly on the region proposal network (RPN) [44], and is usually influenced by the regression accuracy of the bounding box.

Meanwhile, methods without proposal generation have also been developed. The basic idea of these methods [4,15,28,34] is to learn instance level features for each pixel with a CNN, then a clustering method is applied to group the pixels together. Sequential group network (SGN) [37] uses CNN to generate features and makes group decisions based on a series of networks.

In this paper, we focus on proposal-free method and exploit semantic information from a new perspective. Similar to other proposal-free methods, we develop our scheme based on semantic segmentation. In addition to using pixel-wise classification results from semantic segmentation, we propose deriving pixel affinity information that tells if two pixels belong to the same object. We design networks to derive this information for neighboring pixels at various scales. We then take the set of pixels as vertexes and the pixel affinities as the weights of edges, constructing a graph from the output of the network. Then we propose a simple graph merge algorithm to group the pixels into instances. More details will be shown in Sect. 3.4. By doing so, we can achieve state-of-the-art results on the Cityscapes *test* set with only Cityscapes training data.

Our main contributions are as follows:

- We introduce a novel proposal-free instance segmentation scheme, where we use both semantic information and pixel affinity information to derive instance segmentation results.
- We show that even with a simple graph merge algorithm, we can outperform other methods, including proposal-based ones. It clearly shows that proposal-free methods can have comparable or even better performance than proposal-based methods. We hope that our findings will inspire more people to take instance segmentation to new levels along this direction.
- We show that a semantic segmentation network is reasonably suitable for pixel affinity prediction with only the meaning of the output changed.

2 Related Work

Our proposed method is based on CNNs for semantic segmentation, and we adapt this to generate pixel affinities. Thus, we first review previous works on semantic segmentation, followed by discussing the works on instance segmentation, which is further divided into proposal-based and proposal-free methods.

Semantic Segmentation: Replacing fully connected layers with convolution layers, Fully Convolutional Networks (FCN) [46] adapts a classification network for semantic segmentation. Following this, many works try to improve the network to overcome shortcomings [35,40,48]. To preserve spatial resolution and enlarge the corresponding respective field, [5,47] introduce dilated/atrous convolution to the network structure. To explore multi-scale information, PSPNet [48] designs a pyramid pooling structure [20,30,39] and Deeplabv2 [5] proposes Atrous Spatial Pyramid Pooling (ASPP) to embed contextual information. Most recently, Chen *et al.* have proposed Deeplabv3+ [8] by introducing an encoder-decoder structure [16,27,36,41] to [7] which achieves promising performance. In this paper, we do not focus on network structure design. Any CNN for semantic segmentation would be feasible for our work.

Proposal-Based Instance Segmentation: These methods exploit region proposals to locate the object and then obtain corresponding mask exploiting detection models [11,13,38,44]. DeepMask [42] proposes a network to classify whether the patch contains an object and then generates a mask. Multi-task Network Cascades (MNC) [10] provides a cascaded framework and decomposes instance segmentation into three phases including box localization, mask generation and classification. Instance-sensitive FCN [12] extends features to position-sensitive score maps, which contain necessary information for mask proposals, and generates instances combined with objectiveness scores. FCIS [33] takes position-sensitive maps further with inside/outside scores to encode information for instance segmentation. Mask-RCNN [23] adds another branch on top of Faster-RCNN [44] to predict mask outputs together with box prediction and classification, achieving excellent performance. MaskLab [6] combines Mask-RCNN with position-sensitive scores and improves performance.

Proposal-Free Instance Segmentation: These methods often consist of two branches, a segmentation branch and a clustering-purpose branch. Pixel-wise mask prediction is obtained by segmentation output and the clustering process aims to group the pixels that belong to a certain instance together. Liang *et al.* [34] predict the number of instances in an image and instance location for each pixel together with the semantic mask. They then perform a spectral clustering to group pixels. Long *et al.* [28] encode instance relationships to classes and exploit the boundary information when clustering pixels. Alireza *et al.* [15] and Bert *et al.* [4] try to learn the embedding vectors to cluster instances. SGN [37] tends to propose a sequential framework to group the instances gradually from points to lines and finally to instances, which currently achieves the best performance of proposal-free methods.

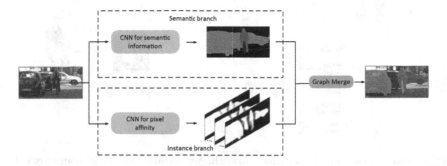

Fig. 1. Basic structure for the proposed framework.

Fig. 2. Illustration for pixel affinity. (a) Locations for proposed neighbors. (b) The yellow point indicates the current pixel. Other points are neighboring pixels, in which red ones indicate pixels of different instances and blue ones indicate the same instance (*rider*). The pixel distance is NOT real but only for an illustration. (c) The derived labels and expected network output. (Color figure online)

3   Our Approach

3.1   Overview

The fundamental framework of our approach is shown in Fig. 1. We propose splitting the task of instance segmentation into two sequential steps. The first step utilizes CNN to obtain class information and pixel affinity of the input image, while the second step applies the graph merge algorithm on those results to generate the pixel-level masks for each instance.

In the first step, we utilize a semantic segmentation network to generate the class information for each pixel. Then, we use another network to generate information which is helpful for instance segmentation. It is not straightforward to make the network output pixel-level instance label directly, as labels of instances are exchangeable. Under this circumstance, we propose learning whether a pair of neighboring pixels belongs to the same instance. It is a binary classification problem that can be handled by the network.

It is impractical to generate affinities between each pixel and all the others in an image. Thus, we carefully select a set of neighboring pixels to generate

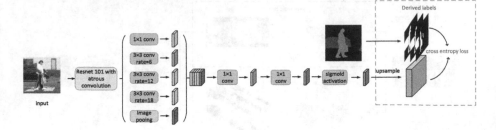

Fig. 3. Basic structure for instance branch, we utilize the basic framework from Deeplabv3 [7] based on Resnet-101 [25].

affinity information. Each channel of the network output represents a probability of whether the neighbor pixel and the current one belong to the same instance, as illustrated in Fig. 2(a). As can be seen from the instance branch in Fig. 1, the pixel affinities apparently indicate the boundary and show the feasibility to represent the instance information.

In the second step, we consider the whole image as a graph and apply the graph merge algorithm on the network output to generate instance segmentation results. For every instance, the class label is determined by voting among all pixels based on semantic labels.

3.2   Semantic Branch

Deeplabv3 [7] is one of the state-of-the-art networks in semantic segmentation. Thus, we use it as the semantic branch in our proposed framework. It should be noted that other semantic segmentation approaches could also be used in our framework.

3.3   Instance Branch

We select several pixel pairs, with the output of instance branch representing whether they belong to the same instance. Theoretically, if an instance is composed of only one connected area, we can merge the instance with only two pairs of pixel affinities, i.e whether $(p(x, y), p(x - 1, y))$ and $(p(x, y), p(x, y - 1))$ belong to the same instance, $p(x, y)$ is the pixel at location (x, y) in an image I. For the robustness to noise and ability to handle fragmented instances, we choose the following pixel set as the neighborhood of the current pixel $p(x, y)$

$$N(x, y) = \bigcup_{d \in D} N_d(x, y), \tag{1}$$

where $N_d(x, y)$ is the set of eight-neighbors of $p(x, y)$ with distance d, which can be expressed as

$$N_d(x, y) = \{p(x + a, y + b), \forall a, b \in \{d, 0, -d\}\} \setminus \{p(x, y)\}, \tag{2}$$

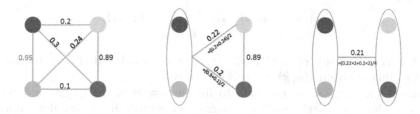

Fig. 4. A brief illustration for the graph merge algorithm

and D is the set of distances. In our implementation, $D = \{1, 2, 4, 8, 16, 32, 64\}$, as illustrated in Fig. 2(a).

We employ the network in Fig. 3 as the instance branch, in which we remove the last softmax activation of the semantic segmentation network and minimize the cross entropy loss after sigmoid activation. There are $8 \times 7 = 56$ elements in the set $N(x, y)$, so we assign 56 channels to the last layer. In the training procedure, the corresponding label is assigned as 1 if the pixel pair belongs to the same instance. In the inference procedure, we treat the network outputs as the probability of the pixel pair belonging to the same instance. We make a simple illustration of the selected neighbors in Fig. 2(b), and the corresponding label is shown in Fig. 2(c).

3.4   Graph Merge

The graph merge algorithm takes the semantic segmentation and pixel affinity results as input to generate instance segmentation results. Let vertex set V be the set of pixels and edge set E be the set of pixel affinities obtained from the network. Then, we have a graph $G = (V, E)$. It should be noted that the output of the instance branch is symmetrical. Pair $(p(x, y), p(x_c, y_c))$ obtained at (x, y) and $(p(x_c, y_c), p(x, y))$ at (x_c, y_c) have same physical meaning, both indicating the probability of these two pixels belonging to a certain instance. We average the corresponding probabilities before using them as the initial E. Thus, G can be considered an undirected graph (Fig. 4).

Let $e(i, j)$ denote an edge connecting vertex i and j. We first find the edge $e(u, v)$ with maximum probability and merge u, v together into a new super-pixel uv. It should be noted that we do not distinguish pixel and super-pixel explicitly, and uv is just a symbol indicating it is merged from u and v. After merging u, v, we need to update the graph G. For vertex set V, two pixels are removed and a new super-pixel is added,

$$V := V \setminus \{u, v\} \cup \{uv\}. \tag{3}$$

Then, the edge set E needs to be updated. We define $E(u) = \bigcup_{k \in K_u} \{e(u, k)\}$ representing all edges connecting with u. K_u is the set of pixels connecting to u. $E(u)$ and $E(v)$ should be discarded as u and v have been removed. $K_{uv} = K_u \cup K_v \setminus \{u, v\}$, E is updated as follows,

$$E := E \setminus E(u) \setminus E(v) \bigcup_{k \in K_{uv}} \{e(uv, k)\}. \tag{4}$$

For $k \in K(u) \cap K(v)$, $e(uv, k)$ is the average of $e(u, k)$ and $e(v, k)$. Otherwise, $e(uv, k)$ inherits from $e(u, k)$ or $e(v, k)$ directly.

After updating G, we continue to find a new maximum edge and repeat the procedure iteratively until the maximum probability is smaller than the threshold r_w. We summarize the procedure above in Algorithm 1. We then obtain a set of V and each pixel/super-pixel represents an instance. We recover the super-pixels to sets of pixels and filter the sets with a cardinality threshold r_c which means we only preserve the instance with pixels more than r_c. We get a set of pixels X as an instance and calculate the confidence of the instance from the initial E. We average all the edges $e(i, j)$ for both $i, j \in X$, and this confidence indicates the probability of X being an instance.

Algorithm 1. Graph Merge Algorithm

Require: Averaged instance branch output $P(u, v)$, thresholds r_w
Ensure: Merge result V, E
 1: Initialize V with pixels and E with $e(u, v) = P(u, v)$
 2: **while** Maximum $e(u, v) \in E \geq r_w$ **do**
 3:     Merge u, v to super-pixel uv
 4:     Update V: $V \Leftarrow V \setminus \{u, v\} \cup \{uv\}$
 5:     $K_{uv} = K_u \cup K_v \setminus \{u, v\}$
 6:     **for** $k \in K_{u,v}$ **do**
 7:         **if** $k \in E(u) \cap E(v)$ **then**
 8:             $e(uv, k)$ is the average of $e(u, k)$ and $e(v, k)$
 9:         **else**
10:             $e(uv, k) = k \in K_u?\ e(u, k) : e(v, k)$
11:         **end if**
12:     **end for**
13:     Update E: $E \Leftarrow E \setminus E(u) \setminus E(v) \bigcup_{k \in K_{uv}} \{e(uv, k)\}$
14: **end while**

We prefer the spatially neighboring pixels to be merged together. For this reason, we divide $D = \{1, 2, 4, 8, 16, 32, 64\}$ as three subsets $D_s = \{1, 2, 4\}$, $D_m = \{8, 16\}$ and $D_l = \{32, 64\}$ with which we do our graph merge sequentially. Firstly, we merge pixels with probabilities in D_s with a large threshold $r_{ws} = 0.97$, and then all edges with distances in D_m are added. We continue our graph merge with a lower threshold $r_{wm} = 0.7$ and repeat the operation for D_l with $r_{wl} = 0.3$.

4   Implementation Details

The fundamental framework of our approach has been introduced in the previous section. In this section, we elaborate on the implementation details.

4.1 Excluding Background

Background pixels do not need to be considered in the graph merge procedure, since they should not be present in any instance. Excluding them decreases the image size and accelerates the whole process. We refer to the interested sub-regions containing foreground objects as ROI in our method. Different from the ROI in the proposal-based method, the ROI in our method may contain multiple objects. In implementation, we look for connected areas of foreground pixels as ROIs. The foreground pixels will be aggregated to super-pixels when generating feasible areas for connecting the separated components belonging to a certain instance. In our implementation, the super-pixel is 32×32, which means if any pixel in a 32×32 region is foreground pixel, we consider the whole 32×32 region as foreground. We extend the connected area with a few pixels (16 in our implementation) and find the tightest bounding boxes, which is used as the input of our approach. Different from thousands of proposals used in the proposal-based instance segmentation algorithms, the number of ROIs in our approach is usually less than 10.

4.2 Pixel Affinity Refinement

Besides determining the instance class, the semantic segmentation results can help more with the graph merge algorithm. Intuitively, if two pixels have different semantic labels, they should not belong to a certain instance. Thus, we propose refining the pixel affinity output from the instance branch in Fig. 1 by scores from the semantic branch. We denote $P(x, y, c)$ as the probability of $p(x, y)$ and $p(x_c, y_c)$ belonging to a certain instance from the instance branch. We refine it by multiplying the semantic similarity of these two pixels.

Let $\mathbf{P}(x, y) = (p_0(x, y), p_1(x, y), \cdots, p_m(x, y))$ denote the probability output of the semantic branch. $m + 1$ denotes the number of classes (including background), $p_i(x, y)$ denotes the probability of the pixel belonging to the i-th class and $p_0(x, y)$ is the background probability. The inner product of the probabilities of two pixels indicates the probability of these two pixels having a certain semantic label. We do not care about background pixels, so we discard the background probability and calculate the inner product of $\mathbf{P}(x, y)$ and $\mathbf{P}(x_c, y_c)$ as $\sum_{i=1}^{m} p_i(x, y)p_i(x_c, y_c)$. We then refine the pixel affinity by

$$P_r(x, y, c) = \sigma(\sum_{i=1}^{m} p_i(x, y)p_i(x_c, y_c))P(x, y, c), \tag{5}$$

where

$$\sigma(x) = 2 \times (\frac{1}{1 + e^{-\alpha x}} - \frac{1}{2})_a. \tag{6}$$

This $\sigma()$ function is modified from the sigmoid function and we set $\alpha = 5$ to weaken the influence of the semantic inner product.

Fig. 5. Illustration for forcing local merge. We simulate the merging process with distance $\{1, 2, 4\}$ and window size 2, we only show edges involved in this process. Pixels with identical colors are merged and we update the new weights for edges. The left graph shows that the new probability in distance $\{2\}$ should only be averaged by the original weights from distance $\{4\}$ in the same direction. However, the right graph shows the new probability for distance $\{1\}$ should be an average of the edges from both distance $\{1\}$ and $\{2\}$.

Despite the information we mentioned above, we find that the semantic segmentation model may confuse different classes. Thus, we define the confusion matrix. The confusion matrix in semantic segmentation means a matrix where c_{ij} represents the count of pixels belonging to class i classified to class j. Given this, we can find that the semantic segmentation model sometimes misclassifies a pixel in a subclass, but rarely across sets. Thus, we combine classes in each set together as a super-class to further weaken the influence on instance segmentation from the semantic term. Moreover, we set the inner product to 0, when the two pixels are in different super-classes, which helps to refine the instance segmentation results.

4.3   Resizing ROIs

Like what ROI pooling does, we enlarge the shortened edge of the proposed boxes to a fixed size and proportionally enlarge the other edge, which we use as the input. For the Cityscapes dataset, we scale the height of each ROI to 513, if the original height is smaller than that. The reason of scaling it to 513 is that the networks are trained with 513×513 patches. Thus, we would like to use the same value for inference. Moreover, we limit the scaling factor to be less than 4. Resizing ROIs is helpful for finding more small instances.

4.4   Forcing Local Merge

We force the neighboring $m \times m$ pixels to be merged before the graph merge. During the process, we recalculate the pixel affinities according to our graph algorithm in Sect. 3.4. Figure 5 shows a simple example. Force merging neighboring pixels not only filters out the noises of the network output by averaging, but also decreases the input size of the graph merge algorithm to save on processing time. We will provide results on different merge window size in Sect. 5.3.

4.5   Semantic Class Partition

To get more exquisite ROIs, we refer to the semantic super-classes in Sect. 4.2 and apply it to the procedure of generating connected areas. We add together the probabilities in each super-class and classify the pixels to super-classes. To find the foreground region of a super-class, we only consider the pixels classified to this super-class as foreground and all the others as background. Detailed experiment results will be provided in Sect. 5.3.

5 Experiment Evaluation

We evaluate our method on the Cityscapes dataset [9], which consists of 5,000 images representing complex urban street scenes with a resolution of 2048×1024. Images in the dataset are split into training, validation, and test sets of 2,975, 500, and 1,525 images, respectively. We use average precision (AP) as our metric to evaluate the results, which is calculated by the mean of the IOU threshold from 0.5 to 0.95 with the step of 0.05.

As most of the images in the Cityscapes dataset are background on top or bottom, we discard the parts with no semantic labeled pixels on the top or bottom for 90% of training images randomly, in order to make our data more effective. To improve semantic segmentation performance, we utilize coarse labeled training data by selecting patches containing *trunk, train,* and *bus* as additional training data to train the semantic branch. We crop 1554 patches from coarse labeled data. To augment data with different scale objects, we also crop several upsampled areas in the fine labeled data. As a result, the final patched fine labeled training data includes 14178 patches, including 2975 original training images with 90% of them having been dropped top and bottom background pixels. The networks are trained with Tensorflow [1] and the graph merge algorithm is implemented in C++.

5.1 Training Strategy

For the basic setting, the network output strides for both semantic and instance branch are set to 16, and they are trained with input images of size 513×513.

For the semantic branch, the network structure is defined as introduced in Sect. 3.2, whose weight is initialized with ImageNet [45] pretrained ResNet-101 model. During training, we use 4 Nvidia P40 GPUs with SGD [31] in the following steps. (1) We use 19-class semantic labeled data in the Cityscapes dataset fine and coarse data together, with an initial learning rate of 0.02 and a batch size of 16 per GPU. The model is trained using 100k iterations and the learning rate is multiplied by 0.7 every 15k iterations. (2) As the instance segmentation only focuses on 8 foreground objects, we then finetune the network with 9 classes labeled data (8 foreground objects and 1 background). Training data for this model contains a mix of 2 times fine labeled patched data and coarse labeled patches. We keep the other training setting unchanged. (3) We finetune the model with 3 times of original fine labeled data together with coarse labeled patches, with other training settings remaining unchanged.

For instance branch, we initialize the network with the ImageNet pretrained model. We train this model with patched fine labeled training data for 120k iterations, with other settings identical to step (1) in semantic model training.

Table 1. Instance segmentation performance on the Cityscapes *test* set. All results listed are trained only with Cityscapes.

Methods	person	rider	car	trunk	bus	train	mcycle	bicycle	AP 50%	AP
InstanceCut [29]	10.0	8.0	23.7	14.0	19.5	15.2	9.3	4.7	27.9	13.0
SAIS [22]	14.6	12.9	35.7	16.0	23.2	19.0	10.3	7.8	36.7	17.4
DWT [3]	15.5	14.1	31.5	22.5	27.0	22.9	13.9	8.0	35.3	19.4
DIN [2]	16.5	16.7	25.7	20.6	30.0	23.4	17.1	10.1	38.8	20.0
SGN [37]	21.8	20.1	39.4	**24.8**	33.2	**30.8**	17.7	12.4	44.9	25.0
Mask RCNN [23]	30.5	23.7	**46.9**	22.8	32.2	18.6	**19.1**	**16.0**	**49.9**	26.2
Ours	**31.5**	**25.2**	42.3	21.8	**37.2**	28.9	18.8	12.8	45.6	**27.3**

5.2 Main Results

As shown in Table 1, our method notably improves the performance and achieves 27.3 AP on the Cityscapes *test* set, which outperforms Mask RCNN trained with only Cityscapes *train* data by 1.1 points (4.2% relatively).

We show qualitive results for our algorithm in Fig. 6. As shown in the figure, we produce high quality results on both semantic and instance masks, where we get precise boundaries. As shown in the last row of results, we can handle the problem of fragmented instances and merge the separated parts together.

Our method outperforms Mask RCNN on AP but gets a relatively lower performance on AP 50%. This could mean we would get a higher score when the IOU threshold is larger. It also means that Mask RCNN could find more instances with relatively less accurate masks (higher AP 50%), but our method achieves more accurate boundaries. The bounding box of proposal-based method may lead to a rough mask, which will be judged as correct with a small IOU.

Utilizing the implementation of Mask RCNN in Detectron[1], we generate the instance masks and compare them with our results. As shown in Fig. 7, our results are finer grained. It can be expected that results will be better if we substitute the mask from Mask RCNN with ours when both approaches have prediction of a certain instance.

5.3 Detailed Results

We report the ablation studies with *val* set and discuss in detail.

Baseline: We take the algorithm we describe in Sect. 4.1 as the baseline, for excluding backgrounds helps to significantly speedup the graph merge algorithm and hardly affects the final results. We get 18.9% AP as our baseline, and we will introduce the results for strategies applied to the graph merge algorithm.

We show the experiment results for graph merge strategies in Table 2. For pixel affinity refinement, we add semantic information to refine the probability and get a 22.8% AP result. As shown in the table, it provides 3.9 points AP improvement. Then we resize the ROIs with a fixed size of 513, and we get a

---

[1] https://github.com/facebookresearch/Detectron.

Fig. 6. Results on Cityscapes *val* dataset, original image, semantic results, instance results and ground truth from left to right. Results in the last two rows are cropped from the original ones for better visualization.

Fig. 7. Results compared with Mask RCNN. The first row is our results and the second row are results from Mask RCNN. As shown in the figure, we generate more fine-grained masks.

Fig. 8. Examples of faliure case

raise of 5.9 points AP, which significantly improve the results. The merge window size influences the results a lot. We have a 0.5 point improvement utilizing window size 2 and a 1.2 point drop with a window size of 4. As we can see, utilizing 2 as the window size not only reduces the complexity of graph merge, but also improves performance. Utilizing 4 causes a loss of detailed information and performs below expectations. Therefore, we utilize 2 in the following experiments. As mentioned in Sect. 4.1, we finally divide semantic classes into 3 subclasses for semantic class partition:{*person, rider*}, {*car, trunk, bus, train*} and {*motorcycle, bicycle*}, finding feasible areas separately. Such separation reduces

Table 2. Graph Merge Strategy: we test for our graph merge strategies for our algorithm including PAR: Pixel Affinity Refinement, RR: Resizing ROIs, FLM: Forcing Local Merge and SCP: Semantic Class Partition. Note that 2 and 4 in FLM represent the merge window size, default as 1.

PAR	RR	FLM	SCP	AP
				18.9
✓				22.8
✓	✓			28.7
✓	✓	2		29.2
✓	✓	4		27.5
✓	✓	2	✓	30.7

the influence across subclasses and makes the ROI resize more effectively. We get a 1.5 improvement by applying this technique from 29.0% to 30.5%, as shown in the table. It should be noted that utilizing larger images can make results better, but it also increases processing time.

Besides the strategies we utilize in the graph merge, we also test our model for different inference strategies referring to [7]. Output stride is always important for segmentation-like tasks. Small output stride usually means more detailed information but more inference time cost and smaller batch size in training. We test our models first trained on output stride 16, then we finetune models on output stride 8 as in [7]. It shows in Table 3 that both semantic and instance model finetuned with output stride 8 improve results by 0.5 point individually. When combined together, we achieve 32.1% AP with 1.4 point improvement compared with output stride 16.

We apply horizontal flips and semantic class refinement as alternative inference strategies. Horizontal flips for semantic inference brings 0.7 point increase in AP, and for instance inference flip, 0.5 point improvement is observed. We then achieve 33.5% AP combining these two flips.

Through observations on the *val* set, we find that instances in *bicycle* and *motorcycle* often fail to be connected when they are fragmented. To improve such situations, we map the pixel affinities between these two classes with Eq. 6 at the distance $d = 64$. As shown in Table 3, semantic class refinement yields 0.6 point improvement, and we get our best result of 34.1% AP on the *val* set.

5.4   Discussions

In our current implementation, the maximum distance of the instance branch output is 64. This means that the graph merge algorithm is not able to merge two non-adjacent parts with distance greater than 64. Adding more output channels can hardly help overall performance. Moreover, using other network structures, which could achieve better results on semantic segmentation may further improve the performance of the proposed graph merge algorithm. Some existing methods,

Table 3. Additional inference strategies: We test for additional inference strategies for our algorithm including Semantic OS: output stride for semantic branch, Instance OS: output stride for instance branch SHF: Semantic horizontal flip inference, IHF: Instance horizontal flip inference and SCR: Semantic Class Refinement. We also list several results from other methods for comparison.

Methods	Semantic OS	Instance OS	SHF	IHF	SCR	AP
DWT [3]						21.2
SGN [37]						29.2
Mask RCNN [23]						31.5
Ours	16	16				30.7
	8	16				31.2
	16	8				31.2
	8	8				32.1
	8	8	✓			32.8
	8	8		✓		32.6
	8	8	✓	✓		33.5
	8	8	✓	✓	✓	34.1

such as [32], could solve the graph merge problem but [32] is much slower than the proposed method. The current graph merge step is implemented on CPU and we believe there is big potential to use a multi-core CPU system for acceleration. Some examples of failure case are shown in Fig. 8. The proposed method may miss some small objects or merge different instances together by mistake.

6   Conclusions

In this paper, we introduce a proposal-free instance segmentation scheme via affinity derivation and graph merge. We generate semantic segmentation results and pixel affinities from two separate networks with a similar structure. Taking this information as input, we regard pixels as vertexes and pixel affinity information as edges to build a graph. The proposed graph merge algorithm is then used to cluster the pixels into instances. Our method outperforms Mask RCNN on the Cityscapes dataset by 1.1 point AP improvement using only Cityscapes training data. It shows that the proposal-free method can achieve state-of-the-art performance. We notice that the performance of semantic segmentation keeps improving with new methods, which can easily lead to performance improvement for instance segmentation via our method. The proposed graph merge algorithm is simple. We believe that more advanced algorithms can lead to even better performance. Improvements along these directions are left for further work.

Acknowledgement. Yiding Liu, Wengang Zhou and Houqiang Li's work was supported in part by 973 Program under Contract 2015CB351803, Natural Science Foundation of China (NSFC) under Contract 61390514 and Contract 61632019.

References

1. Abadi, M., et al.: TensorFlow: large-scale machine learning on heterogeneous distributed systems. arXiv preprint arXiv:1603.04467 (2016)
2. Arnab, A., Torr, P.H.S.: Pixelwise instance segmentation with a dynamically instantiated network. In: 2017 IEEE Conference on Computer Vision and Pattern Recognition (CVPR), pp. 879–888, July 2017. https://doi.org/10.1109/CVPR.2017.100
3. Bai, M., Urtasun, R.: Deep watershed transform for instance segmentation. In: 2017 IEEE Conference on Computer Vision and Pattern Recognition (CVPR), pp. 2858–2866, July 2017. https://doi.org/10.1109/CVPR.2017.305
4. Brabandere, B.D., Neven, D., Gool, L.V.: Semantic instance segmentation for autonomous driving. In: 2017 IEEE Conference on Computer Vision and Pattern Recognition Workshops (CVPRW), pp. 478–480, July 2017. https://doi.org/10.1109/CVPRW.2017.66
5. Chen, L.C., Papandreou, G., Kokkinos, I., Murphy, K., Yuille, A.L.: DeepLab: semantic image segmentation with deep convolutional nets, atrous convolution, and fully connected CRFs. IEEE Trans. Pattern Anal. Mach. Intell. **40**(4), 834–848 (2018). https://doi.org/10.1109/TPAMI.2017.2699184
6. Chen, L.C., Hermans, A., Papandreou, G., Schroff, F., Wang, P., Adam, H.: MaskLab: instance segmentation by refining object detection with semantic and direction features. arXiv preprint arXiv:1712.04837 (2017)
7. Chen, L.C., Papandreou, G., Schroff, F., Adam, H.: Rethinking atrous convolution for semantic image segmentation. arXiv preprint arXiv:1706.05587 (2017)
8. Chen, L.C., Zhu, Y., Papandreou, G., Schroff, F., Adam, H.: Encoder-decoder with atrous separable convolution for semantic image segmentation. arXiv preprint arXiv:1802.02611 (2018)
9. Cordts, M., et al.: The cityscapes dataset for semantic urban scene understanding. In: 2016 IEEE Conference on Computer Vision and Pattern Recognition (CVPR), pp. 3213–3223, June 2016. https://doi.org/10.1109/CVPR.2016.350
10. Dai, J., He, K., Sun, J.: Instance-aware semantic segmentation via multi-task network cascades. In: 2016 IEEE Conference on Computer Vision and Pattern Recognition (CVPR), pp. 3150–3158, June 2016. https://doi.org/10.1109/CVPR.2016.343
11. Dai, J., et al.: Deformable convolutional networks. In: 2017 IEEE International Conference on Computer Vision (ICCV), pp. 764–773, October 2017. https://doi.org/10.1109/ICCV.2017.89
12. Dai, J., He, K., Li, Y., Ren, S., Sun, J.: Instance-sensitive fully convolutional networks. In: Leibe, B., Matas, J., Sebe, N., Welling, M. (eds.) ECCV 2016. LNCS, vol. 9910, pp. 534–549. Springer, Cham (2016). https://doi.org/10.1007/978-3-319-46466-4_32
13. Dai, J., Li, Y., He, K., Sun, J.: R-FCN: object detection via region-based fully convolutional networks. In: Advances in Neural Information Processing Systems, pp. 379–387 (2016)
14. Erhan, D., Szegedy, C., Toshev, A., Anguelov, D.: Scalable object detection using deep neural networks. In: 2014 IEEE Conference on Computer Vision and Pattern Recognition, pp. 2155–2162, June 2014. https://doi.org/10.1109/CVPR.2014.276
15. Fathi, A., et al.: Semantic instance segmentation via deep metric learning. arXiv preprint arXiv:1703.10277 (2017)

16. Fu, J., Liu, J., Wang, Y., Lu, H.: Stacked deconvolutional network for semantic segmentation. arXiv preprint arXiv:1708.04943 (2017)
17. Garcia-Garcia, A., Orts-Escolano, S., Oprea, S., Villena-Martinez, V., Garcia-Rodriguez, J.: A review on deep learning techniques applied to semantic segmentation. arXiv preprint arXiv:1704.06857 (2017)
18. Girshick, R.: Fast R-CNN. In: 2015 IEEE International Conference on Computer Vision (ICCV), pp. 1440–1448, December 2015. https://doi.org/10.1109/ICCV.2015.169
19. Girshick, R., Donahue, J., Darrell, T., Malik, J.: Rich feature hierarchies for accurate object detection and semantic segmentation. In: 2014 IEEE Conference on Computer Vision and Pattern Recognition, pp. 580–587, June 2014. https://doi.org/10.1109/CVPR.2014.81
20. Grauman, K., Darrell, T.: The pyramid match kernel: discriminative classification with sets of image features. In: Tenth IEEE International Conference on Computer Vision (ICCV 2005) Volume 1, vol. 2, pp. 1458–1465, October 2005. https://doi.org/10.1109/ICCV.2005.239
21. Hariharan, B., Arbeláez, P., Girshick, R., Malik, J.: Simultaneous detection and segmentation. In: Fleet, D., Pajdla, T., Schiele, B., Tuytelaars, T. (eds.) ECCV 2014. LNCS, vol. 8695, pp. 297–312. Springer, Cham (2014). https://doi.org/10.1007/978-3-319-10584-0_20
22. Hayder, Z., He, X., Salzmann, M.: Shape-aware instance segmentation. arXiv preprint arXiv:1612.03129 (2016)
23. He, K., Gkioxari, G., Dollr, P., Girshick, R.: Mask R-CNN. In: 2017 IEEE International Conference on Computer Vision (ICCV), pp. 2980–2988, October 2017. https://doi.org/10.1109/ICCV.2017.322
24. He, K., Zhang, X., Ren, S., Sun, J.: Delving deep into rectifiers: surpassing human-level performance on imagenet classification. In: 2015 IEEE International Conference on Computer Vision (ICCV), pp. 1026–1034 (Dec 2015). https://doi.org/10.1109/ICCV.2015.123
25. He, K., Zhang, X., Ren, S., Sun, J.: Deep residual learning for image recognition. In: 2016 IEEE Conference on Computer Vision and Pattern Recognition (CVPR), pp. 770–778 (June 2016). https://doi.org/10.1109/CVPR.2016.90
26. Huang, J., et al.: Speed/accuracy trade-offs for modern convolutional object detectors. In: 2017 IEEE Conference on Computer Vision and Pattern Recognition (CVPR), pp. 3296–3297, July 2017. https://doi.org/10.1109/CVPR.2017.351
27. Islam, M.A., Rochan, M., Bruce, N.D.B., Wang, Y.: Gated feedback refinement network for dense image labeling. In: 2017 IEEE Conference on Computer Vision and Pattern Recognition (CVPR), pp. 4877–4885, July 2017. https://doi.org/10.1109/CVPR.2017.518
28. Jin, L., Chen, Z., Tu, Z.: Object detection free instance segmentation with labeling transformations. arXiv preprint arXiv:1611.08991 (2016)
29. Kirillov, A., Levinkov, E., Andres, B., Savchynskyy, B., Rother, C.: InstanceCut: from edges to instances with MultiCut. In: 2017 IEEE Conference on Computer Vision and Pattern Recognition (CVPR), pp. 7322–7331, July 2017. https://doi.org/10.1109/CVPR.2017.774
30. Lazebnik, S., Schmid, C., Ponce, J.: Beyond bags of features: spatial pyramid matching for recognizing natural scene categories. In: 2006 IEEE Computer Society Conference on Computer Vision and Pattern Recognition (CVPR 2006), vol. 2, pp. 2169–2178 (2006). https://doi.org/10.1109/CVPR.2006.68
31. LeCun, Y., et al.: Backpropagation applied to handwritten zip code recognition. Neural Comput. **1**(4), 541–551 (1989). https://doi.org/10.1162/neco.1989.1.4.541

32. Levinkov, E., et al.: Joint graph decomposition and node labeling: problem, algorithms, applications. In: IEEE Conference on Computer Vision and Pattern Recognition (CVPR) (2017)

33. Li, Y., Qi, H., Dai, J., Ji, X., Wei, Y.: Fully convolutional instance-aware semantic segmentation. In: 2017 IEEE Conference on Computer Vision and Pattern Recognition (CVPR), pp. 4438–4446, July 2017. https://doi.org/10.1109/CVPR.2017.472

34. Liang, X., Wei, Y., Shen, X., Yang, J., Lin, L., Yan, S.: Proposal-free network for instance-level object segmentation. arXiv preprint arXiv:1509.02636 (2015)

35. Lin, G., Shen, C., Van Den Hengel, A., Reid, I.: Efficient piecewise training of deep structured models for semantic segmentation. In: 2016 IEEE Conference on Computer Vision and Pattern Recognition (CVPR), pp. 3194–3203, June 2016. https://doi.org/10.1109/CVPR.2016.348

36. Lin, T.Y., Dollr, P., Girshick, R., He, K., Hariharan, B., Belongie, S.: Feature pyramid networks for object detection. In: 2017 IEEE Conference on Computer Vision and Pattern Recognition (CVPR), pp. 936–944 (July 2017). https://doi.org/10.1109/CVPR.2017.106

37. Liu, S., Jia, J., Fidler, S., Urtasun, R.: SGN: sequential grouping networks for instance segmentation. In: 2017 IEEE International Conference on Computer Vision (ICCV), pp. 3516–3524, October 2017. https://doi.org/10.1109/ICCV.2017.378

38. Liu, W., et al.: SSD: single shot multibox detector. In: Leibe, B., Matas, J., Sebe, N., Welling, M. (eds.) ECCV 2016. LNCS, vol. 9905, pp. 21–37. Springer, Cham (2016). https://doi.org/10.1007/978-3-319-46448-0_2

39. Liu, W., Rabinovich, A., Berg, A.C.: ParseNet: looking wider to see better. arXiv preprint arXiv:1506.04579 (2015)

40. Liu, Z., Li, X., Luo, P., Loy, C.C., Tang, X.: Semantic image segmentation via deep parsing network. In: 2015 IEEE International Conference on Computer Vision (ICCV), pp. 1377–1385, December 2015. https://doi.org/10.1109/ICCV.2015.162

41. Newell, A., Yang, K., Deng, J.: Stacked hourglass networks for human pose estimation. In: Leibe, B., Matas, J., Sebe, N., Welling, M. (eds.) ECCV 2016. LNCS, vol. 9912, pp. 483–499. Springer, Cham (2016). https://doi.org/10.1007/978-3-319-46484-8_29

42. Pinheiro, P.O., Collobert, R., Dollár, P.: Learning to segment object candidates. In: Advances in Neural Information Processing Systems, pp. 1990–1998 (2015)

43. Redmon, J., Divvala, S., Girshick, R., Farhadi, A.: You only look once: unified, real-time object detection. In: 2016 IEEE Conference on Computer Vision and Pattern Recognition (CVPR), pp. 779–788, June 2016. https://doi.org/10.1109/CVPR.2016.91

44. Ren, S., He, K., Girshick, R., Sun, J.: Faster R-CNN: towards real-time object detection with region proposal networks. IEEE Trans. Pattern Anal. Mach. Intell. **39**(6), 1137–1149 (2017). https://doi.org/10.1109/TPAMI.2016.2577031

45. Russakovsky, O., et al.: Imagenet large scale visual recognition challenge. Int. J. Comput. Vis. **115**(3), 211–252 (2015). https://doi.org/10.1007/s11263-015-0816-y

46. Shelhamer, E., Long, J., Darrell, T.: Fully convolutional networks for semantic segmentation. IEEE Trans. Pattern Anal. Mach. Intell. **39**(4), 640–651 (2017). https://doi.org/10.1109/TPAMI.2016.2572683

47. Yu, F., Koltun, V.: Multi-scale context aggregation by dilated convolutions. arXiv preprint arXiv:1511.07122 (2015)

48. Zhao, H., Shi, J., Qi, X., Wang, X., Jia, J.: Pyramid scene parsing network. In: 2017 IEEE Conference on Computer Vision and Pattern Recognition (CVPR), pp. 6230–6239, July 2017. https://doi.org/10.1109/CVPR.2017.660

Generating 3D Faces Using Convolutional Mesh Autoencoders

Anurag Ranjan[(✉)], Timo Bolkart, Soubhik Sanyal, and Michael J. Black

Max Planck Institute for Intelligent Systems, Tübingen, Germany
{aranjan,tbolkart,ssanyal,black}@tuebingen.mpg.de

Abstract. Learned 3D representations of human faces are useful for computer vision problems such as 3D face tracking and reconstruction from images, as well as graphics applications such as character generation and animation. Traditional models learn a latent representation of a face using linear subspaces or higher-order tensor generalizations. Due to this linearity, they can not capture extreme deformations and non-linear expressions. To address this, we introduce a versatile model that learns a non-linear representation of a face using spectral convolutions on a mesh surface. We introduce mesh sampling operations that enable a hierarchical mesh representation that captures non-linear variations in shape and expression at multiple scales within the model. In a variational setting, our model samples diverse realistic 3D faces from a multivariate Gaussian distribution. Our training data consists of 20,466 meshes of extreme expressions captured over 12 different subjects. Despite limited training data, our trained model outperforms state-of-the-art face models with 50% lower reconstruction error, while using 75% fewer parameters. We show that, replacing the expression space of an existing state-of-the-art face model with our model, achieves a lower reconstruction error. Our data, model and code are available at http://coma.is.tue.mpg.de/.

1 Introduction

The human face is highly variable in shape as it is affected by many factors such as age, sex, ethnicity, etc., and deforms significantly with expressions. The existing state of the art 3D face representations mostly use linear transformations [28,41,42] or higher-order tensor generalizations [12,14,46]. These 3D face models have several applications including face recognition [40], generating and animating faces [28] and monocular 3D face reconstruction [44]. Since these models are linear, they do not capture the non-linear deformations due to extreme facial expressions. These expressions are crucial to capture the realism of a 3D face.

Meanwhile, convolutional neural networks (CNNs) have emerged as rich models for generating images [22,35], audio [34], etc. One of the reasons for

Electronic supplementary material The online version of this chapter (https://doi.org/10.1007/978-3-030-01219-9_43) contains supplementary material, which is available to authorized users.

V. Ferrari et al. (Eds.): ECCV 2018, LNCS 11207, pp. 725–741, 2018.
https://doi.org/10.1007/978-3-030-01219-9_43

their success is attributed to the multi-scale hierarchical structure of CNNs that allows them to learn translational-invariant localized features. Recent works have explored volumetric convolutions [8] for 3D representations. However, volumetric operations require a lot of memory and have been limited to low resolution 3D volumes. Modeling convolutions on 3D meshes can be memory efficient and allows for processing high resolution 3D structures. However, CNNs have mostly been successful in Euclidean domains with grid-based structured data and the generalization of CNNs to meshes is not trivial. Extending CNNs to graph structures and meshes has only recently drawn significant attention [10,11,17]. Hierarchical operations in CNNs such as max-pooling and upsampling have not been adapted to meshes. Moreover, training CNNs on 3D facial data is challenging due to the limited size of current 3D datasets. Existing large scale datasets [14,16,38,49,50] do not contain high resolution extreme facial expressions.

To address these problems, we introduce a Convolutional Mesh Autoencoder (CoMA) with novel mesh sampling operations, which preserve the topological structure of the mesh features at different scales in a neural network. We follow the work of Defferrard et al. [17] on generalizing the convolution on graphs using fast Chebyshev filters, and use their formulation for convolving over our facial mesh. We perform spectral decomposition of meshes and apply convolutions directly in frequency space. This makes convolutions memory efficient and feasible to process high resolution meshes. We combine the convolutions and sampling operations to construct our model in the form of a Convolutional Mesh Autoencoder. We show that CoMA performs much better than state of the art face models at capturing highly non-linear extreme facial expressions with fewer model parameters. Having fewer parameters in our model makes it more compact, and easier to train. This reduction in parameters is attributed to the locally invariant convolutional filters that can be shared over the mesh surface.

We address the problem of data limitation by capturing 20,466 high resolution meshes with extreme facial expressions in a multi-camera active stereo system. Our dataset spans 12 subjects performing 12 different expressions. The expressions are chosen to be complex and asymmetric, with significant deformation in the facial tissue.

In summary, our work introduces a representation that models variations on the mesh surface using a hierarchical multi-scale approach and can generalize to other 3D mesh processing applications. Our main contributions are: (1) we introduce a Convolutional Mesh Autoencoder consisting of mesh downsampling and mesh upsampling layers with fast localized convolutional filters defined on the mesh surface; (2) we show that our model accurately represents 3D faces in a low-dimensional latent space performing 50% better than a PCA model that is used in state of the art face models such as [1,7,28,41,47]; (3) our autoencoder uses up to 75% fewer parameters than linear PCA models, while being more accurate in terms of reconstruction error; (4) we show that replacing the expression space of a state of the art face model, FLAME [28], by CoMA improves its reconstruction accuracy; (5) we show that our model can be used in a variational setting to sample a diversity of facial meshes from a known

Gaussian distribution; (6) we provide 20,466 frames of complex 3D head meshes from 12 different subjects for a range of extreme facial expressions along with our code and trained models for research purposes.

2 Related Work

Face Representations. Blanz and Vetter [2] introduced the *morphable model*; the first generic representation for 3D faces based on principal component analysis (PCA) to describe facial shape and texture variations. We also refer the reader to Brunton et al. [13] for a comprehensive overview of 3D face representations. To date, the Basel Face Model (BFM) [36], i.e. the publicly available variant of the morphable model, is the most widely used representation for 3D face shape in a neutral expression. Booth et al. [3] recently proposed another linear neutral expression 3D face model learned from almost 10, 000 face scans of more diverse subjects.

Representing facial expressions with linear spaces, or higher-order generalizations thereof, remains the state-of-the-art. The linear expression basis vectors are either computed using PCA [1, 7, 28, 41, 47], or are manually defined using linear blendshapes (e.g. [6, 27, 42]). Yang et al. [47] use multiple PCA models, one per expression, Amberg et al. [1] combine a neutral shape PCA model with a PCA model on the expression residuals from the neutral shape. A similar model with an additional albedo model was used within the Face2Face framework [43]. The recently published FLAME model [28] additionally models head rotation, and yaw motion with linear blendskinning and achieves state-of-the-art results. Vlasic et al. [46] introduce multilinear models, i.e., a higher-order generalization of PCA to model expressive 3D faces. Recently, Abrevaya et al. [18] propose an autoencoder with a CNN-based encoder and a multilinear model as a decoder. Opposed to our mesh autoencoder, their encoder operates on depth images rather than directly on meshes. For all these methods, the model parameters globally influence the shape; i.e. each parameter affects all the vertices of the face mesh. Our convolutional mesh autoencoder however models localized variations due to the hierarchical multiscale nature of the convolutions combined with the down- and up-sampling.

To capture localized facial details, Neumann et al. [33] and Ferrari et al. [19] use sparse linear models. Brunton et al. [12] use a hierarchical multiscale approach by computing localized multilinear models on wavelet coefficients. While Brunton et al. [12] also used a hierarchical multi-scale representation, their method does not use shared parameters across the entire domain. Note that sampling in localized low-dimensional spaces [12] is difficult due to the locality of the facial features; combinations of localized facial features are unlikely to form plausible global face shapes. One goal of our work is to generate new face meshes by sampling the latent space, thus we design our autoencoder to use a single low-dimensional latent space.

Jackson et al. [25] use a volumetric face representation in their CNN-based framework. In contrast to existing face representation methods, our mesh autoencoder uses convolutional layers to represent faces with significantly fewer parameters. Since it is defined completely on the mesh space, we do not have memory constraints which affect volumetric convolutional methods for representing 3D models.

Convolutional Networks. Brönstein et al. [10] give a comprehensive overview of generalizations of CNNs on non-Euclidean domains, including meshes and graphs. Masci et al. [31] define the first mesh convolutions by locally parameterizing the surface around each point using geodesic polar coordinates, and defining convolutions on the resulting angular bins. In a follow-up work, Boscaini et al. [5] parametrize local intrinsic patches around each point using anisotropic heat kernels. Monti et al. [32] introduce d-dimensional pseudo-coordinates that define a local system around each point with weight functions. This method resembles the intrinsic mesh convolution of [31] and [5] for specific choices of the weight functions. In contrast, Monti el al. [32] use Gaussian kernels with a trainable mean vector and covariance matrix as weight functions.

Verma et al. [45] presente dynamic filtering on graphs where the filter weights depend on the inputs. This work does not focus on reducing the dimensionality of graphs or meshes. Yi et al. [48] also present a spectral CNN for labeling nodes but does not involve any mesh dimensionality reduction. Sinha et al. [39] and Maron et al. [30] embed mesh surfaces into planar images to apply conventional CNNs. Sinha et al. use a robust spherical parametrization to project the surface onto an octahedron, which is then cut and unfolded to form a square image. Maron et al. [30] introduce a conformal mapping from the mesh surface into a flat torus. Litany et al. [29] use graph convolutions for shape completion.

Although, the above methods presented generalizations of convolutions on meshes, they do not use a structure to reduce the meshes to a low dimensional space. Our proposed autoencoder efficiently handles these problems by combining the mesh convolutions with efficient mesh-downsampling and mesh-upsampling operators.

Bruna et al. [11] propose the first generalization of CNNs on graphs by exploiting the connection of the graph Laplacian and the Fourier basis (see Sect. 3 for more details). This leads to spectral filters that generalize graph convolutions. Boscaini et al. [4] extend this using a windowed Fourier transform to localize in frequency space. Henaff et al. [24] build upon the work of Bruna et al. by adding a procedure to estimate the structure of the graph. To reduce the computational complexity of the spectral graph convolutions, Defferrard et al. [17] approximate the spectral filters by truncated Chebyshev poynomials, which avoids explicitly computing the Laplacian eigenvectors, and introduce an efficient pooling operator for graphs. Kipf and Welling [26] simplify this using only first-order Chebyshev polynomials.

However, these graph CNNs are not directly applied to 3D meshes. CoMA uses truncated Chebyshev polynomials [17] as mesh convolutions. In addition, we define mesh down-sampling and up-sampling layers to obtain a complete mesh autoencoder structure to represent highly complex 3D faces, obtaining state of the art results in 3D face modeling.

3   Mesh Operators

We define a 3D facial mesh as a set of vertices and edges, $\mathcal{F} = (\mathcal{V}, A)$, with $|\mathcal{V}| = n$ vertices that lie in 3D Euclidean space, $\mathcal{V} \in \mathbb{R}^{n \times 3}$. The sparse adjacency matrix $A \in \{0, 1\}^{n \times n}$ represents the edge connections, where $A_{ij} = 1$ denotes an edge connecting vertices i and j, and $A_{ij} = 0$ otherwise. The non-normalized graph Laplacian [15] is defined as $L = D - A$, with the diagonal matrix D that represents the degree of each vertex in $\mathcal{V}$ as $D_{ii} = \sum_j A_{ij}$.

The Laplacian is diagonalized by the Fourier basis $U \in \mathbb{R}^{n \times n}$ (as L is a real symmetric matrix) as $L = U \Lambda U^T$, where the columns of $U = [u_0, u_1, ..., u_{n-1}]$ are the orthogonal eigenvectors of L, and $\Lambda = diag([\lambda_0, \lambda_1, ..., \lambda_{n-1}]) \in \mathbb{R}^{n \times n}$ is a diagonal matrix with the associated real, non-negative eigenvalues. The graph Fourier transform [15] of the mesh vertices $x \in \mathbb{R}^{n \times 3}$ is then defined as $x_\omega = U^T x$, and the inverse Fourier transform as $x = U x_\omega$.

3.1   Fast Spectral Convolutions

The convolution operator $*$ can be defined in Fourier space as a Hadamard product, $x * y = U((U^T x) \odot (U^T y))$. This is computationally expensive with large numbers of vertices, since U is not sparse. The problem is addressed by formulating mesh filtering with a kernel g_θ using a recursive Chebyshev polynomial [17,23]. The filter g_θ is parametrized as a Chebyshev polynomial of order K given by

$$g_\theta(L) = \sum_{k=0}^{K-1} \theta_k T_k(\tilde{L}), \tag{1}$$

where $\tilde{L} = 2L/\lambda_{max} - I_n$ is the scaled Laplacian, the parameter $\theta \in \mathbb{R}^K$ is a vector of Chebyshev coefficients, and $T_k \in \mathbb{R}^{n \times n}$ is the Chebyshev polynomial of order k that can be computed recursively as $T_k(x) = 2x T_{k-1}(x) - T_{k-2}(x)$ with $T_0 = 1$ and $T_1 = x$. The spectral convolution can then be defined as in [17]

$$y_j = \sum_{i=1}^{F_{in}} g_{\theta_{i,j}}(L) x_i \in \mathbb{R}^n, \tag{2}$$

where y_j computes the jth feature of $y \in \mathbb{R}^{n \times F_{out}}$. The input $x \in \mathbb{R}^{n \times F_{in}}$ has F_{in} features. The input face mesh has $F_{in} = 3$ features corresponding to its 3D vertex positions. Each convolutional layer has $F_{in} \times F_{out}$ vectors of Chebyshev coefficients, $\theta_{i,j} \in \mathbb{R}^K$, as trainable parameters.

3.2   Mesh Sampling

In order to capture both global and local context, we seek a hierarchical multi-scale representation of the mesh. This allows convolutional kernels to capture local context in the shallow layers and global context in the deeper layers of the network. In order to address this representation problem, we introduce mesh

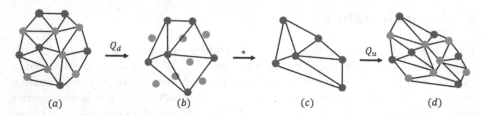

Fig. 1. Mesh sampling operations: a mesh feature (a) is down-sampled by removing red vertices that minimize quadric error [20]. We store the barycentric coordinates of the red vertices w.r.t. the down-sampled mesh (b). The down-sampled mesh can then be transformed using convolutional operations to obtain the transformed mesh (c). The contracted vertices are then added at the barycentric locations (d). (Color figure online)

sampling operators that define the down-sampling and up-sampling of a mesh feature in a neural network. A mesh feature with n vertices can be represented using a $n \times F$ tensor, where F is the dimensionality of each vertex. A 3D mesh is represented with $F = 3$. However, applying convolutions to the mesh can result in features with different dimensionality. The mesh sampling operations define a new topological structure at each layer and maintain the context on neighborhood vertices. We now describe our sampling method with an overview as shown in Fig. 1.

We perform the in-network down-sampling of a mesh with m vertices using transform matrices $Q_d \in \{0,1\}^{n \times m}$, and up-sampling using $Q_u \in \mathbb{R}^{m \times n}$ where $m > n$. The down-sampling is obtained by contracting vertex pairs iteratively that maintain surface error approximations using quadric matrices [20]. In Fig. 1(a), the red vertices are contracted during the down-sampling operation. The (blue) vertices after down-sampling are a subset of the original mesh vertices $\mathcal{V}_d \subset \mathcal{V}$. Each weight $Q_d(p,q) \in \{0,1\}$ denotes whether the q-th vertex is kept during down-sampling, $Q_d(p,q) = 1$, or discarded where $Q_d(p,q) = 0$, $\forall p$.

Since a loss-less down-sampling and up-sampling is not feasible for general surfaces, the up-sampling matrix is built during down-sampling. Vertices retained during down-sampling (blue) undergo convolutional transformations, see Fig. 1(c). These (blue) vertices are retained during up-sampling $Q_u(q,p) = 1$ iff $Q_d(p,q) = 1$. Vertices $v_q \in \mathcal{V}$ discarded during down-sampling (red vertices) where $Q_d(p,q) = 0$ $\forall p$, are mapped into the down-sampled mesh surface using barycentric coordinates. As shown in Figs. 1(b)–(d), this is done by projecting v_q into the closest triangle (i,j,k) in the down-sampled mesh, denoted by $\widetilde{v}_p$, and computing the barycentric coordinates, $\widetilde{v}_p = w_i v_i + w_j v_j + w_k v_k$, such that $v_i, v_j, v_k \in \mathcal{V}_d$ and $w_i + w_j + w_k = 1$. The weights are then updated in Q_u as $Q_u(q,i) = w_i$, $Q_u(q,j) = w_j$, and $Q_u(q,k) = w_k$, and $Q_u(q,l) = 0$ otherwise. The up-sampled mesh with vertices $\mathcal{V}_u$ is obtained using sparse matrix multiplication, $\mathcal{V}_u = Q_u \mathcal{V}_d$.

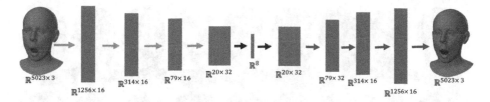

Fig. 2. Convolutional mesh autoencoder: the red and blue arrows indicate down-sampling and up-sampling layers respectively. (Color figure online)

4   Mesh Autoencoder

Network Architecture. Our autoencoder consists of an encoder and a decoder. The structure of the encoder is shown in Table 1. The encoder consists of 4 Chebyshev convolutional filters with $K = 6$ Chebyshev polynomials. Each of the convolutions is followed by a biased ReLU [21]. The down-sampling layers are interleaved between convolutional layers. Each of the down-sampling layers reduce the number of mesh vertices by approximately 4 times. The encoder transforms the face mesh from $\mathbb{R}^{n \times 3}$ to an 8 dimensional latent vector using a fully connected layer at the end.

The structure of the decoder is shown in Table 2. The decoder similarly consists of a fully connected layer that transforms the latent vector from $\mathbb{R}^8$ to $\mathbb{R}^{20 \times 32}$ that can be further up-sampled to reconstruct the mesh. Following the decoder's fully connected layer, 4 convolutional layers with interleaved up-sampling layers generate a 3D mesh in $\mathbb{R}^{5023 \times 3}$. Each of the convolutions is followed by a biased ReLU similar to the encoder network. Each up-sampling layer increases the numbers of vertices by approximately 4 times. Figure 2 shows the complete structure of our mesh autoencoder.

Table 1. Encoder architecture

Layer	Input size	Output size
Convolution	5023×3	5023×16
Down-sampling	5023×16	1256×16
Convolution	1256×16	1256×16
Down-sampling	1256×16	314×16
Convolution	314×16	314×16
Down-sampling	314×16	79×16
Convolution	79×16	79×32
Down-sampling	79×32	20×32
Fully connected	20×32	8

Table 2. Decoder architecture

Layer	Input size	Output size
Fully connected	8	20×32
Up-sampling	20×32	79×32
Convolution	79×32	79×32
Up-sampling	79×32	314×32
Convolution	314×32	314×16
Up-sampling	314×16	1256×16
Convolution	1256×16	1256×16
Up-sampling	1256×16	5023×16
Convolution	5023×16	5023×3

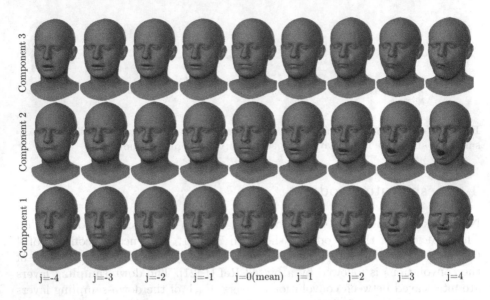

Fig. 3. Sampling from the latent space of the mesh autoencoder around the mean face $j = 0$ along 3 different components.

Training Details. We train our autoencoder for 300 epochs with a learning rate of 8e-3 and a learning rate decay of 0.99 every epoch. We use stochastic gradient descent with a momentum of 0.9 to optimize the L1 loss between predicted mesh vertices and the ground truth samples. We use L1 regularization on the weights of the network using weight decay of 5e-4. The convolutions use Chebyshev filtering with $K = 6$.

5   Experiments

In this section, we evaluate the effectiveness of CoMA on an extreme facial expression dataset. We demonstrate that CoMA allows the synthesis of new expressive faces by sampling from the latent space in Sect. 5.2, including the effect of adding variational loss. Following, we compare CoMA to the widely used PCA representation for reconstructing expressive 3D faces. For this, we evaluate in Sect. 5.3 the ability to reconstruct data similar to the training data (interpolation experiment), and the ability to reconstruct expressions not seen during training (extrapolation experiment). Finally, in Sect. 5.4, we show improved performance by replacing the expression space of state of the art face model, FLAME [28] with our autoencoder.

5.1   Facial Expression Dataset

Our dataset consists of 12 classes of extreme expressions from 12 different subjects. These expressions are complex and asymmetric. The expression sequences

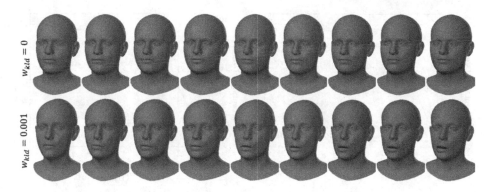

Fig. 4. Sampling using Gaussian noise with variational loss (bottom), and without (top). With $w_{kld} = 0$, the latent representation might not have a Gaussian distribution. Hence, samples on top are not diverse.

in our dataset are – bareteeth, cheeks in, eyebrow, high smile, lips back, lips up, mouth down, mouth extreme, mouth middle, mouth side and mouth up. We show samples from our dataset and the number of frames of each captured sequence in the Supplementary Material.

The data is captured at 60 fps with a multi-camera active stereo system (3dMD LLC, Atlanta) with six stereo camera pairs, five speckle projectors, and six color cameras. Our dataset contains 20,466 3D Meshes, each with about 120,000 vertices. The data is pre-processed using a sequential mesh registration method [28] to reduce the data dimensionality to 5023 vertices.

5.2 Sampling the Latent Space

Let E be the encoder and D be the decoder. We first encode a face mesh from our test set in the latent space to obtain features $z = E(\mathcal{F})$. We then vary each of the components of the latent vector as $\tilde{z}_i = z_i + \epsilon$. We then use the decoder to transform the latent vector into a reconstructed mesh $\tilde{\mathcal{F}} = D(\tilde{z})$. In Fig. 3, we show a diversity of face meshes sampled from the latent space. Here, we extend or contract the latent vector along different dimensions by a factor of 0.3 such that $\tilde{z}_i = (1 + 0.3j)z_i$, where j is the step. In Fig. 3, $j \in [-4, 4]$, and the mean face $\mathcal{F}$ is shown in the middle of the row. More examples are shown in the Supplementary Material.

Variational Convolutional Mesh Autoencoder. Although 3D faces can be sampled from our convolutional mesh autoencoder, the distribution of the latent space is not known. Therefore, sampling requires a mesh to be encoded in that space. In order to constrain the distribution of the latent space, we add a variational loss on our model. Let E be the encoder, D be the decoder, and z be the latent representation of face $\mathcal{F}$. We minimize the loss,

$$l = ||\mathcal{F} - D(z)||_1 + w_{kld} KL(\mathcal{N}(0,1)||Q(z|\mathcal{F})), \qquad (3)$$

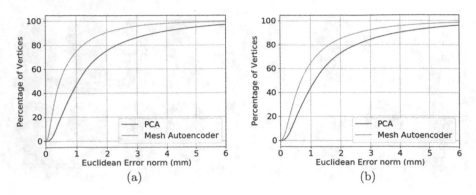

Fig. 5. Cumulative euclidean error between PCA model and mesh autoencoder for interpolation (a) and extrapolation (b) experiments

where $w_{kld} = 0.001$ weights the KL divergence loss. The first term minimizes the L1 reconstruction error, and the second term enforces a unit Gaussian prior $\mathcal{N}(0, 1)$ with zero mean on the distribution of latent vectors $Q(z)$. This enforces the latent space to be a multivariate Gaussian. In Fig. 4, we show visualizations by sampling faces from a Gaussian distribution on this space within $[-3\sigma, 3\sigma]$, where $\sigma = 1$, is the variance of the Gaussian prior. We compare the visualizations by setting $w_{kld} = 0$. We observe that $w_{kld} = 0$ does not enforce any Gaussian prior on $P(z)$, and therefore sampling with Gaussian noise from this distribution results in limited diversity in face meshes. We show more examples in the Supplementary Material.

5.3   Comparison with PCA Spaces

Several face models use PCA space to represent identity and expression variations [1, 7, 28, 41, 47]. We perform interpolation and extrapolation experiments to evaluate our performance. We use Scikit-learn [37] to compute PCA coefficients. We consistently use an 8-dimensional latent space to encode the face mesh using both the PCA model and Mesh Autoencoder.

Interpolation Experiment. In order to evaluate the interpolation capability of the autoencoder, we split the dataset in training and test samples with a ratio of 9:1. The test samples are obtained by picking consecutive frames of length 10 uniformly at random across the sequences. We train CoMA for 300 epochs and evaluate it on the test set. We use Euclidean distance for comparison with the PCA method. The mean error with standard deviation, and median errors are shown in Table 3 for comparison.

We observe that our reconstruction error is 50% lower than PCA. At the same time, the number of parameters in CoMA is about 75% fewer than the PCA model as shown in Table 3. Visual inspection of our qualitative results in Fig. 6 shows that our reconstructions are more realistic and are effective in capturing extreme facial expressions. We also show the histogram of cumulative

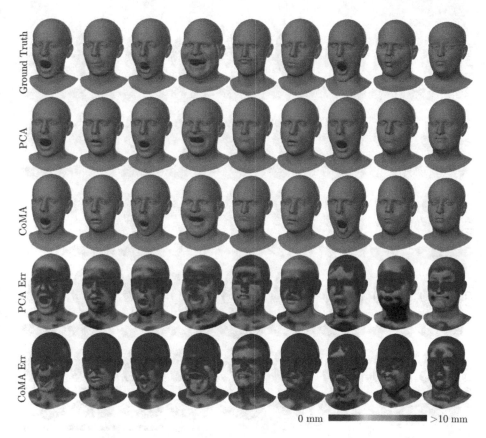

Fig. 6. Comparison with PCA: qualitative results for interpolation experiment

Table 3. Comparison with PCA: interpolation experiments. Errors are in millimeters

	Mean error	Median error	# Parameters
PCA	1.639 ± 1.638	1.101	120,552
Mesh autoencoder	**0.845 ± 0.994**	**0.496**	**33,856**

errors in Fig. 5a. We observe that our Mesh Autoencoder (CoMA) has about 72.6% of the vertices within a Euclidean error of 1 mm, as compared to 47.3% for the PCA model.

Extrapolation Experiment. To measure generalization of our model, we compare the performance of CoMA with the PCA model and FLAME [28]. For comparison, we train the expression model of FLAME on our dataset. The FLAME reconstructions are obtained with latent vector size of 16 with 8 components each for encoding identity and expression. The latent vectors encoded using the PCA model and Mesh autoencoder have a size of 8.

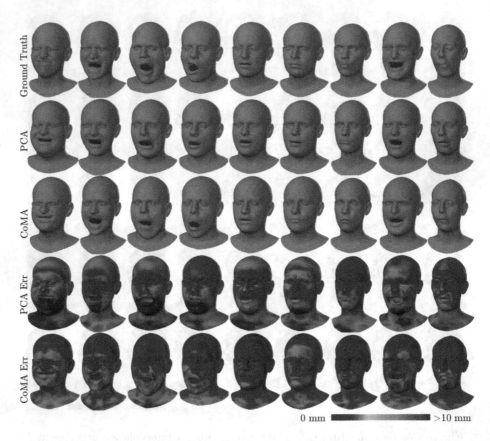

0 mm ■■■■■■■■■■> >10 mm

Fig. 7. Comparison with PCA: qualitative results for extrapolation experiment

Table 4. Comparison with PCA: extrapolation experiment. Errors are in millimeters.

Sequence	Mesh autoencoder Mean error	Median	PCA Mean error	Median	FLAME [28] Mean error	Median
Bareteeth	**1.376 ± 1.536**	**0.856**	1.957 ± 1.888	1.335	2.002 ± 1.456	1.606
Cheeks in	**1.288 ± 1.501**	**0.794**	1.854 ± 1.906	1.179	2.011 ± 1.468	1.609
Eyebrow	**1.053 ± 1.088**	**0.706**	1.609 ± 1.535	1.090	1.862 ± 1.342	1.516
High smile	**1.205 ± 1.252**	**0.772**	1.841 ± 1.831	1.246	1.960 ± 1.370	1.625
Lips back	**1.193 ± 1.476**	**0.708**	1.842 ± 1.947	1.198	2.047 ± 1.485	1.639
Lips up	**1.081 ± 1.192**	**0.656**	1.788 ± 1.764	1.216	1.983 ± 1.427	1.616
Mouth down	**1.050 ± 1.183**	**0.654**	1.618 ± 1.594	1.105	2.029 ± 1.454	1.651
Mouth extreme	**1.336 ± 1.820**	**0.738**	2.011 ± 2.405	1.224	2.028 ± 1.464	1.613
Mouth middle	**1.017 ± 1.192**	**0.610**	1.697 ± 1.715	1.133	2.043 ± 1.496	1.620
Mouth open	**0.961 ± 1.127**	**0.583**	1.612 ± 1.728	1.060	1.894 ± 1.422	1.544
Mouth side	**1.264 ± 1.611**	**0.730**	1.894 ± 2.274	1.132	2.090 ± 1.510	1.659
Mouth up	**1.097 ± 1.212**	**0.683**	1.710 ± 1.680	1.159	2.067 ± 1.485	1.680

To evaluate generalization capability of our model, we reconstruct the expressions that are completely unseen by our model. We perform 12 different experiments for evaluation. For each experiment, we split our dataset by completely excluding one expression set from all the subjects of the dataset. We test our Mesh Autoencoder on the excluded expression. We compare the performance of our model with PCA and FLAME using the Euclidean distance (mean, standard deviation, median). We perform 12 fold cross validation, one for each expression as shown in Table 4. In Table 4, we also show that our model performs better than PCA and FLAME [28] on all expression sequences. We show the qualitative results in Fig. 7. We show the cumulative Euclidean error histogram in Fig. 5b. For a 1 mm accuracy, Mesh Autoencoder captures 63.8% of the vertices while the PCA model captures 45%.

5.4   DeepFLAME

FLAME [28] is a state of the art model for face representation that combines linear blendskinning for head and jaw motion with linear PCA spaces to represent identity and expression shape variations. To improve the reconstruction error of FLAME, we replace the PCA expression space of FLAME with our autoencoder, and refer to the new model as DeepFLAME. We compare the performance of DeepFLAME with FLAME by varying the size of the latent vector for encoding. Head rotations are factored out for comparison since they are well modeled by linear blendskinning in FLAME, and we consider only the expression space. The reconstruction accuracy is measured using Euclidean distance metric. We show the comparisons in Table 5. The median reconstruction of DeepFLAME is lower for all chosen latent space dimensions, while the mean reconstruction error is lower for up to 12 latent variables. This shows that DeepFLAME provides a more compact face representation; i.e., captures more shape variation with fewer latent variables.

Table 5. Comparison of FLAME and DeepFLAME. DeepFLAME is obtained by replacing expression model of FLAME with CoMA. All errors are in millimeters.

#dim of z	DeepFLAME		FLAME [28]	
	Mean error	Median	Mean error	Median
2	**0.610 ± 0.851**	**0.317**	0.668 ± 0.876	0.371
4	**0.509 ± 0.746**	**0.235**	0.589 ± 0.803	0.305
6	**0.464 ± 0.711**	**0.196**	0.525 ± 0.743	0.252
8	**0.432 ± 0.681**	**0.169**	0.477 ± 0.691	0.217
10	**0.421 ± 0.664**	**0.162**	0.439 ± 0.655	0.193
12	**0.388 ± 0.630**	**0.139**	0.403 ± 0.604	0.172
14	0.371 ± 0.605	**0.128**	**0.371 ± 0.567**	0.152
16	0.372 ± 0.611	**0.125**	**0.351 ± 0.543**	0.139

5.5 Discussion

The focus of CoMA is to model facial shape for reconstruction applications. The Laplace-Beltrami operator (LBo) describes the intrinsic surface geometry and is invariant under isometric surface deformations. This isometry invariance of the LBo is beneficial for shape matching and registration. Since changes in facial expression are near isometric deformations [9, Sect. 13.3], applying LBo to expressive faces would result in a loss of most expression-related shape variations, making it infeasible to model such variations. The graph Laplacian used by CoMA in contrast to the LBo is not isometry invariant.

While we evaluate CoMA on face shapes, it is applicable to any class of objects. Similar to existing statistical models however, it requires all meshes in dense vertex correspondence; i.e. all meshes need to share the same topology. A future research direction is to directly learn a 3D face representation from raw 3D face scans or 2D images without requiring vertex correspondence.

As is also true for other deep learning based models, the performance of CoMA could further improve with more training data. The amount of existing 3D face data however is very limited. The data scarcity especially limits our expression model to outperform existing models for higher latent space dimensions (>12 see Table 5). We predict superior quality on larger datasets and plan to evaluate CoMA on significantly more data in the future.

As CoMA is an end-to-end trained model, it could also be combined with some existing image convolutional network to regress the 3D face shape from 2D images. We will explore this in future work.

6 Conclusion

We have introduced CoMA, a new representation for 3D faces of varying shape and expression. We designed CoMA as a hierarchical, multi-scale representation to capture global and local shape and expression variations of multiple scales. To do so, we introduce novel sampling operations and combine these with fast graph convolutions in an autoencoder network. The locally invariant filters, shared across the mesh surface, significantly reduce the number of filter parameters in the network, and the non-linear activation functions capture extreme facial expressions. We evaluated CoMA on a dataset of extreme 3D facial expressions that we will make publicly available for research purposes along with the trained model. We showed that CoMA significantly outperforms state-of-the-art models in 3D face reconstruction applications while using 75% fewer model parameters. CoMA outperforms the linear PCA model by 50% on interpolation experiments and generalizes better on completely unseen facial expressions. We further demonstrated that CoMA in a variational setting allows us to synthesize new expressive faces by sampling the latent space.

Acknowledgement. We thank T. Alexiadis and J. Márquez for data aquisition; H. Feng for rendering the figures; S. Wuhrer for advice on mesh convolutions; and G. Pavlakos, D. Paschalidou and S. Pujades for helping us with paper revisions.

References

1. Amberg, B., Knothe, R., Vetter, T.: Expression invariant 3D face recognition with a morphable model. In: International Conference on Automatic Face Gesture Recognition, pp. 1–6 (2008)
2. Blanz, V., Vetter, T.: A morphable model for the synthesis of 3D faces. In: SIGGRAPH, pp. 187–194 (1999)
3. Booth, J., Roussos, A., Ponniah, A., Dunaway, D., Zafeiriou, S.: Large scale 3D morphable models. Int. J. Comput. Vis. **126**, 1–22 (2017)
4. Boscaini, D., Masci, J., Melzi, S., Bronstein, M.M., Castellani, U., Vandergheynst, P.: Learning class-specific descriptors for deformable shapes using localized spectral convolutional networks. In: Eurographics Symposium on Geometry Processing, pp. 13–23 (2015)
5. Boscaini, D., Masci, J., Rodolà, E., Bronstein, M.: Learning shape correspondence with anisotropic convolutional neural networks. In: Advances in Neural Information Processing Systems, pp. 3189–3197 (2016)
6. Bouaziz, S., Wang, Y., Pauly, M.: Online modeling for realtime facial animation. ACM Trans. Graph. **32**(4), 40 (2013)
7. Breidt, M., Bülthoff, H.H., Curio, C.: Robust semantic analysis by synthesis of 3D facial motion. In: International Conference on Automatic Face and Gesture Recognition and Workshops, pp. 713–719 (2011)
8. Brock, A., Lim, T., Ritchie, J.M., Weston, N.: Generative and discriminative voxel modeling with convolutional neural networks. arXiv preprint arXiv:1608.04236 (2016)
9. Bronstein, A.M., Bronstein, M.M., Kimmel, R.: Numerical Geometry of Non-Rigid Shapes. Springer, Heidelberg (2008). https://doi.org/10.1007/978-0-387-73301-2
10. Bronstein, M.M., Bruna, J., LeCun, Y., Szlam, A., Vandergheynst, P.: Geometric deep learning: going beyond euclidean data. Signal Process. Mag. **34**(4), 18–42 (2017)
11. Bruna, J., Zaremba, W., Szlam, A., LeCun, Y.: Spectral networks and locally connected networks on graphs. CoRR abs/1312.6203 (2013)
12. Brunton, A., Bolkart, T., Wuhrer, S.: Multilinear wavelets: a statistical shape space for human faces. In: Fleet, D., Pajdla, T., Schiele, B., Tuytelaars, T. (eds.) ECCV 2014. LNCS, vol. 8689, pp. 297–312. Springer, Cham (2014). https://doi.org/10.1007/978-3-319-10590-1_20
13. Brunton, A., Salazar, A., Bolkart, T., Wuhrer, S.: Review of statistical shape spaces for 3D data with comparative analysis for human faces. Comput. Vis. Image Underst. **128**, 1–17 (2014)
14. Cao, C., Weng, Y., Zhou, S., Tong, Y., Zhou, K.: Facewarehouse: a 3D facial expression database for visual computing. Trans. Vis. Comput. Graph. **20**(3), 413–425 (2014)
15. Chung, F.R.K.: Spectral Graph Theory, vol. 92. American Mathematical Soc., Providence (1997)
16. Cosker, D., Krumhuber, E., Hilton, A.: A FACS valid 3D dynamic action unit database with applications to 3D dynamic morphable facial modeling. In: International Conference on Computer Vision, pp. 2296–2303 (2011)
17. Defferrard, M., Bresson, X., Vandergheynst, P.: Convolutional neural networks on graphs with fast localized spectral filtering. In: Advances in Neural Information Processing Systems, pp. 3844–3852 (2016)

18. Abrevaya, V.F., Wuhrer, S., Boyer, E.: Multilinear autoencoder for 3D face model learning. In: Winter Conference on Applications of Computer Vision, pp. 1–9 (2018)
19. Ferrari, C., Lisanti, G., Berretti, S., Bimbo, A.D.: Dictionary learning based 3D morphable model construction for face recognition with varying expression and pose. In: International Conference on 3D Vision, pp. 509–517 (2015)
20. Garland, M., Heckbert, P.S.: Surface simplification using quadric error metrics. In: Proceedings of the 24th Annual Conference on Computer Graphics And Interactive Techniques, pp. 209–216. ACM Press/Addison-Wesley Publishing Co. (1997)
21. Glorot, X., Bordes, A., Bengio, Y.: Deep sparse rectifier neural networks. In: Fourteenth International Conference on Artificial Intelligence and Statistics (2011)
22. Goodfellow, I., et al.: Generative adversarial nets. In: Advances in Neural Information Processing Systems, pp. 2672–2680 (2014)
23. Hammond, D.K., Vandergheynst, P., Gribonval, R.: Wavelets on graphs via spectral graph theory. Appl. Comput. Harmonic Anal. $30(2)$, 129–150 (2011)
24. Henaff, M., Bruna, J., LeCun, Y.: Deep convolutional networks on graph-structured data. CoRR abs/1506.05163 (2015)
25. Jackson, A.S., Bulat, A., Argyriou, V., Tzimiropoulos, G.: Large pose 3D face reconstruction from a single image via direct volumetric CNN regression. In: International Conference on Computer Vision (2017)
26. Kipf, T.N., Welling, M.: Semi-supervised classification with graph convolutional networks. In: International Conference on Learning Representations (2016)
27. Li, H., Weise, T., Pauly, M.: Example-based facial rigging. ACM Trans. Graph. $29(4)$, 32 (2010)
28. Li, T., Bolkart, T., Black, M.J., Li, H., Romero, J.: Learning a model of facial shape and expression from 4D scans. ACM Trans. Graph. $36(6)$, 194 (2017)
29. Litany, O., Bronstein, A., Bronstein, M., Makadia, A.: Deformable shape completion with graph convolutional autoencoders. arXiv preprint arXiv:1712.00268 (2017)
30. Maron, H., et al.: Convolutional neural networks on surfaces via seamless toric covers. ACM Trans. Graph. $36(4)$, 71:1–71:10 (2017)
31. Masci, J., Boscaini, D., Bronstein, M., Vandergheynst, P.: Geodesic convolutional neural networks on Riemannian manifolds. In: International Conference on Computer Vision Workshops, pp. 37–45 (2015)
32. Monti, F., Boscaini, D., Masci, J., Rodolà, E., Svoboda, J., Bronstein, M.M.: Geometric deep learning on graphs and manifolds using mixture model CNNs (2017)
33. Neumann, T., Varanasi, K., Wenger, S., Wacker, M., Magnor, M., Theobalt, C.: Sparse localized deformation components. Trans. Graph. (Proc. SIGGRAPH Asia) $32(6)$, 179:1–179:10 (2013)
34. van den Oord, A., et al.: WaveNet: a generative model for raw audio. CoRR abs/1609.03499 (2016)
35. Oord, A.V.D., Kalchbrenner, N., Kavukcuoglu, K.: Pixel recurrent neural networks. arXiv preprint arXiv:1601.06759 (2016)
36. Paysan, P., Knothe, R., Amberg, B., Romdhani, S., Vetter, T.: A 3D face model for pose and illumination invariant face recognition. In: International Conference on Advanced Video and Signal Based Surveillance, pp. 296–301 (2009)
37. Pedregosa, F., et al.: Scikit-learn: machine learning in Python. J. Mach. Learn. Res. 12, 2825–2830 (2011)
38. Savran, A., et al.: Bosphorus database for 3D face analysis. In: Schouten, B., Juul, N.C., Drygajlo, A., Tistarelli, M. (eds.) BioID 2008. LNCS, vol. 5372, pp. 47–56. Springer, Heidelberg (2008). https://doi.org/10.1007/978-3-540-89991-4_6

39. Sinha, A., Bai, J., Ramani, K.: Deep learning 3D shape surfaces using geometry images. In: Leibe, B., Matas, J., Sebe, N., Welling, M. (eds.) ECCV 2016. LNCS, vol. 9910, pp. 223–240. Springer, Cham (2016). https://doi.org/10.1007/978-3-319-46466-4_14

40. Taigman, Y., Yang, M., Ranzato, M., Wolf, L.: DeepFace: closing the gap to human-level performance in face verification. In: Proceedings of the IEEE Conference on Computer Vision and Pattern Recognition, pp. 1701–1708 (2014)

41. Tewari, A., et al.: MoFA: model-based deep convolutional face autoencoder for unsupervised monocular reconstruction. In: International Conference on Computer Vision (2017)

42. Thies, J., Zollhöfer, M., Nießner, M., Valgaerts, L., Stamminger, M., Theobalt, C.: Real-time expression transfer for facial reenactment. Trans. Graph. **34**(6), 183:1–183:14 (2015)

43. Thies, J., Zollhöfer, M., Stamminger, M., Theobalt, C., Nießner, M.: Face2Face: real-time face capture and reenactment of RGB videos. In: Conference on Computer Vision and Pattern Recognition, pp. 2387–2395 (2016)

44. Tran, A.T., Hassner, T., Masi, I., Paz, E., Nirkin, Y., Medioni, G.: Extreme 3D face reconstruction: looking past occlusions. In: IEEE Conference on Computer Vision and Pattern Recognition (CVPR) (2018)

45. Verma, N., Boyer, E., Verbeek, J.: Dynamic filters in graph convolutional networks. CoRR abs/1706.05206 (2017)

46. Vlasic, D., Brand, M., Pfister, H., Popović, J.: Face transfer with multilinear models. Trans. Graph. **24**(3), 426–433 (2005)

47. Yang, F., Wang, J., Shechtman, E., Bourdev, L., Metaxas, D.: Expression flow for 3D-aware face component transfer. Trans. Graph. **30**(4), 60:1–60:10 (2011)

48. Yi, L., Su, H., Guo, X., Guibas, L.J.: SyncSpecCNN: synchronized spectral CNN for 3D shape segmentation (2017)

49. Yin, L., Chen, X., Sun, Y., Worm, T., Reale, M.: A high-resolution 3D dynamic facial expression database. In: International Conference on Automatic Face and Gesture Recognition, pp. 1–6 (2008)

50. Yin, L., Wei, X., Sun, Y., Wang, J., Rosato, M.J.: A 3D facial expression database for facial behavior research. In: International Conference on Automatic Face and Gesture Recognition, pp. 211–216 (2006)

Hierarchical Relational Networks for Group Activity Recognition and Retrieval

Mostafa S. Ibrahim[✉] and Greg Mori[✉]

School of Computing Science, Simon Fraser University, Burnaby, Canada
msibrahi@sfu.ca, mori@cs.sfu.ca

Abstract. Modeling structured relationships between people in a scene is an important step toward visual understanding. We present a Hierarchical Relational Network that computes relational representations of people, given graph structures describing potential interactions. Each relational layer is fed individual person representations and a potential relationship graph. Relational representations of each person are created based on their connections in this particular graph. We demonstrate the efficacy of this model by applying it in both supervised and unsupervised learning paradigms. First, given a video sequence of people doing a collective activity, the relational scene representation is utilized for multi-person activity recognition. Second, we propose a Relational Autoencoder model for unsupervised learning of features for action and scene retrieval. Finally, a Denoising Autoencoder variant is presented to infer missing people in the scene from their context. Empirical results demonstrate that this approach learns relational feature representations that can effectively discriminate person and group activity classes.

1 Introduction

Human activity recognition is a challenging computer vision problem and has received a lot of attention from the research community. Challenges include factors such as the variability within action classes, background clutter, and similarity between different action classes. Group activity recognition arises in the context of multi-person scenes, including in video surveillance, sports analytics, and video search and retrieval. A particular challenge of group activity recognition is the fact that inferring labels for a scene requires contextual reasoning about the people in the scene and their relations. In this paper we develop a novel deep network layer for learning representations for capturing these relations.

Figure 1 provides a schematic of our relational layer and Fig. 2 highlights the processing of a single person inside the layer. Initially, each person in a scene can be represented by a feature, e.g. derived from a standard CNN. We amalgamate these individual representations via stacking multiple relational layers – deep network layers that combine information from a set of (neighbouring) person representations. These layers are utilized in a hierarchy, refining representations for each individual person based on successive integration of information from other people present in the scene.

© Springer Nature Switzerland AG 2018
V. Ferrari et al. (Eds.): ECCV 2018, LNCS 11207, pp. 742–758, 2018.
https://doi.org/10.1007/978-3-030-01219-9_44

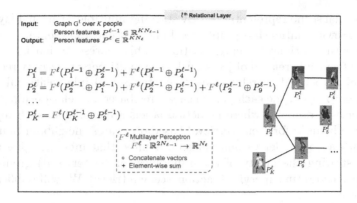

Fig. 1. A single relational layer. The layer can process an arbitrary sized set of people from a scene, and produces new representations for these people that capture their relationships. The input to the layer is a set of K people and a graph G^ℓ encoding their relations. In the relational layer, a shared neural network (F^ℓ) maps each pair of person representations to a new representation that also encodes relationships between them. These are aggregated over all edges emanating from a person node via summation. This process results in a new, relational representation for each of the K people. By stacking multiple relational layers, each with its own relationship graph G^ℓ, we can encode hierarchical relationships for each person and learn a scene representation suitable for group activity recognition or retrieval.

Recent deep learning approaches [9,20,25] for group activity recognition use a 2-stage processing pipeline where first each person is represented using a large feature vector (e.g., fc7 features). Then, the person representations are pooled together to construct the final features for the scene. The typical scene pooling is max/average/attentional pooling over people, which reduces dimensionality, but loses information. First, all spatial and relational information is dropped. Second, features about individual people, which actually define actions, are lost. Finally, although such a scene representation is optimized for group activity recognition, it cannot be used for analysis tasks based on individual *actions*.

Our models utilize a similar 2-stage processing framework, but work on solving these drawbacks in an efficient and effective manner. Given initial feature representations for each person and a relationship graph, we present a relational layer that jointly computes a compact representation for each person that encodes inter-person relations. By stacking multiple relational layers, this hierarchical relational network learns a *compact relational representation per person*.

Our contributions can be summarized as follows:

– A relational layer that jointly infers relational representations for each person based on a relationship graph. The layer can operate on a variable sized set of people in a scene. Given features for K people, the layer maps the given K feature vectors to K new ones, capturing relations and preserving correspondence between each feature vector and each person.

- A relational scene representation. By stacking multiple relational layers, each with its own relationship graph, we build a scene representation encoding hierarchical relationship representations. This representation is suitable for scenes of multiple related objects, such as in multi-person activity recognition.
- A novel autoencoder architecture that stacks multiple relational layers to jointly encode/decode each person's features based on relationship graphs. In unsupervised domains where no action labels are available, such representations can be used for scene retrieval based on nearest neighbour matching. A denoising autoencoder variant is also presented that infers missing people.
- Demonstrating the utility of these modules for (supervised) group activity recognition and (unsupervised) action/scene retrieval. We will publicly release our code[1]

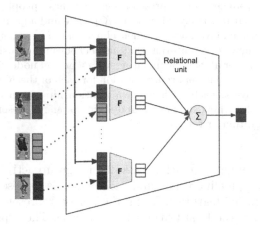

Fig. 2. Relational unit for processing one person inside a relational layer. The feature vector for a person (red) is combined with each of its neighbours'. Resultant vectors are summed to create a new feature vector for the person (dark red). (Color Figure online)

2 Related Work

We develop methods for multi-person activity recognition and retrieval by learning relational features. Below, we review related work in these areas.

Multi-person Activity Recognition: Recent deep learning approaches to multi-person activity recognition include Ibrahim et al. [9], which presents a 2-stage deep model. Person actions are modeled using a long short-term memory (LSTM) temporal layer. Scene dynamics are captured by adding a max-pooling layer which is fed to a higher-level LSTM. Ramanathan et al. [20] formulate an attention model to highlight key players in a scene, resulting in a weighted

---

[1] https://github.com/mostafa-saad/hierarchical-relational-network.

summation of person feature representations. Bagautdinov et al. [1] propose a joint model of action localization and group activity recognition. A multi-person object detection approach finds people and extracts their feature representations, which are linked based on Euclidean distance and fed to temporal recurrent network. Shu et al. [25] extend this pipeline with an energy layer and confidence measure to consider reliability and numerical stability of the inference. Our work follows these 2-stage processing pipelines, but introduces a new relational layer that can learn compact relational representations for each person.

Image Retrieval: Content-based retrieval for structured scenes is an active research area [14,19,23,28]. Siddiquie et al. [26] extract multi-attributes and their correlations from a text query. Lan et al. [16] introduce queries that specify the objects that should be present in the scene, and their spatial relations (e.g., "car on the road"). Kim et al. [12] retrieve video clips that emphasize the progression of the text query. Johnson et al. [11] consider scene graph queries (objects and relationships). Xu et al. [29] generate scene graphs via a message passing neural network. In the realm of multi-person activity recognition, hard-coded representations of spatial relations have been developed previously [2,15]. We show how our relational layers can be used in structured scene image retrieval, by matching frames of similar visual *structure* of people and their *actions*.

Relational Networks: Recent work with deep networks includes capturing object relationships through aggregating with *every-pair-relation* models. Santoro et al. [24] introduce a relational network module that infers relationships between image objects. A multi-layer perceptron (MLP) learns the relationship of two objects, the scene is represented as summation of all object pairs. In a similar manner, Guttenberg et al. [8] use an MLP to learn a permutation-equivariant representation of a group of objects based on the relationship of every pair of objects. Inspired by these simple relation networks, we introduce our hierarchical relational network to build a compact relational scene representation, while preserving the correspondence between the feature representation and each person.

3   Proposed Approach

This paper introduces a Hierarchical Relational Network that builds a compact relational representation per person. Recent approaches [8,9,20] represent people in a scene then directly (max/average) pool all the representations into a single scene representation. This final representation has some drawbacks such as dropping relationships between people and destroying the individual person features. We tackle these challenges through a relational layer that jointly creates K person representations for the K people in a scene. By stacking multiple relational layers, we compactly encode hierarchical relationship representations. In the next subsections, we elaborate on the details of the Relational Network, then show its applications in supervised classification and unsupervised retrieval settings.

3.1   Hierarchical Relational Network

Our relational network for multi-person activity recognition processes a single video frame at a time. An input video frame has K initial person feature vectors (e.g., person detections with features extracted by a CNN) associated with multiple potential relationship graphs (e.g., based on spatial Euclidean distance thresholds). A single relational layer is fed with both K feature vectors and a relationship graph, and maps them to K new relational representations.

The building block for our model is a relational unit that processes an individual person in the scene. Each person's feature vector is mapped to a new representation by aggregating information from each neighbouring person in the relationship graph. This is accomplished via a network that processes the person combined with each neighbour, followed by aggregation. This relational unit is depicted Fig. 2.

Within one relational layer, every person in the scene is processed using this unit. This results in new feature representations for each person in the scene, capturing their individual features as well as those from his/her neighbours.

By stacking multiple layers, each with its own graph and relational unit parameters, we learn hierarchical relationship representations for the people. Pooling of the final person representations is used to construct the scene representation. An overview of our relational network for multi-person activity recognition in a single frame is shown in Fig. 3.

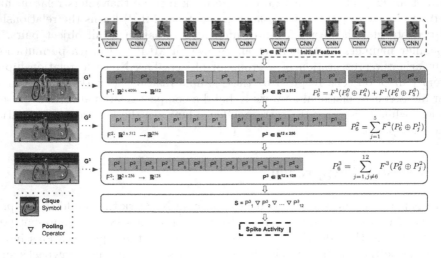

Fig. 3. Our relational network for group activity recognition for a single video frame. Given K people and their initial feature vectors, these vectors are fed to 3 stacked relational layers (of output sizes per person: 512, 256, 128). Each relational layer is associated with a graph G^{ℓ} (disjoint cliques in this example: layer 1 has 4 cliques, each of size 3; layer 3 is a complete graph). The shared MLP F^{ℓ} of each layer computes the representation of 2 neighbouring players. Pooling of the output K feature vectors is used for group activity classification.

Formally, given a video frame, the ith person representation P_i^ℓ in the ℓth relational layer is computed as follows:

$$P_i^0 = CNN(I_i) \tag{1}$$

$$P_i^\ell = \sum_{j \in \mathcal{E}_i^\ell} F^\ell(P_i^{\ell-1} \oplus P_j^{\ell-1}; \theta^\ell) \tag{2}$$

where P_i^0 is the initial i^{th} person representation derived from a CNN on cropped image I_i, $\mathcal{E}_i^\ell$ is the set of relationship edges from the ith person in the graph G^ℓ used for the ℓth layer, and $\oplus$ is the concatenation operator. $P_i^\ell \in \mathbb{R}^{N_\ell}$ where N_ℓ is the output size per-person for the ℓth layer.

The function F^ℓ is a shared MLP for the ℓth network layer with parameters θ^ℓ (end-to-end differentiable model). The MLP has input size $2N_{\ell-1}$ and output size N_ℓ. Given two concatenated vectors, F^ℓ maps them to a new vector capturing the given pair's content and relationship.

The relational layer feeds each edge in G^ℓ through its own shared MLP to compute the K new representations. Equation 2 computes a relationship representation between the ith person and his/her neighbours. This network structure and the use of layer-wise shared parameters results in relationship representations per layer – treating each pair of people within one network layer equivalently. This results in efficient parameter reuse while letting the representation be driven by the graph structure at each layer. Importantly, this representation can also be used with any number of people K, including situations where K can vary per time step due to occlusions or false positive detections.

By stacking multiple compressive *relational layers*, each with its own graph, we can construct reduced dimension person features from one layer to another until a desired compact relational representation has been formed. The final scene representation S is the pooling of person representations from the last relational layer output and defined as:

$$S = P_1^L \triangledown P_2^L \triangledown \ldots \triangledown P_k^L \tag{3}$$

where P_i^L is the ith person output representation of last relational layer L and $\triangledown$ is a pooling operator (such as vector concatenation or element-wise max pooling).

3.2 Supervised Learning: Group Activities

The activity of a group of people is a function of the persons' actions. We can utilize our model to represent each scene and learn its parameters in a supervised fashion. We utilize an Imagenet pre-trained VGG network [27] to represent each single person bounding box. The whole network is fine-tuned using action-labeled bounding boxes. Once trained, each person bounding box can be represented with the last layer in VGG19 (4096-d fc7 features).

Given the bounding boxes of the people in the scene in a video sequence, we recognize the overall multi-person activity. Each bounding box at the tth frame is modeled and represented with an initial feature vector as explained above and fed to the relational network. The relational layer jointly maps the representations to ones that encode the relationship representation of a person based on connections to other people. To capture the temporal dynamics of the video scene, the output of the final *relational layer* is pooled to the tth scene representation S_t and fed to an LSTM layer with a softmax output for group activity classification. Figure 3 illustrates this model for a single frame.

3.3 Unsupervised Learning: Action Retrieval

Detailed annotation of individual person bounding boxes in video is a time-consuming process [7]. As an alternative, one could utilize unsupervised autoencoder mechanisms to learn feature representations for people in scenes. These representations could potentially be general-purpose: allowing comparison of person features based on relations and context for single-person action retrieval, and retrieval of scenes of similarly structured sets of actions.

Recent efforts in object recognition [6,18] and temporal sequence learning [17, 21] aimed to learn effective feature representations in unsupervised encoding frameworks. In a similar vein, we propose unsupervised autoencoders that learn relational representations for all people in the scene.

Our relational layer is well-suited to this task since it: (1) encodes person relationships, (2) preserves action features for individual people, and (3) has compact size, efficient for retrieval. In other words, our scene representation is both efficient (compact size) and effective (relationship-based). Further, the model has the same parameter count as a simple autoencoder of a single person, as each layer has a shared network.

For the encoder, given K feature vectors for the people in the scene, we stack multiple relational layers of decreasing size that encode features to a final compact representation. The decoder is the inverse of these layers. That is, we again stack multiple relational layers of increasing size that decode a compressed feature vector to its original CNN representation. Each relational layer jointly maps a person representation from a given input size to a required output size considering graph connections. An Euclidean loss is computed between the initial K feature vectors and the corresponding decoded ones. An overview of the autoencoder model is shown in Fig. 4.

The reconstruction loss $\mathcal{L}$ of the input scene and its reconstructed one is given by:

$$\mathcal{L}(S_{cnn}, S'_{cnn}) = \sum_{i=1}^{K} \| P_i^0 - P_i^L \|^2 \tag{4}$$

where P_i^0 and P_i^ℓ are similar to Eq. 2 (but for a singel frame), S_{cnn} is the concatenation of the K initial feature vectors P_i^0, and S'_{cnn} is the reconstructed output of our network extracted from the last layer L. This novel autoencoder preserves features for individual people, so can be used for both scene and action retrieval.

Denoising Relational Autoencoder: What if some persons are missing in the scene (e.g., due to person detector failures, fast camera movement, or low image quality)? Denoising the input K feature vectors by dropping the *whole* vector for some of the persons allows our relational autoencoder to construct person representations from incomplete scenes. That is, our model infers the missing people from their context. To implement this, the input layer is followed by a dropout layer that drops a complete vector (not just subset of features) with probability P [22].

Retrieval: Given a single frame of K people, suppose we wish to search a video database for a matching frame with similar action structure. Note, the purpose is not retrieving a scene with the same overall activity, but a similar structured scene of actions. The pooled representation style, such as in [9], fits with group activity classification, but not with scene retrieval based on the matching of the actual actions due to losing person features for sake of a global scene representation. On the contrary, our representation for the scene preserves the individual person actions explicitly in a compact sized feature.

For the retrieval mechanism, we use a simple K-Nearest-Neighbour technique with a brute-force algorithm for comparison. To avoid comparison with each possible permutation, people are ordered based on the top corner (x, y) of a person's bounding box (on x first, and on y if tied). Euclidean distance is used to compare feature vectors.

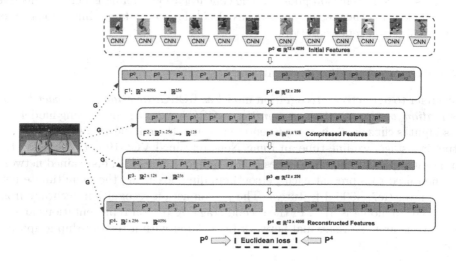

Fig. 4. Our relational autoencoder model. The relationship graph for this volleyball scene is 2 disjoint cliques, one for each team and fixed for all layers. K input person feature vectors, each of length 4096, are fed to a 4-layer relational autoencoder (sizes 256-128-256-4096) to learn a compact representation of size 128 per person.

4   Experiments

To demonstrate the power of our relational network, we evaluate it for two tasks: group activity recognition and action scene retrieval. The results are evaluated on the recent Volleyball Dataset [9]. The dataset consists of 4830 short clips gathered from 55 volleyball games, with 3493 training clips and 1337 for testing. Each clip is classified to one of 8 scene activity labels. Only the middle frame of each clip is fully annotated with the players' bounding boxes and their action labels (out of 9 actions). Clips of 10 frames (centered around the annotated middle frame) are used for the activity recognition task and the middle frame is used for the action scene retrieval task.

Our relational layer accepts free-form graph relationships. For volleyball, one suitable style is graphs of disjoint cliques based on person spatial locations. For example, in volleyball games there might be 3 potential graphs: **(I)** All players are in 1 clique (1C), represents all pairwise relationships; **(II)** each team can be a clique (2C); **(III)** each team can be composed of 2 cliques, a total of 4 cliques (4C). We base our experiments on these clique-based groupings.

For the final scene pooling, instead of just max-pooling all persons, we use a slight variant [10] that reduces confusions between actions of the two team. Specifically, we max-pool each team individually, then concatenate the two representations. This is the default pooling strategy unless otherwise mentioned. In addition, due to the final person features' compact size, we could also do all-persons concatenation pooling. The concatenation pooling is neither effective nor efficient in other recent approaches [9, 25] due to the large dimensionality of the final person representation.

4.1   Group Activity Recognition

We refer to our activity recognition model as RCRG: *Relational Compact Representation for Group activity recognition*. RCRG is a 2-stage processing model and its input is clips of 10 timesteps, centered around the middle annotated frame. In the first stage, we fine-tune an ImageNet-pretrained VGG19 network using the annotated person bounding boxes (not a temporal model). This trained network is then used to represent each person bounding box using the penultimate network layer (fc7, 4096-d features). The person action recognition accuracy from the VGG19 model is 81%. In the second stage, K person representations are fed to our hierarchical relational network (associated with a relationship graph per layer) as in Fig. 3.

Baselines: We perform ablation studies with the following **non-temporal** (single frame) variants of our model to help us understand the performance of the model. The default pooling strategy is max-pooling unless **-conc** postfix is used to indicate concatenation pooling.

Table 1. Volleyball Dataset: Left table is for versions of our model using single frame (last row shows state-of-the-art using a single frame). Right table is for 10-timesteps input clips performance of our best models versus state-of-the-art.

Method	Accuracy
B1-NoRelations	85.1
RCRG-1R-1C	86.5
RCRG-1R-1C-!tuned	75.4
RCRG-2R-11C	86.1
RCRG-2R-21C	87.2
RCRG-3R-421C	86.4
RCRG-2R-11C-conc	**88.3**
RCRG-2R-21C-conc	86.7
RCRG-3R-421C-conc	87.3
Bagautdinov et al. [1]-single	83.8

Method	Accuracy
Bagautdinov et al. [1]	**90.6**
RCRG-2R-11C-conc	89.5
RCRG-2R-21C	89.4
Shu et al. [25]	83.3
Ibrahim et al. [10]	81.9

1. **B1-NoRelations:** In the first stage, the ImageNet-pretrained VGG19 network is fined tuned and a person is represented with fc7, 4096-d features. In the second stage, each person is connected to a shared dense layer of 128 features, then the person representations (each of length 128 features) are pooled, then fed to a softmax layer for group activity classification. This variant compresses person representations and represents the scene without inferring relationship representations.

2. **RCRG-1R-1C:** Same as previous variant, but the shared dense layer is replaced with a single relational layer (1R), all people in 1 clique (1C), i.e. all-pairs relationships. The layer maps each person from input size 4096 to 128 features jointly considering the given relationships.

3. **RCRG-1R-1C-!tuned:** Same as previous variant, but ImageNet-pretrained VGG19 without fine-tuning.

4. **RCRG-2R-11C:** Close to the RCRG-1R-1C variant, but uses 2 relational layers (2R) of sizes 256 and 128. The graphs of these 2 layers are 1 clique (11C) of all people. This variant and the next ones explore stacking layers with different graph structures.

5. **RCRG-2R-21C:** Same as the previous model, but the first layer has 2 cliques, one per team. The second layer is all-pairs relations (1C). **RCRG-2R-21C-conc** replaces the max pool strategy with concatenation pooling.

6. **RCRG-3R-421C:** Close to the previous model, but 3 relational layers (of sizes 512, 256 and 128) with clique sizes of the layers set to (4, 2, 1). The first layer has 4 cliques, with each team divided into 2 cliques. This model is in Fig. 3.

Implementation Details: We utilize the available dataset annotations for implementation. We follow Ibrahim et al. [9] to compute 10-frame tracklets of each person across the video sequence [3].

For training all the models and baselines, the same training protocols are followed using a Tesla K40C GPU (12 GB RAM) and Lasagne Framework [5]. Stochastic gradient descent is used train the model for 200 epochs and initial learning rate 10^{-4} with ADAM [13] optimizer, with fixed hyper-parameters $\beta_1 = 0.9$, $\beta_2 = 0.999$, $\epsilon = 10^{-8}$. We fine-tune the whole pre-trained VGG19 network [27] using batch-size 64 (small due to memory limits). For the relational model, a batch size of 250 is used. The input layer in our relational model is followed by a 50% dropout layer. Two-layer MLP networks are used of sizes N_ℓ. The first layer uses a linear activation function ($f(x) = x$) and the second uses ReLU non-linearities. Note, the models are end-to-end differentiable, but due to memory limits we implement it in a 2-stage style, similar to recent approaches.

In testing, only one shared person network is loaded and used by the K players to extract their features. The time complexity of a relational layer depends on the summation of the nodes degrees in the layer's graph. In other words, for each directed edge, the MLP of a layer is evaluated.

To determine graph cliques, we follow a simple approach [10]. People are ordered based on the upper left corner (x, y) of their bounding box (on x first, and on y if tied). Cliques are generated by sweeping this ordered list. For example, to divide 12 people to 4 cliques of equal size, each 3 consecutive people are grouped as a clique. More sophisticated grouping (e.g., color/motion clustering) or gating functions [4] would be potential extensions.

Results: Table 1 compare the classification performance of our compact representation with the baselines and the state-of-the-art approaches.

Discussion: Our non-temporal models' performance is superior to state-of-the-art corresponding models and outperform compact baselines. Note even without temporal information this model is superior to 2 recent temporal models (In right Table 1). It seems from the results that stacking 2 layers is enough in this domain: in a volleyball scene inter-person relationships are strong. Max-pooling is effective at a scene level. Likely, this is due to the domain; a few players are the key actors, and max-pooling can keep the right features.

4.2 Experiments for Action and Scene Retrieval

We evaluate our retrieval model trained using unsupervised learning, termed RAER (*Relational AutoEncoder for Retrieval*). Our main model is shown in Fig. 4. It consists of 4 relational layers (256-128-256-4096 sizes) and it assumes the graph is 2 cliques (one per team) in all layers. We denote this structure by RAER-4L-2222C. This means, each team is compressed jointly, but all people per layer use the same shared relational MLP. Once the network is trained, each person is represented with 128 features from the compressed layer and used for scene and person retrieval.

Performance Measure: We consider two volleyball dataset frames as a correct match if the IoU (intersection over union) of the distributions of actions of the two frames is ≥ 0.5). For example, if the person actions of frame 1 are 7 people standing and 5 moving, and frame 2 are 4 standing, 6 moving, and 2 jumping then $\text{IoU} = \dfrac{4+5+0}{7+6+2} = 0.6$, hence a match.

Baselines: We compare with the following single-frame baseline models. One naive way to implement such a retrieval system is to learn a person action autoencoder, with its input and output a single person feature vector. Then concatenating the persons in the scene can be used for scene match. However, such direct reduction ignores all relationships in the scene ending with a weak scene representation. Another possibility is a direct concatenation of original persons feature vectors (e.g., 4096). Such a large scene representation may work in some domains, however, this large scene dimensionality is problematic.

1. **B1-Compact128:** Autoencoder with input/output of a single person feature vector of length 4096 from the fc7 layer of a pre-trained VGG19 network. The 4096-d vector is fed to network layers of sizes 256, 128, 256, 4096. The middle layer (128 features) is used as a compressed representation of the person. This network is structured similar to our model and of same compact person size (128 features) for fair comparison.
2. **B2-VGG19:** No autoencoder. Each single person is represented directly with a feature vector of length 4096 from the fc7 layer of a pretrained VGG19 network. Note that this baseline uses a much larger dimensionality (4096 vs. 128 features per person) and is especially problematic for representing scenes of many people.

Implementation Details: The same settings are used as Sect. 4.1 except the following. We trained these models *without* person action labels for 150 epochs and initial learning rate 10^{-4}. The MLP in the last relational layer ends with sigmoid non-linearities instead of ReLU. For person modeling, the ImageNet-pretrained VGG19 network is used as-is, without fine-tuning. The same setup is used for the Denoising Autoencoder, but with initial learning rate 10^{-3}.

Results: In this section we list our results for the retrieval tasks. We present the scene retrieval results, followed by single person retrieval. Then we discuss the performance of the models.

Table 2 compares the scene retrieval performance of our relational autoencoder with the baselines. We compute the Hit@K measure for $K \in \{1, 2, \ldots, 5\}$. Specifically, given a query frame, the frame is encoded using the autoencoder model and the closest K matches in the database are retrieved. Recall, two frames are a match if the IoU of their actions $\geq$ threshold (0.5). Mean average precision is also reported: mean of the average precision values for each image query where Euclidean distance is used as the confidence indicator. The training and testing sets are the ground truth annotated scenes in the Volleyball Dataset. Results indicate how this novel architecture is capable of capturing the context and encoding it within each person. Surprisingly, our model even beats the uncompressed VGG19, though VGG should be much stronger due to its size and sparsity.

Table 2. Scene retrieval compared to baselines.

Method	Hit@1	Hit@2	Hit@3	Hit@4	Hit@5	mAP
B1-Compact128	49.4	68.7	80.4	87.7	91.4	35.4
B2-VGG19	55.0	73.9	82.7	87.5	91.5	36.4
RAER-4L-2222C	**57.4**	**76.7**	**85.3**	**90.4**	**93.3**	**36.8**

In Table 3, we explore variants of our scene retrieval model. Specifically, we try 2 models with only 2 relational layers (128, 4096): One of these models uses 1 clique in all layers (RAER-2L-11C, all pair relationships) and the second uses 2 cliques (RAER-2L-22C, all pairs within a team). The complex version (RAER-4L-4224C) is 2 layers as our main model, but layer cliques are (4, 2, 2, 4). This means the decoder has to learn how to decode such hierarchical information.

Table 3. Scene retrieval compared to model variants.

Method	Hit@1	Hit@2	Hit@3	Hit@4	Hit@5	mAP
RAER-2L-11C	56.8	74.9	84.5	89.8	92.6	**36.8**
RAER-2L-22C	56.9	75.6	84.9	90.0	**93.3**	36.7
RAER-4L-4224C	55.8	76.1	84.0	88.9	92.7	36.6
RAER-4L-2222C	**57.4**	**76.7**	**85.3**	**90.4**	**93.3**	**36.8**

In Table 4, we show the results for the Denoising Autoencoder when a person might be missing with probability 0.5 in the test data.

Table 4. Scene Retrieval using Denoising Autoencoder (-D) with 50% possible drop for people in test data for models and baselines. Our model is robust; the No Autoencoder model performance drops significantly.

Method	Hit@1	Hit@2	Hit@3	Hit@4	Hit@5	mAP
B1-Compact128-D	38.1	58.8	70.5	78.2	84.7	34.6
B2-VGG19-D	34.0	51.1	62.2	70.0	76.0	34.9
RAER-4L-2222C-D	**43.0**	**65.0**	**78.7**	**85.8**	**90.7**	**35.2**

Table 5 compares the person retrieval performance of using the same relational autoencoder model with the baselines. The training and testing sets are the ground truth bounding boxes of annotated actions in the Volleyball Dataset. Note that the Volleyball dataset consists of 9 action labels, with standing class representing ≈70% of the action labels, so a retrieval system that keeps retrieving standing samples will score high results. To avoid that, the standing class is removed from both the training and test sets in the person retrieval task. After training the model, we extract the compressed person representations for each person action and build a retrieval model for them. Results indicate that our compact person representation works well and beats the alternative compression baseline.

Table 5. Person Retrieval on Volleyball Dataset: Hit@K results of our method and baselines. Last column is mean average precision of query results. Our model outperforms the normal autoencoder model, and is competitive with a 32x larger sparse representation.

Method	Hit@1	Hit@2	Hit@3	Hit@4	Hit@5	mAP
B1-Compact128-P	37.7	54.7	64.6	71.7	76.4	22.8
B2-VGG19-P	**47.3**	**63.2**	**72.1**	**77.4**	**81.2**	25.4
RAER-2L-11C-P	45.5	62.2	70.9	76.1	80.1	**25.8**
RAER-4L-2222C-P	42.6	58.3	68.3	73.7	77.8	25.2

Discussion: The high Hit@K results indicate that the autoencoder approach works well for this task. From the scene and action retrieval results, we notice that our relational autoencoder outperforms the normal autoencoder model of the same structure and compression size due to encoding/decoding of person relationships. Of particular note, the autoencdoer outperforms high-dimensional VGG features for scene retrieval. We hypothesize that this is due to the ability of the relational layers to capture contextual information among people in the scene. Figure 5 visualizes scene retrieval results.

Fig. 5. Visualizations of scene retrieval using our relational autoencoder. Each 2 rows are a query: Query image first (blue box), followed by the closest 5 retrievals. Green Framed boxes are correct matches. The last query is for *Right team winpoint event*, and its results are 3 consecutive *Right team winpoint events* followed by 2 *Left team winpoint events*. (Color Figure online)

5 Conclusion

We proposed a hierarchical relational network for learning feature representations. The network can be used in both supervised and unsupervised learning paradigms. We utilized this network for group activity recognition, based on the final compact scene layer. We also showed how the relational layer can be the main building block in novel autoencoder models that jointly encode/decode each person's feature representation using a shared memory. Results in both tasks demonstrate the effectiveness of the relational network. The relationship graph associated with each layer allows explicit relationship consideration that can be applied to other visual understanding tasks.

References

1. Bagautdinov, T.M., Alahi, A., Fleuret, F., Fua, P., Savarese, S.: Social scene understanding: end-to-end multi-person action localization and collective activity recognition. In: IEEE Conference on Computer Vision and Pattern Recognition (CVPR) (2017)
2. Choi, W., Shahid, K., Savarese, S.: Learning context for collective activity recognition. In: Computer Vision and Pattern Recognition (CVPR) (2011)
3. Danelljan, M., Hger, G., Shahbaz Khan, F., Felsberg, M.: Accurate scale estimation for robust visual tracking. In: British Machine Vision Conference (BMVC) (2014)
4. Deng, Z., Vahdat, A., Hu, H., Mori, G.: structure inference machines: recurrent neural networks for analyzing relations in group activity recognition. In: IEEE Conference on Computer Vision and Pattern Recognition (CVPR) (2016)
5. Dieleman, S., et al.: Lasagne: First release, August 2015. https://doi.org/10.5281/zenodo.27878
6. Doersch, C., Gupta, A., Efros, A.A.: Unsupervised visual representation learning by context prediction. In: International Conference on Computer Vision (ICCV) (2015)
7. Gu, C., et al.: Ava: A video dataset of spatio-temporally localized atomic visual actions. In: arXiv (2017)
8. Guttenberg, N., Virgo, N., Witkowski, O., Aoki, H., Kanai, R.: Permutation-equivariant neural networks applied to dynamics prediction. arXiv preprint arXiv:1612.04530 (2016)
9. Ibrahim, M.S., Muralidharan, S., Deng, Z., Vahdat, A., Mori, G.: A hierarchical deep temporal model for group activity recognition. In: IEEE Conference on Computer Vision and Pattern Recognition (CVPR) (2016)
10. Ibrahim, M.S., Muralidharan, S., Deng, Z., Vahdat, A., Mori, G.: Hierarchical deep temporal models for group activity recognition. arXiv preprint arXiv:1607.02643 (2016)
11. Johnson, J., et al.: Image retrieval using scene graphs. In: IEEE Conference on Computer Vision and Pattern Recognition (CVPR) (2015)
12. Kim, G., Moon, S., Sigal, L.: Ranking and retrieval of image sequences from multiple paragraph queries. In: IEEE Conference on Computer Vision and Pattern Recognition (CVPR) (2015)
13. Kingma, D.P., Ba, J.: Adam: a method for stochastic optimization. In: International Conference on Learning Representations (ICLR) (2014)

14. Krishna, R., et al.: Visual genome: connecting language and vision using crowd-sourced dense image annotations. Int. J. Comput. Vis. (IJCV) **123**, 32–73 (2017)

15. Lan, T., Wang, Y., Mori, G., Robinovitch, S.N.: Retrieving actions in group contexts. In: Kutulakos, K.N. (ed.) ECCV 2010. LNCS, vol. 6553, pp. 181–194. Springer, Heidelberg (2012). https://doi.org/10.1007/978-3-642-35749-7_14

16. Lan, T., Yang, W., Wang, Y., Mori, G.: Image retrieval with structured object queries using latent ranking SVM. In: Fitzgibbon, A., Lazebnik, S., Perona, P., Sato, Y., Schmid, C. (eds.) ECCV 2012. LNCS, vol. 7577, pp. 129–142. Springer, Heidelberg (2012). https://doi.org/10.1007/978-3-642-33783-3_10

17. Lee, H.Y., Huang, J.B., Singh, M., Yang, M.H.: Unsupervised representation learning by sorting sequences. In: International Conference on Computer Vision (ICCV) (2017)

18. Pathak, D., Krhenbhl, P., Donahue, J., Darrell, T., Efros, A.A.: Context encoders: feature learning by inpainting. In: Computer Vision and Pattern Recognition (CVPR) (2016)

19. Perronnin, F., Liu, Y., Sánchez, J., Poirier, H.: Large-scale image retrieval with compressed fisher vectors. In: IEEE Conference on Computer Vision and Pattern Recognition (CVPR) (2010)

20. Ramanathan, V., Huang, J., Abu-El-Haija, S., Gorban, A., Murphy, K., Fei-Fei, L.: Detecting events and key actors in multi-person videos. In: IEEE Conference on Computer Vision and Pattern Recognition (CVPR) (2016)

21. Ramanathan, V., Tang, K., Mori, G., Fei-Fei, L.: Learning temporal embeddings for complex video analysis. In: International Conference on Computer Vision (ICCV) (2015)

22. Ravanbakhsh, S., Schneider, J.G., Póczos, B.: Deep learning with sets and point clouds. In: International Conference on Learning Representations (ICLR) - workshop track (2017)

23. Sadeghi, M.A., Farhadi, A.: Recognition using visual phrases. In: IEEE Conference on Computer Vision and Pattern Recognition (CVPR) (2011)

24. Santoro, A., et al.: A simple neural network module for relational reasoning. arXiv preprint arXiv:1706.01427 (2017)

25. Shu, T., Todorovic, S., Zhu, S.: CERN: confidence-energy recurrent network for group activity recognition. In: IEEE Conference on Computer Vision and Pattern Recognition (CVPR) (2017)

26. Siddiquie, B., Feris, R.S., Davis, L.S.: Image ranking and retrieval based on multi-attribute queries. In: IEEE Conference on Computer Vision and Pattern Recognition (CVPR) (2011)

27. Simonyan, K., Zisserman, A.: Very deep convolutional networks for large-scale image recognition. In: International Conference on Learning Representations (ICLR) (2014)

28. Stewénius, H., Gunderson, S.H., Pilet, J.: Size matters: exhaustive geometric verification for image retrieval accepted for ECCV 2012. In: Fitzgibbon, A., Lazebnik, S., Perona, P., Sato, Y., Schmid, C. (eds.) ECCV 2012. LNCS, pp. 674–687. Springer, Heidelberg (2012). https://doi.org/10.1007/978-3-642-33709-3_48

29. Xu, D., Zhu, Y., Choy, C.B., Fei-Fei, L.: Scene graph generation by iterative message passing. In: CVPR (2017)

Neural Procedural Reconstruction
for Residential Buildings

Huayi Zeng[1][✉], Jiaye Wu[1], and Yasutaka Furukawa[2]

[1] Washington University in St. Louis, St. Louis, USA
{zengh,jiaye.wu}@wustl.edu
[2] Simon Fraser University, Burnaby, Canada
furukawa@sfu.ca

Abstract. This paper proposes a novel 3D reconstruction approach, dubbed Neural Procedural Reconstruction (NPR). NPR infers a sequence of shape grammar rule applications and reconstructs CAD-quality models with procedural structure from 3D points. While most existing methods rely on low-level geometry analysis to extract primitive structures, our approach conducts global analysis of entire building structures by deep neural networks (DNNs), enabling the reconstruction even from incomplete and sparse input data. We demonstrate the proposed system for residential buildings with aerial LiDAR as the input. Our 3D models boast compact geometry and semantically segmented architectural components. Qualitative and quantitative evaluations on hundreds of houses demonstrate that the proposed approach makes significant improvements over the existing state-of-the-art.

Keywords: 3D reconstruction · CAD · Deep learning
Procedural modeling

1 Introduction

Procedural modeling (PM) has revolutionized the practice of urban planning, architecture, and entertainment. PM procedurally applies shape transformation rules in a shape grammar to synthesize realistic 3D models, which have CAD quality geometries with procedural structures [8,9,26].

Discovering such procedural structure and reconstructing CAD quality geometry from raw sensor data, such as images or 3D point-clouds, is a similar but completely different problem [27], which we call procedural reconstruction (PR). A successful PR system could turn city-scale LiDAR scans into high-quality 3D city models with procedural structures, opening doors for novel applications in digital mapping, urban study, civil engineering, and entertainment. Unfortunately, most existing PR algorithms start from low-level geometry analysis in

Electronic supplementary material The online version of this chapter (https://doi.org/10.1007/978-3-030-01219-9_45) contains supplementary material, which is available to authorized users.

© Springer Nature Switzerland AG 2018
V. Ferrari et al. (Eds.): ECCV 2018, LNCS 11207, pp. 759–775, 2018.
https://doi.org/10.1007/978-3-030-01219-9_45

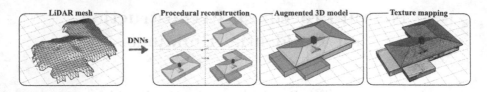

Fig. 1. Neural procedural reconstruction learns to procedurally apply shape grammar rules to reconstruct CAD-quality models from raw 3D points. The procedural representation allows easy geometry augmentation (e.g., roof thickening) and texture mapping.

a bottom-up process (e.g., RANSAC for plane detection), requiring dense and near complete 3D points.

This paper proposes a novel approach, dubbed Neural Procedural Reconstruction (NPR), which trains deep neural networks (DNNs) to procedurally apply shape grammar rules and reconstruct CAD-quality geometry models from 3D points (See Fig. 1). DNNs detect primitive structures via global analysis of entire buildings, making the reconstruction possible even from incomplete and sparse 3D data. We demonstrated the framework for a shape grammar of residential buildings in England, where LiDAR point-clouds are publicly accessible. Qualitative and quantitative evaluations over hundreds of houses demonstrate that our approach makes significant improvements over the state-of-the-art. We will publicly share code and data to promote further research.

2   Related Work

This paper makes contributions at the intersection of architectural reconstruction, procedural modeling, and procedural reconstruction. We focus the description to automated techniques in these fields.

Reconstruction with Geometric Regularities: Geometric regularities, such as planarity or orthogonality, have been effective for architecture reconstruction [3,10,16,28,33,37–39]. Global geometric regularities can further improve the model quality [41]. Their 3D models are clean and compact, but miss procedural structure, limiting the range of applications.

Procedural Modeling and Shape Analysis: Procedural modeling of architectural buildings has been a big success with many commercial products [9,26]. A binary image or a volume guides the procedural modeling process of buildings by Markov Chain Monte Carlo (MCMC) [34]. However, their goal is to synthesize virtual scenes as opposed to faithfully reconstructing existing ones from sensor data. The analysis of man-made shapes through a structured representation has also been presented for objects [18,19], buildings [6], indoor floorplans [24], and raw 3D point-clouds [5]. The analysis further enables model manipulation for interactive modeling [5] or even the discovery of a grammar [21]. Our problem is different: turning noisy sensor data into 3D models with procedural structure.

Procedural Reconstruction: Procedural reconstruction has been an active research topic for building facades [22,27], plants [31], and trees [35]. For building architecture, a seminal work by Dick ct al. [7] employs MCMC to reconstruct structured building models from multiple images. MCMC is also used for the reconstruction of roof structures from laser scanned 3D points [14]. Recent techniques rely on machine learning to incorporate semantics [20,36]. However, these approaches critically rely on low-level geometry analysis for primitive extraction (e.g., RANSAC for plane detection), which is vulnerable to noisy or incomplete input data. Poor data quality is the key challenge for our problem, where the data comes from a country-scale survey [4] with much lower resolution than what has been commonly used [20,36]. Our approach employs DNNs and conducts global analysis of entire buildings to detect primitive structures.

Integrating primitive detection with shape-rule inference robustifies the process [23], but the approach has been only demonstrated on one special building type: Greek temples. Top-down procedural reconstruction without primitive detection was proposed for indoor scenes [15], but the system requires many heuristics and hand-coded algorithms. A Support Vector Machine (SVM) performs roof type classification to generate CAD-quality building models [13], but their method requires rectangular building footprints as input. DNNs are used to guide the reconstruction of stroke-graphics [32]. They have a simple grammar for 2D strokes, while we handle 3D architectural buildings with more complex grammar.

The closest work to ours is the one by Nishida et al. [30], which utilizes DNNs to predict geometric primitives from user-strokes. While the fundamental role of DNNs is the same (i.e., classification of a rule-branch and regression of geometric parameters), our problem is substantially more challenging, requiring a different algorithmic solution. First, their input is clean feature-curves, while ours is raw sensor data. Second, their rules are limited to the generation of a single primitive at a time as an interactive system, while our rules need to generate an arbitrary number of primitives (e.g., multiple foundational blocks, dormers or chimneys). Third, their system infers a single rule application given user strokes, while our system needs to infer a complete sequence of rule applications as an automated reconstruction algorithm. To our knowledge, this work is one of the first[1] to demonstrate the use of DNNs for procedural reconstruction of architectural buildings from raw sensor data.

3   Shape Grammar for Residential Buildings

Our shape-grammar has seven rules, forming five reconstruction phases (See Fig. 2). We modified a default grammar in CityEngine [9] to focus on houses in England. Rules are applied in a fixed sequential order over the phases.

---

[1] About one week before the deadline, we encountered a future publication [29], which utilizes DNNs to reconstruct procedural building models from a RGB image. DNNs are used to parse each rectified facade image. This is not considered to be a prior work, but we cite the paper here for a reference.

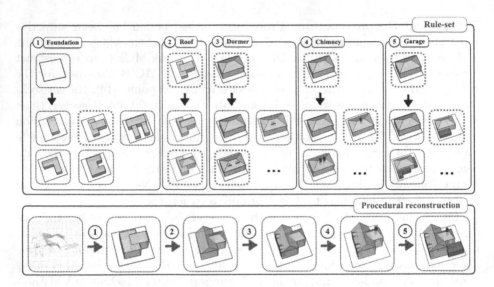

Fig. 2. Our NPR system for residential buildings has 5 stages, consisting of seven shape-grammar rules. The application order of the rules are fixed while DNNs are trained to (1) select a rule-branch and (2) regress geometric parameters for each rule-application.

Each rule is associated with several branches and each branch has its own geometric parameters. We defer the full specification of our parameterization to the supplementary material, as the grammar definition is not our contribution.

- The "foundation-rule" first determines the 2D shape of a house from six types (i.e., rule-branches): I, II, III, L, U, or $\mathcal{C}$. Houses consisting of one, two, and three rectangular blocks have I, II, and III types, respectively. L (or U) types refer to L-shaped (or U-shaped) buildings.
  The last type $\mathcal{C}$ is for houses with complex shapes beyond our grammar or non-architectural structures such as trees, where our system would stop the reconstruction process. Geometric parameters are the position, the shape, and the height of each foundational block.
- Three "roof-rules" determine the roof structures for each foundational block, namely, I-, L-, or U-component. Hip and gable are the two popular types in England, and each rule has two branches. Geometric parameters determine the hip roof shape (i.e. hip ratio) and the roof height.
- The "dormer-rule" adds arbitrary number of dormers to each foundation component. We model dormers as a block primitive plus a gable roof. Therefore, the geometric parameters are the position and the shape of a block plus the roof height. The "chimney-rule" is the same as the dormer except that we assume its roof to be flat and its shape to be square.
- The "garage-rule" adds arbitrary number of surrounding sub-structures such as garages, balconies, or shelters as I- or L-polygons. The roof is fixed to flat.

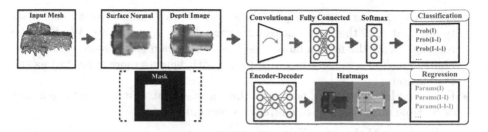

Fig. 3. Typical rule branch classifier and geometric parameter regressor. A variant of the ResNet [12] performs the classification. A standard encoder-decoder performs the regression. The regressors estimate the corners of building foundations for example. Our input is a 4-channel (surface normal + depth) image of resolution 64× 64. The binary mask optionally specifies the region of interests.

4 Neural Procedural Reconstruction

Neural procedural reconstruction (NPR) applies shape-grammar rules in a fixed sequential order to reconstruct 3D models. NPR solves two fundamental tasks at each rule application: (1) classifying a rule-branch, and (2) regressing geometric parameters associated with the branch. DNNs perform all the branch classifications. For the parameter regression, DNNs play important roles, while we also use standard heuristics for some parameters, whose training data collection would require excessive manual work (e.g., 3D model manipulation). For DNNs, our input image has 4 channels encoding the surface normal and the depth, whose values are normalized to the intensity range $[0, 255]$. The resolution is 64×64. As part of pre-processing, we apply the orientation rectification DNN introduced in [25] and assume that building structures are axis-aligned.

4.1 Foundation-Rule

A variant of the ResNet [12] performs the rule branch classification (i.e., I, II, III, L, U, or $\mathcal{C}$) with one modification: We add one more fully-connected layer between the global pooling and the output layers with softmax. A simple one-hot encoding is used with a cross-entropy loss (See Fig. 3). At test time, we simply pick a branch corresponding to the maximum probability.

I-, L-, or U-shaped 2D polygons are the regression targets. Directly regressing the parameters did not work even with DNNs. We borrow a standard encoder-decoder network to detect corner points in the output activation image [2]. We then enumerate possible polygon candidates, and pick the best one with a simple metric. We now explain the details for each rule branch.

- For I-shape, a DNN detects four types of corners in four activation images (i.e., top-left, top-right, bottom-left, or bottom-right). We extract peaks above a certain threshold (0.5 in our experiments) after the non-local max suppression. This process usually results in 2 to 3 corner candidates for each corner type. We then exhaustively pick three corner candidates from three corner types, and find the tight enclosing rectangle as a candidate. We find the rectangle with the maximum intersection over union (IoU) score against the binary mask of a house (the set of pixels with heights more than 2m) as the foundation.

- For II- or III-shapes, the process is the same except that we generate a pair or a triple of rectangles sequentially as one candidate.

- For L- or U-shapes, DNNs also detect four types of corners, whose types are defined in a scheme independent of the rotations (see the right figure). For instance, "internal" concave points are detected in the first activation image regardless of the rotations. We generate candidate polygons as follows. L-polygon has six corners and we exhaustively enumerate the set of six points to make one candidate (i.e., one from type-1, two from type-2, two from type-3, and one from type-4). Adjacent corners must have the

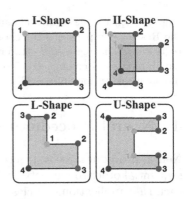

same X or Y coordinate, and we simply take the average to make them consistent. We generate more candidates by enumerating five points (excluding one from the complete set), while inferring the missing one from its neighbors. The same process is used for U.

We extrude 2D polygons vertically after shape regression, while estimating the height by the average of the bottom 10% height values inside the polygon. Note that the final optimization refines all the parameters, and the parameters do not have to be precise in this step.

4.2   Roof-Rules

The same DNN architecture classifies the roof types (i.e., gable or hip). For II- or III-shapes, which consist of multiple I-shaped components with different roof types, a binary mask specifies an I-shaped component of interests by setting the mask values to 1 inside the corresponding I-component. Each height value is estimated by the average of the top 5% of the height values in the corresponding foundation. The ratios for hip-roofs are initialized with a common value 0.1.

4.3   Dormer-Rule and Chimney-Rule

The dormer roof structure is fixed to gable, and the rule has only a regression DNN-branch. The same encoder-decoder network [2] detects the center location of each dormer in a single activation image. We further apply the non-local maxim suppression and remove peaks lower than 0.5. For II- or III-foundations, we use the binary mask to specify I-components to add dormers. Dormers are initialized with an axis-aligned rectangle whose width and length are set to 2.0 m.

The roof height is initialized so that a roof angle is 30° from the horizontal surface. The chimney-rule follows the same process except that its shape is initialized with a 0.7 m × 0.7 m square, and its height is initialized by 2.5 m plus the roof height at the center position.

4.4 Garage-Rule

The garage-rule resembles the foundation-rule. However, we take a different approach, because arbitrary number of sub-structures are to be added, whose candidate enumeration would be challenging. We use the regression branch to infer a set of pixels belonging to the sub-structures in an activation image. More precisely, the encoder-decoder network [2] performs pixel-wise regression. Higher value indicates the higher possibility of garage existence in each pixel. We keep pixels with values at least 0.5, find connected components whose diameters are at least 3 pixels, and try fitting rectangular or L-shaped polygons (with four rotation variants). Specifically, a tight bounding box is calculated for each connected component as a rectangle candidate. Starting from this bounding box, L polygon candidates are composed by replacing one corner by an internal point at least 4 pixels away from the boundary. We enumerate all possible polygon candidates and pick the best one based on the IoU against the binary mask of a house (i.e., same as the foundation-rule).

4.5 Model Refinement

We apply a standard non-linear least squares technique to optimize all the geometric parameters by minimizing the discrepancy against the input height values. We defer the details to the supplementary material.

5 Dataset Creation

The section explains how we generate input depth, surface normal images, and ground-truth annotations.

5.1 Depth and Normal Image Generation

UK Environment Agency provides aerial LiDAR data over England as Digital Terrain Model (DTM) and Digital Surface Model (DSM). DTM only contains the terrain while DSM also contains buildings, vegetation, and other objects. The LiDAR data is arranged on the British National Grid [1]. Each grid covers a roughly square region. 25 cm resolution (i.e., one sample per 25 cm) is the highest resolution but covers only a small portion of the land. We downloaded 50 cm resolution data of all the $10\,km \times 10\,km$ grids. This amounts to roughly 500 grids. A grid with few houses has a small file size in a compressed form. We chose the top twenty grids based on the compressed file sizes, while skipping certain grids manually (e.g., complex mountainous terrains without houses).

For each grid data, we subtract DTM from DSM to remove terrain influences. To isolate houses, we discard points below 2.0 meters, identify connected components, and remove small ones (i.e., areas less than 64 pixels). To further discard outliers, we use building footprints from Ordance Survey (Britain's mapping agency). We enlarge each footprint by a factor of two around the bounding-box center, and keep only components that are fully inside at least one of the expanded footprints. The discarded components in the last step are marked as non-building structures for complex class ($\mathcal{C}$).

For each remaining component, we estimate the rectification angle by an existing DNN-based system [25]. Bilinear interpolation is used for image sampling. We find the tight axis-aligned rectangle, turn it into a square while keeping the center, then add a 20% margin all around. Lastly, we linearly map the height range in each square to [0, 255]. We use a finite-difference to also compute a surface normal image, which directly captures roof orientations. We linearly-map each vector element from its valid range ([−1.0, 1.0] or [0.0, 1.0]) to [0, 255].

5.2   Manual Annotation

The right figure illustrates our typical annotations. For each normal image, we specify its foundational shape type (i.e., I, II, III, L, U, or $\mathcal{C}$) with its 2D polygons and roof type(s) (i.e., hip or gable). Garage structures are annotated with either I- or L-polygons. The center loca-

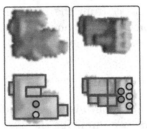

☐ Foundation
   specification

☐ Garage
   specification

○ Dormer
   location

◉ Chimney
   location

tions are annotated for the dormers or chimneys.[2] We do not annotate the remaining geometric parameters, which require time-consuming manual work: (1) shapes of dormers and chimneys; (2) heights of foundations and roofs; and (3) internal roof structures for hip. These parameters are initialized by default values or standard heuristics instead of the regression as described in Sect. 4. We also rectify rotations manually to collect data for the rotation rectification DNN [25]. In total, we annotated 3,210 examples, in particular, 720, 1025, 142, 524, 247, and 552 samples for the foundation types I, II, III, L, U, and $\mathcal{C}$, respectively.

5.3   Data Augmentation

First, we rotate depth images with an increment of 90° with or without mirroring (factor of 8 augmentation). Second, since only a small percentage of houses contain dormers, we synthetically add dormer structures to the depth images, specially for the training of the dormer regression DNN. More concretely, for each house, we synthesize a new depth image by adding 1 to 5 synthetic dormers (the number randomly picked with uniform probabilities). Each dormer has five

---

[2] Dormers are annotated only for II-buildings to save time, as the trained model works on all the other cases. The dormer detection will be evaluated for all building types.

Table 1. Training and testing performance. Accuracies, IoU scores against the ground-truth, and (precision, recalls) are reported for the classification, foundation/garage regressions, and dormer/chimney regressions, respectively.

Dataset	Classification				Regression								
	Foundation	Roof			Foundation					Dormer	Chimney	Garage
		I	L	U	I	II	III	L	U			
Training	99.1%	96.1%	100%	100%	0.832	0.812	0.797	0.817	0.839	(100%, 100%)	(100%, 100%)	0.646
Testing	89.2%	85.0%	89.7%	66.0%	0.831	0.797	0.795	0.779	0.838	(77%, 84%)	(81%, 84%)	0.582

parameters (See supplementary materials) and we randomly specify each parameter with uniform probabilities within a specified range: (1) the center can be anywhere inside an image; (2) each lateral size is from 3 to 6 pixels; and (3) the height is from 0.5 to 2.5 m. We repeat the process until the synthesized dormer is valid: (1) not colliding with any other dormers; and (2) residing inside only one foundational shape (i.e., not at the intersection of multiple I-shapes).

5.4   Synthetic Data Generation

The shape grammar allows generation of synthetic building models with ground-truth annotations via standard procedural modeling. While synthetic examples would not replace real data, it is still interesting to study how much they help training. We use Esri CityEngine [9] to generate synthetic house models, then sample 3D points at every 50 cm to simulate the LiDAR scanning process. More specifically, we manually modify a default shape-grammar in CityEngine to better match the house examples in our data (See the rule-file in the supplementary document). To minimize the appearance gap between the real and synthetic images, we add uniform noise in a range $[-0.3\,\mathrm{m}, 0.3\,\mathrm{m}]$ to the z coordinate (i.e., height) of each 3D point with probability 70%. Synthetic examples are axis-aligned at this point, and we randomly rotate each model around the gravity by uniformly picking an angle in the range $[0, 360]$. We generated 150,000 synthetic examples, in particular, 30,000 examples for each foundation type (i.e., I, II, III, L, or U).

6   Experimental Results

We implemented the proposed system in C++ and PyTorch, using a standard PC with NVIDIA Titan X. We trained 4 classification DNNs (for the foundation and the three roof-rules), 8 regression DNNs (except the roof-rules), and 1 DNN for rotation rectification as pre-processing [25]. We used two thirds of the real data for training and the rest for testing after random sampling. Synthetic and augmented samples are used only for training. The encoder-decoder network has been initialized with a pre-trained model [2]. At test time, the network inference is instant (i.e., 100 to 150 instances per second), while the most expensive step

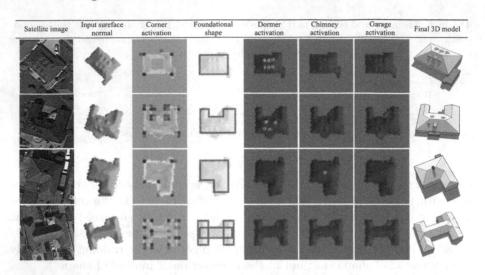

| Satellite image | Input sureface normal | Corner activation | Foundational shape | Dormer activation | Chimney activation | Garage activation | Final 3D model |

Fig. 4. Representative reconstructions with intermediate results. The satellite image is shown for reference from Google Maps.

is the model refinement, which takes about 10 s per house. We show only reconstruction results in the testing set. Please see the supplementary file for more results.

Evaluations: Figure 4 shows some of our representative reconstructions with intermediate results. A satellite image of the corresponding region is also shown at the left for reference. Our method successfully turns noisy raw sensor data into CAD-quality geometries with architectural components, whose segmentations are highlighted in colors in the 3D model renderings.

Table 1 shows the training and testing performance of our trained DNNs. Accuracies, IoU scores against the ground-truth, and precision/recalls are reported for the classification, foundation-garage regressions, and dormer-chimney detections (correct if within 3 pixels from the ground-truth), respectively. The trained networks demonstrate good generalization performance for many tasks, but the testing accuracy suffers for U-roof classification, where U-shapes are rare and lack in real training data.

The confusion matrix of the foundation classification in the right figure also illustrates that U-shapes are one of the challenging cases together with III. The matrix shows confusion between II and L or III and U, where these cases are not clearly distinguishable even to 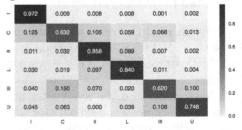 human eyes. We also observe the confusion between III and C, because some III-shaped houses are quite complex.

Figure 5 illustrates a few major failure cases: (1) the misclassification of foundation types; (2) missing dormers or chimneys; (3) local minima in the final refinement; and (4) unique architectural styles beyond our grammar. While the lack of ground-truth 3D models prevents quantitative evaluations, to our eyes, 20 to 25% of the examples fall into those failure modes.

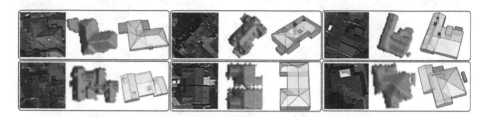

Fig. 5. Major failure modes. Top-left: Foundation mis-classification (II mis-classified as L). Top-middle: Missing dormers/chimneys. Top-right: A local minimum in the final refinement, where an example is correctly classified as III. Bottom: Unique architectural styles beyond our grammar.

Table 2. The average mean absolute distance (MAD) againstor the input depth images and the average number of triangles (#tri) over 250 houses.

	I		II		III		L		U		Average	
	MAD	#tri	MAD	#tri	MAD	#tri	MAD	#tri	MAD	#tri	MAD	#tri
Poisson	2.12	33.1	1.43	39.0	1.24	60.6	1.40	44.3	1.15	50.3	1.47	45.5
Piecewise planar	1.08	33.0	0.92	39.0	0.94	60.6	0.99	44.2	0.80	50.3	0.95	45.4
USC	1.64	166.1	1.36	158.1	1.48	213.3	1.44	154.6	1.10	152.7	1.40	169.0
Kentucky	1.61	12.9	1.81	19.9	3.13	10.0	2.19	12.4	1.90	13.2	2.13	13.7
Ours	0.95	33.1	0.75	39.0	0.88	60.7	0.62	44.4	0.84	50.3	0.81	45.5

Comparative Evaluations: Figure 6 compares our algorithm against four competing methods: Poisson Surface Reconstruction (PSR) [17], piecewise planar reconstruction (PPR) [33], dual-contouring method (USC) [40], and semantic decomposition and reconstruction (Kentucky) [20].[3] For PPR and Kentucky, their software is not publicly available and we used our local implementations.

---

[3] Three more potential competing methods exist. The first work is an old one with MCMC as the optimization engine [7], but we found it difficult to reproduce due to the complex algorithm and many parameters. The second work also utilizes MCMC [34]. While it may appear straight-forward, we found it difficult to adapt to our problem setting. They seek to roughly match the silhouette against a binary image/volume, allowing infinitely many solutions. Our input is noisy raw sensor data, where subtle geometric signals (e.g., small roof surfaces, chimneys and dormers) need to be recognized, allowing only one solution. The third work uses trained models to parse aerial LiDAR into architectural components [36]. We have not empirically compared, because their approach (bottom-up from primitive detection) is well-represented by Kentucky [20].

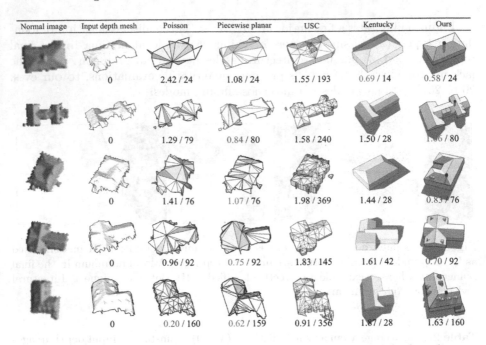

Normal image	Input depth mesh	Poisson	Piecewise planar	USC	Kentucky	Ours
	0	2.42 / 24	1.08 / 24	1.55 / 193	0.69 / 14	0.58 / 24
	0	1.29 / 79	0.84 / 80	1.58 / 240	1.50 / 28	1.96 / 80
	0	1.41 / 76	1.07 / 76	1.98 / 369	1.44 / 28	0.83 / 76
	0	0.96 / 92	0.75 / 92	1.83 / 145	1.61 / 42	0.70 / 92
	0	0.20 / 160	0.62 / 159	0.91 / 356	1.87 / 28	1.63 / 160

Fig. 6. Comparisons against baselines. The numbers show the mean absolute distance against the input depth images and the polygon counts.

Only Kentucky and our method generate semantically segmented CAD-quality geometry. However, Kentucky failed to capture main architectural structures in most cases. Two major failure modes stem from their plane extraction step. First, they often miss planes, especially small roof surfaces with clutter such as dormers. Second, they detect non-existent planes, which cause irreversible mistakes in merging pairs of planes to build high-level components. Note that our LiDAR is aerial and has only 4 samples per sq.m., making the plane-detection challenging. Kentucky uses ground-based LiDAR, which is probably 30 to 50 times denser. Despite challenges, our approach recovers even small architectural structures such as dormers and chimneys through top-down learning instead of bottom-up primitive detection. The other methods produce a mere polygon soup without semantic segmentation or CAD-quality geometry. The figure demonstrates that our method makes significant improvements over the current state-of-the-art.

We quantitatively evaluated the accuracy of the models by taking the mean absolute distance between our model and the input depth images along the gravity direction. PSR and PPR generate dense polygon meshes, and we used a standard mesh simplification software QSlim [11] to make the number of triangles roughly equal to ours for fair comparison. For USC, we tweaked the parameters of their software to make their models as compact as possible, although their polygon counts are still three to five times larger than ours.

The distances and the polygon counts are shown for examples in Fig. 4. Table 2 reports the averages over 250 houses, where we randomly chose 50 samples for each foundation type. Our method consistently outperforms the competing methods in the geometric accuracy. This is a surprise, as PSR+QSlim seeks to decrease the polygon counts with a focus on maintaining the original geometry. Our method not only produces compact 3D models with proper segmentation and semantics, but also achieves the best geometric accuracy.

Table 3. Relative importance of the synthetic data. The first two rows show the classification accuracy of the foundation-rule. "x30" indicates that the number of synthetic examples for training is 30 times more than the real ones. The second row uses only synthetic samples for training. The bottom two rows show the regression accuracy (i.e., the IoU score against the ground-truth) for the II-foundation branch.

	0	× 10	× 20	× 30	× 40	× 50
Accu. (w/ real)	82.2	85.3	85.6	87.7	89.2	88.7
Accu. (w/o real)	(N/A)	40.6	48.8	42.3	42.0	42.3
IoU (w/ real)	0.796	0.814	0.813	0.809	0.815	0.810
IoU (w/o real)	(N/A)	0.796	0.799	0.802	0.803	0.800

Impact of Synthetic and Augmented Data: Table 3 shows how synthetic training samples influence foundation classification and regression. Classification improves with more synthetic data in general, while IoU scores do not improve much. We found that the raw outputs of the regression DNN degrade with fewer synthetic samples, but our post-processing (i.e., polygon candidate enumeration) is robust and yields good IoU scores even from poor corner detections. Augmentation of dormer structures improves the precision and recall from (8% and 17%) to (77% and 84%), where a detection is declared correct if within 3 pixels from a ground-truth.

Applications: The procedural representation easily allows for geometry augmentation and texture association (See Fig. 7). First, roof geometries do not have thickness nor overhang structures. We enlarge the roof geometry by 15%, then thicken the structure by extruding the surface along the gravity direction by 0.35 m. Second, we used CityEngine and its texture-image asset to interactively map textures, while the process can be automated by exploiting the reconstructed procedural structure. Besides content creation, digital mapping is another immediate application, which we demonstrate by importing our models to Google Earth (See Fig. 8). Our models reveal rich architectural information of houses with minimal increase in data size.

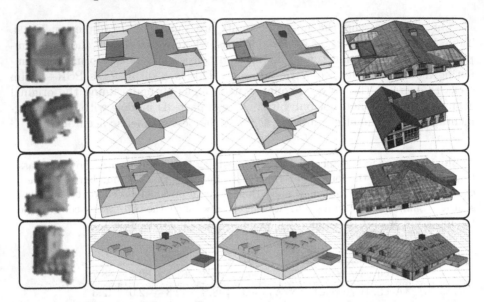

Fig. 7. Model enhancement. The procedural representation allows easy geometry augmentation and texture mapping. From left to right, an input surface normal image, our reconstructed model, an augmented 3D model, and a texture mapped 3D model.

Fig. 8. Digital mapping is one key application domain. We rendered our models in Google Earth while changing the background texture from satellite to map-tiles. Our 3D models reveal rich architectural information with minimal increase in data size.

7 Conclusion

This paper presents a novel computational framework for procedural reconstruction, which turns noisy and sparse 3D points into high-quality 3D models with procedural structure. The qualitative and quantitative evaluations show significant improvements over the existing state-of-the-art. Our 3D models have CAD-quality geometry with semantically segmented architectural components, making them immediately effective for many applications. While the paper demonstrates the system for residential houses with LiDAR 3D points, neural procedural reconstruction is a general computational framework, independent of the particular choice of a shape grammar. This paper has a potential to enable effective procedural reconstruction system in other domains. A future direction of our works will be to make more effective use of synthetic examples and minimize the requirement on human annotations. We will publicly share all the code and data to promote further research.

Acknowledgement. This research is partially supported by National Science Foundation under grant IIS 1540012 and IIS 1618685, and Google Faculty Research Award. We thank Nvidia for a generous GPU donation.

References

1. https://en.wikipedia.org/wiki/Ordnance_Survey_National_Grid (2017)
2. Bulat, A., Tzimiropoulos, G.: Human pose estimation via convolutional part heatmap regression. In: Leibe, B., Matas, J., Sebe, N., Welling, M. (eds.) ECCV 2016. LNCS, vol. 9911, pp. 717–732. Springer, Cham (2016). https://doi.org/10. 1007/978-3-319-46478-7_44
3. Chauve, A.L., Labatut, P., Pons, J.P.: Robust piecewise-planar 3D reconstruction and completion from large-scale unstructured point data. In: IEEE Conference on Computer Vision and Pattern Recognition, pp. 1261–1268. IEEE (2010)
4. Data.gov.uk.   http://environment.data.gov.uk/ds/survey/index.jsp#/survey (2015)
5. Demir, I., Aliaga, D.G., Benes, B.: Procedural editing of 3D building point clouds. In: International Conference on Computer Vision, pp. 2147–2155 (2015)
6. Demir, I., Aliaga, D.G., Benes, B.: Proceduralization for editing 3D architectural models. In: 2016 Fourth International Conference on 3D Vision (3DV), pp. 194–202. IEEE (2016)
7. Dick, A.R., Torr, P.H.S., Cipolla, R.: A bayesian estimation of building shape using MCMC. In: Heyden, A., Sparr, G., Nielsen, M., Johansen, P. (eds.) ECCV 2002. LNCS, vol. 2351, pp. 852–866. Springer, Heidelberg (2002). https://doi.org/10. 1007/3-540-47967-8_57
8. Dylla, K., Frischer, B., Müller, P., Ulmer, A., Haegler, S.: Rome reborn 2.0: a case study of virtual city reconstruction using procedural modeling techniques. Comput. Graph. World **16**(6), 62–66 (2008)
9. EsriCityEngine. http://www.esri.com/software/cityengine (2017)
10. Furukawa, Y., Curless, B., Seitz, S.M., Szeliski, R.: Manhattan-world stereo. In: IEEE Conference on Computer Vision and Pattern Recognition, pp. 1422–1429. IEEE (2009)
11. Garland, M., Heckbert, P.S.: Surface simplification using quadric error metrics. In: Proceedings of the 24th Annual Conference on Computer Graphics and Interactive Techniques, pp. 209–216. ACM Press/Addison-Wesley Publishing Co. (1997)
12. He, K., Zhang, X., Ren, S., Sun, J.: Deep residual learning for image recognition. arXiv preprint arXiv:1512.03385 (2015)
13. Henn, A., Grger, G., Stroh, V., Plmer, L.: Model driven reconstruction of roofs from sparse LiDAR point clouds 76, 17–29, February 2013

14. Huang, H., Brenner, C., Sester, M.: A generative statistical approach to automatic 3D building roof reconstruction from laser scanning data. ISPRS J. Photogramm. Remote Sens. **79**, 29–43 (2013)
15. Ikehata, S., Yang, H., Furukawa, Y.: Structured indoor modeling. In: IEEE International Conference on Computer Vision, pp. 1323–1331 (2015)
16. Jiang, H., Xiao, J.: A linear approach to matching cuboids in RGBD images. In: IEEE Conference on Computer Vision and Pattern Recognition, pp. 2171–2178 (2013)
17. Kazhdan, M., Hoppe, H.: Screened poisson surface reconstruction. ACM Trans. Graph. (TOG) **32**(3), 29 (2013)
18. Kim, V.G., Li, W., Mitra, N.J., Chaudhuri, S., DiVerdi, S., Funkhouser, T.: Learning part-based templates from large collections of 3D shapes. ACM Trans. Graph. (TOG) **32**(4), 70 (2013)
19. Li, Y., Wu, X., Chrysathou, Y., Sharf, A., Cohen-Or, D., Mitra, N.J.: Globfit: consistently fitting primitives by discovering global relations. In: ACM Transactions on Graphics (TOG), vol. 30, p. 52. ACM (2011)
20. Lin, H., Gao, J., Zhou, Y., Lu, G., Ye, M., Zhang, C., Liu, L., Yang, R.: Semantic decomposition and reconstruction of residential scenes from LiDAR data. ACM Trans. Graph. (TOG) **32**(4), 66 (2013)
21. Martinovic, A., Van Gool, L.: Bayesian grammar learning for inverse procedural modeling. In: IEEE Conference on Computer Vision and Pattern Recognition, pp. 201–208 (2013)
22. Martinovic, A., Van Gool, L.: Hierarchical co-segmentation of building facades. In: 2014 2nd International Conference on 3D Vision (3DV), vol. 1, pp. 409–416. IEEE (2014)
23. Mathias, M., Martinovic, A., Weissenberg, J., Van Gool, L.: Procedural 3D building reconstruction using shape grammars and detectors. In: 2011 International Conference on 3D Imaging, Modeling, Processing, Visualization and Transmission (3DIMPVT), pp. 304–311. IEEE (2011)
24. Merrell, P., Schkufza, E., Koltun, V.: Computer-generated residential building layouts. ACM Trans. Graph. (TOG) **29**(6), 181 (2010)
25. Mousavian, A., Anguelov, D., Flynn, J., Kosecka, J.: 3D bounding box estimation using deep learning and geometry. In: IEEE Conference on Computer Vision and Pattern Recognition (2017)
26. Müller, P., Wonka, P., Haegler, S., Ulmer, A., Van Gool, L.: Procedural modeling of buildings. In: Acm Transactions On Graphics (Tog), vol. 25, pp. 614–623. ACM (2006)
27. Müller, P., Zeng, G., Wonka, P., Van Gool, L.: Image-based procedural modeling of facades. ACM Trans. Graph. (TOG) **26**(3), 85 (2007)
28. Nguatem, W., Mayer, H.: Modeling urban scenes from pointclouds. In: 2017 IEEE International Conference on Computer Vision (ICCV), pp. 3857–3866, October 2017. https://doi.org/10.1109/ICCV.2017.414
29. Nishida, G., Bousseau, A., Aliaga, D.G.: Procedural modeling of a building from a single image. Eurographics (2018)
30. Nishida, G., Garcia-Dorado, I., Aliaga, D.G., Benes, B., Bousseau, A.: Interactive sketching of urban procedural models. ACM Trans. Graph. (TOG) **35**(4), 130 (2016)
31. Quan, L., Tan, P., Zeng, G., Yuan, L., Wang, J., Kang, S.B.: Image-based plant modeling. In: ACM Transactions on Graphics (TOG), vol. 25, pp. 599–604. ACM (2006)

32. Ritchie, D., Thomas, A., Hanrahan, P., Goodman, N.: Neurally-guided procedural models: amortized inference for procedural graphics programs using neural networks. In: Advances In Neural Information Processing Systems, pp. 622–630 (2016)

33. Sinha, S., Steedly, D., Szeliski, R.: Piecewise planar stereo for image-based rendering. In: IEEE International Conference on Computer Vision (2009)

34. Talton, J.O., Lou, Y., Lesser, S., Duke, J., Měch, R., Koltun, V.: Metropolis procedural modeling. ACM Trans. Graph. (TOG) **30**(2), 11 (2011)

35. Tan, P., Zeng, G., Wang, J., Kang, S.B., Quan, L.: Image-based tree modeling. In: ACM Transactions on Graphics (TOG), vol. 26, p. 87. ACM (2007)

36. Toshev, A., Mordohai, P., Taskar, B.: Detecting and parsing architecture at city scale from range data. In: IEEE Conference on Computer Vision and Pattern Recognition, pp. 398–405. IEEE (2010)

37. Wang, H., Zhang, W., Chen, Y., Chen, M., Yan, K.: Semantic decomposition and reconstruction of compound buildings with symmetric roofs from LiDAR data and aerial imagery. Remote Sens. **7**(10), 13945–13974 (2015). https://doi.org/10.3390/rs71013945

38. Xiao, J., Furukawa, Y.: Reconstructing the world's museums. Int. J. Comput. Vis. **110**(3), 243–258 (2014)

39. Zebedin, L., Bauer, J., Karner, K., Bischof, H.: Fusion of feature- and area-based information for urban buildings modeling from aerial imagery. In: Forsyth, D., Torr, P., Zisserman, A. (eds.) ECCV 2008. LNCS, vol. 5305, pp. 873–886. Springer, Heidelberg (2008). https://doi.org/10.1007/978-3-540-88693-8_64

40. Zhou, Q.-Y., Neumann, U.: 2.5D dual contouring: a robust approach to creating building models from aerial LiDAR point clouds. In: Daniilidis, K., Maragos, P., Paragios, N. (eds.) ECCV 2010. LNCS, vol. 6313, pp. 115–128. Springer, Heidelberg (2010). https://doi.org/10.1007/978-3-642-15558-1_9

41. Zhou, Q.Y., Neumann, U.: 2.5D building modeling by discovering global regularities. In: IEEE Conference on Computer Vision and Pattern Recognition, pp. 326–333. IEEE (2012)

Simultaneous 3D Reconstruction for Water Surface and Underwater Scene

Yiming Qian[1](✉), Yinqiang Zheng[2], Minglun Gong[3]🆔, and Yee-Hong Yang[1]🆔

[1] University of Alberta, Edmonton, Canada
yqian3@ualberta.ca, yang@cs.ualberta.ca
[2] National Institute of Informatics, Tokyo, Japan
yqzheng@nii.ac.jp
[3] Memorial University of Newfoundland, St. John's, Canada
gong@cs.mun.ca

Abstract. This paper presents the first approach for simultaneously recovering the 3D shape of both the wavy water surface and the moving underwater scene. A portable camera array system is constructed, which captures the scene from multiple viewpoints above the water. The correspondences across these cameras are estimated using an optical flow method and are used to infer the shape of the water surface and the underwater scene. We assume that there is only one refraction occurring at the water interface. Under this assumption, two estimates of the water surface normals should agree: one from Snell's law of light refraction and another from local surface structure. The experimental results using both synthetic and real data demonstrate the effectiveness of the presented approach.

Keywords: 3D reconstruction · Water surface · Underwater imaging

1 Introduction

Consider the imaging scenario of viewing an underwater scene through a water surface. Due to light refraction at the water surface, conventional land-based 3D reconstruction techniques are not directly applicable to recovering the underwater scene. The problem becomes even more challenging when the water surface is wavy and hence constantly changes the light refraction paths. Nevertheless, fishing birds are capable of hunting submerged fish while flying over the water, which suggests that it is possible to estimate the depth for underwater objects in the presence of the water surface.

In this paper, we present a new method to mimic a fishing bird's underwater depth perception capability. This problem is challenging for several reasons. Firstly, the captured images of the underwater scene are distorted due to light refraction through the water. Under the traditional triangulation-based scheme for 3D reconstruction, tracing the poly-linear light path requires the 3D geometry of the water surface. Unfortunately, reconstructing a 3D fluid surface is an even

© Springer Nature Switzerland AG 2018
V. Ferrari et al. (Eds.): ECCV 2018, LNCS 11207, pp. 776–792, 2018.
https://doi.org/10.1007/978-3-030-01219-9_46

harder problem because of its transparent characteristic [23]. Secondly, the water interface is dynamic and the underwater scene may be moving as well. Hence, real-time data capture is required.

In addition to the biological motivation [19] (*e.g.* the above example of fishing birds), the problems of reconstructing underwater scene and of reconstructing water surface both have attracted much attention due to applications in computer graphics [14], oceanography [17] and remote sensing [38]. These two problems are usually tackled separately in computer vision. On the one hand, most previous works reconstruct the underwater scene by assuming the interface between the scene and the imaging sensor is flat [4,7,12]. On the other hand, existing methods for recovering dynamic water surfaces typically assume that the underwater scene is a known flat pattern, for which a checkerboard is commonly used [10,24]. Recently, Zhang *et al.* [44] make the first attempt to solve the two problems simultaneously using depth from defocus. Nevertheless, their approach assumes that the underwater scene is stationary and an image of the underwater scene with a flat water surface is available. Because of the assumptions of the flat water surface or the flat underwater scene, none of the above mentioned methods can be directly applied to solving the problem of jointly recovering the *wavy* water surface and the natural underwater *dynamic* scene. Indeed, the lack of any existing solution to the above problem forms the motivation of our work.

In this paper, we propose to employ multiple viewpoints to tackle such a problem. In particular, we construct a portable camera array to capture the images of the underwater scene distorted by the wavy water surface. Our physical setup does not require any precise positioning and thus is easy to use. Following the conventional multi-view reconstruction framework for on-land objects, we first estimate the correspondences across different views. Then, based on the inter-view correspondences, we impose a normal consistency constraint across all camera views. Suppose that the light is refracted only once while passing through the water surface. We present a refraction-based optimization scheme that works in a frame-by-frame[1] fashion, enabling us to handle the dynamic nature of both the water surface and the underwater scene. More specifically, our approach is able to return the 3D positions and the normals of a dynamic water surface, and the 3D points of a moving underwater scene simultaneously. Encouraging experimental results on both synthetic and real data are obtained.

2 Related Work

Fluid Surface Reconstruction. Reconstructing dynamic 3D fluid surface is a difficult problem because most fluids are transparent and exhibit a view-dependent appearance. Therefore, traditional Lambertian-based shape recovery methods do not work. In the literature, the problem is usually solved by placing a known flat pattern beneath the fluid surface. Single camera [17,26] or multiple cameras [10,24,30] are used to capture the distorted versions of the flat pattern. 3D reconstruction is then performed by analyzing the differences between the captured

---

[1] A frame refers to the pictures captured from all cameras at the same time point.

images and the original pattern. Besides, several methods [39, 43, 45], rather than using a flat board, propose to utilize active illumination for fluid shape acquisition. Precisely positioned devices are usually required in these methods, such as Bokode [43] and light field probes [39]. In contrast, our capturing system uses cameras only and thus is easy to build. More importantly, all of the above methods focus on the fluid surface only, whereas the proposed approach can recover the underwater scene as well.

Underwater Scene Reconstruction. Many works recover the 3D underwater scene by assuming the water surface is flat and static. For example, several land-based 3D reconstruction models, including stereo [12], structure-from-motion [7, 32], photometric stereo [27], have been extended for this task, which is typically achieved by explicitly accounting for light refraction at the flat interface in their methods. The location of the flat water surface is measured beforehand by calibration [12] or parameterization [32]. Asano *et al.* [4] use the water absorption property to recover depths of underwater objects. However, the light rays are assumed to be perpendicular to the flat water surface. In contrast, in our new approach, the water surface can be wavy and is estimated along with the underwater scene.

There are existing methods targeting at obtaining the 3D structure of underwater objects under a wavy surface. Alterman *et al.* [3] present a stochastic method for stereo triangulation through wavy water. However, their method can produce only a likelihood function of the object's 3D location. The dynamic water surface is also not estimated. More recently, Zhang *et al.* [44] treat such a task in monocular view and recover both the water surface and the underwater scene using a co-analysis of refractive distortion and defocus. As mentioned in Sect. 1, their method is limited in practical use. Firstly, to recover the shape of an underwater scene, an undistorted image captured through a flat water surface is required. However, such an image is very hard to obtain in real life, if not impossible. Secondly, the image plane of their camera has to be parallel with the flat water surface in their implementation, which is impractical to achieve. In contrast, our camera array-based setup can be positioned casually and is easy to implement. Thirdly, for the water surface, their method can return the normal information of each surface point only. The final shape is then obtained using surface integration, which is known to be prone to error in the absence of accurate boundary conditions. In comparison, our approach bypasses surface integration by jointly estimating the 3D positions and the normals of the water surface. Besides, the methods in [3] and [44] assume a still underwater scene, while both the water surface and the underwater scene can be dynamic in this paper. Hence, our proposed approach is applicable to a more general scenario.

Our work is also related to other studies on light refraction, *e.g.* environment matting [8, 29], image restoration under refractive distortion [11, 37], shape recovery of transparent objects [16, 21, 28, 36, 40] and gas flows [18, 41], and underwater camera calibration [2, 33, 42].

3   Multi-view Acquisition Setup

As shown in Fig. 1(a), to capture the underwater scene, we build a small-scale, 3×3 camera array (highlighted in the red box) placed above the water surface. The cameras are synchronized and capture video sequences. For clarity, in the following, we refer to the central camera in the array as the *reference* view, and the other cameras as the *side* views. Similar to the traditional multi-view triangulation-based framework for land-based 3D reconstruction, the 3D shapes of both the water surface and the underwater scene are represented in the reference view. Notice that an additional camera, referred to as the *evaluation* camera, is also used to capture the underwater scene at a novel view, which is for accuracy assessment in our real experiments and is presented in detail in Sect. 5.2.

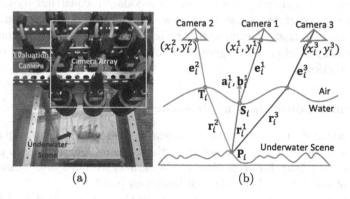

(a)   (b)

Fig. 1. Acquisition setup using a camera array (a) and the corresponding imaging model illustrated in 2D (b). The evaluation camera in (a) is for accuracy evaluation only and is not used for 3D shape recovery.

Figure 1(b) further illustrates the imaging model in 2D. We set Camera 1 as the reference camera and Camera $k \in \Pi$ as the side cameras, where Π is $\{2, 3, \cdots\}$. For each pixel (x_i^1, y_i^1) in Camera 1, the corresponding camera ray $\mathbf{e}_i^1$ gets refracted at the water surface point $\mathbf{S}_i$. Then the refracted ray $\mathbf{r}_i^1$ intersects with the underwater scene at point $\mathbf{P}_i$. The underwater scene point $\mathbf{P}_i$ is also observed by the side cameras through the same water surface but at different interface locations.

Our approach builds upon the correspondences across multiple views. Specifically, we compute the optical flow field between the reference camera and each of the side cameras. Take side Camera 2 for example, for each pixel (x_i^1, y_i^1) of Camera 1, we estimate the corresponding projection (x_i^2, y_i^2) of $\mathbf{P}_i$ in Camera 2, by applying the variational optical flow estimation method [6]. Suppose that the intrinsic and extrinsic parameters of the camera array are calibrated beforehand and fixed during capturing, we can easily compute the corresponding camera ray $\mathbf{e}_i^2$ of ray $\mathbf{e}_i^1$. The same procedure of finding correspondences applies to the other side views and each single frame is processed analogously.

After the above step, we obtain a sequence of the inter-view correspondences of the underwater scene. Below, we present a new reconstruction approach that solves the following problem: *Given the dense correspondences of camera rays* $\{\mathbf{e}^1 \Leftrightarrow \mathbf{e}^k, k \in \Pi\}$ *of each frame, how to recover the point set* $\mathbf{P}$ *of the underwater scene, as well as the depths and the normals of the dynamic water surface?*

4   Multi-view Reconstruction Approach

We tackle the problem using an optimization-based scheme that imposes a normal consistency constraint. Several prior works [24,30] have used such a constraint for water surface reconstruction. Here we show that, based on the similar form of normal consistency, we can simultaneously reconstruct dynamic water and underwater surfaces using multi-view data captured from a camera array. The key insight is that, at each water surface point, the normal estimated using its neighboring points should agree with the normal obtained based on the law of light refraction.

4.1   Normal Consistency at Reference View

As mentioned in Sect. 3, we represent the water surface by a depth map $\mathbf{D}$ and the underwater scene by a 3D point set $\mathbf{P}$, both in the reference view. In particular, as shown in Fig. 1(b), for each pixel in Camera 1, we have *four* unknowns: the depth $\mathbf{D}_i$ of point $\mathbf{S}_i$ and the 3D coordinates of point $\mathbf{P}_i$.

Given the camera ray $\mathbf{e}_i^1$, we can compute the 3D coordinates of $\mathbf{S}_i$ when a depth hypothesis $\mathbf{D}_i$ is assumed. At the same time, connecting the hypothesized point $\mathbf{P}_i$ and point $\mathbf{S}_i$ gives us the refracted ray direction $\mathbf{r}_i^1$. Then, the normal of $\mathbf{S}_i$ can be computed based on Snell's law, which is called the *Snell* normal in this paper and denoted by $\mathbf{a}_i^1$. Here superscript 1 in $\mathbf{a}_i^1$ indicates that $\mathbf{a}_i^1$ is estimated using ray $\mathbf{e}_i^1$ of Camera 1. Consider the normal $\mathbf{a}_i^1$, the camera ray $\mathbf{e}_i^1$ and the refracted ray $\mathbf{r}_i^1$ are co-planar as stated in Snell's law. Hence, we can express $\mathbf{a}_i^1$ as a linear combination of $\mathbf{e}_i^1$ and $\mathbf{r}_i^1$, *i.e.* $\mathbf{a}_i^1 = \Psi(\eta_a \mathbf{e}_i^1 - \eta_f \mathbf{r}_i^1)$, where η_a and η_f are the refractive index of air and fluid, respectively. We fix $\eta_a = 1$ and $\eta_f = 1.33$ in our experiments. $\Psi()$ is a function defining the operation of vector normalization.

On the other hand, the normal of a 3D point can be obtained by analyzing the structure of its nearby points [31]. Specifically, suppose that the water surface is spatially smooth, at each point $\mathbf{S}_i$, we fit a local polynomial surface from its neighborhood and then estimate its normal based on the fitted surface. In practice, for a 3D point (x, y, z), we assume its z component can be represented by a quadratic function of the other two components:

$$z(x, y) = w_1 x^2 + w_2 y^2 + w_3 xy + w_4 x + w_5 y + w_6, \tag{1}$$

where $w_1, w_2 \ldots, w_6$ are unknown parameters. Stacking all quadratic equations of the set $\mathcal{N}_i$ of the neighboring points of $\mathbf{S}_i$ yields:

$$\mathbf{A}(\mathcal{N}_i)\mathbf{w}(\mathcal{N}_i) = \mathbf{z}(\mathcal{N}_i) \Leftrightarrow \begin{bmatrix} x_1^2 & y_1^2 & x_1 y_1 & x_1 & y_1 & 1 \\ & & \cdots & & & \\ x_m^2 & y_m^2 & x_m y_m & x_m & y_m & 1 \\ & & \cdots & & & \end{bmatrix} \times \begin{bmatrix} w_1 \\ w_2 \\ : \\ w_6 \end{bmatrix} = \begin{bmatrix} z_1 \\ : \\ z_m \\ : \end{bmatrix}, \quad (2)$$

where $\mathbf{A}(\mathcal{N}_i)$ is a $|\mathcal{N}_i| \times 6$ matrix calculated from $\mathcal{N}_i$, and $|\mathcal{N}_i|$ the size of $\mathcal{N}_i$. $\mathbf{z}(\mathcal{N}_i)$ is a $|\mathcal{N}_i|$ dimensional vector. After getting the parameter vector $\mathbf{w}(\mathcal{N}_i)$, the normal of point (x, y, z) in this quadratic surface is estimated as the normalized cross product of two vectors: $[1, 0, \frac{\partial}{\partial x} z(x, y)]$ and $[0, 1, \frac{\partial}{\partial y} z(x, y)]$. Plugging in the 3D coordinates of $\mathbf{S}_i$, we obtain its normal $\mathbf{b}_i^1$, which is referred to as the *Quadratic* normal in this paper.

So far, given the camera ray set $\mathbf{e}^1$ of Camera 1, we obtain two types of normals at each water surface point, which should be consistent if the hypothesized depth $\mathbf{D}$ and point set $\mathbf{P}$ are correct. We thus define the normal consistency error as:

$$E_i^1(\mathbf{D}, \mathbf{P}, \mathbf{e}_i^1) = \|\mathbf{a}_i^1 - \mathbf{b}_i^1\|_2^2 \quad (3)$$

at ray $\mathbf{e}_i^1$. Next, we show how to measure the normal consistency term at the side views using their camera ray sets $\{\mathbf{e}^k, k \in \Pi\}$, the point set $\mathbf{S}$ estimated from the depth hypothesis $\mathbf{D}$, and the hypothesized point set $\mathbf{P}$.

4.2   Normal Consistency at Side Views

We take side Camera 2 for illustration and the other side views are analyzed in a similar fashion. As shown in Fig. 1(b), point $\mathbf{P}_i$ is observed by Camera 2 through the water surface point $\mathbf{T}_i$. Similarly, we have the *Snell* normal $\mathbf{a}_i^2$ and the *Quadratic* normal $\mathbf{b}_i^2$ at $\mathbf{T}_i$.

To compute the *Snell* normal $\mathbf{a}_i^2$ via Snell's law, the camera ray $\mathbf{e}_i^2$ and the refracted ray $\mathbf{r}_i^2$ are required. $\mathbf{e}_i^2$ is acquired beforehand in Sect. 3. Considering the point hypothesis $\mathbf{P}_i$ is given, $\mathbf{r}_i^2$ can be obtained if the location of $\mathbf{T}_i$ is known. Hence, the problem of estimating normal $\mathbf{a}_i^2$ is reduced to the problem of locating the first-order intersection between ray $\mathbf{e}_i^2$ and the water surface point set $\mathbf{S}$. A similar problem has been studied in ray tracing [1]. In practice, we first generate a triangular mesh for $\mathbf{S}$ by creating a Delaunay triangulation of 2D pixels of Camera 1. We then apply the Bounding Volume Hierarchy-based ray tracing algorithm [20] to locate the triangle that $\mathbf{e}_i^2$ intersects. Using the neighboring points of that intersecting triangle, we fit a local quadratic surface as described in Sect. 4.1, and the final 3D coordinates of $\mathbf{T}_i$ is obtained by the standard ray-polynomial intersection procedure. Meanwhile, the fitted quadratic surface gives us the *Quadratic* normal $\mathbf{b}_i^2$ of point $\mathbf{T}_i$.

In summary, given each ray $\mathbf{e}_i^k$ of each side Camera k, we obtain two normals $\mathbf{a}_i^k$ and $\mathbf{b}_i^k$. The congruity between them results in the normal consistency error:

$$E_i^k(\mathbf{D}, \mathbf{P}, \mathbf{e}_i^k) = \|\mathbf{a}_i^k - \mathbf{b}_i^k\|_2^2, \ k \in \Pi. \quad (4)$$

4.3   Solution Method

Here we first discuss the feasibility of recovering both the water surface and the underwater scene using normal consistency at multiple views. Combining the error terms Eq. (3) at the reference view and Eq. (4) at the side views, we have:

$$E_i^k(\mathbf{D}, \mathbf{P}, \mathbf{e}_i^k) = 0, \text{ for each } i \in \Omega \text{ and } k \in \Phi, \tag{5}$$

where Ω is the set of all pixels of Camera 1, and $\Phi = \{1\} \cup \Pi$ the set of camera indices. Let $\bar{i} = |\Omega|$ and $\bar{k} = |\Phi|$ be the size of Ω and Φ, respectively. Assume that each camera ray $\mathbf{e}_i^1$ can find a valid correspondence in all side views, we get a total of $\bar{i} \times \bar{k}$ equations. Additionally, recall that we have 4 unknowns at each pixel of Camera 1, so we have $\bar{i} \times 4$ unknowns. Hence, to make the problem solvable, we should have $\bar{i} \times \bar{k} \geq \bar{i} \times 4$, which means that at least 4 cameras are required. In reality, some camera rays (e.g. those at corner pixels) of the reference view cannot locate a reliable correspondence in all side views because of occlusion or of the field of view. We essentially need more than four cameras.

Directly solving Eq. (5) is impractical due to the complex operations involved in computing the *Snell* and *Quadratic* normals. Therefore, we cast the reconstruction problem as minimizing the following objective function:

$$\min_{\mathbf{D}, \mathbf{P}} \sum_{i \in \Omega} \sum_{k \in \Phi} E_i^k(\mathbf{D}, \mathbf{P}, \mathbf{e}_i^k) + \lambda \sum_{i \in \Omega} F_i(\mathbf{D}, \mathbf{e}_i^1), \tag{6}$$

where the first term enforces the proposed normal consistency constraint. The second term ensures the spatial smoothness of the water surface. In particular, we set

$$F_i(\mathbf{D}, \mathbf{e}_i^1) = \|\mathbf{A}(\mathcal{N}_i)\mathbf{w}(\mathcal{N}_i) - \mathbf{z}(\mathcal{N}_i)\|_2^2, \tag{7}$$

which measures the local quadratic surface fitting error using the neighborhood $\mathcal{N}_i$ of the water surface point $\mathbf{S}_i$. Adding such a polynomial regularization term helps to increase the robustness of our multi-view formulation, as demonstrated in our experiments in Sect. 5.1. Please also note that this smoothness term is only defined w.r.t Camera 1 since we represent our 3D shape in that view. λ is a parameter balancing the two terms.

While it may be tempting to enforce the spatial smoothness of underwater surface points $\mathbf{P}$ computed for different pixels as well, it is not imposed in our approach for the fol-

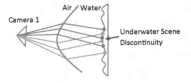

Fig. 2. Discontinuity of underwater scene points. As indicated by the purple arrow, the red points are interlaced with the green points, although the red and green rays are each emitted from contiguous pixels. (Color figure online)

lowing reason. As shown in Fig. 2, when the light paths are refracted at the water surface, the neighborhood relationship among underwater scene points can be different from the neighborhood relationship among observed pixels in Camera 1. Hence, we cannot simply enforce that the 3D underwater surface points computed for adjacent camera rays are also adjacent.

Optimization. Computing the normal consistency errors in Eq. (6) involves some non-invertible operations such as vector normalization, making the analytic derivatives difficult to derive. To handle such a problem, we use the L-BFGS method [47] with numerical differentiation for optimization. However, calculating numerical derivatives is computationally expensive especially for a large-scale problem. We elaborately optimize our implementation by sharing common intermediate variables in derivative computation at different pixels. In addition, solving Eq. (6) is unfortunately a non-convex problem; hence, there is a chance of getting trapped by local minima. Here we adopt a coarse-to-fine optimization procedure commonly used in refractive surface reconstruction [28,30,34]. Specifically, we first downsample the correspondences acquired in Sect. 3 to 1/8 of the original resolution. We then use the results under the coarse resolution to initialize the optimization at the final scale.

Notice that the input of Eq. (6) is the multi-view data of a single time instance. Although it is possible to process all frames in a sequence simultaneously by concatenating them into Eq. (6), a large system with high computational complexity will be produced accordingly. In contrast, we process each frame independently and initialize the current frame using the results of the last one. Such a single-shot method effectively reduces the computational cost in terms of running time and memory consumption and, more importantly, can handle moving underwater scenes.

It is also noteworthy that, even when the underwater scene is strictly static, our recovered point set $\mathbf{P}$ could be different for different frames. This is because each point $\mathbf{P}_i$ can be interpreted as the intersection between the refracted ray $\mathbf{r}_i^1$ and the underwater scene, as shown in Fig. 1(b). When the water surface is flowing, because $\mathbf{S}_i$ relocates, the refracted ray direction is altered, and thus the intersection $\mathbf{P}_i$ is changed. Our frame-by-frame formulation naturally handles such a varying representation of point set $\mathbf{P}$.

5   Experiments

The proposed approach is tested on both synthetic and real-captured data. Here we provide some implementation details. While computing the *Quadratic* normals at both the reference and side views, we set the neighborhood size to 5×5. The parameter λ is fixed at 2 units in the synthetic data and 0.1 mm in the real experiments. During the coarse-to-fine optimization of Eq. (6), the maximum number of L-BFGS iterations at the coarse scale is fixed to 2000 and 200 for synthetic data and real scenes, respectively, and is set to 20 at the full resolution in both cases. The linear least squares system Eq. (2) is solved via normal equations using Eigen [15]. As the *Snell* and *Quadratic* normal computations at different pixels are independent, we implement our algorithm in C++, with parallelizable steps optimized using OpenMP [9], on an 8-core PC with 3.2GHz Intel Core i7 CPU and 32GB RAM.

5.1 Synthetic Data

We use the ray tracing method [20] to generate synthetic data for evaluation. In particular, two scenes are simulated: a static Stanford Bunny observed through a sinusoidal wave: $z(x, y, t) = 2 + 0.1\cos(\pi(t+50)\sqrt{(x-1)^2 + (y-0.5)^2}/80)$, and a moving Stanford Dragon seen through a different water surface: $z(x, y, t) = 2 - 0.1\cos(\pi(t+60)\sqrt{(x+0.05)^2 + (y+0.05)^2}/75)$. The Dragon object moves along a line with a uniform speed of 0.01 units per frame. Because of the different sizes of the two objects, we place the Bunny and Dragon objects on top of a flat backdrop positioned at $z = 3.5$ and $z = 3.8$, respectively. The synthetic scenes are captured using a 3×3 camera array. The reference camera is placed at the origin and the baseline between adjacent cameras in the array system is set to 0.3 and 0.2 for the Bunny and Dragon scene, respectively.

Table 1. Reconstruction errors of the synthetic Bunny scene and the Dragon scene. Here, for each scene, we list the average errors by considering all frames.

Scene	RMSE of $\mathbf{D}$ (*units*)	MAD of $\mathbf{a}^1$ (°)	MAD of $\mathbf{b}^1$ (°)	MED of $\mathbf{P}$ (*units*)
Bunny	0.006	0.76	0.77	0.01
Dragon	0.002	0.36	0.37	0.01

We start with quantitatively evaluating the proposed approach. Since our approach can return the depths and the normals of the water surface, and the 3D point set of the underwater scene, we employ the following measures for accuracy assessment: the root mean square error (RMSE) between the ground truth (GT) depths and the estimated depths $\mathbf{D}$, the mean angular difference (MAD) between the GT normals and the recovered *Snell* normals $\mathbf{a}^1$, the MAD between the true normals and the computed *Quadratic* normals $\mathbf{b}^1$, and the mean Euclidean distance (MED) between the reconstructed point set $\mathbf{P}$ of the underwater scene and the GT one. Table 1 shows our reconstruction accuracy by averaging over all frames. It is noteworthy that the average MAD of the *Snell* normals and that of the *Quadratic* normals are quite similar for both scenes, which coincides with our normal consistency constraint.

Figure 3 visually shows the reconstruction results of several example frames. The complete sequences can be found in the supplementary materials [35]. Compared to the GT, our approach accurately recovers both the dynamic water surfaces and the underwater scenes. We can also observe that, while the underwater scene in the Bunny case is statically positioned in the simulation, different point clouds are obtained at different frames (see the red boxes in Fig. 3(c)), echoing our varying representation $\mathbf{P}$ of underwater points. Besides, with the frame-by-frame reconstruction scheme, our approach successfully captures the movement of the underwater Dragon object. In short, accurate results are obtained for the two scenes generated using different water fluctuations, different underwater objects (static or moving), and data acquisition settings, which demonstrate the robustness of our approach.

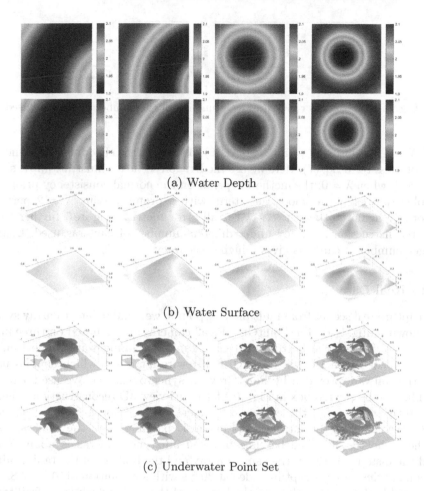

(a) Water Depth

(b) Water Surface

(c) Underwater Point Set

Fig. 3. Visual comparisons with GT on two example frames of the Bunny scene (left two columns) and the Dragon scene (right two columns). In each subfigure, we show the GT and our result in the top and bottom row, respectively. (a) shows the GT water surface depth and the estimated one. (b) shows the GT water surface colored with the GT normal map, and the computed one colored with the *Quadratic* normals. The *Snell* normals are not shown here because they are similar to the *Quadratic* normals. (c) shows the GT point set of the underwater scene and the recovered one, where each point is colored with its z-axis coordinate. The red boxes highlight an obvious different region of the underwater point clouds of two different frames; see text for details. (Color figure online)

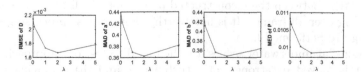

Fig. 4. Different error measures as a function of the balancing parameter λ.

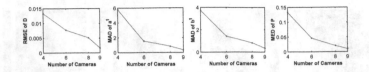

Fig. 5. Different error measures as a function of the number of cameras used.

We then adjust the weight λ in Eq. (6) to validate the effect of the polynomial smoothness term Eq. (7). Here we use the Dragon scene for illustration. As shown in Fig. 4, when $\lambda = 0$, the method depends on the normal consistency prior only. Explicitly applying a smoothness term with a proper setting $\lambda = 2$ performs favorably against other choices w.r.t. all error metrics. Figure 5 further shows our reconstruction accuracy under different number of cameras used. Using a larger number of cameras gives a higher accuracy.

5.2   Real Data

To capture real scenes from multiple viewpoints, we build a camera array system as shown in Fig. 1(a). Ten PointGrey Flea2 cameras are mounted on three metal frames to observe the bottom of a glass tank containing water. The cameras are connected to a PC via two PCI-E Firewire adapters, which enables us to use the software provided by PointGrey for synchronization. We use 9 cameras highlighted by the red box in Fig. 1(a) for multi-view 3D reconstruction, whereas the 10th camera, *i.e.* the evaluation camera, is used for *accuracy evaluation only*. We calibrate the intrinsic and extrinsic parameters of the cameras using a checkerboard [46]. The baseline between adjacent cameras is about 75mm and the distance between the camera array and the bottom of the tank is about 55cm. All the cameras capture video at 30 fps with a resolution of 516×388. Flat textured backdrops are glued to the bottom of the tank, which is for facilitating optical flow estimation.

In order to verify our approach on real data, we first capture a simple scene: a flat textured plane placed at the bottom of the tank, which is referred to as Scene 1. The water surface is perturbed by continuously dripping water drops near one corner of the pattern. As shown in Fig. 6(a), our approach not only faithfully recovers the quarter-annular ripples propagated from the corner with the dripping water, but also accurately returns the 3D underwater plane without any prior knowledge of the flat structure. For accuracy assessment, we also fit a plane for the reconstructed underwater point set of each frame using RANSAC [13]. The MED between the reconstructed points and the fitted plane is 0.44mm by averaging over all frames. It is noteworthy that no post-processing steps like smoothing are performed here.

Two non-flat underwater scenes are then used to test our approach: (i) a toy tiger that is moved by strong water turbulence, and (ii) a moving hand in a textured glove. We refer to the two scenes as Scene 2 and Scene 3, respectively. In both cases, to generate water waves, we randomly disturb the water surface

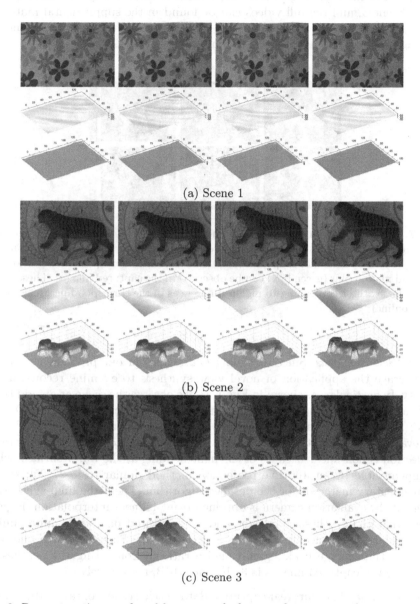

(a) Scene 1

(b) Scene 2

(c) Scene 3

Fig. 6. Reconstruction results of four example frames of our captured scenes. In each subfigure, we show the captured image of the reference camera (top), the point cloud of the water surface colored with the *Quadratic* normals (middle), the point cloud of the underwater scene colored with the z-axis coordinates (bottom). Note that the motion blur (green box) in the captured image may affect the reconstruction result (red box). (Color figure online)

at one end of the tank. Figure 6(b and c) shows several example results on Scene 2 and Scene 3, and the full videos can be found in the supplemental materials. Our approach successfully recovers the 3D shapes of the tiger object and the moving hand, as well as the fast evolving water surfaces.

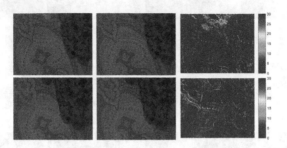

Fig. 7. View synthesis on two example frames (top and bottom) of Scene 3. From left to right, it shows the images captured using the evaluation camera, the synthesized images and the absolute difference maps between them. The effects of specular reflection (red box) and motion blur (green box) can be observed in the captured images. These effects cannot be synthesized, leading to higher differences in the corresponding areas. (Color figure online)

Novel View Synthesis. Since obtaining GT shapes in our problem is difficult, we leverage the application of novel view synthesis to examine reconstruction quality. In particular, as shown in Fig. 1(a), we observe the scene at an additional calibrated view, *i.e.* the evaluation camera. At each frame, given the 3D point set of the underwater scene, we project each scene point to the image plane of the evaluation camera through the recovered water surface. Here such a forward projection is non-linear because of the light bending at the water surface, which is implemented by an iterative projection method similar to [5,22,25]; see the supplementary materials for the detailed algorithm. Then, the final synthesized image at the evaluation camera is obtained using bilinear interpolation. Figure 7 shows that the synthesized images and the captured ones look quite similar, which validates the accuracy of our approach. Take Scene 2 and Scene 3 for example, the average peak signal-to-noise ratio by comparing the synthesized images to the captured images is 30dB and 31dB, respectively.

Running Time. For our real-captured data, each scene contains 100 frames and each frame has 119,808 water surface points and 119,808 underwater scene points. It takes about 5.5 h to process each whole sequence, as shown in Table 2.

Table 2. Average running time of the three real scenes.

Scene	Scene 1	Scene 2	Scene 3
Optical Flow Estimation (minutes per frame)	0.74	0.74	0.77
3D Reconstruction (minutes per frame)	2.55	2.50	2.52

6   Conclusions

This paper presents a novel approach for a 3D reconstruction problem: recovering underwater scenes through dynamic water surfaces. Our approach exploits multiple viewpoints by constructing a portable camera array. After acquiring the correspondences across different views, the unknown water surface and underwater scene can be estimated through minimizing an objective function under a normal consistency constraint. Our approach is validated using both synthetic and real data. To our best knowledge, this is the first approach that can handle both dynamic water surfaces and dynamic underwater scenes, whereas the previous work [44] uses a single view and cannot handle moving underwater scenes.

Our approach works under several assumptions that are also commonly used in state-of-the-art works in shape from refraction. Firstly, we assume that the medium (*i.e.* water in our case) is transparent and homogeneous, and thus light is refracted exactly once from water to air. Secondly, the water surface is assumed to be locally smooth, so that the *Quadratic* normal of each surface point can be reliably estimated based on the local neighborhood. Thirdly, the underwater scene is assumed to be textured so that the optical flow field across views can be accurately estimated. The above assumptions may be violated in real-world scenarios. For example, water phenomena like bubbles, breaking waves, light scattering, may lead to multiple light bending events along a given light path. The observed motion blur and specular reflection in Fig. 7 can affect the accuracy of correspondence matching and the subsequent reconstruction, as highlighted by the red box in Fig. 6(c).

Although promising reconstruction performance is demonstrated in this paper, our approach is just a preliminary attempt to solving such a challenging problem. The obtained results are not perfect, especially at the boundary regions of the surfaces, as shown in Fig. 6. That is because those regions are covered by fewer views compared to other regions. To cope with this issue, we plan to build a larger camera array or use a light-field camera for video capture. In addition, occlusion is a known limitation in a multi-view setup because correspondence matching in occluded areas is not reliable. We plan to accommodate occlusion in our model in the near future.

Finally, our work is inspired by fishing birds' ability of locating underwater fish. Our solution requires 4 or more cameras, whereas a fishing bird uses only two eyes. It would be interesting to further explore additional constraints or cues that the birds use to make this possible. Our hypotheses include that the birds have prior knowledge on the size of the fish and estimate only a rough depth of the fish [3]. Whether the depth of underwater scene can be estimated under these additional assumptions is worthy for further investigation.

Acknowledgments. We thank NSERC, Alberta Innovates and the University of Alberta for the financial support. Yinqiang Zheng is supported by ACT-I, JST and Microsoft Research Asia through the 2017 Collaborative Research Program (Core13).

References

1. Adamson, A., Alexa, M.: Ray tracing point set surfaces. In: Shape Modeling International, 2003, pp. 272–279. IEEE (2003)
2. Agrawal, A., Ramalingam, S., Taguchi, Y., Chari, V.: A theory of multi-layer flat refractive geometry. In: Computer Vision and Pattern Recognition (CVPR), IEEE Conference on 2012, pp. 3346–3353. IEEE (2012)
3. Alterman, M., Schechner, Y.Y., Swirski, Y.: Triangulation in random refractive distortions. In: IEEE International Conference on Computational Photography (ICCP), pp. 1–10. IEEE (2013)
4. Asano, Y., Zheng, Y., Nishino, K., Sato, I.: Shape from water: bispectral light absorption for depth recovery. In: Leibe, B., Matas, J., Sebe, N., Welling, M. (eds.) ECCV 2016. LNCS, vol. 9910, pp. 635–649. Springer, Cham (2016). https://doi.org/10.1007/978-3-319-46466-4_38
5. Belden, J.: Calibration of multi-camera systems with refractive interfaces. Exp. Fluids **54**(2), 1463 (2013)
6. Brox, T., Bruhn, A., Papenberg, N., Weickert, J.: High accuracy optical flow estimation based on a theory for warping. In: Pajdla, T., Matas, J. (eds.) ECCV 2004. LNCS, vol. 3024, pp. 25–36. Springer, Heidelberg (2004). https://doi.org/10.1007/978-3-540-24673-2_3
7. Chang, Y.J., Chen, T.: Multi-view 3D reconstruction for scenes under the refractive plane with known vertical direction. In: IEEE International Conference on Computer Vision (ICCV), pp. 351–358. IEEE (2011)
8. Chuang, Y.Y., Zongker, D.E., Hindorff, J., Curless, B., Salesin, D.H., Szeliski, R.: Environment matting extensions: towards higher accuracy and real-time capture. In: Proceedings of the 27th Annual Conference on Computer Graphics and Interactive Techniques, pp. 121–130. ACM Press/Addison-Wesley Publishing Co. (2000)
9. Dagum, L., Menon, R.: OpenMP: an industry standard API for shared-memory programming. IEEE Comput. Sci. Eng. **5**(1), 46–55 (1998)
10. Ding, Y., Li, F., Ji, Y., Yu, J.: Dynamic fluid surface acquisition using a camera array. In: IEEE International Conference on Computer Vision (ICCV), pp. 2478–2485. IEEE (2011)
11. Efros, A., Isler, V., Shi, J., Visontai, M.: Seeing through water. In: Advances in Neural Information Processing Systems, pp. 393–400 (2005)
12. Ferreira, R., Costeira, J.P., Santos, J.A.: Stereo reconstruction of a submerged scene. In: Marques, J.S., Pérez de la Blanca, N., Pina, P. (eds.) IbPRIA 2005. LNCS, vol. 3522, pp. 102–109. Springer, Heidelberg (2005). https://doi.org/10.1007/11492429_13
13. Fischler, M.A., Bolles, R.C.: Random sample consensus: a paradigm for model fitting with applications to image analysis and automated cartography. In: Readings in computer vision, pp. 726–740. Elsevier (1987)

14. Gregson, J., Ihrke, I., Thuerey, N., Heidrich, W.: From capture to simulation: connecting forward and inverse problems in fluids. ACM Trans. Graph. (TOG) **33**(4), 139 (2014)
15. Guennebaud, G., Jacob, B., et al.: Eigen v3. http://eigen.tuxfamily.org (2010)
16. Han, K., Wong, K.Y.K., Liu, M.: A fixed viewpoint approach for dense reconstruction of transparent objects. In: Proceedings of the IEEE Conference on Computer Vision and Pattern Recognition, pp. 4001–4008 (2015)
17. Jähne, B., Klinke, J., Waas, S.: Imaging of short ocean wind waves: a critical theoretical review. JOSA A **11**(8), 2197–2209 (1994)
18. Ji, Y., Ye, J., Yu, J.: Reconstructing gas flows using light-path approximation. In: Proceedings of the IEEE Conference on Computer Vision and Pattern Recognition, pp. 2507–2514 (2013)
19. Katzir, G., Intrator, N.: Striking of underwater prey by a reef heron, egretta gularis schistacea. J. Comp. Physiol. A **160**(4), 517–523 (1987)
20. Kay, T.L., Kajiya, J.T.: Ray tracing complex scenes. In: ACM SIGGRAPH Computer Graphics, vol. 20, pp. 269–278. ACM (1986)
21. Kim, J., Reshetouski, I., Ghosh, A.: Acquiring axially-symmetric transparent objects using single-view transmission imaging. In: 30th IEEE Conference on Computer Vision and Pattern Recognition (CVPR) (2017)
22. Kudela, L., Frischmann, F., Yossef, O.E., Kollmannsberger, S., Yosibash, Z., Rank, E.: Image-based mesh generation of tubular geometries under circular motion in refractive environments. Mach. Vis. Appl. **29**(5), 719–733 (2018). https://doi.org/10.1007/s00138-018-0921-3
23. Kutulakos, K.N., Steger, E.: A theory of refractive and specular 3D shape by light-path triangulation. Int. J. Comput. Vis. **76**(1), 13–29 (2008)
24. Morris, N.J., Kutulakos, K.N.: Dynamic refraction stereo. IEEE Trans. Pattern Anal. Mach. Intell. **33**(8), 1518–1531 (2011)
25. Mulsow, C.: A flexible multi-media bundle approach. Int. Arch. Photogram. Remote Sens. Spat. Inf. Sci **38**, 472–477 (2010)
26. Murase, H.: Surface shape reconstruction of a nonrigid transparent object using refraction and motion. IEEE Trans. Pattern Anal. Mach. Intell. **14**(10), 1045–1052 (1992)
27. Murez, Z., Treibitz, T., Ramamoorthi, R., Kriegman, D.J.: Photometric stereo in a scattering medium. IEEE Trans. Pattern Anal. Mach. Intell. **39**(9), 1880–1891 (2017)
28. Qian, Y., Gong, M., Hong Yang, Y.: 3D reconstruction of transparent objects with position-normal consistency. In: Proceedings of the IEEE Conference on Computer Vision and Pattern Recognition, pp. 4369–4377 (2016)
29. Qian, Y., Gong, M., Yang, Y.H.: Frequency-based environment matting by compressive sensing. In: Proceedings of the IEEE International Conference on Computer Vision, pp. 3532–3540 (2015)
30. Qian, Y., Gong, M., Yang, Y.H.: Stereo-based 3D reconstruction of dynamic fluid surfaces by global optimization. In: Proceedings of the IEEE Conference on Computer Vision and Pattern Recognition, pp. 1269–1278 (2017)
31. Rusu, R.B.: Semantic 3D object maps for everyday manipulation in human living environments. Ph.D. thesis, Computer Science department, Technische Universitaet Muenchen, Germany, October 2009
32. Saito, H., Kawamura, H., Nakajima, M.: 3D shape measurement of underwater objects using motion stereo. In: Proceedings of the 1995 IEEE IECON 21st International Conference on Industrial Electronics, Control, and Instrumentation, vol. 2, pp. 1231–1235. IEEE (1995)

33. Sedlazeck, A., Koch, R.: Calibration of housing parameters for underwater stereo-camera rigs. In: BMVC, pp. 1–11. Citeseer (2011)
34. Shan, Q., Agarwal, S., Curless, B.: Refractive height fields from single and multiple images. In: IEEE Conference on Computer Vision and Pattern Recognition (CVPR), pp. 286–293. IEEE (2012)
35. Supplemental Materials. http://webdocs.cs.ualberta.ca/~yang/conference.htm
36. Tanaka, K., Mukaigawa, Y., Kubo, H., Matsushita, Y., Yagi, Y.: Recovering transparent shape from time-of-flight distortion. In: Proceedings of the IEEE Conference on Computer Vision and Pattern Recognition, pp. 4387–4395 (2016)
37. Tian, Y., Narasimhan, S.G.: Seeing through water: image restoration using model-based tracking. In: IEEE 12th International Conference on Computer Vision, pp. 2303–2310. IEEE (2009)
38. Westaway, R.M., Lane, S.N., Hicks, D.M.: Remote sensing of clear-water, shallow, gravel-bed rivers using digital photogrammetry. Photogram. Eng. Remote Sens. **67**(11), 1271–1282 (2001)
39. Wetzstein, G., Raskar, R., Heidrich, W.: Hand-held schlieren photography with light field probes. In: IEEE International Conference on Computational Photography (ICCP), pp. 1–8. IEEE (2011)
40. Wu, B., Zhou, Y., Qian, Y., Gong, M., Huang, H.: Full 3D reconstruction of transparent objects. ACM Trans. Graph. (Proc. SIGGRAPH) **37**(4), 103:1–103:11 (2018)
41. Xue, T., Rubinstein, M., Wadhwa, N., Levin, A., Durand, F., Freeman, W.T.: Refraction wiggles for measuring fluid depth and velocity from video. In: Fleet, D., Pajdla, T., Schiele, B., Tuytelaars, T. (eds.) ECCV 2014. LNCS, vol. 8691, pp. 767–782. Springer, Cham (2014). https://doi.org/10.1007/978-3-319-10578-9_50
42. Yau, T., Gong, M., Yang, Y.H.: Underwater camera calibration using wavelength triangulation. In: IEEE Conference on Computer Vision and Pattern Recognition (CVPR), pp. 2499–2506. IEEE (2013)
43. Ye, J., Ji, Y., Li, F., Yu, J.: Angular domain reconstruction of dynamic 3D fluid surfaces. In: IEEE Conference on Computer Vision and Pattern Recognition (CVPR), pp. 310–317. IEEE (2012)
44. Zhang, M., Lin, X., Gupta, M., Suo, J., Dai, Q.: Recovering scene geometry under wavy fluid via distortion and defocus analysis. In: Fleet, D., Pajdla, T., Schiele, B., Tuytelaars, T. (eds.) ECCV 2014. LNCS, vol. 8693, pp. 234–250. Springer, Cham (2014). https://doi.org/10.1007/978-3-319-10602-1_16
45. Zhang, X., Cox, C.S.: Measuring the two-dimensional structure of a wavy water surface optically: a surface gradient detector. Exp. Fluids **17**(4), 225–237 (1994)
46. Zhang, Z.: A flexible new technique for camera calibration. IEEE Trans. Pattern Anal. Mach. Intell. **22**(11), 1330–1334 (2000)
47. Zhu, C., Byrd, R.H., Lu, P., Nocedal, J.: Algorithm 778: L-BFGS-B: Fortran subroutines for large-scale bound-constrained optimization. ACM Trans. Math. Softw. (TOMS) **23**(4), 550–560 (1997)

Women Also Snowboard: Overcoming Bias in Captioning Models

Lisa Anne Hendricks[1]([envelope]) [iD], Kaylee Burns[1] [iD], Kate Saenko[2] [iD],
Trevor Darrell[1] [iD], and Anna Rohrbach[1] [iD]

[1] UC Berkeley, Berkeley, USA
lisa_anne@eecs.berkeley.edu, kayleeburns@berkeley.edu
[2] Boston University, Boston, USA

Abstract. Most machine learning methods are known to capture and
exploit biases of the training data. While some biases are beneficial for
learning, others are harmful. Specifically, image captioning models tend
to exaggerate biases present in training data (e.g., if a word is present in
60% of training sentences, it might be predicted in 70% of sentences at
test time). This can lead to incorrect captions in domains where unbiased captions are desired, or required, due to over-reliance on the learned
prior and image context. In this work we investigate generation of gender-
specific caption words (e.g. man, woman) based on the person's appearance or the image context. We introduce a new *Equalizer* model that
encourages equal gender probability when gender evidence is occluded
in a scene and confident predictions when gender evidence is present.
The resulting model is forced to look at a person rather than use contextual cues to make a gender-specific prediction. The losses that comprise
our model, the *Appearance Confusion Loss* and the *Confident Loss*, are
general, and can be added to any description model in order to mitigate
impacts of unwanted bias in a description dataset. Our proposed model
has lower error than prior work when describing images with people
and mentioning their gender and more closely matches the ground truth
ratio of sentences including women to sentences including men. Finally,
we show that our model more often looks at people when predicting their
gender (https://people.eecs.berkeley.edu/~lisaanne/snowboard.html).

Keywords: Image description · Caption bias
Right for the right reasons

1 Introduction

Exploiting contextual cues can frequently lead to better performance on computer vision tasks [12,34,35]. For example, in the visual description task,

---

L. A. Hendricks and K. Burns—Authors contributed equally.

Electronic supplementary material The online version of this chapter (https://
doi.org/10.1007/978-3-030-01219-9_47) contains supplementary material, which is
available to authorized users.

V. Ferrari et al. (Eds.): ECCV 2018, LNCS 11207, pp. 793–811, 2018.
https://doi.org/10.1007/978-3-030-01219-9_47

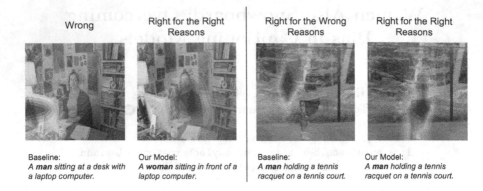

| Wrong | Right for the Right Reasons | Right for the Wrong Reasons | Right for the Right Reasons |

Baseline:
*A **man** sitting at a desk with a laptop computer.*

Our Model:
*A **woman** sitting in front of a laptop computer.*

Baseline:
*A **man** holding a tennis racquet on a tennis court.*

Our Model:
*A **man** holding a tennis racquet on a tennis court.*

Fig. 1. Examples where our proposed model (Equalizer) corrects bias in image captions. The overlaid heatmap indicates which image regions are most important for predicting the gender word. On the left, the baseline predicts gender incorrectly, presumably because it looks at the laptop (not the person). On the right, the baseline predicts the gender correctly but it does not look at the person when predicting gender and is thus not acceptable. In contrast, our model predicts the correct gender word and correctly considers the person when predicting gender.

predicting a "mouse" might be easier given that a computer is also in the image. However, in some cases making decisions based on context can lead to incorrect, and perhaps even offensive, predictions. In this work, we consider one such scenario: generating captions about men and women. We posit that when description models predict gendered words such as "man" or "woman", they should consider visual evidence associated with the described person, and not contextual cues like location (e.g., "kitchen") or other objects in a scene (e.g., "snowboard"). Not only is it important for description systems to avoid egregious errors (e.g., always predicting the word "man" in snowboarding scenes), but it is also important for predictions to be right for the right reason. For example, Fig. 1 (left) shows a case where prior work predicts the incorrect gender, while our model accurately predicts the gender by considering the correct gender evidence. Figure 1 (right) shows an example where both models predict the correct gender, but prior work does not look at the person when describing the image (it is right for the wrong reasons).

Bias in image captioning is particularly challenging to overcome because of the multimodal nature of the task; predicted words are not only influenced by an image, but also biased by the learned language model. Though [47] studied bias for structured prediction tasks (e.g., semantic role labeling), they did not consider the task of image captioning. Furthermore, the solution proposed in [47] requires access to the entire test set in order to rebalance gender predictions to reflect the distribution in the training set. Consequently, [47] relies on the assumption that the distribution of genders is the same at training and test time. We make no such assumptions; we consider a more realistic scenario in which captions are generated for images independent of other test images.

In order to encourage description models to generate less biased captions, we introduce the *Equalizer* Model. Our model includes two complementary loss terms: the *Appearance Confusion Loss (ACL)* and the *Confident Loss (Conf)*. The Appearance Confusion Loss is based on the intuition that, given an image in which evidence of gender is absent, description models should be unable to accurately predict a gendered word. However, it is not enough to confuse the model when gender evidence is absent; we must also encourage the model to consider gender evidence when it is present. Our Confident Loss helps to increase the model's confidence when gender is in the image. These complementary losses allow the Equalizer model to be cautious in the absence of gender information and discriminative in its presence.

Our proposed Equalizer model leads to less biased captions: not only does it lead to lower error when predicting gendered words, but it also performs well when the distribution of genders in the test set is not aligned with the training set. Additionally, we observe that Equalizer generates gender neutral words (like "person") when it is not confident of the gender. Furthermore, we demonstrate that Equalizer focuses on humans when predicting gender words, as opposed to focusing on other image context.

2   Related Work

Unwanted Dataset Bias. Unwanted dataset biases (e.g., gender, ethnic biases) have been studied across a wide variety of AI domains [3–5,23,29,31]. One common theme is the notion of *bias amplification*, in which bias is not only learned, but amplified [4,31,47]. For example, in the image captioning scenario, if 70% of images with umbrellas include a woman and 30% include a man, at test time the model might amplify this bias to 85% and 15%. Eliminating bias amplification is not as simple as balancing across attributes for a specific category. [31] study bias in classification and find that even though white and black people appear in "basketball" images with similar frequency, models learn to classify images as "basketball" based on the presence of a black person. One explanation is that though the data is balanced in regard to the class "basketball", there are many more white people in the dataset. Consequently, to perfectly balance a dataset, one would have to balance across all possible co-occurrences which is infeasible.

Natural language data is subject to *reporting bias* [4,13,21,22] in which people over-report less common co-occurrences, such as "male nurse" [4] or "green banana" [22]. [21] also discuss how visual descriptions reflect cultural biases (e.g., assuming a woman with a child is a mother, even though this cannot be confirmed in an image). We observe that annotators specify gender even when gender cannot be confirmed in an image (e.g., a snowboarder might be labeled as "man" even if gender evidence is occluded).

Our work is most similar to [47] who consider bias in semantic role labeling and multilabel classification (as opposed to image captioning). To avoid bias amplification, [47] rebalance the test time predictions to more accurately reflect the training time word ratios. This solution is unsatisfactory because (i) it requires access to the entire test set and (ii) it assumes that the distribution of objects at test time is the same as at training time. We consider a more realistic scenario in our experiments, and show that the ratio of woman to man in our predicted sentences closely resembles the ratio in ground truth sentences, even when the test distribution is different from the training distribution.

Fairness. Building AI systems which treat *protected attributes* (e.g., age, gender, sexual orientation) in a fair manner is increasingly important [9,14,25,43]. In the machine learning literature, "fairness" generally requires that systems do not use information such as gender or age in a way that disadvantages one group over another. We consider is different scenario as we are trying to *predict* protected attributes.

Distribution matching has been used to build fair systems [25] by encouraging the distribution of decisions to be similar across different protected classes, as well as for other applications such as domain adaption [36,46] and transduction learning [24]. Our Appearance Confusion Loss is similar as it encourages the distribution of predictions to be similar for man and woman classes when gender information is not available.

Right for the Right Reasons. Assuring models are "right for the right reasons," or consider similar evidence as humans when making decisions, helps researchers understand how models will perform in real world applications (e.g., when predicting outcomes for pneumonia patients in [7]) or discover underlying dataset bias [33]. We hypothesize that models which look at appropriate gender evidence will perform better in new scenarios, specifically when the gender distribution at test and training time are different.

Recently, [28] develop a loss function which compares explanations for a decision to ground truth explanations. However, [28] generating explanations for visual decisions is a difficult and active area of research [11,26,27,30,42,48]. Instead of relying on our model to accurately explain itself during training, we verify that our formulation encourages models to be right for the right reason at test time.

Visual Description. Most visual description work (e.g., [1,8,15,37,39]) focuses on improving overall sentence quality, without regard to captured biases. Though we pay special attention to gender in this work, all captioning models trained on visual description data (MSCOCO [20], Flickr30k [41], MSR-VTT [38] to name a few) implicitly learn to classify gender. However current captioning models do not discuss gender the way humans do, but *amplify* gender bias; our intent is to generate descriptions which more accurately reflect human descriptions when discussing this important category.

Gender Classification. Gender classification models frequently focus on facial features [10,18,45]. In contrast, we are mainly concerned about whether contextual clues in complex scenes bias the production of gendered words during sentence generation. Gender classification has also been studied in natural language processing ([2,6,40]).

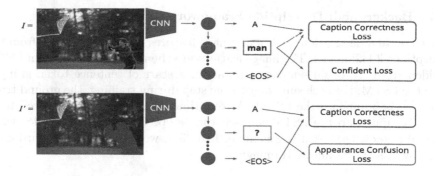

Fig. 2. Equalizer includes two novel loss terms: the Confident Loss on images with men or women (top) and the Appearance Confusion Loss on images where men and women are occluded (bottom). Together these losses encourage our model to make correct predictions when evidence of gender is present, and be cautious in its absence. We also include the Caption Correctness Loss (cross entropy loss) for both image types.

Ethical Considerations. Frequently, gender classification is seen as a binary task: data points are labeled as either "man" or "woman". However, AI practitioners, both in industrial[1] and academic[2] settings, are increasingly concerned that gender classification systems should be inclusive. Our captioning model predicts three gender categories: male, female, and gender neutral (e.g., person) based on visual appearance. When designing gender classification systems, it is important to understand where labels are sourced from [16]. We determine gender labels using a previously collected publicly released dataset in which annotators describe images [20]. Importantly, people in the images are not asked to identify their gender. Thus, we emphasize that we are not classifying biological sex or gender identity, but rather outward gender appearance.

3   Equalizer: Overcoming Bias in Description Models

Equalizer is based on the following intuitions: if evidence to support a specific gender decision is not present in an image, the model should be *confused* about which gender to predict (enforced by an Appearance Confusion Loss term), and if evidence to support a gender decision is in an image, the model should be *confident* in its prediction (enforced by a Confident Loss term). To train our model we require not only pairs of images, I, and sentences, S, but also annotation masks M which indicate which evidence in an image is appropriate for determining gender. Though we use [37] as our base network, Equalizer is general and can be integrated into any deep description framework.

---

[1] https://clarifai.com/blog/socially-responsible-pixels-a-look-inside-clarifais-new-demographics-recognition-model.

[2] https://www.media.mit.edu/projects/gender-shades/faq.

3.1   Background: Description Framework

To generate a description, high level image features are first extracted from the InceptionV3 [32] model. The image features are then used to initialize an LSTM hidden state. To begin sentence generation, a start of sentence token is input into the LSTM. For each subsequent time step during training, the ground truth word w_t is input into the LSTM. At test time, the previously predicted word w_{t-1} is input into the LSTM at each time step. Generation concludes when an end of sequence token is generated. Like [37], we include the standard cross entropy loss ($\mathcal{L}^{CE}$) during training:

$$\mathcal{L}^{CE} = -\frac{1}{N} \sum_{n=0}^{N} \sum_{t=0}^{T} \log(p(w_t|w_{0:t-1}, I)), \tag{1}$$

where N is the batch size, T is the number of words in the sentence, w_t is a ground truth word at time t, and I is an image.

3.2   Appearance Confusion Loss

Our Appearance Confusion Loss encourages the underlying description model to be *confused* when making gender decisions if the input image does not contain appropriate evidence for the decision. To optimize the Appearance Confusion Loss, we require ground truth rationales indicating which evidence is appropriate for a particular gender decision. We expect the resulting rationales to be masks, M, which are 1 for pixels which should not contribute to a gender decision and 0 for pixels which are appropriate to consider when determining gender. The Hadamard product of the mask and the original image, $I \odot M$, yields a new image, I', with gender information that the implementer deems appropriate for classification removed. Intuitively, for an image devoid of gender information, the probability of predicting man or woman should be equal. The Appearance Confusion Loss enforces a fair prior by asserting that this is the case.

To define our Appearance Confusion Loss, we first define a *confusion* function ($\mathcal{C}$) which operates over the predicted distribution of words $p(\tilde{w}_t)$, a set of woman gender words ($\mathcal{G}_w$), and a set of man gender words ($\mathcal{G}_m$):

$$\mathcal{C}(\tilde{w}_t, I') = |\sum_{g_w \in \mathcal{G}_w} p(\tilde{w}_t = g_w|w_{0:t-1}, I') - \sum_{g_m \in \mathcal{G}_m} p(\tilde{w}_t = g_m|w_{0:t-1}, I')|. \tag{2}$$

In practice, the $\mathcal{G}_w$ consists only of the word "woman" and, likewise, the $\mathcal{G}_m$ consists only of the word "man". These are by far the most commonly used gender words in the datasets we consider and we find that using these "sets" results in similar performance as using more complete sets.

We can now define our Appearance Confusion Loss ($\mathcal{L}^{AC}$) as:

$$\mathcal{L}^{AC} = \frac{1}{N} \sum_{n=0}^{N} \sum_{t=0}^{T} \infty(w_t \in \mathcal{G}_w \cup \mathcal{G}_m)\mathcal{C}(\tilde{w}_t, I'), \tag{3}$$

where ∞ is an indicator variable that denotes whether or not w_t is a gendered word.

For the remaining non-gendered words that correspond to images I', we apply the standard cross entropy loss to encourage the model to discuss objects which are still visible in I'. In addition to encouraging sentences to be image relevant even when the gender information has been removed, this also encourages the model to learn representations of words like "dog" and "frisbee" that are not reliant on gender information.

3.3 Confident Loss

In addition to being unsure when gender evidence is occluded, we also encourage our model to be confident when gender evidence is present. Thus, we introduce the Confident Loss term, which encourages the model to predict gender words correctly.

Our Confident Loss encourages the probabilities for predicted gender words to be high on images I in which gender information is present. Given functions $\mathcal{F}^W$ and $\mathcal{F}^M$ which measure how confidently the model predicts woman and man words respectively, we can write the Confident Loss as:

$$\mathcal{L}^{Con} = \frac{1}{N} \sum_{n=0}^{N} \sum_{t=0}^{T} (\infty(w_t \in \mathcal{G}_w)\mathcal{F}^W(\tilde{w}_t, I) + \infty(w_t \in \mathcal{G}_m)\mathcal{F}^M(\tilde{w}_t, I)). \quad (4)$$

To measure the confidence of predicted gender words, we consider the quotient between predicted probabilities for man and gender words ($\mathcal{F}^M$ is of the same form):

$$\mathcal{F}^W(\tilde{w}_t, I) = \frac{\sum_{g_m \in \mathcal{G}_m} p(\tilde{w}_t = g_m | w_{0:t-1}, I)}{(\sum_{g_w \in \mathcal{G}_w} p(\tilde{w}_t = g_w | w_{0:t-1}, I)) + \epsilon} \quad (5)$$

where ϵ is a small epsilon value added for numerical stability.

When the model is confident of a gender prediction (e.g., for the word "woman"), the probability of the word "woman" should be considerably higher than the probability of the word "man", which will result in a small value for $\mathcal{F}^W$ and thus a small loss. One nice property of considering the quotient between predicted probabilities is that we encourage the model to distinguish between gendered words without forcing the model to predict a gendered word. For example, if the model predicts a probability of 0.2 for "man", 0.5 for "woman", and 0.3 for "person" on a "woman" image, our confidence loss will be low. However, the model is still able to predict gender neutral words, like "person" with relatively high probability. This is distinct from other possible losses, like placing a larger weight on gender words in the cross entropy loss, which forces the model to predict "man"/"woman" words and penalizes the gender neutral words.

3.4   The Equalizer Model

Our final model is a linear combination of all aforementioned losses:

$$\mathcal{L} = \alpha\mathcal{L}^{CE} + \beta\mathcal{L}^{AC} + \mu\mathcal{L}^{Con}, \tag{6}$$

where α, β, and μ are hyperparameters chosen on a validation set ($\alpha, \mu = 1$, $\beta = 10$ in our experiments).

Our Equalizer method is general and our base captioning framework can be substituted with any other deep captioning framework. By combining all of these terms, the Equalizer model can not only generate image relevant sentences, but also make confident gender predictions under sufficient evidence. We find that both the Appearance Confusion Loss and the Confident Loss are important in creating a confident yet cautious model. Interestingly, the Equalizer model achieves the lowest misclassification rate only when these two losses are combined, highlighting the complementary nature of these two loss terms.

4   Experiments

4.1   Datasets

MSCOCO-Bias. To evaluate our method, we consider the dataset used by [47] for evaluating bias amplification in structured prediction problems. This dataset consists of images from MSCOCO [20] which are labeled as "man" or "woman". Though "person" is an MSCOCO class, "man" and "woman" are not, so [47] employ ground truth captions to determine if images contain a man or a woman. Images are labeled as "man" if at least one description includes the word "man" and no descriptions include the word "woman". Likewise, images are labeled as "woman" if at least one description includes the word "woman" and no descriptions include the word "man". Images are discarded if both "man" and "woman" are mentioned. We refer to this dataset as MSCOCO-Bias.
MSCOCO-Balanced. We also evaluate on a set where we purposely change the gender ratio. We believe this is representative of real world scenarios in which different distributions of men and women might be present at test time. The MSCOCO-Bias set has a roughly 1:3 woman to man ratio where as this set, called MSCOCO-Balanced, has a 1:1 woman to man ratio. We randomly select 500 images from MSCOCO-Bias set which include the word "woman" and 500 which include "man".
Person Masks. To train Equalizer, we need ground truth human rationales for why a person should be predicted as a man or a woman. We use the person segmentation masks from the MSCOCO dataset. Once the masked image is created, we fill the segmentation mask with the average pixel value in the image. We use the masks both at training time to compute Appearance Confusion Loss and during evaluation to ensure that models are predicting gender words by looking at the person. While for MSCOCO the person annotations are readily available, for other datasets e.g. a person detector could be used.

4.2   Metrics

To evaluate our methods, we rely on the following metrics.

Error. Due to the sensitive nature of prediction for protected classes (gender words in our scenario), we emphasize the importance of a low error. The error rate is the number of man/woman misclassifications, while gender neutral terms are not considered errors. We expect that the best model would rather predict gender neutral words in cases where gender is not obvious.

Gender Ratio. Second, we consider the ratio of sentences which belong to a "woman" set to sentences which belong to a "man" set. We consider a sentence to fall in a "woman" set if it predicts any word from a precompiled list of female gendered words, and respectively fall in a "man" set if it predicts any word from a precompiled list of male gendered words.

Right for the Right Reasons. Finally, to measure if a model is "right for the right reasons" we consider the pointing game [44] evaluation. We first create visual explanations for "woman"/"man" using the Grad-CAM approach [30] as well as saliency maps created by occluding image regions in a sliding window fashion. To measure if our models are right for the right reason, we verify whether the point with the highest activation in the explanation heat map falls in the person segmentation mask.

4.3   Training Details

All models are initialized from the Show and Tell model [37] pre-trained on all of MSCOCO for 1 million iterations (without fine-tuning through the visual representation). Models are trained for additional 500,000 iterations on the MSCOCO-Bias set, fine-tuning through the visual representation (Inception v3 [32]) for 500,000 iterations.

4.4   Baselines and Ablations

Baseline-FT. The simplest baseline is fine-tuning the Show and Tell model through the LSTM and convolutional networks using the standard cross-entropy loss on our target dataset, the MSCOCO-Bias dataset.

Balanced. We train a Balanced baseline in which we re-balance the data distribution at training time to account for the larger number of men instances in the training data. Even though we cannot know the correct distribution of our data at test time, we can enforce our belief that predicting a woman or man should be equally likely. At training time, we re-sample the images of women so that the number of training examples of women is the same as the number of training examples of men.

UpWeight. We also experiment with upweighting the loss value for gender words in the standard cross entropy loss to increase the penalty for a misclassification. For each time step where the ground truth caption says the word

Table 1. Evaluation of predicted gender words based on error rate and ratio of generated sentences which include the "woman" words to sentences which include the "man" words. Equalizer achieves the lowest error rate and predicts sentences with a gender ratio most similar to the corresponding ground truth captions (Ratio Δ), even when the test set has a different distribution of gender words than the training set, as is the case for the MSCOCO-Balanced dataset.

Model	MSCOCO-Bias		MSCOCO-Balanced	
	Error	Ratio Δ	Error	Ratio Δ
Baseline-FT	12.83	0.14	19.30	0.51
Balanced	12.85	0.14	18.30	0.47
UpWeight	13.56	0.08	16.30	0.35
Equalizer w/o ACL	7.57	0.04	10.10	0.26
Equalizer w/o Conf	9.62	0.09	13.90	0.40
Equalizer	**7.02**	**-.03**	**8.10**	**0.13**

"man" or "woman", we multiply that term in the loss by a constant value (10 in reported experiments). Intuitively, upweighting should encourage the models to accurately predict gender words. However, unlike our Confident Loss, upweighting drives the model to make either "man" or "woman" predictions without the opportunity to place a high probability on gender neutral words.

Ablations. To isolate the impact of the two loss terms in Equalizer, we report results with only the Appearance Confusion Loss (Equalizer w/o Conf) and only the Confidence Loss (Equalizer w/o ACL). We then report results of our full Equalizer model.

4.5 Results

Error. Table 1 reports the error rates when describing men and women on the MSCOCO-Bias and MSCOCO-Balanced test sets. Comparing to baselines, Equalizer shows consistent improvements. Importantly, our full model consistently improves upon Equalizer w/o ACL and Equalizer w/o Conf. When comparing Equalizer to baselines, we see a larger performance gain on the MSCOCO-Balanced dataset. As discussed later, this is in part because our model does a particularly good job of decreasing error on the minority class (woman). Unlike baseline models, our model has a similar error rate on each set. This indicates that the error rate of our model is not as sensitive to shifts in the gender distribution at test time.

Interestingly, the results of the Baseline-FT model and Balanced model are not substantially different. One possibility is that the co-occurrences across words are not balanced (e.g., if there is gender imbalance specifically for images with "umbrella" just balancing the dataset based on gender word counts is not sufficient to balance the dataset). We emphasize that balancing across all co-occurring words is difficult in large-scale settings with large vocabularies.

Table 2. Accuracy per class for MSCOCO-Bias dataset. Though UpWeight achieves the highest recall for both men and women images, it also has a high error, especially for women. One criterion of a "fair" system is that it has similar outcomes across classes. We measure outcome similarity by computing the Jensen-Shannon divergence between Correct/Incorrect/Other sentences for men and women images (lower is better) and observe that Equalizer performs best on this metric.

Model	Women			Men			Outcome divergence between genders
	Correct	Incorrect	Other	Correct	Incorrect	Other	
Baseline-FT	46.28	34.11	19.61	75.05	4.23	20.72	0.121
Balanced	47.67	33.80	18.54	75.89	4.38	19.72	0.116
UpWeight	**60.59**	29.82	9.58	**87.84**	6.98	5.17	0.078
Equalizer w/o ACL	56.18	16.02	27.81	67.58	**4.15**	28.26	0.031
Equalizer w/o Conf	46.03	24.84	29.13	61.11	3.47	35.42	0.075
Equalizer (Ours)	57.38	**12.99**	29.63	59.02	4.61	36.37	**0.018**

Gender Ratio. We also consider the ratio of captions which include only female words to captions which include only male words. In Table 1 we report the *difference* between the ground truth ratio and the ratio produced by each captioning model. Impressively, Equalizer achieves the closest ratio to ground truth on both datasets. Again, the ACL and Confident losses are complementary and Equalizer has the best overall performance.

Performance for Each Gender. Images with females comprise a much smaller portion of MSCOCO than images with males. Therefore the overall performance across classes (i.e. man, woman) can be misleading because it downplays the errors in the minority class. Additionally, unlike [47] who consider a classification scenario in which the model is forced to predict a gender, our description models can also discuss gender neutral terms such as "person" or "player". In Table 2 for each gender, we report the percentage of sentences in which gender is predicted correctly or incorrectly and when no gender specific word is generated on the MSCOCO-Bias set.

Across all models, the error for Men is quite low. However, our model significantly improves the error for the minority class, Women. Interestingly, we observe that Equalizer has a similar recall (Correct), error (Incorrect), and Other rate across both genders. A caption model could be considered more "fair" if, for each gender, the possible outcomes (correct gender mentioned, incorrect gender mentioned, gender neutral) are similar. This resembles the notion of equalized odds in fairness literature [14], which requires a system to have similar false positive

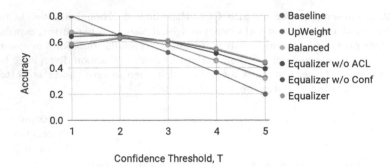

Fig. 3. Accuracy across man, woman, and gender neutral terms for different models as a function of annotator confidence. When only one annotator describes an image with a gendered word, equalizer has a low accuracy as it more likely predicts gender neutral words but when more annotations mention gendered words, equalizer has higher accuracy than other models.

and false negative rates across groups. To formalize this notion of fairness in our captioning systems, we report the outcome type divergence between genders by measuring the Jensen-Shannon [19] divergence between Correct/Incorrect/Other outcomes for Men and Women. Lower divergence indicates that Women and Men classes result in a similar distribution of outcomes, and thus the model can be considered more "fair". Equalizer has the lowest divergence (0.018).

Annotator Confidence. As described above, gender labels are mined from captions provided in the MSCOCO dataset. Each image corresponds to five captions, but not all captions for a single image include a gendered word. Counting the number of sentences which include a gendered word provides a rough estimate of how apparent gender is in an image and how important it is to mention when describing the scene.

To understand how well our model captures the way annotators describe people, instead of labeling images as either "man" or "woman", we label images as "man", "woman", or "gender neutral" based on how many annotators mentioned gender in their description. For a specific threshold value T, we consider an image to belong to the "man" or "woman" class if T or more annotators mention the gender in their description, and "gender neutral" otherwise. We can then measure accuracy over these three classes. Whereas a naive solution which restricts vocabulary to include no gender words would have low error as defined in Table 1, it would not capture the way humans use gender words when describing images. Indeed, the MSCOCO training set includes over 200,000 instances of words which describe people. Over half of all words used to describe people are gendered. By considering accuracy across three classes, we can better measure how well models capture the way humans describe gender.

Figure 3 plots the accuracy of each model with respect to the confidence threshold T. At low threshold values, Equalizer performs worse as it tends to more frequently output gender neutral terms, and the UpWeight model, which

Table 3. *Pointing game* evaluation that measures whether the visual explanations for "man"/"woman" words fall in the person segmentation ground-truth. Evaluation is done for ground-truth captions on the MSCOCO-Balanced.

Accuracy	Woman	Man	All
Random	22.6	19.5	21.0
Baseline-FT	39.8	34.3	37.0
Balanced	37.6	34.1	35.8
UpWeight	43.3	36.4	39.9
Equalizer w/o ACL	48.1	39.6	43.8
Equalizer w/o Conf	43.9	36.8	40.4
Equalizer (Ours)	**49.9**	**45.2**	**47.5**

Accuracy	Woman	Man	All
Random	25.1	17.5	21.3
Baseline-FT	45.3	40.4	42.8
Balanced	48.5	42.2	45.3
UpWeight	54.1	45.5	49.8
Equalizer w/o ACL	54.7	47.5	51.1
Equalizer w/o Conf	48.9	46.7	47.8
Equalizer (Ours)	**56.3**	**51.1**	**53.7**

(a) Visual explanation is a *Grad-CAM* map.   (b) Visual explanation is a *saliency* map.

almost always predicts gendered words, performs best. However, as the threshold value increases, Equalizer performs better than other models, including at a threshold value of 3 which corresponds to classifying images based off the majority vote. This indicates that Equalizer naturally captures when humans describe images with gendered or gender neutral words.

Object Gender Co-occurrence. We analyze how gender prediction influences prediction of other words on the MSCOCO-Bias test set. Specifically, we consider the 80 MSCOCO categories, excluding the category "person". We adopt the bias amplification metric proposed in [47], and compute the following ratios: $\frac{count(man\&object)}{count(person\&object)}$ and $\frac{count(woman\&object)}{count(person\&object)}$, where *man* refers to all male words, *woman* refers to all female words, and *person* refers to all male, female, or gender neutral words. Ideally, these ratios should be similar for generated captions and ground truth captions. However, e.g. for *man* and *motorcycle*, the ground truth ratio is 0.40 and for the Baseline-FT and Equalizer, the ratio is 0.81 and 0.65, respectively. Though Equalizer over-predicts this pair, the ratio is closer to the ground truth than when comparing Baseline-FT to the ground truth. Likewise, for *woman* and *umbrella*, the ground truth ratio is 0.40, Baseline-FT ratio is 0.64, and Equalizer ratio is 0.56. As a more holistic metric, we average the *difference* of ratios between ground truth and generated captions across objects (lower is better). For male words, Equalizer is substantially better than the Baseline-FT (0.147 vs. 0.193) and similar for female words (0.096 vs. 0.99).

Caption Quality. Qualitatively, the sentences from all of our models are linguistically fluent (indeed, comparing sentences in Fig. 4 we note that usually only the word referring to the person changes). However, we do notice a small drop in performance on standard description metrics (25.2 to 24.3 on METEOR [17] when comparing Baseline-FT to our full Equalizer) on MSCOCO-Bias. One possibility is that our model is overly cautious and is penalized for producing gender neutral terms for sentences that humans describe with gendered terms.

Right for the Right Reasons. We hypothesize that many misclassification errors occur due to the model looking at the wrong visual evidence, e.g. conditioning gender prediction on context rather than on the person's appearance. We quantitatively confirm this hypothesis and show that our proposed model improves this behavior by looking at the appropriate evidence, i.e. is being "right for the right reasons". To evaluate this we rely on two visual explanation techniques: Grad-CAM [30] and saliency maps generated by occluding image regions in a sliding window fashion.

Unlike [30] who apply Grad-CAM to an entire caption, we visualize the evidence for generating specific words, i.e. "man" and "woman". Specifically, we apply Grad-CAM to the last convolutional layer of our image processing network, InceptionV3 [32], we obtain 8×8 weight matrices. To obtain saliency maps, we resize an input image to 299×299 and uniformly divide it into 32×32 pixel regions, obtaining a 10×10 grid (the bottom/rightmost cells being smaller). Next, for every cell in the grid, we zero out the respective pixels and feed the obtained "partially blocked out" image through the captioning network (similar to as was done in the occlusion sensitivity experiments in [42]). Then, for the ground-truth caption, we compute the "information loss", i.e. the decrease in predicting the words "man" and "woman" as $-\log(p(w_t = g_m))$ and $-\log(p(w_t = g_w))$, respectively. This is similar to the top-down saliency approach of [26], who zero-out all the intermediate feature descriptors but one.

To evaluate whether the visual explanation for the predicted word is focused on a person, we rely on person masks, obtained from MSCOCO ground-truth person segmentations. We use the *pointing game* evaluation [44]. We upscale visual explanations to the original image size. We define a "hit" to be when the point with the highest weight is contained in the person mask. The accuracy is computed as $\frac{\#hits}{\#hits + \#misses}$.

Results on the MSCOCO-Balanced set are presented in Table 3 (a) and (b), for the Grad-CAM and saliency maps, respectively. For a fair comparison we provide all models with ground-truth captions. For completeness we also report the random baseline, where the point with the highest weight is selected randomly. We see that Equalizer obtains the best accuracy, significantly improving over the Baseline-FT and all model variants. A similar evaluation on the actual generated captions shows the same trends.

Looking at Objects. Using our pointing technique, we can also analyze which MSCOCO objects models are "looking" at when they *do not* point at the person while predicting "man"/"woman". Specifically, we count "hit" if the highest activation is on an object in question. We compute the following ratio for each gender: number of images where an object is "pointed at" to the true number of images with that object. We find that there are differences across genders, e.g. "umbrella", "bench", "suitcase" are more often pointed at when discussing women, while e.g. "truck", "couch", "pizza" -when discussing men. Our model reduces the overall "delta" between genders for ground truth sentences from an average 0.12 to 0.08, compared to the Baseline-FT. E.g. for "dining table" Equalizer decreases the delta from 0.07 to 0.03.

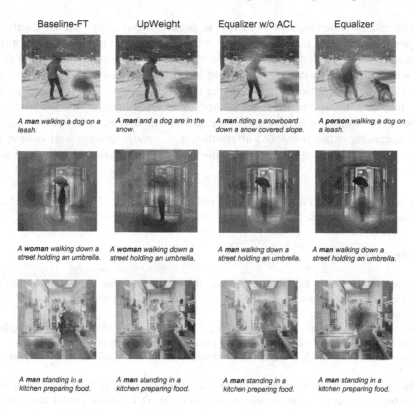

Fig. 4. Qualitative comparison of multiple baselines and our model. In the top example, being conservative ("person") is better than being wrong ("man") as the gender is not obvious. In the bottom example the baselines are looking at the wrong visual evidence.

Qualitative Results. Figure 4 compares Grad-CAM visualizations for predicted gender words from our model to the Baseline-FT, UpWeight, and Equalizer w/o ACL. We consistently see that our model looks at the person when describing gendered words. In Fig. 4 (top), all other models look at the dog rather than the person and predict the gender "man" (ground truth label is "woman"). In this particular example, the gender is somewhat ambiguous, and our model conservatively predicts "person" rather than misclassify the gender. In Fig. 4 (middle), the Baseline-FT and UpWeight example both incorrectly predict the word "woman" and do not look at the person (women occur more frequently with umbrellas). In contrast, both the Equalizer w/o ACL and the Equalizer look at the person and predict the correct gender. Finally, in Fig. 4 (bottom), all models predict the correct gender (man), but our model is the only model which looks at the person and is thus "right for the right reasons."

Discussion. We present the Equalizer model which includes an Appearance Confusion Loss to encourage predictions to be confused when predicting gender if evidence is obscured and the Confident Loss which encourages predictions to be confident when gender evidence is present. Our Appearance Confusion Loss, requires human rationales about what is visual evidence is appropriate to consider when predicting gender. We stress the importance of human judgment when designing models which include protected classes. For example, our model can use information about clothing type (e.g., dresses) to predict a gender which may not be appropriate for all applications. Though we concentrate on gender in this work, we believe the generality of our framework could be applied when describing other protected attributes, e.g., race/ethnicity and believe our results suggest Equalizer can be a valuable tool for overcoming bias in captioning models.

Acknowledgements. This work was partially supported by US DoD, the DARPA XAI program, and the Berkeley Artificial Intelligence Research (BAIR) Lab.

References

1. Anderson, P., et al.: Bottom-up and top-down attention for image captioning and VQA. In: Proceedings of the IEEE Conference on Computer Vision and Pattern Recognition (CVPR) (2018)
2. Argamon, S., Koppel, M., Pennebaker, J.W., Schler, J.: Mining the blogosphere: age, gender and the varieties of self-expression. First Monday 12(9) (2007)
3. Barocas, S., Selbst, A.D.: Big data's disparate impact. Calif. Law Rev. **104**, 671 (2016)
4. Bolukbasi, T., Chang, K.W., Zou, J.Y., Saligrama, V., Kalai, A.T.: Man is to computer programmer as woman is to homemaker? Debiasing word embeddings. In: Advances in Neural Information Processing Systems (NIPS), pp. 4349–4357 (2016)
5. Buolamwini, J.A.: Gender shades: intersectional phenotypic and demographic evaluation of face datasets and gender classifiers. Ph.D. thesis, Massachusetts Institute of Technology (2017)
6. Burger, J.D., Henderson, J., Kim, G., Zarrella, G.: Discriminating gender on Twitter. In: Proceedings of the Conference on Empirical Methods in Natural Language Processing (EMNLP), pp. 1301–1309. Association for Computational Linguistics (2011)
7. Caruana, R., Lou, Y., Gehrke, J., Koch, P., Sturm, M., Elhadad, N.: Intelligible models for healthcare: predicting pneumonia risk and hospital 30-day readmission. In: Proceedings of the 21th ACM SIGKDD International Conference on Knowledge Discovery and Data Mining, pp. 1721–1730. ACM (2015)
8. Donahue, J., et al.: Long-term recurrent convolutional networks for visual recognition and description. In: Proceedings of the IEEE Conference on Computer Vision and Pattern Recognition (CVPR), pp. 2625–2634 (2015)
9. Dwork, C., Hardt, M., Pitassi, T., Reingold, O., Zemel, R.: Fairness through awareness. In: Proceedings of the 3rd Innovations in Theoretical Computer Science Conference, pp. 214–226. ACM (2012)
10. Eidinger, E., Enbar, R., Hassner, T.: Age and gender estimation of unfiltered faces. IEEE Trans. Inf. For. Secur. **9**(12), 2170–2179 (2014)
11. Fong, R.C., Vedaldi, A.: Interpretable explanations of black boxes by meaningful perturbation. In: Proceedings of the IEEE International Conference on Computer Vision (ICCV) (2017)

12. Gkioxari, G., Girshick, R., Malik, J.: Contextual action recognition with R* CNN. In: Proceedings of the IEEE International Conference on Computer Vision (ICCV), pp. 1080–1088 (2015)
13. Gordon, J., Van Durme, B.: Reporting bias and knowledge acquisition. In: Proceedings of the 2013 workshop on Automated Knowledge Base Construction, pp. 25–30. ACM (2013)
14. Hardt, M., Price, E., Srebro, N., et al.: Equality of opportunity in supervised learning. In: Advances in Neural Information Processing Systems (NIPS), pp. 3315–3323 (2016)
15. Karpathy, A., Fei-Fei, L.: Deep visual-semantic alignments for generating image descriptions. In: Proceedings of the IEEE Conference on Computer Vision and Pattern Recognition (CVPR), pp. 3128–3137 (2015)
16. Larson, B.N.: Gender as a variable in natural-language processing: Ethical considerations (2017)
17. Lavie, M.D.A.: Meteor universal: language specific translation evaluation for any target language. In: Proceedings of the Annual Meeting of the Association for Computational Linguistics (ACL), p. 376 (2014)
18. Levi, G., Hassner, T.: Age and gender classification using convolutional neural networks. In: Proceedings of the IEEE Conference on Computer Vision and Pattern Recognition Workshops (CVPR Workshops), pp. 34–42 (2015)
19. Lin, J.: Divergence measures based on the shannon entropy. IEEE Trans. Inf. Theory $37(1)$, 145–151 (1991)
20. Lin, T.-Y., et al.: Microsoft COCO: common objects in context. In: Fleet, D., Pajdla, T., Schiele, B., Tuytelaars, T. (eds.) ECCV 2014. LNCS, vol. 8693, pp. 740–755. Springer, Cham (2014). https://doi.org/10.1007/978-3-319-10602-1_48
21. van Miltenburg, E.: Stereotyping and bias in the Flickr30k dataset. In: Workshop on Multimodal Corpora: Computer Vision and Language Processing (2016)
22. Misra, I., Zitnick, C.L., Mitchell, M., Girshick, R.: Seeing through the human reporting bias: Visual classifiers from noisy human-centric labels. In: Proceedings of the IEEE Conference on Computer Vision and Pattern Recognition (CVPR), pp. 2930–2939. IEEE (2016)
23. President of the United Search Engine Optimization, Podesta, J.: Big data: seizing opportunities, preserving values. White House, Executive Office of the President (2014)
24. Quadrianto, N., Petterson, J., Smola, A.J.: Distribution matching for transduction. In: Advances in Neural Information Processing Systems (NIPS), pp. 1500–1508 (2009)
25. Quadrianto, N., Sharmanska, V.: Recycling privileged learning and distribution matching for fairness. In: Advances in Neural Information Processing Systems (NIPS), pp. 677–688 (2017)
26. Ramanishka, V., Das, A., Zhang, J., Saenko, K.: Top-down visual saliency guided by captions. In: Proceedings of the IEEE Conference on Computer Vision and Pattern Recognition (CVPR), vol. 1, p. 7 (2017)
27. Ribeiro, M.T., Singh, S., Guestrin, C.: Why should i trust you?: Explaining the predictions of any classifier. In: Proceedings of the 22nd ACM SIGKDD International Conference on Knowledge Discovery and Data Mining, pp. 1135–1144. ACM (2016)
28. Ross, A.S., Hughes, M.C., Doshi-Velez, F.: Right for the right reasons: training differentiable models by constraining their explanations. In: Proceedings of the International Joint Conference on Artificial Intelligence (IJCAI) (2017)

29. Ryu, H.J., Adam, H., Mitchell, M.: Inclusivefacenet: Improving face attribute detection with race and gender diversity. In: Workshop on Fairness, Accountability, and Transparency in Machine Learning (FAT/ML) (2018)

30. Selvaraju, R.R., Cogswell, M., Das, A., Vedantam, R., Parikh, D., Batra, D.: Grad-CAM: visual explanations from deep networks via gradient-based localization. In: Proceedings of the IEEE International Conference on Computer Vision (ICCV) (2017)

31. Stock, P., Cisse, M.: ConvNets and imageNet beyond accuracy: explanations, bias detection, adversarial examples and model criticism. arXiv preprint arXiv:1711.11443 (2017)

32. Szegedy, C., Vanhoucke, V., Ioffe, S., Shlens, J., Wojna, Z.: Rethinking the inception architecture for computer vision. In: Proceedings of the IEEE Conference on Computer Vision and Pattern Recognition. pp. 2818–2826 (2016)

33. Tan, S., Caruana, R., Hooker, G., Lou, Y.: Detecting bias in black-box models using transparent model distillation. In: AAAI/ACM Conference on Artificial Intelligence, Ethics, and Society (2018)

34. Torralba, A.: Contextual modulation of target saliency. In: Advances in Neural Information Processing Systems (NIPS), pp. 1303–1310 (2002)

35. Torralba, A., Sinha, P.: Statistical context priming for object detection. In: Proceedings of the IEEE International Conference on Computer Vision (ICCV), vol. 1, pp. 763–770. IEEE (2001)

36. Tzeng, E., Hoffman, J., Darrell, T., Saenko, K.: Simultaneous deep transfer across domains and tasks. In: Proceedings of the IEEE International Conference on Computer Vision (ICCV), pp. 4068–4076. IEEE (2015)

37. Vinyals, O., Toshev, A., Bengio, S., Erhan, D.: Show and tell: a neural image caption generator. In: IEEE Conference on Computer Vision and Pattern Recognition (CVPR), pp. 3156–3164. IEEE (2015)

38. Xu, J., Mei, T., Yao, T., Rui, Y.: MSR-VTT: a large video description dataset for bridging video and language. In: Proceedings of the IEEE Conference on Computer Vision and Pattern Recognition (CVPR), pp. 5288–5296. IEEE (2016)

39. Xu, K., et al.: Show, attend and tell: neural image caption generation with visual attention. In: Proceedings of the International Conference on Machine Learning (ICML), pp. 2048–2057 (2015)

40. Yan, X., Yan, L.: Gender classification of weblog authors. In: AAAI Spring Symposium: computational Approaches to Analyzing Weblogs, pp. 228–230. Palo Alto (2006)

41. Young, P., Lai, A., Hodosh, M., Hockenmaier, J.: From image descriptions to visual denotations: new similarity metrics for semantic inference over event descriptions. Trans. Assoc. Computat. Linguist. (TACL) 2, 67–78 (2014)

42. Zeiler, M.D., Fergus, R.: Visualizing and understanding convolutional networks. In: Fleet, D., Pajdla, T., Schiele, B., Tuytelaars, T. (eds.) ECCV 2014. LNCS, vol. 8689, pp. 818–833. Springer, Cham (2014). https://doi.org/10.1007/978-3-319-10590-1_53

43. Zhang, B.H., Lemoine, B., Mitchell, M.: Mitigating unwanted biases with adversarial learning. In: AAAI/ACM Conference on Artificial Intelligence, Ethics, and Society (AIES) (2018)

44. Zhang, J., Lin, Z., Brandt, J., Shen, X., Sclaroff, S.: Top-down neural attention by excitation backprop. In: Leibe, B., Matas, J., Sebe, N., Welling, M. (eds.) ECCV 2016. LNCS, vol. 9908, pp. 543–559. Springer, Cham (2016). https://doi.org/10.1007/978-3-319-46493-0_33

45. Zhang, K., Tan, L., Li, Z., Qiao, Y.: Gender and smile classification using deep convolutional neural networks. In: Proceedings of the IEEE Conference on Computer Vision and Pattern Recognition Workshops (CVPR Workshops), pp. 34–38 (2016)
46. Zhang, X., Yu, F.X., Chang, S.F., Wang, S.: Deep transfer network: unsupervised domain adaptation. arXiv preprint arXiv:1503.00591 (2015)
47. Zhao, J., Wang, T., Yatskar, M., Ordonez, V., Chang, K.W.: Men also like shopping: reducing gender bias amplification using corpus-level constraints. In: Proceedings of the Conference on Empirical Methods in Natural Language Processing (EMNLP) (2017)
48. Zintgraf, L.M., Cohen, T.S., Adel, T., Welling, M.: Visualizing deep neural network decisions: prediction difference analysis. In: Proceedings of the International Conference on Learning Representations (ICLR) (2017)

Joint Camera Spectral Sensitivity Selection and Hyperspectral Image Recovery

Ying Fu[1], Tao Zhang[1], Yinqiang Zheng[2], Debing Zhang[3],
and Hua Huang[1(✉)]

[1] Beijing Laboratory of Intelligent Information Technology, School of Computer Science and Technology, Beijing Institute of Technology, Beijing 100081, China
huahuang@bit.edu.cn
[2] National Institute of Informatics, Tokyo 101-8430, Japan
[3] DeepGlint, Beijing 100091, China

Abstract. Hyperspectral image (HSI) recovery from a single RGB image has attracted much attention, whose performance has recently been shown to be sensitive to the camera spectral sensitivity (CSS). In this paper, we present an efficient convolutional neural network (CNN) based method, which can jointly select the optimal CSS from a candidate dataset and learn a mapping to recover HSI from a single RGB image captured with this algorithmically selected camera. Given a specific CSS, we first present a HSI recovery network, which accounts for the underlying characteristics of the HSI, including spectral nonlinear mapping and spatial similarity. Later, we append a CSS selection layer onto the recovery network, and the optimal CSS can thus be automatically determined from the network weights under the nonnegative sparse constraint. Experimental results show that our HSI recovery network outperforms state-of-the-art methods in terms of both quantitative metrics and perceptive quality, and the selection layer always returns a CSS consistent to the best one determined by exhaustive search.

Keywords: Camera spectral sensitivity selection
Hyperspectral image recovery · Spectral nonlinear mapping
Spatial similarity

1 Introduction

Compared with ordinary panchromatic and RGB images, the hyperspectral image (HSI) of the natural scene can effectively describe the spectral distribution and provide intrinsic and discriminative spectral information of the scene. It has been proven beneficial to numerous applications, including segmentation [43], classification [49], anomaly detection [50], face recognition [39], document analysis [28], food inspection [48], surveillance [37], earth observation [6], to name a few.

© Springer Nature Switzerland AG 2018
V. Ferrari et al. (Eds.): ECCV 2018, LNCS 11207, pp. 812–828, 2018.
https://doi.org/10.1007/978-3-030-01219-9_48

Hyperspectral cameras are widely used for HSI acquisition, which needs to densely sample the spectral signature across consecutive wavelength bands for every scene point. Such devices often come with a high cost and tend to suffer from the degradation of spatial/temporal resolution.

Recently, some methods [3,22,38,42] have been presented to directly recover the HSI from a single RGB image. Since the mapping from RGB to spectrum is three-to-many, some prior knowledge has been introduced. Examples include radial basis function network mapping [38], K-SVD based sparse coding [3], constrained sparse coding [42], and manifold-based mapping [22]. In particular, Jia et al. [22] disclose the nonlinear characteristics of natural spectra, and show that properly designing nonlinear mapping can significantly boost the recovery accuracy. Inspired by this observation, we propose a spectral convolutional neural network (CNN) to better approximate the underlying nonlinear mapping. In contrast to the pixel-wise operation in [3,22,38], we further propose to better utilize the spatial similarity in HSI via a properly designed spatial CNN. In addition, the input RGB image is employed to guide the HSI reconstruction and residual learning is used to further preserve the spatial structure in our network. Experimental results show that our recovery network outperforms state-of-the-art methods in terms of quantitative metrics and perceptive quality, and both the spectral CNN module and the spatial CNN module have contributed to this performance gain.

Existing methods [3,22,38,42] mainly focus on the HSI recovery under a given camera spectral sensitivity (CSS) function, while [4] shows that the quality of spectral recovery is sensitive to the CSS used. For example, given a CSS dataset, the optimal CSS selection may improve the accuracy by 33%, as shown in [4]. Rather than using exhaustive search, an evolutionary optimization methodology is used in [4] to choose the optimal CSS, which still needs to train the recovery method for multiple times and results in high time complexity.

Through experiments, we have found that the performance of our CNN-based recovery method is dependent on the CSS as well. This motivates us to develop a CNN-based CSS selection method with a single training process, which can jointly work with our HSI recovery method and have low time complexity. In this work, we propose a novel CSS selection layer, which can automatically determine the optimal CSS from the network weights under nonnegative sparse constraint. As illustrated in Fig. 1, this filter selection layer is appended to the recovery network, which jointly selects the proper CSS and learns the mapping for HSI recovery from a single RGB image captured with the algorithmically selected CSS. Experiment results show that the selection layer always gives a CSS that is consistent with the best one determined by exhaustive search. The spectral recovery accuracy can be further boosted by this optimal CSS, compared with using a casually selected CSS. To the best of our knowledge, this work is the first to integrate optimal CSS selection with HSI recovery via a unified CNN-based framework, which boosts HSI recovery fidelity and has much lower complexity.

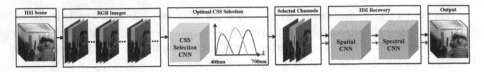

Fig. 1. Overview of the proposed method, which combines optimal CSS selection and HSI recovery into a unified CNN-based framework. The parameters for these two aspects are jointly learned first. Then, the RGB images are captured under the selected optimal CSS as the inputs and the underlying HSIs are reconstructed by using the HSI recovery network. The black arrow shows the training process and the red arrow denotes the testing process. (Color figure online)

Our main contributions are that we

- Design a CNN-based HSI recovery network to account for spectral nonlinear mapping and utilize spatial similarity in the image plane domain;
- Develop a CSS selection layer to retrieve the optimal CSS on the basis of the nonnegative sparse constraint onto the weight factors;
- Jointly determine the optimal CSS and learn an accurate HSI recovery mapping in a single training process.

2   Related Work

Hyperspectral imaging can effectively provide discriminative spectral information of the scene. To obtain HSIs, whiskbroom and pushbroom style scanning systems [5,41] are widely used to capture the scene pointwisely or linewisely. RGB or monochromatic cameras with variant filters [9,10,51] or specific illuminations [19,40] were also used to capture the HSI. But all these methods scanning along the spatial or spectral dimension result in low temporal resolution. To capture dynamic scenes, snapshot hyperspectral cameras [8,14–16] were developed to capture full 3D HSIs, but they sacrificed spatial resolution.

To obtain high-resolution HSIs in real time, some coding-based hyperspectral imaging approaches have been presented, relying on the compressive sensing (CS) theory. CASSI [17,44] employed a coding aperture with the disperser to uniformly encode the spectral signals into 2D space. DCCHI [45,46] incorporated a co-located panchromatic camera to collect more information simultaneously with the CASSI measurement. SSCSI [33] jointly encoded the spatial and spectral dimensions in a single gray image. Besides, fusion-based approaches [1,11,12,25,31,32,35] were presented. These approaches were based on a hybrid camera system, in which a low spatial resolution hyperspectral camera and a high spatial resolution RGB camera were mounted in a coaxial system. The captured two images could be fused into a high resolution HSI, which has the same spatial resolution as the RGB image and same spectral resolution as the input HSI. All these coding-based and fusion-based hyperspectral imaging systems demand either high precision optical design or expensive hyperspectral camera.

To avoid using the above mentioned specialized devices, i.e. multiple illuminations, filters, coding aperture and hyperspectral cameras, HSI recovery from a single RGB image has attracted more attention. The spectral recovery from three values provided by the RGB camera arouses a three-to-many mapping, which is severely underdetermined in general.

To unambiguously determine the spectrum, some prior knowledge on the mapping is introduced. Nguyen *et al.* [38] learned the mapping between white balanced RGB values and illumination-free spectral signals based on a radial basis function network. Arad and Ben-Shahar [3] built a large hyperspectral dataset for natural scenes, and derived the mapping between hyperspectral signatures and their RGB values under a dictionary learned by K-SVD. Robles-Kelly [42] reconstructed the illumination-free HSI based on a constrained sparse coding approach by using a set of prototypes extracted from the training set. Jia *et al.* [22] proposed a two-step manifold-based mapping method, which highlighted the role of nonlinear mapping in spectral recovery. In this work, we present a spectral CNN module to better account for spectral nonlinear mapping, and a spatial CNN module to further incorporate the spatial similarity.

Arad and Ben-Shahar [4] first recognized that the quality of HSI recovery from a single RGB image was sensitive to the CSS selection. To avoid the heavy computational cost of exhaustive search, they proposed an evolutionary optimization based selection strategy. However, the training has still to be conducted multiple times under different CSS instances. In this work, we propose a CSS selection layer under the nonnegative sparse constraint, and jointly select the optimal CSS and learn the mapping for HSI recovery via a unified CNN-based framework. This can be achieved in only one training process, in contrast to repeated training operations in [4].

3   Joint Optimal CSS Selection and HSI Recovery

In this section, we present a CNN-based method for simultaneous optimal CSS selection and HSI recovery from a single RGB image. The overall framework of the proposed method is shown in Fig. 1. In the training stage, given a large set of CSS functions and HSIs, we first synthesize multiple RGB images for each HSI under variant CSS functions, which are the input of the network. The designed optimal CSS selection network is utilized to select the best CSS and the corresponding RGB channels. In the HSI recovery network, we design a spectral CNN to approximate the complex nonlinear mapping between the RGB space and the spectra space, and a spatial CNN for the spatial similarity. The CSS selection network and the spectral recovery network are combined to recover the HSI, which should be close enough to its corresponding HSI in the training dataset. In the testing stage, the input RGB image is obtained under the selected CSS. A HSI will be obtained by feeding this input RGB image into the recovery network, which has been learned in the training stage.

In the following, we first describe the motivation of our network structure by digesting common approaches for HSI recovery from a single RGB image. Then, we introduce our CNN-based method for both HSI recovery and optimal CSS selection. Finally, the learning detail is provided.

3.1 Preliminaries and Motivation

Let $\mathbf{Y} \in \mathbb{R}^{3 \times M}$ and $\mathbf{X} \in \mathbb{R}^{B \times M}$ denote the input RGB image and the recovered HSI, where M and B are the number of pixels and bands in the HSI. The relationship between $\mathbf{Y}$ and $\mathbf{X}$ can be described as

$$\mathbf{Y} = \mathbf{CX}, \tag{1}$$

where $\mathbf{C} \in \mathbb{R}^{3 \times B}$ denotes the RGB CSS function.

Most state-of-the-art methods assume that the CSS function is known and model HSI recovery from a single RGB image as

$$E(\mathbf{X}) = E_d(\mathbf{X}, \mathbf{Y}) + \lambda E_s(\mathbf{X}), \tag{2}$$

where the first term $E_d(\mathbf{X}, \mathbf{Y})$ is the data term, and it guarantees that the recovered $\mathbf{X}$ should be projected to $\mathbf{Y}$ under the CSS function $\mathbf{C}$. The second term $E_s(\mathbf{X})$ is the prior regularization for $\mathbf{X}$.

The models for the first term in the previous works [3,22,38,42] can be generally described as

$$E_d(\mathbf{X}, \mathbf{Y}) = \|f_d(\mathbf{X}) - \mathbf{Y}\|_F^2. \tag{3}$$

where the function f_d is linear mapping for [3,42] and spectral nonlinear mapping for [22,38]. [22] shows that the nonlinear mapping can effectively assist HSI recovery, compared with the linear constraint in [3].

In addition, [3,42] assume that the spectra can be sparsely described by several bases, which means

$$E_s(\mathbf{X}) = \|\mathbf{D}\boldsymbol{\alpha} - \mathbf{X}\|_F^2 + \|\boldsymbol{\alpha}\|_1, \tag{4}$$

where $\mathbf{D}$ is the learned spectral dictionary and $\boldsymbol{\alpha}$ is the corresponding spectral sparse coefficient. [38] and [22] implicitly assume that the spectral information lies in a low dimensional space in the model.

Furthermore, since the neighboring pixels in the recovered HSI $\mathbf{X}$ should be similar, [42] also has the spatial constraint as

$$E_s(\mathbf{X}) = \|f_s(\mathbf{X})\|_F^2, \tag{5}$$

where the function f_s denotes the local spatial operation.

According to these analyzes, we present a CNN-based HSI recovery method from a single RGB image, which can effectively learn the nonlinear spectral mapping and the spatial structure information to improve the recovered HSI.

Besides, from Eq. (1), we can see that the quality of recovered HSI $\mathbf{X}$ is influenced by both the input RGB image $\mathbf{Y}$ and the CSS function $\mathbf{C}$. Meanwhile, [4] shows that the selection of CSS significantly affects the quality of HSI recovery. To boost the accuracy of recovered HSI, it is essential to select the optimal CSS as well. Therefore, our method models the optimal CSS selection and the HSI recovery via a unified CNN-based framework.

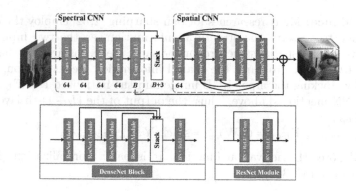

Fig. 2. The architecture of CNN-based HSI recovery from a single RGB image.

3.2 HSI Recovery

Previous works have shown that effectively exploiting the underlying characteristics of the HSI—spectral nonlinear mapping [22,38] and spatial similarity [42]—can reconstruct high quality HSI from a single RGB image. Compared with these approaches, our method utilizes multiple CNN layers in spectral CNN to deeply learn the nonlinear mapping between spectra and RGB space, and employs DenseNet blocks [21] and ResNet modules [20] in the spatial CNN to enlarge the receptive field and obtain more spatial similarity in the space domain. Besides, our method uses the input RGB image to further guide the HSI recovery and residual learning to preserve the spatial structure. Figure 2 shows the HSI recovery network.

Spectral CNN. Previous works for the spectral recovery from a single RGB image [3,22,38,42] mainly consider the spectral mapping between the input RGB image and the recovered HSI. It is well-known that CNN can effectively learn the nonlinear mapping. Thus, we design a spectral CNN to learn the spectral nonlinear mapping between the RGB values and the corresponding spectrum, which consists of L layers. The output of the l-th layer is expressed as

$$\mathbf{F}_l = \text{ReLU}(\mathbf{W}_l * \mathbf{F}_{l-1} + \boldsymbol{b}_l), \quad \text{where} \quad \mathbf{F}_0 = \mathbf{Y}, \tag{6}$$

where $\text{ReLU}(x) = \max\{x, 0\}$, denoting a rectified linear unit [36]. $\mathbf{W}_l$ and $\boldsymbol{b}_l$ represent the filters and biases for the l-th layer, respectively. For the first layer, we compute a_0 feature maps using an $s_1 \times s_1$ receptive field, where $a_0 = 64$ in our network. Filters are of size $3 \times s_1 \times s_1 \times a_0$, when the input is an RGB image. In the 2-nd to $(L-1)$-th layers, we also compute a_0 feature maps using an $s_1 \times s_1$ receptive field and a rectified linear unit. The filters are of size $a_0 \times s_1 \times s_1 \times a_0$. Finally, the last layer uses the same receptive field and the filters are of size $a_0 \times s_1 \times s_1 \times B$. In the experiments, we set $L = 5$.

To perform the spectral nonlinear mapping, $s_1 = 1$ and the receptive field is 1×1 in the spatial domain. It implies that only the spectral nonlinear mapping is learned without any spatial structure.

RGB Guidance. Many researches for pan-sharping [2,52] employ the panchromatic image to preserve the structural information, as the two input images should have similar spatial structure for the same scene. Inspired by this, we use the input RGB image to guide the spatial information reconstruction, which is modeled by stacking the input RGB image and the initialized HSI $\mathbf{F}_L$ from the spectral CNN mentioned above. Thus, the output of the $(L+1)$-th layer can be expressed as

$$\mathbf{F}_{L+1} = \mathcal{C}(\mathbf{W}_{L+1} * \text{stack}(\mathbf{Y}, \mathbf{F}_L) + \boldsymbol{b}_{L+1}), \tag{7}$$

where $\mathcal{C}$ denotes the activation function. It is batch normalization (BN) [34] followed by a ReLU [36].

Spatial CNN. Due to abundant self-repeating patterns in natural images [7,13], the spatial information is usually similar in the neighboring area. To effectively exploit the spatial similarity, we need to obtain abundant spatial correlation in much larger area, which can be carried out by using several DenseNet blocks [21]. We employ N DenseNet blocks into the designed network, and the output of the n-th DenseNet block can be expressed as

$$\mathbf{S}_n = \mathcal{D}_n(\text{stack}(\mathbf{S}_0, \cdots, \mathbf{S}_{n-1})), \quad \text{where} \quad \mathbf{S}_0 = \mathbf{F}_{L+1}, \tag{8}$$

where $\mathcal{D}_n$ denotes the n-th DenseNet block function.

In each DenseNet block, there are K ResNet modules [20]. For the n-th DenseNet block, the input is $\mathbf{S}_{n-1}$ and the k-th ResNet module can be expressed as

$$\mathbf{H}_n^k = \mathcal{R}_n(\mathbf{H}_n^{k-1}) + \mathbf{H}_n^{k-1}, \quad \text{where} \quad \mathbf{H}_n^0 = \mathbf{S}_{n-1}. \tag{9}$$

In our spatial CNN, we set $N = 4$ and $K = 4$.

In addition, since the spatial structural information mainly exists in the high-pass components, we employ the residual learning to efficiently reconstruct detail information like [27]. Thus, the final output can be described as

$$\hat{\mathbf{X}} = \mathbf{S}_N + \mathbf{F}_L. \tag{10}$$

3.3 Optimal CSS Selection

Previous work [4] shows that the quality of HSI recovery is sensitive to the CSS used to generate the input RGB image. As will be shown in Sect. 4.3, we perform our HSI recovery method by using the synthetic RGB images under different CSS functions in a brute force way. From Fig. 5, we can see that the accuracy of HSI recovery has about 10%–25% difference. It means that properly choosing a CSS will contribute to the HSI recovery accuracy as well. The exhaustive search method and the evolutionary optimization method in [4] are not appropriate for our CNN-based HSI recovery method, since they need to train the HSI recovery network multiple times, which is extremely slow. Thus, we propose to design a selection convolution layer to retrieve the optimal CSS, which only needs to train once and has much lower time complexity.

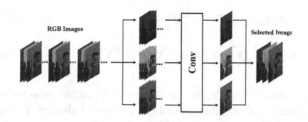

Fig. 3. The illustration of the optimal CSS selection.

To select the optimal CSS function, RGB images for each HSI are first synthesized with all CSS functions in a candidate dataset. Let $\mathbf{C}_j$ $(j = 1, \cdots, J)$ denote the j-th CSS function. Each synthetic RGB image via the j-th CSS function and the t-th HSI in the training dataset can be described as

$$\mathbf{Y}_{j,t} = \mathbf{C}_j \mathbf{X}_t. \tag{11}$$

Thus, for each scene, the input RGB images are obtained by stacking all RGB images under different CSS functions, i.e.,

$$\mathcal{Y}_t = \text{stack}(\mathbf{Y}_{1,t}, \cdots, \mathbf{Y}_{j,t}, \cdots, \mathbf{Y}_{J,t}). \tag{12}$$

Since our work mainly focuses on the HSI recovery from a single RGB image, we will select a CSS from an existing camera, without considering the combination of channels from different cameras. Note that the simulated RGB image cannot be negative, so the weight to select CSS should be nonnegative. To correctly localize the promising CSS, we further add a sparsity constraint. Thus, we design a convolution layer for the optimal CSS selection, which acts as the largest weight learned in the network under the nonnegative sparse constraint. To enforce the nonnegative constraint, the weights in this convolution layer for CSS selection are set to be positive. As for the sparse constraint, the weights are learned under the sparsity promoting l_1-norm.

The optimal CSS selection is equivalent to an RGB image selection in $\mathcal{Y}_t$, which is synthesized with the selected optimal CSS. As shown in Fig. 3, we first separate RGB bands into three branches, which share the same convolution filter $\mathbf{V}$. The size of this filter is $J \times 1 \times 1 \times a_1$, where $a_1 = 1$ is the number of the output band for each branch. Thus, the output of this optimal CSS selection network can be expressed as

$$\hat{\mathbf{Y}}_t = \text{stack}(\mathbf{V} * \mathcal{Y}_t(R), \mathbf{V} * \mathcal{Y}_t(G), \mathbf{V} * \mathcal{Y}_t(B)), \tag{13}$$

where $\mathcal{Y}_t(R)$, $\mathcal{Y}_t(G)$, and $\mathcal{Y}_t(B)$ denote all the red, green, and blue channels in $\mathcal{Y}_t$, respectively.

The values in $\mathbf{V}$ can be determined by minimizing the mean squared error (MSE) under the nonnegative sparse constraint between the selected RGB image

$\hat{\mathbf{Y}}$ and the corresponding ground truth image

$$\mathcal{L}_c(\mathbf{V}) = \frac{1}{T}\sum_{t=1}^{T}\|\hat{\mathbf{Y}}_t(\mathbf{V}) - \mathbf{Y}_t\|^2 + \|\mathbf{V}\|_1, \quad s.t. \quad \mathbf{V} \geq 0, \tag{14}$$

where $\hat{\mathbf{Y}}_t$ is the t-th output, $\mathbf{Y}_t$ is the t-th corresponding selected optimal CSS, and T is the number of training samples. A larger value in $\mathbf{V}$ represents that its corresponding CSS is better for HSI recovery. Consequently, the CSS corresponding to the largest value in $\mathbf{V}$ is selected as the optimal CSS.

3.4 Learning Details

The parameters for the HSI recovery network are denoted as $\mathbf{\Theta}$, and can be achieved by minimizing the MSE between the reconstructed HSI $\hat{\mathbf{X}}$ and the corresponding ground truth image,

$$\mathcal{L}_s(\mathbf{\Theta}) = \frac{1}{T}\sum_{t=1}^{T}\|\hat{\mathbf{X}}_t(\hat{\mathbf{Y}}_t, \mathbf{\Theta}) - \mathbf{X}_t\|^2 + \|\mathbf{\Theta}\|_2^2, \tag{15}$$

where $\hat{\mathbf{X}}_t$ is the t-th output, $\mathbf{X}_t$ is the corresponding ground truth, and $\hat{\mathbf{Y}}_t$ is the corresponding selected RGB image by the CSS selection network.

In our method, since the output of CSS selection network in Eq. (14) is the input of HSI recovery network, it depends on the HSI recovery network training. Thus, we first append the optimal CSS selection network onto the HSI recovery network to select the optimal CSS and learn the mapping for spectral recovery together. In this joint training phase, we train the entire network by minimizing the loss

$$\mathcal{L} = \mathcal{L}_c(\mathbf{V}) + \tau\mathcal{L}_s(\mathbf{\Theta}), \tag{16}$$

where τ is a predefined parameter. Please note that $\mathbf{Y}_t$ needs not to be explicitly labeled in this joint training process, and thus $\|\hat{\mathbf{Y}}_t(\mathbf{V}) - \mathbf{Y}_t\|^2$ can be ignored in Eq. (14). Then, the CSS corresponding to the largest value in $\mathbf{V}$ is selected as the optimal CSS, which is used to synthesize RGB images. These synthetic RGB images act as the input of the recovery network to recover HSIs.

The loss is minimized with the adaptive moment estimation method [29]. For all designed network modules, we set the mini-batch size to 16, momentum parameter to 0.9, and weight decay to 10^{-4}. To fit the nonnegative constraint for the optimal CSS selection, its convolution layer's weights are initialized as random positive numbers and all negative weights are set to zero during the forward and backward propagation. In the HSI recovery network, all convolution layer's weights are initialized by the method in [18]. The network has been trained with the deep learning tool Caffe [23] on a NVIDIA Titan X GPU.

4   Experimental Results

In the following, we will first introduce the datasets used for training and testing of all methods, and the metrics for quantitative evaluation. Then, we compare our method with several state-of-the-art HSI recovery methods under a typical CSS. In addition, the effectiveness of our optimal CSS selection method is evaluated on two CSS datasets.

4.1 Datasets and Metrics

We evaluate our joint CSS selection and CNN-based HSI recovery from a single RGB image on three public hyperspectral datasets, including the ICVL dataset [3], the NUS dataset [38], and the Harvard dataset [9]. The ICVL dataset consists of 201 images, which is by far the most comprehensive natural hyperspectral dataset. We randomly select 101 images in this dataset for training and use the rest for testing. The NUS dataset contains 41 HSIs in the training set and 25 HSIs in the testing set. The Harvard dataset consists of 50 outdoor images captured under daylight illumination. We remove those 6 images with strong highlights, and randomly use 35 images for training and 9 images for testing. All HSIs in these datasets have 31 bands. Two CSS datasets are used to evaluate the optimal CSS selection. The first dataset [24] contains 28 CSS curves and the second dataset [26] contains 12 CSS curves. Both datasets cover different camera types and brands.

We uniformly extract the patch pairs from each HSI and its corresponding RGB images under variant CSS functions with the size of 64×64 and the stride of 61. We randomly select 90% pairs for training and 10% pairs for validation. The RGB patches are regarded as the network's input and the HSI patches are regarded as the ground truth.

Three image quality metrics are utilized to evaluate the performance of all methods, including root-mean-square error (RMSE), structural similarity (SSIM) [47], and spectral angle mapping (SAM) [30]. RMSE and SSIM are calculated on each 2D spatial image, which measure the spatial fidelity between the recovered HSI and the ground truth. SAM is calculated on the 1D spectral vector, which shows the spectral fidelity. Smaller values of RMSE and SAM suggest better performance, while a larger value of SSIM implies better performance.

4.2 Evaluation on HSI Recovery

Here, we first compare our CNN-based HSI recovery method with three state-of-the-art HSI recovery methods from a single RGB image under the known CSS, including radial basis function network based method (RBF) [38], the sparse representation based method (SR) [3], and manifold-based mapping (MM) [22]. The original HSIs in datasets serve as ground truth. To fairly compare with these methods, we use the CSS function of Canon 5D Mark II to synthesize RGB values, which is the same as [22].

Table 1 provides the average results over all HSIs in the testing sets from three HSI datasets, for quantitative comparison of RBF, SR, MM and our method. The best results are highlighted in bold. We observe that MM [22] outperforms the other two methods. The reason is that MM effectively approximates the spectral nonlinear mapping between the RGB values and spectral signatures, compared

Table 1. RMSE, SSIM, and SAM results for different HSI recovery methods on there HSI datasets.

Dataset	Metrics	RBF	SR	MM	Ours
ICVL	RMSE	7.7152	3.0223	2.1245	**1.3533**
	SSIM	0.9546	0.9582	0.9946	**0.9975**
	SAM	0.1419	0.0645	0.0470	**0.0277**
NUS	RMSE	14.8785	8.9766	6.1825	**5.2426**
	SSIM	0.8648	0.8701	0.9555	**0.9649**
	SAM	0.3239	0.2358	0.2114	**0.1712**
Harvard	RMSE	11.8101	4.9534	4.9616	**2.1923**
	SSIM	0.9539	0.9126	0.9541	**0.9924**
	SAM	0.1723	0.1848	0.2273	**0.0956**

Table 2. Time complexity for different HSI recovery methods. (Unit: second)

Size	RBF	SR	MM	Ours(CPU)	Ours(GPU)
$256 \times 256 \times 31$	0.20	2.08	4.13	18.94	**0.09**
$512 \times 512 \times 31$	0.69	8.38	16.27	75.87	**0.36**
$1024 \times 1024 \times 31$	2.55	33.36	65.67	299.04	**1.58**

with RBF and SR. This demonstrates that the spectral nonlinear mapping is much relevant for HSI recovery from a single RGB image. Our method provides substantial improvements over all these methods, in terms of RMSE, SSIM and SAM. This reveals the advantages of deeply exploiting the intrinsic properties of HSIs and verifies the effectiveness of our HSI recovery network.

To visualize the experimental results for all methods, several representative recovered HSIs and the corresponding recovered spectral errors on three datasets are shown in Fig. 4. The ground truth, our results, error images for RBF/SR/MM/our methods, and RMSE results along spectra for all methods are shown from top to bottom. The ground truth and our results are the 16-th band for all scenes. The error images are the average absolution errors between the ground truth and the recovered results across spectra. We can observe that the recovered images from our method are consistently more accurate for all scenes, which verifies that our method can provide higher spatial accuracy. The RMSE results along spectra for all methods show that the results of our method are much closer to the ground truth than other compared methods along spectra, which demonstrates that our approach obtains higher spectral fidelity.

The average testing time among 10 independent trials for HSIs with different sizes of all compared methods is included in Table 2. All results performed on an Intel Core i7-6800K CPU are provided. We can see that our method have higher time complexity on CPU, yet the running time on GPU is much shorter.

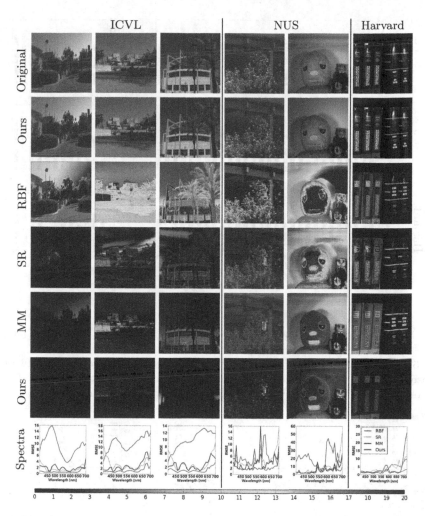

Fig. 4. Visual quality comparison on six typical scenes in HSI datasets. The ground truth, recovered HSI by our method, the error map for RBF/SR/MM/our results, and RMSE results along spectra for all methods are shown from top to bottom.

Compared with the other methods, our method on GPU can reconstruct HSIs more than 10 frames per second for size of $256 \times 256 \times 31$.

4.3 Evaluation on CSS Selection

To evaluate the effect of CSS functions in our spectral recovery network, we have conducted experiments to evaluate the performance of HSI recovery on both CSS datasets [24, 26]. First, we perform all methods on the synthetic RGB images by different CSS functions in a brute force way. As shown in Fig. 5, we can indeed observe that our method is also dependent on the CSS selection. In

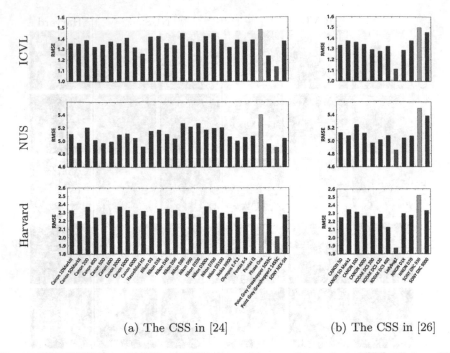

(a) The CSS in [24]   (b) The CSS in [26]

Fig. 5. The RMSE results of our HSI recovery network on three HSI and two CSS datasets. The red and green bars indicate the best and worst CSS functions for the HSI recovery in a brute force way, respectively. (Color figure online)

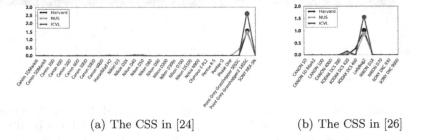

(a) The CSS in [24]   (b) The CSS in [26]

Fig. 6. The selected optimal CSS by our method on three HSI datasets.

spite of that, our method is still superior even with an improper CSS. To obtain an optimal CSS for improved HSI recovery by training once, our method uses a convolutional layer to select the optimal CSS. In Fig. 6, we can see that our method can effectively select the optimal CSS, which is consistent with the best one determined by exhaustive search. In addition, the selected CSS keeps the same for all three HSI dataset, which seems to indicate that this CSS properly encodes the intrinsic spectral information of the physical world.

Figure 7 shows the HSI recovery results of a typical scene under different CSS functions. The recovered HSIs under the worst/middle/best CSS functions in [24]

| Worst | Middle | Best | Worst | Middle | Best |

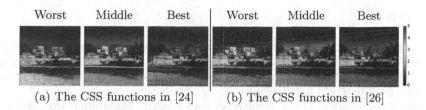

(a) The CSS functions in [24]   (b) The CSS functions in [26]

Fig. 7. Visual quality comparison under different CSS functions on a typical scene. The recovered HSIs under the worst/middle/best CSS functions in [24] and [26] are shown in (a) and (b), respectively.

and [26] in terms of Fig. 5 are shown in (a) and (b), respectively. We can see that the results under the selected optimal CSS are much close to the ground truth, which further demonstrates the effectiveness of joint optimal CSS selection and the accuracy of the learned CNN nonlinear mapping in HSI recovery.

5   Conclusion

In this paper, we have presented an effective CNN-based method to jointly select the optimal camera spectral sensitivity function and learn an accurate mapping to reconstruct hyperspectral image from an RGB image. We first propose a spectral recovery network with properly designed modules to account for the underlying characteristics of the HSI, including spectral nonlinear mapping and spatial similarity. Meanwhile, a camera spectral sensitivity selection layer is developed to append onto the recovery network, which can automatically retrieve the optimal sensitivity functions by using the nonnegative sparse constraint. Experimental results show that our method can provide substantial improvements over the current state-of-the-art methods in terms of both objective metric and subjective visual quality.

Our current network selects the optimal sensitivity from off-the-shelf cameras. Therefore, there is no need to produce a new filter array, which is known to be extremely expensive. However, filter array makers are indeed able to produce novel filter arrays, which might be better for this spectral recovery task than all existing RGB cameras. It is thus worth investigating the limitations of current filter manufacturing techniques and exploring how to incorporate these limitations in a more relaxed filter response designing (rather than selection) process.

Acknowledgments. This work was supported by the National Natural Science Foundation of China under Grants No. 61425013 and No. 61672096.

References

1. Akhtar, N., Shafait, F., Mian, A.: Sparse spatio-spectral representation for hyperspectral image super-resolution. In: Fleet, D., Pajdla, T., Schiele, B., Tuytelaars, T. (eds.) ECCV 2014. LNCS, vol. 8695, pp. 63–78. Springer, Cham (2014). https://doi.org/10.1007/978-3-319-10584-0_5
2. Aly, H.A., Sharma, G.: A regularized model-based optimization framework for pan-sharpening. IEEE Trans. Image Process. **23**(6), 2596–2608 (2014)
3. Arad, B., Ben-Shahar, O.: Sparse recovery of hyperspectral signal from natural RGB images. In: Leibe, B., Matas, J., Sebe, N., Welling, M. (eds.) ECCV 2016. LNCS, vol. 9911, pp. 19–34. Springer, Cham (2016). https://doi.org/10.1007/978-3-319-46478-7_2
4. Arad, B., Ben-Shahar, O.: Filter selection for hyperspectral estimation. In: Proceedings of International Conference on Computer Vision (ICCV), pp. 3172–3180, October 2017
5. Basedow, R.W., Carmer, D.C., Anderson, M.E.: HYDICE system: implementation and performance. In: SPIE's Symposium on OE/Aerospace Sensing and Dual Use Photonics, pp. 258–267 (1995)
6. Bioucas-Dias, J.M., Plaza, A., Camps-Valls, G., Scheunders, P., Nasrabadi, N.M., Chanussot, J.: Hyperspectral remote sensing data analysis and future challenges. IEEE Geosci. Remote Sens. Mag. **1**(2), 6–36 (2013)
7. Buades, A., Coll, B., Morel, J.M.: A non-local algorithm for image denoising. In: Proceedings of IEEE Conference on Computer Vision and Pattern Recognition (CVPR), vol. 2, pp. 60–65, June 2005
8. Cao, X., Du, H., Tong, X., Dai, Q., Lin, S.: A prism-based system for multispectral bideo acquisition. IEEE Trans. Pattern Anal. Mach. Intell. (PAMI) **33**(12), 2423–2435 (2011)
9. Chakrabarti, A., Zickler, T.: Statistics of real-world hyperspectral images. In: Proceedings of IEEE Conference on Computer Vision and Pattern Recognition (CVPR), pp. 193–200, June 2011
10. Chi, C., Yoo, H., Ben-Ezra, M.: Multi-spectral imaging by optimized wide band illumination. Int. J. Comput. Vis. (IJCV) **86**(2–3), 140–151 (2010)
11. Dian, R., Fang, L., Li, S.: Hyperspectral image super-resolution via non-local sparse tensor factorization. In: Proceedings of IEEE Conference on Computer Vision and Pattern Recognition (CVPR), pp. 5344–5353, June 2017
12. Dong, W., et al.: Hyperspectral image super-resolution via non-negative structured sparse representation. IEEE Trans. Image Process. **25**(5), 2337–2352 (2016)
13. Dong, W., Zhang, L., Shi, G.: Centralized sparse representation for image restoration. In: Proceedings of International Conference on Computer Vision (ICCV), pp. 1259–1266, November 2011
14. Ford, B.K., Descour, M.R., Lynch, R.M.: Large-image-format computed tomography imaging spectrometer for fluorescence microscopy. Opt. Express **9**(9), 444–453 (2001)
15. Gao, L., Kester, R.T., Hagen, N., Tkaczyk, T.S.: Snapshot image mapping spectrometer (IMS) with high sampling density for hyperspectral microscopy. Opt. Express **18**(14), 14330–14344 (2010)
16. Gat, N., Scriven, G., Garman, J., Li, M.D., Zhang, J.: Development of four-dimensional imaging spectrometers (4D-IS). In: Proceeding of SPIE Optics + Photonics, vol. 6302, pp. 63020M–63020M-11 (2006)

17. Gehm, M.E., John, R., Brady, D.J., Willett, R.M., Schulz, T.J.: Single-shot compressive spectral imaging with a dual-disperser architecture. Opt. Express **15**(21), 14013–27 (2007)
18. Glorot, X., Bengio, Y.: Understanding the difficulty of training deep feedforward neural networks. In: Proceedings of International Conference on Artificial Intelligence and Statistics, pp. 249–256, May 2010
19. Han, S., Sato, I., Okabe, T., Sato, Y.: Fast spectral reflectance recovery using DLP projector. Int. J. Comput. Vis. (IJCV) **110**(2), 172–184 (2014)
20. He, K., Zhang, X., Ren, S., Sun, J.: Identity mappings in deep residual networks. In: Leibe, B., Matas, J., Sebe, N., Welling, M. (eds.) ECCV 2016. LNCS, vol. 9908, pp. 630–645. Springer, Cham (2016). https://doi.org/10.1007/978-3-319-46493-0_38
21. Huang, G., Liu, Z., van der Maaten, L., Weinberger, K.Q.: Densely connected convolutional networks. In: Proceedings of IEEE Conference on Computer Vision and Pattern Recognition (CVPR), pp. 2261–2269, July 2017
22. Jia, Y., et al.: From RGB to spectrum for natural scenes via manifold-based mapping. In: Proceedings of International Conference on Computer Vision (ICCV), pp. 4715–4723, October 2017
23. Jia, Y., et al.: Caffe: convolutional architecture for fast feature embedding. In: Proceedings of ACM Multimedia Conference (MM), pp. 675–678, November 2014
24. Jiang, J., Liu, D., Gu, J., Süsstrunk, S.: What is the space of spectral sensitivity functions for digital color cameras? In: IEEE Workshop on Applications of Computer Vision (WACV), pp. 168–179 (2013)
25. Kawakami, R., Wright, J., Tai, Y.W., Matsushita, Y., Ben-Ezra, M., Ikeuchi, K.: High-resolution hyperspectral imaging via matrix factorization. In: Proceedings of IEEE Conference on Computer Vision and Pattern Recognition (CVPR), pp. 2329–2336, June 2011
26. Kawakami, R., Zhao, H., Tan, R.T., Ikeuchi, K.: Camera spectral sensitivity and white balance estimation from sky images. Int. J. Comput. Vis. (IJCV) **105**(3), 187–204 (2013)
27. Kim, J., Lee, J.K., Lee, K.M.: Accurate image super-resolution using very deep convolutional networks. In: Proceedings of IEEE Conference on Computer Vision and Pattern Recognition (CVPR), pp. 1646–1654, June 2016
28. Kim, S.J., Deng, F., Brown, M.S.: Visual enhancement of old documents with hyperspectral imaging. Pattern Recogn. **44**(7), 1461–1469 (2011)
29. Kingma, D.P., Ba, J.L.: Adam: a method for stochastic optimization. In: Proceedings of International Conference on Learning Representations (ICLR), May 2015
30. Kruse, F.A., et al.: The spectral image processing system (SIPS)-interactive visualization and analysis of imaging spectrometer data. Remote Sens. Environ. **44**(2–3), 145–163 (1993)
31. Kwon, H., Tai, Y.W.: RGB-guided hyperspectral image upsampling. In: Proceedings of International Conference on Computer Vision (ICCV), pp. 307–315, December 2015
32. Lanaras, C., Baltsavias, E., Schindler, K.: Hyperspectral super-resolution by coupled spectral unmixing. In: Proceedings of International Conference on Computer Vision (ICCV), pp. 3586–3594, December 2015
33. Lin, X., Liu, Y., Wu, J., Dai, Q.: Spatial-spectral encoded compressive hyperspectral imaging. ACM Trans. Graph. **33**(6), 233:1–233:11 (2014). (Proceedings of SIGGRAPH Asia)
34. Ioffe, S., Szegedy, C.: Batch normalization: accelerating deep network training by reducing internal covariate shift. In: Proceedings of International Conference on Machine Learning (ICML), pp. 448–456, June 2015

35. Ma, C., Cao, X., Tong, X., Dai, Q., Lin, S.: Acquisition of high spatial and spectral resolution video with a hybrid camera system. Int. J. Comput. Vis. (IJCV) **110**(2), 141–155 (2014)
36. Nair, V., Hinton, G.E.: Rectified linear units improve restricted Boltzmann machines. In: Proceedings of International Conference on Machine Learning (ICML), pp. 807–814, June 2010
37. Nguyen, H.V., Banerjee, A., Chellappa, R.: Tracking via object reflectance using a hyperspectral video camera. In: IEEE Conference on Computer Vision and Pattern Recognition - Workshops, pp. 44–51, June 2010
38. Nguyen, R.M.H., Prasad, D.K., Brown, M.S.: Training-based spectral reconstruction from a single RGB image. In: Fleet, D., Pajdla, T., Schiele, B., Tuytelaars, T. (eds.) ECCV 2014. LNCS, vol. 8695, pp. 186–201. Springer, Cham (2014). https://doi.org/10.1007/978-3-319-10584-0_13
39. Pan, Z., Healey, G., Prasad, M., Tromberg, B.: Face recognition in hyperspectral images. IEEE Trans. Pattern Anal. Mach. Intell. (PAMI) **25**(12), 1552–1560 (2003)
40. Park, J.I., Lee, M.H., Grossberg, M.D., Nayar, S.K.: Multispectral imaging using multiplexed illumination. In: Proceedings of International Conference on Computer Vision (ICCV), pp. 1–8, October 2007
41. Porter, W.M., Enmark, H.T.: A system overview of the airborne visible/infrared imaging spectrometer (AVIRIS). In: Annual Technical Symposium, pp. 22–31 (1987)
42. Robles-Kelly, A.: Single image spectral reconstruction for multimedia applications. In: Proceedings of ACM Multimedia Conference (MM), pp. 251–260, October 2015
43. Tarabalka, Y., Chanussot, J., Benediktsson, J.A.: Segmentation and classification of hyperspectral images using watershed transformation. Pattern Recogn. **43**(7), 2367–2379 (2010)
44. Wagadarikar, A., John, R., Willett, R., Brady, D.: Single disperser design for coded aperture snapshot spectral imaging. Appl. Opt. **47**(10), 44–51 (2008)
45. Wang, L., Xiong, Z., Gao, D., Shi, G., Wu, F.: Dual-camera design for coded aperture snapshot spectral imaging. Appl. Opt. **54**(4), 848–858 (2015)
46. Wang, L., Xiong, Z., Shi, G., Wu, F., Zeng, W.: Adaptive nonlocal sparse representation for dual-camera compressive hyperspectral imaging. IEEE Trans. Pattern Anal. Mach. Intell. (PAMI) **39**(10), 2104–2111 (2017)
47. Wang, Z., Bovik, A., Sheikh, H., Simoncelli, E.: Image quality assessment: from error visibility to structural similarity. IEEE Trans. Image Process. **13**(4), 600–612 (2004)
48. Wu, D., Sun, D.W.: Advanced applications of hyperspectral imaging technology for food quality and safety analysis and assessment: a reviewpart I: fundamentals. Innov. Food Sci. Emerg. Technol. **19**, 1–14 (2013)
49. Xu, X., Li, J., Huang, X., Dalla Mura, M., Plaza, A.: Multiple morphological component analysis based decomposition for remote sensing image classification. IEEE Trans. Geosci. Remote Sens. **54**(5), 3083–3102 (2016)
50. Xu, X., Wu, Z., Li, J., Plaza, A., Wei, Z.: Anomaly detection in hyperspectral images based on low-rank and sparse representation. IEEE Trans. Geosci. Remote Sens. **54**(4), 1990–2000 (2016)
51. Yamaguchi, M., et al.: High-fidelity video and still-image communication based on spectral information: natural vision system and its applications. In: Electronic Imaging, pp. 60620G–60620G-12 (2006)
52. Yang, J., Fu, X., Hu, Y., Huang, Y., Ding, X., John, P.: PanNet: a deep network architecture for pan-sharpening. In: Proceedings of International Conference on Computer Vision (ICCV), pp. 1753–1761, October 2017

Disentangling Factors of Variation with Cycle-Consistent Variational Auto-encoders

Ananya Harsh Jha[1(✉)], Saket Anand[1], Maneesh Singh[2],
and VSR Veeravasarapu[2]

[1] IIIT-Delhi, Delhi, India
{ananyaharsh12018,anands}@iiitd.ac.in
[2] Verisk Analytics, Jersey City, USA
maneesh.singh@verisk.com, vsr.veera@gmail.com

Abstract. Generative models that learn disentangled representations for different factors of variation in an image can be very useful for targeted data augmentation. By sampling from the disentangled latent subspace of interest, we can efficiently generate new data necessary for a particular task. Learning disentangled representations is a challenging problem, especially when certain factors of variation are difficult to label. In this paper, we introduce a novel architecture that disentangles the latent space into two complementary subspaces by using only weak supervision in form of pairwise similarity labels. Inspired by the recent success of cycle-consistent adversarial architectures, we use cycle-consistency in a variational auto-encoder framework. Our non-adversarial approach is in contrast with the recent works that combine adversarial training with auto-encoders to disentangle representations. We show compelling results of disentangled latent subspaces on three datasets and compare with recent works that leverage adversarial training.

Keywords: Disentangling factors of variation
Cycle-consistent architecture · Variational auto-encoders

1 Introduction

Natural images can be thought of as samples from an unknown distribution conditioned on different factors of variation. The appearance of objects in an image is influenced by these factors that may correspond to shape, geometric attributes, illumination, texture and pose. Based on the task at hand, like image classification, many of these factors serve as a distraction for the prediction

Code for the paper: github.com/ananyahjha93/cycle-consistent-vae.

Electronic supplementary material The online version of this chapter (https://doi.org/10.1007/978-3-030-01219-9_49) contains supplementary material, which is available to authorized users.

© Springer Nature Switzerland AG 2018
V. Ferrari et al. (Eds.): ECCV 2018, LNCS 11207, pp. 829–845, 2018.
https://doi.org/10.1007/978-3-030-01219-9_49

model and are often referred to as nuisance variables. One way to mitigate the confusion caused by uninformative factors of variation is to design representations that ignore all nuisance variables [1,2]. This approach, however, is limited by the quantity and quality of training data available. Another way is to train a classifier to learn representations, invariant to uninformative factors of variation, by providing sufficient diversity via data augmentation [3].

Generative models that are driven by a disentangled latent space can be an efficient way of controlled data augmentation. Although Generative Adversarial Networks (GANs) [4,5] have proven to be excellent at generating new data samples, vanilla GAN architecture does not support inference over latent variables. This prevents control over different factors of variation during data generation. DNA-GANs [6] introduce a fully supervised architecture to disentangle factors of variation, however, acquiring labels for each factor, even when possible, is cumbersome and time consuming.

Recent works [7,8] combine auto-encoders with adversarial training to disentangle informative and uninformative factors of variation and map them onto separate sets of latent variables. The informative factors, typically specified by the task of interest, are associated with the available source of supervision, e.g. class identity or pose, and are referred to as the *specified* factors of variation. The remaining uninformative factors are grouped together as *unspecified* factors of variation. Learning such a model has two benefits: first, the encoder learns to factor out nuisance variables for the task under consideration, and second, the decoder can be used as a generative model that can generate novel samples with controlled specified and randomized unspecified factors of variation.

In context of disentangled latent representations, Mathieu et al. [7] define *degenerate solution* as a failure case, where the specified latent variables are entirely ignored by the decoder and all information (including image identity) is taken from the unspecified latent variables during image generation (Fig. 1(c) and (d)). This degeneracy is expected in auto-encoders unless the latent space is somehow constrained to preserve information about the specified and unspecified factors in the corresponding subspaces. Both [7] and [8] circumvent this issue by using an adversarial loss that trains their auto-encoder to produce images whose identity is defined by the specified latent variables instead of the unspecified latent variables. While this strategy produces good quality novel images, it may train the decoder to *ignore any leakage of information* across the specified and unspecified latent spaces, rather than training the encoder to restrict this leakage.

Szabó et al. [8] have also explored a non-adversarial approach to disentangle factors of variation. They demonstrate that severely restricting the dimensionality of the unspecified latent space discourages the encoder from encoding information related to the specified factors of variation in it. However, the results of this architecture are extremely sensitive to the dimensionality of the unspecified space. As shown in Fig. 1(e), even slightly plausible results require careful selection of dimensionality.

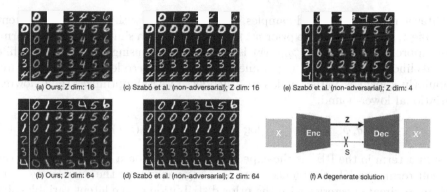

Fig. 1. s: specified factors space (class identity), z: unspecified factors space. In each of the image grids: (a), (b), (c), (d) and (e), the digits in the top row and the first column are taken from the test set. Digits within each grid are generated by taking s from the top row and z from the first column. (a) and (b): results of disentangling factors of variation using our method. (c) and (d): results of the non-adversarial architecture from [8]. (e): dimensionality of z required to produce even a few plausible digits using the non-adversarial approach in [8]. (f): visualization of a degenerate solution in case of auto-encoders.

Based on these observations, we make the following contributions in this work:

- We introduce *cycle-consistent variational auto-encoders*, a weakly supervised generative model, that disentangles specified and unspecified factors of variation using only pairwise similarity labels
- We empirically show that our proposed architecture avoids *degeneracy* and is robust to the choices of dimensionality of both the specified and unspecified latent subspaces
- We claim and empirically verify that cycle-consistent VAEs produce highly disentangled latent representations by explicitly training the encoder to reduce leakage of specified factors of variation into the unspecified subspace.

To our knowledge, cycle-consistency has neither been applied to the problem of disentangling factors of variation nor has been used in combination with variational auto-encoders. The remaining paper is organized as follows: Sect. 2 discusses the previous works relevant in context of this paper, Sect. 3 provides the details of our proposed architecture, Sect. 4 empirically verifies each of our claims using quantitative and qualitative experiments, and Sect. 5 concludes this paper by summarizing our work and providing a scope for further development of the ideas presented.

2   Related Work

Variational Auto-encoders. Kingma et al. [9] present a variational inference approach for an auto-encoder based latent factor model. Let $X = \{x_i\}_{i=1}^N$ be a dataset containing N i.i.d samples, each associated with a continuous latent variable z_i drawn from some prior $p(z)$, usually having a simple parametric form. The approximate posterior $q_\phi(z|x)$ is parameterized using the encoder, while the likelihood term $p_\theta(x|z)$ is parameterized by the decoder. The architecture, popularly known as Variational Auto-Encoders (VAEs), optimizes the following variational lower-bound:

$$\mathcal{L}(\theta, \phi; x) = \mathbb{E}_{q_\phi(z|x)}[\log p_\theta(x|z)] - \mathrm{KL}(q_\phi(z|x)\|p(z)) \tag{1}$$

The first term in the RHS is the expected value of the data likelihood, while the second term, the KL divergence, acts as a regularizer for the encoder to align the approximate posterior with the prior distribution of the latent variables. By employing a clever linear transformation based reparameterization, the authors enable end-to-end training of the VAE using back-propagation. At test time, VAEs can be used as a generative model by sampling from the prior $p(z)$ followed by a forward pass through the decoder. Our architecture uses the VAE framework to model the unspecified latent subspace.

Generative Adversarial Networks. GANs [4] have been shown to model complex, high dimensional data distributions and generate novel samples from it. They comprise of two neural networks, a generator and a discriminator, that are trained together in a min-max game setting, by optimizing the loss in Eq. (2). The discriminator outputs the probability that a given sample belongs to true data distribution as opposed to being a sample from the generator. The generator tries to map random samples from a simple parametric prior distribution in the latent space to samples from the true distribution. The generator is said to be successfully trained when the output of the discriminator is $\frac{1}{2}$ for all generated samples. DCGANs [5] use CNNs to replicate complex image distributions and are an excellent example of the success of adversarial training.

$$\min_G \max_D V(D, G) = \mathbb{E}_{x \sim p_{data}(x)}[\log D(x)] + \mathbb{E}_{z \sim p_z(z)}[\log(1 - D(G(z)))] \tag{2}$$

Despite their ability to generate high quality samples when successfully trained, GANs require carefully designed tricks to stabilize training and avoid issues like mode collapse. We do not use adversarial training in our proposed approach, however, recent works of Mathieu et al. [7] and Szabó et al. [8] have shown interesting application of adversarial training for disentangling latent factors.

Cycle-Consistency. Cycle-consistency has been used to enable a Neural Machine Translation system to learn from unlabeled data by following a closed loop of machine translation [10]. Zhou et al. [11] use cycle-consistency to establish cross-instance correspondences between pairs of images depicting objects of the same category. Cycle-consistent architectures further find applications in depth estimation [12], unpaired image-to-image translation [13] and unsupervised domain adaptation [14]. We leverage the idea of cycle-consistency in the unspecified latent space and explicitly train the encoder to reduce leakage of information associated with specified factors of variation.

Disentangling Factors of Variation. Initial works like [15] utilize the E-M framework to discover independent factors of variation which describe the observed data. Tenenbaum et al. [16] learn bilinear maps from style and content parameters to images. More recently, [17–19] use Restricted Boltzmann Machines to separately map factors of variation in images. Kulkarni et al. [20] model *vision as inverse graphics* problem by proposing a network that disentangles transformation and lighting variations. In [1] and [2], invariant representations are learnt by factoring out the nuisance variables for a given task at hand.

Tran et al. [21] utilize identity and pose labels to disentangle facial identity from pose by using a modified GAN architecture. SD-GANs [22] introduce a siamese network architecture over DC-GANs [5] and BE-GANs [23], that simultaneously generates pairs of images with a common identity but different unspecified factors of variation. However, like vanilla GANs they lack any method for inference over the latent variables. Reed et al. [24] develop a novel architecture for visual analogy making, which transforms a query image according to the relationship between the images of an example pair.

DNA-GANs [6] present a fully supervised approach to learn disentangled representations. Adversarial auto-encoders [25] use a semi-supervised approach to disentangle style and class representations, however, unlike the methods of [7,8] and ours, they cannot generalize to unseen object identities. Hu et al. [26] present an interesting approach that combines auto-encoders with adversarial training to disentangle factors of variation in a fully unsupervised manner. However, the quality of disentanglement still falls short in comparison to [7,8].

Our work builds upon the network architectures introduced by Mathieu et al. [7] and Szabó et al. [8]. Both of them combine auto-encoders with adversarial training to disentangle specified and unspecified factors of variation based on a single source of supervision, like class labels. Our work differs from these two by introducing a non-adversarial approach to disentangle factors of variation under a weaker source of supervision which uses only pairwise similarity labels. Recently, [27] also proposed another non-adversarial approach for disentangling representations based on group-level supervision. However, their architecture does not explicitly train the encoder, thus making it susceptible to degeneracy when randomly selecting latent dimensions.

3   Cycle-Consistent Variational Auto-encoders

In this section, we describe our model architecture, explain all its components and develop its training strategy.

3.1   Cycle-Consistency

The intuition behind a cycle-consistent framework is simple – the forward and reverse transformations composited together in any order should approximate an identity function. For the forward cycle, this translates to a forward transform $F(x_i)$ followed by a reverse transform $G(F(x_i)) = x'_i$, such that $x'_i \simeq x_i$.

The reverse cycle should ensure that a reverse transform followed by a forward transform yields $F(G(y_i)) = y'_i \simeq y_i$. The mappings $F(\cdot)$ and $G(\cdot)$ can be implemented using neural networks with training done by minimizing the ℓ_p norm based *cyclic* loss defined in Eq. (3) (Fig. 2).

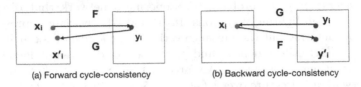

(a) Forward cycle-consistency   (b) Backward cycle-consistency

Fig. 2. (a): Forward cycle in a cycle-consistent framework: $x_i \rightarrow F(x_i) \rightarrow G(F(x_i)) \rightarrow x'_i$. (b): Backward cycle in a cycle-consistent framework: $y_i \rightarrow G(y_i) \rightarrow F(G(y_i)) \rightarrow y'_i$.

Cycle-consistency naturally fits into the (variational) auto-encoder training framework, where the KL divergence regularized reconstruction comprises the $\mathcal{L}_{forward}$. We also use the reverse cycle-consistency loss to train the encoder to disentangle better. As is typical for such loss functions, we train our model by alternating between the forward and reverse losses. We discuss the details in the sections that follow.

$$\mathcal{L}_{cyclic} = \mathcal{L}_{forward} + \mathcal{L}_{reverse}$$
$$\mathcal{L}_{cyclic} = \mathbb{E}_{x \sim p(x)}[||G(F(x)) - x||_p] + \mathbb{E}_{y \sim p(y)}[||F(G(y)) - y||_p] \quad (3)$$

3.2 Model Description

We propose a conditional variational auto-encoder based model, where the latent space is partitioned into two *complementary* subspaces: s, which controls specified factors of variation associated with the available supervision in the dataset, and z, which models the remaining unspecified factors of variation. Similar to Mathieu et al.'s [7] work we keep s as a real valued vector space and z is assumed to have a standard normal prior distribution $p(z) = \mathcal{N}(0, I)$. Such an architecture enables explicit control in the specified subspace, while permitting random sampling from the unspecified subspace. We assume marginal independence between z and s, which implies complete disentanglement between the factors of variation associated with the two latent subspaces.

Encoder. The encoder can be written as a mapping $Enc(x) = (f_z(x), f_s(x))$, where $f_z(x) = (\mu, \sigma) = z$ and $f_s(x) = s$. Function $f_s(x)$ is a standard encoder with real valued vector latent space and $f_z(x)$ is an encoder whose vector outputs parameterize the approximate posterior $q_\phi(z|x)$. Since the same set of features extracted from x be used to create mappings to z and s, we define a single encoder with shared weights for all but the last layer, which branches out to give outputs of the two functions $f_z(x)$ and $f_s(x)$.

Decoder. The decoder, $x' = Dec(z, s)$, in this VAE is represented by the conditional likelihood $p_\theta(x|z, s)$. Maximizing the expectation of this likelihood w.r.t

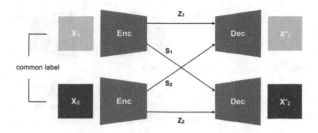

Fig. 3. Image reconstruction using VAEs by swapping the s latent variable between two images from the same class. This process works with pairwise similarity labels, as we do not need to know the actual class label of the sampled image pair.

the approximate posterior and s is equivalent to minimizing the squared reconstruction error.

Forward Cycle. We sample a pair of images, x_1 and x_2, from the dataset that have the same class label. We pass both of them through the encoder to generate the corresponding latent representations $Enc(x_1) = (z_1, s_1)$ and $Enc(x_2) = (z_2, s_2)$. The input to the decoder is constructed by swapping the specified latent variables of the two images. This produces the following reconstructions: $x_1' = Dec(z_1, s_2)$ and $x_2' = Dec(z_2, s_1)$. Since both these images share class labels, swapping the specified latent variables should have no effect on the reconstruction loss function. We can re-write the conditional likelihood of the decoder as $p_\theta(x|z, s^*)$, where $s^* = f_s(x^*)$ and x^* is any image with the same class label as x. The entire forward cycle minimizes the modified variational upper-bound given in Eq. 4. Figure 3 shows a diagrammatic representation of the forward cycle.

$$\min_{Enc, Dec} \mathcal{L}_{forward} = -\mathbb{E}_{q_\phi(z|x, s^*)}[\log p_\theta(x|z, s^*)] + \text{KL}(q_\phi(z|x, s^*)\|p(z)) \qquad (4)$$

It is worth noting that forward cycle does not demand actual class labels at any given time. This results in the requirement of a weaker form of supervision in which images need to be annotated with pairwise similarity labels. This is in contrast with the previous works of Mathieu et al. [7], which requires actual class labels, and Szabó et al. [8], which requires image triplets.

The forward cycle mentioned above is similar to the auto-encoder reconstruction loss presented in [7] and [8]. As discussed in Sect. 1, the forward cycle alone can produce a *degenerate solution* (Fig. 1(c) and (d)) as there is no constraint which prevents the decoder from reconstructing images using only the unspecified latent variables. In [7] and [8], an adversarial loss function has been successfully applied to specifically tackle the *degenerate solution*. The resulting generative model works well, however, adversarial training is challenging in general and has limitations in effectively disentangling the latent space. For now, we defer this discussion to Sect. 4.1. In the next section, we introduce our non-adversarial method, based on reverse cycle-consistency, to avoid learning

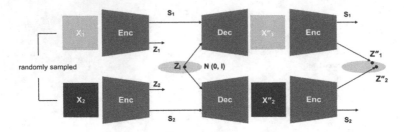

Fig. 4. Reverse cycle of the cycle-consistent VAE architecture. A point sampled from the z latent space, combined with specified factors from two separate sources, forms two different images. However, we should be able to obtain the same sampled point in the z space if we pass the two generated images back through the encoder.

a *degenerate solution* and explicitly train the encoder to prevent information associated with specified factors from leaking into the unspecified subspace.

3.3   Preventing a Degenerate Solution

Reverse Cycle. The reverse cycle shown in Fig. 4 is based on the idea of cyclic-consistency in the unspecified latent space. We sample a point z_i from the Gaussian prior $p(z) = \mathcal{N}(0, I)$ over the unspecified latent space and pass it through the decoder in combination with specified latent variables $s_1 = f_s(x_1)$ and $s_2 = f_s(x_2)$ to obtain reconstructions $x_1'' = Dec(z_i, s_1)$ and $x_2'' = Dec(z_i, s_2)$ respectively. Unlike the forward cycle, x_1 and x_2 need not have the same label and can be sampled independently. Since both images x_1'' and x_2'' are generated using the same z_i, their corresponding unspecified latent embeddings $z_1'' = f_z(x_1'')$ and $z_2'' = f_z(x_2'')$ should be mapped close to each other, regardless of their specified factors. Such a constraint promotes marginal independence of z from s as images generated using different specified factors could potentially be mapped to the same point in the unspecified latent subspace. This step directly drives the encoder to produce disentangled representations by only retaining information related to the unspecified factors in the z latent space.

The variational loss in Eq. (4) enables sampling of the unspecified latent variables and aids the generation of novel images. However, the encoder does not necessarily learn a unique mapping from the image space to the unspecified latent space. In other words, samples with similar unspecified factors are likely to get mapped to significantly different unspecified latent variables. This observation motivates our *pairwise* reverse cycle loss in Eq. (5), which penalizes the encoder if the unspecified latent embeddings z_1'' and z_2'' have a large pairwise distance, but not if they are mapped farther away from the originally sampled point z_i. This modification is in contrast with the typical usage of cycle-consistency in previous works. We found that minimizing the pairwise reverse cycle loss in Eq. (5) was easier than its absolute counterpart ($||z_i - z_1''|| + ||z_i - z_2''||$), both in terms of the loss value and the extent of disentanglement.

$$\min_{Enc} \mathcal{L}_{reverse} = \mathbb{E}_{x_1,x_2 \sim p(x), z_i \sim \mathcal{N}(0,I)}[|||f_z(Dec(z_i, f_s(x_1)))$$
$$-f_z(Dec(z_i, f_s(x_2)))||_1] \tag{5}$$

4 Experiments

We evaluate the performance of our model on three datasets: MNIST [28], 2D Sprites [24,29] and LineMod [30,31]. We divide our experiments into two parts. The first part evaluates the performance of our model in terms of the quality of disentangled representations. The second part evaluates the image generation capabilities of our model. We compare our results with the recent works in [7,8]. The three dataset we use are described below:

Table 1. Quantitative results for the three datasets. Classification accuracies on the z and s latent spaces are a good indicator of the amount of specified factor information present in them. Since we are aiming for disentangled representations for unspecified and specified factors of variation, *lower is better* for the z latent space and *higher is better* the s latent space.

Architecture	z dim	s dim	z train acc.	z test acc.	s train acc.	s test acc.
MNIST						
Szabó et al.	16	16	97.65	96.08	98.89	98.46
Mathieu et al.	16	16	70.85	66.83	99.37	98.52
Ours	16	16	**17.72**	**17.56**	99.72	98.35
Szabó et al.	64	64	99.69	98.14	99.41	98.05
Mathieu et al.	64	64	74.94	72.20	99.94	98.64
Ours	64	64	**26.04**	**26.55**	99.95	98.33
2D Sprites						
Szabó et al.	512	64	99.72	99.63	99.85	99.79
Mathieu et al.	512	64	12.05	11.98	99.18	96.75
Ours	512	64	**11.55**	**11.47**	98.53	97.16
Szabó et al.	1024	512	99.79	99.65	99.87	99.76
Mathieu et al.	1024	512	12.48	12.25	99.22	97.45
Ours	1024	512	**11.27**	**11.61**	98.13	97.22
LineMod						
Szabó et al.	64	256	100.0	100.0	100.0	100.0
Mathieu et al.	64	256	90.14	89.17	100.0	100.0
Ours	64	256	**62.11**	**57.17**	99.99	99.86
Szabó et al.	256	512	100.0	99.97	100.0	100.0
Mathieu et al.	256	512	86.87	86.46	100.0	100.0
Ours	256	512	**60.34**	**57.70**	100.0	100.0

MNIST. The MNIST dataset [28] consists of hand-written digits distributed amongst 10 classes. The specified factors in case of MNIST is the digit identity, while the unspecified factors control digit slant, stroke width etc.

2D Sprites. 2D Sprites consists of game characters (sprites) animated is different poses for use in small scale indie game development. We download the dataset from [29], which consists of 480 unique characters according to variation in gender, hair type, body type, armor type, arm type and greaves type. Each unique character is associated with 298 different poses, 120 of which have weapons and the remaining do not. In total, we have 143040 images in the dataset. The training, validation and the test set contain 320, 80 and 80 unique characters respectively. This implies that character identity in each of the training, validation and test split is mutually exclusive and the dataset presents an opportunity to test our model on completely unseen object identities. The specified factors latent space for 2D Sprites is associated with the character identity, while the pose is associated with the unspecified factors.

Line-MOD. LineMod [30] is an object recognition and 3D pose estimation dataset with 15 unique objects: 'ape', 'benchviseblue', 'bowl', 'cam', 'can', 'cat', 'cup', 'driller', 'duck', 'eggbox', 'glue', 'holepuncher', 'iron', 'lamp' and 'phone', photographed in a highly cluttered environment. We use the synthetic version of the dataset [31], which has the same objects rendered under different viewpoints. There are 1541 images per category and we use a split of 1000 images for training, 241 for validation and 300 for test. The specified factors latent space models the object identity in this dataset. The unspecified factors latent space models the remaining factors of variation in the dataset.

During forward cycle, we randomly pick image pairs defined by the same specified factors of variation. During reverse cycle, the selection of images is completely random. All our models were implemented using PyTorch [32]. Specific details about our architectures are included in the supplementary material.

4.1   Quality of Disentangled Representations

We set up the quantitative evaluation experiments similar to [7]. We train a two layer neural network classifier separately on the specified and unspecified latent embeddings generated by each competing model. Since the specified factors of variation are associated with the available labels in each dataset, the classifier accuracy gives a fair measure of the information related to specified factors of variation present in the two latent subspaces. If the factors were completely disentangled, we expect the classification accuracy in the specified latent space to be perfect, while that in the unspecified latent space to be close to chance. In this experiment, we also investigate the effect of change in the dimensionality of the latent spaces. We report the quantitative comparisons in Table 1.

The quantitative results in Table 1 show consistent trends for our proposed Cycle-Consistent VAE architecture across all the three datasets as well as for different dimensionality of the latent spaces. Classification accuracy in the unspecified latent subspace is the smallest for the proposed architecture, while it is comparable with the others in the specified latent subspace. These trends indicate that among the three competing models, the proposed one leaks the least amount of specified factor information into the unspecified latent subspace. This restricted amount of leakage of specified information can be attributed to the reverse cycle-consistency loss that explicitly trains the encoder to disentangle factors more effectively.

(a) Szabó et al.; Z dim: 16   (b) Mathieu et al.; Z dim: 16   (c) Ours; Z dim: 16

Fig. 5. Comparison between t-SNE plots of the z latent space for MNIST. We can see good cluster formation according to class identities in (a) [8], indicating that adversarial training alone does not promote marginal independence of z from s. Mathieu's work [7] in (b) uses re-parameterization on the encoder output to create confusion regarding the specified factors in the z space while retaining information related to the unspecified factors. Our work (c) combines re-parameterization with reverse cycle loss to create confusion regarding the specified factors.

We also visualize the unspecified latent space as t-SNE plots [33] to check for the presence of any apparent structure based on the available labels with the MNIST dataset. Figure 5 shows the t-SNE plots of the unspecified latent space obtained by each of the competing models. The points are color-coded to indicate specified factor labels, which in case of MNIST are the digit identities. We can see clear cluster structures in Fig. 5(a) indicating strong presence of the specified factor information in the unspecified latent space. This observation is consistent with the quantitative results shown in Table 1. As shown in Fig. 5(b) and (c), the t-SNE plots for Mathieu et al.'s model [7] and our model appear to have similar levels of confusion with respect to the specified factor information. However, since t-SNE plots are approximations, the quantitative results reported in Table 1 better capture the performance comparison.

The architectures in [7,8] utilize adversarial training in combination with a regular and a variational auto-encoder respectively. Despite the significant presence of specified factor information in the unspecified latent embeddings from Szabó et al.'s model [8], it successfully generates novel images by combining the specified and unspecified factors (shown in Sect. 4.2). This apparently conflicting observation suggests that the decoder somehow learns to ignore the specified factor information in the unspecified latent space. We conjecture that since the adversarial loss updates the decoder and the encoder parameters together, and in that order, the encoder remains less likely to disentangle the latent spaces.

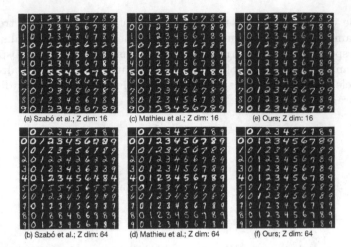

(a) Szabó et al.; Z dim: 16   (c) Mathieu et al.; Z dim: 16   (e) Ours; Z dim: 16

(b) Szabó et al.; Z dim: 64   (d) Mathieu et al.; Z dim: 64   (f) Ours; Z dim: 64

Fig. 6. Image generation results on MNIST by swapping z and s variables. The top row and the first column are randomly selected from the test set. The remaining grid is generated by taking z from the digit in first column and s from the digit in first row. This keeps the unspecified factors constant in rows and the specified factors constant in columns.

A similar argument can be made that Mathieu et al.'s [7] architecture does not explicitly train the encoder to disentangle factors of variation, thus resulting in higher classification accuracy in the unspecified latent space. This behavior, however, is mitigated to a large extent due to the VAE framework, which promotes class confusion in the unspecified latent subspace by performing reparametrization at the time of new image generation. Our approach benefits from the reparametrization as well, however, significantly lower classification accuracies on the unspecified latent space embeddings indicate that the encoder learns to disentangle the factors better by minimizing the reverse cycle-consistency loss.

4.2   Quality of Image Generation

The quality of image generation is evaluated in three different setups. First, we test the capability of our model to combine unspecified and specified factors from different images to generate a new image. The results are shown in the form of a grid of images, where the first row and the first column is taken from the test set. The remaining grid shows images generated by combining the specified factor from images in the first row and the unspecified factors of those in the first column. For this evaluation, we compare our results with prior works [7] and [8]. Unlike the non-adversarial approach proposed by Szabó et al. [8], our model is robust to the choices of dimensionality for both z and s variables. We emphasize that our model avoids *degeneracy* for significantly higher dimensions of latent variables, as compared to the base values, despite being a non-adversarial architecture. Second, we show the effect of linear interpolation in the latent spaces. The images in the top-left and the bottom-right corner are taken from the test set and similar to the first evaluation, the remaining images are generated by keeping z constant across the rows and s constant across the columns. Finally, we check the conditional image generation capability of our model by conditioning on the s variable and sampling data points directly from the Gaussian prior $p(z)$ for the z variable.

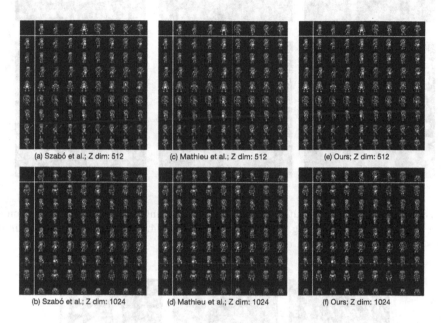

(a) Szabó et al.; Z dim: 512   (c) Mathieu et al.; Z dim: 512   (e) Ours; Z dim: 512

(b) Szabó et al.; Z dim: 1024   (d) Mathieu et al.; Z dim: 1024   (f) Ours; Z dim: 1024

Fig. 7. Image generation results on 2D Sprites by swapping z and s variables. Arrangement of the grid is same as Fig. 6.

The first evaluation of generating new images by combining z and s from different sources is shown in Figs. 6, 7 and 8. LineMod dataset comprises of images with complex geometric structures that do not share a fixed frame of reference. For example, an image of a 'duck' will not be aligned in the same direction as an image of a 'cat' for a common viewpoint. Hence, as is apparent from Fig. 8, interpretation of transfer of unspecified factors as viewpoint transfer does not exactly hold true.

The results for linear interpolation in the latent space and conditional image generation via sampling from $p(z)$ are shown in Figs. 9 and 10 respectively.

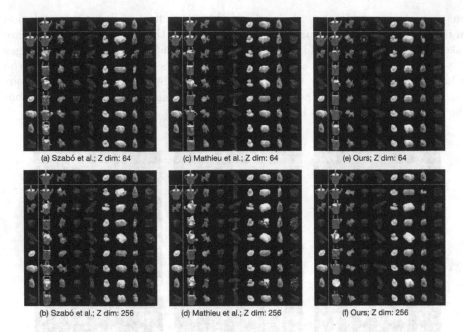

Fig. 8. Image generation results on LineMod by swapping z and s variables. Arrangement of the grid is same as Fig. 6. As explained in Sect. 4.2, we do not observe a direct transfer of viewpoint between the objects.

Fig. 9. Linear interpolation results for our model in the z and s latent spaces. The images in the top-left and the bottom-right corner are taken from the test set. Like Fig. 6, z variable is constant in the rows, while s is constant in the columns.

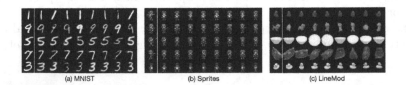

Fig. 10. Image generation by conditioning on s variable, taken from test images, and sampling the z variable from $\mathcal{N}(0, I)$.

5 Conclusion

In this paper we introduced a simple yet effective way to disentangle specified and unspecified factors of variation by leveraging the idea of cycle-consistency. The proposed architecture needs only weak supervision in the form of pairs of data having similar specified factors. The architecture does not produce degenerate solutions and is robust to the choices of dimensionality of the latent space. Through our experimental evaluations, we found that even though adversarial training produces good visual reconstructions, the encoder does not necessarily learn to disentangle the factors of variation effectively. Our model, on the other hand, achieves compelling quantitative results on three different datasets and shows good image generation capabilities as a generative model.

We also note that generative models based on VAEs produce less sharper images compared to GANs and our model is no exception. One way to address this problem could be to train our cycle-consistent VAE as the first step, followed by training the decoder with a combination of adversarial and reverse cycle-consistency loss. This training strategy may improve the sharpness of the generated images while maintaining the disentangling capability of the encoder. Another interesting direction to pursue from here would be to further explore the methods that disentangle factors of variation in an unsupervised manner.

Acknowledgement. We are thankful for the insightful feedback from anonymous ECCV reviewers. We acknowledge Infosys Center for AI at IIIT-Delhi for partially supporting this research. We also appreciate the support from Verisk Analytics for its successful execution.

References

1. Edwards, H., Storkey, A.J.: Censoring representations with an adversary. In: International Conference in Learning Representations, ICLR 2016 (2016)
2. Louizos, C., Swersky, K., Li, Y., Welling, M., Zemel, R.S.: The variational fair autoencoder. In: International Conference in Learning Representations, ICLR 2016 (2016)
3. Krizhevsky, A., Sutskever, I., Hinton, G.E.: ImageNet classification with deep convolutional neural networks. In: Proceedings of the 25th International Conference on Neural Information Processing Systems - NIPS 2012, vol. 1, pp. 1097–1105 (2012)
4. Goodfellow, I.J., et al.: Generative adversarial nets. In: NIPS, pp. 2672–2680 (2014)
5. Radford, A., Metz, L., Chintala, S.: Unsupervised representation learning with deep convolutional generative adversarial networks. In: International Conference in Learning Representations, ICLR 2016 (2016)
6. Xiao, T., Hong, J., Ma, J.: DNA-GAN: learning disentangled representations from multi-attribute images. arXiv preprint arXiv:1711.05415 (2017)
7. Mathieu, M., Zhao, J.J., Sprechmann, P., Ramesh, A., LeCun, Y.: Disentangling factors of variation in deep representation using adversarial training. In: NIPS, pp. 5041–5049 (2016)
8. Szabó, A., Hu, Q., Portenier, T., Zwicker, M., Favaro, P.: Challenges in disentangling independent factors of variation. arXiv preprint arXiv:1711.02245 (2017)

9. Kingma, D.P., Welling, M.: Auto-encoding variational Bayes. In: International Conference in Learning Representations, ICLR 2014 (2014)

10. He, D., et al.: Dual learning for machine translation. Adv. Neural Inf. Process. Syst. **29**, 820–828 (2016)

11. Zhou, T., Krähenbühl, P., Aubry, M., Huang, Q., Efros, A.A.: Learning dense correspondence via 3D-guided cycle consistency. In: CVPR, pp. 117–126. IEEE Computer Society (2016)

12. Godard, C., Mac Aodha, O., Brostow, G.J.: Unsupervised monocular depth estimation with left-right consistency. In: CVPR (2017)

13. Zhu, J., Park, T., Isola, P., Efros, A.A.: Unpaired image-to-image translation using cycle-consistent adversarial networks. In: ICCV, pp. 2242–2251. IEEE Computer Society (2017)

14. Hoffman, J., et al.: CyCADA: cycle-consistent adversarial domain adaptation. arXiv preprint arXiv:1711.03213 (2017)

15. Ghahramani, Z.: Factorial learning and the EM algorithm. In: Proceedings of the 7th International Conference on Neural Information Processing Systems, NIPS 1994, Cambridge, MA, USA, pp. 617–624. MIT Press (1994)

16. Tenenbaum, J.B., Freeman, W.T.: Separating style and content with bilinear models. Neural Comput. **12**(6), 1247–1283 (2000)

17. Desjardins, G., Courville, A.C., Bengio, Y.: Disentangling factors of variation via generative entangling. arXiv preprint arXiv:1210.5474 (2012)

18. Reed, S.E., Sohn, K., Zhang, Y., Lee, H.: Learning to disentangle factors of variation with manifold interaction. In: ICML, Volume 32 of JMLR Workshop and Conference Proceedings, pp. 1431–1439. JMLR.org (2014)

19. Tang, Y., Salakhutdinov, R., Hinton, G.E.: Deep Lambertian networks. In: ICML. icml.cc/Omnipress (2012)

20. Kulkarni, T.D., Whitney, W.F., Kohli, P., Tenenbaum, J.B.: Deep convolutional inverse graphics network. In: Proceedings of the 28th International Conference on Neural Information Processing Systems - Volume 2, NIPS 2015, Cambridge, MA, USA, pp. 2539–2547. MIT Press (2015)

21. Tran, L., Yin, X., Liu, X.: Disentangled representation learning GAN for pose-invariant face recognition. In: The IEEE Conference on Computer Vision and Pattern Recognition (CVPR), July 2017

22. Donahue, C., Balsubramani, A., McAuley, J., Lipton, Z.C.: Semantically decomposing the latent spaces of generative adversarial networks. In: International Conference in Learning Representations, ICLR 2018 (2018)

23. Berthelot, D., Schumm, T., Metz, L.: BEGAN: boundary equilibrium generative adversarial networks. arXiv preprint arXiv:1703.10717 (2017)

24. Reed, S.E., Zhang, Y., Zhang, Y., Lee, H.: Deep visual analogy-making. In: NIPS, pp. 1252–1260 (2015)

25. Makhzani, A., Shlens, J., Jaitly, N., Goodfellow, I.: Adversarial autoencoders. In: International Conference on Learning Representations (2016)

26. Hu, Q., Szabó, A., Portenier, T., Zwicker, M., Favaro, P.: Disentangling factors of variation by mixing them. arXiv preprint arXiv:1711.07410 (2017)

27. Bouchacourt, D., Tomioka, R., Nowozin, S.: Multi-level variational autoencoder: learning disentangled representations from grouped observations. In: Proceedings of the Thirty-Second AAAI Conference on Artificial Intelligence, New Orleans, Louisiana, USA, 2–7 February 2018 (2018)

28. Lecun, Y., Bottou, L., Bengio, Y., Haffner, P.: Gradient-based learning applied to document recognition. In: Proceedings of the IEEE, pp. 2278–2324 (1998)

29. Liberated Pixel Cup. http://lpc.opengameart.org/. Accessed 21 Feb 2018
30. Hinterstoisser, S., et al.: Model based training, detection and pose estimation of texture-less 3D objects in heavily cluttered scenes. In: Lee, K.M., Matsushita, Y., Rehg, J.M., Hu, Z. (eds.) ACCV 2012. LNCS, vol. 7724, pp. 548–562. Springer, Heidelberg (2013). https://doi.org/10.1007/978-3-642-37331-2_42
31. Wohlhart, P., Lepetit, V.: Learning descriptors for object recognition and 3D pose estimation. In: CVPR, pp. 3109–3118. IEEE Computer Society (2015)
32. Paszke, A., et al.: Automatic Differentiation in PyTorch (2017)
33. van der Maaten, L., Hinton, G.: Visualizing high-dimensional data using t-SNE. J. Mach. Learn. Res. **9**, 2579–2605 (2008)

Object-Centered Image Stitching

Charles Herrmann[1], Chen Wang[1,2], Richard Strong Bowen[1], Emil Keyder[2],
and Ramin Zabih[1,2(✉)]

[1] Cornell Tech, New York, NY 10044, USA
{cih,chenwang,rsb,rdz}@cs.cornell.edu
[2] Google Research, New York, NY 10011, USA
{wangch,emilkeyder,raminz}@google.com

Abstract. Image stitching is typically decomposed into three phases:
registration, which aligns the source images with a common target image;
seam finding, which determines for each target pixel the source image it
should come from; and blending, which smooths transitions over the
seams. As described in [1], the seam finding phase attempts to place
seams between pixels where the transition between source images is not
noticeable. Here, we observe that the most problematic failures of this
approach occur when objects are cropped, omitted, or duplicated. We
therefore take an object-centered approach to the problem, leveraging
recent advances in object detection [2–4]. We penalize candidate solutions
with this class of error by modifying the energy function used in the
seam finding stage. This produces substantially more realistic stitching
results on challenging imagery. In addition, these methods can be used
to determine when there is non-recoverable occlusion in the input data,
and also suggest a simple evaluation metric that can be used to evaluate
the output of stitching algorithms.

1 Image Stitching and Object Detection

Image stitching is the creation of a single composite image from a set of images
of the same scene. It is a well-studied problem [5] with many uses in both industry and consumer applications, including Google StreetView, satellite mapping,
and the panorama creation software found in modern cameras and smartphones.
Despite its ubiquitous applications, image stitching cannot be considered solved.
Algorithms frequently produce images that appear obviously unrealistic in the
presence of parallax (Fig. 1(c)) or object motion (Fig. 2(c)), or alternatively indicate that images are too disparate to be stitched when this is not the case. One
of the most visually jarring failure modes is the tearing, cropping, deletion, or
duplication of recognizable objects. Indeed, it has become a popular internet
pastime to post and critique stitching failures of this sort that occur in Google
StreetView or on users' own cameras (most famously, the Google Photos failure
shown in Fig. 1). In this paper, we exploit advances in object detection [2–4] to
improve image stitching algorithms and avoid producing these artifacts.

The image stitching pipeline typically consists of three phases: registration,
in which the images to be stitched are aligned to one another; seam finding, in

© Springer Nature Switzerland AG 2018
V. Ferrari et al. (Eds.): ECCV 2018, LNCS 11207, pp. 846–861, 2018.
https://doi.org/10.1007/978-3-030-01219-9_50

(a) Input images

(b) Our results

(c) Google Photos results

Fig. 1. Example showing object cropping. Google Photos (shown) crops the man's body and blends him into the mountains. APAP [8] and Adobe Photoshop both only include the man's arm, while NIS [9] produces severe ghosting.

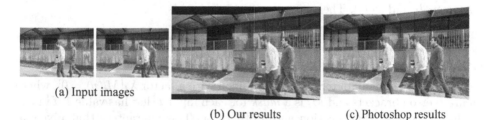

(a) Input images

(b) Our results

(c) Photoshop results

Fig. 2. Example showing object duplication. Photoshop (shown) and APAP give visually similar output, while NIS produces severe ghosting. While we duplicate a shadow on the sidewalk, our object-centered approach preserves the most important elements of the scene.

which a source image is selected for each pixel in the final image; and blending, in which smooths over the transitions between images [5]. In order to avoid introducing object-related errors, we propose modifications to the seam finding step, which typically relies on Markov Random Field (MRF) inference [5,6]. We demonstrate that MRF inference can be naturally extended to prevent the duplication and maintain the integrity of detected objects. In order to evaluate the efficacy of this approach, we experiment with several object detectors on various sets of images, and show that it can substantially improve the perceived quality of the stitching output when objects are found in the inputs.[1] We also show that object detection algorithms can be used to formalize the evaluation of stitching results, improving on previous evaluation techniques [7] that require knowledge of seam locations.

In the remainder of this section, we give a formal description of the stitching problem, and summarize how our approach fits into this framework. Section 2 gives a short review of related work. In Sect. 3, we present our object-centered approach for improving seam finding. We propose an object-centered evaluation

---

[1] In the atypical case of no detected objects, our technique reverts to standard stitching. As object detectors continue to improve their accuracy and coverage, this situation will likely become exceptionally rare.

metric for image stitching algorithms in Sect. 4. Section 5 gives an experimental evaluation of our techniques, and Sect. 6 discusses their limitations and possible extensions.

1.1   Formulating the Stitching Problem

We use the notation from [10] and formalize the perspective stitching problem as follows: given two images[2] I_1, I_2 with an overlap, compute a registration $\omega(I_2)$ of I_2 with respect to I_1, and a *label* x_p for each pixel p that determines whether it gets its value from I_1 or from $\omega(I_2)$.

Following [6], the label selection problem is typically solved with an MRF that uses an energy function that prefers short seams with inconspicuous transitions between I_1 and $\omega(I_2)$. The energy to be minimized is

$$E(x) = \arg\min_{x \in \mathcal{L}} \sum_p E_d(x_p)\lambda_d[M_i(p) = 0] + \sum_{p,q \in \mathcal{N}} V_{p,q} \cdot [x_p \neq x_q].$$

The underlying data term E_d is combined with a factor $\lambda_d[M_i(p) = 0]$, where $[]$ are Iverson brackets and M_i is a *mask* for each input i that has value 1 if image I_i has a value at that location and 0 otherwise. This guarantees that pixels in the output are preferentially drawn from valid regions of the input images.

For a pair of adjacent pixels $p, q \in \mathcal{N}$, the prior term $V_{p,q}$ imposes a penalty for assigning them different labels when the two images have different intensities. A typical choice is $V_{p,q} = |I_1(p) - \omega(I_2)(p)| + |I_1(q) - \omega(I_2)(q)|$.

The generalization to multiple overlapping images is straightforward: with a reference image I_1 and $k-1$ warped images $\{\omega_2(I_2), \omega_3(I_3), \ldots, \omega_k(I_k)\}$, the size of the label set is k instead of 2 and the worst-case computational complexity goes from polynomial to NP-hard [11]. Despite this theoretical complexity, modern MRF inference methods such as graph cuts are very effective at solving these problems [12].

Our Approach. We focus primarily on modifications to the seam finding stage. We introduce three new terms to the traditional energy function that address the cropping, duplication, and occlusion of objects. We also demonstrate that object detection can be used to detect cropping and duplication on the outputs of arbitrary stitching algorithms.

2   Related Work

A long-standing problem in image stitching is the presence of visible seams due to effects such as parallax or movement. Traditionally there have been two ways of mitigating these artifacts: to improve registration by increasing the available degrees of freedom [9,13,14], or to hide misalignments by selecting better seams. We note that artifacts caused by movement *within* the scene cannot be concealed

---

[2] we address the generalization to additional overlapping images shortly.

by better registration, and that improved seams are the only remedy in these cases.

Our work can be seen as continuing the second line of research. Initial approaches here based the pairwise energy term purely on differences in intensity between the reference image and the warped candidate image [6]. This was later improved upon by considering global structure such as color gradients and the presence of edges [15].

A number of papers make use of semantic information in order to penalize seams that cut through entities that human observers are especially likely to notice, such as faces [16]. One more general approach modifies the energy function based on a *saliency* measure defined in terms of the location in the output image and human perceptual properties of colors [7]. Our methods differ from these in that we propose general modifications to the energy function that also cleanly handle occlusion and duplication. [17] uses graphcuts to remove pedestrians from Google StreetView images; their technique bears a strong similarity to our duplication term but addresses a different task.

Evaluation of image stitching methods is very difficult, and has been a major roadblock in the past. Most MRF-based stitching methods report the final energy as a measure of quality [6,12], and therefore cannot be used to compare approaches with different energy functions, or non-MRF based methods. [7] proposes an alternate way to evaluate stitching techniques based on seam quality; their work is perceptually based but similar to MRF energy-based approaches. Our approach, in contrast, takes advantage of more global information provided by object detection.

3   Object-Centered Seam Finding

We use a classic three-stage image stitching pipeline, composed of registration, seam finding, and blending phases. We modify the techniques introduced in [10] to find a single best registration of the candidate image. We then solve a MRF whose energy function incorporates our novel tearing, duplication, and occlusion terms to find seams between the images. Finally, we apply Poisson blending [18] to smooth transitions over stitching boundaries to obtain the final result.

3.1   Registration

Our registration approach largely follows [10], except that we only use a single registration in the seam finding stage. To generate a registration, we first identify a homography that matches a large portion of the image and then run a content-preserving warp (CPW) in order to fix small misalignments [19]. The following provides a high level overview of the registration process.

To create candidate homographies, we run RANSAC on the sparse correspondence between the two input images. In order to limit the set of candidates, homographies that are too different from a similarity transform or too similar to a previously considered one are filtered out at each iteration. The resulting homographies are then refined via CPWs by solving a quadratic program (QP) for each, in which the local terms are populated from the results of an optical flow algorithm run on the reference image and initial candidate registration. This step makes minor non-linear adjustments to the transformation and yields registrations that more closely match portions of the image that would otherwise be slightly misaligned.

We also explored producing multiple registrations and running seam finding on each pair of reference image and candidate registration, and selecting the result by considering both the lowest final energy obtained and the best evaluation score (defined below). This approach is similar to the process used in [14, 20] where homographies are selected based on the final energy from the seam finding phase. We found that this method gave only marginally better results than selecting a single registration.

3.2 Seam Finding

The output of the registration stage is a single proposed warp $\omega(I_2)$. For simplicity, let $I_1^S = I_1$, $I_2^S = \omega(I_2)$ be the input images for the seam finding phase. We denote the set of pixels in the output mosaic by P. In contrast to the traditional seam finding setup, here we assume an additional input consisting of the results of an object detector run on the input images. We write the set of recognized objects in I_ℓ^S as O_ℓ and denote by $\mathcal{M}(O_1, O_2) \subseteq O_1 \times O_2$ the set of corresponding objects between O_1 and O_2. The computation of $\mathcal{M}(O_1, O_2)$ is discussed in Sect. 3.5.

Besides I_1^S and I_2^S, we use an additional label $\perp$, indicating that no value is available for that pixel due to occlusion. The label set for the MRF is then $\mathcal{L} = \{\perp, 1, 2\}$, where $x_p = 1$ or $x_p = 2$ indicate that the pixel is copied from I_1^S or I_2^S, and a label of $x_p = \perp$ indicates that the pixel is occluded by an object in all input images and therefore cannot be accurately reproduced.[3]

Given this MRF, we solve for a labeling x using an objective function that, in addition to the traditional data and smoothness terms E_d and E_s, contains three new terms that we introduce here: a *cropping term* E_c, a *duplication term* E_r, and an *occlusion term* E_o, which are presented in Sect. 3.3, following a brief review of the traditional terms. Using a 4-connected adjacency system $\mathcal{N}$ and tradeoff coefficients $\lambda_d, \lambda_s, \lambda_c, \lambda_r, \lambda_o, \delta$, the final energy is then given by:

$$E(x) = \lambda_d \sum_{p \in P} E_d(x_p) + \lambda_s \sum_{p,q \in \mathcal{N}} E_s(x_p, x_q) + \lambda_c \sum_{\ell \in \mathcal{L}} \sum_{o \in O_\ell} E_c(x; o, \ell) +$$

$$\lambda_r \sum_{(o_1, o_2) \in \mathcal{M}(O_1, O_2)} E_r(x; o_1, o_2) + \lambda_o \sum_{(o_1, o_2) \in \mathcal{M}(O_1, O_2)} E_o(x; o_1, o_2)$$

$$(1)$$

---

[3] Here we present only the two-image case. The generalization to the multi-image case follows directly and does not change any of the terms; it only increases the label space.

Data Term $E_d(x_p)$. This term is given by

$$E_d(x_p) = \begin{cases} 0, & x_p \neq \perp \wedge M_{x_p}(p) = 1, \\ 1, & x_p \neq \perp \wedge M_{x_p}(p) = 0, \\ 1 + \delta, & x_p = \perp \end{cases}$$

This term penalizes choosing a pixel in the output from an input image i if the pixel is not in the mask ($M_i(p) = 0$), or for declaring a pixel occluded. The δ parameter determines how strongly we prefer to leave a pixel empty rather than label it as occluded, and is discussed further in the definition of the occlusion term E_o below. There is no preference between the two source images.

Smoothness Term $E_s(x_p, x_q)$. To define this term we need the following notation: $\mathcal{C}(p, q, r) = \{k \mid \min(\|k - p\|_1, \|k - q\|_1) \leq r\}$ is the set of pixels within L1 distance r of either pixel p or q, describing a local patch around adjacent pixel p and q, while $I_{max} = \max_{p,q} \sum_{k \in \mathcal{C}(p,q,r)} \|I_1^S(k) - I_2^S(k)\|$. Writing exclusive-or as $\oplus$, our smoothness term is

$$E_s(x_p, x_q) = \begin{cases} 0, & x_p = x_q, \\ I_{max}, & x_p = \perp \oplus x_q = \perp, \\ \sum_{k \in \mathcal{C}(p,q,r)} \|I_{x_p}^S(k) - I_{x_q}^S(k)\|, & \text{else.} \end{cases}$$

Note that our term for the case $x_p = \perp \oplus x_q = \perp$ discourages the MRF from transitioning into the occluded label.

In general, E_s penalizes the local photometric difference for a seam between pixels p and q when $x_p \neq x_q$. In the special case where $r = 0$, $\mathcal{C}(p, q, r) = \{p, q\}$, and the cost of the seam here is $\lambda_s(\|I_{x_p}^S(p) - I_{x_q}^S(p)\| + \|I_{x_p}^S(q) - I_{x_q}^S(q)\|)$ as in most seam finding algorithms. Values of $r > 0$ will lead to larger local patches.

3.3 Our New MRF Terms

Cropping Term E_c. We introduce a term that penalizes seams that cut through an object $o \in O_\ell$, with cost proportional to the length of the seam.[4]
$E_c(x; o, \ell) = \sum_{p \in o} \sum_{q \in o} [x_p = \ell, x_q \neq \ell]$
The value of this term is 0 exactly when object o is either drawn entirely from I_ℓ^S, or not present at all in the final stitching result ($x_p = \ell, \forall p \in o$ or $x_p \neq \ell, \forall p \in o$, respectively). As defined, this results in $|o|^2$ pairwise terms, which may cause the optimization to be intractable in practice. As a result, we use an approximation of this term in the experiments, discussed in 3.4.

Note that since this term is a penalty rather than a hard constraint, the tradeoff between the smoothness term E_s and this term E_c will still allow us to cut through an object if it sufficiently benefits photometric consistency (Fig. 3).

---

[4] More precisely, seam means a transition from label ℓ to non-ℓ in particular here, not the transition between two arbitrary labels.

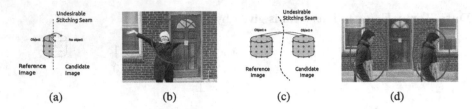

Fig. 3. (a) depicts our crop term. We use pairwise terms to penalize any seam that cuts through an object. (b) depicts a crop error created by Photoshop. (c) depicts our duplication term. We use pairwise terms to penalize any seam that results in the same object appearing in two different locations on the final mosaic. (d) depicts a duplication error created by NIS.

Duplication Term E_r. Our term discourages duplication when o_1 in I_1^S and o_2 in I_2^S are known to refer to the same object, and is defined as

$$E_r(x; o_1, o_2) = \sum_{(p,q) \in m(o_1, o_2)} [x_p = 1 \wedge x_q = 2].$$

Here $m(o_1, o_2) \in o_1 \times o_2$ are the pixel-level correspondences between objects o_1 and o_2. $(p, q) \in m(o_1, o_2)$ represent the same point in the real world, so the final stitching result should not include both pixel p from o_1 and pixel q from o_2. Note that this term includes a potentially complicated function m that calculates dense pixel correspondences; as a result, we use an approximation of this term in the experiments, discussed in 3.4.

Occlusion Term E_o. This term promotes the occlusion label by penalizing the use of out-of-mask labels in areas of the image where duplicate objects were detected:

$$E_o(x; o_1, o_2) = 2\delta \sum_{\ell \in \{1,2\}} \sum_{p \in o_\ell} [M_\ell(p) = 0 \wedge x_p = \ell] \tag{2}$$

where δ is the same parameter used to penalize the selection of the $\perp$ label in E_d. For the intuition behind this term, consider the case where o_1 and o_2 are corresponding objects in I_1^S and I_2^S, and $M_2(p) = 0$ for $p \in o_1$. Then we must either select label 1 for the pixels in o_1 or declare the pixels occluded. The data term E_d ensures that the occlusion label will normally give higher energy than a label which is out of mask. However, in the presence of a duplicated object, the occlusion term E_o increases the energy of the out of mask term since $2\delta > \delta$, resulting in the occlusion label being selected instead. Note, we typically set $\lambda_o = \lambda_d$.

Generalization to 3 or More Images. With multiple inputs, one image acts as the reference and the others become candidates. We then calculate registrations in the same manner as before, then pass to the seam finding phase the reference image and the candidate registrations: I_1 and $\omega_2(I_2), \ldots, \omega_n(I_n)$. We calculate correspondence for all pairs of images. When establishing correspondence between objects, we make sure that correspondence acts as an equivalence relation. The primary difference between the two and three input image case is transitivity. If three objects violate transitivity, we increase the correspondence threshold until the property holds. While other schemes could be imagined to ensure consistency, experimentally, we have yet to see this be violated.

3.4 Optimization

The cropping term E_c above has dense connections between each pixel $p \in I_1^S$ and $q \in I_2^S$, which can lead to computational difficulties. Here we introduce a *local energy term* E_{lc} that has fewer connections and is therefore simpler to compute, while experimentally maintaining the properties of the terms introduced above:

$$E_{lc}(x; o, \ell) = \sum_{p \in o} \sum_{q \in N_p} [x_p = \ell, x_q \neq \ell]$$

where N_p is set of neighbors for p.

Similarly, the duplication term reported above has a complicated structure based on the matching function over detected objects. We define the *local duplication term* E_{lr} in terms of $m_b(o_1, o_2)$, which in contrast to $m(o_1, o_2)$, returns the corresponding points of the two *bounding boxes* around objects o_1 and o_2, where each $p \in o_1$ is bilinearly interpolated to its position in o_2 using the corners of the bounding box.

To solve this MRF, we use alpha-expansion [11] with QPBO [21] for the induced binary subproblems. QPBO has been reported to perform well on a variety of computer vision tasks in practice, even when the induced binary subproblem is supermodular [21].

3.5 Establishing Correspondence Between Objects

Our strategy is to consider pairs of objects o_1, o_2 detected in images I_1, $\omega(I_2)$ respectively and to compute a metric that represents our degree of confidence in their corresponding to the same object. We compute this metric for all object pairs over all images and declare the best-scoring potential correspondence to be a match if it exceeds a specified threshold. In addition to the *correspondence density* metric used in the experiments reported here, we considered and tested several different metrics that we also summarize below. In all cases, the category returned by the object detector was used to filter the set of potential matches to only those in the same category.

Feature Point Matching. We tried running SIFT [22] and DeepMatch [23] directly on the objects identified. These methods gave a large number of correspondences without spatial coherence; for example, comparing a car and bike would result in a reasonable number of matches but the points in image I_1 would match to points very far away in I_2. We tried to produce a metric that captured this by comparing vector difference between feature points p and q from I_1 to their correspondences p' and q' from I_2.

Correspondence Density. We ran DeepMatch [23] on the two input images and counted the matches belonging to the two objects being considered as a match. This number was then divided by the area of the first image. Since DeepMatch feature points are roughly uniformly distributed in the first input image, the density of points in the area of the first input has an upper bound and it is possible to pick a density threshold that is able to distinguish between matching and non-matching objects, regardless of their size. This is the technique used in the experimental section below.

4   Object-Centered Evaluation of Stitching Algorithms

We now discuss the use of object detectors for formalized evaluation of stitching algorithms. In general, we assume access to the input images and the final output. The available object detectors are run on both, and their output used to identify crops, duplication, or omissions introduced by the stitching algorithm. The goal of this evaluation technique is not to quantify pixel-level discontinuities, e.g. slight errors in registration or seam-finding, but rather to determine whether the high-level features of the scene, as indicated by the presence and general integrity of the objects, are preserved.

In the following, F denotes the final output panorama, I the set of input images, and N_X the number of objects detected in an image X. N_F, for instance, would denote the number of objects found by a detector in the stitch result. Note that the techniques we propose can also be applied in parallel for specific categories of objects: instead of a general O and N_F, we might consider O^c and N_F^c for a particular category of objects c, e.g. humans or cats. Separating the consideration of objects in this way makes object analysis more granular and more likely to identify problems with the scene.

4.1   Penalizing Omission and Duplication

We first attempt to evaluate the quality of a stitch through the number of objects N detected in the input images and the final output. We generalize $\mathcal{M}(O_1, \ldots, O_n)$ to apply to an arbitrary number of input images, denoting corresponding object detections across a set of images $I_1, \ldots, I_n$. The techniques discussed above for establishing correspondences between objects can easily be generalized to multiple images and used to formulate an expression for the expected number of objects in the final stitch result. In particular, the expected object count for a hypothetical ideal output image F^* is given by the number of "equivalence classes" of objects found in the input images for the correspondence function under consideration: all detected objects are expected to be represented at least once, and corresponding objects are expected to be represented with a *single* instance.

(a) Input image   (b) Google Photos (0.1140)   (c) Photoshop (no object)

(d) APAP (0.1203)   (e) Our result (left 0.4882, right 0.93380)

Fig. 4. Visualizations for object bounding boxes for humans detected in given source. Final mosaics have been altered for space reasons, but no bounding boxes were removed. The MS-SSIM are listed in parenthesis after the method name. $N_F - N_{F*}$ is as follows (b) -1, (c) -2, (d) -1, and (e) 0.

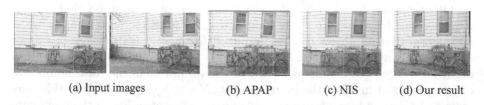

(a) Input images   (b) APAP   (c) NIS   (d) Our result

Fig. 5. Visualizations for object bounding boxes for bikes detected in given source. Final mosaics have been altered for space reasons, but no bounding boxes were removed. Other techniques failed to produce a stitch. The MS-SSIM are as follows: APAP left (0.1608), APAP right (0.1523), NIS left (0.3971), NIS right (0.1771), Ours (**0.8965**). $N_F - N_{F*}$ is as follows (b) 1, (c) 1, and (d) 0

For a good stitching output F, we expect $N_F = N_{F*}$. Note that $N_F > N_{F*}$ or $N_F < N_{F*}$ imply omissions or duplications, respectively. In Fig. 4, a human detector finds objects in only one image and $\mathcal{M}(O_1, O_2) = \emptyset$; therefore, we have that $N_{F*} = 2$ for the category of humans. When run on the output of Photoshop or APAP, however, only one human is found, giving $N_F < N_{F'}$ and indicating an omission.

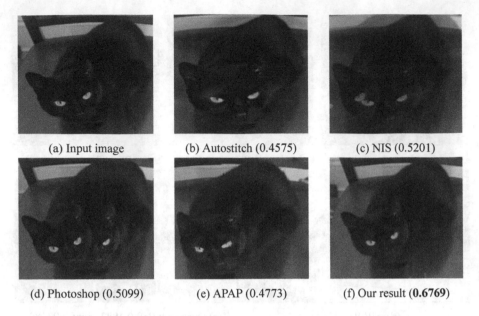

(a) Input image (b) Autostitch (0.4575) (c) NIS (0.5201)

(d) Photoshop (0.5099) (e) APAP (0.4773) (f) Our result (**0.6769**)

Fig. 6. Object bounding boxes for cats detected in given source. MS_SSIM is included in parenthesis. Autostitch applies a warp that alters the cat's facial shape. NIS contains ghosting. Photoshop duplicates part of the cat's face. APAP applies a warp that alters the cat's facial shape.

Other approaches exist for detecting omission or duplication that do not require computing the potentially complicated $\mathcal{M}$ function. For example, it can be inferred that an object has been omitted in the output if it contains fewer objects than any of the inputs: $N_F < \max_{I_i \in I}(|O_i|)$. Similarly, a duplication has occurred if more objects are identified in the output than the total number of objects detected in all of the input images: $N_F > \sum_{I_i \in I} N_{I_i}$. While this may seem to be a weak form of inference, it proves sufficient in Fig. 4: the maximum number of humans in an input image is 2, but only one is found in the Photoshop and APAP results, indicating an omission.

Unfortunately, while duplication almost always indicates an error in an output F, the situation is not as clear-cut with omissions. Objects that are not central to the scene or that are not considered important by humans for whatever reason can often be omitted without any negative effect on the final mosaic.

4.2 Cropping

Object detectors can be used to detect crops in two ways: major crops, which make the object unrecognizable to the detector, are interpreted by our system as omissions, and detected as described above. Even objects that are identifiable in the final output, however, may be partially removed by a seam that cuts through them or undergo unnatural warping. A different approach is therefore needed in order to detect and penalize these cases. Here we consider two options that differ in whether they consider the results of the object detector on the input images: the first directly compares the detected objects from the inputs and output, while the second is less sensitive to the choice of object detector and instead uses more generic template matching methods (Figs. 5 and 6).

For both of the methods, we note that some warping of the input image is usually necessary in order to obtain a good alignment, so image comparison techniques applied to the original input image and the output image are unlikely to be informative. However, given an input image I_i and the output F it is possible to retrospectively compute a set of plausible warps $\omega(I_i)$ and apply image comparison operators to these. Our approach therefore does not require access to the actual warp used to construct the stitch, but it can of course be used to increase the accuracy of our methods if it is available.

Cropping Detection with Direct Object Comparison. This approach implicitly trusts the object detector to give precise results on both the input images and the output image. The object detector is run for F and for all of the plausible registration candidates that have been determined for the various I_i. We then run Multiscale Structural Similarity (MS-SSIM) [24] for all of the correspondences among the detected objects (determined as discussed in Sect. 3.5), and use the average and maximum values of these metrics as our final result. Any reasonable image similarity metric can be used in this approach, including e.g. deep learning techniques.

Cropping Detection with Template Matching. This metric is less sensitive to the choice of object detector. Instead of applying it to all of the warped input images, we apply it only to the result image. The region of the output where the object is detected is then treated as a template, and traditional template matching approaches are used to compare the object to the reference image I_1 and any plausible registrations.

We have experimented with these metrics to confirm that these values match our intuitions about the handling of objects in the stitch result. We provide some examples and their evaluation values (maximum MS-SSIM with direct object comparison) in the captions of the figures above.

5   Experimental Results for Stitching

Our goal is to stitch difficult image sets that give rise to noticeable errors with existing approaches. Unfortunately, there is no standard data set of challenging stitching problems, nor any generally accepted metric to use other than subjective visual evaluation. We therefore follow the experimental setup of [20], who both introduce a stitching technique that is able to stitch a difficult class of images, and also present a set of images that cause previous methods to introduce duplications and cropping. For competitors we consider Photoshop 2018's "Photomerge" stitcher, APAP [8], Autostitch [25], and NIS [9]. Following the approach of [20], we extend APAP with a seam finder.

Experimental Setup. We tried several methods for feature extraction and matching, and found that DeepMatch [23] gave the best results. It was used in all examples shown here. The associated DeepFlow solver was used to generate flows for the optical flow-based warping. The QP problems used to obtain the mesh parameters and determine candidate warpings ω_i were solved with the Ceres solver [26]. For object detection, we experimented with the Mask R-CNN [4] and SSD [3] systems. Both were found to give good performance for different types of objects.

Ablation Study. We performed an ablation study on the pairwise terms in the seam finding stage and found that all terms are necessary and perform as expected. These results are available with the rest of the data as indicated below (Figs. 7, 8, 9 and 10).

In the remainder of this section, we review several images from our test set and highlight the strengths and weaknesses of our technique, as well as those of various methods from the literature. All results shown use the same parameter set. Data, images and additional material omitted here due to lack of space are available online.[5]

(a) Inputs   (b) Photoshop result   (c) Our result

Fig. 7. "Bottle" dataset. Photoshop duplicates the neck of the bottle and the headphones. Our result is plausible.

(a) Inputs   (b) Photoshop result   (c) Our result

Fig. 8. "Walking" dataset

---

[5] See https://sites.google.com/view/oois-eccv18.

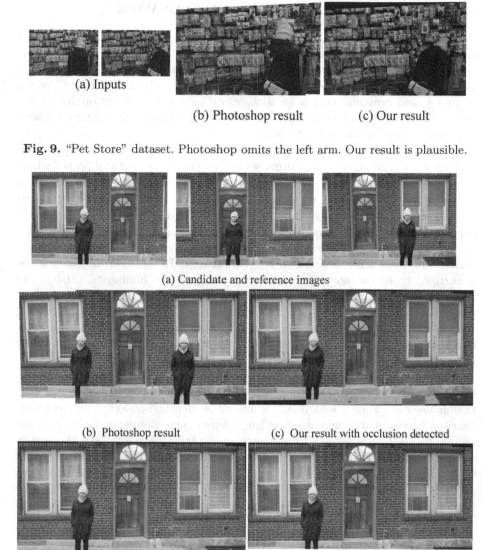

(a) Inputs

(b) Photoshop result   (c) Our result

Fig. 9. "Pet Store" dataset. Photoshop omits the left arm. Our result is plausible.

(a) Candidate and reference images

(b) Photoshop result   (c) Our result with occlusion detected

(d) Our blend result   (e) Our cropped result

Fig. 10. Three image stitching. In (c), we choose to not use the human in the right-most input. However, the legs block any information regarding the sidewalk, making this location occluded. Our algorithm correctly labels it as occluded and colors it magenta. (d) and (e) present ways to fix this occlusion. (Color figure online)

6 Conclusions, Limitations and Future Work

We have demonstrated that object detectors can be used to avoid a large class of visually jarring image stitching errors. Our techniques lead to more realistic and visually pleasing outputs, even in hard problems with perspective changes and differences in object motion, and avoid artifacts such as object duplication, cropping, and omission that arise with other approaches. Additionally, object detectors yield ways of evaluating the output of stitching algorithms without any dependence on the methods used.

One potential drawback to our approach is that it applies only to inputs containing detectable objects, and provides no benefit in e.g. natural scenes where current object detection techniques are unable to generate accurate bounding boxes for elements such as mountains or rivers. We expect, however, that our techniques will become increasingly useful as object detection and scene matching improve. At the other end of the spectrum, we may be unable to find a seam in inputs with a large number of detected objects. We note that our crop, duplication, and omission terms are all soft constraints. In addition, objects can be prioritized based on saliency measures or category (i.e. human vs. other), and crops penalized more highly for objects deemed important. One existing use case where this might apply is for city imagery with pedestrians moving on sidewalks, such as the content of Google Streetview. Traditional seam finding techniques find this setting particularly difficult, and torn or duplicated humans are easily identifiable errors.

False positives from object correspondences are another issue. In this case, matching thresholds can be adjusted to obtain the desired behavior for the particular use case. Scenes with a large number of identical objects, such as traffic cones or similar cars, present a challenge when correspondence techniques are unable to match the objects to one another by taking advantage of the spatial characteristics of the input images. One issue that our technique cannot account for is identical objects with different motions: a pathological example might be pictures of identically-posed twins wearing the same clothing. We consider these false positives to be a reasonable tradeoff for improved performance in the more common use case.

Acknowledgements. This research has been supported by NSF grants IIS-1161860 and IIS-1447473 and by a Google Faculty Research Award. We also thank Connie Choi for help collecting images.

References

1. Szeliski, R.: Image alignment and stitching: a tutorial. Found. Trends Comput. Graph. Vis. **2**(1), 1–104 (2007)
2. Goodfellow, I., Bengio, Y., Courville, A.: Deep Learning. The MIT Press, Cambridge (2016)
3. Liu, W., et al.: SSD: single shot MultiBox detector. In: Leibe, B., Matas, J., Sebe, N., Welling, M. (eds.) ECCV 2016. LNCS, vol. 9905, pp. 21–37. Springer, Cham (2016). https://doi.org/10.1007/978-3-319-46448-0_2

4. Ren, S., He, K., Girshick, R., Sun, J.: Faster R-CNN: towards real-time object detection with region proposal networks. TPAMI **39**(6), 1137–1149 (2017)
5. Szeliski, R.: Computer Vision: Algorithms and Applications. Springer, Berlin (2010). https://doi.org/10.1007/978-3-642-12848-6
6. Kwatra, V., Schödl, A., Essa, I., Turk, G., Bobick, A.: Graphcut textures: image and video synthesis using graph cuts. SIGGRAPH **22**(3), 277–286 (2003)
7. Li, N., Liao, T., Wang, C.: Perception-based seam cutting for image stitching. Signal Image Video Process. **12**, 967–974 (2018)
8. Zaragoza, J., Chin, T.J., Brown, M.S., Suter, D.: As-projective-as-possible image stitching with moving DLT. In: CVPR, pp. 2339–2346 (2013)
9. Chen, Y.-S., Chuang, Y.-Y.: Natural image stitching with the global similarity prior. In: Leibe, B., Matas, J., Sebe, N., Welling, M. (eds.) ECCV 2016. LNCS, vol. 9909, pp. 186–201. Springer, Cham (2016). https://doi.org/10.1007/978-3-319-46454-1_12
10. Herrmann, C., et al.: Robust image stitching using multiple registrations. In: ECCV (2018)
11. Boykov, Y., Veksler, O., Zabih, R.: Fast approximate energy minimization via graph cuts. TPAMI **23**(11), 1222–1239 (2001)
12. Szeliski, R., et al.: A comparative study of energy minimization methods for Markov random fields. TPAMI **30**(6), 1068–1080 (2008)
13. Lin, C.C., Pankanti, S.U., Natesan Ramamurthy, K., Aravkin, A.Y.: Adaptive as-natural-as-possible image stitching. In: CVPR, pp. 1155–1163 (2015)
14. Lin, K., Jiang, N., Cheong, L.-F., Do, M., Lu, J.: SEAGULL: seam-guided local alignment for parallax-tolerant image stitching. In: Leibe, B., Matas, J., Sebe, N., Welling, M. (eds.) ECCV 2016. LNCS, vol. 9907, pp. 370–385. Springer, Cham (2016). https://doi.org/10.1007/978-3-319-46487-9_23
15. Agarwala, A., et al.: Interactive digital photomontage. SIGGRAPH **23**(3), 294–302 (2004)
16. Ozawa, T., Kitani, K.M., Koike, H.: Human-centric panoramic imaging stitching. In: Augmented Human International Conference, pp. 20:1–20:6 (2012)
17. Flores, A., Belongie, S.: Removing pedestrians from google street view images. In: IEEE International Workshop on Mobile Vision, pp. 53–58 (2010)
18. Perez, P., Gangnet, M., Blake, A.: Poisson image editing. In: SIGGRAPH, pp. 313–318 (2003)
19. Liu, F., Gleicher, M., Jin, H., Agarwala, A.: Content-preserving warps for 3D video stabilization. SIGGRAPH **28**(3), 44 (2009)
20. Zhang, F., Liu, F.: Parallax-tolerant image stitching. In: CVPR, pp. 3262–3269 (2014)
21. Kolmogorov, V., Rother, C.: Minimizing nonsubmodular functions with graph cuts-a review. TPAMI **29**(7), 1274–1279 (2007)
22. Lowe, D.: Object recognition from local scale-invariant features. In: ICCV, pp. 1150–1157 (1999)
23. Weinzaepfel, P., Revaud, J., Harchaoui, Z., Schmid, C.: DeepFlow: large displacement optical flow with deep matching. In: ICCV, pp. 1385–1392 (2013)
24. Wang, Z., Simoncelli, E., Bovik, A.: Multiscale structural similarity for image quality assessment. In: Asilomar Conference on Signals, Systems and Computers, pp. 1398–1402 (2004)
25. Brown, M., Lowe, D.G.: Automatic panoramic image stitching using invariant features. IJCV **74**(1), 59–73 (2007)
26. Agarwal, S., Mierle, K., et al.: Ceres solver. http://ceres-solver.org. Accessed 25 Jul 2018

Author Index

Printed in the United States
By Bookmasters